TORTS:
CASES, MATERIALS, QUESTIONS, AND COMMENTS FROM A JUDEO-CHRISTIAN PERSPECTIVE

TORTS: CASES, MATERIALS, QUESTIONS, AND COMMENTS FROM A JUDEO-CHRISTIAN
PERSPECTIVE

Louis W. Hensler III

Published by:

Vandeplas Publishing, LLC – August 2015

801 International Parkway, 5th Floor
Lake Mary, FL. 32746
USA

www.vandeplaspublishing.com

ISBN 978-1-60042-265-2

TORTS:

Cases, Materials, Questions, and Comments from a Judeo-Christian Perspective

Louis W. Hensler III

TABLE OF CONTENTS

ABOUT THIS BOOK

A casual reading of this book might not distinguish it from the many other torts casebooks being published today. It addresses the same tort history and doctrine as all of the others. Also like all of those other texts, this one is written from a particular perspective, and the author of this book happens to be steeped in the Judeo-Christian tradition.

Publishing a torts casebook that is so self-consciously perspectival might seem strange to some, but it will not seem strange to all. By the author's last count, there were forty-nine religiously affiliated law schools in the United States, the overwhelming majority (but by no means all) of them Christian. About a dozen of those law schools are strongly tied to their religion or church. Most of those have a genuine institutional commitment to teaching from a Christian (broadly defined) perspective.

For more than seventeen years, the author of this text has taught Torts at one such school, and teaching from an explicitly Christian perspective has not always been easy. One of the challenges for an explicitly Christian Torts teacher or student is finding teaching materials that reflect (or at least are not hostile to) the perspective to which the torts scholar is committed. This book was developed in response to this challenge. These materials have been collected, edited, and developed over the course of seventeen years to serve as a Torts text in a Christian law school. For the most part, these materials are indistinguishable from any other first-year Torts text, but these materials also are distinctively Christian in at least the following three ways:

1) Case selection – while pedagogy always has come first, where possible, cases have been selected for their particular interest to a student with a moral and/or religious commitment. For example, the subject of premises liability employs an excellent case involving homeowners who opened their house for a private Bible study. The issue of mitigation of damages is taught through a case involving an accident victim who declined treatment for religious reasons. There probably are at least a dozen, perhaps more, cases selected specifically because their fact patterns would be of particular interest to religious students and teachers. Probably as many more cases were selected because either their factual patterns or the court's discussion of the case implicated distinctively moral issues in addition to the strictly legal issues in the case.

2) Probably the most overtly religious characteristic of this book are the several biblical passages included in the materials, sometimes with relevant rhetorical questions. For example, along with

the materials on the duty to rescue is presented Jesus' famous teaching concerning the good Samaritan.

3) Finally, and this would be the most difficult to discern, the materials simply are done from a perspective (a common historical perspective) that sees Torts as being about promoting a transcendent form of justice.

None of this means that this book will be of no use to one who does not share its distinctive perspective. Over the years, probably hundreds of non-Christian students have learned torts by studying these materials. But for those who approach life and law in general and torts in particular from a Christian perspective, it seems that this is the sort of book that ought to be available.

A. What is a Tort?

The Fifth Edition of Black's Law Dictionary defines a "tort" as "[a] private or civil wrong or injury, other than breach of contract, for which the court will provide a remedy in the form of an action for damages." This definition makes torts as a topic quite wide-ranging. While some aspects of this definition may be controversial, it is generally agreed that a tort is conduct for which a court will provide a civil (as opposed to a criminal) remedy.

Tortious conduct can be intentional, reckless, negligent, or innocent. The fact that tort always involves some sort of civil remedy means that every tort must involve a legal injury. In the overwhelming majority of cases, the remedy in a tort case is the payment of money damages.

Tort law overlaps, to some extent, other areas of the law that share some of tort's characteristics. Comparing related but distinct legal fields to torts can be an enlightening exercise, so let us begin to consider the nature of tort law by briefly comparing it with some of its legal competitors.

Criminal Law. The words "private or civil" in Black's definition of tort are very important. Tort law is like criminal law in that both usually are thought to vindicate "wrongs." Because of this overlap, sometimes the same conduct can lead both to criminal and to civil responsibility, but not all torts are crimes, and not all crimes are torts. One way to distinguish tort law from criminal law is that tort law is "private." Other areas of the law, such as criminal law, are said to be "public."

This private/public distinction means that while criminal law vindicates wrongs committed against society at large, the law of torts generally vindicates wrongs suffered by individuals. This difference in emphasis manifests itself in several ways. For example, criminal cases are prosecuted directly by the state at state expense, but tort cases are brought and pursued by private parties at private expense. This difference in parties is reflected in the captions of the cases you will be reading. A typical criminal case will be captioned *United States v. Smith* or *Commonwealth v. Jones*, but a typical tort suit will be captioned, for example, *Smith v. Jones.*

These captions reflect the fact that a criminal case is between the state and a private party while a tort suit is between two private parties.

Another difference between tort law and criminal law relates to the applicable standard of proof. The applicable standard of proof in a tort case usually is proof by a "preponderance of evidence," which means "more likely than not." But the standard of proof in a criminal case is "proof beyond a reasonable doubt."

Furthermore, the "penalty" aspect of criminal and tort cases differ. In a criminal case, the convicted defendant may be punished through loss of property (fine), loss of liberty (imprisonment), or even loss of life (capital punishment). In a civil tort case, there usually is no punishment at all. Tort cases generally are not about punishing wrongdoers – they are about compensating victims for injuries suffered at the hands of others. So while the tort defendant may be required to pay money to the victim or may have his liberty impaired in some way, this usually is not considered a punishment. On the flipside, compensation of the victim is not routinely part of a criminal penalty. Another difference between criminal law and tort is that the victim's responsibility is irrelevant to the criminal case but may bar (in whole or in part) a tort suit.

Contract Law. Like tort law, contract law is private. But unlike tort, contract law does not impose standards on private parties. Rather, contract law enforces the standards voluntarily chosen by the private parties themselves. The question in a contract suit is not whether defendant's conduct measures up to some standard imposed by law but rather whether defendant's conduct measures up to the standard promised by the defendant himself. Moreover, a contract can govern more than standards of conduct relating to safety – compensation for losses also can be covered by first-party insurance contracts. But the state does not always trust private parties to be able to safeguard their own well-being through voluntary contract, and so some contracts are void or voidable.

Direct Compensation. Tort law compensates those who have suffered losses only when a legally responsible private defendant can be found to pay the compensation. The government sometimes provides compensation for those who have suffered certain losses without regard to any private legal responsibility for the loss. A public health insurance program, such as Medicare, is an example.

Direct Regulation. Some view the law of tort as a form of indirect safety regulation – civil liability gives actors incentives to safety. Of course, sometimes the government steps in and regulates safety directly. Two federal "alphabet soup" agencies that are particularly relevant to torts are the Consumer Product Safety Commission (CPSC) and the National Highway and Transportation Safety Administration (NHTSA). There are many others.

States also can directly regulate tort actors. Federal and state safety regulation efforts often run in parallel with private litigation over accidents. Sometimes state and federal regulatory efforts can partially displace private law by "trumping" the common law tort standards of acceptable safety conduct. While state and federal regulations are like tort law in that they provide standards of conduct applicable to private citizens interacting with one another, such regulations, like criminal law (and unlike tort) are public law, not private law. Any regulatory effect of tort law is merely a side-effect (whether intended or not) of the adjudication of private wrongs.

Each of these sorts of law can sometimes work in conjunction with tort law, and sometimes can clash with tort law. These various areas of the law overlap in important ways, and some have questioned whether tort law is any longer needed at all. That is not meant to suggest that tort law has diminished in importance – the United States is the undisputed world leader in tort suits. But most suits are relatively small, and a very small percentage of suits filed actually go to trial.

QUESTIONS

1 What is the significance of the words "private or civil" in the definition of a tort?
2 Why is the standard of proof in a tort case lower than in a criminal case?
3 How is a tort different from a breach of contract?
4 Why should we as a society provide a remedy for harms caused by conduct that is not criminal? In that regard, consider the following passage of Scripture.

FOOD FOR THOUGHT: MATTHEW 5:38-42

Ye have heard that it hath been said, An eye for an eye, and a tooth for a tooth. But I say unto you, That ye resist not evil: but whosoever shall smite thee on thy right cheek, turn to him the other also. And if any man will sue thee at the law, and take away thy coat, let him have thy cloak also. And whosoever shall compel thee to go a mile, go with him twain. Give to him that asketh thee, and from him that would borrow of thee turn not thou away.

COMMENTS AND QUESTIONS

1 The concept underlying the phrase "an eye for an eye, and a tooth for a tooth" is called *lex talionis*. Is there any virtue to this approach?
2 What is Jesus teaching in this passage? Is Jesus' teaching suitable for society at large?
3 Is it "un-Christian" to prosecute or defend a civil lawsuit? Note that because the law of Moses provided an inalienable right to one's cloak (Exodus 22:26-27; Deuteronomy 24:12-13), it could be given only voluntarily. Unlike the coat, it could not be taken through legal process. How does this background fact impact Jesus' teaching?

B. What does Tort Law do?

Tort law makes one party who is legally responsible for an injury compensate with money damages another party who has suffered the injury. As a budding torts scholar, one question you might ask is why society ever should shift a loss from the one on whom it fell to another who is judged to be legally responsible for it? The answerers of this question can be grouped into two camps. The traditional answer has been "corrective justice." A tort creates an "injustice" that the civil law must step in to "correct," usually through the payment of money damages. Defendant is forced to compensate the plaintiff because it is morally right to do so. Under this theory, tort law is a private law topic, and justice or fairness is an end in itself. Some think that corrective justice requires liability only when the defendant is in some sense "at fault." Others think corrective justice is consistent with so-called "strict liability," i.e. liability without fault.

Another group of answers can be labeled "instrumentalism" or "social utility." Under this theory of tort law, justice or fairness may result from a particular tort case, but justice is not an end in itself. Rather, individual losses are shifted to create an incentive environment that leaves all of society better off. This approach to torts makes it much more like a public law topic. Usually, the immediate end of instrumentalism is to provide society's actors with incentives to behave in a productive or socially efficient way. Losses are shifted, not primarily because it is right or fair or just to shift them, but rather because shifting them will deter the parties engaging in risky conduct from causing undue losses. There is less concern with a fair distribution of particular losses than there is with a general minimization of loss to society.

Another possible way to divide the law of torts is into two parts – intentional torts and accidental torts. Intentional torts involve deliberate invasions of protected legal interests. Accidental torts are just that – accidents. Accidental torts can be further divided into negligence and strict liability. Negligence is a fault-based theory of liability. Defendant is liable only if his conduct fails to measure up to some acceptable level. Strict liability permits liability even without any showing of defendant's fault. We will return to all of these terms later.

C. Torts as a Common Law Topic

There are several sources of law in America. The law of tort in this country still is, generally speaking, a "common law" topic. This means that, for the most part, tort rules are made by courts, usually appellate courts, not legislatures, on a case-by-case basis as the courts decide individual cases. Of course, legislatures can, and sometimes do, "trump" judge-made tort law, but that is the exception in American tort law, not the rule.

The decisions of judges in individual cases serve as "precedents" for later cases. And under the doctrine of *stare decisis,* such precedents do more than merely suggest the outcome of later cases. The narrow propositions necessary to an authoritative precedent actually often control the outcome of later cases within the same jurisdiction. Of course, the rule of *stare decisis* is not absolute – precedents sometimes are overruled. Moreover, court decisions often conflict, which presents much of the challenge of lawyering in a common law field. Because tort law actually arises from decided cases, it has a sort of chicken and egg quality to it. Tort suits usually are brought on the authority of previously successful, factually-analogous cases. But for the law to develop over time, some cases must be brought that push the envelope a bit.

Because American tort law has arisen on a case-by-case basis, the subject of torts usually is studied in American law schools using the "case method." The "case method" of studying torts employs a casebook, like this one, that collects edited versions of written appellate opinions (and a few trial court decisions) in cases on various tort topics. These opinions essentially are the judges' written explanations of the reasons for their decisions. In addition to case law, the common law rules of tort are collected and published by the American Law Institute in the Restatement of Torts. Three Restatements of Torts have been published over the years.

Because tort law is dominantly case law, the first skill for the tort student is the ability to read case law, which is harder than it sounds. As you read the cases in this book, you will find that the opinions tend to have certain recurring significant characteristics. The opinions almost always will include the facts that were essential to the court's decision. You should pay attention to the procedural posture of the case because you cannot understand what the court is doing in the case unless you understand precisely what the court has been asked to do. Who is appealing from what decision by the lower court? You also need to be able to distinguish how you feel about what happened to the parties to the case from the precise legal issues that are being decided by the court. You must learn to discern from the opinion the rule of the case, that is, the essential proposition on which the court's decision turns. You should distinguish the rule of the case from its rationale – the rationale is the policy reason that animates the rule adopted by the court. Only the rule of the case will be binding in future cases under the doctrine of *stare decisis*, but the rationale of the decision also may help determine how future cases are decided. Of course, the rules and rationales of appellate decisions will be important to you as a future lawyer because they will drive how you structure the similar cases that you are handling and what arguments you choose to present to future courts. Learning to discern and persuasively deploy holdings and rationales will go a long way toward making you an effective practitioner of the law of tort. Also important will be communication skills, the importance of the ability precisely and persuasively to structure arguments in acceptable English cannot be understated.

Every trial involves multiple questions that must be decided. Some of those questions are decided by the jury – these frequently are called "questions of fact." Other questions are decided by the judge – these are called questions of law. It will be important to your understanding of the cases to be able to distinguish questions of fact from questions of law. Appellate courts technically do not re-visit questions of fact decided by the jury.

I.

Intentional Torts

One way to organize the universe of torts would be to divide torts into three categories – intentional torts, strict liability, and negligence. The law of intentional torts is an excellent place to begin our discussion of tort law because intentional torts are, in some ways, relatively simple – plaintiff recovers only if defendant intentionally invaded a particular protected interest of the plaintiff. A punch in the nose as a battery is very easy to grasp and has been a tort for a very long time. But as we shall see, what appears to be simple on the surface can be deceptively complicated when studied more closely.

All tort causes of action are made up of essential elements that plaintiff bears the burden of pleading and proving. The unifying feature of intentional torts is that each theory requires plaintiff to prove that the interference with plaintiff's protected interest by the defendant was in a meaningful way "intentional." In other words, "intent" is a required element of every intentional tort. Defendant is liable only if he "intended" a particular result (although not necessarily the precise result that he obtained). The precise form of intent required is different for each cause of action. Beyond the common requirement of intent, the elements of the various intentional tort causes of action discussed here differ significantly.

The usual list of intentional torts includes battery, assault, false imprisonment, intentional infliction of emotional distress, trespass to chattels, conversion, and trespass to land. This section also will mention some closely-related causes of action such as malicious prosecution and abuse of process. Intentional torts are relatively rare in practice, but these theories can be attractive to plaintiffs because they often provide advantages over accident-based theories of recovery, e.g., increased availability of punitive damages, reduced defenses, etc. This section will first discuss the elements of the various intentional torts and then will cover common defenses to intentional torts.

A. Introduction To International Torts: Battery

The intentional tort of battery protects a party's interest in being free from unconsented bodily contact. The invasion of plaintiff's bodily integrity is the harm that the tort protects against, not necessarily any physical injury resulting from the invasion. Therefore, battery does not require actual physical harm. In fact, battery comes in two varieties – harmful contact and offensive contact.

The tort of battery often is discussed in conjunction with assault, and frequently the same conduct by defendant will result in both a battery and in the separate tort of assault, but we will delay the full discussion of assault until the next section of these materials. Torts often are understood in terms of their "essential elements," that is, the minimum elements that a plaintiff must prove to recover under the cause of action. Section Thirteen of The Restatement (Second) of Torts sets out the elements of the tort of harmful contact battery: 1) a voluntary act by defendant; 2) intended to cause contact with plaintiff's body (or the body of another); 3) which does in fact cause such contact, and 4) which bodily contact is either harmful or offensive.

1. VOLUNTARY ACT

Every tort begins with one common element that frequently is not discussed by courts – a voluntary act by the defendant. The requirement of an act by the defendant limits the tort of battery to those bodily contacts that flow from defendant's voluntary movement.

2. INTENT

As noted above, intent is an element of each of the intentional torts. Several questions recur with some frequency as courts grapple with whether defendant possessed the intent required for the particular cause of action alleged by plaintiff. In fact, courts have not been entirely consistent on the question of precisely what intent is required for the tort of battery, but more on that in a moment. To begin our consideration of intent, study the court's opinion in *Garratt v. Dailey,* which includes an exceptionally enlightening discussion of the intent requirement.

GARRATT V. DAILEY
279 P.2D 1091 (WASH. 1955)

... Brian Dailey (age five years, nine months) was visiting ... in the backyard of the plaintiff's home .... [Plaintiff Ruth Garratt contends] that she came out into the backyard to talk with Naomi [her sister] and that, as she started to sit down in a ... lawn chair, Brian deliberately pulled it out from under her. The only one of the three persons so testifying was Naomi Garratt. (Ruth Garratt ... did not testify as to how or why she fell.) ....

The authorities generally, but with certain notable exceptions, state that when a minor has committed a tort with force he is liable to be proceeded against as any other person would be....

We have here the conceded volitional act of Brian, i.e., the moving of a chair. Had the plaintiff proved to the satisfaction of the trial court that Brian moved the chair while she was in the act of sitting down, Brian's action would patently have been for the purpose or with the intent of causing the plaintiff's bodily contact with the ground, and she would be entitled to a judgment against him for the resulting damages.

The plaintiff based her case on that theory, and the trial court held that she failed in her proof and accepted Brian's version of the facts rather than that given by the eyewitness who testified for the plaintiff. After the trial court determined that the plaintiff had not established her theory of a battery (i.e., that Brian had pulled the chair out from under the plaintiff while she was in the act of sitting down), it then became concerned with whether a battery was established under the facts as it found them to be.

In this connection, we quote another portion of the comment on the "Character of actor's intention," relating to clause (a) of the rule from the Restatement ... :

It is not enough that the act itself is intentionally done and this, even though the actor realizes or should realize that it contains a very grave risk of bringing about the contact or apprehension. Such realization may make the actor's conduct negligent or even reckless but unless he realizes that to a substantial certainty, the contact or apprehension will result, the actor has not that intention which is necessary to make him liable under the rule stated in this Section.

... If Brian had any of the intents which the trial court found ... that he did not have, he would of course have had the knowledge to which we have referred. The mere absence of any intent to injure the plaintiff or to play a prank on her or to embarrass her, or to commit an assault and battery on her would not absolve him from liability if in fact he had such knowledge. Without such knowledge, there would be nothing wrongful about Brian's act in moving the chair, and ... there would be no liability.

While a finding that Brian had no such knowledge can be inferred from the findings made, we believe that before the plaintiff's action in such a case should be dismissed there should be no question but that the trial court had passed upon that issue; hence, the case should be remanded for clarification of the findings to specifically cover the question of Brian's knowledge, because intent could be inferred therefrom. If the court finds that he had such knowledge the necessary intent will be established and the plaintiff will be entitled to recover, even though there was no purpose to injure or embarrass the plaintiff. . . .

It will be noted that the law of battery as we have discussed it is the law applicable to adults, and no significance has been attached to the fact that Brian was a child less than six years of age when the alleged battery occurred. The only circumstance where Brian's age is of any consequence is in determining what he knew, and there his experience, capacity, and understanding are of course material. . . .

NOTES, QUESTIONS AND COMMENTS

1   *On Remand.* The Trial judge entered judgment in favor of the plaintiff, which the Washington Supreme Court later affirmed. 304 P.2d 681 (Wash. 1956).

2   *Where's the Contact?* If battery requires contact with plaintiff's body, how can moving a chair constitute a battery where neither defendant nor the chair ever touches plaintiff?

3   *Restatements of the Law.* Here the first case in these materials quotes the Restatement of Torts as authority for the nature of the intent necessary for battery liability. The Restatement is published by the American Law Institute ("ALI"), a prestigious group of lawyers, judges and academics that was formed in 1923 and that publishes written summaries of, among other things, each field of the common law, such as Torts, Property and Contracts. The original purpose behind the drafting of the Restatements was to bring some agreement and uniformity to these common law fields. The Restatement drafting process is long and painstaking. The Restatement does not have the binding force of law unless adopted by the courts of a particular jurisdiction, but it has been extremely influential and is frequently cited by courts. While the Restatements mostly reflect majority positions on various legal issues, they do sometimes embrace minority positions if the ALI believes those minority positions are superior to the majority positions. Thus, the Restatement is not merely a useful tool for summarizing majority positions, it also has served as a tool for the development of the common law.

4   *Intentional Torts Under the Third Restatement.* The Restatement (Third) of Torts lumps several intentional torts under a general liability for intentional physical harm.

5   *Proof of Intent.* What is the evidence here of Dailey's intent? How could plaintiff prove intent? Proving a defendant's intent requires the fact finder to "get inside the defendant's head." On rare occasions, a defendant might admit his intent, but almost always, intent must be proven by circumstantial evidence.

6   *Defendant's Age.* Dailey was younger than six years old. The court notes that children can be held responsible for their torts just like adults. When assessing the liability of the child, does the age of the defendant make no difference at all? What if Dailey had been two? One? Some states have adopted a rule that children under a certain age (frequently seven) are conclusively presumed to be incapable of forming the intent to commit an intentional tort and sometimes absolve young children of all tort responsibility.

7   *Parental Responsibility.* Even though children theoretically are legally responsible for their own tortious conduct, because young children rarely possess much in the way of assets, a plaintiff who has been injured by a child sometimes seeks to recover from the child's parents, but there is no general common law rule of vicarious liability by parents for the torts of their children. Most states impose some limited statutory liability on parents for certain malicious or willful tortious conduct by their minor children living with them. Such statutes generally cap the amount of the parents' statutory liability. A couple of jurisdictions go even farther in imposing liability on parents for the torts of their minor children. Should parents be legally responsible for harm caused by their children? Even if a parent is not vicariously liable for a child's tort, sometimes a parent's insurance policy will cover a child, providing a source of compensation for the child's tort victim even if the child tortfeasor has no assets. Note that

holding a parent legally responsible for negligent entrustment of a dangerous instrumentality to the child or for failing to adequately supervise the child may be possible as a direct negligence action against the parent.

8 *Causation.* While frequently not explicitly discussed with regard to the intentional torts, "causation," like "volitional act," is an element of every tort cause of action. The defendant who is found liable for an intentional tort is legally responsible for all the damage (and only the damage) that his tortious conduct causes. Causation will be studied in more detail later in the course, but note for now that courts are more receptive to plaintiffs' arguments concerning causation in the context of intentional torts than in the context of mere negligence.

HYPOTHETICAL SCENARIOS

1. What if the defendant in *Garratt* had been suddenly taken with a violent seizure during which his uncontrollably flailing body bumped the chair away from Garratt?

2. What if Dailey had pulled away the chair to use it, not knowing that Garratt was about to sit down?

3. What if an ordinary reasonable person would have noticed that Garratt was about to sit on the chair and so would not have pulled it out, but Dailey carelessly pulled out the chair without watching what he was doing and so not noticing that Garratt was about to be seated?

4. What if Dailey had pulled out the chair because Dailey wanted to use it, knowing that Garratt was about to sit on the chair and figuring that Garratt almost certainly would hit the ground, but actually hoping that Garratt would not hit the ground?

5. What if Dailey believed that Garratt would find his joke very funny, that she would not be hurt and that she would not be offended?

6. What if Dailey had thought that Garratt should be exercising instead of sitting down and so pulled out the chair for Garratt's benefit?

7. What if Dailey had pulled out the chair figuring that Garratt would be able to avoid contact with the ground but hoping that Garratt would in fact hit the ground?

8. What if a reasonable person would know that Garratt was substantially certain to hit the ground, but little Dailey did not know?

9. What if Dailey guessed correctly and Garratt did not hit the ground?

WAGNER V. STATE
122 P.3D 599 (UTAH 2005)

BACKGROUND

¶ 3 Tracy Wagner was standing in a customer service line at a K-Mart . . . when she was suddenly and inexplicably attacked from behind. The Wagners alleged that Sam Giese, a mentally disabled patient of the Utah State Development Center ("USDC"), "became violent, took [Mrs. Wagner] by the head and hair, threw her to the ground, and otherwise acted in such a way as to cause serious bodily injury to her." . . .

¶ 5 Mrs. Wagner and her husband subsequently filed a complaint against USDC and the Utah Department of Human Services, the state agency under which USDC operates, for failing to "properly supervise the activity of" Mr. Giese while he was in its care. Because the defendants to this matter are all governmental entities, they moved to dismiss the complaint . . . arguing that Mrs. Wagner's injuries arose out of a battery, a tort for which the government is immune from suit. . . . The district court agreed with the government and dismissed the Wagners' complaint, holding that because Giese initiated a contact with "deliberate" intent, his attack constituted a battery and the government was immune under the statute. . . .

ANALYSIS

I. Governmental Immunity Act

¶ 10 . . . At the time of the incident in this case, the Governmental Immunity Act read as follows:
Immunity from suit of all governmental entities is waived for injury proximately caused by a negligent act or omission of an employee committed within the scope of employment except if the injury arises out of . . . :
(2) assault, battery, [or] false imprisonment. . . .
Utah Code Ann. § 63-30-10(2) (Utah 1997) (repealed 2004).

¶ 11 This court has previously held in governmental immunity cases that the State is immunized against a negligence action if the action arises out of an assault or battery. . . .

¶ 14 The Wagners argue that Mr. Giese's attack could not legally constitute a battery because that intentional tort requires the actor to intend harm or offense through his deliberate contact, an intent Mr. Giese was mentally incompetent to form. The State, on the other hand, argues that the only intent required under the statute is simply the intent to make a contact. The contact must be harmful or offensive by law, but the actor need not intend harm so long as he intended contact.

¶ 15 The outcome of this case, then, turns upon which interpretation of the definition of battery is correct. Accordingly, we turn our attention now to the law of battery as defined in the Restatement.

II. The Restatement Definition Of Battery

¶ 16 While there is some variation among the definitions of the tort of battery . . . , Utah has adopted the Second Restatement of Torts to define the elements of this intentional tort, including the element of intent. . . . The Restatement reads:
An actor is subject to liability to another for battery if

(a) he acts intending to cause a harmful or offensive contact with the person of the other or a third person, or an imminent apprehension of such a contact, and

(b) a harmful contact with the person of the other directly or indirectly results.
Restatement (Second) of Torts § 13 (1965).

¶ 17 The only point of dispute in this case is whether the language of the Restatement requires Mr. Giese to have intended not only to make physical contact with Mrs. Wagner, which the Wagners concede he did, but also to have intended the contact to be harmful or offensive. In other words, is a battery committed only when the actor intends for his contact to harm or offend, or is it sufficient that the actor deliberately make physical contact, which contact is harmful or offensive by law? Determining the answer requires a careful dissection of the elements of battery and the meaning of intent.

¶ 18 We conclude that the plain language of the Restatement, the comments to the Restatement, Prosser and Keeton's exhaustive explanation of the meaning of intent as described in the Restatement, and the majority of case law on the subject in all jurisdictions including Utah, compels us to agree with the State that only intent to make contact is necessary.

¶ 19 In order for a contact to constitute a battery at civil law, two elements must be satisfied. First, the contact must have been deliberate. Second, the contact must have been harmful or offensive at law. We hold that the actor need not intend that his contact be harmful or offensive in order to commit a battery so long as he deliberately made the contact and so long as that contact satisfies our legal test for what is harmful or offensive. . . .

¶ 22 The Restatement defines a battery as having occurred where "[an actor] acts intending to cause a harmful or offensive contact." Restatement (Second) of Torts § 13. The comments to the definition of battery refer the reader to the definition of intent in section 8A. *Id.* § 13 cmt. c. Section 8A reads: "The word 'intent' is used throughout the Restatement of this Subject to denote that the actor desires to cause the consequences of his act, or that he believes that the consequences are substantially certain to result from it." *Id.* § 8A (emphasis added).

¶ 23 Although this language might not immediately seem to further inform our analysis, the comments to this section do illustrate the difference between an intentional act and an unintentional one: the existence of intent as to the contact that results from the act. Because much of the confusion surrounding the intent element required in an intentional tort arises from erroneously conflating the act with the consequence intended, we must clarify these basic terms as they are used in our law before we analyze the legal significance of intent as to an act versus intent as to the consequences of that act.

¶ 24 Section 2 of the Restatement (Second) of Torts defines the term "act" as "an external manifestation of the actor's will and does not include any of its results, even the most direct, immediate, and intended." *Id.* § 2. To illustrate this point, the comments clarify that when an actor points a pistol at another person and pulls the trigger, the act is the pulling of the trigger. *Id.* at cmt. c. The consequence of that act is the "impingement of the bullet upon the other's person." *Id.* It would be improper to describe the act as "the shooting," since the shooting is actually the conflation of the act with the consequence. For another example, the act that has taken place when one intentionally strikes another with his fist "is only the movement of the actor's hand and not the contact with the other's body immediately established." *Id.* Thus, presuming that the movement was voluntary rather than spastic, whether an actor has committed an intentional or negligent contact with another, and thus a tort sounding in battery or negligence, depends not upon whether he intended to move his hand, but upon whether he intended to make contact thereby.

¶ 25 The example the Restatement sets forth to illustrate this point is that of an actor firing a gun into the Mojave Desert. Restatement (Second of Torts) § 8A cmt. a. In both accidental and intentional shootings, the actor intended to pull the trigger. *Id.* Battery liability, rather than liability sounding in negligence, will attach only when the actor pulled the trigger in order to shoot another person, or knowing that it was substantially likely that pulling the trigger would lead to that result. *Id.* § 8A cmts. a & b. An actor who intentionally fires a bullet, but who does not realize that the bullet would make contact with another person, as when "the bullet hits a person who is present in the desert without the actor's knowledge," is not liable for an intentional tort. *Id.*

¶ 26 A hunter, for example, may intentionally fire his gun in an attempt to shoot a bird, but may accidentally shoot a person whom he had no reason to know was in the vicinity. He intended his act, pulling the trigger, but not the contact between his bullet and the body of another that resulted from that act. Thus, he intended the act but not the consequence. It is the consequential contact with the other person that the actor must either intend or be substantially certain would result, not the act-pulling the trigger-itself. He is therefore not liable for an intentional tort because his intentional act resulted in an unintended contact. On the other hand, the actor is liable for an intentional tort if he pulled the trigger intending that the bullet released thereby would strike someone, or knowing that it was substantially likely to strike someone as a result of his act. *Id.* at cmts. a & b.

¶ 27 Can an actor who acknowledges that he intentionally pulled the trigger, and did so with the intent that the bullet make contact with the person of another, defeat a battery charge if he can show that he did so only as a joke, or did not intend that the contact between the bullet and the body of the person would cause harm or offense to that person? The Wagners argue that such a showing would provide a full defense to a battery charge because the actor lacked the necessary intent to harm.

¶ 28 We agree with the Wagners that not all intentional contacts are actionable as batteries, and that the contact must be harmful or offensive in order to be actionable. We do not agree, however, that, under our civil law, the actor must appreciate that his act is harmful or offensive in order for his contact to constitute a battery. Before we resort to case law to interpret the language and application of our battery law, we can simply turn first to the plain language of the law itself for a clear refutation of the Wagners' theory.

¶ 29 The plain language of the comments makes clear that the only intent required to commit a battery is the intent to make a contact, not an intent to harm, injure, or offend through that contact. Restatement (Second) of Torts § 13. So long as the actor intended the contact, "it is immaterial that the actor is not inspired by any personal hostility to the other, or a desire to injure him." *Id.* § 13 cmt. c. The actor will be liable for battery even if he honestly but "erroneously believe[d] that ... the other has, in fact, consented to [the contact]." *Id.* In fact, even a healing contact motivated by a helpful intent, as in an act of medical assistance, is actionable as a battery if the actor did not in fact have permission to make the contact. *Id.* The linchpin to liability for battery is not a guilty mind, but rather an intent to make a contact the law forbids. The actor need not appreciate that his contact is forbidden; he need only intend the contact, and the contact must, in fact, be forbidden.

¶ 30 The Restatement comments illustrate this principle using two examples. In the first, an actor playing a good-natured practical joke, under the mistaken belief that he has his victim's consent to make the contact, has committed a battery. *Id.* In the second example, the healing contact of a physician, acting with helpful intent but against the patient's wishes, constituted a battery. *Id.* The fact that the procedure preserved the patient's life does not change the result. *Id.*; *see, e.g., . . .* Mohr v. Williams, 95 Minn. 261, 104 N.W. 12, 16 (1905) . . . .

¶ 31 If a physician who has performed a life-saving act of assistance upon an unconsenting patient with the hope of making that patient whole is liable for battery under the express terms of the Restatement, and a practical joker who makes a contact which he thinks will be taken as a joke or to which he thinks his victim has actually given consent is likewise liable, we cannot then say that other actors must intend harm through their deliberate contact in order to perfect a battery. It is beyond argument that the Restatement itself requires neither a "desire to injure" nor a realization that the contact is injurious or offensive. Restatement (Second) of Torts § 13. Instead, the actor need only intend the contact itself, and that contact must fit the legal definition of harmful or offensive.

¶ 32 Prosser echoed the Restatement when he clarified that "[t]he intent with which tort liability is concerned is not necessarily a hostile intent, or a desire to do harm. Rather, it is an intent to bring about a result which will invade the interests of another in a way that the law forbids." Prosser, *supra,* § 8, at 36. While it may be argued that this statement means that the actor must intend that the contact be forbidden, all ambiguity on the point is eviscerated by Prosser's next comment, in which he lists as one type of intentional tort the act of "intentionally invading the rights of another under a mistaken belief of committing no wrong." *Id.* § 8, at 37.

¶ 33 Though Prosser recognizes that the plaintiff will often recover to the greatest extent "where the [defendant's] motive is a malevolent desire to do harm," he nonetheless ascribes the malevolence to motive, not intent, and labels the less culpable act of innocent invasion of another's rights as an intentional invasion. *Id.* These comments only underscore the point repeated throughout both the Restatement and Prosser's analysis that the only intent required is the intent to make a contact to which the recipient has not consented, and the actor need not appreciate that the victim has not consented.

¶ 34 In Prosser's analysis of battery itself, he states that, in order for the contact to constitute a battery, "[t]he act must cause, and must be intended to cause, an unpermitted contact." *Id.* § 9, at 41. In discussing the difference between battery and mere negligence, he focused upon "the risk that contact will result" from the act, not the risk that harm would result from the contact. *Id.* Yet, if battery required an intent to harm or offend, or to realize that the contact was harmful or offensive or otherwise unpermitted, the proper focus of a discussion distinguishing between negligent and intentional conduct would be upon the risk that harm or offense would result from the contact. Instead, the focus was upon whether the contact itself, not the harm resulting therefrom, was intended or resulted from mere inadvertence.

¶ 35 The Wagners' argument that an actor lacks intent to commit a battery where he deliberately makes physical contact that is harmful or offensive so long as he does not realize his contact is harmful or offensive is simply in direct conflict with the commentaries in the Restatement itself and other commentaries on the law. As Prosser states, "a defendant may be liable [for battery] when intending only a joke, or even a compliment, as where an unappreciated kiss is bestowed without consent, or a misguided effort is made to render assistance." *Id.* § 9, 41-42.

¶ 36 The Wagners' theory is also in conflict with the majority of case law on the subject in both federal and state courts . . . . *See, e.g., . . . Polmatier v. Russ,* 206 Conn. 229, 537 A.2d 468, 469-70 (1988). . . .

¶ 45 Otherwise, the law would err on the side of protecting actors who voluntarily make physical contacts with other people, producing injury or offense, from liability for their deliberate action. The result would be that the victims who were subjected to a harmful or offensive physical contact are at the mercy of those who deliberately come into contact with them, and must bear the costs of the injuries inflicted thereby. The practical consequences of such an interpretation would turn the law of our civil liability on its head.

¶ 46 For example, a man who decides to flatter a woman he spots in a crowd with an unpetitioned-for kiss, one of the examples of battery Prosser provides, Prosser, *supra,* § 9, at 41-42, would find no objection under the Wagners' proposed rule so long as his intentional contact was initiated with no intent to injure or offend. He would be held civilly liable for his conduct only if he intended to harm or offend her through his kiss. A woman in such circumstances would not enjoy the presumption of the law in favor of preserving her bodily integrity; instead, her right to be free from physical contact with strangers would depend upon whether she could prove that the stranger hoped to harm or offend her through his contact. So long as he could show that he meant only flattery and the communication of positive feelings towards her in stroking her, kissing her, or hugging her, she must be subjected to it and will find no protection for her bodily integrity in our civil law.

¶ 47 The law would serve to insulate perpetrators of deliberate contact from the consequences their contact inflicts upon their victims. Bodily integrity would be secondary to protecting a perpetrator's right to deliberately touch another person's body without being accountable for the consequences that contact occasioned. The "harmful or offensive" element would, in essence, be viewed from the perspective of the actor, not the objective eye of the law. Under this rule, so long as the actor does not deem his deliberate contact to be harmful or offensive, he may touch others however he wishes without liability under our law of battery. It is clear that the purpose of our civil law on battery was designed to create the opposite incentive. *See, e.g.,* Restatement (Second) of Torts § 283B cmts. b & c.

¶ 48 The objection can be raised that such a theory of liability as we posit today expands liability beyond all reasonable bounds. Perhaps a handshake or other similar gesture will now expose a person to a lawsuit for battery if he happens to unknowingly shake the hand of an unwilling individual. The Restatement, however, and Prosser's analysis thereof, yields this objection wholly without basis.

¶ 49 We must bear in mind that not all physical contacts deliberately initiated constitute batteries, only harmful or offensive ones. Though it is true that the actor need not appreciate that his contact is, nor need he intend it to be, harmful or offensive in order for it to be so and for him to be accountable for the injuries he inflicted by his intentional contact, the contact must in fact be harmful or offensive in order to constitute a battery.

¶ 50 We now explain that the legal test for harmful or offensive contact preserves the Restatement's purpose of protecting the bodily integrity of individuals from invasion while still recognizing the practical realities of our physical world and the inevitable contacts therein. Because "harmful or offensive contact" is determined objectively by the law, only those deliberate contacts that meet the legal test for harmful or offensive will constitute batteries. . . .

¶ 62 The policy behind the Restatement definition of battery is to allow plaintiffs to recover from individuals who have caused them legal harm or injury, and to lay at the feet of the perpetrators the expense of their own conduct. Lawmakers have specifically declined to exempt mentally handicapped or insane individuals from the list of possible perpetrators of this tort for the express reason that they would prefer that the caretakers of such individuals feel heightened responsibility to ensure that their charges do not attack or otherwise injure members of the public. . . .

¶ 64 Applying the rule we have laid out today to the facts of this case, it is clear that Mr. Giese's attack constituted a battery upon Mrs. Wagner. There is no allegation that his action was the result of an involuntary muscular movement or spasm. Further, the Wagners concede that Mr. Giese affirmatively attacked her; they do not argue that he made muscular movements that inadvertently or accidentally brought him into contact with her.

¶ 65 The fact that the Wagners allege that Mr. Giese could not have intended to harm her, or understood that his attack would inflict injury or offense, is not relevant to the analysis of whether a battery occurred. So long as he intended to make that contact, . . . he committed a battery. Because battery is a tort for which the State has retained immunity, we affirm the court of appeals' decision to dismiss the case for failure to state a claim. . . .

NOTE AND QUESTIONS

1   Ironically, this particular plaintiff is better off from a litigation standpoint if the attacker injured him negligently than if the attack is characterized as an intentional tort. That is due to the impact of the doctrine of sovereign immunity, and is not relevant to our purposes here.

2   Is the court's holding consistent with the language of the cited Restatement provisions? Is it consistent with the new Restatement (Third) of Torts?

3   Some states require the battery plaintiff to prove that defendant both intended to touch the plaintiff's body and intended that the touching cause harm or offense.

a. INCAPACITY

POLMATIER V. RUSS
537 A.2D 468 (CONN. 1988)

The principal issue on this appeal is whether an insane person is liable for an intentional tort. The plaintiff, Dorothy Polmatier, executrix of the estate of her deceased husband, Arthur R. Polmatier, brought this action against the defendant, Norman Russ, seeking to recover damages for wrongful death.

. . . On the afternoon of November 20, 1976, the defendant and his two month old daughter visited the home of Arthur Polmatier, his father-in-law. . . . During the early evening Robert noticed a disturbance in the living room where he saw the defendant astride Polmatier on a couch beating him on the head with a beer bottle . . . . Thereafter, the defendant went into Polmatier's bedroom where he took a box of 30-30 caliber ammunition from the bottom drawer of a dresser and went to his brother-in-law's bedroom where he took a 30-30 caliber Winchester rifle from the closet. He then returned to the living room and shot Polmatier twice, causing his death.

About five hours later, the defendant was found sitting on a stump in a wooded area approximately one half mile from the Polmatier home. The defendant was naked and his daughter was in his arms wrapped in his clothes, and was crying.

. . . The defendant was charged with the crime of murder . . . but was found not guilty by reason of insanity . . . . Dr. Walter Borden, a psychiatrist, . . . testified that, at the time of the homicide, the defendant was suffering from a severe case of paranoid schizophrenia that involved . . . auditory hallucinations. He concluded that the defendant was legally insane and could not form a rational choice but that he could make a schizophrenic or crazy choice. . . . The trial court found that at the time of the homicide the defendant was insane.

The . . . complaint for the wrongful death of Polmatier alleged . . . that the death resulted from an assault, beating and shooting by the defendant . . . . The defendant . . . asserted ... as to all counts, the defendant was non compos mentis at the time . . . and, therefore, not capable of forming the intent necessary for tort liability . . . . After a trial to the court, the court found for the plaintiff on the first count and awarded compensatory damages. . . .

Connecticut has never directly addressed the issue of whether an insane person is civilly liable for an intentional tort.[1] The majority of jurisdictions that have considered this issue have held insane persons liable for their intentional torts. *See* 4 Restatement (Second), Torts § 895J. . . . The majority rule has been applied to cases involving intentional homicide. . . . The majority rule is not . . . without criticism. . . . Nonetheless, we are persuaded by the proponents of the majority rule, especially when the cases in which it has been applied are examined.

A leading case is *Seals* v. *Snow*, 123 Kan. 88, 254 P. 348 (1927). In *Seals*, the widow of Arthur Seals brought a civil action against Martin Snow to recover damages for the death of her husband. Several interrogatories were submitted to the jury, including: "Was Martin Snow insane when he shot Arthur Seals? A. Yes. If you answer the last question in the affirmative, was Martin Snow at the time he shot Arthur Seals able to distinguish right from wrong? A. No." *Id.,* 89. The jury returned a verdict for the plaintiff. In upholding the ensuing judgment, the Kansas Supreme Court stated: "The defendant challenges the doctrine generally sustained by the courts that an insane person is liable to make compensation for his torts. It is conceded that the great weight of authority is that an insane person is civilly liable for his torts. This liability has been based on a number of grounds, one that where one of two innocent persons must suffer a loss, it should be borne by the one who occasioned it. Another, that public policy requires the enforcement of such liability in order that relatives of the insane person shall be led to restrain him and that tort-feasors shall not simulate or pretend insanity to defend their wrongful acts causing damage to others, and that if he was not liable there would be no redress for injuries, and we might have the anomaly of an insane person having abundant wealth depriving another of his rights without compensation." *Id.,* 90.

Like *Seals,* another homicide case applying the majority rule is *McIntyre* v. *Sholty*, 121 Ill. 660, 13 N.E. 239 (1887), where recovery was allowed against an insane person's estate for the wrongful killing of the plaintiff's wife. The court reasoned: "There is, to be sure, an appearance of hardship in compelling one to respond for that which he is unable to avoid for want of the

---

1   Under the Restatement (Second) of Torts § 283B is the following: "Comment:

    a. If the actor is a child, his mental deficiency is taken into account. *See* § 283 A.

    b. The rule that a mentally deficient adult is liable for his torts is an old one, dating back at least to 1616, at a time when the action for trespass rested upon the older basis of strict liability, without regard to any fault of the individual. Apart from mere historical survival, its persistence in modern law has been explained on a number of different grounds. These are as follows:

       1. The difficulty of drawing any satisfactory line between mental deficiency and those variations of temperament, intellect, and emotional balance which cannot, as a practical matter, be taken into account in imposing liability for damage done.

       2. The unsatisfactory character of the evidence of mental deficiency in many cases, together with the ease with which it can be feigned, the difficulties which the triers of fact must encounter in determining its existence, nature, degree, and effect; and some fear of introducing into the law of torts the confusion which has surrounded such a defense in the criminal law. Although this factor may be of decreasing importance with the continued development of medical and psychiatric science, it remains at the present time a major obstacle to any allowance for mental deficiency.

       3. The feeling that if mental defectives are to live in the world they should pay for the damage they do, and that it is better that their wealth, if any, should be used to compensate innocent victims than that it should remain in their hands.

       4. The belief that their liability will mean that those who have charge of them or their estates will be stimulated to look after them, keep them in order, and see that they do not do harm.

    c. Insane persons are commonly held liable for their intentional torts. While there are very few cases, the same rule has been applied to their negligence. As to mental deficiency falling short of insanity, as in the case of stupidity, lack of intelligence, excitability, or proneness to accident, no allowance is made, and the actor is held to the standard of conduct of a reasonable man who is not mentally deficient, even though it is in fact beyond his capacity to conform to it.

control of reason. But the question of liability in these cases is one of public policy. If an insane person is not held liable for his torts, those interested in his estate, as relatives or otherwise, might not have a sufficient motive to so take care of him as to deprive him of opportunities for inflicting injuries upon others. There is more injustice in denying to the injured party the recovery of damages for the wrong suffered by him, than there is in calling upon the relatives or friends of the lunatic to pay the expense of his confinement, if he has an estate ample enough for that purpose. The liability of lunatics for their torts tends to secure a more efficient custody and guardianship of their persons. Again, if parties can escape the consequences of their injurious acts upon the plea of lunacy, there will be a strong temptation to simulate insanity with a view of masking the malice and revenge of an evil heart." *Id.*, 664-65.

Our adoption of the majority rule holding insane persons civilly liable, in appropriate circumstances, for their intentional torts finds support in other Connecticut case law. We have elsewhere recognized the vitality of the common law principle that "'where one of two innocent persons must suffer loss from an act done, it is just that it should fall on the one who caused the loss rather than upon the other who had no agency in producing it and could not by any means have avoided it.'" *Verrilli* v. *Damilowski*, 140 Conn. 358, 360, 100 A.2d 462 (1953), citing *Granniss* v. *Weber*, 107 Conn. 622, 625, 141 A. 877 (1928) . . . .

We now turn to the defendant's claim that the trial court should have applied a two-pronged analysis to his claim. The first prong is whether the defendant intended the act that produced the injury. The defendant argues that for an act to be done with the requisite intent, the act must be an external manifestation of the actor's will. The defendant specifically relies on the Restatement (Second) of Torts §14, comment b, for the definition of what constitutes an "act," where it is stated that "a muscular movement which is purely reflexive or the convulsive movements of an epileptic are not acts in the sense in which that word is used in the Restatement. So too, movements of the body during sleep or while the will is otherwise in abeyance are not acts. An external manifestation of the will is necessary to constitute an act, and an act is necessary to make one liable [for a battery]. . . ." The defendant argues that if his "activities were the external manifestations of irrational and uncontrollable thought disorders these activities cannot be acts for purposes of establishing liability for assault and battery." We disagree.

We note that we have not been referred to any evidence indicating that the defendant's acts were reflexive, convulsive or epileptic. Furthermore, under the Restatement (Second) of Torts § 2, "act" is used "to denote an external manifestation of the actor's will and does not include any of its results, even the most direct, immediate, and intended." Comment b to this section provides in pertinent part: "A muscular reaction is always an act unless it is a purely reflexive reaction in which the mind and will have no share." Although the trial court found that the defendant could not form a rational choice, it did find that he could make a schizophrenic or crazy choice. Moreover, a rational choice is not required since "[a]n insane person may have an intent to invade the interests of another, even though his reasons and motives for forming that intention may be entirely irrational." 4 Restatement (Second), Torts § 895J, comment c. The following example is given in the Restatement to illustrate the application of comment c: "A, who is insane believes that he is Napoleon Bonaparte, and that B, his nurse, who confines him in his room, is an agent of the Duke of Wellington, who is endeavoring to prevent his arrival on the field of Waterloo in time to win the battle. Seeking to escape, he breaks off the leg of a chair, attacks B with it and fractures her skull. A is subject to liability to B for battery."

We recognize that the defendant made conflicting statements about the incident when discussing the homicide. At the hospital on the evening of the homicide the defendant told a police officer that his father-in-law was a heavy drinker and that he used the beer bottle for that reason. He stated he wanted to make his father-in-law suffer for his bad habits and so that he would realize the wrong that he had done. He also told the police officer that he was a supreme being and had the power to rule the destiny of the world and could make his bed fly out of the window. When interviewed by Dr. Borden, the defendant stated that he believed that his father-in-law was a spy for the red Chinese and that he believed his father-in-law was not only going to kill him, but going to harm his infant child so that he killed his father-in-law in self-defense. The explanations given by the defendant for committing the homicide are similar to the illustration of irrational reasons and motives given in comment c to § 895J of the Restatement, set out above.

Under these circumstances we are persuaded that the defendant's behavior at the time of the beating and shooting of Polmatier constituted an "act" within the meaning of comment b, § 2, of the Restatement. Following the majority rule in this case, we conclude that the trial court implicitly determined that the defendant committed an "act" in beating and shooting Polmatier. Accordingly, the trial court did not err. . . .

QUESTIONS

1 How could this insane defendant have the intent that battery requires?
2 Would it have made any difference if defendant had thought that the winchester rifle were a magic wand and that by pulling the trigger he would cause plaintiff to disappear?

b. MISTAKE

RANSON V. KITNER
31 Ill. App. 241 (1889)

This was an action brought . . . to recover the value of a dog killed by appellants, and a judgment rendered for $50.

The defense was that appellants were hunting for wolves, that appellee's dog had a striking resemblance to a wolf, that they in good faith believed it to be one, and killed it as such. . . .

The jury held [Appellants] liable for the value of the dog, and we do not see how they could have done otherwise under the evidence. Appellants are clearly liable for the damages caused by their mistake, notwithstanding they were acting in good faith.

We see no reason for interfering with the conclusion reached by the jury, and the judgment will be affirmed.

c. TRANSFERRED INTENT

ALTEIRI V. COLASSO
362 A.2D 798 (CONN. 1975)

This action is one for battery brought by a minor, the plaintiff Richard Alteiri, to recover for injuries he suffered, and by his mother, the named plaintiff, to recover for expenses incurred. The complaint alleges that while the minor plaintiff was playing in the back yard of a home at which he was visiting, the defendant threw a rock, stone or other missile into the yard and struck the minor plaintiff in the eye and "(a)s a result of said battery by the defendant, the plaintiff Richard Alteiri suffered severe, painful and permanent injuries."

Six interrogatories were submitted to the jury. Two interrogatories were answered in the affirmative as follws: "On April 2, 1966, did the defendant, John Colasso, throw a stone which struck the plaintiff, Richard Alteiri, in the right eye?" Answer: "Yes." "(W)as that stone thrown by John Colasso with the intent to scare any person other than Richard Alteiri?" Answer: "Yes." The jury answered "No" to four other questions concerning whether the defendant had intended to strike either the minor plaintiff or any other person and whether he had thrown the stone either negligently or wantonly and recklessly. A plaintiffs' verdict was returned. The defendant has appealed from the judgment rendered.

. . . The defendant claims that the jury could not have reasonably and logically rendered a verdict under our law when in their answers to the interrogatories they expressly found that the defendant did not throw the stone with intent to strike either the minor plaintiff or any other person and did not throw the stone either negligently or wantonly and recklessly. . . . By their answers to the interrogatories it is clear that the jury found that the battery to the minor plaintiff was one committed willfully. The issue to be determined on this appeal is whether a jury upon finding that the defendant threw the stone with the intent to scare someone other than the one who was struck by the stone can legally and logically return a verdict for the plaintiffs for a willful battery.

. . . The intention of the defendant was not only to throw the stone–the act resulting in the injury was intentional–but his intention was also to cause a resulting injury, that is, an apprehension of bodily harm. If the stone had struck the one whom the defendant had intended to frighten, the defendant would have been liable for a battery. . . . It is not essential that the precise injury which was done be the one intended. . . . An act designed to cause bodily injury to a particular person is actionable as a battery not only by the person intended by the actor to be injured but also by another who is in fact so injured. . . . This principle of "transferred intent" applies as well to the action of assault. . . . And where one intends merely an assault, if bodily injury results to one other than the person whom the actor intended to put in apprehension of bodily harm, it is battery actionable by the injured person. . . .

It follows that the jury could logically and legally return a plaintiffs' verdict for wilful battery, and that the court in accepting that verdict and denying the defendant's motions was not in error.

There is no error.

NOTE

1   *Transferred Intent. Alteiri v. Colasso* is an example of the application of the well-established and generally-accepted doctrine of transferred intent. This doctrine has been carried over to the Restatement (Third) of Torts. Under the doctrine of transferred intent, the intent to invade one protected legal interest of one victim transfers to provide the necessary intent to make out a cause of action for a tort against an actual but unintended victim. In a less well-established application of the doctrine, it is thought to apply among five torts that spring from the ancient writ of trespass *vi et armis*: battery, assault, false imprisonment, trespass to chattels, and trespass to land. Defendant's intent to commit any one supplies the intent necessary to support a cause of action for any of the others. In *Alteiri v. Colasso*, the court found that even if defendant did not intend to cause contact with the body of any person, defendant did intend to put another in imminent apprehension of such contact. Such intent would be sufficient under the doctrine of transferred intent to make out any of the other four transferred intent causes of action. However, this aspect of transferred intent was unnecessary under the Restatement's version of battery because the intent required for battery is precisely the same as the intent required for assault. Here, only the transfer of intent between victims came into play.

3. HARMFUL OR OFFENSIVE CONTACT

The tort of battery requires not only a volitional act by the defendant that is intended to result in contact with the plaintiff. In addition, the intended contact must, in fact, result, either directly or indirectly.

FISHER V. CARROUSEL MOTOR HOTEL
424 SW2D 627 (TEX. 1967)

. . . The plaintiff Fisher was a mathematician with . . . an agency of . . . NASA, near Houston. The defendants were the Carrousel Motor Hotel, Inc., located in Houston, the Brass Ring Club, which is located in the Carrousel, and Robert W. Flynn, who as an employee of the Carrousel was the manager of the Brass Ring Club. . . . Trial was to a jury which found for the plaintiff Fisher. The trial court rendered judgment for the defendants notwithstanding the verdict. . . .

The [question] before this Court [is] whether there was evidence that an actionable battery was committed . . . .

The plaintiff Fisher had been invited by Ampex Corporation and Defense Electronics to a one day's meeting regarding telemetry equipment at the Carrousel. The invitation included a luncheon. . . . The luncheon was buffet style, and Fisher stood in line with others . . . . As Fisher was about to be served, he was approached by Flynn, who snatched the plate from Fisher's hand and shouted that he, a Negro, could not be served in the club. Fisher testified that he was not actually touched, and did not testify that he suffered fear or apprehension of physical injury; but he did testify that he was highly embarrassed and hurt by Flynn's conduct in the presence of his associates. The jury found that Flynn "forcibly dispossessed plaintiff of his dinner plate" and "shouted in a loud and offensive manner" that Fisher could not be served there, thus subjecting Fisher to humiliation and indignity. . . .

> [I]t has long been settled that actual physical contact is not necessary to constitute a battery, so long as there is contact with clothing or an object closely identified with the body. . . . Restatement of Torts 2d, §§ 18 and 19. . . . Under the facts of this case, we have no difficulty in holding that the intentional grabbing of plaintiff's plate constituted a battery. The intentional snatching of an object from one's hand is as clearly an offensive invasion of his person as would be an actual contact with the body. . . .

The rationale for holding an offensive contact with such an object to be a battery is explained in 1 Restatement of Torts 2d § 18 (Comment p. 31) as follows:

> Since the essence of the plaintiff's grievance consists in the offense to the dignity involved in the unpermitted and intentional invasion of the inviolability of his person and not in any physical harm done to his body, it is not necessary that the plaintiff's actual body be disturbed. Unpermitted and intentional contacts with anything so connected with the body as to be customarily regarded as part of the other's person and therefore as partaking of its inviolability is actionable as an offensive contact with his person. There are some things such as clothing or a cane or, indeed, anything directly grasped by the hand which are so intimately connected with one's body as to be universally regarded as part of the person.

We hold, therefore, that the forceful dispossession of plaintiff Fisher's plate in an offensive manner was sufficient to constitute a battery, and the trial court erred in granting judgment notwithstanding the verdict . . . .

NOTES AND QUESTIONS

1   *Vicarious Liability.* This is the first of many examples that we will study where an employer is held "vicariously liable" for the conduct of its employee. We will study this doctrine of vicarious liability in some detail later in the course.

2   *Extended Personality.* This case provides a good illustration of the generous interpretation that courts give to the element of "bodily contact" through what is sometimes called the doctrine of *extended personality.* Essentially, items closely associated with plaintiff's body (here, the dinner plate) are treated as extensions of plaintiff's body for purposes of determining whether defendant has caused a contact with plaintiff's body. The tough question is whether the object that defendant contacts is sufficiently closely associated with plaintiff's body to be fairly treated as an extension of plaintiff's body.

3   What is the harm in this case? What if defendant here had done the very same thing without snatching the plate?

4   *Blowing Smoke.* Some borderline scenarios of physical touching have troubled courts. In the well-known case *Leichtman v. WLW Jacor Communications, Inc.*, 634 N.E.2d 697 (Ohio App. 1994), the plaintiff Leichtman, who claimed to be "a nationally known" antismoking advocate, alleged that "he was invited to appear on the WLW Bill Cunningham radio talk show" and "that, while he was in the studio, Furman, another WLW talk-show host, lit a cigar and repeatedly blew smoke in Leichtman's face 'for the purpose of causing physical discomfort, humiliation and distress.'" Leichtman contended that Furman's intentional act constituted a battery. The Ohio Court of Appeals held that "tobacco smoke, as 'particulate matter,' has the physical properties capable of making contact" and that "when Furman intentionally blew cigar smoke in Leichtman's face, . . . he committed a battery. No matter how trivial the incident, a battery is actionable, even if damages are only one dollar." The holding in *Leichtman* is consistent with holdings in other jurisdictions that have found a battery when one party intentionally blows tobacco smoke at another. The *Leichtman* court left open a more troubling question, which the court called "the theory of a 'smoker's battery,' which imposes liability if there is substantial certainty that exhaled smoke will predictably contact a nonsmoker." The Court worried over the potential implications if "the 'substantial certainty' prong of intent from the Restatement of Torts translates to liability for secondary smoke via the intentional tort." But the Court did not resolve those more difficult questions since "Leichtman's claim for battery is based exclusively on Furman's commission of a deliberate act." Other scenarios raise similar questions. For example, it has been held that injury caused by rapid increase in air pressure from an explosion constitutes an actionable bodily contact.

5   *Harmful or Offensive Contact.* What if the defendant in the above case had gently grasped the plate to take it from plaintiff's hand because defendant noticed that the plate was dirty? Would this constitute a battery? What if plaintiff had an irrational fear of anyone touching his plate and so was deeply disturbed by the touching? Would the irrational fear affect the potential battery case? What if defendant knew of plaintiff's irrational fear and so gently touched the plate for the very purpose of causing distress to plaintiff?

6   What constitutes harmful contact is fairly straightforward – any contact that results in injury to the body is harmful. However, judging the "offensiveness" of contact can be more challenging. The standard is an "objective" one, that is, the question is whether the contact, in the words of the Restatement, "offends a reasonable sense of personal dignity." The mere fact that the plaintiff in fact found the contact to be offensive is insufficient if most people would find the contact socially acceptable. The offensiveness inquiry is fact specific – all of the circumstances of the factual scenario must be taken into account in making the offensiveness judgment.

PAUL V. HOLBROOK
696 SO.2D 1311 (1997)

Meredith A. Paul ("Paul") appeals an order of the trial court granting summary judgment in favor of Professional Medical Products, Inc. ("PMP") and Paul Holbrook ("Holbrook") on Paul's claims against Holbrook and PMP for . . . battery . . . .

Paul and Holbrook are former employees of PMP. Paul testified that Holbrook was her co-worker and not her supervisor. On various occasions, Paul worked alone with Holbrook. During some of these times, Paul alleges that Holbrook harassed her by asking that she wear revealing clothing and suggesting that they engage in sexual relations. Paul claims that on two occasions, Holbrook came up behind her while she was working and tried to massage her shoulders. On both occasions, Paul immediately pulled away and told Holbrook to leave, which he did. After Paul complained to PMP's management, she and Holbrook never again worked the same shifts and his improper behavior toward her ended.

While Paul takes issue with the trial court's judgment in its entirety, we find merit only in Paul's contention that the trial judge erred in granting summary judgment on her battery claim against Holbrook . . . . A battery consists of the infliction of a harmful or offensive contact upon another with the intent to cause such contact or the apprehension that such contact is imminent. . . . Professor Prosser's treatise explains that the tort of battery exists to protect the integrity of the person. As Prosser & Keeton wrote in section 9:

> Proof of the technical invasion of the integrity of the plaintiff's person by even an entirely harm-less, but offensive contact entitles the plaintiff to vindication of the legal right by an award of nominal damages, and the establishment of the tort cause of action entitles the plaintiff also to compensation for the resulting mental disturbance, such as fright, revulsion or humiliation.

Id. (footnotes omitted). Once a contact has been established, its character becomes the focus:

> The element of personal indignity involved always has been given considerable weight. Consequently, the defendant is liable not only for contacts which do actual harm, but also for those relatively trivial ones which are merely offensive and insulting....

The time and place, and the circumstances under which the act is done, will necessarily affect its unpermitted character, and so will the relations between the parties. A stranger is not to be expected to tolerate liberties which would be allowed by an intimate friend. But unless the defendant has special reason to believe that more or less will be permitted by the individual plaintiff, the test is what would be offensive to an ordinary person not unduly sensitive to personal dignity.

Id. (footnotes omitted). Offensiveness is an essential element of the tort. The trial court . . . . concluded that, as a matter of law, Holbrook's actions were not offensive. . . . But, the act of approaching a co-worker from behind while on the job and attempting to massage her shoulders is, in the circumstances of this case, not capable of such summary treatment. On these facts, offensiveness is a question for the trier of fact to decide. . . .

The trial court also found that Paul failed to produce evidence establishing Holbrook's intent to commit a battery. Proof of intent to commit battery is rarely subject to direct proof, but must be established based on surrounding circumstances. . . . Based on the record before this court, a jury could reasonably infer that Holbrook intended to touch Paul in a matter that would constitute a battery. No evidence of an intention to cause harm is necessary.

The trial court properly granted summary judgment against Paul in all respects except with regard to the battery claim against Holbrook. On that claim, we reverse. In all other respects, we affirm the trial court's judgment. . . .

COHEN V. SMITH
648 N.E.2d 329 (Ill. App. 1995)

. . . Patricia Cohen was admitted to St. Joseph Memorial Hospital ("Hospital") to deliver her baby. After an examination, Cohen was informed that it would be necessary for her to have a cesarean section. Cohen and her husband allegedly informed her physician, who in turn advised the Hospital staff, that the couple's religious beliefs prohibited Cohen from being seen unclothed by a male. Cohen's doctor assured her husband that their religious convictions would be respected.

During Cohen's cesarean section, Roger Smith, a male nurse on staff at the Hospital, allegedly observed and touched Cohen's naked body. Cohen and her husband filed suit against Nurse Smith and the Hospital. The trial court allowed defendants' motions to dismiss. We reverse. . . .

The Restatement (Second) of Torts provides that an actor commits a battery if:

"(a) he acts intending to cause a harmful or offensive contact with the person of the other or a third person, or an imminent apprehension of such a contact, and

(b) a harmful contact with the person of the other directly or indirectly results." (Restatement (Second) of Torts, § 13 (1965).)

. . . "Offensive contact" is said to occur when the contact "offends a reasonable sense of personal dignity." Restatement (Second) of Torts § 19 (1965).

Historically, battery was first and foremost a systematic substitution for private retribution. Protecting personal integrity has always been viewed as an important basis for battery. "Consequently, the defendant is liable not only for contacts which do actual physical harm, but also for those relatively trivial ones which are merely offensive and insulting." (Prosser, §9, at 41.) This application of battery to remedy offensive and insulting conduct is deeply ingrained in our legal history. . . . Causing actual physical harm is not an element of battery. "A plaintiff is entitled to demand that the defendant refrain from the offensive touching, although the contact results in no visible injury." Prosser, §9, at 41.

With these definitions in mind, we examine plaintiffs' allegations against Nurse Smith. . . . The plaintiffs' complaint against Nurse Smith alleges that Smith touched Cohen's naked body after being informed of her moral and religious beliefs against such touching by a male. Similarly, the plaintiffs' complaint against the Hospital alleges that the doctor performing the surgery told Nurse Smith that the operation was to be performed without any male seeing Cohen naked.

According to the complaint, despite being informed of Cohen's religious beliefs, Nurse Smith, an agent and employee of the Hospital, intentionally saw and touched Cohen's naked body. . . .

The allegation that both Nurse Smith and the Hospital were informed in advance of plaintiffs' religious beliefs is important in this case, because the religious convictions of plaintiffs might not be those of most people who enter the hospital to give birth. As a matter of fact, plaintiffs' counsel candidly conceded that there would be no cause of action for battery if Patricia Cohen had been placed in Nurse Smith's and the Hospital's care in an emergency situation in which Patricia had been unable to inform the Hospital or its agents of her beliefs. Plaintiffs' attorney acknowledged that his clients' moral and religious views are not widely held in the community and, because of this, plaintiffs could state a claim against defendants only if the plaintiffs plead that the defendants had knowledge of those beliefs. . . .

The fact that the plaintiffs hold deeply ingrained religious beliefs which are not shared by the majority of society does not mean that those beliefs deserve less protection than more mainstream religious beliefs. The plaintiffs were not trying to force their religion on other people; they were only insisting that their beliefs be respected by the Hospital and the Hospital staff. As we have stated previously, Patricia Cohen was not trying to, and was not entitled to, impose her religious beliefs on others. When she informed the Hospital of her moral and religious beliefs against being viewed and touched by males, the Hospital was free to refuse to accede to those demands. But, according to her complaint, when Cohen made her wishes known to the Hospital, it, at least implicitly, agreed to provide her with treatment within the restrictions placed by her beliefs.

Although most people in modern society have come to accept the necessity of being seen unclothed and being touched by members of the opposite sex during medical treatment, the plaintiffs had not accepted these procedures and, according to their complaint, had informed defendants of their convictions. This case is similar to cases involving Jehovah's Witnesses who were unwilling to accept blood transfusions because of religious convictions. Although most people do not share the Jehovah's Witnesses' beliefs about blood transfusions, our society, and our courts, accept their right to have that belief. Similarly, the courts have consistently recognized individuals' rights to refuse medical treatment even if such a refusal would result in an increased likelihood of the individual's death.

A person's right to refuse or accept medical care is not one to be interfered with lightly. As Justice Cardozo stated, "Every human being of adult years and sound mind has a right to determine what shall be done with his own body; and a surgeon who performs an operation without his patient's consent commits an assault, for which he is liable in damages." *Schloendorff v. Society of New York Hospital* (1914), 211 N.Y. 125, 105 N.E. 92.

Knowing interference with the right of determination is battery. Our examination of the record reveals that facts charging that interference are pleaded in plaintiffs' complaint against Nurse Smith and against the Hospital. For purposes of a motion on the pleadings, a court must accept these facts as true. [Case omitted.] Accepting as true the plaintiffs' allegations that they informed defendants of their religious beliefs and that defendants persisted in treating Patricia

Cohen as they would have treated a patient without those beliefs, we conclude that the trial court erred in dismissing . . . the battery . . . coun[t] . . . .

QUESTION

1   Does the appellate court's decision here mean that plaintiff wins the case?

B. ASSAULT

The tort law doctrine of assault protects the plaintiff's right to be free from the apprehension of an imminent battery. Thus, the intentional torts of battery and assault frequently go hand-in-hand. It may be useful to think of assault as either a threatened battery or a failed battery. Some authorities even confusingly use the terms "assault and battery" as a single phrase.

The tort of assault is an example of a trend in tort law that started hundreds of years ago and continues to this day. At the earliest recorded common law, the general rule was that if there was no physical contact, there was no tort. But some causes of action gradually developed to protect a plaintiff's dignity or right to be free from mental or emotional harm, even apart from any physical harm.

VETTER V. MORGAN
913 P.2d 1200 (Kan. App. 1995)

Laura Vetter . . . was alone at 1:30 or 1:45 a.m. when she stopped her van in the right-hand westbound lane of an intersection at a stoplight. [Chad] Morgan and [Dana] Gaither drove up beside Vetter. Morgan began screaming vile and threatening obscenities at Vetter, shaking his fist, and making obscene gestures in a violent manner. According to Vetter, Gaither revved the engine of the car and moved the car back and forth while Morgan was threatening Vetter. Vetter testified that Morgan threatened to remove her from her van and spat on her van door when the traffic light turned green. Vetter stated she was very frightened and thought Morgan was under the influence of drugs or alcohol. She was able to write down the license tag number of the car. Morgan stated he did not intend to scare, upset, or harm Vetter, but "didn't really care" how she felt. He was trying to amuse his friends, who were laughing at his antics.

When the traffic light changed to green, both vehicles drove forward. According to Vetter, after they had driven approximately 10 feet, the car driven by Gaither veered suddenly into her lane, and she reacted by steering her van sharply to the right. Vetter's van struck the curb, causing her head to hit the steering wheel and snap back against the seat, after which she fell to the floor of the van. Morgan and Gaither denied that the car veered into Vetter's lane, stating they drove straight away from the intersection and did not see Vetter's collision with the curb.

Vetter filed this action against Morgan and Gaither, alleging their . . . actions had caused her injuries. The trial court . . . concluded Morgan's actions did not constitute assault . . . and dismissed all claims against Morgan. . . .

The trial court concluded there was no evidence that Morgan threatened or attempted to harm Vetter, that he had no apparent ability to harm her because her van was locked and the windows were rolled up, and there was no claim of immediate apprehension of bodily harm. Vetter contends all of these conclusions involved questions of fact that should have been resolved by a jury.

There was evidence of a threat. Vetter testified in her deposition that Morgan verbally threatened to take her from her van. Ordinarily, words alone cannot be an assault. However, words can constitute assault if "together with other acts or circumstances they put the other in reasonable apprehension of imminent harmful or offensive contact with his person." Restatement (Second) of Torts § 31 (1964).

The record is sufficient to support an inference that Morgan's threat and the acts and circumstances surrounding it could reasonably put someone in Vetter's position in apprehension of imminent or immediate bodily harm. Morgan's behavior was so extreme that Vetter could reasonably have believed he would immediately try to carry out his threat. It is not necessary that the victim be placed in apprehension of instantaneous harm. It is sufficient if it appears there will be no significant delay. *See* Restatement (Second) of Torts § 29(1), comment b (1964).

The record also supports an inference that Morgan had the apparent ability to harm Vetter. Although Vetter's van was locked and the windows rolled up, the windows could be broken. The two vehicles were only six feet apart, and Morgan was accompanied by two other males. It was late at night, so witnesses and potential rescuers were unlikely. Although Vetter may have had the ability to flee by turning right, backing up, or running the red light, her ability to prevent the threatened harm by flight or self-defense does not preclude an assault. It is enough that Vetter believed that Morgan was capable of immediately inflicting the contact unless prevented by self-defense, flight, or intervention by others.

The trial court erred in concluding there was no evidence that Vetter was placed in apprehension of bodily harm. Whether Morgan's actions constituted an assault was a question of fact for the jury.

QUESTIONS AND COMMENTS

1   *Nature of Harm.* How was Plaintiff allegedly harmed? What if Plaintiff had taken no notice of Defendant's antics? Would the answer to the previous question differ if this were a case of criminal assault instead of civil assault? Should the answer be different? Why or why not?

2   *Intent Required.* Does it matter whether Defendant actually intended to touch Plaintiff? What intent is required for assault?

3　*"Assault and Battery."* As noted above, some courts use the words "assault" and "battery" together in one phrase as though there is no distinction between the two. This can cause confusion. The concepts of "assault" and "battery" are distinct, and the two tort causes of action guard different protected interests. Battery protects the plaintiff's right to bodily integrity. Assault protects the plaintiff's right to be free from threats of battery.

4　*Apprehension v. Fear.* Fear is not a necessarily element of assault. The meaning of the word "apprehension" required in the assault context is more like "expectation."

5　*Sticks and Stones.* Courts frequently have stated that words alone cannot constitute an assault. The Second Restatement says the same thing. What does this mean? Did Defendant's conduct here go beyond mere words?

6　*Imminent apprehension.* To allege an assault, plaintiff must plead that the apprehension that plaintiff suffered was of an "imminent" contact. What does "imminent" mean in this context?

7　*Reasonableness of Apprehension.* Some authorities say that only if plaintiff's apprehension is reasonable does defendant's conduct constitute an assault. Other authorities do not include "reasonableness" of the apprehension in the formulation of what constitutes an assault. Do you think that this makes much difference? Try to imagine an assault in which the apprehension is unreasonable. In your imagined scenario, are all of the other elements of assault present? In this case, was Vetter's apprehension reasonable?

TROGDON V. TERRY
90 S.E. 583 (N.C. 1916)

. . . In July, 1915, the plaintiff was in the hotel dining-room at Draper eating his dinner. The defendant finding that he was there, wrote out a so-called retraxit and went into the dining-room with his cane and compelled the plaintiff, by threats to do him bodily harm, to sign the paper against his will. . . . The defendant admitted that when he learned that the plaintiff was to take dinner in the hotel he wrote the paper which he called "an apology and retraction," and that then he picked up his walking stick and hung it on his arm, walked down to where the plaintiff was sitting; that he said to the plaintiff, "I want you to read this paper"; that plaintiff read it and asked, "What do you want me to do?" Defendant said: "I want you to sign it." Plaintiff said: "I will think about it." Defendant says: "No, you won't think about it; you are going to sign it now!" Plaintiff said: "Suppose I do not sign it?" Defendant says: "I will whip hell out of you!" Plaintiff says: "I have not read it, but I will sign it." Defendant says: "No, you are lying when you say you have not read it; but you can sign it that way."

Defendant picked up the paper and read it to plaintiff. Plaintiff signed it. Mr. Lindsay witnessed it. Defendant says: "Trogdon, I do not want to ever hear of your writing or saying anything else about me, you damned, contemptible puppy!"

There is evidence that while this was going on at the table the defendant had his walking stick on his arm or in his hand, ready for action.

. . . The contention that these facts do not constitute an assault cannot be maintained. It is well settled that where one person, by a show of violence and force, puts another in fear and forces him to leave a place where he has a right to be, or to commit some act which he otherwise would not perform, is guilty of an assault. . . . In the case under consideration the defendant approached the plaintiff in a public dining-room and with a walking stick, evidently with the purpose of using it unless the defendant signed the paper-writing. In a most violent and abusive manner, with his stick in view, he forced the plaintiff against his will to sign the paper. In our judgment, according to the defendant's own evidence, he was guilty of an unjustifiable assault upon the plaintiff . . . .

QUESTION

1   Wasn't Terry essentially assuring Trogdon that no harm would come to Trogdon so long as Trogdon signed the retraction?

C. FALSE IMPRISONMENT

The cause of action known as "false imprisonment" provides redress to the victim who has been wrongfully subjected to the indignity of confinement by another. The existence of a false imprisonment frequently turns on whether plaintiff has been confined within a bounded area. Like the other torts we have already studied, assault and battery, false imprisonment is considered a "trespassory" tort because it grew out of the ancient writ of trespass vi et armis.

False imprisonment is more like assault than like battery in at least one way. While the tort of battery guards the plaintiff's right to be free from unwanted touching, assault guards against a harm that is more dignitary than actual – the threat of unwanted touching. It often is suggested that the tort of false imprisonment protects the plaintiff's legal interest in freedom of movement, but this is inaccurate. The tort is perhaps better understood as protecting plaintiff's interest in being free from the indignity of being confined within a bounded area, as illustrated by the following case.

WEBBER V. FROEDTERT MEMORIAL LUTHERAN HOSPITAL
468 N.W.2D 211 (WIS. APP. 1991)

Lester Webber appeals from judgments dismissing his complaint alleging false imprisonment . . . against Dr. James A. Cerletty and Froedtert Memorial Lutheran Hospital (Froedtert Memorial). We affirm the judgments. . . . Mr. Webber's wife, Katherine Webber, was initially admitted to the Milwaukee County Medical Complex pursuant to a petition and order entered on March 27, 1987 by the circuit court . . . . The petition alleged that Mrs. Webber was in need of protective services in light of her husband's neglect in procuring medical treatment for her.

At the hearing on the petition, the trial court found that Mrs. Webber was in substantial danger of irreparable injury or harm because of her serious medical condition and her husband's neglect in arranging for the delivery of medical treatment to her. The court ordered that any hospital accepting Mrs. Webber as a patient for purposes of treatment was authorized to prevent Mr. Webber from visiting her if, in the opinion of the treating physician, his visitation was medically contra-indicated.

On March 31, 1987, Mrs. Webber was transferred to Froedtert Memorial. . . . Dr. Cerletty, Mrs. Webber's treating physician at Froedtert Memorial, did not issue an order barring Mr. Webber from his wife's room. Nevertheless, three members of the hospital's staff, two receptionists and one social worker, barred Mr. Webber from visiting his wife during her hospitalization. These staff members informed Mr. Webber that there were orders in the medical records forbidding him from seeing his wife.

On May 9, 1990, Mrs. Webber was transferred to a nursing home. She died there thirteen days later. Mr. Webber then initiated this lawsuit to challenge his exclusion from his wife's room at Froedtert Memorial. The trial court granted the defendants' respective motions for summary judgment.

. . . Our analysis of the tort of false imprisonment is governed by the Restatement (Second) of Torts sec. 35:

False Imprisonment

(1) An actor is subject to liability to another for false imprisonment if
   (a) he acts intending to confine the other or a third person within the boundaries fixed by the actor, and
   (b) his act directly or indirectly results in such a confinement of the other, and
   (c) the other is conscious of the confinement or is harmed by it.

Dupler v. Seubert, 69 Wis.2d 373, 382, 230 N.W.2d 626, 631 (1975). The essence of false imprisonment is unlawful and nonconsensual restraint. *Id.* at 381, 230 N.W.2d at 631.

The record before the trial court contained no evidence to show that Mr. Webber was confined in any way by either defendant. Absent entering his wife's hospital room, Mr. Webber was free to go where he pleased. Accordingly, Mr. Webber failed to submit *prima facie* proof in support of a key element necessary to his claim of false imprisonment. . . .

NOTE

1 *Confinement Within Bounded Area.* A key issue in some false imprisonment cases, as in *Webber,* is whether the facts that the plaintiff alleges actually constitute a "confinement" within the meaning of the false imprisonment tort. On this subject, consider the following Restatement definition of "confinement":

Restatement (Second) Torts §36. What Constitutes Confinement

(1) To make the actor liable for false imprisonment, the other's confinement within the boundaries fixed by the actor must be complete.

(2) The confinement is complete although there is a reasonable means of escape, unless the other knows of it.

(3) The actor does not become liable for false imprisonment by intentionally preventing another from going in a particular direction in which he has a right or privilege to go.

> A confinement for false imprisonment purposes can be within even very large boundaries, such as the boundaries of a county or even a state. Also, the confinement need not be accomplished by literal barriers to exit. However, if there is a reasonable avenue of escape apparently available to the victim, then there is no confinement and no false imprisonment.

DUPLER V. SEUBERT
230 N.W.2D 626 (WIS. 1975)

This is a false imprisonment action. On April 23, 1971, plaintiff-appellant Ethel M. Dupler was fired from her job . . . . She was informed of her discharge during an hour-and-a-half session with her two superiors, defendants-respondents Keith Peterson and Helen Seubert, who, Dupler claims, falsely imprisoned her during a portion of this time period. A jury found that Peterson and Seubert did falsely imprison Dupler . . . .

At approximately 4:30 on April 23rd, Seubert asked Dupler to come to Peterson's office. When all three were inside, sitting down, with the door closed, Seubert told Dupler the telephone company would no longer employ her and that she could choose either to resign or be fired. Dupler testified that she refused to resign and that in the conversation that followed, Peterson discussed several alternatives short of dismissal, all of which had been considered but rejected.

At approximately 5 o'clock, Dupler testified, she began to feel sick to her stomach and said "You have already fired me. Why don't you just let me go." She made a motion to get up but Peterson told her to sit down in "a very loud harsh voice." Then, Dupler testified, she began to feel violently ill and stated "I got to go. I can't take this anymore. I'm sick to my stomach. I know I'm going to throw up." She got up and started for the door but Seubert also arose and stood in front of the door. After Dupler repeated that she was sick, Seubert allowed her to exit, but followed her to the men's washroom, where Dupler did throw up. Following this, at approximately 5:25, Seubert asked Dupler to return to Peterson's office where she had left her purse to discuss the situation further. Dupler testified that she went back to the office and reached for her purse; Seubert again closed the door and Peterson said "[i]n a loud voice 'Sit down. I'm still your boss. I'm not through with you." At approximately 5:40 Dupler told Peterson her husband was waiting for her outside in a car and Peterson told her to go outside and ask her husband to come inside. Dupler then went outside and explained the situation to her husband who said "You get back in there and get your coat and if you aren't right out I'll call the police." Dupler returned to Peterson's office and was again told in a loud tone of voice to sit down. She said Seubert and Peterson were trying to convince her to resign rather than be fired and again reviewed the alternatives that had been considered. Dupler then said: "What's the sense of all this. Why keep torturing me. Let me go. Let me go." She stated that Peterson replied "No, we still aren't finished. We have a lot of things to discuss, your retirement pay, your vacation, other things." Finally, at approximately 6 o'clock Peterson told Dupler they could talk further on the phone or at her house, and Dupler left. . . . Peterson and Seubert did not dispute that Dupler had been fired on April 23rd, or that the conference lasted from 4:30 to 6 p.m., or that Dupler became very upset and sick to her stomach and had to leave to throw up. Peterson admitted that Dupler had asked to leave and that he requested that she stay and continue talking so she could indicate whether she wished to resign or be fired. . . .

The issue raised by a motion for review filed by defendants-respondents is: *Is the jury's verdict, finding that Dupler was falsely imprisoned, supported by the evidence?* . . . In *Maniaci v. Marquette University*, . . . the court adopted the definition of false imprisonment contained in sec. 35 of the Restatement of Torts 2d. . . . Secs. 39 . . . and 40 . . . provide that the confinement may be caused by physical force or the threat of physical force, and the comment to sec. 40 indicates the threat may either be express, or inferred from the person's conduct. . . .

[W]e conclude that the record contains sufficient evidence from which the jury could have concluded that Mrs. Dupler was intentionally confined, against her will, by an implied threat of actual physical restraint. She testified that defendant Peterson ordered her in a loud voice to remain seated several times, after she expressed the desire to leave. She reported being "berated, screamed and hollered at," and said the reason she did not just walk out of the room was that "Mrs. Seubert had blocked the door, and tempers had been raised with all the shouting and screaming, I was just plain scared to make an effort. There were two against one." The jury obviously believed Mrs. Dupler's rather than the defendants' account of what transpired, as it had the right to do, and we conclude her testimony was sufficient to support the jury's verdict. . . .

HERBST V. WUENNENBERG
266 N.W.2D 391 (WIS. 1978)

Carol Wuennenberg appeals from a judgment entered by the trial court on a jury's special verdict finding that she falsely imprisoned Jason A. Herbst, Ronald B. Nadel, and Robert A. Ritholz ("plaintiffs"). . . . On September 19, 1974, the plaintiffs were comparing the voter registration list for the City of Madison with names on the mailboxes in multi-unit residential dwellings in Wuennenberg's aldermanic district. Plaintiffs' ultimate purpose was to "purge the voter lists" by challenging the registrations of people whose names were not on mailboxes at the addresses from which they were registered to vote. The plaintiffs and Wuennenberg gave somewhat differing accounts of the incident which gave rise to the action for false imprisonment, but the dispositive facts are not in dispute.

. . . [W]hen the plaintiffs reached Wuennenberg's house at approximately 4:30 p.m. they entered unannounced through the outer door into a vestibule area which lies between the inner and outer doors to Wuennenberg's building. The plaintiffs stood in the vestibule near the mailboxes, which were on a wall in the vestibule approximately two feet inside the front door to the building. Neither he nor the other plaintiffs touched the mailboxes, stated Ritholz; he simply read the names listed for Wuennenberg's address from a computer printout of the registered voters in Wuennenberg's district, and the others checked to see if those names appeared on the mailboxes.

When they were half way through checking, testified Ritholz, Wuennenberg entered the vestibule from an inner door and asked plaintiffs what they were doing. Ritholz replied that they were working for the Republican party, purging voter lists. According to Ritholz, Wuennenberg became very agitated and told the plaintiffs that she did not want them in her district. "At first she told us to leave," testified Ritholz, "and we agreed to leave, but she very quickly changed her mind and wanted to know who we were. Since we already agreed to leave, we didn't think this was necessary."

After the plaintiffs had refused to identify themselves to her, Wuennenberg asked them whether they would be willing to identify themselves to the police. Ritholz replied that they would be willing to do so. Nonetheless, testified Ritholz, he would have preferred to leave, and several times he offered to leave. Both Nadel and Herbst, who agreed that Ritholz was acting as spokesman for the group, testified to Ritholz's statement to Wuennenberg that the plaintiffs were willing to identify themselves to the police.

Subsequently, Wuennenberg's husband came to the vestibule to see what was going on, and Wuennenberg asked him to call the police. About this time Wuennenberg moved from the inner door to a position in front of the outer door. According to Nadel, Wuennenberg blocked the outer door by "standing there with her arms on the pillars to the door to block our exit." The plaintiffs agreed that Wuennenberg had not threatened or intimidated them and that they neither asked her permission to leave nor made any attempt to get her to move away from the doorway. When asked why he had not attempted to leave the vestibule, each of the plaintiffs answered, in effect, that he assumed he would have had to push Wuennenberg out of the way in order to do so.

The plaintiffs waited in the vestibule, stated Ritholz, until the police came some five minutes later. They gave their names and explained their errand to a police officer who told them that they were not doing anything wrong and that they could continue checking the mailboxes in the district.

Wuennenberg testified that . . . [a]fter Ritholz told Wuennenberg that the plaintiffs would not identify themselves to her, but that they would identify themselves to the police, Wuennenberg's husband came out to see what was happening. She explained and then told him, "It looks like you'll have to call the police." Her husband looked at the plaintiffs, and they "nodded their approval to this."

After her husband left to call the police, testified Wuennenberg, she positioned herself in front of the outer doorway because she could watch for the arrival of the police from that vantage and because "I didn't want someone trying to run away at that point." She stated she did not brace her arms against the door frame. She would not have made any effort to stop the plaintiffs had they attempted to leave, stated Wuennenberg, because "I'm not physically capable of stopping anybody." . . . The jury returned a special verdict finding that Wuennenberg had falsely imprisoned the plaintiffs and awarded Herbst, Nadel and Ritholz a total of $1,500 in actual damages.

. . . We hold that the evidence adduced in the case before us does not support a finding that the plaintiffs were falsely imprisoned, and accordingly we reverse the judgment of the trial court. . . . The essence of false imprisonment is the intentional, unlawful, and unconsented restraint by one person of the physical liberty of another. . . . There is no cause of action unless the confinement is contrary to the will of the "prisoner.". . .

In *Maniaci v. Marquette University*, 50 Wis.2d 287, 295, 184 N.W.2d 168 (1971) and in *Dupler v. Seubert, supra* 69 Wis.2d at 381, we adopted the definition of false imprisonment given by the Restatement of Torts, Second, sec. 35:

1. An actor is subject to liability to another for false imprisonment if
    a. he acts intending to confine the other or a third person within boundaries fixed by the actor, and
    b. his act directly or indirectly results in such a confinement of the other, and
    c. the other is conscious of the confinement or is harmed by it.

After review of the record we conclude that the evidence is not sufficient to support the conclusion that Wuennenberg's acts "directly or indirectly result[ed] in . . . a confinement of the [plaintiffs]," a required element of the cause of action. The Restatement lists the ways in which an actor may bring about a "confinement": "by actual or apparent physical barriers" [Sec. 38, Comment a]; "by overpowering physical force, or by submission to physical force" [Sec. 39]; "by submission to a threat to apply physical force to the other's person immediately upon the other's going or attempting to go beyond the area in which the actor intends to confine him" [Sec. 40]; "by submission to duress other than threats of physical force, where such duress is sufficient to make the consent given ineffective to bar the action" (as by a threat to inflict harm upon a member of the other's immediate family, or his property) [Sec. 40A]; "by taking a person into custody under an asserted legal authority" [Sec. 41].

The plaintiffs do not contend that confinement was brought about by an actual or apparent physical barrier, or by overpowering physical force, or by submission to duress, or by taking a person into custody under an asserted legal authority. The parties agree that the central issue is whether there was confinement by threat of physical force and thus argue only as to the applicability of section 40 of the Restatement, which we cited and applied in *Dupler v. Seubert, supra* 69 Wis.2d at 382. Section 40 provides:

"40. Confinement by Threats of Physical Force

The confinement may be by submission to a threat to apply physical force to the other's person immediately upon the other's going or attempting to go beyond the area in which the actor intends to confine him."

The comments to section 40 provide that a person has not been confined by "threats of physical force" unless by words or other acts the actor "threatens to apply" and "has the apparent intention and ability to apply" force to his person.[2] It is not a sufficient basis for an action for false imprisonment that the "prisoner" remained within the limits set by the actor. Remaining within such limits is not a submission to the threat of force unless the "prisoner" believed that the actor had the ability to carry his threat into effect. . . .

Dean Prosser comments on the elements of false imprisonment as follows:

Character of Defendant's Act

The restraint may be by means of physical barriers, or by threats of force which intimidate the plaintiff into compliance with orders. It is sufficient that he submits to an apprehension of force reasonably to be understood from the conduct of the defendant, although no force is used or even expressly threatened. The plaintiff is not required to incur the risk of personal violence by resisting until it actually is used. It is essential, however, that the restraint be against the plaintiff's will; and if he agrees of his own free choice to surrender his freedom of motion, as by remaining in a room or accompanying the defendant voluntarily, to clear himself of suspicion or to accommodate the desires of another, rather than yielding to the constraint of a threat, then there is no imprisonment. This gives rise, in borderline cases, to questions of fact, turning upon the details of the testimony, as to what was reasonably to be understood and implied from the defendant's conduct, tone of voice and the like, which seldom can be reflected accurately in an appellate record, and normally are for the jury.[4]

As plaintiffs state in their brief, the question before this court is whether there is any credible evidence which supports a conclusion that the plaintiffs did not consent to the confinement and that they remained in the vestibule only because Wuennenberg indicated by standing in the doorway that she had "the apparent intention and ability to apply" force to their persons should they attempt to leave. We have reviewed the record, and we find that it does not support this conclusion. Ritholz testified that Wuennenberg had not verbally threatened the plaintiffs, and since none of the plaintiffs asked Wuennenberg to step aside, it could be no more than speculation to conclude that Wuennenberg would not only have refused this request but also would have physically resisted had the plaintiffs attempted to leave. At best, the evidence supports

---

2   Restatement of Torts, Second, Section 40, Comments:

    a.   Under the rule stated in sec. 35, the actor's threat may be by words as well as by other acts. It is not necessary that he do any act actually or apparently effectual in carrying a threat into immediate execution. It is enough that he threatens to apply and has the apparent intention and ability to apply force to the other's person immediately upon the other's attempting to escape from the area within which it is the actor's intention to confine him. . . .

    b.   The submission must be made to a threat to apply the physical force immediately upon the other's going or attempting to go beyond the area within which the threat is intended to confine him. Submission to the threat to apply physical force at a time appreciably later than that at which the other attempts to go beyond the given area is not confinement. . . .

    c.   *Submission to threats.* The other must submit to the threat by remaining within the limits fixed by the actor in order to avoid or avert force threatened to the other. The other's remaining within such limits is not a submission to the threat unless the other believes that the actor has the ability to carry his threat into effect unless prevented by the other's self-defensive action or otherwise, and that it is, therefore, necessary to remain within these limits in order to escape or avert the violence threatened. . . .

    d.   It is not necessary that the force threatened be such that a reasonable man would submit to confinement rather than sustain the harm threatened; it is sufficient that the actor threatens physical force with the intention of confining the other and that the other submits to the threat.

4   Prosser, Torts sec. 11, p. 44 (4th ed. 1971).

an inference that plaintiffs remained in the vestibule because they *assumed* they would have to push Wuennenberg out of the way in order to leave. This assumption is not sufficient to support a claim for false imprisonment.

We do not intend to suggest that false imprisonment will not lie unless a "prisoner" attempts to assault his captor or unless he fails to make such attempt only because he fears harm. The plaintiffs in the case at bar were not required to obtain their freedom by taking steps dangerous to themselves or offensive to their reasonable sense of decency or personal dignity. *See* Restatement of Torts, Second, sec. 36. At a minimum, however, plaintiffs should have attempted to ascertain whether there was any basis to their assumption that their freedom of movement had been curtailed. False imprisonment may not be predicated upon a person's unfounded belief that he was restrained. . . .

Viewed in the light most favorable to plaintiffs, the evidence shows that the plaintiffs were willing to identify themselves to the police, but that they would have preferred to leave Wuennenberg's premises. It is not a sufficient basis for an action for false imprisonment that the plaintiffs remained on the premises although they would have preferred not to do so. Because plaintiffs did not submit to an apprehension of force, they were not imprisoned. . . .

NOTE AND QUESTIONS

1 *Motive irrelevant.* Notice again that evil or good motive is irrelevant. Even if the confinement is thought to be for the good of the confined, it still can be a tort.

2 *Special Verdict.* The trial court entered judgment on the jury's special verdict. This means that the trial court determined the outcome of the case based upon the jury's answers to specific questions about what happened as a matter of fact.

3 Assume that Mrs. Wuennenberg had simply closed the door. How would that factual change impact the analysis? Would it have made any difference if Mrs. Wuennenberg had been built like Arnold Schwartzenegger? Would it have made any difference if the ratio had been reversed – three to one instead of one to three? Would it have made any difference if plaintiffs had asked to leave, and defendant had screamed "you're not going anywhere"?

4 *Awareness of Confinement.* The text introducing this section of the materials notes that false imprisonment is like assault in that both compensate the victim for dignitary harm rather than for actual physical harm. This aspect of the tort of false imprisonment is evidenced by the Restatement's requirement that to recover for false imprisonment, the victim must have been aware of the confinement at the time. Similarly, recovery for assault requires an awareness by the victim at the time of the assault. If plaintiff is not aware of the confinement, then she must prove that she suffered actual physical harm.

5 *Accidental Confinement.* False imprisonment is an intentional tort, which means that if a defendant did not intend to confine the victim but the defendant's carelessness led to the victim's confinement, defendant is not responsible for false imprisonment. However, a negligence cause of action may be available to the plaintiff in such circumstances.

As the preceding cases have demonstrated, a false imprisonment can arise in a variety of circumstances, but one particular scenario – the shopkeeper's holding of a suspected shoplifter – arises with special frequency and merits special attention. We will look at defenses to intentional torts in some detail soon, but a particular defense, frequently called the "shopkeeper's privilege" often arises in the false imprisonment context. The shopkeeper's privilege is an often statutory version of the broader common law privilege to recapture chattels. The protection afforded to shopkeepers by the privilege is somewhat more generous than the protection provided by the common law privilege for recapture of chattels in that shopkeepers usually are protected even for reasonable mistakes.

COBLYN V. KENNEDY'S, INC.
268 N.E.2D 860 (MASS. 1971)

. . . [P]laintiff went to Kennedy's, Inc. (Kennedy's), a store in Boston. He was seventy years of age and about five feet four inches in height. He was wearing a woolen shirt, which was "open at the neck," a topcoat and a hat. "[A]round his neck" he wore an ascot which he had "purchased . . . previously . . . ." He proceeded to the second floor of Kennedy's to purchase a sport coat. He removed his hat, topcoat and ascot, putting the ascot in his pocket. After purchasing a sport coat and leaving it for alterations, he put on his hat and coat and walked downstairs. Just prior to exiting through the outside door of the store, he stopped, took the ascot out of his pocket, put it around his neck, and knotted it. . . .

Just as the plaintiff stepped out of the door, the defendant Goss, an employee, "loomed up" in front of him with his hand up and said: "Stop. Where did you get that scarf?" The plaintiff responded, "[W]hy?" Goss firmly grasped the plaintiff's arm and said: "[Y]ou better go back and see the manager." Another employee was standing next to him. Eight or ten other people were standing around and were staring at the plaintiff. The plaintiff then said, "Yes, I'll go back in the store" and proceeded to do so. As he and Goss went upstairs to the second floor, the plaintiff paused twice because of chest and back pains. After reaching the second floor, the salesman from whom he had purchased the coat . . . confirmed that the plaintiff had purchased a sport coat and that the ascot belonged to him. . . . As a direct result of the emotional upset caused by the incident, the plaintiff was hospitalized and treated for a "myocardial infarct."

Initially, the defendants . . . argue that no unlawful restraint was imposed by either force or threat upon the plaintiff's freedom of movement. . . . However, "[t]he law is well settled that '[a]ny general restraint is sufficient to constitute an imprisonment . . .' and '[a]ny demonstration of physical power which, to all appearances, can be avoided only by submission, operates as effectually to constitute an imprisonment, if submitted to, as if any amount of force had been exercised.' . . . *Jacques* v. *Childs Dining Hall Co.* 244 Mass. 438, 438-439. We think it is clear that there was sufficient evidence of unlawful restraint to submit this question to the jury. Just as the plaintiff had stepped out of the door of the store, the defendant Goss stopped him, firmly grasped his arm and told him that he had "better go back and see the manager." There was another employee at his side. The plaintiff was an elderly man and there were other people standing around staring at him. Considering the plaintiff's age and his heart condition, it is hardly to be expected that with one employee in front of him firmly grasping his arm and another at his side the plaintiff could do other than comply with Goss's "request" that he go back and see the manager. . . .

The defendants next contend that the detention of the plaintiff was sanctioned by G.L. c. 231, §94B . . . . This statute provides as follows: "In an action for false arrest or false imprisonment brought by any person by reason of having been detained for questioning on or in the immediate vicinity of the premises of a merchant, if such person was detained in a reasonable manner and for not more than a reasonable length of time by a person authorized to make arrests or by the merchant or his agent or servant authorized for such purpose and if there were reasonable grounds to believe that the person so detained was committing or attempting to commit larceny of goods for sale on such premises, it shall be a defense to such action. If such goods had not been purchased and were concealed on or amongst the belongings of a person so detained it shall be presumed that there were reasonable grounds for such belief."

The defendants argue in accordance with the conditions imposed in the statute that the plaintiff was detained in a reasonable manner for a reasonable length of time and that Goss had reasonable grounds for believing that the plaintiff was attempting to commit larceny of goods held for sale.

It is conceded that the detention was for a reasonable length of time. . . . We need not decide whether the detention was effected in a reasonable manner for we are of opinion that there were no reasonable grounds for believing that the plaintiff was committing larceny and, therefore, he should not have been detained at all. However, we observe that Goss's failure to identify himself as an employee of Kennedy's and to disclose the reasons for his inquiry and actions, coupled with the physical restraint in a public place imposed upon the plaintiff, an elderly man, who had exhibited no aggressive intention to depart, could be said to constitute an unreasonable method by which to effect detention. . . .

The pivotal question before us as in most cases of this character is whether the evidence shows that there were reasonable grounds for the detention. At common law in an action for false imprisonment, the defense of probable cause, as measured by the prudent and cautious man standard, was available to a merchant. . . . In enacting G. L. c. 231, § 94B, the Legislature inserted the words, "reasonable grounds." Historically, the words "reasonable grounds" and "probable cause" have been given the same meaning by the courts. . . . Applying the standard of reasonable grounds as measured by the reasonably prudent man test . . . to the evidence in the instant case, we are of opinion that the evidence warranted the conclusion that Goss was not reasonably justified in believing that the plaintiff was engaged in shoplifting. There was no error in denying the motion for directed verdicts and in the refusal to give the requested instructions.

Exceptions overruled.

NOTES AND QUESTIONS

1   On the facts of this case, what evidence here would tend to support a finding of coercion of the plaintiff by defendant's employees?

2 How should the appellate court have ruled if the jury had found for defendant and plaintiff had appealed the finding?

3 Many jurisdictions have codified the common law shopkeeper's privilege. Here is an example:

Va. Code Ann. § 8.01-226.9

§ 8.01-226.9. Exemption from civil liability in connection with arrest or detention of person suspected of shoplifting.

A merchant, agent or employee of the merchant, who causes the arrest or detention of any person pursuant to the provisions of §§ 18.2-95, 18.2-96 or § 18.2-103, shall not be held civilly liable for unlawful detention, if such detention does not exceed one hour, slander, malicious prosecution, false imprisonment, false arrest, or assault and battery of the person so arrested or detained, whether such arrest or detention takes place on the premises of the merchant, or after close pursuit from such premises by such merchant, his agent or employee, provided that, in causing the arrest or detention of such person, the merchant, agent or employee of the merchant, had at the time of such arrest or detention probable cause to believe that the person had shoplifted or committed willful concealment of goods or merchandise. The activation of an electronic article surveillance device as a result of a person exiting the premises or an area within the premises of a merchant where an electronic article surveillance device is located shall constitute probable cause for the detention of such person by such merchant, his agent or employee, provided such person is detained only in a reasonable manner and only for such time as is necessary for an inquiry into the circumstances surrounding the activation of the device, and provided that clear and visible notice is posted at each exit and location within the premises where such a device is located indicating the presence of an antishoplifting or inventory control device. For purposes of this section, "electronic article surveillance device" means an electronic device designed and operated for the purpose of detecting the removal from the premises, or a protected area within such premises, of specially marked or tagged merchandise.

TEEL V. MAY DEP'T STORES
155 S.W.2D 74 (MO. 1941)

Plaintiff's sister-in-law Leona Teel, who was separated from plaintiff's brother and had a divorce suit pending against him, . . . met Mr. A. F. Foster . . . and he frequently came to see her. . . . Foster . . . told Leona he would buy her a fur coat. She selected a coat at defendant's store, paid $3 on it, and had it "placed in the Will Call." Foster went with her on October 27th, got the coat, and had it . . . charged to his account. Plaintiff rode down town with them on that trip. Foster was married and lived with his wife and thirteen-year-old son. However, Foster showed Leona a clipping from an Alton newspaper stating that a divorce suit had been filed by Fred Foster against Mary Foster (which was his wife's name) and Leona showed this to plaintiff. Foster testified that these were other parties and that he carried it "for quite a while and got many a laugh out of it." (Foster and his wife were never separated and were still living together at the time of the trial.) He did not say whether he told Leona that it did not refer to him, and it may be inferred that she and plaintiff thought it did, and believed that they would be married when both were divorced. Foster also gave Leona a letter addressed to "To Whom It May Concern," which stated that Leona Nesslein was authorized to buy on his account . . . , and stated a limit of $150 per month. Plaintiff said she saw this letter, but it was never presented to defendant and no notice of any such authorization was given to defendant. . . . Foster told Leona to tell them, at defendant's store, she was Miss Foster because "if she bought something and wanted to take it with her she could not give her name." (Unless she showed the letter.) He said he told Leona that the letter "was not to be used unless she was required to;" that "if anybody questioned it (her right to buy on his account) to produce this letter;" because, if she did not take her purchase with her, "it would have to come to the house, and she would have to come up here and get it." (It is not difficult to understand why that might prove an unworkable arrangement.) After the purchase of the coat, . . . Leona did buy, on Foster's account, such items as "shoes, women's gloves, women's hose, handkerchiefs, two bridge sets, luncheon cloth, pot holder and six towels," amounting to between thirty and forty dollars. . . .

On November 29, Leona asked plaintiff to accompany her to defendant's store. Leona purchased items there amounting to a total of $93.39. She told each of defendant's clerks from whom she purchased goods that she was Mrs. A. F. Foster. Plaintiff said that of course she knew Leona was not Mrs. Foster. Leona had left her car in a parking lot nearby and she and plaintiff carried some of the packages there and put them in her automobile, making at least two trips with packages to the car. The largest amount of the purchases were in the bedding department where she bought blankets and linens amounting to $53.26. When they went back to the bedding department to get these purchases defendant's detective Mr. Zytowski came over to plaintiff and asked her if she was charging on the Foster account and she motioned to Leona. Plaintiff testified as to what occurred thereafter as follows:

He stepped over and asked her if she was charging on the Foster account, and she said that she was, and he said, "Are you Mrs. Foster?" and she said, "Yes;" . . . and then Mr. Zytowski said, "Now, you will have to come along with me." . . . I was afraid if we didn't go, we would be forced to go, so I didn't want a scene, so I went with him. . . . He took us up to the eighth floor, credit department. . . . Two lady detectives were seated directly behind us, and there were a couple of girls right in front of us at typewriters that looked at us. . . . Mr. Jackson (the credit manager, who had already called the Foster home, talked to Mrs. Foster, and had been advised by her that no one was authorized to buy on their account) asked Leona then if she was Mrs. Foster, and she said again that she was, and he said, "You know you are not telling the truth and might as well admit that you are not Mrs. Foster, because I know Mrs. Foster. . . . Then Leona had asked to use the telephone to call Mr. Foster. . . . They said no . . . . She said if she could call Mr. Foster she could straighten things out with them. . . . Mr. Jackson said, "Well, you are not telling the truth; you are not Mrs. Foster; you might as well admit the truth;" and Mr. Zytowski looked at me then and he said, "You are just as guilty as this woman; you were carrying one of the packages, and you might as well tell the truth and save yourself a lot of trouble." . . . I didn't say anything; and then Mr. Jackson became furious, and he said "As far as I am concerned, you may turn those girls over to the proper authorities." . . . Mr. Zytowski called me and was talking privately and he told me I better tell him who she was; he said I could make it mighty easy on myself; he said, "You two girls are in terrible trouble; you are in an awful mess, and I don't know how you are going to get out of it." . . . I told him I couldn't see where I was in any trouble at all, because Leona had written authorization to use the charge account, and I told him all about her supposed to be married to Mr. Foster, and I also told him that I had a charge account there, that I had it for years, and if I wanted anything I could use my own charge account; and I asked him if I could go, and he said no; and I asked him if I could use the phone and he said no; . . . and also told him who Leona was . . . ; and I told him all that and told him my address, and then he called her over. . . . I said to her, "Well, Leona, I told Mr. Zytowski who you are and where you are from," and . . . she admitted right up there in the credit department that she . . . was charging on Mr. Foster's account because she had permission to.

They then were taken to Zytowski's office, and he "told Leona where she made her great mistake was posing as Mrs. Foster. He said that was a very serious offense." Leona then showed him a love letter (but not the authorization letter) she had from Foster . . . which made reference to his expectation that she would get some things from defendant's store, and stated . . . that soon "we can both be with each other and always enjoy each other's companionship." Zytowski, read it and said, "Well, I am very sorry, but this doesn't mean a thing; it is only signed 'Fred.'" Leona also showed him a picture of Mr. Foster, but he said, "This picture doesn't mean anything; it could be anybody." Leona then told him that "about a month ago Mr. Foster bought me a fur coat here and put it on his charge account," and that the amount was $119. Zytowski said, "Well, Leona, I may have to have that fur coat back. Would you be willing to give that fur coat back? Would you be willing to give it up?" and she said, "Yes." . . . Zytowski then made another call to Mrs. Foster . . . . While talking to Mrs. Foster, he said to Leona, "'Mrs. Foster doesn't know you,' and then he said, 'Mr. Foster doesn't know you either;' and Leona was sort of surprised at that, because she did not know that Mr. and Mrs. Foster were living together; she thought they were divorced. . . . She said, 'Can I talk to Mr. Foster?' Mrs. Foster was supposed to have said that Mr. Foster was sick in bed and he couldn't answer the phone." Mrs. Foster corroborated this at the trial, saying that she called Foster at the County Highway office and told him of the credit manager's call; that he said "don't let anyone have anything and don't call me because we are very busy here;" and that to keep him from being disturbed she told Zytowski he was sick and could not answer the phone. . . . After further conversation, . . . Zytowski . . . asked two of the lady detectives to accompany me to the machine and get the packages." Plaintiff did go with them to the parking lot and helped them bring back the packages from the car. The store was closed when they returned. Plaintiff said they "were first taken into custody at 4:30 and we were released about 6:20 (p.m.)." . . .

[I]t is well established . . . that the owner of property has the right to take action (by force or confinement reasonable under the circumstances) in defense of his property. . . . In such cases, probable cause may be an important element of the defense of justification. Therefore, it has been recognized that an owner of a store or other premises has the right to detain a person therein, for a reasonable time for a reasonable investigation, whom he has reasonable grounds to believe has not paid for what he has received or is attempting to take goods without payment. . . .

Plaintiff helped to carry some of the goods to the car, so knew where they were, when, at the credit department, Leona continued to insist that she was Mrs. Foster, and she (plaintiff) was refusing to answer when first asked there who Leona was. Finally, when Zytowski took her to one side, she did tell him the truth about her identity, and explained about her understanding of Leona's relation with Foster. Even then, in view of the fact that defendant had no notice from Foster of any such authority to buy on his credit, and had found the real Mrs. Foster at the Foster home, defendant's agents were undoubtedly justified in not accepting this explanation as the complete truth, and at least demanding the return of the goods. . . . Defendant's agents certainly made a reasonable investigation because Mr. Jackson called Mrs. Foster and learned that she was at home before any action was taken; and Mr. Zytowski, after talking to plaintiff and Leona, again talked to Mrs. Foster and attempted to talk to Mr. Foster. To be considered also is the fact of the large purchases made at this time and the earlier and still unpaid charges upon the account of a man whose only income was a salary of $130 per month. Under all these circumstances . . . , our conclusion is that defendant's agents were within their rights in demanding and thus obtaining the return of the merchandise obtained from defendant by means of such false personation. We would not be willing to hold that the evidence shows unreasonable or unlawful detention of plaintiff and Leona by defendant's agents up to the time of obtaining the return of the goods.

However, we do not think we can say that there could be no jury case of false imprisonment after the goods were returned. Defendant's agents, if they did not believe the explanation made by plaintiff and Leona (and there was evidence of reasonable grounds after investigation for not believing it), might have been within their rights if they had called the authorities to take them into custody and preferred charges against them. . . . Instead of doing this (accepting plaintiff's evidence as true) Zytowski undertook to do something that not even the public authorities had any right to do, namely: to compel them to sign confessions under threat of not permitting them to leave his office until they did so. Plaintiff said that after she got back with the merchandise from the car, Zytowski was writing a confession for Leona, and that it was "about twenty-five minutes" after she got back, "before he got it finished," then "he gave it to Leona and wanted her to sign it," but "she said she didn't want to sign it." Plaintiff further testified: "He told us before we would have to sign those statements, or we would not be permitted to leave. . . . He called me over and started writing some sort of a confession for me, . . . it took him quite a little time to write it out, and he handed it to me, and I signed it right away, thinking I would be permitted to leave. . . . He told me I was very smart in signing mine, and he said, 'Now, go over and tell her what kind of a fool she is.' And I went over and told her I thought she was foolish; that we would be permitted to leave; and she said, 'Mabel, I don't want to sign it; it doesn't seem right.' And I said, 'Well, sign it anyway, so we will be permitted to leave,' and she signed it very reluctantly. . . ."

It is well settled that unreasonable delay in releasing a person, who is entitled to be released, or such delay in calling, taking him before or turning him over to proper authorities, or in wrongfully denying opportunity to give bond would thereafter amount to false imprisonment. . . . Although defendant was within its rights in doing what it did to obtain the return of the goods, . . . Zytowski was "not privileged to use the power, which his custody of another (here held for the purpose of obtaining return of its goods) gives him over the other, to force the other to comply with any demand which has no relation to accomplishing the purpose for which the custody is privileged." Certainly, neither the privilege to restrain plaintiff for the purpose of obtaining return of the goods or in order to turn her over to the proper authorities charged with a felony . . . would give defendant any authority to hold plaintiff to compel her to give a confession in violation of her civil rights under the Constitution of this State. . . .

QUESTIONS AND NOTE

1   The detention in *Coblyn* was held to be unreasonable because there was no "probable cause" to believe that plaintiff had shoplifted. What evidence supported a finding of probable cause in *Teel*?

2   Assuming that there was probable cause in *Teel,* why was the detention nevertheless found to be unreasonable?

3   Similar to false imprisonment is the tort of false arrest, where the defendant confines plaintiff by asserting legal arrest authority. Would the facts of this case support a finding of false arrest?

MANIACI V. MARQUETTE UNIV.
184 N.W.2D 168 (WIS. 1971)

In September of 1966, Saralee Maniaci left her home in . . . Canada, to attend school at Marquette University in Milwaukee. She was sixteen years old at the time. She arrived at the airport in Milwaukee carrying a check for $2,000, which was to be used to pay the year's expenses. She was met at the airport by Father Thomas A. Stemper, a Jesuit priest employed by the university and an old Maniaci family friend. He took her to Heraty Hall, which was to be her dormitory.

In the following months Saralee Maniaci became very dissatisfied with life at Marquette. . . . She spent three of the first seven weekends at her parents' home in Windsor. She travelled from Milwaukee to Windsor with Leonard McGravey, a thirty-two-year-old former priest, whom she had known since she was in high school. Each time she went home, she told her parents of her desire to leave Marquette. Her father each time convinced her that things would get better and that she should give the school another chance. She returned to Marquette on October 30, 1966, with the idea that she would give Marquette one more chance, but that if things did not work out, she would have her parents' permission to quit.

On Wednesday, November 2, 1966, she decided to quit school. She told her closest friend, Jean Huby, that she was leaving, and Jean said she wanted to leave, too. Jean asked to go home with Saralee to Windsor, because Jean thought her father would send her back to Marquette if she tried to go to her own home. Saralee agreed to this request. Jean got Saralee to promise, however, that she would not tell anyone where they were going.

On Thursday, November 3, 1966, Saralee went to the Student Credit Bank and withdrew the $1,300 she had remaining on deposit there. She then went to the railroad station and purchased two tickets to Detroit, which was across the river from Windsor, and as close as she could get to Windsor by train. She then returned to Heraty Hall and began packing.

A representative of the student bank notified the dean of women's office that Saralee had said that she was leaving school. Assistant Dean of Women Patricia Watson notified Esther Morgan, the head resident at Heraty Hall. Esther Morgan notified Joseph Maniaci that his daughter Saralee was intending to run away from school to marry an older man. When Maniaci learned that the man was Leonard McGravey, he said there must be some mistake and gave his approval of whatever plans Leonard McGravey had.

Esther Morgan told Saralee that on Friday morning, November 4, 1966, she was to report to the office of the dean of women. When Saralee failed to report, Dean of Women Mary Alice Cannon went with Assistant Dean Watson to Heraty Hall to persuade Saralee to remain at the school. Saralee admitted that she intended to leave Milwaukee that evening and refused to state her destination. She stated a number of reasons for leaving, including hostility toward her parents, dissatisfaction with education at the university, a desire to act, sing, and write, and a belief that she was more mature than the other students she knew. She insisted that she was going to leave by train at 8 o'clock that evening and that she would notify her father later. She did not state that she had, in fact, received her father's permission to leave. The discussion continued through the morning.

Father Stemper was called about 11:30 a.m. to help persuade Saralee to remain at the school until her parents could be notified. Dean Cannon concluded that Student Health Physician Dean D. Miller should be called. Dr. Miller arrived at Heraty Hall at about 1:30 p.m. accompanied by Nurse June B. Steiner. Dr. Miller conferred with Saralee for about two hours. During that time, Dean Cannon and Assistant Dean Watson persuaded Jean not to leave with Saralee. Throughout the afternoon, unsuccessful attempts were made by Saralee and the dean of women to contact Saralee's father. At 3:30 p.m., Dr. Miller suggested to Dean Cannon that Saralee be hospitalized. Father Stemper saw nothing abnormal about Saralee's conduct and disagreed with Dr. Miller, although he did not know Dr. Miller proposed commitment to a mental hospital.

Milwaukee police officers were called and asked to bring the proper papers for temporary detention of Saralee Maniaci . . . . The officers arrived at about 4:30 p.m. The "Application for Temporary Custody" was filled out by Dr. Miller and signed by him, by Dean Cannon, and by Nurse Steiner. The "Application for Temporary Custody" stated:

That each of the applicants is an adult resident of the State of Wisconsin, and that one of the applicants, Dean D. Miller M.D., is a physician licensed to practice medicine and surgery in this state.

That Sara Lee Maniaci of the City of Milwaukee, in said county, hereinafter called the patient, is believed to be mentally ill for the reason (state facts observed or information known tending to show existence of mental illness, mental infirmity, or mental deficiency): Sara Lee is a 16 yr. old freshman at Marquette University, wishes to leave the University without the consent of the University officials or her parents, to an unknown destination. Her plans for the future are indefinite and it is obvious that she cannot give *rational* reasons for leaving.

That the patient is in need of hospitalization and is irresponsible and dangerous to self or others, so as to require immediate temporary detention by reason of she has persuaded other girls to leave the University with her for reasons which are illogical to us. As a minor we cannot permit her to leave, and feel that she should be confined until her parents have been informed of the situation, and appear on her behalf, and until she has been thoroughly evaluated by a psychiatrist.

WHEREFORE, your applicants pray for immediate temporary detention of the patient in the custody of the sheriff or other police officer, not exceeding five days, and for a judicial inquiry to determine the mental condition of the patient and for such orders of temporary or permanent nature as may be necessary.

Dean D. Miller M.D.	1945 Wauwatosa Ave.	Wauwatosa, Wisc.
Mary Alice Cannon	731 Glenview Ave.	Wauwatosa
June B. Steiner RN.	3731 W. Linden Pl.	Milwaukee

The police officers took Saralee to the Milwaukee County General Hospital, where she was taken to a locked ward on the fifth floor for mental observation. The officers said they had an intelligent conversation with Saralee and that she was cooperative and displayed no tendencies toward violence.

At the hospital her clothes were removed and she was given a bath. She was checked for scars or bruises and given a housecoat to wear. She stated that while confined to a room with several other female persons, she saw what appeared to her to be shocking conduct by two female persons in the same bed.

She persuaded a social worker at the hospital to notify Leonard McGravey what had happened to her. At about 11 p.m., McGravey arrived at the hospital and was permitted to talk to Saralee after she told the nurse he was her fiance. She told him what had happened, and he relayed the message to her father. Her father contacted Dr. Miller and insisted that his daughter be released. Dr. Miller was unable to have Saralee released at that time of night, but he arranged to have Saralee transferred from a larger ward on the fifth floor to a locked private room. Dr. Miller did not tell Joseph Maniaci that Saralee would continue to be confined in a mental hospital. She was, however, released from the hospital at about 9 o'clock the next morning. She returned to her dormitory, gathered up her belongings, and went to Windsor. She never returned to Marquette.

On November 29, 1967, an action was commenced by Saralee Maniaci . . . against Marquette University, Dr. Dean D. Miller, Dean Mary Alice Cannon, and Nurse June B. Steiner . . . for false imprisonment. That matter was submitted to the jury, and it returned a general verdict for the plaintiff and assessed her damages as follows: (1) Compensatory damages — $5,000; (2) punitive damages: Marquette University — $35,000; Dr. Miller — $2,000; Dean Cannon — $5,000; and Nurse Steiner — $1. . . .

Plaintiffs, respondents herein, take the position that the facts spelled out a cause of action for false imprisonment . . . . We agree with the defendants in their contention that no cause of action has been proved under the theory of false imprisonment.

This court has defined the tort of false imprisonment as, "'The unlawful restraint by one person of the physical liberty of another.'" *Lane v. Collins* (1965), 29 Wis. 2d 66, 69, 138 N. W. 2d

264. It is apparent, therefore, that a "lawful" restraint does not constitute false imprisonment, though it may well constitute some other tort. Restatement, Torts 2d . . . sec. 35, points out: "(1) An actor is subject to liability to another for false imprisonment if (a) he acts intending to confine the other or a third person within boundaries fixed by the actor, and (b) his act directly or indirectly results in such a confinement of the other . . . ."

The commentary on this section states, however, that an act which makes an actor liable for confinement by a lawful arrest is not false imprisonment, but may be malicious prosecution or abuse of process.

Restatement, Torts 2d . . . sec. 45A, points out that, "One who instigates or participates in the unlawful confinement of another is subject to liability to the other for false imprisonment." Comment (b) to the chapter states in part:

In order for this Section to be applicable to an arrest, it must be a false arrest, made without legal authority. One who instigates or participates in a lawful arrest, as for example an arrest made under a properly issued warrant by an officer charged with the duty of enforcing it, may become liable for malicious prosecution, as stated in Chapter 29, or for abuse of process, as stated in Chapter 31, but he is not liable for false imprisonment, since no false imprisonment has occurred.

Prosser points out that no cause of action for false imprisonment will lie: If the defendant complies with the formal requirements of the law, as by swearing out a valid warrant, so that the arrest of the plaintiff is legally authorized . . . . He is therefore liable, if at all, only for a misuse of legal process to effect a valid arrest for an improper purpose. Prosser, *Law of Torts* (hornbook series, 3d ed.) . . . sec. 12. . . .

In the instant case it is clear that the type of tort that the concept of "false imprisonment" encompasses did not take place. There was not an "*unlawful*" restraint of freedom.

Since the plaintiff Saralee was confined pursuant to . . . a petition that conformed, prima facie at least, to the jurisdictional requirements of the statute, the confinement was pursuant to law. She was arrested by legal process in the sense that the document executed by the defendants under the statute conferred authority or jurisdiction upon the police officers to take physical custody of the plaintiff's person and to deliver her to the mental hospital.

Although the tort committed was not that of false imprisonment as contended by the plaintiff, neither can we agree with defendants' contention that the insult to plaintiff's liberty can properly be denominated as "malicious prosecution." The reason why defendants assert plaintiff's only cause of action is malicious prosecution is clear, for defendants point out, after setting up the "strawman" of malicious prosecution, that plaintiff cannot prove significant facts to maintain her action. In this contention they are correct, but their argument proves too much . . . .

Prosser, *supra*, page 852, sec. 113, explains that the cause of action for malicious prosecution is designed to afford redress for invasions of the right to be free from unjustifiable litigation. Four elements originally were requisite to a cause of action for malicious prosecution:

1. A criminal proceeding instituted or continued by the defendant against the plaintiff.

2. Termination of the proceeding in favor of the accused.

3. Absence of probable cause for the proceeding.

4. "Malice," or a primary purpose other than that of bringing an offender to justice.

Prosser, *supra*, p. 853, sec. 113.

Prosser demonstrates that malicious prosecution lies only when a plaintiff's interests are invaded by an ostensibly legal process. The essence of the tort is the "perversion of proper legal procedure." (P. 853) He distinguishes it from false imprisonment in that the latter tort occurs only when a plaintiff is arrested or confined without a warrant or legal authority. As stated above, the tort alleged here is clearly not that of false arrest. . . . In the instant case, however, elements that must be present to characterize the action as one of malicious prosecution are absent.

Here . . . the petition was never presented to a court, and no order of a court ever provided for the institution of a mental inquiry. Whatever proceedings antedated this action did not terminate in favor of the plaintiff. In the instant case the defendants simply chose not to proceed and released Saralee from the mental hospital. . . .

Other elements of malicious prosecution are arguably present. Although the plaintiff would contend that no probable cause existed for the confinement, and defendants would argue that no injury or damage resulted as the result of the occurrence, these are determinations that need not be made in view of the disposition we make of this appeal. Suffice it to say that the plaintiff failed to properly prove up a cause of action in either false imprisonment or malicious prosecution. We, however, do not for that reason dismiss her complaint, for we are satisfied that the proof submitted would, skeletally at least, support an alternate cause of action -- that of abuse of process.

Abuse of process is defined by the Restatement, Torts . . . sec. 682, in the following terms: "One who uses a legal process, whether criminal or civil, against another to accomplish a purpose for which it is not designed is liable to the other for the pecuniary loss caused thereby."

Prosser, *supra* . . . sec. 115, points out that abuse of process supplies a remedy that is denied under the theory of malicious prosecution. Abuse of process lies even in those instances where: ". . . legal procedure has been set in motion in proper form, with probable cause, and even with ultimate success, but nevertheless has been perverted to accomplish an ulterior purpose for which it was not designed."

The gist of the tort is: ". . . misusing or misapplying process justified in itself for an end other than that which it was designed to accomplish. The purpose for which the process is used . . . is the only thing of importance." Prosser, *supra* . . . sec. 115.

Malice is not required. Probable cause does not defeat the plaintiff's action, and there need not have been a termination in the plaintiff's favor.

Our appraisal of the evidence leads to the conclusion that the plaintiff's proof spells out a cause of action for abuse of process. It is clear that the purpose of all the individual defendants was not essentially to have inquiry into Saralee's mental condition, though Dean Cannon, at least, was concerned about her "illogical" state of mind. Rather, the purpose of the three defendants was to detain her until such time as her parent had been notified and he had either given his permission for Saralee to leave or had directed Saralee to stay at school. The purpose was to have her physically detained until the problem of her withdrawal from school was resolved to the satisfaction of the school authorities. Dr. Miller acknowledged that he told Saralee he could not release her without her parent's permission. To assure her nonrelease until that time, he struck upon the idea of using the statute that permits the temporary detention of persons who demonstrate symptoms of dangerous mental illness.

On the facts before us, this was a perversion of the purpose of the law and constituted an abuse of process. After Saralee's father was contacted, Saralee was released — all interest in her mental condition vanished, and the pretense of proceeding with a mental inquiry was abandoned.

The trial judge made the specific finding that the purpose of the petition was to detain the plaintiff and not to examine the condition of her mental health. These facts, which appear in the record on the instant appeal, are facts which would support a cause of action for abuse of process. . . .

NOTE

1   A false imprisonment can be indirect, such as when defendant intentionally causes a third-party to confine the victim without legal justification. One of two other tort causes of action (malicious prosecution or abuse of process) also sometimes arises under such circumstances.

EXODUS 20:12

Honour thy father and thy mother: that thy days may be long upon the land which the LORD thy God giveth thee.

MATTHEW 10:34-39

Think not that I am come to send peace on earth: I came not to send peace, but a sword. For I am come to set a man at variance against his father, and the daughter against her mother, and the daughter in law against her mother in law. And a man's foes shall be they of his own household. He that loveth father or mother more than me is not worthy of me: and he that loveth son or daughter more than me is not worthy of me. And he that taketh not his cross, and followeth after me, is not worthy of me. He that findeth his life shall lose it: and he that loseth his life for my sake shall find it.

1. Note the radical language here, so contrary to the prevailing view of the character of Jesus' teachings. What did Jesus mean when He said that he came to send a sword on earth?

2. In what way is the follower who has a greater affection for his family than for Jesus therefore not "worthy" of Jesus?

3. What does it mean for the follower of Jesus to "take up his cross"?

4. Imagine these same words on the lips of a religious leader other than Jesus. Do these sound like the words of the leader of a "cult" as that term is defined by the court in the following case?

PETERSON V. SORLIEN
299 N.W.2D 123 (MINN. 1980)

This action by plaintiff Susan Jungclaus Peterson for false imprisonment and intentional infliction of emotional distress arises from an effort by her parents, in conjunction with other individuals named as defendants, to prompt her disaffiliation from an organization known as The Way Ministry. . . .

Viewing the evidence in the light most favorable to the prevailing defendants, this case marks the emergence of a new cultural phenomenon: youth-oriented religious or psuedo-religious groups which utilize the techniques of what has been termed "coercive persuasion" or "mind control" to cultivate an uncritical and devoted following. Commentators have used the term "coercive persuasion," originally coined to identify the experience of American prisoners of war during the Korean conflict to describe the cult-induction process. The word "cult" is not used pejoratively but in its dictionary sense to describe an unorthodox system of belief characterized by "(g)reat or excessive devotion or dedication to some person, idea, or thing." Webster's New International Dictionary of the English Language Unabridged 552 (1976). Coercive persuasion is fostered through the creation of a controlled environment that heightens the susceptibility of a subject to suggestion and manipulation through sensory deprivation, physiological depletion, cognitive dissonance, peer pressure, and a clear assertion of authority and dominion. The aftermath of indoctrination is a severe impairment of autonomy and the ability to think independently, which induces a subject's unyielding compliance and the rupture of past connections, affiliations and associations. . . .

At the time of the events in question, Susan Jungclaus Peterson was 21 years old. For most of her life, she lived with her family on a farm near Bird Island, Minnesota. In 1973, she graduated with honors from high school, ranking second in her class. She matriculated that fall at Moorhead State College. A dean's list student during her first year, her academic performance declined and her interests narrowed after she joined the local chapter of a group organized internationally and identified locally as The Way of Minnesota, Inc.

The operation of The Way is predicated on the fund-raising activities of its members. The Way's fund-raising strategy centers upon the sale of pre-recorded learning programs. Members are instructed to elicit the interest of a group of ten or twelve people and then play for them, at a charge of $85 per participant, a taped introductory course produced by The Way International. Advanced tape courses are then offered to the participants at additional cost, and training sessions are conducted to more fully acquaint recruits with the orientation of the group and the obligations of membership. Recruits must contribute a minimum of 10 percent of their earnings to the organization; to meet the tithe, student members are expected to obtain part-time employment. Members are also required to purchase books and other materials published by the ministry, and are encouraged to make larger financial contributions and to engage in more sustained efforts at solicitation.

By the end of her freshman year, Susan was devoting many hours to The Way, listening to instructional tapes, soliciting new members and assisting in training sessions. As her sophomore year began, Susan committed herself significantly, selling the car her father had given her and working part-time as a waitress to finance her contributions to The Way. Susan spent the following summer in South Dakota, living in conditions described as appalling and overcrowded, while recruiting, raising money and conducting training sessions for The Way.

As her junior year in college drew to a close, the Jungclauses grew increasingly alarmed by the personality changes they witnessed in their daughter; overly tired, unusually pale, distraught and irritable, she exhibited an increasing alienation from family, diminished interest in education and decline in academic performance. The Jungclauses, versed in the literature of youth cults and based on conversations with former members of The Way, concluded that through a calculated process of manipulation and exploitation Susan had been reduced to a condition of psychological bondage.

On May 24, 1976, defendant Norman Jungclaus, father of plaintiff, arrived at Moorhead to pick up Susan following the end of the third college quarter. Instead of returning to their family home, defendant drove with Susan to Minneapolis to the home of Veronica Morgel. Entering the home of Mrs. Morgel, Susan was greeted by Kathy Mills and several young people who wished to discuss Susan's involvement in the ministry. Each of those present had been in some way touched by the cult phenomenon. Kathy Mills, the leader of the group, had treated a number of former cult members, including Veronica Morgel's son. It was Kathy Mills a self-styled professional deprogrammer, to whom the Jungclauses turned, and intermittently for the next sixteen days, it was in the home of Veronica Morgel that Susan stayed.

The avowed purpose of deprogramming is to break the hold of the cult over the individual through reason and confrontation. Initially, Susan was unwilling to discuss her involvement; she lay curled in a fetal position, in the downstairs bedroom where she first stayed, plugging her ears and crying while her father pleaded with her to listen to what was being said. This behavior persisted for two days during which she intermittently engaged in conversation, at one point screaming hysterically and flailing at her father. But by Wednesday Susan's demeanor had changed completely; she was friendly and vivacious and that night slept in an upstairs bedroom. Susan spent all day Thursday reading and conversing with her father and on Saturday night went roller-skating. On Sunday she played softball at a nearby park, afterwards enjoying a picnic lunch. The next week Susan spent in Columbus, Ohio, flying there with a former cult member who had shared with her the experiences of the previous week. While in Columbus, she spoke every day by telephone to her fiance who, playing tapes and songs from the ministry's headquarters in Minneapolis, begged that she return to the fold. Susan expressed the desire to extricate her fiance from the dominion of the cult.

Susan returned to Minneapolis on June 9. Unable to arrange a controlled meeting so that Susan could see her fiance outside the presence of other members of the ministry, her parents asked that she sign an agreement releasing them from liability for their past weeks' actions. Refusing to do so, Susan stepped outside the Morgel residence with the puppy she had purchased in Ohio, motioned to a passing police car and shortly thereafter was reunited with her fiance in the Minneapolis headquarters of The Way. Following her return to the ministry, she was directed to counsel and initiated the present action.

Plaintiff seeks a judgment notwithstanding the verdict on the issue of false imprisonment, alleging that defendants unlawfully interfered with her personal liberty by words or acts which induced a reasonable apprehension that force would be used against her if she did not otherwise comply. . . .

The period in question began on Monday, May 24, 1976, and ceased on Wednesday, June 9, 1976, a period of 16 days. The record clearly demonstrates that Susan willingly remained in the company of defendants for at least 13 of those days. During that time she took many excursions into the public sphere, playing softball and picnicking in a city park, roller-skating at a public rink, flying aboard public aircraft and shopping and swimming while relaxing in Ohio. Had Susan desired, manifold opportunities existed for her to alert the authorities of her allegedly unlawful detention; in Minneapolis, two police officers observed at close range the softball game in which she engaged; en route to Ohio, she passed through the security areas of the Twin Cities and Columbus airports in the presence of security guards and uniformed police; in Columbus she transacted business at a bank, went for walks in solitude and was interviewed by an F.B.I. agent who sought assurances of her safety. At no time during the 13-day period did she complain of her treatment or suggest that defendants were holding her against her will. If one is aware of a reasonable means of escape that does not present a danger of bodily or material harm, a restriction is not total and complete and does not constitute unlawful imprisonment. Damages may not be assessed for any period of detention to which one freely consents. *See* . . . Restatement (Second) of Torts s 36, Comment a (1965) . . . .

In light of our examination of the record and rules of construction providing that upon review the evidence must be viewed in a manner most favorable to the prevailing party, . . . we find that a reasonable basis existed for the verdict exonerating defendants of the charge of false imprisonment. Although carried out under colorably religious auspices, the method of cult indoctrination, viewed in a light most favorable to the prevailing party, is predicated on a strategy of coercive persuasion that undermines the capacity for informed consent. While we acknowledge that other social institutions may utilize a degree of coercion in promoting their objectives, none do so to the same extent or intend the same consequences. Society, therefore, has a compelling interest favoring intervention. The facts in this case support the conclusion that plaintiff only regained her volitional capacity to consent after engaging in the first three days of the deprogramming process. As such, we hold that when parents, or their agents, acting under the conviction that the judgmental capacity of their adult child is impaired, seek to extricate that child from what they reasonably believe to be a religious or psuedo-religious cult, and the child at some juncture assents to the actions in question, limitations upon the child's mobility do not constitute meaningful deprivations of personal liberty sufficient to support a judgment for false imprisonment.

WAHL, Justice (dissenting in part, concurring in part).

I must respectfully dissent. In every generation, parents have viewed their children's religious and political beliefs with alarm and dismay if those beliefs were different from their own. Under the First Amendment, however, adults in our society enjoy freedoms of association and belief. In my view, it is unwise to tamper with those freedoms and with longstanding principles of tort law out of sympathy for parents seeking to help their "misguided" offspring, however well-intentioned and loving their acts may be. Whether or not, as the majority opinion asserts, The Way of Minnesota, Inc. is a "youth-oriented," "pseudo-religious group" which pursues its "fundraising strategy" in such a way as to inflict physical and psychological harm on its members, emphasis on this characterization beclouds the purely legal issues which are presented by this appeal.

The first of those legal issues is whether, as a matter of law, any of the defendants in this case are guilty of false imprisonment of the plaintiff. The elements of the tort of false imprisonment are (1) words or acts by defendant intended to confine plaintiff, (2) actual confinement, and (3) awareness by plaintiff that she is being confined. . . . Any imprisonment "which is not legally justifiable" is false imprisonment, . . . therefore, the fact that the tortfeasor acted in good faith is no defense to a charge of false imprisonment. . . . Thus, . . . evidence concerning the activities of The Way and the impact of those activities upon plaintiff . . . has little bearing on the issue of defendants' liability for false imprisonment.

The unrebutted evidence shows that defendant Norman Jungclaus, the father of the 21-year-old plaintiff in this case, took his adult daughter, kicking and screaming, to a small bedroom in the basement of the Morgel home on Monday, May 23. Norman Jungclaus admitted that she did not go with him willingly. Plaintiff curled up on the bed, plugged her ears, and cried. Defendant Perkins testified that plaintiff screamed and cried and pleaded with several people to let her go, but her pleas were ignored. This situation continued until 3 a.m. Tuesday. At one point that morning, plaintiff flew at her father, and he held her arms around her from the back, in his words, "for maybe a half an hour, until she calmed down again." Plaintiff testified that defendant Mills told her papers had been drafted to commit her to Anoka State Hospital if she continued to refuse to cooperate with the "deprogramming."

In its memorandum accompanying the order denying plaintiff's motion for judgment notwithstanding the verdict, the trial court stated:

It should be noted that there must be considerable room for doubt concerning that portion of the verdict finding that Norman Jungclaus did not participate in a false imprisonment. The evidence is unrebutted that he picked up his 21-year-old daughter Susan and took her into the basement without her permission or consent, and against her will. . . .

Certainly, parents who disapprove of or disagree with the religious beliefs of their adult offspring are free to exercise their own First Amendment rights in an attempt, by speech and persuasion without physical restraints, to change their adult children's minds. But parents who engage in tortious conduct in their "deprogramming" attempts do so at the risk that the deprogramming will be unsuccessful and the adult children will pursue tort remedies against their parents. To allow parents' "conviction that the judgmental capacity of their (adult) child is impaired (by her religious indoctrination)" to excuse their tortious conduct sets a dangerous precedent.

Here, the evidence clearly supported a verdict against Norman Jungclaus on the false imprisonment claim, and no reasonable basis existed for denying judgment notwithstanding the verdict. The trial court's holding in this regard should be reversed. . . .

OTIS, Justice (dissenting in part).

I join in the views expressed by Justice Wahl, and particularly take issue with a rule which authorizes what is euphemistically described as "limitations upon the adult child's mobility" whenever a parent, or indeed a stranger acting for a parent, subjectively decides, without the benefit of a professional opinion or judicial intervention, that the adult child's "judgmental capacity" is impaired and that she should be "extricated" from what is deemed to be a religious or pseudo-religious cult.

The rule adopted by the majority states:

We hold that where parents, or their agents, acting under the conviction that the judgmental capacity of their adult child is impaired, seek to extricate that child from what they reasonably believe to be a religious or pseudo-religious cult, and the child at some juncture assents to the actions in question, limitations upon the child's mobility do not constitute meaningful deprivations of personal liberty sufficient to support a judgment for false imprisonment.

We furnish no guidelines or criteria for what constitutes "impaired judgmental capacity" other than the fact that the adult child has embraced an unorthodox doctrine with a zeal which has given the intervenor cause for alarm, a concern which may be well-founded, ill-founded, or unfounded.

Nor do we specify whether the "cult" must be for a benign or a malevolent purpose. It is enough that the intervenor has reason to believe it is a cult i.e. "an unorthodox system of belief" and that at some juncture during the adult child's involuntary confinement, she "assents," that is to say, yields or surrenders, possibly from exhaustion or fatigue, and possibly for a period only long enough to regain her composure.

If there is any constitutional protection we should be slow to erode it is the right of serious-minded people, young or old, well-adjusted, or maladjusted, to search for religious or philosophical fulfillment in their own way and in their own time without the interference of meddling friends or relatives, however well-intentioned they may be.

At age 21, a daughter is no longer a child. She is an adult. Susan Peterson was not only an adult in 1976 but she was a bright, well-educated adult. For whatever reason, she was experiencing a period of restlessness and insecurity which is by no means uncommon in students of that age. But to hold that for seeking companionship and identity in a group whose proselytizing tactics may well be suspect, she must endure without a remedy the degrading and humiliating treatment she received at the hands of her parents, is, in my opinion, totally at odds with the basic rights of young people to think unorthodox thoughts, join unorthodox groups, and proclaim unorthodox views. I would reverse the denial of recovery as to that cause of action.

QUESTIONS

1   What if the defendants in *Maniaci* had not bothered to use a civil commitment process? Would their actions then have constituted a false imprisonment as a matter of law? If so, are the facts of *Maniaci* distinguishable from the facts of *Peterson*?

2   Can the influence of a "cult" ever overcome a person's volition? If so, should there be a special privilege for those who would rescue others from "cults"?

3   What is a "cult"? In the light of the New Testament, including Matthew 10:34-39, is Jesus the founder of a "cult"? If not, what is the difference?

SCOTT V. ROSS
140 F.3D 1275 (9TH CIR. 1998)

... In 1991, Kathy Tonkin and her six children joined the Life Tabernacle Church ("Life Tabernacle"), a branch of the United Pentecostal Church International. Tonkin remained a member for over a year before withdrawing. She urged her sons to withdraw from Life Tabernacle, but her three oldest sons, appellant Jason Scott ("Scott"), Thysen and Matthew, refused. At the time Scott was 18 years of age, Thysen, 16 and Matthew, 13.

Tonkin believed Life Tabernacle had a destructive effect on her sons and sought help in having them removed from the church's influence. Tonkin contacted Shirley Landa after a referral from the Seattle Community Service hotline. Landa was involved in various "anti-cult" activities and worked as CAN's Washington state "contact." ... CAN [Cult Awareness Network] has described itself as "a national nonprofit organization founded to educate the public about the harmful effects of mind control as used by destructive cults." ...

Landa referred Tonkin to Rick Ross, whom Tonkin hired to "deprogram" her three sons. Although the record is somewhat unclear as to the specific nature or origin of Landa's relationship with Ross, it is clear that Landa was aware Ross performed involuntary deprogrammings because she had seen Ross do so on the television program "48 Hours." Ross was known to, and received referrals from, other CAN members as well.

Ross performed "successful" involuntary deprogrammings on Thysen and Matthew, who were minors and therefore within their mother's control. Tonkin, Landa and Ross knew that to deprogram Scott would be more difficult legally because Scott was 18 years of age. Nonetheless, Ross, with the aid of defendants Simpson, Workman and Rotfroff, attempted to deprogram Scott. They abducted Scott and held him captive for five days, during which Ross "debated" Life Tabernacle's teachings with Scott. Tonkin planned to send Scott to a deprogramming rehabilitation center in Ohio after Ross completed the deprogramming. After several days, Scott feigned acceptance of Ross' positions, escaped and filed this suit. . . . After a six-day trial, a jury . . . awarded Scott $875,000 in compensatory damages and $4 million in punitive damages. . . .

CAN argues that even if it is [liable] for Landa's acts, the evidence fails to establish that Landa was aware of any plan to deprogram or abduct Scott, and that even if she was aware of this plan, she did not participate in it. The record shows otherwise.

. . . The record shows Landa was involved in the agreement to deprogram Scott . . . . Landa referred Tonkin to Ross, and Landa was aware of Ross' methods. Tonkin indicated that Landa referred to Ross as "a very successful deprogrammer" with a "very, very high success rate." Landa knew Ross conducted involuntary deprogramming, as indicated by the fact she saw the "48 Hours" program in which Ross involuntarily deprogrammed a minor. Landa was involved in the deprogramming of Scott's younger brothers. Tonkin discussed and planned the deprogramming of Scott with Landa. Landa advised Tonkin of the possible legal problems involved in Scott's deprogramming. Landa told Tonkin that the only way properly to deprogram Scott was to abduct and deprogram him. The fact Ross contacted Landa for "legal advice" after his arrest is further evidence of her complicity. . . .

The judgment of the district court is AFFIRMED.

D. INTENTIONAL INFLICTION OF EMOTIONAL DISTRESS

PROVERBS 26:18-19

As a mad man who casteth firebrands, arrows, and death, So is the man that deceiveth his neighbour, and saith, Am not I in sport?

1. History

One of the things that sets liability for the intentional infliction of emotional distress apart from other intentional torts is those last two words – emotional distress. Recovery for pure emotional distress is a relatively recent innovation in tort law. The earliest torts involved some kind of actual or threatened physical invasion, either of person or property. In fact, courts generally were not willing to entertain a freestanding cause of action for emotional distress until the twentieth century. Before that time, a claim for economic harm or for emotional distress was cognizable only if accompanied by an allegation of physical injury. However, in an influential law review article published in 1936, Professor Calvert Magruder noted that, in reality, some courts had been awarding damages for intentional infliction of emotional distress in cases where defendant's conduct was particularly outrageous. This recognition was followed by the American Law Institute in 1948 when it recognized the inentional inflication of mental distress cause of action in the first Restatement of Torts.

One of the reasons courts hesitated to permit recovery for pure emotional distress was the fear that if plaintiffs could recover for emotional distress alone, apart from any physical invasion or injury, this would encourage frivolous claims for trivial indignities. Therefore, early emotional distress cases required that the emotional distress be accompanied by some form of physical injury. This requirement was swept away by the Supreme Court of California in the leading case of *State Rubbish Collectors Ass'n v. Siliznoff.* Since the California Court's groundbreaking work in *Siliznoff,* the freestanding tort of intentional infliction of emotional distress has become widely accepted, although the emotional distress plaintiff continues to face significant hurdles to recovery, as illustrated by the cases below.

STATE RUBBISH COLLECTORS ASS'N V. SILIZNOFF
240 P.2d 282 (Cal. 1952)

On February 1, 1948, Peter Kobzeff signed a contract with the Acme Brewing Company to collect rubbish from the latter's brewery. Kobzeff . . . was able to secure the contract because Acme was dissatisfied with the service then being provided by another collector, one Abramoff. Although Kobzeff signed the contract, it was understood that the work should be done by John Siliznoff, Kobzeff's son-in-law. . . .

Both Kobzeff and Abramoff were members of the plaintiff State Rubbish Collectors Association, but Siliznoff was not. The by-laws of the association provided that one member should not take an account from another member without paying for it . . . . After Abramoff lost the Acme account he complained to the association, and Kobzeff was called upon to settle the matter. Kobzeff and Siliznoff took the position that the Acme account belonged to Siliznoff, and that he was under no obligation to pay for it. . . .

Defendant testified that shortly after he secured the Acme account, the president of the association and its inspector, John Andikian, called on him and Kobzeff. They suggested that either a settlement be made with Abramoff or that the job be dropped, and requested Kobzeff and defendant to attend a meeting of the association. At this meeting defendant was told that the association "ran all the rubbish from that office, all the rubbish hauling," and that if he did not pay for the job they would take it away from him. . . . Thereafter, . . . Andikian told defendant that "'We will give you up till tonight to get down to the board meeting and make some kind of arrangements or agreements about the Acme Brewery, or otherwise we are going to beat you up.' . . . He says he either would hire somebody or do it himself. And I says, 'Well, what would they do to me?' He says, well, they would physically beat me up first, cut up the truck tires or burn the truck, or otherwise put me out of business completely. He said if I didn't appear at that meeting and make some kind of an agreement that they would do that, but he says up to then they would let me alone, but if I walked out of that meeting that night they would beat me up for sure." Defendant attended the meeting and protested that he owed nothing for the Acme account and in any event could not pay the amount demanded. . . . After two hours of further discussion defendant agreed to join the association and pay for the Acme account. . . . He testified that the only reason "they let me go home, is that I promised that I would sign the notes the very next morning." The president "made me promise on my honor and everything else, and I was scared, and I knew I had to come back, so I believe he knew I was scared and that I would come back. That's the only reason they let me go home." Defendant also testified that because of the fright he suffered during his dispute with the association he became ill and vomited several times and had to remain away from work for a period of several days.

Plaintiff contends that the evidence does not establish an assault against defendant because the threats made all related to action that might take place in the future; that neither Andikian nor members of the board of directors threatened immediate physical harm to defendant. [Citations omitted.] We have concluded, however, that a cause of action is established when it is shown that one, in the absence of any privilege, intentionally subjects another to the mental suffering incident to serious threats to his physical well-being, whether or not the threats are made under such circumstances as to constitute a technical assault.

In the past it has frequently been stated that the interest in emotional and mental tranquillity is not one that the law will protect from invasion in its own right. [Citations omitted.] As late as 1934 the Restatement of Torts took the position that "The interest in mental and emotional tranquillity and, therefore, in freedom from mental and emotional disturbance is not, as a thing in itself, regarded as of sufficient importance to require others to refrain from conduct intended or recognizably likely to cause such a disturbance." (Restatement, Torts, § 46, comment c.) The Restatement explained the rule allowing recovery for the mere apprehension of bodily harm in traditional assault cases as an historical anomaly . . . .

The view has been forcefully advocated that the law should protect emotional and mental tranquillity as such against serious and intentional invasions [citations omitted], and there is a growing body of case law supporting this position. [Citations omitted.] In recognition of this development the American Law Institute amended section 46 of the Restatement of Torts in 1947 to provide: "One who, without a privilege to do so, intentionally causes severe emotional distress to another is liable (a) for such emotional distress, and (b) for bodily harm resulting from it."

In explanation it stated that "The interest in freedom from severe emotional distress is regarded as of sufficient importance to require others to refrain from conduct intended to invade it. Such conduct is tortious. The injury suffered by the one whose interest is invaded is frequently far more serious to him than certain tortious invasions of the interest in bodily integrity and other legally protected interests. In the absence of a privilege, the actor's conduct has no social utility; indeed it is anti-social. No reason or policy requires such an actor to be protected from the liability which usually attaches to the wilful wrongdoer whose efforts are successful." (Restatement of the Law, 1948 Supplement, Torts, § 46, comment d.)

There are persuasive arguments and analogies that support the recognition of a right to be free from serious, intentional, and unprivileged invasions of mental and emotional tranquillity. If a cause of action is otherwise established, it is settled that damages may be given for mental suffering naturally ensuing from the acts complained of [citation omitted], and in the case of many torts, such as assault, battery, false imprisonment, and defamation, mental suffering will frequently constitute the principal element of damages. [Citations omitted.] In cases where mental suffering constitutes a major element of damages it is anomalous to deny recovery because the defendant's intentional misconduct fell short of producing some physical injury.

It may be contended that to allow recovery in the absence of physical injury will open the door to unfounded claims and a flood of litigation, and that the requirement that there be physical injury is necessary to insure that serious mental suffering actually occurred. The jury is ordinarily in a better position, however, to determine whether outrageous conduct results in mental distress than whether that distress in turn results in physical injury. From their own experience jurors are aware of the extent and character of the disagreeable emotions that may result from the defendant's conduct, but a difficult medical question is presented when it must be determined if emotional distress resulted in physical injury. [Citations omitted.] Greater proof that mental suffering occurred is found in the defendant's conduct designed to bring it about than in physical injury that may or may not have resulted therefrom. . . .

QUESTIONS

1   Why does the plaintiff here resort to the novel theory of intentional infliction of emotional distress? Would Siliznoff have a cause of action for the more traditional theories of assault or false imprisonment?

2   *Physical Injury Requirement.* As noted above, the tort of intentional infliction of emotional distress originally applied only to infliction of emotional distress when accompanied by physical injury such as heart attack. Would this be a sensible requirement? Why or why not? In this regard, the court in *Siliznoff* suggested that a finder of fact would be more competent to evaluate a claim for emotional distress alone than a claim for actual physical injury caused by emotional distress. Do you agree?

2. Elements

The Restatement (Second) of Torts substantially altered the description of the tort of intentional inflication of emotional distress.

FIGUEIREDO-TORRES V. NICKEL
584 A.2d 69 (Md. 1991)

Appellant Silvio Figueiredo-Torres (Torres) filed a complaint on March 2, 1989 . . . against Appellee Herbert J. Nickel (Nickel) seeking damages for negligence, gross negligence, intentional infliction of emotional distress and "outrage." The complaint alleged the following facts: In July 1985, Torres and his wife sought the counsel of Nickel, a licensed psychologist, for the purpose of preserving and improving their marital relationship. Most of the therapy sessions with Nickel were joint sessions attended by both Torres and his wife; however, Torres also attended some individual sessions with Nickel. Apparently, Nickel conducted individual sessions with Mrs. Torres as well, for the complaint maintains that, during the course of Nickel's treatment of Torres and his wife, Nickel commenced a romantic relationship with Mrs. Torres, . . . which culminated in the dissolution of the Torres' marriage. In therapy sessions with Torres, Nickel "consistently advised [him] to be distant from his wife, not to engage in intimate and/or sexual contact with her, and ultimately to separate from her." The complaint further alleged that, as a result of his psychologist-patient relationship with Torres, Nickel knew that Torres was particularly sensitive emotionally. Torres also set forth numerous injuries, both emotional and physical, and damages allegedly sustained as a result of Nickel's conduct.

Nickel filed a . . . motion to dismiss the complaint for failure to state a claim upon which relief can be granted . . . . The motion was granted by the circuit court as to the gross negligence, intentional infliction of emotional distress, and "outrage" counts . . . . Torres . . . appealed to the Court of Special Appeals challenging the dismissal of the professional negligence and intentional infliction of emotional distress counts. We issued a writ of certiorari before the intermediate court ruled on the case. . . .

We recognized the tort of intentional infliction of emotional distress in *Harris v. Jones*, 281 Md. 560, 380 A.2d 611 (1977). . . . We emphasized that close adherence to [the] elements would assure that "two problems which are inherent in recognizing a tort of this character can be minimized: (1) distinguishing the true from the false claim, and (2) distinguishing the trifling annoyance from the serious wrong." *Id.* These inherent problems are of no less concern to us today; and we acknowledge the view expressed by Judge Bloom in *Hamilton v. Ford Motor Credit Co.*, 66 Md.App. 46, 61, 502 A.2d 1057, 1065 . . . that "[i]n developing the tort of intentional infliction of emotional distress, whatever the relationship between the parties, recovery will be meted out sparingly, its balm reserved for those wounds that are truly severe and incapable of healing themselves." With these qualifications firmly in mind, we consider Nickel's argument that Torres' complaint has not sufficiently pled the elements of extreme and outrageous conduct and severe emotional distress.

Torres avers that Nickel was a psychologist engaged to treat him for the purpose of bettering his mental and emotional health and to assist in resolving marital problems he was having with his wife. Despite the goals of this therapy and Nickel's knowledge that Torres was "particularly susceptible to emotional upset, anxiety and distress," Torres maintains that Nickel "developed a romantic relationship with [Torres'] wife, . . . and engaged in improper affectionate conduct and repeated sexual intercourse with her." Nickel contends that, because Torres' wife was a consenting adult and sexual relations between consenting adults in modern society is not extreme and outrageous conduct, the intentional infliction of emotional distress count was properly dismissed. Nickel's analysis neglects one important detail. Nickel was not "the milkman, the mailman, or the guy next door"; he was Torres' psychologist and marriage counselor.

As we recognized in *Harris*, "the extreme and outrageous character of the defendant's conduct may arise from his abuse of a position, or relation with another person, which gives him actual or apparent authority over him, or power to affect his interests." 281 Md. at 569, 380 A.2d at 616 (citing Restatement (Second) of Torts § 46 comment e (1965)). Furthermore, "[i]n cases where the defendant is in a peculiar position to harass the plaintiff, and cause emotional distress, his conduct will be carefully scrutinized by the courts." 281 Md. at 569, 380 A.2d at 615 . . . . A psychologist-patient relationship, by its nature, focuses on the psyche of the patient; and a psychologist is in a unique position to influence the patient's emotional well-being. For this reason, a psychologist-patient relationship falls squarely into the category of relationships which are carefully scrutinized by the courts. That is not to say that any patient who is unhappy with the results of psychotherapy has a cause of action against the therapist for intentional infliction of emotional distress; however, a jury may find extreme and outrageous conduct where a psychologist who is retained to improve a marital relationship implements a course of extreme conduct which is injurious to the patient and designed to facilitate a romantic, sexual relationship between the therapist and the patient's spouse.

In addition to the allegations of sexual misconduct, Torres further alleges that, despite his knowledge that Torres "was particularly susceptible to emotional upset, anxiety and distress" and "emotionally and mentally unstable," Nickel "demoralized [Torres] by making statements, and engaging in conduct that was destructive to [Torres'] ego development and self-respect," and "caused further and greater feelings of helplessness, discouragement, shame, guilt, fear and confusion by telling him he was a 'codfish' and that his wife deserved a 'fillet'; by telling him he had bad breath and should not go near his wife, and by falsely and systematically telling [Torres] that the deterioration of [Torres'] relationship with his wife was exclusively the result of [Torres'] conduct." As we stated in *Harris*, "'mere insults, indignities, threats, annoyances, petty oppressions, or other trivialities'" are insufficient to support a claim for intentional infliction of emotional distress, *Harris*, 281 Md. at 567, 380 A.2d at 614 (quoting Restatement (Second) of Torts § 46 comment d). Nevertheless, we repeat our conviction that "[i]n determining whether conduct is extreme and outrageous, it should not be considered in a sterile setting, detached from the surroundings in which it occurred." Coming from a stranger, or even a friend, this conduct may not be outrageous; but we are not prepared to state as a matter of law that such behavior by a psychologist which takes advantage of the patient's known emotional problems is not extreme and outrageous conduct sufficient to support an intentional infliction of emotional distress claim.

As to the question of severity, Nickel argues that Torres "has not alleged that he has been unable to attend to his daily activities or that no person would be expected to endure such a situation." That degree of severity was found in *Moniodis v. Cook*, 64 Md.App. 1, 494 A.2d 212 ... , where the Court of Special Appeals upheld a verdict for intentional infliction of emotional distress. This Court has since discussed the degree of severity of emotional distress required to sustain a claim for intentional infliction of emotional distress in *B.N. v. K.K.*, 312 Md. 135, 538 A.2d 1175 (1988), a case posing the certified question "Does Maryland Recognize A Cause of Action for ... Intentional Infliction of Emotional Distress, ... Resulting From the Sexual Transmission Of A Dangerous, Contagious, and Incurable Disease, Such As Genital Herpes?" We stated,

> We do not believe, however, that a showing like that in *Moniodis* is essential to recovery. While the emotional distress must be severe, it need not produce total emotional or physical disablement.... And severity must be measured in light of the outrageousness of the conduct and the other elements of the tort. (Citations omitted.)

Id. at 148, 538 A.2d at 1181-82 ....

> The complaint in this case alleges that Torres suffered systemic hypertension and loss of visual acuity in his left eye, required hospitalization for severe emotional distress, shock and fright to his nervous system; he suffered depression, anxiety, obsession ... and impairment of his ability to form intimate relationships with women, all said injuries requiring psychological therapy and counseling; he lost the benefit received from prior psychological counseling....

While we are mindful that Torres must prove both that he suffered severe injury and that the injury was proximately caused by Nickel's tortious conduct, we believe that the complaint is sufficient to survive a ... motion [to dismiss]. ...

NOTE AND QUESTIONS

1   What is the evidence of defendant's intent here? Do you think that a reasonable jury could find that defendant wanted to cause plaintiff severe emotional distress?

2   Comment d to Restatement (Second) Sec. 46 states as follows:
Liability has been found only where the conduct has been so outrageous in character, and so extreme in degree, as to go beyond all possible bounds of decency, and to be regarded as atrocious, and utterly intolerable in a civilized community. Generally, the case is one in which the recitation of the facts to an average member of the community would arouse his resentment against the actor, and lead him to exclaim "Outrageous!"

3   Would you say that defendant's alleged conduct in this case goes "beyond all possible bounds of decency"? The plaintiff emphasized that he was emotionally sensitive. Does this make a difference?

4   Consider the following hypothetical scenarios. Assume that Student A and Student B are students at Prestigious University Law School. Student B is a fundamentalist Christian, and each time Student A sees Student B in the hall

or at an informal law school gathering, Student A greets Student B by shouting, "Hey, here comes the right wing reactionary fundamentalist fruitcake!" Does Student B have a cause of action against Student A for intentional infliction of emotional distress? Would your analysis differ if it were Professor C who called Student B a "right-wing reactionary, fundamentalist fruitcake" in Torts class?

JONES V. CLINTON
990 F. SUPP. 657 (E.D. ARK. 1998)

The plaintiff in this lawsuit, Paula Corbin Jones, seeks civil damages from William Jefferson Clinton, President of the United States, and Danny Ferguson, a former Arkansas State Police Officer, for alleged actions beginning with an incident in a hotel suite in Little Rock, Arkansas. . . . For the reasons that follow, the Court finds that the President's and Ferguson's motions for summary judgment should both be and hereby are granted. . . .

I.

This lawsuit is based on an incident that is said to have taken place on the afternoon of May 8, 1991, in a suite at the Excelsior Hotel in Little Rock, Arkansas. President Clinton was Governor of the State of Arkansas at the time, and plaintiff was a State employee with the Arkansas Industrial Development Commission ("AIDC") . . . . Ferguson was an Arkansas State Police officer assigned to the Governor's security detail.

According to the record, then-Governor Clinton was at the Excelsior Hotel on the day in question delivering a speech at an official conference being sponsored by the AIDC. . . . Plaintiff states that she and another AIDC employee, Pamela Blackard, were working at a registration desk for the AIDC when a man approached the desk and informed her and Blackard that he was Trooper Danny Ferguson, the Governor's bodyguard. . . . The conversation between plaintiff, Blackard, and Ferguson lasted approximately five minutes and consisted of light, friendly banter; there was nothing intimidating, threatening, or coercive about it. . . .

Upon leaving the registration desk, Ferguson apparently had a conversation with the Governor about the possibility of meeting with plaintiff, during which Ferguson states the Governor remarked that plaintiff had "that come-hither look," i.e. "a sort of [sexually] suggestive appearance from the look or dress." . . . He states that "some time later" the Governor asked him to "get him a room, that he was expecting a call from the White House and . . . had several phone calls that he needed to make," and asked him to go to the car and get his briefcase containing the phone messages. . . . Ferguson states that upon obtaining the room, the Governor told him that if plaintiff wanted to meet him, she could "come up" . . . .

Plaintiff states that Ferguson later reappeared at the registration desk, delivered a piece of paper to her with a four-digit number written on it, and said that the Governor would like to meet with her in this suite number. . . . She states that she, Blackard, and Ferguson talked about what the Governor could want and that Ferguson stated, among other things, "We do this all the time." *Id.* Thinking that it was an honor to be asked to meet the Governor and that it might lead to an enhanced employment opportunity, plaintiff states that she agreed to the meeting and that Ferguson escorted her to the floor of the hotel upon which the Governor's suite was located. . . .

Plaintiff states that upon arriving at the suite and announcing herself, the Governor shook her hand, invited her in, and closed the door. . . . She states that a few minutes of small talk ensued, which included the Governor asking her about her job and him mentioning that Dave Harrington, plaintiff's ultimate superior within the AIDC and a Clinton appointee, was his "good friend." . . . Plaintiff states that the Governor then "unexpectedly reached over to [her], took her hand, and pulled her toward him, so that their bodies were close to each other." . . . She states she removed her hand from his and retreated several feet, but that the Governor approached her again and, while saying, "I love the way your hair flows down your back" and "I love your curves," put his hand on her leg, started sliding it toward her pelvic area, and bent down to attempt to kiss her on the neck, all without her consent. . . . Plaintiff states that she exclaimed, "What are you doing?," told the Governor that she was "not that kind of girl," and "escaped" from the Governor's reach "by walking away from him." . . . She states she was extremely upset and confused and, not knowing what to do, attempted to distract the Governor by chatting about his wife. . . . Plaintiff states that she sat down at the end of the sofa nearest the door, but that the Governor approached the sofa where she had taken a seat and, as he sat down, "lowered his trousers and underwear, exposed [himself] and told [her] to 'kiss it.'" . . . She states that she was "horrified" by this and that she "jumped up from the couch" and told the Governor that she had to go, saying something to the effect that she had to get back to the registration desk. . . . Plaintiff states that the Governor, "while fondling [himself]," said, "Well, I don't want to make you do anything you don't want to do," and then pulled up his pants and said, "If you get in trouble for leaving work, have Dave call me immediately and I'll take care of it." . . . She states that as she left the room (the door of which was not locked), the Governor "detained" her momentarily, "looked sternly" at her, and said, "You are smart. Let's keep this between ourselves." . . .

Plaintiff states that the Governor's advances to her were unwelcome, that she never said or did anything to suggest to the Governor that she was willing to have sex with him, and that during the time they were together in the hotel suite, she resisted his advances although she was "stunned by them and intimidated by who he was." . . . She states that when the Governor referred to Dave Harrington, she "understood that he was telling her that he had control over Mr. Harrington and over her job, and that he was willing to use that power." . . . She states that from that point on, she was "very fearful" that her refusal to submit to the Governor's advances could damage her career and even jeopardize her employment. . . .

Plaintiff states she returned to the registration desk and told Blackard some of what had happened. . . . Blackard states that plaintiff was shaking and embarrassed. . . . Following the Conference, plaintiff states she went to the workplace of a friend, Debra Ballentine, and told her of the incident as well. . . . Ballentine states that plaintiff was upset and crying. . . . Later that same day, plaintiff states she told her sister, Charlotte Corbin Brown, what had happened and, within the next two days, also told her other sister, Lydia Corbin Cathey, of the incident. . . . Brown's observations of plaintiff's demeanor apparently are not included in the record. Cathey, however, states that plaintiff was "bawling" and "squalling," and that she appeared scared, embarrassed, and ashamed. . . .

Ballentine states that she encouraged plaintiff to report the incident to her boss or to the police, but that plaintiff declined, pointing out that her boss was friends with the Governor and that the police were the ones who took her to the hotel suite. . . . Plaintiff states that what the Governor and Ferguson had said and done made her "afraid" to file charges. . . . Plaintiff's amended complaint contains several claims . . . . The third is a state law claim in which plaintiff asserts a claim of intentional infliction of emotional distress . . . against Governor Clinton, based primarily on the alleged incident at the hotel . . . .

II.

The President moves for summary judgment on the following grounds: . . . plaintiff's claim of intentional infliction of emotional distress or outrage fails because (a) by plaintiff's own testimony, the conduct at issue does not constitute intentional infliction of emotional distress . . . under Arkansas law, and (b) plaintiff did not as a result of the alleged conduct suffer emotional distress so severe that no reasonable person could endure it. . . . To establish a claim of intentional infliction of emotional distress, a plaintiff must prove that: (1) the defendant intended to inflict emotional distress or knew . . . that emotional distress was the likely result of his conduct; (2) the conduct was extreme and outrageous and utterly intolerable in a civilized community; (3) the defendant's conduct was the cause of the plaintiff's distress; and (4) the plaintiff's emotional distress was so severe in nature that no reasonable person could be expected to endure it. . . .

The President argues that the alleged conduct of which plaintiff complains was brief and isolated; did not result in any physical harm or objective symptoms of the requisite severe distress; did not result in distress so severe that no reasonable person could be expected to endure it; and he had no knowledge of any special condition of plaintiff that would render her particularly susceptible to distress. . . . The Court agrees. . . . While the Court will certainly agree that plaintiff's allegations describe offensive conduct, the Court, as previously noted, has found that the Governor's alleged conduct . . . describes a mere sexual proposition or encounter, albeit an odious one, that was relatively brief in duration, did not involve any coercion or threats of reprisal, and was abandoned as soon as plaintiff made clear that the advance was not welcome. The Court is not aware of any authority holding that such a sexual encounter or proposition of the type alleged in this case, without more, gives rise to a claim . . . .

Moreover, notwithstanding the offensive nature of the Governor's alleged conduct, plaintiff admits that she never missed a day of work following the alleged incident, she continued to work at AIDC another nineteen months (leaving only because of her husband's job transfer), she continued to go on a daily basis to the Governor's Office to deliver items and never asked to be relieved of that duty, she never filed a formal complaint or told her supervisors of the incident while at AIDC, she never consulted a psychiatrist, psychologist, or incurred medical bills as a result of the alleged incident, and she acknowledges that her two subsequent contacts with the

Governor involved comments made "in a light vein" and nonsexual contact that was done in a "friendly fashion." . . . Plaintiff's actions and statements in this case do not portray someone who experienced emotional distress so severe in nature that no reasonable person could be expected to endure it. . . . In sum, plaintiff's allegations fall far short of the rigorous standards for establishing a claim of outrage under Arkansas law and the Court therefore grants the President's motion for summary judgment on this claim. . . .

NOTES AND QUESTIONS

1   In *Jones* the court held that plaintiff had not pled a *prima facie* case of outrage or intentional infliction of emotional distress, but the appellate court in *Figuereido-Torres* reversed a similar holding by the trial court. What facts distinguish the two cases?

2   Intentional infliction of emotional distress is unique among the intentional torts in that intent is not required – recklessness with regard to causing emotional distress is sufficient.

3   Claims of intentional infliction of emotional distress frequently involve distress allegedly cause by something defendant said or wrote. Where the alleged intentional infliction of emotional distress involves speech, the First Amendment protection of the freedom of speech can be implicated, especially where the plaintiff is a public figure. First Amendment protection of speech is discussed, *infra*, in the section on defamation.

3. Third Party Claims

DORNFELD V. OBERG
503 N.W.2D 115 (MINN. 1993)

This case raises the issue of whether a cause of action exists for intentional or reckless infliction of emotional distress where a person claims to have suffered severe emotional distress as a result of being present at the death of a family member.

Respondent Barbara Dornfeld brought suit against appellants Scott Oberg and American Family Insurance Company, claiming . . . intentional infliction of emotional distress arising out of a motor vehicle accident in which her husband was killed. Following a jury trial, the jury awarded respondent damages for reckless infliction of emotional distress, finding that appellant Oberg's conduct was extreme and outrageous, was reckless, and resulted in severe emotional distress in respondent. . . .

On November 15, 1985, Don Dornfeld and his wife, respondent Barbara Dornfeld, were driving home after an evening of dancing. Around 11:00, . . . the Dornfelds' car had a flat tire. They pulled off the road onto the right shoulder, and Don Dornfeld put on the warning flashers before going to change the rear tire on the driver's side. Mrs. Dornfeld remained in the car.

While changing the tire, Mr. Dornfeld was hit by a car driven by appellant Scott Oberg. Oberg, whose blood alcohol content was .224 at the time of the accident, dragged Dornfeld's body over 200 feet, leaving him in the right roadside ditch. Oberg claimed that he never saw the Dornfeld vehicle prior to impact. Mr. Dornfeld was pronounced dead at the scene.

Respondent, who remained inside the car on the passenger side, felt but did not see the Oberg vehicle or the resulting collision. She testified that although she felt the impact, she "just had no idea what hit or where it came from." She suffered no significant physical injuries as a result of the crash.

After the collision, respondent got out of the car and asked where her husband was. Witnesses and police officers told her that her husband had been found in a roadside ditch and that he was dead. When she asked to see him one last time, police led her to his body, where she bent over to kiss him goodbye.

As a result of the accident, respondent claims that she began to suffer from post-traumatic stress syndrome/disorder (PTSS/PTSD). She claims that she suffered from memory deterioration, inability to retain jobs, and terrible nightmares as a result of the accident. A psychiatrist testified at trial that the accident triggered the onset of Mrs. Dornfeld's PTSS. After hearing this evidence, the jury found that Oberg's extreme and outrageous conduct had been reckless and that it resulted in respondent suffering severe emotional distress. . . . Appellants Oberg and American Family Insurance . . . appealed to this court, claiming that neither the facts of this case nor existing Minnesota law supports a cause of action for intentional . . . infliction of emotional distress.

In determining whether to recognize this cause of action, we must look to past precedent and the language of the Restatement (Second) of Torts § 46 (1965). In *Hubbard v. United Press Int'l, Inc.*, 330 N.W.2d 428 (Minn.1983), this court adopted the formulation set forth in section 46(1) of the Restatement (Second) of Torts with respect to the elements necessary to prove intentional infliction of emotional distress. Specifically, this section provides as follows: "One who by extreme and outrageous conduct intentionally or recklessly causes severe emotional distress to another is subject to liability for such emotional distress, and if bodily harm to the other results from it, for such bodily harm." Restatement (Second) of Torts § 46(1) (1965). . . . The Restatement emphasizes that "[t]he law intervenes only where the distress inflicted is so severe that no reasonable man could be expected to endure it." Restatement (Second) of Torts § 46 cmt. j (1965). . . .

Despite recognizing a new cause of action for intentional infliction of emotional distress, this court specifically refused to answer the question of whether third parties or bystanders could avail themselves of this remedy, stating, "While we adopt the theory of Restatement (Second) of Torts § 46(1) (1965), the third party issues reflected by subsection (2) are not before us and we do not pass upon them." [*Hubbard*, 330 N.W.2d] at 439 n. 8. This latter section, which addresses the issue of liability to third parties for emotional distress, provides:

> (2) Where such conduct is directed at a third person, the actor is subject to liability if he intentionally or recklessly causes severe emotional distress
> (a) to a member of such person's immediate family who is present at the time, whether or not such distress results in bodily harm, or (b) to any other person who is present at the time, if such distress results in bodily harm.

Restatement (Second) of Torts § 46(2) (1965). It is precisely the issues addressed in subsection (2) which this case raises. Thus, this court must determine whether the facts of this case justify recognizing such an action.

The court of appeals held that respondent's recovery was justified by existing Minnesota tort law. To reach this conclusion, the court of appeals added the requirement that a plaintiff must be within the "zone of danger." *Dornfeld*, 491 N.W.2d at 300; *see Stadler v. Cross*, 295 N.W.2d 552 (Minn.1980). The court of appeals stated, "Minnesota has long allowed recovery to persons within the zone of danger. . . ." *Dornfeld*, 491 N.W.2d at 300 (footnote omitted).

We believe the analysis by the court of appeals blurs the distinction between two independent torts-intentional infliction of emotional distress and negligent infliction of emotional distress. While the court of appeals is correct in noting that Minnesota has allowed recovery for injuries resulting from fear for one's own safety for those within the zone of danger, . . . these cases have arisen under the theory of negligent infliction of emotional distress, not under intentional infliction of emotional distress. In addition, the cases cited above also require persons to prove that they suffered severe emotional distress with resultant physical injury before recovery is permitted, *Stadler*, 295 N.W.2d at 553, and proof of physical injury is only a requirement for negligent infliction of emotional distress, not for intentional infliction. *See* Restatement (Second) of Torts § 436A (1965). . . .

Under section 46(2) of the Restatement (Second) of Torts, one is liable for reckless infliction of emotional distress only if some intentional action is taken toward the third party. While Minnesota courts have found that a cause of action exists when a wall suddenly collapses, *Okrina v. Midwestern Corp.*, 282 Minn. 400, 165 N.W.2d 259 (1969), or when a plane drops 34,000 feet, *Quill v. Trans World Airlines, Inc.*, 361 N.W.2d 438 (Minn.App.1985), *pet. for rev. denied* (Minn., Apr. 18, 1985), these actions have arisen under negligent infliction of emotional distress, not intentional infliction of emotional distress, in part because there was no intent or no intended victim.

In contrast, section 46(2) clearly requires that the reckless conduct be "directed at" a third party, thereby requiring some intentional act on the part of the actor. Restatement (Second) of Torts § 46(2) (1965). . . . Thus, in order to hold Oberg liable for reckless infliction of emotional distress, this court must find that his actions were intentionally "directed at" respondent's husband.

Under the facts of this case, it is difficult to construe Oberg's conduct as being "directed at" any third person. While reckless driving or driving while intoxicated is morally reprehensible and is punishable by criminal sanctions, it is difficult to see how that reckless driving is "directed at" any particular motorist within the meaning of the Restatement (Second) of Torts § 46(2). Mere reckless driving is directed, if at all, only at the driving community generally rather than at a particular individual, and, therefore, such conduct would be insufficient to give rise to a claim for intentional or reckless infliction of emotional distress. Allowing recovery under the present facts would raise the specter that any surviving family member in a car crash caused by a drunk or reckless driver could maintain an action against the driver for intentional infliction of emotional distress.

Instead, the Restatement contemplates that recovery should be permitted only when the extreme and outrageous conduct is directed at a third person, such as when a husband is murdered in the presence of his wife. In such cases, "the actor may know that it is substantially certain, or at least highly probable, that it will cause severe emotional distress to the plaintiff." Restatement (Second) of Torts § 46 cmt. 1 (1965). . . .

Thus, the available evidence indicates that in order to recover for intentional or reckless infliction of emotional distress, the conduct must be "directed at" a particular third person and the defendant must know of the plaintiff's presence so that the mental effect upon the plaintiff can be anticipated by the defendant. Here, Oberg's reckless driving was not "directed at" any particular third person, and Oberg was not aware of respondent's presence.[5] Thus, under the facts of this case, Oberg's conduct was not "directed at" respondent's husband within the meaning of the Restatement (Second) of Torts § 46(2) (1965), and respondent's claim for intentional or reckless infliction of emotional distress must therefore fail.

Reversed.

QUESTIONS

1. What is the nature of the intent required to establish a cause of action for intentional infliction of emotional distress? Why does not the jury's finding of reckless driving by the defendant sufficiently establish the intent required for intentional infliction of emotional distress?

4. Fighting Words

HUTCHINS V. CECIL
44 VA. CIR. 380 (1998)

I. Procedural History

Following an acquittal of criminal charges, Mr. Thomas Hutchins sued Mr. David and Mrs. Kelli Cecil for malicious prosecution. The Cecils counterclaimed against Hutchins. Count I of the Counterclaim, titled "Insulting Words Directed at Kelli A. Cecil," alleges Hutchins called Mrs. Cecil a "bitch" in public. Mrs. Cecil claims the words were insulting, tended to violence

---

5   Respondent's failure to observe the fatal accident is not directly relevant to her claim for intentional or reckless infliction of emotional distress but could be relevant in a claim for negligent infliction of emotional distress. Whether respondent was inside the car unaware of the accident, or outside the car observing the entire incident, she would not be entitled to recover in either instance, because the conduct was not "directed at" her. If respondent had actually observed the accident while standing on the roadside, this factor might be relevant to establishing one element of negligent infliction of emotional distress (i.e., that she had some "fear for her own safety"), but this would not affect the intentional or reckless infliction of emotional distress claim, which requires that the conduct actually be directed at that third person. If, however, the "directed at" element had been established, the Restatement then merely requires that the family member be "present at the time," which was certainly met in this case, whether or not Mrs. Dornfeld actually "observed" the fatal accident.

and breaches of the peace, and she was insulted, offended and frightened. . . . Count II of the Counterclaim, titled "Insulting Words Directed at David B. Cecil," alleges Mr. Hutchins called Mr. Cecil a "motherfucker" in public. Mr. Cecil claims the words were insulting, tended to violence and breaches of the peace, and he was insulted, offended and frightened. . . .

Hutchins demurs to Counts I and II of the counterclaim . . . .

II. Discussion

. . . Virginia Code '8.01-45 states "[a]ll words shall be actionable which from their usual construction and common acceptance are construed as insults and tend to violence and breach of the peace." The insulting words statute was originally enacted as an anti-dueling statute. . . . Although the statute's original purpose is obsolete, it continues today to "prevent breaches of the peace, to discourage offensive and excessive freedom in the use of that unruly member, the tongue, to inflict punishment . . . by subjecting those who are so hasty of temper and inconsiderate of the feelings of others as to insult them to such actual and punitive damages as may be awarded by a jury." *Hines v. Gravins*, 136 Va. 313 (1922), *cert. denied*, 265 U.S. 583 (1924). In *Wright v. Cofield*, 146 Va. 637 (1926), the Court stated the purpose of the statute is to prevent the use of language by one towards another likely to bring about a personal encounter. (citing Hines). . . .

We are a society that places significant value in permitting citizens a wide range of individual expressive freedom, not the least of which is the freedom of speech. This freedom is not limited to political and scientific discussion, but also includes speech that is controversial, unpopular, pornographic, and offensive. The First Amendment states Congress shall make no law abridging freedom of speech. In fact, the United States Supreme Court has struck down as vague and overbroad state laws designed to penalize insulting words. . . . However, no Constitutional right is unqualified, and freedom of speech is no exception. There are several classes of speech which can be punished without violating the First Amendment. In both *Gooding* and *Lewis*, the majority struck down the laws as the state courts had not adopted precise definitions of the statutory terms restricting their application to true "fighting words," as required by *Chaplinsky v. New Hampshire*, 315 U.S. 568 (1942). In *Chaplinsky*, the United States Supreme Court held that the Constitution does not protect insulting or "fighting words"– those which by their very utterance inflict injury or tend to incite an immediate breach of the peace. *Gooding*, at 240, citing *Chaplinsky*, at 572-73. The "fighting words" doctrine articulated in *Chaplinsky* . . . remains alive today. A state may criminally penalize a verbal attack directed at a particular individual in a face to face confrontation that presents a clear and present danger of violent physical reaction. . . . Accordingly, there is no constitutional infirmity in a statute which affords a civil remedy to anyone who is aggrieved by such speech. . . .

I find that Va. Code '8.01-45 . . . encompasses an action for fighting words. . . . I construe the statute to only penalize words used in a verbal attack directed at a particular individual in a face to face confrontation that presents a clear and present danger of a violent physical reaction. This statute is therefore constitutional under *Chaplinsky* and *Cohen*, and does not suffer from being a vague or overbroad statute such as the laws in *Gooding* and *Lewis*. If the words uttered could be "fighting words" under the circumstances alleged, that is, if they could reasonably be construed to have been insults provoking imminent violence and a breach of the peace, it is for the jury as representatives of the community to decide if an individual's words have violated the insulting words statute, and then determine what damages, if any, to award. . . .

E. TRESPASS TO CHATTELS

Of course, the law of intentional torts protects more than merely plaintiff's own bodily integrity – plaintiff's property also is protected. The next three causes of action that we will consider (trespass to chattels, conversion of chattels, and trespass to land) are analogous to the other three intentional torts that used to fit under the old common law umbrella of "trespass" (battery, assault, and false imprisonment) in that all six involve the direct application of force or the threat of force by the defendant.

Considering trespass to chattels first, a trespass to chattels is an unauthorized exercise of dominion or control over or intermeddling with plaintiff's chattel (personal property). Most authorities indicate that the interference must result in either damage to the chattel, substantial deprivation of use, or dispossession. Many of the trespass to chattels cases in recent years have been fought, not over the basic elements of the tort, but rather over precisely what constitutes "intermeddling" with a "chattel" in this technological age. Does electronic contact with an internet connected device count as physical contact? The clear trend has been toward considering the application of traditional tort causes of action to conduct on the internet.

REGISTER.COM, INC. V. VERIO, INC.
126 F. SUPP.2D 238 (S.D.N.Y. 2000)

I. Findings of Fact

The Parties

Plaintiff Register.com is one of over fifty domain name registrars . . . . In addition to its domain name registration services, Register.com offers . . . a variety of other related services, such as (i) web site creation tools; (ii) web site hosting; (iii) electronic mail; (iv) domain name hosting; (v) domain name forwarding, and (vi) real-time domain name management. Register.com has invested over $15 million dollars in equipment, software, service fees, and human resources in designing, developing, and maintaining its website and the computer systems necessary to host

Register.com's Internet-based services. . . . It has also spent in excess of $25 million on advertising and brand promotion in the year 2000 alone, including through print, radio, and television media. . . .

In order to give its customers control over their receipt of commercial solicitations, Register.com provides them with the opportunity to "opt-in" during the domain name registration process to receiving sales and marketing communications from Register.com or its co-brand or private label partners. Customers who do not opt-in to such communications are not solicited by Register.com or its co-brands. . . .

Defendant Verio is one of the largest operators of web sites for businesses and a leading provider of comprehensive Internet services. Although not a registrar of domain names, Verio directly competes with Register.com and its partners to provide registration services and a variety of other Internet services including website hosting and development. . . .

The WHOIS database

To become an accredited domain name registrar for the .com, .net, and .org domains, all registrars, including Register.com are required to enter into a registrar Accreditation Agreement ("Agreement") with the Internet Corporation for Assigned Names and Numbers ("ICANN"). . . . Under that Agreement, Register.com, as well as all other registrars, is required to provide an on-line, interactive WHOIS database. This database contains the names and contact information-postal address, telephone number, electronic mail address and in some cases facsimile number-for customers who register domain names through the registrar. The Agreement also requires Register.com to make the database freely accessible to the public via its web page and through an independent access port . . . . These query-based channels of access to the WHOIS database allow the user to collect registrant contact information for one domain name at a time by entering the domain name into the provided search engine. . . . The primary purpose of the WHOIS database is to provide necessary information in the event of domain name disputes, such as those arising from cybersquatting or trademark infringement. . . . The parties also agree that the WHOIS data may be used for market research.

Specifically, . . . Register.com's Accreditation Agreement with ICANN requires that:

> In providing query-based public access to registration data . . . , Registrar shall not impose terms and conditions on use of the data provided except as permitted by ICANN-adopted policy. Unless and until ICANN adopts a different policy, Registrar shall permit use of data it provides in response to queries *for any lawful purposes except to: (a) allow, enable, or otherwise support the transmission of mass unsolicited, commercial advertising or solicitations via e-mail (spam); or (b) enable high volume, automated, electronic processes that apply to Registrar (or its systems).* . . .

Originally Register.com's terms and conditions for users of its WHOIS database were substantially the same. In April 2000, however, Register.com implemented the following more restrictive terms of use governing its WHOIS database:

> By submitting a WHOIS query, you agree that you will use this data *only for lawful purposes* and that, *under no circumstances will you use this data to: (1) allow, enable, or otherwise support the transmission of mass unsolicited, commercial advertising or solicitations **via direct mail, electronic mail, or by telephone;*** or (2) enable high volume, automated, electronic processes that apply to Register.com (or its systems). The compilation, repackaging, dissemination or other use of this data is expressly prohibited without the prior written consent of Register.com. Register.com reserves the right to modify these terms at any time. By submitting this query, you agree to abide by these terms. . . . (emphasis added). . . .

Verio's Project Henhouse

In late 1999, to better target their marketing and sales efforts toward customers in need of web hosting services and to reach those customers more quickly, Verio developed an automated software program or "robot." . . . With its search robot, Verio accessed the WHOIS database maintained by the accredited registrars, including Register.com, and collected the contact information of customers who had recently registered a domain name. Then, despite the marketing prohibitions in Register.com's terms of use, Verio utilized this data in a marketing initiative known as Project Henhouse and began to contact and solicit Register.com's customers, within the first several days after their registration, by e-mail, regular mail, and telephone.

Verio's Search Robots

In general, the process worked as follows: first, each day Verio downloaded, in compressed format, a list of all currently registered domain names, of all registrars, ending in .com, .net, and .org. . . . The registry list is updated twice daily and provides the domain name, the sponsoring registrar, and the nameservers for all registered names. Using a computer program, Verio then compared the newly downloaded NSI registry with the NSI registry it downloaded a day earlier in order to isolate the domain names that had been registered in the last day and the names that had been removed. After downloading the list of new domain names, only then was a search robot used to query the NSI database to extract the name of the accredited registrar of each new name. . . . That search robot then automatically made successive queries to the various registrars' WHOIS databases, via the . . . access channels, to harvest the relevant contact information for each new domain name registered. . . . Once retrieved, the WHOIS data was deposited into an information database maintained by Verio. The resulting database of sales leads was then provided to Verio's telemarketing staff.

Marketing History

Beginning in January, 2000, Register.com learned that Verio was e-mailing its customers to solicit business. . . . Register.com continued to get complaints about e-mail and telephone solicitations by Verio from its customers and co-brand partners through January. In March 2000 [Register.com] . . . contacted [Verio] to complain that Register.com was . . . receiving numerous complaints, including that a number of telephone messages similar to the following were left with Register.com customers: "This is [name of telemarketer] calling from Verio regarding the registration of [customer's domain name]. Please contact me at your earliest convenience." . . .

On May 5, 2000 Register.com's lawyers wrote to Verio's General Counsel requesting that Verio immediately cease and desist from this marketing conduct. Register.com complained generally that the use of its mark as well as the timing of the solicitations was harming its good will and specifically warned Verio that it was violating the terms of use it had agreed to in submitting its WHOIS queries by sending "mass unsolicited, commercial advertising or solicitations via e-mail (spam)." . . .

Register.com's lawyers sent Verio a terms letter for it to sign and acknowledge. In that letter Register.com specifically required Verio to cease use of the WHOIS database for not just e-mail marketing, but also direct mail and telemarketing. Verio refused to sign and although it ceased e-mail solicitation, it continued to use the WHOIS contact information for telemarketing purposes into July 2000. . . . Accordingly, Register.com commenced this lawsuit and moved for a temporary restraining order and preliminary injunction on August 3, 2000. . . .

II. Discussion

. . . While Register.com acknowledges its obligation to provide public access to its customers' contact information, it has developed "terms of use" which prohibit third parties, such as Verio, from using the contact information for any mass marketing purpose-whether by e-mail, regular mail or telephone. Register.com also argues that the use of automated software to access the WHOIS database violates its terms of use and harms its computer systems.

Verio admits both the use of the WHOIS data for marketing purposes and the use of the search robot. . . . Verio also . . . claims that Register.com has not proven that the robot causes any harm, let alone irreparable harm, to Register.com's computer systems. . . .

IV. Register.com's Claim

. . . Register.com argues that Verio's use of an automated software robot to search the "WHOIS" database constitutes trespass to chattels. Register.com states that it has made its computer system available on the Internet, and that "Verio has used 'software automation' to flood that computer system with traffic in order to retrieve the contact information of Register.com customers for the purpose of solicitation in knowing violation of Register.com's posted policies and terms of use." (Pl.'s Mem. of Law at 36.)

The standard for trespass to chattels in New York is based upon the standard set forth in the Restatement of Torts: "One who uses a chattel with the consent of another is subject to liability in trespass for any harm to the chattel which is caused by or occurs in the course of any use exceeding the consent, even though such use is not a conversion." *City of Amsterdam v. Goldreyer, Ltd.*, 882 F.Supp. 1273 (E.D.N.Y.1995) (citing Restatement (Second) of Torts, § 256 (1965)).

. . . [I]t is clear since at least the date this lawsuit was filed that Register.com does not consent to Verio's use of a search robot, and Verio is on notice that its search robot is unwelcome. . . . Accordingly, Verio's future use of a search robot to access the database exceeds the scope of Register.com's consent, and Verio is liable for any harm to the chattel (Register.com's computer systems) caused by that unauthorized access. *See CompuServe*, 962 F.Supp. at 1024 (holding that defendants' continued use after CompuServe notified defendants that it no longer consented to the use of its proprietary computer equipment was a trespass) (citing Restatement (Second) of Torts §§252 and 892A(5)).

Having established that Verio's access to its WHOIS database by robot is unauthorized, Register.com must next demonstrate that Verio's unauthorized access caused harm to its chattels, namely its computer system. To that end, Robert Gardos, Register.com's Vice President for Technology, submitted a declaration estimating that Verio's searching of Register.com's WHOIS database has resulted in a diminishment of 2.3% of Register.com's system resources. . . .

Although Register.com's evidence of any burden or harm to its computer system caused by the successive queries performed by search robots is imprecise, evidence of mere possessory interference is sufficient to demonstrate the quantum of harm necessary to establish a claim for trespass to chattels. "A trespasser is liable when the trespass diminishes the condition, quality, or value of personal property." *EBay, Inc. v. Bidder's Edge, Inc.*, 100 F.Supp.2d 1058, 1071 (N.D.Cal.2000) (citing *CompuServe*, 962 F.Supp. at 1022). "The quality or value of personal property may be 'diminished even though it is not physically damaged by defendant's conduct.'" *Id.* Though it does correctly dispute the trustworthiness and accuracy of Mr. Gardos' calculations, Verio does not dispute that its search robot occupies some of Register.com's systems capacity.

Although Register.com was unable to directly measure the amount by which its systems capacity was reduced, the record evidence is sufficient to establish the possessory interference necessary to establish a trespass to chattels claim. As the *eBay* Court wrote:

BE argues that its searches present a negligible load on plaintiff's computer systems, and do not rise to the level of impairment to the condition or value of eBay's computer system required to constitute a trespass. *However, it is undisputed that eBay's server and its capacity are personal property, and that BE's searches use a portion of this property. Even if, as BE argues, its searches only use a small amount of eBay's computer system capacity, BE has nonetheless deprived eBay of the ability to use that portion of its personal property for its own purposes. The law recognizes no such right to use another's personal property.* Accordingly, BE's actions appear to have caused injury to eBay and appear likely to continue to cause injury to eBay.

(100 F.Supp.2d at 1071.) (emphasis added).

Furthermore, Gardos also noted in his declaration "if the strain on Register.com's resources generated by Verio's searches becomes large enough, it could cause Register.com's computer systems to malfunction or crash" and "I believe that if Verio's searching of Register.com's WHOIS database were determined to be lawful, then every purveryor of Internet-based services would engage in similar conduct." (Gardos Decl. ¶¶ 33, 34). Gardos' concerns are supported by Verio's testimony that it sees no need to place a limit on the number of other companies that should be allowed to harvest data from Register.com's computers. . . . Furthermore, Verio's own internal documents reveal that Verio was aware that its robotic queries could slow the response times of the registrars' databases and even overload them. . . .

Accordingly, Register.com's evidence that Verio's search robots have presented and will continue to present an unwelcome interference with, and a risk of interruption to, its computer system and servers is sufficient to demonstrate a likelihood of success on the merits of its trespass to chattels claim. . . .

QUESTION

1 Trespass to chattels is an intentional tort. Would Verio commit a trespass to chattels if it mistakenly thought that it had permission to access the data on Register.com's computer system?

F. CONVERSION

Like trespass to chattels, the law of conversion protects a person's interest in possessing personal property free from interference. In fact, conversion is a trespass to chattels that so seriously interferes with plaintiff's right to exclusive control that defendant is justly required to pay for the entire value of the chattel. In this way, conversion is a subset of trespass to chattels – in other words, all conversions involve a trespass, but minor trespasses do not amount to conversions. Restatement § 222A identifies several factors used to determine what constitutes a conversion.

The clearest case of conversion is where defendant destroys plaintiff's property, but complete destruction of the property is not necessary to find a conversion. Another distinction between trespass to chattels and conversion is in the available remedy. Unlike trespass, conversion gives plaintiff the option to accept the chattel's return in mitigation of damages.

PEARSON V. DODD

410 F.2D 701 (D.C. CIR. 1969)

J. SKELLY WRIGHT, Circuit Judge:

This case arises out of the exposure of the alleged misdeeds of Senator Thomas Dodd of Connecticut by newspaper columnists Drew Pearson and Jack Anderson. . . . The undisputed facts in the case were stated by the District Court as follows:

> * * * On several occasions in June and July, 1965, two former employees of the plaintiff, at times with the assistance of two members of the plaintiff's staff, entered the plaintiff's office without authority and unbeknownst to him, removed numerous documents from his files, made copies of them, replaced the originals, and turned over the copies to the defendant Anderson, who was aware of the manner in which the copies had been obtained. The defendants Pearson and Anderson thereafter published articles containing information gleaned from these documents. . . .

The District Court ruled that appellants' receipt and subsequent use of photocopies of documents which appellants knew had been removed from appellee's files without authorization established appellants' liability for conversion. We conclude that appellants are not guilty of conversion on the facts shown.

. . . Conversion is the substantive tort theory which underlay the ancient common law form of action for trover. A plaintiff in trover alleged that he had lost a chattel which he rightfully possessed, . . . and that the defendant had found it and converted it to his own use. With time, the allegations of losing and finding became fictional, leaving the question of whether the defendant had "converted" the property the only operative one. . . .

The most distinctive feature of conversion is its measure of damages, which is the value of the goods converted. . . . The theory is that the "converting" defendant has in some way treated the goods as if they were his own, so that the plaintiff can properly ask the court to decree a forced sale of the property from the rightful possessor to the converter. . . . Because of this stringent measure of damages, it has long been recognized that not every wrongful interference with the personal property of another is a conversion. . . . Where the intermeddling falls short of the complete or very substantial deprivation of possessory rights in the property, the tort committed is not conversion, but the lesser wrong of trespass to chattels. . . .

The Second Restatement of Torts has marked the distinction by defining conversion as: "* * * An intentional exercise of dominion or control over a chattel which so seriously interferes with the right of another to control it that the actor may justly be required to pay the other the full value of the chattel." . . . Less serious interferences fall under the Restatement's definition of trespass. . . . The difference is more than a semantic one. The measure of damages in trespass is not the whole value of the property interfered with, but rather the actual diminution in its value caused by the interference. . . . More important for this case, a judgment for conversion can be obtained with only nominal damages, whereas liability for trespass to chattels exists only on a showing of actual damage to the property interfered with. . . . Here the District Court granted partial summary judgment on the issue of liability alone, while conceding that possibly no more than nominal damages might be awarded on subsequent trial. Partial summary judgment for liability could not have been granted on a theory of trespass to chattels without an undisputed showing of actual damages to the property in question.

It is clear that on the agreed facts appellants committed no conversion of the physical documents taken from appellee's files. Those documents were removed from the files at night, photocopied, and returned to the files undamaged before office operations resumed in the morning. Insofar as the documents' value to appellee resided in their usefulness as records of the business of his office, appellee was clearly not substantially deprived of his use of them.

This of course is not an end of the matter. It has long been recognized that documents often have value above and beyond that springing from their physical possession. . . . They may embody information or ideas whose economic value depends in part or in whole upon being kept secret. The question then arises whether the information taken by means of copying appellee's office files is of the type which the law of conversion protects. The general rule has been that ideas or information are not subject to legal protection, . . . but the law has developed exceptions to this rule. Where information is gathered and arranged at some cost and sold as a commodity on the market, it is properly protected as property. . . . Where ideas are formulated with labor and inventive genius, as in the case of literary works . . . or scientific researches, . . . they are protected. Where they constitute instruments of fair and effective commercial competition, those who develop them may gather their fruits under the protection of the law. . . .

The question here is not whether appellee had a right to keep his files from prying eyes, but whether the information taken from those files falls under the protection of the law of property, enforceable by a suit for conversion. In our view, it does not. The information included the contents of letters to appellee from supplicants, and office records of other kinds, the nature of which is not fully revealed by the record. Insofar as we can tell, none of it amounts to literary property, to scientific invention, or to secret plans formulated by appellee for the conduct of commerce. Nor does it appear to be information held in any way for sale by appellee, analogous to the fresh news copy produced by a wire service. . . .

Appellee complains, not of the misappropriation of property bought or created by him, but of the exposure of information either (1) injurious to his reputation or (2) revelatory of matters which he believes he has a right to keep to himself. Injuries of this type are redressed at law by suit for libel and invasion of privacy respectively . . . .

Because no conversion of the physical contents of appellee's files took place, and because the information copied from the documents in those files has not been shown to be property subject to protection by suit for conversion, the District Court's ruling that appellants are guilty of conversion must be reversed.

G. TRESPASS TO LAND

The tort of trespass to land protects the interest of the legal possessor of real property to be free from unconsented tangible intrusions onto the property. The trespassing defendant is liable without regard to whether plaintiff suffers any tangible harm. Modern science has muddied the waters a bit on what constitutes a tangible intrusion onto real property.

BRADLEY V. AMERICAN SMELTING AND REFINING CO.
709 P.2D 782 (WASH. 1985)

. . . Plaintiffs, landowners on Vashon Island, had sued for damages in trespass and nuisance from the deposit on their property of microscopic, airborne particles of heavy metals which came from the American Smelting and Refining Company (ASARCO) copper smelter at Ruston, Washington. The issues certified for answer are as follows:

1. Did the defendant have the requisite intent to commit intentional trespass as a matter of law?
2. Does an intentional deposit of microscopic particulates, undetectable by the human senses, upon a person's property give rise to a cause of action for trespassory invasion of the person's right to exclusive possession of property as well as a claim of nuisance?
3. Does the cause of action for trespassory invasion require proof of actual damages? . . .

The parties have stipulated to the facts as follows: Plaintiffs Michael O. Bradley and Marie A. Bradley, husband and wife, are owners and occupiers of real property on the southern end of Vashon Island in King County, Washington. The Bradleys purchased their property in 1978. Defendant ASARCO, a New Jersey corporation doing business in Washington, operates a primary copper smelter on real property it owns in Rushton, which is . . . surrounded by the city of Tacoma, Washington.

On October 3, 1983, plaintiffs brought this action against defendant alleging a cause of action for intentional trespass and for nuisance.

Plaintiffs' property is located some 4 miles north of defendant's smelter. Defendant's primary copper smelter (also referred to as the Tacoma smelter), has operated in its present location since 1890. It has operated as a copper smelter since 1902, and in 1905 it was purchased and operated by a corporate entity which is now ASARCO. As a part of the industrial process of smelting copper at the Tacoma smelter, various gases such as sulfur dioxide and particulate matter, including arsenic, cadmium and other metals, are emitted. Particulate matter is composed of distinct particles of matter other than water, which cannot be detected by the human senses. . . . It was apparently stipulated that the record contains no proof of actual damages. . . .

1. Did the defendant have the requisite intent to commit intentional trespass as a matter of law?

The parties stipulated that as a part of the smelting process, particulate matter including arsenic and cadmium was emitted, that some of the emissions had been deposited on the plaintiffs' land and that the defendant has been aware since 1905 that the wind, on occasion, caused these emissions to be blown over the plaintiffs' land. The defendant cannot and does not deny that whenever the smelter was in operation the whim of the winds could bring these deleterious substances to the plaintiffs' premises. We are asked if the defendant, knowing what it had to know from the facts it admits, had the legal intent to commit trespass.

The Restatement (Second) of Torts § 158 (1965) states:

> One is subject to liability to another for trespass, irrespective of whether he thereby causes harm to any legally protected interest of the other, if he intentionally
>
> a. enters land in the possession of the other, or causes a thing or a third person to do so, or
> b. remains on the land, or
> c. fails to remove from the land a thing which he is under a duty to remove.

In the comment on Clause (a) of § 158 . . . it is stated in part:

> i. *Causing entry of a thing.* The actor, without himself entering the land, may invade another's interest in its exclusive possession by throwing, propelling, or placing a thing, either on or beneath the surface of the land or in the air space above it. Thus, in the absence of the possessor's consent or other privilege to do so, it is an actionable trespass to throw rubbish on another's land ... In order that there may be a trespass under the rule stated in this Section, it is not necessary that the foreign matter should be thrown directly and immediately upon the other's land. It is enough that an act is done with knowledge that it will to a substantial certainty result in the entry of the foreign matter.

Addressing the definition, scope and meaning of "intent", section 8A of the Restatement (Second) of Torts says: "The word 'intent' is used ... to denote that the actor desires to cause consequences of his act, or that he believes that the consequences are substantially certain to result from it." . . . [A]nd we find in comment b at 15: "Intent is not, however, limited to consequences which are desired. If the actor knows that the consequences are certain, or substantially certain, to result from his act, and still goes ahead, he is treated by the law as if he had in fact desired to produce the result."

The defendant has known for decades that sulfur dioxide and particulates of arsenic, cadmium and other metals were being emitted from the tall smokestack. It had to know that the solids propelled into the air by the warm gases would settle back to earth somewhere. It had to know that a purpose of the tall stack was to disperse the gas, smoke and minute solids over as large an area as possible and as far away as possible, but that while any resulting contamination would be diminished as to any one area or landowner, that nonetheless contamination, though slight, would follow.

In W. Prosser, *Torts* § 8, at 31-32 (4th ed. 1971) intent is defined as follows:

> The intent with which tort liability is concerned is not necessarily a hostile intent, or a desire to do any harm. Rather it is an intent to bring about a result which will invade the interests of another in a way that the law will not sanction. The defendant may be liable although he has meant nothing more than a good-natured practical joke . . . .
>
> Intent, however, is broader than a desire to bring about physical results. It must extend not only to those consequences which are desired, but also to those which the actor believes are substantially certain to follow from what he does.... The man who fires a bullet into a dense crowd may fervently pray that he will hit no one, but since he must believe and know that he cannot avoid doing so, he intends it. The practical application of this principle has meant that where a reasonable man in the defendant's position would believe that a particular result was substantially certain to follow, he will be dealt with by the jury, or even by the court, as though he had intended it.
>
> (Footnotes omitted.) . . . .

It is patent that the defendant acted on its own volition and had to appreciate with substantial certainty that the law of gravity would visit the effluence upon someone, somewhere.

We find that the defendant had the requisite intent to commit intentional trespass as a matter of law.

2. Does an intentional deposit of microscopic particulates, undetectable by the human senses, upon a person's property give rise to a cause of action for trespassory invasion of the person's right to exclusive possession of property as well as a claim of nuisance?

The courts have been groping for a reconciliation of the doctrines of trespass and nuisance over a long period of time and, to a great extent, have concluded that little of substance remains to any distinction between the two when air pollution is involved. . . . The basic distinction is that trespass can be defined as any intentional invasion of the plaintiff's interest in the exclusive possession of property, whereas a nuisance requires a substantial and unreasonable interference with his use and enjoyment of it. That is to say, in trespass cases defendant's conduct typically results in an encroachment by "something" upon plaintiff's exclusive rights of possession. . . .

It is also true that in the environmental arena both nuisance and trespass cases typically involve intentional conduct by the defendant who knows that his activities are substantially certain to result in an invasion of plaintiff's interests. The principal difference in theories is that the tort of trespass is complete upon a tangible invasion of plaintiff's property, however slight, whereas a nuisance requires proof that the interference with use and enjoyment is "substantial and unreasonable." This burden of proof advantage in a trespass case is accompanied by a slight remedial advantage as well. Upon proof of a technical trespass plaintiff always is entitled to nominal damages. It is possible also that a plaintiff could get injunctive relief against a technical trespass—for example, the deposit of particles of air pollutant on his property causing no known adverse effects. The protection of the integrity of his possessory interests might justify the injunction even without proof of the substantial injury necessary to establish a nuisance. Of course absent proof of injury, or at least a reasonable suspicion of it, courts are unlikely to invoke their equitable powers to require expensive control efforts.

. . . Just as there may be proof advantages in a trespass theory, there may be disadvantages also. Potential problems lurk in the ancient requirements that a trespassory invasion be "direct or immediate" and that an "object" or "something tangible" be deposited upon plaintiff's land. Some courts . . . define "object" as requiring something larger or more substantial than smoke, dust, gas, or fumes. . . .

The insistence that a trespass involve an invasion by a "thing" or "object" was repudiated in the well-known (but not particularly influential) case of *Martin v. Reynolds Metals Co.*, [221 Or. 86, 342 P.2d 790 (1959)], which held that gaseous and particulate fluorides from an aluminum smelter constituted a trespass for purposes of the statute of limitations:

> [L]iability on the theory of trespass has been recognized where the harm was produced by the vibration of the soil or by the concussion of the air which, of course, is nothing more than the movement of molecules one against the other.

> The view recognizing a trespassory invasion where there is no 'thing' which can be seen with the naked eye undoubtedly runs counter to the definition of trespass expressed in some quarters. [Citing the Restatement (First), Torts and Prosser]. It is quite possible that in an earlier day when science had not yet peered into the molecular and atomic world of small particles, the courts could not fit an invasion through unseen physical instrumentalities into the requirement that a trespass can result only from a *direct* invasion. But in this atomic age even the uneducated know the great and awful force contained in the atom and what it can do to a man's property if it is released. In fact, the now famous equation $E=MC_2$ has taught us that mass and energy are equivalents and that our concept of 'things' must be reframed. If these observations on science in relation to the law of trespass should appear theoretical and unreal in the abstract, they become very practical and real to the possessor of land when the unseen force cracks the foundation of his house. The force is just as real if it is chemical in nature and must be awakened by the intervention of another agency before it does harm.

Martin is quite right in hastening the demise of the "direct" and "tangible" limitations on the law of trespass. . . .

The Restatement (Second) of Torts § 821D, comment *d*, at 102 (1979) states:

For an intentional trespass, there is liability without harm; for a private nuisance, there is no liability without significant harm. In trespass an intentional invasion of the plaintiff's possession is of itself a tort, and liability follows unless the defendant can show a privilege. In private nuisance an intentional interference with the plaintiff's use or enjoyment is not of itself a tort, and unreasonableness of the interference is necessary for liability.

Comment *e* at 102 states:

> There may, however, be some overlapping of the causes of action for trespass and private nuisance. An invasion of the possession of land normally involves some degree of interference with its use and enjoyment and this is true particularly when some harm is inflicted upon the land itself. The cause of action for trespass has traditionally included liability for incidental harms of this nature. If the interference with the use and enjoyment of the land is a significant one, sufficient in itself to amount to a private nuisance, the fact that it arises out of or is accompanied by a trespass will not prevent recovery for the nuisance, and the action may be maintained upon either basis as the plaintiff elects or both....

The two actions, trespass and private nuisance, are thus not entirely exclusive or inconsistent, and in a proper case in which the elements of both actions are fully present, the plaintiff may have his choice of one or the other, or may proceed upon both. . . .

3. Does the cause of action for trespassory invasion require proof of actual damages?

When airborn particles are transitory or quickly dissipate, they do not interfere with a property owner's possessory rights and, therefore, are properly denominated as nuisances. When, however, the particle or substance accumulates on the land and does not pass away, then a trespass has occurred. . . . While at common law any trespass entitled a landowner to recover nominal or punitive damages for the invasion of his property, such a rule is not appropriate under the circumstances before us. No useful purpose would be served by sanctioning actions in trespass by every landowner within a hundred miles of a manufacturing plant. Manufacturers would be harassed and the litigious few would cause escalation of costs to the detriment of the many. . . .

NOTES

1   *Intent.* The only intent required is the intention to enter, remain or cause another to enter where not permitted. Intentional entry onto land is required, but the defendant need not know that the entry constitutes a trespass.
2   *Ad coelum.* The rule at common law was "*cujus est solum emus est usque ad coelum*" (he who owns the soil also owns upward unto heaven). And today the real property owner's right to exclude still extends to the space above (and below) the surface of his land but is limited to the space of which the landowner can make practical use.
3   *Nuisance.* As this case and the following section will demonstrate, there is some overlap between trespass and nuisance.

4 *Damages.* The tort of trespass is cognizable without respect to whether the trespass causes any actual harm so long as there is an intentional, physical invasion of plaintiff's real property. Of course, if the trespass does cause harm, plaintiff can recover for her loss. Punitive damages may be available for deliberate trespass.

H. NUISANCE

Nuisance law is divided into "private" nuisance and "public" nuisance. The two causes of action are not very closely related. A defendant's "private" nuisance unreasonably interferes with his neighbor's quiet use and enjoyment of real property. A public nuisance interferes more broadly with the rights of the community at large.

1. PRIVATE NUISANCE

Private nuisance and trespass both vindicate real property interests. While the tort of trespass to land narrowly but rigorously protects the possessor's right to be free from unwanted physical intrusions, the law of private nuisance protects the broader, but less concrete, interest of the lawful occupier of property, in the "use and enjoyment" of that property. Such interferences frequently, but do not always, involve some sort of pollution.

The evaluation of a potential nuisance cause of action is almost devoid of bright lines. A defendant is subject to liability for private nuisance if his conduct causes a (1) substantial and unreasonable; (2) interference with plaintiff's use and enjoyment of land; and the interference is (3) intentional, reckless, negligent, or the product of an abnormally dangerous activity. Most torts writers treat the law of nuisance outside the context of intentional tort. It is a category unto itself that is closely related to property law.

a. NATURE OF LIABILITY

CLINIC & HOSPITAL, INC. V. MCCONNELL
236 S.W.2D 384 (MO. APP. 1951)

. . . [P]laintiff corporation operates the McCleary Clinic and Hospital in Excelsior Springs, Missouri. Since 1925, its main hospital building has been located at the northwest corner of the intersection of St. Louis Avenue . . . and Thompson Avenue . . . . The defendants . . . have operated the 'Tune In' music shop since November, 1947. This shop . . . is located . . . diagonally across the street from plaintiff's main building . . . . In February, 1948, the defendants installed a so-called loud speaker in the shop . . . . This loud speaker is located in an opening in the front window of the shop and pointed in the general direction of plaintiff's main building . . . . It is connected with and operated by an electric record player which is inside the shop. The volume of the sounds which emanate from the loud speaker can be regulated by turning a knob on the record player.

. . . Plaintiff's evidence was that defendants operated the record player and loud speaker every day from 8:00 or 9:00 a.m. until 7:00 or 8:00 p.m.; that on many occasions the machine was operated as late as 10:00 or 11:00 p.m.; and that during the hours mentioned the records were played almost continuously. The music reproduced through the loud speaker was distinctly audible in plaintiff's main hospital and clinic building, in the operating and recovery rooms . . . , above the usual noises of the street traffic.

. . . [O]ne of plaintiff's surgeons, and two surgical nurses connected with plaintiff's hospital, testified that music emanating from defendants' loud speaker disturbed patients in the recovery rooms, causing them to become very restless and nervous, and that it was necessary to give some of them additional sedatives. The nurses stated that the music was "loud" and could be heard "above the traffic." Dr. Kepler said that while the music disturbed some patients it did not disturb all of them. . . .

B. C. Hedges, president of plaintiff corporation, testified that on two occasions he called on defendants and requested them to reduce the volume of the music and explained that it was disturbing the patients; that he "reasoned with them from the standpoint of business people, fair play, fair dealing, and not only the economic side of the clinic, but the inhuman side to suffering people"; that defendants continued to broadcast the music "just as they had always done," and on several occasions he complained to the city officials. He said he had been in "various parts of the clinic at the time when the broadcasting was coming from across the street and heard the broadcasting." . . .

A. L. Forsythe testified that in June, 1949, he was a patient in Annex "C" for ten days; that during the time he was hospitalized defendants operated the record player every day, beginning about nine o'clock in the morning and continuing throughout the day and evening; that he was in a "bad condition and highly nervous" when he entered the hospital, and the music made him more nervous. He further stated that he had been employed at the post office located at the intersection of St. Louis Avenue and Thompson Avenue, some 200 feet south of defendants' music shop; that the music could be heard inside the post office when the windows were open, and "in a modified form" when the windows were closed. . . .

Generally speaking a person has the right to the exclusive control of his property and the right to devote it to such uses as will best subserve his interests; but these rights are not absolute. There are certain uses to which property may be put which so seriously interfere with the use and enjoyment by others of their property or with the rights of the public that they must be forbidden. . . . Noise is not a nuisance per se, but it may be of such a character as to constitute a nuisance, even though it arises from the operation of a lawful business. . . .

[A] business which is lawful in itself may become a nuisance where it is not operated in a fair and reasonable way with regard to the rights of others in the use and enjoyment of their property. The courts have made it clear that in every case the question is one of reasonableness. What is a reasonable use of one's property and whether a particular use is an unreasonable invasion of another's use and enjoyment of his property cannot be determined by exact rules, but must necessarily depend upon the circumstances of each case, such as locality and the character of the surroundings, the nature, utility and social value of the use, the extent and nature of the harm involved, the nature, utility and social value of the use or enjoyment invaded, and the like. *See* Restatement, Torts, Vol. IV, secs. 822, 831, pp. 214, 265. The use of property for a particular purpose and in a particular way in one locality may be reasonable and lawful, but such use may be unreasonable, unlawful and a nuisance in another locality. . . . While the weight of authority is that priority of occupation is not a defense as to one maintaining a nuisance, some courts have expressed the view that it is a factor to be considered in determining the character of the locality. . . . It is true, of course, that persons who live or work in thickly populated communities or in business districts must necessarily endure the usual annoyances and discomforts incident to the conduct of those trades and businesses which are properly located and carried on in the neighborhood where they live or work. But these annoyances and discomforts must not be more than those ordinarily to be expected in the community or district, and which are incident to the lawful conduct of such trades and businesses. If they exceed what might be reasonably expected and cause unnecessary harm, then the court will grant relief.

The evidence shows that plaintiff's hospital was established on Thompson Avenue in 1925, about 22 years before defendants opened their music shop. It is true that stores and shops were being operated on Thompson Avenue at the time the hospital was established, but the sounds complained of are not inherent in the character of that locality. There is nothing in the record to show that any merchants in that vicinity, except the defendants herein, have ever broadcast music for any purpose. On the contrary, it appears that the sounds broadcast by defendants are substantially different from all other sounds and noises incident to the usual activities in that district. The record does not show that the other noises are harmful to the patients or that they interfere with the operation of the clinic and hospital. Under these circumstances, it cannot be said that plaintiff's business is unsuited to the character of the locality.

. . . There can be no doubt that defendants have the right to operate their music shop in its present location so long as the business is conducted in a reasonable manner with regard to the rights of others. We think, however, that the broadcasting of the music in the manner described and with the results set forth in our findings is an unusual, unreasonable, and unlawful use of defendants' property, in the particular location and under the conditions with which we are here confronted. Furthermore, defendant Richard McConnell testified that he intended to continue the broadcasting "the way it is now." It is clear, therefore, that plaintiff is entitled to equitable relief.

On the other hand, freedom of action on the part of one person ought not to be curtailed more than is necessary for the public welfare or the protection of the rights of some other person. In the present case, the chancellor should have entered a judgment perpetually enjoining the defendants, and each of them, from operating any loud speaker or sound amplifier, or any record player or phonograph, or permitting the same to be operated in or about their place of business, in such manner as to cause the music or sounds produced by any such device to be audible in any part of plaintiff's said clinic and hospital buildings devoted to the care and treatment of patients.

For the reasons stated, it is the recommendation of the Commissioner that the judgment be reversed and the cause remanded with directions to enter a judgment to the above effect.

NOTE

1   Some activities have attained almost *per se* status as nuisances when conducted in a purely residential area, e.g., funeral homes.

ENSIGN V. WALLS
34 N.W.2D 549 (MICH. 1948)

Defendant herein has for some years past carried on at 13949 Dacosta Street, in the city of Detroit, the business of raising, breeding and boarding St. Bernard dogs. Plaintiffs are property owners and residents in the immediate neighborhood. Claiming that the business conducted by defendant constituted a nuisance as to them and their property, plaintiffs brought suit for injunctive relief. The bill of complaint alleged that obnoxious odors came from defendant's premises at all times, that the continual barking of the dogs interfered with and disturbed plaintiffs in the use and enjoyment of their respective properties, that the premises were infested with rats and flies, and that on occasions dogs escaped from defendant's premises and roamed about the neighborhood. Defendant in her answer denied that her business was conducted in such a manner as to constitute a nuisance, and claimed further that she had carried on the business at the premises in question since 1926, that she had invested a considerable sum of money in the purchase of the property and in the subsequent erection of buildings thereon, and that under the circumstances plaintiffs were not entitled to the relief sought. . . . The trial judge inspected the premises of the defendant, and it appears from the record that his observations confirmed, in many respects at least, the proofs offered by plaintiffs with reference to the existing conditions. Decree was entered enjoining the carrying on of the business at the location in question after the expiration of 90 days from the entry of the decree, and requiring defendant to abate, within the period of time stated, the nuisance found to exist.

. . . The record discloses that the plaintiffs, or the majority of them at least, have moved into the neighborhood in recent years. In view of this situation it is claimed by defendant that, inasmuch as she was carrying on her business of raising, breeding and boarding dogs on her premises at the time plaintiffs established their residences in the neighborhood, they cannot now be heard to complain. Such circumstance may properly be taken into account in a proceeding of this nature in determining whether the relief sought ought, in equity and good conscience, to be granted. Doubtless under such circumstances courts of equity are more reluctant to restrain the continued operation of a lawful business than in instances where it is sought to begin in a residential district a business of such character that it will constitute a nuisance. The supreme court of Pennsylvania in *Wier's Appeal,* 74 Pa. 230, declared the commonly accepted rule as follows:

> There is a very marked distinction to be observed in reason and equity between the case of a business long established in a particular locality, which has become a nuisance from the growth of population and the erection of dwellings in proximity to it, and that of a new erection threatened in such a vicinity. Carrying on an offensive trade for any number of years in a place remote from buildings and public roads, does not entitle the owner to continue it in the same place after houses have been built and roads laid out in the neighborhood, to the occupants of which and travelers upon which it is a nuisance. As the city extends, such nuisances should be removed to the vacant grounds beyond the immediate neighborhood of the residences of the citizens. This, public policy, as well as the health and comfort of the population of the city, demand. . . . It certainly ought to be a much clearer case, however, to justify a court of equity in stretching forth the strong arm of injunction to compel a man to remove an establishment in which he has invested his capital and been carrying on business for a long period of time, from that of one who comes into a neighborhood proposing to establish such a business for the first time, and who is met at the threshold of his enterprise by a remonstrance and notice that if he persists in his purpose, application will be made to a court of equity to prevent him.

. . . Defendant cites and relies on prior decisions of this Court in each of which consideration was given to the circumstance that the parties seeking relief had established residences near the business the operation of which was sought to be enjoined. That such a circumstance may properly be considered in any case of this character in determining whether equitable relief should be granted is scarcely open to question. However it is not necessarily controlling. Looking to all the facts and circumstances involved, the question invariably presented is whether the discretion of the court should be exercised in favor of the parties seeking relief. In the case at bar the trial court came to the conclusion that the nuisance found by him to exist ought to be abated, and that such action was necessary . . . to protect the plaintiffs in their rights and in the use and enjoyment of their homes. It may be assumed that new residences will be built in the community in the future, as they have been in the past, and that in consequence the community will become more and more thickly populated. This means of course that the injurious results of the carrying on of defendant's business, if the nuisance is not abated, will be greater in the future than it has been in the past. Such was obviously the view of the trial judge, and we cannot say that he abused his discretion in granting relief. On the contrary we think his conclusions were fully justified by the record. . . .

QUESTIONS

1   This case reflects the majority rule that a plaintiff's "coming to the nuisance" is not a complete defense. Is it unfair that defendant's activity was barred even though defendant was in business before plaintiffs moved into the neighborhood?

2   Would the analysis of this scenario change at all if the surrounding residential neighborhood had been there first? What if when defendant started her business, she was the first occupant of a sub-division with lots for sale with streets, sidewalks and utilities all ready to go, but the developer could not sell any other lots with the St. Bernard farm in place? Would it be fair to enjoin defendant's business then? What if the surrounding land were owned by a developer who has written plans for a developed sub-division but who cannot get financing because of this St. Bernard farm? What if the surrounding land were vacant, and the owner were seeking a developer to buy it, but none was interested because of the St. Bernard farm? Should the business be enjoined? If your answers to these four questions differ, what's the difference?

ROGERS V. ELLIOTT
15 N.E. 768 (MASS. 1888)

The defendant was the custodian and authorized manager of property of the Roman Catholic Church used for religious worship. The acts for which the plaintiff seeks to hold him responsible were done in the use of this property . . . . The plaintiff's case rests upon the proposition that the ringing of the bell was a nuisance. The consideration of this proposition involves an inquiry into what the defendant could properly do in the use of the real estate which he had in charge, and what was the standard by which his rights were to be measured. . . .

In an action of this kind, a fundamental question is, by what standard, as against the interests of a neighbor, is one's right to use his real estate to be measured. In densely populated communities the use of property in many ways which are legitimate and proper necessarily affects in greater or less degree the property or persons of others in the vicinity. In such cases the inquiry always is, when rights are called in question, what is reasonable under the circumstances. If a use of property is objectionable solely on account of the noise which it makes, it is a nuisance, if at all, by reason of its effect upon the health or comfort of those who are within hearing. The right to make a noise for a proper purpose must be measured in reference to the degree of annoyance which others may reasonably be required to submit to. In connection with the importance of the business from which it proceeds, that must be determined by the effect of noise upon people generally, and not upon those, on the one hand, who are peculiarly susceptible to it, or those, on the other, who by long experience have learned to endure it without inconvenience; not upon those whose strong nerves and robust health enable them to endure the greatest disturbances without suffering, nor upon those whose mental or physical condition makes them painfully sensitive to everything about them.

. . . Upon a question whether one can lawfully ring his factory bell, or run his noisy machinery, or whether the noise will be a private nuisance to the occupant of a house nearby, it is necessary to ascertain the natural and probable effect of the sound upon ordinary persons in that house – not how it will affect a particular person, who happens to be there to-day, or who may chance to come tomorrow. . . . If one's right to use his property were to depend upon the effect of the use upon a person of peculiar temperament or disposition, or upon one suffering from an uncommon disease, the standard for measuring it would be so uncertain and fluctuating as to paralyze industrial enterprises. The owner of a factory containing noisy machinery, with dwelling-houses all about it, might find his business lawful as to all but one of the tenants of the houses, and as to that one, who dwelt no nearer than the others, it might be a nuisance. The character of his business might change from legal to illegal, or illegal to legal, with every change of tenants of an adjacent estate; or with an arrival or departure of a guest or boarder at a house nearby; or even with the wakefulness or the tranquil repose of an invalid neighbor on a particular night. Legal rights to the use of property cannot be left to such uncertainty. . . .

In the case at bar it is not contended that the ringing of the bell for church services in the manner shown by the evidence materially affected the health or comfort of ordinary people in the vicinity, but the plaintiff's claim rests upon the injury done him on account of his peculiar condition. However his request should have been treated by the defendant upon considerations of humanity, we think he could not put himself in a place of exposure to noise, and demand as of legal right that the bell should not be used.

b. REMEDIES

Courts exercise broad discretion in formulating remedies for private nuisance, but the most common remedies are damages, injunctive relief, or both. The following case discusses the choice between these two potential remedies.

BOOMER V. ATLANTIC CEMENT CO.
257 N.E.2D 870 (N.Y. 1970)

Defendant operates a large cement plant near Albany. These are actions for injunction and damages by neighboring land owners alleging injury to property from dirt, smoke and vibration emanating from the plant. A nuisance has been found after trial, temporary damages have been allowed; but an injunction has been denied. . . .

The cement making operations of defendant have been found by the court at Special Term to have damaged the nearby properties of plaintiffs in these two actions. That court, as it has been noted, accordingly found defendant maintained a nuisance and this has been affirmed at the Appellate Division. The total damage to plaintiffs' properties is, however, relatively small in comparison with the value of defendant's operation and with the consequences of the injunction which plaintiffs seek.

The ground for the denial of injunction, notwithstanding the finding both that there is a nuisance and that plaintiffs have been damaged substantially, is the large disparity in economic consequences of the nuisance and of the injunction. This theory cannot, however, be sustained without overruling a doctrine which has been consistently reaffirmed in several leading cases in this court and which has never been disavowed here, namely that where a nuisance has been found and where there has been any substantial damage shown by the party complaining an injunction will be granted. The rule in New York has been that such a nuisance will be enjoined although marked disparity be shown in economic consequence between the effect of the injunction and the effect of the nuisance. . . .

Although the court at Special Term and the Appellate Division held that injunction should be denied, it was found that plaintiffs had been damaged in various specific amounts up to the time of the trial and damages to the respective plaintiffs were awarded for those amounts. The effect of this was, injunction having been denied, plaintiffs could maintain successive actions at law for damages thereafter as further damage was incurred.

The court at Special Term also found the amount of permanent damage attributable to each plaintiff, for the guidance of the parties in the event both sides stipulated to the payment and acceptance of such permanent damage as a settlement of all the controversies among the parties. The total of permanent damages to all plaintiffs thus found was $185,000. This basis of adjustment has not resulted in any stipulation by the parties.

This result at Special Term and at the Appellate Division is a departure from a rule that has become settled; but to follow the rule literally in these cases would be to close down the plant at once. This court is fully agreed to avoid that immediately drastic remedy; the difference in view is how best to avoid it.[*]

One alternative is to grant the injunction but postpone its effect to a specified future date to give opportunity for technical advances to permit defendant to eliminate the nuisance; another is to grant the injunction conditioned on the payment of permanent damages to plaintiffs which would compensate them for the total economic loss to their property present and future caused by defendant's operations. For reasons which will be developed the court chooses the latter alternative.

If the injunction were to be granted unless within a short period – e.g., 18 months – the nuisance be abated by improved methods, there would be no assurance that any significant technical improvement would occur. . . . For obvious reasons the rate of the research is beyond control of defendant. If at the end of 18 months the whole industry has not found a technical solution a court would be hard put to close down this one cement plant if due regard be given to equitable principles.

On the other hand, to grant the injunction unless defendant pays plaintiffs such permanent damages as may be fixed by the court seems to do justice between the contending parties. All of the attributions of economic loss to the properties on which plaintiffs' complaints are based will have been redressed. The nuisance complained of by these plaintiffs may have other public or private consequences, but these particular parties are the only ones who have sought remedies and the judgment proposed will fully redress them. . . .

---

[*] Respondent's investment in the plant is in excess of $45,000,000. There are over 300 people employed there.

It seems reasonable to think that the risk of being required to pay permanent damages to injured property owners by cement plant owners would itself be a reasonable effective spur to research for improved techniques to minimize nuisance. . . . Thus it seems fair to both sides to grant permanent damages to plaintiffs which will terminate this private litigation. The theory of damage is the "servitude on land" of plaintiffs imposed by defendant's nuisance. . . . The judgment, by allowance of permanent damages imposing a servitude on land, which is the basis of the actions, would preclude future recovery by plaintiffs or their grantees. This should be placed beyond debate by a provision of the judgment that the payment by defendant and the acceptance by plaintiffs of permanent damages found by the court shall be in compensation for a servitude on the land. . . .

Jasen, Judge (dissenting).

I agree with the majority that a reversal is required here, but I do not subscribe to the newly enunciated doctrine of assessment of permanent damages, in lieu of an injunction, where substantial property rights have been impaired by the creation of a nuisance. . . . I see grave dangers in overruling our long-established rule of granting an injunction where a nuisance results in substantial continuing damage. In permitting the injunction to become inoperative upon the payment of permanent damages, the majority is, in effect, licensing a continuing wrong. It is the same as saying to the cement company, you may continue to do harm to your neighbors so long as you pay a fee for it. Furthermore, once such permanent damages are assessed and paid, the incentive to alleviate the wrong would be eliminated, thereby continuing air pollution of an area without abatement. . . .

This kind of inverse condemnation may not be invoked by a private person or corporation for private gain or advantage. Inverse condemnation should only be permitted when the public is primarily served in the taking or impairment of property. The promotion of the interests of the polluting cement company has, in my opinion, no public use or benefit. . . .

I would enjoin the defendant cement company from continuing the discharge of dust particles upon its neighbors' properties unless, within 18 months, the cement company abated this nuisance.

It is not my intention to cause the removal of the cement plant from the Albany area, but to recognize the urgency of the problem stemming from this stationary source of air pollution, and to allow the company a specified period of time to develop a means to alleviate this nuisance.

I am aware that the trial court found that the most modern dust control devices available have been installed in defendant's plant, but, I submit, this does not mean that *better* and more effective dust control devices could not be developed within the time allowed to abate the pollution. Moreover, I believe it is incumbent upon the defendant to develop such devices, since the cement company, at the time the plant commenced production (1962), was well aware of the plaintiffs' presence in the area, as well as the probable consequences of its contemplated operation. Yet, it still chose to build and operate the plant at this site. . . .

1   What do you think of the one-time payment of permanent damages instead of an immediate injunction from a policy perspective?
2   Do you think an injunction in a case like *Boomer* likely would result in the shutdown of the cement plant?
3   The *Boomer* court chose between awarding a single lump sum for future damages and allowing periodic actions for actual damages as they arise. What are the pros and cons of each approach?

SPUR INDUSTRIES, INC. V. DEL E. WEBB DEVELOPMENT CO.
494 P.2D 700 (ARIZ. 1972)

From a judgment permanently enjoining the defendant, Spur Industries, Inc., from operating a cattle feedlot near the plaintiff Del E. Webb Development Company's Sun City, Spur appeals. Webb cross-appeals. Although numerous issues are raised, we feel that it is necessary to answer only two questions. They are:

> Where the operation of a business, such as a cattle feedlot, is lawful in the first instance but becomes a nuisance by reason of a nearby residential area, may the feedlot operation be enjoined in an action brought by the developer of the residential area?
>
> Assuming that the nuisance may be enjoined, may the developer of a completely new town or urban area in a previously agricultural area be required to indemnify the operator of the feedlot who must move or cease operation because of the presence of the residential area created by the developer?

... The area in question is ... some 14 to 15 miles west of the urban area of Phoenix, on ... Grand Avenue. ... In 1956, Spur's predecessors in interest, H. Marion Welborn and the Northside Hay Mill and Trading Company, developed feed-lots ... in an area between the confluence of the usually dry Agua Fria and New Rivers. The area is well suited for cattle feeding and in 1959, there were 25 cattle feeding pens or dairy operations within a 7 mile radius of the location developed by Spur's predecessors. In April and May of 1959, the Northside Hay Mill was feeding between 6,000 and 7,000 head of cattle and Welborn approximately 1,500 head on a combined area of 35 acres.

In May of 1959, Del Webb began to plan the development of an urban area to be known as Sun City. For this purpose, ... some 20,000 acres of farmland, were purchased for $15,000,000 or $750.00 per acre. This price was considerably less than the price of land located near the urban area of Phoenix, and ... was a factor influencing the decision to purchase the property in question.

By September 1959, Del Webb had started construction of a golf course south of Grand Avenue and Spur's predecessors had started to level ground for more feedlot area. In 1960, Spur purchased the property in question and began a rebuilding and expansion program extending both to the north and south of the original facilities. By 1962, Spur's expansion program was completed and had expanded from approximately 35 acres to 114 acres. . . .

Accompanied by an extensive advertising campaign, homes were first offered by Del Webb in January 1960 and the first unit to be completed was south of Grand Avenue and approximately 2 1/2 miles north of Spur. By 2 May 1960, there were 450 to 500 houses completed or under construction. At this time, Del Webb did not consider odors from the Spur feed pens a problem and Del Webb continued to develop in a southerly direction, until sales resistance became so great that the parcels were difficult if not impossible to sell. . . . By December 1967, Del Webb's property had extended south to Olive Avenue and Spur was within 500 feet of Olive Avenue to the north. . . . Del Webb filed its original complaint alleging that in excess of 1,300 lots in the southwest portion were unfit for development for sale as residential lots because of the operation of the Spur feedlot.

Del Webb's suit complained that the Spur feeding operation was a public nuisance because of the flies and the odor which were drifting or being blown by the prevailing south to north wind over the southern portion of Sun City. At the time of the suit, Spur was feeding between 20,000 and 30,000 head of cattle, and the facts amply support the finding of the trial court that the feed pens had become a nuisance to the people who resided in the southern part of Del Webb's development. The testimony indicated that cattle in a commercial feedlot will produce 35 to 40 pounds of wet manure per day, per head, or over a million pounds of wet manure per day for 30,000 head of cattle, and that despite the admittedly good feedlot management and good housekeeping practices by Spur, the resulting odor and flies produced an annoying if not unhealthy situation as far as the senior citizens of southern Sun City were concerned. There is no doubt that some of the citizens of Sun City were unable to enjoy the outdoor living which Del Webb had advertised and that Del Webb was faced with sales resistance from prospective purchasers as well as strong and persistent complaints from the people who had purchased homes in that area. . . .

MAY SPUR BE ENJOINED?

. . . Where the injury is slight, the remedy for minor inconveniences lies in an action for damages rather than in one for an injunction. . . . Moreover, some courts have held, in the "balancing of conveniences" cases, that damages may be the sole remedy. *See Boomer v. Atlantic Cement Co.,* . . . . (1970) . . . . It is clear that as to the citizens of Sun City, the operation of Spur's feedlot was both a public and a private nuisance. They could have successfully maintained an action to abate the nuisance. Del Webb, having shown a special injury in the loss of sales, had a standing to bring suit to enjoin the nuisance. . . . The judgment of the trial court permanently enjoining the operation of the feedlot is affirmed.

MUST DEL WEBB INDEMNIFY SPUR?

A suit to enjoin a nuisance sounds in equity and the courts have long recognized a special responsibility to the public when acting as a court of equity . . . . In addition to protecting the public interest, . . . courts of equity are concerned with protecting the operator of a lawfully, albeit noxious, business from the result of a knowing and willful encroachment by others near his business. . . . Were Webb the only party injured, we would feel justified in holding that the doctrine of "coming to the nuisance" would have been a bar to the relief asked by Webb, and, on the other hand, had Spur located the feedlot near the outskirts of a city and had the city grown toward the feedlot, Spur would have to suffer the cost of abating the nuisance as to those people locating within the growth pattern of the expanding city . . . . We agree, however, with the Massachusetts court that:

> The law of nuisance affords no rigid rule to be applied in all instances. It is elastic. It undertakes
> to require only that which is fair and reasonable under all the circumstances. In a common-
> wealth like this, which depends for its material prosperity so largely on the continued growth
> and enlargement of manufacturing of diverse varieties, "extreme rights" cannot be enforced. * * *.

Stevens v. Rockport Granite Co., 216 Mass. 486, 488, 104 N.E. 371, 373 (1914).

There was no indication in the instant case at the time Spur and its predecessors located in western Maricopa County that a new city would spring up, full-blown, alongside the feeding operation and that the developer of that city would ask the court to order Spur to move because of the new city. Spur is required to move not because of any wrongdoing on the part of Spur, but because of a proper and legitimate regard of the courts for the rights and interests of the public.

Del Webb, on the other hand, is entitled to the relief prayed for (a permanent injunction), not because Webb is blameless, but because of the damage to the people who have been encouraged to purchase homes in Sun City. It does not equitably or legally follow, however, that Webb, being entitled to the injunction, is then free of any liability to Spur if Webb has in fact been the cause of the damage Spur has sustained. It does not seem harsh to require a developer, who has taken advantage of the lesser land values in a rural area as well as the availability of large tracts of land on which to build and develop a new town or city in the area, to indemnify those who are forced to leave as a result.

Having brought people to the nuisance to the foreseeable detriment of Spur, Webb must indemnify Spur for a reasonable amount of the cost of moving or shutting down. It should be noted that this relief to Spur is limited to a case wherein a developer has, with foreseeability, brought into a previously agricultural or industrial area the population which makes necessary the granting of an injunction against a lawful business and for which the business has no adequate relief.

It is therefore the decision of this court that the matter be remanded to the trial court for a hearing upon the damages sustained by the defendant Spur as a reasonable and direct result of the granting of the permanent injunction. Since the result of the appeal may appear novel and both sides have obtained a measure of relief, it is ordered that each side will bear its own costs. Affirmed in part, reversed in part, and remanded for further proceedings consistent with this opinion.

2. PUBLIC NUISANCE

The line that divides public from private nuisance is somewhat vague – according to the Restatement (Second) of Torts, the interest protected by the law of public nuisance is freedom from an unreasonable interference with a right common to the general public. Public nuisance applies only to an interference with a common right, frequently in air, water or streets. The distinction between public and private nuisance that may have the greatest practical significance is that not just anyone may sue for damages to remedy a public nuisance. Traditionally, courts have distinguished between a private citizen who has sustained a harm of the same kind as that suffered by the general public, for which there is no civil damages remedy, and a private citizen whose harm is different in kind from that suffered by other members of the public (frequently personal injury), which citizen may sue for the harm caused by the public nuisance. Also, public officials or agencies may sue for damages. In the vast majority of public nuisance cases, suit is brought by government bodies, as in the following case.

STATE V. LEAD INDUSTRIES ASS'N
951 A.2D 428 (R.I. 2008)

It is undisputed that lead poisoning constitutes a public health crisis that has plagued and continues to plague this country, particularly its children. . . . There seems to be little public debate that exposure to lead can have a wide range of effects on a child's development and behavior. . . . Lead was widely used in residential paints in the United States until the mid-1970s. There is no doubt that lead-based paint is the primary source of childhood lead exposure. In the United States, children most often are lead-poisoned by ingesting lead paint chips from deteriorating walls or inhaling lead-contaminated surface dust.

Children under six years of age are the most susceptible to lead poisoning for two primary reasons. First, children are more likely to encounter lead; young children spend a significant portion of their time on the floor, among the dust and chips of lead paint. Second, because they are young, children's growing bodies have a tendency to absorb more lead, and their brains and nervous systems are more sensitive to the lead. Most lead pigment manufacturers belonged to the LIA as early as 1928, but the length of each company's membership varied considerably. . . .

On October 12, 1999, the Attorney General, on behalf of the state filed a ten-count complaint against eight former lead pigment manufacturers, John Doe corporations, and the LIA. . . . The state alleged that the manufacturers or their predecessors-in-interest had manufactured, promoted, distributed, and sold lead pigment for use in residential paint, despite that they knew or should have known, since the early 1900s, that lead is hazardous to human health. The state also contended that the LIA was, in essence, a coconspirator or aider and abettor of one or more of the manufacturers from at least 1928 to the present. . . . The state further alleged that defendants' actions caused it to incur substantial damages. As such, the state asserted, defendants were liable for public nuisance . . . . In January 2000, defendants moved to dismiss all counts of the state's complaint pursuant to Rule 12(b)(6) of the Superior Court Rules of Civil Procedure. . . . . The trial justice, agreeing with the state, denied defendants' motion. . . .

The trial justice provided the jury with the law applicable to the case and instructed the jury to apply that law to the facts as it found them based on the evidence presented. First, the trial justice explained that the jury was being asked to determine "whether the cumulative presence of lead pigment in paints and coatings in or on buildings throughout the state of Rhode Island constitutes a public nuisance." He defined public nuisance as "something that unreasonably interferes with a right common to the general public. It is something that unreasonably interferes with the health, safety, peace, comfort or convenience of the general community." He further explained that the right common to the general public is collective in nature and belongs to the community at large. The trial justice then clarified that "an interference is an injury, invasion, disruption, or obstruction of a right held by the general public." He added that an interference "is unreasonable when persons have suffered harm or are threatened with injuries that they ought not have to bear." . . . The jury began deliberations on February 14, 2006, and returned its verdict on February 22, 2006; it found that the "cumulative presence of lead pigment in paints and coatings on buildings throughout the State of Rhode Island" constituted a public nuisance. . . .

The defendants first argue that the trial justice erred in refusing to dismiss the public nuisance count set forth in the state's complaint. . . . We agree with defendants that the public nuisance claim should have been dismissed at the outset because the state has not and cannot allege that defendants' conduct interfered with a public right or that defendants were in control of lead pigment at the time it caused harm to children in Rhode Island. . . . Today, public nuisance and private nuisance are separate and distinct causes of action, but both torts are inextricably linked by their joint origin as a common writ, dating to twelfth-century English common law. . . . In its earliest form, nuisance was a criminal writ used to prosecute individuals or require abatement of activities considered to "be . . . a nuisance by reason of the common and public welfare." Gifford, 71 U. Cin. L. Rev. at 793-94 (citing Henry de Bracton, 3 *Bracton on the Laws and Customs of England* 191, f. 232b (Samuel E. Thorne ed., 1977)). Public nuisance, or common nuisance as it originally was called, was "an infringement of the rights of the Crown." 4 Restatement (Second) Torts § 821B, cmt. a at 87 (1979). Although the earliest cases involved encroachments on the royal domain, public nuisance law evolved to include "the invasion of the rights of the public." *Id.*

By the fourteenth century, courts began to apply public nuisance principles to protect rights common to the public, including "roadway safety, air and water pollution, disorderly conduct, and public health * * *." Faulk & Gray, 2007 Mich. St. L. Rev. at 951. Nuisance became a "flexible judicial remedy" that allowed courts to address conflicts between land use and social welfare at a time when government regulations had not yet made their debut. *Id.*

It was not until the sixteenth century that the crime of public nuisance largely was transformed into the tort that is familiar in our courts today. Faulk & Gray, 2007 Mich. St. L. Rev. at 952. However, additional parameters were necessary to limit the reach of the new tort. A private party seeking to bring a public nuisance claim was required to demonstrate that he or she had "suffered a `particular' or `special' injury that was not common to the public." *Id.; see also* 4 Restatement (Second) Torts § 821B, cmt. a at 87-88 (explaining that public nuisance had remained a crime until the sixteenth century, when it first was determined that a private individual, suffering a particularized harm different in kind from that suffered by the public, had the right, in tort, to recover damages for his injury). Ultimately, "[a]t common law public nuisance came to cover a large, miscellaneous and diversified group of minor offenses * * *." 4 Restatement (Second) Torts § 821B, cmt. b at 40. Notably, all these offenses involved an "interference with the interests of the community at large—interests that were recognized as rights of the general public entitled to protection." *Id.*

Public nuisance as it existed in English common law made its way to Colonial America without change. . . . In time, public nuisance became better known as a tort, and its criminal counterpart began to fade away in American jurisprudence. As state legislatures started enacting statutes prohibiting particular conduct and setting forth criminal penalties there was little need for the broad, vague, and anachronistic crime of nuisance. 4 Restatement (Second) Torts § 821B, cmt. c at 88. . . .

This Court has defined public nuisance as "an unreasonable interference with a right common to the general public." *Citizens for Preservation of Waterman Lake v. Davis,* 420 A.2d 53, 59 (R.I. 1980). . . . Although this Court previously has not had the opportunity to address all the elements of public nuisance, to the extent that we have addressed this common law cause of action, our definition largely is consistent with that of many other jurisdictions, the Restatement (Second) of Torts, and several scholarly commentators.

The Restatement (Second) defines public nuisance, in relevant part, as follows:

(1) A public nuisance is an unreasonable interference with a right common to the general public.

(2) Circumstances that may sustain a holding that an interference with a public right is unreasonable include the following:
    a. Whether the conduct involves a significant interference with the public health, the public safety, the public peace, the public comfort or the public convenience * * *.

4 Restatement (Second) Torts § 821B at 87. . . . This Court recognizes three principal elements that are essential to establish public nuisance: (1) an unreasonable interference; (2) with a right

common to the general public; (3) by a person or people with control over the instrumentality alleged to have created the nuisance when the damage occurred. . . .

Unreasonable Interference

Whether an interference with a public right is unreasonable will depend upon the activity in question and the magnitude of the interference it creates. Activities carried out in violation of state laws or local ordinances generally have been considered unreasonable if they interfere with a public right. . . . Activities that do not violate the law but that nonetheless create a substantial and continuing interference with a public right also generally have been considered unreasonable. . . . The plaintiff bears the burden of showing that a legal activity is unreasonable.

Public Right

A respected legal authority has identified "[t]he interference with a public right [as] the *sine qua non* of a cause of action for public nuisance." 58 Am.Jur.2d *Nuisances* § 39 at 598-99 (2002) (emphasis added). This Court also has emphasized the requirement that "the nuisance must affect an interest common to the general public, rather than peculiar to one individual, or several." *Iafrate,* 96 R.I. at 222, 190 A.2d at 476 (quoting Prosser, *Torts,* ch. 14, § 72 at 402). . . . This is not to say that public nuisance only is actionable if it occurs on public property. Rather, public nuisance is actionable even when the nuisance itself is present on private property, so long as the alleged nuisance *affects* the rights of the general public. . . .

The Restatement (Second) provides further assistance in defining a public right:

> A public right is *one common to all members of the general public.* It is collective in nature and not like the individual right that everyone has not to be assaulted or defamed or defrauded or negligently injured. Thus the pollution of a stream that merely deprives fifty or a hundred lower riparian owners of the use of the water for purposes connected with their land does not for that reason alone become a public nuisance. If, however, the pollution prevents the use of a public bathing beach or kills the fish in a navigable stream and so deprives all members of the community of the right to fish, it becomes a public nuisance.

4 Restatement (Second) Torts § 821B, cmt. g at 92 (emphasis added). . . .

As the Restatement (Second) makes clear, a public right is more than an aggregate of private rights by a large number of injured people. . . . Rather, a public right is the right to a public good, such as "an indivisible resource shared by the public at large, like air, water, or public rights of way." *Am. Cyanamid Co.,* 291 Ill. Dec. at 215, 823 N.E.2d at 131. . . .

Control

As an additional prerequisite to the imposition of liability for public nuisance, a defendant must have *control* over the instrumentality causing the alleged nuisance *at the time the damage occurs.* . . . Indeed, control at the time the damage occurs is critical in public nuisance cases, especially because the principal remedy for the harm caused by the nuisance is abatement. . . .

Causation

The party alleging the existence of a public nuisance not only must demonstrate the existence of the nuisance, but also must demonstrate "that injury has been caused by the nuisance complained of." *Citizens for Preservation of Waterman Lake,* 420 A.2d at 59 (citing *McClellan v. Thompson,* 114 R.I. 334, 344, 333 A.2d 424, 429 (1975)). Causation is a basic requirement in any public nuisance action; such a requirement is consistent with the law of torts generally. . . .

Another Attribute of Public Nuisance

In concluding this discussion of the elements necessary to establish a public nuisance, we also believe that it is advisable to mention the following. A common feature of public nuisance is the occurrence of a dangerous condition at a specific location. This Court has recognized that the existence of a nuisance depends in large part on its location, and, to date, the actions for nuisance in this jurisdiction have been related to *land.* . . . The United States Supreme Court has remarked that "the question [of] whether * * * a particular thing is a nuisance, is to be determined, not by an abstract consideration of the building or of the thing considered apart, but by considering it in connection with the circumstances and the locality." *Village of Euclid v. Ambler Realty Co.,* 272 U.S. 365, 388, 47 S.Ct. 114, 71 L.Ed. 303 (1926) (citing *Sturgis v. Bridgeman,* L.R. 11 Ch. 852, 865). Professor William L. Prosser, the highly respected authority on the law of torts, remarked that "[i]f `nuisance' is to have any meaning at all, it is necessary to dismiss a considerable number of cases which have applied the term to matters not connected either with land or with any public right, as mere aberration * * *." *Prosser and Keeton on the Law of Torts,* § 86 at 618 . . . . Unlike private nuisance, public nuisance does not necessarily involve an interference with a particular *individual's* use and enjoyment of his or her land. *In re Lead Paint Litigation,* 924 A.2d at 495-96 (citing 4 Restatement (Second) Torts § 821B, cmt. h at 93). Rather, public nuisance typically arises on a defendant's land and interferes with a public right. . . .

Whether the Presence of Lead Paint Constitutes a Public Nuisance

After thoroughly reviewing the complaint filed by the state in this case, we are of the opinion that the trial justice erred in denying defendants' motion to dismiss under Rule 12(b)(6) of the Superior Court Rules of Civil Procedure.

As the foregoing analysis demonstrates, under Rhode Island law, a complaint for public nuisance minimally must allege: (1) an unreasonable interference; (2) with a right common to the general public; (3) by a person or people with control over the instrumentality alleged to have created the nuisance when the damage occurred; and (4) causation.

Even considering the allegations of fact as set forth in the complaint, we cannot ascertain allegations in the complaint that support each of these elements. The state's complaint alleges simply that "[d]efendants created an environmental hazard that continues and will continue to unreasonably interfere with the health, safety, peace, comfort or convenience of the residents of the [s]tate, thereby constituting a public nuisance." Absent from the state's complaint is any allegation that defendants have interfered with a public right as that term long has been understood in the law of public nuisance. Equally problematic is the absence of any allegation that defendants had control over the lead pigment at the time it caused harm to children.

. . . A necessary element of public nuisance is an interference with a public right — those indivisible resources shared by the public at large, such as air, water, or public rights of way. The interference must deprive all members of the community of a right to some resource to which they otherwise are entitled. *See* 4 Restatement (Second) Torts § 821B, cmt. g at 92. The Restatement (Second) provides much guidance in ascertaining the fine distinction between a public right and an aggregation of private rights. "Conduct does not become a public nuisance merely because it interferes with the use and enjoyment of land by a large number of persons." *Id.* . . .

Although the state asserts that the public's right to be free from the hazards of unabated lead had been infringed, this contention falls far short of alleging an interference with a public right as that term traditionally has been understood in the law of public nuisance. The state's allegation that defendants have interfered with the "health, safety, peace, comfort or convenience of the residents of the [s]tate" standing alone does not constitute an allegation of interference with a public right. . . . The term public right is reserved more appropriately for those indivisible resources shared by the public at large, such as air, water, or public rights of way. . . . Expanding the definition of public right based on the allegations in the complaint would be antithetical to the common law and would lead to a widespread expansion of public nuisance law that never was intended, as we discuss *infra*. . . . The right of an individual child not to be poisoned by lead paint is strikingly similar to other examples of nonpublic rights cited by courts, the Restatement (Second), and several leading commentators. *See* . . . 4 Restatement (Second) *Torts* § 821B, cmt. g at 92 (the individual right that everyone has not to be assaulted or defamed or defrauded or negligently injured is not a public right) . . . .

Even had the state adequately alleged an interference with a right common to the general public, which we conclude it did not, the state's complaint also fails to allege any facts that would support a conclusion that defendants were in control of the lead pigment at the time it harmed Rhode Island's children. The state filed suit against defendants in their capacity "either as the manufacturer of * * * lead pigment * * * or as the successors in interest to such manufacturers" for "the cumulative presence of lead pigment in paints and coatings in or on buildings throughout the [s]tate of Rhode Island." For the alleged public nuisance to be actionable, the state would have had to assert that defendants not only manufactured the lead pigment but also controlled that pigment at the time it caused injury to children in Rhode Island — and there is no allegation of such control. . . .

We conclude, therefore, that there was no set of facts alleged in the state's complaint that, even if proven, could have demonstrated that defendants' conduct, however unreasonable, interfered with a public right or that defendants had control over the product causing the alleged nuisance at the time children were injured. . . . Public nuisance focuses on the abatement of annoying or bothersome activities. Products liability law, on the other hand, has its own well-defined structure, which is designed specifically to hold manufacturers liable for harmful products that the manufacturers have caused to enter the stream of commerce.

Undoubtedly, public nuisance and products liability are two distinct causes of action, each with rational boundaries that are not intended to overlap. . . . It is essential that these two causes of action remain just that — two separate and distinct causes of action. . . . For the foregoing reasons, we conclude that the trial justice erred in denying defendants' motion to dismiss.

I. PRIVILEGES/DEFENSES TO INTENTIONAL TORTS

So far, we have been focusing on the several legal interests protected by the law of intentional tort and the elements that a plaintiff must plead and prove to make out a prima facie case of liability. When a plaintiff makes out a *prima facie* case, she has come forward with sufficient evidence on each element of her cause of action to permit a reasonable jury to find in her favor. Once plaintiff establishes a *prima facie* case, the burden of persuasion then shifts to the defendant, who still can prevail in one of two ways: (1) defendant may rebut plaintiff's *prima facie* case by coming forward with evidence sufficient to convince the trier of fact that one of the essential elements of plaintiff's cause of action is not established by a preponderance of the evidence, or (2) defendant may come forward with *prima facie* evidence of some affirmative defense. An affirmative defense permits the defendant to prevail despite plaintiff's proof by a preponderance of the evidence of all the elements of her cause of action. While plaintiff bears the burden of pleading and proving all the elements of her cause of action, the burden to plead and prove any affirmative defense is on the defendant. In the following section of these materials, we will explore the most commonly discussed defenses to intentional torts.

Several affirmative defenses in the intentional tort context are in the nature of "privileges." A privilege generally is a justification (as opposed to an excuse) and permits a tort defendant to do legally what would otherwise be tortious, generally because defendant's conduct serves some legitimate interest that outweighs the interest served by plaintiff's cause of action. These materials will at least touch on several such privileges including defense of self and others, defense of property (including recapture of chattels), public and private necessity, legal authority, and discipline of children. But the first defense that we consider is consent.

1. CONSENT

The idea here is simple. Tort law gives parties wide latitude to make their own decisions, even decisions that might result in harm to them. Therefore, even if defendant's conduct otherwise would constitute a valid intentional tort claim, defendant is not liable to the plaintiff if plaintiff has agreed to the conduct. The maxim *volenti non fit injuria* – to the willing, there is no wrong – embodies the privilege of consent. Harmful conduct, when voluntarily encountered, provides no basis for a cause of action. We will see an essentially similar concept later when we study the defense of assumption of risk in the context of a negligence action.

a. NATURE AND SCOPE OF CONSENT

The question of consent can be relatively simple when the consent is expressed. But consent may also be implied, and implied consent can be quite difficult to sort out. Several issues can arise, including what constitutes implied consent and when implied consent exists, precisely to what does the plaintiff consent? Some of the difficulties that can arise in the implied consent context are illustrated by the following case.

O'BRIEN V. CUNARD STEAMSHIP CO.
28 N.E. 266 (MASS. 1891)

. . . [Plaintiff passenger appeals from a directed verdict against her battery action. P]laintiff relied on the fact that the surgeon who was employed by the defendant vaccinated her on shipboard . . . . [T]he surgeon's conduct must be considered in connection with the circumstances. If the plaintiff's behavior was such as to indicate consent on her part, he was justified in his act, whatever her unexpressed feelings may have been. In determining whether she consented, he could be guided only by her overt acts and the manifestations of her feelings. [Cases omitted.] It is undisputed that at Boston there are strict quarantine regulations in regard to the examination of emigrants, to see that they are protected from small-pox by vaccination, and that only those persons who hold a certificate from the medical officer of the steamship, stating that they are so protected, are permitted to land without detention in quarantine or vaccination by the port physician. It appears that the defendant is accustomed to have its surgeons vaccinate all emigrants who desire it, and who are not protected by previous vaccination, and give them a certificate which is accepted at quarantine as evidence of their protection. Notices of the regulations at quarantine, and of the willingness of the ship's medical officer to vaccinate such as needed vaccination, were posted about the ship, in various languages, and on the day when the operation was performed the surgeon had a right to presume that she and the other women who were vaccinated understood the importance and purpose of vaccination for those who bore no marks to show that they were protected.

By the plaintiff's testimony, which in this particular is undisputed, it appears that about two hundred women passengers were assembled below, and she understood from conversation with them that they were to be vaccinated; that she stood about fifteen feet from the surgeon, and saw them form in a line and pass in turn before him; that he "examined their arms, and, passing some of them by, proceeded to vaccinate those that had no mark"; that she did not hear him say anything to any of them; that upon being passed by they each received a card and went on deck; that when her turn came she showed him her arm, and he looked at it and said there was no mark, and that she should be vaccinated; that she told him she had been vaccinated before and it left no mark; "that he then said nothing, that he should vaccinate her again"; that she held up her arm to be vaccinated; that no one touched her; that she did not tell him that she did not want to be vaccinated; and that she took the ticket which he gave her certifying that he had vaccinated her, and used it at quarantine. She was one of a large number of women who were vaccinated on that occasion, without, so far as appears, a word of objection from any of them. They all indicated by their conduct that they desired to avail themselves of the provisions made for their benefit. There was nothing in the conduct of the plaintiff to indicate to the surgeon that she did not wish to obtain a card which would save her from detention at quarantine, and to be vaccinated, if necessary, for that purpose. Viewing his conduct in the light of the circumstances, it was lawful; and there was no evidence tending to show that it was not. . . .

NOTES AND QUESTIONS

1   *Unanticipated Injury.* Would it have made any difference if the vaccination had resulted in a severe reaction such as paralysis?

2   *Privilege or part of prima facie case?* The majority and best-reasoned authorities treat consent as a privilege on which defendant bears the burden of pleading and proof while a minority of others treat absence of consent as an element of plaintiff's *prima facie* case.

3   *Capacity to Consent.* Consent must be given by one having capacity to consent or by one authorized to act on behalf of one lacking capacity to consent. Infancy, intoxication or mental incapacity, known or obvious to Defendant, can vitiate otherwise effective consent. While the cases are split, most courts permit minors to consent to conduct appropriate to their age. One special case is abortion – the Supreme Court has held that even minor women have a right to an abortion, without regard to parental consent, under certain circumstances.

4   *Consent Implied in Fact.* Many activities of life cannot reasonably be undertaken without expecting some bodily contact that might, in other contexts, be tortious. The most common example may be participation in "contact" sports. Under such circumstances, the voluntary participant in the activity impliedly consents to contacts incident to the activity.

5   *Consent Implied by Law.* In *O'Brien*, the question was not whether plaintiff had, in fact, impliedly consented to the vaccination. Rather, the court held that plaintiff's objective manifestation of assent resulted in legal consent, without regard to whether she had consented in fact. Does it make sense to thus place the burden on the plaintiff to assure that it is abundantly clear that she has *not* consented?

GRABOWSKI V. QUIGLEY
684 A.2D 610 (PA. SUPER. 1996)

. . . The facts and procedural history may be summarized as follows: Appellant was injured on January 4, 1989, when he slipped and fell on ice, injuring his lower back. Because his symptoms became progressively worse, Appellant sought treatment from Appellee Matthew R. Quigley, M.D. (Quigley). At the time that Appellant sought treatment, he had complaints of low back pain radiating into his left leg with numbness and tingling of his left foot, particularly between two toes. . . . Quigley recommended to Appellant that he undergo corrective surgery. Quigley told Appellant that he would perform the necessary surgery and that he would schedule it. . . . Appellant agreed to undergo the surgery and to have Quigley perform it. Quigley's secretary then scheduled the surgery for April 17, 1989.

The night before the scheduled surgery Appellant received a phone call rescheduling the surgery for April 18, 1989. Although not given a surgical time, Appellant was told to report to Allegheny General Hospital (AGH) at 6:00 a.m. Appellant went to AGH as directed. After his arrival, he was taken to a room, changed his clothes and was placed on a gurney. An anesthesiologist then came to meet with him. After the anesthesiologist left, a nurse came in and handed Appellant a form entitled "Consent to Operation, Anesthetics, and Special Procedures." Appellant was told to sign the form so that Quigley could perform the surgery. The nurse stood by while Appellant signed the form. No other explanation was given. Appellant was then taken to the operating room and placed under anesthesia.

Following surgery, Appellant had continuing back pain. He also noticed a problem with his left foot-he noticed that it would "drag" whenever he walked. When Appellant asked Quigley about the problem, Quigley told him that he had developed a drop foot which was a result of the surgery. Quigley ordered physical therapy, but there was no real improvement in Appellant's condition. Thus, Quigley ordered additional diagnostic tests and discussed the results with Appellant and told him that additional surgery was required. Appellant decided to get a second opinion and, therefore, requested his medical records.

After obtaining the records, Appellant reviewed them. Included within the records was a letter from Quigley to David Torpey, Chief, Division of Anesthesia, dated April 19, 1989. From this letter, Appellant learned for the first time that Quigley was in Somerset County at the time that he was placed under anesthesia and that Appellee Julian E. Bailes, M.D. (Bailes), rather than Quigley, had performed a major portion of his surgery. A review of the anesthesia records revealed that Appellant was placed under anesthesia at 8:15 a.m. Quigley was then paged at 8:35 a.m. and then several times over the next twenty minutes. Quigley's office was then called at 8:50 a.m. and 9:15 a.m. Appellee Joseph C. Maroon, M.D. (Maroon) was made aware of Quigley's absence, and at approximately 9:15 a.m. the anesthesiologist spoke with Maroon. The anesthesia record further revealed that Bailes began the surgical procedure, at the request of Maroon, at 10:20 a.m. Finally, the anesthesia record stated that Quigley arrived in the operating room at 11:25 a.m. and surgery was completed at 12:30 p.m.

Appellant was extremely upset to learn physicians that he did not know and had not authorized performed surgery on him and/or directed a physician to perform surgery on him. Appellant was also upset to learn that Quigley did not perform his surgery. According to Appellant, he would not have undergone the surgery had he known Quigley would not be performing the procedure in its entirety. Appellant sought a second opinion from Frances T. Ferraro, M.D. (Ferraro), who performed surgery on him in April of 1990 for excision of disc fragments at the site of the April, 1989, surgery. According to Appellant, he was informed by Ferraro that the fragments that were removed were lying on a nerve and that this fact caused his continued back pain and drop foot.

Appellant commenced the instant action . . . . In Count I, Appellant alleges that he did not consent to the manner in which he was operated upon by Bailes and/or Quigley and argues that the record evinces a genuine issue of material fact as to the doctors' liability under a theory of battery. The facts asserted by Appellant on the issue of consent are largely set out above. Generally, Appellant has asserted facts which demonstrate that he consented to an operation to be performed in its entirety by Quigley, not by Bailes, or a combination of Bailes and Quigley. Appellee doctors counter by noting that the consent form which Appellant signed stated that the surgery would be "performed under the direction of Dr. Quigley, et al." Appellant testified that "et al," which was handwritten, looked to him like "ETOL," and that he did not know what the words meant until counsel explained them to him on the morning of his deposition.

In addition, Appellant argues that the evidence demonstrates that he was not the only one who was of the belief that Quigley would be performing the operation. He points to the anesthesia record which shows that Quigley had been paged and called numerous times in an attempt to locate him while Appellant was under anesthesia. He also notes that Quigley wrote a letter to his superior detailing the events of that morning. The letter takes an apologetic tone in which Quigley appears to acknowledge that he was to operate on Appellant that morning. A significant excerpt of the letter reads as follows:

[Y]ou can imagine my chagrin when [approximately one hour after anesthesia had been introduced] I received a phone call that my first case was on the table already asleep. At this point we faced two options, one of reawakening [Appellant] and informing him of the mishap or having another physician starting the case and allowing time to return and finish it. We elected to do the latter.·····

Appellee doctors argue that Appellant admitted in his deposition testimony that he likely expected that Quigley would be assisted during the operation. Because Quigley did arrive in time to finish the operation, they urge that Bailes merely assisted in the procedure. Nevertheless, examining the record in a light most favorable to Appellant, as the non-moving party, we conclude that a genuine issue of material fact exists with respect to Appellant's consent. . . . Since Appellant has alleged facts which, if true, established that consent was not given to Bailes and/ or Quigley to perform the surgery in the manner in which it occurred, he has thereby alleged sufficient facts to establish a cause of action for battery against them. . . .

Where it is proven that an unauthorized invasion of a person's personal integrity has occurred, even if harmless, the person is entitled to nominal damages. . . . The dispositive issue in this battery claim is the nature and scope of Appellant's consent. Appellant contends that as a result of his dealings with Quigley, his consent extended to an operation to be performed by Quigley only. He claims that the consent form which he signed on the morning of the operation was ambiguous on its face, and that he believed by signing he was providing his consent to Quigley only. . . . On these facts we find that genuine issues of material fact exist with respect to Count I . . . such that summary judgment is inappropriate. Thus, we reverse the trial court's grant of summary judgment in favor of Bailes and Quigley as to Count I of Appellant's complaint and remand that count for trial. . . .

NOTES

1   *Express v. Implied Consent.* One significant distinction between the consent in *O'Brien* and the consent in *Grabowski* is that the consent in *O'Brien* was implicit while the consent in *Grabowski* was explicit. In *O'Brien*, it was necessary for the Court to look at plaintiff's objective manifestation of her apparent assent to determine whether she had consented at all. In *Grabowski*, consent in fact was not at issue – the only question was the scope of plaintiff's explicit consent. In the medical context, patients generally are required by health care providers to consent in writing to their treatment.

MOHR V. WILLIAMS
104 N.W. 12 (MINN. 1905)

Defendant is a physician and surgeon of standing and character, making disorders of the ear a specialty . . . . He was consulted by plaintiff, who complained to him of trouble with her right ear, and, at her request, made an examination of that organ for the purpose of ascertaining its condition. He also at the same time examined her left ear, but, owing to foreign substances therein, was unable to make a full and complete diagnosis at that time. The examination of her right ear disclosed a large perforation in the lower portion of the drum membrane, and a large polyp in the middle ear, which indicated that some of the small bones of the middle ear (ossicles) were probably diseased. He informed plaintiff of the result of his examination, and advised an operation for the purpose of removing the polyp and diseased ossicles. After consultation with her family physician, and one or two further consultations with defendant, plaintiff decided to submit to the proposed operation. She was not informed that her left ear was in any way diseased, and understood that the necessity for an operation applied to her right ear only. She repaired to the hospital, and was placed under the influence of anaesthetics; and, after being made unconscious, defendant made a thorough examination of her left ear, and found it in a more serious condition than her right one. . . . He called this discovery to the attention of Dr. Davis – plaintiff's family physician, who attended the operation at her request – who also examined the ear, and confirmed defendant in his diagnosis. Defendant also further examined the right ear, and found its condition less serious than expected, and finally concluded that the left, instead of the right, should be operated upon; devoting to the right ear other treatment. He then performed the operation of ossiculectomy on plaintiff's left ear . . . . The operation was in every way successful and skillfully performed. It is claimed by plaintiff that the operation greatly impaired her hearing, seriously injured her person, and, not having been consented to by her, was wrongful and unlawful, constituting a . . . battery; and she brought this action to recover damages therefor. The trial in the court below resulted in a verdict for plaintiff . . . .

It is contended that final judgment should be ordered in [defendant's] favor for the following reasons: (a) That it appears from the evidence received on the trial that plaintiff consented to the operation on her left ear. (b) If the court shall find that no such consent was given, that, under the circumstances disclosed by the record, no consent was necessary. (c) That, under the facts disclosed, an action for . . . battery will not lie; it appearing conclusively, as counsel urge, that there is a total lack of evidence showing or tending to show malice or evil intent on the part of defendant, or that the operation was negligently performed.

We shall consider first the question whether, under the circumstances shown in the record, the consent of plaintiff to the operation was necessary. . . . It cannot be doubted that ordinarily the patient must be consulted, and his consent given, before a physician may operate upon him. . . . If the physician advises his patient to submit to a particular operation, and the patient weighs the dangers and risks incident to its performance, and finally consents, he thereby, in effect, enters into a contract authorizing his physician to operate to the extent of the consent given, but no further. It is not, however, contended by defendant that under ordinary circumstances consent is unnecessary, but that, under the particular circumstances of this case, consent was implied; that it was an emergency case, such as to authorize the operation without express consent or permission. . . . If a person should be injured to the extent of rendering him unconscious, and his injuries were of such a nature as to require prompt surgical attention, a physician called to attend him would be justified in applying such medical or surgical treatment as might reasonably be necessary for the preservation of his life or limb, and consent on the part of the injured person would be implied. And again, if, in the course of an operation to which the patient consented, the physician should discover conditions not anticipated before the operation was commenced, and which, if not removed, would endanger the life or health of the patient, he would, though no express consent was obtained or given, be justified in extending the operation to remove and overcome them. But such is not the case at bar. The diseased condition of plaintiff's left ear was not discovered in the course of an operation on the right, which was authorized, but upon an independent examination of that organ, made after the authorized operation was found unnecessary. Nor is the evidence such as to justify the court in holding, as a matter of law, that it was such an affection as would result immediately in the serious injury of plaintiff, or such an emergency as to justify proceeding without her consent. . . .

The contention of defendant that the operation was consented to by plaintiff is not sustained by the evidence. At least, the evidence was such as to take the question to the jury. This contention is based upon the fact that she was represented on the occasion in question by her family physician; that the condition of her left ear was made known to him, and the propriety of an operation thereon suggested, to which he made no objection. It is urged that by his conduct he assented to it, and that plaintiff was bound thereby. It is not claimed that he gave his express consent. It is not disputed but that the family physician of plaintiff was present on the occasion of the operation, and at her request. But the purpose of his presence was not that he might participate in the operation, nor does it appear that he was authorized to consent to any change in the one originally proposed to be made. Plaintiff was naturally nervous and fearful of the consequences of being placed under the influence of anaesthetics, and the presence of her family physician was requested under the impression that it would allay and calm her fears. The evidence made the question one of fact for the jury to determine.

The last contention of defendant is that the act complained of did not amount to . . . battery. This is based upon the theory that, as plaintiff's left ear was in fact diseased, in a condition dangerous and threatening to her health, the operation was necessary, and, having been skillfully performed at a time when plaintiff had requested a like operation on the other ear, the charge of . . . battery cannot be sustained; that, in view of these conditions, and the claim that there was no negligence on the part of defendant, and an entire absence of any evidence tending to show an evil intent, the court should say, as a matter of law, that no . . . battery was committed, even though she did not consent to the operation. In other words, that the absence of a showing that defendant was actuated by a wrongful intent, or guilty of negligence, relieves the act of defendant from the charge of an unlawful . . . battery. We are unable to reach that conclusion . . . . It would seem to follow from what has been said on the other features of the case that the act of defendant amounted at least to a technical . . . battery. . . . [E]very person has a right to complete immunity of his person from physical interference of others, except in so far as contact may be necessary under the general doctrine of privilege . . . . In the case at bar, as we have already seen, the question whether defendant's act in performing the operation upon plaintiff was authorized was a question for the jury to determine. If it was unauthorized, then it was . . . a violent assault, not a mere pleasantry; and, even though no negligence is shown, it was wrongful and unlawful. . . .

QUESTIONS AND NOTE

1   Did defendant here intend harm or offense to plaintiff? If not, how can there be a cause of action for battery?
2   Even if the requisite intent by defendant can be established, how can a beneficial touching constitute a battery?

3   Presumably, plaintiff testified that she would not have consented to surgery on her left ear. But what if she secretly were willing at the time of the surgery to allow Dr. Williams to perform the surgery on either ear, at his discretion, but had never expressed that willingness because the issue never came up?

4   *Emergency.* Courts frequently hold that consent is implied when serious harm is threatened and an emergency precludes a reasonable opportunity to obtain consent. Others say that the medical treatment is privileged. Either way, defendant is not liable for battery. Why did this emergency doctrine not apply on the facts of this case? Note that the emergency doctrine is quite narrowly limited to circumstances where consent is impracticable and does not apply generally to all circumstances in which the contact is for plaintiff's benefit.

5   With the emergence and general acceptance of the negligence cause of action for failure to obtain informed consent (*see Canterbury* and *Largey, infra*), courts have become extremely reluctant to permit a finding of battery in cases of medical treatment unless consent is completely lacking.

6   One recurring consent issue is the scope of a party's right to refuse consent to medical treatment on religious grounds. While medical personnel may provide treatment without consent in emergency circumstances where it is impracticable to obtain consent, a conscious plaintiff generally has the right to refuse even life-prolonging treatment. Sometimes such treatment is refused on religious grounds, e.g., Jehovah's Witnesses often refuse blood transfusions, and Christian Scientists sometimes refuse standard treatments as well. Courts are less willing to honor religious scruples when a parent refuses, on religious grounds, life-prolonging treatment on behalf of a child.

NEAL V. NEAL
873 P.2D 871 (IDAHO 1994)

In January of 1990, defendant Thomas A. Neal filed for divorce after his wife became aware that he was having an extramarital affair. Mary Neal, his wife, counterclaimed for divorce and also asserted tort claims against Thomas Neal . . . . Mary Neal contends that she has alleged a prima facie case of battery against Thomas Neal. Her battery claim is founded on her assertion that although she consented to sexual intercourse with her husband during the time of his affair, had she known of his sexual involvement with another woman, she would not have consented, as sexual relations under those circumstances would have been offensive to her. Therefore, she contends that his failure to disclose the fact of the affair rendered her consent ineffective and subjects him to liability for battery.

   Civil battery consists of an intentional, unpermitted contact upon the person of another . . . . The intent necessary for battery is the intent to commit the act, not the intent to cause harm. . . . Consent obtained by fraud or misrepresentation vitiates the consent and can render the offending party liable for a battery. . . . Mary Neal may have engaged in a sexual act based upon a substantial mistake concerning the nature of the contact or the harm to be expected from it, and . . . she did not become aware of the offensiveness until well after the act had occurred. Mary Neal's affidavit at least raises a genuine issue of material fact as to whether there was indeed consent to the alleged act of battery.

1   Would this case be materially different if instead of having an extra-marital affair, Mr. Neal had been verbally flirting with women at the office? If this is different, how is it different?

2   *STDs.* What result if Mr. Neal had been faithful to his wife during the marriage, but, unknown to him, had contracted a sexually transmitted disease during a pre-marital affair? What if he did know about the disease but kept it a secret from his wife? Several courts have imposed liability for battery on defendants who know that they are infected with an STD but fail to inform their sexual partner.

3   *Fraud.* The actor who extracts "consent" through duress, as well as fraud, obtains no privilege thereby. *See, e.g.,* Restatement (Second) Torts, Sec. 892B, comment j. Does this principle apply to the facts of this case? One difficult question is what constitutes duress?

NABOZNY V. BARNHILL
334 N.E.2D 258 (ILL. APP. 1975)

Plaintiff, Julian Claudio Nabozny, a minor, . . . commenced this action to recover damages for personal injuries allegedly caused by . . . defendant, David Barnhill. . . . At the close of plaintiff's case on motion of defendant, the trial court directed a verdict in favor of the defendant. . . . Plaintiff contends on appeal . . . that plaintiff's actions as a participant do not prohibit the establishment of a prima facie case . . . .

A soccer match began between two amateur teams . . . . Plaintiff was playing the position of goalkeeper for the Hansa team. Defendant was playing the position of forward for the Winnetka team. Members of both teams were of high-school age. Approximately twenty minutes after play had begun, a Winnetka player kicked the ball over the midfield line. Two players, Jim Gallos (for Hansa) and the defendant (for Winnetka) chased the free ball. Gallos reached the ball first. Since he was closely pursued by the defendant, Gallos passed the ball to the plaintiff, the Hansa goalkeeper. Gallos then turned away and prepared to receive a pass from the plaintiff. The plaintiff, in the meantime, went down on his left knee, received the pass, and pulled the ball to his chest. The defendant did not turn away when Gallos did, but continued to run in the direction of the plaintiff and kicked the left side of plaintiff's head causing plaintiff severe injuries.

All of the occurrence witnesses agreed that the defendant had time to avoid contact with plaintiff and that the plaintiff remained at all times within the "penalty area," a rectangular area between the eighteenth yard line and the goal. Four witnesses testified that they saw plaintiff in a crouched position on his left knee inside the penalty zone. Plaintiff testified that he actually had possession of the ball when he was struck by defendant. One witness, Marie Shekem, stated that plaintiff had the ball when he was kicked. All other occurrence witnesses stated that they thought plaintiff was in possession of the ball.

Plaintiff called three expert witnesses. Julius Roth, coach of the Hansa team, testified that the game in question was being played under "F.I.F.A." rules. The three experts agreed that those rules prohibited all players from making contact with the goalkeeper when he is in possession of the ball in the penalty area. Possession is defined in the Chicago area as referring to the goalkeeper having his hands on the ball. Under "F.I.F.A." rules, any contact with a goalkeeper in possession in the penalty area is an infraction of the rules, even if such contact is unintentional. The goalkeeper is the only member of a team who is allowed to touch a ball in play so long as he remains in the penalty area. The only legal contact permitted in soccer is shoulder to shoulder contact between players going for a ball within playing distance. The three experts agreed that the contact in question in this case should not have occurred. Additionally, goalkeeper head injuries are extremely rare in soccer. As a result of being struck, plaintiff suffered permanent damage to his skull and brain. . . .

Individual sports are advanced and competition enhanced by a comprehensive set of rules. Some rules secure the better playing of the game as a test of skill. Other rules are primarily designed to protect participants from serious injury. (Restatement (Second) of Torts, Sec. 50, comment B.) . . . The defendant contends he is immune from tort action for any injury to another player that happens during the course of a game, to which theory we do not subscribe. . . .

While playing his position, [plaintiff] remained in the penalty area and took possession of the ball in a proper manner. Plaintiff had no reason to know of the danger created by defendant. . . . The facts in evidence revealed that the play in question was of a kind commonly executed in this sport. Frank Longo, one of plaintiff's expert witnesses, testified that once the goalkeeper gets possession of the ball in the penalty area, "the instinct should be there (in an opposing player pursuing the ball) through training and knowledge of the rules to avoid contact (with the goalkeeper)." All of plaintiff's expert witnesses agreed that a player charging an opposition goaltender under circumstances similar to those which existed during the play in question should be able to avoid all contact. Furthermore, it is a violation of the rules for a player simply to kick at the ball when a goalkeeper has possession in the penalty area even if no contact is made with the goalkeeper. . . .

This cause, therefore, is reversed and remanded to the Circuit Court of Cook County for a new trial consistent with the views expressed in this opinion.

Reversed and remanded.

b. CONSENT TO ILLEGALITY – MUTUAL COMBAT

HUDSON V. CRAFT
204 P.2D 1 (CAL. 1949)

. . . Plaintiff . . . alleges that he is 18 years of age; that defendants were conducting a carnival where one of the concessions . . . consisted of boxing exhibitions; that such concession was conducted in violation of . . . the Penal Code . . . in that prizes . . . were given to contestants and no license to conduct the same had been obtained from the State Athletic Commission, and they were not conducted in accordance with the rules of the Commission; that plaintiff, on the solicitation of defendants, and a promise of receiving $5, engaged in a boxing match and suffered personal injuries as the result of being struck by his opponent. Plaintiff's opponent in the match was also made a party defendant but was not served with process.

The basis and theory of liability, if any, in mutual combat cases has been the subject of considerable controversy. Proceeding from the premise that, as between the combatants, the tort involved is that of assault and battery, many courts have held that, inasmuch as each contestant has committed a battery on the other, each may hold the other liable for any injury inflicted although both consented to the contest. . . . Being contrary to the maxim volente non fit injuria, . . . the courts have endeavored to rationalize the rule by reasoning . . . that no one may consent to such breach. There are cases expressing a minority view and severe criticism has been levelled at the majority rule, such as, that it . . . encourages rather than deters mutual combat. . . . The Restatement adopts the minority view. An assent which satisfies the rules stated "prevents an invasion from being tortious and, therefore, actionable, although the invasion assented to constitutes a crime." Rest.Torts, sec. 60. An example given thereunder is a boxing match where no license was had as required by law. . . .

There is an exception to the rule stated in the Restatement, reading: "Where it is a crime to inflict a particular invasion of an interest . . . upon a particular class of persons, irrespective of their assent, and the policy of the law is primarily to protect the interest of such a class of persons from their inability to appreciate the consequences of such an invasion, and it is not solely to protect the interests of the public, the assent of such a person to such an invasion is not a consent thereto." Rest.Torts, sec. 61. . . . Concerning the bearing of the factor of consent or assumption of risk on liability, the instant case, as will more fully appear from the later discussion herein, clearly falls within the exception stated in section 61 (*supra*) by reason of the declared public policy of the state. . . . From the beginning, this state has taken an uncompromising stand against uncontrolled prize fights and boxing matches. . . . While there are other purposes underlying that policy, it is manifest that one of the chief goals is to provide safeguards for the protection of persons engaging in the activity. . . . [I]nsofar as the purpose is protection from physical harm, the chief offender would be the promoter the activating force in procuring the occurrence of such exhibitions. It is from his uncontrolled conduct that the combatants are protected. Secondarily, the contestants are protected against their own ill-advised participation in an unregulated match. This is especially true in the case at bar where plaintiff is a lad of eighteen years. . . .

c. WITHDRAWAL OF CONSENT

STATE V. WILLIAMS
75 N.C. 134 (1876)

. . . The defendants and the prosecutrix were members of a benevolent society . . . known as the "Good Samaritans," which society had certain rules and ceremonies known as the ceremonies of initiation into and expulsion from the Society. The prosecutrix, having been remiss in some of her obligations, and having been called upon to explain, became violent.

The defendants, with others, proceeded to perform the ceremony of expulsion, which consisted in suspending her from the wall by means of a cord fastened around her waist. This ceremony had been performed upon others theretofore, in the presence of the prosecutrix. She resisted to the extent of her ability. . . .

There was a verdict of guilty and judgment thereupon. The defendants appealed.

BYNUM, J. When the prosecutrix refused to submit to the ceremony of expulsion established by this benevolent society, it could not be lawfully inflicted . . . . The punishment inflicted upon the person of the prosecutrix was willful, violent and against her consent. . . . There is no error. . . . Judgment affirmed.

QUESTIONS

1   By voluntarily joining this society knowing what would happen if she were to be expelled, did plaintiff not impliedly consent to this bodily contact? If not, what would have been required to establish consent? If so, then, can this be a battery?

d. INFORMED CONSENT

CANTERBURY V. SPENCE
464 F.2D 772 (D.C. CIR. 1972)

I

The record we review tells a depressing tale. A youth troubled only by back pain submitted to an operation without being informed of a risk of paralysis incidental thereto. . . . Despite extensive medical care, he has never been what he was before. Instead of the back pain, even years later, he hobbled about on crutches, a victim of paralysis of the bowels and urinary incontinence. In a very real sense this lawsuit is an understandable search for reasons.

At the time of the events which gave rise to this litigation, appellant was nineteen years of age . . . . In December, 1958, he began to experience severe pain between his shoulder blades. . . . Dr. Spence examined appellant in his office at some length but found nothing amiss. On Dr. Spence's advice appellant was x-rayed, but the films did not identify any abnormality. Dr. Spence then recommended that appellant undergo a myelogram—a procedure in which dye is injected into the spinal column and traced to find evidence of disease or other disorder—at the Washington Hospital Center.

. . . The myelogram revealed a "filling defect" in the region of the fourth thoracic vertebra. . . . . Dr. Spence told appellant that he would have to undergo a laminectomy—the excision of the posterior arch of the vertebra—to correct what he suspected was a ruptured disc. Appellant did not raise any objection to the proposed operation nor did he probe into its exact nature. . . . Dr. Spence told [appellant's mother] that the surgery was occasioned by a suspected ruptured disc. Mrs. Canterbury then asked if the recommended operation was serious and Dr. Spence replied "not any more than any other operation." . . . Dr. Spence performed the laminectomy . . . .

For approximately the first day after the operation appellant recuperated normally, but then suffered a fall and an almost immediate setback. . . . [L]ater, appellant began to complain that he could not move his legs and that he was having trouble breathing; paralysis seems to have been virtually total from the waist down. . . . At the time of the trial in April, 1968, appellant required crutches to walk [and] still suffered from urinal incontinence and paralysis of the bowels . . . .

II

Appellant filed suit . . . . Against Dr. Spence [the Complaint] alleged, among other things, . . . failure to inform him beforehand of the risk involved. . . . Dr. Spence . . . testified that . . . paralysis can be anticipated "somewhere in the nature of one percent" of the laminectomies performed, a risk he termed "a very slight possibility." He felt that communication of that risk to the patient is not good medical practice because it might deter patients from undergoing needed surgery and might produce adverse psychological reactions which could preclude the success of the operation.

At the close of appellant's case in chief, each defendant moved for a directed verdict and the trial judge granted both motions. . . . We reverse. The testimony of appellant and his mother that Dr. Spence did not reveal the risk of paralysis from the laminectomy made out a prima facie case of violation of the physician's duty to disclose which Dr. Spence's explanation did not negate as a matter of law. . . .

III

Suits charging failure by a physician adequately to disclose the risks and alternatives of proposed treatment are not innovations in American law. They date back a good half-century, and in the last decade they have multiplied rapidly. There is, nonetheless, disagreement among the courts and the commentators on many major questions . . . . For the tools enabling resolution of the issues on this appeal, we are forced to begin at first principles.

The root premise is the concept, fundamental in American jurisprudence, that "[e]very human being of adult years and sound mind has a right to determine what shall be done with his own body." . . . True consent to what happens to one's self is the informed exercise of a choice, and that entails an opportunity to evaluate knowledgeably the options available and the risks attendant upon each. The average patient has little or no understanding of the medical arts, and ordinarily has only his physician to whom he can look for enlightenment with which to reach an intelligent decision. From these almost axiomatic considerations springs the need, and in turn the requirement, of a reasonable divulgence by physician to patient to make such a decision possible. . . .

In duty-to-disclose cases, the focus of attention is more properly upon the nature and content of the physician's divulgence than the patient's understanding or consent. Adequate disclosure and informed consent are, of course, two sides of the same coin—the former a *sine qua non* of the latter. But the vital inquiry on duty to disclose relates to the physician's performance of an obligation, while one of the difficulties with analysis in terms of "informed consent" is its tendency to imply that what is decisive is the degree of the patient's comprehension. As we later emphasize, the physician discharges the duty when he makes a reasonable effort to convey sufficient information although the patient, without fault of the physician, may not fully grasp it. . . . Even though the factfinder may have occasion to draw an inference on the state of the patient's enlightenment, the factfinding process on performance of the duty ultimately reaches back to what the physician actually said or failed to say. And while the factual conclusion on adequacy of the revelation will vary as between patients—as, for example, between a lay patient and a physician-patient—the fluctuations are attributable to the kind of divulgence which may be reasonable under the circumstances.

A physician is under a duty to treat his patient skillfully . . . but proficiency in diagnosis and therapy is not the full measure of his responsibility. The cases demonstrate that the physician is under an obligation to communicate specific information to the patient when the exigencies of reasonable care call for it. . . . Due care may . . . call upon the physician confronting an ailment which does not respond to his ministrations to inform the patient thereof. . . . It may command the physician to instruct the patient as to any limitations to be presently observed for his own welfare . . . and as to any precautionary therapy he should seek in the future. . . . It may oblige the physician to advise the patient of the need for or desirability of any alternative treatment promising greater benefit than that being pursued. . . . Just as plainly, due care normally demands that the physician warn the patient of any risks to his well-being which contemplated therapy may involve. . . .

The context in which the duty of risk-disclosure arises is invariably the occasion for decision as to whether a particular treatment procedure is to be undertaken. To the physician, whose training enables a self-satisfying evaluation, the answer may seem clear, but it is the prerogative of the patient, not the physician, to determine for himself the direction in which his interests seem to lie. . . . To enable the patient to chart his course understandably, some familiarity with the therapeutic alternatives and their hazards becomes essential. . . .

A reasonable revelation in these respects is not only a necessity but, as we see it, is as much a matter of the physician's duty. It is a duty to warn of the dangers lurking in the proposed treatment, and that is surely a facet of due care. . . . It is, too, a duty to impart information which the patient has every right to expect. . . . The patient's reliance upon the physician is a trust of the kind which traditionally has exacted obligations beyond those associated with arms-length transactions. . . . His dependence upon the physician for information affecting his well-being, in terms of contemplated treatment, is well-nigh abject. As earlier noted, long before the instant litigation arose, courts had recognized that the physician had the responsibility of satisfying the vital informational needs of the patient. . . . We now find, as a part of the physician's overall obligation to the patient, a similar duty of reasonable disclosure of the choices with respect to proposed therapy and the dangers inherently and potentially involved. . . .

It is well established that the physician must seek and secure his patient's consent before commencing an operation or other course of treatment. It is also clear that the consent, to be efficacious, must be free from imposition upon the patient. It is the settled rule that therapy not authorized by the patient may amount to a tort—a common law battery—by the physician. . . . And it is evident that it is normally impossible to obtain a consent worthy of the name unless the physician first elucidates the options and the perils for the patient's edification. . . . Thus the physician has long borne a duty, on pain of liability for unauthorized treatment, to make adequate disclosure to the patient.

IV

Duty to disclose has gained recognition in a large number of American jurisdictions, but more largely on a different rationale. The majority of courts dealing with the problem have made the duty depend on whether it was the custom of physicians practicing in the community to make the particular disclosure to the patient. If so, the physician may be held liable for an unreasonable and injurious failure to divulge, but there can be no recovery unless the omission forsakes a practice prevalent in the profession. . . . We agree that the physician's noncompliance with a professional custom to reveal, like any other departure from prevailing medical practice, . . . may give rise to liability to the patient. We do not agree that the patient's cause of action is dependent upon the existence and nonperformance of a relevant professional tradition.

There are, in our view, formidable obstacles to acceptance of the notion that the physician's obligation to disclose is either germinated or limited by medical practice. To begin with, the reality of any discernible custom reflecting a professional consensus on communication of option and risk information to patients is open to serious doubt. We sense the danger that what in fact is no custom at all may be taken as an affirmative custom to maintain silence . . . . We cannot gloss over the inconsistency between reliance on a general practice respecting divulgence and, on the other hand, realization that the myriad of variables among patients makes each case so different that its omission can rationally be justified only by the effect of its individual circumstances. Nor can we ignore the fact that to bind the disclosure obligation to medical usage is to arrogate the decision on revelation to the physician alone. Respect for the patient's right of self-determination on particular therapy demands a standard set by law for physicians rather than one which physicians may or may not impose upon themselves. . . .

V

Once the circumstances give rise to a duty on the physician's part to inform his patient, the next inquiry is the scope of the disclosure the physician is legally obliged to make. The courts have frequently confronted this problem but no uniform standard defining the adequacy of the divulgence emerges from the decisions. Some have said "full" disclosure, a norm we are unwilling to adopt literally. It seems obviously prohibitive and unrealistic to expect physicians to discuss with their patients every risk of proposed treatment—no matter how small or remote—and generally unnecessary from the patient's viewpoint as well. Indeed, the cases speaking in terms of "full" disclosure appear to envision something less than total disclosure, leaving unanswered the question of just how much.

The larger number of courts . . . have applied tests framed with reference to prevailing fashion within the medical profession. Some have measured the disclosure by "good medical practice," others by what a reasonable practitioner would have bared under the circumstances, and still others by what medical custom in the community would demand. We have explored this rather considerable body of law but are unprepared to follow it. The duty to disclose, we have reasoned, arises from phenomena apart from medical custom and practice. The latter, we think, should no more establish the scope of the duty than its existence. Any definition of scope in terms purely of a professional standard is at odds with the patient's prerogative to decide on projected therapy himself. That prerogative, we have said, is at the very foundation of the duty to disclose, and both the patient's right to know and the physician's correlative obligation to tell him are diluted to the extent that its compass is dictated by the medical profession.

In our view, the patient's right of self-decision shapes the boundaries of the duty to reveal. That right can be effectively exercised only if the patient possesses enough information to enable an intelligent choice. The scope of the physician's communications to the patient, then, must be measured by the patient's need, and that need is the information material to the decision. Thus the test for determining whether a particular peril must be divulged is its materiality to the patient's decision: all risks potentially affecting the decision must be unmasked. And to safeguard the patient's interest in achieving his own determination on treatment, the law must itself set the standard for adequate disclosure.

Optimally for the patient, exposure of a risk would be mandatory whenever the patient would deem it significant to his decision, either singly or in combination with other risks. Such a requirement, however, would summon the physician to second-guess the patient, whose ideas on materiality could hardly be known to the physician. That would make an undue demand upon medical practitioners, whose conduct, like that of others, is to be measured in terms of reasonableness. Consonantly with orthodox negligence doctrine, the physician's liability for nondisclosure is to be determined on the basis of foresight, not hindsight; no less than any other aspect of negligence, the issue on nondisclosure must be approached from the viewpoint of the reasonableness of the physician's divulgence in terms of what he knows or should know to be the patient's informational needs. If, but only if, the fact-finder can say that the physician's communication was unreasonably inadequate is an imposition of liability legally or morally justified. . . .

From these considerations we derive the breadth of the disclosure of risks legally to be required. The scope of the standard is not subjective as to either the physician or the patient; it remains objective with due regard for the patient's informational needs . . . . The category of risks which the physician should communicate is, of course, no broader than the complement he could communicate. . . . The duty to divulge may extend to any risk he actually knows, but he obviously cannot divulge any of which he may be unaware. Nondisclosure of an unknown risk does not, strictly speaking, present a problem in terms of the duty to disclose although it very well might pose problems in terms of the physician's duties to have known of it and to have acted accordingly. . . .

The topics importantly demanding a communication of information are the inherent and potential hazards of the proposed treatment, the alternatives to that treatment, if any, and the results likely if the patient remains untreated. The factors contributing significance to the dangerousness of a medical technique are, of course, the incidence of injury and the degree of the harm threatened. A very small chance of death or serious disablement may well be significant; a potential disability which dramatically outweighs the potential benefit of the therapy or the detriments of the existing malady may summons discussion with the patient.

There is no bright line separating the significant from the insignificant; the answer in any case must abide a rule of reason. Some dangers—infection, for example—are inherent in any operation; there is no obligation to communicate those of which persons of average sophistication are aware. Even more clearly, the physician bears no responsibility for discussion of hazards the patient has already discovered or those having no apparent materiality to patients' decision on therapy. The disclosure doctrine, like others marking lines between permissible and impermissible behavior in medical practice, is in essence a requirement of conduct prudent under the circumstances. Whenever nondisclosure of particular risk information is open to debate by reasonable-minded men, the issue is for the finder of the facts.

VI

Two exceptions to the general rule of disclosure have been noted by the courts. Each is in the nature of a physician's privilege not to disclose, and the reasoning underlying them is appealing. . . . The first comes into play when the patient is unconscious or otherwise incapable of consenting, and harm from a failure to treat is imminent and outweighs any harm threatened by the proposed treatment. When a genuine emergency of that sort arises, it is settled that the impracticality of conferring with the patient dispenses with need for it. . . . Even in situations of that character the physician should, as current law requires, attempt to secure a relative's consent if possible. . . . But if time is too short to accommodate discussion, obviously the physician should proceed with the treatment. . . .

The second exception obtains when risk-disclosure poses such a threat of detriment to the patient as to become unfeasible or contraindicated from a medical point of view. It is recognized that patients occasionally become so ill or emotionally distraught on disclosure as to . . . complicate or hinder the treatment, or perhaps even pose psychological damage to the patient. Where that is so, the cases have generally held that the physician is armed with a privilege to keep the information from the patient, and we think it clear that portents of that type may justify the physician in action he deems medically warranted. The critical inquiry is whether the physician responded to a sound medical judgment that communication of the risk information would present a threat to the patient's well-being.

The physician's privilege to withhold information for therapeutic reasons must be carefully circumscribed, however, for otherwise it might devour the disclosure rule itself. The privilege does not accept the paternalistic notion that the physician may remain silent simply because divulgence might prompt the patient to forego therapy the physician feels the patient really needs. That attitude presumes instability or perversity for even the normal patient, and runs counter to the foundation principle that the patient should and ordinarily can make the choice for himself. Nor does the privilege contemplate operation save where the patient's reaction to risk information, as reasonable foreseen by the physician, is menacing. And even in a situation of that kind, disclosure to a close relative with a view to securing consent to the proposed treatment may be the only alternative open to the physician.

VII

No more than breach of any other legal duty does nonfulfillment of the physician's obligation to disclose alone establish liability to the patient. An unrevealed risk that should have been made known must materialize, for otherwise the omission, however unpardonable, is legally without consequence. Occurrence of the risk must be harmful to the patient, for negligence unrelated to injury is nonactionable. And, as in malpractice actions generally, there must be a causal relationship between the physician's failure to adequately divulge and damage to the patient.

A causal connection exists when, but only when, disclosure of significant risks incidental to treatment would have resulted in a decision against it. . . . The patient obviously has no complaint if he would have submitted to the therapy notwithstanding awareness that the risk was one of its perils. On the other hand, the very purpose of the disclosure rule is to protect the patient against consequences which, if known, he would have avoided by foregoing the treatment. . . . The more difficult question is whether the factual issue on causality calls for an objective or a subjective determination.

It has been assumed that the issue is to be resolved according to whether the fact-finder believes the patient's testimony that he would not have agreed to the treatment if he had known of the danger which later ripened into injury. . . . We think a technique which ties the factual conclusion on causation simply to the assessment of the patient's credibility is unsatisfactory. To be sure, the objective of risk-disclosure is preservation of the patient's interest in intelligent self-choice on proposed treatment, a matter the patient is free to decide for any reason that appeals to him. . . . But when causality is explored at a post injury trial with a professedly uninformed patient, the question whether he actually would have turned the treatment down if he had known the risks is purely hypothetical . . . . And the answer which the patient supplies hardly represents more than a guess, perhaps tinged by the circumstance that the uncommunicated hazard has in fact materialized. . . .

In our view, this method of dealing with the issue on causation comes in second-best. It places the physician in jeopardy of the patient's hindsight and bitterness. It places the fact-finder in the position of deciding whether a speculative answer to a hypothetical question is to be credited. It calls for a subjective determination solely on testimony of a patient-witness shadowed by the occurrence of the undisclosed risk.

Better it is, we believe, to resolve the causality issue on an objective basis: in terms of what a prudent person in the patient's position would have decided if suitably informed of all perils bearing significance. If adequate disclosure could reasonably be expected to have caused that person to decline the treatment because of the revelation of the kind of risk or danger that resulted in harm, causation is shown, but otherwise not. The patient's testimony is relevant on that score of course but it would not threaten to dominate the findings. And since that testimony would probably be appraised congruently with the fact-finder's belief in its reasonableness, the case for a wholly objective standard for passing on causation is strengthened. . . .

VIII

In the context of trial of a suit claiming inadequate disclosure of risk information by a physician, the patient has the burden of going forward with evidence tending to establish prima facie the essential elements of the cause of action, and ultimately the burden of proof . . . on those elements. . . . The burden of going forward with evidence pertaining to a privilege not to disclose, . . . however, rests properly upon the physician. . . .

There are obviously important roles for medical testimony in such cases, and some roles which only medical evidence can fill. Experts are ordinarily indispensable to identify and elucidate for the fact-finder the risks of therapy and the consequences of leaving existing maladies untreated. They are normally needed on issues as to the cause of any injury or disability suffered by the patient and, where privileges are asserted, as to the existence of any emergency claimed and the nature and seriousness of any impact upon the patient from risk-disclosure. Save for relative infrequent instances where questions of this type are resolvable wholly within the realm of ordinary human knowledge and experience, the need for the expert is clear. . . .

It is evident that many of the issues typically involved in nondisclosure cases do not reside peculiarly within the medical domain. . . . Experts are unnecessary to a showing of the materiality of a risk to a patient's decision on treatment, or to the reasonably expectable effect of risk disclosure on the decision. . . .

X

This brings us to the remaining question . . . : whether appellant's evidence was of such caliber as to require a submission to the jury. On the first, the evidence was clearly sufficient to raise an issue as to whether Dr. Spence's obligation to disclose information on risks was reasonably met or was excused by the surrounding circumstances. Appellant testified that Dr. Spence revealed to him nothing suggesting a hazard associated with the laminectomy. His mother testified that, in response to her specific inquiry, Dr. Spence informed her that the laminectomy was no more serious than any other operation. When, at trial, it developed from Dr. Spence's testimony that paralysis can be expected in one percent of laminectomies, it became the jury's responsibility to decide whether that peril was of sufficient magnitude to bring the disclosure duty into play. There was no emergency to frustrate an opportunity to disclose, and Dr. Spence's expressed opinion that disclosure would have been unwise did not foreclose a contrary conclusion by the jury. There was no evidence that appellant's emotional makeup was such that concealment of the risk of paralysis was medically sound. Even if disclosure to appellant himself might have bred ill consequences, no reason appears for the omission to communicate the information to his mother, particularly in view of his minority. The jury, not Dr. Spence, was the final arbiter of whether nondisclosure was reasonable under the circumstances. . . .

LARGEY V. ROTHMAN
540 A.2D 504 (N.J. 1988)

This medical malpractice case raises an issue of a patient's informed consent to treatment. The jury found that plaintiff Janice Largey had consented to an operative procedure performed by the defendant physician. The single question presented goes to the correctness of the standard by which the jury was instructed to determine whether the defendant, Dr. Rothman, had adequately informed his patient of the risks of that operation.

The trial court told the jury that when informing the plaintiff Janice Largey of the risks of undergoing a certain biopsy procedure, described below, defendant was required to tell her "what reasonable medical practitioners in the same or similar circumstances would have told their patients undertaking the same type of operation." By answer to a specific interrogatory on this point, the jurors responded that defendant had not "fail[ed] to provide Janice Largey with sufficient information so that she could give informed consent" for the operative procedure. . . .

Plaintiffs argued below, and repeat the contention here, that the proper standard is one that focuses not on what information a reasonable doctor should impart to the patient (the "professional" standard) but rather on what the physician should disclose to a reasonable patient in order that the patient might make an informed decision (the "prudent patient" or "materiality of risk" standard). The latter is the standard announced in *Canterbury v. Spence*, 464 F.2d 772 (D.C.Cir.), *cert. den.*, 409 U.S. 1064 (1972). . . . We now discard [the] "reasonable physician" standard and adopt instead the *Canterbury* "reasonable patient" rule. Hence, we reverse and remand for a new trial.

I

. . . In the course of a routine physical examination plaintiff's gynecologist, Dr. Glassman, detected a "vague mass" in her right breast. The doctor arranged for mammograms to be taken. The radiologist reported two anomalies to the doctor: an "ill-defined density" in the subareola region and an enlarged lymph node or nodes, measuring four-by-two centimeters, in the right axilla (armpit). The doctor referred plaintiff to defendant, a surgeon. Defendant expressed concern that the anomalies on the mammograms might be cancer and recommended a biopsy. There was a sharp dispute at trial over whether he stated that the biopsy would include the lymph nodes as well as the breast tissue. Plaintiff claims that defendant never mentioned the nodes.

Plaintiff submitted to the biopsy procedure after receiving a confirmatory second opinion from a Dr. Slattery. During the procedure defendant removed a piece of the suspect mass from plaintiff's breast and excised the nodes. The biopsies showed that both specimens were benign. About six weeks after the operation, plaintiff developed a right arm and hand lymphedema, a swelling caused by inadequate drainage in the lymphatic system. The condition resulted from the excision of the lymph nodes. Defendant did not advise plaintiff of this risk. Plaintiff's experts testified that defendant should have informed plaintiff that lymphedema was a risk of the operation. Defendant's experts testified that it was too rare to be discussed with a patient. Plaintiff[s] . . . claimed that even if they had authorized the node excision, defendant was negligent in failing to warn them of the risk of lymphedema and therefore their consent was uninformed. . . .

II

The origins of the requirement that a physician obtain the patient's consent before surgery may be traced back at least two centuries. The doctrine is now well-embedded in our law. . . . [T]here is no "battery" claim implicated in this appeal because the jury determined as a matter of fact that plaintiff had given consent to the node excision performed by Dr. Rothman.

Although the requirement that a patient give consent before the physician can operate is of long standing, the doctrine of *informed* consent is one of relatively recent development in our jurisprudence. It is essentially a negligence concept, predicated on the duty of a physician to disclose to a patient such information as will enable the patient to make an evaluation of the nature of the treatment and of any attendant substantial risks, as well as of available options in the form of alternative therapies.

. . . In 1972 a new standard of disclosure for "informed consent" was established in *Canterbury v. Spence.* . . . The case raised a question of the defendant physician's duty to warn the patient beforehand of the risk involved in a laminectomy, a surgical procedure the purpose of which was to relieve pain in plaintiff's lower back, and particularly the risk attendant on a myelogram, the diagnostic procedure preceding the surgery. . . . The *Canterbury* court announced a duty on the part of a physician to "warn of the dangers lurking in the proposed treatment" and to "impart information [that] the patient has every right to expect," as well as a duty of "reasonable disclosure of the choices with respect to proposed therapy and the dangers inherently and potentially involved." *Id.* at 782. The court held that the scope of the duty to disclose must be measured by the patient's need, and that need is the information material to the decision. Thus the test for determining whether a particular peril must be divulged is its materiality to the patient's decision: all risks potentially affecting the decision must be unmasked. And to safeguard the patient's interest in achieving his own determination on treatment, the law must itself set the standard for adequate disclosure. . . .

The breadth of the disclosure of the risks legally to be required is measured, under *Canterbury*, by a standard whose scope is "not subjective as to either the physician or the patient," *id.* at 787; rather, "it remains *objective* with due regard for the patient's informational needs and with suitable leeway for the physician's situation." *Ibid.* (emphasis added). A risk would be deemed "material" when a reasonable patient, in what the physician knows or should know to be the patient's position, would be "likely to attach significance to the risk or cluster of risks" in deciding whether to forego the proposed therapy or to submit to it. *Ibid.*

The foregoing standard for adequate disclosure, known as the "prudent patient" or "materiality of risk" standard, has been adopted in a number of jurisdictions. . . . [T]he policy considerations are clear-cut. At the outset we are entirely unimpressed with the argument, made by those favoring the "professional" standard, that the "prudent patient" rule would compel disclosure of *every* risk (not just *material* risks) to *any* patient (rather than the *reasonable* patient). As *Canterbury* makes clear,

> [t]he topics importantly demanding a communication of information are the inherent and potential hazards of the proposed treatment, the alternatives to that treatment, if any, and the results likely if the patient remains untreated. The factors contributing significance to the dangerousness of a medical technique are, of course, the incidence of injury and the degree of harm threatened.

[464 F.2d at 787-88.] The court in *Canterbury* did not presume to draw a "bright line separating the significant [risks] from the insignificant"; rather, it resorted to a "rule of reason," *id.* at 788, concluding that "[w]henever non-disclosure of particular risk information is open to debate by reasonable-minded men, the issue is one for the finder of facts." *Ibid.* The point assumes significance in this case because defendant argues that the risk of lymphedema from an axillary node biopsy is remote, not material. Plaintiff's experts disagree, contending that she should have been informed of that risk. Thus there will be presented on the retrial a factual issue for the jury's resolution: would the risk of lymphedema influence a prudent patient in reaching a decision on whether to submit to the surgery?

Perhaps the strongest consideration that influences our decision in favor of the "prudent patient" standard lies in the notion that the physician's duty of disclosure "arises from phenomena apart from medical custom and practice": the patient's right of self-determination. *Canterbury, supra,* 464 F.2d at 786-87. The foundation for the physician's duty to disclose in the first place is found in the idea that "it is the prerogative of the patient, not the physician, to determine for himself the direction in which his interests seem to lie." *Id.* at 781. In contrast the arguments for the "professional" standard smack of an anachronistic paternalism that is at odds with any strong conception of a patient's right of self-determination. . . .

III

Finally, we address the issue of proximate cause. As with other medical malpractice actions, informed-consent cases require that plaintiff prove not only that the physician failed to comply with the applicable standard for disclosure but also that such failure was the proximate cause of plaintiff's injuries.

. . . As *Canterbury* observes,

> [t]he patient obviously has no complaint if he would have submitted to the therapy notwithstanding awareness that the risk was one of its perils. On the other hand, the very purpose of the disclosure rule is to protect the patient against consequences which, if known, he would have avoided by foregoing the treatment. The more difficult question is whether the factual issue on causality calls for an objective or a subjective determination.

[464 F.2d at 790.] *Canterbury* decided its own question in favor of an objective determination. The subjective approach, which the court rejected, inquires whether, if the patient had been informed of the risks that in fact materialized, he or she would have consented to the treatment. The shortcoming of this approach, according to *Canterbury*, is that it places the physician in jeopardy of the patient's hindsight and bitterness. It places the factfinder in the position of deciding whether a speculative answer to a hypothetical question is to be credited. It calls for a subjective determination solely on testimony of a patient-witness shadowed by the occurrence of the undisclosed risk. [*Id.* at 790-91.]

The court therefore elected to adopt an objective test, as do we. Because we would not presume to attempt an improvement in its articulation of the reasons, we quote once again the *Canterbury* court:

> Better it is, we believe, to resolve the causality issue on an objective basis: in terms of what a prudent person in the patient's position would have decided if suitably informed of all perils bearing significance. If adequate disclosure could reasonably be expected to have caused that person to decline the treatment because of the revelation of the kind of risk or danger that resulted in harm, causation is shown, but otherwise not. The patient's testimony is relevant on that score of course but it would not threaten to dominate the findings. And since that testimony would probably be appraised congruently with the factfinder's belief in its reasonableness, the case for a wholly objective standard for passing on causation is strengthened. Such a standard would in any event ease the fact-finding process and better assure the truth as its product. [*Id.* at 791.]

. . . The judgment of the Appellate Division is reversed. The cause is remanded for a new trial consistent with this opinion.

1 *Why not battery?* Why are these negligence cases and not battery cases? Would the result on the battery claim in *Largey* have been different if defendant had assured plaintiff that the surgery would be exploratory only and that nothing would be removed?

2 *Materiality.* Beginning with *Canterbury*, courts started to replace the "medical professional standard" for the duty of disclosure with the "materiality" standard of the duty. The materiality standard now is dominant.

3 *Causation.* Even assuming that defendants here failed to provide sufficient information to allow plaintiffs to make an informed decision whether to consent, is plaintiff harmed? What is the harm, and how is it connected to the alleged lack of information? One of the most controversial aspects of the court's decision in *Canterbury* is the so-called "objective test" of causation that the *Largey* court also employed. The effect of this objective standard is that plaintiff must prove, not only that plaintiff would have declined the procedure if sufficient information had been provided, but that the hypothetical reasonable patient also would have declined the procedure. While this is the majority approach, some courts, including one that will be discussed in the medical malpractice part of the materials, have rejected this approach.

What if a physician warns that a particular treatment carries a 1% likelihood of death but fails to warn that non-treatment carries a 50% likelihood of death and the patient decides against treatment. If the patient dies, is the physician subject to liability?

What if a physician warns that a particular treatment carries a .0001% likelihood of death, that non-treatment carries a 100% likelihood of death, and that even with the treatment, the patient has only a .0002% chance of survival. The physician fails to warn that the treatment entails a 100% likelihood of extreme pain and discomfort until the patient is cured or dies, whichever comes first. The patient consents to the treatment and spends her remaining days in pain and discomfort, before finally dying, as expected. Is the physician subject to liability?

4 *Minors.* Generally, parents are authorized to consent to treatment on behalf of their minor children.

5 *Exceptions.* There are two widely-accepted exceptions to the requirement that a physician must provide information sufficient to permit the patient to make an informed decision whether to consent. First, if emergency circumstances (such as unconsciousness of the patient) make it impossible to provide information, then the physician may proceed with a life-saving procedure. However, frequently this exception merely shifts the physician's duty to provide information to the next of kin. A second exception applies when the provision of material information is itself medically contraindicated. Again, though, if the patient is not physically able to receive material information, the information still should be provided to the patient's next of kin.

2. DEFENSE

a. DEFENSE OF PERSON

MATTHEW 5:38-39

Ye have heard that it hath been said, An eye for an eye, and a tooth for a tooth: But I say unto you, That ye resist not evil: but whosoever shall smite thee on thy right cheek, turn to him the other also.

1   Does Jesus here condemn self-defense? Defense of others?

The privilege of self-defense permits a party to protect her right to bodily integrity by using reasonable force to ward off an attack.

(1) SELF-DEFENSE

The concept of "reasonableness" appears twice in Restatement (Second) Torts §63(1). First, an actor is privileged to use only "reasonable" force. Second, the privilege to use such reasonable force applies only when the actor "reasonably" believes that another is about to intentionally inflict on him unprivileged bodily harm or offensive contact. But what if the actor mistakenly believes that the other is about to inflict unprivileged bodily harm or offensive contact? Usually "deadly force" may be used in self-defense only to prevent death, serious bodily injury, or sexual assault, but sometimes a defendant may be privileged to *threaten* force in self-defense that the defendant would not be privileged to *use.*

SLAYTON V. MCDONALD
690 SO.2D 914 (LA. CT. APP. 1997)

The plaintiff, Jimmy V. Slayton, appeals a trial court judgment rendered in favor of the defendant, A. S. McDonald, rejecting plaintiff's claim for personal injuries sustained as the result of a shooting incident. For the reasons assigned below, we affirm the trial court's judgment.

FACTS

On the afternoon of May 20, 1994, fourteen-year-old Daniel McDonald and fourteen-year-old James Slayton had a disagreement while riding the school bus . . . . Slayton was the larger of the two boys . . . . The disagreement began when Slayton threw a piece of paper at McDonald. After McDonald threw the paper back at Slayton, Slayton threatened to come to McDonald's house. McDonald told Slayton not to come to his house. When asked about Slayton's reputation as a fighter, McDonald testified he had heard that Slayton had won fights against people larger than himself, and that Slayton could "take care of himself pretty good."

    Later that afternoon, after McDonald arrived at home, he went outside his house and saw Slayton walking up the long driveway toward him. Slayton testified that he went to McDonald's house because he wanted to talk to McDonald about "kicking and punching on little kids and about messing with me and stuff." There were no adults present at McDonald's home when

Slayton arrived at the residence. McDonald yelled at Slayton to go home. However, Slayton kept walking up McDonald's driveway. Slayton testified that he did not hear McDonald's warning. After shouting the warning to Slayton, McDonald went into his house, got his twelve-gauge shotgun, came back outside and loaded the gun with #7 1/2 shot shells. McDonald testified that Slayton saw him load the gun; Slayton said that he did not. Again, McDonald asked Slayton to leave[.] Slayton refused.

McDonald then retreated into his home and called 911 to request help. McDonald testified that he closed the front door of his house after retreating inside. Slayton testified that the door was open. However, it is undisputed that the front door of the McDonald home did not have a lock and anyone could open it from the outside.

As McDonald spoke to the 911 operator, Slayton came inside McDonald's house. The transcript of the 911 conversation reveals that McDonald told Slayton to leave several times, to no avail. McDonald can be heard to say: "I think he's like sixteen. He's a lot bigger than me and he's in my house"; "Don't take another step towards me"; and, "If he keeps coming toward me I'm going to shoot him." (*See* Appendix A)

McDonald testified that Slayton pointed at his own leg, dared McDonald to shoot, and said that McDonald "didn't have the guts" to shoot. McDonald also stated that Slayton told him he was going to teach him a lesson and "kick my [McDonald's] ass." Slayton testified that after McDonald threatened to shoot him, he told McDonald that if McDonald shot him, he would get up and beat McDonald.

When asked if he was afraid when Slayton came into his house, McDonald testified that Slayton frightened him because "he [Slayton] had a crazy look in his eye. I didn't know what he was going to do after he didn't stop for the gun, I thought he must have been crazy." McDonald also told the 911 operator that "he's kinda crazy, I think." McDonald testified that Slayton "asked me if I could get him before he got to me and got the gun first. I was afraid that if he came past the gun that he was crazy enough to kill me."

At some point during the encounter, Slayton's younger sister, Amanda, arrived at the McDonald home and asked Slayton to leave because McDonald was armed. According to McDonald, Slayton refused to leave by saying "he's too scared to shoot me. He's about to cry." The 911 operator told McDonald several times not to shoot Slayton; McDonald said "I ain't gonna shoot him but in the leg. But I have to defend myself." Slayton testified that McDonald never pointed the shotgun at his head or chest.

What happened next was a matter of some dispute. On the 911 transcript, McDonald tells Slayton that "I might just count to three." Slayton testified that he was kneeling down because he was "resting waiting for the cops to get there so I could tell my story." However, Amanda Slayton and McDonald testified that Slayton was standing. Both Amanda and James Slayton testified that Slayton did not make a move toward McDonald, and Slayton testified that at all times during the incident, he was never more than two feet inside the McDonald home. However, McDonald testified that Slayton then began to count and to move "eight feet at least" into the home. On the tape of the 911 conversation, most of what Slayton says is inaudible, but, at the point where McDonald states that he might count to three, Slayton can be heard to count "one-- two-- three." McDonald then shot Slayton once in the left knee. Slayton's grandmother arrived shortly thereafter, pulled Slayton out of the McDonald home and waited for the paramedics and law enforcement authorities to arrive.

McDonald testified that from his experience, a load of #7 1/2 shot did not do a great deal of damage to animals at ordinary hunting distance, but he had never fired his shotgun at anything so close before. On the 911 tape, McDonald can be heard saying, "I ain't got but squirrel shot in here . . . ."

Nevertheless, according to one of Slayton's doctors, Dr. Richard I. Ballard, the shot charge caused Slayton a "devastating" and "severe" injury that will require knee fusion rendering his knee permanently stiff and the injured leg at least an inch shorter than the other leg. . . .

In written reasons for judgment, the court found that Slayton, "a much larger opponent who had a reputation for fighting," was the aggressor in the encounter and that McDonald acted reasonably under the circumstances in protecting himself using only that force necessary to prevent a forcible offense against his person. From this adverse judgment, plaintiff appeals.

DISCUSSION

The plaintiff contends the trial court erred in finding that the defendant's son acted reasonably under the circumstances surrounding this incident, and thus, was justified in shooting the plaintiff's son in the leg. We do not find that the trial court erred. . . .

Even when another party is the initial aggressor, the victim may use only so much force as is reasonably necessary to repel the attack and if the victim goes beyond that point, he is liable for damages. In determining the amount of force which is justified in repelling an attack, all facts and circumstances at the scene of the incident must be considered.

Generally, one is not justified in using a dangerous weapon in self-defense if the attacking party is not armed but only commits battery with his fists or in some manner not inherently dangerous to life. However, resort to dangerous weapons to repel an attack may be justifiable in certain cases when the fear of danger of the person attacked is genuine and founded on facts likely to produce similar emotions in reasonable men. Under this rule, it is only necessary that the actor have grounds which would lead a reasonable man to believe that the employment of a dangerous weapon is necessary, and that he actually so believes. All facts and circumstances must be taken into account to determine the reasonableness of the actor's belief, but detached reflections or a pause for consideration cannot be demanded under circumstances which by their nature require split second decisions. Various factors relied upon by the courts to determine the reasonableness of the actions of the party being attacked are the character and reputation of the attacker, the belligerence of the attacker, a large difference in size and strength between the parties, an overt act by the attacker, threats of serious bodily harm, and the impossibility of a peaceful retreat. . . .

In the instant case, McDonald testified that he believed that Slayton had beaten up people larger than himself, and, in essence, was capable of giving McDonald a beating as well; Slayton admitted that he had been in two fights while attending junior high school but gave no details of those altercations. Moreover, Slayton exhibited marked belligerence by refusing to leave McDonald's home despite repeated demands by McDonald while the latter was on the telephone with law enforcement authorities and was armed with a loaded twelve-gauge shotgun. This combination of reputation and belligerence evidence provides support for the trial court's conclusion that "the presence of the shotgun and defendant's threats were insufficient to thwart plaintiff's advances." It is undisputed that Slayton was considerably physically larger than McDonald, and the trial court accepted McDonald's testimony that Slayton had threatened to harm him. Indeed, Slayton himself admitted that he told McDonald that if McDonald shot him, he was going to get up and beat McDonald.

The trial court's finding that McDonald shot Slayton "to stop the plaintiff's advance" is a decision based upon the court's judgment of the credibility of the witnesses. Although both Slayton and his sister contradicted McDonald's testimony that Slayton was advancing when he was shot, Slayton's testimony that he was kneeling down when he was shot is contradicted by that of his sister and McDonald. Additionally, Slayton's testimony that he never came more than two feet into the house is contradicted by A.S. McDonald's testimony that he found blood about ten feet inside his home. Finally, the 911 tape, on which Slayton's voice became clearly audible only seconds before McDonald shot him, is further support for the conclusion that Slayton was advancing upon McDonald when shot. From its reasons for judgment, it is apparent that the trial court chose to credit McDonald's version of events over Slayton's version. Because the record supports this decision, it will not be disturbed on appeal.

Finally, it is evident that McDonald was simply unable to retreat from the encounter. While retreat is not a condition precedent for a finding of self-defense using justifiable force, in our opinion, the retreat of a lawful occupant of a home into a position in his home from which he cannot escape an attacker except by the use of force is strong evidence that the occupant's use of force to prevent the attack is proper. Although a shotgun may be a deadly weapon, McDonald used the gun in a way that he calculated would stop the attack without fatally injuring Slayton. Further, as recited above, McDonald testified that he was "afraid that if he came past the gun that he was crazy enough to kill me." Under these circumstances, where McDonald was on the telephone with law enforcement authorities and had repeatedly demanded that Slayton leave, and Slayton continued to advance and threaten McDonald, we cannot disagree with the trial court's conclusion that McDonald used reasonable force to repel Slayton's attack.

APPENDIX

RH: 911, what is your emergency?

A: Ah, there's a trespasser in my house.

RH: A trespasser?

A: Well, never mind.

RH: Is there-

A: I think he's leaving.

RH: Okay

A: Okay, I'm sorry about that, okay, well no, no he's here.

RH: Who is it?

A: 120 Cardinal Hill.

RH: Who's the guy there?

A: JAMES SLATON.

RH: What's he doing?

A: He's coming in my house and I got a shotgun in my hand.

RH: 120 Cardinal Hill Road? Where's Cardinal Hill Road? Where's Cardinal Hill Road?

A: Go ahead and go on home.

RH: Do what?

A: It's in Pea Ridge.

RH: Pea Ridge?

A: Off eight, twenty-two.

RH: Okay, what's his problem?

A: I don't know. He threw a piece of paper at me on the school bus and now he's in my house.

RH: He's in your house?

A: He's standing right in front of me.

RH: Hold on just a second. Okay.

A: Okay. (inaudible). Go, get your foot out of my house or you won't have a foot to get out of my house. Go and get out of my house. The cops are on the phone right here.

RH: You still there?

A: Yeah he's still in here.

RH: He's still in there.

A: Yeah, the only thing holding him back is

RH: How old are you?

A: I'm fourteen.

RH: How old is he?

A: I think he's like sixteen. He's alot bigger than me and he's in my house.

RH: He's in your house? Is there anyone else there?

A: Yes. Huh?

RH: Is anyone else there?

A: No, just me.

RH: Okay, hold on just a second okay?

A: Okay.
(pause)

A: Go and go home. Now, go on home man.

JS: (inaudible)

A: Yeah, you're in my house.
(Pause)

A: Don't take another step towards me.

RH: Okay, what's your name?

A: DANIEL MCDONALD.

RH: DANIEL MCDONALD?

A: Yes.

RH: Okay, where exactly do you live?

A: You go down Farmerville Highway, you go down eight, twenty-two and it will be the second road on the right.

RH: Second road on the right?

A: Yeah and then you take the first road on the right once you go down there----

RH: Ah, huh.

A: It'll be the first driveway on the right.

RH: First driveway on the right?

A: Yes.

RH: Okay.

A: He's standing here telling me to shoot him.

RH: On eight, twenty-two, take a right I think and then you turn on Cardinal Hill.

A: Yeah.

RH: Okay. Do you come in on Virgil Road or the other little road, off Rock Corner Road?

A: You come in off Cardinal Hill. You go down Virgil--

RH: Ah, huh. It comes off of Virgil?

A: Yeah it comes off of Virgil.

RH: Ah, huh. How far down?

A: Ah, not real far.

RH: On the left or the right?

A: It's on the right. The road is on the right. Cardinal Hill will be the first driveway on that road.

RH: First Driveway on Cardinal Hill?

A: Yeah.

RH: Okay, hold on just a second.

A: Huh?

RH: Hold on just a second okay?

A: Well he, if he comes towards me I'm gonna have to shoot him.

RH: Hold on just a second okay. Calm down.

A: And he's over here saying that he's gonna get up and get me after that, but I

RH: Okay---

A: ain't got but squirrel shot in here, but------

RH: Hold on just a second okay?

A: Okay.
(pause)

RH: On the left?

A: On the right.

RH: You live on---

A: Yeah.

RH: When you turn off of Virgil onto Cardinal Hill, do you live on the left or the right?

A: The right.

RH: On the right?

A: Yeah.

RH: Okay, hold on.

A: Yeah I can, because you're in my house and I'm pressing charges on you too.

RH: Did he break in?

A: Yeah, I told him, I told him to get off my land and not to come up here or I would press charges and then I was calling the police and now he's in my house, standing in the doorway.

RH: He's in your house. What's his name?

A: JAMES SLATON.

RH: JAMES SLATON, has he been drinking or anything?

A: No he's kinda crazy I think. I don't know, but see, he threw a piece of paper at me on the bus.

RH: Ah, huh.

A: And so I threw it back at him and now he decides to come up here and come in my house.

RH: Okay, my deputies are enrout up there.

A: You move your foot around and come toward me, I'm gonna shoot you.

JS: (inaudible)

A: I can hit a running target, yeah.

JS: (inaudible)

A: I'm positive. I am positive.

RH: DANIEL where are your parents at?

A: They're not here right now.

RH: They're at work?

A: Ah, huh.

RH: Okay what's your Dad's name?

A: TREY MCDONALD, work at UNR Sink Plant.

JS: (inaudible)

A: You better get out of my house.

JS: (inaudible)

A: If I have to shoot you I will.

JS: (inaudible)

RH: DANIEL is your phone number two, five, one, nine, four, two, zero?

A: Yes.

RH: Okay.

A: That's my phone number.

RH: That's your phone number?

A: Yes sir.

RH: You live a 120 Cardinal Hill Road?

A: Yes sir.

RH: Okay.

A: Well you need to tell them to hurry because if he keeps coming toward me I'm gonna shoot him.

RH: Okay.

A: I ain't gonna shoot him but in the leg.

RH: Okay.

A: But I have to defend myself. 120 Cardinal Hill is my address.

RH: 120 Cardinal Hill.

A: Yeah.

RH: Okay.

JS: (inaudible)

A: Put my stuff down! Put my stuff down! I'm fixing to shoot him. I swear.

RH: Don't shoot him.

A: I'm gonna have to.

RH: Don't shoot him.

A: Put my shit down right now.

RH: Don't shoot him. Okay.

A: If I have to.

JS: (inaudible)

A: I'm not gonna let him come over here. You keep pointing at your knee and I'm gonna shoot you damn knee boy!

JS: (inaudible) boy!

A: I'm gonna have to shoot him! It's in self defense. He's in my f--- house! That is self-defense. You better get out.

RH: DANIEL is anyone else there beside you and him?

A: His sister.

RH: His sister?

A: Yeah.

RH: How old is his sister?

A: Yeah

RH: How old is his sister?

A: I don't know.

RH: Is she older or younger?

A: She's younger than him.

RH: Okay.

A: She's young, she's like in fifth grade, in elementary school.

RH: Okay.

A: And he's in high school and I'm in junior high.

RH: Okay, where do you go to school?

A: Ruston Junior High.

RH: Ruston Junior High. Okay.

A: They gonna have to bring a stretcher too if you don't get out of my damn house! I might just count to three! You don't know that! I'm crazy man! You better leave!

JS: One, two, three. (gun fire)

JS: Oh, (inaudible)

RH: Did you shoot him? DANIEL? DANIEL?

JS: Oh God! Oh God! God! Help!

RH: Hello, Hello, Hello, Hello, DANIEL? Hello, DANIEL are you there? Hello. Hello, hello.

NOTES AND QUESTIONS

1   What facts made McDonald's belief that self-defense was necessary a reasonable belief under the circumstances?
2   In the next case, if Courviosier's shooting of a police officer in the street was arguably privileged, is not this case – where plaintiff pursued defendant into defendant's own house, threatening him all the while – an extremely easy one? *See* Restatement (Second) of Torts Section 65(2).

3 Even where force is warranted, deadly force is justified only where plaintiff intentionally places defendant in reasonable apprehension of imminent death or serious bodily injury. What facts support the reasonableness of the force used by defendant?

4 What if Slayton had approached McDonald on the street on the way to school and said, "If you give me your lunch money, nobody needs to get hurt here." Unknown to Slayton, McDonald had a gun in his pocket. Would McDonald be privileged to resist Slayton with force? Would he be privileged to use the gun?

COURVOISIER V. RAYMOND
47 P. 284 (COLO. 1896)

It is admitted . . . that appellee received a gunshot wound at the hands of the appellant . . . . It is further shown that the shooting occurred under the following circumstances: That Mr. Courvoisier, on the night in question, was asleep in his bed in the second story of a brick building . . . ; that he occupied a portion of the lower floor of this building as a jewelry store. He was aroused from his bed shortly after midnight by parties shaking or trying to open the door of the jewelry store. These parties, when asked by him as to what they wanted, insisted upon being admitted, and upon his refusal to comply with this request, they used profane and abusive epithets toward him. Being unable to gain admission, they broke some signs upon the front of the building, and then entered the building by another entrance, and passing upstairs commenced knocking upon the door of a room where defendant's sister was sleeping. Courvoisier partly dressed himself, and, taking his revolver, went upstairs and expelled the intruders from the building. In doing this he passed downstairs and out on the sidewalk as far as the entrance to his store, which was at the corner of the building. The parties expelled from the building, upon reaching the rear of the store, were joined by two or three others. In order to frighten these parties away, the defendant fired a shot in the air, but instead of retreating they passed around to the street in front, throwing stones and brickbats at the defendant, whereupon he fired a second and perhaps a third shot. The first shot fired attracted the attention of plaintiff Raymond and two deputy sheriffs, who were . . . across the street. These officers started toward Mr. Courvoisier, who still continued to shoot, but two of them stopped when they reached the men in the street, for the purpose of arresting them, Mr. Raymond alone proceeding towards the defendant, calling out to him that he was an officer and to stop shooting. Although the night was dark, the street was well lighted by electricity, and when the officer approached him defendant shaded his eyes, and, taking deliberate aim, fired, causing the injury complained of. . . . The defendant claims that the plaintiff was approaching him at the time in a threatening attitude, and that the surrounding circumstances were such as to cause a reasonable man to believe that his life was in danger, and that it was necessary to shoot in self-defense, and that defendant did so believe at the time of firing the shot. . . . [The plaintiff prevailed at trial.]

The [issue on appeal] relates to the instructions given by the court to the jury and to those requested by the defendant and refused by the court. The second instruction given by the court was clearly erroneous. The instruction is as follows: "The court instructs you that if you believe

from the evidence, that, at the time the defendant shot the plaintiff, the plaintiff was not assaulting the defendant, then your verdict should be for the plaintiff."

The vice of this instruction is that it excluded from the jury a full consideration of the justification claimed by the defendant. The . . . evidence for the defendant tends to show that the circumstances surrounding him at the time of the shooting were such as to lead a reasonable man
to believe that his life was in danger, or that he was in danger of receiving great bodily harm at
the hands of the plaintiff, and the defendant testified that he did so believe. He swears that his
house was invaded shortly after midnight by two men, whom he supposed to be burglars; that
when ejected, they were joined on the outside by three or four others; that the crowd so formed
assaulted him with stones and other missiles, when, to frighten them away, he shot into the air;
that instead of going away someone approached him from the direction of the crowd; that he
supposed this person to be one of the rioters, and did not ascertain that it was the plaintiff until
after the shooting. He says that he had had no previous acquaintance with plaintiff; that he did
not know that he was a police officer, or that there were any police officers in the town . . . ;
that he heard nothing said at the time by the plaintiff or anyone else that caused him to think
the plaintiff was an officer; that his eyesight was greatly impaired, so that he was obliged to use
glasses, and that he was without glasses at the time of the shooting, and for this reason could
not see distinctly. He then adds: "I saw a man come away from the bunch of men and come up
towards me, and as I looked around I saw this man put his hand to his hip pocket. I didn't think
I had time to jump aside, and therefore turned around and fired at him. . . ."

. . . The defendant's justification did not rest entirely upon the proof of assault by the plaintiff. A riot was in progress, and the defendant swears that he was attacked with missiles, hit with
stones, brickbats, etc.; that he shot plaintiff, supposing him to be one of the rioters. We must
assume these facts as established in reviewing the instruction, as we cannot say what the jury
might have found had this evidence been submitted to them under a proper charge.

By the second instruction the conduct of those who started the fracas was eliminated from
the consideration of the jury. If the jury believed from the evidence that the defendant would
have been justified in shooting one of the rioters had such person advanced towards him as did
the plaintiff, then it became important to determine whether the defendant mistook plaintiff for
one of the rioters, and if such a mistake was in fact made, was it excusable in the light of all the
circumstances leading up to and surrounding the commission of the act? If these issues had been
resolved by the jury in favor of the defendant, he would have been entitled to a judgment. . . .

Where a defendant in a civil action like the one before us attempts to justify on a plea of necessary self-defense, he must satisfy the jury not only that he acted honestly in using force, but
that his fears were reasonable under the circumstances; and also as to the reasonableness of the
means made use of. In this case perhaps the verdict would not have been different had the jury
been properly instructed, but it might have been, and therefore the judgment must be reversed.

Reversed.

1   Here the trial court erred by giving an improper instruction to the jury. What would a proper jury instruction look like?

2   Does it matter that plaintiff is a police officer? Of what significance, if any, are the unusual surrounding circumstances, e.g., time of night, the break-in, the hurling of stones and brickbats? What if a reasonable person in defendant's position would have known that plaintiff here was a police officer? Would plaintiff's mistake still provide a potential defense?

3   What if a uniformed officer had approached plaintiff with hands raised saying "I'm a police officer. Calm down. Nobody's going to hurt you." Assume further that defendant was paranoid and actually believed that the officer was about to kill him. Would defendant be privileged to shoot the officer in self-defense?

4   What if Mr. Courvoisier had merely grazed Raymond with a bullet and then dropped his gun and put his hands in the air. Assume that Raymond then, in a rage, shot Courvoisier, and Courvoisier sues Raymond for battery. What result?

5   What if Courvoisier shoots at and misses Raymond then drops his gun and reaches for the sky. Raymond then draws his gun saying, "If you're gonna take a shot at me, you'd better kill me, and if you don't, you've gotta pay the price." Courvoisier, who has seen lots of Hollywood movies, then dives for his gun, snatches it from the ground, rolls and fires injuring Raymond. Battery?

6   Assume the same facts as the immediately preceding scenario except that when Courvoisier fired his first shot, he missed and hit innocent bystander A, and when Courvoisier rolled and fired his second shot, he missed again, striking innocent bystander B. Has he battered the bystanders?

7   Assume the same facts as in the immediately preceding scenario except that after Courvoisier fires and misses, Raymond does not draw his gun but rather says "you better watch your back Courvoisier, because when you least expect it, I'll be there to take you out." As Raymond turns to walk away, Courvoisier, fearing that Raymond will kill him at some point, shoots Raymond in the back. Does Courvoisier have a potential self-defense claim?

8   What if when Raymond approached, he made a disparaging remark about Courvoisier's mother, and Courvoisier punched him in the nose? What if after Raymond made the disparaging remark about Courvoisier's mother, Courvoisier said, "You're just a coward hiding behind a badge. If you were half a man, you'd take off that badge and gun, and then we'd see how tough you are." Raymond obliges, takes off the badge and gun, and punches Courvoisier in the nose. Battery?

DUPRE V. MARYLAND MANAGEMENT CORP.
127 N.Y.S.2D 615 (1954)

. . . Plaintiff was a guest in the hotel of the corporate defendant. He has recovered damages for an assault committed by one Jones, a bellboy. The trial court found that plaintiff initiated the encounter in which he received his injuries, but that Jones used more than sufficient force to repel an attack by plaintiff, and, therefore, found defendant liable to plaintiff in damages.

We agree with the basic findings of the trial court in all respects except the finding that an excess of force was used by Jones in self-defense. We find from the record that Jones struck plaintiff after he had twice tried to avoid a physical encounter and after he had been assaulted and threatened with further assault. He struck plaintiff with his fist in self-defense fracturing plaintiff's jaw. There is no credible evidence that Jones persisted in an attack after plaintiff was incapacitated. That the blow or blows . . . resulted in more serious injury than might have been sufficient to stall the attack is not the test of use of excessive force. One must know that what he does will be excessive . . . . "Detached reflection cannot be demanded" of one facing a dangerous attack (*Brown v. United States*, 256 U.S. 335, 343). At least, he is not to be held liable in damages if he fails to anticipate the precise effect of a blow with the fist . . . .

NOTES

1   *Battered wife syndrome.* A controversial topic in the criminal law context is whether an abused spouse may claim self-defense when she kills her abuser at a moment (often while he slept) at which he posed no imminent threat of harm to her. Courts have uniformly held that she may not.

(2) DEFENSE OF THIRD PARTY

Generally, the law permits one to defend any third party to the same extent as the third party would be permitted to defend himself. In considering this privilege, a metaphor frequently is used: defendant "steps into the shoes" of the third party and acquires the same privilege. The difficult question is whether defendant is privileged to use force in defense of a third party when defendant reasonably but mistakenly believes that force is necessary in defense of the other.

YOUNG V. WARREN
383 S.E.2D 381 (N.C. APP. 1989)

. . . The evidence introduced at trial showed that defendant shot and killed Lewis Reid Young ("Young") on 12 May 1986. The death occurred as a result of a 20-gauge shotgun blast fired at close range into the deceased's back. Prior to the shooting, in the early morning hours of 12 May 1986, Young, who had been dating defendant's daughter for several months, went to the home of defendant's daughter who lived with her two children within sight of the defendant's residence. Upon arriving at the defendant's daughter's home, Young threw a large piece of wood through the glass in the front door. He then entered the home by reaching through the broken window and unlocking the door. Once inside the house Young argued with the defendant's daughter and "jerked" her arm. At that point, the defendant arrived with his loaded shotgun, having been awakened by a telephone call from a neighbor, his ex-wife, who had told him "something bad is going on" at his daughter's house. When the defendant arrived at his daughter's house, he heard screaming and saw Young standing inside the door. The defendant then testified:

> . . . I told him like, "Come on out. This doesn't make any sense," and he kind of came forward,
> you know, kind of had his hands up like that. (Indicating) I backed away from the door and I told

him to get on out. "This can be taken care of tomorrow," or something to that effect. Q. You told him to get the hell out, didn't you? A. Well, okay; something like that. Q. Okay. And then what happened? A. Then he walked out the door and I just backed up like he came out the door and he walked over about six feet. There is a cement porch there, and he stepped right there, and I was behind him anywhere from a foot to eighteen inches, maybe even two foot, and he stopped. And in my opinion, he started to turn around. . . . Q. What did he do? A. He stopped and started to lower his hands and started to turn around.

. . . We first determine whether a defendant in a civil action may assert defense of family to justify assault on a third party. While self-defense and defense of family are seen more often in the context of criminal law, these defenses are nonetheless appropriate in civil actions. If the defenses apply, the defendant's conduct is considered "privileged" and the defendant is not subject to tort liability for actions taken within the privilege. . . . The defenses, as they result in avoidance of liability, are considered affirmative defenses and must be affirmatively pled. . . . The burden of proof is on the defendant to prove the defenses by a preponderance of the evidence. . . .

An assault on a third party in defense of a family member is privileged only if the "defendant had a well-grounded belief that an assault was about to be committed by another on the family member . . . ." However, in no event may defendant's action be in excess of the privilege of self-defense granted by law to the family member. . . . The privilege protects the defendant from liability only to the extent that the defendant did not use more force than was necessary or reasonable. . . . Finally, the necessity for the defense must "be immediate, and attacks made in the past, or threats for the future, will not justify" the privilege. . . .

The record contains no evidence that the defendant reasonably believed his daughter was, at the time of the shooting of the plaintiff, in peril of death or serious bodily harm. At that time, the plaintiff stood outside the house with his back to the defendant. Defendant's daughter and children were inside the house, removed from any likely harm from plaintiff. Accordingly, . . . the evidence in this trial did not support the submission of the issue to the jury, and the plaintiff is entitled to a new trial.

QUESTIONS

1   Distinguish the facts in *Slayton* from the facts in *Young*. Why might the cases have come out differently? Is it important that the defendant in *Slayton* was defending himself while defendant in *Young* was defending his daughter?

. . . [O]n May 17, 1989, a group of some forty-five to fifty persons entered . . . the West Texas Professional Building. Among the tenants of that building was James Morris, M.D. Entrance to his office was blocked by this group of people, among whom was appellant. After being requested to leave, appellant refused to do so, giving rise to this prosecution. . . . [A]ppellant testified that on the day in question he had been informed that the doctor in question had abortions scheduled. His stated belief was that, by the performance of the abortions, there would be "harm taking place to the life that was inside of them."

In his first point, appellant contends that this testimony was admissible, and under it, he was entitled to a charge on necessity, justification, and defense of a third person. . . . Texas Penal Code Annotated, § 9.33 (Vernon 1974) provides:

A person is justified in using force or deadly force against another to protect a third person if:

1. under the circumstances as the actor reasonably believes them to be, the actor would be justified . . . in using force or deadly force to protect himself against the unlawful force or unlawful deadly force he reasonably believes to be threatening the third person he seeks to protect; and

2. the actor reasonably believes that his intervention is immediately necessary to protect the third person.

. . . [F]etuses are not persons under established Texas law. . . . Section 1.07(a)(17) of the Texas Penal Code Annotated (Vernon 1974) defines an individual as "a human being who has been born and is alive." . . . To establish that he was entitled to submission of the protection of a third person, justification, or the necessity defenses, the record and the bill of exception testimony must demonstrate that it met all elements of those theories. They do not do so. Accordingly, the trial court did not err by excluding the tendered testimony nor did it err in refusing the charge in question. . . .

b. DEFENSE OF PROPERTY

In some ways, the privilege to defend property by doing what would otherwise be considered tortious is like the privilege of self-defense. A defendant is privileged to use reasonable force in defense of property. But the right to use force in defense of property is more circumscribed than the right of self-defense.

One difference between self-defense and defense of property is the treatment of mistaken beliefs that force is necessary. In most jurisdictions, reasonable mistakes in self-defense are privileged, but defense of property is universally like the majority position on defense of third-parties. A mistake, even if reasonable, negates the privilege to use force in defense of property unless plaintiff induced the mistake.

(1) Deadly Force

Another difference between defense of person and defense of property is in the level of force that can reasonably be used in the two contexts – more force is justifiable in defense of person. The limits on the use of force in defense of property are discussed in the following case.

M'ILVOY V. COCKRAN
2 A.K.MARSH. 271 (KY. CT. APP. 1820)

This is an appeal from a judgment recovered by Cockran in an action of trespass, assault and battery, brought by him against M'Ilvoy.

The declaration charges M'Ilvoy of having . . . with sticks, clubs, fists, hands and feet, made an assault upon, and beat, wounded and illy treated Cockran . . . . M'Ilvoy . . . alleged [that Cockran's] action against him ought not to . . . maintain, because he says that he M'Ilvoy . . . was lawfully possessed of . . . a certain tract and parcel of land . . . , and . . . Cockran, . . . without . . . permission, but against the will of . . . M'Ilvoy, did force and break down some of the . . . posts, intending thereby to demolish said fence, and . . . did . . . endeavor forcibly to break down and demolish . . . the posts and rails of . . . M'Ilvoy . . . , being with an intention . . . unlawfully to pull up and throw down . . . M'Ilvoy's posts, . . . and would . . . have . . . accomplished such unlawful attempt . . . had not [M'Ilvoy] . . . defended his . . . fence and posts, whereupon . . . M'Ilvoy . . . did . . . defend his . . . possession of his . . . close, posts and rails, and . . . resist the . . . attempt . . . of . . . Cockran, . . . and in so doing he did . . . unavoidably assault, beat and ill treat . . . Cockran . . . . M'Ilvoy saith that . . . any damage or injury . . . to . . . Cockran . . . happened of the wrong of . . . Cockran and in the lawful and necessary defence of . . . M'Ilvoy's . . . close, posts and rails . . . .

During the . . . trial before the jury, and after the evidence was closed on both sides, . . . the court . . . instructed the jury that . . . not every trespass . . . would justify so enormous a battery . . . . The jury, after retiring . . . to consult of their verdict, returned a verdict . . . in favor of Cockran; whereupon the counsel of M'Ilvoy moved the court for a new trial . . . for an error in the court's . . . giving the instructions it did to the jury. The motion was, however, overruled, and judgment rendered in conformity with the verdict. . . .

. . . [I]t must be borne in mind that the declaration contains a charge of assault, battery and wounding; and the plea alleges the injury to have been occasioned by M'Ilvoy . . . in defence of a close of which he was possessed, and in resisting the attempt of Cockran forcibly to enter and demolish the fence . . . . An assault and battery may be justified in defense of real or personal property; but except the assailant uses force in fact, resort is not to be had to violence before a request to depart . . . .

There are certainly cases where force may be employed in defence of the possession without a previous request to depart. Thus in the case of Green against Godard, . . . the court said, in cases of actual force, as breaking open a gate or door, it is lawful to oppose force with force; and if one breaks down a gate, or comes into a close with force . . . , the possessor need not request him to depart, but may lay hands upon him immediately, for it is but returning violence with violence; so if one comes forcibly and takes away my goods, he may be opposed immediately, for there is no time to make a request; but say the court, where one enters the close without actual force, . . . there must be a request to depart before the possessor can lay hands upon him and turn him out.

. . . Where the possession is invaded by force . . . , force may be employed by the possessor, and . . . an assault and battery may be justified.

Notwithstanding, however, an assault and battery may be justified . . . , we apprehend a wounding cannot be; for it is well settled that in defense of possession a wounding cannot be justified. . . . But although a wounding can not be justified barely in defence of possession, yet, if in attempting to remove the intruder, or prevent his forcible entry, he should commit an assault upon the person of the possessor or his family, and the owner should, in defence of himself or family, wound him, the wounding may no doubt be justified . . . but then as the personal assault would form the grounds of justification, the plea should set out specifically the assault in justification.

Though an assault and battery may be justified in defense of possession, yet a wounding in no case can; but if the intruder in his attempt assaults the possessor or his family, the possessor resisting the attempt may wound the intruder; the plea in this case should specially set out and rely on the assault and not on the intrusion.

From what has been said it will be perceived, that the plea of M'Ilvoy, as it contains allegations of actual force on the part of Cockran, imports a defence to the assault and battery charged in the declaration, but as it contains no allegation of a personal assault by Cockran, it furnishes no justification to the wounding stated in the declaration. . . .

The judgment must be affirmed with cost and damages.

HYPOTHETICAL SCENARIOS

1. A mugger approaches with palms out and says, "Give me your wallet." You have a gun. May you use the gun?

2. If someone tries to pick your pocket, may you resist with force? May you use the gun?

BIRD V. HOLBROOK

4 BING. 628 (C.P. 1828)

Before, and at the time of; the Plaintiff's sustaining the injury complained of, the Defendant rented and occupied a walled garden . . . in which the Defendant grew valuable flower-roots, and particularly tulips, of the choicest and most expensive description. The garden was at the distance of near a mile from the Defendant's dwelling-house, and above one hundred yards from the road. In it there was a summer-house, consisting of a single room, in which the defendant and his wife had some considerable time before slept, and intended in a few days after the accident again to have slept, for the greater protection of their property. The garden was surrounded by a wall, by which it was separated on the south from a footway up to some houses, on the east and west from other gardens, and on the north from a field which had no path through it, and was itself fenced against the highway, at a considerable distance from the garden, by a wall. On the north side of the garden the wall adjoining the field was seven or eight feet high. The other walls were somewhat lower. The garden was entered by a door in the wall. The Defendant had been, shortly before the accident, robbed of flowers and roots from his garden . . . in consequence of which, . . . he placed in the garden a spring gun, the wires connected with which were made to pass from the doorway of the summer-house to some tulip beds, at the height of about fifteen inches from the ground, and across three or four of the garden paths; which wires were visible from all parts of the garden or the garden wall; but it was admitted by the Defendant, that the Plaintiff had not seen them, and that he had no notice of the spring gun and the wires being there; and that the Plaintiff had gone into the garden for an innocent purpose, to get back a pea-fowl that had strayed.

A witness to whom the Defendant mentioned the fact of his having been robbed, and of having set a spring gun, proved that he had asked the Defendant if he had put up a notice of such gun being set, to which the Defendant answered, that "he did not conceive that there was any law to oblige him to do so," and the Defendant desired such person not to mention to any one that the gun was set, "lest the villain should not be detected." The Defendant stated to the same person that the garden was very secure, and that he and his wife were going to sleep in the summer-house in a few days.

No notice was given of the spring gun being placed in the garden . . . .

On the 21st March 1825, between the hours of six and seven in the afternoon, it being then light, a pea-hen belonging to the occupier of a house in the neighbourhood had escaped, and . . . alighted in the Defendant's garden. A female servant of the owner of the bird was in pursuit of it, and the Plaintiff (a youth of the age of nineteen years), seeing her in distress from the fear of losing the bird, said he would go after it for her: he accordingly got upon the wall at the back of the garden, next to the field, and having called out two or three times to ascertain whether any person was in the garden, and waiting a short space of time without receiving any answer, jumped down into the garden.

The bird took shelter near the summer-house, and the boy's foot coming in contact with one of the wires, close to the spot where the gun was set, it was thereby discharged, and a great part of its contents, consisting of large swan shot, were lodged in and about his knee-joint, and caused a severe wound.

The question for the opinion of the Court was, Whether the Plaintiff was entitled to recover:
. . .

BEST C. J. I am of opinion that this action is maintainable. . . . "Humanity requires that the fullest notice possible should be given, and the law of England will not sanction what is inconsistent with humanity."

It has been argued that the law does not compel every line of conduct which humanity or religion may require; but there is no act which Christianity forbids, that the law will not reach: if it were otherwise, Christianity would not be, as it has always been held to be, part of the law of England. I am, therefore, clearly of opinion that he who sets spring guns, without giving notice, is guilty of an inhuman act, and that, if injurious consequences ensue, he is liable to yield redress to the sufferer. But this case stands on grounds distinct from any that have preceded it. In general, spring guns have been set for the purpose of deterring; the Defendant placed his for the express purpose of doing injury; for, when called on to give notice, be said, "If - I give notice, I shall not catch him." He intended, therefore, that the gun should be discharged, and that the contents should be lodged in the body of his victim, for he could not be caught in any other way. . . . As to the case of *Brock v. Copeland,* Lord Kenyon proceeded on the ground that the defendant had a right to keep a dog for the preservation of his house, and the Plaintiff, who was his foreman, knew where the dog was stationed. . . .

Those cases, therefore, do not apply to one, where an instrument is placed solely for a bad purpose. . . . But we want no authority in a case like the present; we put it on the principle that it is inhuman to catch a man by means which may maim him or endanger his life, and, as far as human means can go, it is the object of English law to uphold humanity, and the sanctions of religion. It would be, indeed, a subject of regret, if a party were not liable in damages, who, instead of giving notice of the employment of a destructive engine, or removing it, at least, during the day, expressed a resolution to withhold notice, lest, by affording it, he should fail to entrap his victim.

PARK J. . . . [I]n the present case, I found my decision on the circumstance of the Defendant having omitted to give notice of what he had done, and his even expressing a desire to conceal it. . . .

BURROUGH J. The common understanding of mankind shews that notice ought to be given when these means of protection are resorted to; and it was formerly the practice upon such occasions to give public notice in market towns. But the present case is of a worse complexion than those which have preceded it; for if the Defendant had proposed merely to protect his property from thieves, he would have set the spring guns only by night. The Plaintiff was only a trespasser: if the Defendant had been present, he would not have been authorised even in taking him into custody, and no man can do indirectly that which he is forbidden to do directly. . . .

Here, no notice whatever was given, but the Defendant artfully abstained from giving it, and he must take the consequence. . . .

Judgment for the Plaintiff.

NOTES

1   The form of English judicial opinions sometimes can confuse new American law students. Instead of the familiar majority and dissenting opinions used by American appellate courts, English judges frequently each write their own opinions.

2   *Guard Dogs.* Courts usually have held that use of guard dogs to protect property is not excessive force. This result is not surprising since a dog usually would be more naturally characterized as a deterrent than as a trap.

With regard to breaking into a dwelling, American law distinguishes between breaking in at night and breaking in during the day. Some jurisdictions limit the definition of the crime of burglary to nighttime break-ins, and case law has privileged a homeowner to use deadly force in defense of his living quarters at night, even against an unarmed intruder. Some of the reasons for this distinction are obvious. First, people with legitimate purposes on the premises almost always come during the day. Second, it is more difficult for the homeowner to be discriminating at night when visibility is bad and most are asleep. This distinction can also be seen in the law of Moses:

EXODUS 22:2-3

If a thief be found breaking up, and be smitten that he die, there shall no blood be shed for him. If the sun be risen upon him, there shall be blood shed for him . . . .

(2) Recapture of Chattels

The common law developed a privilege allowing a property owner, under certain circumstances, to use otherwise tortious means to "recapture" her personal property. We have already considered a subset of this privilege (the shopkeeper's privilege) in conjunction with our consideration of false imprisonment.

HODGEDEN V. HUBBARD
18 vt. 504 (1846)

. . . [P]laintiff gave evidence . . . that . . . he purchased . . . in Montpelier, a stove, and gave his promissory note therefore, . . . that on the same day, and soon after the sale, the defendants learned, that the plaintiff was irresponsible as to property, and started in pursuit of him, and overtook him about two miles from Montpelier and took the stove from him by force; . . . it did appear, that, in the attempt to dispossess the plaintiff of the stove, [plaintiff] drew his knife, and that he was then forcibly held by one of the defendants, while the other took possession of the stove; and the testimony tended to prove, that the resistance of the plaintiff was such, that the defendants used violence and applied force to his person with great rudeness and outrage. The defendants then gave evidence, tending to prove that the purchase of the stove by the plaintiff was effected by means of his false and fraudulent representations as to his ability to pay, and as to the amount of his property; that, among other things, the plaintiff represented, that he owned a farm in Cabot and considerable stock upon it, that he owned the team that he then had with him, and that he carried on a large business manufacturing butter firkins, &c.; that it was only by means of these representations, and others of like character, that [defendant] was induced to sell the stove to the plaintiff on credit; that soon after the delivery of the stove, on the same day, [defendant] learned, upon inquiry, from a person whom he saw from Cabot, that the plaintiff was entirely irresponsible, and that his representations as to his property were wholly false; and that the defendants immediately followed the plaintiff, and took the stove from him . . . .

The court charged the jury, that, although the plaintiff was guilty of misrepresentation and fraud, in obtaining the stove, in the manner attempted to be proved by the defendants, yet this would not justify the defendants in forcibly taking the property from him that . . . the defendants might take it peaceably, wherever they could find it; but that the defendants, having delivered the stove to the plaintiff, could not justify taking it from him by blows inflicted upon his person, or by holding him, but should resort to redress by legal process.

. . .Verdict for plaintiff for one dollar damages. . . .

In the present case the defendants had clearly a right to retake the property . . . thus fraudulently obtained from them, if it could be done without unnecessary violence to the person, or without breach of the peace. It is admitted by the counsel for the plaintiff, that a right to recapture existed in the defendants, if it could be done without violence, or breach of the peace. And how far this qualification of the right to retake property, thus taken, was intended for the security, or benefit, of the fraudulent possessor may admit of some doubt. . . . The plaintiff had no lawful possession, nor any right to resist the attempt of the defendants to regain the property, of which he had unlawfully and fraudulently obtained the possession.

. . . The judgment of the county court is reversed.

NOTE AND QUESTIONS

1   If Hubbard had reasonably suspected Hodgeden of shoplifting a lighter from Hubbard's shop, would Hodgeden have been justified in forcibly detaining Hodgeden as he was leaving long enough to investigate? Is this shoplifting scenario materially different from the facts of this case? If so, how?

2   Assume defendants had shot and killed Hodgeden? Would that use of force have been privileged?

3   Assume the source of the information in this case were mistaken and Hodgeden actually were as creditworthy as he claimed? Would this change the privilege analysis?

4   Reconsider the holding in *M'Ilvoy*. Why was the physical violence in *M'Ilvoy* held not to be privileged while this violence is held to be privileged?

5   The Court here notes that plaintiff had no legal right to resist the retaking of the stove. This common holding – that a party has no right to oppose a properly asserted privilege, is important both in recapture cases and, as we will see in *Ploof v. Putnam, infra,* in necessity cases.

LAMB V. WOODRY

58 P.2D 1257 (ORE. 1936)

. . . On October 30, 1934, plaintiff purchased a heating stove at the agreed price of $8.50. . . . Plaintiff issued two checks to defendant, F. N. Woodry, in the sum of $4.25 each. On November 14, 1934, one of these checks was paid. The other bears the superscription, "Hold till Dec. 3." On January 15, 1935, defendant, F. N. Woodry, tendered it for deposit, but on the following day, in the process of clearing, the bank . . . refused payment and the check was returned to defendant . . . .

On the 8th day of April, 1935, defendant, Don Woodry, went to the home of plaintiff. The testimony is conflicting as to what then occurred. In effect, plaintiff's version of the occurrence is that she first asked said defendant to wait until her husband would return from his day's work in order that he might make a satisfactory adjustment and when defendant declined to do that plaintiff refused to accord said defendant the privilege of taking the stove unless and until he should return to plaintiff the unpaid check above mentioned. Plaintiff claims that when defendant, Don Woodry, took hold of the stove . . . , Don Woodry shoved plaintiff up against a bedroom door near which she was standing. . . .

Defendants argue that defendant, Don Woodry, in taking the stove was in the performance of a lawful act and if plaintiff interfered with that lawful act by force she became the aggressor, and in that state of the case the mere fact that the bodies of defendant . . . and plaintiff may have come in contact one with the other, would not constitute an assault, or an assault and battery.

. . . The jury heard the testimony and found for the plaintiff. There is substantial testimony supporting the claim that plaintiff refused to assent to the taking and objected thereto. . . . We find no reversible error and for that reason the judgment of the circuit court is affirmed.

NOTES AND QUESTION

1   *Conditional Sales Contract.* This case has been edited to exclude references to the fact that this stove was sold pursuant to a conditional sales contract. The Uniform Commercial Code provides that when a sales contract provides for repossession by the seller, such repossession may be effected privately only if the repossession can be accomplished without a breach of the peace. Does that fact help to distinguish *Lamb* from *Hodgeden*?

2   Putting to one side the legal effect of the conditional sales contract, are the facts of *Lamb* nevertheless sufficiently distinct from those of *Hodgeden* to justify the different result?

3   *Shopkeepers' Privilege.* The shopkeepers' privilege, discussed, *supra,* in the section on false imprisonment, which allows a shopkeeper who reasonably believes that a customer is shoplifting to detain that customer for a reasonable length of time under reasonable circumstances, really is a particular, usually statutory, application of the privilege to use reasonable force in defense of property.

4   *Repossession of Land.* Many jurisdictions, by statute, reverse the common law rule and prohibit the use of force to retake possession of real property.

3. NECESSITY

PROVERBS 6:30-31

Men do not despise a thief, if he steal to satisfy his soul when he is hungry; But if he be found, he shall restore sevenfold; he shall give all the substance of his house.

The common law of tort recognized that, in some emergency circumstances, the right of the property owner had to give way to the necessity of the situation, and so the law recognized the privilege of necessity. The privilege of necessity is divided into two categories, private necessity and public necessity. Private necessity is a qualified privilege that permits the actor to commit a trespass or conversion, if necessary, to avoid a greater harm to the actor or his property, or to that of a small group of people. The privilege is "qualified" in that the actor is liable to make the property owner whole for any harm done. The privilege of public necessity applies when an actor reasonably commits what would otherwise be a trespass or conversion to avoid a greater harm to the community at large. In contrast to private necessity, public necessity is an absolute privilege – the actor is privileged to commit the trespass or conversion free of any liability.

a. PRIVATE NECESSITY

The following two cases are among the most famous cases in Anglo-American law, probably because their factual similarity and surface inconsistency have made them irresistible to almost every torts teacher. Part of the interest in the *Vincent* case may stem from a scholarly fascination with its apparent contradiction of the general contemporary American tort law rule that a party is liable for harm that the party causes only when that party is at fault.

PLOOF V. PUTNAM
71 A. 188 (VT. 1908)

It is alleged . . . that . . . defendant was the owner of a certain island in Lake Champlain, and of a certain dock attached thereto, which island and dock were then in charge of the defendant's servant; that the plaintiff was then possessed of and sailing upon said lake a certain loaded sloop, on which were the plaintiff and his wife and two minor children; that there then arose a sudden and violent tempest, whereby the sloop and the property and persons therein were placed in great danger of destruction; that to save these from destruction or injury the plaintiff was compelled to, and did, moor the sloop to defendant's dock; that the defendant by his servant unmoored the sloop, whereupon it was driven upon the shore by the tempest, without the plaintiff's fault; and that the sloop and its contents were thereby destroyed, and the plaintiff and his wife and children cast into the lake and upon the shore, receiving injuries. This claim is set forth . . . in trespass, charging that the defendant by his servant . . . willfully and designedly unmoored the sloop . . . .

There are many cases in the books which hold that necessity . . . will justify entries upon land and interferences with personal property that would otherwise have been trespasses. . . . If one have a way over the land of another for his beasts to pass, and the beasts, being properly driven, feed the grass by morsels in passing or run out of the way and are promptly pursued and brought back, trespass will not lie. A traveler on a highway, who finds it obstructed from a sudden and temporary cause, may pass upon the adjoining land without becoming a trespasser, because of the necessity. An entry upon land to save goods which are in danger of being lost or destroyed by water or fire is not a trespass. . . .

This doctrine of necessity applies with special force to the preservation of human life. One assaulted and in peril of his life may run through the close of another to escape from his assailant. One may sacrifice the personal property of another to save his life or the lives of his fellows. . . . It is clear that an entry upon the land of another may be justified by necessity, and that the declaration before us discloses a necessity for mooring the sloop. . . . The allegations are, in substance, that the stress of a sudden and violent tempest compelled the plaintiff to moor to defendant's dock to save his sloop and the people in it. The averment of necessity is complete, for it covers not only the necessity of mooring to the dock; and the details of the situation which created this necessity, whatever the legal requirements regarding them, are matters of proof, and need not be alleged. It is certain that the rule suggested cannot be held applicable irrespective of circumstance, and the question must be left for adjudication upon proceedings had with reference to the evidence or the charge. . . .

NOTES

1   *On Remand.* The jury awarded plaintiff $650.
2   *Necessity as Cause of Action.* Ordinarily, the privilege of necessity is an affirmative defense. Here, though, the plaintiff, not the defendant, pleads necessity. Thus, this case illustrates the principle that sometimes the effect of the privilege is to render tortious a property owner's otherwise ordinary resistance to the privileged invasion. However, if the privilege is based on a mistake of fact, then the privilege to resist the invasion offsets the privileged invasion. Moreover, a privilege frequently confers with it the privilege to use reasonable force to effectuate the privilege.
3   *Duty to Rescue.* What if instead of casting plaintiffs' sloop off defendant had merely installed a fence and gate on his dock that prevented plaintiffs from mooring? What if defendant's servant had merely failed to help the plaintiffs moor to the dock?

VINCENT V. LAKE ERIE TRANSPORTATION CO.
124 N.W. 221 (MINN. 1910)

The steamship Reynolds, owned by the defendant, was for the purpose of discharging her cargo on November 27, 1905, moored to plaintiffs' dock in Duluth. While the unloading of the boat was taking place a storm from the northeast developed, which at about ten o'clock p.m., when the unloading was completed, had so grown in violence that the wind was then moving at fifty miles per hour and continued to increase during the night. There is some evidence that one, and perhaps two, boats were able to enter the harbor that night, but it is plain that navigation was practically suspended from the hour mentioned until the morning of the 29th, when the storm abated, and during that time no master would have been justified in attempting to navigate his vessel, if he could avoid doing so. After the discharge of the cargo the Reynolds signaled for a tug to tow her from the dock, but none could be obtained because of the severity of the storm. If the lines holding the ship to the dock had been cast off, she would doubtless have drifted away; but, instead, the lines were kept fast, and as soon as one parted or chafed it was replaced, sometimes with a larger one. The vessel lay upon the outside of the dock, . . . the wind and waves striking her . . . with such force that she was constantly being lifted and thrown against the dock, resulting in its damage, as found by the jury . . . .

We are satisfied that the character of the storm was such that it would have been highly imprudent for the master of the Reynolds to have attempted to leave the dock or to have permitted his vessel to drift away from it. . . . [T]hose in charge of the dock and the vessel at the time of the storm were not required to use the highest human intelligence, nor were they required to resort to every possible experiment which could be suggested for the preservation of their property. Nothing more was demanded of them than ordinary prudence and care, and the record in this case fully sustains the contention of the appellant that, in holding the vessel fast to the dock, those in charge of her exercised good judgment and prudent seamanship.

The appellant contends by ample assignments of error that, because its conduct during the storm was rendered necessary by prudence and good seamanship under conditions over which it had no control, it cannot be held liable for any injury resulting to the property of others, and claims that the jury should have been so instructed. . . . The situation was one in which the ordinary rules regulating property rights were suspended by forces beyond human control, and if, without the direct intervention of some act by the one sought to be held liable, the property of another was injured, such injury must be attributed to the act of God, and not to the wrongful act of the person sought to be charged. If during the storm the Reynolds had entered the harbor, and while there had become disabled and been thrown against the plaintiffs' dock, the plaintiffs could not have recovered. Again, if while attempting to hold fast to the dock the lines had parted, without any negligence, and the vessel carried against some other boat or dock in the harbor, there would be no liability upon her owner. But here those in charge of the vessel deliberately and by their direct efforts held her in such a position that the damage to the dock resulted, and, having thus preserved the ship at the expense of the dock, it seems to us that her owners are responsible to the dock owners to the extent of the injury inflicted.

In *Ploof v. Putnam . . . ,* the Supreme Court of Vermont held that where, under stress of weather, a vessel was without permission moored to a private dock at an island in Lake Champlain owned by the defendant, the plaintiff was not guilty of trespass, and that the defendant was responsible in damages because his representative upon the island unmoored the vessel, permitting it to drift upon the shore, with resultant injuries to it. If, in that case, the vessel had been permitted to remain, and the dock had suffered an injury, we believe the shipowner would have been held liable for the injury done.

Theologians hold that a starving man may, without moral guilt, take what is necessary to sustain life; but it could hardly be said that the obligation would not be upon such person to pay the value of the property so taken when he became able to do so. And so public necessity, in times of war or peace, may require the taking of private property for public purposes; but under our system of jurisprudence compensation must be made.

Let us imagine in this case that for the better mooring of the vessel those in charge of her had appropriated a valuable cable lying upon the dock. No matter how justifiable such appropriation might have been, it would not be claimed that, because of the overwhelming necessity of the situation, the owner of the cable could not recover its value.

This is not a case where life or property was menaced by any object or thing belonging to the plaintiffs, the destruction of which became necessary to prevent the threatened disaster. Nor is it a case where, because of the act of God, or unavoidable accident, the infliction of the injury was beyond the control of the defendant, but is one where the defendant prudently and advisedly availed itself of the plaintiffs' property for the purpose of preserving its own more valuable property, and the plaintiffs are entitled to compensation for the injury done.

Order affirmed.

QUESTIONS

1   These cases address the fundamental nature of the law of tort. The careful student will spend some time thinking about why the real property owner in *Ploof* is liable while the personal property owner in *Vincent* also is liable. Conceptually, why should the defendant in *Vincent* be held responsible for the loss when he did nothing wrong?

2   *Incomplete Privilege.* The rule in *Vincent* is that while necessity can temporarily override a real property owner's right to exclude and privilege a party to enter the property for the protection of the party or his property, the party so privileged must, nevertheless, compensate the real property owner for any harm done. Because defendant must compensate the plaintiff, the privilege is said to be "incomplete." This private necessity privilege contrasts with the complete privilege of public necessity, which requires no compensation of the property owner.

3   Note that the court in *Vincent* cited the earlier decision in *Ploof.* Is there any tension between the holding here and the holding in *Ploof?*

4   The court in *Vincent* asserts that "[i]f during the storm the Reynolds had entered the harbor, and while there had become disabled and been thrown against the plaintiffs' dock, the plaintiffs could not have recovered." Why should there be no recovery in this hypothetical scenario? How are these facts materially different from those of the instant case?

5   If the court is correct that there is no moral guilt to one who steals to avoid starvation, then why should the thief be forced to pay?

6   Is there anything wrong with the state's allowing one party to destroy the property of another for his own benefit even if he is forced to pay for it? Is this "forced sale" just?

7   Why not require defendant here to negotiate with plaintiff before (re)lashing the ship to the dock?

8   What would you think of a rule that defendant is privileged to damage plaintiff's property in case of necessity, but must pay double the harm caused? Would this rule be superior or inferior to the common law rule, and why?

b. PUBLIC NECESSITY

RESPUBLICA V. SPARHAWK
1 U.S. 357 (PA. 1788)

. . . It is a rule . . . that it is better to suffer a private mischief, than a public inconvenience; and the rights of necessity, form a part of our law. Of this principle, there are many striking illustrations. If a road be out of repair, a passenger may lawfully go through a private enclosure . . . . So, if a man is assaulted, he may fly through another's close. . . . In time of war, bulwarks may be built on private ground . . . and the reason assigned is particularly applicable to the present case, because it is for the public safety. . . . Thus, also, every man may, of common right, justify the going of his servants, or horses, upon the banks of navigable rivers, for towing barges, &c. to whomsoever the right of the soil belongs . . . . The pursuit of foxes through another's ground is allowed, because the destruction of such animals is for the public good . . . . Houses may be razed to prevent the spreading of fire, because for the public good. . . . We find, indeed, a memorable instance of folly recorded in the 3 Vol. of Clarendon's History, where it is mentioned, that the Lord Mayor of London, in 1666, when that city was on fire, would not give directions for, or consent to, the pulling down forty wooden houses, or to the removing the furniture, &c. belonging to the Lawyers of the Temple, then on the Circuit, for fear he should be answerable for a trespass; and in consequence of this conduct half that great city was burnt. . . .

UNITED STATES V. CALTEX, INC.
344 U.S. 149 (1952)

Each of the respondent oil companies owned terminal facilities in the Pandacan district of Manila at the time of the Japanese attack upon Pearl Harbor. . . . News of the Pearl Harbor attack reached Manila early in the morning of December 8, 1941. On the same day, enemy air attacks were mounted against our forces in the Philippines, and thereafter the enemy launched his amphibious assault. . . .

The military situation in the Philippines grew worse. In the face of the Japanese advance, the Commanding General on December 23, 1941, ordered the withdrawal of all troops on Luzon . . . . On December 25, 1941, he declared Manila to be an open city. On that same day, the Chief Engineer on the staff of the Commanding General addressed to each of the oil companies letters stating that the Pandacan oil deposits "are requisitioned by the U.S. Army." The letters further stated: "Any action deemed necessary for the destruction of this property will be handled by the U.S. Army." An engineer in the employ of one of the companies was commissioned a first lieutenant in the Army Corps of Engineers to facilitate this design.

On December 26, he received orders to prepare the facilities for demolition. On December 27, 1941, while enemy planes were bombing the area, this officer met with representatives of the companies. The orders of the Chief Engineer had been transmitted to the companies. Letters from the Deputy Chief of Staff, by command of General MacArthur, also had been sent to each of the oil companies, directing the destruction of all remaining petroleum products and the vital parts of the plants. Plans were laid to carry out these instructions, to expedite the removal of products which might still be of use to the troops in the field, and to lay a demolition network about the terminals. The representatives of Caltex were given, at their insistence, a penciled receipt for all the terminal facilities and stocks of Caltex.

At 5:40 p.m., December 31, 1941, while Japanese troops were entering Manila, Army personnel completed a successful demolition. All unused petroleum products were destroyed, and the facilities were rendered useless to the enemy. The enemy was deprived of a valuable logistic weapon.

After the war, respondents demanded compensation for all of the property which had been used or destroyed by the Army. The Government paid for the petroleum stocks and transportation equipment which were either used or destroyed by the Army, but it refused to compensate respondents for the destruction of the Pandacan terminal facilities. Claiming a constitutional right under the Fifth Amendment to just compensation for these terminal facilities, respondents sued in the court of Claims. Recovery was allowed. We granted certiorari to review this judgment.

. . . Respondents concede that the Army had a right to destroy the installations. But they insist that the destruction created a right in themselves to exact fair compensation from the United States for what was destroyed. . . . *United States v. Pacific R. Co.,* . . . involved bridges which had been destroyed during the War Between the States by a retreating Northern Army to impede the advance of the Confederate Army. Though the point was not directly involved, the Court raised the question of whether this act constituted a compensable taking by the United States and answered it in the negative:

> The destruction or injury of private property in battle, or in the bombardment of cities and towns, and in many other ways in the war, had to be borne by the sufferers alone as one of its consequences. Whatever would embarrass or impede the advance of the enemy, as the breaking up of roads, or the burning of bridges, or would cripple and defeat him, as destroying his means of subsistence, were lawfully ordered by the commanding general. Indeed, it was his imperative duty to direct their destruction. The necessities of the war called for and justified this. The safety of the state in such cases overrides all considerations of private loss.

[120 U.S. at 234.] . . . Had the Army hesitated, had the facilities only been destroyed after retreat, respondents would certainly have no claims to compensation. . . . [W]e conclude that the court below erred in holding that respondents have a constitutional right to compensation on the claims presented to this Court.

Reversed.

QUESTION AND NOTE

1 How can the holding here be reconciled with the result in *Vincent?*
2 Many public necessity cases involve destruction of private property by the government. In the United States, the government enjoys sovereign immunity against tort suits. In 1946, Congress enacted the Federal Tort Claims Act whereby the federal government agreed to be liable for harm caused by the negligence of its employees. There are exceptions, however, including the exception for suits against the government based upon the exercise of a "discretionary function" of a government employee. State governments also enjoy general "sovereign immunity" from suit, but the immunity of municipalities is more limited. Most states govern their own immunity by statute.

MONONGAHELA NAVIGATION CO. V. UNITED STATES
148 U.S. 312 (1893)

. . . [T]he Monongahela Company had . . . expended large sums of money in improving the Monongahela River, by means of locks and dams . . . . By means of these improvements, the Monongahela River, which theretofore was only navigable for boats of small tonnage, and at certain seasons of the year, now carries steamboats at all seasons, and an extensive commerce by means thereof. The question presented is not whether the United States has the power to condemn and appropriate this property of the Monongahela Company, for that is conceded, but how much it must pay as compensation therefor. Obviously, this question, as all others which run along the line of the extent of the protection the individual has under the Constitution against the demands of the government, is of importance; for in any society the fullness and sufficiency of the securities which surround the individual in the use and enjoyment of his property constitute one of the most certain tests of the character and value of the government. . . .

In the case of *Sinnickson v. Johnson,* . . . it was said that "this power to take private property reaches back of all constitutional provisions; and it seems to have been considered a settled principle of universal law that the right to compensation is an incident to the exercise of that power; that the one is so inseparably connected with the other, that they may be said to exist not as separate and distinct principles, but as parts of one and the same principle." . . . And in this there is a natural equity which commends it to everyone. It in no wise detracts from the power of the public to take whatever may be necessary for its uses; while, on the other hand, it prevents the public from loading upon one individual more than his just share of the burdens of government and says that when he surrenders to the public something more and different from that which is exacted from other members of the public, a full and just equivalent shall be returned to him. . . . [C]onstitutional provisions for the security of person and property should be liberally construed. . . . It is the duty of courts to be watchful for the constitutional rights of the citizen, and against any stealthy encroachments thereon.

. . . Our conclusions are, that the Navigation Company rightfully placed this lock and dam in the Monongahela River; that, . . . it has a franchise to receive tolls for its use; that such franchise was as much a vested right of property as the ownership of the tangible property; that the right of the national government, under its grant of power to regulate commerce, to condemn and appropriate this lock and dam belonging to the Navigation Company, is subject to the limitations imposed by the Fifth Amendment, that private property shall not be taken for public uses without just compensation; that just compensation requires payment for the franchise to take tolls, as well as for the value of the tangible property; and that the assertion by Congress of its purpose to take the property does not destroy the state franchise.

The judgment, therefore, will be

Reversed, and the case remanded with instructions to grant a new trial.

QUESTIONS

1   Can you reconcile this holding with the holding in *Caltex*?
2   If the Constitution requires "just compensation" when the government takes a house to build a road for the public good, why should a party who destroys a house for the public good avoid all liability?

4. LEGAL AUTHORITY

Some public officials, particularly the police, are privileged by law to take actions, e.g., effect a lawful arrest or pursue a suspect through private property, that would otherwise constitute an intentional tort, e.g., battery or trespass. In fact, to apprehend a fleeing felon, the common law allows police officers to use even deadly force. The privilege of a private citizen to use force to effect an arrest is more limited.

5. DISCIPLINE

PROVERBS 13:24

He that spareth his rod hateth his son: but he that loveth him chasteneth him betimes.

PROVERBS 22:15

Foolishness is bound in the heart of a child; but the rod of correction shall drive it far from him.

PROVERBS 23:13-14

Withhold not correction from the child: for if thou beatest him with the rod, he shall not die. Thou shalt beat him with the rod, and shalt deliver his soul from hell.

PROVERBS 29:15

The rod and reproof give wisdom: but a child left to himself bringeth his mother to shame.

Parents and those acting *in loco parentis* are privileged to employ reasonable steps in the discipline of a child, even if those steps otherwise would constitute an intentional tort such as battery or false imprisonment. The privilege is limited by the vague "reasonableness" standard. While non-parents in charge of children (usually teachers) possess a similar privilege, discipline that might be considered "reasonable" if inflicted by a parent may well not be considered reasonable for a teacher or another non-parent adult in charge of a child.

STEBER V. NORRIS
206 N.W. 173 (WIS. 1925)

The plaintiff in this action at the time of the alleged assault was an 11 year old boy, whose parents had sent him to the farm of the defendant in the summer of 1923, and upon request he was permitted to return in 1924, when the mother signed a written statement giving the defendant authority to discipline the plaintiff, if and when he broke the rules and regulations enforced upon the farm. The plaintiff was supposed to work at assigned tasks about the farm for six hours a day, and for this labor received his board and room.

The undisputed testimony shows that the plaintiff had failed to perform some of the tasks assigned to him, and had told several falsehoods, and that upon July 23, 1924, the defendant took the plaintiff to his office, and there, after asking him why he had not performed his work, and receiving no answer, inflicted corporal punishment by means of a crude rubber whip about 30 inches long. The clothing of the boy had been so removed that the punishment was inflicted upon the nude body of the boy, who swore that he was undressed and stripped by the defendant, though the defendant testified that the plaintiff removed his clothing voluntarily.

The boy testified that while he was being whipped he pleaded to be allowed to go, and cried and promised "not to do it any more"; that he was struck about 40 or 50 times. He was required to work overtime for 6 days after the whipping, and on the seventh day he found a way to escape and went home. The day after the whipping he wrote his mother, asking her to write the defendant to let him come home, but at the bottom of the letter the defendant wrote, requesting the mother not to comply. The boy's testimony was somewhat confused and not entirely consistent, but he testified that he had much pain and suffering, and that his back still pained him at the time of the trial when the weather was damp. He claimed that he was not well upon the days when he did not work. Five or six days after his return home he was examined by two physicians, who testified, in substance, that there were stripes on his back reaching down to the middle of the thighs; that there were several crusts where abrasions were in the process of healing and scabs on numerous parts of the body; that there were marked swellings and discoloration of the right lumbar region. One of the physicians testified that there were a good many stripes on the back, possibly 20. There were five other witnesses, mostly members of the plaintiff's family, who gave testimony as to the bruises and contusions and scabs which they found when the boy returned home from the defendant's farm.

The defendant testified . . . that he used the whip in question because he expected to find a strap which was missing, and the whip was the only thing convenient; that he did not count the strokes, but they could not have exceeded 10, giving the boy 10 lashes he thought was punishment enough of that kind; that in inflicting the blows there was not more than a 3-foot swing. He swore that he inflicted only light punishment; that he struck the lad only with the idea of punishing him for his disobedience and untruthfulness; that the boy proceeded to play with a dog in the yard as soon as he was dismissed from the office; that he showed no marks such as was testified to by the plaintiff's witnesses; and that he slept normally after this whipping. During the summer of 1924 the defendant had with him between 90 and 100 boys who were required to work from 8 to 11:30 and from 1 to 4 o'clock. There were two large farms on which there were many kinds of work to be done. The defendant was an officer of the juvenile court of Milwaukee county serving without pay, and there was testimony to the effect that the institution is maintained as a charitable one from which no profit is made. On the contrary, it is operated at a loss. Many of the boys were delinquent, and sent there by court orders. Others, including the plaintiff, were sent there by their parents. In the evening recreation of various kinds was furnished.

The defendant produced one witness, a minister, who examined the plaintiff's back on or about the 9th of August and said that he saw no marks or scars. Three physicians were called by the defendant. One testified that he examined the plaintiff about September 20th, and "at that time Dr. Corcoran called to my attention two or three brown spots which I had noticed over the right hip. Aside from that I could find nothing." Dr. Corcoran, one of the physicians called by the plaintiff, testified that at that time the marks had somewhat disappeared, but that marks were then present, although they did not look nearly as bad as on his former examination. The two other physicians called for the defendant testified that on May 27, 1925, and May 28, 1925, they examined the plaintiff and found no evidence of trouble.

Among other instructions to the jury the following were given:

That the principal of a school, and a person situated as was the defendant at the time and place in question, has the right, and it is his duty, to adopt reasonable rules to promote good order and discipline, and may, acting in a proper spirit, and on proper occasions, administer reasonable corporal punishment to the pupil or a boy under his care and in his charge and custody, having regard to the character of the misconduct or offense, and the age, sex, size, and strength of the child. Such reasonable corporal punishment may be administered for an infraction of the rules, and to maintain proper discipline in the school or institution. The principal may exact compliance with all reasonable commands, and may, in a reasonable spirit, inflict corporal punishment upon a pupil or child under his care and in his charge and custody for disobedience or other misconduct. The principal or person, situated as was the defendant at the time and place in question, stands for the time being in loco parentis, or in the place of parents to his pupils and children under his care and in his charge and custody, and because of that relation he must necessarily exercise authority over them in so far as good order and discipline may reasonably require. In the school, as in the family, there exists on the part of the pupils and children the obligation of obedience to lawful and reasonable commands, subordination, civil deportment, respect for the rights of other pupils, and fidelity to duty. In inflicting corporal punishment the principal or guardian may take into consideration habitual disobedience of the pupil, but the corporal punishment should not be excessive, unreasonable, or cruel, and must always be measured and apportioned to the gravity of the misconduct or offense, and be within the bounds of moderation.

If you are satisfied by a preponderance of the evidence to a reasonable certainty that the punishment administered by the defendant to the plaintiff was excessive, unreasonable, or cruel, then your verdict will be for the plaintiff. If you are not satisfied by a preponderance of the evidence to a reasonable certainty that the punishment administered by the defendant to the plaintiff was excessive, unreasonable, or cruel, but within the bounds of moderation, then your verdict will be for the defendant.

The jury, made up of eight men and four women, all of whom upon the voir dire examination had stated they were opposed to the infliction of corporal punishment upon children, found the defendant guilty of assault and battery, and allowed the plaintiff damages in the sum of $1 and costs, refusing to assess punitive damages. The court refused to increase the amount of damages, and denied a motion for a new trial, and entered judgment upon the verdict, and from that judgment the plaintiff appeals.

Counsel for the parties do not challenge the correctness of the instructions as to the relation which plaintiff and defendant sustained to each other, and we shall assume that the defendant had the right to inflict corporal punishment. . . . It may be said to be the general rule that one standing in loco parentis has the right to punish a child under his care, if the punishment is moderate and reasonable, and for the welfare of the child. Necessarily the propriety of inflicting corporal punishment to a considerable extent rests in the discretion of the person holding such relation. But whether the correction is reasonable and proper, or whether it is immoderate or excessive, does not rest absolutely in the discretion of the teacher or other person inflicting the punishment. It is a matter for judicial investigation. It is not to be assumed that, although a teacher or the defendant in this case stands in the relation of a parent, he has the same right to inflict punishment as a parent.

> This parental power is little liable to abuse, for it is continually restrained by natural affection, the tenderness which the parent feels for his offspring, an affection ever on the alert, and acting rather by instinct than reasoning.
>
> The schoolmaster has no such natural restraint. Hence he may not safely be trusted with all a parent's authority, for he does not act from the instinct of parental affection. He should be guided and restrained by judgment and wise discretion, and hence is responsible for their reasonable exercise.

Lander v. Seaver, 32 Vt. 122, 76 Am. Dec. 156.

In determining whether the punishment has been excessive, the conduct of the child, the nature of his misconduct, the nature of the whip or instrument used for punishment, the kind of marks or wounds left on the body, are all subjects to be considered. . . . It is argued by counsel for respondent that there was ample testimony to sustain the verdict, and that the plaintiff sustained only nominal damages. It is true there is some conflict in the testimony, and it becomes necessary to consider the nature of that conflict. There was a large mass of testimony, part of it by disinterested witnesses showing a condition of the boy's body one week after the assault, which could only have resulted from severe blows. That evidence is undisputed except by the statement of the defendant that he inflicted only a light punishment. One of the defendant's experts testified that at a time nearly 2 months after the assault complained of he made an examination and found only two or three brown spots. Two other experts called by the defendant testified as to a time about 10 months after the assault complained of. Their testimony was relevant on the question whether there had been such lasting injury as was claimed, but could have little or no bearing on the boy's condition in July, 1924. The witness of the defendant who saw no marks about 2 weeks after July 23, 1924, was contradicted by one of defendant's experts, who did see marks more than a month after the examination by this witness, and, in view of the overwhelming evidence to the contrary, we cannot regard the testimony of this witness as convincing. We see no reason to doubt the truthfulness of the two experts called by the plaintiff who testified to the condition of the boy's person about 1 week after the assault. Their testimony, and that of other witnesses called by the plaintiff, is corroborated by the nature of the lash which was used. It was one bought by the defendant in South America, and it does not appear for what general purpose it was used. It was described by the defendant as follows:

> The whip was made out of not very well refined rubber, and was twisted. The whip was about 2 feet 6 or 8 inches in length. There was a ring made of the rubber itself at the end of it. The whip varies from about 1 1/4 inch down to about 1/4 of an inch.
>
> It is one of the exhibits in the case. Being twisted and rather heavy, it has great possibilities when applied to the bare flesh.

The only misconduct of the boy which was objected to was that he had not worked as directed and that he had lied. Those things deserve correction, but they were not unpardonable sins, nor did they call for such a lashing as left marks, which, according to the almost undisputed testimony, were found on the boy on his return to his home. The jury found the defendant guilty of assault, and we do not see how on the testimony they could avoid so finding. It follows that under the instructions given by the court the jury must have believed that the punishment was excessive, but they measured the excess by the sum of $1, although they were given the usual instruction that, if they found for the plaintiff, they should assess such compensatory damages as they found from the preponderance of the evidence to a reasonable certainty would be required to reasonably compensate the plaintiff for his mental and physical suffering. . . . Our duty to direct new trials when damages are claimed to be excessive is very often invoked, and is frequently exercised. Appeals on the ground that damages are inadequate are much less frequent, probably because juries are . . . likely to be liberal . . . in the assessment of damages. But the power of the court in both classes of cases rests on the same grounds, because it is quite as unjust that one person should receive too little compensation for a wrong done as that another should receive too much.

We are convinced that in this case the jury disregarded both the strongly preponderating and almost undisputed testimony given for the plaintiff on the question of damages and the instruction of the court. We cannot understand how on finding the assault they arrived at their verdict, except as an improper compromise. We appreciate the weight to be given to the finding of a jury on the question of damages, especially when it is approved by the trial judge. We have considered the argument of counsel that in carrying on his farms in the manner he did the defendant was doing a laudable work. But we cannot sanction the view that in this generation it is permissible for a teacher or other person in loco parentis, for such misconduct as was proven in this instance, to inflict such blows as were given in this case with such a whip as was used, on the bare body of a child. . . .

We consider that the jury disregarded the instructions of the court, that the award of damages was grossly inadequate, and therefore perverse within the meaning of the decisions; and that the verdict should have been set aside and a new trial granted. [Cases omitted.] Judgment reversed, and the cause is remanded, with directions that a new trial be ordered.

[Dissenting opinion omitted.]

Historic Foundations of Strict Liability and Negligence

Now for some Anglo-American torts history. So far, these materials have addressed intentional torts, which involve a defendant's intentional invasion of a protected legal interest, but such cases are relatively rare in practice today. Now we turn our attention to a much more common tort scenario – the accident. Cases of accidental harm can be governed by one of two types of rules. One possible sort of rule is a "strict" liability rule – liability is called "strict" because the defendant is responsible for the consequences of his voluntary conduct without regard to his fault.

Thus, contemporary tort causes of action fall into three broad categories: intentional torts, negligence, and strict liability. But this division is a relatively recent innovation. A number of prominent tort scholars (and I) believe that the normal rule of tort liability in Anglo-American law before the nineteenth century was a form of strict liability, at least for direct, forcible injuries, without regard to defendant's intent or negligence. These direct, forcible injuries were compensated through a form of action called the writ of Trespass, which came in three forms, and this writ formed the basis for our modern causes of action of battery, assault, trespass to land, trespass to chattels, and false imprisonment. Note that most of the intentional tort liability rules that we have been studying so far, including those just listed, can fairly be characterized as "strict liability" rules.

Despite this history, the dominant form of liability rule in the accident context today is the negligence rule, a rule that bases defendant's liability in fault. Negligence likely came into Anglo-American tort law through a second early common law writ applicable to indirect harms called the writ of "Trespass on the Case" or simply "Case." To recover under Case, the plaintiff had to prove defendant's intent or fault. By contrast, under the strict liability rule of Trespass, plaintiff need only show that defendant's conduct caused plaintiff's harm directly. Under a negligence rule, plaintiff would have to show also that defendant's conduct was in some sense blameworthy, which makes negligence like Case. Courts increasingly distinguished between Trespass and Case in this way – Case was used for negligence.

The adoption of negligence instead of strict liability as the background rule in cases of accidental injury is significant on a practical level. Some seem to entertain the mistaken notion that someone always is at fault when harm results, but this is not so – sometimes accidents just happen. In those cases, a negligence rule can leave the injured plaintiff to bear his own loss as best he can, even if that loss was caused by someone else's voluntary act.

Just before turning to the dominant contemporary negligence rule of liability for accidental injury, this section of the material will illustrate briefly the development of theories of tort liability in Anglo-American law beginning in the seventeenth century with what some would call the simple rule of strict liability and gradually moving to the now dominant fault-based rule. We will then explore the remaining pockets of common law strict liability before moving on to study negligence.

GIBBONS V. PEPPER
91 ENG. REP. 922 (1695)

... The defendant pleads, that he rode upon a horse in the King's highway, and that his horse being affrighted ran away with him ... so that he could not stop the horse; that there were several persons standing in the way, among whom the plaintiff stood; and that he called to them to take care, but that notwithstanding, the plaintiff did not go out of the way, but continued there; so that the defendant's horse ran over the plaintiff against the will of the defendant .... [D]efendant argued, that if the defendant in his justification shews that the accident was inevitable, and that the negligence of the defendant did not cause it, judgment shall be given for him... . [P]laintiff said, that in all [the cases cited by defendant,] the defendant confessed a battery, which he afterwards justified; but in this case he justified a battery, which is no battery. Of which opinion was the whole Court; for if I ride upon a horse, and J. S. whips the horse, so that he runs away with me and runs over any other person, he who whipped the horse is guilty of the battery, and not me. But if I by spurring was the cause of such accident then I am guilty. In the same manner if A. takes the hand of B. and with it strikes C., A. is the trespasser, and not B. ... And therefore judgment was given for the plaintiff.

QUESTIONS

1 *Gibbons v. Pepper* is the first of several English cases that will appear in these materials. Upon America's independence from the British Empire, American courts adopted the English common law. Therefore, prerevolutionary English cases like *Gibbons* are part of the American common law of torts. Even some postrevolutionary English cases have had persuasive authority in the United States.

2 *Negligence.* The word "negligence" appears in this opinion, but it probably does not mean what that word would mean to an American lawyer today. As we will see later in these materials, "negligence" today means failure to exercise reasonable care. In the seventeenth century, "negligence" probably meant something like engaging in some conduct without taking every possible precaution against harm.

3 Under the rule of this case, what is the basis of liability? What must plaintiff show to prove a case against defendant? How can defendant avoid liability for battery? What would you infer is the purpose of tort liability in late seventeenth century England?

4   In light of defendant's call to plaintiff to "take care," presumably by getting out of the way, why is this not a case in which plaintiff caused his own injury?

For almost 200 years following *Gibbons v. Pepper,* the writ of "Case" gradually became more popular than the writ of "Trespass," and then a legal breakthrough took place. Although the following opinion does not use the label "negligence" for the theory of liability employed, *Brown v. Kendall* frequently is cited as the beginning of the fault-based liability rule in Anglo-American law that soon came to be known as negligence because the court required some showing of fault even for a sort of harm that previously would have been considered under the writ of "Trespass":

BROWN V. KENDALL
60 MASS. 292 (1850)

This was an action of trespass for assault and battery . . . . [T]wo dogs, belonging to the plaintiff and the defendant, respectively, were fighting in the presence of their masters; . . . defendant took a stick about four feet long, and commenced beating the dogs . . . to separate them; . . . plaintiff was looking on . . . and . . . advanced a step or two towards the dogs. In their struggle, the dogs approached the place where the plaintiff was standing. The defendant retreated backwards from before the dogs, striking them as he retreated; and as he approached the plaintiff, with his back towards him, in raising his stick over his shoulder, in order to strike the dogs, he accidentally hit the plaintiff in the eye, inflicting upon him a severe injury.

[The judge declined to instruct the jury as requested by the defendant and instead instructed the jury that liability depended on whether defendant's conduct was a "necessary act" (one which it was his duty to do). Defendant was required to exercise ordinary care for a necessary act, but extraordinary care for an unnecessary act (an act that he was not duty-bound to undertake). The plaintiff bore the burden of proving lack of ordinary care for a necessary act, but defendant bore the burden of proving extraordinary care for an unnecessary act.]

The jury under these instructions returned a verdict for the plaintiff; whereupon the defendant alleged exceptions. . . .

This is an action of trespass . . . brought by George Brown against George K. Kendall . . . . The facts set forth in the bill of exceptions preclude the supposition, that the blow, inflicted by the hand of the defendant upon the person of the plaintiff, was intentional. The whole case proceeds on the assumption, that the damage sustained by the plaintiff, from the stick held by the defendant, was inadvertent and unintentional; and the case involves the question how far, and under what qualifications, the party by whose . . . act the damage was done is responsible for it. We use the term "unintentional" rather than involuntary, because in some of the cases, it is stated, that the act of holding and using a weapon or instrument, the movement of which is the immediate cause of hurt to another, is a voluntary act, although its particular effect in hitting and hurting another is not within the purpose or intention of the party doing the act.

It appears to us, that some of the confusion in the cases on this subject has grown out of the long-vexed question, under the rule of the common law, whether a party's remedy, where he has one, should be sought in an action of the case, or of trespass. . . . The result of these cases is, that if the damage complained of is the immediate effect of the act of the defendant, trespass . . . lies; if consequential only, and not immediate, case is the proper remedy. . . .

We think, as the result of all the authorities, the rule is correctly stated that the plaintiff must come prepared with evidence to show either that the *intention* was unlawful, or that the defendant was *in fault;* for if the injury was unavoidable, and the conduct of the defendant was free from blame, he will not be liable. In applying these rules to the present case, we can perceive no reason why the instructions asked for by the defendant ought not to have been given; to this effect, that if both plaintiff and defendant at the time of the blow were using ordinary care, or if at that time the defendant was using ordinary care, and the plaintiff was not, or if at that time, both the plaintiff and the defendant were not using ordinary care, then the plaintiff could not recover.

In using this term, ordinary care, it may be proper to state, that what constitutes ordinary care will vary with the circumstances of cases. In general, it means that kind and degree of care, which prudent and cautious men would use, such as is required by the exigency of the case, and such as is necessary to guard against probable danger. A man, who should have occasion to discharge a gun, on an open and extensive marsh, or in a forest, would be required to use less circumspection and care, than if he were to do the same thing in an inhabited town, village, or city. To make an accident, or casualty, or as the law sometimes states it, inevitable accident, it must be such an accident as the defendant could not have avoided by the use of the kind and degree of care necessary to the exigency, and in the circumstances in which he was placed.

. . . We can have no doubt that the act of the defendant in attempting to part the fighting dogs, one of which was his own, and for the injurious acts of which he might be responsible, was a lawful and proper act, which he might do by proper and safe means. If, then, in doing this act, using due care and all proper precautions necessary to the exigency of the case, to avoid hurt to others, in raising his stick for that purpose, he accidentally hit the plaintiff in his eye, and wounded him, this was the result of pure accident, or was involuntary and unavoidable, and therefore the action would not lie. . . .

If the act of hitting the plaintiff was unintentional, on the part of the defendant, and done in the doing of a lawful act, then the defendant was not liable, unless it was done in the want of exercise of due care, adapted to the exigency of the case, and therefore such want of due care became part of the plaintiff's case, and the burden of proof was on the plaintiff to establish it. . . . [I]f it appears that the defendant was doing a lawful act, and unintentionally hit and hurt the plaintiff, then unless it also appears to the satisfaction of the jury, that the defendant is charge-able with some fault, negligence, carelessness, or want of prudence, the plaintiff fails to sustain the burden of proof, and is not entitled to recover.

New trial ordered.

1   The holding in *Brown v. Kendall* is a result of the "flowering" of the negligence standard of liability in America in the first half of the nineteenth century, replacing a more strict form of liability. By the middle of the nineteenth century, the negligence standard had become dominant.

2   According to the court, what must the plaintiff prove to prevail? Is the rule announced in *Brown v. Kendall* different from that seen in *Gibbons v. Pepper*? If so, how?

3   *Ordinary Care.* The court here seeks to define and apply a standard of conduct that it calls "ordinary care." What conduct would the exercise of ordinary care dictate in these circumstances?

4   The court here repeatedly uses language suggesting that this injury was "unavoidable." Was it? Is this accident unavoidable like a lightning strike is unavoidable?

BROWN V. COLLINS
53 N.H. 442 (1873)

It is agreed that the defendant was in the use of ordinary care and skill in managing his horses, until they were frightened; and that they then became unmanageable, and ran against and broke a post on the plaintiff's land.... We take the case as one where, without actual fault in the defendant, his horses broke from his control, ran away with him, went upon the plaintiff's land, and did damage there, against the will, intent, and desire of the defendant.... [In the *Thorns Case* (1466), t]he defendant pleads that he hath an acre lying next the [plaintiff's] acres, and upon it a hedge of thorns, and he cut the thorns, and they ... fell upon the plaintiff's land, and the defendant took them off as soon as he could, which is the same trespass; ... adjudged for the plaintiff; for though a man doth a lawful thing, yet, if any damage do thereby befall another, he shall answer for it, if he could have avoided it. As if a man lop a tree, and the boughs fall upon another, ... yet an action lies. If a man shoot at buts, and hurt another unawares, an action lies. I have land through which a river runs to your mill, and I lop the fallows ..., which accidentally stop the water, so as your mill is hindered, an action lies. If I am building my own house, and a piece of timber falls on my neighbor's house, and breaks part of it, an action lies. If a man assault me, and I lift up my staff to defend myself, and, in lifting it up, hit another, an action lies by that person, and yet I did a lawful thing....

[T]he drift of the ancient English authorities on the law of torts seems to differ materially from the view now prevailing in this country. For formerly, in England, there seems to have been no well-defined test of an actionable tort. Defendants were often held liable "because," as Raymond says, "he that is damaged ought to be recompensed;" and not because, upon some clearly stated principle of law founded on actual culpability, public policy, or natural justice, he was entitled to compensation from the defendant. The law was supposed to regard "the loss and damage of the party suffering," more than the negligence and blameworthiness of the defendant: but how much more it regarded the former than the latter, was a question not settled, and very little investigated. "The loss and damage of the party suffering," if without relief, would be a hardship to him; relief compulsorily furnished by the other party would often be a hardship to him: when and why the "loss and damage" should, and when and why they should not, be transferred from one to the other, by process of law, were problems not solved in a philosophical manner. There were precedents, established upon superficial, crude, and undigested notions; but no application of the general system of legal reason to this subject.

Mr. Holmes says,—"It may safely be stated that all the more ancient examples are traceable to conceptions of a much ruder sort (than actual fault), and in modern times to more or less definitely thought-out views of public policy. The old writs in trespass did not allege, nor was it necessary to show, anything savoring of culpability. It was enough that a certain event had happened, and it was not even necessary that the act should be done intentionally, though innocently. An accidental blow was as good a cause of action as an intentional one. . . .

It would seem that some of the early English decisions were based on a view as narrow as that which regards nothing but the hardship "of the party suffering;" disregards the question whether, by transferring the hardship to the other party, anything more will be done than substitute one suffering party for another; and does not consider what legal reason can be given for relieving the party who has suffered, by making another suffer the expense of his relief. For some of those decisions, better reasons may now be given than were thought of when the decisions were announced: but whether a satisfactory test of an actionable tort can be extracted from the ancient authorities, and whether the few modern cases that carry out the doctrine of those authorities . . . can be sustained, is very doubtful. The current of American authority is very strongly against some of the leading English cases. . . .

It is not improbable that the rules of liability for damage done by brutes or by fire, found in the early English cases, were introduced, by sacerdotal influence, from what was supposed to be the Roman or the Hebrew law. . . . They were introduced when the development of many of the rational rules now universally recognized as principles of the common law had not been demanded by the growth of intelligence, trade, and productive enterprise,—when the common law had not been set forth in the precedents, as a coherent and logical system on many subjects other than the tenures of real estate. . . . To extend [those rules] to the present case would be contrary to American authority, as well as to our understanding of legal principles. . . .

There are many cases where a man is held liable for taking, converting . . . or destroying property, or doing something else, or causing it to be done, intentionally, under a claim of right, and without any actual fault. . . . But when there was no fault on his part, and the damage was not caused by his voluntary and intended act; or by an act of which he knew, or ought to have known, the damage would be a necessary, probable, or natural consequence; or by an act which he knew, or ought to have known, to be unlawful,—we understand the general rule to be, that he is not liable. . . . In *Brown* v. *Kendall*, . . . the defendant, having interfered to part his dog and the plaintiff's which were fighting, in raising a stick for that purpose, accidentally struck the plaintiff, and injured him. It was held, that parting the dogs was a lawful and proper act which the defendant might do by the use of proper and safe means; and that if the plaintiff's injury was caused by such an act done with due care and all proper precautions, the defendant was not liable. . . . Judge Shaw, delivering the opinion of the court, said,—"We think, as the result of all the authorities, the rule is correctly stated . . . that the plaintiff must come prepared with evidence to show either that the *intention* was unlawful, or that the defendant was *in fault*; for if the injury was unavoidable, and the conduct of the defendant was free from blame, he will not be liable. . . . If, in the prosecution of a lawful act, a casualty purely accidental arises, no action can be supported for an injury arising therefrom. . . ."

Whatever . . . may be the full legal definitions of necessity, inevitable danger, and unavoidable accident, the occurrence complained of in this case was one for which the defendant is not liable, unless everyone is liable for all damage done by superior force overpowering him, and using him or his property as an instrument of violence. The defendant, being without fault, was as innocent as if . . . his wagon had been hurled on the plaintiff's land by a whirlwind, or he himself, by a stronger man, had been thrown through the plaintiff's window. Upon the facts stated, taken in the sense in which we understand them, the defendant is entitled to judgment. . . .

QUESTIONS

1   Here the court opines that the early English cases set out above were based upon the principle that a plaintiff who suffered a loss must be recompensed. The court noted the obvious bankruptcy of that idea – by forcing defendant to pay for plaintiff's loss, the law merely creates another victim requiring compensation. Do you think this idea of compensation at all cost really is behind the early cases? Is that what the courts themselves said? Can you articulate a more accurate basis for the decisions in those cases?

2   The court compares the facts here to a case in which defendant's "wagon had been hurled on the plaintiff's land by a whirlwind, or he himself, by a stronger man, had been thrown through the plaintiff's window." The analogy to the ancient hypothetical of "A striking with B's hand" is obvious. Is the analogy apt?

HAMMONTREE V. JENNER
97 CAL. RPTR. 739 (CAL. CT. APP. 1971)

Plaintiffs Maxine Hammontree and her husband sued defendant for personal injuries and property damage arising out of an automobile accident. The cause was tried to a jury. Plaintiffs appeal from judgment entered on a jury verdict returned against them and in favor of defendant.

The evidence shows that on the afternoon of April 25, 1967, defendant was driving his 1959 Chevrolet home from work; at the same time plaintiff Maxine Hammontree was working in a bicycle shop owned and operated by her and her husband; without warning defendant's car crashed through the wall of the shop, struck Maxine and caused personal injuries and damage to the shop.

Defendant claimed he became unconscious during an epileptic seizure losing control of his car. He did not recall the accident but his last recollection before it, was leaving a stop light after his last stop, and his first recollection after the accident was being taken out of his car in plaintiffs' shop. Defendant testified he has a medical history of epilepsy and knows of no other reason for his loss of consciousness except an epileptic seizure; . . . in 1953 . . . [he] was told he was an epileptic . . . ; in . . . 1955 Dr. Hyatt prescribed phelantin; from 1955 until the accident occurred

(1967) defendant had used phelantin on a regular basis which controlled his condition; defendant has continued to take medication as prescribed by his physician and has done everything his doctors told him to do to avoid a seizure; he had no inkling or warning that he was about to have a seizure prior to the occurrence of the accident.

In 1955 or 1956 the Department of Motor Vehicles was advised that defendant was an epileptic and placed him on probation under which every six months he had to report to the doctor who was required to advise it in writing of defendant's condition. In 1960 his probation was changed to a once-a-year report.

Dr. Hyatt testified that during the times he saw defendant, and according to his history, defendant "was doing normally" and that . . . he believed it was safe for defendant to drive.

Appellants' contentions that the trial court erred in refusing to grant their motion for summary judgment on the issue of liability and their motion for directed verdict on the pleadings and counsel's opening argument are answered by the disposition of their third claim that the trial court committed prejudicial error in refusing to give their jury instruction on absolute liability.[1]

Under the present state of the law. . . the trial judge properly refused the instruction. The . . . cases generally hold that liability of a driver, suddenly stricken by an illness rendering him unconscious, for injury resulting from an accident occurring during that time rests on principles of negligence. . . .

The judgment is affirmed.

---

1   [Appellants' proposed jury instruction read as follows:] When the evidence shows that a driver of a motor vehicle on a public street or highway loses his ability to safely operate and control such vehicle because of some seizure or health failure, that driver is nevertheless legally liable for all injuries and property damage which an innocent person may suffer as a proximate result of the defendant's inability to so control or operate his motor vehicle.

This is true even if you find the defendant driver had no warning of any such impending seizure or health failure.

TRADITIONAL STRICT LIABILITY

A. INTRODUCTION

As we just saw, Anglo-American tort liability seems to have started out as a simple rule of strict liability for harm caused by defendant's volitional act, but since the nineteenth century, negligence has been the dominant rule of American tort liability. The concept of strict liability is that the actor is liable for the consequences of certain activities of the actor, without regard to whether the actor has behaved reasonably under the circumstances. By contrast, the negligence rule requires that an actor is held liable for harm caused by the actor's conduct only when the actor's conduct is "unreasonable" in that it creates too great a risk of harm to others. While the rising tide of this negligence rule of liability has covered much of the American torts landscape, negligence is not the exclusive rule of liability in American tort law – islands of "strict liability" remain. The next two cases will introduce the general concept of strict liability before we proceed to explore in more detail the major remaining areas of common law strict liability – liability for harm caused by defendant's animals and liability for harm caused by defendant's "abnormally dangerous" activities. These cases are included to get the student thinking about the concept of strict liability before turning to the more mundane doctrine.

VAUGHAN V. MILLER BROS. "101" RANCH WILD WEST SHOW
153 S.E. 289 (W. VA. 1930)

The plaintiff's demand in brief is this: He attended a circus, and a vicious ape on exhibition there bit off his finger. There is no allegation of negligence. The plaintiff takes the position that none is requisite; that the gravamen of the action is not in the negligent keeping of a vicious animal, but in keeping it at all. Much authority supports his position. . . . American authorities are all based directly or indirectly upon English decisions. *May v. Burdett,* 9 Q. B. 101, 115 E. R. 1213, decided in 1846, is the leading English case. Lord Denman, in delivering the judgment of the court said: "The precedents, both ancient and modern, with scarcely an exception, merely state the ferocity of the animal and the knowledge of the defendant without any allegation of negligence or want of care. *** The conclusion to be drawn from an examination of all the authorities appears to us to be this: That a person keeping a mischievous animal with knowledge of its propensities is bound to keep it secure at his peril . . . ." Bramwell, J., in *Nichols v. Marsland,* . . . said: "I am by no means sure that if a man kept a tiger, and lightning broke his chain, and he got loose and did mischief, that the man who kept him would not be liable." . . .

Based on the pronouncement in *May v. Burdett,* judicial dicta followed that the owner of animals ferae naturae "is an insurer for," "is liable under all circumstances for," and "is absolutely liable for" all injuries done by them. . . . It is true that animals ferae naturae constantly seek to escape confinement, and, if successful, become a menace to mankind. But the tiger, unrestrained, is no more dangerous than fire, water, electricity, or gas uncontrolled. The liability of the owner of these has never been declared absolute, nor his negligence presumed from mere ownership. Why discriminate against the owner of the animate menace? . . .

INDIANA HARBOR BELT R.R. V. AMERICAN CYANAMID CO.
916 F.2D 1174 (7TH CIR. 1990)

POSNER, Circuit Judge

American Cyanamid Company, the defendant . . . , is a major manufacturer of chemicals, including acrylonitrile . . . . On January 2, 1979, at its manufacturing plant in Louisiana, Cyanamid loaded 20,000 gallons of liquid acrylonitrile into a railroad tank car that it had leased from the North American Car Corporation. The next day, a train of the Missouri Pacific Railroad picked up the car at Cyanamid's siding. The car's ultimate destination was a Cyanamid plant in New Jersey . . . . The Missouri Pacific train carried the car north to the Blue Island railroad yard of Indiana Harbor Belt Railroad, the plaintiff in this case, a small switching line . . . . The Blue Island yard is in the Village of Riverdale, which is just south of Chicago and part of the Chicago metropolitan area.

The car arrived in the Blue Island yard on the morning of January 9, 1979. Several hours after it arrived, employees of the switching line noticed fluid gushing from the bottom outlet of the car. The lid on the outlet was broken. After two hours, the line's supervisor of equipment was able to stop the leak by closing a shut-off valve controlled from the top of the car. No one was sure at the time just how much of the contents of the car had leaked, but it was feared that all 20,000 gallons had, and since acrylonitrile is flammable at a temperature of 30 degrees Fahrenheit or above, highly toxic, and possibly carcinogenic, the local authorities ordered the homes near the yard evacuated. The evacuation lasted only a few hours, until the car was moved to a remote part of the yard and it was discovered that only about a quarter of the acrylonitrile had leaked. Concerned nevertheless that there had been some contamination of soil and water, the Illinois Department of Environmental Protection ordered the switching line to take decontamination measures that cost the line $981,022.75, which it sought to recover by this suit.

One count of the two-count complaint charges Cyanamid with having maintained the leased tank car negligently. The other count asserts that the transportation of acrylonitrile in bulk through the Chicago metropolitan area is an abnormally dangerous activity, for the consequences of which the shipper (Cyanamid) is strictly liable to the switching line, which bore the financial brunt of those consequences because of the decontamination measures that it was forced to take. After the district judge denied Cyanamid's motion to dismiss the strict liability count, the switching line moved for summary judgment on that count – and won. . . .

The question whether the shipper of a hazardous chemical by rail should be strictly liable for the consequences of a spill or other accident to the shipment en route is a novel one in Illinois. The parties agree . . . that the Supreme Court of Illinois would treat as authoritative the provisions of the Restatement governing abnormally dangerous activities. The key provision is section 520, which sets forth six factors to be considered in deciding whether an activity is abnormally dangerous and the actor therefore strictly liable.

The roots of section 520 are in nineteenth-century cases. The most famous one is *Rylands v. Fletcher*, but a more illuminating one in the present context is *Guille v. Swan* . . . . A man took off in a hot-air balloon and landed, without intending to, in a vegetable garden in New York City. A crowd that had been anxiously watching his involuntary descent trampled the vegetables in their endeavor to rescue him when he landed. The owner of the garden sued the balloonist for the resulting damage, and won. Yet the balloonist had not been careless. In the then state of ballooning it was impossible to make a pinpoint landing.

Guille is a paradigmatic case for strict liability. (a) The risk (probability) of harm was great, and (b) the harm that would ensue if the risk materialized could be, although luckily was not, great (the balloonist could have crashed into the crowd rather than into the vegetables). The confluence of these two factors established the urgency of seeking to prevent such accidents. (c) Yet such accidents could not be prevented by the exercise of due care; the technology of care in ballooning was insufficiently developed. (d) The activity was not a matter of common usage, so there was no presumption that it was a highly valuable activity despite its unavoidable riskiness. (e) The activity was inappropriate to the place in which it took place – densely populated New York City. The risk of serious harm to others (other than the balloonist himself, that is) could have been reduced by shifting the activity to the sparsely inhabited areas that surrounded the city in those days. (f) Reinforcing (d), the value to the community of the activity of recreational ballooning did not appear to be great enough to offset its unavoidable risks.

These are, of course, the six factors in section 520. They are related to each other in that each is a different facet of a common quest for a proper legal regime to govern accidents that negligence liability cannot adequately control. The interrelations might be more perspicuous if the six factors were reordered. One might for example start with (c), inability to eliminate the risk of accident by the exercise of due care. The baseline common law regime of tort liability is negligence. When it is a workable regime, because the hazards of an activity can be avoided by being careful (which is to say, non-negligent), there is no need to switch to strict liability. Sometimes, however, a particular type of accident cannot be prevented by taking care but can be avoided, or its consequences minimized, by shifting the activity in which the accident occurs to another locale, where the risk of harm of an accident will be less (e), or by reducing the scale of the activity in order to minimize the number of accidents caused by it (f). By making the actor strictly liable – by denying him in other words an excuse based on his inability to avoid accidents by being more careful – we give him an incentive, missing in a negligence regime, to experiment with methods of preventing accidents that involve not greater exertions of care, assumed to be futile, but instead relocating, changing, or reducing (perhaps to the vanishing point) the activity giving rise to the accident. The greater the risk of an accident (a) and the costs of an accident if one occurs (b), the more we want the actor to consider the possibility of making accident-reducing activity changes; the stronger, therefore, is the case for strict liability. Finally, if an activity is extremely common (d), like driving an automobile, it is unlikely either that its hazards are perceived as great or that there is no technology of care available to minimize them; so the case for strict liability is weakened.

The largest class of cases in which strict liability has been imposed under the standard codified in the Second Restatement of Torts involves the use of dynamite and other explosives for demolition in residential or urban areas. Explosives are dangerous even when handled carefully, and we therefore want blasters to choose the location of the activity with care and also to explore the feasibility of using safer substitutes (such as a wrecking ball), as well as to be careful in the blasting itself. Blasting is not a commonplace activity like driving a car, or so superior to substitute methods of demolition that the imposition of liability is unlikely to have any effect except to raise the activity's costs.

Against this background we turn to the particulars of acrylonitrile. Acrylonitrile is one of a large number of chemicals that are hazardous in the sense of being flammable, toxic, or both; acrylonitrile is both, as are many others. A table in the record contains a list of the 125 hazardous materials that are shipped in highest volume on the nation's railroads. Acrylonitrile is the fifty-third most hazardous on the list. Number 1 is phosphorus (white or yellow), and among the other materials that rank higher than acrylonitrile on the hazard scale are anhydrous ammonia, liquified petroleum gas, vinyl chloride, gasoline, crude petroleum, motor fuel antiknock compound, methyl and ethyl chloride, sulphuric acid, sodium metal, and chloroform. The plaintiff's lawyer acknowledged at argument that the logic of the district court's opinion dictated strict liability for all 52 materials that rank higher than acrylonitrile on the list, and quite possibly for the 72 that rank lower as well, since all are hazardous if spilled in quantity while being shipped by rail. Every shipper of any of these materials would therefore be strictly liable for the consequences of a spill or other accident that occurred while the material was being shipped through a metropolitan area. . . . No cases recognize so sweeping a liability. Several reject it, though none has facts much like those of the present case. . . .

So we can get little help from precedent, and might as well apply section 520 to the acrylonitrile problem from the ground up. To begin with, we have been given no reason . . . for believing that a negligence regime is not perfectly adequate to remedy and deter, at reasonable cost, the accidental spillage of acrylonitrile from rail cars. . . . More important, although acrylonitrile is flammable even at relatively low temperatures, and toxic, it is not so corrosive or otherwise destructive that it will eat through or otherwise damage or weaken a tank car's valves although they are maintained with due (which essentially means, with average) care. No one suggests, therefore, that the leak in this case was caused by the *inherent* properties of acrylonitrile. It was caused by carelessness – whether that of the North American Car Corporation in failing to maintain or inspect the car properly, or that of Cyanamid in failing to maintain or inspect it, or that of the Missouri Pacific when it had custody of the car, or that of the switching line itself in failing to notice the ruptured lid, or some combination of these possible failures of care. Accidents that are due to a lack of care can be prevented by taking care; and when a lack of care can . . . be shown in court, such accidents are adequately deterred by the threat of liability for negligence.

It is true that the district court purported to find as a fact that there is an inevitable risk of derailment or other calamity in transporting "large quantities of anything." This is not a finding of fact, but a truism: anything can happen. The question is, how likely is this type of accident if the actor uses due care? For all that appears from the record of the case or any other sources of information that we have found, if a tank car is carefully maintained the danger of a spill of acrylonitrile is negligible. If this is right, there is no compelling reason to move to a regime of strict liability, especially one that might embrace all other hazardous materials shipped by rail as well. This also means, however, that the amici curiae who have filed briefs in support of Cyanamid cry wolf in predicting "devastating" effects on the chemical industry if the district court's decision is affirmed. If the vast majority of chemical spills by railroads are preventable by due care, the imposition of strict liability should cause only a slight, not as they argue a substantial, rise in liability insurance rates, because the incremental liability should be slight. The amici have momentarily lost sight of the fact that the feasibility of avoiding accidents simply by being careful is an argument *against* strict liability. . . .

In emphasizing the flammability and toxicity of acrylonitrile rather than the hazards of transporting it, as in failing to distinguish between the active and the passive shipper, the plaintiff overlooks the fact that ultrahazardousness or abnormal dangerousness is, in the contemplation of the law at least, a property not of substances, but of activities: not of acrylonitrile, but of the transportation of acrylonitrile by rail through populated areas. Natural gas is both flammable and poisonous, but the operation of a natural gas well is not an ultrahazardous activity. Whatever the situation under products liability law (section 402A of the Restatement), the manufacturer of a product is not considered to be engaged in an abnormally dangerous activity merely because the product becomes dangerous when it is handled or used in some way after it leaves his premises, even if the danger is foreseeable. The plaintiff does not suggest that Cyanamid should switch to making some less hazardous chemical that would substitute for acrylonitrile in the textiles and other goods in which acrylonitrile is used. Were this a feasible method of accident avoidance, there would be an argument for making manufacturers strictly liable for accidents that occur during the shipment of their products (how strong an argument we need not decide). Apparently it is not a feasible method.

The relevant activity is transportation, not manufacturing and shipping. This essential distinction the plaintiff ignores. But even if the plaintiff is treated as a transporter and not merely a shipper, it has not shown that the transportation of acrylonitrile in bulk by rail through populated areas is so hazardous an activity, even when due care is exercised, that the law should seek to create – perhaps quixotically – incentives to relocate the activity to nonpopulated areas, or to reduce the scale of the activity, or to switch to transporting acrylonitrile by road rather than by rail . . . . It is no more realistic to propose to reroute the shipment of all hazardous materials around Chicago than it is to propose the relocation of homes adjacent to the Blue Island switching yard to more distant suburbs. It may be less realistic. Brutal though it may seem to say it, the inappropriate use to which land is being put in the Blue Island yard and neighborhood may be, not the transportation of hazardous chemicals, but residential living. The analogy is to building your home between the runways at O'Hare.

The briefs hew closely to the Restatement, whose approach to the issue of strict liability is mainly *allocative* rather than *distributive*. By this we mean that the emphasis is on picking a liability regime (negligence or strict liability) that will control the particular class of accidents in question most effectively, rather than on finding the deepest pocket and placing liability there. At argument, however, the plaintiff's lawyer invoked distributive considerations by pointing out that Cyanamid is a huge firm and the Indiana Harbor Belt Railroad a fifty-mile-long switching line that almost went broke in the winter of 1979, when the accident occurred. Well, so what? A corporation is not a living person but a set of contracts the terms of which determine who will bear the brunt of liability. Tracing the incidence of a cost is a complex undertaking which the plaintiff sensibly has made no effort to assume, since its legal relevance would be dubious. We add only that however small the plaintiff may be, it has mighty parents: it is a jointly owned subsidiary of Conrail and the Soo line.

The case for strict liability has not been made. Not in this suit in any event. . . .

B. ANIMALS

EXODUS 21:28-22:5

If an ox gore a man or a woman, that they die: then the ox shall be surely stoned, and his flesh shall not be eaten; but the owner of the ox shall be quit. But if the ox were wont to push with his horn in time past, and it hath been testified to his owner, and he hath not kept him in, but that he hath killed a man or a woman; the ox shall be stoned, and his owner also shall be put to death. If there be laid on him a sum of money, then he shall give for the ransom of his life whatsoever is laid upon him. Whether he have gored a son, or have gored a daughter, according to this judgment shall it be done unto him. If the ox shall push a manservant or a maidservant; he shall give unto their master thirty shekels of silver, and the ox shall be stoned.

And if a man shall open a pit, or if a man shall dig a pit, and not cover it, and an ox or an ass fall therein; The owner of the pit shall make it good, and give money unto the owner of them; and the dead beast shall be his.

And if one man's ox hurt another's, that he die; then they shall sell the live ox, and divide the money of it; and the dead ox also they shall divide. Or if it be known that the ox hath used to push in time past, and his owner hath not kept him in; he shall surely pay ox for ox; and the dead shall be his own.

If a man shall steal an ox, or a sheep, and kill it, or sell it; he shall restore five oxen for an ox, and four sheep for a sheep.

If a thief be found breaking up, and be smitten that he die, there shall no blood be shed for him. If the sun be risen upon him, there shall be blood shed for him; for he should make full restitution; if he have nothing, then he shall be sold for his theft.

If the theft be certainly found in his hand alive, whether it be ox, or ass, or sheep; he shall restore double.

If a man shall cause a field or vineyard to be eaten, and shall put in his beast, and shall feed in another man's field; of the best of his own field, and of the best of his own vineyard, shall he make restitution.

THE MISHNA
BABA KAMMA, 4.9

If its owner had tied it with a halter, or shut it in properly, but it nevertheless came out and caused damage, the owner is culpable whether it was an attested danger or accounted harmless. So R. Meir. R. Judah says: If it was accounted harmless he is liable, but if an attested danger he is not culpable, for it is written, *[And it hath been testified to his owner] and he hath not kept him in;*[1] *but this one was "kept in."* R. Eleazar says: Its only safe-keeping is the knife.

The rules stated in the Restatement (Second) of Torts are consistent with the traditional rules governing the liability of possessors of animals for harm caused by those animals, which differ according to the categorization of the animals as livestock, wild, or domestic. Domestic animals are those customarily kept by people in that particular geographic area and culture. Possessors of wild animals are strictly liable for harm that such an animal has a propensity to cause, while possessors of domestic animals are strictly liable only if the animal has an abnormally dangerous propensity of which the possessor knows or should know. Most domestic animal strict liability cases involve dogs, but some, like the following case, involve personal injuries caused by livestock. The issue in the following case is a common one – had the domesticated animal sufficiently demonstrated vicious propensities that knowledge of those propensities can be attributed to the possesser of the animal?

---

1   Ex. 21:29.

BANKS V. MAXWELL
171 s.e. 70 (n.c. 1933)

Plaintiff instituted this action to recover damages for serious injuries sustained by being gored by a bull owned by the defendant. The plaintiff was a boy 18 years of age, and had been raised on a farm, and on July 10, 1931, was working on the farm of defendant.

The narrative of the injury is substantially as follows:

Mr. Maxwell had a bull on the place, but prior to July 10, 1931, I had never been called upon to perform any service whatever in regard to the bull. I had never had any experience and did not know anything about handling bulls. Mr. Maxwell never told me or gave me any instructions about how to handle the bull. *** The bull was kept in a pen back of the dairy barn, and the pen was between twenty and thirty by sixty feet. *** The lot was enclosed and made out of rails and poles and was built on one side of the barn. *** The bull was in this lot or pen on the morning of July 10, 1931 . . . . The pen had a gate leading into it. On the morning of July 10, 1931, after I had finished milking, Mr. Maxwell told me to take the bull out of the lot and drive him to the pasture. He told me to go into the pen and run him out. When he told me to go into the pen I at first hesitated. I had no idea what the brute was. *** I picked up a club and started in, but he told me not to hit the brute with the club and I dropped it. I had not any more than dropped it until he turned on me, knocked me down and gored me. He rolled me around and gored me. *** He was rolling me with his head. He pushed me to the lower side of the pen and I got out of the pen. *** In the thirty days prior to July, 1931, I worked for Mr. Maxwell not less than ten days. I suppose I worked for him more than a third of the time. *** Sometimes when I came in early I saw them driving the bull in and I had seen them driving him out. Sometimes my brother drove him out. He is eighteen years old. *** I never saw anybody have trouble taking him out. I had never seen anybody put the dogs on him and drive him to the pasture. *** I had seen Arthur Lance drive him. He is about twenty-five years old. He was just coming on behind him and the bull was just going on into the pen. *** I have heard some people talk about bulls, but I did not know anything about that one. *** Before going into the pen I picked up a stick. The stick was about the size of my arm and about eighteen inches long. *** Mr. Maxwell told me not to hit him. I don't know how close I was to him when I raised the stick. I sent to draw it back and when I did he told me not to hit the bull. *** My brother had not been attending to the bull very long – not more than a month and a half, if that long. *** After the bull had me down and was goring me Mr. Maxwell hissed the dog on the bull. I don't know if the dog was there when I went into the pen, but while the bull had me down the dog commenced barking and I suppose Mr. Maxwell hissed him on.

Another witness for plaintiff said:

I drove the bull from the pen to the pasture and drove him back in. Sometimes Lance would drive the bull, but I drove it most of the time. *** When I would drive the bull from the pen down to the pasture he would bellow and paw the ground and burrow in the ground with his head all the way down the pathway. Sometimes he would stop and refuse to go on. *** When I would drive the bull from the pen to the pasture he behaved all the way down and almost every day as I have described already.

At the conclusion of plaintiff's evidence there was judgment of nonsuit, and the plaintiff appealed.

What are the essentials of liability for injury inflicted by a bull?

The ancestry and social standing of a bull antedates the pyramids of Egypt. . . . It is true that his fighting qualities have often been used for describing fear. For instance, the Sweet Singer of Israel, attempting to describe his sense of fear and depression, wrote: "Many bulls have compassed me; strong bulls of Bashan have beset me round. They gaped upon me with their mouths as a ravening and roaring lion." Psalms 22:12-13.

The familiar rule of liability for injuries inflicted by cattle has remained approximately constant for more than 3,000 years. This rule of liability was expressed by Moses in the following words:

> If an ox gore a man or a woman that they die; then the ox shall be surely stoned and his flesh shall not be eaten, but the owner of the ox shall be quit. But if the ox were wont to push with his horn in time past, and it hath been testified to his owner, and he hath not kept him in, but that he hath killed a man or a woman; the ox shall be stoned, and his owner also shall be put to death. If there be laid on him a sum of money, then he shall give for the ransom of his life whatsoever is laid upon him. Ex. 21:28-30.

This court declared in *Rector v. Coal Co.*, 192 N. C. 804, 136 S. E. 113, that a person injured by a domestic animal, in order to recover damages, must show two essential facts: (1) "The animal inflicting the injury must be dangerous, vicious, mischievous or ferocious, or one termed in the law as possessing a vicious propensity." (2) "The owner must have actual or constructive knowledge of the vicious propensity, character and habits of the animal." . . .

In the case at bar there was no evidence offered tending to show that the bull had ever attacked a person or threatened to do so, nor that he was "wont to push with his horn in time past"; nor was there evidence that the owner had actual or constructive knowledge of any vicious propensity of the animal. It is true that a witness said that each morning when the bull was turned out of the pen "he would bellow, paw the ground, and burrow in the ground with his head." Those bred to the soil perhaps know that such acts on the part of a normal bull constituted per se no more than boastful publicity or propaganda, doubtless designed by the animal to inform his bovine friends and admirers that he was arriving upon the scene.

At any rate the trial judge correctly interpreted the prevailing principle of law as held and promulgated in this state.

Affirmed.

1   *Wild animals.* The common law rule is strict liability for animals that are "wild by nature."

2   *Domesticated animals.* At common law, the background rule is no strict liability for personal injury caused by a domesticated animal, so long as the owner has no reason to know of the animal's vicious propensity. However, some jurisdictions have altered this common law rule by statute to make, especially, dog owners strictly liable for dog bites without regard to whether the owner has reason to know of the dog's vicious propensities.

3   *Trespassing livestock.* The common law rule generally has been that owners are strictly liable for damage caused when defendant's livestock trespass onto plaintiff's land, but only to the extent that such damage is reasonably to be expected from such trespass including, in rare cases, personal injury.

4   *Property damage along highway.* Restatement (Second) Torts Sec. 504(3)(b) provides that people who lawfully drive livestock along the highway are not strictly liable for incidental harm to abutting landowners.

5   *Fencing out statutes.* Restatement (Second) Torts Sec. 504(4) provides that the application of strict liability for trespassing livestock can depend on compliance with fencing in or fencing out statutes, which apply mostly in western states. Can you guess why?

MARSHALL V. RANNE
511 S.W.2D 255 (TEX. 1974)

. . . [Plaintiff] and defendant . . . owned neighboring farms . . . . Plaintiff's principal occupation was raising hogs. . . . The hog in question was a boar which had escaped from defendant's farm and had been seen on plaintiff's land during several weeks before the day of the injury. According to plaintiff, defendant's boar had charged him ten to twelve times before this occurrence, had held him prisoner in his outhouse several times, and had attacked his wife on four or five occasions. On the day of the injury plaintiff had hauled in several barrels of old bread in his pickup and had put it out for his hogs at the barn. At that time he saw defendant's boar about a hundred yards behind the barn, but it came no nearer. After feeding his hogs, he went into the house and changed clothes . . . . On emerging from the house, he looked for the boar because, as he testified, he always had to look before he made a move, but he did not see it. He started toward his pickup, and when he was about thirty feet from it, near the outhouse, he heard a noise behind him, turned around and saw the boar charging toward him. He put out his hand defensively, but the boar grabbed it and bit it severely.

Plaintiff testified that the first time the hog had jeopardized his safety was about a week or ten days before he was hurt. He did not shoot the hog because he did not consider that the neighborly thing to do, although he was an expert with a gun and had two available. He made no complaint about the hog to defendant until the day of the injury, when he wrote a note and put it on defendant's gate. The note read: "John, your boar has gone bad. He is trying to chase me off the farm. He stalks us just like a cat stalks a mouse every time he catches us out of the house. We are going to have to get him out before he hurts someone."

This note did not come to defendant's attention until he came in late that afternoon, and the evidence does not reveal whether he saw it before plaintiff was injured. Plaintiff testified that he and defendant had previously discussed the hog's viciousness on several occasions.

The [jury's] answers to the special issues were: (1) defendant's boar hog bit the plaintiff's right hand on January 21, 1970, (2) immediately prior to that date, the boar hog had vicious propensities and was likely to cause injury to persons, (3) refused to find that at any time before plaintiff's injury, the defendant actually knew that the defendant's boar hog was vicious and was likely to cause injury to persons, (4) the defendant prior to plaintiff's injury in the exercise of ordinary care should have known that the boar hog was vicious and likely to cause injury to persons, (5) defendant permitted his boar hog to run at large after he knew or should have known that the hog was vicious and likely to cause injury to persons, (6) plaintiff, Paul Marshall, had knowledge of the vicious propensities of the defendant's boar hog and that it was likely to cause injury to persons at and prior to the time the hog bit him, (7) plaintiff, Paul Marshall, with knowledge of the nature of defendant's boar hog voluntarily exposed himself to the risk of attack by the animal, (8) plaintiff's failure to shoot the defendant's boar hog prior to the time the hog bit plaintiff was negligence, (9) which failure was a proximate cause of plaintiff's injuries, (10) plaintiff failed to maintain a fence about his premises sufficiently close to prevent hogs passing through, (11) which was negligence, and (12) a proximate cause of plaintiff's injuries, (13) plaintiff was damaged in the amount of $4,146.00.

The questions presented by this cause are (1) the true nature of an action for damages caused by a vicious animal, (2) whether contributory negligence is a defense to this action, and (3) whether plaintiff Marshall was, as a matter of law, deprived of a voluntary and free choice in confronting the risk.

Nature of Vicious Animal Cases

A correct classification of this case is important, since that decision also controls the nature of the acceptable defenses to the action. . . . We approve the rule . . . that suits for damages caused by vicious animals should be governed by principles of strict liability . . . . The correct rule is expressed in RESTATEMENT OF TORTS §§507, 509 (1938):

§ 507. LIABILITY OF POSSESSOR OF WILD ANIMAL.

Except as stated in §§ 508 and 517, a possessor of a wild animal is subject to liability to others, . . . on his land, for such harm done by the animal to their persons, lands or chattels as results from a dangerous propensity which is characteristic of wild animals of its class or of which the possessor has reason to know, although he has exercised the utmost care to confine the animal or otherwise prevent it from doing harm.

§ 509. HARM DONE BY ABNORMALLY DANGEROUS DOMESTIC ANIMALS.

Except as stated in § 517, a possessor of a domestic animal which he has reason to know has dangerous propensities abnormal to its class, is subject to liability for harm caused thereby to others, except trespassers on his land, although he has exercised the utmost care to prevent it from doing the harm.

The jury in this case refused to find that the defendant actually knew that the hog was vicious and was likely to cause injury to persons, but it did find in answer to special issue four that the defendant prior to plaintiff's injury should have known that fact. Defendant Ranne does not challenge the finding to issue four. . . .

Contributory Negligence is No Defense To Strict Liability

The . . . jury found that plaintiff Marshall was negligent in several particulars. We hold that contributory negligence is not a defense to this action. . . . This is also the view expressed in RESTATEMENT (SECOND) OF TORTS § 515, Comment b (Tent. Draft No. 10, 1964):

> *b.* Since the strict liability of the possessor of an animal is not founded on his negligence, the ordinary contributory negligence of the plaintiff is not a defense to such an action. The reason is the policy of the law which places the full responsibility for preventing the harm upon the defendant. Thus where the plaintiff merely fails to exercise reasonable care to discover the presence of the animal, or to take precautions against the harm which may result from it, his recovery on the basis of strict liability is not barred.

We conclude that the findings of plaintiff's contributory negligence as contained in the answers to special issues eight through twelve have no place in this case and did not bar the plaintiff from recovery. . . . We do not hold that negligence and contributory negligence can never be a correct theory in a case which concerns animals. All animals are not vicious and a possessor of a non-vicious animal may be subject to liability for his negligent handling of such an animal . . . .

Did Marshall Voluntarily Assume the Risk?

Plaintiff Marshall does not contend that voluntary assumption of risk is no defense to an action which asserts the defendant's strict liability. . . . Marshall's argument is that he did not, as a matter of law voluntarily expose himself to the risk of the attack by the hog. The jury found that plaintiff Marshall had knowledge of the vicious propensities of the hog and that it was likely to cause injury to persons, and also found that plaintiff, with knowledge of the nature of defendant's boar hog, voluntarily exposed himself to the risk of attack by the animal. We hold that there was no proof that plaintiff had a free and voluntary choice, because he did not have a free choice of alternatives. He had, instead, only a choice of evils, both of which were wrongfully imposed upon him by the defendant. He could remain a prisoner inside his own house or he could take the risk of reaching his car before defendant's hog attacked him. Plaintiff could have remained inside his house, but in doing so, he would have surrendered his legal right to proceed over his own property to his car so he could return to his home in Dallas. The latter alternative was forced upon him against his will and was a choice he was not legally required to accept . . . . We approve and follow the rule expressed in RESTATEMENT (SECOND) OF TORTS § 496E (1965):

1. A plaintiff does not assume a risk of harm unless he voluntarily accepts the risk.

2. The plaintiff's acceptance of a risk is not voluntary if the defendant's tortious conduct has left him no reasonable alternative course of conduct in order to
    a. avert harm to himself or another, or
    b. exercise or protect a right or privilege of which the defendant has no right to deprive him.

The dilemma which defendant forced upon plaintiff was that of facing the danger or surrendering his rights with respect to his own real property, and that was not, as a matter of law the voluntary choice to which the law entitled him. . . . Defendant Ranne argues also that the plaintiff Marshall had yet another alternative, that of shooting the hog. . . . We do not regard the slaughter of the animal as a reasonable alternative . . . . We accordingly hold that contributory negligence is not a defense in a strict liability action. Voluntary assumption of risk, if established, would be a valid defense. In this case as a matter of law, the proof shows that plaintiff Marshall did not voluntarily encounter the vicious hog. We, therefore, reverse the judgments of the courts below and render judgment that plaintiff recover the sum of $4,146.00 the amount of damages found by the jury.

C. ABNORMALLY DANGEROUS ACTIVITIES

A concept to keep in mind while studying strict liability for abnormally dangerous activities is that the strict liability is not a form of sanction for engaging in dangerous conduct. To the contrary, the strict liability is imposed on admittedly innocent defendants.

FLETCHER V. RYLANDS
L.R. 1 EX. 265 (1866)

BLACKBURN J.

. . . In the Court of Exchequer, the Chief Baron and Martin, B., were of opinion that the plaintiff was not entitled to recover at all, Bramwell, B., being of a different opinion. The judgment in the

Exchequer was consequently given for the defendants, in conformity with the opinion of the majority of the court. . . . We have come to the conclusion that the opinion of Bramwell, B., was right, and that the answer to the question should be that the plaintiff was entitled to recover damages from the defendants, by reason of the matters stated in the case, and consequently, that the judgment below should be reversed . . . .

It appears from the statement in the case that the plaintiff was damaged by his property being flooded by water, which, without any fault on his part, broke out of a reservoir constructed on the defendants' land by the defendants' orders, and maintained by the defendants.

It appears from the statement in the case that the coal under the defendants' land had, at some remote period, been worked out; but this was unknown at the time when the defendants gave directions to erect the reservoir, and the water in the reservoir would not have escaped from the defendants' land, and no mischief would have been done to the plaintiff, but for this latent defect in the defendants' subsoil. And it further appears that the defendant selected competent engineers and contractors to make his reservoir, and himself personally continued in total ignorance of what we have called the latent defect in the subsoil . . . . It is found that the defendants, personally, were free from all blame . . . . The consequence was, that the reservoir when filled with water burst into the shafts, the water flowed down through them into the old workings, and thence into the plaintiff's mine, and there did the mischief. . . .

The plaintiff, though free from all blame on his part, must bear the loss, unless he can establish that it was the consequence of some default for which the defendants are responsible. The question of law therefore arises, what is the obligation which the law casts on a person who, like the defendants, lawfully brings on his land something which, though harmless whilst it remains there, will naturally do mischief if it escape out of his land. It is agreed on all hands that he must take care to keep in that which he has brought on the land and keeps there, in order that it may not escape and damage his neighbours, but the question arises whether the duty which the law casts upon him, under such circumstances, is an absolute duty to keep it in at his peril, or is, as the majority of the Court of Exchequer have thought, merely a duty to take all reasonable and prudent precautions, in order to keep it in, but no more. If the first be the law, the person who has brought on his land and kept there something dangerous, and failed to keep it in, is responsible for all the natural consequences of its escape. If the second be the limit of his duty, he would not be answerable except on proof of negligence, and consequently would not be answerable for escape arising from any latent defect which ordinary prudence and skill could not detect. . . .

We think that the true rule of law is, that the person who for his own purposes brings on his lands and collects and keeps there anything likely to do mischief if it escapes, must keep it in at his peril, and, if he does not do so, is prima facie answerable for all the damage which is the natural consequence of its escape. He can excuse himself by showing that the escape was owing to the plaintiff's default; or perhaps that the escape was the consequence of vis major, or the act of God; but as nothing of this sort exists here, it is unnecessary to inquire what excuse would be sufficient. The general rule, as above stated, seems on principle just. The person whose grass or corn is eaten down by the escaping cattle of his neighbour, or whose mine is flooded by the water from his neighbour's reservoir, or whose cellar is invaded by the filth of his neighbour's privy, or whose habitation is made unhealthy by the fumes and noisome vapours of his neighbour's alkali works, is damnified without any fault of his own; and it seems but reasonable and just that the neighbour, who has brought something on his own property which was not naturally there, harmless to others so long as it is confined to his own property, but which he knows to be mischievous if it gets on his neighbour's, should be obliged to make good the damage which ensues if he does not succeed in confining it to his own property. But for his act in bringing it there no mischief could have accrued, and it seems but just that he should at his peril keep it there so that no mischief may accrue, or answer for the natural and anticipated consequences. And upon authority, this we think is established to be the law whether the things so brought be beasts, or water, or filth, or stenches.

The case that has most commonly occurred, and which is most frequently to be found in the books, is as to the obligation of the owner of cattle which he has brought on his land, to prevent their escaping and doing mischief. The law as to them seems to be perfectly settled from early times; the owner must keep them in at his peril, or he will be answerable for the natural consequences of their escape; that is with regard to tame beasts, for the grass they eat and trample upon, though not for any injury to the person of others, for our ancestors have settled that it is not the general nature of horses to kick, or bulls to gore; but if the owner knows that the beast has a vicious propensity to attack man, he will be answerable for that too. . . .

NOTES

1   *Other Theories.* Could the plaintiff recover on a trespass theory? A nuisance theory? Why or why not?

2   *American Reception.* By the turn of the twentieth century, most American jurisdictions had accepted the rule in *Rylands.*

3   *Nonreciprocal Risk.* Professor George Fletcher has very influentially theorized that strict liability is imposed where defendant's activity imposes a "nonreciprocal" risk. *See* George P. Fletcher, *Fairness and Utility in Tort Law,* 85 Harv. L. Rev. 537 (1972). Ordinary activities result in the imposition of reciprocal risk, and it is fair to require those living in society to bear the reciprocal risk generated by those acting with reasonable care around them. Such risks are shared by all who create and are exposed to them. By contrast, unconventional activities produce non-reciprocal risks. Strict liability prevents a party who engages in an activity that produces an unusual risk from foisting that risk off on his neighbors without bearing any roughly equivalent risk in return.

4   *Restatement Terminology.* Notice the variant terminology used in the cases and the Restatements: "ultrahazardous" v. "abnormally dangerous." The First Restatement identified strict liability activites using the term "ultrahazardous," which focuses on the abstract level of danger involved in the activity. The Second Restatement uses the term "abnormally dangerous," which focuses more on the "non-reciprocal" nature of the risk created by the activity.

SPANO V. PERINI CORP.
250 N.E.2D 31 (N.Y. 1969)

The principal question posed on this appeal is whether a person who has sustained property damage caused by blasting on nearby property can maintain an action for damages without a showing that the blaster was negligent. . . . The plaintiff Spano is the owner of a garage in Brooklyn which was wrecked by a blast occurring on November 27, 1962. . . . It is undisputed that, on the day in question . . . , the defendants had set off a total of 194 sticks of dynamite at a construction site . . . 125 feet away from the damaged premises. Although both plaintiffs alleged negligence in their complaints, no attempt was made to show that the defendants had failed to exercise reasonable care or to take necessary precautions when they were blasting. Instead, they chose to rely, at the trial, solely on the principle of absolute liability. . . . At the close of the plaintiff Spano's case, when defendants' attorney moved to dismiss the action on the ground . . . that no negligence had been proved, the trial judge expressed the view that the defendants could be held liable even though they were not shown to have been careless. The case then proceeded, with evidence being introduced solely on the question of damages and proximate cause. Following the trial, the court awarded damages of some $4,400 to Spano . . . .

In our view, the time has come for this court to . . . declare that one who engages in blasting must assume responsibility, and be liable without fault, for any injury he causes to neighboring property. The concept of absolute liability in blasting cases is hardly a novel one. The overwhelming majority of American jurisdictions have adopted such a rule. (*See* . . . Restatement, Torts, §§ 519, 520, comment *e*; Ann. . . .). . . .

NOTES

1   *Blasting.* Blasting is, by far, the most common scenario to which modern courts have applied the rule of traditional strict liability for abnormally dangerous activities. In fact, a majority of such cases involve blasting, poison (including the storage of toxic materials), or both.

2   *Defenses to Strict Liability.* Traditionally, contributory negligence was not a defense to strict liability for abnormally dangerous activities. As in the case of wild or vicious animals, it was thought that it made no sense to apply a fault-based defense to a non-fault-based cause of action. Assumption of risk was a defense to a strict liability action. The widespread adoption of principles of comparative responsibility has left up in the air the applicability of defenses to strict liability claims based upon plaintiff's own conduct, but the trend is in the direction of permitting at least a partial defense.

CROSBY V. COX AIRCRAFT CO.
746 P.2D 1198 (WASH. 1987)

Quaere: Should owners and operators of flying aircraft be held strictly liable for ground damage caused by operation of the aircraft, or should their liability depend on a finding of negligence?
. . .

I

The case involves a claim for property damage caused when a plane owned by Cox Aircraft . . . crash-landed onto Douglas Crosby's property. . . . On December 19, 1984, the pilot flew the airplane over the Olympic Peninsula and then turned back to Seattle, intending to land at Boeing Field. However, the engine ran out of fuel in mid-flight, and the pilot was forced to crash-land the plane at Alki Point in West Seattle. The plane landed on the roof of Crosby's garage, causing $3,199.89 in damages.

. . . The trial court granted partial summary judgment for Crosby, holding that both the pilot and Cox Aircraft were strictly liable for all damage done to Crosby's property. . . . The pilot and Cox Aircraft appealed. We accepted certification. . . . We hold that the general principles of negligence control.

II

This is the first case in this State to directly deal with the standard of liability governing ground damage caused by aircraft. . . . Plaintiff Crosby and amicus party . . . urge us to adopt Restatement (Second) of Torts § 520A (1977):

§ 520A. Ground Damage From Aircraft
If physical harm to land or to persons or chattels on the ground is caused by the ascent, descent or flight of aircraft, or by the dropping or falling of an object from the aircraft,
a. the operator of the aircraft is subject to liability for the harm, even though he has exercised the utmost care to prevent it, and
b. the owner of the aircraft is subject to similar liability if he has authorized or permitted the operation.

This provision establishing strict liability is said to be a "special application" of §§ 519-520, the Restatement sections governing liability for "abnormally dangerous" activities. (*See* § 520A, comment *a*). Sections 519-520 provide:

§ 519. General Principle

1. One who carries on an abnormally dangerous activity is subject to liability for harm to the person, land or chattels of another resulting from the activity, although he has exercised the utmost care to prevent the harm.

2. This strict liability is limited to the kind of harm, the possibility of which makes the activity abnormally dangerous.

§ 520. Abnormally Dangerous Activities

In determining whether an activity is abnormally dangerous, the following factors are to be considered:

a. existence of a high degree of risk of some harm to the person, land or chattels of others;

b. likelihood that the harm that results from it will be great;

c. inability to eliminate the risk by the exercise of reasonable care;

d. extent to which the activity is not a matter of common usage;

e. inappropriateness of the activity to the place where it is carried on; and

f. extent to which its value to the community is outweighed by its dangerous attributes.

The defendants urge us to reject Restatement §520A. They contend that aviation can no longer be designated an "abnormally dangerous activity" requiring special rules of liability. We agree.

In the early days of aviation, the cases and treatises were replete with references to the hazards of "aeroplanes." The following assessment is typical:

[E]ven the best constructed and maintained aeroplane is so incapable of complete control that flying creates a risk that the plane even though carefully constructed, maintained and operated, may crash to the injury of persons, structures and chattels on the land over which the flight is made.

Restatement of Torts §520, comment *b* (1938). . . .

. . . In 1922 the Commission on Uniform State Laws proposed a new Uniform Aeronautics Act which, *inter alia*, made owners of aircraft strictly liable for all ground damage caused by the "ascent, descent or flight of the aircraft." Twenty-three states originally adopted this act by statute. By 1943, however, the Commissioners recognized that the act had become "obsolete," and it was removed from the list of uniform laws. . . .

The number of states imposing strict liability has diminished significantly. At present, only six states retain the rule, and even these states apply it only to the owner of the aircraft. The aircraft operator remains liable only for damages caused by his own negligence. . . .

The modern trend followed by a majority of states is to impose liability only upon a showing of negligence by either the aircraft owner or operator. . . . Several states have legislated this rule by providing that ordinary tort law (or the law applicable to torts on land) applies to aviation accidents. . . . Other jurisdictions have case law to this effect. . . . Moreover, a number of courts have expressly disavowed the notion that aviation is an "ultrahazardous activity" requiring special rules of liability. . . .

We have discovered no cases relying on Restatement (Second) of Torts §520A. That section is said to be a "special application" of §519 and §520(a)-(f), which impose strict liability on persons engaging in abnormally dangerous activities. An analysis of the individual factors listed in §520 further persuades us that strict liability is inappropriate here.

Factor (a) of §520 requires that the activity in question contain a "high degree of risk of some harm to the person, land or chattels of others." No such showing has been made. Indeed, statistics indicate that air transportation is far safer than automobile transportation. . . . Factor (b) speaks to the gravity of the harm – that is, in the unlikely event that an airplane accident occurs, whether there is a "likelihood that the [resulting harm] will be great" it is apparent that this possibility is present. However, this must be further evaluated in light of factor (c), which speaks of the "inability to eliminate the risk by the exercise of reasonable care." Given the extensive governmental regulation of aviation . . . and the continuing technological improvements in aircraft manufacture, maintenance and operation, we conclude that the *overall* risk of serious injury from ground damage can be sufficiently reduced by the exercise of due care. Finally, factors (d), (e), and (f) do not favor the imposition of strict liability. Aviation is an activity of "common usage," it is appropriately conducted over populated areas, and its value to the community outweighs its dangerous attributes. Indeed, aviation is an integral part of modern society.

The causes of aircraft accidents are legion and can come from a myriad of sources. Every aircraft that flies is at risk from every bird, projectile and other aircraft. Accidents may be caused by improper placement of wires or buildings or from failure to properly mark and light such obstructions. The injury to the ground dweller may have been caused by faulty engineering, construction, repair, maintenance, metal fatigue, operation or ground control. Lightning, wind shear and other acts of God may have brought about a crash. Any listing of the causes of such accidents undoubtedly would fall short of the possibilities. In such circumstances the imposition of liability should be upon the blameworthy party who can be shown to be at fault. . . .

There are no special statutory provisions that regulate or govern the responsibility of persons owning and operating airplanes. In the absence of such statutes, the rules of law applicable generally to torts govern. The ordinary rules of negligence and due care are invoked. . . .

We are not persuaded that we should create a special rule of liability governing only ground damage caused by aircraft accidents.

NOTE

1   *Restatement Factors.* The multi-factor analysis provided for in Restatement §520 always has been controversial. Perhaps the most controversial are factors (e) (appropriateness of activity to location) and (f) (concerning the value of the activity to the community). Why is it that the inherent high risk of an activity should be shifted to others if the activity is valuable to the community? The Restatement (Third) of Torts would distill the six factors in section 520 down to two factors focusing on the magnitude of the risk created by the activity and its common usage and eliminating consideration of appropriateness of activity to location and the social value of the activity.

HERMAN V. WELLAND CHEMICAL, LTD.
580 F. SUPP. 823 (M.D. PA. 1984)

The plaintiffs in the above-captioned actions seek to recover damages for injuries arising from an automobile accident during which defendant Orrach's car struck plaintiffs Daniel Herman and John Curtis. . . . Defendant Welland Chemical, Ltd. (Welland) has moved to dismiss the claims asserted against it . . . . In considering Welland's motion to dismiss, the court is bound to accept as true the allegations set forth in the plaintiffs' complaints. According to the plaintiffs' allegations, Welland agreed to sell, and to ship from its plant in Canada, 18 tons of aluminum chloride anhydrous to a company in New Jersey. Welland obtained a truck, a flatbed trailer and a driver and loaded the chemical into 12 polyethylene pallet hoppers. The hoppers were placed on the trailer and were secured with chains, binders and hooks. On or about February 1, 1982, the truck began its journey from Canada to New Jersey.

Proceeding eastbound on Interstate Highway 80, the truck had reached Stroud Township in Monroe County, Pennsylvania at approximately 4:30 a.m. on February 3, 1982. According to the complaint, the driver lost control of the truck at about this point. The rear portion of the trailer allegedly struck the concrete barrier dividing the east and westbound lanes of the highway. Eight hoppers fell from the trailer, and several of the containers ruptured, causing the chemical to spill on the roadway. Because it had been raining that morning, the pavement was wet. The chemical reacted with the water from the rain, creating a cloud of hydrochloric gas.

State, County and Stroud Township officials assembled a task force to respond to the danger posed by the hydrochloric gas. A ten mile stretch of Route 80 was closed in both directions. A few miles east of the disabled truck, in East Stroudsburg, some volunteer firemen were dispatched and told to help reroute motorists off the westbound lane of the highway. Plaintiffs Daniel Herman and John Curtis were among this group of firemen. Lit flares were placed along the road to aid the firemen in merging traffic into the right-hand lane and eventually off the highway. The complaint asserts that plaintiff Herman was directing traffic by holding a flare in his hand and waving it in the desired direction.

Six hours after the chemical spill and at least one hour after the flares had been placed along the highway, defendant Orrach approached the firemen in his automobile, traveling westerly in the center lane. According to the complaint, Orrach "caused his vehicle to run over several flares, proceed[ed] upon a closed area of highway, and str[uck] the [p]laintiff[s] where [they] stood" directing traffic. Both plaintiffs were injured severely. . . .

The absolute liability counts can be dismissed without extended discussion, for a valid claim clearly is not stated under that theory. The Pennsylvania Supreme Court has adopted the doctrine embodied in § 519 of the Restatement of Torts which states that one who carries on an ultrahazardous activity may be held absolutely liable for injuries resulting from that activity. [Citations omitted.] While the parties have cited no case holding that the activity of Welland falls within § 519 of the Restatement ("ultrahazardous" activities) or § 519 of the Restatement Second ("abnormally dangerous" activities), the court will assume for the plaintiffs' benefit that a Pennsylvania court would so decide. Even assuming that the doctrine of absolute liability could be applied to the shipment of chemicals, the plaintiffs' claims must fail, for such responsibility "is limited to the kind of harm, the possibility of which makes the activity abnormally dangerous." Restatement (Second) of Torts § 519 & Comment e. The kind of harm suffered in the present case does not, as a matter of law, fall within the scope of the risks making the shipment of chemicals abnormally dangerous. Accordingly, no valid claim is stated. . . .

The court will grant Welland's motion to dismiss . . . . An appropriate Order will enter.

IV.

A. INTRODUCTION

As has already been discussed, tort cases can be divided into three categories: intentional torts, strict liability, and negligence. Now we turn to the third and most important of those categories. Unlike the intentional torts, with which we started our study of tort law, negligence focuses on the risk created by defendant's conduct.

The word "negligence" is a common part of Americans' everyday speech, but some confusion can stem from the fact that the word "negligence" can be used in at least two senses. In one sense, the term refers to the tort cause of action consisting of the five elements of voluntary act, duty, breach, causation (cause in fact and proximate cause), and damages. This use of the word "negligence" to refer to a cause of action has been around since the nineteenth century. Before that time, the word "negligence" was used (and sometimes still is used) in a second sense, to refer to the second of the four elements of the negligence cause of action – breach of duty. In this latter sense, the word is a close synonym with "carelessness."

While negligence as a cause of action has been around for only a couple hundred years, it is the dominant form of tort liability in America today. The popularity of the negligence cause of action probably is due to its breadth – it does not guard only specific protected interests, as the intentional torts do, and it is not limited to certain activities, as strict liability is. Rather, negligence more broadly protects against all tangible harm caused by defendant's careless conduct, whatever form that conduct might take. In one way, the negligence cause of action is more like strict liability than like intentional torts – both negligence and strict liability involve accidental harm. But in another way, negligence has more in common with intentional torts than with strict liability – both intentional torts and negligence involve a form of wrongdoing or fault on the part of the liable defendant.

As already noted, the negligence cause of action consists of five elements. First, plaintiff must show that defendant engaged in a voluntary act. Second, defendant must owe plaintiff a legal duty of care to guard against the sort of harm suffered by the plaintiff. Third, that duty must have been breached by defendant – negligence liability extends only to the defendant who is at fault, where the word "fault" is used in the sense of carelessness. Fourth, defendant is responsible for plaintiff's injury only if the injury was "proximately caused" (which includes actual causation) by defendant's breach of duty. The final element, the occurrence of harm to the plaintiff, usually is the event that launches a tort suit. Plaintiff must prove that she actually suffered some compensable detriment, usually bodily injury and/or property damage – the rule in the negligence context is "no harm, no foul." The variety of harms that can constitute a compensable injury under a negligence cause of action has been gradually expanding. (We will discuss damages at greater detail later in the materials.)

These five elements sometimes are stated slightly differently from court to court, but there is no significant substantive deviation among the American jurisdictions. For example, the fourth element of "causation" frequently is broken into the two separate elements of "cause in fact" and "proximate cause." Also, these five elements sometimes are collapsed to four by ignoring the first element of defendant's "voluntary act," but as the following case illustrates, it is necessary to the negligence cause of action.

LOBERT V. PACK
9 A.2D 365 (PA. 1939)

Plaintiff was injured in the early morning of July 8, 1936, while driving a two-door sedan owned by the defendant, who at the time of the accident was riding on the rear seat, immediately behind her. . . . The parties had visited several cafes and clubs during the course of the preceding evening, and had partaken liberally of beer and other refreshments. From an agreed statement of facts it appears "that . . . the defendant had been 'kicking the seat' * * * which in this type of car can be moved forward in order to permit access to the rear seat. * * * The accident happened about two miles beyond Hays Borough and plaintiff testified that during the two mile drive defendant was asleep, * * * that suddenly the back of the seat was forced against her, throwing her arms off the wheel and causing her to cross the road, crash into the culvert and upset. . . . Defendant testified that he had been resting his feet on the back of the seat . . . but had removed them at her request, after which he went to sleep, and knew nothing more until he awoke in the hospital. To his knowledge he neither replaced his feet on the back of the seat nor pushed it again after her request to remove them."

The jury returned a verdict for defendant, and from the refusal of the court in banc to grant a new trial the plaintiff has taken this appeal. The sole error alleged is the following excerpt from the charge of the trial judge: "If, on the other hand, you believe that the defendant was asleep, then the defendant would be entitled to a verdict because if he actually was asleep then he was unconscious of what occurred and could not have intentionally done anything to bring about the accident." While plaintiff concedes that the alleged tortious conduct of defendant was involuntary and unintentional, it is her contention that defendant should be held liable for the injuries she sustained to the same extent as though he had been awake when the accident happened.[1] . . . The question therefore, is whether a person is responsible for a tort involuntarily committed while he was sleeping or unconscious.

. . . [F]undamentally to create liability for an act alleged to be negligent, it must be shown to have been the conscious act of a person's volition. He must have done that which he ought not to have done, or omitted that which he ought to have done, as a conscious being endowed with a will. [Citation omitted.] The Restatement, Torts, Vol. 1, Section 2 (comment a), expresses the same thought in these words: "There cannot be an act without volition. Therefore, a contraction of a person's muscles which is purely a reaction to some outside force, * * * or the convulsive movements of an epileptic, are not acts of that person. So too, movements of the body during sleep when the will is in abeyance are not acts * * * some outward manifestation of the defendant's will is necessary to the existence of an act which can subject him to liability * * *." Nowhere in cases dealing with the subject of torts do we find the suggestion that a person should be held responsible for injuries inflicted during periods of unconsciousness.

In the present case there was no duty on the part of defendant to remain awake, as he had no part in the operation of the automobile. It is not charged by plaintiff that he was negligent in going to sleep. . . . He could not foresee that after he had fallen asleep some sudden movement of his body might throw the plaintiff against the steering wheel and thus endanger the occupants of the car. Such an extraordinary occurrence is not within the realm of every day experience, and the mere fact that it happened in the present case is no indication that it was reasonably to be anticipated. The defendant was required to exercise foresight, not clairvoyance.

Once asleep, defendant was no longer capable of voluntary action or of conscious behavior. Therefore, whatever happened while he was in that condition could have no significance, so far as defendant's liability was concerned, except as it might properly be designated a natural and probable consequence of some previous wrongful act. Since the record shows that his conduct prior to the accident involved no breach of duty toward plaintiff, it is clear that the instruction to the jury assigned as error was not improper.

Judgment affirmed.

CADORETTE V. SUMNER COUNTY BOARD OF EDUCATION
1996 WL 187586 (TENN. CT. APP. APRIL 19, 1996)

Todd Cadorette suffered a head injury on April 15, 1993, during an art class at Beech High School in Sumner County, Tennessee. . . . On the day of his fall, Todd's art teacher, Vicki Yeary, sought a volunteer to stand up on a four foot high table and model for the class. Todd, a fifteen year old ninth-grade student, agreed. Ms. Yeary instructed Todd to stand on the table while trying, "not to move too much," with his hands in his pockets. Todd stood on the desk for approximately ten

---

[1]   Plaintiff relies upon the principle that where a loss must be borne by one of two innocent parties it shall be borne by him who occasioned it, and cites as authority the case of *Mutual Fire Ins. Co. v. Showalter,* 3 Pa. Super. 452, where an insane person was held liable for his tort. . . .

minutes, but proceeded to faint and fall off the desk, injuring his head when he landed on the classroom floor.

Ms. Yeary, Todd's instructor, had been a teacher for twenty-five years, including twenty-four in the Sumner County School System. She testified that she had used this modeling technique throughout her career and had been taught the method herself in college. Todd had never modeled prior to the accident, and by all accounts was a very healthy young man. When Todd fell, Ms. Yeary was instructing a student on the other side of the room, and was not close to Todd.

. . . Todd's parents filed an action on his behalf . . . against the Sumner County Board of Education, as well as Sumner County. The Cadorettes alleged in their complaint . . . that Todd's injury resulted from the negligence of his teacher. . . . [A] bench trial ensued . . . . The court found . . . that the Defendants were not negligent . . . . The court dismissed the matter, and this appeal followed. . . .

Since the essential facts in this case are not in dispute, the questions raised by this appeal relate chiefly to the application of law to those facts. . . . In order to establish liability on the part of Sumner County . . . for any damages in this lawsuit, it is the Appellant's burden to prove the following elements: (1) the duty of care owed by the Defendant to the Plaintiff; (2) conduct on the part of the Defendant falling below the applicable standard of care amounting to a breach of that duty; (3) an injury or loss; (4) causation in fact; (5) proximate or legal cause. . . .

This Court begins its assessment of negligence claims by reviewing whether the defendant owed a duty to the Plaintiff. [Citation omitted.] The existence or non-existence of a duty owed to the Plaintiff by the Defendant is entirely a question of law for the court. . . . While school teachers and administrators have a duty to supervise their students in order to protect them from injury, the fact that an injury to a student has occurred does not, in and of itself, prove that a teacher's supervision was negligent. . . .

Negligence can be established only upon a showing that the teacher's or supervisor's actions amounted to a deviation from what a reasonable and prudent person would do under the same or similar circumstances. . . . We believe that Ms. Yeary owed Todd Cadorette, as well as all of her pupils, a duty to act reasonably under the circumstances. More specifically, in order for Ms. Yeary to discharge this duty she must instruct and supervise her students in a manner which recognizes their age and maturity.

After the trial court determines that the defendant owed the plaintiff a duty, then it must be proven that the defendant's actions or inaction constituted a breach of that duty. The failure of proper supervision of students is not sufficient to fix liability on the school unless it is also shown that such failure was the proximate cause of the plaintiff's injuries. . . . Ms. Yeary taught art classes for 25 years, and studied art as a college student. In her tenure she estimated that nine-hundred to one thousand high school students like Todd Cadorette modeled on tables in her classrooms. Ms. Yeary testified that she had never known a subject to faint as Cadorette did. This court readily concedes, as the trial court did, that proof that a person acts in a manner that is consistent with custom, or a long-standing practice, does not necessarily mean that their action is not negligent. Thus, the fact that modeling on tables might be widespread practice in high school art classrooms in Tennessee does not prevent us from deciding she was negligent.

. . . Here, we have an outgoing and vigorously healthy fifteen year old who volunteered to stand on a table and model for his art class. There is no evidence that the table was unsteady, nor is there any proof that Todd Cadorette indicated to his teacher that he was in any way ill, or physically unable to perform the task. Even after taking into consideration the fact that Cadorette stood on a four foot high table, thereby increasing the "gravity of the possible harm," we cannot say that a "falling type injury," is foreseeable when viewing the record as a whole.

. . . At trial expert medical testimony explained the phenomena which caused Todd Cadorette to faint, that is that his locked knees prevented the normal flow of blood to the head. While comprehending this expert testimony is not too difficult for a layman, we do not think it can be considered to be a matter of common knowledge. The . . . evidence supports the trial court's finding that Ms. Yeary was not negligent in permitting Todd Cadorette to stand on a four foot high table in order to provide a model for an art class. . . .

The judgment of the trial court is affirmed. . . .

LUBITZ V. WELLS
113 A.2D 147 (CONN. SUPER. CT. 1955)

The complaint alleges that James Wells was the owner of a golf club and that he left it for some time lying on the ground in the backyard of his home. That thereafter his son, the defendant James Wells, Jr., aged eleven years, while playing in the yard with the plaintiff, Judith Lubitz, aged nine years, picked up the golf club and proceeded to swing at a stone lying on the ground. In swinging the golf club, James Wells, Jr., caused the club to strike the plaintiff about the jaw and chin. . . .

In an attempt to hold the boy's father, James Wells, liable . . . , it is alleged that James Wells was negligent because although he knew the golf club was on the ground in his backyard and that his children would play with it, and that although he knew or "should have known" that the negligent use of the golf club by children would cause injury to a child, he neglected to remove the golf club from the backyard or to caution James Wells, Jr., against the use of the same.

The demurrer challenges the sufficiency of the allegations of the complaint to state a cause of action or to support a judgment against the father, James Wells.

It would hardly be good sense to hold that this golf club is so obviously and intrinsically dangerous that it is negligence to leave it lying on the ground in the yard. The father cannot be held liable on the allegations of this complaint. [Cases omitted.]

The demurrer is sustained.

QUESTIONS

1   Would the analysis of this case have differed if plaintiff had been struck with a baseball bat instead of with a golf club? With a stick? A boomerang? Bow and arrow? A gun? Why or why not?

B. DUTY

"Duty" usually is listed as the first element in a negligence cause of action. Defendant is responsible for harm that his conduct causes to plaintiff only if he owed plaintiff a duty to guard against that harm. It has often been said that the duty that a defendant owes to a plaintiff depends on the nature of the relationship between the defendant and the plaintiff. Frequently, the necessary relationship is created by defendant's decision to engage in conduct that presents a risk of harm to the plaintiff.

1. AFFIRMATIVE ACT

The most common starting point for any analysis of tort duty is the proposition that there is no general duty to act. (Of course, there are exceptions.) One traditional way to think of the idea that there is no general duty to act is to divide the universe of harms to plaintiffs into two broad categories – harms resulting from defendant's misfeasance and harms resulting from defendant's nonfeasance. "Misfeasance" is harm caused by defendant's affirmative act that leaves plaintiff worse off, and "nonfeasance" is harm caused by defendant's failure to act that leaves plaintiff no worse off but merely fails to confer a benefit or protection.

Most tort cases involve "misfeasance" i.e. defendant's alleged breach of duty is based on defendant's affirmative act, not on defendant's failure to act. In this sort of case, the question of duty is easy – tort law imposes a general duty on one who chooses to act. Any time a party chooses to act in a way that creates a foreseeable risk of harm to others, the acting party undertakes the duty to act in such a way that the risk thereby created is a reasonable one. If defendant's affirmative act has caused harm to another, it is certain that defendant owed plaintiff a duty of care – only breach, causation and damage would be at issue.

WEIRUM V. RKO GENERAL, INC.
539 P.2D 36 (CAL. 1975)

. . . The facts are not disputed. Radio station KHJ is a successful Los Angeles broadcaster with a large teenage following. . . . In order to attract an even larger portion of the available audience and thus increase advertising revenue, KHJ inaugurated in July of 1970 a promotion entitled "The Super Summer Spectacular." The "spectacular," with a budget of approximately $40,000 for the month, was specifically designed to make the radio station "more exciting." Among the programs included in the "spectacular" was a contest broadcast on July 16, 1970, the date of the accident.

On that day, Donald Steele Revert, known professionally as "The Real Don Steele," a KHJ disc jockey and television personality, traveled in a conspicuous red automobile to a number of locations in the Los Angeles metropolitan area. Periodically, he apprised KHJ of his where-abouts and his intended destination, and the station broadcast the information to its listeners. The first person to physically locate Steele and fulfill a specified condition received a cash prize. . . . In addition, the winning contestant participated in a brief interview on the air with "The Real Don Steele." . . .

17-year-old Robert Sentner was listening to KHJ in his car while searching for "The Real Don Steele." Upon hearing that "The Real Don Steele" was proceeding to Canoga Park, he immediately drove to that vicinity. Meanwhile . . . , 19-year-old Marsha Baime heard and responded to the same information. Both of them arrived at the Holiday Theater in Canoga Park to find that someone had already claimed the prize. Without knowledge of the other, each decided to follow the Steele vehicle to its next stop and thus be the first to arrive when the next contest question or condition was announced.

For the next few miles the Sentner and Baime cars jockeyed for position closest to the Steele vehicle, reaching speeds up to 80 miles an hour.[2] About a mile and a half from the Westlake off ramp the two teenagers heard the following broadcast: "11:13-The Real Don Steele with bread is heading for Thousand Oaks to give it away. Keep listening to KHJ . . . The Real Don Steele out on the highway-with bread to give away-be on the lookout, he may stop in Thousand Oaks and may stop along the way . . . . Looks like it may be a good stop Steele-drop some bread to those folks."

The Steele vehicle left the freeway at the Westlake off ramp. Either Baime or Sentner, in attempting to follow, forced decedent's car onto the center divider, where it overturned. Baime stopped to report the accident. Sentner, after pausing momentarily to relate the tragedy to a passing peace officer, continued to pursue Steele, successfully located him and collected a cash prize.

Decedent's wife and children brought an action for wrongful death against Sentner, Baime, PKO General, Inc. as owner of KHJ, and the maker of decedent's car. Sentner settled prior to the commencement of trial for the limits of his insurance policy. The jury returned a verdict against Baime and KHJ in the amount of $300,000 and found in favor of the manufacturer of decedent's car. KHJ appeals . . . . Baime did not appeal. . . . The primary question for our determination is whether defendant owed a duty to decedent arising out of its broadcast of the giveaway contest. The determination of duty is primarily a question of law. . . . Any number of considerations may justify the imposition of duty in particular circumstances, including the guidance of history, our continually refined concepts of morals and justice, the convenience of the rule, and social judgment as to where the loss should fall. . . . While the question whether one owes a duty to another must be decided on a case-by-case basis, every case is governed by the rule of general application that all persons are required to use ordinary care to prevent others from being injured as the result of their conduct. . . .

It is of no consequence that the harm to decedent was inflicted by third parties acting negligently. Defendant invokes the maxim that an actor is entitled to assume that others will not act negligently. This concept is valid, however, only to the extent the intervening conduct was

---

2   It is not contended that the Steele vehicle at any time exceeded the speed limit.

not to be anticipated. If the likelihood that a third person may react in a particular manner is a hazard which makes the actor negligent, such reaction whether innocent or negligent does not prevent the actor from being liable for the harm caused thereby. Here, reckless conduct by youthful contestants, stimulated by defendant's broadcast, constituted the hazard to which decedent was exposed.

It is true, of course, that virtually every act involves some conceivable danger. Liability is imposed only if the risk of harm resulting from the act is deemed unreasonable-i.e., if the gravity and likelihood of the danger outweigh the utility of the conduct involved. . . . We need not belabor the grave risk inherent in the contest broadcast by defendant. . . . Obviously, neither the entertainment afforded by the contest nor its commercial rewards can justify the creation of such a grave risk. . . .

Defendant, relying upon the rule stated in section 315 of the Restatement Second of Torts, urges that it owed no duty of care to decedent. The section provides that, absent a special relationship, an actor is under no duty to control the conduct of third parties. As explained hereinafter, this rule has no application if the plaintiff's complaint, as here, is grounded upon an affirmative act of defendant which created an undue risk of harm.

The rule stated in section 315 is merely a refinement of the general principle embodied in section 314[5] that one is not obligated to act as a "good samaritan." (Rest.2d Torts, s 314, com. (a). . .) This doctrine is rooted in the common law distinction between action and inaction, or misfeasance and nonfeasance. Misfeasance exists when the defendant is responsible for making the plaintiff's position worse, i.e., defendant has created a risk. Conversely, nonfeasance is found when the defendant has failed to aid plaintiff through beneficial intervention. As section 315 illustrates, liability for nonfeasance is largely limited to those circumstances in which some special relationship can be established. If, on the other hand, the act complained of is one of misfeasance, the question of duty is governed by the standards of ordinary care discussed above.

Here, there can be little doubt that we review an act of misfeasance to which section 315 is inapplicable. Liability is not predicated upon defendant's failure to intervene for the benefit of decedent but rather upon its creation of an unreasonable risk of harm to him. . . . Defendant's reliance upon cases which involve the failure to prevent harm to another is therefore misplaced
. . . .

The judgment and the orders appealed from are affirmed. . . .

NOTE

1   *Question of Law.* As stated by the *Weirum* Corut, whether defendant owes plaintiff a duty on a particular set of facts is treated as a question of law for the court, not a question of fact for the jury. But disputed factual questions that the jury must answer may impact the court's determination whether a duty exists.

---

5   Section 314, states: "The fact that the actor realizes or should realize that action on his part is necessary for another's aid or protection does not of itself impose upon him a duty to take such action."

2. DUTY TO RESCUE

LUKE 10:25-37

And, behold, a certain lawyer stood up, and tempted him, saying, Master, what shall I do to inherit eternal life? He said unto him, What is written in the law? how readest thou? And he answering said, Thou shalt love the Lord thy God with all thy heart, and with all thy soul, and with all thy strength, and with all thy mind; and thy neighbour as thyself. And he said unto him, Thou hast answered right: this do, and thou shalt live. But he, willing to justify himself, said unto Jesus, And who is my neighbour? And Jesus answering said, A certain man went down from Jerusalem to Jericho, and fell among thieves, which stripped him of his raiment, and wounded him, and departed, leaving him half dead. And by chance there came down a certain priest that way: and when he saw him, he passed by on the other side. And likewise a Levite, when he was at the place, came and looked on him, and passed by on the other side. But a certain Samaritan, as he journeyed, came where he was: and when he saw him, he had compassion on him, And went to him, and bound up his wounds, pouring in oil and wine, and set him on his own beast, and brought him to an inn, and took care of him. And on the morrow when he departed, he took out two pence, and gave them to the host, and said unto him, Take care of him; and whatsoever thou spendest more, when I come again, I will repay thee. Which now of these three, thinkest thou, was neighbour unto him that fell among the thieves? And he said, He that shewed mercy on him. Then said Jesus unto him, Go, and do thou likewise.

QUESTIONS

1   What does Jesus teach in this passage about moral obligation?
2   Should the civil law demand this sort of moral obligation?
3   Should the civil law include all moral obligations?
4   Should the civil law include any moral obligations as such?
5   If the civil law is to include some subset of moral obligation, how should that subset be defined?

American common law has not yet recognized a general duty to be a "Good Samaritan." To the extent that such a duty may exist, it is a moral duty only, not a legal one. Under Anglo-American law, there is no general civil duty to confer a benefit on another. But in recent decades, courts have somewhat eroded the general rule that there is no duty to rescue. A difficult question that advocates of an affirmative duty to render aid must answer is how to measure when the duty "kicks in."

Since there is no general duty to come to the aid of another, a legal duty owed by one to another usually depends on some relationship between the parties. Such a relationship can be formed in a number of ways. The most basic and common way is, as discussed in the immediately preceding section, through the voluntary act of defendant, which creates a duty toward those to whom defendant's act poses a foreseeable risk of harm. Such scenarios involve clear cases of misfeasance.

But not all breach of duty scenarios involve clear cases of misfeasance. The more difficult duty cases are those cases where plaintiff is not harmed by defendant's affirmative act – in other words, cases of mere nonfeasance. These generally will be cases of no liability unless the plaintiff can establish some relationship between the parties that supports an affirmative duty to rescue. Some cases will be clear, while others will be close calls.

A defendant's conduct that could sensibly be characterized as a nonfeasance may be treated as a misfeasance by taking into consideration other conduct by the defendant that necessitates further action on his part. The key may be whether defendant's conduct, taken as a whole, leaves plaintiff worse off. As you review the following cases involving questions of duty, think about whether defendant's conduct is more naturally characterized as a misfeasance or as a nonfeasance.

a. The No Duty Rule

YANIA V. BIGAN
155 A.2D 343 (PA. 1959)

. . . On September 25, 1957 John E. Bigan was engaged in a coal strip-mining operation . . . . On the property being stripped were large cuts or trenches created by Bigan when he removed the earthen overburden for the purpose of removing the coal underneath. One cut contained water 8 to 10 feet in depth with side walls or embankments 16 to 18 feet in height; at this cut Bigan had installed a pump to remove the water.

At approximately 4 p.m. on that date, Joseph F. Yania, the operator of another coal strip-mining operation, and one Boyd M. Ross went upon Bigan's property for the purpose of discussing a business matter with Bigan, and, while there, were asked by Bigan to aid him in starting the pump. Ross and Bigan entered the cut and stood at the point where the pump was located. Yania stood at the top of one of the cut's side walls and then jumped from the side wall—a height of 16 to 18 feet—into the water and was drowned.

Yania's widow, in her own right and on behalf of her three children, instituted wrongful death and survival actions against Bigan contending Bigan was responsible for Yania's death. [The trial judge dismissed the complaint.]

. . . Summarized, Bigan stands charged with three-fold negligence: (1) by urging, enticing, taunting and inveigling Yania to jump into the water; (2) by failing to warn Yania of a dangerous condition on the land, i.e., the cut wherein law 8 to 10 feet of water; (3) by failing to go to Yania's rescue after he had jumped into the water. . . . The complaint does not allege that Yania slipped or that he was pushed or that Bigan made any physical impact upon Yania. . . . Had Yania been a child of tender years or a person mentally deficient then it is conceivable that taunting and enticement could constitute actionable negligence if it resulted in harm. However to contend that such conduct directed to an adult in full possessionof all his mental faculties constitututes actionable negligence is not only without precedent but completely without merit.

. . . *The only* condition on Bigan's land which could possibly have contributed in any manner to Yania's death was the water-filled cut with its high embankment. Of this condition there was neither concealment nor failure to warn, but, on the contrary, the complaint specifically avers that Bigan not only requested Yania and Boyd to assist him in started the pump to remove the water from the cut but "led" them to the cut itself. If this cut possessed any potentiality of danger, such a condition was as obvious and apparent to Yania as to Bigan, both coal strip-mine operators. Under the circumstances herein depicted Bigan could not be held liable in this respect.

Lastly, it is urged that Bigan failed to take the necessary steps to rescue Yania from the water. The mere fact that Bigan saw Yania in a position of peril in the water imposed upon him no legal, although a moral, obligation or duty to go to his rescue unless Bigan was legally responsible, in whole or in part, for placing Yania in the perilous position. . . . The complaint does not aver any facts which impose upon Bigan legal responsibility for placing Yania in the dangerous position in the water and, absent such legal responsibility, the law imposes on Bigan no duty of rescue. . . .

NOTES

1   Some states by statute criminally punish one who fails to help another in distress.

2   In a fascinating study, Professor David Hyman concludes that cases of non-rescue in America are exceptionally rare. David A. Hyman, Rescue Without Law: An Empirical Perspective on the Duty to Rescue, 84 Tex. L. Rev. 653 (2006).

3   *"Good Samaritan" Statutes.* Although the rule at common law is that there is no general duty to rescue, some jurisdictions have adopted by statute a limited requirement to render aid in an emergency. All American jurisdictions have adopted some form of "Good Samaritan" Statute, which insulates some classes of rescuers, or even rescuers generally, from civil suits that claim the rescue attempts were negligent.

b. Defendant Created Peril

One exception to the no-duty-to-rescue rule that arguably might have applied in *Yania v. Bigan* is that defendant sometimes owes a duty to rescue plaintiff from a peril created by defendant.

MONTGOMERY V. NATIONAL CONVOY & TRUCKING CO.
195 s.e. 247 (s.c. 1938)

. . . There are thirteen specifications of negligence . . . contained in the complaint . . . . The case was . . . submitted to the jury, and it found in favor of respondent against both appellants in the full amount demanded in the complaint, $3,000.00, as actual damage. . . . [C]ounsel for appellants have reduced the issues to . . . (2) Was it error not to hold as a matter of law . . . that there was no actionable negligence on the part of this appellant? . . .

December 1, 1936, the day on which the collision occurred and respondent received her injuries, was a cold, disagreeable day, and on various sections of the main highway leading from Spartanburg, S.C. to Charlotte, N.C., rain and sleet fell, causing the highways to become quite slick in places. Respondent, whose home was in Spartanburg, S.C. had gone to Charlotte that morning . . . . Returning, they . . . proceeded to drive slowly in the direction of Spartanburg. . . . [A]s respondent's automobile came around a curve at the crest of a long hill, and when the car was sufficiently around the curve on the crest of the hill for the lights of the car to focus on the highway leading down the hill, respondent's chauffeur observed the trucks of appellants, which had completely blocked the highway, said trucks being about fifty-one feet from the point where he could see them. The chauffeur at the time was operating the car at not more than 20 miles per hour, due to the condition of the highway. He applied his brakes and put the car in reverse gear, but by reason of the ice on the highway and decline the car slid on . . . into the truck of the appellant, Frank G. North, Inc., which was stalled on the highway, a little to the north of where the truck of appellant National Convoy & Trucking Company was stalled, completely blocking the traffic line of the highway . . . . In this collision, respondent received her injuries. There is evidence that the lights of one of the trucks were burning, and fuses or flares burning at the location where the trucks were stalled, but that at the crest of the hill and curve in the highway there were no lights or other warning attempted to be given the public using the highway traveling in a southerly direction. The agents of appellants operating the trucks knew, or had every reason to know, that once a car had passed the crest of the hill and started down the decline, . . . it would be impossible to stop such automobile or motor vehicle due to the icy condition of the highway, regardless of the rate of speed at which such automobile may be traveling. The trucks of appellant had entirely blocked the highway for fifteen minutes prior to the automobile of respondent reaching the point of the collision, and as aforesaid, there was evidence that appellants failed to warn travelers approaching from the north by the putting out of lights or flares or the flagging of such traffic at the crest of the hill and the curve of the road, the only place, under the conditions of the road on that day, a warning would be of any avail. Several people had congregated at the place where the trucks were stalled, but none was requested to flag oncoming vehicles from the north.

. . . [W]e will briefly relate the circumstances under which the road was blocked. As the truck of appellant National Convoy & Trucking Company undertook to negotiate the hill, . . . due to the icy condition of the highway, it stalled and commenced to slide backward down the hill, and it was necessary to jackknife the tractor of the truck in order to avoid sliding down the hill, which entirely blocked the right-hand side of the road traveling in a northerly direction; and there is some testimony that a portion of the tractor extended across the middle of the highway thereby partially blocking travel to the south. The operators of this truck put out a . . . flare to the rear of the truck and left the scene for help, and there is some testimony that the lights of the truck were left burning. A little later the truck of appellant Frank G. North, Inc., heavily loaded and traveling towards Charlotte, reached the point where the truck of its co-appellant was stalled, and attempted to drive around same although it was necessary that the left-hand wheels of the truck leave the pavement in order to get around it; and as this last truck reached a point a little to the north of the truck it was undertaking to pass, it also stalled and commenced to slide down the hill, and it was necessary for the driver thereof to jackknife the tractor on this truck in order to prevent it from sliding down the hill. . . .

One may be negligent by acts of omission as well as of commission, and liability therefore will attach if the act of omission of a duty owed another, under the circumstances, is the . . . cause of the injury. . . . One of the acts of negligence alleged in the complaint is the failure of the appellants to warn approaching vehicles of the conditions existing, and this necessarily means that the warning should be given at a point where it would be effective. . . . [I]f appellants owed a duty to others using the highway, . . . the performance of such duty was not met by merely having lights at the point where the trucks blocked the highway, but it was incumbent on the appellants to take such precautions as would reasonably be calculated to prevent injury.

For the moment let us repeat some of the facts. There is a curve in the highway at the crest of a long hill. A short distance to the south of the curve and crest of the hill two trucks are stalled and block the entire road. It is a much-traveled highway. Respondent's chauffeur testified that due to the curve in the road and the hill, the lights of an automobile approaching from the north would not focus on the trucks until the automobile was within a little over fifty feet from the trucks. Once a car passed the crest of the hill and commenced to descend on the south side, it could not be stopped due to the ice on the highway—the slippery condition thereof, which was known or should have been known to appellants. No flagman nor warning of any description was placed at the crest of the hill to warn approaching cars. That a warning at the crest of the hill would have been effective and prevented the injury is fully demonstrated from other evidence had upon the trial. . . .

And the judgment of the Circuit Court is affirmed.

NOTES AND QUESTIONS

1   Is plaintiff seeking to hold defendant liable for a nonfeasance?
2   Is it possible to distinguish the result in *Montgomery* from the result in *Yania*? Can you articulate a rule that would impose a duty on defendant here but that would not impose a general duty to rescue motorists in plaintiff's position?

TUBBS V. ARGUS
225 N.E.2D 841 (1967)

. . . On January 28, 1959 at approximately 12:00 Noon, the appellant was riding as a guest passenger in the right front seat of an automobile owned and operated by the appellee in the 100 block west of West Hampton Drive in the City of Indianapolis, Indiana. While traveling in an easterly direction the automobile was driven over the south curb of West Hampton Drive and into a tree, resulting in injury to the appellant. After the said collision, the appellee abandoned the automobile and did not render reasonable aid and assistance to the injured appellant. Appellant alleges that she suffered additional injuries as a result of appellee's failure to render reasonable aid and assistance and seeks to recover only for these additional injuries. In her assignment of errors, the appellant . . . alleges that appellee's failure to render reasonable aid and assistance constituted a breach of a common law duty. The appellee contends that throughout the appellant's occupancy of the said motor vehicle, she was a guest as defined under the "Guest Statute", which limited liability to those injuries resulting from wanton and willful misconduct and thus precluded liability for negligence. . . .

A literal interpretation of this statute leads this court to the conclusion that the motor vehicle operator is not liable for injuries resulting from the operation of said vehicle, unless caused by his wanton and willful misconduct.

Before the appellee in the case at bar can invoke this statute to preclude herself from liability for negligence, the injuries must result from the operation of said motor vehicle.

The appellant herein is seeking recovery for additional injuries arising from the appellee's failure to render reasonable aid and assistance, and not for the initial injuries which resulted from the operation of the automobile. It is the opinion of this Court that appellant's cause of action for additional injuries is outside the scope of Sec. 47-1021 because these additional injuries did not arise until after the operation of the said automobile had ceased. Sec. 47-1021 is only applicable to those injuries resulting from the operation of the said vehicle. Thus the appellee cannot invoke Sec. 47-1021, *supra,* to limit his liability for these additional injuries to acts of wanton and willful misconduct.

At common law, there is no general duty to aid a person who is in peril. . . . However, in *L. S. Ayres & Company,* . . . 40 N.E.2d page 337, the Supreme Court of Indiana held that "under some circumstances, moral and humanitarian considerations may require one to render assistance to another who has been injured, even though the injury was not due to negligence on his part and may have been caused by the negligence of the injured person. Failure to render assistance in such a situation may constitute actionable negligence if the injury is aggravated through lack of due care." *Tippecanoe Loan, etc., Co. v. Cleveland, etc. R. Co.* (1915), 57 Ind.App. 644, 104 N.E. 866, 106 N.E. 739 . . . .

In *Tippecanoe Loan, etc., Co. v. Cleveland, etc. R. Co., supra,* this court held that a railroad company was liable for failing to provide medical assistance to an employee who was injured through no fault of the railroad company, but who was rendered helpless and by reason of which the employee's injuries were aggravated.

The Supreme Court of Indiana in *L. S. Ayres, supra,* found the appellant liable for aggravation of injuries when it failed to extricate the appellee, a six year old boy, whose fingers were caught in the moving parts of an escalator, even though the jury conclusively established that the appellant was not negligent with respect to the choice, construction, or manner of operating the elevator. In so holding, the Supreme Court stated that it may be deduced from *Tippecanoe*

Loan, etc. Co. v. Cleveland, etc. R. Co., supra, "that there may be a legal obligation to take positive or affirmative steps to effect the rescue of a person who is helpless and in a situation of peril, when the one proceeded against is a master or an invitor or when the injury resulted from use of an instrumentality under the control of the defendant."

The doctrine of law as set forth in Restatement (Second) of Torts, s 322 . . . adds credence to these two Indiana cases. "* * * If the actor knows or has reason to know that by his conduct, whether tortious or innocent, he has caused such bodily harm to another as to make him helpless and in danger of future harm, the actor is under a duty to exercise reasonable care to prevent such further harm."

One distinction between the *Ayres, supra,* and *Tippecanoe, supra,* cases and the case at bar is that both of the former cases involve situations where an economic advantage flows to the defendant, while the case at bar does not. It is the opinion of this Court that an affirmative duty to render reasonable aid and assistance is not limited to those cases involving the flow of an economic advantage to the alleged defendant. The court, in both the above mentioned cases, stated that other relationship may impose a like obligation and it is the opinion of the Court that the case at bar presents a situation in which an affirmative duty arises to render reasonable aid and assistance to one who is helpless and in a situation of peril, when the injury resulted from use of an instrumentality under the control of the defendant.

In the case at bar, the appellant received her injuries from an instrumentality under the control of the appellee. Under the rule stated above and on the authority of the cases cited, this was a sufficient relationship to impose a duty to render reasonable aid and assistance, a duty for the breach of which the appellee is liable for the additional injuries suffered.

We are of the opinion that the court below erred in sustaining the demurrer to appellant's Second Amended Complaint.

This cause is reversed and remanded for proceedings not inconsistent with this opinion. . . .

NOTE

1 Remember, of course, that the plaintiff's ability to establish the existence of a duty does not necessarily mean that plaintiff's suit will succeed – plaintiff must also prove breach (negligence), causation, and damages.

3. VOLUNTARY UNDERTAKING

When defendant chooses to do something that defendant otherwise had no legal obligation to do, the law may impose on defendant the obligation to act with reasonable care, even if defendant's carelessness leaves plaintiff no worse off than if defendant had declined to act at all, a choice that defendant was legally entitled to make.

OCOTILLO WEST JOINT VENTURE V. SUPERIOR COURT FOR THE COUNTY OF MARICOPA
844 P.2D 653 (1992)

FACTS

. . . In 1989 Joseph Zylka and William Easley played golf and consumed alcoholic beverages at the Ocotillo Golf Course ("Ocotillo") which is operated by the petitioners. Because Zylka appeared intoxicated, two Ocotillo employees took possession of Zylka's car keys. At that time, Easley stepped forward and offered to drive Zylka home. With that assurance, and observing Easley's apparent lack of impairment, the two employees gave Zylka's keys to Easley. Once in the parking lot, Easley returned the keys to Zylka. Zylka left the golf course in his own automobile and was involved in a one car accident. He subsequently died from his injuries.

The respondents brought a wrongful death action against the golf course alleging that Ocotillo's sale of alcohol to Zylka was the cause of the accident. The petitioners filed a notice of nonparty at fault . . . alleging that Easley was at least partially at fault because he volunteered to drive Zylka home and then gave the car keys back to Zylka. The respondents filed a motion for summary judgment asking the court to dismiss the petitioners' allegation of a nonparty at fault. The trial judge treated the motion for summary judgment as a motion to strike the notice of nonparty at fault and granted it. The petitioners then brought this special action. . . .

DISCUSSION

. . . To find a person at fault in a negligence action, four elements must be shown: 1) duty, 2) breach of duty, 3) causation, and 4) damages. . . . Whether a duty exists is usually a question of law for the court to decide. [Cases omitted.] The petitioners argue that Easley had a duty to Zylka under the good samaritan doctrine. The doctrine . . . is set forth in two sections of the Restatement (Second) of Torts (1986) . . . . Restatement § 323 provides:

> One who undertakes, gratuitously or for consideration to render services to another which he should recognize as necessary for the protection of the other's person or things, is subject to liability to the other for physical harm resulting from his failure to exercise reasonable care to perform his undertaking, if
> a. his failure to exercise such care increases the risk of harm, or
> b. the harm is suffered because of the other's reliance upon the undertaking.

Restatement § 324 provides:

> One who, being under no duty to do so, takes charge of another who is helpless adequately to aid or protect himself is subject to liability to the other for any bodily harm caused to him by

a. the failure of the actor to exercise reasonable care to secure the safety of the other while within the actor's charge, or

b. the actor's discontinuing his aid or protection, if by so doing he leaves the other in a worse position than when the actor took charge of him.

Although the trial judge focused on § 324 in his order, we find that both sections of the Restatement are applicable to the facts of this case. The only difference between the two sections is the particular feature of § 324 that the plaintiff is in a helpless position. Section 323 has no such requirement. In either event, we believe the good samaritan doctrine applies when an actor, otherwise without any duty to do so, voluntarily takes charge of an intoxicated person who is attempting to drive a vehicle and, because of the actor's failure to exercise reasonable care, has changed the other's position for the worse. Restatement § 323 and § 324 cmts. b and c. The rule applies to this situation because if Easley had not said that he would see that Zylka got home safely, the petitioners might have taken steps that would have avoided the accident. . . .

When Easley took charge of Zylka for reasons of safety he thereby assumed a duty to use reasonable care. Zylka was too drunk to drive. Under one version of the facts Ocotillo's employees had taken charge of Zylka and effectively stopped him from driving. Easley's offer deterred the employees from their efforts to keep Zylka out of his automobile. Rather than use reasonable care to drive Zylka home or make alternative arrangements, Easley discontinued his assistance and put Zylka in a worse position than he was in when Ocotillo's employees had possession of his keys. A reasonable fact finder could conclude that Easley's actions contributed to Zylka's death, rendering Easley wholly or partially at fault.

We conclude that the trial court erred in striking Easley as a nonparty at fault and therefore reverse and remand for further proceedings.

H. R. MOCH CO. V. RENSSELAER WATER CO.
159 N.E. 896 (N.Y. 1928)

The defendant . . . made a contract with the city of Rensselaer for the supply of water during a term of years. . . . While this contract was in force, a building caught fire. The flames, spreading to the plaintiff's warehouse nearby, destroyed it and its contents. The defendant according to the complaint was promptly notified of the fire, "but omitted and neglected after such notice, to supply or furnish sufficient or adequate quantity of water, with adequate pressure to stay, suppress or extinguish the fire before it reached the warehouse of the plaintiff, although the pressure and supply which the defendant was equipped to supply and furnish, and had agreed by said contract to supply and furnish, was adequate and sufficient to prevent the spread of the fire to and the destruction of the plaintiff's warehouse and its contents." By reason of the failure of the defendant to "fulfill the provisions of the contract between it and the city of Rensselaer," the plaintiff is said to have suffered damage, for which judgment is demanded. A motion, in the nature of a demurrer, to dismiss the complaint, was denied at Special Term. The Appellate Division reversed by a divided court. . . .

"It is ancient learning that one who assumes to act, even though gratuitously, may thereby become subject to the duty of acting carefully, if he acts at all" (*Glanzer v. Shepard*, 233 N.Y. 236, 239 . . .). The plaintiff would bring its case within the orbit of that principle. The hand once set to a task may not always be withdrawn with impunity though liability would fail if it had never been applied at all. A time-honored formula often phrases the distinction as one between misfeasance and nonfeasance. Incomplete the formula is, and so at times misleading. Given a relation involving in its existence a duty of care irrespective of a contract, a tort may result as well from acts of omission as of commission in the fulfillment of the duty thus recognized by law . . . . What we need to know is not so much the conduct to be avoided when the relation and its attendant duty are established as existing. What we need to know is the conduct that engenders the relation. It is here that the formula, however incomplete, has its value and significance. If conduct has gone forward to such a stage that inaction would commonly result, not negatively merely in withholding a benefit, but positively or actively in working an injury, there exists a relation out of which arises a duty to go forward . . . . The query always is whether the putative wrongdoer has advanced to such a point as to have launched a force or instrument of harm, or has stopped where inaction is at most a refusal to become an instrument for good . . . .

The plaintiff would have us hold that the defendant, when once it entered upon the performance of its contract with the city, was brought into such a relation with everyone who might potentially be benefited through the supply of water at the hydrants as to give to negligent performance, without reasonable notice of a refusal to continue, the quality of a tort. . . . We are satisfied that liability would be unduly and indeed indefinitely extended by this enlargement of the zone of duty. . . . The failure in such circumstances to furnish an adequate supply of water is at most the denial of a benefit. It is not the commission of a wrong. . . .

The judgment should be affirmed with costs.

ERIE RR. CO. V. STEWART
40 F.2D 855 (6TH CIR. 1930)

Stewart, plaintiff below, was a passenger in an automobile truck . . . . He recovered a judgment in the District Court for injuries received when the truck was struck by one of the defendant's trains at the 123d Street crossing in the city of Cleveland. Defendant maintained a watchman at this crossing, which was admittedly heavily traveled, but the watchman was either within the shanty or just outside of it as the train approached, and he gave no warning until too late to avoid the accident. . . .

The . . . appellant presents the question whether the court erred in charging the jury that the absence of the watchman, where one had been maintained by the defendant company at a highway crossing over a long period of time to the knowledge of the plaintiff, would constitute negligence . . . . In the present case it is conceded that the employment of the watchman by the defendant was voluntary upon its part, there being no statute or ordinance requiring the same, and that plaintiff had knowledge of this practice and relied upon the absence of the watchman as an assurance of safety and implied invitation to cross. We are not now concerned with the extent of the duty owing to one who had no notice of the prior practice . . . . The question is simply whether there was any positive duty owing to the plaintiff in respect to the maintenance of such watchman . . . .

Where . . . there is no duty prescribed by statute or ordinance, it is usually a question for the jury whether the circumstances made the employment of a watchman necessary in the exercise of due care. Where the voluntary employment of a watchman was unknown to the traveler upon the highway, the mere absence of such watchman could probably not be considered as negligence toward him as a matter of law, for in such case[, he had not] . . . been led into reliance upon the custom. The question would remain simply whether the circumstances demanded such employment. But where the practice is known to the traveler upon the highway, and such traveler has been educated into reliance upon it, some positive duty must rest upon the railway with reference thereto. . . . The company has established for itself a standard of due care while operating its trains across the highway, and, having led the traveler into reliance upon such standard, it should not be permitted thereafter to say that no duty required, arose from, or attached to these precautions.

This duty has been recognized as not only actual and positive, but as absolute, in the sense that the practice may not be discontinued without exercising reasonable care to give warning of such discontinuance, although the company may thereafter do all that would otherwise be reasonably necessary. Conceding for the purposes of this opinion that, in cases where a watchman is voluntarily employed by the railway in an abundance of precaution, the duty is not absolute, . . . still, if there be some duty, it cannot be less than that the company must use reasonable care to see that reliance by members of the educated public upon its representation of safety is not converted into a trap. Responsibility for injury will arise if the service be negligently performed or abandoned without other notice of that fact. . . .

The judgment of the District Court is affirmed.

NOTES AND QUESTIONS

1   Explain how plaintiff here is left worse off in the case of the missing watchman than plaintiff would have been in the case in which defendant never provided a watchman in the first place.

2   If defendant here breached a duty to maintain an adequate watch that it voluntarily provided, is it ever possible to discontinue such a voluntary watch without a breach of duty? If defendant reasonably determined that a watchman at this intersection was no longer warranted, is there anything that defendant can do to discontinue the watch without running the risk of liability?

3   Section 90 of the Restatement of Contracts famously provides that a promise by defendant plus reasonable reliance by plaintiff supplies the consideration necessary to make defendant's promise enforceable.

4. SPECIAL RELATIONSHIPS

The clearest case for the general rule of no duty to act for the protection of others is that a defendant owes no affirmative duty to a pure stranger. But where the defendant bears a special relationship either to the plaintiff or to some third-party wrongdoer, the rule can be quite different. For example, it is generally recognized that parents owe a duty to their children by virtue of that special relationship. Courts have found several other types of relationships to give rise to a "duty to rescue" plaintiff from a third party, e.g., common carrier-passenger relationships, custodial relationships, and landlord-tenant relationships.

a. DEFENDANT'S RELATIONSHIP TO PLAINTIFF

APPLEBAUM V. NEMON
678 s.w.2d 533 (1984)

This wrongful death and survival action was brought by appellees, David Nemon and Suzanne Nemon, for the death of their two year old son, Howard Nemon against appellants, Montessori Educational Corp. of Texas, d/b/a Houston Children's Center, and its officers and employees, Sanford Applebaum, Marilyn Applebaum, Noreen DeBoy, and Jackie Jones. Appellees delivered Howard into the care and custody of Houston Children's Center on December 19, 1980.

The testimony concerning the circumstances of Howard Nemon's death was as follows. After Howard was delivered to the day care center on December 19, 1980 by his parents, he was taken outdoors for twenty to twenty-five minutes of free play. Jackie Jones observed Howard playing on various equipment. A short time later, Jackie Jones began lining the children up to return inside and discovered Howard with his head on the playground equipment known as the platform, feet touching the ground with his hands near his head. After Howard did not respond to clapping hands, she went over and picked Howard up and laid him on the platform. She then summoned Sanford Applebaum who examined Howard for ten seconds and then called the operator to obtain an ambulance. Applebaum returned to Howard and rendered mouth-to-mouth resuscitation for two to three minutes. He then telephoned the fire department direct for an ambulance a second time, because the ambulance had not yet arrived. He returned to Howard and continued mouth-to-mouth resuscitation until the ambulance arrived. Howard was transported by the ambulance to Southwest Memorial Hospital. He was later transported to Texas Children's Hospital where he was pronounced dead at 2:59 p.m. on December 22, 1980. Howard was brain dead at the time he first received treatment at the hospital.

By special issues the jury (1) failed to find that Howard Nemon was injured on the playground; (2) found that the day care center's failure to provide adequate life-saving aid to Howard was negligence proximately causing his death; (3) found that the day care center's failure to instruct its employees in proper measures to be taken in an emergency was negligence proximately causing Howard's death; and (4) assessed values for various types of damages. The trial court rendered judgment on the verdict for appellees in the amount of $304,822.53 against appellees. ... We find no evidence to support the jury findings of negligence and proximate cause against appellants. We therefore reverse and render.

Appellant contends . . . that the jury's findings that appellant was negligent in (1) failing to provide adequate and proper life-saving aid to Howard Nemon and (2) failing to instruct its employees as to the proper measures to be taken in the event of an emergency on its premises are immaterial because appellant did not owe a duty to provide adequate life-saving aid or to instruct its employees in emergency procedures. There can be no liability if the defendant has not breached a duty which he owed to the plaintiff. . . .

There is no Texas statute or regulation which imposes on day care centers these specific duties. We must determine whether these duties arise from the common law.

Deeply rooted in the common law is the doctrine that a person owes no duty to render aid to one for whose initial injury he is not liable. . . . However, in other jurisdictions, it has been held that certain relationships may impose a duty to render assistance to one for whose initial injury he is not liable.

The relationship between Howard Nemon and appellants was that which exists between a child and the day care center to which the care of the child has been entrusted. The relationship is an economic one in which the day care center in exchange for a fee agrees to care for the child and to protect the child from harm during the time the child is in the custody of the day care center. We hold this relationship includes both an implied agreement and a duty to render reasonable assistance to a child in its custody who becomes imperiled.

Restatement of the Law of Torts, Second, § 314 provides in part:

1. A common carrier is under a duty to its passengers to take reasonable action...

   b. to give them first aid after it knows or has reason to know that they are ill or injured, and to care for them until they can be cared for by others.

3. A possessor of land who holds it open to the public is under a similar duty to members of the public who enter in response to his invitation.

4. One who is required by law to take or who voluntarily takes custody of another under circumstances such as to deprive the other of his normal opportunities for protection is under a similar duty to the other.

Appellants, as the day care center with custody of Howard Nemon, would come under either subsection three or four of § 314. Illustration seven under § 314 demonstrates the duty and liability which can arise from the relationship which existed between appellants and Howard Nemon.

7. A is a small child sent by his parents for the day to B's kindergarten. In the course of the day A becomes ill with scarlet fever. Although recognizing that A is seriously ill, B does nothing to obtain medical assistance, or to take the child home or remove him to a place where help can be obtained. As a result, A's illness is aggravated in a manner which proper medical attention would have avoided.

The relationship giving rise to the duty to render aid in this cause is analogous to the relationship between a student and the school which he attends. The courts have been quick to recognize that this relationship gives rise to a duty to render assistance to a student initially injured without the fault of the school. . . . Although there is no authority in this state which applies the duty to render aid to a day care center we choose to follow the Restatement of the Law of Torts 2d Ed. and the law of other jurisdictions which hold that day care centers have a duty to render aid to children in their custody. The imposition of this duty is consistent with the Minimum Standards for Day Care Centers promulgated by the Texas Department of Human Resources. These standards require day care centers to give first aid when needed, to call the physician named by the child's parents in the case of critical injury or illness, and to take the child to the nearest emergency room when necessary.

The standard of care imposed on one with a duty to render aid is explained in Comment f. of § 314, Restatement of the Law of Torts 2d.

f. The defendant is not required to take any action until he knows or has reason to know that the plaintiff is endangered, or is ill or injured. He is not required to take any action beyond that which is reasonable under the circumstances. In the case of an ill or injured person, he will seldom be required to do more than give such first aid as he reasonably can, and take reasonable steps to turn the sick man over to a physician, or to those who will look after him and see that medical assistance is obtained. He is not required to give any aid to one who is in the hands of apparently competent persons who have taken charge of him, or whose friends are present and apparently in a position to give him all necessary assistance.

The standard of care which appellants were under was whether they acted reasonably under all the circumstances in their rendition of aid. Appellants were not insurers of the life of Howard Nemon. In most circumstances a defendant will not be required to do more than administer whatever initial aid he reasonably can and knows how to do, and take reasonable steps to place the injured person in the hands of a competent physician. . . .

In fact, if the person who is charged with the duty to render aid is not possessed with medical training and he undertakes to render medical assistance, he may be liable if such assistance is found to be detrimental. . . . Courts do not expect school personnel to possess a physician's knowledge nor do they want school personnel to assume the role of physician. . . .

ISEBERG V. GROSS

879 N.E.2D 278 (ILL. 2007)

In this interlocutory appeal, plaintiffs, Mitchell Iseberg (Iseberg) and his wife, Carol, seek reversal of the order dismissing with prejudice count I of their third amended complaint, brought against defendants, Sheldon Gross (Gross) and Henry Frank (Frank). In count I, plaintiffs alleged that Gross and Frank were negligent because they failed to warn Iseberg that a former mutual business partner, Edward Slavin (Slavin), had made threats against Iseberg's life. Slavin later acted on his threats and shot Iseberg, rendering him a paraplegic.

The circuit court of Cook County dismissed the claim . . . , finding that plaintiffs failed to state a cause of action because, under the facts alleged, Gross and Frank owed no duty to warn Iseberg or to protect him from the criminal conduct of Slavin. A divided appellate court affirmed the dismissal. . . .

BACKGROUND

The facts of this case are . . . not materially in dispute.

In 1995, Slavin and Gross formed the Vernonshire Auto Laundry Group, Inc. (VAL), an Illinois corporation created for the purpose of developing Slavin's idea of building a car wash . . . . Thereafter, Gross contacted Iseberg, an attorney and real estate broker, who Gross had learned was in the process of purchasing land in the Vernon Hills area (the Leikam Farm property). Iseberg planned to purchase the Leikam Farm property and develop it into a strip mall. To that end, Iseberg had joined with Frank to form the Leikam Farm Development Corporation (LFD).

In October 1996, VAL and LFD entered into a partnership agreement, with each contributing funds toward the purchase of the Leikam Farm property. . . . On April 14, 1997, VAL tendered an offer to purchase LFD's beneficial interest in the trust. LFD refused to sell. Previously LFD, without VAL's knowledge, had assigned its 50% beneficial interest in the land trust to Frank and executed a promissory note in the amount of $352,000 in Frank's favor. VAL filed suit against LFD to enforce its rights under the partnership agreement. This legal suit was settled in September 1997 when the parties entered into a "Settlement and Joint Venture Agreement."

Pursuant to the agreement, Frank, VAL, Gross and Slavin wanted "to eliminate all Iseberg involvement with respect to the Property." Therefore, the settlement provided for the termination of the VAL-LFD partnership and the creation of the Leikam Farm Joint Venture (Venture), which had as its sole purpose the sale of the Leikam Farm property. The settlement agreement specifically provided that Iseberg was not to be a party to the Venture, that LFD's and Iseberg's interests, if any, in the property and the land trust were terminated. . . .

Despite the Venture's efforts, the Property was not sold by December 31, 1998, when monthly interest payments on the mortgage note for the property came due. Slavin, having already invested all of his savings in the project, was unable to meet his share of the monthly interest obligation. As a result, in February 1999, Slavin was forced to surrender his interest in the property, losing his entire investment.

Plaintiffs alleged that Slavin's financial demise caused him to become mentally unbalanced and that Slavin focused his anger on Iseberg, whom he blamed for his financial situation. According to statements Gross gave to the Lake County police, Slavin spoke to Gross on several occasions between the fall of 1998 and the early months of 1999 about wanting to harm Iseberg. In the beginning, Slavin talked about punching Iseberg in the face with brass knuckles. But as time passed and Slavin became more agitated, he talked about wanting to find a "hit man" and, later, he outlined a plan for killing Iseberg himself and then committing suicide. Slavin told Gross that, once the suicide exemption clause in his life insurance policy was no longer in effect, he would go to Iseberg's home, ring the doorbell, shoot Iseberg, and then kill himself so his family could collect his insurance. On at least one occasion, Slavin spoke about a plan that included killing Frank as well. Slavin also told Gross that he had purchased a gun and asked whether the caliber was large enough to kill someone.

Gross contacted Slavin's brother, Earl, to express his concerns about Slavin's threats. Gross suggested, more than once, that Earl obtain psychiatric help for his brother. Earl always demurred, assuring Gross that Slavin would never act on his threats. Gross told Frank about the threats, but neither Gross nor Frank told Iseberg.

According to Gross' statements to the police, after Slavin surrendered his interest in the Leikam Farm property in February 1999, Gross had almost no contact with Slavin. Gross said he spoke to Slavin on only three occasions over the next 11 months. Although Slavin voiced no more threats against Iseberg during this time, on one occasion Slavin asked Gross if he knew Iseberg's new address. Gross said he told Slavin he did not know the address and would not give it to him if he did.

On January 24, 2000, Slavin rang the doorbell at Iseberg's residence. When Iseberg answered the door, Slavin shot him four times. Iseberg was not killed, but was rendered a paraplegic.

In October 2001, Mitchell and Carol Iseberg filed a complaint, which was later amended to include claims against Gross and Frank. . . . In an order dated August 13, 2004, the trial court dismissed with prejudice the counts alleging negligence, negligent performance of a voluntary undertaking, and civil conspiracy. . . . Thereafter, plaintiffs brought an interlocutory appeal in the appellate court seeking reversal of the dismissal order with respect to counts I (negligence) and II (negligent performance of a voluntary undertaking). . . . On appeal, the appellate court affirmed the dismissals, with one justice dissenting. . . .

ANALYSIS

Before this court, plaintiffs' only challenge is to the dismissal of count I, the claim charging Gross and Frank with negligence for their failure to warn Iseberg of Slavin's threats. The circuit court dismissed this count . . . , finding that the facts alleged in the complaint failed to establish any basis for imposing a duty on defendants to warn or protect Iseberg from the criminal conduct of Slavin. . . . To state a legally sufficient claim of negligence, the complaint must allege facts establishing the existence of a duty of care owed by the defendants to the plaintiffs, a breach of that duty, and an injury proximately caused by that breach. . . . Whether a duty is owed is a question of law for the court to decide, while breach and proximate cause are factual matters for the jury. . . .

Because of the procedural posture of this case, the only issue before us is whether a legal duty existed. Plaintiffs do not allege that defendants owed a duty by virtue of any contract or statute. Rather, they seek to hold defendants liable for negligence under common law principles.

This case presents a question of "duty" in its most basic or "primary" sense, i.e., duty as obligation. . . . What we must decide is whether Iseberg and defendants stood in such a relationship to one another that the law imposed on defendants an obligation of reasonable conduct for the benefit of Iseberg. . . . Under common law, the universally accepted rule, articulated in section 314 of the Restatement (Second) of Torts, and long adhered to by this court, is that a private person has no duty to act affirmatively to protect another from criminal attack by a third person absent a "special relationship" between the parties. . . . When one of these special relationships exists between the parties and an unreasonable risk of physical harm arises within the scope of that relationship, an obligation may be imposed on the one to exercise reasonable care to protect the other from such risk, if the risk is reasonably foreseeable, or to render first aid when it is known that such aid is needed. *See* . . . Restatement (Second) of Torts § 314A (1965). The existence of one of these . . . "special relationships" has typically been the basis for imposing an affirmative duty to act where one would not ordinarily exist.

In the case at bar, plaintiffs do not allege that one of the above-listed "special relationships" existed. . . . Plaintiffs contend that decisions of this court have demonstrated that the "special relationship" doctrine is no longer the *sine qua non* for determining whether to impose an affirmative duty to protect against the tortious acts of a third party. Rather, plaintiffs . . . argue that, if we find that the "special relationship" analysis has not already been discarded, we should take this opportunity to do so now because the no-affirmative-duty rule is out of step with modern notions of morality. . . .

Abandoning the "Special Relationship" Doctrine

As noted above, in arguing that their negligence claim should not have been dismissed, plaintiffs offer an alternative argument. They contend that our recent case law demonstrates that the "special relationship" doctrine has been eroded in this state and that "the evolution of our case law has clearly been away from the formulaic application of the special relationship doctrine." Plaintiffs argue that the "special relationship" doctrine, in particular, and the no-duty rule, in general, are "antiquated" and out of step with contemporary societal morals. Thus, according to plaintiffs, the existence of an affirmative duty to warn or protect, particularly in situations where the parties are not strangers, should be a policy determination, made on a case-by-case basis, upon consideration of factors commonly used to determine the existence of a duty in ordinary negligence situations . . . . Plaintiffs urge us to abandon the "special relationship" framework for determining whether to impose an affirmative duty to protect against third-party attacks and to find a duty in the case at bar by applying the above four-factor negligence test.

Earlier in this opinion, we noted this court's long history of adherence to the rule that private persons owe no duty to act affirmatively to protect others from criminal attack by third persons absent a "special relationship" between the parties. . . . Plaintiffs contend that we would not be straying very far from the path of *stare decisis* because the "special relationship" doctrine has already been eroded by Illinois courts, including this court, which have eschewed the "special relationship" analysis and, instead, applied the traditional negligence factors when deciding whether a duty exists. . . . However, we find that these cases do not support plaintiffs' erosion theory. In none of these cases was the question at issue whether an affirmative duty should be imposed on a person to warn or protect another against the criminal acts of a third party. . . . Accordingly, we reject plaintiffs' claim that the "special relationship" doctrine has been eroded in Illinois.

Plaintiffs only remaining argument for abandoning the "special relationship" doctrine is that the doctrine and the no-duty rule, in general, are antiquated and out of step with today's morality. While it is true that the no-duty rule has suffered criticism from a number of legal scholars, criticism of the rule is not new. Legal pundits have assailed the rule, citing its lack of social conscience, for as long as it has existed. *See* Restatement (Third) of Torts: Liability for Physical Harm § 37, Comment *e,* Proposed Final Draft No. 1 (April 6, 2005) . . . .

Contrary to plaintiffs' assertions, the no-affirmative-duty rule, as a common law tort principle, has been retained in every jurisdiction. *See* Restatement (Third) of Torts: Liability for Physical Harm § 37, Reporter's Note, at 719, Proposed Final Draft No. 1 (April 6, 2005) ("no court has adopted an affirmative duty to assist in a rescue"). . . . Some states have legislatively created narrow exceptions to the no-affirmative-duty rule, imposing criminal sanctions if a person who is present when certain violent crimes are taking place fails to notify police or, in some instances, fails to render assistance to the victim. However, none of these statutes provide for a civil cause of action. Thus, given the wide acceptance of the no-duty rule and the "special relationship" doctrine, it cannot be said that they are "antiquated" or "outmoded."

Moreover, abandonment of the no-duty rule would create a number of practical difficulties—defining the parameters of an affirmative obligation and enforcement, to name just two. . . . In the case at bar, plaintiffs have not provided good cause or compelling reasons to judicially abandon the "special relationship" doctrine for finding an exception to the no-affirmative-duty rule. We will continue to adhere to its principles.

CONCLUSION

The no-affirmative-duty rule and the "special relationship" doctrine stand as the law of this state. Accordingly, an affirmative duty to warn or protect against the criminal conduct of a third party may be imposed on one for the benefit of another only if there exists a special relationship between them. In the case at bar, no such relationship existed between the defendants and Iseberg. . . . For these reasons, we affirm the judgment of the appellate court.

1   Section 40 of the Third Restatement of Torts lists several relationships that give rise to a duty: employer-employee, school-student, landlord-tenant, and one who holds its premises open to the public with those lawfully on the premises.

2   *Third-party negligence.* If a duty exists by virtue of a particular relationship, the duty likely extends to all foreseeable harm, including the risk of harm from the negligence of third-parties.

b. RELATIONSHIP TO PERSON CAUSING HARM

DEUTERONOMY 24:16

The fathers shall not be put to death for the children, neither shall the children be put to death for the fathers: every man shall be put to death for his own sin.

TARASOFF V. REGENTS OF THE UNIVERSITY OF CALIFORNIA
551 P.2D 334 (CAL. 1976)

On October 27, 1969, Prosenjit Poddar killed Tatiana Tarasoff. Plaintiffs, Tatiana's parents, allege that two months earlier Poddar confided his intention to kill Tatiana to Dr. Lawrence Moore, a psychologist employed by the Cowell Memorial Hospital at the University of California at Berkeley. They allege that on Moore's request, the campus police briefly detained Poddar, but released him when he appeared rational. They further claim that Dr. Harvey Powelson, Moore's superior, then directed that no further action be taken to detain Poddar. No one warned plaintiffs of Tatiana's peril. Concluding that these facts set forth causes of action against neither therapists and policemen involved, nor against the Regents of the University of California as their employer, the superior court sustained defendants' demurrers to plaintiffs' second amended complaints without leave to amend. This appeal ensued. . . .

When a therapist determines, or pursuant to the standards of his profession should determine, that his patient presents a serious danger of violence to another, he incurs an obligation to use reasonable care to protect the intended victim against such danger. The discharge of this duty may require the therapist to take one or more of various steps, depending upon the nature of the case. Thus it may call for him to warn the intended victim or others likely to apprise the victim of the danger, to notify the police, or to take whatever other steps are reasonably necessary under the circumstances.

. . . [Plaintiffs allege] that on August 20, 1969, Poddar was a voluntary outpatient receiving therapy at Cowell Memorial Hospital. Poddar informed Moore, his therapist, that he was going to kill an unnamed girl, readily identifiable as Tatiana, when she returned home from spending the summer in Brazil. Moore . . . decided that Poddar should be committed for observation in a mental hospital. Moore orally notified Officers Atkinson and Teel of the campus police that he would request commitment. He then sent a letter to Police Chief William Beall requesting the assistance of the police department in securing Poddar's confinement.

Officers Atkinson, Brownrigg, and Halleran took Poddar into custody, but, satisfied that Poddar was rational, released him on his promise to stay away from Tatiana. Powelson, director of the department of psychiatry at Cowell Memorial Hospital, then asked the police to return Moore's letter, directed that all copies of the letter and notes that Moore had taken as therapist be destroyed, and "ordered no action to place Prosenjit Poddar in 72-hour treatment and evaluation facility."

Plaintiffs' second cause of action . . . can be amended to allege that Tatiana's death proximately resulted from defendants' negligent failure to warn Tatiana or others likely to apprise her of her danger. Plaintiffs contend that as amended, such allegations of negligence and proximate causation, with resulting damages, establish a cause of action. Defendants, however, contend that in the circumstances of the present case they owed no duty of care to Tatiana or her parents and that, in the absence of such duty, they were free to act in careless disregard of Tatiana's life and safety.

In analyzing this issue, we bear in mind that legal duties are not discoverable facts of nature, but merely conclusory expressions that, in cases of a particular type, liability should be imposed for damage done. As stated in *Dillon* v. *Legg* (1968) . . . :

> The assertion that liability must . . . be denied because defendant bears no "duty" to plaintiff "begs the essential question – whether the plaintiff's interests are entitled to legal protection against the defendant's conduct. . . . [Duty] is not sacrosanct in itself, but only an expression of the sum total of those considerations of policy which lead the law to say that the particular plaintiff is entitled to protection."

In the landmark case of *Rowland* v. *Christian* . . . , Justice Peters recognized that liability should be imposed "for injury occasioned to another by his want of ordinary care or skill" . . . . Thus, Justice Peters, quoting from *Heaven* v. *Pender*, . . . stated: "whenever one person is by circumstances placed in such a position with regard to another . . . that if he did not use ordinary care and skill in his own conduct . . . he would cause danger of injury to the person or property of the other, a duty arises to use ordinary care and skill to avoid such danger."

. . . As a general principle, a "defendant owes a duty of care to all persons who are foreseeably endangered by his conduct, with respect to all risks which make the conduct unreasonably dangerous." As we shall explain, however, when the avoidance of foreseeable harm requires a defendant to control the conduct of another person, or to warn of such conduct, the common law has traditionally imposed liability only if the defendant bears some special relationship to the dangerous person or to the potential victim. . . . [T]he relationship between a therapist and his patient satisfies this requirement . . . .

Although . . . under the common law, as a general rule, one person owed no duty to control the conduct of another . . . (Rest.2d Torts (1965) §315), nor to warn those endangered by such conduct (Rest.2d Torts, *supra*, §314, com. c. . . .), the courts have carved out an exception to this rule in cases in which the defendant stands in some special relationship to either the person whose conduct needs to be controlled or in a relationship to the foreseeable victim of that conduct (*see* Rest.2d Torts, *supra*, §§315-320). Applying this exception to the present case, we note that a relationship of defendant therapists to either Tatiana or Poddar will suffice to establish a duty of care; as explained in section 315 of the Restatement Second of Torts, a duty of care may arise from either "(a) a special relation . . . between the actor and the third person which imposes a duty upon the actor to control the third person's conduct, or (b) a special relation . . . between the actor and the other which gives to the other a right of protection."

Although plaintiffs' pleadings assert no special relation between Tatiana and defendant therapists, they establish as between Poddar and defendant therapists the special relation that arises between a patient and his doctor or psychotherapist. Such a relationship may support affirmative duties for the benefit of third persons. Thus, for example, a hospital must exercise reasonable care to control the behavior of a patient which may endanger other persons. A doctor must also warn a patient if the patient's condition or medication renders certain conduct, such as driving a car, dangerous to others.

Although the California decisions that recognize this duty have involved cases in which the defendant stood in a special relationship *both* to the victim and to the person whose conduct created the danger, we do not think that the duty should logically be constricted to such situations. Decisions of other jurisdictions hold that the single relationship of a doctor to his patient is sufficient to support the duty to exercise reasonable care to protect others against dangers emanating from the patient's illness. . . .

Defendants contend . . . that imposition of a duty to exercise reasonable care to protect third persons is unworkable because therapists cannot accurately predict whether or not a patient will resort to violence. In support of this argument amicus representing the American Psychiatric Association and other professional societies cites numerous articles which indicate that therapists, in the present state of the art, are unable reliably to predict violent acts; their forecasts, amicus claims, tend consistently to overpredict violence, and indeed are more often wrong than right. Since predictions of violence are often erroneous, amicus concludes, the courts should not render rulings that predicate the liability of therapists upon the validity of such predictions. . . .

We recognize the difficulty that a therapist encounters in attempting to forecast whether a patient presents a serious danger of violence. Obviously, we do not require that the therapist, in making that determination, render a perfect performance; the therapist need only exercise "that reasonable degree of skill, knowledge, and care ordinarily possessed and exercised by members of [that professional specialty] under similar circumstances." Within the broad range of reasonable practice and treatment in which professional opinion and judgment may differ, the therapist is free to exercise his or her own best judgment without liability; proof, aided by hindsight, that he or she judged wrongly is insufficient to establish negligence.

In the instant case, however, the pleadings do not raise any question as to failure of defendant therapists to predict that Poddar presented a serious danger of violence. On the contrary, the present complaints allege that defendant therapists did in fact predict that Poddar would kill, but were negligent in failing to warn.

Amicus contends, however, that even when a therapist does in fact predict that a patient poses a serious danger of violence to others, the therapist should be absolved of any responsibility for failing to act to protect the potential victim. In our view, however, once a therapist does in fact determine, or under applicable professional standards reasonably should have determined, that a patient poses a serious danger of violence to others, he bears a duty to exercise reasonable care to protect the foreseeable victim of that danger. While the discharge of this duty of due care will necessarily vary with the facts of each case, in each instance the adequacy of the therapist's conduct must be measured against the traditional negligence standard of the rendition of reasonable care under the circumstances. . . .

The risk that unnecessary warnings may be given is a reasonable price to pay for the lives of possible victims that may be saved. We would hesitate to hold that the therapist who is aware that his patient expects to attempt to assassinate the President of the United States would not be obligated to warn the authorities because the therapist cannot predict with accuracy that his patient will commit the crime.

Defendants further argue that free and open communication is essential to psychotherapy. . . . The giving of a warning, defendants contend, constitutes a breach of trust which entails the revelation of confidential communications.

We recognize the public interest in supporting effective treatment of mental illness and in protecting the rights of patients to privacy, and the consequent public importance of safeguarding the confidential character of psychotherapeutic communication. Against this interest, however, we must weigh the public interest in safety from violent assault. . . .

We realize that the open and confidential character of psychotherapeutic dialogue encourages patients to express threats of violence, few of which are ever executed. Certainly a therapist should not be encouraged routinely to reveal such threats; such disclosures could seriously disrupt the patient's relationship with his therapist and with the persons threatened. To the contrary, the therapist's obligations to his patient require that he not disclose a confidence unless such disclosure is necessary to avert danger to others, and even then that he do so discreetly, and in a fashion that would preserve the privacy of his patient to the fullest extent compatible with the prevention of the threatened danger. . . .

Our current crowded and computerized society compels the interdependence of its members. In this risk-infested society we can hardly tolerate the further exposure to danger that would result from a concealed knowledge of the therapist that his patient was lethal. If the exercise of reasonable care to protect the threatened victim requires the therapist to warn the endangered party or those who can reasonably be expected to notify him, we see no sufficient societal interest that would protect and justify concealment. The containment of such risks lies in the public interest. . . .

1   The California Supreme Court begins its analysis by asserting that "legal duties are not discoverable facts of nature, but merely conclusory expressions that, in cases of a particular type, liability should be imposed for damage done." Do you agree? Is the court admitting that its imposition of legal duty is arbitrary? If the existence of duty is not a "discoverable fact of nature," then on what basis can a court ever conclude that "liability should be imposed for damage done"? Does nature explain why a parent owes a duty to control the conduct of her child?

2   The California Supreme Court based the duty to plaintiffs here on the special patient-doctor/phsycotherapist relation between Poddar and the defendant therapist. Would this rationale require a doctor to warn family members or fellow employees of a leprosy patient? An AIDS patient? An alcoholic patient? If not, how are these situations different?

3   Most American courts to address the issue have followed the result in *Tarasoff*. A noteworthy exception is the Commonwealth of Virginia, which has rejected *Tarasoff*. *See Nasser v. Parker*, 249 Va. 172, 455 S.E.2d 502 (1995).

5. PREMISES LIABILITY: DUTIES OF POSSESSORS OF LAND

The duty of a possessor of real property is different from most tort duties in that the duty arises, not based upon something defendant actively does (unless owning or possessing land is considered affirmative conduct), but rather based upon a condition that exists on defendant's property. Ordinarily, the defendant is the master of her own duty in that she can avoid any duty by declining to act. The idea that the owner or occupier of real property owes, by virtue of her status as owner, a "duty" to protect those coming on the property from dangerous conditions on the property is in tension both with the general "no duty" rule and with the tendency at common law to give the property owner *carte blanche* on her own property. Indeed, foundational to tort law is the cause of action in trespass, which protects the property owner's right to exclude.

As the common law developed, the duty of care owed by the owner or occupier of real property to those coming on the property eventually came to depend on the status of the person coming on the property. The highest duty was owed to the "invitee." Little or no duty was owed to the mere "trespasser." And the duty owed to a "licensee" fell somewhere in the middle.

These three common law status categories might best be understood as an attempt to square the possessor's duty with the traditional distinction between nonfeasance and misfeasance. If plaintiff is on the property by defendant's invitation, then collapsing the invitation with the failure to correct the dangerous condition on the property makes it possible to characterize defendant's failure to protect the plaintiff as a misfeasance by omission rather than a pure nonfeasance. The possessor of real property remains the master of her duty – she may avoid any duty by declining to give others permission to enter the property. Thus, the historical categories discussed in the following cases might make sense as an attempt to divide between a misfeasance and a nonfeasance.

Whatever its theoretical underpinnings, the three-category system of duty for occupiers of real property generally has persisted, even in the face of significant criticism that it produces somewhat arbitrary results. This general persistence has been despite some erosion at the edges. For example, many jurisdictions developed what amount to sub-categories for "tolerated" or "discovered" trespassers. But, again, this softening of the "no duty to trespassers" rule may have roughly corresponded with a general questioning of the broader "no affirmative duty" rule.

a. COMMON LAW CATEGORIES

As noted above, the common law duty owed by an owner of real property to an entrant on that property has turned on the "status" of the entrant on the land. The following case discusses these traditional common law categories and the varying duties owed to each.

CARTER V. KINNEY
896 s.w.2d 926 (mo. 1995)

I.

Ronald and Mary Kinney hosted a Bible study at their home for members of the Northwest Bible Church. Appellant Jonathan Carter, a member of the Northwest Bible Church, attended the early morning Bible study at the Kinney's home on February 3, 1990. Mr. Kinney had shoveled snow from his driveway the previous evening, but was not aware that ice had formed overnight. Mr. Carter arrived shortly after 7:00 a.m., slipped on a patch of ice in the Kinneys' driveway, and broke his leg. The Carters filed suit against the Kinneys.

The parties agree that the Kinneys offered their home for the Bible study as part of a series sponsored by their church; that some Bible studies took place at the church and others were held at the homes of church members; that interested church members signed up for the studies on a sheet at the church, which actively encouraged enrollment but did not solicit contributions through the classes or issue an invitation to the general public to attend the studies; that the Kinneys and the Carters had not engaged in any social interaction outside of church prior to Mr. Carter's injury, and that Mr. Carter had no social relationship with the other participants in the class. Finally, the parties agree that the Kinneys received neither a financial nor other tangible benefit from Mr. Carter in connection with the Bible study class.

They disagree, however, as to Mr. Carter's status. Mr. Carter claims he was an invitee; the Kinneys say he was a licensee. And the parties dispute certain facts bearing on the purpose of his visit, specifically, whether the parties intended a future social relationship, and whether the Kinneys held the Bible study class in order to confer some intangible benefit on themselves and others.

On the basis of these facts, the Kinneys moved for summary judgment. The trial court sustained the Kinneys' summary judgment motion on the ground that Mr. Carter was a licensee and that the Kinneys did not have a duty to a licensee with respect to a dangerous condition of which they had no knowledge. This appeal followed.

II.

... [W]hether Mr. Carter was an invitee, as he claims, or a licensee is a question of law and summary judgment is appropriate if the defendants' conduct conforms to the standard of care Mr. Carter's status imposes on them. ... Historically, premises liability cases recognize three broad classes of plaintiffs: trespassers, licensees and invitees. All entrants to land are trespassers until the possessor of the land gives them permission to enter. All persons who enter a premises with permission are licensees until the possessor has an interest in the visit such that the visitor "has reason to believe that the premises have been made safe to receive him." 65 C.J.S. Negligence, § 63(41), 719. That makes the visitor an invitee. The possessor's intention in offering the invitation determines the status of the visitor and establishes the duty of care the possessor owes the visitor. ...

A social guest is a person who has received a social invitation. ... In Missouri, social guests are but a subclass of licensees. The fact that an invitation underlies a visit does not render the visitor an invitee for purposes of premises liability law. ...

It does not follow from this that a person invited for purposes not strictly social is perforce an invitee. ... [A]n entrant becomes an invitee when the possessor invites with the expectation of a material benefit from the visit or extends an invitation to the public generally. *See also* Restatement (Second) of Torts, § 332 (defining an invitee for business purposes) .... Absent the sort of invitation from the possessor that lifts a licensee to invitee status, the visitor remains a licensee as a matter of law.

The record shows beyond cavil that Mr. Carter did not enter the Kinneys' land to afford the Kinneys any material benefit. He is therefore not an invitee under the definition of invitee contained in Section 332 of the Restatement. The record also demonstrates that the Kinneys did not "throw open" their premises to the public in such a way as would imply a warranty of safety. The Kinneys took no steps to encourage general attendance by some undefined portion of the public; they invited only church members who signed up at church. They did nothing more than give permission to a limited class of persons – church members – to enter their property.

Mr. Carter's response to the Kinneys' motion for summary judgment includes Mr. Carter's affidavit in which he says that he did not intend to socialize with the Kinneys and that the Kinneys would obtain an intangible benefit, albeit mutual, from Mr. Carter's participation in the class. Mr. Carter's affidavit attempts to create an issue of fact for the purpose of defeating summary judgment. But taking Mr. Carter's statement of the facts as true in all respects, he argues a factual distinction that has no meaning under Missouri law. Human intercourse and the intangible benefits of sharing one's property with others for a mutual purpose are hallmarks of a licensee's permission to enter. Mr. Carter's factual argument makes the legal point he wishes to avoid: his invitation is not of the sort that makes an invitee. He is a licensee.

The trial court concluded as a matter of law that Mr. Carter was a licensee, that the Kinneys had no duty to protect him from unknown dangerous conditions, and that the defendants were entitled to summary judgment as a matter of law. In that conclusion, the trial court was eminently correct. . . .

The Carters next argue that this Court should abolish the distinction between licensees and invitees and hold all possessors to a standard of reasonable care under the circumstances. They argue that the current system that recognizes a lower standard of care for licensees than invitees is arbitrary and denies deserving plaintiffs compensation for their injuries. . . . The Carters note that twenty states have abolished the distinction since 1968 and encourage Missouri to join this "trend."

The Kinneys claim that the trend is little more than a fad. They note that twelve states have expressly rejected the abolition of the distinction since the "trend" began in 1968 and that the remaining eighteen states, including Missouri, have not directly addressed the issue and maintain the common law distinctions.

We are not persuaded that the licensee/invitee distinction no longer serves. The possessor's intentions in issuing the invitation determine not only the status of the entrant but the possessor's duty of care to that entrant. The contours of the legal relationship that results from the possessor's invitation reflect a careful and patient effort by courts over time to balance the interests of persons injured by conditions of land against the interests of possessors of land to enjoy and employ their land for the purposes they wish. Moreover, and despite the exceptions courts have developed to the general rules, the maintenance of the distinction between licensee and invitee creates fairly predictable rules within which entrants and possessors can determine appropriate conduct and juries can assess liability. To abandon the careful work of generations for an amorphous "reasonable care under the circumstances" standard seems – to put it kindly – improvident. . . . The experience of the states that have abolished the distinction between licensee and invitee does not convince us that their idea is a better one. Indeed, we are convinced that they have chosen wrongly.

III.

The judgment of the trial court is affirmed.

QUESTIONS AND NOTES

1 If the same injury had happened on the church premises shortly before public Sunday morning services, would the same result have obtained? Should the two situations be treated the same or differently?

2 *Trespassers.* Under the common law tri-partite categories, trespasser is one who enters premises without permission. (As the preceding case demonstrates, there is no intent requirement to trespasser status.) It has frequently been said that the possessor of real property owes "no duty" to the mere trespasser. Actually, the duty is to avoid "willful or wanton" injury to the trespasser. As illustrated by Restatement (Second) Section 334, this sort of liability has been especially likely when the possessor knows or has reason to know of constant trespassing on the property at that place. Not only does the property owner owe only a very limited duty to trespassers, but, as

we discussed in the section on defenses to intentional torts, the occupier actually has a privilege to use reasonable force to expel the trespasser.

3 *Licensees.* "Licensees" are all who enter premises with legal permission but who are not "invitees." Perhaps somewhat confusing is the fact that "social guests" have traditionally been treated as licensees, not invitees, even though they may be on the premises by the express invitation of the owner. The duty to licensees also is quite limited – merely the duty to warn of known but hidden dangers on the premises.

4 *Invitees.* The highest duty is owed to "invitees." Invitees come in two varieties – business invitees and public invitees. A business invitee is one who is on the premises for the business purposes of the owner. A public invitee is one who has permission to be on the premises because the premises are open to the general public. The duty owed to invitees is "reasonable care under the circumstances." The duty of reasonable care includes not only the duty to warn imposed for the benefit of licensees, but also the affirmative duty to make reasonable inspections and to take reasonable steps to make the premises reasonably safe for the invitee.

5 *Changing categories.* The status of an entrant on land may change with the circumstances. For example, permission to remain on the premises may be granted or revoked, resulting in a change of status either to or from the category of trespasser. It is important to assess the status of the entrant at the precise moment of the accident.

6 *Ownership and Possession.* Premises liability applies to occupiers of land even if they do not own the land in fee simple absolute. A defendant need not own property to be a possessor of property for purposes of premises liability. For example, a tenant can be a defendant in a premises liability case. The traditional rule is that the premises liability duty for leased premises is owed by the lessee, not by the lessor. The lessor's (landlord's) duty usually arises by contract (by the terms of the lease), not by tort. Of course, tort duties still sometimes are imposed on landlords by statute as public safety measures.

7 *Conditions v. Activities.* The plaintiff categories address the fact that harm resulting from dangerous conditions on land is not clearly either a misfeasance or a nonfeasance. The same uncertainty does not necessarily apply to harm resulting from dangerous activities on land. The possessor of land is much more likely to be held legally responsible for harm resulting from activities on the land than for harm resulting from mere conditions on the land. For example, a possessor of real property who carelessly and dangerously sets off fireworks on his property resulting in injuries to social guests likely will be held to a reasonableness standard of care. The harm fairly clearly results from a misfeasance (an activity on the land), not a nonfeasance (a condition of the land). This does not mean that plaintiff's status on the property is completely immaterial in the case of harmful activities on land. For example, more care may be reasonable when the possessor knows that guests are present than when unknown trespassers are present.

GLADON V. GREATER CLEVELAND REGIONAL TRANSIT AUTHORITY
662 N.E.2D 287 (OHIO 1996)

Greater Cleveland Regional Transit Authority ("RTA") appeals from a jury verdict awarding Robert M. Gladon $2,736,915.35 in damages arising from RTA's operation of a rapid transit train.

Gladon purchased a passenger ticket and boarded an RTA rapid transit train at Terminal Tower after attending a Cleveland Indians' night game with friends. During the baseball game, Gladon consumed about five 16-ounce beers. He left his friends at the stadium in search of a restroom, and ended up traveling alone on the RTA trains. Because there were no witnesses, the jury heard only Gladon's account of events. According to Gladon, he mistakenly exited the train at the West 65th Street Station and, once on the platform, was chased and attacked by two unknown males. Gladon testified that he remembered being "rolled up in a ball" on the tracks but he could not recall if he had jumped onto the tracks or had been pushed onto the tracks. While there, however, he did recall being kicked in the head.

While Gladon lay on the tracks with his legs draped over the rail, an RTA rapid train approached the West 65th Street Station. Mary Bell, the train's operator, had the train in braking mode when she observed first a tennis shoe and then Gladon's leg on the tracks. The operator pulled the cinestar, or control handle, back and hit the "mushroom," or emergency brake. Unfortunately, the train struck Gladon, causing him serious and permanent injuries.

. . . The trial court overruled RTA's motion for a directed verdict at the close of Gladon's case-in-chief. . . . The jury returned a verdict for Gladon . . . . We determine that the trial court erred in instructing the jury about plaintiff's legal status and RTA's corresponding duty. The trial court instructed the jury "as a matter of law that * * * the plaintiff was an invitee," and that as a result RTA was "required to use ordinary care to discover and to avoid danger." . . . Given the evidence presented in the trial of this case, the erroneous instruction was prejudicial. Accordingly, we reverse the judgment of the trial court and remand the cause for a new trial. . . .

Ohio adheres to the common-law classifications of invitee, licensee, and trespasser in cases of premises liability. . . . Although there was a movement in many jurisdictions in the 1970s to abolish these traditional duty classification schemes, it quite abruptly lost its steam late in that decade. . . . In Ohio, the status of the person who enters upon the land of another (i.e., trespasser, licensee, or invitee) continues to define the scope of the legal duty that the landowner owes the entrant. . . . Invitees are persons who rightfully come upon the premises of another by invitation, express or implied, for some purpose which is beneficial to the owner. . . .

The status of an invitee is not absolute but is limited by the landowner's invitation. " * * * [T]he visitor has the status of an invitee only while he is on the part of the land to which his invitation extends--or in other words, the part of the land upon which the possessor gives him reason to believe that his presence is desired for the purpose for which he has come." * * *

"If the invitee goes outside of the area of his invitation, he becomes a trespasser or a licensee, depending upon whether he goes there without the consent of the possessor, or with such consent." 2 Restatement of the Law 2d, Torts (1965) 181-182, Section 332, Comment *l.*

In the present case, Gladon was an invitee when he purchased an RTA ticket, rode the rapid transit train and waited at RTA's platform. However, RTA's invitation to Gladon to use its premises did not extend to the area on or near the tracks. In fact, Gladon acknowledged that RTA did not permit the public in the area on or near the tracks.

Although the result seems harsh, the common law on this subject is well grounded and we are not inclined to reject it. Accordingly, we hold that where an entrant upon another's land exceeds the scope of the landowner's invitation, the entrant will lose the status of an invitee, and become either a licensee or trespasser. *See* . . . Restatement of Torts 2d, *supra* Section 332, Comment *l.*

Gladon contends that he retained his invitee status because there was no evidence that he "intentionally or purposely entered upon the track area." According to the Restatement, "so far as the liability of the possessor of the land to the intruder is concerned, however, the possessor's duty, and liability, will be the same regardless of the manner of entry, so long as the entry itself is not privileged." Restatement of Torts 2d, 171–172, *supra,* Section 329, Comment c.

In determining whether the person is a trespasser within the meaning of this section, the question whether his entry has been intentional, negligent or purely accidental is not material, except as it may bear on the existence of a privilege. *Id.* at 171. Without the consent or privilege to enter the area of the tracks, the law views such entry from the aspect of the landowner whose duties to the entrant flow from the parameters of his permission to be there. As a result, "the determining fact is the presence or absence of a privilege to enter or to remain on the land, and the status of an accidental trespasser is still that of a trespasser." *Id.* at 172.

The illustration employed by the Restatement to explain the duties owed to a trespasser is remarkably similar to Gladon's situation. "Without any negligence on his part A, standing on the platform of a subway station of the X Company, slips and falls onto the tracks. While there he is run over by the train of X Company, and injured. A is a trespasser, and the liability to him is determined by the rules stated in sections 333 and 336, notwithstanding the accidental character of his intrusion." *Id.* at 171, Illustration 1.[2]

Furthermore, whether Gladon was privileged to enter the tracks is immaterial. A person privileged to enter the land is owed the same duties as a licensee. Restatement of Torts 2d, *supra,* at Section 345. . . . Even though his entry may have been unintentional and against Gladon's wishes, once on the tracks, Gladon exceeded the scope of his invitation and lost his status as an invitee. . . .[T]he trial court erred in instructing the jury that he was an invitee as a matter of law.

We now turn to the duty owed to Gladon by RTA as a result of Gladon's change in status . . . . A landowner owes a duty to an invitee to exercise ordinary care for the invitee's safety and protection. . . . Having instructed the jury as a matter of law that Gladon was an invitee, the trial court assigned RTA a duty of ordinary care "to discover and to avoid danger." These instructions erred in two respects. First, the instructions imposed upon RTA a duty to use ordinary care to discover Gladon's presence. To the contrary, RTA was under no duty to anticipate trespassers and could only be liable for injuries resulting from willful or wanton conduct. Second, the instructions imposed upon RTA a duty to use ordinary care to avoid injuring Gladon prior to the operator's discovery of him. . . . Given that the instructions were erroneous and prejudicial, we reverse the judgment of the court of appeals and remand this cause for a new trial. . . .

---

2   Section 333 states generally that "a possessor of land is not liable to trespassers for physical harm caused by his failure to exercise reasonable care (a) to put the land in a condition reasonably safe for their reception, or (b) to carry on his activities so as not to endanger them." Restatement of the Law 2d, Torts (1965) 183, Section 333. Section 336 generally prescribes the duty of ordinary care from a possessor of land who knows or has reason to know of the presence of another who is trespassing on the land. Restatement of the Law 2d, *supra,* at Section 336. Again, the example cited by the Restatement for this duty is identical to the situation when the train driver saw Gladon and his shoe on the tracks. "The engineer of the X & Y Railroad Company sees lying upon the track a pile of clothing such as would give a reasonable man cause to suspect that it might contain a human being. Under these circumstances the engineer is not entitled to assume that it is not a human being but is required to keep the engine under control until he is certain that it is not." *Id.* at 191–192, Comment *b,* Illustration 1.

b. SPECIAL ENTRANTS

The common law long has recognized that certain entrants onto land warrant special treatment. These situations are exceptional and are not governed strictly by the traditional tripartite division of entrants among trespassers, licensees and invitees.

(1) TRESPASSING CHILDREN

Children are notorious trespassers. The traditional rule of "no duty" to trespassers frequently appeared to be particularly harsh toward children, who might not appreciate the danger to which they were subjecting themselves. To soften these harsh results, the courts developed the doctrine of "attractive nuisance" whereby a defendant owed trespassing children a duty of reasonable care when defendant had reason to know that children were likely to trespass and nevertheless maintained an artificial condition on defendant's property, which condition was likely to attract children. The idea was that the condition acted as a lure or a trap for children, which justified holding defendant responsible. But even this doctrine came to be seen as too harsh toward trespassing children and eventually evolved into the widely adopted Restatement (Second) Sec. 339, which eliminated the "lure" or "trap" aspect of the former "attractive nuisance" doctrine.

Restatement (Second) Torts § 339. Artificial Conditions Highly Dangerous To Trespassing Children

A possessor of land is subject to liability for physical harm to children trespassing thereon caused by an artificial condition upon the land if

a. the place where the condition exists is one upon which the possessor knows or has reason to know that children are likely to trespass, and

b. the condition is one of which the possessor knows or has reason to know and which he realizes or should realize will involve an unreasonable risk of death or serious bodily harm to such children, and

c. the children because of their youth do not discover the condition or realize the risk involved in intermeddling with it or in coming within the area made dangerous by it, and

d. the utility to the possessor of maintaining the condition and the burden of eliminating the danger are slight as compared with the risk to children involved, and

e. the possessor fails to exercise reasonable care to eliminate the danger or otherwise to protect the children.

1   *Natural Conditions.* The doctrine of enhanced duty to trespassing children generally does not apply to natural conditions such as streams, ponds and the like.

2   *Lure.* The modern doctrine eliminates the requirement that the dangerous condition "lured" the child onto the property. A minority of jurisdictions still retain this aspect of the older "attractive nuisance" doctrine.

3   *"Reason to Know."* Defendant generally will not be responsible for harm caused to a trespassing child by a dangerous condition on defendant's property unless defendant had a specific reason to know that a child was likely to be trespassing and that a condition is likely to be dangerous to such trespassing child.

4   *Assumption of risk.* The doctrine applicable to trespassing children does not eliminate traditional defenses such as assumption of risk, but assumption of risk requires a subjective appreciation of the danger that generally may not exist for very young children. Thus, the primary benefit of Section 339 applies to children of grade school age or younger.

5   *Common Hazards.* The rule applicable to trespassing children is not a doctrine of strict liability, and even the trespassing child would need to show that defendant could have reasonably avoided the danger. This is a difficult showing for plaintiffs in the case of so-called "common hazards" such as ponds.

6   The Restatement (Third) of Torts, Sec. 51 would impose a unitary duty of reasonable care on property occupiers toward all entrants on the land, including ordinary trespassers, eliminating the need for a special rule for childhood trespassers. However, both trespasser status and childhood status still might be particular circumstances taken into account in determining what care is warranted under the circumstances.

(2) THE "FIREFIGHTER'S RULE"

Postal delivery workers, trash collectors, and most other public employees who enter property pursuant to their official duties ordinarily are treated as "invitees" for purposes of premises liability. While the jurisdictions are far from uniform on this issue, firefighters who enter the premises under emergency circumstances frequently are treated as mere "licensees." While this principle is commonly called the "firefighters rule," most jurisdictions have extended it to other professional risk-takers, including police officers and even EMTs. But this limitation applies only to professionals – as we will see later, the firefighter's rule does not apply to private rescuers, only to those who are paid to rescue. Dangers faced by such emergency personnel are essentially treated as occupational hazards so long as the risks are inherent to the job and are, in fact, the very reason the emergency responder is on the scene to begin with.

Note that the firefighter's rule protects only the property occupier who creates a dangerous risk through negligence, not the intentional wrongdoer. The Restatement (Third) of Torts, Sec. 51 purports to take no position with regard to the firefighter's rule; however, its elimination of the category of "licensee" eliminates the historical rationale typically applied by the firefighter's rule. As the following statutory provision illustrates, some jurisdictions, such as Virginia, have adopted a rule by statute:

§ 8.01-226. Duty of care to law-enforcement officers and firefighters, etc.

An owner or occupant of real property containing premises normally open to the public shall, with respect to such premises, owe to firefighters, Department of Emergency Management hazardous materials officers, non-firefighter regional hazardous materials emergency response team members, and law-enforcement officers who in the performance of their duties come upon that portion of the premises normally open to the public the duty to maintain the same in a reasonably safe condition or to warn of dangers thereon of which he knows or has reason to know, whether or not such premises are at the time open to the public.

An owner or occupant of real property containing premises not normally open to the public shall, with respect to such premises, owe the same duty to firefighters, Department of Emergency Management hazardous materials officers, non-firefighter regional hazardous materials emergency response team members, and law-enforcement officers who he knows or has reason to know are upon, about to come upon or imminently likely to come upon that portion of the premises not normally open to the public.

While otherwise engaged in the performance of his duties, a law-enforcement officer, Department of Emergency Management hazardous materials officer, non-firefighter regional hazardous materials emergency response team member, or firefighter shall be owed a duty of ordinary care.

For purposes of this section, the term "law-enforcement officers" shall mean only police officers, sheriffs and deputy sheriffs and the term "firefighter" includes (i) emergency medical personnel and (ii) special forest wardens designated pursuant to § 10.1-1135.

c. THE UNITARY STANDARD

ROWLAND V. CHRISTIAN
443 P.2D 561 (CAL. 1968)

Plaintiff . . . alleged that about November 1, 1963, Miss Christian told the lessors of her apartment that the knob of the cold water faucet on the bathroom basin was cracked and should be replaced; that on November 30, 1963, plaintiff entered the apartment at the invitation of Miss Christian; that he was injured while using the bathroom fixtures . . . . Miss Christian's affidavit and admissions made by plaintiff show that plaintiff was a social guest and that he suffered injury when the faucet handle broke; they do not show that the faucet handle crack was obvious or even non-concealed. Without in any way contradicting her affidavit or his own admissions, plaintiff at trial could establish that [defendant] was aware of the condition and realized or should have realized that it involved an unreasonable risk of harm to him, that defendant should have expected that he would not discover the danger, that she did not exercise reasonable care to eliminate the danger or warn him of it, and that he did not know or have reason to know of the danger. Plaintiff also could establish . . . that the crack was not obvious . . . .

One of the areas where this court and other courts have departed from the fundamental concept that a man is liable for injuries caused by his carelessness is with regard to the liability of a possessor of land for injuries to persons who have entered upon that land. . . . The departure from the fundamental rule of liability for negligence has been accomplished by classifying the plaintiff either as a trespasser, licensee, or invitee and then adopting special rules as to the duty owed by the possessor to each of the classifications. Generally speaking a trespasser is a person who enters or remains upon land of another without a privilege to do so; a licensee is a person like a social guest who is not an invitee and who is privileged to enter or remain upon land by virtue of the possessor's consent, and an invitee is a business visitor who is invited or permitted to enter or remain on the land for a purpose directly or indirectly connected with business dealings between them. Although the invitor owes the invitee a duty to exercise ordinary care to avoid injuring him, the general rule is that a trespasser and licensee or social guest are obliged to take the premises as they find them insofar as any alleged defective condition thereon may exist . . . . The ordinary justification for the general rule severely restricting the occupier's liability to social guests is based on the theory that the guest should not expect special precautions to be made on his account and that if the host does not inspect and maintain his property the guest should not expect this to be done on his account. . . .

Without attempting to labor all of the rules relating to the possessor's liability, it is apparent that the classifications of trespasser, licensee, and invitee, the immunities from liability predicated upon those classifications, and the exceptions to those immunities, often do not reflect the major factors which should determine whether immunity should be conferred upon the possessor of land. . . . Although in general there may be a relationship between the remaining factors and the classifications of trespasser, licensee, and invitee, there are many cases in which no such relationship may exist. Thus, although the foreseeability of harm to an invitee would ordinarily seem greater than the foreseeability of harm to a trespasser, in a particular case the opposite may be true. The same may be said of the issue of certainty of injury. The burden to the defendant and consequences to the community of imposing a duty to exercise care with resulting liability for breach may often be greater with respect to trespassers than with respect to invitees, but it by no means follows that this is true in every case. In many situations, the burden will be the same, i.e., the conduct necessary upon the defendant's part to meet the burden of exercising due care as to invitees will also meet his burden with respect to licensees and trespassers. The last of the major factors, the cost of insurance, will, of course, vary depending upon the rules of liability adopted, but there is no persuasive evidence that applying ordinary principles of negligence law to the land occupier's liability will materially reduce the prevalence of insurance due to increased cost or even substantially increase the cost.

Considerations such as these have led some courts in particular situations to reject the rigid common law classifications and to approach the issue of the duty of the occupier on the basis of ordinary principles of negligence.

A man's life or limb does not become less worthy of protection by the law nor a loss less worthy of compensation under the law because he has come upon the land of another without permission or with permission but without a business purpose. Reasonable people do not ordinarily vary their conduct depending upon such matters, and to focus upon the status of the injured party as a trespasser, licensee, or invitee in order to determine the question whether the landowner has a duty of care, is contrary to our modern social mores and humanitarian values.

The common law rules obscure rather than illuminate the proper considerations which should govern determination of the question of duty.

It bears repetition that the basic policy of this state . . . is that everyone is responsible for an injury caused to another by his want of ordinary care or skill in the management of his property. The factors which may in particular cases warrant departure from this fundamental principle do not warrant the wholesale immunities resulting from the common law classifications, and we are satisfied that continued adherence to the common law distinctions can only lead to injustice or, if we are to avoid injustice, further fictions with the resulting complexity and confusion. We decline to follow and perpetuate such rigid classifications. The proper test to be applied to the liability of the possessor of land . . . is whether in the management of his property he has acted as a reasonable man in view of the probability of injury to others, and, although the plaintiff's status as a trespasser, licensee, or invitee may in the light of the facts giving rise to such status have some bearing on the question of liability, the status is not determinative.

Once the ancient concepts as to the liability of the occupier of land are stripped away, the status of the plaintiff relegated to its proper place in determining such liability, and ordinary principles of negligence applied, the result in the instant case presents no substantial difficulties. As we have seen, when we view the matters presented on the motion for summary judgment as we must, we must assume defendant Miss Christian was aware that the faucet handle was defective and dangerous, that the defect was not obvious, and that plaintiff was about to come in contact with the defective condition, and under the undisputed facts she neither remedied the condition nor warned plaintiff of it. Where the occupier of land is aware of a concealed condition involving in the absence of precautions an unreasonable risk of harm to those coming in contact with it and is aware that a person on the premises is about to come in contact with it, the trier of fact can reasonably conclude that a failure to warn or to repair the condition constitutes negligence. Whether or not a guest has a right to expect that his host will remedy dangerous conditions on his account, he should reasonably be entitled to rely upon a warning of the dangerous condition so that he, like the host, will be in a position to take special precautions when he comes in contact with it. . . .

The judgment is reversed.

BURKE, J. I dissent. In determining the liability of the occupier or owner of land for injuries, the distinctions between trespassers, licensees and invitees have been developed and applied by the courts over a period of many years. They supply a reasonable and workable approach to the problems involved, and one which provides the degree of stability and predictability so highly prized in the law. The unfortunate alternative, it appears to me, is the route taken by the majority in their opinion in this case; that such issues are to be decided on a case by case basis under the application of the basic law of negligence, bereft of the guiding principles and precedent which the law has heretofore attached by virtue of the relationship of the parties to one another.

Liability for negligence turns upon whether a duty of care is owed, and if so, the extent thereof. Who can doubt that the corner grocery, the large department store, or the financial institution owes a greater duty of care to one whom it has invited to enter its premises as a prospective customer of its wares or services than it owes to a trespasser seeking to enter after the close of business hours and for a nonbusiness or even an antagonistic purpose? I do not think it unreasonable or unfair that a social guest (classified by the law as a licensee, as was plaintiff here) should be obliged to take the premises in the same condition as his host finds them or permits them to be. . . . Yet today's decision appears to open the door to potentially unlimited liability despite the purpose and circumstances motivating the plaintiff in entering the premises of another, and despite the caveat of the majority that the status of the parties may "have some bearing on the question of liability . . . ," whatever the future may show that language to mean. . . .

I would affirm the judgment for defendant.

NOTES AND QUESTIONS

1   Contrary to most common law jurisdictions at the time, the *Rowland* Court treats the common law duty owed to licensees as identical to the duty owed to trespassers. Precisely what would the newly-announced unitary standard require of defendant on these facts? How does this differ from what the common law standard would require in the landowner-licensee context?

2   Under the *Rowland* Court's new unitary standard, would it have made any difference if plaintiff had been a mere trespasser?

3   Assume instead of a broken faucet there had been a tiger in the bathroom. Would that change defendant's duty to the mere trespasser under the unitary standard?

4   The effect of the unitary standard is to allow the jury to judge each situation on a case-by-case basis. Perhaps some predictability is sacrificed in exchange for more flexibility. The jury can do case-by-case justice as it sees fit instead of applying a one-size-fits-all standard of care. A related effect may be that fewer cases can be decided by the judge as a matter of law, resulting in more jury trials. *See* Carl S. Hawkins, *Premises Liability After Repudiation of the Status Categories: Allocation of Judge and Jury Functions*, 1981 Utah L. Rev 15. However, Comment c.(1) to the Restatement (Third) of Torts, Sec. 51 calls this view into question.

5   The *Rowland* decision's immediate impact on American tort law was felt in the 1960s and 1970s when several jurisdictions followed California's lead. The movement stalled out in the 1980s, and few states have adopted the *Rowland* court's unitary standard since. However, quite a few jurisdictions have eliminated the distinction between licensee and invitee. Despite this erosion, several jurisdictions retain the common law tri-partite division of duty.

6   A unitary standard that the property occupier owes a duty of reasonable care for the protection of all entrants on the land does not mean that the occupier is strictly liable for all injuries resulting from dangerous conditions on the land.

7   The Restatement (Third) of Torts adopts a unitary standard of reasonable care (Sec. 51) for the duty owed by property occupiers to all entrants on the property, with the exception of so-called "flagrant trespassers" (Sec. 52), to whom a more limited duty is owed. Here "flagrant" means "egregious," not "conspicuous."

8   For harm caused to those outside the property due to conditions on the property, the dividing line between liability and no liability usually is whether the condition is natural or artificial. Generally, there is no duty to guard against harm posed to those outside the land from natural conditions occurring on the land.

9   *Recreational Use Statutes.* Practically all jurisdictions have adopted some form of "Recreational Use Statute." The purpose of such statutes is to give occupiers of usually rural tracts of land an incentive to make that land available to the public for "recreational uses," frequently hunting, by limiting the duty of the property owner to those coming on the property to take advantage of the recreational use. Where such statute applies, it trumps common law liability rules. In those jurisdictions that have eliminated the common law categories, recreational use statutes restore the limited duty owed to mere trespassers and implied licensees.

C. BREACH

In this section, we will explore, first, under what standard a defendant's conduct is judged in a negligence suit, and then what tools are available to apply that standard in particular cases.

1. REASONABLE PERSON STANDARD

When a defendant owes a duty to the plaintiff, the substance of that duty is defined by the standard of "reasonableness under the circumstances." The Restatement (Second) of Torts used to call this the "reasonable man" standard, but it now usually is called the "reasonably prudent person standard." Both monikers mean the same thing. As we will see, this standard is said to be an "objective" standard, that is, it is a general standard for all people, not tailored to the individual person. But what does it mean to say that the negligence standard is an "objective" standard when it is applied "under the circumstances"? Depending upon what "circumstances" are taken into account, the "objective" negligence standard can appear to be quite subjective.

Clearly, among the "circumstances" taken into account when deciding whether a defendant has behaved reasonably are factors entirely external to the defendant such as atmospheric conditions, and so forth. But do the "circumstances" taken into account when judging a defendant's conduct also include factors internal to the defendant, such as physical, mental, and or emotional characteristics of the defendant? If so, in what sense is the standard objective? If not, then is the reasonableness standard morally flawed? These and other questions are addressed in the cases that follow.

LUKE 12:41-48

Then Peter said unto him, Lord, speakest thou this parable unto us, or even to all?

And the Lord said, Who then is that faithful and wise steward, whom his lord shall make ruler over his household, to give them their portion of meat in due season? Blessed is that servant, whom his lord when he cometh shall find so doing. Of a truth I say unto you, that he will make him ruler over all that he hath. But and if that servant say in his heart, My lord delayeth his coming; and shall begin to beat the menservants and maidens, and to eat and drink, and to be drunken; The lord of that servant will come in a day when he looketh not for him, and at an hour when he is not aware, and will cut him in sunder, and will appoint him his portion with the unbelievers.

And that servant, which knew his lord's will, and prepared not himself, neither did according to his will, shall be beaten with many stripes. But he that knew not, and did commit things worthy of stripes, shall be beaten with few stripes. For unto whomsoever much is given, of him shall be much required: and to whom men have committed much, of him they will ask the more.

QUESTION

Here Jesus appears to advocate varying punishments based upon the knowledge of the offender. In this parable, the servant who possesses more knowledge is held to a higher standard of performance. We know from the writings of the great Jewish Rabbi Maimonides that the Jewish society, which was Jesus' audience here, developed a tradition of tailoring punishments to the individual. What are the requirements of ideal justice? Is justice ideally tailored to the individual? If so, should our tort system seek to tailor standards of expected conduct to the abilities of the individual? If not, why not?

a. INTELLECTUAL DISABILITY

VAUGHAN V. MENLOVE
132 ENG. REP. 490 (C.P. 1837)

[Defendant stacked hay near the border of his property. Because of the way the hay was stacked, it caught fire; the fire spread to Defendant's barn and stables, and from there it spread to Plaintiff's cottages, which were destroyed.]

Patteson, J. before whom the cause was tried, told the jury that the question for them to consider, was, whether the fire had been occasioned by . . . negligence on the part of the defendant; adding, that he was bound to proceed with such reasonable caution as a prudent man would have exercised under such circumstances.

A verdict having been found for the Plaintiff, . . . a new trial was obtained, on the ground that the jury should have been directed to consider, not, whether the Defendant had been guilty of . . . . negligence with reference to the standard of ordinary prudence, . . . but whether he had acted bona fide to the best of his judgment; if he had, he ought not to be responsible for the misfortune of not possessing the highest order of intelligence. . . .

Tindal C. J.

. . . It is contended . . . that the question of negligence was so mixed up with reference to what would be the conduct of a man of ordinary prudence that the jury might have thought the latter the rule by which they were to decide; that such a rule would be too uncertain to act upon; and that the question ought to have been whether the Defendant had acted honestly and bona fide to the best of his own judgment. That, however, would leave so vague a line as to afford no rule at all, the degree of judgment belonging to each individual being infinitely various: and though it has been urged that the care which a prudent man would take, is not an intelligible proposition as a rule of law, yet such has always been the rule adopted in cases of bailment, as laid down in *Coggs* v. *Bernard* . . . . The care taken by a prudent man has always been the rule laid down; and as to the supposed difficulty of applying it, a jury has always been able to say, whether, taking that rule as their guide, there has been negligence on the occasion in question. Instead, therefore, of saying that the liability for negligence should be co-extensive with the judgment of each individual, which would be as variable as the length of the foot of each individual, we ought rather to adhere to the rule which requires in all cases a regard to caution such as a man of ordinary prudence would observe. That was in substance the criterion presented to the jury in this case, and therefore the present rule must be discharged. . . .

Vaughan J.

The principle on which this action proceeds, is by no means new. It has been urged that the Defendant in such a case takes no duty on himself; but I do not agree in that position: everyone takes upon himself the duty of so dealing with his own property as not to injure the property of others. It was, if anything, too favourable to the Defendant to leave it to the jury whether he had been guilty of . . . negligence . . . . The conduct of a prudent man has always been the criterion for the jury in such cases . . . . Here, there was not a single witness whose testimony did not go to establish . . . negligence in the Defendant. . . .

NOTES AND QUESTIONS

1   *Vaughan* probably is the most celebrated and perhaps the first example of a court holding that the negligence standard of care is an "objective" standard. What different standard of care did defendant advocate? What would a "subjective" standard of care look like?

2   Why did defendant in *Vaughan* contend that he should be excused from the ordinary standard of care? Is defendant's argument right? Assume for a moment that the defendant's mental ability was so low that he simply was incapable of living up to a standard of "average" care. Should the law hold defendant to an unattainable standard of care?

3   Perhaps the most persuasive advocate of the objective standard of care was Justice Oliver Wendell Holmes:

> The standards of the law are standards of general application. The law takes no account of the infinite varieties of temperament, intellect, and education which make the internal character of a given act so different in different men. It does not attempt to see men as God sees them, for more than one sufficient reason. In the first place, the impossibility of nicely measuring a man's powers and limitations is [clear]. But a more satisfactory explanation is, that, when men live in society, a certain average of conduct, a sacrifice of individual peculiarities going beyond a certain point, is necessary to the general welfare. If, for instance, a man is born hasty and awkward, is always having accidents and hurting himself or his neighbors, no doubt his congenital defects will be allowed for in the courts of Heaven, but his slips are no less troublesome to his neighbors than if they sprang from guilty neglect. His neighbors accordingly require him, at his proper peril, to come up to their standard, and the courts which they establish decline to take his personal equation into account.

Oliver Wendell Holmes, Jr., *The Common Law* 108 (1881). Do you agree that "the courts of Heaven" will make allowance for our congenital limitations? If so, why should the courts of earth ignore them? Holmes says that it is impossible for courts to "nicely measure a man's powers and limitations." Even so, is it entirely impossible to measure them? Even if individual limitations cannot be measured "nicely" or perfectly, should we abandon the project altogether? What do you think of Holmes' "more satisfactory" explanation of the objective standard of care? Is he saying that some individual justice must be sacrificed on the altar of society's general welfare?

4   *Knowledge of the Reasonable Person.* The conduct of the reasonably prudent person is judged assuming that the person knows what a reasonably prudent person would know. This includes knowing the law.

b. MENTAL ILLNESS

CREASY V. RUSK
730 N.E.2D 659 (IND. 2000)

Carol Creasy, a certified nursing assistant, sued Lloyd Rusk, an Alzheimer's patient, for injuries she suffered when he kicked her while she was trying to put him to bed. We hold that adults with mental disabilities have the same general duty of care toward others as those without. . . .

Background

In July, 1992, Lloyd Rusk's wife admitted Rusk to the Brethren Healthcare Center ("BHC") because he suffered from memory loss and confusion and Rusk's wife was unable to care for him. Rusk's primary diagnosis was Alzheimer's disease. Over the course of three years at BHC, Rusk experienced periods of anxiousness, confusion, depression, disorientation, and agitation. Rusk often resisted when staff members attempted to remove him from prohibited areas of the facility. On several occasions, Rusk was belligerent with both staff and other residents. In particular, Rusk was often combative, agitated, and aggressive and would hit staff members when they tried to care for him.

. . . On May 16, 1995, Creasy and another certified nursing assistant, Linda Davis, were working through their routine of putting Rusk and other residents to bed. Creasy knew that Rusk had been "very agitated and combative that evening." (R. at 228.) By Creasy's account:

> [Davis] was helping me put Mr. Rusk to bed. She was holding his wrists to keep him from hitting us and I was trying to get his legs to put him to bed. He was hitting and kicking wildly. During this time, he kicked me several times in my left knee and hip area. My lower back popped and I yelled out with pain from my lower back and left knee.

(*Id.*)

Creasy filed a civil negligence suit against Rusk, seeking monetary damages for the injuries she suffered as a result of Rusk's conduct. Rusk moved for summary judgment and the trial court granted his motion. Creasy appealed. The Court of Appeals reversed . . . .

Discussion

This case requires us to decide two distinct questions of Indiana common law:

1. Whether the general duty of care imposed upon adults with mental disabilities is the same as that for adults without mental disabilities?

2. Whether the circumstances of Rusk's case are such that the general duty of care imposed upon adults with mental disabilities should be imposed upon him?

. . . In many, if not most, jurisdictions, the general duty of care imposed on adults with mental disabilities is the same as that for adults without mental disabilities. *See* Restatement (Second) of Torts § 283B (1965). . . . Adults with mental disabilities are held to the same standard of care as that of a reasonable person under the same circumstances without regard to the alleged tortfeasor's capacity to control or understand the consequences of his or her actions. *See id.* . . .

[T]he generally accepted rule in jurisdictions other than Indiana is that . . . mental disability does not excuse a person from liability for "conduct which does not conform to the standard of a reasonable man under like circumstances." Restatement (Second) of Torts § 283B; *accord* Restatement (Third) of Torts § 9(c) (Discussion Draft Apr. 5, 1999) ("Unless the actor is a child, the actor's mental or emotional disability is not considered in determining whether conduct is negligent."). . . . People with mental disabilities are commonly held liable for their intentional and negligent torts. No allowance is made for lack of intelligence, ignorance, excitability, or proneness to accident. *See* Restatement (Second) of Torts § 283B cmt. c.

. . . [T]he Restatement rule holding people with mental disabilities liable for their torts was founded upon public policy considerations. The public policy reasons most often cited for holding individuals with mental disabilities to a standard of reasonable care in negligence claims include the following.

(1) Allocates losses between two innocent parties to the one who caused or occasioned the loss. . . . Under this rationale, the one who experienced the loss or injury as a result of the conduct of a person with a mental disability is presumed not to have assumed risks or to have been contributorily negligent with respect to the cause of the injury. This policy is also intended to protect even negligent third parties from bearing excessive liabilities. *See* Restatement (Third) of Torts § 9 cmt. e (Discussion Draft Apr. 5, 1999).

(2) Provides incentive to those responsible for people with disabilities and interested in their estates to prevent harm and "restrain" those who are potentially dangerous. . . .

(3) Removes inducements for alleged tort-feasors to fake a mental disability in order to escape liability. *See, e.g., id.* The Restatement mentions the ease with which mental disability can be feigned as one possible basis for this policy concern. *See* Restatement (Second) of Torts § 283B cmt. B.

(4) Avoids administrative problems involved in courts and juries attempting to identify and assess the significance of an actor's disability. . . . As a practical matter, it is arguably too difficult to account for or draw any "satisfactory line between mental deficiency and those variations of temperament, intellect, and emotional balance." . . .

(5) Forces persons with disabilities to pay for the damage they do if they "are to live in the world." . . . The Restatement adds that it is better that the assets, if any, of the one with the mental deficiency be used "to compensate innocent victims than that [the assets] remain in their hands." *Id.* A discussion draft for the Restatement (Third) of Torts rephrases this policy rationale and concludes: "If a person is suffering from a mental disorder so serious as to make it likely that the person will engage in substandard conduct that threatens the safety of others, there can be doubts as to whether this person should be allowed to engage in the normal range of society's activities; given these doubts, there is nothing especially harsh in at least holding the person responsible for the harms the person may cause by substandard conduct." Restatement (Third) of Torts § 9 cmt. e (Discussion Draft April 5, 1999). . . .

In balancing the considerations presented in the foregoing analysis, we reject the Court of Appeals's approach and adopt the Restatement rule. We hold that a person with mental disabilities is generally held to the same standard of care as that of a reasonable person under the same circumstances without regard to the alleged tort-feasor's capacity to control or understand the consequences of his or her actions. . . .

NOTES AND QUESTIONS

1 Is this case like *Vaughan v. Menlove*? How might *Vaughan* be distinguished?

2 *Sudden Incapacitation.* Can this case be distinguished from *Hammontree v. Jenner*?

3 One of the policy justifications cited for the general rule that insanity usually is no defense to a negligence cause of action is avoiding any incentive for defendant to feign mental illness. There is a biblical precedent for this concern. I Samuel 21:10-22:1 records the account of David's sojourn among Israel's enemies, the Philistines. David had been anointed the second king of Israel by Samuel the prophet and judge and was on the run from the wrath of Saul, the first, and still living, king of Israel. David fled to Gath, which was within enemy territory where David's discovery

by the natives of Gath was, understandably, viewed with alarm. David was renowned for his exploits against the Philistines as a soldier. Finding himself between the "rock" of Saul's wrath and the "hard place" of the wrath of Achish, king of Gath, David "changed his behaviour before them, and feigned himself mad in their hands, and scrabbled on the doors of the gate, and let his spittle fall down upon his beard." This performance had the desired effect when Achish responded "Lo, ye see the man is mad: wherefore then have ye brought him to me? Have I need of mad men, that ye have brought this fellow to play the mad man in my presence? shall this fellow come into my house?" The "madman" David was released by the servants of Achish, and David escaped with his life.

c. CHILDHOOD

It is well-established that defendant's childhood status is one of the "circumstances" that ordinarily is taken into account when determining whether defendant has behaved reasonably under the circumstances.

WILLIAMSON V. GARLAND
402 S.W.2D 80 (KY. 1966)

Dennis Neal Williamson, a minor nearly 12 years old, was injured when he was riding a bicycle which collided under the automobile of appellee Raymond Garland. . . . The accident occurred on a clear day in August . . . . Appellant was riding a bicycle northwardly on 29th Street just before the accident. He was "ahead" in a bicycle race being engaged in between Bruce Johnson, also 11, and himself. Appellee was driving his car eastwardly on Jackson at about 20-25 mph; he was driving in the lane nearest the right curb of Jackson. A hedge and slight embankment on the west side of 29th Street partially obstructed the views for travelers going north on 29th and east on Jackson. According to Bruce Johnson, who was trailing appellant on his bicycle, appellant applied his brake as he approached Jackson Street, but skidded in some loose gravel, entered Jackson Street, turned eastwardly on Jackson, and started "pumping" the bike down Jackson. Bruce expressed the opinion that appellant "tried to outrun" the approaching car of appellee. . . .

The appellant sustained a fractured skull and brain injury in the collision; he was unable to recall the details of the accident with any degree of certainty. The appellee was called to testify briefly on cross-examination, and said that he did not see appellant before impact. Appellee said that in his best judgment the collision occurred at the extreme east side of 29th Street at its intersection with Jackson.

During the trial appellant was not able to recall details of the accident, although appellee's counsel elicited answers from him in which he stated that he knew traffic was heavy along Jackson Street, that he should have stopped before entering Jackson, he should have looked to his left but did not think he had, and the accident would not have occurred if he had stopped and looked for traffic. In another portion of the cross-examination appellant spoke of having observed the hedge on his left — to this extent, at least, contradicting his statement that he had not looked to the left.

We examine the question of contributory negligence. Appellant's counsel concedes that the act of appellant would constitute contributory negligence as a matter of law if done by an adult, but asserts that the same rule is not applicable here because of appellant's age.

It is observed that virtually all authorities agree that the child's conduct is to be measured by the standard of care to be expected under the same or similar circumstances from the *ordinary* child of like age . . . . It seems to us that the [best] rule would be to impose on the child-plaintiff the duty to exercise that degree of care reasonably to be expected from the ordinary child of like age . . . under like or similar circumstances. It is quite obvious that the normal seven year old child should not be charged with the same degree of care to be expected of the normal 14 year old child.

. . . [W]e consider it appropriate in cases involving [children] that they be charged with contributory negligence to the extent that their acts may be deemed violative of the degree of care usually exercised by ordinarily prudent children of the same age . . . under like or similar circumstances. This is not to say that no case could arise in which it would be proper to find a child in the 7-14 age group guilty or free of contributory negligence as a matter of law, but it is to say that the case at bar is not such a one. . . . Henceforth, when an issue is presented respecting the contributory negligence of a minor plaintiff . . . , the jury shall be instructed that the minor is charged with the duty to exercise care for his own safety, commensurate with that degree of care usually exercised by an ordinarily prudent minor of the same age . . . of the plaintiff.

. . . The judgment is reversed for further proceedings consistent with this opinion.

DANIELS V. EVANS
224 A.2D 63 (N.H. 1966)

As to the standard of care to be applied to the conduct of the decedent Robert E. Daniels, 19 years of age, the Trial Court charged the jury in part as follows:

> Now, he is considered a minor, being under the age of twenty-one, and a minor child must exercise the care of the average child of his or her age, experience and stage of mental development.
> In other words, he is not held to the same degree of care as an adult.

Concededly these instructions substantially reflect the rule by which the care of a minor has been judged heretofore in the courts of our state. . . . However an examination of the cases will reveal that in most the minors therein were engaged in activities appropriate to their age, experience and wisdom. These included being a pedestrian, riding a bicycle, riding a horse, and coasting.

We agree that minors are entitled to be judged by standards commensurate with their age, experience, and wisdom when engaged in activities appropriate to their age, experience, and wisdom. Hence when children are walking, running, playing with toys, throwing balls, operating bicycles, sliding or engaging in other childhood activities their conduct should be judged by the rule of what is reasonable conduct under the circumstances among which are the age, experience, and stage of mental development of the minor involved.

However, the question is raised by the defendant in this case whether the standard of care applied to minors in such cases should prevail when the minor is engaged in activities normally undertaken by adults. In other words, when a minor undertakes an adult activity which can result in grave danger to others and to the minor himself if the care used in the course of the activity drops below that care which the reasonable and prudent adult would use, the defendant maintains that the minor's conduct in that instance, should meet the same standards as that of an adult.

Many recent cases have held that when a minor assumes responsibility for the operation of so potentially dangerous an instrument as an automobile, he should assume responsibility for its careful and safe operation in the light of adult standards. . . . The rule has been recognized in Restatement (Second), Torts, s. 283A, comment c.

One of the reasons for such a rule has been stated thusly in *Dellwo* v. *Pearson, supra,* 458: "To give legal sanction to the operation of automobiles by teen-agers with less than ordinary care for the safety of others is impractical today, to say the least. We may take judicial notice of the hazards of automobile traffic, the frequency of accidents, the often catastrophic results of accidents, and the fact that immature individuals are no less prone to accidents than adults. . . . [I]t would be unfair to the public to permit a minor in the operation of a motor vehicle to observe any other standards of care and conduct than those expected of all others. A person observing children at play [may] anticipate conduct that does not reach an adult standard of care or prudence. However, one cannot know whether the operator of an approaching automobile [is] a minor or an adult, and usually cannot protect himself against youthful imprudence even if warned." . . .

We are of the opinion that to apply to minors a more lenient standard in the operation of motor vehicles, whether an automobile or a motorcycle, than that applied to adults is unrealistic, contrary to the expressed legislative policy, and inimical to public safety. . . . We hold therefore that a minor operating a motor vehicle, whether an automobile or a motorcycle, must be judged by the same standard of care as an adult and the defendant's objection to the Trial Court's charge applying a different standard to the conduct of plaintiff's intestate was valid.

NOTES

1 The Restatement (Third) of Torts adopts the overwhelming majority position that children are held to the standard of a child of like age unless engaged in an "adult" activity.

2 Some jurisdictions decline as a matter of law to permit very young children to be treated as negligent, and the Restatement (Third) of Torts provides that children under the age of four cannot be negligent as a matter of law.

3 The leading case for the rule that children engaged in adult activities is *Dellwo* v. *Pearson*, which is cited in *Daniels* v. *Evans*. The critical issue in subsequent cases has been whether the particular activity in which the child was engaged should be considered an "adult" activity. Perhaps because *Dellwo* involved a child driving a power boat, many, perhaps even most, cases applying an adult standard of care to a child engaged in an "adult" activity involve the child's use of a motorized vehicle.

4 Why should children engaged in adult activities be judged by an adult standard of care?

d. PHYSICAL DISABILITY

ROBERTS V. LOUISIANA
396 SO. 2D 566 (LA. CT. APP. 1981)

In this tort suit, William C. Roberts sued to recover damages for injuries he sustained in an accident in the lobby of the U. S. Post Office Building in Alexandria, Louisiana. Roberts fell after being bumped into by Mike Burson, the blind operator of the concession stand located in the building. Plaintiff sued the State of Louisiana . . . [for] negligent failure by the State to properly supervise and oversee the safe operation of the concession stand. The stand's blind operator, Mike Burson, is not a party to this suit although he is charged with negligence. . . . The trial court . . . dismissed [plaintiff's suit] . . . . We affirm the trial court's decision for the reasons which follow.

On September 1, 1977, at about 12:45 in the afternoon, operator Mike Burson left his concession stand to go to the men's bathroom located in the building. As he was walking down the hall, he bumped into plaintiff who fell to the floor and injured his hip. Plaintiff was 75 years old, stood 5'6" and weighed approximately 100 pounds. Burson, on the other hand, was 25 to 26 years old, stood approximately 6' and weighed 165 pounds.

. . . Even though Burson was not joined as a defendant, his negligence or lack thereof is crucial to a determination of the State's liability. Because of its importance, we begin with it.

Plaintiff contends that operator Mike Burson traversed the area from his concession stand to the men's bathroom in a negligent manner. To be more specific, he focuses on the operator's failure to use his cane even though he had it with him in his concession stand.

In determining an actor's negligence, various courts have imposed differing standards of care to which handicapped persons are expected to perform. Professor William L. Prosser expresses one generally recognized modern standard of care as follows:

> As to his physical characteristics, the reasonable man may be said to be identical with the actor. The man who is blind . . . is entitled to live in the world and to have allowance made by others for his disability, and he cannot be required to do the impossible by conforming to physical standards which he cannot meet . . . At the same time, the conduct of the handicapped individual must be reasonable in the light of his knowledge of his infirmity, which is treated merely as one of the circumstances under which he acts . . . It is sometimes said that a blind man must use a greater degree of care than one who can see; but it is now generally agreed that as a fixed rule this is inaccurate, and that the correct statement is merely that he must take the precautions, be they more or less, which the ordinary reasonable man would take if he were blind.

W. Prosser, *The Law of Torts*, Section 32, at Page 151-52 (4th ed. 1971).

A careful review of the record in this instance reveals that Burson was acting as a reasonably prudent blind person would under these particular circumstances.

Mike Burson is totally blind. Since 1974, he has operated the concession stand located in the lobby of the post office building. . . . Prior to running the vending stand in Alexandria, Burson attended Arkansas Enterprises for the blind where he received mobility training. In 1972, he took a refresher course in mobility followed by a course on vending stand training. . . .

On the date of the incident in question, Mike Burson testified that he left his concession stand and was on his way to the men's bathroom when he bumped into plaintiff. He, without hesitancy, admitted that at the time he was not using his cane, explaining that he relies on his facial sense which he feels is an adequate technique for short trips inside the familiar building. Burson testified that he does use a cane to get to and from work. Plaintiff makes much of Burson's failure to use a cane when traversing the halls of the post office building. Yet, our review of the testimony received at trial indicates that it is not uncommon for blind people to rely on other techniques when moving around in a familiar setting. . . .

Upon our review of the record, we feel that plaintiff has failed to show that Burson was negligent. Burson testified that he was very familiar with his surroundings, having worked there for three and a half years. He had special mobility training and his reports introduced into evidence indicate good mobility skills. He explained his decision to rely on his facial sense instead of his cane for these short trips in a manner which convinces us that it was a reasoned decision. Not only was Burson's explanation adequate, there was additional testimony from other persons indicating that such a decision is not an unreasonable one. Also important is the total lack of any evidence in the record showing that at the time of the incident, Burson engaged in any acts which may be characterized as negligence on his part. For example, there is nothing showing that Burson was walking too fast, not paying attention, et cetera. Under all of these circumstances, we conclude that Mike Burson was not negligent.

Our determination that Mike Burson was not negligent disposes of our need to discuss liability on the part of the State.

For the above and foregoing reasons, the judgment of the trial court dismissing plaintiff's claims against defendant is affirmed and all costs of this appeal are assessed against the plaintiff-appellant.

Affirmed.

NOTES

1   *Roberts* is an example of the usual rule with regard to defendants with physical disabilities, which is precisely the opposite of that applied with regard to the impact of mental or emotional characteristics on the standard of care. Why should physical characteristics be taken into account when judging a party's conduct but not mental or emotional characteristics?

2   One who knows that he or she is subject to a disability may be negligent in deciding to undertake some activities at all. In *Roberts v. Ring*, (Minn. 1919), the Court pointed out that if the jury were to take the elderly defendant's old age into account in determining whether he drove negligently, that infirmity must be taken into account in judging whether defendant had exercised ordinary care in deciding whether to take to the road in the first place. (Most cases have held that old age, as such, is not taken into account when determining whether defendant has exercised due care.) In other words, even if an aged defendant were not held to the driving standard of a younger,

well-sighted person, then he still would be required to exercise the ordinary judgment that an aged, poorly-sighted person would exercise in deciding whether to drive at all. *See also* Restatement Torts (Second) Sec. 283C, Comment c.

3   Disability produced by voluntary intoxication does not adjust the standard of care by which a defendant's conduct is judged.

e. SPECIAL SKILL

HEATH V. SWIFT WINGS
252 S.E.2D 526 (N.C. APP. 1979)

Assignment of error No. 4 is directed to the trial court's charge concerning the definition of negligence and the applicable standard of care:

> Negligence, ladies and gentlemen of the jury, is the failure of someone to act as a reasonably and careful and prudent person would under the same or similar circumstances. Obviously, this could be the doing of something or the failure to do something, depending on the circumstances. With respect to aviation negligence could be more specifically defined as the failure to exercise that degree of ordinary care and caution, which an ordinary prudent pilot having the same training and experience as Fred Heath, would have used in the same or similar circumstances.

It is a familiar rule of law that the standard of care required of an individual, unless altered by statute, is the conduct of the reasonably prudent man under the same or similar circumstances. . . . While the standard of care of the reasonably prudent man remains constant, the quantity or degree of care required varies significantly with the attendant circumstances. . . .

The trial court improperly introduced a subjective standard of care into the definition of negligence by referring to the "ordinary care and caution, which an ordinary prudent pilot having the same training and experience as Fred Heath, would have used in the same or similar circumstances." We are aware of the authorities which support the application of a greater standard of care than that of the ordinary prudent man for persons shown to possess special skill in a particular endeavor. . . . Indeed, our courts have long recognized that one who engages in a business, occupation, or profession must exercise the requisite degree of learning, skill, and ability of that calling with reasonable and ordinary care. . . . Furthermore, the specialist within a profession may be held to a standard of care greater than that required of the general practitioner. . . . Nevertheless, the professional standard remains an objective standard. . . .

Such objective standards avoid the evil of imposing a different standard of care upon each individual. The instructions in this case concerning the pilot's standard of care are misleading at best, and a misapplication of the law. They permit the jury to consider Fred Heath's own particular experience and training, whether outstanding or inferior, in determining the requisite standard of conduct, rather than applying a minimum standard generally applicable to all pilots.

The plaintiff is entitled to an instruction holding Fred Heath to the objective minimum standard of care applicable to all pilots.

. . . This matter was well tried by both counsel for plaintiff and counsel for defendants, and several days were consumed in its trial. Nevertheless, for prejudicial errors in the charge, there must be a

New trial.

NOTE

1   The Restatement of Torts provides that a defendant's superior knowledge or skill is taken into account in determining whether the actor has exercised reasonable care under the circumstances.

f. EMERGENCY

CORDAS V. PEERLESS TRANSP. CO.
27 N.Y.S.2D 198 (N.Y. CITY CT. 1941)

CARLIN, Justice.

This case presents the ordinary man – that problem child of the law – in a most bizarre setting. As a lowly chauffeur in defendant's employ he became in a trice the protagonist in a breach-bating drama with a denouement almost tragic. It appears that a man, whose identity it would be indelicate to divulge was feloniously relieved of his portable goods by two nondescript highwaymen in an alley near 26th Street and Third Avenue, Manhattan; they induced him to relinquish his possessions by a strong argument ad hominem couched in the convincing cant of the criminal and pressed at the point of a most persuasive pistol. Laden with their loot, but not thereby impeded, they took an abrupt departure and he, shuffling off the coil of that discretion which enmeshed him in the alley, quickly gave chase through 26th Street toward 2d Avenue, whether they were resorting "with expedition swift as thought" for most obvious reasons. Somewhere on that thoroughfare of escape they indulged the stratagem of separation ostensibly to disconcert their pursuer and allay the ardor of his pursuit. He then centered on for capture the man with the pistol whom he saw board defendant's taxicab, which quickly veered south toward 25th Street on 2d Avenue where he saw the chauffeur jump out while the cab, still in motion, continued toward 24th Street; after the chauffeur relieved himself of the cumbersome burden of his fare the latter also is said to have similarly departed from the cab before it reached 24th Street.

The chauffeur's story is substantially the same except that he states that his uninvited guest boarded the cab at 25th Street while it was at a standstill waiting for a less colorful fare; that his "passenger" immediately advised him "to stand not upon the order of his going but to go at once" and added finality to his command by an appropriate gesture with a pistol addressed to his sacroiliac. The chauffeur in reluctant acquiescence proceeded about fifteen feet, when his hair, like unto the quills of the fretful porcupine, was made to stand on end by the hue and cry of the man despoiled accompanied by a clamorous concourse of the law-abiding which paced him as he ran; the concatenation of "stop thief," to which the patter of persistent feet did maddingly beat time, rang in his ears as the pursuing posse all the while gained on the receding cab with its quarry therein contained. The hold-up man sensing his insecurity suggested to the chauffeur that in the event there was the slightest lapse in obedience to his curt command that he, the chauffeur, would suffer the loss of his brains, a prospect as horrible to an humble chauffeur as it undoubtedly would be to one of the intelligentsia. The chauffeur apprehensive of certain dissolution from either Scylla, the pursuers, or Charybdis, the pursued, quickly threw his car out of first speed in which he was proceeding, pulled on the emergency, jammed on his brakes and, although he thinks the motor was still running, swung open the door to his left and jumped out of his car. He confesses that the only act that smacked of intelligence was that by which he jammed the brakes in order to throw off balance the hold-up man who was half-standing and half-sitting with his pistol menacingly poised. Thus abandoning his car and passenger the chauffeur sped toward 26th Street and then turned to look; he saw the cab proceeding south toward 24th Street where it mounted the sidewalk. The plaintiff-mother and her two infant children were there injured by the cab which, at the time, appeared to be also minus its passenger who, it appears, was apprehended in the cellar of a local hospital where he was pointed out to a police officer by a remnant of the posse, hereinbefore mentioned. He did not appear at the trial. The three aforesaid plaintiffs and the husband-father sue the defendant for damages predicating their respective causes of action upon the contention that the chauffeur was negligent in abandoning the cab under the aforesaid circumstances. Fortunately the injuries sustained were comparatively slight.

Negligence has been variously defined but the common legal acceptation is the failure to exercise that care and caution which a reasonable and prudent person ordinarily would exercise under like conditions or circumstances. . . . Negligence is "not absolute or intrinsic," but "is always relevant to some circumstances of time, place or person." In slight paraphrase of the world's first bard it may be truly observed that the expedition of the chauffeur's violent love of his own security outran the pauser, reason, when he was suddenly confronted with unusual emergency which "took his reason prisoner." The learned attorney for the plaintiffs concedes that the chauffeur acted in an emergency but claims a right to recovery upon the following proposition taken verbatim from his brief: "It is respectfully submitted that the value of the interests of the public at large to be immune from being injured by a dangerous instrumentality such as a car unattended while in motion is very superior to the right of a driver of a motor vehicle to abandon same while it is in motion even when acting under the belief that his life is in danger and by abandoning same he will save his life." To hold thus under the facts adduced herein would be tantamount to a repeal by implication of the primal law of nature written in indelible characters upon the fleshy tablets of sentient creation by the Almighty Law-giver, "the supernal Judge who sits on high."

There are those who stem the turbulent current for bubble fame, or who bridge the yawning chasm with a leap for the leap's sake or who "outstare the sternest eyes that look outbrave the heart most daring on the earth, pluck the young sucking cubs from the she-bear, yea, mock the lion when he roars for prey" to win a fair lady and these are the admiration of the generality of men; but they are made of sterner stuff than the ordinary man upon whom the law places no duty of emulation. The law would indeed be fond if it imposed upon the ordinary man the obligation to so demean himself when suddenly confronted with a danger, not of his creation, disregarding the likelihood that such a contingency may darken the intellect and palsy the will of the common legion of the earth, the fraternity of ordinary men, – whose acts or omissions under certain conditions or circumstances make the yardstick by which the law measures culpability or innocence, negligence or care. If a person is placed in a sudden peril from which death might ensue, the law does not impel another to the rescue of the person endangered nor does it condemn him for his unmoral failure to rescue when he can; this is in recognition of the immutable law written in frail flesh.

Returning to our chauffeur. If the philosophic Horatio and the martial companions of his watch were "distilled almost to jelly with the act of fear" when they beheld "in the dead vast and middle of the night" the disembodied spirit of Hamlet's father stalk majestically by "with a countenance more in sorrow than in anger" was not the chauffeur, though unacquainted with the example of these eminent men-at-arms, more amply justified in his fearsome reactions when he was more palpably confronted by a thing of flesh and blood bearing in its hand an engine of destruction which depended for its lethal purpose upon the quiver of a hair? When Macbeth was cross-examined by Macduff as to any reason he could advance for his sudden despatch of Duncan's grooms he said in plausible answer "Who can be wise, amazed, temperate and furious, loyal and neutral, in a moment? No man." Macbeth did not by a "tricksy word" thereby stand justified as he criminally created the emergency from which he sought escape by indulgence in added felonies to divert suspicion to the innocent. . . . *Kolanka v. Erie Railroad Co.,* 212 N.Y.S. 714, 717, says: "The law in this state does not hold one in an emergency to the exercise of that mature judgment required of him under circumstances where he has an opportunity for deliberate action. He is not required to exercise unerring judgment, which would be expected of him, were he not confronted with an emergency requiring prompt action." The circumstances provide the foil by which the act is brought into relief to determine whether it is or is not negligent. If under normal circumstances an act is done which might be considered negligent it does not follow as a corollary that a similar act is negligent if performed by a person acting under an emergency, not of his own making, in which he suddenly is faced with a patent danger with a moment left to adopt a means of extrication. The chauffeur – the ordinary man in this case – acted in a split second in a most harrowing experience. To call him negligent would be to brand him coward; the court does not do so in spite of what those swaggering heroes, "whose valor plucks dead lions by the beard," may bluster to the contrary. The court is loathe to see the plaintiffs go without recovery even though their damages were slight, but cannot hold the defendant liable upon the facts adduced at the trial. . . . Judgment for defendant against plaintiffs dismissing their complaint upon the merits. . . .

NOTE

1   Courts commonly used to give an "emergency circumstances" instruction when the facts of the case warranted it. Some courts now have held that a separate jury instruction is either unnecessary and/or confusing. A simple instruction that the applicable standard of care is "reasonableness under the circumstances" adequately covers emergencies.

g. RELIGIOUS BELIEF

WILLIAMS V. BRIGHT
658 N.Y.S.2D 910 (N.Y. APP. DIV. 1997)

Plaintiff Robbins was a passenger in an automobile driven by her 70-year-old father on an upstate highway. An eyewitness saw the car veer off the road at about 65 mph and turn over in a culvert on adjoining farmland. There was circumstantial evidence that the driver, who had driven with this plaintiff and other family members early that morning from New York City to Plattsburgh and was returning the same day, had fallen asleep at the wheel. This was conduct that the jury found to be both negligent and a proximate cause of the accident. On this appeal, defendants . . . do not seriously contest liability; the main issue is the trial court's treatment of plaintiff Robbins' alleged failure to mitigate damages due to her religious beliefs as a Jehovah's Witness. . . .

I.

For a hundred years it has been settled law in this state that a party who claims to have suffered damage by the tort of another is bound "to use reasonable and proper efforts to make the damage as small as practicable" (*Blate v. Third Ave. R.R. Co.,* 44 App.Div. 163, 167, 60 N.Y.S. 732), and if an injured party allows the damages to be unnecessarily enhanced, the incurred loss justly falls upon him . . . . Plaintiff Robbins suffered a severely damaged left hip, as well as a painful injury to her right knee. Her own expert testified that if these injuries were not alleviated by well recognized and universally accepted surgical procedures, her prognosis was for a wheelchair-bound life because of the inevitability of necrotic development in the bone structure of these limbs. Moreover, all the experts agreed that the surgical intervention available to this plaintiff (52 years of age at the time of the accident) offered her the prospect of a good recovery and a near normal life. However, Robbins, a devout Jehovah's Witness, presented proof (chiefly from her own hospital records) that she was obliged to refuse these recommended surgeries because her church prohibits the blood transfusions they would necessarily entail.

In accordance with settled law, the New York pattern jury instruction on the subject of damage mitigation refers to the actions of "a reasonably prudent person" . . . and measures the duty to mitigate in accordance with that standard. . . . Although the trial court acquainted the jury with the existence of that standard, it charged that in this case the standard to be applied was something very different (our emphasis added):

> You have to accept as a given that the dictates of her religion forbid blood transfusions.
> And so you have to determine ⋯ whether she ⋯ *acted reasonably as a Jehovah's Witness in refusing surgery which would involve blood transfusions.*
> Was it reasonable for her, not what you would do or your friends or family, *was it reasonable for her given her beliefs, without questioning the validity or the propriety of her beliefs?*

In abandoning the "reasonably prudent person" test in favor of a "reasonable Jehovah's Witness" standard, over defendants' objection, the trial court perceived the issue as involving this plaintiff's fundamental right to the free exercise of her religion, protected by the First Amendment of the United States Constitution . . . . Virtually all of the handful of jurisdictions to have considered the question have adopted the test of the reasonably prudent person instead of the formulation employed here. . . .

In our view, the analysis of the trial court contained many flaws. The first error was in defining the fundamental issue as whether any jury verdict could be permitted to conflict with this plaintiff's "religious belief that it may be better to suffer present pain than to be barred from entering the Kingdom of Heaven" . . . . With all due deference, this is not the question that should have been presented; to put it in this manner inevitably skews the result. . . .

No one suggests that the State, or, for that matter, anyone else, has the right to interfere with that religious belief. But the real issue here is whether the consequences of that belief must be fully paid for here on earth by someone other than the injured believer. According to the trial court, the State has little interest in enforcing its general rule of damage mitigation simply to rescue a wrongdoer from the full consequences of his tortious conduct. . . .

Of course, the State does not have any interest in the question of who wins this lawsuit, or the extent to which one party prevails over the other. But the State *does* have a compelling interest in assuring that the proceedings before its civil tribunals are fair, and that any litigant is not improperly advantaged or disadvantaged by adherence to a particular set of religious principles. The State also has a compelling interest, by constitutional command under the Fourteenth Amendment, to extend equal protection of the law to every person haled before its courts. . . .

Under the Religious Freedom Restoration Act of 1993 . . . a State's effort to impose a substantial burden upon an individual's free exercise of religion may only be justified in the presence of a compelling governmental interest. For example, a State's interest in establishing eligibility rules for unemployment compensation cannot justify forcing a Sabbatarian applicant to accept work on her day of rest ... or requiring Amish children to attend public school in contravention of their religious tenets and practice ....

An order emanating from a State court constitutes "state action" which, under the Fourteenth Amendment, would trigger First Amendment protections .... The trial court's instruction to the jurors on mitigation directed them to pass upon the reasonableness of plaintiff Robbins' objection, on religious grounds, to a blood transfusion. The fallacy in this instruction was that the jury never received any evidence pertaining to the rationale of her religious convictions, nor how universally accepted they may have been by members of her faith. True, there were entries in her medical records that she refused blood transfusions because she was a Jehovah's Witness, and there was brief testimony (in the context of presenting her diminished physical capabilities) that she attended Jehovah's Witness prayer services. But there was no evidence of the basis for the religious prohibition of blood transfusions. The charge thus created a sham inquiry; instead of framing an issue on how plaintiff Robbins' religious beliefs impacted on mitigation, the court foreclosed the issue in her favor without any supporting evidence. Let us recall, the jurors were told that they must ask themselves whether this plaintiff's refusal to accept a blood transfusion was reasonable, "given her beliefs, *without questioning the validity*" of those beliefs (emphasis added). Having thus removed from the jury's consideration any question as to the validity (that is to say, the reasonableness) of plaintiff Robbins' religious convictions, the court effectively directed a verdict on the issue.

Of course, the alternative—the receipt of "expert" testimony on this subject—presents an even worse prospect. Such evidence, if any conflict developed, would present a triable issue as to whether the conviction against transfusions was heretical—or orthodox ... —within the Jehovah's Witness faith. ... Heresy trials are foreign to our Constitution. Men may believe what they cannot prove. They may not be put to the proof of their religious doctrines or beliefs. ... [I]f those doctrines are subject to trial before a jury charged with finding their truth or falsity, then the same can be done with the religious beliefs of any sect. When the triers of fact undertake that task, they enter a forbidden domain." ...

An extraordinary example of the perils of such an excursion is the recent Minnesota case of *Lundman v McKown* ... , where damages were awarded against a Christian Scientist stepfather who blocked conventional treatment that, to a medical certainty, would have saved a young child's life. ... Here was a healthy 11-year-old boy who succumbed to a sudden onset of juvenile diabetes, a disease that is easily diagnosable and treatable by conventional medical practice. Instead, his mother and stepfather enlisted the services of Christian Science practitioners who provided only "spiritual treatment." The child's condition deteriorated rapidly, and he died three days later. There was evidence that a shot of insulin administered as late as two hours before death could have saved him. A wrongful death action was commenced by the child's natural father and older sister against the mother and stepfather, the various spiritual practitioners and the Christian Science Church itself. A jury awarded compensatory damages against all defendants in the amount of $5.2 million (reduced on posttrial motion to $1.5 million), and $9 million in punitive damages against the church.

The Minnesota Court of Appeals overturned the verdict against the church and its officials, but upheld the portion of the award against the mother, stepfather and local practitioners. In reaching that conclusion, the appellate court allowed itself to become deeply entangled in ecclesiastical matters regarding the tenets of the Christian Science faith. The trial court, in awarding damages against the mother and stepfather, had applied the reasonable person standard of care. The Court of Appeals ruled, to the contrary, that the proper standard was that of the "reasonable Christian Scientist," but then went on to hold, as a matter of law, that a new trial was not warranted because the reasonable Christian Scientist would necessarily have concluded (as did the jury under the reasonable person standard) that the life-or-death interest of the child should have prevailed and dictated conventional medical treatment . . . . In other words, the appellate court undertook to evaluate the reasonableness of various practices and tenets of the Christian Science faith; by doing so as a matter of law, it proceeded deep into the very "forbidden domain" . . . . We should firmly decline to follow that rarely trodden and perilous path.

II.

In espousing the objective standard and remanding this matter for a new trial, we take note of an obvious problem with strict adherence to the pattern jury instruction that is provided as a general guide . . . . We conclude that the unmodified application of that formulation would work an injustice in this case, as well as in others of a similar nature. It seems apparent to us that a person in plaintiff Robbins' position must be permitted to present to the jury the basis for her refusal of medical treatment; otherwise, the jury would simply be left with the fact of her refusal, without any explanation at all. Once such evidence is (as it should be) received, the court is called upon to instruct the jurors as to how such evidence should affect their deliberations. Addressing this issue, we hold that the pattern jury instruction must be supplemented here with the following direction: "In considering whether the plaintiff acted as a reasonably prudent person, you may consider the plaintiff's testimony that she is a believer in the Jehovah's Witness faith, and that as an adherent of that faith, she cannot accept any medical treatment which requires a blood transfusion. I charge you that such belief is a factor for you to consider, together with all the other evidence you have heard, in determining whether the plaintiff acted reasonably in caring for her injuries, keeping in mind, however, that the overriding test is whether the plaintiff acted as a reasonably prudent person, under all the circumstances confronting her."

The so-called "reasonable believer" charge . . . has found some support in other jurisdictions . . . . Our modification of the PJI charge is intended to strike a fair balance between the competing interests of these parties. And in pursuit of that goal, we reiterate that the court is *not* to permit the introduction of any "theological" proof, by way of either expert or lay testimony, as to the validity of religious doctrine, nor should the court issue any instructions whatsoever on that score. . . .

And whatsoever man there be of the house of Israel, or of the strangers that sojourn among you, that eateth any manner of blood; I will even set my face against that soul that eateth blood, and will cut him off from among his people. For the life of the flesh is in the blood: and I have given it to you upon the altar to make an atonement for your souls: for it is the blood that maketh an atonement for the soul. Therefore I said unto the children of Israel, No soul of you shall eat blood, neither shall any stranger that sojourneth among you eat blood. And whatsoever man there be of the children of Israel, or of the strangers that sojourn among you, which hunteth and catcheth any beast or fowl that may be eaten; he shall even pour out the blood thereof, and cover it with dust. For it is the life of all flesh; the blood of it is for the life thereof: therefore I said unto the children of Israel, Ye shall eat the blood of no manner of flesh: for the life of all flesh is the blood thereof: whosoever eateth it shall be cut off.

And certain men which came down from Judaea taught the brethren, and said, Except ye be circumcised after the manner of Moses, ye cannot be saved. When therefore Paul and Barnabas had no small dissension and disputation with them, they determined that Paul and Barnabas, and certain other of them, should go up to Jerusalem unto the apostles and elders about this question. And being brought on their way by the church, they passed through Phenice and Samaria, declaring the conversion of the Gentiles: and they caused great joy unto all the brethren. And when they were come to Jerusalem, they were received of the church, and of the apostles and elders, and they declared all things that God had done with them. But there rose up certain of the sect of the Pharisees which believed, saying, That it was needful to circumcise them, and to command them to keep the law of Moses.

And the apostles and elders came together for to consider of this matter. And when there had been much disputing, Peter rose up, and said unto them, Men and brethren, ye know how that a good while ago God made choice among us, that the Gentiles by my mouth should hear the word of the gospel, and believe. And God, which knoweth the hearts, bare them witness, giving them the Holy Ghost, even as he did unto us; And put no difference between us and them, purifying their hearts by faith. Now therefore why tempt ye God, to put a yoke upon the neck of the disciples, which neither our fathers nor we were able to bear? But we believe that through the grace of the Lord Jesus Christ we shall be saved, even as they. Then all the multitude kept silence, and gave audience to Barnabas and Paul, declaring what miracles and wonders God had wrought among the Gentiles by them. And after they had held their peace, James answered, saying, Men and brethren, hearken unto me: Simeon hath declared how God at the first did visit the Gentiles, to take out of them a people for his name. And to this agree the words of the prophets; as it is written, After this I will return, and will build again the tabernacle of David, which is fallen down; and I will build again the ruins thereof, and I will set it up: That the residue of men might seek after the Lord, and all the Gentiles, upon whom my name is called, saith the Lord, who doeth all these things. Known unto God are all his works from the beginning of the world. Wherefore my sentence is, that we trouble not them, which from among the Gentiles are turned to God: But that we write unto them, that they abstain from pollutions of idols, and from fornication, and from things strangled, and from blood. For Moses of old time hath in every city them that preach him, being read in the synagogues every sabbath day.

Then pleased it the apostles and elders, with the whole church, to send chosen men of their own company to Antioch with Paul and Barnabas; namely, Judas surnamed Barsabas, and Silas, chief men among the brethren: And they wrote letters by them after this manner; The apostles and elders and brethren send greeting unto the brethren which are of the Gentiles in Antioch and Syria and Cilicia: Forasmuch as we have heard, that certain which went out from us have troubled you with words, subverting your souls, saying, Ye must be circumcised, and keep the law: to whom we gave no such commandment: It seemed good unto us, being assembled with one accord, to send chosen men unto you with our beloved Barnabas and Paul, Men that have hazarded their lives for the name of our Lord Jesus Christ. We have sent therefore Judas and Silas, who shall also tell you the same things by mouth. For it seemed good to the Holy Ghost, and to us, to lay upon you no greater burden than these necessary things; That ye abstain from meats offered to idols, and from blood, and from things strangled, and from fornication: from which if ye keep yourselves, ye shall do well. Fare ye well. So when they were dismissed, they came to Antioch: and when they had gathered the multitude together, they delivered the epistle: Which when they had read, they rejoiced for the consolation.

2. COST/BENEFIT BALANCING

Having spent some time examining the applicable standard of due care in a negligence action – reasonableness under the circumstances – we turn now to the more practical question of how to determine what is reasonable under the circumstances? Scholars and courts have spilled gallons of ink trying to bring more concrete content to the otherwise vague and general reasonableness inquiry. One method for assessing reasonableness that has become generally accepted is to perform some form of risk/utility or cost/benefit balancing. The common-sense idea here is that there is a correlative relationship between the care that is reasonable and the risk to be avoided. Greater risk warrants greater care. In this regard, section 291 of the Restatement (Second) of Torts sets out a widely-adopted balancing "test": "the risk is unreasonable and the act is negligent if the risk is of such magnitude as to outweigh what the law regards as the utility of the act or of the particular manner in which it is done."

In defining "Negligence," the Restatement (Third) Torts Sec. 3 provides similarly that "[p]rimary factors to consider in ascertaining whether the person's conduct lacks reasonable care are the foreseeable likelihood that the person's conduct will result in harm, the foreseeable severity of any harm that may ensue, and the burden of precautions to eliminate or reduce the risk of harm." Of course, risk/utility balancing was around in one form or another long before either Restatement was drafted. In the following case, the celebrated American jurist, Learned Hand, articulated the most famous expression of the risk/utility principle, which has come to be known as "the Hand formula" or "the calculus of risk":

UNITED STATES V. CARROLL TOWING CO.
159 F.2D 169 (2D CIR. 1947)

These appeals concern the sinking of the barge, "Anna C," on January 4, 1944 . . . . [T]he Conners Company chartered the barge, "Anna C," to the Pennsylvania Railroad Company . . . , which included the services of a bargee, apparently limited to the hours 8 A.M. to 4 P.M. . . . [F]ive other barges were moored outside her, extending into the river . . . . The Grace Line, which had chartered the tug, "Carroll," sent her down to . . . "drill" out one of the barges which lay at the end of the Public Pier . . . . The captain of the "Carroll" put a deckhand and the "harbormaster" on the barges, [and] told them to . . . make sure that the . . . [barges] on Pier 52 [were] safely moored, as there was a strong northerly wind blowing down the river. The "harbormaster" and the deckhand went aboard the barges and readjusted all the fasts to their satisfaction, including those from the "Anna C." to the pier.

After doing so, they . . . again boarded the "Carroll," which backed away from the outside barge . . . . She had only got about seventy-five feet away when the [barges] . . . broke adrift because the fasts from the "Anna C," either rendered, or carried away. The tide and wind carried down the six barges, still holding together, until the "Anna C" fetched up against a tanker, . . . whose propeller broke a hole in her at or near her bottom. Shortly thereafter . . . , she careened, dumped her cargo of flour and sank. The tug, "Grace," owned by the Grace Line, and the "Carroll," came to the help of the flotilla after it broke loose; and, as both had syphon pumps on board, they could have kept the "Anna C" afloat, had they learned of her condition; but the bargee had left her on the evening before, and nobody was on board to observe that she was leaking. . . .

L. HAND, J.

We cannot . . . excuse the Conners Company for the bargee's failure to care for the barge, and we think that this prevents full recovery. . . . [I]f the bargee had been on board, and had done his duty to his employer, he would have gone below at once, examined the injury, and called for help from the "Carroll" and the Grace Line tug. Moreover, it is clear that these tugs could have kept the barge afloat, until they had safely beached her, and saved her cargo. This would have avoided what we shall call the "sinking damages." . . . For this reason the question arises whether a barge owner is slack in the care of his barge if the bargee is absent.

. . . [T]here is no general rule to determine when the absence of a bargee or other attendant will make the owner of the barge liable for injuries to other vessels if she breaks away from her moorings. . . . It becomes apparent why there can be no such general rule, when we consider the grounds for such a liability. Since there are occasions when every vessel will break from her moorings, and since, if she does, she becomes a menace to those about her; the owner's duty, as in other similar situations, to provide against resulting injuries is a function of three variables: (1) The probability that she will break away; (2) the gravity of the resulting injury, if she does; (3) the burden of adequate precautions. Possibly it serves to bring this notion into relief to state it in algebraic terms: if the probability be called P; the injury, L; and the burden, B; liability depends upon whether B is less than L multiplied by P: i.e., whether $B < PL$.

Applied to the situation at bar, the likelihood that a barge will break from her fasts and the damage she will do, vary with the place and time; for example, if a storm threatens, the danger is greater; so it is, if she is in a crowded harbor where moored barges are constantly being shifted about. On the other hand, the barge must not be the bargee's prison, even though he lives aboard; he must go ashore at times. . . . [W]e hold that it is not in all cases a sufficient answer to a bargee's absence without excuse, during working hours, that he has properly made fast his barge to a pier, when he leaves her. In the case at bar the bargee left at five o'clock in the afternoon of January 3rd, and the flotilla broke away at about two o'clock in the afternoon of the following day, twenty-one hours afterwards. The bargee had been away all the time, and we hold that his fabricated story was affirmative evidence that he had no excuse for his absence. At the locus in quo—especially during the short January days and in the full tide of war activity—barges were being constantly "drilled" in and out. Certainly it was not beyond reasonable expectation that, with the inevitable haste and bustle, the work might not be done with adequate care. In such circumstances we hold—and it is all that we do hold—that it was a fair requirement that the Conners Company should have a bargee aboard (unless he had some excuse for his absence), during the working hours of daylight.

NOTES

1   How does the court go about determining what the barge owner should have done to satisfy due care?

2   *Duty v. Breach.* Note that the Hand formula does not address the question whether a duty is owed at all. Rather, the Hand formula provides a method for analyzing what reasonable care requires, assuming that a duty exists.

3   *Risk/benefit at the margin.* Precaution should be assessed under the Hand formula at the margin. While a particular "set" of care might, in some sense seem "efficient," when analyzed as a set and compared with "no care," some lesser-included level of care might be even more efficient. For example, when measured as a set, the benefit of wearing both a belt and suspenders might seem "worth" the cost – the risk of losing one's trousers could be reduced to near zero. But once either the belt or suspenders is worn, the cost of adding the other might not be worthwhile since the risk of losing one's trousers is reduced to near zero by the first protective measure so that little additional protection is gained by adding the second. Likewise, risk must by analyzed marginally. Returning to *Krayenbuhl* for an illustration, note that even dangerous turntables probably are an economic plus, but we do not analyze the risk as a set. Rather we compare the incremental cost of a particular element of care against the incremental gains in safety to determine whether the *status quo* is reasonable.

Perhaps no one has done more to expand consideration and/or application of the "Hand formula" than contemporary jurist and "law and economics" scholar, Richard Posner, whose book, The Economic Analysis of Law, practically builds an entire jurisprudence on the Hand Formula. The following is one of Judge Posner's opinions applying a Hand analysis.

UNITED STATES FID. & GUAR. CO. V. PLOVIDBA
683 F.2D 1022 (7TH CIR. 1982)

POSNER, Circuit Judge.

This is an appeal from a judgment exonerating the defendant, a Yugoslavian enterprise that owns the M/V *Makarska*, from negligence in connection with the death of a longshoreman, Patrick Huck, who fell into a hold.

The *Makarska* has five holds, numbered 1 through 5 from bow to stern . . . . Holds 2 through 5 are identical . . . . Each has three decks. From top to bottom they are the weather deck, the upper 'tween deck, and the lower 'tween deck. Below the lower 'tween deck is the main cargo area of the hold. Each deck contains a hatch roughly 30 feet across. When all three hatches in a hold are open, cargo can be loaded into (or unloaded from) the main cargo area. Hatchways of the typical maritime type (smaller than regular doorways, and with high thresholds) connect the holds laterally at each deck.

Hold number 1 is different from the others: its top is raised to form a forecastle. As a result the weather deck of hold number 1 is at a higher level than the weather deck of the other four holds, its upper 'tween deck is flush with the weather decks of the other holds, and its lower 'tween deck is flush with the upper 'tween decks of the other holds.

On the morning of the day he was killed, Huck was working with a party of longshoremen on the upper 'tween deck of hold number 1. The hatch above them (in the weather deck) was open to give them light, and the hatch beneath their feet (in the upper 'tween deck) was closed. The longshoremen completed their work in hold number 1 at noon and took their lunch break. When work resumed it was in hold number 4, but by the end of the afternoon the longshoremen were working on the weather deck of hold number 2, which is to say on the same level as, and adjacent to, the upper 'tween deck of hold number 1.

After the longshoremen had completed their work in hold number 1 and broken for lunch, the ship's crew had come in and closed the hatch in the weather deck but opened the two hatches below it (the hatches in the upper 'tween and lower 'tween decks). This is a customary practice to facilitate a prompt start on loading and unloading cargo at the next port of call, for it can take as long as 30 minutes to open each hatch.

The closing of the hatch in the weather deck of hold number 1 plunged the entire hold into pitch darkness. Sometime during the late afternoon Huck, unobserved, entered hold number 1. He did so by stepping through the hatchway between the weather deck of hold number 2, where the longshoremen were then working, and the upper 'tween deck of hold number 1, now in darkness. It is unclear whether he opened the door in the hatchway or whether it was open already. It would not have been locked, but only latched, so if it was not already open he could easily have opened it. The hatch in the upper 'tween deck of hold number 1 – now open, but in darkness – begins about 6 to 10 feet in from the hatchway where Huck entered. But Huck's body was found at the bottom of the forward part of hold number 1, some 40 feet in from the hatchway. This suggests that he had not walked directly into the open hatch, but rather had fallen in from the forward part of the upper 'tween deck after having successfully skirted the open hatch when he first entered.

The other longshoremen left the ship without noticing that Huck was not among them. His body was not found till the next morning. No one knows why Huck was in hold number 1. But it was stipulated that crates of liquor were stored in the forward part of the hold on the upper 'tween deck, the part from which Huck apparently fell, and it is conjectured that he was planning to steal some of the liquor on his way off the ship. The jury . . . found that the ship owner had not been negligent . . . .

[T]he negligence formula proposed in *Johnson v. A/S Ivarans Rederi*, . . . 613 F.2d at 348, . . . requires "balancing the usefulness to the ship of the dangerous condition and the burden involved in curing it against the probability and severity of the harm it poses." This formula echoes that of Judge Learned Hand in *United States v. Carroll Towing Co.*, 159 F.2d 169, 173 (2d Cir. 1947), also a maritime negligence case, though *Johnson* does not cite *Carroll Towing*. Judge Hand, designating by "B" the burden of the precautions necessary to avert an accident, by "L" the magnitude of the loss if the accident occurred, and by "P" the probability that if the precautions were not taken the accident would occur, reasoned that a ship owner or other alleged tortfeasor was negligent if B<PL, that is, if the burden of precautions was less than the harm if the accident occurred discounted (i.e., multiplied) by the probability that it would occur. The higher P and L are, and the lower B is, the likelier is a finding of negligence.

Though mathematical in form, the Hand formula does not yield mathematically precise results in practice; that would require that B, P, and L all be quantified, which so far as we know has never been done in an actual lawsuit. Nevertheless, the formula is a valuable aid to clear thinking about the factors that are relevant to a judgment of negligence and about the relationship among those factors. . . . We do not want to force the district courts into a straitjacket, so we do not hold that they must use the Hand formula in all maritime negligence cases. We merely commend it to them as a useful tool – one we have found helpful in this case in evaluating the plaintiff's . . . contention that negligence was shown as a matter of law. . . .

The plaintiff . . . contends that . . . the undisputed facts showed negligence by the ship owner as a matter of law. We again use the Hand formula to frame this issue. L, the loss if the accident occurred, was large. There was a 25 foot drop from the upper 'tween deck of hold number 1 to the bottom of the hold, and a fall from that height was very likely to cause serious injury or, as in this case, death. As to B, the burden of precautions, there were various ways the ship owner could have prevented the accident. He could have lit the hold, locked the hatchway leading to it from the weather deck of hold number 2, roped off the open hatch, or placed a sign at the hatchway (though the effectiveness of this last precaution may be doubted). Probably the cheapest way of avoiding the accident, however, would have been for the ship's crew not to open the hatches until all the longshoremen had left the ship. This would have meant either the crew's working after normal working hours, or, if the opening of the hatches was postponed till the following morning, delay in beginning stevedoring operations at the next port of call. We doubt that either alternative would be very costly so we judge B in this case to have been, at most, moderate, and possibly small.

If P, the probability of an accident if the precautions that would avert it were not taken, was high, then it would appear, in light of our discussion of L and B, that the ship owner was negligent in failing to take one of the precautions that we have mentioned. But probably P was low. There was no reason for a longshoreman to reenter a hold after he had completed his work there and moved on to another part of the ship. The plaintiff speculates that Huck may have left a piece of clothing in hold number 1 and gone back to retrieve it. It does not seem very likely that anyone would enter a pitch-black hold to retrieve a glove or a sock or a jacket, when he could easily ask for light. It is far more likely that Huck entered for an illicit purpose. . . . Huck's motive in entering hold number 1 bears on the probability of the accident and hence on the cost-justified level of precautions by the ship owner. . . . Unless it is common for longshoremen to try to pilfer from darkened holds – and it was the plaintiff's burden to show that it is – the ship owner would have no reason to think it so likely that a longshoreman would be in a darkened hold as to require precautions against his falling through an open hatch.

Moreover, the relevant probability, so far as the Hand formula is concerned, is not the probability that a longshoreman would enter a darkened hold but the probability that he would fall into an open hatch in such a hold. The probability was small. The darkness was as effective a warning of danger as a sign would have been. Any longshoreman would know that there was a hatch on the floor and he could not rationally assume that it was closed. Only a reckless person would walk about in the hold in these circumstances, especially if he had no flashlight; Huck had none. There are reckless people as there are dishonest people; but the plaintiff did not try to prove that there are so many reckless dishonest longshoremen as to require the precautions that the defendant in this case would have had to take to avert injury to them.

We do not know whether Huck was aware of the custom of opening the hatches after the longshoremen left the hold, and for the reasons just suggested it is not critical whether he was or not. But probably he was. His body was found well forward of where he would have fallen had he walked straight into the hold. No doubt he was trying to skirt what he knew to be an open hatch. The ship owner was not required to anticipate that a longshoreman knowing of the open shaft would not be able to avoid it; this was possible – it happened – but the probability was too remote to warrant precautions beyond the implicit warning of darkness itself.

Another factor bearing on the probability of an accident is that Huck was under the general supervision of the stevedore company that employed him. Even if the defendant should have regarded Huck as no better than a sheep wandering about the ship with no rational concern for his own safety, it was entitled to regard the stevedore as his principal shepherd. The stevedore had a work rule forbidding longshoremen to be anywhere on the ship except where stevedoring operations were actually in progress. The ship owner was entitled to rely on the stevedore to enforce this rule, if not 100 percent at least enough to make it highly improbable, in light of the other circumstances that we have discussed, that one of the longshoremen would stray away from the rest and fall into a darkened hold.

The fact that the practice of leaving the hatches open in darkened holds was customary (or so the jury could find) and not just an idiosyncrasy of this Yugoslavian ship or ship owner has additional relevance to this case. Although custom is not a defense to a charge of negligence, *The T. J. Hooper*, 60 F.2d 737, 740 (2d Cir. 1932), it is a material consideration in evaluating the charge . . . . If a ship owner were to follow a practice that flunked the Hand formula – that in other words was not cost-justified, because the expected accident costs associated with the practice exceeded the costs of abandoning the practice and so preventing any accident from happening – then he would have to pay his stevedores higher rates, to compensate them for the additional risk to their employees, the longshoremen, whom the stevedores must compensate . . . for any injury the longshoremen sustain in the course of their employment. And since by hypothesis the cost to the stevedores of the additional compensation – the expected accident cost, in other words – would exceed the cost of abandoning the practice (for otherwise the practice would be cost-justified), it would pay the ship owner to abandon it. . . . Hence if the ship owner persists in a dangerous practice – if the whole trade persists in the practice – that is some evidence, though not conclusive, that the practice is cost-justified, and not negligent.

But all this is not to say that the defendant's conduct in this case was, in fact, non-negligent. We are not the triers of fact. The jury found the defendant non-negligent and our job is just to decide whether a reasonable jury could have so found. Obviously we think the jury's finding was reasonable . . . .

The judgment appealed from is
AFFIRMED.

MOISAN V. LOFTUS
178 F.2D 148 (2D CIR. 1949)

. . . On the evening of April 19, 1948, the defendant, Robert F. Loftus, invited the plaintiff to drive with him from Burlington, Vermont, to St. Albans in a truck . . . . The accident happened near midnight on a road, leading north from Burlington, at a point where the highway was close to Lake Champion, whose waters for some unexplained reason had overflowed the road and frozen. The truck skidded on the frozen patch, left the road and injured the plaintiff. . . . Taking the evidence most favorable to [plaintiff], the facts, which a jury might have found, were as follows. After crossing a culvert or bridge the highway going north curved gently to the right, after which it ran unobstructed to the place of the accident. Loftus, the driver, who had been over the road once before, increased his speed to over fifty miles after he had passed the bridge, and put his headlights on "low beam, notwithstanding there were no other vehicles or vehicle lights in sight." The night was cold and windy and the temperature "very close to freezing," although it did not appear how cold it had been during the day. Loftus saw the patch of ice when he was 200 or 300 feet away, and mistook it for water until the truck was upon it, when he applied his brakes hard, which made the truck skid for about 125 feet, strike a tree and upset. The only question we need decide is whether there was enough evidence . . . to support a verdict. The judge thought not, and directed a verdict for the driver.

. . . The difficulties . . . arise from the necessity of applying a quantitative test to an incommensurable subject matter; and the same difficulties inhere in the concept of "ordinary" negligence. It is indeed possible to state an equation for negligence in the form, C equals P times D, in which the C is the care required to avoid risk, D, the possible injuries, and P, the probability that the injuries will occur, if the requisite care is not taken. But of these factors care is the only one ever susceptible of quantitative estimate, and often that is not. The injuries are always a variable within limits, which do not admit of even approximate ascertainment; and, although probability might theoretically be estimated, if any statistics were available, they never are; and, besides, probability varies with the severity of the injuries. It follows that all such attempts are illusory; and, if serviceable at all, are so only to center attention upon which one of the factors may be determinative in any given situation. . . . Confining ourselves therefore to the factor of probability, it appears to us that the chance that the truck would leave the road that night was slight . . . .

Judgment affirmed.

QUESTIONS

1 Is the Court here correct that the elements of a Hand analysis are almost never amenable to quantitative analysis? If so, why is the Hand analysis ever discussed at all? Should it be used?

ANDREWS V. UNITED AIRLINES
24 F.3D 39 (9TH CIR. 1994)

KOZINSKI, Circuit Judge.

We are called upon to determine whether United Airlines took adequate measures to deal with that elementary notion of physics - what goes up, must come down. For, while the skies are friendly enough, the ground can be a mighty dangerous place when heavy objects tumble from overhead compartments.

I

During the mad scramble that usually follows hard upon an airplane's arrival at the gate, a briefcase fell from an overhead compartment and seriously injured plaintiff Billie Jean Andrews. No one knows who opened the compartment or what caused the briefcase to fall, and Andrews doesn't claim that airline personnel were involved in stowing the object or opening the bin. Her claim, rather, is that the injury was foreseeable and the airline didn't prevent it.

The district court dismissed the suit on summary judgment, and we review de novo. . . .

II

. . . To show that United did not satisfy its duty of care toward its passengers, Ms. Andrews presented the testimony of two witnesses. The first was Janice Northcott, United's Manager of Inflight Safety, who disclosed that in 1987 the airline had received 135 reports of items falling from overhead bins. As a result of these incidents, Ms. Northcott testified, United decided to add a warning to its arrival announcements, to wit, that items stored overhead might have shifted during flight and passengers should use caution in opening the bins. . . . This announcement later became the industry standard. . . .

Ms. Andrews's second witness was safety and human factors expert Dr. David Thompson, who testified that United's announcement was ineffective because passengers opening overhead bins couldn't see objects poised to fall until the bins were opened, by which time it was too late. Dr. Thompson also testified that United could have taken additional steps to prevent the hazard, such as retrofitting its overhead bins with baggage nets, as some airlines had already done, . . . or by requiring passengers to store only lightweight items overhead . . . .

United argues that Andrews presented too little proof to satisfy her burden . . . . One hundred thirty-five reported incidents, United points out, are trivial when spread over the millions of passengers travelling on its 175,000 flights every year. . . . Even that number overstates the problem, according to United, because it includes events where passengers merely observed items falling from overhead bins but no one was struck or injured. . . . Indeed, United sees the low incidence of injuries as incontrovertible proof that the safety measures suggested by plaintiff's expert would not merit the additional cost and inconvenience to airline passengers.

III

It is a close question, but we conclude that plaintiff has made a sufficient case to overcome summary judgment. United is hard-pressed to dispute that its passengers are subject to a hazard from objects falling out of overhead bins, considering the warning its flight crews give hundreds of times each day. The case then turns on whether the hazard is serious enough to warrant more than a warning. . . . United has demonstrated neither that retrofitting overhead bins with netting (or other means) would be prohibitively expensive, nor that such steps would grossly interfere with the convenience of its passengers. . . .

The reality, with which airline passengers are only too familiar, is that airline travel has changed significantly in recent years. As harried travelers try to avoid the agonizing ritual of checked baggage, they hand-carry more and larger items - computers, musical instruments, an occasional deceased relative. . . . The airlines have coped with this trend, but perhaps not well enough. Given its awareness of the hazard, United may not have done everything technology permits and prudence dictates to eliminate it. . . .

Jurors, many of whom will have been airline passengers, will be well equipped to decide whether United had a duty to do more than warn passengers about the possibility of falling baggage. A reasonable jury might conclude United should have done more; it might also find that United did enough. Either decision would be rational on the record presented to the district court which, of course, means summary judgment was not appropriate.

REVERSED AND REMANDED.

NOTE

1   *Question of Fact.* Ordinarily, whether the "balance" of the risk calculus tilts toward reasonableness or unreasonableness is a "question of fact," that is, the jury decides. Judges can, sometimes, decide that defendant either was or was not negligent "as a matter of law," which means that no reasonable jury could find to the contrary, but judicial determinations of negligence, or due care, "as a matter of law" are quite rare, especially after the jury already has spoken on the matter. In *Andrews*, for example, Judge Kozinski indicates that a jury decision either way would have been reasonable and not subject to interference by the court.

ANDREWS PROBLEM

Assume that under the status quo, there will be five overhead bin accidents per 100,000 flights, with expected harm of $1,000 per accident. Assume further that the airline can reduce these expected accidents by exercising care according to the following schedule. Which of the following steps would a reasonable airline take? Would the airline's decision change if a strict liability rule were applied?

Care	Expected Accidents	Cumulative Accident Cost Reduction	Marginal Cost of Care	Cumulative Cost of Care	Total Social Cost
Status Quo	5	0	0	0	$5,000
Warning	4	$1,000	$500	$500	$4,500
Above Plus Weight Limit on Overhead Baggage	3	$2,000	$700	$1,200	$4,200
Above Plus Baggage Net	2	$3,000	$1,200	$2,400	$4,400
Above Plus Restricting Access to Bins	1	$4,000	$1,500	$3,900	$4,900

1   *Negligence v. Strict liability.* What will be the total cost to the defendant airline under a negligence rule? What would be the total cost to the defendant under a strict liability rule? Which rule will induce the airline to invest more in care? The contemporary king of the economic analysis of law, Judge Richard Posner, has suggested that the Hand formula promotes "economic efficiency" because it quantifies the social costs of care on the one hand and accidents on the other and induces the actor to incur the costs of care only when it makes economic sense to do so. However, notice that imposing this "efficient" result through a negligence rule instead of through a strict liability rule merely substitutes the court's calculation of risk and reward for that of the market. Assuming that both the court and the market calculate correctly, defendant will make the same choice whether to exercise care under either a strict liability rule or under a negligence rule. Perhaps the choice between which rule is "better" depends upon whether one believes that courts or defendants are more accurate calculators of risk and reward? It has been suggested that the negligence rule might actually cause defendants to exceed the optimum level of care because of the all-or-nothing nature of liability. Can you see how that might be?

3. CUSTOM

As we have seen, "reasonable care" can be a very vague and uncertain standard. One way courts and commentators have tried to bring more certainty to the negligence analysis is by employing the Hand formula that we just studied. However, as Learned Hand himself recognized, the risk/benefit analysis can be difficult to apply at best. Another way courts have brought more concrete substantive content to the general "reasonable care" standard is by importing an external standard of care developed through custom in the industry, culture, or area. One way to think of custom is as the real life result of all the participants in an area of culture calculating risk and acting on that calculus.

In its most definite manifestation, the custom becomes a specific application of reasonable care that amounts to a rule of reasonable care for that circumstance, but the common law eventually came to reject such a strong role for custom in ordinary cases. After all, the famous jurist in the *T.J. Hooper* case asked, what if the entire industry adopts a deficient custom?

Interestingly, in the law of tort, we see custom used both as a "sword" and as a "shield." Defendants try to use custom as a shield i.e. to show that defendant's conduct was reasonable because defendant complied with the applicable custom. Plaintiffs try to use custom as a sword i.e. defendant's conduct was unreasonable because defendant failed to comply with custom. As you work through the cases in this section, notice whether custom is being used as a sword or as a shield, and ask whether the use made of custom affects the deference given to custom by the court. These materials will examine the use of custom in two contexts – first in the ordinary negligence case, then in the professional malpractice case.

a. ORDINARY NEGLIGENCE

THE T. J. HOOPER

60 F.2D 737 (2D CIR. 1932)

LEARNED HAND, *Circuit Judge.*

The barges . . . belonging to the Northern Barge Company, had lifted cargoes of coal at Norfolk, Virginia, for New York in March, 1928. They were towed by two tugs of the petitioner, the "Montrose" and the "Hooper," and were lost off the Jersey Coast on March tenth, in an easterly gale. The cargo owners sued the barges . . . ; the owner of the barges sued the tugs . . . . All the suits were joined and heard together, and the judge found that all the vessels were unseaworthy; the tugs, because they did not carry radio receiving sets by which they could have seasonably got warnings of a change in the weather which should have caused them to seek shelter . . . . The petitioner appealed . . . .

The weather was fair without ominous symptoms, as the tows passed the Delaware Breakwater about midnight of March eighth, and the barges did not get into serious trouble until they were about opposite Atlantic City some sixty or seventy miles to the north. The wind began to freshen in the morning of the ninth and rose to a gale before noon; by afternoon the second barge of the Hooper's tow was out of hand and signaled the tug, which found that not only this barge needed help, but that the No. 30 was aleak. Both barges anchored and the crew of the No. 30 rode out the storm until the afternoon of the tenth, when she sank, her crew having been meanwhile taken off. The No. 17 sprang a leak about the same time; she too anchored at the Montrose's command and sank on the next morning after her crew also had been rescued. . . .

The evidence of the condition of the barges was very extensive . . . . As to each, the fact remains that she foundered in weather that she was bound to withstand. A more difficult issue is as to the tugs. . . .

The weather bureau at Arlington broadcasts two predictions daily, at ten in the morning and ten in the evening. Apparently there are other reports floating about, which come at uncertain hours but which can also be picked up. The Arlington report of the morning read as follows: "Moderate north, shifting to east and southeast winds, increasing Friday, fair weather to-night."
. . .

Moreover, the "Montrose" and the "Hooper" would have had the benefit of the evening report from Arlington had they had proper receiving sets. This predicted worse weather; it read: "Increasing east and southeast winds, becoming fresh to strong . . . ." The bare "increase" of the morning had become "fresh to strong." To be sure this scarcely foretold a gale of from forty to fifty miles for five hours or more, rising at one time to fifty-six; but if . . . [some] thought the first report enough, the second ought to have laid any doubts. The master of the "Montrose" himself, when asked what he would have done had he received a substantially similar report, said that he would certainly have put in. The master of the "Hooper" was also asked for his opinion, and said that he would have turned back also, but this admission is somewhat vitiated by the incorporation in the question of the statement that it was a "storm warning," which the witness seized upon in his answer. All this seems to us to support the conclusion of the judge that prudent masters, who had received the second warning, would have found the risk more than the exigency warranted; they would have been amply vindicated by what followed. . . . Taking the situation as a whole, it seems to us that these masters would have taken undue chances, had they got the broadcasts.

They did not, because their private radio receiving sets, which were on board, were not in working order. These belonged to them personally, and were partly a toy, partly a part of the equipment, but neither furnished by the owner, nor supervised by it. It is not fair to say that there was a general custom among coastwise carriers so as to equip their tugs. One line alone did it; as for the rest, they relied upon their crews, so far as they can be said to have relied at all. An adequate receiving set suitable for a coastwise tug can now be got at small cost and is reasonably reliable if kept up; obviously it is a source of great protection to their tows. Twice every day they can receive these predictions, based upon the widest possible information, available to every vessel within two or three hundred miles and more. Such a set is the ears of the tug to catch the spoken word, just as the master's binoculars are her eyes to see a storm signal ashore. Whatever may be said as to other vessels, tugs towing heavy coal laden barges, strung out for half a mile, have little power to manoeuvre, and do not, as this case proves, expose themselves to weather which would not turn back stauncher craft. They can have at hand protection against dangers of which they can learn in no other way.

Is it then a final answer that the business had not yet generally adopted receiving sets? There are yet, no doubt, cases where courts seem to make the general practice of the calling the standard of proper diligence; we have indeed given some currency to the notion ourselves. Indeed in most cases reasonable prudence is in fact common prudence; but strictly it is never its measure; a whole calling may have unduly lagged in the adoption of new and available devices. It may never set its own tests, however persuasive be its usages. Courts must in the end say what is required; there are precautions so imperative that even their universal disregard will not excuse their omission. [Citations omitted.] But here there was no custom at all as to receiving sets; some had them, some did not; the most that can be urged is that they had not yet become general. Certainly in such a case we need not pause; when some have thought a device necessary, at least we may say that they were right, and the others too slack. . . . We hold the tugs [liable] therefore because had they been properly equipped, they would have got the Arlington reports. The injury was a direct consequence of this unseaworthiness.

Decree affirmed.

QUESTIONS

1   Is it surprising that Judge Hand did not use the "Hand formula" to try to resolve this case?

2   Was custom sought to be used here as a sword or as a shield? Was the attempt to use custom successful? Would the same result have obtained if the Restatement (Third) of Torts had been applied on these facts?

LA SELL V. TRI-STATES THEATRE CORP.
11 N.W.2D 36 (IOWA 1943)

. . . The appellant, aged 64 years, weighing at the time about 223 pounds, accompanied by her daughter, and the latter's daughter, having paid the required admission, entered the Des Moines Theater, operated by the appellee, about 5 o'clock in the afternoon of June 8, 1941, to attend a moving picture show. Patrons, after passing through the entrance, traverse the lobby, foyer, and promenade, in succession, before taking their seats in the auditorium. The auditorium is approximately 100 feet east and west, and probably somewhat farther, north and south, from its rear to the screen at the north end. The main or ground floor of the auditorium consists of four sections of seats, the two center sections having 40 rows of seats, and the side sections having two or three rows less. There are five aisles extending from the rear, north, to the screen aisle number one being along the west wall, and the other aisles being numbered consecutively to the aisle along the east wall. The entire floor of the auditorium extends from the stage toward the rear, south, on a gradually rising gradient or incline, until it reaches the third row of seats from the rear wall of the auditorium. From the elevation of this line, the level of the aisles gradually slopes downward toward the aisle entrances and coincides with the floor level of the prome- nade. But the level of the floor under the last three rows of seats in the auditorium, and between those parts of the aisles which slope southward and down, continues on a rising incline to the rear wall. As a result of this method of construction the passageway to the seats in the third row from the rear is on the same level as the aisle, and there is no step-up from the aisle into this passageway. But to enter the passageway to the seats in the second row from the back there is a step-up of approximately five inches, which continues as a ramp or upward-sloping way for a short distance into the passageway. Entrance from the aisle into the last row at the rear of the auditorium is in like manner except that the step-up is somewhat higher.

Appellant and her daughter and granddaughter entered the auditorium at aisle two, the second from the west wall. An usher, with a flashlight, seated them in the second row from the rear, in the section of seats on the left or west of this aisle. The granddaughter sat in the third seat from the aisle, and the daughter in the seat on the aisle and just over the step-up. None of them had any difficulty in taking her seat, and the appellant testified that she did not notice the step-up. The usher did not call their attention to the step-up. Other patrons were passing along the aisle as they came in. Patrons were entering and leaving the auditorium throughout the entertainment. The picture was shown, as is customary, in partial darkness. After they had been in the theater for about three hours, the daughter went to the rest room. She almost fell in stepping to the aisle, but retained her balance. About five or ten minutes later, the appel- lant took hold of the granddaughter's hand with her left hand, and stepped toward the aisle. Not seeing the step-down because of darkness, and not knowing of its presence, and thinking there was no change in level of the floor on which she was walking, she lost her balance when her foot went to the aisle floor, and she fell forward, striking her head on the metal seat across the aisle. She had never been in this theater before. Her petition alleged negligence thus: "The proximate cause of the plaintiff's injuries and damages was the negligence of the defendant in negligently permitting an uneven condition in its floor to exist, over which patrons would be likely to stumble and fall, with insufficient lighting and without warning of the danger." . . . The answer was a general denial.

There was uncontradicted evidence that the riser of this step and about two inches in width of its tread had been repainted with white enamel paint about the end of April, 1941. There was also evidence that it was repainted as it became soiled, darkened, or worn off, but no evidence of its being painted between April, 1941 and June 8, 1941, the day of the injury. . . . There is a conflict in the evidence as to the existence and the adequacy of the lighting, and as to the visibility of any painting on the step. The appellant and her daughter testified that it was so dark that neither the floor nor the step was seen by them. Two strangers to the appellant testified to facts supporting the testimony of appellant and her daughter respecting the absence of lighting and the non-visibility of any painting, and also, without objection, gave their opinions as to the inadequacy of the lighting at the step and vicinity. . . . Respecting the allegation of negligence in maintaining the uneven floor, or step, there is no denial other than might be in the general denial of the answer. Appellee, by evidence and by argument, admits the existence of the step, and asserts that it was necessary, and was an approved method of construction. . . .

One ground of appellee's peremptory motion for a directed verdict is: "4. The theatre is constructed and lighted in an approved manner, and in accordance with the customary method of lighting and constructing theatres of similar character and nature." . . . We do not agree with the contention of appellee that because its lighting and construction was in accord with the customary or standard practice of theaters generally, in these respects, that these issues of alleged negligence were issues of law for the court, rather than issues of fact for the jury. The standard of custom cannot be substituted for the legal standard of reasonable or ordinary care under the circumstances. Following an approved method is merely evidentiary and is not conclusive on the question of ordinary care. The standard of care is ordinary care under the circumstances, and not what others have done under like circumstances. Habitual practice of any number, for any period of time, cannot make a negligent act an act of due care and caution. . . . The rule is aptly stated by the able court of the Second Circuit speaking through Learned Hand, J., in *The T. J. Hooper*, 60 F.2d 737, 739, 740 . . . : "Is then a final answer that the business had not yet generally adopted receiving sets? There are, no doubt, cases where courts seem to make the general practice of the calling the standard of proper diligence; we have indeed given some currency to the notion ourselves. . . . Indeed in most cases reasonable prudence is in fact common prudence; but strictly it is never its measure; a whole calling may have unduly lagged in the adoption of new and available devices. It never may set its own tests, however persuasive may be its usages. Courts must in the end say what is required; there are precautions so imperative that even their universal disregard will not excuse their omission." . . . We have held that what others in the same line of business have been accustomed to do in any particular is not in itself a standard of care, but is evidence only of that standard, which the jury may consider under proper instructions, in determining whether the defendant exercised ordinary care. . . .

The appellant was rightfully upon the premises. Appellee had received its admission charge for her, and she was in the theater as its invitee. It is a general rule, recognized without dissent, that an owner or occupant of buildings or premises, who directly or impliedly invites or induces others to enter therein, owes an active, affirmative duty to such persons to use reasonable, ordinary, care to keep such premises in a reasonably safe condition, so as not to unreasonably or unnecessarily expose them to danger. . . . The impracticability and the probative weakness of the standard practice test of negligence is made manifest when you consider the great variety of theater construction, the diversity of lighting in capacity and shading, the variety, presence, and absence of balconies, pillars, etc., which cast shadows, the reflecting powers of the carpeting, tapestries, wall coloring, and numerous other factors. There is ordinarily no absolute test, where human conduct is a controlling factor, of either negligence or due care, in a particular instance, unless it is by statute or statutory construction. . . .

The issue of appellee's negligence was for the jury. . . . For all of the reasons given the judgment is reversed and the cause is remanded for new trial. Reversed and remanded. . . .

NOTE

1   *Evidence of due care.* The universal rule in ordinary negligence cases now is that custom is evidence of due care, but not due care itself.

b. PROFESSIONAL MALPRACTICE

A malpractice action is a special sort of negligence case. The most common form of malpractice action is the medical malpractice case brought by a patient against her doctor.

LAMA V. BORRAS
16 F.3D 473 (1ST CIR. 1994)

Defendants-appellants Dr. Pedro Borras . . . and Asociacion Hospital del Maestro, Inc. (Hospital) appeal from a jury verdict finding them liable for medical malpractice to plaintiffs Roberto Romero Lama (Romero) and his wife, Norma. . . . Defendants principally argue that the district court erred in denying their post-verdict motions for judgment as a matter of law . . . because the evidence at trial was legally insufficient to prove the prima facie elements of negligence. For the same reason, the Borras Defendants also argue that the court erred in denying their motion for a new trial . . . . Finding no error, we affirm.

I.

BACKGROUND

. . . In 1985, Romero was suffering from back pain and searching for solutions. Dr. Nancy Alfonso, Romero's family physician, provided some treatment but then referred him to Dr. Borras, a neurosurgeon. Dr. Borras concluded that Romero had a herniated disc and scheduled surgery. Prior to surgery, Dr. Borras neither prescribed nor enforced a regime of absolute bed rest, nor did he offer other key components of "conservative treatment." . . .

While operating on April 9, 1986, Dr. Borras discovered that Romero had an "extruded" disc and attempted to remove the extruding material. Either because Dr. Borras failed to remove the offending material or because he operated at the wrong level, Romero's original symptoms returned in full force several days after the operation. Dr. Borras concluded that a second operation was necessary to remedy the "recurrence."

Dr. Borras operated again on May 15, 1986. Dr. Borras did not order pre- or post-operative antibiotics. It is unclear whether the second operation was successful in curing the herniated disc. In any event, as early as May 17, a nurse's note indicates that the bandage covering Romero's surgical wound was "very bloody," a symptom which, according to expert testimony, indicates the possibility of infection. On May 18, Romero was experiencing local pain at the site of the incision, another symptom consistent with an infection. On May 19, the bandage was "soiled again." . . .

On the night of May 20, Romero began to experience severe discomfort in his back. He passed the night screaming in pain. At some point on May 21, Dr. Edwin Lugo Piazza, an attending physician, diagnosed the problem as discitis – an infection of the space between discs – and responded by initiating antibiotic treatment. Discitis is extremely painful and, since it occurs in a location with little blood circulation, very slow to cure. Romero was hospitalized for several additional months while undergoing treatment for the infection.

. . . Plaintiffs alleged that Dr. Borras was negligent in four general areas: (1) failure to provide proper conservative medical treatment; (2) premature and otherwise improper discharge after surgery; (3) negligent performance of surgery; and (4) failure to provide proper management for the infection. While plaintiffs did not claim that the Hospital was vicariously liable for any negligence on the part of Dr. Borras, they alleged that the Hospital was itself negligent in two respects: (1) failure to prepare, use, and monitor proper medical records; and (2) failure to provide proper hygiene at the hospital premises.

At each appropriate moment, defendants attempted to remove the case from the jury. Before trial they moved for summary judgment. . . . At the close of plaintiffs' case and at the close of all the evidence, defendants moved for judgment as a matter of law. . . . After the jury returned a verdict awarding plaintiffs $600,000 in compensatory damages, defendants again sought judgment as a matter of law. . . . Additionally, the Borras Defendants requested either a new trial or remittitur. . . . At each procedural step and with respect to each allegation of negligence, defendants' primary argument was that plaintiffs had failed to establish the required elements of duty, breach, and causation.

The district court rebuffed all of defendants' entreaties, ruling that the evidence was legally sufficient to fuel the jury's deliberations and ultimately to support its findings. Because our analysis necessarily focuses on the denial of the post-verdict motions for judgment as a matter of law, . . . we quote at length from the district court's order denying those motions:

> In reference to Dr. Borras, the evidence, seen in the light most favorable to the plaintiffs, allowed the jury to at least conclude that Dr. Borras failed to pursue a well-planned and managed, conservative treatment course for Roberto Romero Lama's back ailment before exposing him to the inherent dangers of a herniated disc operation. Had such conservative treatment been successful, then the post-surgical complications that unfortunately took place in the operated vertebral interspace [including the infection following the second surgery] would not have occurred. A reasonable jury could have concluded that the negligent act was the recommendation of a first operation without the benefit of additional conservative treatment . . . . As to Hospital del Maestro, it was entirely possible for the jury to conclude that the particular way in which the medical and nursing records were kept constituted evidence of carelessness in monitoring the patient after the second operation. Perhaps the infection would have been reported and documented earlier. Perhaps the hospital was negligent in not dealing appropriately with wound inspection and cleaning, [and] bandage changing . . . .

Romero Lama v. Borras, No. 91-1055, slip op. at 1-2 (D.P.R. Sept. 1, 1992) (order denying post-verdict motions). We find the reasoning of the district court to be substantially sound and therefore affirm the result. . . .

III.

DISCUSSION

A. Medical Malpractice under Puerto Rico Law

We begin our analysis by laying out the substantive law of Puerto Rico governing this diversity suit. . . . To establish a prima facie case of medical malpractice in Puerto Rico, a plaintiff must demonstrate: (1) the basic norms of knowledge and medical care applicable to general practitioners or specialists; (2) proof that the medical personnel failed to follow these basic norms in the treatment of the patient; and (3) a causal relation between the act or omission of the physician and the injury suffered by the patient. . . .

The burden of a medical malpractice plaintiff in establishing the physician's duty is more complicated than that of an ordinary tort plaintiff. Instead of simply appealing to the jury's view of what is reasonable under the circumstances, a medical malpractice plaintiff must establish the relevant national standard of care. . . . Naturally, the trier of fact can rarely determine the applicable standard of care without the assistance of expert testimony. . . . The predictable battle of the experts then creates a curious predicament for the fact-finder, because an error of judgment regarding diagnosis or treatment does not lead to liability when expert opinion suggests that the physician's conduct fell within a range of acceptable alternatives. . . . While not allowed to speculate, the fact-finder is of course free to find some experts more credible than others. . . .

B. Negligence of Dr. Borras

The Borras Defendants claim that plaintiffs failed to introduce any evidence sufficient to prove . . . the relevant standards of acceptable medical practice . . . . While plaintiffs may not have been able to substantiate the broad attack outlined in their complaint, we focus here on only one allegation of negligence: Dr. Borras' failure to provide conservative treatment prior to the first operation. Defendants argue that plaintiffs failed to prove a general medical standard governing the need for conservative treatment in a case like that of Romero. We disagree. Plaintiffs' chief expert witness, Dr. George Udvarhelyi, testified that, absent an indication of neurological impairment, the standard practice is for a neurosurgeon to postpone lumbar disc surgery while the patient undergoes conservative treatment, with a period of absolute bed rest as the prime ingredient. . . . In these respects, the views of defendants' neurosurgery experts did not diverge from those of Dr. Udvarhelyi. . . . Indeed, when called by plaintiffs, Dr. Borras (who also testified as a neurosurgery expert) agreed on cross-examination with the statement that "bed rest is normally recommended before surgery is decided in a patient like Mr. Romero," and claimed that he did give conservative treatment to Romero.

In spite of Dr. Borras' testimony to the contrary, there was also sufficient evidence for the jury to find that Dr. Borras failed to provide the customary conservative treatment. Dr. Alfonso, Romero's family physician, testified that Dr. Borras, while aware that Romero had not followed a program of absolute bed rest, proceeded with surgery anyway. Although Romero was admitted to the hospital one week before surgery, there was evidence that Dr. Borras neither prescribed nor attempted to enforce a conservative treatment regime. In fact, there was evidence that Dr. Borras' main goal was simply to admit Romero for a week of smoke-free relaxation, not absolute bed rest, because Romero's heavy smoking and mild hypertension made him a high-risk surgery patient. In short, we agree with the district court that the jury could reasonably have concluded that Dr. Borras failed to institute and manage a proper conservative treatment plan. . . . We conclude that plaintiffs introduced legally sufficient evidence to support each element of at least one major allegation of negligence on the part of Dr. Borras. We therefore hold that the district court properly denied the Borras Defendants' . . . motions. . . .

IV.

CONCLUSION

. . . For the foregoing reasons, the order of the district court denying defendants' motions for judgment as a matter of law and the Borras Defendants' motions for new trial is Affirmed.

1   How are the elements of this medical malpractice cause of action different from an ordinary negligence action?
2   What if plaintiff's expert had testified merely that he would have tried the conservative practice of bed rest before operating and that he believed that the failure to try the bed rest was the cause of plaintiff's injuries? Would this constitute a prima facie case for plaintiff?
3   *Standard of care in malpractice cases.* In a medical malpractice case, the "standard" of care is not really a standard, but more like a rule of customary practice in that particular situation. A necessary implication of using custom as the standard of care in the medical malpractice case is that a defendant who complies with the accepted standard of care in the medical field has not been negligent. In fact, compliance with any one of several accepted "schools of thought" in the relevant medical field shields defendant from liability.
4   *Medical Custom v. Reasonable Care.* In the medical malpractice case, courts do not follow the rule in *TJ Hooper* that custom is merely evidence of due care. Frequently medical custom may equal due care, but even if the entire medical industry and therefore the medical custom is demonstrably deficient, then the doctor who follows medical custom still has exercised "due care." Is there any reason to place more weight on custom in the medical field?
5   *Expert testimony.* Because the applicable standard of care in a medical malpractice case is the medical custom in the particular medical field, and plaintiff therefore bears the burden of establishing that custom, a medical malpractice plaintiff almost always must present expert testimony to establish a *prima facie* case of malpractice. While expert testimony is practically necessary to establish the standard of care in almost all medical malpractice cases, it may also be very useful in establishing other elements of the case such as breach and causation.

VERGARA V. DOAN
593 N.E.2D 185 (IND. 1992)

Javier Vergara was born on May 31, 1979, at the Adams Memorial Hospital in Decatur, Indiana. His parents, Jose and Concepcion, claimed that negligence on the part of Dr. John Doan during Javier's delivery caused him severe and permanent injuries. A jury returned a verdict for Dr. Doan and the plaintiffs appealed. The Court of Appeals affirmed. . . .

In most negligence cases, the defendant's conduct is tested against the hypothetical reasonable and prudent person acting under the same or similar circumstances. In medical malpractice cases, however, Indiana has applied a more specific articulation of this standard. It has become known as the modified locality rule: "The standard of care . . . is that degree of care, skill, and proficiency which is commonly exercised by ordinarily careful, skillful, and prudent [physicians], at the time of the operation and in similar localities." *Burke v. Capello* (1988), Ind., 520 N.E.2d 439, 441. Appellants have urged us to abandon this standard, arguing that the reasons for the modified locality rule are no longer applicable in today's society. We agree.

The modified locality rule is a less stringent version of the strict locality rule, which measured the defendant's conduct against that of other doctors in the same community. When the strict locality rule originated in the late 19th century, there was great disparity between the medical opportunities, equipment, facilities, and training in rural and urban communities. Travel and communication between rural and urban communities were difficult. The locality rule was intended to prevent the inequity that would result from holding rural doctors to the same standards as doctors in large cities.

With advances in communication, travel, and medical education, the disparity between rural and urban health care diminished and justification for the locality rule waned. The strict locality rule also had two major drawbacks, especially as applied to smaller communities. First, there was a scarcity of local doctors to serve as expert witnesses against other local doctors. Second, there was the possibility that practices among a small group of doctors would establish a local standard of care below that which the law required. In response to these changes and criticisms, many courts adopted a modified locality rule, expanding the area of comparison to similar localities. . . .

Use of a modified locality rule has not quelled the criticism. Many of the common criticisms seem valid. The modified locality rule still permits a lower standard of care to be exercised in smaller communities because other similar communities are likely to have the same care. We also spend time and money on the difficulty of defining what is a similar community. The rule also seems inconsistent with the reality of modern medical practice. The disparity between small town and urban medicine continues to lessen with advances in communication, transportation, and education. In addition, widespread insurance coverage has provided patients with more choice of doctors and hospitals by reducing the financial constraints on the consumer in selecting caregivers. These reasons and others have led our Court of Appeals to observe that the modified locality rule has fallen into disfavor. . . .

Many states describe the care a physician owes without emphasizing the locality of practice. Today we join these states and adopt the following: a physician must exercise that degree of care, skill, and proficiency exercised by reasonably careful, skillful, and prudent practitioners in the same class to which he belongs, acting under the same or similar circumstances. Rather than focusing on different standards for different communities, this standard uses locality as but one of the factors to be considered in determining whether the doctor acted reasonably. Other relevant considerations would include advances in the profession, availability of facilities, and whether the doctor is a specialist or general practitioner. . . .

NOTES

1   While there has been a trend away from any sort of "locality rule," some form of "modified locality rule" probably still is the majority rule in the United States, at least for general practitioners.

2   The medical profession is organized into specialties. Specialists are held to the national custom within their specialty.

3   Non-medical practitioners, e.g., chiropractors, are permitted to practice within their schools of belief.

4   Nurses are held to a professional standard for nurses.

SCOTT V. BRADFORD
606 P.2D 554 (OKLA. 1979)

This appeal is taken by plaintiffs in trial below, from a judgment in favor of defendant rendered on a jury verdict in a medical malpractice action.

Mrs. Scott's physician advised her she had several fibroid tumors on her uterus. He referred her to defendant surgeon. Defendant admitted her to the hospital where she signed a routine consent form prior to defendant's performing a hysterectomy. After surgery, Mrs. Scott experienced problems with incontinence. She visited another physician . . . . This physician referred her to an urologist who, after three surgeries, succeeded in correcting her problems.

Mrs. Scott, joined by her husband, filed the present action alleging medical malpractice, claiming defendant failed to advise her of the risks involved or of available alternatives to surgery. She further maintained had she been properly informed she would have refused the surgery. The case was submitted to the jury with instructions to which plaintiffs objected. The jury found for defendant and plaintiffs appeal. . . .

Plaintiffs complain of three instructions and submit the following instruction should have been given:

> The law requires physician to disclose to his patient the material risks of a proposed treatment, the material risks of foregoing any treatment, the existence of any alternatives and the material risks of choosing these alternatives. *The failure to disclose these things is negligence.*
>
> A risk is "material" when a reasonable person, in what the physician knows or should know to be the patient's position, would be likely to attach significance to the risk or cluster of risks in deciding whether or not to forego the proposed therapy.
>
> If you find from the evidence in this case that the defendant failed to make disclosures to the plaintiff, NORMA JO SCOTT, as required by law, then your verdict would be for the plaintiffs, for the amount of their damages proximately caused thereby.

This instruction refers to the doctrine of "informed consent."

The issue involved is whether Oklahoma adheres to the doctrine of informed consent as the basis of an action for medical malpractice, and if so did the present instructions adequately advise the jury of defendant's duty.

Anglo-American law starts with the premise of thoroughgoing self-determination, each man considered to be his own master. This law does not permit a physician to substitute his judgment for that of the patient by any form of artifice. The doctrine of informed consent arises out of this premise.

Consent to medical treatment . . . should stem from an understanding decision based on adequate information about the treatment, the available alternatives, and the collateral risks. This requirement, labeled "informed consent," is, legally speaking, as essential as a physician's care and skill in the *performance* of the therapy. The doctrine imposes a duty on a physician or surgeon to inform a patient of his options and their attendant risks. . . .

If treatment is completely unauthorized and performed without any consent at all, there has been a battery. However, if the physician obtains a patient's consent but has breached his duty to inform, the patient has a cause of action sounding in negligence for failure to inform the patient of his options, regardless of the due care exercised at treatment, assuming there is injury.

Until today, Oklahoma has not officially adopted this doctrine. . . . In perhaps one of the most influential informed consent decisions, *Canterbury v. Spence,* . . . 464 F.2d 772 (D.C. Cir. 1972), . . . the doctrine received perdurable impetus. Judge Robinson . . . emphasized the fundamental concept in American jurisprudence that every human being of adult years and sound mind has a right to determine what shall be done with his own body. True consent to what happens to one's self is the informed exercise of a choice. This entails an opportunity to evaluate knowledgeably the options available and the risks attendant upon each. It is the prerogative of every patient to chart his own course and determine which direction he will take.

The decision in *Canterbury* recognized the tendency of some jurisdictions to turn this duty on whether it is the custom of physicians practicing in the community to make the particular disclosure to the patient. That court rejected this standard and held the standard measuring performance of the duty of disclosure is conduct which is reasonable under the circumstances: "[We cannot] ignore the fact that to bind disclosure obligations to medical usage is to arrogate the decision on revelation to the physician alone." We agree. A patient's right to make up his mind whether to undergo treatment should not be delegated to the local medical group. What is reasonable disclosure in one instance may not be reasonable in another. We decline to adopt a standard based on the professional standard. We, therefore, hold the scope of a physician's communications must be measured by his patient's need to know enough to enable him to make an intelligent choice. In other words, full disclosure of all *material risks* incident to treatment must be made. There is no bright line separating the material from the immaterial; it is a question of fact. A risk is material if it would be likely to affect patient's decision. When non-disclosure of a particular risk is open to debate, the issue is for the finder of facts. . . .

This duty to disclose is the first element of the cause of action in negligence based on lack of informed consent. However, there are exceptions creating a privilege of a physician not to disclose. There is no need to disclose risks that either ought to be known by everyone or are already known to the patient. Further, the primary duty of a physician is to do what is best for his patient and where full disclosure would be detrimental to a patient's total care and best interests a physician may withhold such disclosure, for example, where disclosure would alarm an emotionally upset or apprehensive patient. Certainly too, where there is an emergency and the patient is in no condition to determine for himself whether treatment should be administered, the privilege may be invoked. . . .

The patient has the burden of going forward with evidence tending to establish prima facie the essential elements of the cause of action. The burden of proving an exception to his duty, and thus a privilege not to disclose, rests upon the physician as an affirmative defense.

The cause of action, based on lack of informed consent, is divided into three elements: the duty to inform being the first, the second is causation, and the third is injury. The second element, that of causation, requires that plaintiff patient would have chosen no treatment or a different course of treatment had the alternatives and material risks of each been made known to him. If the patient would have elected to proceed with treatment had he been duly informed of its risks, then the element of causation is missing. In other words, a causal connection exists between physician's breach of the duty to disclose and patient's injury when and only when disclosure of material risks incidental to treatment would have resulted in a decision against it. . . . A patient obviously has no complaint if he would have submitted to the treatment if the physician had complied with his duty and informed him of the risks. This fact decision raises the difficult question of the correct standard on which to instruct the jury.

The court in *Canterbury v. Spence, supra,* although emphasizing principles of self-determination permits liability only if non-disclosure would have affected the decision of a fictitious "reasonable patient," even though actual patient testifies he would have elected to forego therapy had he been fully informed.

Decisions discussing informed consent have emphasized the *disclosure* element but paid scant attention to the consent element of the concept, although this is the root of causation. Language in some decisions suggests the standard to be applied is a subjective one, i.e., whether that particular patient would still have consented to the treatment, reasonable choice or otherwise. . . . Although the *Canterbury* rule is probably that of the majority, its "reasonable man" approach has been criticized by some commentators as backtracking on its own theory of self-determination. The *Canterbury* view certainly severely limits the protection granted an injured patient. To the extent the plaintiff, given an adequate disclosure, would have declined the proposed treatment, and a reasonable person in similar circumstances would have consented, a patient's right of self-determination is *irrevocably lost.* This basic right to know and decide is the reason for the . . . rule. Accordingly, we decline to jeopardize this right by the imposition of the "reasonable man" standard.

If a plaintiff testifies he would have continued with the proposed treatment had he been adequately informed, the trial is over under either the subjective or objective approach. If he testifies he would not, then the causation problem must be resolved by examining the credibility of plaintiff's testimony. The jury must be instructed that it must find plaintiff would have refused the treatment if he is to prevail.

Although it might be said this approach places a physician at the mercy of a patient's hindsight, a careful practitioner can always protect himself by insuring that he has adequately informed each patient he treats. If he does not breach this duty, a causation problem will not arise.

The final element of this cause of action is that of injury. The risk must actually materialize and plaintiff must have been injured as a result of submitting to the treatment. Absent occurrence of the undisclosed risk, a physician's failure to reveal its possibility is not actionable. . . .

In summary, in a medical malpractice action a patient suing under the theory of informed consent must allege and prove:

1. defendant physician failed to inform him adequately of a material risk before securing his consent to the proposed treatment;

2. if he had been informed of the risks he would not have consented to the treatment;

3. the adverse consequences that were not made known did in fact occur and he was injured as a result of submitting to the treatment.

As a defense, a physician may plead and prove plaintiff knew of the risks, full disclosure would be detrimental to patient's best interests or that an emergency existed requiring prompt treatment and patient was in no condition to decide for himself. . . .

BARNES, J.: CONCURRING IN PART: DISSENTING IN PART:

I concur with the majority opinion in all respects except I would adopt the reasonable man test set out in *Canterbury v. Spence* . . . .

4. NEGLIGENCE *PER SE*

ROMANS 13:1-7

Let every soul be subject unto the higher powers. For there is no power but of God: the powers that be are ordained of God. Whosoever therefore resisteth the power, resisteth the ordinance of God: and they that resist shall receive to themselves damnation. For rulers are not a terror to good works, but to the evil. Wilt thou then not be afraid of the power? do that which is good, and thou shalt have praise of the same: For he is the minister of God to thee for good. But if thou do that which is evil, be afraid; for he beareth not the sword in vain: for he is the minister of God, a revenger to execute wrath upon him that doeth evil. Wherefore ye must needs be subject, not only for wrath, but also for conscience sake. For for this cause pay ye tribute also: for they are God's ministers, attending continually upon this very thing. Render therefore to all their dues: tribute to whom tribute is due; custom to whom custom; fear to whom fear; honour to whom honour.

1 What is St. Paul the Apostle teaching here?
2 Is it wrong to disobey the positive law? If so, is it always wrong?
3 Is it wrong to disobey a law that is obsolete, unreasonable, or unfair?
4 Should the believer submit to a law that seeks to punish the believer's faith?

a. VIOLATIONS OF STATUTE

While the question of what conduct is "reasonable under the circumstances" usually is left to the jury, sometimes the Court provides an answer to that question. One recurring situation in which courts frequently do not permit the jury to decide what conduct is reasonable under the circumstances is when the conduct in question is governed by a legislative enactment. Courts frequently will simply "adopt" the statute as the standard of reasonable conduct under the circumstances. Violation of the statute is treated as "negligence *per se*." Courts might apply negligence per se without regard to whether the statute itself expressly or impliedly provides a statutory right of action, which most statutes do not.

Historically, at least two ideas have provided the theoretical underpinning for this deference to statutes in a private civil suit. First, the judgment of the legislature concerning what conduct is "reasonable" trumps the judgment of a particular jury on that subject. Second, it is thought that without regard to the reasonableness of the statute in the abstract, reasonable people obey the law so that a law breaker is acting unreasonably *per se*.

OSBORNE V MCMASTERS
41 N.W. 543 (MINN. 1889)

Upon the record in this case it must be taken as the facts that defendant's clerk in his drug-store, in the course of his employment as such, sold to plaintiff's intestate a deadly poison without labeling it "Poison," as required by statute; that she, in ignorance of its deadly qualities, partook of the poison which caused her death. Except for the ability of counsel and the earnestness with which they have argued the case, we would not have supposed that there could be any serious doubt of defendant's liability on this state of facts. . . . It is now well settled, certainly in this state, that where a statute or municipal ordinance imposes upon any person a specific duty for the protection or benefit of others, if he neglects to perform that duty he is liable to those for whose protection or benefit it was imposed for any injuries of the character which the statute or ordinance was designed to prevent, and which were proximately produced by such neglect. . . . The common law gives a right of action to every one sustaining injuries caused proximately by the negligence of another. The present is a common-law action, the gist of which is defendant's negligence, resulting in the death of plaintiff's intestate. Negligence is the breach of legal duty. It is immaterial whether the duty is one imposed by the rule of common law requiring the exercise of ordinary care not to injure another, or is imposed by a statute designed for the protection of others. In either case the failure to perform the duty constitutes negligence, and renders the party liable for injuries resulting from it. The only difference is that in the one case the measure of legal duty is to be determined upon common-law principles, while in the other the statute fixes it, so that the violation of the statute constitutes conclusive evidence of negligence, or, in other words, negligence per se. The action in the latter case is not a statutory one, nor does the statute give the right of action in any other sense, except that it makes an act negligent which otherwise might not be such, or at least only evidence of negligence. All that the statute does is to establish a fixed standard by which the fact of negligence may be determined. The gist of the action is still negligence, or the non-performance of a legal duty to the person injured. . . . Judgment affirmed.

One issue that has splintered courts applying the negligence *per se* doctrine is what is the effect of a finding of negligence *per se*? In the following case, the lower court instructed the jury that the violation of statute should be given one effect, but the appellate court found that another effect was appropriate.

MARTIN V. HERZOG
126 N.E. 814 (N.Y. 1920)

Cardozo, J.

. . . Plaintiff and her husband, while driving toward Tarrytown in a buggy on the night of August 21, 1915, were struck by the defendant's automobile coming in the opposite direction. They were thrown to the ground, and the man was killed. At the point of the collision the highway makes a curve. The car was rounding the curve when suddenly it came upon the buggy, emerging, the defendant tells us, from the gloom. Negligence is charged against the defendant, the driver of the car, in that he did not keep to the right of the center of the highway . . . . Negligence is charged against the plaintiff's intestate, the driver of the wagon, in that he was traveling without lights . . . . There is no evidence that the defendant was moving at an excessive speed. There is none of any defect in the equipment of his car. . . . The case against him must stand, therefore, if at all, upon the divergence of his course from the center of the highway. The jury found him delinquent and his victim blameless. The Appellate Division reversed, and ordered a new trial.

We agree with the Appellate Division that the charge to the jury was erroneous and misleading. . . . In the body of the charge the trial judge said that the jury could consider the absence of light "in determining whether the plaintiff's intestate was guilty of contributory negligence in failing to have a light upon the buggy as provided by law. I do not mean to say that the absence of light necessarily makes him negligent, but it is a fact for your consideration." The defendant requested a ruling that the absence of a light on the plaintiff's vehicle was "*prima facie* evidence of contributory negligence." This request was refused, and the jury were again instructed that they might consider the absence of lights as some evidence of negligence, but that it was not conclusive evidence. The plaintiff then requested a charge that "the fact that the plaintiff's intestate was driving without a light is not negligence in itself," and to this the court acceded. . . .

We think the unexcused omission of the statutory signals is more than some evidence of negligence. It *is* negligence in itself. Lights are intended for the guidance and protection of other travelers on the highway . . . . By the very terms of the hypothesis, to omit, willfully or heedlessly, the safeguards prescribed by law for the benefit of another that he may be preserved in life or limb, is to fall short of the standard of diligence to which those who live in organized society are under a duty to conform. . . . Whether the omission of an absolute duty, not willfully or heedlessly, but through unavoidable accident, is also to be characterized as negligence, is a question of nomenclature into which we need not enter, for it does not touch the case before us. . . . A rule less rigid has been applied where the one who complains of the omission is not a member of the class for whose protection the safeguard is designed. . . .

In the case at hand, we have an instance of the admitted violation of a statute intended for the protection of travelers on the highway, of whom the defendant at the time was one. Yet the jurors were instructed in effect that they were at liberty in their discretion to treat the omission of lights either as innocent or as culpable. They were allowed to "consider the default as lightly or gravely" as they would. . . . Jurors have no dispensing power by which they may relax the duty that one traveler on the highway owes under the statute to another. It is error to tell them that they have. The omission of these lights was a wrong, and being wholly unexcused was also a negligent wrong. No license should have been conceded to the triers of the facts to find it anything else.

We must be on our guard, however, against confusing the question of negligence with that of the causal connection between the negligence and the injury. A defendant who travels without lights is not to pay damages for his fault unless the absence of lights is the cause of the disaster. A plaintiff who travels without them is not to forfeit the right to damages unless the absence of lights is at least a contributing cause of the disaster. . . .

We think, however, that evidence of a collision occurring more than an hour after sundown between a car and an unseen buggy, proceeding without lights, is evidence from which a causal connection may be inferred between the collision and the lack of signals . . . . [The jury] should have been told not only that the omission of the lights was negligence, but that it was "*prima facie* evidence of contributory negligence," i.e., that it was sufficient in itself unless its probative force was overcome to sustain a verdict that the decedent was at fault. . . .

We are persuaded that the tendency of the charge and of all the rulings following it, was to minimize unduly, in the minds of the triers of the facts, the gravity of the decedent's fault. . . . A statute designed for the protection of human life is not to be brushed aside as a form of words, its commands reduced to the level of cautions, and the duty to obey attenuated into an option to conform.

1   How would this case have been different if there had been no statute requiring lights on the buggy?

2   Is it possible to comply with all laws all of the time? Is such compliance desirable? Would it have made any difference here if the buggy were not ordinarily used on the highway but was taken out this time to get a seriously ill child to the hospital?

3   Would it have made any difference here if plaintiff's buggy had lights but was in technical violation of the statute because the bulb prematurely burned out just before the collision and before plaintiff took notice? Is it possible to argue that a plaintiff's failure to comply with a statute constituted a breach of duty when plaintiff had no reasonable opportunity to comply?

4   What effect did plaintiff contend that the violation should have on the negligence inquiry? What effect was defendant advocating? What rule did the court adopt?

5   Is it possible to articulate a general principle encompassing which violations of statute are negligence *per se* and which are not? If some violations of statute are not treated as negligence *per se*, what then is the practical effect of a showing of a statutory violation?

6   *Legislative Intent.* Sometimes the legislature announces its intent on the negligence *per se* issue, and such clear statements are controlling. If the legislature had expressly addressed whether failing to use lights was negligence *per se* under the circumstances, what do you think the legislature would have determined? If the legislature explicitly provides a private right of action, this is not an example of negligence *per se*. A statutory right of action is its own cause of action. Under negligence *per se* the statute merely displaces only part of a pre-existing common law negligence action – breach of duty. Negligence *per se* comes into play only when the legislature does not explicitly provide a right of action.

7   Assume that plaintiff's buggy included only one small light, and assume that would be in technical compliance with the statute. Could plaintiff argue persuasively that he was careful *per se* because he obeyed the statute?

8   Restatement (Second) of Torts Section 288A would excuse violations of statute in cases of necessity, emergency, and incapacity. Restatement (Third) Section 15 is similar.

ZENI V. ANDERSON
243 N.W.2D 270 (MICH. 1976)

. . . The first [issue] is the effect of an alleged violation of statute by plaintiff. . . . We hold that violation of a statute by plaintiff or defendant creates a prima facie case from which a jury may draw an inference of negligence. The jury may also consider whether a legally sufficient excuse has been presented to refute this inference. . . .

I – Facts

The accident which precipitated this action occurred one snowy morning, March 7, 1969, when the temperature was 11 degrees F, the sky was clear and the average snow depth was 21 inches. Plaintiff Eleanor Zeni, then a 56-year-old registered nurse, was walking to her work . . . . Instead of using the snow-covered sidewalk, which in any event would have required her to walk across the street twice to get to her job, she traveled along a well-used pedestrian snowpath, with her back to oncoming traffic.

Defendant Karen Anderson, a college student, was driving within the speed limit in a steady stream of traffic on the same street. Ms. Anderson testified that she had turned on the defroster in the car and her passenger said she had scraped the windshield. An eyewitness whose deposition was read at trial, however, testified that defendant's windshield was clouded and he doubted that the occupants could see out. He also testified that the car was traveling too close to the curb and that he could tell plaintiff was going to be hit.

Defendant's car struck the plaintiff on the driver's right side. Ms. Anderson testified she first saw the plaintiff between a car parked on the right-hand side of the road and defendant's car, and that she did not hear nor feel her car strike Ms. Zeni. The eyewitness reported seeing plaintiff flip over the fender and hood. He said when he went over to help her his knees were on or inside the white line delineating a parking space. A security officer observed blood stains on the pavement approximately 13 feet from the curb.

Ms. Zeni's injuries were serious . . . . She has retrograde amnesia and therefore, because she does not remember anything from the time she began walking that morning until sometime after the impact, there is no way to determine whether she knew defendant was behind her.

Testimony at trial indicated that it was common for nurses to use the roadway to reach the health center, and a security officer testified that in the wintertime it was safer to walk there than on the one sidewalk. Apparently, several days before the accident, Ms. Zeni had indeed fallen on the sidewalk. Although she was not hurt when she fell, the Director of University Security was hospitalized when he fell on the walk.

Defendant, however, maintained that plaintiff's failure to use that sidewalk constituted contributory negligence because, she said, it violated . . . MSA 9.2355, which requires: "Where sidewalks are provided, it shall be unlawful for pedestrians to walk upon the main traveled portion of the highway. Where sidewalks are not provided, pedestrians shall, when practicable, walk on the left side of the highway facing traffic which passes nearest."

The trial court instructed the jury on this point:

Now, it is for you to decide whether on the evidence presented in this case, sidewalks were provided for the plaintiff, Mrs. Zeni, to go from parking lot "X" [where she parked her car before beginning her walk] to her place of work. Then, as to this statute, you shall then decide whether or not it was practicable for her to walk on the left side of the highway facing traffic which passes nearest. If you find that the plaintiff, Mrs. Zeni, violated this statute before or at the time of the occurrence, then Mrs. Zeni was negligent as a matter of law, which, of course, would bar her claim under count I, providing that her negligence was a proximate contributing cause of the occurrence.

. . . The jury . . . awarded plaintiff damages of $30,000.

II – Effect of Violation of Statute

An analysis of the Michigan cases indicates that the real Michigan rule as to the effect of violation of a penal statute in a negligence action is that such violation creates only a prima facie case from which the jury may draw an inference of negligence. It is true that a number of passages in cases speak of negligence per se almost in terms of strict liability, but closer examination of the application of the rule reveals that Michigan does not subscribe to such a harsh dogma.

A. *Violation of Statute as Rebuttable Presumption*

In a growing number of states, the rule concerning the proper role of a penal statute in a civil action for damages is that violation of the statute which has been found to apply to a particular set of facts establishes only a prima facie case of negligence, a presumption which may be rebutted . . . by a showing on the part of the party violating the statute of an adequate excuse[2] under the facts and circumstances of the case. . . . The approach is logical. Liability without fault is not truly negligence, and in the absence of a clear legislative mandate to so extend liability, the courts should be hesitant to do so on their own. Because these are, after all, criminal statutes, a court is limited in how far it may go in plucking a statute from its criminal milieu and inserting it into the civil arena. The rule of rebuttable presumption has arisen in part in response to this concern, and in part because of the reluctance to go to the other extreme and in effect, discard or disregard the legislative standard. . . .

B. *Violation of Statute as Negligence Per Se*

[T]he judge-made rule of negligence per se has . . . proved to be too inflexible and mechanical to satisfy thoughtful commentators and judges. It is forcefully argued that no matter how a court may attempt to confine the negligence per se doctrine, if defendant is liable despite the exercise of due care and the availability of a reasonable excuse, this is really strict liability, and not negligence. . . . Since it is always possible that the Legislature's failure to deal specifically with the question of private rights was not accidental, and that there might have been no legislative intent to change the law of torts . . . such treatment of the statute may well be a gross perversion of the legislative will. . . . It is troublesome, too, that "potentially ruinous civil liability" may follow from a "minor infraction of petty criminal regulations", 49 Colum L Rev 21, 23, or may,

---

2   Although not intended to be exclusive, the Restatement Torts, 2d, suggests some possible excuses:

       (a) [T]he violation is reasonable because of the actor's incapacity;

       (b) he neither knows nor should know of the occasion for compliance;

       (c) he is unable after reasonable diligence or care to comply;

       (d) he is confronted by an emergency not due to his own misconduct;

       (e) compliance would involve a greater risk of harm to the actor or to others.

      2 Restatement of Torts 2d, § 288A . . . .

in a jurisdiction burdened by contributory negligence, serve to deprive an otherwise deserving plaintiff of a much-needed recovery.

C. Violation of Statute as Evidence of Negligence

Just as the rebuttable presumption approach to statutory violations in a negligence context apparently arose, at least in part, from dissatisfaction with the result of a mechanical application of the per se rule, a parallel development in our state with respect to infractions of ordinances, and of administrative regulations, has been that violations of these amount to only evidence of negligence. . . . In view of the fairness and ease with which the rebuttable presumption standard has been and can be administered, we believe the litigants are thereby well served and the Legislature is given appropriate respect.

D. Application of Statutory Standard to This Case

We have seen, therefore, that while some of our Michigan cases seem to present negligence per se as an unqualified rule, the fact of the matter is that there are a number of qualifications which make application of this rule not really a per se approach at all. . . . Not only must the statutory purpose doctrine and the requirement of proximate cause be satisfied, but the alleged wrongdoer has an opportunity to come forward with evidence rebutting the presumption of negligence.

An accurate statement of our law is that when a court adopts a penal statute as the standard of care in an action for negligence, violation of that statute establishes a prima facie case of negligence, with the determination to be made by the finder of fact whether the party accused of violating the statute has established a legally sufficient excuse. If the finder of fact determines such an excuse exists, the appropriate standard of care then becomes that established by the common law. Such excuses shall include, but shall not be limited to, those suggested by the Restatement Torts, 2d, §288A, and shall be determined by the circumstances of each case.

In the case at bar, moreover, the statute itself provides a guideline for the jury, for a violation will not occur when it is impracticable to use the sidewalk or to walk on the left side of a highway. This is ordinarily a question for the finder of fact . . . , and thus the statute itself provides not only a legislative standard of care which may be accepted by the court, but a legislatively mandated excuse as well.

In the instant case the court charged the jury:

> Now, it is for you to decide whether on the evidence presented in this case, sidewalks were provided for the plaintiff, Mrs. Zeni, to go from parking lot "X" to her place of work. Then, as to this statute, you shall then decide whether or not it was practicable for her to walk on the left side of the highway facing traffic which passes nearest. If you find that the plaintiff, Mrs. Zeni, violated this statute before or at the time of the occurrence, then Mrs. Zeni was negligent as a matter of

law, which, of course, would bar her claim . . . , providing that her negligence was a proximate contributing cause of the occurrence.

Thus, we find the jury was adequately instructed as to the effect of the violation of this particular statute on plaintiff's case. . . . The Court of Appeals is reversed and the trial court is affirmed.

NOTES

1   Most jurisdictions state that an unexcused violation of statute creates an irrebuttable presumption of breach of duty. Does this make any sense? What is an "excuse" if not a rebuttal of the presumption of breach? A minority of jurisdictions treat the violation merely as evidence of negligence. Note that the failure to establish negligence *per se* does not impact plaintiff's case at all – the trier of fact still would be free to find negligence (or not) as usual.

2   Some jurisdictions hold that the violation of a mere local ordinance, as opposed to a statute, does not give rise to negligence *per se*.

BAUMAN V. CRAWFORD
704 P.2D 1181 (WASH.1985)

This appeal requires us to decide whether the negligence per se doctrine should be applicable to minors, or whether minors should instead be judged only by the special child's standard of care in a civil negligence action. We hold that a minor's violation of a statute does not constitute proof of negligence per se, but may, in proper cases, be introduced as evidence of a minor's negligence. . . .

On April 24, 1979, at approximately 9:30 p.m., the bicycle ridden by petitioner Donald Bauman collided with the automobile driven by respondent. Petitioner was 14 years 4 months old at that time. The collision occurred after dark on a public street in Seattle. Petitioner was riding his bicycle down a steep hill; as he reached the base of the hill, respondent turned left in front of petitioner and the collision resulted. Petitioner's bicycle was equipped with reflectors, but had no headlight. Seattle Municipal Code 11.44.160 and RCW 46.61.780(1) each require a headlight on a bicycle operated after dark. . . .

Petitioner, through his guardian ad litem, sued respondent for damages. Respondent's answer alleged contributory negligence by petitioner as an affirmative defense.

The trial court instructed the jury that violation of an ordinance is negligence per se. The court also instructed the jury that the standard of ordinary care for a child is the care that a reasonably careful child of the same age, intelligence, maturity, training and experience would exercise under similar circumstances.

The jury rendered a verdict of $8,000 for petitioner, reduced by 95 percent for petitioner's contributory negligence. Thus, the final verdict was $400 for petitioner.

Petitioner contends it was reversible error for the court to instruct on negligence per se because he is a minor. He further contends that it was reversible error for the court to give the negligence per se instruction in combination with the special child's standard of care instruction because these instructions are contradictory to one another. . . .

Washington has long recognized the special standard of care applicable to children: a child's conduct is measured by the conduct of a reasonably careful child of the same age, intelligence, maturity, training and experience. . . . The rationale for the special child's standard of care is that a child is lacking in the judgment, discretion, and experience of an adult; thus, the child's standard of care allows for the normal incapacities and indiscretions of youth. . . . Most significantly, the child's standard was created because public policy dictates that it would be unfair to predicate legal fault upon a standard most children are incapable of meeting. Thus, the fact of minority is not what lowers the standard; rather, the child's immaturity of judgment and lack of capacity to appreciate dangers justifies a special child's standard. . . .

A primary rationale for the negligence per se doctrine is that the Legislature has determined the standard of conduct expected of an ordinary, reasonable person; if one violates a statute, he is no longer a reasonably prudent person. . . . Negligence per se exists when a statute or ordinance is violated, and that law is designed to (a) protect a class of persons which includes the person whose interest is invaded, (b) protect the particular interest which is invaded, (c) protect against the kind of harm which resulted, and (d) protect that interest against the particular hazard from which the harm results. . . .

A majority of courts in states which apply the negligence per se doctrine to adults have recognized a fundamental conflict between that doctrine and the special child's standard of care. . . . Scholarly commentary also overwhelmingly supports the view that negligence per se is inapplicable to children. . . .

The majority rule is based upon the policy considerations underlying each doctrine. These courts and commentators recognize that application of negligence per se to children abrogates the special standard of care for children; such abrogation violates the public policy inherent in the special child's standard. These courts and commentators also recognize that refusal to consider a child's minority in effect substitutes a standard of strict liability for the criterion of the reasonable child. . . .

A significant number of the courts which decline to apply negligence per se to minors have determined that violation of a statute by a minor may be introduced as evidence of negligence, as long as the jury is clearly instructed that the minor's behavior is ultimately to be judged by the special child's standard of care. . . .

We agree with these courts that allowing a statutory violation to be introduced simply as one factor to be considered by the trier of fact is an equitable resolution of the dilemma created by a minor's violation of law. We therefore remand for a new trial on the issue of liability under proper instructions. At that trial the jury must be instructed as to the special child's standard of care. The jury may then be instructed that violation of a relevant statute[3] may be considered as evidence of negligence only if the jury finds that a reasonable child of the same age, intelligence, maturity and experience as petitioner would not have acted in violation of the statute under the same circumstances. . . .

[The decision of the Court of Appeals is reversed].

Finally, we hold that our ruling today, which exempts minors from the operation of the negligence per se doctrine, shall apply prospectively. However, the rule shall also apply to any case already tried where the issue of the doctrine's application to a minor was preserved for appeal.

Brachtenbach, J. (concurring)

I concur in the rationale and result of the majority but I am convinced that in the appropriate case this court should reexamine the entire theory of negligence per se arising from the alleged violation of a statute, an ordinance or an administrative regulation.

This court has long been committed to the rule that violation of a positive statute constitutes negligence per se. . . . This rule has been applied to violations of statutes, ordinances and regulations, . . . , in determining both the liability of defendants and the contributory negligence of plaintiffs. . . . The Restatement (Second) of Torts § 286 (1965) adopted the test of the relevancy of the statute to the tortious action. Where the relevancy test is met and where there exists prima facie a discernible causal connection between the violation of the statute and the injury, the jury is properly advised that the violation amounts to negligence per se and proximate cause then becomes the sole issue of fact to be resolved by the trier of fact. . . .

The rule, however, has not been applied with relentless indifference to actual fault. A violation of statute has been held not to constitute negligence per se where the violation is due to some cause beyond the violator's control, and which reasonable prudence could not have guarded against. . . ; where the violation is due to an emergency . . . ; where the violation is merely technical . . . ; where the violation is perpetuated out of necessity . . . ; or where the violator is not given notice that his actions were in violation of the law . . . .

This 77-year-old doctrine has been the subject of exceptions almost since its adoption. Perhaps it is time we stopped selectively placing the negligence question within "rational judicial control" and place it, in all cases, in the rational control of the trier of fact, where it belongs.

The finding of negligence is normally a task for the trier of fact. Through the application of the negligence per se doctrine we have taken that task away from the jury and the court now decides when a violation of statute constitutes negligence. It is evident from the numerous exceptions to the doctrine that the court is not merely applying a statute to the tortious action, but determining from the total factual circumstances whether or not the statute violator was negligent at all. I, therefore, advocate true rational control of the negligence doctrine through the return of the negligence question to the trier of fact in cases involving evidence of a violation of statute.

---

3   A statute must still be shown to be applicable under the negligence per se test before its violation may be introduced even as mere evidence of negligence. That is, the statute must be designed to protect the proper class of persons, to protect the particular interest involved, and to protect against the harm which results. . . Thus, only relevant statutory violations will be admitted.

Currently, the majority of American jurisdictions follow the negligence per se doctrine and find that a breach of statutory duty is a breach of standard of care for civil negligence cases. Seven states follow the theory that a breach of a statutory duty is evidence of negligence in civil action, . . . while five states hold that a violation of a statute is prima facie negligence which may be rebutted by competent evidence. . . . Such cases seem to indicate a desire to leave some leeway for cases where a violation may not be necessarily unreasonable. . . .

The most widely accepted rationale for the negligence per se rule is that the reasonable man always obeys the criminal law, thus, a breach of the criminal law must be unreasonable and, therefore, negligent. . . . The basic flaw in this rationale and in inferring legislative intent is the fact that the criminal proscriptions may be ill conceived, hastily drawn with inadequate investigation or obsolete and, yet, the validity of the statute will not be before the court in the negligence action. The Legislature has not considered the policy problems peculiar to civil liability nor has it composed the legislation in terms of a standard of due care in damage suits or for judging negligence. . . . Reliance on the Legislature for a standard of reasonableness under these circumstances would not make for the wisest decision.

A second rationale for finding legislative intent to create a standard of care in civil cases is that the Legislature recognizes that the negligence per se rule is needed to promote and fulfill reliance by others on uniform obedience to statutes. However, where the Legislature does not explicitly impose automatic liability in a civil action as a sanction, the court is encroaching on legislative territory when it adds such a sanction for the purposes of law enforcement. . . .

Criticism is also made because of the imposition of liability without fault. As noted above, the Washington courts have joined in this criticism and produced multiple exceptions in order to avoid this aspect of the doctrine. This exception-finding approach produces a weakened doctrine and ultimately places the jury's task of determining negligence with the court under all circumstances. Such an approach also leads to distorted statutory construction which affects the criminal law as well.

The defect in our prior reasoning is that the negligence per se doctrine removes the determination of negligence from the fact-finding function of the jury, or the court sitting as a fact finder. While it is a convenient method to affix liability, it runs counter to the basic notion of determining tort liability. I would prospectively limit the doctrine to an evidence of negligence standard.

POTTS V. FIDELITY FRUIT & PRODUCE CO.
301 s.e.2d 903 (ga. app. 1983)

The appellant sued to recover for personal injuries which he allegedly sustained when he was bitten by a spider while unloading bananas from a truck. The incident occurred during the course of his employment with Colonial Stores. The defendants are the local distributor of the bananas, Fidelity Fruit and Produce Co., Inc., and the transporter, Refrigerated Transport Co., Inc. Liability was originally predicated both on ordinary negligence and negligence *per se* under the Georgia Food Act . . . . However, the appellant has since conceded that the evidence would not sustain a finding of ordinary negligence. This appeal is from a grant of summary judgment in favor of Fidelity Fruit and Produce Co., Inc., as to the negligence *per se* claim, based on a determination that the appellant is not among the class of persons whom the Georgia Food Act was designed to protect. *Held:*

In determining whether the violation of a statute or ordinance is negligence *per se* as to a particular person, it is necessary to examine the purposes of the legislation and decide (1) whether the injured person falls within the class of persons it was intended to protect and (2) whether the harm complained of was the harm it was intended to guard against. . . . Having examined the provisions of the Georgia Food Act, we agree fully with the following analysis made by the trial court: "Clearly, the Act is a consumer protection act, designed not to render the workplace a safer environment, but to prevent the sale and distribution of adulterated or misbranded foods to consumers. While safety in the workplace, and compensation for injuries arising out of work activities, are indeed matters of contemporary concern, they are the subject of other legislative enactments on both the state and federal level." Because the appellant's alleged injuries did not arise incident to his consumption of the bananas, we hold that the trial court was correct in concluding that the Act affords him no basis for recovery.

Judgment affirmed.

b. JUDGE-MADE RULES

BALTIMORE & OHIO R. CO. V. GOODMAN
275 U.S. 66 (1927)

Mr. Justice HOLMES delivered the opinion of the Court.

This is a suit brought by the widow and administratrix of Nathan Goodman against the petitioner for causing his death by running him down at a grade crossing. The defense is that Goodman's own negligence caused the death. . . . Goodman was driving an automobile truck in an easterly direction and was killed by a train running southwesterly across the road at a rate of not less than 60 miles an hour. The line was straight but it is said by the respondent that Goodman "had no practical view" beyond a section house 243 feet north of the crossing until he was about 20 feet from the first rail, or, as the respondent argues, 12 feet from danger, and that then the engine was still obscured by the section house. He had been driving at the rate of 10 or 12 miles an hour but had cut down his rate to 5 or 6 miles at about 40 feet from the crossing. It is thought that there was an emergency in which, so far as appears, Goodman did all that he could.

We do not go into further details as to Goodman's precise situation, beyond mentioning that it was daylight and that he was familiar with the crossing, for it appears to us plain that nothing is suggested by the evidence to relieve Goodman from responsibility for his own death. When a man goes upon a railroad track he knows that he goes to a place where he will be killed if a train comes upon him before he is clear of the track. He knows that he must stop for the train not the train stop for him. In such circumstances it seems to us that if a driver cannot be sure otherwise whether a train is dangerously near he must stop and get out of his vehicle, although obviously he will not often be required to do more than to stop and look. It seems to us that if he relies upon not hearing the train or any signal and takes no further precaution he does so at his own risk. If at the last moment Goodman found himself in an emergency it was his own fault that he did not reduce his speed earlier or come to a stop. It is true . . . that the question of due care very generally is left to the jury. But we are dealing with a standard of conduct, and when the standard is clear it should be laid down once for all by the Courts. . . .

Judgment reversed.

POKORA V. WABASH RY. CO.
292 u.s. 98 (1934)

Mr. Justice CARDOZO delivered the opinion of the Court.

John Pokora, driving his truck across a railway grade crossing . . . was struck by a train and injured. Upon the trial of his suit for damages, the District Court held that he had been guilty of contributory negligence, and directed a verdict for the defendant. The Circuit Court of Appeals (one judge dissenting) affirmed . . . , resting its judgment on the opinion of this court in *B. & O.R. Co. v. Goodman*, 275 U.S. 66 . . . . A writ of certiorari brings the case here.

Pokora was an ice dealer, and had come to the crossing to load his truck with ice. The tracks of the Wabash Railway are laid along Tenth Street, which runs north and south. There is a crossing at Edwards Street running east and west. . . .

The defendant has four tracks on Tenth Street; a switch track on the east, then the main track, and then two switches. Pokora, as he left the northeast corner where his truck had been stopped, looked to the north for approaching trains. He did this at a point about ten or fifteen feet east of the switch ahead of him. A string of box cars standing on the switch, about five to ten feet from the north line of Edwards street, cut off his view of the tracks beyond him to the north. At the same time he listened. There was neither bell nor whistle. Still listening, he crossed the switch, and reaching the main track was struck by a passenger train coming from the north at a speed of twenty-five to thirty miles an hour.

The burden of proof was on the defendant to make out the defense of contributory negligence. . . . The record does not show in any conclusive way that the train was visible to Pokora while there was still time to stop. . . . In such circumstances the question, we think, was for the jury whether reasonable caution forbade his going forward in reliance on the sense of hearing, unaided by that of sight. No doubt it was his duty to look along the track from his seat, if looking would avail to warn him of the danger. This does not mean, however, that if vision was cut off by obstacles, there was negligence in going on, any more than there would have been in trusting to his ears if vision had been cut off by the darkness of the night. . . . Pokora made his crossing in the daytime, but like the traveler by night he used the faculties available to one in his position. . . . A jury, but not the court, might say that with faculties thus limited he should have found some other means of assuring himself of safety before venturing to cross. The crossing was a frequented highway in a populous city. Behind him was a line of other cars, making ready to follow him. To some extent, at least, there was assurance in the thought that the defendant would not run its train at such a time and place without sounding bell or whistle. . . . All this the plaintiff, like any other reasonable traveler, might fairly take into account. All this must be taken into account by us in comparing what he did with the conduct reasonably to be expected of reasonable men. . . .

The argument is made, however, that our decision in . . . *Goodman, supra,* is a barrier in the plaintiff's path, irrespective of the conclusion that might commend itself if the question were at large. There is no doubt that the opinion in that case is correct in its result. Goodman, the driver, traveling only five or six miles an hour, had, before reaching the track, a clear space of eighteen feet within which the train was plainly visible. With that opportunity, he fell short of the legal standard of duty established for a traveler when he failed to look and see. This was decisive of the case. But the court did not stop there. It added a remark, unnecessary upon the facts before it, which has been a fertile source of controversy. "In such circumstances it seems to us that if a driver cannot be sure otherwise whether a train is dangerously near he must stop and get out of his vehicle, although obviously he will not often be required to do more than to stop and look."

There is need at this stage to clear the ground of brushwood that may obscure the point at issue. We do not now inquire into the existence of a duty to stop, disconnected from a duty to get out and reconnoiter. The inquiry, if pursued, would lead us into the thickets of conflicting judgments. Some courts apply what is often spoken of as the Pennsylvania rule, and impose an unyielding duty to stop, as well as to look and listen, no matter how clear the crossing or the tracks on either side. . . . Other courts, the majority, adopt the rule that the traveler must look and listen, but that the existence of a duty to stop depends upon the circumstances, and hence generally, even if not invariably, upon the judgment of the jury. . . . The subject has been less considered in this court, but in none of its opinions is there a suggestion that at any and every crossing the duty to stop is absolute, irrespective of the danger. Not even in . . . *Goodman, supra,* which goes farther than the earlier cases, is there support for such a rule. To the contrary, the opinion makes it clear that the duty is conditioned upon the presence of impediments whereby sight and hearing become inadequate for the traveler's protection. . . .

Choice between these diversities of doctrine is unnecessary for the decision of the case at hand. Here the fact is not disputed that the plaintiff did stop before he started to cross the tracks. If we assume that by reason of the box cars, there was a duty to stop again when the obstructions had been cleared, that duty did not arise unless a stop could be made safely after the point of clearance had been reached. . . . For reasons already stated, the testimony permits the inference that the truck was in the zone of danger by the time the field of vision was enlarged. No stop would then have helped the plaintiff if he remained seated on his truck, or so the triers of the facts might find. His case was for the jury, unless as a matter of law he was subject to a duty to get out of the vehicle before it crossed the switch, walk forward to the front, and then, afoot, survey the scene. We must say whether his failure to do this was negligence so obvious and certain that one conclusion and one only is permissible for rational and candid minds. . . .

Standards of prudent conduct are declared at times by courts, but they are taken over from the facts of life. To get out of a vehicle and reconnoiter is an uncommon precaution, as everyday experience informs us. Besides being uncommon, it is very likely to be futile, and sometimes even dangerous. If the driver leaves his vehicle when he nears a cut or curve, he will learn nothing by getting out about the perils that lurk beyond. By the time he regains his seat and sets his car in motion, the hidden train may be upon him. . . . Often the added safeguard will be dubious though the track happens to be straight, as it seems that this one was, at all events as far as the station, about five blocks to the north. A train traveling at a speed of thirty miles an hour will cover a quarter of a mile in the space of thirty seconds. It may thus emerge out of obscurity as the driver turns his back to regain the waiting car, and may then descend upon him suddenly when his car is on the track. Instead of helping himself by getting out, he might do better to press forward with all his faculties alert. So a train at a neighboring station, apparently at rest and harmless, may be transformed in a few seconds into an instrument of destruction. At times the course of safety may be different. One can figure to oneself a roadbed so level and unbroken that getting out will be a gain. Even then the balance of advantage depends on many circumstances and can be easily disturbed. Where was Pokora to leave his truck after getting out to reconnoiter? If he was to leave it on the switch, there was the possibility that the box cars would be shunted down upon him before he could regain his seat. The defendant did not show whether there was a locomotive at the forward end, or whether the cars were so few that a locomotive could be seen. If he was to leave his vehicle near the curb, there was even stronger reason to believe that the space to be covered in going back and forth would make his observations worthless. One must remember that while the traveler turns his eyes in one direction, a train or a loose engine may be approaching from the other.

Illustrations such as these bear witness to the need for caution in framing standards of behavior that amount to rules of law. The need is the more urgent when there is no background of experience out of which the standards have emerged. They are then, not the natural flowerings of behavior in its customary forms, but rules artificially developed, and imposed from without. Extraordinary situations may not wisely or fairly be subjected to tests or regulations that are fitting for the commonplace or normal. In default of the guide of customary conduct, what is suitable for the traveler caught in a mesh where the ordinary safeguards fail him is for the judgment of a jury. . . . The opinion in Goodman's Case has been a source of confusion in the federal courts to the extent that it imposes a standard for application by the judge, and has had only wavering support in the courts of the states. We limit it accordingly.

The judgment should be reversed, and the cause remanded for further proceedings in accordance with this opinion.

It is so ordered.

AKINS V. GLENS FALLS CITY SCHOOL DIST.

424 N.E.2D 531 (N.Y. 1981)

On this appeal, we are called upon to define the scope of the duty owed by a proprietor of a baseball field to the spectators attending its games. The specific question presented is whether such an owner, having provided protective screening for the area behind home plate, is liable in negligence for the injuries sustained by a spectator as a result of being struck by a foul ball while standing in an unscreened section of the field. . . .

In the early afternoon of April 14, 1976, plaintiff attended a high school baseball game that was being played on a field owned and maintained by defendant Glens Falls City School District. The field was equipped with a backstop 24 feet high and 50 feet wide. This backstop was located 60 feet behind home plate and was positioned in front of bleachers that could seat approximately 120 adults. There was additional standing room behind the backstop as well. Two chain link fences, three feet in height, ran from each end of the backstop along the base lines to a distance approximately 60 feet behind first and third base.

Plaintiff arrived while the game was in progress and elected to view the contest from a position behind the three-foot fence along the third base line, approximately 10 to 15 feet from the end of the backstop and 60 feet from home plate. As there were no seating facilities for spectators along the base lines, plaintiff had to stand in order to watch the game. At the time, other spectators were also standing along the base lines behind the three-foot fence. There was, however, no proof that the screened bleachers behind home plate were filled or that plaintiff was prevented from watching the game from behind the backstop. Approximately 10 minutes after arriving at the baseball field, plaintiff was struck in the eye by a sharply hit foul ball, causing her serious and permanent injury.

The present action was then commenced by the plaintiff against the defendant school district. Alleging that the school district was negligent in failing to provide safe and proper screening devices along the base lines of its field, plaintiff sought judgment against the school district in the sum of $250,000. After trial, the jury returned a verdict in plaintiff's favor, assessing damages in the amount of $100,000 and apportioning fault at 65% to the school district and 35% to plaintiff. . . .

Cases involving the liability of an owner of a baseball field for the injuries sustained by those attending its games are not altogether foreign to the courts of this State. Indeed, the doctrine of assumption of risk has had extensive application in a number of cases involving spectators struck by misguided baseballs. . . . As was aptly summarized by Chief Judge Cardozo, the spectator at a sporting event, no less than the participant, "accepts the dangers that inhere in it so far as they are obvious and necessary, just as a fencer accepts the risk of a thrust by his antagonist or a spectator at a ball game the chance of contact with the ball * * * The timorous may stay at home." (*Murphy v Steeplechase Amusement Co.*, 250 NY 479, 482-483.) However . . . , there is no case law in this State which defines the duty of care owed by a proprietor of a baseball field to its spectators. We now define that duty.

At the outset, it should be stated that an owner of a baseball field is not an insurer of the safety of its spectators. Rather, like any other owner or occupier of land, it is only under a duty to exercise "reasonable care under the circumstances" to prevent injury to those who come to watch the games played on its field. *(Basso v Miller . . . .)* The perils of the game of baseball, however, are not so imminent that due care on the part of the owner requires that the entire playing field be screened. Indeed, many spectators prefer to sit where their view of the game is unobstructed by fences or protective netting and the proprietor of a ball park has a legitimate interest in catering to these desires. Thus, the critical question becomes what amount of screening must be provided by an owner of a baseball field before it will be found to have discharged its duty of care to its spectators.

Other jurisdictions addressing this question have adopted various standards in defining the duty of a ball park proprietor to protect its spectators from stray balls. Some courts have held that an owner merely has a duty to screen such seats as are adequate to provide its spectators with an opportunity to sit in a protected area if they so desire. . . . Other courts have stated that a proprietor of a baseball field need only screen as many seats as may reasonably be expected to be applied for on an ordinary occasion by those desiring such protection. . . . Most courts, however, have adopted a two-prong standard in defining the scope of an owner's duty to provide protective screening for its patrons. Under the majority rule, the owner must screen the most dangerous section of the field – the area behind home plate – and the screening that is provided must be sufficient for those spectators who may be reasonably anticipated to desire protected seats on an ordinary occasion. . . . We believe this to be the better rule and adopt this definition of the duty owed by an owner of a baseball field to provide protective screening for its spectators.

We hold that, in the exercise of reasonable care, the proprietor of a ball park need only provide screening for the area of the field behind home plate where the danger of being struck by a ball is the greatest. Moreover, such screening must be of sufficient extent to provide adequate protection for as many spectators as may reasonably be expected to desire such seating in the course of an ordinary game. In so holding, we merely recognize the practical realities of this sporting event. As mentioned earlier, many spectators attending such exhibitions desire to watch the contest taking place on the playing field without having their view obstructed or obscured by a fence or a protective net. In ministering to these desires, while at the same time providing adequate protection in the most dangerous area of the field for those spectators who wish to avail themselves of it, a proprietor fulfills its duty of reasonable care under such circumstances.

This is not to say that, by adequately screening the area of the field where the incidence of foul balls is the greatest, the risks inherent in viewing the game are completely eliminated. Rather, even after the exercise of reasonable care, some risk of being struck by a ball will continue to exist. Moreover, contrary to the supposition of the dissent, we do not attempt to prescribe precisely what, as a matter of law, are the required dimensions of a baseball field backstop. Nor do we suggest that where the adequacy of the screening in terms of protecting the area behind home plate properly is put in issue, the case should not be submitted to the jury. We merely hold that where a proprietor of a ball park furnishes screening for the area of the field behind home plate where the danger of being struck by a ball is the greatest and that screening is of sufficient extent to provide adequate protection for as many spectators as may reasonably be expected to desire such seating in the course of an ordinary game, the proprietor fulfills the duty of care imposed by law and, therefore, cannot be liable in negligence. Indeed, to adopt the view urged by the dissent would mean that every spectator injured by a foul ball, no matter where he is seated or standing in the ball park, would have an absolute right to go to the jury on every claim of negligence, regardless of the owner's efforts to provide reasonable protection and despite the spectator's failure to utilize the protection made available. . . .

In this case, it is undisputed that the school district equipped its field with a backstop which was 24 feet high and 50 feet wide. Plaintiff presented no evidence that this backstop was inadequate in terms of providing protection for the area behind home plate where there was a substantial likelihood of spectators being struck by misguided balls or that there was an insufficient number of screened seats for those who might reasonably be expected to desire such protection. Under these circumstances, having provided adequate protection for those spectators seated, or standing, in the area behind home plate, liability may not be imposed on the school district for failing to provide additional screening along the baselines of its field where the risk of being struck by a stray ball was considerably less. . . .

As the dissent correctly notes, what constitutes reasonable care under the circumstances ordinarily is a question for the jury. This is not to say, however, that in every case involving a landowner's liability in negligence the question whether reasonable care was exercised must be determined by the jury. As we have only recently stated, "before it becomes appropriate for the jury to consider * * * such questions, the court, as it would in the usual negligence action, must make the threshold determination as to whether the plaintiff, by introducing adequate evidence on each element, has made out a case sufficient in law to support a favorable jury verdict. Only in those cases where there arises a real question as to the landowner's negligence should the jury be permitted to proceed. In all others, where proof of any essential element falls short, the case should go no further." *(Basso v Miller, 40 NY2d 233, 241-242, supra . . . .)*

In short, a court always is required to undertake an initial evaluation of the evidence to determine whether the plaintiff has established the elements necessary to a cause of action in negligence, to wit: (1) the existence of a duty on defendant's part as to plaintiff; (2) a breach of this duty; and (3) injury to the plaintiff as a result thereof. . . . In this regard, this court, on more than one occasion, has held that a defendant fulfilled its duty of care notwithstanding a jury verdict to the contrary. . . . Similarly, on the record before us and the undisputed facts of this case, the school district fulfilled its *duty* of reasonable care to plaintiff as a matter of law and, therefore, no question of negligence remained for the jury's consideration. . . .

Accordingly, the order of the Appellate Division should be reversed, with costs, and the complaint dismissed.

Chief Judge Cooke (dissenting). The majority today engages in an unfortunate exercise in judicial rule making in an area that should be left to the jury. This attempt to precisely prescribe what steps the proprietor of a baseball field must take to fulfill its duty of reasonable care is unwarranted and unwise. . . . I therefore dissent and vote to affirm.

As the majority recognizes, the proprietor of a baseball field owes the same duty to spectators that any landowner owes to a person who comes onto the owner's property – "reasonable care under the circumstances" *(Basso v Miller,* 40 NY2d 233, 241. . .). This duty requires that the landowner "must act as a reasonable man in maintaining his property in a reasonably safe condition in view of all the circumstances, including the likelihood of injury to others, the seriousness of the injury, and the burden of avoiding the risk" *(Basso v Miller,* 40 NY2d 233, 241 . . .).

The majority errs, however, in deciding as a matter of law exactly what steps by a baseball field proprietor will constitute reasonable care under the circumstances. Such a determination, by its very dependence upon the "circumstances," hinges upon the facts of the individual situation and should be left for the jury. Indeed, those exceptions to this rule that have been made by courts occur only in those narrow classes of cases where an identical set of facts is likely to recur with regularity . . . .

The majority has in effect undertaken the task of prescribing the size, shape and location of backstops and other protective devices that will satisfy a baseball field owner's duty of reasonable care under the circumstances. This attempt to impose a straightjacket upon the relationship between a baseball field proprietor and spectators, regardless of the particular circumstances, is arbitrary and unrealistic. It is reminiscent of the Supreme Court's attempt, in the early years of the automobile, to impose upon the operator the duty of leaving the vehicle and examining each railroad grade crossing on foot, if necessary for a better view of the tracks *(Baltimore & Ohio R. R. v Goodman,* 275 U.S. 66 [per Holmes, J.]). This standard enjoyed little favor among State courts, engendered confusion among lower Federal courts attempting to apply it and was quickly repudiated by the Supreme Court *(Pokora v Wabash Ry. Co.,* 292 U.S. 98).

In *Pokora,* Justice Cardozo noted that the problems springing from the grade-crossing rule emphasized "the need for caution in framing standards of behavior that amount to rules of law" (*id.,* at p 105). Indeed, railroad crossing cases provide a good example of this court's reluctance to impose blanket rules of conduct divorced from actual events. . . .

The wisdom of eschewing such blanket rules where negligence is concerned is obvious. In the present context, the majority had held as a matter of law that the proprietor of the baseball field fulfilled his duty of reasonable care by erecting a backstop that was 24 feet high and 50 feet wide. The court issues this rule with no more expertise available to it than Justice Holmes had in 1927 when he recommended that motorists venture on foot onto railroad grade crossings for a better view. It has selected one of a variety of forms of protection currently in use at professional ballparks and school playgrounds – what in reality is nothing more than a straight, high fence behind home plate – and has designated it as sufficient protection as a matter of law.

Such a ruling robs the jury of its ability to pass on whether the circumstances here might have made this type of backstop inadequate. In the present case, the majority has taken from the jury its ability to consider the following evidence: that the cost of placing "wings" on the backstop extending to first and third base would have been only $209 when the backstop was built; that other baseball diamonds do have such wings; that the type of game being played at the field was not a softball game between young tykes but rather a varsity high school hardball game involving players such as the batter in this incident, who was six-foot two-inches tall, weighed 190 pounds and was advanced enough in ability to later play professional ball; that school authorities were aware that line drives "frequently" went over the low fence that ran along the base lines, and that there were no signs or other warnings of the dangers of standing behind this fence. Because of public familiarity with the "national pastime," no expert testimony would generally be required to make out a showing of failure to exercise due care in such a case . . . . In this case, however, the jury even had before it the testimony of a civil engineer as to the feasibility and minimal cost of ensuring greater safety for spectators. This makes an even stronger argument for sending this case to the jury.

The court's ruling will also foreclose juries in the future from considering the wide range of circumstances of individual cases, as well as new developments in safety devices or procedures. Unless the court plans to periodically take up such cases in the future to adjust its rule, it has frozen a position that is certain to become outdated, if it is not already. It would make as much sense for the court to decree, as a matter of law, what sort of batting helmet or catcher's mask a school district should supply to its baseball team. Baseball may be a sport steeped in tradition, but it is hardly immune from technological change and shifts in public perception of what constitute reasonable safety measures. It has traditionally been the jury that reflects these shifts and changes. . . .

5. RES IPSA LOQUITUR

In a negligence case, as in tort cases generally, plaintiff bears the burden of pleading and proving each essential element of the cause of action, including that defendant breached a duty. (Defendant bears the burden of proving each element of any affirmative defense.) The burden of proof really is two burdens in one: First, plaintiff bears the burden of production, i.e. coming forward with evidence from which a reasonable finder of fact could find for the plaintiff under the applicable standard of proof on each element of the cause of action. (If plaintiff fails to carry this burden of production, she will be vulnerable to a motion for judgment as a matter of law – there is no reason to require the jury to deliberate over a matter that could not reasonably be resolved in plaintiff's favor.) This burden of production can shift back and forth between the parties as the process of proof proceeds through the case. The court determines whether a burden of production has been carried. Finally, plaintiff bears the burden of persuasion, i.e. actually convincing the finder of fact of each element of the cause of action under the applicable standard of proof (usually by a preponderance of evidence). The trier of fact (usually a jury) determines whether the burden of persuasion has been carried.

Frequently, breach of duty is proven directly, using evidence of precisely how defendant's conduct failed to live up to the standard of reasonableness under the circumstances. Sometimes, however, it may be apparent that defendant (or someone) has breached a duty to plaintiff, but plaintiff is unable, due to the precise circumstances of the case, to prove with specificity the nature of that breach of duty. How then can plaintiff carry her burden of proof? At such times, the doctrine of *res ipsa loquitur* ("the thing speaks for itself") can step in to provide a way for plaintiff to prove a *prima facie* case. Thus, the doctrine of *res ipsa loquitur* allows the plaintiff to prove negligence circumstantially and to survive defendant's dispositive motion in circumstances where the facts "speak for themselves."

BYRNE V. BOADLE
159 eng. rep. 299 (ex. 1863)

A witness named Critchley said: "On the 18th July, I was in Scotland Road, on the right side going north, defendant's shop is on that side. When I was opposite to his shop, a barrel of flour fell from a window above in defendant's house and shop, and knocked the plaintiff down. . . . A horse and cart came opposite the defendant's door. Barrels of flour were in the cart. I do not think the barrel was being lowered by a rope. . . . I did not see the barrel until it struck the plaintiff. It was not swinging when it struck the plaintiff. It struck him on the shoulder and knocked him towards the shop. No one called out until after the accident." [In fact, defendant had a hoist for the lowering of barrels over the window in question.] The plaintiff said: "On approaching Scotland Place and defendant's shop, I lost all recollection. I felt no blow. I saw nothing to warn me of danger. I was taken home in a cab. I was helpless for a fortnight." . . . It was admitted that the defendant was a dealer in flour.

It was submitted, on the part of the defendant, that there was no evidence of negligence for the jury. The learned Assessor was of that opinion, and nonsuited the plaintiff . . . .

[The court commented: "There are certain cases of which it may be said *res ipsa loquitur* and this seems one of them.]

Pollock, C. B. We are all of opinion . . . to enter the verdict for the plaintiff. The learned counsel was quite right in saying that there are many accidents from which no presumption of negligence can arise, but I think it would be wrong to lay down as a rule that in no case can presumption of negligence arise from the fact of an accident. Suppose in this case the barrel had rolled out of the warehouse and fallen on the plaintiff, how could he possibly ascertain from what cause it occurred? It is the duty of persons who keep barrels in a warehouse to take care that they do not roll out, and I think that such a case would, beyond all doubt, afford prima facie evidence of negligence. A barrel could not roll out of a warehouse without some negligence, and to say that a plaintiff who is injured by it must call witnesses from the warehouse to prove negligence seems to me preposterous. So in the building or repairing a house, or putting pots on the chimneys, if a person passing along the road is injured by something falling upon him, I think the accident alone would be prima facie evidence of negligence. Or if an article calculated to cause damage is put in a wrong place and does mischief, I think that those whose duty it was to put it in the right place are prima facie responsible, and if there is any state of facts to rebut the presumption of negligence, they must prove them. The present case upon the evidence comes to this, a man is passing in front of the premises of a dealer in flour, and there falls down upon him a barrel of flour. I think it apparent that the barrel was in the custody of the defendant who occupied the premises, and who is responsible for the acts of his servants who had control of it; and in my opinion the fact of its falling is prima facie evidence of negligence, and the plaintiff who was injured by it is not bound to shew that it could not fall without negligence, but if there are any facts inconsistent with negligence it is for the defendant to prove them. . . .

QUESTIONS

1   Would this case have been materially different if a witness had testified that he saw defendant's employee secure the barrel using only two of four connecting straps on the hoisting mechanism? Would such testimony provide *prima facie* evidence of a want of the exercise of due care?

2   What if a witness testified that examination of the condition of the straps after the accident revealed that two obviously had been well-used, but the other two were in like-new condition? Would such testimony create a jury question on defendant's exercise of due care? How is this case different from the case outlined in the previous question?

3   How was the evidence in *Byrne* different from both of these hypothetical cases? What was plaintiff's evidence of defendant's negligence in *Byrne*?

COMBUSTION ENGINEERING CO. V. HUNSBERGER
187 A. 825 (MD. 1936)

An employee of a subcontractor on construction work in a building . . . has sued over and recovered a judgment against another subcontractor on the ground of negligence of the defendant causing the injury. . . . The work was reconstruction of a boiler room for the United States Industrial Alcohol Company, and it had been going on for three months or more. The Combustion Engineering Company was finishing erecting on each side of the boiler, from the first floor up to a height of 30 to 35 feet, an iron air duct . . . . Within the preheater there were plates extending throughout the length, 27 in number, spaced about an inch or an inch and a half apart, and supported by angle irons at intervals. Inside the top were shelves for workmen to lie on when cleaning out. The plates, or elements, as they were called, were to be welded at the top, and that was the work being done at the time of the accident. Below the preheaters, in the basement, the plaintiff's employer . . . had recently started work of constructing connections of the preheaters with the boiler. The basement was open, no floor boards having been laid above it.

At the beginning of the day's work on the morning of the accident, Walter Durdella, one of the Combustion Company's workmen, climbed the ladder to the top of the particular preheater they had been working on at the close of the last preceding working day, and began work of forcing the tops of the plates, or elements, in position for his brother to weld them together from outside the box. The force was applied by means of a metal wedge, in size about a quarter of an inch by about one inch and a half, and ten or eleven inches long, hammered in between two plates. The restriction on the space required Durdella to do the work lying on his stomach. While he was doing this, twenty to thirty minutes after starting work, a wedge fell down through the preheater and struck and injured the plaintiff working underneath it. Durdella's explanation of the occurrence—and he was the only man who had knowledge of what occurred at the top—was that he first drove the wedge in until he was sure it was held fast in place, then, resting his weight on one arm, with the other gave it a hard stroke; and as he did so the wedge jumped out and found its way down through the preheater. At the time Durdella supposed that it must have lodged in the preheater somewhere.

The plaintiff's case was rested on an assumption that the mere fact of the falling of the wedge afforded evidence of negligence, and the trial court, on a prayer of the plaintiffs instructed the jury that this was true. But this court does not agree in that view. There must be evidence from which the jury might reasonably and properly conclude that there was negligence. . . . And apart from any question of the effect on a prima facie presumption, if there should be one, of evidence of the facts produced by a defendant (*Byrne v. Boadle* . . .), the court is of opinion that the mere fall of a tool being used within the building, in work of construction, cannot be presumed to result from negligence, because it cannot be supposed that such a thing is probably the result of negligence every time it occurs. On the contrary, it would seem likely that with workmen handling loose tools continually, the falling of some of them at times must be expected despite all precautions. To presume otherwise would be to presume a perfection in men's work which we know does not exist. . . . But as stated, it seems to the court plain that there must be some falling of small tools and other objects handled with ordinary care in the course of the work, and that therefore a particular fall cannot, of itself and without more, afford proof of negligence. Unless facts appear to indicate negligence, it must be taken as no more than one of the incidents of the work, to be expected. Error is found in the instruction to the contrary in this case.

The facts given in Durdella's evidence leave it open to speculation whether despite his belief that the wedge was held fast he had driven it in more lightly than usual, or whether the plates offered unusual and unexpected resistance. That the wedge jumped out when struck would seem to indicate unexpected resistance. If there was a miscalculation on Durdella's part as to the resistance, or otherwise, that fact alone would not indicate negligence unless it could be said that every such miscalculation on the part of a workman is probably due to lack of ordinary care. And plainly, we think, it cannot. It is conceivable that with the greatest practicable care a workman might be surprised at the resistance of metal, and evidence would be needed to show the contrary in this instance. . . .

In the opinion of the court, negligence, if there was any, causing the accident, must have consisted in doing the work above without some adjustment of the two jobs of work, with due care for the safety of men working below in case of a fall. There is evidence that pieces or rods of heated metal were expected to fall down through the preheater, and that fall of a tool was anticipated as a possibility, although apparently not so likely in view of the obstruction by plates and angles inside a preheater. . . . Judgment reversed, without a new trial, with costs.

QUESTION

1   Why did this attempt to use *res ipsa loquitur* fail?

Plaintiffs sued for damages for the death of their adult son, Robert Sullivan, who was killed while a guest in a motor truck which swerved off the highway and overturned down a steep embankment. Suit was brought against . . . the driver of the truck . . . . There was a verdict and judgment in his favor, and plaintiffs appealed in error.

The truck was a large trailer-tractor truck owned by Hoover Motor Express Company, Inc., and used by it in its business as a carrier of freight. Its driver, Crabtree, was driving the truck with a load of freight from Nashville to Atlanta, and he permitted Sullivan to ride with him as a guest in the cab of the truck. He drove from Nashville to Monteagle, arriving there in the afternoon. He then decided to drive back some ten miles to his home at Pelham, eat supper there, and go on to Atlanta that night. It was on his way back to Pelham that the accident happened.

The road on which he was driving was a paved first-class Federal-state highway . . . , but coming down the mountain from Monteagle to Pelham it had a number of moderate grades and pretty sharp curves. It was midafternoon, and the weather was dry and clear. As Crabtree was approaching a curve another truck overtook and passed him, and just after it did so, Crabtree's truck suddenly swerved from his right side over to his left, ran off the left shoulder, overturned down a steep embankment, and crushed Sullivan to death.

Defendant testified that there was some loose gravel on the road, which had perhaps been spilled there by trucks hauling gravel, and the pavement was broken a little on the right-hand side; and that when he "hit the edge of the curve on the right-hand side" he "lost control of the truck," and it turned from his right side across to the left, and ran off the left shoulder of the highway. On cross-examination he further said:

Q. Can you tell the Jury now what caused you to lose control of the truck and permit it to run off the road down the embankment?
A. No. The brakes could have gave way, or the brakes could have grabbed or it could have been a particular wheel grabbed, because on a tractor, if the brakes happen to grab on it, the load is so much heavier than the tractor, it whips either way and takes control of the tractor and you have nothing to do with it.
Q. Did that happen in this case?
A. It is possible.
* * *

Q. You can't tell us just what did cause the accident or cause you to lose control of the truck?
A. Probably hitting the edge of the pavement or it could have been several different things. Like one going off the mountain, if it is pulled out with the wrecker, you don't know whether a hose got connected up in there and when you turned the curve break it loose. The brakes are cut on and off with a catch there like that, and it is easy for a hose to get loose.

Such being the undisputed facts, plaintiffs contend that defendant was guilty, as a matter of law, of negligence causing the death sued for, and that there was no evidence to support a verdict for defendant. They show a duty of care owing by defendant to the deceased under our rule that a driver must use ordinary care for the safety of his guest, . . . and to make out a breach of that duty, or proximate negligence, they invoke the rule of *res ipsa loquitur.* They insist that the facts of this case brought it within the rule of *res ipsa loquitur* requiring a finding of negligence, in the absence of an explanation disproving negligence; that since there was no such explanation, since defendant did not know why he lost control of the truck or what caused the accident, the jury were bound to find that it was caused by his negligence and could not reasonably render a verdict in his favor.

The classic statement of the doctrine of *res ipsa loquitur* is this: "[W]here the thing [causing the harm] is shown to be under the management of defendant or his servants, and the accident is such as in the ordinary course of things does not happen if those who have the management use proper care, it affords reasonable evidence, in the absence of explanation by the defendants, that the accident arose from want of care." *Erle, C. J., Scott v. London and St. Katherine Docks Co.* (1865), 3 H. & C. 596, 159 Eng. Reprint 665, 667. . . . The maxim *res ipsa loquitur* means that the facts of the occurrence evidence negligence; the circumstances unexplained justify an inference of negligence. In the principle of proof employed, a case of *res ipsa loquitur* does not differ from an ordinary case of circumstantial evidence. . . . This maxim does not generally apply to motor vehicle accidents, but it may apply to such an accident where the circumstances causing it were within the driver's control and the accident was such as does not usually occur without negligence. So where a motor vehicle, without apparent cause, runs off the road and causes harm, the normal inference is that the driver was negligent, and *res ipsa loquitur* is usually held to apply. . . .

[W]e agree with learned counsel for plaintiffs that the facts of this case brought it within the maxim *res ipsa loquitur.* The accident was such as does not usually occur without negligence, and the cause of it was in control of the driver, or rather it resulted from his loss of control of the truck, which he could not explain. While we agree that these facts made a case of *res ipsa loquitur,* we do not agree that they, though unexplained, required an inference or finding of negligence, or that the jury could not reasonably refuse to find negligence and return a verdict for defendant, or that there was no evidence to support their verdict for him.

It is true there has been confusion in the cases as to the procedural effect of *res ipsa loquitur,* some cases giving it one and some another of these three different effects:

1. It warrants an *inference* of negligence which the jury may draw or not, as their judgment dictates. . . .

2. It raises a *presumption* of negligence which requires the jury to find negligence if defendant does not produce evidence sufficient to rebut the presumption. . . .

3. It not only raises such a presumption but also *shifts the ultimate burden of proof* to defendant and requires him to prove by a preponderance of all the evidence that the injury was not caused by his negligence. . . .

The effect of a case of *res ipsa loquitur*, like that of any other case of circumstantial evidence, varies from case to case, depending on the particular facts of each case; and therefore such effect can no more be fitted into a fixed formula or reduced to a rigid rule than can the effect of other cases of circumstantial evidence. The only generalization that can be safely made is that, in the words of the definition of *res ipsa loquitur*, it affords "reasonable evidence," in the absence of an explanation by defendant, that the accident arose from his negligence.

The weight or strength of such "reasonable evidence" will necessarily depend on the particular facts of each case, and the cogency of the inference of negligence from such facts may of course vary in degree all the way from practical certainty in one case to reasonable probability in another. In exceptional cases the inference may be so strong as to require a directed verdict for plaintiff, as in cases of objects falling from defendant's premises on persons in the highway, such as *Byrne v. Boadle* (1863) . . . . In the ordinary case, however, *res ipsa loquitur* merely makes a case for the jury – merely permits the jury to choose the inference of defendant's negligence in preference to other permissible or reasonable inferences. . . .

We think this is true in the case before us. The cause of the death sued for was defendant's loss of control of the truck. This may have been due to his own negligence, or it may have been due to no fault of his – an unavoidable accident resulting from the brakes giving way or the breaking of some part of the control mechanism of the truck. Since such conflicting inferences might be reasonably drawn from the evidence, it was for the jury to choose the inference they thought most probable; and we cannot say that there was no evidence to support their verdict for defendant. . . .

QUESTIONS

1 How did the Court here formulate the showing necessary for the *res ipsa loquitur* inference? How is this formulation of the rule different here from the Restatement formulation at the beginning of this section? Do you think this makes any difference in the application of the rule? Note the reformulation of the doctrine in the Restatement (Third) of Torts, Section 17 seems to collapse the two-step analysis into a single step.

A. PLAINTIFF'S CONDUCT

We now turn our attention to the effect of plaintiff's own conduct on his or her right to recover. Courts long have recognized that a plaintiff's conduct should affect plaintiff's right to recover from a negligent defendant. Originally, the idea that an at-fault plaintiff should not be allowed to recover for injuries to which his own negligence contributed was grounded in the moral notion that the court should not be solicitous of an at-fault plaintiff. More recently, law and economics scholarship has stripped much of the moral content out of this notion, replacing it with concepts of efficient incentives to care.

Plaintiff's conduct comes into the torts suit in the form of an affirmative defense. The defendant bears the burden of pleading and proving applicable affirmative defenses. Two defenses of historical significance relating to plaintiff's conduct are contributory negligence and assumption of risk. While these two historical defenses are based on distinct concepts, both have merged, somewhat, into the new concept of comparative negligence, comparative fault, or comparative responsibility. As you read through these cases, consider why plaintiff's conduct should matter at all. If defendant has been negligent, why not hold that blameworthy defendant responsible without regard to plaintiff's conduct?

1. CONTRIBUTORY NEGLIGENCE

Simply put, contributory negligence is plaintiff's own negligence that is a substantial contributing cause of her injury. Until relatively recently, contributory negligence was a complete defense to a negligence cause of action. Under the contributory negligence rule, a plaintiff whose own negligence was a substantial contributing cause of his own harm, and combined with the negligence of defendant to create that harm, recovered nothing. As an affirmative defense, the defendant would bear the burden of pleading and proving each element of negligence against the plaintiff. While the contributory negligence defense has been replaced in all but five American jurisdictions with a comparative responsibility rule, the contributory negligence rule still is the law in Virginia, Maryland, North Carolina, Alabama, and the District of Columbia.

BUTTERFIELD V. FORRESTER
103 ENG. REP. 926 (K.B. 1809)

. . . At the trial, . . . it appeared that the defendant, for the purpose of making some repairs to his house, which was close by the road side . . ., had put up a pole across this part of the road, a free passage being left by another branch or street in the same direction. That the plaintiff left a public house not far distant from the place in question at 8 o'clock in the evening in August, when they were just beginning to light candles, but while there was light enough left to discern the obstruction at 100 yards distance: and the witness . . . said that if the plaintiff had not been riding very hard he might have observed and avoided it: the plaintiff however, who was riding violently, did not observe it, but rode against it, and fell with his horse and was much hurt in consequence of the accident; and there was no evidence of his being intoxicated at the time. On this evidence Bayley J. directed the jury, that if a person riding with reasonable and ordinary care could have seen and avoided the obstruction; and if they were satisfied that the plaintiff was riding along the street extremely hard, and without ordinary care, they should find a verdict for the defendant: which they accordingly did. . . .

BAYLEY, J. The plaintiff was proved to be riding as fast as his horse could go, and this was through the streets of Derby. If he had used ordinary care he must have seen the obstruction; so that the accident appeared to happen entirely from his own fault.

LORD ELLENBOROUGH C.J. A party is not to cast himself upon an obstruction which has been made by the fault of another, and avail himself of it, if he do not himself use common and ordinary caution to be in the right. In cases of persons riding upon what is considered to be the wrong side of the road, that would not authorize another purposely to ride up against them. One person being in fault will not dispense with another's using ordinary care for himself. Two things must concur to support this action, an obstruction in the road by the fault of the defendant, and a want of ordinary care to avoid it on the part of the plaintiff.

NOTES AND QUESTIONS

1   *Multiple Causes. Butterfield v. Forrester* is historically significant as the first case in which contributory negligence emerges as a distinct doctrine. Before *Butterfield*, plaintiff's conduct was analyzed as a question of causation – a question of whose conduct caused the harm, defendant's or plaintiff's. This was seen as an either/or proposition, as illustrated by Bayley's opinion here. Is Bayley correct when he writes that the accident happened "entirely" from plaintiff's "own fault"? Courts have since accepted the idea that more than one party can be considered to have "caused" a particular harm, and this has been a significant development. With the acceptance of this idea came the need to decide how to apportion responsibility for the harm caused by more than one party. The initial choice of the common law, as reflected in Ellenborough's opinion, was to let the defendant off the liability hook altogether when plaintiff's own negligence contributed to his harm. The courts applied the defense of contributory negligence

very stringently – the contributorily negligent plaintiff, no matter how slight, could recover nothing even if defendant's negligence had been quite severe.

2   Lord Ellenborough opined that plaintiffs are not entitled negligently to "cast" themselves against a danger, even if created by defendant's negligence. What does this mean? As a policy matter, what is the court worried about? Is this concern warranted? Is it realistic to think that a plaintiff will fail to exercise care for his own protection in the hope that if he is injured, a financially responsible defendant will appear? Even if a plaintiff has reason to believe that a responsible defendant will be available, are there nevertheless good reasons for plaintiff to exercise care for his or her protection? What impact do you think that the contributory negligence rule could be expected to have on the level of care exercised by plaintiffs? Do you think that the typical plaintiff probably knows about, understands and adjusts activities to the rule?

3   Do not be confused by the tenor of Lord Ellenborough's opinion – courts applying the contributory negligence doctrine long have treated it as an affirmative defense. Defendant bears the burden of pleading and proving all of the elements of plaintiff's contributory negligence. This includes all of the elements of duty, breach, causation, and harm.

4   Should it make any difference to the outcome of a case like *Butterfield* if, instead of riding too fast, plaintiff had crashed into the obstruction because of old age and slow reaction time? Should it make any difference if plaintiff had crashed into the obstruction because he were a child who did not appreciate appropriate speed for the conditions? Why or why not?

5   Should it make any difference to the outcome of the case if instead of negligently leaving an obstruction in the road, defendant had purposely pushed the obstruction in front of plaintiff at the last minute? Why or why not?

6   Should it make any difference to the outcome of the case if there were a thick fog at the time so that plaintiff could not have avoided this obstruction if he had ridden reasonably carefully?

7   Should it make any difference to the outcome of the case if the jury could not determine whether the accident would have occurred in the absence of plaintiff's negligence? Why or why not?

8   Should it make any difference to the outcome of the case if plaintiff were riding carefully, crashed into the obstruction, but failed to wear a helmet and therefore suffered serious injuries that would have been prevented if plaintiff had worn a helmet?

2. AVOIDABLE CONSEQUENCES

Plaintiff owes a duty of reasonable care to avoid creating unreasonable risk of accidental harm to herself. Plaintiff also owes a post-accident duty to take reasonable steps to mitigate the harm caused by defendant's negligence.

SPIER V. BARKER
323 N.E.2D 164 (N.Y. 1974)

Presented for our consideration, for the first time, is the question of what effect, if any, the failure of a plaintiff to wear a seat belt has upon his right to recovery in an action for personal injuries incurred in a motor vehicle accident. . . . The facts are simply stated. At approximately 6:30 p.m. on the evening of March 10, 1970, the plaintiff was operating her 1964 Ford convertible . . . on a two-lane . . . highway known as New York State Route 31 toward her son's home located on an intersecting road. The weather was cool, clear and dry; and the visibility, though it was near dusk, was good. Route 31 is a 24-foot-wide divided highway with a speed limit of 50 miles per hour. Plaintiff testified that when she neared the intersection, she reduced the speed of her automobile from 40 to 20 miles per hour and simultaneously turned on her left directional indicator; and as she was doing this, plaintiff looked in her rear view mirror and saw a set of headlights "way back"; she then neared the center line of Route 31, and, while she was turning left to enter Camp Road, was struck in the westbound lane of Route 31 by the defendants' tractor-trailer which was in the process of attempting to pass her automobile. The right front fender of the tractor-trailer came into contact with the left front portion of the plaintiff's automobile, and, as a result of the initial impact, the plaintiff was ejected from her vehicle, which then rolled over her in such a way that her legs were pinned under the left rear wheel. Although the plaintiff's automobile was equipped with seat belts, she was not using the device at the time of the accident.

. . . Upon the trial, defendants called, as an expert witness, a professor of mechanical and aerospace engineering, who had also been previously employed as a consulting engineer in the field of accident analysis and reconstruction. He testified to an extensive background in the use of seat belts in both the aircraft and automotive industries. Over plaintiff's objection, the expert was permitted to give his opinion that "The seat belt is an extremely effective device in either preventing or alleviating injury." More specifically, he stated that the seat belt is the most effective improvement that has been made in the automobile in the last 20 years. After viewing photographs of the vehicles and the accident scene, the expert opined that had the plaintiff been wearing a seat belt, she would not have been ejected from her automobile; and that had she not been ejected, she probably would not have been seriously injured. When asked on cross-examination if the fact that plaintiff was ejected from her automobile might have saved her life, the engineer stated that "the worst thing that could have happened to her [was] being ejected from the vehicle."

. . . [W]e do not subscribe to the holdings of those cases in which the plaintiff's failure to fasten his seat belt may be determined by the jury to constitute contributory negligence as a matter of common law . . . . In our view, the doctrine of contributory negligence is applicable only if the plaintiff's failure to exercise due care causes, in whole or in part, the accident, rather than when it merely exacerbates or enhances the severity of his injuries . . . . That being the case, holding a nonuser contributorily negligent would be improper since it would impose liability upon the plaintiff for all his injuries though use of a seat belt might have prevented none or only a portion of them. . . . Having disapproved of these . . . variations of the seat belt defense, we address ourselves to the defendants' contention that nonuse of an available seat belt may be considered by the jury in assessing the plaintiff's damages where it is shown that the seat belt would have prevented at least a portion of the injuries.

As Prosser has indicated, the plaintiff's duty to mitigate his damages is equivalent to the doctrine of avoidable consequences, which precludes recovery for any damages which could have been eliminated by reasonable conduct on the part of the plaintiff . . . . Traditionally both of these concepts have been applied only to post-accident conduct, such as a plaintiff's failure to obtain medical treatment after he has sustained an injury. To do otherwise, it has been argued, would impose a pre-accident obligation upon the plaintiff and would deny him the right to assume the due care of others. . . . We concede that the opportunity to mitigate damages prior to the occurrence of an accident does not ordinarily arise, and that the chronological distinction, on which the concept of mitigation of damages rests, is justified in most cases. However, in our opinion, the seat belt affords the automobile occupant an unusual and ordinarily unavailable means by which he or she may minimize his or her damages *prior* to the accident. . . . When an automobile occupant may readily protect himself, at least partially, from the consequences of a collision, we think that the burden of buckling an available seat belt may, under the facts of the particular case, be found by the jury to be less than the likelihood of injury when multiplied by its accompanying severity. . . .

Another objection frequently raised is that the jury will be unable to segregate the injuries caused by the initial impact from the injuries caused by the plaintiff's failure to fasten his seat belt. In addition to underestimating the abilities of those trained in the field of accident reconstruction, this argument fails to consider other instances in which the jury is permitted to apportion damages (i.e., as between an original tort-feasor and a physician who negligently treats the original injury). Furthermore, if the defendant is unable to show that the seat belt would have prevented some of the plaintiff's injuries, then the trial court ought not submit the issue to the jury.

In the instant case, the plaintiff was ejected from her car, which subsequently rolled over her body causing a broken leg. . . . The defense expert stated that she would have remained in the car had she used her seat belt, and that she would have sustained only minor injuries had she not been ejected. On cross-examination, plaintiff's counsel was unsuccessful in his attempts to undermine either of these opinions of the expert. In view of what has previously been stated, we hold that the trial court properly submitted this issue to the jury. . . .

3. LAST CLEAR CHANCE

Common law courts developed several doctrines to ameliorate the harsh effects of the draconian contributory negligence defense, including the doctrine of "last clear chance." The idea behind the last clear chance doctrine was to permit a negligent plaintiff a full recovery if his negligence left him in a helpless position, and the defendant, who had the "last clear chance" to avoid the injury, negligently inflicted it anyway. The following case illustrates the application of the doctrine.

WASHINGTON METROPOLITAN AREA TRANSIT AUTHORITY V. YOUNG
731 A.2D 389 (D.C. 1999)

This case involves a collision between a bus and a bicycle in a District of Columbia intersection. The two impacted when the bus driver, while making a right turn, cut off the bicyclist, who was in the lane to the right of the bus. . . . The jury returned a verdict for the bicyclist, awarding him $925,000 in damages. Through the use of a special verdict form, the jury found that the bus driver was negligent and that the bicyclist was contributorily negligent. However, because the jury concluded that the bus driver had the last clear chance to avoid the accident, it found the driver ultimately responsible for what happened.

Appellant, the Washington Metropolitan Area Transit Authority ("WMATA" or "Metro"), maintains that the trial court erred in denying its motion for judgment notwithstanding the verdict. It argues that appellee Young, the bicyclist and plaintiff below, did not present sufficient evidence of last clear chance, and hence that the case should not have gone to the jury on that theory. . . . Although the question is a close one, we hold that appellee presented sufficient evidence to go to the jury on the issue of last clear chance. Finding WMATA's other arguments unpersuasive, we affirm.

I

. . . The westbound portion of Calvert Street, upon which both the bus and the bicycle were proceeding just before the accident, consists of two lanes. By means of a channeling line painted in the roadway, traffic in the left lane is directed to make a wide-angle right turn (about 135 degrees) onto Cleveland Avenue unless turning left. Traffic in the right lane can make either a wide-angle right turn onto Cleveland or a sharp right turn (90 degrees) onto 29th Street. Mr. Young testified that on September 9, 1994, at approximately 9:20 a.m., he was traveling westbound on Calvert Street, approaching its intersection with Cleveland Avenue and 29th Street. He had ridden through that intersection on his bicycle many times on his way to and from work and intended as usual to proceed through the intersection and head northwest on Cleveland. When he was approximately four hundred feet away, he noticed a Metro bus ahead of him at the intersection. The bus was in the left lane and was stopped at a red light.

Mr. Young rode his bicycle toward the intersection in the right lane, which was clear of traffic. As he neared the intersection, the light turned green. The bus accelerated quickly, and Young continued pedaling at a steady rate, anticipating the upcoming hill on Cleveland Avenue. As they entered the intersection, the bus was slightly ahead and to the left of Young. Once in the intersection, the bus began to bear slightly to the right, indicating to Mr. Young that it was continuing forward onto Cleveland Avenue. The bus then made a sudden sharp right turn into the northbound lane of 29th Street, cutting across Young's path in the curb lane. Young tried to avoid the bus by braking and turning to the right, but he was unable to elude its continuing encroachment, and his bicycle struck the middle of the right side of the bus. The initial contact caused him to lose his balance and collide with the bus a second time. He was then propelled over the handlebars and landed under the bus, where he was dragged for a short distance. When the bus came to a stop, its right rear wheel was on top of his left leg, pinning him there until, nearly an hour later, rescue workers raised the bus and pulled him out. Mr. Young suffered a number of severe injuries as a result of this accident. . . .

II

A. The General Rule and the Limited Exception

... [O]n facts very similar to those in the case at bar, this court denied recovery to a bicyclist who collided with a truck when the truck made a right turn in front of him. . . . But there is a narrow exception to the rule barring recovery when there is contributory negligence—an exception not raised by the parties . . . . Under the doctrine of last clear chance, a plaintiff may recover, despite his own contributory negligence, if he can demonstrate that "the defendant had a superior opportunity to avoid the accident." *Phillips v. D.C. Transit System, Inc.,* 198 A.2d 740, 741–742 (D.C.1964). The doctrine "presupposes a perilous situation caused by the negligence of both the plaintiff and the defendant; it assumes that after the situation had been created there was a time when the defendant could, and the plaintiff could not, avoid the accident." *Griffin v. Anderson,* 148 A.2d 713, 714 (D.C.1959). To recover under the last clear chance doctrine, therefore, the plaintiff must prove by a preponderance of the evidence:

> (1) that the plaintiff was in a position of danger caused by the negligence of both plaintiff and defendant; (2) that the plaintiff was oblivious to the danger, or unable to extricate [himself] from the position of danger; (3) that the defendant was aware, or by the exercise of reasonable care should have been aware, of the plaintiff's danger and of [his] oblivion to it or [his] inability to extricate [himself] from it; and (4) that the defendant, with means available to him, could have avoided injuring the plaintiff after becoming aware of the danger and the plaintiff's inability to extricate [himself] from it, but failed to do so.

Felton, 512 A.2d at 296 (citations omitted) . . . .

B. Last Clear Chance and the Facts of This Case

The outcome of this appeal depends on whether Mr. Young adequately proved the second, third, and fourth elements of last clear chance as outlined in Felton. . . . Therefore, it is important to emphasize that the second element may be proved in either of two ways. The plaintiff needs to show either that he was oblivious to the danger or that he was unable to extricate himself from his position of peril, but not both. Equally important is the objective standard inherent in the third element. The defendant need not have actually known of the plaintiff's danger and his obliviousness to it or inability to extricate himself from it, provided that the defendant should reasonably have been aware of those facts. This court has also clarified that the same is true of the fourth element, which "pertains to a defendant who, with means available to him, could have avoided injuring the plaintiff after he became aware of, or reasonably should have become aware of, the danger and the plaintiff's inability to extricate himself from it." *Robinson,* 580 A.2d at 1258; *accord, Huysman,* 650 A.2d at 1326. . . .

The evidence showed that Young reached that point when he negligently rode up alongside a bus that was going to make an improper right turn from the left lane. Prior to that moment, the possibility of danger existed, but there was still an opportunity for Young to avoid it. Once he arrived at the side of the bus, however, he was in a dangerous position.

Turning to the second element, we are reluctant to suggest that Young was oblivious to the danger posed by the bus. Although Young testified that the bus made no indication that it was going to turn right before it suddenly crossed his path, he had seen the bus long before he rode up beside it. The specific danger posed by the bus was not obvious until it abruptly turned right, but any vehicle as big as a bus poses a threat to smaller vehicles, especially bicycles. . . .

But the evidence, particularly Mr. Young's own testimony, would permit a reasonable jury to find that he was in an inextricable position of peril when he rode up alongside the bus. Young stated that when the bus suddenly turned in front of him, he tried to avoid running into it by braking and turning to the right. That attempt, as it turned out, was unsuccessful. In addition, from her vantage point just a few feet away, Colleen Morgan concluded that Young could not have done anything to avoid the accident. Young's inextricability from his position of peril is further evidenced by the accident itself. While such an inference may not always be possible, one can reasonably infer from the circumstances presented here that if Young had been able to avoid the accident, he would have done so. The jury was not obliged to accept Herman Adkins' assertion that Young had means available to avoid colliding with the bus. . . .

Whether there was sufficient evidence of the third element is an equally close question. Nevertheless, viewing the evidence in the light most favorable to Mr. Young, we conclude that a reasonable jury could find that the bus driver knew or should have known that Young was in a position of peril and was unable to extricate himself from that position. The diagrams contained in WMATA's SOP for the positioning of mirrors on a bus indicate that the right exterior mirror should be positioned so that the driver can see objects that are near the rear of the bus. Accepting Colleen Morgan's testimony that Young was four to five feet from the rear of the bus and on the right side of the bus when he entered the intersection, the jury could find that the driver saw or (more likely) reasonably should have seen Young in the right exterior mirror if it were properly positioned. From such a finding, the jury could also conclude that the bus driver should have been aware of Young's peril.

Furthermore, even if the mirror did not provide a view of Young as he rode up next to the bus, the driver testified that he saw Young in his interior mirror just as he was "going into" his turn. Although he also said that he thought Young was on the sidewalk and hence out of harm's way, a trier of fact could reasonably conclude that the driver should have checked his mirrors again and, if no view of what was behind the bus was available, taken other precautions to ensure that the bicycle was not in a dangerous position. WMATA's SOP for right turns instructs a bus driver to "[u]se [the] right side view and [the] inside mirror to determine that [the] right side of [the] bus will clear the corner curb and vehicles or pedestrians. If unsure of clearance, stop the bus and check." . . .

Having thus concluded that Mr. Young sufficiently proved the third element of last clear chance, we turn to the fourth element and conclude that, because the driver reasonably should have seen Young before initiating the right turn, he could have avoided the accident by stopping or otherwise aborting the turn. Colleen Morgan specifically testified that, as the situation appeared to her, the bus could have avoided the accident by stopping if the driver had seen Mr. Young. WMATA's claim that the driver would have had to act "instantaneously" to avoid the accident, *see Huysman*, 650 A.2d at 1326; *Phillips*, 198 A.2d at 742, is unpersuasive because it assumes that the driver was under no duty to act until after he began the turn. The jury could reasonably find, however, that the driver could and should have avoided the accident by stopping before he began his turn. Moreover, WMATA's SOP instructs drivers to ensure that the right side of the bus is clear before attempting a right turn. The jury could have found that, had the driver followed the SOP, he would have seen Mr. Young riding his bicycle to the right of the bus and would have been able to avoid the accident by simply not turning. . . .

V

Our holding today is a narrow one, dependent on the particular facts of this case, and should not be read as a retreat from anything we said in *Washington v. A. & H Garcias Trash Hauling Co.* In *Washington* we held, on facts very similar to those presented here, that the plaintiff bicyclist was contributorily negligent as a matter of law. Nevertheless, in the instant case we are persuaded that, although the evidence was far from overwhelming, Mr. Young did present sufficient evidence of last clear chance to justify the jury's verdict in his favor. In the absence of other errors, we must uphold the jury's decision. Accordingly, the judgment is

Affirmed.

NOTES

1   Under the last clear chance doctrine, most courts treated the "helpless" plaintiff more favorably than the merely "inattentive" plaintiff.

2   Some courts applied a somewhat less generous version of last clear chance, sometimes called the "discovered peril" doctrine, only defendant actually knew or should have known of plaintiff's position of peril.

3   Most jurisdictions have abandoned last clear chance along with contributory negligence.

4. COMPARATIVE NEGLIGENCE

By the mid-twentieth century, the contributory negligence defense had come under severe attack on a number of fronts and grounds. Perhaps chief among the bases of attack was the perceived unfairness of the "all or nothing" character of the defense. It was at least theoretically possible that a plaintiff who was only slightly responsible for her own injury could recover nothing while the defendant, whose negligence dominated the situation, avoided liability completely. The principal response to these concerns was a widespread adoption of the doctrine of comparative negligence.

LI V. YELLOW CAB CO.
532 P.2D 1226 (CAL. 1975)

In this case we address the grave and recurrent question whether we should judicially declare no longer applicable in California courts the doctrine of contributory negligence, which bars all recovery when the plaintiff's negligent conduct has contributed as a legal cause in any degree to the harm suffered by him, and hold that it must give way to a system of comparative negligence, which assesses liability in direct proportion to fault. . . . [P]laintiff Nga Li was proceeding northbound on Alvarado in her 1967 Oldsmobile. She was in the inside lane, and about 70 feet before she reached the Third Street intersection she stopped and then began a left turn across the three southbound lanes of Alvarado, intending to enter the driveway of a service station. At this time defendant Robert Phillips, an employee of defendant Yellow Cab Company, was driving a company-owned taxicab southbound in the middle lane on Alvarado. He came over the crest of the hill, passed through the intersection, and collided with the right rear portion of plaintiff's automobile, resulting in personal injuries to plaintiff as well as considerable damage to the automobile.

The court, sitting without a jury, found as facts that defendant Phillips was traveling at approximately 30 miles per hour when he entered the intersection, that such speed was unsafe at that time and place, and that the traffic light controlling southbound traffic at the intersection was yellow when defendant Phillips drove into the intersection. It also found, however, that plaintiff's left turn across the southbound lanes of Alvarado "was made at a time when a vehicle was approaching from the opposite direction so close as to constitute an immediate hazard." The dispositive conclusion of law was as follows: "That the driving of Nga Li was negligent, that such negligence was a proximate cause of the collision, and that she is barred from recovery by reason of such contributory negligence." Judgment for defendants was entered accordingly.

"Contributory negligence is conduct on the part of the plaintiff which falls below the standard to which he should conform for his own protection, and which is a legally contributing cause cooperating with the negligence of the defendant in bringing about the plaintiff's harm." (Rest.2d Torts, s 463.) Thus the American Law Institute, in its second restatement of the law, describes the kind of conduct on the part of one seeking recovery for damage caused by negligence which renders him subject to the doctrine of contributory negligence. What the effect of such conduct will be is left to a further section, which states the doctrine in its clearest essence: "Except where the defendant has the last clear chance, the plaintiff's contributory negligence bars recovery against a defendant whose negligent conduct would otherwise make him liable to the plaintiff for the harm sustained by him." (Rest.2d Torts, s 467.) . . .

This rule, rooted in the long-standing principle that one should not recover from another for damages brought upon oneself . . . , has been the law of this state from its beginning. . . . Although criticized almost from the outset for the harshness of its operation, it has weathered numerous attacks . . . . We have undertaken a thorough reexamination of the matter . . . . [T]his reexamination leads us to the conclusion that the "all-or-nothing" rule of contributory negligence can be and ought to be superseded by a rule which assesses liability in proportion to fault.

It is unnecessary for us to catalogue the enormous amount of critical comment that has been directed over the years against the "all-or-nothing" approach of the doctrine of contributory negligence. The essence of that criticism has been constant and clear: the doctrine is inequitable in its operation because it fails to distribute responsibility in proportion to fault. Against this have been raised several arguments in justification, but none have proved even remotely adequate to the task. The basic objection to the doctrine—grounded in the primal concept that in a system in which liability is based on fault, the extent of fault should govern the extent of liability—remains irresistible to reason and all intelligent notions of fairness.

Furthermore, practical experience with the application by juries of the doctrine of contributory negligence has added its weight to analyses of its inherent shortcomings: "Every trial lawyer is well aware that juries often do in fact allow recovery in cases of contributory negligence, and that the compromise in the jury room does result in some diminution of the damages because of the plaintiff's fault. But the process is at best a haphazard and most unsatisfactory one." (Prosser, *Comparative Negligence*) . . . . It is manifest that this state of affairs, viewed from the standpoint of the health and vitality of the legal process, can only detract from public confidence in the ability of law and legal institutions to assign liability on a just and consistent basis. . . . It is in view of these theoretical and practical considerations that to this date 25 states, have abrogated the "all or nothing" rule of contributory negligence and have enacted in its place general apportionment statutes calculated in one manner or another to assess liability in proportion to fault. . . . We are likewise persuaded that logic, practical experience, and fundamental justice counsel against the retention of the doctrine rendering contributory negligence a complete bar to recovery—and that it should be replaced in this state by a system under which liability for damage will be borne by those whose negligence caused it in direct proportion to their respective fault. . . .

We are thus brought to the second group of arguments which have been advanced by defendants and the amici curiae supporting their position. Generally speaking, such arguments expose considerations of a practical nature which, it is urged, counsel against the adoption of a rule of comparative negligence in this state . . . . The most serious of these considerations are those attendant upon the administration of a rule of comparative negligence in cases involving multiple parties. One such problem may arise when all responsible parties are not brought before the court: it may be difficult for the jury to evaluate relative negligence in such circumstances . . . . Problems of contribution and indemnity among joint tortfeasors lurk in the background. . . .

A second and related major area of concern involves the administration of the actual process of fact-finding in a comparative negligence system. The assigning of a specific percentage factor to the amount of negligence attributable to a particular party, while in theory a matter of little difficulty, can become a matter of perplexity in the face of hard facts. . . . These inherent difficulties are not, however, insurmountable. Guidelines might be provided the jury which will assist it in keeping focused upon the true inquiry . . . , and the utilization of special verdicts or jury interrogatories can be of invaluable assistance in assuring that the jury has approached its sensitive and often complex task with proper standards and appropriate reverence. . . .

The third area of concern, the status of the doctrines of last clear chance and assumption of risk, involves less the practical problems of administering a particular form of comparative negligence than it does a definition of the theoretical outline of the specific form to be adopted. Although several states which apply comparative negligence concepts retain the last clear chance doctrine . . . , the better reasoned position seems to be that when true comparative negligence is adopted, the need for last clear chance as a palliative of the hardships of the "all-or-nothing" rule disappears and its retention results only in a windfall to the plaintiff in direct contravention of the principle of liability in proportion to fault. . . . As for assumption of risk, we have recognized in this state that this defense overlaps that of contributory negligence to some extent . . . . We think it clear that the adoption of a system of comparative negligence should entail the merger of the defense of assumption of risk into the general scheme of assessment of liability in proportion to fault in those particular cases in which the form of assumption of risk involved is no more than a variant of contributory negligence. . . .

It remains to identify the precise form of comparative negligence which we now adopt for application in this state. Although there are many variants, only the two basic forms need be considered here. The first of these, the so-called "pure" form of comparative negligence, apportions liability in direct proportion to fault in all cases. This . . . is the form favored by most scholars and commentators. The second basic form of comparative negligence, of which there are several variants, applies apportionment based on fault up to the point at which the plaintiff's negligence is equal to or greater than that of the defendant—when that point is reached, plaintiff is barred from recovery. . . . The principal argument advanced in its favor is moral in nature: that it is not morally right to permit one more at fault in an accident to recover from one less at fault. . . . We have concluded that the "pure" form of comparative negligence is that which should be adopted in this state. In our view the "50 percent" system simply shifts the lottery aspect of the contributory negligence rule to a different ground. . . .

For all of the foregoing reasons we conclude that the "all-or-nothing" rule of contributory negligence as it presently exists in this state should be and is herewith superseded by a system of "pure" comparative negligence, the fundamental purpose of which shall be to assign responsibility and liability for damage in direct proportion to the amount of negligence of each of the parties. Therefore, in all actions for negligence resulting in injury to person or property, the contributory negligence of the person injured in person or property shall not bar recovery, but the damages awarded shall be diminished in proportion to the amount of negligence attributable to the person recovering. The doctrine of last clear chance is abolished, and the defense of assumption of risk is also abolished to the extent that it is merely a variant of the former doctrine of contributory negligence; both of these are to be subsumed under the general process of assessing liability in proportion to negligence. . . .

1   *Li* was decided when American jurisdictions rapidly were replacing the contributory negligence defense with a comparative fault rule. Today only five American jurisdictions retain the all-or-nothing contributory negligence defense.

2   As the cases in this section illustrate, comparative negligence rules come in two basic forms – pure and modified. The modified form of the rule bars plaintiff's recovery altogether if plaintiff's share of the negligence meets a certain threshold, usually about 50%. Application of this threshold requires a basis for comparison, and there are two basic approaches to this question. The "unit rule" compares plaintiff's negligence to that of all defendants combined while the "individual rule" compares plaintiff's negligence to that of each defendant on an individual basis.

MCINTYRE V. BALENTINE
833 s.w.2d 52 (tenn. 1992)

In this personal injury action, we granted Plaintiff's application for permission to appeal in order to decide whether to adopt a system of comparative fault in Tennessee. . . .

In the early morning darkness of November 2, 1986, Plaintiff-Harry Douglas McIntyre and Defendant-Clifford Balentine were involved in a motor vehicle accident resulting in severe injuries to Plaintiff. . . . Shortly after Plaintiff entered the highway, his pickup truck was struck by Defendant's Peterbilt tractor. At trial, the parties disputed the exact chronology of events immediately preceding the accident.

Both men had consumed alcohol the evening of the accident. After the accident, Plaintiff's blood alcohol level was measured at .17 percent by weight. Testimony suggested that Defendant was traveling in excess of the posted speed limit.

Plaintiff brought a negligence action against Defendant-Balentine . . . . Defendants answered that Plaintiff was contributorially negligent, in part due to operating his vehicle while intoxicated. After trial, the jury returned a verdict stating: "We, the jury, find the plaintiff and the defendant equally at fault in this accident; therefore, we rule in favor of the defendant."

After judgment was entered for Defendants, Plaintiff brought an appeal alleging the trial court erred by refusing to instruct the jury regarding the doctrine of comparative negligence . . . . The Court of Appeals affirmed, holding that comparative negligence is not the law in Tennessee. . . .

I.

The common law contributory negligence doctrine has traditionally been traced to Lord Ellenborough's opinion in *Butterfield v. Forrester*. . . . There, plaintiff, "riding as fast as his horse would go," was injured after running into an obstruction defendant had placed in the road. Stating as the rule that "one person being in fault will not dispense with another's using ordinary care," plaintiff was denied recovery on the basis that he did not use ordinary care to avoid the obstruction. The contributory negligence bar was soon brought to America as part of the common law . . . and proceeded to spread throughout the states. . . .

In Tennessee, . . . we have continued to follow the general rule that a plaintiff's contributory negligence completely bars recovery. . . . Equally entrenched in Tennessee jurisprudence are exceptions to the general all-or-nothing rule: contributory negligence does not absolutely bar recovery where defendant's conduct was intentional, . . . where defendant had the "last clear chance" with which, through the exercise of ordinary care, to avoid plaintiff's injury, . . . or where plaintiff's negligence may be classified as "remote." . . .

Between 1920 and 1969, a few states began utilizing the principles of comparative fault in all tort litigation. . . . Then, between 1969 and 1984, comparative fault replaced contributory negligence in 37 additional states. . . . In 1991, South Carolina became the 45th state to adopt comparative fault, . . . leaving Alabama, Maryland, North Carolina, Virginia, and Tennessee as the only remaining common law contributory negligence jurisdictions. . . .

II.

. . . After exhaustive deliberation that was facilitated by extensive briefing and argument by the parties, amicus curiae, and Tennessee's scholastic community, we conclude that it is time to abandon the outmoded and unjust common law doctrine of contributory negligence and adopt in its place a system of comparative fault. Justice simply will not permit our continued adherence to a rule that, in the face of a judicial determination that others bear primary responsibility, nevertheless completely denies injured litigants recompense for their damages. . . .

III.

Two basic forms of comparative fault are utilized by 45 of our sister jurisdictions, these variants being commonly referred to as either "pure" or "modified." In the "pure" form,[4] a plaintiff's damages are reduced in proportion to the percentage negligence attributed to him; for example, a plaintiff responsible for 90 percent of the negligence that caused his injuries nevertheless may recover 10 percent of his damages. In the "modified" form,[5] plaintiffs recover as in pure jurisdictions, but only if the plaintiff's negligence either (1) does not exceed ("50 percent" jurisdictions) or (2) is less than ("49 percent" jurisdictions) the defendant's negligence. . . .

Although we conclude that the all-or-nothing rule of contributory negligence must be replaced, we nevertheless decline to abandon totally our fault-based tort system. We do not

---

4   The 13 states utilizing pure comparative fault are Alaska, Arizona, California, Florida, Kentucky, Louisiana, Mississippi, Missouri, Michigan, New Mexico, New York, Rhode Island, and Washington. . . .

5   The 21 states using the "50 percent" modified form: Connecticut, Delaware, Hawaii, Illinois, Indiana, Iowa, Massachusetts, Minnesota, Montana, Nevada, New Hampshire, New Jersey, Ohio, Oklahoma, Oregon, Pennsylvania, South Carolina, Texas, Vermont, Wisconsin, and Wyoming. The 9 states using the "49 percent" form: Arkansas, Colorado, Georgia, Idaho, Kansas, Maine, North Dakota, Utah, and West Virginia. Two states, Nebraska and South Dakota, use a slight-gross system of comparative fault. . . .

agree that a party should necessarily be able to recover in tort even though he may be 80, 90, or 95 percent at fault. We therefore reject the pure form of comparative fault.

We recognize that modified comparative fault systems have been criticized as merely shifting the arbitrary contributory negligence bar to a new ground. *See, e.g., Li v. Yellow Cab Co.,* . . . 532 P.2d 1226 . . . (1975). However, we feel the "49 percent rule" ameliorates the harshness of the common law rule while remaining compatible with a fault-based tort system. . . . We therefore hold that so long as a plaintiff's negligence remains less than the defendant's negligence the plaintiff may recover; in such a case, plaintiff's damages are to be reduced in proportion to the percentage of the total negligence attributable to the plaintiff.

In all trials where the issue of comparative fault is before a jury, the trial court shall instruct the jury on the effect of the jury's finding as to the percentage of negligence as between the plaintiff or plaintiffs and the defendant or defendants. . . . The attorneys for each party shall be allowed to argue how this instruction affects a plaintiff's ability to recover.

IV.

Turning to the case at bar, the jury found that "the plaintiff and defendant [were] equally at fault." Because the jury, without the benefit of proper instructions by the trial court, made a gratuitous apportionment of fault, we find that their "equal" apportionment is not sufficiently trustworthy to form the basis of a final determination between these parties. Therefore, the case is remanded for a new trial in accordance with the dictates of this opinion.

V.

We recognize that today's decision affects numerous legal principles surrounding tort litigation. For the most part, harmonizing these principles with comparative fault must await another day. However, we feel compelled to provide some guidance to the trial courts charged with implementing this new system.

First, and most obviously, the new rule makes the doctrines of remote contributory negligence and last clear chance obsolete. The circumstances formerly taken into account by those two doctrines will henceforth be addressed when assessing relative degrees of fault.

Second, in cases of multiple tortfeasors, plaintiff will be entitled to recover so long as plaintiff's fault is less than the combined fault of all tortfeasors.

Third, today's holding renders the doctrine of joint and several liability obsolete. Our adoption of comparative fault is due largely to considerations of fairness: the contributory negligence doctrine unjustly allowed the entire loss to be borne by a negligent plaintiff, notwithstanding that the plaintiff's fault was minor in comparison to defendant's. Having thus adopted a rule more closely linking liability and fault, it would be inconsistent to simultaneously retain a rule, joint and several liability, which may fortuitously impose a degree of liability that is out of all proportion to fault.

Further, because a particular defendant will henceforth be liable only for the percentage of a plaintiff's damages occasioned by that defendant's negligence, situations where a defendant has paid more than his "share" of a judgment will no longer arise, and therefore the Uniform Contribution Among Tort-feasors Act . . . will no longer determine the apportionment of liability between codefendants.

Fourth, fairness and efficiency require that defendants called upon to answer allegations in negligence be permitted to allege, as an affirmative defense, that a nonparty caused or contributed to the injury or damage for which recovery is sought. In cases where such a defense is raised, the trial court shall instruct the jury to assign this nonparty the percentage of the total negligence for which he is responsible. However, in order for a plaintiff to recover a judgment against such additional person, the plaintiff must have made a timely amendment to his complaint and caused process to be served on such additional person. Thereafter, the additional party will be required to answer the amended complaint. The procedures shall be in accordance with the Tennessee Rules of Civil Procedure.

Fifth, until such time as the Tennessee Judicial Conference Committee on Civil Pattern Jury Instructions promulgates new standard jury instructions, we direct trial courts' attention to the suggested instructions and special verdict form set forth in the appendix to this opinion.

APPENDIX

The following instructions may be used in cases where the negligence of the plaintiff is at issue. These instructions are intended for two-party litigation. Appropriate modifications would be necessary for more complex litigation.

Suggested Jury Instructions

[The following instructions should be preceded by instructions on negligence, proximate cause, damages, etc.]

1. If you find that defendant was not negligent or that defendant's negligence was not a proximate cause of plaintiff's injury, you will find for defendant.

2. If you find that defendant was negligent and that defendant's negligence was a proximate cause of plaintiff's injury, you must then determine whether plaintiff was also negligent and whether plaintiff's negligence was a proximate cause of his/her injury.

3. In this state, negligence on the part of a plaintiff has an impact on a plaintiff's right to recover damages. Accordingly, if you find that each party was negligent and that the negligence of each party was a proximate cause of plaintiff's damages, then you must determine the degree of such negligence, expressed as a percentage, attributable to each party.

4. If you find from all the evidence that the percentage of negligence attributable to plaintiff was equal to, or greater than, the percentage of negligence attributable to defendant, then you are instructed that plaintiff will not be entitled to recover any damages for his/her injuries. If, on the other hand, you determine from the evidence that the percentage of negligence attributable to plaintiff was less than the percentage of negligence attributable to defendant, then plaintiff will be entitled to recover that portion of his/her damages not caused by plaintiff's own negligence.

5. The court will provide you with a special verdict form that will assist you in your duties. This is the form on which you will record, if appropriate, the percentage of negligence assigned to each party and plaintiff's total damages. The court will then take your findings and either (1) enter judgment for defendant if you have found that defendant was not negligent or that plaintiff's own negligence accounted for 50 percent or more of the total negligence proximately causing his/her injuries or (2) enter judgment against defendant in accordance with defendant's percentage of negligence.

SPECIAL VERDICT FORM

We, the jury, make the following answers to the questions submitted by the court:

1. Was the defendant negligent?

Answer: (Yes or No)

(If your answer is "No," do not answer any further questions. Sign this form and return it to the court.)

2. Was the defendant's negligence a proximate cause of injury or damage to the plaintiff?

Answer: (Yes or No)

(If your answer is "No," do not answer any further questions. Sign this form and return it to the court.)

3. Did the plaintiff's own negligence account for 50 percent or more of the total negligence that proximately caused his/her injuries or damages?

Answer: (Yes or No)

(If your answer is "Yes," do not answer any further questions. Sign this form and return it to the court.)

4. What is the total amount of plaintiff's damages, determined without reference to the amount of plaintiff's negligence? Amount in dollars: $

5. Using 100 percent as the total combined negligence which proximately caused the injuries or damages to the plaintiff, what are the percentages of such negligence to be allocated to the plaintiff and defendant?

Plaintiff %

Defendant %

(Total must equal 100%)

Signature of Foreman

1   *Special Verdict Form.* The Special Verdict Form provided by the Court here for the benefit of the Tennessee
    trial courts is especially helpful to an understanding of precisely what the jury is asked to do in a comparative
    negligence case.

2   *Comparative What?* The first cases to replace the complete contributory negligence defense with a partial defense
    based on comparative principles naturally adopted the label "comparative negligence" for the new doctrine. Later,
    some jurisdiction adopted the term "comparative fault." But as the doctrine has expanded to consider more and
    more conduct, including assumption of risk and strict liability, the drafters of the Restatement of Torts have settled
    on the term "comparative responsibility."

3   *Basis of Comparison.* What is compared in a comparative negligence analysis? Does it apply to cases of strict
    liability? The various American jurisdictions have not yet reached a consensus on this question. The Restatment
    (Third) of Torts, Apportionment of Liability, Section 8 would include at least the egregiousness of each party's
    conduct and the strength of the causal connection between each party's conduct and the harm. Maine takes a
    unique approach and simply asks the jury to reduce damages in a proportion that it considers "equitable and just."

4   *Telling Jury of Consequences of Allocation.* The Court here held that the lawyers could argue to the jury the effect of
    their allocation of fault. Is that a good idea? Courts have split over the question.

5   *Leglislating from the bench.* Note the legislative tenor of this opinion. The Court considers and chooses among
    various policy options in adopting its new rule, and the questions are many. For example, what should be done
    with joint and several liability? What happens to last clear chance? Is assumption of risk subsumed within the new
    doctrine? Each of these questions will be considered in the sections that follow.

5. ASSUMPTION OF RISK

We now consider another form of defense based upon plaintiff's conduct, assumption of risk.
Assumption of risk is fundamentally different from contributory or comparative neglience.
While contributory and comparative negligence are grounded in plaintiff's carelessness,
assumption of risk is grounded in plaintiff's exercise of volition. Like the defense of consent in
the intentional tort context, the defense of assumption of risk is based upon the notion that "to
the volunteer, no wrong is done."

The doctrine of assumption of risk can be variously divided, but the fundamental division is
between those cases in which the voluntary assumption of risk is explicit, usually written, and
those cases in which the assumption of risk is implied by the circumstances. The former cases
tend to be contractual, while the latter are more purely a matter of tort. Originally, plaintiff's
implied assumption of the risk was a complete defense to defendant's liability. However, despite
the distinction between negligence and assumption of risk, with the widespread adoption of
comparative negligence, the desireability of a separate assumption of risk defense has been
questioned, and some jurisdictions have merged the defense with comparative responsibility.

a. EXPRESS ASSUMPTION OF RISK

We will first look at a recurring assumption of risk scenario in which a party engaged in an inherently risky business will agree to do business with a potential plaintiff only if the plaintiff will explicitly agree in advance to absolve defendant from liability for negligence. The question in such cases typically is whether enforcing the agreement of the parties would impermissibly undermine tort policy.

WINTERSTEIN V. WILCOM
293 A.2D 821 (MD. 1972)

> REQUEST AND RELEASE I, the undersigned, hereby request permission to enter the premises of 75-80 DRAG-A-WAY, PIT AREA, STAGING AREA, and participate in auto timing and acceleration runs, tests, contests and exhibitions to be held this day. I have inspected the premises and I know the risks and dangers involved in the said activities, and that unanticipated and unexpected dangers may arise during such activities and I assume all risks of injury to my person and property that may be sustained in connection with the stated and associated activities, in and about the premises. In consideration of the permission granted to me to enter the premises and participate in the stated activities, and in further consideration of the provisions of a insurance medical plan, I do hereby, for myself, my heirs, administrators and assigns, release, remise and discharge the owners, operators, and sponsors of the said premises, of the activities, of the vehicles, and of the equipment therein, and their respective servants, agents, officers, and officials, and all other participants in the stated activities of and from all claims, demands, actions, and causes of action of any sort, for injuries sustained by my person and/or property during my presence in said premises and participation in the stated activities due to negligence or any other fault. I represent and certify that my true age is stated below, and if I am under the age of 21 years, I do represent and certify that I have the permission of my parents and/or guardians to participate in the stated activities, and that they have full knowledge thereof. I certify that my attendance and participation in the stated activities is voluntary, and that I am not, in any way, the employee, servant, or agent of the owners, operators or sponsors of the premises and the activities therein. I HAVE READ AND UNDERSTAND THE FOREGOING REQUEST AND RELEASE. In Witness Whereof, I have hereunto set my hand and seal. . . .

The effectiveness of this document to hold harmless WILLIAM A. WILCOM, trading as 75-80 Drag-A-Way, . . . is the crux of the case before us. ROLAND C. WINTERSTEIN and BARBARA WINTERSTEIN, his wife . . . (Winterstein), claim that it is void as against public policy and not "conclusively binding upon them as their intentional and unreasonable exposure to danger, which [Wilcom] knew or had reason to know." Wilcom asserts it was a binding contract relieving him of responsibility for damages in accordance with its terms. The lower court agreed with Wilcom and so do we.

II

The case arose by the filing of an action in tort by Winterstein against Wilcom . . . [who] operated a business called 75-80 Drag-A-Way. Automobile timing and acceleration runs were conducted on two racing lanes. Wilcom's employees were in a tower to watch "for any hazards on the track," in the pits to inspect participating vehicles prior to each run, and at the end of the course to time the run. Roland Winterstein saw an advertisement of the runs and on 9 June 1967 went to the track to participate in speed contests in the "C gas class." He paid the stated fee. Near the end of his run his car "hit a cylinder head approximately 36" long, 6" wide and 4" high, weighing approximately 100 pounds * * * which was not visible to him when he commenced the race" but was visible to Wilcom's employees in the tower. He lost control of his car, jumped a ditch, drove up an embankment and turned over. . . . The declaration claimed that the crash and resulting injuries were due solely to the negligence of Wilcom and specified acts of omission and commission demonstrating that Wilcom had been careless. . . .

III

The first question is whether the releases were void as against public policy. . . .

The General Rule of Law Regarding Exculpatory Clauses

In the absence of legislation to the contrary, the law, by the great weight of authority, is that there is ordinarily no public policy which prevents the parties from contracting as they see fit, as to whether the plaintiff will undertake the responsibility of looking out for himself. . . . In other words, the parties may agree that there shall be no obligation to take precautions and hence no liability for negligence.

Exceptions to the General Rule

There is a proviso to the general rule. The relationship of the parties must be such that their bargaining be free and open. When one party is at such an obvious disadvantage in bargaining power that the effect of the contract is to put him at the mercy of the other's negligence, the agreement is void as against public policy. The proviso is applicable on this basis between employer and employee.

It is also against public policy to permit exculpatory agreements as to transactions involving the public interest, as for example with regard to public utilities, common carriers, innkeepers and public warehousemen. Prosser feels that there has been a definite tendency to expand the exception raised by the proviso to other professional bailees who are under no public duty but deal with the public, such as garagemen, owners of parking lots, and parcel checkrooms, because the indispensable need for their services deprives the customer of all real equal bargaining power. He finds decisions divided as to other private, bailees for hire, the decision likely to turn upon the extent to which it is considered that the public interest is involved. . . .

Generally, exculpatory agreements otherwise valid are not construed to cover the more extreme forms of negligence — wilful, wanton, reckless or gross. Nor do they encompass any conduct which constitutes an intentional tort. . . . And, of course, it is fundamental that if an agreement exempting a defendant from liability for his negligence is to be sustained, it must appear that its terms were known to the plaintiff, and "if he did not know of the provision in his contract and a reasonable person in his position would not have known of it, it is not binding upon him, and the agreement fails for want of mutual consent." . . .

Transactions Affected with a Public Interest

Because an exculpatory provision may not stand if it involves the public interest, . . . our inquiry turns to what transactions are affected with a public interest. In *Tunkl v. Regents of the University of California,* 383 P. 2d 441 (1963) the Supreme Court of California, . . . found that in placing particular contracts within or without the category of those affected with a public interest, the courts have revealed a rough outline of that type of transaction in which exculpatory provisions will be held invalid. "Thus the attempted but invalid exemption involves a transaction which exhibits some or all of the following characteristics. It concerns a business of a type generally thought suitable for public regulation. The party seeking exculpation is engaged in performing a service of great importance to the public, which is often a matter of practical necessity for some members of the public. The party holds himself out as willing to perform this service for any member of the public who seeks it, or at least for any member coming within certain established standards. As a result of the essential nature of the service, in the economic setting of the transaction, the party invoking exculpation possesses a decisive advantage of bargaining strength against any member of the public who seeks his services. In exercising a superior bargaining power the party confronts the public with a standardized adhesion contract of exculpation, and makes no provision whereby a purchaser may pay additional reasonable fees and obtain protection against negligence. Finally, as a result of the transaction, the person or property of the purchaser is placed under the control of the seller, subject to the risk of carelessness by the seller or his agents." At 445-456 (footnotes citing authorities omitted).

We note a further refinement. Although the traditional view has been that where the defendant's negligence consists of the violation of a statute, the plaintiff may still assume the risk, there is a growing tendency to the contrary where a safety statute enacted for the protection of the public is violated. The rationale is that the obligation and the right so created are public ones which it is not within the power of any private individual to waive. . . .

IV

It is clear that the exculpatory provisions involved in the case before us whereby Winterstein expressly agreed in advance that Wilcom would not be liable for the consequences of conduct which would otherwise be negligent were under the general rule recognizing the validity of such provisions. There was not the slightest disadvantage in bargaining power between the parties. Winterstein was under no compulsion, economic or otherwise, to race his car. He obviously participated in the speed runs simply because he wanted to do so, perhaps to demonstrate the superiority of his car and probably with the hope of winning a prize. This put him in no bargaining disadvantage.

The business operated by Wilcom had none of the characteristics of one affected with the public interest. The legislature has not thought it suitable for public regulation for it has not sought to regulate it. Wilcom is not engaged in performing a service of great importance to the public which is a matter of practical necessity for any member of the public. Wilcom does not hold himself out as willing to perform the service for any member of the public coming within certain established standards; we see nothing to indicate that he may not arbitrarily refuse to permit any person to participate in the speed runs. Since the service is not of an essential nature Wilcom had no decisive advantage of bargaining strength against any member of the public seeking to participate. Nor was Winterstein so placed under the control of Wilcom that he was subject to the risk of carelessness by Wilcom or his agents; Winterstein was under no obligation whatsoever to race his car.

We do not believe that any safety statute of this State, enacted for the protection of the public, was involved. Our attention has not been called to, nor are we aware of, such a statute dealing with activities of the nature conducted by Wilcom.

We observe that Winterstein did not allege that the negligence he attributed to Wilcom was other than simple negligence; he characterized Wilcom's omissions and commissions as careless, not wilful, wanton, reckless or gross; he does not say that he was wronged by an intentional tort.

The short of it is that as to the releases here the effect of the exemptive clauses upon the public interest was nil. We find that each release was merely an agreement between persons relating entirely to their private affairs. In the absence of a legislative declaration, we hold that they were not void as against public policy. . . .

VI

Winterstein contends that the releases executed "did not conclusively establish the voluntary assumption of risk in which there was an intentional and unreasonable exposure to danger which the plaintiffs-appellants knew or had reason to know as a matter of law." . . . [T]he premise of the contention is faulty because the rule of law on which Winterstein relies is not invoked in the factual posture of the case before us. Winterstein relies on the statement in *Powers v. State*, 178 Md. 23, 31: "The test in determining voluntary assumption of risk is whether there was an intentional and unreasonable exposure to danger which the plaintiff either knew or had reason to know." That rule deals with implied acceptance of risk, the basis which is not contract but consent. There can be no valid implied and voluntary consent to assume a risk without the knowledge of the risk. . . . But here there was an express agreement admittedly executed by each of Roland Winterstein and Barbara Winterstein. We have found that the release was not void as against public policy and it is not claimed to be otherwise invalid. In it Winterstein not only acknowledged the risks and dangers involved and recognized that unanticipated and unexpected dangers might arise but expressly released Wilcom "from all claims, demands, actions and causes of action of any sort, for injuries sustained by my person and/or property during my presence in said premises and participation in the stated activities due to negligence or any other fault." This exculpatory language is thorough and comprehensive. It encompassed the claim, demand and action here and effectively released Wilcom. The intent of the parties was expressed in clear and unequivocal terms. The document anticipated the alleged negligence of Wilcom and held him harmless. The contention is without merit. . . .

Judgment affirmed with costs.

QUESTION

1   Why should a party ever be permitted to disclaim liability?

TUNKL V. THE REGENTS OF THE UNIVERSITY OF CALIFORNIA
383 P.2D 441 (CAL. 1963)

. . . Hugo Tunkl brought this action to recover damages for personal injuries alleged to have resulted from the negligence of two physicians in the employ of the University of California Los Angeles Medical Center, a hospital operated and maintained by the Regents of the University of California . . . . The University of California at Los Angeles Medical Center admitted Tunkl as a patient on June 11, 1956. The Regents maintain the hospital for the primary purpose of aiding and developing a program of research and education in the field of medicine; patients are selected and admitted if the study and treatment of their condition would tend to achieve these purposes. Upon his entry to the hospital, Tunkl signed a document setting forth certain "Conditions of Admission." The crucial condition number six reads as follows:

> RELEASE: The hospital is a nonprofit, charitable institution. In consideration of the hospital and allied services to be rendered and the rates charged therefor, the patient or his legal representative agrees to and hereby releases The Regents of the University of California, and the hospital from any and all liability for the negligent or wrongful acts or omissions of its employees, if the hospital has used due care in selecting its employees.

Plaintiff stipulated that the hospital had selected its employees with due care. . . .

The cases have consistently held that the exculpatory provision may stand only if it does not involve "the public interest." . . . If, then, the exculpatory clause which affects the public interest cannot stand, we must ascertain those factors or characteristics which constitute the public interest. The social forces that have led to such characterization are volatile and dynamic. No definition of the concept of public interest can be contained within the four corners of a formula. The concept, always the subject of great debate, has ranged over the whole course of the common law; rather than attempt to prescribe its nature, we can only designate the situations in which it has been applied. We can determine whether the instant contract does or does not manifest the characteristics which have been held to stamp a contract as one affected with a public interest.

In placing particular contracts within or without the category of those affected with a public interest, the courts have revealed a rough outline of that type of transaction in which exculpatory provisions will be held invalid. Thus the attempted but invalid exemption involves a transaction which exhibits some or all of the following characteristics. It concerns a business of a type generally thought suitable for public regulation. . . . The party seeking exculpation is engaged in performing a service of great importance to the public, . . . which is often a matter of practical necessity for some members of the public. . . . The party holds himself out as willing to perform this service for any member of the public who seeks it, or at least for any member coming within certain established standards. . . . As a result of the essential nature of the service, in the economic setting of the transaction, the party invoking exculpation possesses a decisive advantage of bargaining strength against any member of the public who seeks his services. . . . In exercising a superior bargaining power the party confronts the public with a standardized adhesion contract of exculpation . . . and makes no provision whereby a purchaser may pay additional reasonable fees and obtain protection against negligence. . . . Finally, as a result of the transaction, the person or property of the purchaser is placed under the control of the seller, . . . subject to the risk of carelessness by the seller or his agents. . . .

While obviously no public policy opposes private, voluntary transactions in which one party, for a consideration, agrees to shoulder a risk which the law would otherwise have placed upon the other party, the above circumstances pose a different situation. In this situation the releasing party does not really acquiesce voluntarily in the contractual shifting of the risk, nor can we be reasonably certain that he receives an adequate consideration for the transfer. Since the service is one which each member of the public, presently or potentially, may find essential to him, he faces, despite his economic inability to do so, the prospect of a compulsory assumption of the risk of another's negligence. The public policy of this state has been, in substance, to posit the risk of negligence upon the actor; in instances in which this policy has been abandoned, it has generally been to allow or require that the risk shift to another party better or equally able to bear it, not to shift the risk to the weak bargainer.

In the light of the decisions, we think that the hospital-patient contract clearly falls within the category of agreements affecting the public interest. To meet that test, the agreement need only fulfill some of the characteristics above outlined; here, the relationship fulfills all of them.

Thus the contract of exculpation involves an institution suitable for, and a subject of, public regulation. . . . That the services of the hospital to those members of the public who are in special need of the particular skill of its staff and facilities constitute a practical and crucial necessity is hardly open to question. . . .

The hospital, likewise, holds itself out as willing to perform its services for those members of the public who qualify for its research and training facilities. While it is true that the hospital is selective as to the patients it will accept, such selectivity does not negate its public aspect or the public interest in it. The hospital is selective only in the sense that it accepts from the public at large certain types of cases which qualify for the research and training in which it specializes. But the hospital does hold itself out to the public as an institution which performs such services for those members of the public who can qualify for them. . . .

In insisting that the patient accept the provision of waiver in the contract, the hospital certainly exercises a decisive advantage in bargaining. The would-be patient is in no position to reject the proffered agreement, to bargain with the hospital, or in lieu of agreement to find another hospital. The admission room of a hospital contains no bargaining table where, as in a private business transaction, the parties can debate the terms of their contract. As a result, we cannot but conclude that the instant agreement manifested the characteristics of the so-called adhesion contract. Finally, when the patient signed the contract, he completely placed himself in the control of the hospital; he subjected himself to the risk of its carelessness.

In brief, the patient here sought the services which the hospital offered to a selective portion of the public; the patient, as the price of admission and as a result of his inferior bargaining position, accepted a clause in a contract of adhesion waiving the hospital's negligence; the patient thereby subjected himself to control of the hospital and the possible infliction of the negligence which he had thus been compelled to waive. The hospital, under such circumstances, occupied a status different than a mere private party; its contract with the patient affected the public interest. . . .

We must note, finally, that the integrated and specialized society of today, structured upon mutual dependency, cannot rigidly narrow the concept of the public interest. From the observance of simple standards of due care in the driving of a car to the performance of the high standards of hospital practice, the individual citizen must be completely dependent upon the responsibility of others. The fabric of this pattern is so closely woven that the snarling of a single thread affects the whole. We cannot lightly accept a sought immunity from careless failure to provide the hospital service upon which many must depend. Even if the hospital's doors are open only to those in a specialized category, the hospital cannot claim isolated immunity in the interdependent community of our time. It, too, is part of the social fabric, and prearranged exculpation from its negligence must partly rend the pattern and necessarily affect the public interest.

The judgment is reversed.

1 Is the result in *Tunkl* consistent with the result in *Wilcom*? Note that releases in the recreational context usually are upheld.

2 Two hurdles that must be surmounted by the defendant seeking to enforce an express assumption of risk are the following: 1) Is the agreement enforceable? 2) Does the agreement cover the risk at issue in the case?

3 Most courts have held that express assumptions of risk barring recovery for reckless or intentional harm are unenforceable.

b. IMPLIED ASSUMPTION OF RISK

It probably goes without saying that cases of implied assumption of risk include at least one complicating wrinkle that usually is not present in cases of express assumption of risk – the need to discern whether plaintiff has chosen to encounter a risk. Much of the modern scholarship on the subject of implied assumption of risk has focused on whether this topic should be treated as a question that is distinct from the comparative negligence doctrine.

WOODALL V. WAYNE STEFFNER PROD., INC.
20 CAL. RPTR. 572 (CAL. CT. APP. 1962)

. . . Plaintiff had a stunt in which he was lifted over water while suspended by and sitting on the framework of a kite which he had constructed. This he had done often. In March 1959, he made a deal with defendant corporation to come from his Cleveland home to the Los Angeles area and for a consideration of $500 to do the same act, known as "The Human Kite," over land, being drawn by an automobile instead of a boat. It was to be a sequence for a television production entitled "You Asked For It." Briefly, the setup was this: He stood on roller skates with the kite in position, it was tied to the rear axle of an automobile by a 150 foot rope; the auto was to start slowly and increase its speed to 27-30 miles an hour, at which time the kite would take to the air with plaintiff sitting in it. His experience had been such that he was able to control all features of the flight except forward speed; on that he had to rely on the operator of the boat or automobile; it was imperative that the speed be reduced as soon as the kite became airborne; the object of this is to stop the upward climb, when that happens the kite goes forward and can be maneuvered successfully; if the take-off speed is maintained the wind in the back will override the forward speed and cause the kite to dive. . . . Though plaintiff had made but one exhibition flight over land, he had found in 10 or 11 trial flights that the land job was steadier than the one over water. He had one expert driver whom he used for the land flight . . . . When making the deal with Mr. Chamberlin (television producer for defendant corporation) plaintiff said his main requirement in a driver was that he had been on stunts of that nature before. Asked if it was absolutely necessary for his own driver to come to California he said,

I knew my kite and I could take care of the kite if the man on the ground will listen to instructions, if he was a qualified driver. So at that he said "We have one of the best stunt drivers in Hollywood," . . . in fact better than my drivers back in Cleveland and I said "Well, in that case, it would be all right to use your drivers." . . . Q. Was there any discussion in the second conversation again about the qualifications of the driver? A. Yes, we went over that again and he had contacted the drivers that would be used on the program and again he assured me, I reminded him that the man would have to be a top qualified driver and able to listen to orders when given to him, and what not to do. Q. He again assured you, you say? A. Yes.

Likewise, Don Henderson (defendant's . . . director-cameraman) "assured me that the drivers they had were qualified drivers." So plaintiff left his own driver at home.

Soon after his arrival in Los Angeles on March 22, 1959, one Hochman drove plaintiff from his hotel to the drag strip where the stunt was to be put on. Hochman said he was to be plaintiff's driver but when plaintiff discovered he had been driving with his emergency brake partially on he refused to have Hochman. So Welo was assigned by defendant to drive in the exhibition flight. Plaintiff gave Welo explicit and repeated instructions as to speed, signals, etc., and Welo was told to slow the car after reaching a speed of 27-30 miles; he agreed to do so. Plaintiff's last word to Welo before the flight was, "Remember, now, don't go over 30 miles an hour," to which Welo agreed. Welo himself testified by deposition: "I have never represented myself to Mr. Woodall or anybody else as being a driver because I am not." In fact Welo never held himself out to Henderson as a stunt driver, had never been used as such by defendant, but had been assigned to this stunt notwithstanding the assurances previously given to plaintiff.

On the occasion in question, according to plaintiff, Welo started too slowly, was given a signal to go faster and was supposed to accelerate at once; the kite jumped along and did not take off; then Welo gave a quick surge forward and the kite rocketed up. Plaintiff started giving the wave-off signal (for an emergency stop); the kite reversed itself, but plaintiff still felt a forward motion, the kite began to fall and he could no longer control it. They were jerked along the ground and plaintiff could feel the rope taut and could feel the forward motion. His estimate was that the car got up to 45 miles [per hour].

Welo testified: "Q. Do you recall anything that Mr. Woodall told you with respect to the importance of slowing down after a certain point when he took to the air? A. Yes, I know all that. Q. You know all that? A. Yes. Q. You accelerated, though, is that correct? A. No, I did not. Q. Well, did you slow down when he got into the air? A. Did I slow down? Q. Did you slow the speed of the car down when he got in the air? A. I stopped immediately. Q. How far into the air did he get then? A. I would say 70, 75, maybe 80 feet. I am not sure. Q. While he was getting 70, 75 or 80 feet in the air, during that period from the time he left the ground until he got 75 feet in the air, did you slow down any before you made an immediate stop? A. Look, fellow. There wasn't time, it happened so fast." "I said we had a prearranged signal but it happened so fast that I never got the signal. Q. Then you didn't see any signal; is that right? A. That is right." "Q. You were the driver on that day, weren't you? A. I was the driver, if you want to call it that, but I am looking backwards and he [Carlson] is watching the speedometer and everything else. Q. Who is holding the wheel? A. Pardon? Q. Who is holding the wheel? A. I don't remember."

The kite turned over on plaintiff and he was seriously injured. He began to yell, "Too fast, too fast, I told him too fast." A boy who was about five feet from plaintiff when on the ground heard him, less than a minute after the accident, repeating, "I told him not to go too fast." Welo said the car got up to 33-34 miles [per hour]. Kenneth Carlson, who was in the tow car with Welo assigned to the job of watching the speedometer, testified that when plaintiff was lying on the ground he heard him say, "Too fast" and "My leg, my leg."

An expert witness, William D. Bridgeman, who viewed the film of this unfortunate flight and made computations based thereon, testified that "speed was the cause of the accident"; also, "Speed caused it to come down, that is right." Another expert, Sergeant Donald M. MacLean, of the Los Angeles Police Department, upon the basis of like calculations expressed the opinion that the speed of the tow car got up to 46.5 miles an hour. . . .

Appellants' . . . first point is that there was no substantial evidence that appellants were negligent or that the negligence of appellants, if any, was a proximate cause of plaintiff's injuries. The foregoing statement of facts seems to answer this contention sufficiently. Actually the burden of the argument is that this was an inherently hazardous stunt and one who engaged in it was negligent as a matter of law or assumed any risks involved in it. . . .

Appellants urge that they were released from liability by an instrument reading as follows: "Release Agreement. Pursuant to our telephone conversation, this written agreement hereby releases the Wayne Steffner Productions and any or all of its agents or representatives from any and all responsibility, liability or claims resulting from the performance of my act. /s/ Alphonse Woodall, Human Kite." Without any previous discussion, this document was presented to plaintiff upon his arrival at defendant's office, he was requested to sign, he read it and signed it; there was no further talk about it. The deal was oral, completed by telephone, nothing had been said on this subject, and plaintiff relying upon the deal as made had paid or incurred transportation costs of $224. Without any additional consideration he signed this instrument after arriving in California.

There is in it no mention of negligence and the writing must be strictly construed, with the result that it does not cover defendant's own negligence. . . .

The issue of assumption of risk, upon which appellants heavily rely, was left to the jury as one of fact by the instructions, which were as favorable to defendants as they reasonably could expect.

It is doubtless true that plaintiff assumed any risk growing out of inexpert manipulation of the kite, a sudden windstorm, breaking loose of the tow rope which he had fastened, the kite splitting in the air, or any one of many eventualities that were not properly attributable to the two defendants' own activities. Respondent's brief says, at page 63: "Respondent may have assumed the risk of his kite's breaking, his landing's being imperfect, a pothole in the road, a gust of wind. But that respondent assumed the risk of the ridiculous and callous lead-foot on the accelerator, which *in fact* caused the accident, is denied by a mass of testimony. Every case cited by appellants simply underlines this concept. In each and every one of them, the cause of the injury was inherent in the very nature of the thing." . . . The parties had a fair trial and the judgment is affirmed; the attempted appeal from the verdict of the jury is dismissed; the order denying the motion of defendants Wayne Productions, Inc., and Jerome Welo for judgment notwithstanding the verdict is affirmed.

QUESTIONS

1   Why did the release in *Winterstein* absolve the defendants of liability while the release in *Woodall* did not?

MURPHY V. STEEPLECHASE AMUSEMENT CO.
166 N.E. 173 (N.Y. 1929)

CARDOZO, C.J.

The defendant, Steeplechase Amusement Company, maintains an amusement park at Coney Island, New York. One of the supposed attractions is known as "The Flopper." It is a moving belt, running upward on an inclined plane, on which passengers sit or stand. Many of them are unable to keep their feet because of the movement of the belt, and are thrown backward or aside. The belt runs in a groove, with padded walls on either side to a height of four feet, and with padded flooring beyond the walls at the same angle as the belt. An electric motor . . . supplies the needed power.

Plaintiff, a vigorous young man, visited the park with friends. One of them, a young woman, now his wife, stepped upon the moving belt. Plaintiff followed and stepped behind her. As he did so, he felt what he describes as a sudden jerk, and was thrown to the floor. His wife in front and also friends behind him were thrown at the same time. Something more was here, as everyone understood, than the slowly-moving escalator that is common in shops and public places. A fall was foreseen as one of the risks of the adventure. There would have been no point to the whole thing, no adventure about it, if the risk had not been there. The very name above the gate, the Flopper, was warning to the timid. If the name was not enough, there was warning more distinct in the experience of others. We are told by the plaintiff's wife that the members of her party stood looking at the sport before joining in it themselves. Some aboard the belt were able, as she viewed them, to sit down with decorum or even to stand and keep their footing; others jumped or fell. The tumbling bodies and the screams and laughter supplied the merriment and fun. "I took a chance," she said when asked whether she thought that a fall might be expected.

Plaintiff took the chance with her, but, less lucky than his companions, suffered a fracture of a knee cap. He states in his complaint that the belt was dangerous to life and limb in that it stopped and started violently and suddenly and was not properly equipped to prevent injuries to persons who were using it without knowledge of its dangers, and in a bill of particulars he adds that it was operated at a fast and dangerous rate of speed and was not supplied with a proper railing, guard or other device to prevent a fall therefrom. No other negligence is charged.

We see no adequate basis for a finding that the belt was out of order. It was already in motion when the plaintiff put his foot on it. He cannot help himself to a verdict in such circumstances by the addition of the facile comment that it threw him with a jerk. One who steps upon a moving belt and finds his heels above his head is in no position to discriminate with nicety between the successive stages of the shock, between the jerk which is a cause and the jerk, accompanying the fall, as an instantaneous effect. . . . But the jerk, if it were established, would add little to the case. Whether the movement of the belt was uniform or irregular, the risk at greatest was a fall. This was the very hazard that was invited and foreseen.

Volenti non fit injuria. One who takes part in such a sport accepts the dangers that inhere in it so far as they are obvious and necessary, just as a fencer accepts the risk of a thrust by his antagonist or a spectator at a ball game the chance of contact with the ball. The antics of the clown are not the paces of the cloistered cleric. The rough and boisterous joke, the horseplay of the crowd, evokes its own guffaws, but they are not the pleasures of tranquility. The plaintiff was not seeking a retreat for meditation. Visitors were tumbling about the belt to the merriment of onlookers when he made his choice to join them. He took the chance of a like fate, with whatever damage to his body might ensue from such a fall. The timorous may stay at home.

A different case would be here if the dangers inherent in the sport were obscure or unobserved, or so serious as to justify the belief that precautions of some kind must have been taken to avert them. Nothing happened to the plaintiff except what common experience tells us may happen at any time as the consequence of a sudden fall. Many a skater or a horseman can rehearse a tale of equal woe. . . . According to the defendant's estimate, 250,000 visitors were at the Flopper in a year. Some quota of accidents was to be looked for in so great a mass. One might as well say that a skating rink should be abandoned because skaters sometimes fall. . . .

The judgment of the Appellate Division and that of the Trial Term should be reversed, and a new trial granted, with costs to abide the event.

QUESTIONS

1 What is the distinction between *Murphy* and *Woodall?*
2 Why is the defendant in *Murphy* not legally responsible for plaintiff's injury? Is it because defendant was not negligent? Is it because plaintiff's own negligence was a substantial contributing cause of this injury? Is it because plaintiff has voluntarily chosen to accept the unreasonable risk created by defendant's negligence? What language in the opinion supports your theory of the basis for the court's decision?

BLACKBURN V. DORTA
348 SO. 2D 287 (FLA. 1977)

. . . Since our decision in *Hoffman v. Jones,* contributory negligence no longer serves as a complete bar to plaintiff's recovery but is to be considered in apportioning damages according to the principles of comparative negligence. We are now asked to determine the effect of the *Hoffman* decision on the common law doctrine of assumption of risk. If assumption of risk is equivalent to contributory negligence, then *Hoffman* mandates that it can no longer operate as a complete bar to recovery. However, if it has a distinct purpose apart from contributory negligence, its continued existence remains unaffected by *Hoffman*. . . .

At the outset, we note that assumption of risk is not a favored defense. There is a puissant drift toward abrogating the defense. . . . The argument is that assumption of risk serves no purpose which is not subsumed by either the doctrine of contributory negligence or the common law concept of duty. . . . It is said that this redundancy results in confusion and, in some cases, denies recovery unjustly. . . . The issue is most salient in states which have enacted comparative negligence legislation. Those statutes provide that the common law defense of contributory negligence no longer necessarily acts as a complete bar to recovery. The effect of these statutes upon the doctrine of assumption of risk has proved to be controversial. Joining the intensifying assault upon the doctrine, a number of comparative negligence jurisdictions have abrogated assumption of risk. . . . Those jurisdictions hold that assumption of risk is interchangeable with contributory negligence and should be treated equivalently. Today we are invited to join this trend of dissatisfaction with the doctrine. For the reasons herein expressed, we accept the invitation

At the commencement of any analysis of the doctrine of assumption of risk, we must recognize that we deal with a potpourri of labels, concepts, definitions, thoughts, and doctrines. The confusion of labels does not end with the indiscriminate and interchangeable use of the terms "contributory negligence" and "assumption of risk." In the case law and among text writers, there have developed categories of assumption of risk. Distinctions exist between express and implied; . . . between primary and secondary; . . . and between reasonable and unreasonable or, as sometimes expressed, strict and qualified. . . . It will be our task to analyze these various labels and to trace the historical basis of the doctrine to unravel what has been in the law an "enigma wrapped in a mystery."

It should be pointed out that we are not here concerned with express assumption of risk which is a contractual concept outside the purview of this inquiry and upon which we express no opinion herein. . . . Included within the definition of express assumption of risk are express contracts not to sue for injury or loss which may thereafter be occasioned by the covenantee's negligence as well as situations in which actual consent exists such as where one voluntarily participates in a contact sport. The breed of assumption of risk with which we deal here is that which arises by implication or *implied* assumption of risk. Initially it may be divided into the categories of *primary* and *secondary*. The term primary assumption of risk is simply another means of stating that the defendant was not negligent, either because he owed no duty to the plaintiff in the first instance, or because he did not breach the duty owed. Secondary assumption of risk is an affirmative defense to an established breach of a duty owed by the defendant to the plaintiff. . . .

The concept of primary assumption of risk is the basis for the historical doctrine which arose in the master-servant relationship during the late nineteenth century. . . . The master was held not to be negligent if he provided a reasonably safe place to work; the servant was said to have assumed the inherent risks that remained. In this context assumption of risk was not an affirmative defense at all. Rather, it was another way of expressing that the master was not negligent, for the servant had the burden of proving that his injury resulted from a risk other than one inherent in a facility or location that was a reasonably safe place to work. . . . As is often the case in the common law, however, the doctrine mutated into an affirmative defense, with the burden of pleading and proof upon the master. Consequently, even if the servant could show that the master owed and had breached a duty to provide a reasonably safe place to work, the master could escape liability if he could establish that the servant had voluntarily exposed himself to a risk negligently created by the master. Thus, two distinct concepts came to bear the same label with inevitable confusion which has persisted to the present. . . .

It is apparent that no useful purpose is served by retaining terminology which expresses the thought embodied in primary assumption of risk. This branch (or trunk) of the tree of assumption of risk is subsumed in the principle of negligence itself. Under our Florida jury instructions, the jury is directed first to determine whether the defendant has been negligent, i.e., did he owe a duty to the plaintiff and, if so, did he breach that duty? To sprinkle the term assumption of risk into the equation can only lead to confusion of a jury. . . . An example of this concept is presented in the operation of a passenger train. It can be said that a passenger assumes the risk of lurches and jerks which are ordinary and usual to the proper operation of the train, but that he does not assume the risk of extraordinary or unusual lurches and jerks resulting from substandard operation of the train. The same issue can be characterized in terms of the standard of care of the railroad. Thus, it can be said that the railroad owes a duty to operate its train with the degree of care of an ordinary prudent person under similar circumstances which includes some lurching and jerking while a train is in motion or commencing to move under ideal circumstances. So long as the lurching or jerking is not extraordinary due to substandard conduct of the railroad, there is no breach of duty and, hence, no negligence on the part of the railroad. The latter characterization of the issue clearly seems preferable and is consistent with the manner in which the jury is instructed under our standard jury instructions.

Having dispensed with *express* and *primary-implied* assumption of risk, we recur to *secondary-implied* assumption of risk which is the affirmative defense variety that has been such a thorn in the judicial side. The affirmative defense brand of assumption of risk can be subdivided into the type of conduct which is reasonable but nonetheless bars recovery (sometimes called *pure* or *strict* assumption of risk), and the type of conduct which is unreasonable and bars recovery (sometimes referred to as *qualified* assumption of risk). . . . Application of pure or strict assumption of risk is exemplified by the hypothetical situation in which a landlord has negligently permitted his tenant's premises to become highly flammable and a fire ensues. The tenant returns from work to find the premises a blazing inferno with his infant child trapped within. He rushes in to retrieve the child and is injured in so doing. Under the pure doctrine of assumption of risk, the tenant is barred from recovery because it can be said he voluntarily exposed himself to a known risk. Under this view of assumption of risk, the tenant is precluded from recovery notwithstanding the fact that his conduct could be said to be entirely reasonable under the circumstances. . . . There is little to commend this doctrine of implied-pure or strict assumption of risk, and our research discloses no Florida case in which it has been applied. Certainly, in light of *Hoffman v. Jones*, there is no reason supported by law or justice in this state to give credence to such a principle of law.

There remains, then, for analysis only the principle of implied-qualified assumption of risk, and it can be demonstrated in the hypothetical recited above with the minor alteration that the tenant rushes into the blazing premises to retrieve his favorite fedora. Such conduct on the tenant's part clearly would be unreasonable. Consequently, his conduct can just as readily be characterized as contributory negligence. It is the failure to exercise the care of a reasonably prudent man under similar circumstances. It is this last category of assumption of risk which has caused persistent confusion in the law of torts because of the lack of analytic difference between it and contributory negligence. If the only significant form of assumption of risk (implied-qualified) is so readily characterized, conceptualized, and verbalized as contributory negligence, can there be any sound rationale for retaining it as a separate affirmative defense to negligent conduct which bars recovery altogether? In the absence of any historical imperative, the answer must be no. We are persuaded that there is no historical significance to the doctrine of implied-secondary assumption of risk. . . .

We find no discernible basis analytically or historically to maintain a distinction between the affirmative defense of contributory negligence and assumption of risk. The latter appears to be a viable, rational doctrine only in the sense described herein as implied-qualified assumption of risk which connotes unreasonable conduct on the part of the plaintiff. This result comports with the definition of contributory negligence appearing in Restatement (Second) of Torts, § 466 (1965). Furthermore, were we not otherwise persuaded to elimination of assumption of risk as a separate affirmative defense in the context herein described, the decision of this Court in *Hoffman v. Jones* would dictate such a result. As stated therein:

> . . . A primary function of a court is to see that legal conflicts are equitably resolved. In the field of tort law, the most equitable result that can ever be reached by a court is the equation of liability with fault. Comparative negligence does this more completely than contributory negligence, and we would be shirking our duty if we did not adopt the better doctrine.

280 So.2d 431, 438.

Is liability equated with fault under a doctrine which would totally bar recovery by one who voluntarily, but reasonably, assumes a known risk while one whose conduct is unreasonable but denominated "contributory negligence" is permitted to recover a proportionate amount of his damages for injury? Certainly not. Therefore, we hold that the affirmative defense of implied assumption of risk is merged into the defense of contributory negligence and the principles of comparative negligence enunciated in *Hoffman v. Jones* shall apply in all cases where such defense is asserted. . . .

1   *Primary v. Secondary.* The phrase "implied assumption of risk" can be used to describe two different scenarios. Sometimes, the phrase is used to describe a situation in which defendant has breached no duty because the risk that came to fruition was inherent in the activity. This is called "primary" implied assumption of risk. *Murphy* may be an example of primary implied assumption of risk. In "secondary" implied assumption of risk, defendant has breached a duty, but plaintiff was aware of the risk created by defendant's breach and voluntarily chooses to encounter that risk.

2   *Third Restatement of Torts.* The Restatement (Third) of Torts appears largely to have abandoned implied assumption of risk, perhaps merging it with comparative responsibility.

B. MULTIPLE DEFENDANTS

So far, these materials have focused mainly on the single plaintiff/single defendant scenario. We just finished considering how a plaitiff's own partial responsibility for her harm might affect her ability to recover. Now we turn to the question of how to apportion responsibility among multiple potentially responsible defendants. It has been abundantly clear for a very long time that the liability of one tortfeasor does not necessarily preclude the simultaneous liability of another.

We first consider the doctrine of joint and several liability, which the common law developed for situations involving "joint tortfeasors," in other words, situations where multiple defendants' conduct combined to cause an indivisible harm to the plaintiff. Under the doctrine of joint and several liability, each defendant was responsible for the entire indivisible harm. But this doctrine of joint and several liability led to another question: What happens when a plaintiff forces one defendant to pay for the entire harm that was caused jointly with another defendant? Can the defendant who has compensated plaintiff for the entire loss obtain "contribution" from any other jointly responsible defendants? The common law's initial answer was "no," but that has changed, as we shall see. Finally, we will consider the doctrine of vicarious liability – holding one person responsible for harms caused by another person's negligence.

1. JOINT LIABILITY

Here we address the question of how to allocate liability among multiple defendants. The majority answer to that question has, for some time, been captured by the phrase "joint and several liability." This label is made up of two very different concepts that address the scenario where one defendant is, for one reason or another, not required to pay for his share of a loss.

Under the concept of "joint" liability, the other liable defendants make up that missing share in the plaintiff's recovery. When defendants are "jointly" liable for a loss, plaintiff takes a judgement against each defendant for the entire loss. Plaintiff can obtain her entire recovery from any one of jointly liable tortfeasors, but she can collect only one complete recovery. If plaintiff does recover all of her damages against only one of a group of jointly liable tortfeasors, then plaintiff may not seek any additional recovery from any other tortfeasor. The full recovery from one defendant "extinguishes" plaintiff's entire claim against all others. However, the defendant who is made to pay the entire claim may, in most cases, pursue "contribution" from the other tortfeasors who have paid nothing, or less than their share of the loss.

The now traditional doctrine of joint liability has relatively recently been modified in some jurisdictions toward a more "several" form of liability. Under the concept of "several" liability (sometimes called individual liability), each defendant is responsible only for his respective share so that the injured plaintiff ends up bearing any portion of her loss that cannot be collected from one of the responsible defendants. To illustrate, imagine that plaintiff suffers a $100,000 loss, and the jury apportions 50% responsibility for the loss to each of two defendants A and B. Under joint liability, plaintiff would take a $100,000 judgment against A and a $100,000 judgment against B (although only one complete recovery will be allowed). Under several liability, plaintiff would take a $50,000 judgment against A and a $50,000 judgment against B.

a. CONCERTED ACTION

As illustrated by the following case, defendants who act in concert are jointly liable for harm done by those with whom they act in concert. Restatement (Second) Torts § 876 sets out the circumstances under which one will be held jointly liable for harm caused while acting in concert with another:

> For harm resulting to a third person from the tortious conduct of another, one is subject to
> liability if he
> a.   does a tortious act in concert with the other or pursuant to a common design with him, or
> b.   knows that the other's conduct constitutes a breach of duty and gives substantial assistance or encouragement to the other so to conduct himself, or
> c.   gives substantial assistance to the other in accomplishing a tortious result and his own conduct, separately considered, constitutes a breach of duty to the third person.

BIERCZYNSKI V. ROGERS
239 A.2D 218 (DEL. 1968)

This appeal involves an automobile accident in which the plaintiffs claim that the defendant motorists were racing on the public highway, as the result of which the accident occurred. [Cecil Rogers] brought this action against Robert C. Race and Ronald Bierczynski, ages 18 and 17 respectively, alleging concurrent negligences in that they violated various speed statutes and various other statutory rules of the road, and in that they failed to keep a proper lookout and failed to keep their vehicles under proper control. The jury, by answer to interrogatories in its special verdict, expressly found that Race and Bierczynski were each negligent and that the negligence of each was a proximate cause of the accident. Substantial verdicts were entered in favor of the plaintiffs against both defendants jointly. The defendant Bierczynski appeals therefrom. The defendant Race does not appeal; rather, he joins with the plaintiffs in upholding the judgment below.

. . . . The Trial Court had before it the following evidence:

Bierczynski and Race worked at the same place, located . . . near Lore Avenue. They lived near each other in the southerly part of Wilmington. On the day before the accident, Bierczynski drove Race to work. On the day of the accident, Bierczynski intended to pick Race up again; but, upon meeting, Race told Bierczynski he would take his own automobile too, because he intended to leave work early. Thereupon, one following the other, they drove toward their place of employment northerly . . . to Lore Avenue in a suburban area . . . . The accident occurred on Lore Avenue about 300 feet east of its intersection with River Road. . . . Lore Avenue was 18 feet wide, macadam surfaces, without a marked center line, and was lined by guard rails at various places. For a distance of about 1,000 feet west of its intersection with River Road, Lore Avenue is a moderately steep hill; after crossing River Road, it levels off. The speed limit at the scene was 25 m.p.h.

Cecil Rogers testified as follows: He was returning from a Girl Scout trip with his daughter, headed for their home located about three blocks from the scene of the accident. He entered Lore Avenue . . . driving in a westerly direction . . . . At a point about 300 feet east of River Road, Rogers' car was struck by Race's car which approached him sideways, moving in an easterly direction on the westbound lane. Rogers saw Race's car coming at him; he stopped in the westbound lane; but he was unable to move out of the way because there was a guard rail along that part of the road and no shoulder. Rogers first saw the Race vehicle when it was about 550 feet up Lore Avenue – or about 250 feet west of River Road. At that point, the Race car was being driven easterly on Lore Avenue in the westbound lane, almost along-side the Bierczynski car which was moving easterly in the eastbound lane. The front bumper of the Race car was opposite the back bumper of the Bierczynski car. Both cars were moving at about 55 or 60 m.p.h. down the hill. Before reaching River Road, Race swerved back into the eastbound lane behind Bierczynski, who was about a car length in front. As it crossed River Road, the Race automobile "bottomed on the road;" and it "careened down against the pavement and gave an impression of an explosion"; dust "flew everywhere" sufficiently to obscure the Race car momentarily from Rogers' view. At that point, the Race and Bierczynski automobiles were only "inches apart." The Race car then emerged from behind the Bierczynski car and careened sideways, at about 70 m.p.h., a distance of about 300 feet to the Rogers car standing in the westbound lane. The left side of the Race car struck the front of the Rogers car. Meanwhile, the Bierczynski car was brought to a stop in the eastbound lane, about 35 feet from the area of impact. The Bierczynski car did not come into contact with the Rogers vehicle.

Bierczynski's contention as to lack of proximate cause is based mainly upon the facts that his automobile remained in the proper lane at all times and was stopped about 35 feet before reaching the area of impact, without coming into contact with the Rogers car. . . .

In many States, automobile racing on a public highway is prohibited by statute, the violation of which is negligence *per se*. Delaware has no such statute. Nevertheless, speed competition in automobiles on the public highway is negligence in this State, for the reason that a reasonably prudent person would not engage in such conduct. This conclusion is in accord with the general rule, prevailing in other jurisdictions which lack statutes on the subject, that racing motor vehicles on a public highway is negligence.

It is also generally held that all who engage in a race on the highway do so at their peril, and are liable for injury or damage sustained by a third person as a result thereof, regardless of which of the racing cars directly inflicted the injury or damage. The authorities reflect generally accepted rules of causation that all parties engaged in a motor vehicle race on the highway are wrongdoers acting in concert, and that each participant is liable for harm to a third person arising from the tortious conduct of the other, because he has induced and encouraged the tort. . . .

We subscribe to those rules; and hold that, as a general rule, participation in a motor vehicle race on a public highway is an act of concurrent negligence imposing liability on each participant for any injury to a non-participant resulting from the race. If, therefore, Race and Bierczynski were engaged in a speed competition, each was liable for the damages and injuries to the plaintiffs herein, even though Bierczynski was not directly involved in the collision itself. Bierczynski apparently concedes liability if a race had, in fact, been in progress.

. . . We find no error as asserted by the appellant. The judgments below are affirmed.

b. INDIVISIBLE INJURY

AMERICAN MOTORCYCLE ASSN. V. SUPERIOR COURT OF LOS ANGELES CO.
578 p.2d 899 (cal. 1978)

Three years ago, in *Li* v. *Yellow Cab Co.* . . . , we concluded that the harsh and much criticized contributory negligence doctrine, which totally barred an injured person from recovering damages whenever his own negligence had contributed in any degree to the injury, should be replaced in this state by a rule of comparative negligence, under which an injured individual's recovery is simply proportionately diminished, rather than completely eliminated, when he is partially responsible for the injury. In reaching the conclusion to adopt comparative negligence in *Li*, we explicitly recognized that our innovation inevitably raised numerous collateral issues, "[the] most serious [of which] are those attendant upon the administration of a rule of comparative negligence in cases involving multiple parties." . . . The present mandamus proceeding . . . requires us to resolve a number of the thorny multiple party problems to which *Li* adverted.

For the reasons explained below, we have reached the following conclusions with respect to the multiple party issues presented by this case. First, we conclude that our adoption of comparative negligence to ameliorate the inequitable consequences of the contributory negligence rule does not warrant the abolition or contraction of the established "joint and several liability" doctrine; each tortfeasor whose negligence is a proximate cause of an indivisible injury remains individually liable for all compensable damages attributable to that injury. Contrary to petitioner's contention, we conclude that joint and several liability does not logically conflict with a comparative negligence regime. . . . The joint and several liability doctrine continues, after *Li*, to play an important and legitimate role in protecting the ability of a negligently injured person to obtain adequate compensation for his injuries from those tortfeasors who have negligently inflicted the harm.

Second, although we have determined that *Li* does not mandate a diminution of the rights of injured persons through the elimination of the joint and several liability rule, we conclude that the general principles embodied in *Li* do warrant a reevaluation of . . . the allocation of loss *among* multiple tortfeasors. . . . Prior to *Li*, of course, the notion of apportioning liability on the basis of comparative fault was completely alien to California common law. In light of *Li*, however, we think that . . . liability among multiple tortfeasors may be apportioned on a comparative negligence basis. As we explain, many jurisdictions which have adopted comparative negligence have embraced similar comparative contribution or comparative indemnity systems by judicial decision. Such a doctrine conforms to *Li's* objective of establishing "a system under which liability for damage will be borne by those whose negligence caused it in direct proportion to their respective fault. . . ."

1. *The facts*

In the underlying action in this case, plaintiff Glen Gregos, a teenage boy, seeks to recover damages for serious injuries which he incurred while participating in a cross-country motorcycle race for novices. Glen's second amended complaint alleges, in relevant part, that defendants American Motorcycle Association (AMA) and the Viking Motorcycle Club (Viking) – the organizations that sponsored and collected the entry fee for the race – negligently designed, managed, supervised and administered the race, and negligently solicited the entrants for the race. The . . . complaint . . . alleges that as a direct and proximate cause of such negligence, Glen suffered a crushing of his spine . . . .

AMA filed an answer to the complaint, denying the charging allegations and asserting a number of affirmative defenses, including a claim that Glen's own negligence was a proximate cause of his injuries. Thereafter, AMA sought leave of court to file a cross-complaint, which purported to state two causes of action against Glen's parents. . . .

. . . AMA . . . reasserts Glen's parents' negligence . . . and asks for a declaration of the "allocable negligence" of Glen's parents so that "the damages awarded [against AMA], if any, [may] be reduced by the percentage of damages allocable to cross-defendants' negligence." As more fully explained in the accompanying points and authorities, this . . . cause of action is based on an implicit assumption that the *Li* decision abrogates the rule of joint and several liability of concurrent tortfeasors and establishes in its stead a new rule of "proportionate liability," under which each concurrent tortfeasor who has proximately caused an indivisible harm may be held liable only for a *portion* of plaintiff's recovery, determined on a comparative fault basis. . . .

2. The adoption of comparative negligence in Li does not warrant the abolition of joint and several liability of concurrent tortfeasors.

. . . Under well-established common law principles, a negligent tortfeasor is generally liable for all damage of which his negligence is *a* proximate cause; stated another way, in order to recover damages sustained as a result of an indivisible injury, a plaintiff is not required to prove that a tortfeasor's conduct was *the sole* proximate cause of the injury, but only that such negligence was *a* proximate cause. . . .

In cases involving multiple tortfeasors, the principle that each tortfeasor is personally liable for any indivisible injury of which his negligence is a proximate cause has commonly been expressed in terms of "joint and several liability." As many commentators have noted, the "joint and several liability" concept has sometimes caused confusion because the terminology has been used with reference to a number of distinct situations. . . . The terminology originated with respect to tortfeasors who acted in concert to commit a tort, and in that context it reflected the principle . . . that all members of a "conspiracy" or partnership are equally responsible for the acts of each member in furtherance of such conspiracy. . . .

In the concurrent tortfeasor context, however, the "joint and several liability" label . . . simply embodies the general common law principle, noted above, that a tortfeasor is liable for any injury of which his negligence is *a* proximate cause. Liability attaches to a concurrent tortfeasor in this situation not because he is responsible for the acts of other independent tortfeasors who may also have caused the injury, but because he is responsible for all damage of which his own negligence was a proximate cause. When independent negligent actions of a number of tortfeasors are each a proximate cause of a single injury, each tortfeasor is thus personally liable for the damage sustained, and the injured person may sue one or all of the tortfeasors to obtain a recovery for his injuries; the fact that one of the tortfeasors is impecunious or otherwise immune from suit does not relieve another tortfeasor of his liability for damage which he himself has proximately caused.

Prior to *Li*, of course, a negligent tortfeasor's liability was limited by the draconian contributory negligence doctrine; under that doctrine, a negligent tortfeasor escaped liability for injuries which he had proximately caused to another whenever the injured person's lack of due care for his own safety was also a proximate cause of the injury. In *Li*, however, we repudiated the contributory negligence rule . . . .

In the instant case AMA argues that the *Li* decision, by repudiating the all-or-nothing contributory negligence rule and replacing it by a rule which simply diminishes an injured party's recovery on the basis of his comparative fault, in effect undermined the fundamental rationale of the entire joint and several liability doctrine as applied to concurrent tortfeasors. . . . AMA argues that after *Li* (1) there *is* a basis for dividing damages, namely on a comparative negligence basis, and (2) a plaintiff is no longer necessarily "innocent," for *Li* permits a negligent plaintiff to recover damages. AMA maintains that in light of these two factors it is logically inconsistent to retain joint and several liability of concurrent tortfeasors after *Li*. As we explain, for a number of reasons we cannot accept AMA's argument.

First, the simple feasibility of apportioning fault on a comparative negligence basis does not render an indivisible injury "divisible" for purposes of the joint and several liability rule. As we have already explained, a concurrent tortfeasor is liable for the whole of an indivisible injury whenever his negligence is a proximate cause of that injury. In many instances, the negligence of each of several concurrent tortfeasors may be sufficient, in itself, to cause the entire injury; in other instances, it is simply impossible to determine whether or not a particular concurrent tortfeasor's negligence, acting alone, would have caused the same injury. Under such circumstances, a defendant has no equitable claim vis-a-vis an injured plaintiff to be relieved of liability for damage which he has proximately caused simply because some other tortfeasor's negligence may also have caused the same harm. In other words, the mere fact that it may be possible to assign some percentage figure to the relative culpability of one negligent defendant as compared to another does not in any way suggest that each defendant's negligence is not a proximate cause of the entire indivisible injury.

Second, abandonment of the joint and several liability rule is not warranted by AMA's claim that, after *Li*, a plaintiff is no longer "innocent." Initially, of course, it is by no means invariably true that after *Li* injured plaintiffs will be guilty of negligence. In many instances a plaintiff will be completely free of all responsibility for the accident, and yet, under the proposed abolition of joint and several liability, such a completely faultless plaintiff, rather than a wrongdoing defendant, would be forced to bear a portion of the loss if any one of the concurrent tortfeasors should prove financially unable to satisfy his proportioned share of the damages.

Moreover, even when a plaintiff is partially at fault for his own injury, a plaintiff's culpability is not equivalent to that of a defendant. In this setting, a plaintiff's negligence relates only to a failure to use due care for his own protection, while a defendant's negligence relates to a lack of due care for the safety of others. Although we recognized in *Li* that a plaintiff's self-directed negligence would justify reducing his recovery in proportion to his degree of fault for the accident, the fact remains that insofar as the plaintiff's conduct creates only a risk of self-injury, such conduct, unlike that of a negligent defendant, is not tortious. . . .

Finally, from a realistic standpoint, we think that AMA's suggested abandonment of the joint and several liability rule would work a serious and unwarranted deleterious effect on the practical ability of negligently injured persons to receive adequate compensation for their injuries. One of the principal by-products of the joint and several liability rule is that it frequently permits an injured person to obtain full recovery for his injuries even when one or more of the responsible parties do not have the financial resources to cover their liability. In such a case the rule recognizes that fairness dictates that the "wronged party should not be deprived of his right to redress," but that "[the] wrongdoers should be left to work out between themselves any apportionment." (*Summers* v. *Tice* (1948) . . . 199 P.2d 1, ...) The *Li* decision does not detract in the slightest from this pragmatic policy determination.

For all of the foregoing reasons, we reject AMA's suggestion that our adoption of comparative negligence logically compels the abolition of joint and several liability of concurrent tortfeasors. Indeed, although AMA fervently asserts that the joint and several liability concept is totally incompatible with a comparative negligence regime, the simple truth is that the overwhelming majority of jurisdictions which have adopted comparative negligence have retained the joint and several liability doctrine. . . . AMA has not cited a single judicial authority to support its contention that the advent of comparative negligence rationally compels the demise of the joint and several liability rule. Under the circumstances, we hold that after *Li*, a concurrent tortfeasor whose negligence is a proximate cause of an indivisible injury remains liable for the total amount of damages, diminished only "in proportion to the amount of negligence attributable to the person recovering." (13 Cal.3d at p. 829.)

3. Upon reexamination of the common law equitable indemnity doctrine in light of the principles underlying Li, we conclude that the doctrine should be modified to permit partial indemnity among concurrent tortfeasors on a comparative fault basis.

Although, as discussed above, we are not persuaded that our decision in *Li* calls for a fundamental alteration of the rights of injured plaintiffs vis-a-vis concurrent tortfeasors through the abolition of joint and several liability, the question remains whether the broad principles underlying *Li* warrant any modification of this state's common law rules governing the allocation of loss *among* multiple tortfeasors. . . . Taking our cue from a recent decision of the highest court of one of our sister states, we conclude – in line with *Li's* objectives – that the California common law . . . should . . . permit a concurrent tortfeasor to obtain partial indemnity from other concurrent tortfeasors on a comparative fault basis.

In California, as in most other American jurisdictions, the allocation of damages among multiple tortfeasors has historically been analyzed in terms of two, ostensibly mutually exclusive, doctrines: contribution and indemnification. In traditional terms, the apportionment of loss between multiple tortfeasors has been thought to present a question of contribution; indemnity, by contrast, has traditionally been viewed as concerned solely with whether a loss should be entirely shifted from one tortfeasor to another, rather than whether the loss should be shared between the two. . . .

Early California decisions, relying on the ancient saw that "the law will not aid a wrongdoer," embraced the then ascendant common law rule denying a tortfeasor any right to contribution whatsoever. . . .

In *Li*, after concluding "that logic, practical experience, and fundamental justice counsel against the retention of the doctrine rendering contributory negligence a complete bar to recovery" (13 Cal.3d at pp. 812-813), we made clear our conviction that the discarded doctrine "should be replaced in this state *by a system under which liability for damage will be borne by those whose negligence caused it in direct proportion to their respective fault.*" (Italics added.) (*Id.*, at p. 813.)

In order to attain such a system, in which liability for an indivisible injury caused by concurrent tortfeasors will be borne by each individual tortfeasor "in direct proportion to [his] respective fault," we conclude that the current . . . rule should be modified to permit a concurrent tortfeasor to obtain partial indemnity from other concurrent tortfeasors on a comparative fault basis. In reaching this conclusion, we point out that in recent years a great number of courts, particularly in jurisdictions which follow the comparative negligence rule, have for similar reasons adopted, as a matter of common law, comparable rules providing for comparative contribution . . . .

6. Conclusion

In *Li* v. *Yellow Cab Co., supra,* this court examined and abandoned the time-worn contributory negligence rule which completely exonerated a negligent defendant whenever an injured plaintiff was partially at fault for the accident . . . .

In the instant case we have concluded that the force of *Li's* rationale applies equally to the allocation of responsibility between two or more negligent defendants . . . . From the crude all-or-nothing rule of traditional indemnity doctrine, and the similarly inflexible per capita division of the narrowly circumscribed contribution statute, we have progressed to the more refined stage of permitting the jury to apportion liability in accordance with the tortfeasors' comparative fault.

Accordingly, we hold that under the common law equitable indemnity doctrine a concurrent tortfeasor may obtain partial indemnity from cotortfeasors on a comparative fault basis. . . .

CLARK, J., Dissenting.

I

Repudiating the existing contributory negligence system and adopting a system of comparative negligence, this court in *Li* v. *Yellow Cab Co.* (1975) 13 Cal.3d 804 repeatedly – like the tolling bell – enunciated the principle that the extent of liability must be governed by the extent of fault. Thus, the court stated, "the extent of fault should govern the extent of liability" (*id.*, at p. 811), "liability for damage will be borne by those whose negligence caused it in direct proportion to their respective fault" (*id.*, at p. 813), and "the fundamental purpose of [the rule of pure comparative negligence] shall be to assign responsibility and liability for damage in direct proportion to the amount of negligence of each of the parties" (*id.*, at p. 829). And in a cacophony of emphasis this court explained that the "basic objection to the doctrine [of contributory negligence] – grounded in the primal concept that in a system in which liability is based on fault, the extent of fault should govern the extent of liability – remains irresistible to reason and all intelligent notions of fairness." (*Id.*, at p. 811.)

Now, only three years later, the majority of my colleagues conclude that the *Li* principle is not irresistible after all. Today, in the first decision of this court since *Li* explaining the operation of the *Li* principle, they reject it for almost all cases involving multiple parties.

The majority reject the *Li* principle in two ways. First, they reject it by adopting joint and several liability holding that each defendant – including the marginally negligent one – will be responsible for the loss attributable to his codefendant's negligence. To illustrate, if we assume that the plaintiff is found 30 percent at fault, the first defendant 60 percent, and a second defendant 10 percent, the plaintiff under the majority's decision is entitled to a judgment for 70 percent of the loss against each defendant, and the defendant found only 10 percent at fault may have to pay 70 percent of the loss if his codefendant is unable to respond in damages.

The second way in which the majority reject *Li's* irresistible principle is by its settlement rules. Under the majority opinion, a good faith settlement releases the settling tortfeasor from further liability, and the "plaintiff's recovery from nonsettling tortfeasors should be diminished only by the amount that the plaintiff has actually recovered in a good faith settlement, rather than by an amount measured by the settling tortfeasor's proportionate responsibility for the injury." . . . The settlement rules announced today may turn *Li's* principle upside down – the extent of dollar liability may end up in inverse relation to fault.

Whereas the joint and several liability rules violate the *Li* principle when one or more defendants are absent or unable to respond in damages, the settlement rules will ordinarily preclude effecting the majority's principle in cases when all defendants are involved in the litigation and are solvent. To return to my 30-60-10 illustration and further assuming both defendants are solvent, the plaintiff is ordinarily eager to settle quickly to avoid the long delay incident to trial. Further, he will be willing to settle with either defendant because under the majority's suggested rules, he may then pursue the remaining defendant for the balance of the recoverable loss (70 percent) irrespective whether the remaining defendant was 10 percent at fault or 60 percent at fault. The defendants' settlement postures will differ substantially. Realizing the plaintiff is eager for quick recovery and is capable of pursuing the codefendant, the defendant 60 percent liable for the loss will be prompted to offer a sum substantially below his share of fault, probably paying 20 to 40 percent of the loss. The defendant only 10 percent at fault will be opposed to such settlement, wishing to limit his liability. To compete with his codefendant in settlement offers he will be required to offer substantially in excess of his 10 percent share of the loss, again frustrating the *Li* principle that the extent of liability should be governed by the extent of fault. Should he fail to settle, the 10 percent at fault defendant runs the risk that his codefendant will settle early for perhaps half of his own liability, while the lesser negligent person must eventually pay the remainder, not only frustrating the *Li* principle but turning it upside down. In any event, it is extremely unlikely he can settle for his 10 percent share. . . .

The foregoing demonstrates that under the majority's joint and several liability and settlement rules, only rarely will the *Li* principle be carried out in multi-party litigation. The principle will be frustrated if one or more defendants are unavailable, insolvent, or have settled. Prior to *Li*, the overwhelming majority of accident cases were settled in whole or in part, and assuming this practice continues, the *Li* principle will not be realized in those cases. In a substantial number of the remaining cases it can be expected that one of the tortfeasors will not be able to respond in damages, again frustrating the *Li* principle. In sum, although the majority devote approximately half of their opinion to asserted maintenance of the *Li* principle . . . , in only a very small number of multiple party cases will the loss be shared in accordance with that principle.

Attempting to justify their repudiation of the *Li* principle in favor of joint and several liability, the majority suggest three rationales. First, we are told that the feasibility of apportioning fault on a comparative basis does not "render an indivisible injury 'divisible,'" each defendant's negligence remaining a proximate cause of the entire indivisible injury. . . . The argument proves too much. Plaintiff negligence is also a proximate cause of the entire indivisible injury, and the argument, if meritorious, would warrant repudiation of *Li* not only in the multiple party case but in all cases.

The second rationale of the majority lies in two parts. First, we are told that after *Li* there is no reason to assume that plaintiffs will "invariably" be guilty of negligence. . . . Obviously this is true. The basis of joint and several liability prior to *Li* was that between an innocent plaintiff and two or more negligent defendants, it was proper to hold the defendants jointly and severally liable. The innocent plaintiff should not suffer as against a wrongdoing defendant. . . . Accordingly, it is not unreasonable to reject the *Li* principle when we are comparing the plaintiff's innocence and defendants' negligence. But the issue presented by this case is whether joint and several liability shall be extended to *Li* cases, cases where the plaintiff *by definition* is negligent. While we cannot know whether a plaintiff will be found negligent until trial, we also cannot know whether any given defendant will be found at fault until trial. Since liability is not to be determined until after trial, there is no reason not to deal with the real issue before us whether joint and several liability should be applied in cases where the plaintiff is found negligent – i.e., cases where by definition the plaintiff is "invariably" found negligent.

As a second part of the second rationale for joint and several liability we are told that a plaintiff's culpability is not equivalent to that of a defendant. This is obviously true – this is what *Li* is all about. The plaintiff may have been driving 50 miles in excess of the speed limit while the defendants may have been driving 10 miles in excess. The converse may also be true. But the differences warrant departure from the *Li* principle in toto or not at all.

The majority's third rationale for rejecting the *Li* principle is an asserted public policy for fully compensating accident victims. The majority state that joint and several liability "recognizes that fairness dictates that the 'wronged party should not be deprived of his right to redress,' but that '[the] wrongdoers should be left to work out between themselves any apportionment.' (*Summers* v. *Tice* (1948) [199 P.2d 1 . . .].)" . . . The quoted language is not helpful to the majority when the plaintiff is also negligent because he is himself a wrongdoer.

Until today neither policy nor law called for fully compensating the negligent plaintiff. Prior to *Li*, the negligent plaintiff was denied all recovery under the contributory negligence doctrine – the policy reflected being directly contrary to that asserted today. *Li*, of course, repudiated that doctrine replacing it with a policy permitting compensation of the negligent accident victim but only on the basis of comparative fault. Moreover, *Li* cannot be twisted to establish a public policy requiring rejection of its own irresistible principle. In sum, the majority are establishing a new policy both contrary to that existing prior to *Li* and going further than that reflected by the comparative principle enunciated in *Li*.

. . . In my view the majority's effort to resist the irresistible fails. They have furnished no substantial reason for refusing to apply the *Li* principle to multi-party litigation.

II

Adherence to the *Li* principle that the extent of liability is governed by the extent of fault requires that only a limited form of joint and several liability be retained in cases where the plaintiff is negligent.[4] The issue of joint and several liability presents the problem whether the plaintiff or the solvent defendants should bear the portion of the loss attributable to unknown defendants or defendants who will not respond in damages due to lack of funds.

Consistent with the *Li* principle – the extent of liability is governed by the extent of fault – the loss attributable to the inability of one defendant to respond in damages should be apportioned between the negligent plaintiff and the solvent negligent defendant in relation to their fault. . . . Returning to my 30-60-10 illustration, if the 60 percent at fault defendant is unable to respond, the 30 percent at fault plaintiff should be permitted to recover 25 percent of the entire loss from the 10 percent at fault solvent defendant based on the 3 to 1 ratio of fault between them. (The solvent defendant would have added to his 10 percent liability one-fourth of the 60 percent or 15 percent to reach the 25 percent figure.) To the extent that anything is recovered from the 60 percent at fault defendant, the money should be apportioned on the basis of the 3 to 1 ratio. The system is based on simple mechanical calculations from the jury findings.

Placing the entire loss attributable to the insolvent defendant solely on the negligent plaintiff or solely on the solvent negligent defendant is not only contrary to the *Li* principle, but also undermines the entire system of comparative fault. If the portion attributable to the insolvent defendant is placed upon the negligent plaintiff, the solvent defendant will attempt to reduce his liability by magnifying the fault of the insolvent defendant. Should the insolvent's portion be placed solely upon the solvent defendant – as done by the majority's application of joint and several liability – the plaintiff will have an incentive to magnify the fault of the insolvent defendant. . . . Because the insolvent – and therefore disinterested – defendant will usually not be present at trial to defend himself, any semblance to comparative fault will be destroyed.

Similarly, settlement rules should also reflect the *Li* principle. When a defendant settles, he should be deemed to have settled his share of the total liability and the pleadings and releases should so reflect. The nonsettling defendant should be liable only for the portion of the loss attributable to him – deducting from the total loss the amount attributable to the plaintiff's negligence . . . and the amount attributable to the settling defendant's negligence. This rule . . . would force a plaintiff to demand settlements reasonably commensurate to the fault of the

---

4   When the plaintiff is free of fault he is entitled to a joint and several judgment against each defendant in accordance with common law rule. The Li principle is inapplicable because there is simply no plaintiff fault for comparing with defendants' fault.

settling defendant because he will no longer be able to settle quickly and cheaply, then holding the remaining defendants for part of his codefendant's share of the loss. Granted, the nonsettling defendant will have an incentive to magnify the fault of the settling defendant, but it is not unfair to place the burden of defending the settling defendant upon the plaintiff for three reasons: He is the one who chose to settle, the settlement has eliminated any right of contribution or partial indemnity of the nonsettling defendant, and the plaintiff in obtaining his settlement may secure the cooperation of the settling defendant for the later trial.

III

"[Irresistible] to reason and all intelligent notions of fairness" (13 Cal.3d 804, 811), this court created a policy three years ago the majority today cavalierly reject without real explanation. Their attempted rationale for rejection of the *Li* principle insofar as it is based on a newly discovered public policy is entitled to little weight. The public has no such policy and any attack on the principle based on logic or abstract notions of fairness fail. The principle is transparently irresistible in the abstract.

If not applied across the board the *Li* principle should be abandoned. The reason for abandonment applies not only to multi-party cases but also to two-party cases, warranting total repudiation of the principle, not merely the majority's partial rejection.

While logically reasonable and fair in the abstract, the *Li* principle is generally unworkable, producing unpredictable and inconsistent results. Implementation of the principle requires judgment beyond the ability of human judges and juries. The point is easily illustrated. If the first party to an accident drove 10 miles in excess of the speed limit, the second 50 miles in excess, it is clear that the second should suffer the lion's share of the loss. But should he pay 55 percent of the loss, 95 percent or something in between? That question cannot be answered with any precision, and human beings will not answer it consistently. Yet that is the easiest question presented in comparing fault because we are dealing only with apples. When we add oranges to the comparison, there are no guidelines. If the first driver also was driving under the influence of Jack Daniels, reasonable judges and juries will disagree as to who shall bear the lion's share of the loss, much less the percentages. Finally, when the case is pure apples and oranges – one party speeds, the other runs a stop signal – there is no guide post, much less guidelines, and acting in furtherance of the *Li* principle, reasonable judges and juries can be expected to come up with radically different evaluations. . . .

In short, the pure comparative fault system adopted by *Li* not only invites but demands arbitrary determinations by judges and juries, turning them free to allocate the loss as their sympathies direct. We may expect that allocation of the loss will be based upon the parties' appearance and personality and the abilities of their respective counsel. The system is a nonlaw system. . . .

I do not suggest return to the old contributory negligence system. The true criticism of that system remains valid: one party should not be required to bear a loss which by definition two have caused. However, in departing from the old system of contributory negligence numerous approaches are open, but the Legislature rather than this court is the proper institution in a democratic society to choose the course. To accommodate the true criticism, for example, it might be proper to take the position that a negligent plaintiff forfeits part – but not all – of his recovery in a percentage fixed by the Legislature. A fixed percentage approach would eliminate the impossible task of comparing apples and oranges placed upon the trier of fact by *Li* and would provide the consistency, certainty and predictability which foster compromise and settlement. Although the percentage would be arbitrary, the allocation of loss as demonstrated above is necessarily arbitrary under the present system. . . .

NOTES

1   *Indivisible Harm.* In addition to joint liability for harm caused by defendants acting in concert (discussed in the immediately preceding section of these materials), here we have an example of joint liability for harm caused by two defendants acting independently but causing a single, indivisible harm.

2   *Contribution.* While defendants' liability to plaintiff has for decades now tended to be joint, this does not necessarily mean that one defendant can be saddled with the entire liability. While defendants are jointly liable to the plaintiff, defendants are severally liable between and among each other and may seek contribution from each other on a several basis. Since the widespread adoption of comparative responsibility, contribution between and among defendants generally has been on a comparative basis. If a defendant desires to have the contribution question decided in the same lawsuit in which defendant's liability to plaintiff is determined, the procedural devices of cross-claim and/or impleader are available. The contribution doctrine is discussed in more detail, *infra.*

3   *Joint v. Several Liability.* Under the approach adopted by the majority of the Supreme Court of California in this case, liability among defendants is "joint" whereas, by virtue of the Court's earlier decision in the *Li v. Yellow Cab, supra,* liability as between plaintiff and defendants is several. This is not the approach taken by every jurisdiction. Some jurisdictions have adopted the approach outlined by the dissent in this case.

4   *Intentional Torts.* Joint liability generally does not apply to intentional tortfeasors.

5   *Joint Liability in Retreat.* Especially with the widespread adoption of comparative responsibility, there has been a gradual retreat from joint and several liability. Some states, both by statute and by judicial decision, have done away with joint liability altogether, sometimes in conjunction with the adoption of comparative fault, resulting in pure several liability. *See, e.g., McIntyre v. Balentine, supra.* While most jurisdictions retain some form of joint and several liability, in most cases the doctrine has been modified (limited) in one way or another, often by statute. A number of states (e.g., California and New York) have limited joint liability for non-economic losses (usually pain and suffering damages) but retained it for economic losses. Some jurisdictions have applied a modified form of joint and several liability, applying joint liability to defendants whose share of comparative fault meets or exceeds a threshold (often 50%) and only several liability to those defendants whose comparative fault comes below the threshold. Some jurisdictions (e.g., New York and Illinois) tie joint liability to the degree of plaintiff's fault, applying joint liability only where plaintiff is either completely or nearly without fault. The effect of eliminating or limiting joint and several liability is to shift the risk of an insolvent defendant from other responsible defendants to the plaintiff.

2. SEVERAL/INDIVIDUAL APPORTIONED LIABILITY

When it is possible to divide a particular loss (causally) between or among multiple defendants (in other words, when the loss is "divisible"), then the responsible defendants will be held to be only "severally liable.

BARTLETT V. NEW MEXICO WELDING SUPPLY, INC.
646 p.2d 579 (n.m 1982)

This comparative negligence case presents two issues: (1) whether a tortfeasor is liable for all of the damages caused by concurrent tortfeasors under a theory of joint and several liability; and (2) whether the percentage of fault of a nonparty concurrent tortfeasor is to be determined by the fact finder.

The automobile accident involved three vehicles. The car in front of plaintiffs' car signaled a right hand turn. This lead car turned into and then pulled out of a service station in a very fast motion. Plaintiff Jane Bartlett slammed on her brakes to avoid hitting the lead car. Defendant's truck was behind plaintiffs' car. Defendant's driver applied his brakes; however, the truck skidded into the rear of plaintiffs' car.

The driver of the lead car is unknown. Plaintiff sued defendant on a theory of negligence. Defendant contended that the negligence of the unknown driver "caused or contributed to cause" the accident and resulting damages.

The trial court instructed the jury:

> If you find for the plaintiff but also find that the negligence of the plaintiff and/or the unknown
> third party contributed to cause the accident and resulting damages, then you must decide how
> much each party was at fault. The defendant is liable only for defendant's percentage of fault
> in causing the accident and any resulting damages and the total amount of damages to which
> plaintiff would otherwise be entitled shall be reduced in proportion to the percentage of plain-
> tiff's negligence and/or the negligence of the unknown third party.

The jury answered "special questions." It determined that plaintiffs' damages were $100,000.00, that plaintiffs were not negligent, that defendant was negligent, that defendant's negligence contributed to the accident and plaintiffs' damages to the extent of 30%, that the unknown driver was negligent and this negligence contributed to the accident and plaintiffs' damages to the extent of 70%.

Plaintiffs moved that judgment be entered in their favor in the amount of $100,000.00. This motion was not granted. Instead, the trial court ordered a new trial. The trial court was of the view that: (a) the above quoted instruction should not have been given; (b) that the case should not have been tried between plaintiffs, defendant, and the unknown driver; (c) that defendant is jointly and severally liable for the damages to plaintiffs caused by defendant and the unknown driver; and (d) "that a different result would have occurred had the jury known that this Defendant would have been responsible for the total damages under joint and several liability."

We granted defendant's application for an interlocutory appeal.

Joint and Several Liability

In this case, in using the term "joint and several liability," we mean that either of two persons whose concurrent negligence contributed to cause plaintiffs' injury and damage may be held liable for the entire amount of the damage caused by them. . . . It is not disputed that this is a common law rule which existed in New Mexico prior to . . . *Claymore v. City of Albuquerque*. In *Claymore*, this Court adopted pure comparative negligence. . . . It is not disputed that defendant and the unknown driver were concurrent tortfeasors.

The question is whether, in a comparative negligence case, a concurrent tortfeasor is liable for the entire damage caused by concurrent tortfeasors. . . . [J]oint and several liability, for concurrent tortfeasors, has been retained by judicial decision in pure comparative negligence states. We recognize that this retention accords with 2 Restatement of Torts, Second (1965), § 433A. *See*, Comment h to § 433A. Retention also accords with the Uniform Comparative Fault Act, § 2. . . . The retention of joint and several liability ultimately rests on two grounds; neither ground is defensible.

The first ground is the concept that a plaintiff's injury is "indivisible." The California Supreme Court, in *American Motorcycle Ass'n, supra*, followed this ground when it stated:

> [T]he simple feasibility of apportioning fault on a comparative negligence basis does not render an indivisible injury "divisible" for purposes of the joint and several liability. * * * In other words, the mere fact that it may be possible to assign some percentage figure to the relative culpability of one negligent defendant as compared to another does not in any way suggest that each defendant's negligence is not a proximate cause of the entire indivisible injury.

Thus, under the California Supreme Court decision, a concurrent tortfeasor, 1% at fault, is liable for 100% of the damage caused by concurrent tortfeasors, on the basis that the tortfeasor, 1% at fault, caused the entire damage. . . . The California Court of Appeal stated in *American Motorcycle Ass'n, supra*: "*Li* [where pure comparative negligence was adopted] accepts the ability of the fact finding process to apportion degrees of negligence. In so doing, it eliminates the previously assumed inability to apportion fault among tortfeasors as the foundation of joint and several liability." We are unwilling, as was the California Supreme Court, to say that although fault may be apportioned, causation cannot. If the jury can do one, it can do the other. . . . Joint and several liability is not to be retained in our pure comparative negligence system on a theory of one indivisible wrong. The concept of one indivisible wrong, based on common law technicalities, is obsolete, and is not to be applied in comparative negligence cases in New Mexico. . . .

The second ground is that joint and several liability must be retained in order to favor plaintiffs; a plaintiff should not bear the risk of being unable to collect his judgment. We fail to understand the argument. Between one plaintiff and one defendant, the plaintiff bears the risk of the defendant being insolvent; on what basis does the risk shift if there are two defendants, and one is insolvent? In our case, the risk factor arises because the concurrent tortfeasor, 70% at fault, is unknown. . . . Joint and several liability is not to be retained in our pure comparative negligence system on the basis that a plaintiff must be favored.

We hold that defendant is not liable for the entire damage caused by defendant and the unknown driver. Defendant, as a concurrent tortfeasor, is not liable on a theory of joint and several liability.

Non-Party Concurrent Tortfeasor

. . . *Brown v. Keill, supra*, stated in connection with the Kansas statute that:

> [T]he intent and purpose of the legislature * * * was to impose individual liability for damages based on the proportionate fault of all parties to the occurrence which gave rise to the injuries and damages even though one or more parties cannot be joined formally as a litigant or be held legally responsible for his or her proportionate fault.

Claymore, supra, had the same intent and purpose. . . . The trial court properly instructed the jury to consider the negligence and damage resulting from the negligence of the unknown driver.

The order granting a new trial is reversed. The cause is remanded with instructions to enter judgment in favor of plaintiffs, against defendant, for the 30% of plaintiffs' damages caused by defendant.

IT IS SO ORDERED.

3. CONTRIBUTION AND INDEMNITY

In those jurisdictions that retain joint and several liability in any form, it sometimes will be possible that plaintiff can require one defendant to pay more than his "share" of a judgment. In such situations, most jurisdictions permit the overpaying defendant to seek "contribution" from other defendants who have paid less than their "share." This was a change from the older common law rule, which foreclosed a blameworthy defendant from seeking to shift any part of the loss. Of course, in those few jurisdictions that have completely done away with joint and several liability, no defendant ever is required to pay more than his share of the judgment, so there is no occasion for contribution.

The first cases to permit a defendant to recover contribution from other defendants permitted contribution on a "pro rata" or "ratable share" basis. In other words, the liability was divided equally among the defendants. But with the widespread adoption of comparative responsibility, contribution now is more commonly permitted on a comparative basis.

UNIFORM COMPARATIVE FAULT ACT

§ 1. [Effect of Contributory Fault].

(a) In an action based on fault seeking to recover damages for injury or death to person or harm to property, any contributory fault chargeable to the claimant diminishes proportionately the amount awarded as compensatory damages for an injury attributable to the claimant's contributory fault, but does not bar recovery. This rule applies whether or not under prior law the claimant's contributory fault constituted a defense or was disregarded under applicable legal doctrines, such as last clear chance.

(b) "Fault" includes acts or omissions that are in any measure negligent or reckless toward the person or property of the actor or others, or that subject a person to strict tort liability. The term also includes breach of warranty, unreasonable assumption of risk not constituting an enforceable express consent, misuse of a product for which the defendant otherwise would be liable, and unreasonable failure to avoid an injury or to mitigate damages. Legal requirements of causal relation apply both to fault as the basis for liability and to contributory fault.

§ 2. [Apportionment of Damages].

(a) In all actions involving fault of more than one party to the action, including third-party defendants and persons who have been released under Section 6, the court, unless otherwise agreed by all parties, shall instruct the jury to answer special interrogatories or, if there is no jury, shall make findings, indicating:
    (1) the amount of damages each claimant would be entitled to recover if contributory fault is disregarded; and
    (2) the percentage of the total fault of all of the parties to each claim that is allocated to each claimant, defendant, third-party defendant, and person who has been released from liability under Section 6. For this purpose the court may determine that two or more persons are to be treated as a single party.

(b)   In determining the percentages of fault, the trier of fact shall consider both the nature of the conduct of each party at fault and the extent of the causal relation between the conduct and the damages claimed.

(c)   The court shall determine the award of damages to each claimant in accordance with the findings, subject to any reduction under Section 6, and enter judgment against each party liable on the basis of rules of joint-and-several liability. For purposes of contribution under Sections 4 and 5, the court also shall determine and state in the judgment each party's equitable share of the obligation to each claimant in accordance with the respective percentages of fault.

(d)   Upon motion made not later than [one year] after judgment is entered, the court shall determine whether all or part of a party's equitable share of the obligation is uncollectible from that party, and shall reallocate any uncollectible amount among the other parties, including a claimant at fault, according to their respective percentages of fault. The party whose liability is reallocated is nonetheless subject to contribution and to any continuing liability to the claimant on the judgment.

...

§ 4. [Right of Contribution].

(a)   A right of contribution exists between or among two or more persons who are jointly and severally liable upon the same indivisible claim for the same injury, death, or harm, whether or not judgment has been recovered against all or any of them. It may be enforced either in the original action or by a separate action brought for that purpose. The basis for contribution is each person's equitable share of the obligation, including the equitable share of a claimant at fault, as determined in accordance with the provisions of Section 2.

(b)   Contribution is available to a person who enters into a settlement with a claimant only (1) if the liability of the person against whom contribution is sought has been extinguished and (2) to the extent that the amount paid in settlement was reasonable.

§ 5. [Enforcement of Contribution].

(a)   If the proportionate fault of the parties to a claim for contribution has been established previously by the court, as provided by Section 2, a party paying more than his equitable share of the obligation, upon motion, may recover judgment for contribution.

(b)   If the proportionate fault of the parties to the claim for contribution has not been established by the court, contribution may be enforced in a separate action, whether or not a judgment has been rendered against either the person seeking contribution or the person from whom contribution is being sought.

(c)   If a judgment has been rendered, the action for contribution must be commenced within [one year] after the judgment becomes final. If no judgment has been rendered, the person bringing the action for contribution either must have (1) discharged by payment the common liability within the period of the statute of limitations applicable to the claimant's right of action against him and commenced the action for contribution within [one year] after payment, or (2) agreed while action was pending to discharge the common liability and, within [one year] after the agreement, have paid the liability and commenced an action for contribution.

§ 6. [Effect of Release].

A release, covenant not to sue, or similar agreement entered into by a claimant and a person liable discharges that person from all liability for contribution, but it does not discharge any other persons liable upon the same claim unless it so provides. However, the claim of the releasing person against other persons is reduced by the amount of the released person's equitable share of the obligation, determined in accordance with the provisions of Section 2. . . .

NOTE

1   Most jurisdictions have adopted a statute permitting some form of contribution among joint tortfeasors.

HYPOTHETICAL SCENARIO

Two neighbors independently start fires, both of which spread to plaintiff's property, one destroying the $100,000 house and the other destroying the $100,000 barn. Plaintiff successfully sues both. Defendant B is insolvent. What result under traditional joint and several liability? What if the fires merged to destroy both the house and barn? What result in jurisdiction that has eliminated joint and several liability?

This action was brought on behalf of Douglas Hillman, a minor, (hereafter plaintiff) to recover for personal injuries resulting from the horseplay of other students on a schoolbus .... The suit was against Lyle Wallin, the driver of the schoolbus, and LaDon Ellingson and Ronald Kleven, the student passengers who caused the injury. Defendant Wallin cross-claimed against both Ellingson and Kleven, seeking indemnity or contribution. The jury apportioned the negligence of Wallin at 76 percent and Ellingson and Kleven at 12 percent each. Wallin appeals from denial of his motion for a new trial. We reverse and remand.

The incident causing plaintiff's injury occurred during the regular bus trip carrying students to their homes after school .... Shortly after this trip began, a number of students on the bus began playing with a 1/4-inch plastic hose about 3 feet in length. Ellingson, an 18-year-old high school student, had brought the hose onto the bus concealed in his pocket. Ellingson and Kleven were seated near the rear of the bus while plaintiff was seated nearer the front. Kleven walked toward the front of the bus, stretching the hose with Ellingson holding the other end. When Kleven got to within 3 or 4 feet of the driver, the hose broke and struck plaintiff in the eye.

Wallin became aware of the plastic hose after the bus trip had begun. The bus was equipped with a large interior mirror which enabled the driver to see most students in the bus. Wallin observed Kleven stretching the hose down the aisle. Wallin, who ... had driven this same route for 3 years, knew it was his responsibility to maintain discipline on the bus but made no effort to do so until reaching the stopping point at the grade school. He testified that at the time of the injury, his attention was directed at semitractor traffic approaching him and a line of vehicles following him. ...

Contribution and indemnity are both equitable remedies to provide restitution to a tortfeasor based on the degree of his culpability for a negligent act. The remedies differ in the character and amount of restitution allowed a joint tortfeasor. "* * * Contribution is appropriate where there is a common liability among the parties, whereas indemnity is appropriate where one party has a primary or greater liability or duty which justly requires him to bear the whole of the burden as between the parties." *Hendrickson v. Minnesota Power & Light Co.* 258 Minn. 368, 371, 104 N.W. 2d 843, 847 (1960). ...

Wallin is liable only because of his failure to exercise reasonable care to prevent injuries caused by his student passengers. In *Hendrickson v. Minnesota Power & Light Co.* 258 Minn. 368, 373, 104 N.W. 2d 843, 848 (1960), we approved of a tortfeasor's receiving indemnity "[w]here the one seeking indemnity has incurred liability merely because of failure, even though negligent, to discover or prevent the misconduct of the one sought to be charged." Indemnity is permitted in some instances in favor of one wrongdoer because his negligence is imputed or vicarious. ...

In the case before us, the jury found that the bus driver was negligent in failing to properly supervise the children on the bus. Although he is legally responsible for injuries caused by student passengers which he could have prevented by using ordinary care, he is only secondarily liable for their negligent acts. We regard Ellingson and Kleven as being primarily liable. .

. . We might also characterize the negligence of the driver as "passive" and the wrongdoing of Ellingson and Kleven as "active." . . .

Thus, given the facts of this case, if we look to one of the guidelines of *Hendrickson*, or describe the duty and hence the liability of the bus driver as "secondary" and that of the two students as "primary," or characterize the negligence of the bus driver as passive and that of the two students as active, or determine that the wrongdoers are not *in pari delicto*, or if we look to the relative culpability of the parties, we conclude that indemnity should be awarded. All of these principles are merely attempts to establish guidelines leading to the ultimate goal of doing justice. So far, no one has come up with a complete answer and we will have to permit indemnity on a case-by-case basis where our sense of fundamental fairness seems to require it.

It follows from our decision on the indemnity issue that because of the difference in the nature of the legal responsibility of defendants for plaintiff's injuries, it was improper for the trial court to permit the jury to compare the negligence of Wallin with that of the students. In a claim for contribution between joint tortfeasors under a common liability, the respective liability is now apportioned under the comparative negligence statute according to their respective degrees of negligence. But in cases of indemnity, the comparison of negligence of parties who are primarily and secondarily liable for the injury is improper. . . . Speaking to this point, we said in *Keefer v. Al Johnson Const. Co.,* . . . 193 N.W. 2d 305, 311 (1971):

> . . . [T]he trial court was in error to instruct with reference to comparative negligence as it
> related to the third-party actions [for indemnity] between contractor and the subcontractor and
> to submit questions in the special verdict which would cast them in the situation of joint tortfea-
> sors, as if they were both liable in contribution. . . . Where there are elements of primary and
> secondary liability – which is ordinarily a question of law for the court – indemnity shifts the
> entire loss from one tortfeasor, who has been compelled to pay, to the shoulders of another who
> should bear it instead. . . . It should also be kept in mind that the difference between primary and
> secondary liabilty, as used in determining the right of indemnity, is based, not on a difference in
> degrees of negligence or on any doctrine of comparative negligence, but on the difference in the
> character or kind of wrongs which caused the injury and in the nature of the legal obligation
> owed by each wrongdoer to the injured person.

In the present case, the jury should not have been permitted to compare the negligence of the bus driver with the negligence of those primarily liable for plaintiff's injuries. Once the jury found the bus driver negligent, he is 100 percent responsible for his negligence but only in the posture of secondary liability. Although the jury was improperly comparing the negligence of these three defendants, it found each student defendant equally negligent at 12 percent each. Under these circumstances, the only fair and reasonable conclusion is that, had the jury not been comparing the negligence of Wallin, they would have found each student 50 percent primarily responsible for plaintiff's injuries.

We reverse and remand the case to the trial court with directions to amend its findings so as to find Ellingson and Kleven each 50 percent primarily negligent and Wallin 100 percent secondarily negligent. We also direct that Wallin is entitled to complete indemnity on his cross-claim against the student defendants, who shall be jointly liable on the indemnification claim. If either of the defendants Ellingson or Kleven fails to pay his share of the plaintiff's judgment and the other thereby becomes liable to indemnify Wallin for more than his share of the indemnification, such defendant shall be entitled to contribution from the other.

Reversed and remanded with directions.

IN RE OIL SPILL BY THE AMOCO CADIZ
954 F.2D 1279 (7TH CIR. 1992)

PER CURIAM. On the morning of March 16, 1978, the supertanker AMOCO CADIZ broke apart in a severe storm, spewing most of its load of 220,000 tons of Iranian crude into the seas off Brittany. The wreck resulted in one of the largest oil spills in history, damaging approximately 180 miles of coastline in one of the most important tourist and fishing regions in France. The clean up took more than six months and involved equipment and resources from all over the country. The disaster has had lasting effects on the environment, the economy, and the people of Brittany, and has resulted in numerous lawsuits. Thirteen years later, the matter is before us. . . . Before we begin, a brief history of the litigation and its cast of characters is in order.

I.

A.

The origins of the AMOCO CADIZ are not difficult to trace. The vessel was born of discussions that began in Madrid, Spain in May 1970 between Astilleros Espanoles, S.A., the shipbuilder who constructed the fleet in which Columbus voyaged to the New World, and Standard Oil Company of Indiana ("Standard") (now called Amoco) . . . . (For simplicity's sake, we generally will refer to Amoco and its various subsidiaries . . . as "the Amoco parties" or "Amoco.") . . . On May 30, Astilleros confirmed the content of the negotiations and submitted a bid to build . . . the AMOCO CADIZ . . . . Amoco accepted the bid by letter on June 18, and the parties signed off on the final contract and ship specifications in Chicago on July 31, 1970.

The contract required that the ship be built according to the American Bureau of Shipping's ("ABS") Rules for Building and Classing Steel Vessels. The ABS is a not-for-profit maritime classification society headquartered in New York that promulgates rules and sets standards for shipbuilding, design, and seaworthiness. The ABS's technical staff in London reviewed Astilleros's proposed plan for the AMOCO CADIZ to ensure that it complied with the ABS's Rules. The ABS examined the "general arrangement" plans – plans featuring the layout and list of components used in the various parts of the ship – as well as drawings related to the detailed design of the ship. (By "detailed design," we mean items as small as nuts and bolts.) The ABS stamped the plans and drawings with its Maltese cross emblem to signify its approval. The Amoco-Astilleros contract incorporated the general arrangement plans and required Astilleros to submit them to Amoco for acceptance prior to construction. Astilleros did so, but did not pass along to Amoco its detailed design drawings, calculations, or fabrication drawings showing the mechanical details of the steering mechanism's component parts. Amoco reviewed the design of the steering gear system and approved it on October 19, 1971. Amoco later made two modifications to the system: it designed a low fluid level alarm for the replenishment gravity tank and increased the size of the rudder. It chose not to include an optional hand charging pump. . . .

Pursuant to the contract, Astilleros built the behemoth at its shipyards in Cadiz, Spain. It took four years to complete the job. Throughout the construction process, both Amoco and the ABS had representatives on the scene at the shipyard. The Amoco representatives were concerned with deadlines and whether construction conformed to the contract specifications and general arrangement drawings. They also were present to witness tests of equipment and gear and to catch any problems that might have been missed in the plan approval process. The ABS representatives monitored the progress of the ship to ensure that construction was in conformity with the ABS's Rules. The Amoco representatives deferred to the ABS representatives' technical and engineering expertise in evaluating whether construction was proceeding as it should.

At long last, the vessel was finished. It measured 1095 feet long and 167 feet wide – the size of three football fields – and weighed 230,000 deadweight tons. It was powered by a 30,000 horsepower diesel engine driving a single screw and was equipped with a single rudder driven by a hydraulic steering engine. It had a hydraulic steering gear with movement of the rudder controlled by two pairs of rams contained in four cylinders that were filled with hydraulic fluid. The four rams were made of rolled steel and their heads were cast steel. Ram isolation valves controlled the flow of oil through the passages in the distribution block. These valves were a critical safety component. They could capture the remaining hydraulic fluid in the rams in the event of a rupture in the piping. The valves also could be closed to isolate the various lines from the rest of the system or to block the passage of oil to or from the cylinder.

The AMOCO CADIZ's steering system was supposed to work in the following manner. When the helmsman turned the steering wheel or when the ship operated on autopilot, an electronic signal was generated. In response to the signal, hydraulic fluid was moved by a series of pumps, which in turn moved the rams and, eventually, the rudder. The hydraulic fluid in the cylinders kept the rudder restrained and in the desired position by exerting pressure against the rams. There was no device aboard that could be used to steer the ship if the primary system failed. The ship was not equipped with twin screws, twin rudders, or bow thrusters that could be used to steer in an emergency. The anchor was underdesigned and could not be used as a stopping device in a crisis situation.

The ABS certified the ship – and its steering gear – as being in compliance with the ABS's Rules. Even after delivery, the ABS periodically conducted inspections of the AMOCO CADIZ to determine if it still was in seaworthy condition. Three times – June 1975, April 1976, and May 1977 – the ABS inspected the steering gear and pronounced it in working order.

B.

Amoco Tankers ("Tankers") . . . took delivery of the AMOCO CADIZ on May 11, 1974. Two weeks later, Tankers sold the vessel to Amoco Transport ("Transport") . . . . In June 1974, Transport entered into a consulting agreement with AIOC. The agreement provided that AIOC was responsible for the operation of the AMOCO CADIZ, including maintenance, repair, and train-ing of its crew. Transport remained the owner of the vessel. Long after delivery, in August 1975, representatives from Astilleros met with Amoco in Chicago to discuss contract guarantee terms. . . . Just like a home appliance, the AMOCO CADIZ came with a one-year guarantee. Astilleros agreed to repair or replace any defects in the ship or its equipment during its first year of opera-tion, 1974-75. Consequently, during that first year, the ship always had on board an engineer from Astilleros who was attuned to any problem that arose. After the one-year guarantee period had expired, AIOC took care of maintenance problems.

In June 1974, the AMOCO CADIZ was chartered to Shell International Petroleum. "Charter hire" is the expense charterers pay owners of vessels per long ton per day. During off-hire periods, such as when the vessel is in for repairs, charter hire payments stop. It thus is in the pecuniary interest of a chartered ship's owner to keep the vessel running. The Amoco-Shell time charter required annual drydocking of the tanker for maintenance, but for reasons of economy, Amoco unilaterally lengthened the interval between drydockings to eighteen months and made plans to extend the interval to two years. . . . The ABS rules required two-year intervals between drydockings unless the owner received special permission from the ABS. By January 1976, Amoco decided that time-chartered vessels would be drydocked every two and one-half years.

C.

In February 1978, the fully-staffed AMOCO CADIZ took on a load of crude oil . . . destined for Rotterdam around the Cape of Good Hope. The Italian crew was experienced and the officers all were properly licensed. With regard to training, Captain Pasquale Bardari and his officers and crew participated in on-shore classes and on-board safety exercises. The latter were con-ducted by representatives of Marine Safety Services, a British organization. In addition, the ship's library contained a collection of films, videos, and technical information pertaining to ship operations.

As the tanker approached western Europe, it sailed into a storm. Retired Royal Navy officer Leslie Maynard, an on-board representative of Marine Safety Services, later testified that he had seen worse weather only once, during a typhoon. The AMOCO CADIZ had the capacity to weather severe storm conditions and heavy seas if she was in seaworthy condition. Buffeted by the rough seas and high winds, the ship rolled heavily on March 15 and through the night of March 16. Despite the bad weather, the helmsman reported no difficulty with the steering mechanism. During their normal inspection rounds, the crew members reported no abnormali-ties in the steering room.

In the morning, while the AMOCO CADIZ was approximately nine miles off the French island of Ushant, its steering gear completely failed. The helmsman informed Captain Bardari, who broadcast a message to nearby ships giving the AMOCO CADIZ's position and a caution to stay clear. The crew raised "not-under-command" flags as an additional warning. Almost immediately, the ship's engineers examined the steering gear only to find that the "De" flange, which had held a pipe that carried oil from the port steering gear pump to the hydraulic oil distribution block, had come off. Oil was spurting everywhere.

The crew members discovered that five of the six steel studs holding the De flange and pipe to the distribution block had broken; no other studs had failed in the system. The failure of the studs allowed the rapid escape of hydraulic fluid out of the steering system and the immediate entry of air. One of the engineers futilely tried to stop the flow of oil by closing the port steering gear pump and the isolation valves on the distribution block. The chief engineer tried to replenish the system by adding hydraulic fluid to the steering gear gravity replacement tank, but the fluid level in the gravity tank did not drop as it should have if the steering mechanism had been functioning normally.

Because of the lack of hydraulic pressure, the rudder was unrestrained. Some of the crew unsuccessfully tried to control the swinging rudder with a block and tackle, while others tried to repair the flange connection and purge the air from the system. As the crew worked, a relief valve pipe blew off, and oil hit the ceiling of the steering compartment. With the relief valve blown, the rudder's unchecked movement became more violent until it crashed into its stops, breaking apart the steering gear and hurling metal parts in every direction. The chief engineer ordered an evacuation of the compartment after one of the crewmen was struck in the head with a piece of metal. The chief engineer then reported to Captain Bardari that the steering gear could not be repaired.

About two hours after the steering failure, Captain Bardari called for salvage tugboats. In response, the PACIFIC, a salvage tug in the fleet of Bugsier Reederei und Bergungs, A.G., a corporation organized under the laws of the then Federal Republic of Germany, arrived on the scene. Bugsier undertook salvage jobs only under a "Lloyd's Open Form" ("LOF") "No-Cure-No Pay" salvage contract. The tug did not begin operations immediately because Bardari had to call Chicago to find out if he could enter into such a deal. While the AMOCO CADIZ foundered, Amoco and the tug's captain, Hartmut Weinert, haggled over the LOF. Finally, Amoco and Captain Weinert came to terms. By then, the island of Ushant was less than six miles dead ahead, the shallow Chenal du Four on the port bow, and the rocky Finistere coast on the port beam. The wind was fierce, the seas high, and the AMOCO CADIZ pitched so wildly that her bow repeatedly plunged beneath the surface.

The PACIFIC approached and secured a fairlead on the bow of the AMOCO CADIZ intending to turn the ship to her starboard, head her out to sea, and then tow her in to shore. In hindsight, this strategy proved unfortunate. The PACIFIC was incapable of turning a ship the size of the AMOCO CADIZ into the wind and the towing chain broke. The PACIFIC made a second tow attempt by connecting to the stern of the tanker. By then, tidal currents and heavy winds had carried the AMOCO CADIZ dangerously close to the rocky and irregular Finistere coastline.

The tanker continued to roll on the rocks and sink into the shoals. As the PACIFIC continued its futile maneuvers, its captain received the following message from Marine Safety Services representative Leslie Maynard, "Sir, we are grounded." The AMOCO CADIZ began tearing in two and the PACIFIC lost contact altogether. Soon, the telltale odor of oil filled the air. Fifteen million gallons spilled into the sea during the first night alone.

D.

The resulting oil slick was eighteen miles wide and eighty miles long, one-fourth of the Breton coast. Over the weeks following the grounding of the AMOCO CADIZ 4,400 men and 50 vessels (which included ships and personnel from the British Royal Navy) were dispatched to aid in the clean up operations at sea. France sought more than 30 million francs for the cost of the clean up at sea . . . . The clean up on land took over six months and involved the participation of the French army. Heavy machinery and volunteers were recruited from all over France. Approximately 220,000 tons of oily waste the color and consistency of chocolate mousse were recovered from the beaches along the Cotes du Nord. The infusion of oil upset the delicate ecosystem along the coastline, destroying algae and ruining oyster and lobster beds. Especially hard hit was the Breton economy. Brittany is France's second most important tourist region after the Riviera. The claimed overall cost to France was an estimated $100,000,000 at the 1978 rate of exchange.

II.

In the aftermath of the environmental disaster, various parties brought lawsuits. The Republic of France ("France") sued Amoco to recover for pollution damages and clean up costs. Similar actions were brought by the French administrative departments of Cotes du Nord and Finistere ("the Cotes du Nord parties"), numerous municipalities called "communes, and various French individuals, businesses, and associations, including hoteliers and fisherman who lost business as a result of the oil spill ("the French claimants"). The Cotes du Nord parties and the French claimants charged Astilleros with negligence in designing and constructing the tanker. . . . Both the Cotes du Nord parties and Amoco sued Bugsier, the owner of the tug PACIFIC, claiming that it was negligent in attempting to tow the AMOCO CADIZ. . . .

In addition, the Amoco parties filed a third-party claim and cross-claims against Astilleros. Amoco filed for contribution from the ABS to the extent that the grounding was caused by ABS's negligence and breach of contract in approving the vessel design, inspecting it, and certifying its seaworthiness. The Cotes du Nord parties and French claimants also sued the ABS. The ABS settled these claims and sued the Amoco parties in New York, seeking reimbursement for expenses in connection with the settlement. Amoco . . . counterclaimed. Petroleum Insurance Limited ("PIL"), Royal Dutch Shell's subrogee, sought to recover from Amoco for loss of the oil cargo, claiming loss occurred through Amoco's lack of due diligence in making the vessel seaworthy and through Amoco's breach of the charter contract.

The various federal actions were bifurcated and brought before Judge Frank J. McGarr of the Northern District of Illinois. After consolidating the liability issues, Judge McGarr opened the bench trial on May 4, 1982. The liability phase would not end until late November of the same year. In an April 18, 1984 opinion, the court held Amoco Corporation, Astilleros (who neither participated in discovery nor in the trial), and Amoco Production Company jointly and severally liable to France, the Cotes du Nord parties, the French claimants, and to PIL. . . . Bugsier was exonerated on the claims brought against it by the Cotes du Nord parties. . . . Because of its settlement with France and the Cotes du Nord parties, the ABS did not participate in the liability trial. It still is part of a pending "tag-along" action in federal district court in Chicago in which Amoco is seeking contribution from the ABS.

The court subsequently held a second bench trial on the consolidated damages issues. . . . On October 5, 1987, the court awarded PIL 11,212,349.50 pounds sterling for the loss of Shell's oil cargo. . . . With regard to the other plaintiffs' damages, on January 11, 1988, the district court applied French law and ordered an award to cover costs of clean up and restoration incurred by France, the Cotes du Nord parties, and the French claimants. The court awarded statutory costs as well as compound prejudgment interest . . . for a total of nearly 600 million French francs.

When Judge McGarr retired in late January 1988, the case was reassigned to Judge Charles R. Norgle, Sr., who appointed Judge McGarr as a Special Master to resolve any remaining issues. Special Master McGarr issued his Final Report and Recommendations on October 31, 1989. Pursuant to Rule 53 of the Federal Rules of Civil Procedure, the Amoco Parties, France, the Cotes du Nord parties, Astilleros, and PIL filed objections. In March 1990, a hearing was held on those objections. Following the hearing, the district court adopted all of the Special Master's Recommendations relating to liability and damages and, on July 24, 1990, issued four separate final judgments awarding claimants damages in French francs and pounds sterling against the Amoco parties and Astilleros, jointly and severally. These consolidated appeals followed.

. . . The American Bureau of Shipping (ABS) certified that the AMOCO CADIZ was properly designed and constructed. Every year the ABS re-certified the AMOCO CADIZ as seaworthy. Amoco believes that the ABS accordingly bears some of the responsibility for the loss; so do the Cotes du Nord parties, which sued the ABS and settled their claims against it. After settling with the Cotes du Nord parties, the ABS paid the French State for a release in advance of litigation. The district court deducted from the judgment against Amoco the amounts the plaintiffs have received from the ABS.

Amoco is dissatisfied with this approach and wants either contribution from the ABS or a reduction in the plaintiffs' claims by the amount of the ABS's responsibility. It cannot have the former in this action, for the ABS is not a party. Amoco's suit seeking contribution from the ABS remains on the district court's docket. (We express no opinion on the question whether Amoco ultimately will be entitled to contribution.) Far better, from Amoco's perspective, would be a decision that it is not liable at all for that portion of the loss reflecting the ABS's share of the fault. A reduction in the allowable claims would eliminate Amoco's risk that it will lose the litigation against the ABS (or be unable to collect any judgment it receives); it also would reduce the headaches Amoco will confront as it tries to enforce its judgment for indemnity from

Astilleros. Such a reduction is appropriate, Amoco submits, because the plaintiffs settled their claims against the ABS on terms satisfactory to themselves. Amoco asks: if the ABS bears 20% of the fault and the plaintiffs settled for 10 centimes on the franc for that share of the damages, why should they be able to collect the other 90 from Amoco? According to Amoco, maritime law enforces a general comparative fault approach under which each party is responsible only for its own share. . . .

There are four potential rules:

No contribution: All defendants are jointly and severally liable for the full damages. A plaintiff may decide to collect any part of an award from any of the defendants. No one may obtain contribution from another person.

Contribution: All defendants are jointly and severally liable for the full damages. The prevailing plaintiff may decide to collect any part of the award from any of the defendants. A party called on to pay more of the award than its share of fault implies may obtain contribution from a party called on to pay less than its share.

Contribution plus settlement bar: The same as the contribution rule, except that one party may obtain contribution only from another that proceeds to judgment. By settling, a party escapes any liability for contribution. (Variant: By settling in good faith, that is, for a bona fide estimate of liability at trial, a party escapes any liability for contribution.)

Claim reduction: Defendants are jointly and severally liable, unless one or more settles. By accepting a settlement from any party, the plaintiff forgoes the ability to collect from the remaining defendants any damages attributable to the settling party's share of fault. The remaining defendants are not entitled to contribution from the settling party – because after claim reduction there is no excess payment for which contribution would be appropriate. This is sometimes called the "comparative fault" rule.

. . . *Cooper Stevedoring* adopted a contribution rule for admiralty cases. When contribution is authorized, the norm is ability to collect from any other party, including those who have settled. Contracts affect only the rights of the parties, yet a settlement-bar rule allows the plaintiff and one defendant to extinguish the rights of another defendant by a settlement contract to which that defendant is a stranger. . . . Many states have adopted the settlement-bar rule by statute. Uniform Contribution Among Tortfeasors Act § 4(b) (1955 rev.).

Amoco asks us to adopt the fourth approach, claim reduction. No case in the Supreme Court has done so for any subject. For that matter, the Court has never used a settlement-bar rule. . . .

These assessments are in concord on the following conclusions about the different rules in any system where liability is based on fault (we disregard the complications introduced by strict liability):

No contribution: This approach promotes settlements, not only because by settling a party buys peace but also because, by concentrating full liability on those who hold out through trial and judgment, it creates a distinct possibility that those who settle first will pay a lower share of the total damages. This effect magnifies the plaintiffs' total recoveries, for every dollar from a settling defendant is recovered with certainty even if the plaintiff would have failed at trial, and if the plaintiff succeeds at trial it always obtains full compensation. The magnification effect ensures adequate deterrence as well as full compensation; indeed it may over-compensate and thus over-deter. No contribution is also the cheapest for the courts, as there is no collateral litigation.

Contribution: Instead of the rush to settle under the no-contribution rule there is competition not to settle – for a settling defendant pays cash with certainty but does not buy peace, and may be called on to pay a full share if the plaintiff wins at trial, while a party going to trial may be able to obtain contribution from another defendant. Plaintiffs receive the actuarially correct amount of damages (the magnification effect discussed above disappears). Costs of administering the legal system rise, for courts must apportion damages. The costs of doing this may be steep, if the parties cannot agree on who should be responsible.

Contribution plus settlement bar: This removes the disincentive to settlement (now the settling defendant buys peace) but is otherwise similar to contribution. Administrative costs are higher than under no contribution, for even though it will not generally be necessary to decide on degrees of fault, it may be essential to inquire into the bona fides of a settlement, which extinguishes other defendants' right of contribution. Determining bona fides may require a mini-trial of the merits, to see whether the settling party indeed made a payment reasonably related to the strength of the plaintiff's claim.

Claim reduction: The effect on settlement is uncertain – defendants would love to settle (for they can buy peace, just as under no contribution), but settlement is costly for the plaintiffs, who get cash but relinquish not only their claim against the settling party but also a share of the claims against other parties. Bargaining should lead to actuarially fair settlements (if all defendants are solvent, an important qualification), and thus claim reduction has no *ex ante* effect on total compensation and deterrence . . . . Claim reduction may require substantial ancillary litigation to fix the amount of the carve-out. Further complications arise if the plaintiff settled with one party because of doubts about solvency, perhaps for the limit of insurance. Would claims against other defendants be reduced by the settling party's fault or only by the extent the settling party could have chipped into the pot after trial?

It should be clear from this recitation that none of the four approaches is without its problems, and that claim reduction in particular is no panacea. It creates a substantial possibility of extended collateral litigation. Take this case as an example. Thirteen years have passed since the grounding, almost two of them spent in trials on liability and damages. The record still does not permit a confident assessment of the ABS's proportionate fault (if any). A trial between the plaintiffs and Amoco over ABS's fault would be a curious adventure. ABS itself, the party with the best knowledge of its activities, would be on the sidelines (for it has settled); Amoco would try to magnify the ABS's contributions (to reduce its own liability) and the plaintiffs to belittle the ABS's role. Such a contest would make more sense if the ABS were brought back in, but as its own liability is fixed it would have no incentive to litigate (and such post-settlement litigation would remove the principal incentive to settle – the prospect of saving the costs of litigation). And the ABS is not necessarily the end. Amoco might point a finger at Bugsier, the owner of the tug PACIFIC. . . We are confident that the case would at last come to an end, but maybe not in this century. At all events, why should the judicial system invest so heavily in adjusting accounts among wrongdoers? Neither justification for the tort system – compensation of victims and the creation of incentives to take care – would be served by this collateral litigation. Conducting such cases would detract from the time courts have available to handle new claims by deserving persons.

. . . Only the claim reduction alternative would have required the district court to determine in this proceeding the degree of fault, if any, attributable to the ABS, and we approve the district court's decision not to adopt that alternative.

. . . The case is remanded for the entry of judgment in accordance with this opinion.

QUESTION AND NOTE

1   Which of the possible approaches to the contribution question do you think is best, and why?
2   *"Mary Carter" Agreements.* A "Mary Carter" agreement is a settlement with fewer than all defendants that guarantees plaintiff a minimum recovery and gives the settling defendant an offset to the settlement amount proportional to the sum that plaintiff recovers from any non-settling defendant(s). The settling defendant remains in the case and works to increase plaintiff's recovery against the other defendants. Quite a few courts have disapproved such agreements.

4. VICARIOUS LIABILITY

DEUTERONOMY 24:16

The fathers shall not be put to death for the children, neither shall the children be put to death for the fathers: every man shall be put to death for his own sin.

ROMANS 5:15-19

But not as the offence, so also is the free gift. For if through the offence of one many be dead, much more the grace of God, and the gift by grace, which is by one man, Jesus Christ, hath abounded unto many. And not as it was by one that sinned, so is the gift: for the judgment was by one to condemnation, but the free gift is of many offences unto justification. For if by one man's offence death reigned by one; much more they which receive abundance of grace and of the gift of righteousness shall reign in life by one, Jesus Christ.)

Therefore as by the offence of one judgment came upon all men to condemnation; even so by the righteousness of one the free gift came upon all men unto justification of life. For as by one man's disobedience many were made sinners, so by the obedience of one shall many be made righteous.

Many, if not most, of the cases included in these materials involve suits against deep pocket defendants, e.g., corporations. Frequently, this is accomplished through the doctrine of vicarious liability. Vicarious liability is a legal doctrine whereby one party is held liable for harm caused by the tortious conduct (usually negligence) of another. This counter-intuitive result usually is justified by pointing to some agency-like relationship (e.g., the employer/employee relationship) between the tortious actor and the vicariously liable party – the relationship is thought to make vicarious liability appropriate under the circumstances.

To understand vicarious liability, it is important to resist the natural inclination to think of the liability as being imposed because the vicariously liable party has somehow been "at fault." In a sense, vicarious liability is a form of strict liability, it has nothing to do with fault. Rather, it is a policy choice.

a. RESPONDEAT SUPERIOR

Respondeat superior (literally, "let the superior respond") is the most common application of vicarious liability – the employer is held responsible for the tortious conduct of the employee (who also is liable) when the conduct occurs during the course of and within the scope of the employment.

FRUIT V. SCHREINER
502 P.2D 133 (ALASKA 1972)

. . . At the time of the accident, Fruit, a life insurance salesman, was attending a sales convention of his employer, Equitable Life Assurance Society (Equitable). . . . Sales employees of the company were required to attend the convention. After discussing with district managers the possibility of transporting the Anchorage insurance salesmen to the convention by bus, the agency manager decided that participants should travel by private transportation, and . . . be reimbursed a lump sum for their expenses. Clay Fruit chose to drive his own automobile . . . . Insurance experts from California and Washington were also invited as guests to the convention, and the Alaska salesmen were encouraged to mix freely with these guests to learn as much as possible about sales techniques during the three-day gathering. Scheduled events included business meetings during morning hours, evening dinners and at least two cocktail parties. . . . A desk clerk . . . testified that loud and sometimes disorderly partying continued around the room of the agency manager and the adjoining porch and stairway until the early hours of the morning on Friday, July 11 . . . . A business meeting on Friday morning proceeded on schedule followed by a cocktail party and hors d'oeuvres in the room and adjoining spaces of the agency manager. Fruit went to the room of an out-of-state guest with whom he talked business and had drinks. Testimony indicates that by mid-afternoon Fruit was asleep on the floor. That evening, a scheduled cocktail party and seafood dinner on the beach proceeded without Fruit who was still asleep in a room adjacent to that of the out-of-state guest. At some time between 10:00 and 11:30 p.m. . . . other members of the group awoke Fruit who . . . walked to the Salty Dawg Bar and returned shortly. The others were tired and went to bed but Fruit decided to go to Homer as he was under the impression that the out-of-state guests were at the Waterfront Bar and Restaurant. Fruit then drove his car to Homer but departed when he did not find any of his colleagues.

His return . . . took him past the Salty Dawg Bar where Schreiner's automobile was disabled on or immediately off the side of the road opposite Fruit's lane. While the facts of the particular moment of the accident which occurred at approximately 2:00 a.m. on July 12, 1969, are unclear, it appears that Fruit applied his brakes and skidded across the dividing line of the highway, colliding with the front of Schreiner's car. The hood of Schreiner's automobile had been raised and Schreiner was standing in front of his car. The collision crushed his legs.

The subsequent amputation and crippling of Schreiner was exacerbated by a urinary disorder resulting from exploratory surgery necessitated by the accident. Schreiner sued Fruit and his employer, Equitable . . . . The jury found on special interrogatories that Fruit's negligence was the proximate cause of the accident; that he was acting within the course and scope of his employment for Equitable . . . and that Schreiner was not contributorily negligent. The jury awarded damages of $635,000 against both defendants. Both moved for a judgment notwithstanding the verdict and presently appeal from the respective denials of the motions. Equitable contends that the evidence was insufficient to establish that Fruit was acting within the course and scope of his employment at the time of the accident . . . .

EQUITABLE'S LIABILITY UNDER THE DOCTRINE OF RESPONDEAT SUPERIOR

. . . Under the doctrine of *respondeat superior* (which simply means "let the employer answer") Equitable would . . . be liable for Fruit's acts of negligence despite lack of fault on Equitable's part. Equitable argues, however, that the evidence was insufficient to establish that Fruit was acting within the course and scope of his employment. Equitable contends that any business purpose was completed when Fruit left the Waterfront Bar and Restaurant. It cites cases holding that an employee traveling to his home or other personal destination cannot ordinarily be regarded as acting in the scope of his employment. But Fruit was not returning to his home. He was traveling to the convention headquarters where he was attending meetings as a part of his employment.

In addition, Equitable seeks to narrow the scope of *respondeat superior* to those situations where the master has exercised control over the activities of employees. Disposition of this issue requires an analysis of the doctrine of *respondeat superior,* one of the few anomalies to the general tort doctrine of no liability without fault.

The origins of the principle whereby an employer may be held vicariously liable for the injuries wrought by his employee are in dispute. Justice Holmes traces the concept to Roman law while Wigmore finds it to be of Germanic origin. The doctrine emerged in English law in the 17th Century. Initially a master was held liable for those acts which he commanded or to which he expressly assented. This was expanded to include acts by implied command or authority and eventually to acts within the scope of employment. The modern theory evolved with the growth of England's industry and commerce.

A truly imaginative variety of rationales have been advanced by courts and glossators in justification of this imposition of liability on employers. Among the suggestions are the employer's duty to hire and maintain a responsible staff of employees, to "control" the activities of his employees and thus to insist upon appropriate safety measures; the belief that the employer should pay for the inherent risks which result from hiring others to carry on his business; the observation that the employer most often has easier access to evidence of the facts surrounding the injury; and the metaphysical identification of the employer and employee as a single "persona" jointly liable for the injury which occurred in the context of the business. [A commentator] cynically states: "In hard fact, the reason for the employers' liability is the damages are taken from a deep pocket."

The two theories which carry the greatest weight in contemporary legal thought are respectively, the "control" theory which finds liability whenever the act of the employee was committed with the implied authority, acquiescence or subsequent ratification of the employer, and the "enterprise" theory which finds liability whenever the enterprise of the employer would have benefited by the context of the act of the employee but for the unfortunate injury.

Since we are dealing with vicarious liability, justification may not be found on theories involving the employer's personal fault such as his failure to exercise proper control over the activities of his employees or his failure to take proper precautions in firing or hiring them. Lack of care on the employer's part would subject him to direct liability without the necessity of involving *respondeat superior*. The concept of vicarious liability . . . arises from the relationship of the enterprise to society rather than from a misfeasance on the part of the employer.

The aspect of the relationship most commonly advanced to delimit the theory is the "scope of employment" of the employee-tortfeasor. . . . To assist in delineating the areas of tortious conduct imposing liability, it is helpful to consider what we believe to be the correct philosophical basis for the doctrine. There was a time when the artisans, shopkeepers and master craftsmen could directly oversee the activities of their apprentices and journeymen. Small, isolated communities or feudal estates evinced a provincial sense of social interaction which ensured that many enterprises would conduct their businesses with a careful concern for the community of its patrons. But in the present day when hundreds of persons divide labors under the same corporate roof and produce a single product for market to an unidentified consumer, the communal spirit and shared commitment of enterprises from another age is sacrificed to other efficiencies. At the same time, the impersonal nature of such complex enterprises and their mechanization make third parties considerably more vulnerable to injury incidentally arising from the pursuit of the business. Business corporations are granted a personal identification in legal fiction to limit liability of the investors, but not to insulate the corporate entity itself from liability for the unfortunate consequences of its enterprise.

"Scope of employment" as a test for application of *respondeat superior* would be insufficient if it failed to encompass the duty of every enterprise to the social community which gives it life and contributes to its prosperity. . . . The basis of *respondeat superior* has been correctly stated as "the desire to include in the costs of operation inevitable losses to third persons incident to carrying on an enterprise, and thus distribute the burden among those benefited by the enterprise."[19]

The desirability of the result is readily discernible when an employee obviously engaged in his employer's business causes injury to a third party as a result of the employee's negligence. Thus, if an employee is engaged in trucking merchandise for an employer and through negligence in driving injures a pedestrian, it appears more socially desirable for the employer, although faultless itself, to bear the loss than the individual harmed. Insurance is readily available for the employer so that the risk may be distributed among many like insureds paying premiums and the extra cost of doing business may be reflected in the price of the product.

The principle has been recognized by every state in the enactment of workmen's compensation laws whereby employees may recover compensation for injuries arising out of and in the course of their employment without reference to negligence on the part of employers. The costs to the employers are distributed to the public in the price of the product.

Indeed the concept whereby the enterprise bears the loss caused by it has been recently extended to cover any loss caused by a defect in a manufactured product even without fault of employees or employers. The rule of *respondeat superior,* however, has not been extended to that length and is limited to requiring an enterprise to bear the loss incurred as a result of the employee's negligence. The acts of the employee need be so connected to his employment as to justify requiring that the employer bear that loss.

Although not usually enunciated as a basis for liability, in essence the enterprise may be regarded as a unit for tort as opposed to contract liability purposes. Employees' acts sufficiently connected with the enterprise are in effect considered as deeds of the enterprise itself. Where through negligence such acts cause injury to others it is appropriate that the enterprise bear the loss incurred.

Consistent with these considerations, it is apparent that no categorical statement can delimit the meaning of "scope of employment" once and for all times. Applicability of *respondeat superior* will depend primarily on the findings of fact in each case. In this particular case, Clay Fruit's employment contract required that he attend the sales conference. Each employee was left to his own resources for transportation, and many of the agents, including Fruit, chose to drive their own automobiles. By the admission of Equitable's agency manager, the scope of the conference included informal socializing as well as formal meetings. Social contact with the out-of-state guests was encouraged, and there is undisputed evidence that such associations were not limited to the conference headquarters . . . . Some agents, including Fruit, gathered with the guests in Homer the evening before the accident, and groups of agents and their wives visited the Salty Dawg on various occasions.

When Fruit left for the Waterfront Bar and Restaurant his principal purpose was to join the out-of-state guests. This testimony of his was further confirmed by the fact that once he discovered that they were not present at the Waterfront he departed immediately. Had he been engaged in a "frolic of his own" it would appear likely that he would have remained there. There was evidence from which the jury would find that he was at least motivated in part by his desire

---

19   Smith, *Frolic and Detour*, 23 Col.L.Rev. 716, 718 (1923).

to meet with the out-of-state guests and thus to benefit from their experience so as to improve his abilities as a salesman.

Because we find that fair-minded men in the exercise of reasonable judgment could differ as to whether Fruit's activities in returning from Homer to the convention headquarters were within the scope of his employment, we are not disposed to upset the jury's conclusion that liability for damages may be vicariously imputed to Equitable.

. . . The judgment below is affirmed.

QUESTIONS

1   Did the employer want the employee to engage in this particular conduct? Should it make any difference if the employer had specifically told salesmen to drive carefully and not to drink and drive? If not, why not? If so, why and how?
2   Should it make any difference if the salesman had been motivated by personal animus toward plaintiff?
3   *Direct v. Vicarious Liability.* If an employer has been careless in screening, training, or supervising its employees, the employer may be directly liable to parties injured by the employees' negligence. Vicarious liability attaches to the employer for tortious harm caused by its employees within the scope of employment even if the employer has exercised reasonable care in hiring, training and supervising. Of course, if the employee in question is an officer or director of the employer, that employee's conduct may be attributable directly to the corporation in support of a direct liability action without the assistance of vicarious liability.
4   *Frolic and Detour.* These words frequently are used to distinguish between a minor deviation from the employer's business (a mere detour) that does not destroy vicarious liability and an entirely new activity (frolic) that does. As one might imagine, the line between the two is not always particularly bright.

b. INDEPENDENT CONTRACTORS

The "rule" concerning the vicarious liability of independent contractors is quite simple – there is no vicarious liability. *Respondeat Superior* generally is limited to the employer/employee relationship. But exceptions make the analysis much more complicated, as illustrated by the following case.

MAVRIKIDIS V. PETULLO
707 A.2D 977 (N.J. 1998)

In this case, we revisit the parameters of the vicarious liability doctrine as it pertains to whether a contractee may be vicariously liable for the negligence of its independent contractor . . . .

I

This case arose from an automobile accident that resulted in severe injury to plaintiff Alice Mavrikidis . . . (Mavrikidis or plaintiff) . . . . On September 11, 1990, the intersection collision occurred after defendant Gerald Petullo, . . . operating a dump truck registered to Petullo Brothers, Inc. (Petullo Brothers), drove through a red light, struck plaintiff's car, hit a telephone pole, and then overturned, spilling the truck's contents onto Mavrikidis's car. At the time of the accident, Gerald was transporting 10.99 tons of hot asphalt, which had been loaded onto the truck . . . , to his job site at Clar Pine Servicenter (Clar Pine) . . . .

Prior to the accident, Clar Pine's owner, Karl Pascarello (Pascarello), decided to renovate the station . . . . Because Pascarello had no experience in the construction or paving business, he hired Gerald's father, Angelo Petullo, to perform the asphalt and concrete work as part of the renovation of his service station. . . . Pascarello hired Angelo by verbal agreement to participate in the station's renovations based on Angelo's reputation as an excellent mason and, to a lesser extent, the debt owed Clar Pine under the Petullo Brothers account. Over the years, Angelo and Gerald had charged gas and small repairs to their company account. In exchange for the asphalt work, both parties orally agreed that the Petullos would receive a $6,800 credit toward a $12,000 to $20,000 debt that Petullo Brothers had accumulated.

At trial, there was conflicting testimony whether Angelo or Gerald operated Petullo Brothers, a corporation that had been dissolved in 1978 by the New Jersey Secretary of State for nonpayment of annual fees. Although Angelo and Gerald both testified that Gerald had been running the company since 1982 and that Angelo formally transferred ownership to his son in 1989, Pascarello testified that he considered Angelo to be the company head and Gerald to be an employee who worked "hand in hand" with his father. Furthermore, a police officer testified that, at the accident site Angelo identified himself as the owner of Petullo Brothers. The jury concluded that Pascarello hired Angelo and Petullo Brothers to complete the asphalt and concrete work at the Clar Pine job site.

The Petullos supplied the labor, equipment, concrete, and most of the asphalt needed for the job, until Angelo "ran out of money" in the midst of the renovations. As a result, Pascarello provided him with a blank check made out to Newark Asphalt to purchase the asphalt on the day of the accident. Pascarello testified that he supplied Angelo with a check because he "[was] the type of person you don't give cash to." Nevertheless, it is undisputed that Pascarello was not involved in supervising the Petullos' work on a daily basis. Other than general supervision and periodic consultation, Pascarello's limited participation in the asphalt work consisted of payment for three loads of asphalt, including the one involved in this accident, as well as his direction to lay the asphalt in front of the service station's bay doors first to enable him to continue his automotive repairs while the gas station was out of service. . . .

On the morning of the accident, Gerald ordered twenty tons of asphalt from Newark Asphalt's plant. The employees of Newark Asphalt loaded 10.99 tons of asphalt, at a temperature between 300 and 310 degrees Fahrenheit, onto Gerald's truck and 9 tons onto a second truck. The vice-president of the asphalt supplier, Michael Manno, testified that its workers did not physically inspect its customers' vehicles to ensure their ability to carry a given load. Rather, he explained, Newark Asphalt is "like a grocery store." Its employees "are not policemen, we don't inspect anything." If the customer is able to pay, the customer will receive what is ordered.

The employees at Newark Asphalt, however, do conduct visual inspections of a truck to determine whether it can accommodate the requested load. According to Manno's testimony, such a visual inspection of Gerald's truck would lead to the conclusion that it could haul up to fifteen tons of asphalt in its truck bed. Yet, at the scene of the accident, Gerald admitted to the responding police officer that he was unable to stop at the red light because of the load on his truck.

The police also learned at the scene of the accident that Gerald's driver's license had been suspended. The officer issued two summonses to Gerald – one for failure to stop at a red light and the other for driving while on the suspended list. Shortly after the collision, Angelo arrived on the scene to assist in cleaning up the asphalt before it cooled and stuck to the roadway. The officer issued three summonses to Angelo, whose license had also been suspended – one for driving while suspended, one for having no vehicle insurance, and one for allowing an unlicensed driver (Gerald) to operate a vehicle. At trial, the officer explained that he issued the second and third tickets to Angelo because, as noted before, he identified himself as the owner of Petullo Brothers. Although Gerald and Angelo dispute their speaking with the officer at the scene of the accident, it was stipulated at trial that on February 26, 1991, both Petullos pleaded guilty in Bloomfield Municipal Court to driving while on the suspended list on September 11, 1990. At that same municipal hearing, Gerald also pleaded guilty to disregarding a traffic signal and failing to have insurance on the date of the accident. Furthermore, Petullo Brothers, through Gerald, pleaded guilty to operating an unsafe and overweight vehicle on September 11, 1990.

As a result of an inspection of Gerald's truck, conducted two days after the accident by a member of the commercial vehicle inspection unit of the Essex County Police Department, two weight violations were uncovered: (1) the truck's weight at the time of the accident exceeded the gross vehicle weight (GVW) of 32,000 pounds, for which it was registered with the Division of Motor Vehicles, by 866 pounds . . . and (2) the combined weight of the cargo plus the axle exceeded the statutory limit by 5,106 pounds. . . . Moreover, the testimony of plaintiff's expert indicated that the cause of the accident was primarily due to the truck being excessively overloaded by eighty-two percent. His calculation was based on Gerald's deposition testimony that the actual GVW for the truck was 18,000 pounds. The expert further testified that had the truck not been overloaded, Gerald would have maintained better control and required a shorter braking distance.

Pascarello testified that the Petullos' trucks appeared to be "junks" and would run for three to five days before breaking down. Specifically, Pascarello observed that the trucks had dents in the bumpers and fenders, loosened grills and tailgates, and frequent bald tires. None of those observations, however, implicated faulty brakes. Pascarello never repaired or inspected the dump trucks that the Petullos used to transport asphalt. He did not know that the trucks were uninsured. He also did not know that Angelo and Gerald had suspended licenses or that Gerald was a reckless or careless driver.

On December 6, 1990, Mavrikidis and her husband filed a complaint against Gerald, Angelo, Petullo Brothers, Geraldine Petullo (Angelo's wife), Ottavio Petullo (Angelo's brother), Newark Asphalt, and Clar Pine. . . .

In special interrogatories, the jury found that Gerald operated his truck negligently on September 11, 1990 and that his negligence was a proximate cause of the accident. The jurors further found that Gerald was acting as an agent, servant and/or employee of Angelo at the time of the accident. In addition, the jury found that Newark Asphalt was negligent in overloading the truck and that its negligence was also a proximate cause of plaintiff's injuries. . . . Furthermore, the panel found that Clar Pine retained control of the "manner and means" of performing the paving work at the station and that such work, "i.e. the transport and/or paving of hot asphalt, [was] an inherently dangerous activity."

Specifically, the jury determined that Gerald was 48% negligent; Angelo was 24% negligent; Newark Asphalt was 11% negligent; and Clar Pine was 17% negligent. The jury awarded $750,000 in damages to plaintiff and $30,000 to her husband. . . . Subsequently, the trial court molded the verdict. In that verdict, the court found Angelo vicariously liable for all of Gerald's negligence. Therefore, Angelo was liable for the 24% share attributed to him by the jury as well as the 48% attributed to Gerald. Based on the finding that Clar Pine was vicariously liable for its independent contractor, Angelo, the court entered a judgment against Clar Pine for 89% of the total damages awarded, including the 17% attributed directly to Clar Pine by the jury, the 24% attributed to Angelo, and the 48% attributed to Gerald. The court also entered judgment against Newark Asphalt for eleven percent of the total damages awarded. Clar Pine and Newark Asphalt appealed. The Appellate Division reversed with respect to Clar Pine, holding there was insufficient evidence to support a finding of vicarious liability on the part of Clar Pine . . . .

II

The first question is whether Clar Pine is vicariously liable for plaintiff's injuries. As we explained in *Majestic, supra*, the resolution of this issue

> must be approached with an awareness of the long settled doctrine that ordinarily where a
> person engages a contractor, who conducts an independent business by means of his own
> employees, to do work not in itself a nuisance (as our cases put it), he is not liable for the negli-
> gent acts of the contractor in the performance of the contract.

[*Id.* at 430-31].

. . . The initial inquiry in our analysis is to examine the status of the Petullos in relation to Clar Pine. Despite plaintiff's alternate theories to the contrary, the Petullos were independent contractors rather than servants of Clar Pine. The important difference between an employee and an independent contractor is that one who hires an independent contractor "has no right of control over the manner in which the work is to be done, it is to be regarded as the contractor's own enterprise, and he, rather than the employer is the proper party to be charged with the responsibility for preventing the risk, and administering and distributing it." (quoting *Prosser & Keeton on the Law of Torts* § 71 (5th ed. 1984). . . .

In contrast, a servant is traditionally one who is "employed to perform services in the affairs of another, whose physical conduct in the performance of the service is controlled, or is subject to a right of control, by the other." W. Page Keeton, *Prosser & Keeton on the Law of Torts* § 70 at 501 (5th ed. 1984).

In determining whether a contractee maintains the right of control, several factors are to be considered. The Restatement (Second) of Agency sets forth these factors, including:

    a.   the extent of control which, by the agreement, the master may exercise over the details of the work;

    b.   whether or not the one employed is engaged in a distinct occupation or business;

                      * * *

    d.   the skill required in the particular occupation;

    e.   whether the employer or the workman supplies the instrumentalities, tools, and the place of work for the person doing the work;

    f.   the length of time for which the person is employed;

    g.   the method of payment, whether by the time or by the job;

    h.   whether or not the work is a part of the regular business of the employer; [and]

    i.   whether or not the parties believe they are creating the relation of master and servant

    . . . .

[Restatement (Second) of Agency § 220(2) (1958).]

Applying those Restatement factors, it is evident that neither Angelo nor Gerald was a servant of Clar Pine. The masonry work required a skilled individual. Although Pascarello paid for three loads of asphalt, the Petullos provided their own tools and the remainder of the needed materials, other than bolts and plywood supplied by Pascarello to install the canopies. Their work did not involve the regular business of Clar Pine. In addition, the period of employment spanned only the time it took to lay the asphalt and concrete. Following the accident, the Petullos continued the job for which they were hired, which was approved by the Building Inspector of Montclair. In exchange for their services, the Petullos were not paid by the hour or month; instead, they received a discharge of the portion of their debt.

Based on that threshold determination, we now must determine whether this case falls within any exceptions to the general rule of nonliability of principals/contractees for the negligence of their independent contractors. There are three such exceptions, as delineated by the Majestic Court: "(a) where the landowner [or principal] retains control of the manner and means of the doing of the work which is the subject of the contract; (b) where he engages an incompetent contractor; or (c) where . . . the activity contracted for constitutes a nuisance per se." *Majestic, supra,* 30 N.J. at 431. . . .

V

Next, we consider the application of the third Majestic exception – whether the work engaged in by Petullo Brothers was inherently dangerous. . . . The definition of inherently dangerous set forth in *Majestic* comports with the discussion in sections 413, 416, and 427 of the Restatement (Second) of Torts (1965) regarding a contractee's nondelegable duty to take special precautions against dangers that arise from inherently dangerous work. The comments and illustrations following those sections explain that in cases in which the work relates to the transport of materials, the contractee is not responsible for the ordinary risks or dangers associated with faulty brakes or poor driving. In discussing the meaning of "peculiar risk and special precautions," comment b to section 413 states:

> It is obvious that an employer of an independent contractor may always anticipate that if the contractor is in any way negligent toward third persons, some harm to such persons may result. Thus one who hires a trucker to transport his goods must, as a reasonable man, always realize that if the truck is driven at an excessive speed, or with defective brakes, some collision or other harm to persons on the highway is likely to occur. . . . [Routine] precautions are the responsibility of the contractor . . . .

[Restatement (Second) of Torts, (1965), § 413 comment b.] A peculiar risk is different "from the common risks to which persons in general are commonly subjected by the ordinary forms of negligence." *Id.* § 416 comment d. As a result, "the [contractee] is not liable for the contractor's failure to inspect the brakes on his truck, or for his driving in excess of the speed limit, because the risk is in no way a peculiar one, and only an ordinary precaution is called for." *Ibid.* . . .

[I]n this case, neither Gerald's negligent driving nor overloading the truck were inherent in the work being performed by Petullo Brothers. Clar Pine was justified in presuming that the Petullos would operate their vehicles safely and in accordance with the traffic laws; Clar Pine was further justified in presuming that the Petullos and their supplier would not overload their trucks. The risk of an accident between Gerald and an innocent third party was unrelated to the transportation of asphalt. Rather, the risk was directly connected to his negligent and careless driving (running the red light) as well as the failure of the brakes, which resulted from the overloading of the truck and/or its disrepair. Although the consequences of the accident were more severe due to the contents of the truck at the time of the accident, the accident itself did not arise out of any peculiar risk inherent to the transportation of asphalt.

Poor driving, faulty brakes, and overloading are ordinary risks associated with motor vehicles and the transport of materials, and as such, are the responsibility of the contractor. Clar Pine did not have a nondelegable duty to take special precautions to prevent those risks. Absent proof that the contractee was aware of an enhanced risk that Petullo Brothers would drive negligently or would overload their vehicles, Clar Pine will not be held vicariously or independently liable for the ordinary dangers that arise from normal human activity, in this case, driving. . . . In this case, reasonable men could not differ that the work for which Clar Pine contracted with

Petullo Brothers, paving, was not inherently dangerous. As a matter of law, Clar Pine was not vicariously liable under that exception. . . .

VIII

We affirm the Appellate Division's judgment and remand for a reallocation trial to determine the appropriate percentage of liability to be attributed to the Petullos and Newark Asphalt. . . .

c. JOINT ENTERPRISE

Probably the second most common scenario for applying vicarious liability is where defendant is held liable for the tortious conduct of another with whom defendant is engaged in a joint enterprise.

POPEJOY V. STEINLE
820 P.2D 545 (WYO. 1991)

Appellants Ronald L. and Doris J. Popejoy (Popejoys) appeal the trial court's order granting summary judgment to appellees Carl Steinle and the Converse County Bank as personal representatives of the William E. Steinle Estate (Estate). Claiming that a joint venture relationship existed between William and his wife Constance E. (Connie) Steinle, the Popejoys seek to hold William's estate vicariously liable for Connie's alleged negligence in causing a traffic accident in which Ronald Popejoy was injured. We affirm the trial court's order granting summary judgment.

FACTS

On the morning of May 8, 1986, Connie Steinle, accompanied by her seven-year-old daughter and a niece, left the family ranch for Douglas, Wyoming. The purpose of the trip was to purchase a calf for the daughter to raise on the ranch. While en route to Douglas, the truck Connie was driving collided with a vehicle driven by Ronald Popejoy. Connie died as a result of the accident and Ronald sustained injuries initially diagnosed as a muscle strain. As a result of his injuries, Ronald received outpatient medical treatment at a local hospital. One week after the accident William Steinle completed the calf purchase for his daughter. The calf was raised on the Steinle ranch and sold the following year. The daughter received the proceeds from the sale.

Approximately fifteen months after the accident Ronald Popejoy began experiencing severe pain in his neck and back. Because other treatments failed to correct the problem, he underwent two separate neurosurgeries to fuse cervical vertebrae. Following the second surgical procedure, Ronald attempted unsuccessfully to reopen Connie Steinle's estate which had been probated and closed more than a year earlier. The Popejoys then filed a creditor's claim against William's estate as he had died in the interim following Connie's death. After the Popejoys' creditor's claim was rejected, they filed a complaint against the personal representatives of William's estate. The complaint was premised on the theory that William and Connie Steinle were engaged in a joint venture when Connie embarked on her May 8, 1986 "business trip" to pick up the daughter's calf.

After answering the complaint, the Estate filed a motion for summary judgment. The motion, supported by the affidavits of three Steinle family members, was heard by the trial court and subsequently denied. In his decision letter denying summary judgment, the trial court judge stated in part: "There is in my mind a geuine [sic] issue of material fact as to the financial and business structure of the Steinle Ranch operation."

. . . The Estate then filed a second motion for summary judgment accompanied by additional supporting documents. This motion was heard and granted by the trial court on June 6, 1990. In its decision letter, the trial court stated:

> It is the decision of the Court that there is not a genuine issue of material fact to present to a jury in this case and I will award summary judgment to the Defendants.
>
> It has been the hope of the Court that since the date of the last argument on Defendant's Motion For Summary Judgment, that discovery would reveal facts which could be determined as genuine issues involving the relationship between the Defendant, his wife and children.
>
> In a careful reading of the depositions and affidavits, it appears that there was not a financial[,] pecuniary or other interest which would result in a contingent liability upon the Defendant and present a genuine issue of material fact for presentation to a jury. . . .

DISCUSSION

The Popejoys seek to impute Connie Steinle's alleged negligence to her husband William's estate by claiming that the Steinles were engaged in a joint venture relationship at the time of the accident. . . . Consequently, the Popejoys are required to . . . show that the joint venture relationship existed at the time of Connie's alleged negligent conduct. . . . [I]n *Holliday v. Bannister*, 741 P.2d 89, 93 n.1 (Wyo. 1987), this court suggested that the statement of the elements of a joint enterprise set forth in *Endresen* appeared to be a "chopped version" of the elements as stated by the Restatement (Second) of Torts §491 comment c at 548 (1965), [which defines] the four elements of a joint enterprise as:

> (1) an agreement, express or implied, among the members of the group; (2) a common purpose to be carried out by the group; (3) a community of pecuniary interest in that purpose, among the members; and (4) an equal right to a voice in the direction of the enterprise, which gives an equal right of control.

Id. . . . The Popejoys' claim in this case is premised on a theory of joint venture and the contention that William and Connie Steinle were engaged in securing an appreciable business asset for their family business at the time of the accident. . . . Thus, in determining the existence or nonexistence of a joint venture relationship in this case, we apply the same four-pronged joint enterprise test . . . .

In support of its second motion for summary judgment, the . . . daughter who was accompanying her mother at the time of the accident and who was the intended recipient of the calf they were on their way to buy submitted an affidavit stating that her father did not ordinarily have any ownership interest in the cattle that she, her sisters and mother raised and owned. She also stated that she, her mother and sisters were primarily responsible for caring for the "pets" and other domestic animals raised on the ranch. Carl Steinle, William's brother and one of two personal representatives of the Estate, submitted an affidavit indicating that Connie and the Steinle daughters regularly kept numerous farm animals as their own and that William would not have had any interest in the calf that was to be purchased. Further, he stated that the purpose of the trip was to purchase a calf for the daughter to raise as her own. A second Steinle daughter also submitted an affidavit confirming the purpose of the trip.

Other materials submitted with the motion supplemented the affidavits described above and included the affidavit and deposition of Roger Wesnitzer, a certified public accountant. After reviewing Steinle tax records, ranch journal books, bank records, livestock sales receipts and the other affidavits and depositions, Wesnitzer stated that other livestock raised by the Steinle daughters in the past had been given directly to the children by the parents. Further, he stated that while William Steinle bore the costs of raising such livestock on his ranch, sale proceeds went directly to the children. Similar "nonranch" cattle owned by the Steinle daughters in the past had been separately identified by brands owned by the daughters and sale proceeds had gone directly to the children. He stated that William and Connie did not share in any portion of livestock sale proceeds of their daughters' cattle. . . .

Though Wesnitzer did not offer his opinion as to the specific intention of the parties in attempting to purchase the particular calf on the day of the accident (the same calf which was eventually purchased by William for his daughter a week after the accident), evidence exists that the calf in question would have been purchased, branded, raised and sold in identical fashion to other similar "nonranch" livestock. In other words, the calf that Connie was on her way to purchase at the time of the accident would have been paid for by the parents; it would have been branded with a brand registered and owned by one of the daughter's older sisters; it would have been raised with other livestock on the family ranch; and any profits from the eventual sale of the animal would have gone directly to the daughter. Neither side submitted any evidence or argument to the contrary. . . .

In attempting to demonstrate existence of a joint venture relationship, the Popejoys relied extensively on the affidavits provided by Ted Grooms, a certified public accountant. Grooms stated in his first affidavit that William and Connie Steinle did not separate their income and expenses with respect to their ranching activities and that Connie did much of the work around the ranch because of William's poor health. In his second affidavit, Grooms maintained that after reviewing all the depositions, affidavits, business and tax records submitted by the Steinles for the years 1982-1986 he was convinced that William and Connie were involved in a joint venture at the time of Connie's trip on May 8, 1986. Grooms stated that William's eventual purchase of the calf for his daughter a week after the accident, his efforts in raising and selling the calf, and the fact that the calf bore the brand of the daughter's older sister led him to the conclusion that a joint venture relationship existed between Connie and William. Finally, and significantly, he stated that it was his understanding that only a pecuniary interest and not an interest in profit was needed to show existence of a joint venture.

Noticeably missing from Grooms' testimony is any evidence that proceeds from the sale of the calf that Connie and the daughter were on their way to purchase on May 8, 1986, would not have gone solely to the daughter. Along the same lines, he found no evidence that proceeds from the actual sale of the calf that was eventually purchased for the daughter following the accident went to anyone other than the daughter. Thus, it appears that only the daughter had an actual pecuniary or financial interest in the profits of the sale of the calf that was to be purchased at the time of the accident.

The record in this case shows that Connie's trip to Douglas to purchase a calf for the couple's seven-year-old daughter was a family undertaking. Assuming, *arguendo,* that William agreed with his wife to share in the expense of purchasing and raising the calf in question, this only demonstrates that, at most, the couple may have had an agreement with a common purpose and that they shared a substantially equal right of control in decision making (the first, second and fourth elements of the four-part *Holliday* "test" for joint enterprise).

That William may ultimately have shared in some or all of the expenses of purchasing and raising his daughter's calf does not mandate existence of a joint venture. "The mere sharing of incidental expenses *** does not, however, constitute the business purpose essential to a joint venture * * *." *Galliher v. Holloway,* 130 Ill.App.3d 628, 85 Ill.Dec. 837, 474 N.E.2d 797, 802 (1985). Also, the materials submitted by the Estate with its second motion for summary judgment support the conclusion that it was the intent of both parents to brand the calf with an older sister's brand rather than the brand used for regular ranch livestock. The calf was to be accounted for separately from other cattle on the ranch and the daughter was to receive the full benefit of the proceeds from the eventual sale of the calf. This contention is strengthened by unrefuted evidence that William and Connie Steinle had helped purchase, raise and sell calves for their offspring under identical circumstances in the past. It is further strengthened by the manner in which the surviving family members handled the calf when the purchase was actually completed a week after Connie's accident.

Thus, though three of the four essential elements of a joint venture may have been present at the time of the accident, the record in this case does not demonstrate that William and Connie Steinle shared the requisite financial, pecuniary or profit motive interest in this particular calf. The Popejoys failed to refute evidence that the parents intended for the calf to belong to the daughter and that although the daughter would raise the calf on the family ranch, it would still be her own and she would enjoy all proceeds from the eventual sale of the calf. This example of parental nurturing, familial accommodation and generosity does not justify imputing negligence from one parent to the other.

Regardless of whether or not William and Connie were engaged in a joint venture in the course of their other ranching activities, Connie's trip to purchase a calf for their daughter was a separate, distinguishable event and not a part of the general course of the commercial ranching business in which William and Connie were otherwise associated. We recognize the possibility that in other aspects of their ranch operation William and Connie Steinle may have been joint venturers. Under circumstances not present in this case, vicarious liability might attach to a non-negligent spouse engaged in a family-owned business venture.

In the present case, however, there was no evidence presented at the summary judgment stage to show that William and Connie were engaged in a joint venture at the time of the accident. The events and circumstances preceding Connie's accident dictate that the relationship between the parents involved only the common purpose of child rearing and teaching the responsibility of caring for livestock. . . .

CONCLUSION

In *Holliday,* this court adopted and applied a narrow definition of joint enterprise. . . . By limiting the application of the doctrine to a venture having a distinct business or pecuniary purpose, we avoid the imposition of a basically commercial concept upon relationships not having this characteristic. . . . With our decision in this case, we . . . continue to restrict application of the joint venture/joint enterprise doctrine in Wyoming.

After a careful review of the record, we hold that the Popejoys failed to demonstrate the existence of a genuine issue of material fact [,] which would preclude summary judgment as a matter of law. William and Connie Steinle were not engaged in a joint venture when Connie attempted to drive to Douglas to purchase the calf for their daughter.

The decision of the trial court is affirmed.

d. BAILMENTS

SHUCK V. MEANS
226 N.W.2D 285 (MINN. 1974)

One of these actions was brought by Carol L. Shuck to recover for personal injuries sustained in an automobile accident involving a vehicle owned by defendant Hertz Rent-A-Car and driven by defendant David Means, age 18. . . .

The parties to these suits stipulated to plaintiff Shuck's damages, to the negligence of Means, and also to the liability of Hertz conditioned on a finding that Means' use of the vehicle was with Hertz' permission and consent. The issues were then submitted to the court upon the record without oral testimony other than depositions, resulting in findings . . . . Means' use of the Hertz vehicle at the time of the accident was with the permission and consent of Hertz. . . . We affirm.

On March 27, 1967, an automobile owned by Hertz, leased to one George A. Codling, and driven by Means, collided with an automobile in which plaintiff Shuck was a passenger. Means was uninsured at the time of the accident and the parties later stipulated that he had been negligent. The rental agreement signed by Codling was a standard form which provided that persons under 21 years of age were not allowed to operate the vehicle. The Hertz employee who had rented the car to Codling was deposed on the subject of Hertz' policy regarding minors, but she had no recollection of that particular rental transaction. In its answer to plaintiff's complaint, Hertz denied that its vehicle was being used with permission, and alleged that its possession by Means was obtained by fraud through a conspiracy between Means and Codling. And in a cross-claim against Means, Hertz alleged that Means, who could not himself obtain a vehicle from Hertz because of his age, conspired with Codling to have the latter obtain the vehicle ostensibly for his own use but in fact for the use of Means. Despite these allegations, the record is completely devoid of anything which could directly support a finding of fraud, leaving for our consideration only the following issue: Whether a car rental agency is liable under the Minnesota Safety Responsibility Act when one of its cars is leased by one person, but operated by another in violation of the rental agreement.

The applicable owner-consent statute, Minn. St. 1965, § 170.54, provides as follows: "Whenever any motor vehicle * * * shall be operated upon any public street or highway of this state, by any person other than the owner, with the consent of the owner, express or implied, the operator thereof shall in case of accident, be deemed the agent of the owner of such motor vehicle in the operation thereof."

This provision, enacted as part of the Safety Responsibility Act, was intended to make the owners of motor vehicles liable to those injured by their operation where no such liability would otherwise exist, giving such injured persons more certainty of recovery by encouraging owners to obtain appropriate liability insurance. And to that end, the statute is to be given a liberal construction. . . .

Proving lack of consent in these situations requires a strong showing that the car was being used by the permittee without the owner's knowledge and contrary to his explicit instructions, or that the subpermittee was driving without the permission of the first permittee under conditions which approach the status of conversion or a theft. . . . Neither of these situations is shown by the facts of the instant case, and the trial court's finding that implied consent existed is justified under the aforementioned cases unless the holdings of those cases are confined to situations involving permittees who are minor children of the owners. Such a narrow application of those cases would be inappropriate in light of the purpose of the owner-consent statute and the commercial nature of the transaction here involved.

. . . Accordingly, the trial court was correct in concluding that Means was operating the vehicle with the implied consent of Hertz.

Affirmed.

VI.

CAUSATION

Even if plaintiff can prove that defendant breached a duty of due care to her and that she suffered an injury, she still has no cause of action against defendant unless she can prove a connection between that breach of duty and that injury. We call that necessary link between defendant's negligent conduct and plaintiff's injury "causation." The causation question is not as simple as it sounds. In the most general terms, the concept of causation assures that defendants are held legally responsible only for harm that they brought about, a proposition that usually is not very controversial. But the causation requirement can produce results that seem somewhat arbitrary – two defendants can engage in identical conduct, but if the conduct of one happens to cause harm in fact while the conduct of the other does not, the resulting legal implications of the identical conduct of the two defendants can be vastly different.

The causation inquiry usually is divided into two parts: 1) cause in fact; and 2) proximate cause. (The Restatement (Third) of Torts would substitute for the phrase "proximate cause" another phrase that is thought to be more descriptive – "scope of liability.") A defendant's conduct is the "cause in fact," "actual cause," or "but-for cause" of plaintiff's injury if defendant's conduct is one of the links in the chain of events that in fact led to plaintiff's harm. The list of events that are causes in fact of any particular injury is quite long. Essentially, the jury must imagine a world in which everything was the same except that defendant was not negligent and ask whether plaintiff's injury would have occurred anyway. The concept of "proximate" or "legal" cause shortens this lengthy list by separating those causes in fact that are merely "remote" causes from those that are sufficiently closely connected with plaintiff's injury to warrant holding defendant legally responsible. Drawing this line between "proximate" causes, which are held responsible for plaintiff's injury, and "remote" causes, which are not, is thought to be a matter of public policy.

Perhaps the most commonly-cited illustration of the distinction between cause in fact and proximate cause is the Great Chicago Fire. By tradition, the first started when Mrs. O'Leary's cow kicked over a lantern. If so, Mrs. O'Leary's livestock operations were a "cause in fact" of the

Great Chicago Fire. This is a separate question from whether Mrs. O'Leary will be responsible for the entire massive loss – that question will be governed by concepts of proximate cause.

A. CAUSE IN FACT

There is no liability in negligence unless defendant's failure to exercise due care was a cause in fact of plaintiff's loss. The cause in fact inquiry analyzes whether the exercise of due care by the defendant would have prevented the harm. Simply put, would plaintiff's harm have occurred, with or without defendant's allegedly negligent conduct? Put yet another way, would the same result have obtained "but for" defendant's substandard care? For this reason, cause in fact frequently is called "but for" causation. Because the "but for" test requires the imagination of a scenario in which the defendant did not breach a duty and a determination whether the harm would have resulted anyway, the test sometimes has been called the "counterfactual" test. If the same harm results in that imaginary scenario in which defendant did not breach a duty, then defendant's breach of duty is not a cause in fact of plaintiff's injury.

It is important to remember that the causation question is independent of the question of blame. In a negligence inquiry, blame is addressed by the elements of duty and breach. Frequently, a defendant's reasonable conduct will be a cause in fact of a particular harm. In such circumstances, the defendant is not liable despite having caused the harm in fact because the defendant did not breach a duty. After all, in every case of harm, that harm has many causes in fact, most of them (probably) innocent. Defendant's decision to get out of bed in the morning always is a cause in fact of any harm that result's from defendant's conduct that day, but getting out of bed almost never would support a finding of breach of duty.

1. "BUT FOR" TEST

The best-known "test" for cause in fact is the "but for" test.

NEW YORK CENTRAL R.R. V. GRIMSTAD
264 F. 334 (2D CIR. 1920)

This is an action . . . to recover damages for the death of Angell Grimstad, captain of the covered barge Grayton, owned by the defendant railroad company. The charge of negligence is failure to equip the barge with proper life-preservers and other necessary and proper appliances, for want of which the decedent, having fallen into the water, was drowned.

The barge was lying ... on the north side of Pier 2, ... Brooklyn .... The tug Mary M, entering the slip ... bumped against the barge. The decedent's wife, feeling the shock, came out from the cabin, looked on one side of the barge, and saw nothing, and then went across the deck to the other side, and discovered her husband in the water about 100 feet from the barge holding up his hands out of the water. He did not know how to swim. She immediately ran back into the cabin for a small line, and when she returned with it he had disappeared.... The jury found as a fact that the defendant was negligent in not equipping the barge with life-preservers....

... On the ... question, whether a life buoy would have saved the decedent from drowning, we think the jury were left to pure conjecture and speculation. A jury might well conclude that a light near an open hatch or a rail on the side of a vessel's deck would have prevented a person's falling into the hatch or into the water, in the dark. But there is nothing whatever to show ... that, if there had been a life buoy on board, the decedent's wife would have got it in time, that is, sooner than she got the small line, or, if she had, that she would have thrown it so that her husband could have seized it, or, if she did, that he would have seized it, or that, if he did, it would have prevented him from drowning.

The court erred in denying the defendant's motion to dismiss the complaint at the end of the case.

Judgment reversed.

NOTES AND QUESTIONS

1. But-for causation requires plaintiff to prove a hypothetical scenario i.e. what would (or would not) have happened without defendant's negligence. Is this burden of proof fair?

2. What evidence supported plaintiff's contention of causation in fact? Whatever the evidence of cause in fact, the evidence apparently was insufficient to present a question for the jury. What sorts of evidence, if offered at trial, might have sufficed to prove cause in fact, or at least present a jury question? Modern American courts tend to leave the question of cause in fact to the trier of fact.

3. Only the part of defendant's conduct that allegedly gives rise to liability is considered in a causation analysis. The question is not whether defendant's conduct caused plaintiff's injury but rather whether defendant's negligence caused plaintiff's injury. For example, there is no question that the *Grimstad* defendant's participation in the barge business was a cause in fact of plaintiff's injury, but this is not the question at hand. There is nothing negligent about operating a barge. Defendant's allegedly negligent conduct was failing to have a "life bouy" on board the barge. Therefore, the causation analysis focuses on whether plaintiff's harm would have occurred if this aspect of defendant's conduct had been different. In other words, if defendant had supplied life preservers, would plaintiff still have drowned?

4. The previous note raises the following question. Might plaintiff have avoided this result by adjusting her allegation of negligence? Suppose that plaintiff had alleged that the defendant had been negligent in failing to erect a tall chain link fence around the entire perimeter of the barge. Would defendant then be able to argue as persuasively that the alleged breach was not a cause in fact of the drowning? Would plaintiff's case then have been strengthened by such a shift in the alleged breach of duty?

2. SUBSTANTIAL FACTOR TEST

The "substantial factor test" of but-for causation can help to determine cause-in-fact, especially in situations in which the traditional "but for" test will not work.

NORTHINGTON V. MARIN
102 F.3D 1564 (10TH CIR. 1996)

Deputy Sheriff Jesse Marin appeals the judgment entered against him in this . . . action brought by Craig Northington, a Denver County jail inmate, claiming Marin caused other inmates to assault Northington by labeling him a snitch. . . . We affirm. . . .

In February 1990, Northington was serving a sentence at the Denver County Jail . . . . Although it was against department regulations for deputies to engage in business relationships with inmates, a deputy sold Northington a truck on contract. Northington cooperated in the subsequent department internal affairs investigation, which led to dismissal of the deputy. . . . Northington . . . alleged Deputy Marin caused other inmates to assault him by labeling him a snitch or an informer.

Northington brought this action . . . alleging the internal affairs officers, Marin, various other deputies, correction officers, and the Denver Sheriff Department violated his civil rights. . . . Counsel was appointed to represent Northington, and the case went to trial before a magistrate judge sitting as a special master. The magistrate . . . recommended a $5,000 judgment in favor of Northington on the claim against Marin. The magistrate believed the testimony of several inmates that Deputy Marin had spread a rumor among inmates that Northington was a snitch, and found Northington was assaulted several times by inmates who accused him of being a snitch. Although Marin denied spreading the rumor, he testified that an inmate labeled a snitch would most likely be beaten. There was evidence that other deputies spread the snitch rumor about Northington, and the magistrate found there was no evidence that Marin rather than another deputy originated the rumor heard by the inmates who assaulted Northington. . . .

The district court reviewed the magistrate's report and concluded "the facts in this case present a concurrent cause situation; inmates and guards were spreading rumors regarding Northington. The spreading of the rumor is akin to starting a fire. Over time the sources from which the statements were heard become muddled and often indistinguishable." Appellant's append. II at 223. . . . We agree.

Under the "but for" test of causation, Marin could not be the cause of Northington's beating. Had Marin not spread the rumor, the statements of other deputies to inmates would have spread rapidly with the probable result that Northington would have been beaten. However, Restatement (Second) of Torts §432(2) states: "If two forces are actively operating, one because of the actor's negligence, the other not because of any misconduct on his part, and each of itself is sufficient to bring about harm to another, the actor's negligence may be found to be a substantial factor in bringing it about."[2] . . .

Here, two forces were actively operating to spread the rumor—Marin and the other deputies. Because, as the magistrate found, rumors about snitches spread rapidly and inmates rumored to be snitches will probably be beaten, the conduct of each (Marin's circulation of the rumor, or the other deputies' circulation of the rumor) by itself was sufficient to cause Northington to be beaten.

The magistrate's findings also established that Marin's spreading of the rumor was a substantial factor in bringing about harm to Northington. Marin's actions were not insignificant in relation to those of the other deputies. The magistrate found Marin repeated the rumor to inmates on four occasions. There was no evidence of more than four other instances in which other deputies spread the rumor. . . . The magistrate's findings therefore established that Marin and the other deputies were substantial factors in bringing about harm to Northington, and thus were concurrent causes of the harm.

Multiple tortfeasors who concurrently cause an indivisible injury are jointly and severally liable; each can be held liable for the entire injury. . . . Consequently, a tortfeasor who cannot prove the extent to which the harm resulted from other concurrent causes is liable for the entire harm. . . .

AFFIRMED.

NOTES AND QUESTIONS

1. Was defendant's spreading the rumor that plaintiff was a "snitch" a "but for" cause of plaintiff's beating? What would have happened to plaintiff if defendant had not called him a "snitch"?

2. *Northington v. Marin* involved multiple causes combining to cause injury to plaintiff, and either cause, in and of itself, would have been sufficient to cause the harm. Therefore, the "but for" test does not work well in *Northington* because the multiple sources of the rumor that resulted in plaintiff's beating can point to each other claiming, not without logic, that the harm would have resulted even "but for" their spreading of the dangerous rumor. To avoid this type of dilemma, the drafters of the Restatement adopted the "substantial factor" test of causation set out in Restatement (Second) of Torts, Section 431 instead of a "but for" test. In Section 432(2), the Restatement explicitly provides that "[i]f two forces are actively operating, one because of the actor's negligence, . . . and each of itself is sufficient to bring about harm to another, the actor's negligence may be found to be a substantial factor in bringing it about."

3. The trial court analogized that "The spreading of the rumor is akin to starting a fire." The court, no doubt, had in mind a line of cases involving destruction of property from multiple fires started by different sources. Such converging fire cases probably provide the most common example of concurrent sufficient causes of damage. *See, e.g., Kingston v. Chicago & N.W. Ry.*, 211 N.W. 913 (Wis. 1927). The result applied by the court in the case of defendant's starting a rumor is consistent with the results in cases involving fires started by defendants. The rumor/fire analogy appears also in the epistle of James:

---

2   This rule also applies to reckless and intentional acts. *See* Restatement (Second) of Torts §§ 501 and 870, comment 1.

Even so the tongue is a little member, and boasteth great things. Behold, how great a matter a little fire kindleth! And the tongue is a fire, a world of iniquity: so is the tongue among our members, that it defileth the whole body, and setteth on fire the course of nature; and it is set on fire of hell.

3. ALTERNATIVE LIABILITY

A unique problem is presented when more than one party has breached a duty to the plaintiff but only one of those parties actually caused harm to plaintiff, and plaintiff is unable to prove which party caused the harm.

SUMMERS V. TICE
199 P.2D 1 (CAL. 1948)

. . . Plaintiff's action was against both defendants for an injury to his right eye and face as the result of being struck by bird shot discharged from a shotgun. The case was tried by the court without a jury and the court found that on November 20, 1945, plaintiff and the two defendants were hunting quail on the open range. Each of the defendants was armed with a 12 gauge shotgun loaded with shells containing 7 1/2 size shot. Prior to going hunting plaintiff discussed the hunting procedure with defendants, indicating that they were to exercise care when shooting and to "keep in line." In the course of hunting plaintiff proceeded up a hill, thus placing the hunters at the points of a triangle. The view of defendants with reference to plaintiff was unobstructed and they knew his location. Defendant Tice flushed a quail which rose in flight to a 10-foot elevation and flew between plaintiff and defendants. Both defendants shot at the quail, shooting in plaintiff's direction. At that time defendants were 75 yards from plaintiff. One shot struck plaintiff in his eye and another in his upper lip. Finally it was found by the court that as the direct result of the shooting by defendants the shots struck plaintiff as above mentioned and that defendants were negligent in so shooting and plaintiff was not contributorily negligent.

First, on the subject of negligence, . . . [t]here is evidence that both defendants, at about the same time or one immediately after the other, shot at a quail and in so doing shot toward plaintiff who was uphill from them, and that they knew his location. That is sufficient from which the trial court could conclude that they acted with respect to plaintiff other than as persons of ordinary prudence. . . . The problem presented in this case is whether the judgment against both defendants may stand. It is argued by defendants that they are not joint tortfeasors, and thus jointly and severally liable, as they were not acting in concert, and that there is not sufficient evidence to show which defendant was guilty of the negligence which caused the injuries . . . .

[W]e believe it is clear that the court sufficiently found on the issue that defendants were jointly liable and that thus the negligence of both was the cause of the injury or to that legal effect. It found that both defendants were negligent and "That as a direct and proximate result of the shots fired by *defendants, and each of them*, a birdshot pellet was caused to and did lodge in plaintiff's right eye and that another birdshot pellet was caused to and did lodge in plaintiff's upper lip." . . . Implicit in such finding is the assumption that the court was unable to ascertain whether the shots were from the gun of one defendant or the other . . . . The one shot that entered plaintiff's eye was the major factor in assessing damages and that shot could not have come from the gun of both defendants. It was from one or the other only. . . .

When we consider the relative position of the parties and the results that would flow if plaintiff was required to pin the injury on one of the defendants only, a requirement that the burden of proof on that subject be shifted to defendants becomes manifest. They are both wrongdoers – both negligent toward plaintiff. They brought about a situation where the negligence of one of them injured the plaintiff, hence it should rest with them each to absolve himself if he can. The injured party has been placed by defendants in the unfair position of pointing to which defendant caused the harm. If one can escape the other may also and plaintiff is remediless. Ordinarily defendants are in a far better position to offer evidence to determine which one caused the injury. . . .

If defendants are independent tortfeasors and thus each liable for the damage caused by him alone, and, at least, where the matter of apportionment is incapable of proof, the innocent wronged party should not be deprived of his right to redress. The wrongdoers should be left to work out between themselves any apportionment. . . .

NOTE

1 *Liability Without Causation.* The innovation of *Summers v. Tice* is that the court contemplates liability for a defendant whom the Court knows did not in fact cause the harm. In essence, the Court sacrifices cause in fact to avoid the perceived injustice of permitting two blameworthy defendants to avoid liability altogether while an innocent plaintiff goes uncompensated. As you will see, the Court's decision in *Summers v. Tice* plays a starring role in the *Sindell v. Abbott Laboratories* decision that follows.

4. LOST OPPORTUNITY

HERSKOVITS V. GROUP HEALTH COOPERATIVE
664 P.2D 474 (WASH. 1983)

This appeal raises the issue of whether an estate can maintain an action for professional negligence as a result of failure to timely diagnose lung cancer, where the estate can show probable reduction in statistical chance for survival but cannot show and/or prove that with timely diagnosis and treatment, decedent probably would have lived to normal life expectancy.

Both counsel advised that for the purpose of this appeal we are to *assume* that the respondent Group Health Cooperative of Puget Sound and Dr. William Spencer negligently failed to diagnose Herskovits' cancer on his first visit to the hospital and *proximately* caused a 14 percent reduction in his chances of survival. It is undisputed that Herskovits had less than a 50 percent chance of survival at all times herein.

The main issue we will address in this opinion is whether a patient, with less than a 50 percent chance of survival, has a cause of action against the hospital and its employees if they are negligent in diagnosing a lung cancer which reduces his chances of survival by 14 percent.

The personal representative of Leslie Herskovits' estate initiated this survivorship action against Group Health Cooperative of Puget Sound (Group Health), alleging failure to make an early diagnosis of her husband's lung cancer. Group Health moved for summary judgment for dismissal on the basis that Herskovits *probably* would have died from lung cancer even if the diagnosis had been made earlier, which the trial court granted.

The complaint alleged that Herskovits came to Group Health Hospital in 1974 with complaints of pain and coughing. In early 1974, chest x-rays revealed infiltrate in the left lung. Rales and coughing were present. In mid-1974, there were chest pains and coughing, which became persistent and chronic by fall of 1974. A December 5, 1974 entry in the medical records confirms the cough problem. Plaintiff contends that Herskovits was treated thereafter only with cough medicine. No further effort or inquiry was made by Group Health concerning his symptoms, other than an occasional chest x-ray. In the early spring of 1975, Mr. and Mrs. Herskovits went south in the hope that the warm weather would help. Upon his return to the Seattle area with no improvement in his health, Herskovits visited Dr. Jonathan Ostrow on a private basis for another medical opinion. Within 3 weeks, Dr. Ostrow's evaluation and direction to Group Health led to the diagnosis of cancer. In July of 1975, Herskovits' lung was removed, but no radiation or chemotherapy treatments were instituted. Herskovits died 20 months later, on March 22, 1977, at the age of 60.

At hearing on the motion for summary judgment, plaintiff was unable to produce expert testimony that the delay in diagnosis "probably" or "more likely than not" caused her husband's death. The affidavit and deposition of plaintiff's expert witness, Dr. Jonathan Ostrow, construed in the most favorable light possible to plaintiff, indicated that had the diagnosis of lung cancer been made in December 1974, the patient's possibility of 5-year survival was 39 percent. At the time of initial diagnosis of cancer 6 months later, the possibility of a 5-year survival was reduced to 25 percent. Dr. Ostrow testified he felt a diagnosis perhaps could have been made as early as December 1974, or January 1975, about 6 months before the surgery to remove Mr. Herskovits' lung in June 1975.

Dr. Ostrow testified that if the tumor was a "stage 1" tumor in December 1974, Herskovits' chance of a 5-year survival would have been 39 percent. In June 1975, his chances of survival were 25 percent assuming the tumor had progressed to "stage 2." Thus, the delay in diagnosis may have reduced the chance of a 5-year survival by 14 percent.

Dr. William Spencer, the physician from Group Health Hospital who cared for the deceased Herskovits, testified that in his opinion, based upon a reasonable medical probability, earlier diagnosis of the lung cancer that afflicted Herskovits would not have prevented his death, nor would it have lengthened his life. He testified that nothing the doctors at Group Health could have done would have prevented Herskovits' death, as death within several years is a virtual certainty with this type of lung cancer regardless of how early the diagnosis is made.

Plaintiff contends that medical testimony of a reduction of chance of survival from 39 percent to 25 percent is sufficient evidence to allow the proximate cause issue to go to the jury. Defendant Group Health argues conversely that Washington law does not permit such testimony on the issue of medical causation and requires that medical testimony must be at least sufficiently definite to establish that the act complained of "probably" or "more likely than not" caused the subsequent disability. It is Group Health's contention that plaintiff must prove that Herskovits "probably" would have survived had the defendant not been allegedly negligent; that is, the plaintiff must prove there was at least a 51 percent chance of survival. . . .

This court has held that a person who negligently renders aid and consequently increases the risk of harm to those he is trying to assist is liable for any physical damages he causes. *Brown v. MacPherson's, Inc.*, 86 Wash.2d 293, 299, 545 P.2d 13 (1975). In *Brown*, the court cited Restatement (Second) of Torts § 323 (1965), which reads:

> One who undertakes ... to render services to another which he should recognize as necessary for the protection of the other's person or things, is subject to liability to the other for physical harm resulting from his failure to exercise reasonable care to perform his undertaking, if
>> (a) his failure to exercise such care increases the risk of such harm,...

This court heretofore has not faced the issue of whether, under § 323(a), proof that the defendant's conduct increased the risk of death by decreasing the chances of survival is sufficient to take the issue of proximate cause to the jury. Some courts in other jurisdictions have allowed the proximate cause issue to go to the jury on this type of proof. . . . These courts emphasized the fact that defendants' conduct deprived the decedents of a "significant" chance to survive or recover, rather than requiring proof that with absolute certainty the defendants' conduct caused the physical injury. The underlying reason is that it is not for the wrongdoer, who put the possibility of recovery beyond realization, to say afterward that the result was inevitable. . . .

Other jurisdictions have rejected this approach, generally holding that unless the plaintiff is able to show that it was more likely than not that the harm was caused by the defendant's negligence, proof of a decreased chance of survival is not enough to take the proximate cause question to the jury. . . . These courts have concluded that the defendant should not be liable where the decedent more than likely would have died anyway.

The ultimate question raised here is whether the relationship between the increased risk of harm and Herskovits' death is sufficient to hold Group Health responsible. Is a 36 percent (from 39 percent to 25 percent) reduction in the decedent's chance for survival sufficient evidence of causation to allow the jury to consider the possibility that the physician's failure to timely diagnose the illness was the proximate cause of his death? We answer in the affirmative. To decide otherwise would be a blanket release from liability for doctors and hospitals any time there was less than a 50 percent chance of survival, regardless of how flagrant the negligence. . . .

We are persuaded by the reasoning of the Pennsylvania Supreme Court in *Hamil v. Bashline, supra.* While *Hamil* involved an original survival chance of greater than 50 percent, we find the rationale used by the *Hamil* court to apply equally to cases such as the present one, where the original survival chance is less than 50 percent. The plaintiff's decedent was suffering from severe chest pains. His wife transported him to the hospital where he was negligently treated in the emergency unit. The wife, because of the lack of help, took her husband to a private physician's office, where he died. In an action brought under the wrongful death and survivorship statutes, the main medical witness testified that if the hospital had employed proper treatment, the decedent would have had a substantial chance of surviving the attack. The medical expert expressed his opinion in terms of a 75 percent chance of survival. It was also the doctor's opinion that the substantial loss of a chance of recovery was the result of the defendant hospital's failure to provide prompt treatment. The defendant's expert witness testified that the patient would have died regardless of any treatment provided by the defendant hospital.

The *Hamil* court reiterated the oft-repeated principle of tort law that the mere occurrence of an injury does not prove negligence, but the defendant's conduct must be a proximate cause of the plaintiff's injury. The court also referred to the traditional "but for" test, with the qualification that multiple causes may culminate in injury. *Hamil,* 481 Pa. at 266, 392 A.2d 1280.

The court then cited Restatement (Second) of Torts § 323 (1965) as authority to relax the degree of certitude normally required of plaintiff's evidence in order to make a case for the jury. The court held that once a plaintiff has introduced evidence that a defendant's negligent act or omission increased the risk of harm to a person in plaintiff's position, and that the harm was in fact sustained, "it becomes a question for the jury as to whether or not that increased risk was a substantial factor in producing the harm." *Hamil,* 481 Pa. at 269, 392 A.2d 1280. . . .

The *Hamil* court distinguished the facts of that case from the general tort case in which a plaintiff alleges that a defendant's act or omission set in motion a force which resulted in harm. In the typical tort case, the "but for" test, requiring proof that damages or death probably would not have occurred "but for" the negligent conduct of the defendant, is appropriate. In *Hamil* and the instant case, however, the defendant's act or omission failed in a duty to protect against harm from another source. Thus, as the *Hamil* court noted, the fact finder is put in the position of having to consider not only what did occur, but also what might have occurred. *Hamil* states at 271, 392 A.2d 1280:

> Such cases by their very nature elude the degree of certainty one would prefer and upon which the law normally insists before a person may be held liable. Nevertheless, in order that an actor is not completely insulated because of uncertainties as to the consequences of his negligent conduct, Section 323(a) tacitly acknowledges this difficulty and permits the issue to go to the jury upon a less than normal threshold of proof.

(Footnote omitted.) The *Hamil* court held that once a plaintiff has demonstrated that the defendant's acts or omissions have increased the risk of harm to another, such evidence furnishes a basis for the jury to make a determination as to whether such increased risk was in turn a substantial factor in bringing about the resultant harm. . . .

Under the *Hamil* decision, once a plaintiff has demonstrated that defendant's acts or omissions in a situation to which § 323(a) applies have increased the risk of harm to another, such evidence furnishes a basis for the fact finder to go further and find that such increased risk was in turn a substantial factor in bringing about the resultant harm. The necessary proximate cause will be established if the jury finds such cause. It is not necessary for a plaintiff to introduce evidence to establish that the negligence resulted in the injury or death, but simply that the negligence increased the risk of injury or death. The step from the increased risk to causation is one for the jury to make. *Hamil*, 481 Pa. at 272, 392 A.2d 1280. . . .

Both counsel have agreed for the purpose of arguing this summary judgment, that the defendants were negligent in failing to make a diagnosis of cancer on Herskovits' initial visit in December 1974, and that such negligence was the proximate cause of reducing his chances of survival by 14 percent. It is undisputed that Herskovits had less than a 50 percent chance of survival at that time. Based on this agreement and Dr. Ostrow's deposition and affidavit, a prima facie case is shown. We reject Group Health's argument that plaintiffs must show that Herskovits "probably" would have had a 51 percent chance of survival if the hospital had not been negligent. We hold that medical testimony of a reduction of chance of survival from 39 percent to 25 percent is sufficient evidence to allow the proximate cause issue to go to the jury.

Causing reduction of the opportunity to recover (loss of chance) by one's negligence, however, does not necessitate a total recovery against the negligent party for all damages caused by the victim's death. Damages should be awarded to the injured party or his family based only on damages caused directly by premature death, such as lost earnings and additional medical expenses, etc.

We reverse the trial court and reinstate the cause of action.

ROSELLINI, J., concurs.

PEARSON, Justice (concurring).

I agree with the majority that the trial court erred in granting defendant's motion for summary judgment. I cannot, however, agree with the majority's reasoning in reaching this decision. The majority's reliance on *Hamil v. Bashline*, 481 Pa. 256, 392 A.2d 1280 (1978) and *Hicks v. United States*, 368 F.2d 626 (4th Cir.1966) is inappropriate for the reasons identified in the dissent of Justice Dolliver. Moreover, the issue before us is considerably more complex than the apparently straightforward policy choice suggested by the interaction of the majority opinion and Justice Dolliver's dissent. I therefore agree with Justice Brachtenbach that those opinions fail to focus on the key issue. I decline to join Justice Brachtenbach's dissent, however, because the result he advocates is harsh, as he recognizes at page 491. In an effort to achieve a fair result by means of sound analysis, I offer the following approach.

This action began in July 1979 with a complaint alleging that defendant Group Health Cooperative had negligently treated the decedent Leslie Herskovits. Plaintiff, the widow of decedent Herskovits, alleged in this complaint that defendant's failure to diagnose the decedent's lung cancer "led to and caused his death". The complaint sought damages for the medical expenses, disability, and pain and suffering of the decedent, together with pecuniary loss suffered by plaintiff, including loss of support, affection, and consortium.

As discovery progressed, some undisputed facts were established. Mr. Herskovits had been a patient of the Group Health Cooperative for more than 20 years. In December 1974, he consulted a physician at Group Health for the treatment of a persistent cough. The physician prescribed cough medicine. Obtaining no relief from his cough, Mr. Herskovits consulted a physician outside Group Health, Dr. Jonathan Ostrow. Dr. Ostrow suspected that Mr. Herskovits had lung cancer, and recommended a medical procedure be undertaken to confirm his suspicions. The procedure was performed in June 1975, and revealed that Mr. Herskovits had cancer in the bronchus of his left lung. The lung was removed on July 1, 1975. Mr. Herskovits died of cancer on March 22, 1977, at the age of 60 years.

Defendant moved for summary judgment in May 1981, on the ground that plaintiff was unable to produce testimony that earlier diagnosis would probably have prevented Mr. Herskovits' death from cancer. The trial court granted the motion and dismissed the action, holding that plaintiff had "failed to produce expert testimony which would establish that the decedent probably would not have died on or about March, 1977 but for the conduct of the defendant". This holding was based on the court's conclusion that "under Washington law the loss of a possibility of survival is not compensable".

Plaintiff's case was based on the testimony of the expert witness, Dr. Ostrow. This court's enquiry, therefore, is whether Dr. Ostrow's testimony, together with reasonable inferences therefrom, creates a prima facie issue of causation. . . . The critical testimony of Dr. Ostrow, from his affidavit and deposition, may fairly be summarized as follows:

1. There is a reasonable medical probability that defendant failed to take necessary steps to diagnose Mr. Herskovits' condition, and defendant therefore failed to meet the appropriate standard of care.

2. Had reasonable care been exercised, Mr. Herskovits' cancer could have been diagnosed in December 1974 instead of June 1975.

3. Unless removed, a cancerous tumor can be expected to increase in size over time, and the patient's chances of survival decline accordingly.

4. There is no way of knowing how far the tumor in Mr. Herskovits' lung had developed by December 1974.

5. If the tumor had been a Stage 1 tumor in December 1974, decedent's statistical chance of surviving 5 years was 39 percent.

6. When the tumor was discovered in June 1975, it was a Stage 2 tumor. The statistical chance of surviving 5 years when the tumor has reached Stage 2 is 25 percent.

7. Dr. Ostrow summed up his opinion as follows: "By failing to properly evaluate Mr. Herskovits' condition as late as December 1974, Group Health probably caused Mr. Herskovits' chance for long-term survival to be substantially reduced".

Dr. Ostrow's testimony does not, therefore, establish a prima facie case that defendant's alleged negligence probably (or more likely than not) caused Mr. Herskovits' death. Rather, the testimony establishes only that the alleged negligence caused a substantial reduction in Mr. Herskovits' long-term chance of survival. Dr. Ostrow testified that if the tumor was at Stage 1 in December 1974, the chance of survival was reduced from 39 percent to 25 percent. He did not, however, indicate the likelihood of the tumor's being at Stage 1 in December 1974, either in terms of certainty, probability, or statistical chance. Therefore, the only indications from the record of the extent of the reduction in Mr. Herskovits' chance of long-term survival are that it was "substantial" and that it was at most a 14 percent reduction (from 39 percent to 25 percent).

I turn now to consider whether this testimony is sufficient to create a material issue whether defendant's alleged negligence was a proximate cause of harm to plaintiff.

. . .

In medical malpractice cases such as the one before us, cause in fact must usually be established by expert medical testimony, and must be established beyond the balance of probabilities.

In a case such as this, medical testimony must be relied upon to establish the causal relationship between the liability-producing situation and the claimed physical disability resulting therefrom. The evidence will be deemed insufficient to support the jury's verdict, if it can be said that considering the whole of the medical testimony the jury must resort to speculation or conjecture in determining such causal relationship. In many recent decisions of this court we have held that such determination is deemed based on speculation and conjecture if the medical testimony does not go beyond the expression of an opinion that the physical disability "might have" or "possibly did" result from the hypothesized cause. To remove the issue from the realm of speculation, the medical testimony must at least be sufficiently definite to establish that the act complained of "probably" or "more likely than not" caused the subsequent disability. . . .

The issue before the court, quite simply, is whether Dr. Ostrow's testimony . . . established that the act complained of (the alleged delay in diagnosis) "probably" or "more likely than not" caused Mr. Herskovits' subsequent disability. In order to make this determination, we must first define the "subsequent disability" suffered by Mr. Herskovits. Therein lies the crux of this case, for it is possible to define the injury or "disability" to Mr. Herskovits in at least two different ways. First, and most obviously, the injury to Mr. Herskovits might be viewed as his death. Alternatively, however, the injury or disability may be seen as the reduction of Mr. Herskovits' chance of surviving the cancer from which he suffered.

Therefore, although the issue before us is primarily one of causation, resolution of that issue requires us to identify the nature of the injury to the decedent. Our conception of the injury will substantially affect our analysis. If the injury is determined to be the death of Mr. Herskovits, then under the established principles of proximate cause plaintiff has failed to make a prima facie case. Dr. Ostrow was unable to state that probably, or more likely than not, Mr. Herskovits' death was caused by defendant's negligence. On the contrary, it is clear from Dr. Ostrow's testimony that Mr. Herskovits would have probably died from cancer even with the exercise of reasonable care by defendant.

Accordingly, if we perceive the death of Mr. Herskovits as the injury in this case, we must affirm the trial court, unless we determine that it is proper to depart substantially from the traditional requirements of establishing proximate cause in this type of case.

If, on the other hand, we view the injury to be the reduction of Mr. Herskovits' chance of survival, our analysis might well be different. Dr. Ostrow testified that the failure to diagnose cancer in December 1974 probably caused a substantial reduction in Mr. Herskovits' chance of survival. . . .

I note here that two other problems are created by the latter analysis. First, we have never before considered whether the loss or reduction of a chance of survival is a compensable injury. And second, this analysis raises the issue of whether an action for reduction of the chance of survival can be brought under the wrongful death statute, RCW 4.20.010.

Confronted with these problems, and with the first impression choice between the two approaches to the issue before us, I turn to consider how other jurisdictions have dealt with similar cases.

One approach, and that urged by defendant, is to deny recovery in wrongful death cases unless the plaintiff establishes that decedent would probably have survived but for defendant's negligence. . . .

On the other hand, plaintiff cites seven cases in support of her position. . . . [T]he critical element in each of the cases is that the defendant's negligence either deprived a decedent of a chance of surviving a potentially fatal condition or reduced that chance. To summarize, in *Hicks v. United States* the decedent was deprived of a probability of survival; in *Jeanes v. Milner* the decedent's chance of survival was reduced from 35 percent to 24 percent; in *O'Brien v. Stover*, the decedent's 30 percent chance of survival was reduced by an indeterminate amount; in *McBride v. United States* the decedent was deprived of the probability of survival; in *Kallenberg v. Beth Israel Hosp.* the decedent was deprived of a 20 percent to 40 percent chance of survival; in *Hamil v. Bashline* the decedent was deprived of a 75 percent chance of survival; and in *James v. United States* the decedent was deprived of an indeterminate chance of survival, no matter how small.

The three cases where the chance of survival was greater than 50 percent (*Hicks, McBride,* and *Hamil*) are unexceptional in that they focus on the death of the decedent as the injury, and they require proximate cause to be shown beyond the balance of probabilities. Such a result is consistent with existing principles in this state, and with cases from other jurisdictions cited by defendant.

The remaining four cases allowed recovery despite the plaintiffs' failure to prove a probability of survival. Three of these cases (*Jeanes, O'Brien,* and *James*) differ significantly from the *Hicks, McBride,* and *Hamil* group in that they view the reduction in or loss of the chance of survival, rather than the death itself, as the injury. Under these cases, the defendant is liable, not for all damages arising from the death, but only for damages to the extent of the diminished or lost chance of survival. The fourth of these cases, *Kallenberg*, differs from the other three in that it focuses on the death as the compensable injury. This is clearly a distortion of traditional principles of proximate causation. In effect, *Kallenberg* held that a 40 percent possibility of causation (rather than the 51 percent required by a probability standard) was sufficient to establish liability for the death. Under this loosened standard of proof of causation, the defendant would be liable for all damages resulting from the death for which he was at most 40 percent responsible.

My review of these cases persuades me that the preferable approach to the problem before us is that taken (at least implicitly) in *Jeanes*, *O'Brien*, and *James*. I acknowledge that the principal predicate for these cases is the passage of obiter dictum in *Hicks*, a case which more directly supports the defendant's position. I am nevertheless convinced that these cases reflect a trend to the most rational, least arbitrary, rule by which to regulate cases of this kind. I am persuaded to this conclusion not so much by the reasoning of these cases themselves, but by the thoughtful discussion of a recent commentator. King, *Causation, Valuation, and Chance in Personal Injury Torts Involving Preexisting Conditions and Future Consequences,* 90 Yale L.J. 1353 (1981).

King's basic thesis is explained in the following passage, which is particularly pertinent to the case before us.

> Causation has for the most part been treated as an all-or-nothing proposition. Either a loss was caused by the defendant or it was not.... A plaintiff ordinarily should be required to prove by the applicable standard of proof that the defendant caused the loss in question. What caused a loss, however, should be a separate question from what the nature and extent of the loss are. This distinction seems to have eluded the courts, with the result that lost chances in many respects are compensated either as certainties or not at all.
>
> To illustrate, consider the case in which a doctor negligently fails to diagnose a patient's cancerous condition until it has become inoperable. Assume further that even with a timely diagnosis the patient would have had only a 30% chance of recovering from the disease and surviving over the long term. There are two ways of handling such a case. Under the traditional approach, this loss of a not-better-than-even chance of recovering from the cancer would not be compensable because it did not appear more likely [than] not that the patient would have survived with proper care. Recoverable damages, if any, would depend on the extent to which it appeared that cancer killed the patient sooner than it would have with timely diagnosis and treatment, and on the extent to which the delay in diagnosis aggravated the patient's condition, such as by causing additional pain. A more rational approach, however, would allow recovery for the loss of the chance of cure even though the chance was not better than even. The probability of long-term survival would be reflected in the amount of damages awarded for the loss of the chance. While the plaintiff here could not prove by a preponderance of the evidence that he was denied a cure by the defendant's negligence, he could show by a preponderance that he was deprived of a 30% chance of a cure.

90 Yale L.J. at 1363-64.

Under the all or nothing approach, typified by *Cooper v. Sisters of Charity of Cincinnati, Inc.*, 27 Ohio St.2d 242, 272 N.E.2d 97 (1971), a plaintiff who establishes that but for the defendant's negligence the decedent had a 51 percent chance of survival may maintain an action for that death. The defendant will be liable for all damages arising from the death, even though there was a 49 percent chance it would have occurred despite his negligence. On the other hand, a plaintiff who establishes that but for the defendant's negligence the decedent had a 49 percent chance of survival recovers nothing.

This all or nothing approach to recovery is criticized by King on several grounds, 90 Yale L.J. at 1376-78. First, the all or nothing approach is arbitrary. Second, it

> subverts the deterrence objectives of tort law by denying recovery for the effects of conduct that causes statistically demonstrable losses.... A failure to allocate the cost of these losses to their tortious sources ... strikes at the integrity of the torts system of loss allocation.

90 Yale L.J. at 1377. Third, the all or nothing approach creates pressure to manipulate and distort other rules affecting causation and damages in an attempt to mitigate perceived injustices. (*Kallenberg v. Beth Israel Hosp.* appears to be a good illustration of this tendency.) Fourth, the all or nothing approach gives certain defendants the benefit of an uncertainty which, were it not for their tortious conduct, would not exist. (This is reminiscent of the reasoning in the fertile dictum in *Hicks v. United States*.) Finally, King argues that the loss of a less than even chance is a loss worthy of redress.

These reasons persuade me that the best resolution of the issue before us is to recognize the loss of a less than even chance as an actionable injury. Therefore, I would hold that plaintiff has established a prima facie issue of proximate cause by producing testimony that defendant probably caused a substantial reduction in Mr. Herskovits' chance of survival. . . .

Finally, it is necessary to consider the amount of damages recoverable in the event that a loss of a chance of recovery is established. Once again, King's discussion provides a useful illustration of the principles which should be applied.

> To illustrate, consider a patient who suffers a heart attack and dies as a result. Assume that the defendant-physician negligently misdiagnosed the patient's condition, but that the patient would have had only a 40% chance of survival even with a timely diagnosis and proper care. Regardless of whether it could be said that the defendant caused the decedent's death, he caused the loss of a chance, and that chance-interest should be completely redressed in its own right. Under the proposed rule, the plaintiff's compensation for the loss of the victim's chance of surviving the heart attack would be 40% of the compensable value of the victim's life had he survived (including what his earning capacity would otherwise have been in the years following death). The value placed on the patient's life would reflect such factors as his age, health, and earning potential, including the fact that he had suffered the heart attack and the assumption that he had survived it. The 40% computation would be applied to that base figure.

(Footnote omitted.) 90 Yale L.J. at 1382. . . .

I would remand to the trial court for proceedings consistent with this opinion.
WILLIAM H. WILLIAMS, C.J., and UTTER and STAFFORD, JJ., concur. . . .

5. MARKET SHARE LIABILITY

SINDELL V. ABBOTT LABORATORIES
607 P.2D 924 (CAL. 1980)

This case involves a complex problem both timely and significant: may a plaintiff, injured as the result of a drug administered to her mother during pregnancy, who knows the type of drug involved but cannot identify the manufacturer of the precise product, hold liable for her injuries a maker of a drug produced from an identical formula?

Plaintiff Judith Sindell brought an action against eleven drug companies and Does 1 through 100 . . . . The complaint alleges as follows:

Between 1941 and 1971, defendants were engaged in the business of manufacturing, promoting, and marketing diethylstilbesterol (DES), a drug which is a synthetic compound of the female hormone estrogen. The drug was administered to plaintiff's mother and the mothers of the class she represents . . . for the purpose of preventing miscarriage. In 1947, the Food and Drug Administration authorized the marketing of DES as a miscarriage preventative, but only on an experimental basis, with a requirement that the drug contain a warning label to that effect.

DES may cause cancerous vaginal and cervical growths in the daughters exposed to it before birth, because their mothers took the drug during pregnancy. The form of cancer from which these daughters suffer is known as adenocarcinoma, and it manifests itself after a minimum latent period of 10 or 12 years. . . .

In 1971, the Food and Drug Administration ordered defendants to cease marketing and promoting DES for the purpose of preventing miscarriages, and to warn physicians and the public that the drug should not be used by pregnant women because of the danger to their unborn children.

During the period defendants marketed DES, they knew or should have known that it was a carcinogenic substance, that there was a grave danger after varying periods of latency it would cause cancerous and precancerous growths in the daughters of the mothers who took it, and that it was ineffective to prevent miscarriage. Nevertheless, defendants continued to advertise and market the drug as a miscarriage preventative. They failed to test DES for efficacy and safety; the tests performed by others, upon which they relied, indicated that it was not safe or effective. . . .

Because of defendants' advertised assurances that DES was safe and effective to prevent miscarriage, plaintiff was exposed to the drug prior to her birth. . . . As a result of the DES ingested by her mother, plaintiff developed a malignant bladder tumor which was removed by surgery. She suffers from adenosis and must constantly be monitored by biopsy or coloscopy to insure early warning of further malignancy.

The first cause of action alleges that defendants were jointly and individually negligent in that they manufactured, marketed and promoted DES as a safe and efficacious drug to prevent miscarriage, without adequate testing or warning, and without monitoring or reporting its effects. . . . DES was produced from a common and mutually agreed upon formula as a fungible drug interchangeable with other brands of the same product; defendants knew or should have known that it was customary for doctors to prescribe the drug by its generic rather than its brand name and that pharmacists filled prescriptions from whatever brand of the drug happened to be in stock. . . .

Defendants demurred to the complaint. While the complaint did not expressly allege that plaintiff could not identify the manufacturer of the precise drug ingested by her mother, she stated in her points and authorities in opposition to the demurrers filed by some of the defendants that she was unable to make the identification, and the trial court sustained the demurrers of these defendants without leave to amend on the ground that plaintiff did not and stated she could not identify which defendant had manufactured the drug responsible for her injuries. Thereupon, the court dismissed the action. . . .

We begin with the proposition that, as a general rule, the imposition of liability depends upon a showing by the plaintiff that his or her injuries were caused by the act of the defendant or by an instrumentality under the defendant's control. The rule applies whether the injury resulted from an accidental event or from the use of a defective product.

There are, however, exceptions to this rule. Plaintiff's complaint suggests several bases upon which defendants may be held liable for her injuries even though she cannot demonstrate the name of the manufacturer which produced the DES actually taken by her mother. The first of these theories, classically illustrated by *Summers* v. *Tice* (1948) 33 Cal.2d 80, places the burden of proof of causation upon tortious defendants in certain circumstances. The second basis of liability emerging from the complaint is that defendants acted in concert to cause injury to plaintiff. There is a third and novel approach to the problem, sometimes called the theory of "enterprise liability," but which we prefer to designate by the more accurate term of "industry-wide" liability, which might obviate the necessity for identifying the manufacturer of the injury-causing drug. We shall conclude that these doctrines, as previously interpreted, may not be applied to hold defendants liable under the allegations of this complaint. However, we shall propose and adopt a fourth basis for permitting the action to be tried, grounded upon an extension of the *Summers* doctrine.

I

Plaintiff places primary reliance upon cases which hold that if a party cannot identify which of two or more defendants caused an injury, the burden of proof may shift to the defendants to show that they were not responsible for the harm. This principle is sometimes referred to as the "alternative liability" theory.

The celebrated case of *Summers* v. *Tice, supra,* 33 Cal.2d 80, a unanimous opinion of this court, best exemplifies the rule. In *Summers*, the plaintiff was injured when two hunters negligently shot in his direction. It could not be determined which of them had fired the shot that actually caused the injury to the plaintiff's eye, but both defendants were nevertheless held jointly and severally liable for the whole of the damages. . . . [P]laintiff may not prevail in her claim that the *Summers* rationale should be employed to fix the whole liability for her injuries upon defendants, at least as those principles have previously been applied. There is an important difference between the situation involved in *Summers* and the present case. There, all the parties who were or could have been responsible for the harm to the plaintiff were joined as defendants. Here, by contrast, there are approximately 200 drug companies which made DES, any of which might have manufactured the injury-producing drug.[16]

Defendants maintain that, while in *Summers* there was a 50 percent chance that one of the two defendants was responsible for the plaintiff's injuries, here since any one of 200 companies which manufactured DES might have made the product that harmed plaintiff, there is no rational basis upon which to infer that any defendant in this action caused plaintiff's injuries, nor even a reasonable possibility that they were responsible. These arguments are persuasive if we measure the chance that any one of the defendants supplied the injury-causing drug by the number of possible tortfeasors. In such a context, the possibility that any of the five defendants supplied the DES to plaintiff's mother is so remote that it would be unfair to require each defendant to exonerate itself. There may be a substantial likelihood that none of the five defendants joined in the action made the DES which caused the injury, and that the offending producer not named would escape liability altogether. While we propose, *infra*, an adaptation of the rule in *Summers* which will substantially overcome these difficulties, defendants appear to be correct that the rule, as previously applied, cannot relieve plaintiff of the burden of proving the identity of the manufacturer which made the drug causing her injuries.

II

The second principle upon which plaintiff relies is the so-called "concert of action" theory. . . .
. . . The gravamen of the charge of concert is that defendants failed to adequately test the drug or to give sufficient warning of its dangers and that they relied upon the tests performed by one another and took advantage of each others' promotional and marketing techniques. These allegations do not amount to a charge that there was a tacit understanding or a common plan

---

16 According to the Restatement, the burden of proof shifts to the defendants only if the plaintiff can demonstrate that all defendants acted tortiously and that the harm resulted from the conduct of one of them. (Rest.2d Torts, § 433B, com. g . . . .) It goes on to state that the rule thus far has been applied only where all the actors involved are joined as defendants and where the conduct of all is simultaneous in time, but cases might arise in which some modification of the rule would be necessary if one of the actors is or cannot be joined, or because of the effects of lapse of time, or other circumstances. (*Id.*, com. h . . . .)

among defendants to fail to conduct adequate tests or give sufficient warnings, and that they substantially aided and encouraged one another in these omissions. . . .

What the complaint appears to charge is defendants' parallel or imitative conduct in that they relied upon each others' testing and promotion methods. But such conduct describes a common practice in industry: a producer avails himself of the experience and methods of others making the same or similar products. Application of the concept of concert of action to this situation would expand the doctrine far beyond its intended scope and would render virtually any manufacturer liable for the defective products of an entire industry, even if it could be demonstrated that the product which caused the injury was not made by the defendant. . . .

III

A third theory upon which plaintiff relies is the concept of industry-wide liability, or according to the terminology of the parties, "enterprise liability." This theory was suggested in *Hall* v. *E. I. Du Pont de Nemours & Co., Inc.* (E.D.N.Y. 1972) 345 F.Supp. 353. In that case, plaintiffs were 13 children injured by the explosion of blasting caps in 12 separate incidents which occurred in 10 different states between 1955 and 1959. The defendants were six blasting cap manufacturers, comprising virtually the entire blasting cap industry in the United States, and their trade association. . . . The gravamen of the complaint was that the practice of the industry of omitting a warning on individual blasting caps and of failing to take other safety measures created an unreasonable risk of harm, resulting in the plaintiffs' injuries. The complaint did not identify a particular manufacturer of a cap which caused a particular injury.

The court reasoned as follows: there was evidence that defendants, acting independently, had adhered to an industry-wide standard with regard to the safety features of blasting caps, that they had in effect delegated some functions of safety investigation and design, such as labelling, to their trade association, and that there was industry-wide cooperation in the manufacture and design of blasting caps. In these circumstances, the evidence supported a conclusion that all the defendants jointly controlled the risk. Thus, if plaintiffs could establish by a preponderance of the evidence that the caps were manufactured by one of the defendants, the burden of proof as to causation would shift to all the defendants. The court noted that this theory of liability applied to industries composed of a small number of units, and that what would be fair and reasonable with regard to an industry of five or ten producers might be manifestly unreasonable if applied to a decentralized industry composed of countless small producers.

Plaintiff attempts to state a cause of action under the rationale of *Hall.* She alleges joint enterprise and collaboration among defendants in the production, marketing, promotion and testing of DES, and "concerted promulgation and adherence to industry-wide testing, safety, warning and efficacy standards" for the drug. . . . We decline to apply this theory in the present case. At least 200 manufacturers produced DES; *Hall*, which involved 6 manufacturers representing the entire blasting cap industry in the United States, cautioned against application of the doctrine espoused therein to a large number of producers. . . . Moreover, in *Hall*, the conclusion that the defendants jointly controlled the risk was based upon allegations that they had delegated some functions relating to safety to a trade association. There are no such allegations here, and we have concluded above that plaintiff has failed to allege liability on a concert of action theory. . . .

IV

If we were confined to the theories of *Summers* and *Hall*, we would be constrained to hold that the judgment must be sustained. Should we require that plaintiff identify the manufacturer which supplied the DES used by her mother or that all DES manufacturers be joined in the action, she would effectively be precluded from any recovery. As defendants candidly admit, there is little likelihood that all the manufacturers who made DES at the time in question are still in business or that they are subject to the jurisdiction of the California courts. There are, however, forceful arguments in favor of holding that plaintiff has a cause of action. In our contemporary complex industrialized society, advances in science and technology create fungible goods which may harm consumers and which cannot be traced to any specific producer. The response of the courts can be either to adhere rigidly to prior doctrine, denying recovery to those injured by such products, or to fashion remedies to meet these changing needs. . . .

The most persuasive reason for finding plaintiff states a cause of action is that advanced in *Summers*: as between an innocent plaintiff and negligent defendants, the latter should bear the cost of the injury. Here, as in *Summers*, plaintiff is not at fault in failing to provide evidence of causation, and although the absence of such evidence is not attributable to the defendants either, their conduct in marketing a drug the effects of which are delayed for many years played a significant role in creating the unavailability of proof.

From a broader policy standpoint, defendants are better able to bear the cost of injury resulting from the manufacture of a defective product. . . . The manufacturer is in the best position to discover and guard against defects in its products and to warn of harmful effects; thus, holding it liable for defects and failure to warn of harmful effects will provide an incentive to product safety. These considerations are particularly significant where medication is involved, for the consumer is virtually helpless to protect himself from serious, sometimes permanent, sometimes fatal, injuries caused by deleterious drugs.

Where, as here, all defendants produced a drug from an identical formula and the manufacturer of the DES which caused plaintiff's injuries cannot be identified through no fault of plaintiff, a modification of the rule of *Summers* is warranted. As we have seen, an undiluted *Summers* rationale is inappropriate to shift the burden of proof of causation to defendants because if we measure the chance that any particular manufacturer supplied the injury-causing product by the number of producers of DES, there is a possibility that none of the five defendants in this case produced the offending substance and that the responsible manufacturer, not named in the action, will escape liability.

But we approach the issue of causation from a different perspective: we hold it to be reasonable in the present context to measure the likelihood that any of the defendants supplied the product which allegedly injured plaintiff by the percentage which the DES sold by each of them for the purpose of preventing miscarriage bears to the entire production of the drug sold by all for that purpose. . . . If plaintiff joins in the action the manufacturers of a substantial share of the DES which her mother might have taken, the injustice of shifting the burden of proof to defendants to demonstrate that they could not have made the substance which injured plaintiff is significantly diminished. While 75 to 80 percent of the market is suggested as the requirement . . . , we hold only that a substantial percentage is required.

The presence in the action of a substantial share of the appropriate market also provides a ready means to apportion damages among the defendants. Each defendant will be held liable for the proportion of the judgment represented by its share of that market unless it demonstrates that it could not have made the product which caused plaintiff's injuries. In the present case, . . . one DES manufacturer was dismissed from the action upon filing a declaration that it had not manufactured DES until after plaintiff was born. Once plaintiff has met her burden of joining the required defendants, they in turn may cross-complaint against other DES manufacturers, not joined in the action, which they can allege might have supplied the injury-causing product.

Under this approach, each manufacturer's liability would approximate its responsibility for the injuries caused by its own products. Some minor discrepancy in the correlation between market share and liability is inevitable; therefore, a defendant may be held liable for a somewhat different percentage of the damage than its share of the appropriate market would justify. It is probably impossible, with the passage of time, to determine market share with mathematical exactitude. But just as a jury cannot be expected to determine the precise relationship between fault and liability in applying the doctrine of comparative fault (*Li* v. *Yellow Cab Co.* (1975) 13 Cal.3d 804) or partial indemnity (*American Motorcycle Assn.* v. *Superior Court* (1978) 20 Cal.3d 578), the difficulty of apportioning damages among the defendant producers in exact relation to their market share does not seriously militate against the rule we adopt. As we said in *Summers* with regard to the liability of independent tortfeasors, where a correct division of liability cannot be made "the trier of fact may make it the best it can." (33 Cal.2d at p. 88.)

We are not unmindful of the practical problems involved in defining the market and determining market share, but these are largely matters of proof which properly cannot be determined at the pleading stage of these proceedings. Defendants urge that it would be both unfair and contrary to public policy to hold them liable for plaintiff's injuries in the absence of proof that one of them supplied the drug responsible for the damage. Most of their arguments, however, are based upon the assumption that one manufacturer would be held responsible for the products of another or for those of all other manufacturers if plaintiff ultimately prevails. But under the rule we adopt, each manufacturer's liability for an injury would be approximately equivalent to the damage caused by the DES it manufactured.

The judgments are reversed.

RICHARDSON, J.

I respectfully dissent. In these consolidated cases the majority adopts a wholly new theory which contains these ingredients: The plaintiffs were not alive at the time of the commission of the tortious acts. They sue a generation later. They are permitted to receive substantial damages from multiple defendants without any proof that any defendant caused or even probably caused plaintiffs' injuries.

Although the majority purports to change only the required burden of proof by shifting it from plaintiffs to defendants, the effect of its holding is to guarantee that plaintiffs will prevail on the causation issue because defendants are no more capable of disproving factual causation than plaintiffs are of proving it. "Market share" liability thus represents a new high water mark in tort law. . . . In my view, the majority's departure from traditional tort doctrine is unwise.

The applicable principles of causation are very well established. . . . According to the majority, in the present case plaintiffs have openly conceded that they are unable to identify the particular entity which manufactured the drug consumed by their mothers. In fact, plaintiffs have joined only *five* of the approximately *two hundred* drug companies which manufactured DES. Thus, the case constitutes far more than a mere factual variant upon the theme composed in *Summers* v. *Tice* (1948) 33 Cal.2d 80, wherein plaintiff joined as codefendants the *only* two persons who could have injured him. As the majority must acknowledge, our *Summers* rule applies only to cases in which ". . . it is proved that harm has been caused to the plaintiff by . . . one of [the named defendants], but there is uncertainty as to which one has caused it . . . ." (Rest.2d Torts, § 433B, subd. (3).) In the present case, in stark contrast, it remains wholly speculative and conjectural whether *any* of the five named defendants actually caused plaintiffs' injuries.

The fact that plaintiffs cannot tie defendants to the injury-producing drug does not trouble the majority for it declares that the *Summers* requirement of proof of actual causation by a named defendant is satisfied by a joinder of those defendants who have *together* manufactured "*a substantial percentage*" of the DES which has been marketed. Notably lacking from the majority's expression of its new rule, unfortunately, is any definition or guidance as to what should constitute a "substantial" share of the relevant market. The issue is entirely open-ended and the answer, presumably, is anyone's guess.

Much more significant, however, is the consequence of this unprecedented extension of liability. Recovery is permitted from a handful of defendants *each* of whom *individually* may account for a comparatively small share of the relevant market, so long as the *aggregate* business of those who have been sued is deemed "substantial." In other words, a particular defendant may be held proportionately liable *even though mathematically it is much more likely than not that it played no role whatever in causing plaintiffs' injuries.* Plaintiffs have strikingly capsulated their reasoning by insisting ". . . that while one manufacturer's product may not have injured a particular plaintiff, we can assume that it injured a different plaintiff and all we are talking about is a mere matching of plaintiffs and defendants." (Counsel's letter (Oct. 16, 1979) p. 3.) In adopting the foregoing rationale the majority rejects over 100 years of tort law which required that before tort liability was imposed a "matching" of defendant's conduct and plaintiff's injury was absolutely essential. . . .

The "market share" thesis may be paraphrased. Plaintiffs have been hurt by *someone* who made DES. Because of the lapse of time no one can prove who made it. Perhaps it was not the named defendants who made it, but they did make some. . . . There should be a remedy. Strict products liability is unavailable because the element of causation is lacking. Strike that requirement and label what remains "alternative" liability, "industry-wide" liability, or "market share" liability, proving thereby that if you hit the square peg hard and often enough the round holes will really become square, although you may splinter the board in the process.

The foregoing result is directly contrary to long established tort principles. Once again, in the words of Dean Prosser, the applicable rule is: "[Plaintiff] must introduce evidence which affords a reasonable basis for the conclusion that it is more likely than not that the conduct of the defendant was a substantial factor in bringing about the result. *A mere possibility of such causation is not enough*; and when the matter remains one of pure speculation or conjecture, or the probabilities are at best evenly balanced, it becomes the duty of the court to direct a verdict for the defendant." (*Prosser, supra*, § 41, . . . italics added, fns. omitted.) Under the majority's new reasoning, however, a defendant is fair game if it happens to be engaged in a similar business and causation is *possible*, even though remote. . . .

Although seeming to acknowledge that imposition of liability upon defendants who probably did not cause plaintiffs' injuries is unfair, the majority justifies this inequity on the ground that "each manufacturer's liability for an injury would be approximately equivalent to the damages caused by the DES it manufactured." . . . In other words, because each defendant's liability is proportionate to its market share, supposedly "each manufacturer's liability would approximate its responsibility for the injuries caused by his own products." . . .

Furthermore, several other important policy considerations persuade me that the majority holding is both inequitable and improper. The injustice inherent in the majority's new theory of liability is compounded by the fact that plaintiffs who use it are treated far more favorably than are the plaintiffs in routine tort actions. In most tort cases plaintiff knows the identity of the person who has caused his injuries. In such a case, plaintiff, of course, has no option to seek recovery from an entire industry or a "substantial" segment thereof, but in the usual instance can recover, if at all, only from the particular defendant causing injury. Such a defendant may or may not be either solvent or amenable to process. Plaintiff in the ordinary tort case must take a chance that defendant can be reached and can respond financially. On what principle should those plaintiffs who wholly fail to prove any causation, an essential element of the traditional tort cause of action, be rewarded by being offered both a wider selection of potential defendants and a greater opportunity for recovery?

The majority attempts to justify its new liability on the ground that defendants herein are "better able to bear the cost of injury resulting from the manufacture of a defective product." . . . This "deep pocket" theory of liability, fastening liability on defendants presumably because they are rich, has understandable popular appeal and might be tolerable in a case disclosing substantially stronger evidence of causation than herein appears. But as a general proposition, a defendant's wealth is an unreliable indicator of fault, and should play no part, at least consciously, in the legal analysis of the problem. In the absence of proof that a particular defendant caused or at least probably caused plaintiff's injuries, a defendant's ability to bear the cost thereof is no more pertinent to the underlying issue of liability than its "substantial" share of the relevant market. A system priding itself on "*equal* justice under law" does not flower when the *liability* as well as the *damage* aspect of a tort action is determined by a defendant's wealth.

The inevitable consequence of such a result is to create and perpetuate two rules of law – one applicable to wealthy defendants, and another standard pertaining to defendants who are poor or who have modest means. . . .

Given the grave and sweeping economic, social, and medical effects of "market share" liability, the policy decision to introduce and define it should rest not with us, but with the Legislature which is currently considering not only major statutory reform of California product liability law in general, but the DES problem in particular. . . .

NOTES

1 Despite the alarming predictions of the *Sindell* dissent, the market share doctrine has had a very limited impact. Market share is a minority doctrine that has not been extended very successfully anywhere beyond the DES scenario.

2 Most jurisdictions adopting the doctrine have come to agree that liability is several only, not joint, and divided according to market share, not according to relative fault.

3 In those few jurisdictions that have adopted market share, how to determine market share has been a perplexing problem. The jurisdictions have varied considerably in the details of the doctrine.

4 Like the court's decision in *Sindell*, most other courts have likewise declined to apply concert of action theory or enterprise liability to product liability cases.

B. PROXIMATE CAUSE

"Causation" frequently is listed as the third element of a negligence cause of action. As we have already observed, to recover, plaintiff must prove that defendant's conduct was an actual cause or "cause in fact" of plaintiff's injury, but such proof is not sufficient on the question of causation. (Should it be? If not, why not?) Many harms that are "caused in fact" by a defendant's breach of duty are thought to be too tenuously connected with defendant's conduct to warrant liability. After all, the chain of "but for" causation can be quite long. Struggling to find some principle by which to sever the potentially endless chain of causes in fact, courts have held that plaintiff must prove that the causal connection between defendant's conduct and plaintiff's harm is sufficiently "proximate" to warrant liability. While this inquiry is treated as a question of fact, it tends to be more of a subjective judgment call.

The word "proximate" means "close." Thus, one way to think of the proximate cause inquiry is that it answers when the defendant will be legally responsible for harm that his negligence has caused in fact because the causal connection is sufficiently close or proximate. This has come to be known as "proximate cause." Use of the term "proximate cause" dates back at least to the seventeenth-century scientist and politician, Francis Bacon, who said, "*In jure non remota causa, sed proxima, spectator*" (in law not the remote cause, but the proximate, is looked to). In twenty-first century America, we do not use the word "proximate" very much, and commentators have criticized the use of the term, sometimes offering to replace it with another term such as "legal cause." Use of the word "proximate" has been criticized as potentially misleading – to be "proximate," a cause need not necessarily be close to the harm caused either geographically or temporally. But while the proximate cause inquiry is not literally temporal or spatial, keeping the literal meaning of the word "proximate" in mind can the help the student avoid the trap of losing track of the fundamental nature of the proximate cause inquiry while wading through the quagmire of the proximate cause case law. Most recently, the drafters of the Restatement (Third) of Torts replace the term "proximate casue" with the phrase "scope of liability." But for now, the new Restatement's attempt to shift the language away from the word "causation" has not yet widely caught on, and most American courts still speak in terms of "proximate cause." Whatever terminology is used, the point of the proximate cause inquiry is to determine that subset of causes in fact for which defendant will be liable.

Proximate cause cases have tended to fall into two categories. One approach toward proximate cause is to ask whether defendant's negligence was a "direct cause" of plaintiff's injury in unbroken sequence. The second approach asks whether plaintiff's injury was a "foreseeable" consequence of defendant's conduct. First we will look at a few general proximate cause cases under the heading of "causal link" to get a feeling for proximate cause concepts. Then the two methods of analyzing proximate cause will be considered in turn. Finally, the topic of superceding cause will be considered.

1. INTRODUCTION – CAUSAL LINK

BERRY V. BOROUGH OF SUGAR NOTCH
43 A. 240 (PA. 1899)

The plaintiff was a motorman in the employ of the Wilkes-Barre and Wyoming Valley Traction Company on its line running from Wilkes-Barre to the borough of Sugar Notch. The ordinance by virtue of which the company was permitted to lay its track and operate its cars in the borough of Sugar Notch contained a provision that the speed of the cars while on the streets of the borough should not exceed eight miles an hour. On the line of the road, and within the borough limits, there was a large chestnut tree, as to the condition of which there was some dispute at the trial. The question of the negligence of the borough in permitting it to remain must, however, be considered as set at rest by the verdict. On the day of the accident the plaintiff was running his car on the borough street in a violent wind-storm, and as he passed under the tree it was blown down, crushing the roof of the car and causing the plaintiff's injury.

There is some conflict of testimony as to the speed at which the car was running, but it seems to be fairly well established that it was considerably in excess of the rate permitted by the borough ordinance. We do not think that the fact that the plaintiff was running his car at a higher rate of speed than eight miles an hour affects his right to recover. It may be that in doing so he violated the ordinance by virtue of which the company was permitted to operate its cars in the streets of the borough, but he certainly was not for that reason without rights upon the streets. Nor can it be said that the speed was the cause of the accident, or contributed to it. It might have been otherwise if the tree had fallen before the car reached it; for in that case a high rate of speed might have rendered it impossible for the plaintiff to avoid a collision which he either foresaw or should have foreseen. . . . The testimony however shows that the tree fell upon the car as it passed beneath. With this phase of the case in view, it was urged on behalf of the appellant that the speed was the immediate cause of the plaintiff's injury, inasmuch as it was the particular speed at which he was running which brought the car to the place of the accident at the moment when the tree blew down. This argument, while we cannot deny its ingenuity, strikes us, to say the least, as being somewhat sophistical. That his speed brought him to the place of the accident at the moment of the accident was the merest chance, and a thing which no foresight could have predicted. The same thing might as readily have happened to a car running slowly, or it might have been that a high speed alone would have carried him beyond the tree to a place of safety. . . .

The judgment is affirmed.

CENTRAL OF GEORGIA RY. CO. V. PRICE
32 S.E. 77 (GA. 1898)

. . . The record discloses that Mrs. Price was a passenger on a train of the defendant company, and that her destination was Winchester, Georgia. Through the negligence of the conductor, she was not put off at Winchester, but was carried on to Montezuma. Upon her arrival at the latter place, the conductor advised her to go to the hotel and spend the night, he agreeing to carry her back to Winchester in the morning when his train made the return trip. He accompanied her to a hotel where a room was assigned her, the conductor agreeing with the proprietor to pay her expenses. She was taken to her room by the proprietor or his servants, and furnished with a kerosene lamp which she left burning after she had retired to bed. Sometime during the night the lamp, she claims, exploded and set fire to a mosquito net which covered the bed, and in her efforts to extinguish the flames her hands were badly burned. She sued the railway company for damages, and, under the charge of the court, the jury returned a verdict in her favor for $400. . . . To this the company excepted. . . .

The negligence of the company consisted in passing the station where the passenger desired to alight, without giving her an opportunity to get off. . . . The negligence of the company in passing her station was . . . not the natural and proximate cause of her injury. . . . The injuries to the plaintiff were not the natural and proximate consequences of carrying her beyond her station, but were unusual and could not have been foreseen or provided against by the highest practicable care. The plaintiff was not entitled to recover for such injuries, and the court erred in overruling the motion for new trial.

Judgment reversed. All the Justices concurring.

The plaintiff is a young girl, between eighteen and nineteen years of age, and the object of the suit is to hold the defendant, director general of railroads, liable in damages for two acts of rape upon her person, committed by two men shortly after she had been, as she alleges, negligently required to leave the defendant's train in a dangerous and unprotected place.

. . . The occurrences complained of transpired in daylight, but very shortly before dark, on the 2nd day of February, 1919. The plaintiff was a passenger on the defendant's train and held a ticket from the city of Washington, D.C., to a station called Seminary, in Fairfax county. The train failed to stop at Seminary, and thereupon another passenger, one W. L. Garnett, who also held a ticket for that station, called the attention of a flagman to the fact that he had bought a ticket for that place and wanted to get off. The train was then stopped, and Garnett alighted and walked by a near way to his home. About that time the plaintiff told the conductor she had a ticket to Seminary, and she was about to get off, but he directed her to wait, as he intended to back the train to the station. . . . He then said that he could not go back because he was afraid he would run into another train, and that she would, therefore, have to go on through and be sent back to Seminary on the next train, or else get off at that point. She testified that the conductor's manner was very rough, and that he seemed indifferent to what happened to her; and . . . she understood him to mean that if she did not get off at that point he would carry her on all the way through to Richmond before starting her on the return journey, which would involve a long trip in the night and much discomfort and inconvenience. Thereupon, she said to him: "Let me off," and he stopped the train and she left the car. About the same time, a man wearing a United States army uniform, generally referred to in the record as a soldier, got off the train on the opposite side. The plaintiff started back in the direction of Seminary, walking alongside the track. The soldier followed, and shortly overtook her, taking hold of her arm and asking if he might accompany her home. She denied this request, and he thereupon forcibly carried her across the track and down a high embankment to an obscure spot, where he pushed her to the ground and ravished her. After accomplishing his fiendish purpose, he left her, and has never been identified. Within a few moments thereafter, and while she was still trying to arise from the ground, a man dressed in citizen's clothes, described by her as a civilian, appeared and ravished her the second time. He likewise disappeared, and has never been identified. . . . After both of these horrible occurrences, she struggled to her feet, came back to the surface of the railroad grade, and was then met by two citizens living in the neighborhood, who escorted her to her home. One of these parties, a Mr. Cockrell, had, from his home a few hundred yards away, seen the plaintiff leave the train, with the soldier following. His attention was diverted, and he did not see them leave the railroad grade, but a few minutes later saw that they had disappeared. This fact aroused his suspicion, and he called a companion and they set out to see what had become of the young woman. They testified that when they met her she was in a most pitiable condition – her clothing soiled and disarranged, her mouth bleeding, her face dirty, and her mental condition plainly evidencing that she had been subjected to some horrible treatment. . . .

The point at which the plaintiff left the train was about four-fifths of a mile from the flag-station known as Seminary, and there was abundant evidence to show that on the right-hand side of the railroad track, leading back from that point to Seminary, there was a ravine or depression, locally known as "Hoboes' Hollow," "Tramps' Hollow," and "Tramps' Den," which was then, and had been for at least a year (during the whole of the regime of the director general of railroads), habitually frequented and infested by hoboes, tramps and questionable characters. . . .

In the case of *N. & W. Ry. Co. v. Whitehurst,* 125 Va. 260, 263, 99 S.E. 568, 569, Judge Burks, delivering the opinion of this court, said: "The 'foreseeableness,' or reasonable anticipation of the consequences of a wrongful or negligent act is not the measure of liability of the guilty party, though it may be determinative of the question of his negligence. When once it has been determined that the act is wrongful or negligent, the guilty party is liable for all the consequences which naturally flow therefrom, whether they were reasonably to have been anticipated or not, and in determining whether or not the consequences do naturally flow from the wrongful act or neglect, the case should be viewed retrospectively; that is to say, looking at the consequences, were they so improbable or unlikely to occur that it would not be fair and just to charge a reasonably prudent man with them. If not, he is liable. This is the test of liability, but when liability has been established, its extent is to be measured by the natural consequences of the negligent or wrongful act. The precise injury need not have been anticipated. It is enough if the act is such that the party ought to have anticipated that it was liable to result in injury to others. . . .

Applying the rule above quoted, . . . the case, to say the least of it, was clearly one in which the jury might have properly found in her favor. It requires no resort to a retrospective view of the facts to reach this conclusion. The consequences which overtook this young woman were sufficiently probable to charge any responsible party with the duty of guarding against them. No eighteen-year-old girl should be required to set out alone, near nightfall, to walk along an unprotected route, passing a spot which is physically so situated as to lend itself to the perpetration of a criminal assault, and which is infested by worthless, irresponsible and questionable characters known as tramps and hoboes; and no prudent man, charged with her care, would willingly cause her to do so. The very danger to which this unfortunate girl fell a victim is the one which would at once suggest itself to the average and normal mind as a danger liable to overtake her under these circumstances. It is no answer to the proposition to say that the presumption is that crimes of this character will not be committed. The presumption applies under ordinary circumstances, but it is not to be indulged, and ordinarily prudent men do not indulge it, to the extent of regarding it safe to expose a young woman to such a risk as the plaintiff in this case incurred in passing "Hobo Hollow" as the shades of night were approaching. The fact that there were numerous houses within a few hundred yards of the place does not relieve the situation, if . . . the place itself was dangerous and unprotected. . . .

The chief defense under this branch of the case seems to be based upon the proposition that even if the plaintiff was negligently required to leave the train, the assaults upon her cannot be regarded as the proximate result of that negligence, because they resulted from an independent act of third persons over whom the defendant had no control and with whom it had no relation. Numerous authorities are cited in support of this proposition. We shall content ourselves, in the main, by saying that only a few of the cases relied upon appear to us difficult of substantial distinction from the present case, and that to such as are in conflict with the views herein expressed we are unable to give our approval. . . .

We do not wish to be understood as questioning the general proposition that no responsibility for a wrong attaches whenever an independent act of a third person intervenes between the negligence complained of and the injury. But, as pointed out by Judge Keith in *Connell v. C. & O. Ry. Co.,* 93 Va. 44, 57 . . . , this proposition does not apply where the very negligence alleged consists of exposing the injured party to the act causing the injury. It is perfectly well settled and will not be seriously denied that wherever a carrier has reason to anticipate the danger of an assault upon one of its passengers, it rests under the duty of protecting such passenger against the same. . . .

ATLANTIC COAST LINE R.R. V. DANIELS
70 S.E. 203 (GA. 1911)

. . . The plaintiff was driving an automobile on one of the streets of Savannah, and came to a place where the railroad company's tracks cross the street on an embankment several feet higher than the usual street level, so that the approaches to the crossing are on an incline. At this point the company maintains crossing bars, controlled from a signal-tower located near the crossing. When a train approaches the crossing the bars are lowered, thus excluding travelers from the tracks. When the bars are up, this is a signal to the public that they may cross without danger from the trains. The tracks approach the crossing on a curve, and persons traveling upon the street cannot tell when a train is coming, otherwise than through observing the condition of the crossing bars. The man in the tower who controlled the bars had a view of the tracks, of the crossing, and of persons approaching the crossing from either direction. The plaintiff, as he approached the crossing, saw that the bars were up, indicating that the way was clear. . . . As he came upon the tracks the towerman suddenly lowered the bars on both sides of the crossing, thus penning him in upon the tracks. He threw his brakes on in full emergency and stopped the machine (the gasoline engine, as well as the automobile itself), but did not change the . . . levers. There were three tracks. He stopped on the first. The towerman cried out to him to move the machine, that a train was coming. He released the brakes, and, getting behind the machine, with an abnormal degree of strength caused by the excitement of the emergency, pushed the machine from the first track to the second track. The towerman cried to him again, telling him to move the machine, that the train was coming on the middle track. He gave it another shove, and just as he got it on to the third track the engine and cars dashed by on the middle track. The bars were then raised so that the plaintiff could proceed; but, according to the allegations of the petition, he was so unnerved and robbed of his ordinary senses by the fright which the situation had produced that he forgot the condition in which he had left his levers, and attempted to start the machine with the maximum power turned on. The result was that when he turned the crank, the engine "kicked back," threw him against the radiator of the machine, broke out several of his teeth, and inflicted other severe injuries upon his mouth and face. . . . The defendant filed a general demurrer to the petition, insisting that under the allegations, the defendant's negligence cannot be considered as the proximate cause of the plaintiff's injury; that the injury was not a natural or a reasonably to be anticipated effect of the defendant's act . . . . The trial court overruled the demurrer, and the defendant brings error.

. . . We have read and reread a multitude of cases on the subject of what relation must exist between a negligent act and an injury that follows, in order that the author of the one may be held liable in damages to the sufferer of the other. We have read of "proximate cause" and of "natural consequence," and of other phrases expressing the same general idea, until eyes have grown weak with reading and brain fagged out with trying to understand what learned judge after learned judge and learned law-writer after learned law-writer have said on the subject; and yet we realize that we have not pursued the subject further than to examine only a small percentage of the cases and of the text-books that we might have read. But the thought comes to us, that one may live in sight of the ocean for a lifetime, may sail upon it, may know its moods in the calm and in the storm, and yet not be able to answer some simple question as to a cup of cold water. He who so oft had studied with most critical and intelligent eyes the profusion of flowers in which England's gardens and fields abound confessed how little he knew of the "all in all" of the single and insignificant flower which he plucked from the crannied wall. Thus much we have said by way of explaining why in this opinion there is absence of citation of cases on a subject as to which cases so abound.

Cause and effect find their beginning and end in the limitless and unknowable. Therefore, courts, in their finitude, do not attempt to deal with cause and effect in any absolute degree, but only in such a limited way as is practical and as is within the scope of ordinary human understanding. Hence, arbitrary limits have been set; and such qualifying words as "proximate" and "natural" have come into use as setting the limits beyond which the courts will not look, in the attempt to trace the connection between a given cause and a given effect. A plaintiff comes into court alleging, as an effect, some injury that has been done to his person or to his property. He shows that antecedent to the injury a wrongful act of another person occurred, and that if this wrongful act had not occurred, the injury complained of would not (as human probabilities go) have occurred. We then say, in common speech, that the wrong was a cause of the injury. But to make such a standard (that if the cause had not existed, the effect would not have occurred) the basis of legal responsibility would soon prove very unsatisfactory; for a reductio ad absurdum may be promptly established by calling to mind that if the injured person had never been born, the injury would not have happened. So the courts ask another question: Was the wrongful act the proximate cause?

All the past is a part of the cause of every present effect. The courts can deal with that great body of cause only as it relates to human activity; and a particular court dealing with a particular case must as a practical necessity isolate the activities nearby to the effect in question, and from these must make the juridic determination of responsibility. Now, as activities are viewed by the courts in administering the law, they divide themselves into two classes—proper or non-negligent activities and wrongful or negligent activities. (The word "activity" is here used in a sense broad enough to include both omission and commission.) The normal course of things which the law seeks to establish, and for a violation of which the law professes to give redress, is for all men to regulate their activities properly,—that is to say, non-negligently; and whether a man has so regulated his activities is usually determined by comparing what he did under the circumstances with what an ordinary man of common prudence would have done under the same circumstances. If hurt comes to a person, and by looking back through the near-by causes which concentrated and became effectual in the hurtful thing, it appears that all those whose activities were concerned acted lawfully and as ordinarily prudent men would have acted, we say that the person so hurt has suffered an accident, and no legal responsibility can be asserted against any one. But if, in examining the causes which joined in producing the effect, we find that one or more of them consisted in somebody's having violated the standard and having done something which an ordinarily prudent man would not have done, the first step toward the declaration of legal responsibility is established. We then say that the injury was the result of negligence . . . .

Though negligence is discovered in relation to one of the causes which have preceded the injurious effect, it does not follow that the author of the negligence is to be held legally responsible for the injury. In the first place, to judge the transaction according to the natural probabilities which men's minds take as the basis for passing judgment upon the course of human affairs, it may appear that causes other than the negligent one referred to so preponderated in bringing about the result as to lead us to say, from a human point of view, that the injury was just as likely to have ensued (with only its details somewhat varied, perhaps) if the negligent thing had not occurred. In such cases we exempt the author of the negligence from liability.

Again, it may appear that the negligent act in question was not the only one of the near causes which was negligent. In case two or more near and preponderating negligent causes are found to have become effectuated in the same injurious result, the question as to which of the two or more negligent actors is to be held responsible is determined usually in this wise: If the two negligent acts are so related that the first would not probably have resulted in injury if the other had not occurred, and the latter amounts to such a preponderating cause that it probably would have produced the injury even if the first negligence had not occurred, or if the author of the latter negligence, with the intermediate effects of the former negligence consciously before him, is guilty of a new negligent act which preponderates in producing the injurious effect, we say that the first negligent cause is not the proximate cause, that the intervention of the latter negligence breaks the chain of causal connection so far as juridic purposes are concerned. But if two negligent causes stand so related that neither would have produced a harmful result but for the other, and both of them consist of such acts as, according to the general course of human probabilities, produce some such injurious effect as that which did in fact ensue,—i.e., if both the negligent causes are material factors in producing the injury, and are closely connected with it, and one has not so intervened as to make it the preponderating cause, we say that the two negligent actors are guilty of concurring negligence; or if one of the two negligent actors is himself the complaining party, we speak of his conduct as contributory negligence. Hence, the proximate cause of an injury may not, even in juridic contemplation, be sole or single.

Now if it appears that the injury resulted from a condition into which there entered both negligent and non-negligent activities, and that according to the laws of human probability the injury would not have resulted but for the negligent activities, and that when the negligent and non-negligent activities united, the injury naturally followed, the law disregards the non-negligent activities as causes, considers them as but a part of the normal environment, and considers the negligent actor as disturbing that normality, and, therefore, as being the juridic cause of the injury. The law looks upon the ordinary current of prudently and lawfully conducted human activity as an ever moving stream of energy which may do hurt to those who come within its way, but which can never cause legal injury. Disturb it with negligence, and it flows on; and if the disturbance produced by the negligence causes it to flow in such a way as that it does a hurt which it otherwise would not have done, the negligence, and not the normal stream, is, in legal contemplation, the cause of the injury.

Now, call one other thing to mind, and we will proceed to apply the principles we are discussing to the facts of the case. In every case where a personal injury is complained of, the activities of the injured person are, of necessity, a part of the general conditions attendant upon the particular effect asserted. If his conduct at the time of the injury and precedent thereto has conformed to the normal standard of prudence, his activities are considered as merely a part of the ordinary flow of human activity. If he has been guilty of negligence, then, in determining the proximate cause of the injury, his negligence counts just as if it were anybody else's. It may itself be the proximate cause. It may so intervene between prior negligence of some other person and the injurious effect as to break the line of causal connection. It may concur with the negligence of another person.

In this case the injurious effect was the personal harm done to the plaintiff by the gasoline engine of an automobile kicking back when the plaintiff attempted to crank it. The activities of inanimate things are of course mere conditions, and not causes. The immediate cause of the kicking was the fact that the plaintiff attempted to crank the machine when the spark and gasoline regulators were turned on at full power. Here we find a human activity. Was it a juridic cause? If the plaintiff acted just as the ordinarily prudent man (whom the law takes as its standard) would have acted under similar circumstances, his conduct is to be considered as a part of the normal course of human affairs, and therefore as a medium instead of a cause. The defendant, through its able and earnest counsel, says that an ordinarily prudent man would not have cranked the automobile, knowing that the spark and gasoline were on the machine at their maximum. Counsel for the plaintiff, equally able, equally earnest, assert that while an ordinarily prudent man would not usually attempt to crank an automobile with the spark and gasoline thus on, still that an ordinarily prudent man is likely to do just this very thing if placed in the situation in which the plaintiff was placed—that the plaintiff had just passed through such a terrifying experience as would rob a man of ordinary prudence of the quality of judgment which he usually possesses and which usually guides his conduct. We recognize the principle that if a man has been robbed of his power of judgment by some act not within his control, his resulting lack of judgment becomes a part of the circumstances to be considered; it is in accordance with the rule we have stated, to compare his conduct with the conduct of an ordinarily prudent man *under similar circumstances*. . . . It is true that in the case of a frightened person we have the preliminary question as to whether an ordinarily prudent person would have become so frightened as the particular person was under the circumstances; for we think that it is the part of prudence not to allow one's self to become unduly frightened at causes normally insufficient to produce such an effect. The issue thus made as to what an ordinarily prudent man would have done if he had been circumstanced as the plaintiff was—frightened out of his senses, as he says he was and as the demurrer admits he was—is one that we as judges have no right to decide. It is a matter as to which fair and intelligent minds may easily differ, and is a question of fact. Such questions are for the jury to decide. Since the questions as to whether a reasonably prudent man frightened as the plaintiff was would have attempted to crank his machine with the power on at a maximum, and whether a reasonably prudent man would have experienced such fright as the plaintiff experienced from the circumstances in which he was placed, are jury questions, we must, on demurrer, give the plaintiff the advantage of this point, and consider them as conditions of the injury, rather than causes of the injury.

Thus considering the fright of the plaintiff as a condition rather than a cause of his injury, we must further inquire if the alleged negligent act of the defendant bore such relation to this fright as to be considered as having caused it from the legal point of view. (It may be stated here that it is conceded that, in an abstract sense, the act alleged against the defendant was a negligent act; and the question before this court is whether such a causal connection exists between that act and the plaintiff's injury as that the one may be held to be the juridic or proximate cause of the other.) We will test this by the standards stated above. If the negligence had not occurred, the fright would not have ensued. So, in the broad sense, the negligence was the cause of the fright. It is likewise fair to say that if it is conceded or established that a normally prudent man would have been similarly frightened under the conditions which surrounded the plaintiff as the immediate result of the defendant's negligence, it follows as a necessary logical consequence that the negligence is to be considered as the preponderating cause in producing the fright.

Nothing appears in the case made by the facts stated in the petition to require a belief that, according to the ordinary course of human probability, the fright and the consequent injury would have occurred if the negligence had not operated in a direct causal way upon the conditions surrounding the transaction. We find the plaintiff coming lawfully and prudently within the range of the defendant's activities; as he comes he is uninjured; while he is within the range of those activities the defendant violates the normal standard—acts as a reasonably prudent person would not have acted under the circumstances (for we are assuming the defendant's negligence); and before the plaintiff gets from within the range of these activities he is hurt as the result of a condition to the creation of which these activities contributed in a causal way; wherever else we look among the sum total of the general causes which joined to create the condition and to characterize it, we find no other variation from the normal course of prudence; we except all these other causes, class them as merely a part of the condition or innocuous medium through which the defendant's negligent activities became effectual, and say that the defendant's negligence was, therefore, the sole, direct, and proximate cause of the plaintiff's injury.

To view the case in this way makes it seem simpler than when we try to decide it by any direct application of such undigested, ambiguous, and often misleading general terms as "proximate cause," "natural and probable cause," "controlling and preponderating cause," "chief preponderating cause," "remote consequence," "what a reasonably prudent man should have foreseen under the circumstances," "what follows as a natural result in the ordinary course of nature," "interposition of separate, independent agencies," and all those other phrases which swarm in the reports of negligence cases; but we think that in this more elemental view is reflected the true essence of all these law phrases.

Before the jury can find the defendant liable in this case, they must find that the act of the defendant in allowing the plaintiff to come on the tracks and in shutting him in there while the train was coming was an act of negligence. If they find that this was negligence they must further find that the situation produced by this negligence was such as to frighten a normal person, and to frighten him to such a degree as so to rob him of memory and judgment that if he had been in the plaintiff's situation, he (the normal person) would have likely forgotten the condition in which he left the spark and gasoline levers on his automobile, and would have had no better sense than to attempt to crank the machine without first examining the levers. If they find that the plaintiff experienced such a fright from the negligence of the defendant, and that the fright was natural and normal under the circumstances, and that the impulse and effect of this fright caused him to forget that his machine had been left in a dangerous condition, and caused him to omit such acts of prudence as an ordinarily prudent man would have performed before attempting to crank it, in order to move it off the track, and that while in this state of mind, thus temporarily rendered abnormal, he forgot the condition of the levers and attempted to crank the machine, unconscious of the danger, and was injured, such causal connection between the negligence and the damages is established as to authorize the jury to find the defendant liable. On the other hand, if the jury should find that the defendant's acts were not negligent, or that, if negligent, they were not such as to produce such a sense-robbing degree of fright in a normal person as to cause him to forget the condition of his machine or to neglect to take usual and ordinary precaution before attempting to crank it, or that the defendant's forgetfulness of the dangerous condition of his machine, or his neglect to examine into its condition before attempting to crank it, was the result of his own carelessness more largely than of any fright which he had normally experienced, the jury should find for the defendant. Thus the question is one for the jury; and the court properly declined to solve it on demurrer.

Judgment affirmed.

2. DIRECT CAUSE TEST

IN RE POLEMIS AND FURNESS, WITHY & CO.
3 KB 560 (C.A. 1921)

. . . [T]he respondents charted their vessel to the appellants. The vessel was employed by the charterers to carry a cargo to Casablanca in Morocco. The cargo included a quantity of benzene or petrol in cases. While discharging at Casablanca a heavy plank fell into the hold in which petrol was stowed, and caused an explosion, which set fire to the vessel and completely destroyed her. The owners claimed the value of the vessel from the charterers, alleging that the loss of the vessel was due to the negligence of the charterers' servants. The charterers contended that . . . the damages claimed were too remote. The claim was referred to arbitration . . . .

The three arbitrators made the following findings of fact:–

a. That the ship was lost by fire.

b. That the fire arose from a spark igniting petrol vapour in the hold.

c. That the spark was caused by the falling board coming into contact with some substance in the hold.

d. That the fall of the board was caused by the negligence of the Arabs (other than the winchmen) engaged in the work of discharging.

e. That the said Arabs were employed by the charterers or their agents the Cie. Transatlantique on behalf of the charterers, and that the said Arabs were the servants of the charterers.

f. That the causing of the spark could not reasonably have been anticipated from the falling of the board, though some damage to the ship might reasonably have been anticipated.

g. There was no evidence before us that the Arabs chosen were known or likely to be negligent. . . .

Bankes, L.J.

. . . According to the one view, the consequences which may reasonably be expected to result from a particular act are material only in reference to the question whether the act is or is not a negligent act; according to the other view, those consequences are the test whether the damages resulting from the act, assuming it to be negligent, are or are not too remote to be recoverable. . . . In *Smith v. London and South Western Ry. Co.* . . . Blackburn J. . . . said: "What the defendants might reasonably anticipate is only material with reference to the question, whether the defendants were negligent or not, and cannot alter their liability if they were guilty of negligence." . . .

In the present case the arbitrators have found as a fact that the falling of the plank was due to the negligence of the defendants' servants. The fire appears to me to have been directly caused by the falling of the plank. Under these circumstances I consider that it is immaterial that the causing of the spark by the falling of the plank could not have been reasonably anticipated. The appellants' junior counsel sought to draw a distinction between the anticipation of the extent of damage resulting from a negligent act, and the anticipation of the type of damage resulting from such an act. He admitted that it could not lie in the mouth of a person whose negligent act had caused damage to say that he could not reasonably have foreseen the extent of the damage, but he contended that the negligent person was entitled to rely upon the fact that he could not reasonably have anticipated the type of damage which resulted from his negligent act. I do not think that the distinction can be admitted. Given the breach of duty which constitutes the negligence, and given the damage as a direct result of that negligence, the anticipations of the person whose negligent act has produced the damage appear to me to be irrelevant. I consider that the damages claimed are not too remote.

For these reasons I think that the appeal fails, and must be dismissed with costs.

Warrington L.J.

. . . The presence or absence of reasonable anticipation of damage determines the legal quality of the act as negligent or innocent. If it be thus determined to be negligent, then the question whether particular damages are recoverable depends only on the answer to the question whether they are the direct consequence of the act. . . .

In the present case it is clear that the act causing the plank to fall was in law a negligent act, because some damage to the ship might reasonably be anticipated. If this is so then the appellants are liable for the actual loss, that being on the finds of the arbitrators the direct result of the falling board. . . .

On the whole in my opinion the appeal fails and must be dismissed with costs.

Scrutton L.J. . . .

The second defence is that the damage is too remote from the negligence, as it could not be reasonably foreseen as a consequence. On this head we were referred to a number of well-known cases in which vague language, which I cannot think to be really helpful, has been used in an attempt to define the point at which damage becomes too remote from, or not sufficiently directly caused by, the breach of duty, which is the original cause of action, to be recoverable. For instance, I cannot think it useful to say the damage must be the natural and probable result. This suggests that there are results which are natural but not probable, and other results which are probable but not natural. I am not sure what either adjective means in this connection; if they mean the same things, the difference between them should be defined. And as to many cases of fact in which the distinction has been drawn, it is difficult to see why one case should be decided one way and one another. . . . To determine whether an act is negligent, it is relevant to determine whether any reasonable person would foresee that the act would cause damage: if he would not, the act is not negligent. But if the act would or might probably cause damage, the fact that the damage it in fact causes is not the exact kind of damage one would expect is immaterial, so long as the damage is in fact directly traceable to the negligent act, and not due to the operation of independent causes having no connection with the negligent act, except that they could not avoid its results. Once the act is negligent, the fact that its exact operation was not foreseen is immaterial. In the present case it was negligent in discharging cargo to knock down the planks of the temporary staging, for they might easily cause some damage either to workmen, or cargo, or the ship. The fact that they did directly produce an unexpected result, a spark in an atmosphere of petrol vapour which caused a fire, does not relieve the person who was negligent from the damage which his negligent act directly caused.

For these reasons the experienced arbitrators and the judge appealed from came, in my opinion, to a correct decision, and the appeal must be dismissed with costs.

QUESTION

1   Assuming that the Great Chicago Fire started when Mrs. O'Leary's cow kicked over a lantern and that Mrs. O'Leary was negligent in her use and supervision of the cow and lantern, under the approach to proximate cause exemplified in *Polemis*, for how much of the damage would Mrs. O'Leary be responsible?

VIRGINIA MODEL JURY INSTRUCTIONS
CIVIL. VOL I, INSTRUCTIONS NO. 5.000 (1-93)(2006)

Definition of Proximate Cause

"A proximate cause of an accident, injury, or damage is a cause which in natural and continuous sequence produces the accident, injury, or damage. It is a cause without which the accident, injury, or damage would not have occurred."

3. FORSEEABILITY / SCOPE OF THE RISK TEST

The "direct cause" test has been criticized as both over—and under—inclusive. Under that approach, many very remote causes of harm would be considered "proximate," so long as there is no intervening, unnatural force. On the other hand, many very foreseeable causes will be considered not proximate, merely because some very predictable force, sometimes the action of a third party, intervenes. The "foreseeability" or "scope of the risk" approach is intended to "remedy" some of the problems with the direct cause approach.

The following case involves a scenario analogous to the Great Chicago Fire scenario presented in the note above. This type of scenario was central to the famous debate between Cardozo and Andrews in the *Palsgraf* case that follows. *Palsgraf* is the most famous American proximate cause case.

RYAN V. NEW YORK CENTAL R.R.
35 N.Y. 210 (1866)

On the 15th day of July, 1854, in the city of Syracuse, the defendant, by the careless management, or through the insufficient condition, of one of its engines, set fire to its woodshed, and a large quantity of wood therein. The plaintiff's house, situated at a distance of one hundred and thirty feet from the shed, soon took fire from the heat and sparks, and was entirely consumed . . . . A number of other houses were also burned by the spreading of the fire. The plaintiff brings this action to recover from the railroad company the value of his building thus destroyed. . . .

The question may be thus stated: A house in a populous city takes fire, through the negligence of the owner or his servant; the flames extend to and destroy an adjacent building: Is the owner of the first building liable to the second owner for the damage sustained by such burning?

It is a general principle that every person is liable for the consequences of his own acts. He is thus liable in damages for the proximate results of his own acts, but not for remote damages. It is not easy at all times to determine what are proximate and what are remote damages. In *Thomas* v. *Winchester* . . . Judge Ruggles defines the damages for which a party is liable, as those which are the natural or necessary consequences of his acts. Thus, the owner of a loaded gun, who puts it in the hands of a child, by whose indiscretion it is discharged, is liable for the injury sustained by a third person from such discharge . . . . The injury is a natural and ordinary result of the folly of placing a loaded gun in the hands of one ignorant of the manner of using it, and incapable of appreciating its effects. The owner of a horse and cart, who leaves them unattended in the street, is liable for an injury done to a person or his property, by the running away of the horse . . . . The injury is the natural result of the negligence. If the party thus injured had, however, by the delay or confinement from his injury, been prevented from completing a valuable contract, from which he expected to make large profits, he could not recover such expected profits from the negligent party, in the cases supposed. Such damages would not be the necessary or natural consequences, nor the results ordinarily to be anticipated, from the negligence committed. . . . So if an engineer upon a steamboat or locomotive, in passing the house of A., so carelessly manages its machinery that the coals and sparks from its fires fall upon and consume the house of A., the railroad company or the steamboat proprietors are liable to pay the value of the property thus destroyed. . . . Thus far the law is settled and the principle is apparent. If, however, the fire communicates from the house of A. to that of B., and that is destroyed, is the negligent party liable for his loss? And if it spreads thence to the house of C., and thence to the house of D., and thence consecutively through the other houses, until it reaches and consumes the house of Z., is the party liable to pay the damages sustained by these twenty-four sufferers? The counsel for the plaintiff does not distinctly claim this, and I think it would not be seriously insisted that the sufferers could recover in such case. Where, then, is the principle upon which A. recovers and Z. fails?

. . . [I]n the one case, . . . the destruction of the building upon which the sparks were thrown by the negligent act of the party sought to be charged, the result was to have been anticipated the moment the fire was communicated to the building; that its destruction was the ordinary and natural result of its being fired. In the second, third or twenty-fourth case, as supposed, the destruction of the building was not a natural and expected result of the first firing. That a building upon which sparks and cinders fall should be destroyed or seriously injured must be expected, but that the fire should spread and other buildings be consumed, is not a necessary or an usual result. That it is possible, and that it is not unfrequent, cannot be denied. The result, however, depends, not upon any necessity of a further communication of the fire, but upon a concurrence of accidental circumstances, such as the degree of the heat, the state of the atmosphere, the condition and materials of the adjoining structures and the direction of the wind. These are accidental and varying circumstances. The party has no control over them, and is not responsible for their effects.

My opinion, therefore, is that this action cannot be sustained, for the reason that the damages incurred are not the immediate but the remote result of the negligence of the defendants. The immediate result was the destruction of their own wood and sheds; beyond that, it was remote.

There are some cases which, from the frequency of their citation, and their apparent inconsistency with the view I have taken, should be considered in this connection. The case of *Scott* v. *Shepherd* . . . is that of the celebrated squib case. On the evening of a fair day at Melborneport, the defendant, a lad, threw a lighted squib, or serpent, made of gunpowder, from the street into the market house, which was a covered building, supported by arches, inclosed at one end, but open at the other and at both sides. A large concourse of people were assembled in the market house. The lighted squib, so thrown by the defendant, fell upon the stand of one Yates, where gingerbread, cakes and pies were sold. To prevent injury to himself and the wares of Yates, one Willis instantly took up the squib from the stand and threw it across the market house, when it fell upon another stand of one Ryal, who sold the same sort of wares. Ryal instantly took up the squib, to save his own goods, and threw it to another part of the market house. In its passage, it struck the plaintiff, then in the market house, in the face, and bursting, put out one of his eyes. A recovery . . . by the plaintiff was sustained by the English Court of Common Pleas. . . .

De Grey, Ch. J. . . . says that . . . the true question is, whether the injury was the direct and immediate act of the defendant. He says, also, "I look upon all that was done, subsequent to the original throwing, as a continuation of the first force and first act, which will continue until the squib was spent by bursting. It has been urged, he says, that the intervention of a free agent will make a difference, but I do not consider Willis and Ryal as free agents in the present case, but acting under a compulsive necessity for their own safety and self-preservation." . . . Neither was the continuance of the fire in the present case a "compulsive necessity," such as was imputed to Ryal and Willis in the case under discussion. . . .

The same principle was announced in *Guille* v. *Swaan* . . . , where the defendant's balloon descended into the plaintiff's garden, and a crowd of people rushing in to relieve him, as well as from motives of curiosity, trod down the plaintiff's vegetables and flowers. For the injury done by himself, as well as by the crowd, the defendant was held to be answerable. He was held to have substantially requested the presence of the crowd there, and, therefore, to have been responsible for the results of their action.

Without determining its effect, it will be observed, that the fact exists in each of these cases, that the first act or impulse was voluntary and intentional on the part of the defendant. Scott intentionally threw his squib . . . and Swan intentionally descended into the plaintiff's garden and invoked the aid of the multitude. In each case, too, the result was deemed by the court to be the inevitable consequence of the original unlawful or improper act. There would seem to be no inconsistency in principle between either of these cases and the conclusion already announced in the present case. Whether the principle has been always correctly applied, it is not necessary to determine. . . .

To sustain such a claim as the present, and to follow the same to its legitimate consequences, would subject to a liability against which no prudence could guard, and to meet which no private fortune would be adequate. Nearly all fires are caused by negligence, in its extended sense. In a country where wood, coal, gas and oils are universally used, where men are crowded into cities and villages, where servants are employed, and where children find their home in all houses, it is impossible that the most vigilant prudence should guard against the occurrence of accidental or negligent fires. A man may insure his own house or his own furniture, but he cannot insure his neighbor's building or furniture, for the reason that he has no interest in them. To hold that the owner must not only meet his own loss by fire, but that he must guarantee the security of his neighbors on both sides, and to an unlimited extent, would be to create a liability which would be the destruction of all civilized society. No community could long exist, under the operation of such a principle. In a commercial country, each man, to some extent, runs the hazard of his neighbor's conduct, and each, by insurance against such hazards, is enabled to obtain a reasonable security against loss. . . . The remoteness of the damage, in my judgment, forms the true rule on which the question should be decided, and which prohibits a recovery by the plaintiff in this case. . . .

PALSGRAF V. LONG ISLAND R.R. CO.
162 N.E. 99 (N.Y. 1928)

Cardozo, C.J.

Plaintiff was standing on a platform of defendant's railroad after buying a ticket to go to Rockaway Beach. A train stopped at the station, bound for another place. Two men ran forward to catch it. One of the men reached the platform of the car without mishap, though the train was already moving. The other man, carrying a package, jumped aboard the car, but seemed unsteady as if about to fall. A guard on the car, who had held the door open, reached forward to help him in, and another guard on the platform pushed him from behind. In this act, the package was dislodged, and fell upon the rails. It was a package of small size, about fifteen inches long, and was covered by a newspaper. In fact it contained fireworks, but there was nothing in its appearance to give notice of its contents. The fireworks when they fell exploded. The shock of the explosion threw down some scales at the other end of the platform, many feet away. The scales struck the plaintiff, causing injuries for which she sues.

The conduct of the defendant's guard, if a wrong in its relation to the holder of the package, was not a wrong in its relation to the plaintiff, standing far away. Relatively to her it was not negligence at all. Nothing in the situation gave notice that the falling package had in it the potency of peril to persons thus removed. Negligence is not actionable unless it involves the invasion of a legally protected interest, the violation of a right. . . . The plaintiff as she stood upon the platform of the station might claim to be protected against intentional invasion of her bodily security. Such invasion is not charged. She might claim to be protected against unintentional invasion by conduct involving in the thought of reasonable men an unreasonable hazard that such invasion would ensue. These, from the point of view of the law, were the bounds of her immunity, with perhaps some rare exceptions, survivals for the most part of ancient forms of liability, where conduct is held to be at the peril of the actor. . . . If no hazard was apparent to the eye of ordinary vigilance, an act innocent and harmless, at least to outward seeming, with reference to her, did not take to itself the quality of a tort because it happened to be a wrong, though apparently not one involving the risk of bodily insecurity, with reference to someone else. . . . The plaintiff sues in her own right for a wrong personal to her, and not as the vicarious beneficiary of a breach of duty to another.

A different conclusion will involve us, and swiftly too, in a maze of contradictions. A guard stumbles over a package which has been left upon a platform. It seems to be a bundle of newspapers. It turns out to be a can of dynamite. To the eye of ordinary vigilance, the bundle is abandoned waste, which may be kicked or trod on with impunity. Is a passenger at the other end of the platform protected by the law against the unsuspected hazard concealed beneath the waste? If not, is the result to be any different, so far as the distant passenger is concerned, when the guard stumbles over a valise which a truckman or a porter has left upon the walk? . . . In this case, the rights that are said to have been violated, the interests said to have been invaded, are not even of the same order. The man was not injured in his person nor even put in danger. The purpose of the act, as well as its effect, was to make his person safe. If there was a wrong to him at all, which may very well be doubted, it was a wrong to a property interest only, the safety of his package. Out of this wrong to property, which threatened injury to nothing else, there has passed, we are told, to the plaintiff by derivation or succession a right of action for the invasion of an interest of another order, the right to bodily security. The diversity of interests emphasizes the futility of the effort to build the plaintiff's right upon the basis of a wrong to someone else. The gain is one of emphasis, for a like result would follow if the interests were the same. Even then, the orbit of the danger as disclosed to the eye of reasonable vigilance would be the orbit of the duty. One who jostles one's neighbor in a crowd does not invade the rights of others standing at the outer fringe when the unintended contact casts a bomb upon the ground. The wrongdoer as to them is the man who carries the bomb, not the one who explodes it without suspicion of the danger. . . .

The argument for the plaintiff is built upon the shifting meanings of such words as "wrong" and "wrongful," and shares their instability. What the plaintiff must show is "a wrong" to herself, i.e., a violation of her own right, and not merely a wrong to someone else, nor conduct "wrongful" because unsocial, but not "a wrong" to anyone. We are told that one who drives at reckless speed through a crowded city street is guilty of a negligent act and, therefore, of a wrongful one irrespective of the consequences. Negligent the act is, and wrongful in the sense that it is unsocial, but wrongful and unsocial in relation to other travelers, only because the eye of vigilance perceives the risk of damage. If the same act were to be committed on a speedway or a race course, it would lose its wrongful quality.

The risk reasonably to be perceived defines the duty to be obeyed, and risk imports relation; it is risk to another or to others within the range of apprehension . . . . This does not mean, of course, that one who launches a destructive force is always relieved of liability if the force, though known to be destructive, pursues an unexpected path. . . . The range of reasonable apprehension is at times a question for the court, and at times, if varying inferences are possible, a question for the jury. Here, by concession, there was nothing in the situation to suggest to the most cautious mind that the parcel wrapped in newspaper would spread wreckage through the station. If the guard had thrown it down knowingly and willfully, he would not have threatened the plaintiff's safety, so far as appearances could warn him. His conduct would not have involved, even then, an unreasonable probability of invasion of her bodily security. Liability can be no greater where the act is inadvertent.

Negligence, like risk, is thus a term of relation. Negligence in the abstract, apart from things related, is surely not a tort, if indeed it is understandable at all . . . . Negligence is not a tort unless it results in the commission of a wrong, and the commission of a wrong imports the violation of a right, in this case, we are told, the right to be protected against interference with one's bodily security. But bodily security is protected, not against all forms of interference or aggression, but only against some. One who seeks redress at law does not make out a cause of action by showing without more that there has been damage to his person. If the harm was not willful, he must show that the act as to him had possibilities of danger so many and apparent as to entitle him to be protected against the doing of it though the harm was unintended. Affront to personality is still the keynote of the wrong. . . .

The law of causation, remote or proximate, is thus foreign to the case before us. The question of liability is always anterior to the question of the measure of the consequences that go with liability. If there is no tort to be redressed, there is no occasion to consider what damage might be recovered if there were a finding of a tort. We may assume, without deciding, that negligence, not at large or in the abstract, but in relation to the plaintiff, would entail liability for any and all consequences, however novel or extraordinary. . . . We do not go into the question now. The consequences to be followed must first be rooted in a wrong.

The judgment of the Appellate Division and that of the Trial Term should be reversed, and the complaint dismissed, with costs in all courts.

Andrews, J. (dissenting).

. . . The result we shall reach depends upon our theory as to the nature of negligence. Is it a relative concept – the breach of some duty owing to a particular person or to particular persons? Or where there is an act which unreasonably threatens the safety of others, is the doer liable for all its proximate consequences, even where they result in injury to one who would generally be thought to be outside the radius of danger? This is not a mere dispute as to words. We might not believe that to the average mind the dropping of the bundle would seem to involve the probability of harm to the plaintiff standing many feet away whatever might be the case as to the owner or to one so near as to be likely to be struck by its fall. If, however, we adopt the second hypothesis we have to inquire only as to the relation between cause and effect. We deal in terms of proximate cause, not of negligence.

Negligence may be defined roughly as an act or omission which unreasonably does or may affect the rights of others, or which unreasonably fails to protect oneself from the dangers resulting from such acts. Here I confine myself to the first branch of the definition. Nor do I comment on the word "unreasonable." For present purposes it sufficiently describes that average of conduct that society requires of its members.

There must be both the act or omission, and the right. It is the act itself, not the intent of the actor, that is important. . . . In criminal law both the intent and the result are to be considered. . . .

Where there is the unreasonable act, and some right that may be affected there is negligence whether damage does or does not result. That is immaterial. Should we drive down Broadway at a reckless speed, we are negligent whether we strike an approaching car or miss it by an inch. The act itself is wrongful. It is a wrong not only to those who happen to be within the radius of danger but to all who might have been there – a wrong to the public at large. Such is the language of the street. . . . Due care is a duty imposed on each one of us to protect society from unnecessary danger, not to protect A, B or C alone.

It may well be that there is no such thing as negligence in the abstract. "Proof of negligence in the air, so to speak, will not do." In an empty world negligence would not exist. It does involve a relationship between man and his fellows. But not merely a relationship between man and those whom he might reasonably expect his act would injure. Rather, a relationship between him and those whom he does in fact injure. If his act has a tendency to harm someone, it harms him a mile away as surely as it does those on the scene. We now permit children to recover for the negligent killing of the father. It was never prevented on the theory that no duty was owing to them. A husband may be compensated the loss of his wife's services. To say that the wrong-doer was negligent as to the husband as well as to the wife is merely an attempt to fit facts to theory. An insurance company paying a fire loss recovers its payment of the negligent incendiary. We speak of subrogation – of suing in the right of the insured. Behind the cloud of words is the fact they hide, that the act, wrongful as to the insured, has also injured the company. . . .

In the well-known *Polemis Case* . . . , Scrutton, L. J., said that the dropping of a plank was negligent for it might injure "workman or cargo or ship." Because of either possibility the owner of the vessel was to be made good for his loss. The act being wrongful the doer was liable for its proximate results. Criticized and explained as this statement may have been, I think it states the law as it should be and as it is. . . .

The proposition is this. Everyone owes to the world at large the duty of refraining from those acts that may unreasonably threaten the safety of others. Such an act occurs. Not only is he wronged to whom harm might reasonably be expected to result, but he also who is in fact injured, even if he be outside what would generally be thought the danger zone. There needs be duty due the one complaining but this is not a duty to a particular individual because as to him harm might be expected. Harm to someone being the natural result of the act, not only that one alone, but all those in fact injured may complain. We have never, I think, held otherwise. . . . Unreasonable risk being taken, its consequences are not confined to those who might probably be hurt.

If this be so, we do not have a plaintiff suing by "derivation or succession." Her action is original and primary. Her claim is for a breach of duty to herself – not that she is subrogated to any right of action of the owner of the parcel or of a passenger standing at the scene of the explosion.

The right to recover damages rests on additional considerations. The plaintiff's rights must be injured, and this injury must be caused by the negligence. We build a dam, but are negligent as to its foundations. Breaking, it injures property downstream. We are not liable if all this happened because of some reason other than the insecure foundation. But when injuries do result from our unlawful act we are liable for the consequences. It does not matter that they are unusual, unexpected, unforeseen and unforeseeable. But there is one limitation. The damages must be so connected with the negligence that the latter may be said to be the proximate cause of the former.

These two words have never been given an inclusive definition. What is a cause in a legal sense, still more what is a proximate cause, depend in each case upon many considerations, as does the existence of negligence itself. Any philosophical doctrine of causation does not help us. A boy throws a stone into a pond. The ripples spread. The water level rises. The history of that pond is altered to all eternity. It will be altered by other causes also. Yet it will be forever the resultant of all causes combined. Each one will have an influence. How great only omniscience can say. You may speak of a chain, or if you please, a net. An analogy is of little aid. Each cause brings about future events. Without each the future would not be the same. Each is proximate in the sense it is essential. But that is not what we mean by the word. Nor on the other hand do we mean sole cause. There is no such thing.

Should analogy be thought helpful, however, I prefer that of a stream. The spring, starting on its journey, is joined by tributary after tributary. The river, reaching the ocean, comes from a hundred sources. No man may say whence any drop of water is derived. Yet for a time distinction may be possible. Into the clear creek, brown swamp water flows from the left. Later, from the right comes water stained by its clay bed. The three may remain for a space, sharply divided. But at last, inevitably no trace of separation remains. They are so commingled that all distinction is lost.

As we have said, we cannot trace the effect of an act to the end, if end there is. Again, however, we may trace it part of the way. A murder at Serajevo may be the necessary antecedent to an assassination in London twenty years hence. An overturned lantern may burn all Chicago. We may follow the fire from the shed to the last building. We rightly say the fire started by the lantern caused its destruction.

A cause, but not the proximate cause. What we do mean by the word "proximate" is that, because of convenience, of public policy, of a rough sense of justice, the law arbitrarily declines to trace a series of events beyond a certain point. This is not logic. It is practical politics. Take our rule as to fires. Sparks from my burning haystack set on fire my house and my neighbor's. I may recover from a negligent railroad. He may not. Yet the wrongful act as directly harmed the one as the other. We may regret that the line was drawn just where it was, but drawn somewhere it had to be. We said the act of the railroad was not the proximate cause of our neighbor's fire. Cause it surely was. The words we used were simply indicative of our notions of public policy. Other courts think differently. But somewhere they reach the point where they cannot say the stream comes from any one source.

Take the illustration given in an unpublished manuscript by a distinguished and helpful writer on the law of torts. A chauffeur negligently collides with another car which is filled with dynamite, although he could not know it. An explosion follows. A, walking on the sidewalk nearby, is killed. B, sitting in a window of a building opposite, is cut by flying glass. C, likewise sitting in a window a block away, is similarly injured. And a further illustration: A nursemaid, ten blocks away, startled by the noise, involuntarily drops a baby from her arms to the walk. We are told that C may not recover while A may. As to B it is a question for court or jury. We will all agree that the baby might not. Because, we are again told, the chauffeur had no reason to believe his conduct involved any risk of injuring either C or the baby. As to them he was not negligent.

But the chauffeur, being negligent in risking the collision, his belief that the scope of the harm he might do would be limited is immaterial. His act unreasonably jeopardized the safety of any one who might be affected by it. C's injury and that of the baby were directly traceable to the collision. Without that, the injury would not have happened. C had the right to sit in his office, secure from such dangers. The baby was entitled to use the sidewalk with reasonable safety.

The true theory is, it seems to me, that the injury to C, if in truth he is to be denied recovery, and the injury to the baby is that their several injuries were not the proximate result of the negligence. And here not what the chauffeur had reason to believe would be the result of his conduct, but what the prudent would foresee, may have a bearing. May have some bearing, for the problem of proximate cause is not to be solved by any one consideration.

It is all a question of expediency. There are no fixed rules to govern our judgment. There are simply matters of which we may take account. We have in a somewhat different connection spoken of "the stream of events." We have asked whether that stream was deflected – whether it was forced into new and unexpected channels. . . . This is rather rhetoric than law. There is in truth little to guide us other than common sense.

There are some hints that may help us. The proximate cause, involved as it may be with many other causes, must be, at the least, something without which the event would not happen. The court must ask itself whether there was a natural and continuous sequence between cause and effect. Was the one a substantial factor in producing the other? Was there a direct connection between them, without too many intervening causes? Is the effect of cause on result not too attenuated? Is the cause likely, in the usual judgment of mankind, to produce the result? Or by the exercise of prudent foresight could the result be foreseen? Is the result too remote from the cause, and here we consider remoteness in time and space. . . . Clearly we must so consider, for the greater the distance either in time or space, the more surely do other causes intervene to affect the result. When a lantern is overturned the firing of a shed is a fairly direct consequence. Many things contribute to the spread of the conflagration – the force of the wind, the direction and width of streets, the character of intervening structures, other factors. We draw an uncertain and wavering line, but draw it we must as best we can.

Once again, it is all a question of fair judgment, always keeping in mind the fact that we endeavor to make a rule in each case that will be practical and in keeping with the general understanding of mankind.

Here another question must be answered. In the case supposed it is said, and said correctly, that the chauffeur is liable for the direct effect of the explosion although he had no reason to suppose it would follow a collision. "The fact that the injury occurred in a different manner than that which might have been expected does not prevent the chauffeur's negligence from being in law the cause of the injury." But the natural results of a negligent act – the results which a prudent man would or should foresee – do have a bearing upon the decision as to proximate cause. We have said so repeatedly. What should be foreseen? No human foresight would suggest that a collision itself might injure one a block away. On the contrary, given an explosion, such a possibility might be reasonably expected. I think the direct connection, the foresight of which the courts speak, assumes prevision of the explosion, for the immediate results of which, at least, the chauffeur is responsible.

It may be said this is unjust. Why? In fairness he should make good every injury flowing from his negligence. Not because of tenderness toward him we say he need not answer for all that follows his wrong. We look back to the catastrophe, the fire kindled by the spark, or the explosion. We trace the consequences – not indefinitely, but to a certain point. And to aid us in fixing that point we ask what might ordinarily be expected to follow the fire or the explosion.

This last suggestion is the factor which must determine the case before us. The act upon which defendant's liability rests is knocking an apparently harmless package onto the platform. The act was negligent. For its proximate consequences the defendant is liable. If its contents were broken, to the owner; if it fell upon and crushed a passenger's foot, then to him; if it exploded and injured one in the immediate vicinity, to him also as to A in the illustration. Mrs. Palsgraf was standing some distance away. How far cannot be told from the record – apparently twenty-five or thirty feet, perhaps less. Except for the explosion, she would not have been injured. We are told by the appellant in his brief "it cannot be denied that the explosion was the direct cause of the plaintiff's injuries." So it was a substantial factor in producing the result – there was here a natural and continuous sequence – direct connection. The only intervening cause was that instead of blowing her to the ground the concussion smashed the weighing machine which in turn fell upon her. There was no remoteness in time, little in space. And surely, given such an explosion as here, it needed no great foresight to predict that the natural result would be to injure one on the platform at no greater distance from its scene than was the plaintiff. Just how no one might be able to predict. Whether by flying fragments, by broken glass, by wreckage of machines or structures no one could say. But injury in some form was most probable.

Under these circumstances I cannot say as a matter of law that the plaintiff's injuries were not the proximate result of the negligence. That is all we have before us. The court refused to so charge. No request was made to submit the matter to the jury as a question of fact, even would that have been proper upon the record before us.

The judgment appealed from should be affirmed, with costs.

1   *Question of Fact.* Proximate cause or whether the harm is within the "scope of the risk" created by defendant's
     breach of duty generally is treated as a question of fact.

2   *Duty v. Proximate Cause.* While *Palsgraf* generally is understood as a proximate cause case, Cardozo spoke, not in
     terms of proximate cause, but rather in terms of duty.

MARSHALL V. NUGENT
222 F.2D 604 (1ST CIR. 1955)

On the morning of December 17, 1951, a Chevrolet car owned and operated by Walter G.
Harriman was proceeding on a public highway . . . . Marshall was riding as a passenger in
the front seat of the Chevrolet. . . . As Harriman was driving his car on the right-hand side, or
westerly lane of the highway, at 30 to 35 miles per hour, he approached a curve in the road. At
this point the highway ran uphill and curved rather sharply to Harriman's right. The curve was
heavily banked, the east side being higher than the west side. On the day in question the road
was covered with hard-packed snow and ice and was quite slippery. Proceeding in the opposite
direction . . . was a heavy oil truck owned by Socony-Vacuum Oil Co., Inc., and driven by its
servant, Warren K. Prince, undoubtedly then in the scope of his employment. Upon ample testimony the jury were warranted in finding that after the oil truck loomed over the crest of the
hill it "cut the corner" by swinging over to the westerly side of the highway (to Prince's left) and
proceeded down the banked curve in that manner. In this situation the truck and the Chevrolet,
then approximately 300 ft. or more apart, were headed for a collision. There was credible evidence that Harriman let up on his accelerator and blew his horn, but as the truck did not get
back promptly to its side of the road Harriman turned to the right into the snowbank at the west
side of the road to slow down; the Chevrolet went into a skid for about 50 ft. and came to a stop
completely off the highway on the westerly side and at right angles with the road.

Prince stopped his oil truck . . . about opposite the stalled Chevrolet. Harriman and Marshall
got out of the car. Prince inquired if they were "okay" – which they were at that time – and
offered to yank the Chevrolet back into the highway if Harriman had a chain.

At this time the oil truck, blocking as it was the eastern lane of the highway, was stopped
in a dangerous place. . . . Drivers in cars proceeding in a northerly direction could not see the
truck standing in the "blind spot" below until they arrived almost at the crest of the hill, when
they would realize that there was not room to pass the truck on the right-hand or easterly side,
and the risk was obvious that in the existing weather conditions they might go into a skid while
attempting to swing over to the left on the banked curve in order to pass between the Chevrolet
and the truck. Also there would be danger from northbound traffic during the blocking of the
highway by the anticipated operation of towing the Chevrolet back into the highway.

Prince, who was very familiar with this particular portion of the highway, recognized the
danger inherent in the situation, for he remarked to Messrs. Harriman and Marshall that his

truck was stopped in a rather dangerous position and that someone ought to go up the grade to warn any approaching northbound traffic.

In response to this obviously reasonable suggestion from Prince, Marshall undertook to go up the hill to warn any cars that might be approaching the crest in a northerly direction. Harriman continued the operation of getting out his chain and affixing it to . . . his car. Meanwhile, Prince let the truck stand still on the east side of the highway, when it might have been safer to have pulled over in a matter of moments to the other side of the highway to await the towing operation. Having proceeded southerly for perhaps 75 or 80 ft., walking on his right-hand side of the highway, about 4 ft. from the snowbank on the westerly side, Marshall perceived coming over the crest of the hill a car driven by Robert H. Nugent. This car would have presented no danger to Marshall if it could have proceeded on its right-hand or easterly lane, but this was impossible because the oil truck was blocking this lane. Marshall waved his arms in warning. Nugent turned his car toward the left. It soon went into a skid, crossing to the left-hand side of the banked curve, crashing into a plank guard fence on the westerly side of the highway, and immediately thereafter striking and severely injuring Marshall. It all happened so quickly that Marshall was unable to get out of the way. Nugent's car continued more or less out of control until its front bumper guard struck and dented the rear fender of Harriman's stalled Chevrolet, and there Nugent's car stopped. The injury to Marshall occurred a very short time, perhaps a minute or two, or maybe less, after Marshall had started up the hill in response to Prince's suggestion.

Marshall filed his complaint in the court below against both Socony-Vacuum Oil Co., Inc., and Nugent, charging them as joint tortfeasors, each legally responsible for the plaintiff's personal injuries. . . . After a rather lengthy trial, the jury reported a verdict in favor of Marshall as against Socony in the sum of $25,000, and a verdict in favor of the defendant Nugent. The district court entered judgments against Socony and in favor of Nugent in accordance with the verdict. . . .

This is an appeal by Socony from the judgment against it in favor of Marshall. Appellant has presented a great number of points, most of which do not merit extended discussion.

The most seriously pressed contentions are that the district court was in error in refusing Socony's motion for a directed verdict in its favor, made at the close of all the evidence. The motion was based on several grounds, chief of which were . . . that if Socony's servant Prince were found to have been negligent in "cutting the corner" on the wrong side of the road, and thus forcing Harriman's car off the highway, Marshall suffered no hurt from this, and such negligent conduct . . . was not the proximate cause of Marshall's subsequent injuries when he was run into by Nugent's car. . . .

[T]his has to do with the doctrine of proximate causation, a doctrine which appellant's arguments tend to make out to be more complex and esoteric than it really is. To say that the situation created by the defendant's culpable acts constituted "merely a condition," not a cause of plaintiff's harm, is to indulge in mere verbiage, which does not solve the question at issue, but is simply a way of stating the conclusion, arrived at from other considerations, that the causal relation between the defendant's act and the plaintiff's injury is not strong enough to warrant holding the defendant legally responsible for the injury.

The adjective "proximate," as commonly used in this connection, is perhaps misleading, since to establish liability it is not necessarily true that the defendant's culpable act must be shown to have been the next or immediate cause of the plaintiff's injury. In many familiar instances, the defendant's act may be more remote in the chain of events; and the plaintiff's injury may more immediately have been caused by an intervening force of nature, or an intervening act of a third person whether culpable or not, or even an act by the plaintiff bringing himself in contact with the dangerous situation resulting from the defendant's negligence. . . . Therefore, perhaps, the phrase "legal cause," as used in . . . Rest. of Torts §431, is preferable to "proximate cause;" but the courts continue generally to use "proximate cause," and it is pretty well-understood what is meant.

Back of the requirement that the defendant's culpable act must have been a proximate cause of the plaintiff's harm is no doubt the widespread conviction that it would be disproportionately burdensome to hold a culpable actor potentially liable for all the injurious consequences that may flow from his act, i.e., that would not have been inflicted "but for" the occurrence of the act. This is especially so where the injurious consequence was the result of negligence merely. And so, speaking in general terms, the effort of the courts has been, in the development of this doctrine of proximate causation, to confine the liability of a negligent actor to those harmful consequences which result from the operation of the risk, or of a risk, the foreseeability of which rendered the defendant's conduct negligent.

Of course, putting the inquiry in these terms does not furnish a formula which automatically decides each of an infinite variety of cases. Flexibility is still preserved by the further need of defining the risk, or risks, either narrowly, or more broadly, as seems appropriate and just in the special type of case.

Regarding motor vehicle accidents in particular, one should contemplate a variety of risks which are created by negligent driving. There may be injuries resulting from a direct collision between the carelessly driven car and another vehicle. But such direct collision may be avoided, yet the plaintiff may fall and injure himself in frantically racing out of the way of the errant car. Or the plaintiff may be knocked down and injured by a human stampede as the car rushes toward a crowded safety zone. Or the plaintiff may faint from intense excitement stimulated by the near collision, and in falling sustain a fractured skull. Or the plaintiff may suffer a miscarriage or other physical illness as a result of intense nervous shock incident to a hair-raising escape. This bundle of risks could be enlarged indefinitely with a little imagination. In a traffic mix-up due to negligence, before the disturbed waters have become placid and normal again, the unfolding of events between the culpable act and the plaintiff's eventual injury may be bizarre indeed; yet the defendant may be liable for the result. In such a situation, it would be impossible for a person in the defendant's position to predict in advance just how his negligent act would work out to another's injury. Yet this in itself is no bar to recovery.

When an issue of proximate cause arises in a borderline case, as not infrequently happens, we leave it to the jury with appropriate instructions. We do this because it is deemed wise to obtain the judgment of the jury, reflecting as it does the earthy viewpoint of the common man – the prevalent sense of the community – as to whether the causal relation between the negligent act and the plaintiff's harm which in fact was a consequence of the tortious act is sufficiently close to make it just and expedient to hold the defendant answerable in damages. That is what the courts have in mind when they say the question of proximate causation is one of fact for the jury. It is similar to the issue of negligence, which is left to the jury as an issue of fact. Even where on the evidence the facts are undisputed, if fair-minded men might honestly and reasonably draw contrary inferences as to whether the facts do or do not establish negligence, the court leaves such issue to the determination of the jury, who are required to decide, as a matter of common-sense judgment, whether the defendant's course of conduct subjected others to a reasonable or unreasonable risk, i.e., whether under all the circumstances the defendant ought to be recognized as privileged to do the act in question or to pursue his course of conduct with immunity from liability for harm to others which might result.

In dealing with these issues of negligence and proximate causation, the trial judge has to make a preliminary decision whether the issues are such that reasonable men might differ on the inferences to be drawn. . . . Exercising that judgment on the facts in the case at bar, we have to conclude that the district court committed no error in refusing to direct a verdict for the defendant Socony on the issue of proximate cause. . . .[I]t is held in most jurisdictions that when the defendant is negligent in that he puts X or X's property in undue peril, he may at the same time be deemed to be negligent with relation to potential rescuers as a class, i.e., to persons who, though not in a position of primary danger from defendant's negligent conduct, nevertheless may be stimulated to undertake the rescue of X, or X's property, from the perils created by defendant's negligent conduct, as defendant ought to have foreseen. . . .

Whatever may be the New Hampshire law in the foregoing respect, the case at bar presents a quite different situation. Plaintiff Marshall was a passenger in the oncoming Chevrolet car, and thus was one of the persons whose bodily safety was primarily endangered by the negligence of Prince, as might have been found by the jury, in "cutting the corner" with the Socony truck in the circumstances above related. In that view, Prince's negligence constituted an irretrievable breach of duty to the plaintiff. Though this particular act of negligence was over and done with when the truck pulled up alongside of the stalled Chevrolet without having actually collided with it, still the consequences of such past negligence were in the bosom of time, as yet unrevealed.

If the Chevrolet had been pulled back onto the highway, and Harriman and Marshall, having got in it again, had resumed their journey and had had a collision with another car five miles down the road, in which Marshall suffered bodily injuries, it could truly be said that such subsequent injury to Marshall was a consequence in fact of the earlier delay caused by the defendant's negligence, in the sense that but for such delay the Chevrolet car would not have been at the fatal intersection at the moment the other car ran into it. But on such assumed state of facts, the courts would no doubt conclude, "as a matter of law," that Prince's earlier negligence in cutting the corner was not the "proximate cause" of this later injury received by the plaintiff. That would be because the extra risks to which such negligence by Prince had subjected the passengers in the Chevrolet car were obviously entirely over; the situation had been stabilized and become normal, and, so far as one could foresee, whatever subsequent risks the Chevrolet might have to encounter in its resumed journey were simply the inseparable risks, no more and no less, that were incident to the Chevrolet's being out on the highway at all. But in the case at bar, the circumstances under which Marshall received the personal injuries complained of presented no such clear-cut situation.

As we have indicated, the extra risks created by Prince's negligence were not all over at the moment the primary risk of collision between the truck and the Chevrolet was successfully surmounted. Many cases have held a defendant, whose negligence caused a traffic tie-up, legally liable for subsequent property damage or personal injuries more immediately caused by an oncoming motorist. This would particularly be so where, as in the present case, the negligent traffic tie-up and delay occurred in a dangerous blind spot, and where the occupants of the stalled Chevrolet, having got out onto the highway to assist in the operation of getting the Chevrolet going again, were necessarily subject to risks of injury from cars in the stream of northbound traffic coming over the crest of the hill. It is true, the Chevrolet car was not owned by the plaintiff Marshall, and no doubt, without violating any legal duty to Harriman, Marshall could have crawled up onto the snowbank at the side of the road out of harm's way and awaited there, passive and inert, until his journey was resumed. But the plaintiff, who as a passenger in the Chevrolet car had already been subjected to a collision risk by the negligent operation of the Socony truck, could reasonably be expected to get out onto the highway and lend a hand to his host in getting the Chevrolet started again .... Marshall was therefore certainly not an "officious intermeddler," and whether or not he was barred by contributory negligence in what he did was a question for the jury, as we have already held. The injury Marshall received by being struck by the Nugent car was not remote, either in time or place, from the negligent conduct of defendant Socony's servant, and it occurred while the traffic mix-up occasioned by defendant's negligence was still persisting, not after the traffic flow had become normal again. In the circumstances presented we conclude that the district court committed no error in leaving the issue of proximate cause to the jury for determination.

Of course, the essential notion of what is meant by "proximate cause" may be expressed to the jury in a variety of ways. We are satisfied in the present case that the charge to the jury accurately enough acquainted them with the nature of the factual judgment they were called upon to exercise in their determination of the issue of proximate cause. . . .

QUESTIONS

1   What result if the parties got the cars back on the road and the Chevy were involved in a separate accident one mile down the road?

2   *Thin-Skulled (Eggshell) Plaintiff Rule.* What result if the plaintiff had been a young and famous professional athlete whose career were ruined by defendant's negligence? Is it foreseeable that "cutting the corner" as defendant's driver did will result in multiple millions of dollars in damages? The rule always has been that "defendant takes his victim as he finds him." The idea is that even if a defendant's tortious conduct causes more harm than would be foreseeable due to some unknown and unusual vulnerability of the plaintiff, defendant is, nevertheless, liable for plaintiff's losses. Of course, defendant is liable only if his conduct would have caused some foreseeable harm even to an average plaintiff.

3 What if this were an extremely lightly traveled highway so that the possibility of colliding with anyone coming the opposite direction were extremely remote? If only one car per month travels that way, is it foreseeable that another car would be coming the opposite direction just at the moment that defendant cuts the corner?

UNITED NOVELTY CO. V. DANIELS
42 SO. 2D 395 (MISS. 1949)

The decisive principles here involved are, while important, not novel. Appellees include the members of the family of William Daniels, a minor aged nineteen years, who was fatally burned while cleaning coin-operated machines as an employee of appellant.

The work was being performed in a room eight by ten feet in area, in which there was a gas heater then lighted with an open flame. The cleaning was being done with gasoline. The testimony yields the unique circumstance that the immediate activating cause of a resultant explosion was the escape of a rat from the machine, and its disappointing attempt to seek sanctuary beneath the heater whereat it overexposed itself and its impregnated coat, and returned in haste and flames to its original hideout. Even though such be a fact, it is not a controlling fact, and serves chiefly to ratify the conclusion that the room was permeated with gasoline vapors. Negligence would be predicated on the juxtaposition of the gasoline and the open flame. Under similar circumstances, the particular detonating agency, whether, as here, an animate version of the classic lighted squib, or . . . a bolt of lightning, was incidental except as illustrating the range of foreseeability. . . .

Affirmed.

THE WAGON MOUND I
OVERSEAS TANKSHIP LTD. V. MORTS DOCK & ENGINEERING CO. LTD.
[1961] A.C. 388

. . . In the action the respondents sought to recover from the appellants compensation for the damage which its property known as the Sheerlegs Wharf, in Sydney Harbour, . . . had suffered by reason of fire which broke out on November 1, 1951. . . . The respondents at the relevant time . . . owned and used for their business the Sheerlegs Wharf . . . . In October and November, 1951, a vessel known as the *Corrimel* was moored alongside the wharf and was being refitted by the respondents. Her mast was lying on the wharf and a number of the respondents' employees were working both upon it and upon the vessel itself, using for that purpose electric and oxy-acetylene welding equipment. At the same time the appellants were charterers by demise of the *s.s. Wagon Mound*, an oil-burning vessel, which was moored at the Caltex Wharf on the northern shore of the harbour at a distance of about 600 feet from the Sheerlegs Wharf. . . .

During the early hours of October 30, 1951, a large quantity of bunkering oil was, through the carelessness of the appellants' servants, allowed to spill into the bay, and by 10.30 on the morning of that day it had spread over a considerable part of the bay, being thickly concentrated in some places and particularly along the foreshore near the respondents' property. The appellants made no attempt to disperse the oil. The *Wagon Mound* unberthed and set sail very shortly after.

When the respondents' works manager became aware of the condition of things in the vicinity of the wharf he instructed their workmen that no welding or burning was to be carried on until further orders. He inquired of the manager of the Caltex Oil Company, at whose wharf the *Wagon Mound* was then still berthed, whether they could safely continue their operations on the wharf or upon the *Corrimel*. The results of the inquiry coupled with his own belief as to the inflammability of the furnace oil in the open led him to think that the respondents could safely carry on their operations. He gave instructions accordingly, but directed that all safety precautions should be taken to prevent inflammable material falling off the wharf into the oil.

For the remainder of October 30 and until about 2 p.m. on November 1 work was carried on as usual, the condition and congestion of the oil remaining substantially unaltered. But at about that time the oil remaining substantially unaltered. But at about that time the oil under or near the wharf was ignited and a fire, fed initially by the oil, spread rapidly and burned with great intensity. The wharf and the *Corrimel* caught fire and considerable damage was done to the wharf and the equipment upon it.

The outbreak of fire was due, as the judge found, to the fact that there was floating in the oil underneath the wharf a piece of debris on which lay some smouldering cotton waste or rag which had been set on fire by molten metal falling from the wharf: that the cotton waste or rag burst into flames: that the flames from the cotton waste set the floating oil afire either directly or by first setting fire to a wooden pile coated with oil, and that after the floating oil became ignited the flames spread rapidly over the surface of the oil and quickly developed into a conflagration which severely damaged the wharf.

. . . The judgment of their Lordships was delivered by VISCOUNT SIMONDS, who stated the facts set out above and continued: The trial judge also made the all-important finding, which must be set out in his own words: "The *raison d'etre* of furnace oil is, of course, that it shall burn, but I find the defendant did not know and could not reasonably be expected to have known that it was capable of being set afire when spread on water." . . . One other finding must be mentioned. The judge held that apart from damage by fire the respondents had suffered some damage from the spillage of oil in that it had got upon their slipways and congealed upon them and interfered with their use of the slips. He said: "The evidence of this damage is slight and no claim for compensation is made in respect of it. Nevertheless it does establish some damage, which may be insignificant in comparison with the magnitude of the damage by fire, but which nevertheless is damage which, beyond question, was a direct result of the escape of the oil." . . .

It is inevitable that first consideration should be given to the case *In re Polemis and Furness Withy & Co. Ltd.* . . . which will henceforth be referred to as *Polemis.* . . . What, then, did *Polemis* decide? . . . The negligent act was nothing more than the carelessness of stevedores (for whom the charterers were assumed to be responsible) in allowing a sling or rope by which it was hoisted to come into contact with certain boards, causing one of them to fall into the hold. The falling board hit some substances in the hold and caused a spark: the spark ignited petrol vapour in the hold: there was a rush of flames, and the ship was destroyed. The special case submitted by the arbitrators found that the causing of the spark could not reasonably have been anticipated from the falling of the board, though some damage to the ship might reasonably have been anticipated. They did not indicate what damage might have been so anticipated.

There can be no doubt that the decision of the Court of Appeal in *Polemis* plainly asserts that, if the defendant is guilty of negligence, he is responsible for all the consequences whether reasonably foreseeable or not. The generality of the proposition is perhaps qualified by the fact that each of the Lords Justices refers to the outbreak of fire as the direct result of the negligent act. There is thus introduced the conception that the negligent actor is not responsible for consequences which are not "direct," whatever that may mean. . . .

[T]he authority of *Polemis* has been severely shaken though lip-service has from time to time been paid to it. In their Lordships' opinion it should no longer be regarded as good law. It is not probable that many cases will for that reason have a different result, though it is hoped that the law will be thereby simplified, and that in some cases, at least, palpable injustice will be avoided. For it does not seem consonant with current ideas of justice or morality that for an act of negligence, however slight or venial, which results in some trivial foreseeable damage the actor should be liable for all consequences however unforeseeable and however grave, so long as they can be said to be "direct." It is a principle of civil liability, subject only to qualifications which have no present relevance, that a man must be considered to be responsible for the probable consequences of his act. To demand more of him is too harsh a rule, to demand less is to ignore that civilised order requires the observance of a minimum standard of behaviour.

This concept applied to the slowly developing law of negligence has led to a great variety of expressions which can, as it appears to their Lordship, be harmonised with little difficulty with the single exception of the so-called rule in *Polemis*. For, if it is asked why a man should be responsible for the natural or necessary or probable consequences of his act (or any other similar description of them) the answer is that it is not because they are natural or necessary or probable, but because, since they have this quality, it is judged by the standard of the reasonable man that he ought to have foreseen them. Thus it is that over and over again it has happened that in different judgments in the same case, and sometimes in a single judgment, liability for a consequence has been imposed on the ground that it was reasonably foreseeable or, alternatively, on the ground that it was natural or necessary or probable. The two grounds have been treated as coterminous, and so they largely are. But, where they are not, the question arises to which the wrong answer was given in *Polemis*. For, if some limitation must be imposed upon the consequences for which the negligent actor is to be held responsible—and all are agreed that some limitation there must be—why should that test (reasonable foreseeability) be rejected which, since he is judged by what the reasonable man ought to foresee, corresponds with the common conscience of mankind, and a test (the "direct" consequence) be substituted which leads to nowhere but the never-ending and insoluble problems of causation. "The lawyer," said Sir Frederick Pollock, "cannot afford to adventure himself with philosophers in the logical and metaphysical controversies that beset the idea of cause." Yet this is just what he had most unfortunately done and must continue to do if the rule in *Polemis* is to prevail. . . .

The validity of a rule or principle can sometimes be tested by observing it in operation. . . . Applying the rule in *Polemis* and holding therefore that the unforeseeability of the damage by fire afforded no defence, [the Full Court in the present case] went on to consider the remaining question. Was it a "direct" consequence? Upon this Manning J. said: "Notwithstanding that, if regard is had separately to each individual occurrence in the chain of events that led to this fire, each occurrence was improbable and, in one sense, improbability was heaped upon improbability, I cannot escape from the conclusion that if the ordinary man in the street had been asked as a matter of common sense, without any detailed analysis of the circumstances, to state the cause of the fire at Mort's Dock, he would unhesitatingly have assigned such cause to spillage of oil by the appellant's employees." Perhaps he would, and probably he would have added: "I never should have thought it possible." But with great respect to the Full Court this is surely irrelevant, or, if it is relevant, only serves to show that the *Polemis* rule works in a very strange way. After the event even a fool is wise. But it is not the hindsight of a fool; it is the foresight of the reasonable man which alone can determine responsibility. The *Polemis* rule by substituting "direct" for "reasonably foreseeable" consequence leads to a conclusion equally illogical and unjust.

Their Lordships conclude this part of the case with some general observations. They have been concerned primarily to displace the proposition that unforeseeability is irrelevant if damage is "direct." In doing so they have inevitably insisted that the essential factor in determining liability is whether the damage is of such a kind as the reasonable man should have foreseen. This . . . is a departure from this sovereign principle if liability is made to depend solely on the damage being the "direct" or "natural" consequence of the precedent act. Who knows or can be assumed to know all the processes of nature? But if it would be wrong that a man should be held liable for damage unpredictable by a reasonable man because it was "direct" or "natural," equally it would be wrong that he should escape liability, however "indirect" the damage, if he foresaw or could reasonably foresee the intervening events which led to its being done . . . . Thus foreseeability becomes the effective test. . . .

NOTE

1   As the "scope of the risk" approach has gradually replaced the "direct cause" approach, authorities have increasingly sought to separate the concept of "scope of the risk" from the cause in fact question as a separate element of a negligence cause of action.

4. SUPERCEDING CAUSE

Sometimes tortfeasors act in sequence. In fact, it almost always is possible for defendant to point to some "intervening" force that came between defendant's alleged negligence and plaintiff's injury, and contributed thereto. Therefore, the earlier tortfeasor can argue that the later tortfeasor was a "superceding cause" of plaintiff's injury. It is possible to decide such cases simply by analyzing whether the resulting harm was within the "scope of the risk" created by the earlier defendant's conduct. Nevertheless, courts sometimes undertake a more complicated analysis in such circumstances.

Restatement (Second) Torts § 442. Considerations Important In Determining Whether An Intervening Force Is A Superseding Cause

The following considerations are of importance in determining whether an intervening force is a superseding cause of harm to another:

a. the fact that its intervention brings about harm different in kind from that which would otherwise have resulted from the actor's negligence;

b. the fact that its operation or the consequences thereof appear after the event to be extraordinary rather than normal in view of the circumstances existing at the time of its operation;

c. the fact that the intervening force is operating independently of any situation created by the actor's negligence, or, on the other hand, is or is not a normal result of such a situation;

d. the fact that the operation of the intervening force is due to a third person's act or to his failure to act;

e. the fact that the intervening force is due to an act of a third person which is wrongful toward the other and as such subjects the third person to liability to him;

f. the degree of culpability of a wrongful act of a third person which sets the intervening force in motion.

NOTE

1 Subsections (a), (b), and even (c) of Restatement (Second) Section 442 appear to bear on whether harm is within the "scope of the risk" of an actor's negligence. But subsections (d) – (f) appear to be driven by a different consideration. What is it?

BRAUER V. NEW YORK CENTRAL & HUDSON RIVER R.R.
103 A. 166 (N.J. APP. 1918)

SWAYZE, J. This is a case of a grade-crossing collision. . . . The only question that has caused us difficulty is that of the extent of the defendant's liability. The complaint avers that the horse was killed, the wagon and harness, and the cider and barrels with which the wagon was loaded, were destroyed. What happened was that as a result of the collision, aside from the death of the horse and the destruction of the wagon, the contents of the wagon, consisting of empty barrels and a keg of cider, were scattered and probably stolen by people at the scene of the accident. The driver, who was alone in charge for the plaintiff, was so stunned that one of the railroad detectives found him immediately after the collision in a fit. . . . The controversy on the question of damages is as to the right of the plaintiff to recover the value of the barrels, cider and blanket. . . .

It is now argued that the defendant's negligence was not in any event the proximate cause of the loss of this property since the act of the thieves intervened. The rule of law which exempts the one guilty of the original negligence from damage due to an intervening cause is well settled. The difficulty lies in the application. Like the question of proximate cause, this is ordinarily a jury question. . . .

The negligence which caused the collision resulted immediately in such a condition of the driver of the wagon that he was no longer able to protect his employer's property; the natural and probable result of his enforced abandonment of it in the street of a large city was its disappearance; and the wrongdoer cannot escape making reparation for the loss caused by depriving the plaintiff of the protection which the presence of the driver in his right senses would have afforded.

. . . A railroad company which found it necessary or desirable to have its freight train guarded by two detectives against thieves is surely chargeable with knowledge that portable property left without a guard was likely to be made off with. Again, strictly speaking, the act of the thieves did not intervene between defendant's negligence and the plaintiff's loss; the two causes were to all practical intent simultaneous and concurrent; it is rather a case of a joint tort than an intervening cause. . . . An illustration will perhaps clarify the case. Suppose a fruit vendor at his stand along the street is rendered unconscious by the negligence of the defendant, who disappears, and boys in the street appropriate the unfortunate vendor's stock in trade; could the defendant escape liability for their value? We can hardly imagine a court answering in the affirmative. Yet the case is but little more extreme than the jury might have found the present case.

The judgment is affirmed, with costs.

GARRISON, J. (dissenting). The collision afforded an opportunity for theft of which a thief took advantage, but I cannot agree that the collision was therefore the proximate cause of loss of the stolen articles. Proximate cause imports unbroken continuity between cause and effect, which, both in law and in logic, is broken by the active intervention of an independent criminal actor. This established rule of law is defeated if proximate cause be confounded with mere opportunity for crime. A maladjusted switch may be the proximate cause of the death of a passenger who was killed by the derailment of the train, or by the fire or collision that ensued, but it is not the proximate cause of the death of a passenger who was murdered by a bandit who boarded the train because of the opportunity afforded by its derailment. This clear distinction is not met by saying that criminal intervention should be foreseen, for this implies that crime is to be presumed and the law is directly otherwise.

1   Sometimes the risk of a criminal act by a third-party is the very risk that makes defendant's conduct negligent in the first place. *See, e.g., Hines v. Garrett, supra.* This is the position taken by the drafters of the Restatement (Second) of Torts, Section 449, comment b.

2   Is the dissent correct? Is the hypothetical cited by the dissent in which a passenger is murdered by a bandit who boards a derailed train distinguishable from the facts of this case?

3   How can the result in this case be distinguished from that in *Central of Georgia Railway Co. v. Price?*

4   Intervening v. Superseding. According to Restatement (Second) Torts, Sections 440 and 442, a "superseding cause" is an "intervening force" that prevents an actor from being liable for harm, even when his negligence is a substantial factor in bringing it about. In other words, the superseding cause "breaks the chain" of causation. Not all intervening forces are superseding causes, and only when an intervening force is deemed to be a "superceding cause" is defendant absolved of liability.

5   Most states hold that a plaintiff's suicide attempt is a superceding cause as a matter of law.

WAGNER V. INTERNATIONAL RAILWAY
133 N.E. 437 (N.Y. 1921)

CARDOZO, J. . . .

Plaintiff and his cousin Herbert boarded a car at a station near the bottom of one of the trestles. . . . The platform was provided with doors, but the conductor did not close them. Moving at from six to eight miles an hour, the car, without slackening, turned the curve. There was a violent lurch, and Herbert Wagner was thrown out, near the point where the trestle changes to a bridge. The cry was raised, "Man overboard." The car went on across the bridge, and stopped near the foot of the incline. Night and darkness had come on. Plaintiff walked along the trestle, a distance of four hundred and forty-five feet, until he arrived at the bridge, where he thought to find his cousin's body. . . . Several other persons, instead of ascending the trestle, went beneath it, and discovered under the bridge the body they were seeking. As they stood there, the plaintiff's body struck the ground beside them. Reaching the bridge, he had found upon a beam his cousin's hat, but nothing else. About him, there was darkness. He missed his footing, and fell. . . .

Danger invites rescue. The cry of distress is the summons to relief. The law does not ignore these reactions of the mind in tracing conduct to its consequences. It recognizes them as normal. It places their effects within the range of the natural and probable. The wrong that imperils life is a wrong to the imperiled victim; it is a wrong also to his rescuer. The state that leaves an opening in a bridge is liable to the child that falls into the stream, but liable also to the parent who plunges to its aid . . . . The railroad company whose train approaches without signal is a wrongdoer toward the traveler surprised between the rails, but a wrongdoer also to the bystander who drags him from the path . . . . The risk of rescue, if only it be not wanton, is born of the occasion.

The emergency begets the man. The wrongdoer may not have foreseen the coming of a deliverer. He is accountable as if he had.

The defendant says that we must stop, in following the chain of causes, when action ceases to be "instinctive." By this, is meant, it seems, that rescue is at the peril of the rescuer, unless spontaneous and immediate. If there has been time to deliberate, if impulse has given way to judgment, one cause, it is said, has spent its force, and another has intervened. In this case, the plaintiff walked more than four hundred feet in going to Herbert's aid. He had time to reflect and weigh; impulse had been followed by choice; and choice, in the defendant's view, intercepts and breaks the sequence. We find no warrant for thus shortening the chain of jural causes. We may assume, though we are not required to decide, that peril and rescue must be in substance one transaction; that the sight of the one must have aroused the impulse to the other; in short, that there must be unbroken continuity between the commission of the wrong and the effort to avert its consequences. If all this be assumed, the defendant is not aided. Continuity in such circumstances is not broken by the exercise of volition . . . . So sweeping an exception, if recognized, would leave little of the rule. . . . The law does not discriminate between the rescuer oblivious of peril and the one who counts the cost. It is enough that the act, whether impulsive or deliberate, is the child of the occasion.

The defendant finds another obstacle, however, in the futility of the plaintiff's sacrifice. He should have gone, it is said, below the trestle with the others; he should have known, in view of the overhang of the cars, that the body would not be found above; his conduct was not responsive to the call of the emergency; it was a wanton exposure to a danger that was useless. We think the quality of his acts in the situation that confronted him was to be determined by the jury. Certainly he believed that good would come of his search upon the bridge. He was not going there to view the landscape. The law cannot say of his belief that a reasonable man would have been unable to share it. He could not know the precise point at which his cousin had fallen from the car. If the fall was from the bridge, there was no reason why the body, caught by some projection, might not be hanging on high, athwart the tie rods or the beams. Certainly no such reason was then apparent to the plaintiff, or so a jury might have found. Indeed, his judgment was confirmed by the finding of the hat. There was little time for delay, if the facts were as he states them. Another car was due, and the body, if not removed, might be ground beneath the wheels. The plaintiff had to choose at once, in agitation and with imperfect knowledge. He had seen his kinsman and companion thrown out into the darkness. Rescue could not charge the company with liability if rescue was condemned by reason. "Errors of judgment," however, would not count against him, if they resulted "from the excitement and confusion of the moment" (*Corbin v. Philadelphia*, 195 Penn. St. 461, 472). The reason that was exacted of him was not the reason of the morrow. It was reason fitted and proportioned to the time and the event.

Whether Herbert Wagner's fall was due to the defendant's negligence, and whether plaintiff in going to the rescue, as he did, was foolhardy or reasonable in the light of the emergency confronting him, were questions for the jury. . . .

UNION PUMP CO. V. ALLBRITTON

898 s.w.2d 773 (tex. 1995)

The issue in this case is whether the condition, act, or omission of which a personal injury plaintiff complains was, as a matter of law, too remote to constitute legal causation. Plaintiff brought suit alleging negligence . . . , and the trial court granted summary judgment for the defendant. . . . Because we conclude that there was no legal causation as a matter of law, we . . . render judgment that plaintiff take nothing.

On the night of September 4, 1989, a fire occurred at Texaco Chemical Company's facility in Port Arthur, Texas. A pump manufactured by Union Pump Company caught fire and ignited the surrounding area. This particular pump had caught on fire twice before. Sue Allbritton, a trainee employee of Texaco Chemical, had just finished her shift and was about to leave the plant when the fire erupted. She and her supervisor Felipe Subia, Jr., were directed to and did assist in abating the fire.

Approximately two hours later, the fire was extinguished. However, there appeared to be a problem with a nitrogen purge valve, and Subia was instructed to block in the valve. Viewing the facts in a light most favorable to Allbritton, there was some evidence that an emergency situation existed at that point in time. Allbritton asked if she could accompany Subia and was allowed to do so. To get to the nitrogen purge valve, Allbritton followed Subia over an aboveground pipe rack, which was approximately two and one-half feet high, rather than going around it. It is undisputed that this was not the safer route, but it was the shorter one. Upon reaching the valve, Subia and Allbritton were notified that it was not necessary to block it off. Instead of returning by the route around the pipe rack, Subia chose to walk across it, and Allbritton followed. Allbritton was injured when she hopped or slipped off the pipe rack. There is evidence that the pipe rack was wet because of the fire and that Allbritton and Subia were still wearing fireman's hip boots and other firefighting gear when the injury occurred. Subia admitted that he chose to walk over the pipe rack rather than taking a safer alternative route because he had a "bad habit" of doing so.

Allbritton sued Union Pump, alleging . . . that the defective pump was a proximate or producing cause of her injuries. But for the pump fire, she asserts, she would never have walked over the pipe rack, which was wet with water or firefighting foam.

. . . The question before this Court is whether Union Pump established as a matter of law that neither its conduct nor its product was a legal cause of Allbritton's injuries. Stated another way, was Union Pump correct in contending that there was no causative link between the defective pump and Allbritton's injuries as a matter of law?

Negligence requires a showing of proximate cause. . . . Proximate cause consists of both cause in fact and foreseeability. . . .

At some point in the causal chain, the defendant's conduct or product may be too remotely connected with the plaintiff's injury to constitute legal causation. . . .

Even if the pump fire were in some sense a "philosophic" or "but for" cause of Allbritton's injuries, the forces generated by the fire had come to rest when she fell off the pipe rack. The fire had been extinguished, and Allbritton was walking away from the scene. Viewing the evidence in the light most favorable to Allbritton, the pump fire did no more than create the condition that made Allbritton's injuries possible. We conclude that the circumstances surrounding her injuries are too remotely connected with Union Pump's conduct or pump to constitute a legal cause of her injuries.

VII.

PRODUCT LIABILITY

No area of the common law in America has experienced more growth in the last fifty years than that of product liability. Much of the now familiar vocabulary of this area of tort law is an invention of relatively recent decades. Speaking most generally, as a torts law topic, the label "product liability" applies to all suits for damages allegedly caused by a defective "product." While such cases are today dominated by one theory of recovery – strict product liability, strict liability is not the only theory available to the product liability plaintiff and her lawyer – negligence, breach of warranty (express and implied), and even misrepresentation, among other theories, all are possibilities. However, because strict product liability is a unique theory of recovery that dominates the field, in this chapter of the materials, we will focus on this particular theory, while recognizing that other possible theories of recovery still are available.

A. TORT DEVELOPMENT FROM PRIVITY TO STRICT LIABILITY THEORY

The law of product liability is overwhelmingly a child of the twentieth century. Here we begin with a snapshot of the state of the law at the end of the nineteenth century and then review several important cases marking milestones in the development of modern doctrine since that time. At the end of the nineteenth century, an injured plaintiff's ability to recover from the seller of a defective product was narrowly circumscribed by the doctrine of "privity." The gist of the privity doctrine, as reflected most famously (or infamously?) in the following case, was that parties to a contract for the provision of a product owed a duty only to the other parties to the contract, not to third-party users of the product.

WINTERBOTTOM V. WRIGHT
152 ENG. REP. 402 (EXCH. 1842)

[T]he defendant . . . had . . . contracted . . . with the Postmaster-General, to provide the mail-coach for . . . conveying the mail-bags . . . . [T]he defendant, under . . . said contract, had agreed with the said Postmaster-General that the . . . mail-coach should . . . be kept in a fit, proper, safe, and secure state and condition . . . . [T]he plaintiff, being a mail-coachman, and . . . believing that the . . . coach was in a fit, safe, secure, and proper state and condition . . . hired himself to . . . drive . . . the said mail-coach . . . . [T]he defendant . . . so wholly neglected and failed to perform . . . , that . . . on the 8th of August, 1840, whilst the plaintiff . . . was driving the . . . mail-coach . . . , the . . . coach . . . being then in a frail, weak, and infirm, and dangerous state and condition . . . through certain latent defects in the state and condition thereof, and unsafe and unfit . . . gave way and broke down, whereby the plaintiff was thrown from his seat, and in consequence of injuries then received, had become lamed for life. . . .

LORD ABINGER, C. B. I am clearly of opinion that the defendant is entitled to our judgment. We ought not to permit a doubt to rest upon this subject, for our doing so might be the means of letting in upon us infinity of actions. . . . Here the action is brought simply because the defendant was a contractor with a third person; and it is contended that thereupon he became liable to every body who might use the carriage. . . . It is however contended, that this contract being made on the behalf of the public by the Postmaster-General, no action could be maintained against him, and therefore the plaintiff must have a remedy against the defendant. But that is by no means a necessary consequence — he may be remediless altogether. There is no privity of contract between these parties; and if the plaintiff can sue, every passenger, or even any person passing along the road, who was injured by the upsetting of the coach, might bring a similar action. Unless we confine the operation of such contracts as this to the parties who entered into them, the most absurd and outrageous consequences, to which I can see no limit, would ensue. . . . By permitting this action, we should be working this injustice, that after the defendant had done every thing to the satisfaction of his employer, and after all matters between had been adjusted, and all accounts settled on the footing of their contract, we should subject them to be ripped open by this action of tort being brought against them.

ALDERSON, B. I am of the same opinion. The contract in this case was made with the Postmaster-General alone . . . . If we were to hold that the plaintiff could sue in such a case, there is no point at which such actions would stop. The only safe rule is to confine the right to recover to those who enter into the contract: if we go one step beyond that, there is no reason why we should not go fifty. The only real argument in favour of the action is, that this is a case of hardship; but that might have been obviated, if the plaintiff had made himself a party to the contract. . . .

ROLF, B. The breach of the defendant's duty, stated in this declaration, is his omission to keep the carriage in a safe condition; and when we examine the mode in which that duty is alleged to have arisen, we find a statement that the defendant took upon himself . . . the said contract, the sole and exclusive duty, charge, care, and burden of the repairs, state and condition of the .

. . mail-coach, and, during all the time aforesaid, it had become and was the sole and exclusive duty of the defendant . . . under . . . his said contract, to keep and maintain the . . . mail-coach in a fit, proper, safe, and secure state and condition. The duty, therefore, is shewn to have arisen solely from the contract; and the fallacy consists in the use of that word "duty." If a duty to the Postmaster-General be meant, that is true; but if a duty to the plaintiff be intended (and in that sense the word is evidently used), there was none. This is one of those unfortunate cases in which there certainly has been damnum, but it is damnum absque injuria; it is, no doubt, a hardship upon the plaintiff to be without a remedy, but by that consideration we ought not to be influenced. Hard cases, it has been frequently observed, are apt to introduce bad law.

Judgment for the defendant.

QUESTIONS AND NOTE

1   If defendant's only dealings were with the Post Master General, and the Post Master General is satisfied, and if plaintiff has no direct dealings with the defendant, what did defendant do to subject itself to potential liability to the plaintiff, with whom defendant had no dealings or contact?

2   What if defendant had no contractual arrangement with anyone? What if defendant voluntarily manufactured and maintained a dangerously defective carriage and left it on the street for anyone to use? Should the defendant then owe a duty of due care to the users of the carriage? Is this scenario materially different from *Winterbottom*?

3   As the following cases will illustrate, *Winterbottom* has been overruled essentially everywhere.

Shortly after the decision in *Winterbottom,* courts started to develop exceptions to the privity limitation. Among these exceptions was the rule that where defendant's negligence puts "human life in imminent danger," privity would not bar recovery. *See Thomas v. Winchester,* 6 N.Y. 307 (1852) (defendant liable for harm caused by mislabeled drug even though not in privity with plaintiff). Thus, it became very important whether defendant's alleged negligence was of a sort to put human life in "imminent danger." Ultimately, the courts completely did away with plaintiff's need to plead and prove an exception to the privity limitation. The following case is the landmark case for the beating back of the privity limitation in America.

MACPHERSON V. BUICK MOTOR CO.
111 N.E. 1050 (N.Y. 1916)

Cardozo, J.

The defendant is a manufacturer of automobiles. It sold an automobile to a retail dealer. The retail dealer resold to the plaintiff. While the plaintiff was in the car, it suddenly collapsed. He was thrown out and injured. One of the wheels was made of defective wood, and its spokes crumbled into fragments. The wheel was not made by the defendant; it was bought from another manufacturer. There is evidence, however, that its defects could have been discovered by reasonable inspection, and that inspection was omitted. There is no claim that the defendant knew of the defect and willfully concealed it. . . . The charge is one, not of fraud, but of negligence. The question to be determined is whether the defendant owed a duty of care and vigilance to any one but the immediate purchaser.

The foundations of this branch of the law, at least in this state, were laid in *Thomas* v. *Winchester*. A poison was falsely labeled. The sale was made to a druggist, who in turn sold to a customer. The customer recovered damages from the seller who affixed the label. "The defendant's negligence," it was said, "put human life in imminent danger." A poison falsely labeled is likely to injure any one who gets it. Because the danger is to be foreseen, there is a duty to avoid the injury. . . .

We hold, then, that the principle of *Thomas* v. *Winchester* is not limited to poisons, explosives, and things of like nature, to things which in their normal operation are implements of destruction. If the nature of a thing is such that it is reasonably certain to place life and limb in peril when negligently made, it is then a thing of danger. Its nature gives warning of the consequences to be expected. If to the element of danger there is added knowledge that the thing will be used by persons other than the purchaser, and used without new tests, then, irrespective of contract, the manufacturer of this thing of danger is under a duty to make it carefully. That is as far as we are required to go for the decision of this case. There must be knowledge of a danger, not merely possible, but probable. It is *possible* to use almost anything in a way that will make it dangerous if defective. That is not enough to charge the manufacturer with a duty independent of his contract. Whether a given thing is dangerous may be sometimes a question for the court and sometimes a question for the jury. There must also be knowledge that in the usual course of events the danger will be shared by others than the buyer. Such knowledge may often be inferred from the nature of the transaction. . . . We are dealing now with the liability of the manufacturer of the finished product, who puts it on the market to be used without inspection by his customers. If he is negligent, where danger is to be foreseen, a liability will follow.

. . . We have put aside the notion that the duty to safeguard life and limb, when the consequences of negligence may be foreseen, grows out of contract and nothing else. We have put the source of the obligation where it ought to be. We have put its source in the law.

. . . Beyond all question, the nature of an automobile gives warning of probable danger if its construction is defective. This automobile was designed to go fifty miles an hour. Unless its wheels were sound and strong, injury was almost certain. It was as much a thing of danger as a defective engine for a railroad. The defendant knew the danger. It knew also that the car would be used by persons other than the buyer. This was apparent from its size; there were seats for three persons. It was apparent also from the fact that the buyer was a dealer in cars, who bought to resell. The maker of this car supplied it for the use of purchasers from the dealer . . . . The dealer was indeed the one person of whom it might be said with some approach to certainty that by him the car would not be used. Yet the defendant would have us say that he was the one person whom it was under a legal duty to protect. The law does not lead us to so inconsequent a conclusion. . . .

There is nothing anomalous in a rule which imposes upon A, who has contracted with B, a duty to C and D and others according as he knows or does not know that the subject-matter of the contract is intended for their use. . . .

NOTE AND QUESTION

1   In setting out its holding, the *MacPherson* court emphasized that defendant knew that the product would be used by someone other than the purchaser, "without new tests." What is the significance of the fact that the defendant knew that there would be no further testing of the product before plaintiff used it?

B. CONTRACT THEORIES AND PRIVITY

In no American jurisdiction today is a negligence cause of action any longer barred because of a lack of privity between plaintiff and defendant. But negligence is not the only theory on which a plaintiff may recover in a product liability case, and while the *MacPherson* decision did away with the privity requirement in negligence cases, product liability plaintiffs in the early twentieth century still faced a steep uphill climb. To recover under a negligence theory, plaintiff had to prove that defendant breached a duty of due care, but showing that a manufacturing defendant breached a duty of reasonable care is no easy task.

Breach of contract theories of recovery were potentially available and did not require a showing of defendant's carelessness, but contract theories still required (and frequently still do require) a showing of privity, along with other practical limitations, such as a statute of limitation that started to run at the date of sale. One advantage (from the plaintiff's point of view) of a contract theory of recovery in a product liability case is that plaintiff need not prove defendant's fault – if defendant breached the contract, liability is essentially "strict." While an actionable promise can be provided by the express words of the product seller, a plaintiff who pursues a contract theory of recovery in a product liability case usually alleges the breach of one or more implied warranties, the most common of which are the implied warranty of merchantability and the implied warranty of fitness for a particular purpose. The following case is illustrative.

MCCABE V. L. K. LIGGETT DRUG CO.
112 N.E.2D 254 (MASS. 1953)

This is an action of contract to recover compensation for personal injuries resulting from the use of a metal coffee maker purchased from the defendant. The declaration is in one count and alleges breaches of implied warranties of fitness and merchantability. After a verdict for the plaintiff, the judge, on motion of the defendant and subject to the plaintiff's exception, entered a verdict for the defendant . . . .

There was evidence that on or about May 20, 1949, one Huwe, acting . . . for the plaintiff, purchased a metal coffee maker, called "Lucifer 'Lifetime,'" from the defendant at its store . . . . Huwe had seen "this type of appliance displayed or on sale in that particular store about a week before." He had told the plaintiff about it and she had asked him to buy one of the coffee makers for her. On the following day, he went to the store and asked the clerk "if there were any more of the metal coffee makers that . . . [he] had seen on sale." . . . The clerk handed Huwe a coffee maker packed in a sealed cardboard carton which he took away and delivered to the plaintiff.

This coffee maker . . . consists of three parts, a lower bowl, an upper bowl, and a filter . . . . Water is boiled in the lower bowl and under pressure of the steam which is generated rises through a tube into the upper bowl where ground coffee is placed. The water is there mixed with the coffee and forms the beverage which . . . flows down into the lower bowl. . . .

The plaintiff used the appliance two or three times and noticed that the water was slow in coming up into the upper bowl. On the morning of June 9, 1949, she again used it, complying with the written instructions which came with it. . . . "It was taking quite a while" and she "looked over it and noticed it was not coming up. It had stopped, [and] then it blew up" in her face. The water and coffee grounds were thrown over her and over the floor, walls, and ceiling by the force of the explosion. The upper bowl which she had inserted firmly into the neck of the lower bowl "flew onto the floor." The plaintiff was burned.

The defendant was notified of the occurrence by letter from the plaintiff's attorney dated June 16, 1949. Therein it was stated that the plaintiff was injured on June 9, 1949, "when the top part of a coffee maker apparently having the trademark 'Lucifer Lifetime' exploded and flew off while being used by her in her home according to the instructions in the circular which accompanied the purchase thereof made at your store on or about May 20, 1949," and that damages were claimed "because the appliance was not fit for the purposes for which it was sold and purchased."

. . . The sale carried an implied warranty by the seller that the appliance was a coffee maker of merchantable quality. . . . Merchantable quality means that goods are reasonably suitable for the ordinary uses for which goods of that description are sold. . . . Whether this coffee maker was of such quality depended on its capability, when properly used, to make coffee. This presented a question of fact for the jury. The evidence consisted of the coffee maker and the testimony of the plaintiff concerning the so called explosion. . . . The plaintiff offered in evidence the opinion of an expert that the area of the notches of the filter was inadequate to provide for the release of the pressure which developed from the boiling water; that this area would be further decreased by the "congealing" of the coffee grounds; and that the pressure in the bottom section, having inadequate release, would build up to a point where it would have an explosive effect. . . .

The fact that the apparatus violently burst apart in the manner described showed that the accumulating pressure was not being released and in the absence of explanation was itself evidence of a defective condition. . . . The jury could find that the explosion was caused by the failure of the water to rise into the upper bowl and from an examination of the notches in the filter that this failure was due to an inadequate outlet and the clogging effect of coffee grounds which would collect around the notches.

If the coffee maker was so imperfect in design that it could not be used without the likelihood of an explosion it could be found that the appliance was not reasonably fit for making coffee and therefore not merchantable. . . .

The plaintiff's exceptions are sustained. The verdict for the defendant . . . is set aside. The original verdict for the plaintiff is to stand and judgment is to be entered for the plaintiff on that verdict.

So ordered.

The next case was the first American case to provide a product liability recovery without privity and without proof of defendant's fault.

HENNINGSEN V. BLOOMFIELD MOTORS, INC.
161 A.2D 69 (N.J. 1960)

Plaintiff Claus H. Henningsen purchased a Plymouth automobile, manufactured by defendant Chrysler Corporation, from defendant Bloomfield Motors, Inc. His wife, plaintiff Helen Henningsen, was injured while driving it and instituted suit against both defendants to recover damages on account of her injuries. . . . The complaint was predicated upon breach of express and implied warranties and upon negligence. At the trial the negligence counts were dismissed by the court and the cause was submitted to the jury for determination solely on the issues of implied warranty of merchantability. Verdicts were returned against both defendants and in favor of the plaintiffs. Defendants appealed and plaintiffs cross-appealed from the dismissal of their negligence claim. . . .

On May 7, 1955 Mr. and Mrs. Henningsen visited the place of business of Bloomfield Motors, Inc., an authorized De Soto and Plymouth dealer, to look at a Plymouth. . . . They were shown a Plymouth which appealed to them and the purchase followed. The record indicates that Mr. Henningsen intended the car as a Mother's Day gift to his wife. He said the intention was communicated to the dealer. When the purchase order or contract was prepared and presented, the husband executed it alone. His wife did not join as a party.

The purchase order was a printed form of one page. . . . The type used in the printed parts of the form became smaller in size, different in style, and less readable toward the bottom where the line for the purchaser's signature was placed. The smallest type on the page appears in the two paragraphs, one of two and one-quarter lines and the second of one and one-half lines, on which great stress is laid by the defense in the case. These two paragraphs are the least legible and the most difficult to read in the instrument, but they are most important in the evaluation of the rights of the contesting parties. They do not attract attention and there is nothing about the format which would draw the reader's eye to them. In fact, a studied and concentrated effort would have to be made to read them. De-emphasis seems the motif rather than emphasis. More particularly, most of the printing in the body of the order appears to be 12 point block type, and easy to read. In the short paragraphs under discussion, however, the type appears to be six point script and the print is solid, that is, the lines are very close together.

The two paragraphs are:

The front and back of this Order comprise the entire agreement affecting this purchase and no other agreement or understanding of any nature concerning same has been made or entered into, or will be recognized. I hereby certify that no credit has been extended to me for the purchase of this motor vehicle except as appears in writing on the face of this agreement.

I have read the matter printed on the back hereof and agree to it as a part of this order the same as if it were printed above my signature. I certify that I am 21 years of age, or older, and hereby acknowledge receipt of a copy of this order.

. . . The testimony of Claus Henningsen justifies the conclusion that he did not read the two fine print paragraphs referring to the back of the purchase contract. And it is uncontradicted that no one made any reference to them, or called them to his attention. With respect to the matter appearing on the back, it is likewise uncontradicted that he did not read it and that no one called it to his attention.

The reverse side of the contract contains 8 1/2 inches of fine print. It is not as small, however, as the two critical paragraphs described above. The page is headed "Conditions" and contains ten separate paragraphs consisting of 65 lines in all. The paragraphs do not have head-notes or margin notes denoting their particular subject, as in the case of the "Owner Service Certificate" to be referred to later. In the seventh paragraph, about two-thirds of the way down the page, the warranty, which is the focal point of the case, is set forth. It is as follows:

7. It is expressly agreed that there are no warranties, express or implied, made by either the dealer or the manufacturer on the motor vehicle, chassis, or parts furnished hereunder except as follows:

The manufacturer warrants each new motor vehicle (including original equipment placed thereon by the manufacturer except tires), chassis or parts manufactured by it to be free from defects in material or workmanship under normal use and service. Its obligation under this warranty being limited to making good at its factory any part or parts thereof which shall, within ninety (90) days after delivery of such vehicle *to the original purchaser* or before such vehicle has been driven 4,000 miles, whichever event shall first occur, be returned to it with transportation charges prepaid and which its examination shall disclose to its satisfaction to have been thus defective; *this warranty being expressly in lieu of all other warranties expressed or implied, and all other obligations or liabilities on its part,* and it neither assumes nor authorizes any other person to assume for it any other liability in connection with the sale of its vehicles. . . . (Emphasis ours)

The new Plymouth was turned over to the Henningsens on May 9, 1955. . . . Mr. Henningsen drove it from the dealer's place of business in Bloomfield to their home in Keansburg. On the trip nothing unusual appeared in the way in which it operated. Thereafter, it was used for short trips on paved streets about the town. It had no servicing and no mishaps of any kind before the event of May 19. That day, Mrs. Henningsen drove to Asbury Park. On the way down and in returning the car performed in normal fashion until the accident occurred. She was proceeding . . . at 20-22 miles per hour. The highway was paved and smooth, and contained two lanes for northbound travel. She was riding in the right-hand lane. Suddenly she heard a loud noise "from the bottom, by the hood." It "felt as if something cracked." The steering wheel spun in her hands; the car veered sharply to the right and crashed into a highway sign and a brick wall. No other vehicle was in any way involved. A bus operator driving in the left-hand lane testified that he observed plaintiffs' car approaching in normal fashion in the opposite direction; "all of a sudden [it] veered at 90 degrees * * * and right into this wall." As a result of the impact, the front of the car was so badly damaged that it was impossible to determine if any of the parts of the steering wheel mechanism or workmanship or assembly were defective or improper prior to the accident. The condition was such that the collision insurance carrier, after inspection, declared the vehicle a total loss. It had 468 miles on the speedometer at the time.

The insurance carrier's inspector and appraiser of damaged cars, with 11 years of experience, advanced the opinion, based on the history and his examination, that something definitely went "wrong from the steering wheel down to the front wheels" and that the untoward happening must have been due to mechanical defect or failure; "something down there had to drop off or break loose to cause the car" to act in the manner described.

As has been indicated, the trial court felt that the proof was not sufficient to make out a *prima facie* case as to the negligence of either the manufacturer or the dealer. The case was given to the jury, therefore, solely on the warranty theory, with results favorable to the plaintiffs against both defendants.

I.

THE CLAIM OF IMPLIED WARRANTY AGAINST THE MANUFACTURER.

In the ordinary case of sale of goods by description an implied warranty of merchantability is an integral part of the transaction. . . . The former type of warranty simply means that the thing sold is reasonably fit for the general purpose for which it is manufactured and sold. . . .

Of course such sales, whether oral or written, may be accompanied by an express warranty. Under the broad terms of the Uniform Sale of Goods Law any affirmation of fact relating to the goods is an express warranty if the natural tendency of the statement is to induce the buyer to make the purchase. . . . And over the years since the almost universal adoption of the act, a growing awareness of the tremendous development of modern business methods has prompted the courts to administer that provision with a liberal hand. . . . Solicitude toward the buyer plainly harmonizes with the intention of the Legislature. That fact is manifested further by the later section of the act which preserves and continues any permissible implied warranty, despite an express warranty, unless the two are inconsistent. . . .

The uniform act codified, extended and liberalized the common law of sales. The motivation in part was to ameliorate the harsh doctrine of *caveat emptor*, and in some measure to impose a reciprocal obligation on the seller to beware. The transcendent value of the legislation, particularly with respect to implied warranties, rests in the fact that obligations on the part of the seller were imposed by operation of law, and did not depend for their existence upon express agreement of the parties. And of tremendous significance in a rapidly expanding commercial society was the recognition of the right to recover damages on account of personal injuries arising from a breach of warranty. . . . The particular importance of this advance resides in the fact that under such circumstances strict liability is imposed upon the maker or seller of the product. Recovery of damages does not depend upon proof of negligence or knowledge of the defect. . . .

Chrysler points out that an implied warranty of merchantability is an incident of a contract of sale. It concedes, of course, the making of the original sale to Bloomfield Motors, Inc., but maintains that this transaction marked the terminal point of its contractual connection with the car. Then Chrysler urges that since it was not a party to the sale by the dealer to Henningsen, there is no privity of contract between it and the plaintiffs, and the absence of this privity eliminates any such implied warranty.

There is no doubt that under early common-law concepts of contractual liability only those persons who were parties to the bargain could sue for a breach of it. In more recent times a noticeable disposition has appeared in a number of jurisdictions to break through the narrow barrier of privity when dealing with sales of goods in order to give realistic recognition to a universally accepted fact. The fact is that the dealer and the ordinary buyer do not, and are not expected to, buy goods, whether they be foodstuffs or automobiles, exclusively for their own consumption or use. Makers and manufacturers know this and advertise and market their products on that assumption . . . . The limitations of privity in contracts for the sale of goods developed their place in the law when marketing conditions were simple, when maker and buyer frequently met face to face on an equal bargaining plane and when many of the products were relatively uncomplicated and conducive to inspection by a buyer competent to evaluate quality. . . . With the advent of mass marketing, the manufacturer became remote from the purchaser, sales were accomplished through intermediaries, and the demand for the product was created by advertising media. In such an economy it became obvious that the consumer was the person being cultivated. Manifestly, the connotation of "consumer" was broader than that of "buyer." He signified such a person who, in the reasonable contemplation of the parties to the sale, might be expected to use the product. Thus, where the commodities sold are such that if defectively manufactured they will be dangerous to life or limb, then society's interests can only be protected by eliminating the requirement of privity between the maker and his dealers and the reasonably expected ultimate consumer. In that way the burden of losses consequent upon use of defective articles is borne by those who are in a position to either control the danger or make an equitable distribution of the losses when they do occur. . . .

Although only a minority of jurisdictions have thus far departed from the requirement of privity, the movement in that direction is most certainly gathering momentum. Liability to the ultimate consumer in the absence of direct contractual connection has been predicated upon a variety of theories. Some courts hold that the warranty runs with the article like a covenant running with land; others recognize a third-party beneficiary thesis; still others rest their decision on the ground that public policy requires recognition of a warranty made directly to the consumer. . . .

Under modern conditions the ordinary layman, on responding to the importuning of colorful advertising, has neither the opportunity nor the capacity to inspect or to determine the fitness of an automobile for use; he must rely on the manufacturer who has control of its construction, and to some degree on the dealer who, to the limited extent called for by the manufacturer's instructions, inspects and services it before delivery. In such a marketing milieu his remedies and those of persons who properly claim through him should not depend "upon the intricacies of the law of sales. The obligation of the manufacturer should not be based alone on privity of contract. It should rest, as was once said, upon "the demands of social justice." . . .

Accordingly, we hold that under modern marketing conditions, when a manufacturer puts a new automobile in the stream of trade and promotes its purchase by the public, an implied warranty that it is reasonably suitable for use as such accompanies it into the hands of the ultimate purchaser. Absence of agency between the manufacturer and the dealer who makes the ultimate sale is immaterial. . . .

IV.

PROOF OF BREACH OF IMPLIED WARRANTY OF MERCHANTABILITY.

Both defendants argue that the proof adduced by plaintiffs as to the happening of the accident was not sufficient to demonstrate a breach of warranty. . . . We cannot agree. In our view, the total effect of the circumstances shown from purchase to accident is adequate to raise an inference that the car was defective and that such condition was causally related to the mishap. . . .

V.

THE DEFENSE OF LACK OF PRIVITY AGAINST MRS. HENNINGSEN.

Both defendants contend that since there was no privity of contract between them and Mrs. Henningsen, she cannot recover for breach of any warranty made by either of them. On the facts, as they were developed, we agree that she was not a party to the purchase agreement. . . . Her right to maintain the action, therefore, depends upon whether she occupies such legal status thereunder as to permit her to take advantage of a breach of defendants' implied warranties.

For the most part the cases that have been considered dealt with the right of the buyer or consumer to maintain an action against the manufacturer where the contract of sale was with a dealer and the buyer had no contractual relationship with the manufacturer. In the present matter, the basic contractual relationship is between Claus Henningsen, Chrysler, and Bloomfield Motors, Inc. The precise issue presented is whether Mrs. Henningsen, who is not a party to their respective warranties, may claim under them. . . . We are convinced that the cause of justice in this area of the law can be served only by recognizing that she is such a person who, in the reasonable contemplation of the parties to the warranty, might be expected to become a user of the automobile. Accordingly, her lack of privity does not stand in the way of prosecution of the injury suit against the defendant Chrysler.

. . . Defendant Bloomfield Motors is chargeable with an implied warranty of merchantability to Claus Henningsen. . . . The manufacturer establishes the network of trade and the dealer is a unit utilized in that network to accomplish sales. He is the beneficiary of the same express and implied warranties from the manufacturer as he extends to the buyer of the automobile. . . . His understanding of the expected use of the car by persons other than the buyer is the same as that of the manufacturer. And so, his claim to the doctrine of privity should rise no higher than that of the manufacturer. . . .

[I]t is our opinion that an implied warranty of merchantability chargeable to either an automobile manufacturer or a dealer extends to the purchaser of the car, members of his family, and to other persons occupying or using it with his consent. It would be wholly opposed to reality to say that use by such persons is not within the anticipation of parties to such a warranty of reasonable suitability of an automobile for ordinary highway operation. Those persons must be considered within the distributive chain.

. . . Section 2-318 of the Uniform Commercial Code proposes that the warranty be extended to "any natural person who is in the family or household of his buyer or who is a guest in his home if it is reasonable to expect that such person may use, consume or be affected by the goods and who is injured in person by breach of the warranty." And the section provides also that "A seller may not exclude or limit the operation" of the extension. . . .

In his charge as to Mrs. Henningsen's right to recover on the implied warranty, the trial court referred to her husband's testimony that he was buying the car for her use, and then instructed the jury that on such facts the warranty extended to her. In view of our holding, obviously the protection of the warranty runs to her as an incident of the sale without regard to such testimony. Accordingly, the contention that the instruction was reversible error must be rejected. . . .

VII.

Under all of the circumstances outlined above, the judgments in favor of the plaintiffs and against defendants are affirmed.

1. All states except Louisiana have enacted some form of the Uniform Commercial Code, which codifies the law of express and implied warranties.
2. Once implied warranty liability is recognized and stripped of the privity limitation and the seller's ability to disclaim warranty is narrowly circumscribed, the form of warranty liability employed in *Henningsen* comes close to modern strict products liability. It is not surprising, then, that a mere three years after the Court's decision in *Henningsen*, California became the first state formally to adopt strict products liability in *Greenman v. Yuba Power Products, Inc.*

SELECT WARRANTY PROVISIONS FROM VIRGINIA COMMERCIAL CODE

§ 8.2-313. Express warranties by affirmation, promise, description, sample

1. Express warranties by the seller are created as follows:
   (a) Any affirmation of fact or promise made by the seller to the buyer which relates to the goods and becomes part of the basis of the bargain creates an express warranty that the goods shall conform to the affirmation or promise.
   (b) Any description of the goods which is made part of the basis of the bargain creates an express warranty that the goods shall conform to the description.
   (c) Any sample or model which is made part of the basis of the bargain creates an express warranty that the whole of the goods shall conform to the sample or model.

2. It is not necessary to the creation of an express warranty that the seller use formal words such as "warrant" or "guarantee" or that he have a specific intention to make a warranty, but an affirmation merely of the value of the goods or a statement purporting to be merely the seller's opinion or commendation of the goods does not create a warranty.

§ 8.2-314. Implied warranty: Merchantability; usage of trade

1. Unless excluded or modified (§ 8.2-316), a warranty that the goods shall be merchantable is implied in a contract for their sale if the seller is a merchant with respect to goods of that kind. Under this section the serving for value of food or drink to be consumed either on the premises or elsewhere is a sale.

2. Goods to be merchantable must be at least such as
   (a) pass without objection in the trade under the contract description; and

(b) in the case of fungible goods, are of fair average quality within the description; and

(c) are fit for the ordinary purposes for which such goods are used; and

(d) run, within the variations permitted by the agreement, of even kind, quality and quantity within each unit and among all units involved; and

(e) are adequately contained, packaged, and labeled as the agreement may require; and

(f) conform to the promises or affirmations of fact made on the container or label if any.

3. Unless excluded or modified (§ 8.2-316) other implied warranties may arise from course of dealing or usage of trade.

§ 8.2-315. Implied warranty: Fitness for particular purpose

Where the seller at the time of contracting has reason to know any particular purpose for which the goods are required and that the buyer is relying on the seller's skill or judgment to select or furnish suitable goods, there is unless excluded or modified under the next section [§ 8.2-316] an implied warranty that the goods shall be fit for such purpose.

§ 8.2-316. Exclusion or modification of warranties

1. Words or conduct relevant to the creation of an express warranty and words or conduct tending to negate or limit warranty shall be construed wherever reasonable as consistent with each other; but subject to the provisions of this title on parol or extrinsic evidence (§ 8.2-202) negation or limitation is inoperative to the extent that such construction is unreasonable.

2. Subject to subsection (3), to exclude or modify the implied warranty of merchantability or any part of it the language must mention merchantability and in case of a writing must be conspicuous, and to exclude or modify any implied warranty of fitness the exclusion must be by a writing and conspicuous. Language to exclude all implied warranties of fitness is sufficient if it states, for example, that "There are no warranties which extend beyond the description on the face hereof."
(3) Notwithstanding subsection (2)
(a) unless the circumstances indicate otherwise, all implied warranties are excluded by expressions like "as is," "with all faults" or other language which in common understanding calls the buyer's attention to the exclusion of warranties and makes plain that there is no implied warranty; and
(b) when the buyer before entering into the contract has examined the goods or the sample or model as fully as he desired or has refused to examine the goods there

is no implied warranty with regard to defects which an examination ought in the circumstances to have revealed to him; and

(c) an implied warranty can also be excluded or modified by course of dealing or course of performance or usage of trade.

4. Remedies for breach of warranty can be limited in accordance with the provisions of this title on liquidation or limitation of damages and on contractual modification of remedy (§§ 8.2-718 and 8.2-719).

§ 8.2-318. When lack of privity no defense in action against manufacturer or seller of goods

Lack of privity between plaintiff and defendant shall be no defense in any action brought against the manufacturer or seller of goods to recover damages for **breach of warranty,** express or implied, or for negligence, although the plaintiff did not purchase the goods from the defendant, if the plaintiff was a person whom the manufacturer or seller might reasonably have expected to use, consume, or be affected by the goods; however, this section shall not be construed to affect any litigation pending on June 29, 1962.

§ 8.2-719. Contractual modification or limitation of remedy

1. Subject to the provisions of subsections (2) and (3) of this section and of the preceding section [§ 8.2-718] on liquidation and limitation of damages,
   (a) the agreement may provide for remedies in addition to or in substitution for those provided in this title and may limit or alter the measure of damages recoverable under this title, as by limiting the buyer's remedies to return of the goods and repayment of the price or to repair and replacement of nonconforming goods or parts; and
   (b) resort to a remedy as provided is optional unless the remedy is expressly agreed to be exclusive, in which case it is the sole remedy.

2. Where circumstances cause an exclusive or limited remedy to fail of its essential purpose, remedy may be had as provided in this act.

3. Consequential damages may be limited or excluded unless the limitation or exclusion is unconscionable. Limitation of consequential damages for injury to the person in the case of consumer goods is prima facie unconscionable but limitation of damages where the loss is commercial is not.

C. STRICT LIABILITY IN TORT FOR DEFECTIVE PRODUCTS

1. ADOPTION OF STRICT PRODUCT LIABILITY

To surmount the difficulties that the plaintiff faced under negligence and contract theories, Justice Traynor's opinion in the following case seriously proposed for the first time allowing the product liability plaintiff to recover in tort without proving negligence, thus freeing the plaintiff both from the need to prove fault and from the limitations on existing contract-based remedies.

ESCOLA V. COCA-COLA BOTTLING CO.
150 P.2D 436 (CAL. 1944)

GIBSON, C.J.

Plaintiff, a waitress in a restaurant, was injured when a bottle of Coca Cola broke in her hand. She alleged that defendant company, which had bottled and delivered the alleged defective bottle to her employer, was negligent . . . . This appeal is from a judgment upon a jury verdict in favor of plaintiff.

Defendant's driver delivered several cases of Coca Cola to the restaurant, placing them on the floor . . . where they remained at least thirty-six hours. Immediately before the accident, plaintiff picked up the top case and set it upon a near-by ice cream cabinet . . . . She then proceeded to take the bottles from the case with her right hand, one at a time, and put them into the refrigerator. Plaintiff testified that after she had placed three bottles in the refrigerator and had moved the fourth bottle about eighteen inches from the case "it exploded in my hand." The bottle broke into two jagged pieces and inflicted a deep five-inch cut . . . . Plaintiff further testified that when the bottle exploded, "It made a sound similar to an electric light bulb that would have dropped. It made a loud pop." . . . A fellow employee, on the opposite side of the counter, testified that plaintiff "had the bottle, I should judge, waist high, and I know that it didn't bang either the case or the door or another bottle . . . when it popped. It sounded just like a fruit jar would blow up. . . ." The witness further testified that the contents of the bottle "flew all over herself and myself and the walls and one thing and another." . . .

Plaintiff then . . . announced to the court that being unable to show any specific acts of negligence she relied completely on the doctrine of res ipsa loquitur. . . .

Res ipsa loquitur does not apply unless (1) defendant had exclusive control of the thing causing the injury and (2) the accident is of such a nature that it ordinarily would not occur in the absence of negligence by the defendant. . . .

Many authorities state that the happening of the accident does not speak for itself where it took place some time after defendant had relinquished control of the instrumentality causing the injury. Under the more logical view, however, the doctrine may be applied upon the theory that defendant had control at the time of the alleged negligent act, although not at the time of the accident, *provided* plaintiff first proves that the condition of the instrumentality had not been changed after it left the defendant's possession. . . . It is not necessary, of course, that plaintiff eliminate every remote possibility of injury to the bottle after defendant lost control, and the requirement is satisfied if there is evidence permitting a reasonable inference that it was not accessible to extraneous harmful forces and that it was carefully handled by plaintiff or any third person who may have moved or touched it. . . . If such evidence is presented, the question becomes one for the trier of fact . . . . Upon an examination of the record, the evidence appears sufficient to support a reasonable inference that the bottle here involved was not damaged by any extraneous force after delivery to the restaurant by defendant. It follows, therefore, that the bottle was in some manner defective at the time defendant relinquished control, because sound and properly prepared bottles of carbonated liquids do not ordinarily explode when carefully handled. . . .

The bottle was admittedly charged with gas under pressure, and the charging of the bottle was within the exclusive control of defendant. As it is a matter of common knowledge that an overcharge would not ordinarily result without negligence, it follows under the doctrine of res ipsa loquitur that if the bottle was in fact excessively charged an inference of defendant's negligence would arise. If the explosion resulted from a defective bottle containing a safe pressure, the defendant would be liable if it negligently failed to discover such flaw. If the defect were visible, an inference of negligence would arise from the failure of defendant to discover it. Where defects are discoverable, it may be assumed that they will not ordinarily escape detection if a reasonable inspection is made, and if such a defect is overlooked an inference arises that a proper inspection was not made. . . .

A chemical engineer for the Owens-Illinois Glass Company and its Pacific Coast subsidiary, maker of Coca Cola bottles, explained how glass is manufactured and the methods used in testing and inspecting bottles. He testified that his company is the largest manufacturer of glass containers in the United States, and that it uses the standard methods for testing bottles recommended by the glass containers association. . . . The witness stated that these tests are "pretty near" infallible.

It thus appears that there is available to the industry a commonly-used method of testing bottles for defects not apparent to the eye, which is almost infallible. Since Coca Cola bottles are subjected to these tests by the manufacturer, it is not likely that they contain defects when delivered to the bottler which are not discoverable by visual inspection. . . . It follows that a defect which would make the bottle unsound could be discovered by reasonable and practicable tests.

Although it is not clear in this case whether the explosion was caused by an excessive charge or a defect in the glass, there is a sufficient showing that neither cause would ordinarily have been present if due care had been used. Further, defendant had exclusive control over both the charging and inspection of the bottles. Accordingly, all the requirements necessary to entitle plaintiff to rely on the doctrine of res ipsa loquitur to supply an inference of negligence are present.

It is true that defendant presented evidence tending to show that it exercised considerable precaution by carefully regulating and checking the pressure in the bottles and by making visual inspections for defects in the glass at several stages during the bottling process. It is well settled, however, that when a defendant produces evidence to rebut the inference of negligence which arises upon application of the doctrine of res ipsa loquitur, it is ordinarily a question of fact for the jury to determine whether the inference has been dispelled. . . .

The judgment is affirmed.

TRAYNOR, J.

I concur in the judgment, but I believe the manufacturer's negligence should no longer be singled out as the basis of a plaintiff's right to recover in cases like the present one. In my opinion it should now be recognized that a manufacturer incurs an absolute liability when an article that he has placed on the market, knowing that it is to be used without inspection, proves to have a defect that causes injury to human beings. *McPherson* v. *Buick Motor Co.* . . . established the principle, recognized by this court, that irrespective of privity of contract, the manufacturer is responsible for an injury caused by such an article to any person who comes in lawful contact with it. In these cases the source of the manufacturer's liability was his negligence in the manufacturing process or in the inspection of component parts supplied by others. Even if there is no negligence, however, public policy demands that responsibility be fixed wherever it will most effectively reduce the hazards to life and health inherent in defective products that reach the market. It is evident that the manufacturer can anticipate some hazards and guard against the recurrence of others, as the public cannot. Those who suffer injury from defective products are unprepared to meet its consequences. The cost of an injury and the loss of time or health may be an overwhelming misfortune to the person injured, and a needless one, for the risk of injury can be insured by the manufacturer and distributed among the public as a cost of doing business. It is to the public interest to discourage the marketing of products having defects that are a menace to the public. If such products nevertheless find their way into the market it is to the public interest to place the responsibility for whatever injury they may cause upon the manufacturer, who, even if he is not negligent in the manufacture of the product, is responsible for its reaching the market. However intermittently such injuries may occur and however haphazardly they may strike, the risk of their occurrence is a constant risk and a general one. Against such a risk there should be general and constant protection and the manufacturer is best situated to afford such protection.

The injury from a defective product does not become a matter of indifference because the defect arises from causes other than the negligence of the manufacturer, such as negligence of a submanufacturer of a component part whose defects could not be revealed by inspection, or unknown causes that even by the device of res ipsa loquitur cannot be classified as negligence of the manufacturer. The inference of negligence may be dispelled by an affirmative showing of proper care. . . . An injured person, however, is not ordinarily in a position to refute such evidence or identify the cause of the defect, for he can hardly be familiar with the manufacturing process as the manufacturer himself is. In leaving it to the jury to decide whether the inference has been dispelled, regardless of the evidence against it, the negligence rule approaches the rule of strict liability. It is needlessly circuitous to make negligence the basis of recovery and impose what is in reality liability without negligence. If public policy demands that a manufacturer of goods be responsible for their quality regardless of negligence there is no reason not to fix that responsibility openly. . . .

[I]t is to the public interest to prevent injury to the public from any defective goods by the imposition of civil liability generally.

The retailer, even though not equipped to test a product, is under an absolute liability to his customer, for the implied warranties of fitness for proposed use and merchantable quality include a warranty of safety of the product. This warranty is not necessarily a contractual one, for public policy requires that the buyer be insured at the seller's expense against injury. The courts recognize, however, that the retailer cannot bear the burden of this warranty, and allow him to recoup any losses by means of the warranty of safety attending the wholesaler's or manufacturer's sale to him. Such a procedure, however, is needlessly circuitous and engenders wasteful litigation. Much would be gained if the injured person could base his action directly on the manufacturer's warranty.

The liability of the manufacturer to an immediate buyer injured by a defective product follows without proof of negligence from the implied warranty of safety attending the sale. Ordinarily, however, the immediate buyer is a dealer who does not intend to use the product himself, and if the warranty of safety is to serve the purpose of protecting health and safety it must give rights to others than the dealer. In the words of Judge Cardozo in the McPherson case: "The dealer was indeed the one person of whom it might be said with some approach to certainty that by him the car would not be used. Yet, the defendant would have us say that he was the one person whom it was under a legal duty to protect. The law does not lead us to so inconsequent a solution." While the defendant's negligence in the McPherson case made it unnecessary for the court to base liability on warranty, Judge Cardozo's reasoning recognized the injured person as the real party in interest and effectively disposed of the theory that the liability of the manufacturer incurred by his warranty should apply only to the immediate purchaser. It thus paves the way for a standard of liability that would make the manufacturer guarantee the safety of his product even when there is no negligence. . . .

As handicrafts have been replaced by mass production with its great markets and transportation facilities, the close relationship between the producer and consumer of a product has been altered. Manufacturing processes, frequently valuable secrets, are ordinarily either inaccessible to or beyond the ken of the general public. The consumer no longer has means or skill enough to investigate for himself the soundness of a product, even when it is not contained in a sealed package, and his erstwhile vigilance has been lulled by the steady efforts of manufacturers to build up confidence by advertising and marketing devices such as trade-marks. Consumers no longer approach products warily but accept them on faith, relying on the reputation of the manufacturer or the trade-mark. Manufacturers have sought to justify that faith by increasingly high standards of inspection and a readiness to make good on defective products by way of replacements and refunds. The manufacturer's obligation to the consumer must keep pace with the changing relationship between them; it cannot be escaped because the marketing of a product has become so complicated as to require one or more intermediaries. Certainly there is greater reason to impose liability on the manufacturer than on the retailer who is but a conduit of a product that he is not himself able to test.

The manufacturer's liability should, of course, be defined in terms of the safety of the product in normal and proper use, and should not extend to injuries that cannot be traced to the product as it reached the market.

NOTES AND QUESTIONS

1   *Escola* provides a good example of the difficulties faced by a products liability plaintiff who must rely on a
     negligence theory of liability. The plaintiff in *Escola* faced the challenge of establishing negligence by one defendant
     in relation to a product without knowing precisely how the defect came into the product. To meet this challenge,
     plaintiff employed the now familiar doctrine of *res ipsa loquitur*. But application of this established doctrine was
     not trouble free. Since the product had passed through the hands of several parties, how did plaintiff establish that
     the defect in the bottle was introduced into the product while it was within defendant's control? Can you think of a
     theory of negligence that would have permitted plaintiff to avoid the need to prove that defendant was in exclusive
     control of the bottle when the defect was introduced?
2   What policy justifications does Traynor advance for the elimination of the requirement that plaintiff prove
     negligence? Do you find these policy justifications persuasive?

GREENMAN V. YUBA POWER PRODUCTS, INC.
377 P.2D 897 (CAL. 1962)

Plaintiff brought this action for damages against the retailer and the manufacturer of a Shopsmith, a combination power tool that could be used as a saw, drill, and wood lathe. . . . He decided he wanted a Shopsmith for his home workshop, and his wife bought and gave him one for Christmas in 1955. In 1957 he bought the necessary attachments to use the Shopsmith as a lathe for turning a large piece of wood he wished to make into a chalice. After he had worked on the piece of wood several times without difficulty, it suddenly flew out of the machine and struck him on the forehead, inflicting serious injuries. About 10 1/2 months later, he gave the retailer and the manufacturer written notice of claimed breaches of warranties and filed a complaint against them alleging such breaches and negligence.

After a trial before a jury, the court ruled that there was no evidence that the retailer was negligent or had breached any express warranty and that the manufacturer was not liable for the breach of any implied warranty. Accordingly, it submitted to the jury only the cause of action alleging breach of implied warranties against the retailer and the causes of action alleging negligence and breach of express warranties against the manufacturer. The jury returned a verdict for the retailer against plaintiff and for plaintiff against the manufacturer in the amount of $65,000. . . . The manufacturer and plaintiff appeal. Plaintiff seeks a reversal of the part of the judgment in favor of the retailer, however, only in the event that the part of the judgment against the manufacturer is reversed.

Plaintiff introduced substantial evidence that his injuries were caused by defective design and construction of the Shopsmith. His expert witnesses testified that inadequate set screws were used to hold parts of the machine together so that normal vibration caused the tailstock of the lathe to move away from the piece of wood being turned permitting it to fly out of the lathe. They also testified that there were other more positive ways of fastening the parts of the machine together, the use of which would have prevented the accident. . . .

A manufacturer is strictly liable in tort when an article he places on the market, knowing that it is to be used without inspection for defects, proves to have a defect that causes injury to a human being. Recognized first in the case of unwholesome food products, such liability has now been extended to a variety of other products that create as great or greater hazards if defective. . . . Although in these cases strict liability has usually been based on the theory of an express or implied warranty running from the manufacturer to the plaintiff, the abandonment of the requirement of a contract between them, the recognition that the liability is not assumed by agreement but imposed by law, and the refusal to permit the manufacturer to define the scope of its own responsibility for defective products (*Henningsen* v. *Bloomfield Motors, Inc.* . . .) make clear that the liability is not one governed by the law of contract warranties but by the law of strict liability in tort. Accordingly, rules defining and governing warranties that were developed to meet the needs of commercial transactions cannot properly be invoked to govern the manufacturer's liability to those injured by its defective products unless those rules also serve the purposes for which such liability is imposed.

We need not recanvass the reasons for imposing strict liability on the manufacturer. They have been fully articulated in the cases cited above. (*See* . . . *Escola* v. *Coca Cola Bottling Co.* . . . concurring opinion.) The purpose of such liability is to insure that the costs of injuries resulting from defective products are borne by the manufacturers that put such products on the market rather than by the injured persons who are powerless to protect themselves. Sales warranties serve this purpose fitfully at best. . . . In the present case, for example, plaintiff was able to plead and prove an express warranty only because he read and relied on the representations of the Shopsmith's ruggedness contained in the manufacturer's brochure. Implicit in the machine's presence on the market, however, was a representation that it would safely do the jobs for which it was built. Under these circumstances, it should not be controlling whether plaintiff selected the machine because of the statements in the brochure, or because of the machine's own appearance of excellence that belied the defect lurking beneath the surface, or because he merely assumed that it would safely do the jobs it was built to do. It should not be controlling whether the details of the sales from manufacturer to retailer and from retailer to plaintiff's wife were such that one or more of the implied warranties of the sales act arose. . . . To establish the manufacturer's liability it was sufficient that plaintiff proved that he was injured while using the

Shopsmith in a way it was intended to be used as a result of a defect in design and manufacture of which plaintiff was not aware that made the Shopsmith unsafe for its intended use. . . .

The following section of the Restatement (Second) of Torts was quickly accepted by the overwhelming majority of American jurisdictions:

Restatement (Second) Torts § 402A. Special Liability Of Seller Of Product For Physical Harm To User Or Consumer

1. One who sells any product in a defective condition unreasonably dangerous to the user or consumer or to his property is subject to liability for physical harm thereby caused to the ultimate user or consumer, or to his property, if
   (a) the seller is engaged in the business of selling such a product, and
   (b) it is expected to and does reach the user or consumer without substantial change in the condition in which it is sold.

2. The rule stated in Subsection (1) applies although
   (a) the seller has exercised all possible care in the preparation and sale of his product, and
   (b) the user or consumer has not bought the product from or entered into any contractual relation with the seller.

   i. *Unreasonably dangerous.* The rule stated in this Section applies only where the defective condition of the product makes it unreasonably dangerous to the user or consumer. Many products cannot possibly be made entirely safe for all consumption, and any food or drug necessarily involves some risk of harm, if only from over-consumption. Ordinary sugar is a deadly poison to diabetics, and castor oil found use under Mussolini as an instrument of torture. That is not what is meant by "unreasonably dangerous" in this Section. The article sold must be dangerous to an extent beyond that which would be contemplated by the ordinary consumer who purchases it, with the ordinary knowledge common to the community as to its characteristics. Good whiskey is not unreasonably dangerous merely because it will make some people drunk, and is especially dangerous to alcoholics; but bad whiskey, containing a dangerous amount of fuel oil, is unreasonably dangerous. Good tobacco is not unreasonably dangerous merely because the effects of smoking may be harmful; but tobacco containing something like marijuana may be unreasonably dangerous. Good butter is not unreasonably dangerous merely because, if such be the case, it deposits cholesterol in the arteries and leads to heart attacks; but bad butter, contaminated with poisonous fish oil, is unreasonably dangerous.

1. As will be demonstrated by the cases that follow, the form of strict products liability that eventually emerged from judicial interpretations of Restatement (Second) Section 402A was broader than a literal application of this relatively simple provision would suggest.

2. In 1998, the American Law Institute replaced Section 402A with the Restatement (Third) of Torts: Products Liability (1998).

2. DUTY – PROPER DEFENDANTS

The idea behind the old privity cases was that a defendant owed a "duty" only to the parties with whom that defendant was in privity. With the elimination of the privity requirement, the duty limitation has not disappeared completely from strict products liability. While the strict product liability duty extends broadly to all users or consumers of products, the duty is owed only by a limited universe of defendants – professional sellers.

Restatement (Third) Torts: Products Liability § 1. Liability Of Commercial Seller Or Distributor For Harm Caused By Defective Products

One engaged in the business of selling or otherwise distributing products who sells or distributes a defective product is subject to liability for harm to persons or property caused by the defect.

HYPOTHETICAL SCENARIOS

Assume that Mrs. Jones goes to Rattles R Us and buys a Toyco infant rattle. Toyco distributes the rattle under its own name even though the rattle was manufactured by the Tianamin Lead Company, a Chinese manufacturer of several products including industrial tools and children's toys. Unknown to Mrs. Jones, the infant rattle is painted with lead-based paint. Once her child outgrows the rattle, Mrs. Jones sells the rattle at a yard sale to Mr. Smith, whose child uses the rattle and suffers from lead poisoning after chewing on it. Under Restatement Section 402A, against whom, if anyone, does the Smith child have a potential products liability claim?

What if the rattle as originally manufactured was coated with a non-toxic material, but before the yard sale, Mrs. Jones noticed that some of the paint had chipped off and so sprayed it with a can of industrial metal primer, which happened to be lead-based. Putting the paint manufacturer to one side for a moment, against whom does Smith now have a potential products liability claim under 402A?

Now assume that the rattle had lead paint on it when Mrs. Jones bought it, but nobody knows whether it was the Tianamin Lead Company, Toyco or Rattles R Us who put the lead there. Against whom might Smith have a Section 402A cause of action now?

CAFAZZO V. CENTRAL MEDICAL HEALTH SERVICES, INC.
668 A.2D 521 (PA. 1995)

. . .

In 1986, appellant Albert Cafazzo underwent surgery for implantation of a mandibular prosthesis. In 1992, some time after it was discovered that this device was defective, a complaint . . . . was filed against appellees, the physician who performed the surgery and the hospital where the operation took place, claiming that "all defendants sell, provide or use certain prosthetic devices," and that they should be held strictly liable as having "provided, sold or otherwise placed in the stream of commerce products manufactured by Vitek, Inc., known as Proplast TMJ Implants." The complaint alleged that the prosthesis was defectively designed, unsafe for its intended use, and lacked any warning necessary in order to ensure safety.

. . .

Section 402A of the Restatement (Second) of Torts, provides in relevant part as follows:

1. One who sells any product in a defective condition unreasonably dangerous to the user or consumer or to his property is subject to liability for physical harm thereby caused to the ultimate user or consumer, or to his property, if:
   (a) the seller is engaged in the business of selling such a product, and
   (b) it is expected to and does reach the consumer without substantial change in the condition in which it is sold.

. . .

In this instance, the manufacturer is in bankruptcy, and unable to sustain liability. Thus, an alternative, and solvent, payor was sought. All other considerations were subordinated to this objective, hence the unequivocal necessity, in appellants' view, for appellees to be designated as sellers irrespective of the actual facts of this matter. However, to ignore the ancillary nature of the association of product with activity is to posit surgery, or indeed any medical service requiring the use of a physical object, as a marketing device for the incorporated object. This is tantamount to deciding that the surgical skills necessary for the implantation of, e.g., mandibular prostheses, are an adjunct to the sale of the implants. Moreover, under such a theory, no product of which a patient in any medical setting is the ultimate consumer, from CT scanners to cotton balls, could escape the assignment of strict liability. Clearly, the relationship of hospital and/or doctor to patients is not dictated by the distribution of such products, even if there is some surcharge on the price of the product. As the New York Court of Appeals has aptly stated,

Concepts of purchase and sale cannot be separately attached to the healing materials . . . supplied by the hospital for a price as part of the medical services. That the property or title to certain items of medical material may be transferred, so to speak, from the hospital to the patient during the course of medical treatment does not serve to make such a transaction a sale. "Sale" and "transfer" are not synonymous, and not every transfer of personal property constitutes a sale.

. . .

The thrust of the inquiry is thus not on whether a separate consideration is charged for the physical material used in the exercise of medical skill, but what service is performed to restore or maintain the patient's health. The determinative question becomes not what is being charged, but what is being done. . . .

The cases cited above have been labeled by some the exponents of a "service exception" to 402A. However, the very term "service exception" is misleading, since it presupposes that the distinction drawn where medical personnel/hospitals are involved is an artificial one. The cases, however, make clear that provision of medical services is regarded as qualitatively different from the sale of products, and, rather than being an exception to 402A, is unaffected by it. . . .

This distinction is made clearer by the fact that case law also supports the application of 402A where what has been provided is not medical service or products connected with diagnosis and treatment, but rather materials related to mechanical or administrative functions. . . .

In this connection, it must be noted that the "seller" need not be engaged solely in the business of selling products such as the defective one to be held strictly liable. An example supporting this proposition appears in comment f of the Restatement (Second) of Torts, §402A and concerns the owner of a motion picture theater who offers edibles such as popcorn and candy for sale to movie patrons. The analogue to the instant case is valid in one respect only: both the candy and the TMJ implant are ancillary to the primary activity, viewing a film or undergoing surgery respectively. However, beyond that any comparison is specious. A movie audience is free to purchase or not any food items on offer, and regardless of which option is exercised the primary activity is unaffected. On the other hand, while the implant was incidental to the surgical procedure here, it was a necessary adjunct to the treatment administered, as were the scalpel used to make the incision, and any other material objects involved in performing the operation, all of which fulfill a particular role in provision of medical service, the primary activity. Once the illness became evident, treatment of some kind became a matter of necessity to regain health. [W]hen one enters the hospital as a patient[,] he goes there, not to buy medicines or pills, not to purchase bandages or iodine or serum or blood, but to obtain a course of treatment in the hope of being cured of what ails him.

. . .

We find, consistent with the decisions cited above which distinguish medical services from merchandising, that in the first instance, appellees are not sellers, providers, suppliers or distributors of products such as to activate 402A.

. . .

[Affirmed.]

1   The court discusses the example of the movie theater that sells popcorn. How is the *Cafazzo* scenario materially different?

2   Would the policies underlying the doctrine of strict products liability fit the *Cafazzo* scenario? Is the surgeon in a better position than the plaintiff to discover risks of the implant? Is the surgeon in any worse position than the retail seller of a product to discover risks in the product? Can the surgeon "spread" the loss?

3   One recurring issue is whether the seller of used products is "one who sells," subject to strict liability for harm caused by a defect in the product. The cases have been split, but most have not held the seller of used products to be subject to strict liability. The Restatement Third section 8 would hold the commercial seller of a used product strictly liable for harm caused by a defect in the product if the seller is negligent, or the defect is a manufacturing defect, or the seller has marketed the product so as to convince the buyer that the product presents no greater risk than a new product, or the seller has engaged in substantial remanufacture of the used product, or the seller fails to comply with an applicable safety statute.

MURPHY V. E. R. SQUIBB & SONS, INC.
710 P.2D 247 (CAL. 1985)

We consider issues relating to the liability of a manufacturer and a pharmacy for the production and sale of an allegedly defective drug, . . . (DES). We will decide whether a pharmacy at which the drug was purchased may be held strictly liable for alleged defects in the product (as distinguished from ordinary negligence), and whether a manufacturer which sold 10 percent of DES nationwide may be found to have had a "substantial" share of the market for the purpose of applying the "market share" doctrine enunciated in *Sindell* v. *Abbott Laboratories* (1980) . . . .

Plaintiff filed an action for personal injuries allegedly resulting from DES taken by her mother in 1951 and 1952 during pregnancy for the purpose of reducing the risk of miscarriage. The complaint sought damages on the theory of strict liability, alleging that the drug was defectively designed, with the result that plaintiff developed clear cell adenocarcinoma at the age of 23. As defendants, plaintiff joined Exclusive Prescription Pharmacy Corporation (Exclusive) where plaintiff's mother purchased the DES, and E.R. Squibb & Sons, Inc. (Squibb). The first cause of action alleged that Squibb was the manufacturer of the DES used by plaintiff's mother. The second count, added after our decision in *Sindell*, alleged that plaintiff was unable to identify the manufacturer, but that Squibb supplied a "substantial percentage" of DES for use by pregnant women to prevent miscarriage.

Before jury selection began, the court granted Exclusive's motion for judgment on the pleadings, holding that a pharmacy may not be held strictly liable for dispensing a prescription drug. The court determined that Exclusive rendered a professional service in supplying the DES, that the consumer of the drug was the doctor who prescribed it rather than plaintiff's mother, and that as a matter of policy the doctrine of strict liability should not be extended to a pharmacy.

In support of her second cause of action plaintiff offered to prove that Squibb sold 10 percent of the DES in the national market. The court ruled that as a matter of law 10 percent of the national market was not a "substantial percentage" within the meaning of *Sindell*, and it dismissed the second cause of action. The matter went to trial against Squibb on the first cause of action alleging that Squibb had actually supplied the DES taken by plaintiff's mother. . . . The parties introduced evidence on whether Squibb was the manufacturer of the offending drug, and the trial court instructed the jury that plaintiff had the burden of proof on this issue. The jury returned a special verdict, finding that plaintiff's mother had purchased the DES at Exclusive, and that the DES which she purchased was not manufactured by Squibb. The trial court entered judgment in favor of defendants, and plaintiff appeals.

The Action Against Exclusive

In the seminal case of *Greenman* v. *Yuba Power Products, Inc.* (1963) . . . , Justice Traynor, writing for the court, held a manufacturer strictly liable in tort for injuries caused by a defective product which it knew would be used without inspection for defects. In *Vandermark* v. *Ford Motor Co.* (1964) . . . , the strict liability doctrine was extended to retailers of defective products.

Plaintiff asserts that a pharmacy which sells prescription drugs is in the same position as a retailer of any other consumer product, and that the reasons advanced in *Greenman* . . . for imposing strict liability necessarily apply to a pharmacy. Exclusive counters that a pharmacist who dispenses a prescription drug is primarily furnishing a service rather than selling a product, and that the rationale underlying imposition of strict liability does not justify application of the doctrine to him. . . .

It is critical to the issue posed to determine if the dominant role of a pharmacist in supplying a prescription drug should be characterized as the performance of a service or the sale of a product. Both parties accept as a general rule that "those who sell their services for the guidance of others . . . are not liable in the absence of negligence or intentional misconduct." (*Gagne* v. *Bertran* (1954) 43 Cal.2d 481, 487.) . . .

Magrine v. *Krasnica* (1967) 94 N.J.Super. 228, held that a dentist was not strictly liable for injuries caused by a needle which broke during the course of treatment due to a latent defect. The court characterized the difference between a sale and a service as follows: "[The] *essence* of the transaction between the retail seller and the consumer relates to the *article sold*. The seller is *in the business* of supplying the product to the consumer. It is that, and that alone, for which he is paid. A dentist or physician offers, and is paid for, his professional services and skill. That is the *essence* of the relationship between him and his patient." (*Id.*, at p. 543.) . . .

As might be anticipated, the parties differ sharply as to whether the main function of a pharmacist is to provide a service or to sell a product. Plaintiff asserts that the duties of a pharmacist in filling a prescription do not differ from those of any other retailer: he reads the prescription, fills the container with the proper type and dosage of the medication required, types up a label, attaches it to the container, and exchanges the medication for payment by the customer. In essence, argues plaintiff, a pharmacist is the functional equivalent of "an experienced clerk at a hardware store."

Exclusive and amici curiae . . . paint a dramatically different picture of the role of the pharmacist, characterizing him as a professional who provides an important health service. They point out that with a few exceptions specified by statute, only a physician or a licensed pharmacist may compound or dispense prescription drugs . . . . In order to obtain a license, a pharmacist must have graduated from a four-year college of pharmacy or the department of pharmacy of a university, have one year of practical experience under the supervision of a registered pharmacist, and pass a written examination given by the California State Board of Pharmacy . . . . He must comply with continuing education requirements as a condition to renewal of his license . . . and is subject to rules of professional responsibility and to disciplinary proceedings for violation of those rules . . . .

A pharmacist is required not only to assure that the drug prescribed is properly selected, measured and labelled but, according to the Board, he must be alert to errors in prescriptions written by doctors, and contact the doctor in case of doubts or questions regarding the drug prescribed. In addition, the pharmacist may discuss with the patient the proper use of the drug and the potential side effects, and must be aware of the possibility of harmful interaction between various medications which the pharmacist knows the patient is using. According to the Board, about 22 percent of patients are counseled by the pharmacist, who spends one and one-half to two hours a day in such consultation. . . .

It seems clear to us that the pharmacist is engaged in a hybrid enterprise, combining the performance of services and the sale of prescription drugs. It is pure hyperbole to suggest, as does plaintiff, that the role of the pharmacist is similar to that of a clerk in an ordinary retail store. With a few exceptions, only a licensed pharmacist may dispense prescription drugs, and as indicated above there are stringent educational and professional requirements for obtaining and retaining a license. A pharmacist must not only use skill and care in accurately filling and labelling a prescribed drug, but he must be aware of problems regarding the medication, and on occasion he provides doctors as well as patients with advice regarding such problems. In counseling patients, he imparts the same kind of information as would a medical doctor about the effects of the drugs prescribed. A key factor is that the pharmacist who fills a prescription is in a different position from the ordinary retailer because he cannot offer a prescription for sale except by order of the doctor. In this respect, he is providing a service to the doctor and acting as an extension of the doctor in the same sense as a technician who takes an X-ray or analyzes a blood sample on a doctor's order.

Nevertheless, it cannot be disputed that a sale in fact occurs. There is an obvious distinction between the doctor who provides a patient with a prescription for a defective drug . . . , a dentist who uses a faulty drill . . . or a hospital that uses a defective needle during surgery . . . , and a pharmacist who fills a prescription. The pharmacist is in the business of selling prescription drugs, and his role begins and ends with the sale. His services are rendered only in connection with the sale, and a patient who goes to a pharmacy to have a prescription filled generally is seeking to purchase the drug rather than to obtain the advice of the pharmacist.

By contrast, the doctor, dentist and hospital in the cases cited above are not in the business of selling the drug or device; they use the product in the course of treatment as one element in their efforts to effect a cure, and furnishing the services does not depend on sale of a product. . . .

The Action Against Squibb

Plaintiff alleged in her second cause of action that she could not identify the specific manufacturer of the drug taken by her mother and that Squibb "supplied a substantial percentage" of the drug to prevent miscarriage.

By these allegations, plaintiff sought recovery under the "market share" theory advanced in *Sindell* v. *Abbott Laboratories* . . . . In that case, the plaintiff charged in her complaint that defendant manufacturers of DES, with knowledge that it might cause cancer in the daughters of the mothers who took the drug, failed to adequately test it for safety or to warn of its dangers. She could not identify the producer of the drug actually ingested by her mother, and for that reason the trial court sustained defendants' demurrers to the complaint.

We reversed the judgment, reasoning substantially as follows: The general rule is that the burden of proof is on the plaintiff to establish that the injuries she suffered were caused by the conduct of the defendant. This rule is not without its exceptions, however, including the doctrine of "alternative liability" applied in *Summers* v. *Tice* (1948) . . . . In *Summers*, the plaintiff had suffered an injury to his eye after the two defendants had each shot a gun in his direction. The plaintiff was unable to demonstrate which of the defendants was responsible for his injury. It was held that he was not barred from pursuing the action, because the circumstances justified shifting the burden of proof to the two defendants to absolve themselves if they could. This would not be unfair, it was reasoned, because both had acted negligently toward the plaintiff, and they would both escape liability if the plaintiff were forced to choose between them and was unable to isolate which was responsible. We declined to apply this holding without modification to the drug manufacturer defendants in *Sindell.*

Nevertheless, we held in *Sindell*, because of policy considerations spelled out in our opinion, that plaintiff and those in her position should not be bereft of a remedy. We stated that the likelihood that any of the defendants caused the plaintiff's injuries should be measured not by the number of DES manufacturers joined as defendants – only five of two hundred manufacturers were defendants in the action – but by the percentage which the DES sold by each of them for the purpose of preventing miscarriage bore to the entire production of the drug sold by all producers of the identical formula for that purpose. If plaintiff joined in the action the manufacturers of "a substantial share of the DES which her mother might have taken, the injustice of shifting the burden of proof to defendants to demonstrate that they could not have made the substance which injured plaintiff" would be considerably diminished. . . . We recognized that there were practical problems involved in defining the market and determining market share, but held that these were matters of proof which could not be determined at the pleading stage.

. . .

At the trial level here, plaintiff confined her offer of proof to a national market for DES. Our only inquiry, therefore, is whether, as the trial court determined, a 10 percent share of this market is insufficient as a matter of law to allow plaintiff to proceed on the basis of the market share doctrine.

Plaintiff appears to contend that the doctrine was designed to accomplish a fair approximation of the damages which each defendant DES manufacturer would be required to pay under the principles of comparative fault (*American Motorcycle Assn. v. Superior Court* (1978) . . .), and that its applicability is unrelated to whether plaintiff has joined as defendants the manufacturers of a substantial share of the DES market. This claim lacks merit. The major issue decided in *Sindell* was whether and the circumstances under which a plaintiff in a DES case could avoid application of the usual rule that she had the burden of proving the defendant manufacturer produced the DES which caused her injuries. The opinion makes it clear that in order to shift the burden of proof on the issue of causation in fact, a plaintiff must join in the action the manufacturers of "a substantial share of the DES which her mother might have taken." (26 Cal.3d at p. 612.) Although we stated that the defendant manufacturers could cross-complain against other DES manufacturers not joined in the action, which might have supplied the injury-causing product, we were careful to qualify the statement with the observation that such pleadings would be filed by defendants only after "plaintiff has met her burden of joining the required defendants." (*Ibid.*)

We must determine, therefore, whether Squibb's 10 percent market share is a substantial percentage of the market for the application of the rule laid down in *Sindell.* Plaintiff, relying on general definitions of the word "substantial" asserts that the term must be defined in the context of a particular case, . . . and since Squibb was alleged to be the second largest seller of DES in the country, its 10 percent market share must be deemed substantial in the framework of DES litigation.

We reject this contention because it is contrary to the theoretical justification underlying the market share doctrine. We pointed out in *Sindell* that a major reason why shifting the burden of proof from plaintiff to defendants was warranted in *Summers* was that both parties who were or could have been responsible for the harm to the plaintiff were joined as defendants. Thus, there was a 50 percent chance that one of the defendants was responsible for the injury. . . . We declined to apply an unmodified *Summers* rationale to the facts in *Sindell*, because only five of the two hundred manufacturers of the DES which could have harmed plaintiff were before the court, and therefore there was "no rational basis upon which to infer that any defendant in this action caused plaintiff's injuries, nor even a reasonable possibility that they were responsible." (*Id.*, at pp. 602-603.) Instead, we concluded that the likelihood that one of the defendants supplied the DES should be determined not by the number of manufacturers joined in the action but by the percentage which the DES sold by each to prevent miscarriage bore to the entire production of the drug sold for that purpose. We held that if the plaintiff joined in the action the manufacturers of a substantial share of the DES which her mother might have taken, the injustice of shifting the burden of proof to defendants to exonerate themselves would be significantly diminished. We declined to declare a specific percentage of the market which would satisfy application of the doctrine, but stated only that it must be substantial.

Since Squibb had only a 10 percent share of the DES market, there is only a 10 percent chance that it produced the drug causing plaintiff's injuries, and a 90 percent chance that another manufacturer was the producer. In this circumstance, it must be concluded that she failed to meet the threshold requirement for the application of the market share doctrine. The trial court was justified in ruling, therefore, that she could not proceed to trial on the second cause of action.

The trial of the first cause of action, which was confined to the question whether Squibb was in fact the manufacturer of the drug taken by plaintiff's mother, concluded with a jury verdict in Squibb's favor. Since plaintiff had the burden of proof on this issue, her contention that the trial court erred in instructing the jury to that effect is without merit. . . .

QUESTIONS

1   In what ways is a pharmacy like a service provider?
2   In what ways is a pharmacy like a product seller?

WINTER V. G. P. PUTNAM'S SONS
938 F.2D 1033 (9TH CIR. 1991)

Plaintiffs are mushroom enthusiasts who became severely ill from picking and eating mushrooms after relying on information in *The Encyclopedia of Mushrooms*, a book published by the defendant. . . .

I.

FACTS AND PROCEEDINGS BELOW

The Encyclopedia of Mushrooms is a reference guide containing information on the habitat, collection, and cooking of mushrooms. It was written by two British authors and originally published by a British publishing company. Defendant Putnam, an American book publisher, purchased copies of the book from the British publisher and distributed the finished product in the United States. Putnam neither wrote nor edited the book.

Plaintiffs purchased the book to help them collect and eat wild mushrooms. In 1988, plaintiffs went mushroom hunting and relied on the descriptions in the book in determining which mushrooms were safe to eat. After cooking and eating their harvest, plaintiffs became critically ill. Both have required liver transplants.

Plaintiffs allege that the book contained erroneous and misleading information concerning the identification of the most deadly species of mushrooms. In their suit against the book publisher, plaintiffs allege liability based on products liability, breach of warranty, negligence, negligent misrepresentation, and false representations. Defendant moved for summary judgment asserting that plaintiffs' claims failed as a matter of law because 1) the information contained in a book is not a product for the purposes of strict liability under products liability law; and 2) defendant is not liable under any remaining theories because a publisher does not have a duty to investigate the accuracy of the text it publishes. The district court granted summary judgment for the defendant. Plaintiffs appeal. We affirm. . . .

II.

DISCUSSION

A book containing Shakespeare's sonnets consists of two parts, the material and print therein, and the ideas and expression thereof. The first may be a product, but the second is not. The latter, were Shakespeare alive, would be governed by copyright laws; the laws of libel, to the extent consistent with the First Amendment; and the laws of misrepresentation, negligent misrepresentation, negligence, and mistake. These doctrines applicable to the second part are aimed at the delicate issues that arise with respect to intangibles such as ideas and expression. Products liability law is geared to the tangible world.

A. Products Liability

The language of products liability law reflects its focus on tangible items. In describing the scope of products liability law, the Restatement (Second) of Torts lists examples of items that are covered. All of these are tangible items, such as tires, automobiles, and insecticides. The American Law Institute clearly was concerned with including all physical items but gave no indication that the doctrine should be expanded beyond that area.

The purposes served by products liability law also are focused on the tangible world and do not take into consideration the unique characteristics of ideas and expression. . . . [B]ecause of the difficulty of establishing fault or negligence in products liability cases, strict liability is the appropriate legal theory to hold manufacturers liable for defective products. . . . Thus, the seller is subject to liability "even though he has exercised all possible care in the preparation and sale of the product." Restatement §402A comment a. It is not a question of fault but simply a determination of how society wishes to assess certain costs that arise from the creation and distribution of products in a complex technological society in which the consumer thereof is unable to protect himself against certain product defects. . . .

Plaintiffs' argument is stronger when they assert that *The Encyclopedia of Mushrooms* should be analogized to aeronautical charts. Several jurisdictions have held that charts which graphically depict geographic features or instrument approach information for airplanes are "products" for the purpose of products liability law. . . . Plaintiffs suggest that *The Encyclopedia of Mushrooms* can be compared to aeronautical charts because both items contain representations of natural features and both are intended to be used while engaging in a hazardous activity. We are not persuaded.

Aeronautical charts are highly technical tools. They are graphic depictions of technical, mechanical data. The best analogy to an aeronautical chart is a compass. Both may be used to guide an individual who is engaged in an activity requiring certain knowledge of natural features. Computer software that fails to yield the result for which it was designed may be another. In contrast, *The Encyclopedia of Mushrooms* is like a book on how to use a compass or an aeronautical chart. The chart itself is like a physical "product" while the "How to Use" book is pure thought and expression. . . .

Given these considerations, we decline to expand products liability law to embrace the ideas and expression in a book. . . . We know of no court that has chosen the path to which the plaintiffs point. . . .

For the reasons outlined above, the decision of the district court is AFFIRMED.

QUESTIONS

1   What is the strongest argument that defendant should be subject to strict products liability?

2   If a radio personality were to go on the air and disseminate his favorite wild mushroom recipes, including where to find, how to identify, and how to pick and prepare the mushrooms, and some listeners were poisoned, would this be a case of strict products liability? Why or why not?

3   Can the *Winter* case be distinguished from the hypothetical case of the radio show? On the ground that a book is a product?

4   Would plaintiffs' case in *Winter* have been materially different if plaintiffs had been poisoned by the ink on the pages of the encyclopedia? If so, how would such a hypothetical case be distinguishable from *Winter*?

5   Is it possible to distinguish *Winter* from the scenario cited in the court's opinion involving erroneous aeronautical charts?

3. BREACH — PRODUCT DEFECTS

"Strict" products liability is not absolute liability. While plaintiff need not prove that defendant's behavior was in any way substandard, as plaintiff would have to do in a negligence action, plaintiff in a strict liability action under Restatement Section 402A still bears the burden of proving that the product is in a "defective condition unreasonably dangerous to the user or consumer or to his property," and this burden can be a serious roadblock to recovery. The word "defective" implies that the offending product is in some sense "sub-normal."

Where the product admittedly does not comply with the seller's own intended design for the product, it is easy to characterize the product as "sub-normal" or "defective" – if the product has a "screw loose" somewhere, then of course the product is defective. In such situations, something has gone wrong in the manufacturing process to allow the product to escape the manufacturer's control in a condition that the manufacturer never intended. It was with this simple type of defect in mind that the Restatement (Second) Section 402A was drafted.

But what if the product is precisely as the seller intended it to be? Can a plaintiff ever successfully claim that such a product is "defective"? The case law that developed answered this question in the affirmative and expanded the definition of product "defect" to encompass categories in addition to the simple "manufacturing" defect described above. Accordingly, in 1998 the American Law Institute approved The Restatement (Third) of Torts: Products Liability, which divides product defects into three categories:

§ 2. Categories Of Product Defect

> A product is defective when, at the time of sale or distribution, it contains a manufacturing defect, is defective in design, or is defective because of inadequate instructions or warnings. A product:
>
> a. contains a manufacturing defect when the product departs from its intended design even though all possible care was exercised in the preparation and marketing of the product;
>
> b. is defective in design when the foreseeable risks of harm posed by the product could have been reduced or avoided by the adoption of a reasonable alternative design by the seller or other distributor, or a predecessor in the commercial chain of distribution, and the omission of the alternative design renders the product not reasonably safe;
>
> c. is defective because of inadequate instructions or warnings when the foreseeable risks of harm posed by the product could have been reduced or avoided by the provision of reasonable instructions or warnings by the seller or other distributor, or a predecessor in the commercial chain of distribution, and the omission of the instructions or warnings renders the product not reasonably safe.

While what constitutes a manufacturing defect is fairly straightforward and uncontroversial, the other two categories of product defect, and especially design defect, are quite difficult and controversial.

a. MANUFACTURING DEFECT

A "manufacturing defect" is a departure from the product's intended design. A pratical example of a case involving an alleged design defect is *Pouncey v. Ford Motor Co.*, 464 F.2d 957 (5th Cir. 1972), where plaintiff was injured while putting antifreeze in his 1966 Ford automobile when a blade broke off the radiator fan and struck him in the face. The main thrust of Pouncey's case was that the fan blade failure occurred because of a fatigue fracture in the metal fan blade. It was Pouncey's theory that the premature fatigue failure was caused by an excessive number of inclusions in the metal of the blade. An inclusion is a non-metallic impurity in the steel which weakens the metal. A product that departs from its intended design is, without question, defective. Strict liability for harm caused by a product's departure from its intended design is not controversial legally; however, as a practical matter, plaintiffs frequently find it difficult to prove that the alleged manufacturing defect in the product existed when the product left the defendant's control.

b. DESIGN DEFECT

How to determine whether a particular product is defective in design has been one of the most perplexing questions in the field of products liability. Over the years, courts have employed various "tests" for design defect. The first was the "consumer expectations" test.

(1) CONSUMER EXPECTATIONS TEST

The consumer expectations test for product defect would find a product defective in design when it disappoints the consumer's reasonable expectations.

POTTER V. CHICAGO PNEUMATIC TOOL CO.
694 A.2D 1319 (CONN. 1997)

This appeal arises from a products liability action brought by the plaintiffs against the defendants, Chicago Pneumatic Tool Company (Chicago Pneumatic), Stanley Works and Dresser Industries, Inc. (Dresser). The plaintiffs claim that they were injured in the course of their employment as shipyard workers at the General Dynamics Corporation Electric Boat facility (Electric Boat) in Groton as a result of using pneumatic hand tools manufactured by the defendants. Specifically, the plaintiffs allege that the tools were defectively designed because they exposed the plaintiffs to excessive vibration . . . .

The defendants appeal from the judgment rendered on jury verdicts in favor of the plaintiffs, claiming [that] . . . there was insufficient evidence that the tools were defective in that the plaintiffs had presented no evidence of a feasible alternative design. . . .

The trial record reveals the following facts, which are undisputed for purposes of this appeal. The plaintiffs were employed at Electric Boat as "grinders," positions which required use of pneumatic hand tools to smooth welds and metal surfaces. In the course of their employment, the plaintiffs used various pneumatic hand tools, including chipping and grinding tools, which were manufactured and sold by the defendants. The plaintiffs' use of the defendants' tools at Electric Boat spanned approximately twenty-five years, from the mid-1960s until 1987. The plaintiffs suffer from permanent vascular and neurological impairment of their hands . . . . As a result, the plaintiffs have been unable to continue their employment as grinders and their performance of other activities has been restricted. The plaintiffs' symptoms are consistent with a diagnosis of hand arm vibration syndrome. Expert testimony confirmed that exposure to vibration is a significant contributing factor to the development of hand arm vibration syndrome, and that a clear relationship exists between the level of vibration exposure and the risk of developing the syndrome.

. . . Richard Alexander, a mechanical engineering professor at Texas A & M University, testified that because machinery vibration has harmful effects on machines and on people, engineers routinely research ways to reduce or to eliminate the amount of vibration that a machine produces when operated. Alexander discussed various methods available to control vibration, including isolation (the use of springs or mass to isolate vibration), dampening (adding weights to dampen vibrational effects), and balancing (adding weights to counterbalance machine imbalances that cause vibration). Alexander testified that each of these methods has been available to manufacturers for at least thirty-five years. . . .

After a six week trial, the trial court rendered judgment on jury verdicts in favor of the plaintiffs. Finding that the defendants' tools had been defectively designed so as to render them unreasonably dangerous, the jury awarded the plaintiffs compensatory damages. . . .

We first address the defendants' argument that the trial court improperly failed to render judgment for the defendants notwithstanding the verdicts because there was insufficient evidence for the jury to have found that the tools had been defectively designed. Specifically, the defendants claim that, in order to establish a prima facie design defect case, the plaintiffs were required to prove that there was a feasible alternative design available at the time that the defendants put their tools into the stream of commerce. We disagree.

In order properly to evaluate the parties' arguments, we begin our analysis with a review of the development of strict tort liability, focusing specifically on design defect liability. At common law, a person injured by a product had no cause of action against the manufacturer of the product unless that person was in privity of contract with the manufacturer. This rule, established in *Winterbottom* v. *Wright* . . . made privity a condition precedent to actions against manufacturers grounded in negligence. American courts widely adopted this rule and, for the next one-half century, the privity requirement remained steadfast in American jurisprudence. . . .

The evolution of modern products liability law began with the landmark case of *MacPherson* v. *Buick Motor Co.,* . . . in which the New York Court of Appeals extended the manufacturer's duty to all persons in fact harmed by products that were reasonably certain to cause injury when negligently made. . . . Similarly, the New Jersey Supreme Court in *Henningsen* v. *Bloomfield Motors, Inc.* . . . imposed "strict liability" upon the manufacturer of a defective product, but on a warranty basis. Discarding the antiquated notions of privity of contract, the court imposed upon the manufacturer an implied warranty of merchantability to a third party. . . .

The next major development in products liability law did not attempt to modify the negligence rule any further, but, rather, urged its replacement. In *Escola* v. *Coca Cola Bottling Co. of Fresno,* . . . Justice Roger Traynor, in a now famous concurring opinion, first suggested that courts should hold manufacturers liable without fault when defective products cause personal injury. Justice Traynor asserted that strict liability would serve several policy justifications: (1) manufacturers could readily absorb or pass on the cost of liability to consumers as a cost of doing business; (2) manufacturers would be deterred from marketing defective products; and (3) injured persons, who lack familiarity with the manufacturing process, would no longer shoulder the burden of proving negligence. . . .

Although Justice Traynor's argument did not prevail in *Escola*, nearly twenty years later he wrote for the majority in *Greenman* v. *Yuba Power Products, Inc.*, . . . holding a manufacturer strictly liable because its defective product caused injury to the plaintiff. The *Greenman* court stated that "[a] manufacturer is strictly liable in tort when an article he places on the market, knowing that it is to be used without inspection for defects, proves to have a defect that causes injury to a human being." . . . The court explained that the purpose of this rule "is to insure that the costs of injuries resulting from defective products are borne by the manufacturers that put such products on the market rather than by the injured persons who are powerless to protect themselves." . . .

Two years later, §402A of the Restatement (Second) of Torts adopted, with slight variation, . . . the doctrine of strict tort liability espoused in *Greenman*. Section 402A provides:

1. One who sells any product in a defective condition unreasonably dangerous to the user or consumer or to his property is subject to liability for physical harm thereby caused to the ultimate user or consumer, or to his property, if
   (a) the seller is engaged in the business of selling such a product, and
   (b) it is expected to and does reach the user or consumer without substantial change in the condition in which it is sold.

2. The rule stated in Subsection (1) applies although
   (a) the seller has exercised all possible care in the preparation and sale of his product, and
   (b) the user or consumer has not bought the product from or entered into any contractual relation with the seller.

2 Restatement (Second), Torts §402A (1965).

Products liability law has thus evolved to hold manufacturers . . . strictly liable for unreasonably dangerous products that cause injury to ultimate users. Nevertheless, strict tort liability does not transform manufacturers into insurers, nor does it impose absolute liability. . . . Strict tort liability merely relieves the plaintiff from proving that the manufacturer was negligent and allows the plaintiff to establish instead the defective condition of the product as the principal basis of liability. . . .

Although courts have widely accepted the concept of strict tort liability, some of the specifics of strict tort liability remain in question. In particular, courts have sharply disagreed over the appropriate definition of defectiveness in design cases. . . . Section 402A imposes liability only for those defective products that are "unreasonably dangerous" to "the ordinary consumer who purchases it, with the ordinary knowledge common to the community as to its characteristics." 2 Restatement (Second), *supra*, §402A, comment (i). Under this formulation, known as the "consumer expectation" test, a manufacturer is strictly liable for any condition not contemplated by the ultimate consumer that will be unreasonably dangerous to the consumer. . . . Other jurisdictions apply only a risk-utility test in determining whether a manufacturer is liable for a design defect. . . . To assist the jury in evaluating the product's risks and utility, these courts have set forth a list of nonexclusive factors to consider when deciding whether a product has been defectively designed. . . .

This court has long held that in order to prevail in a design defect claim, "the plaintiff must prove that the product is unreasonably dangerous." *Id.* We have derived our definition of "unreasonably dangerous" from comment (i) to §402A, which provides that "the article sold must be dangerous to an extent beyond that which would be contemplated by the ordinary consumer who purchases it, with the ordinary knowledge common to the community as to its characteristics." 2 Restatement (Second), *supra*, §402A, comment (i). This "consumer expectation" standard is now well established in Connecticut strict products liability decisions. . . .

The defendants propose that it is time for this court to abandon the consumer expectation standard and adopt the requirement that the plaintiff must prove the existence of a reasonable alternative design in order to prevail on a design defect claim. We decline to accept the defendants' invitation.

In support of their position, the defendants point to the second tentative draft of the Restatement (Third) of Torts: Products Liability (1995) (Draft Restatement [Third]), which provides that, as part of a plaintiff's prima facie case, the plaintiff must establish the availability of a reasonable alternative design. Specifically, §2 (b) of the Draft Restatement (Third) provides:

[A] product is defective in design when the foreseeable risks of harm posed by the product could have been reduced or avoided by the adoption of a reasonable alternative design by the seller or other distributor, or a predecessor in the commercial chain of distribution, and the omission of the alternative design renders the product not reasonably safe.

The reporters to the Draft Restatement (Third) state that "very substantial authority supports the proposition that [the] plaintiff must establish a reasonable alternative design in order for a product to be adjudged defective in design." Draft Restatement (Third), *supra*, §2, reporters' note to comment (c) . . . .

We point out that this provision of the Draft Restatement (Third) has been a source of substantial controversy among commentators. . . . In our view, the feasible alternative design requirement imposes an undue burden on plaintiffs that might preclude otherwise valid claims from jury consideration. Such a rule would require plaintiffs to retain an expert witness even in cases in which lay jurors can infer a design defect from circumstantial evidence. . . .

Although today we continue to adhere to our long-standing rule that a product's defectiveness is to be determined by the expectations of an ordinary consumer, we nevertheless recognize that there may be instances involving complex product designs in which an ordinary consumer may not be able to form expectations of safety. . . . In such cases, a consumer's expectations may be viewed in light of various factors that balance the utility of the product's design with the magnitude of its risks. We find persuasive the reasoning of those jurisdictions that have modified their formulation of the consumer expectation test by incorporating risk-utility factors into the ordinary consumer expectation analysis. . . . Thus, the modified consumer expectation test provides the jury with the product's risks and utility and then inquires whether a reasonable consumer would consider the product unreasonably dangerous. As the Supreme Court of Washington stated in *Seattle-First National Bank v. Tabert, supra*, at 154, 542 P.2d 774, "[i]n determining the reasonable expectations of the ordinary consumer, a number of factors must be considered. The relative cost of the product, the gravity of the potential harm from the claimed defect and the cost and feasibility of eliminating or minimizing the risk may be relevant in a particular case. In other instances the nature of the product or the nature of the claimed defect may make other factors relevant to the issue." Accordingly, under this modified formulation, the consumer expectation test would establish the product's risks and utility, and the inquiry would then be whether a reasonable consumer would consider the product design unreasonably dangerous.

In our view, the relevant factors that a jury *may* consider include, but are not limited to, the usefulness of the product, the likelihood and severity of the danger posed by the design, the feasibility of an alternative design, the financial cost of an improved design, the ability to reduce the product's danger without impairing its usefulness or making it too expensive, and the feasibility of spreading the loss by increasing the product's price. . . . The availability of a feasible alternative design is a factor that the plaintiff may, rather than must, prove in order to establish that a product's risks outweigh its utility. . . . Furthermore, we emphasize that our adoption of a risk-utility balancing component to our consumer expectation test does not signal a retreat from strict tort liability. In weighing a product's risks against its utility, the focus of the jury should be on the product itself, and not on the conduct of the manufacturer. . . .

Although today we adopt a modified formulation of the consumer expectation test, we emphasize that we do not require a plaintiff to present evidence relating to the product's risks and utility in every case. . . . Accordingly, the ordinary consumer expectation test is appropriate when the everyday experience of the particular product's users permits the inference that the product did not meet minimum safety expectations. . . .

Conversely, the jury should engage in the risk-utility balancing required by our modified consumer expectation test when the particular facts do not reasonably permit the inference that the product did not meet the safety expectations of the ordinary consumer. . . .

QUESTIONS

1   The Court here purports to employ a consumer expectations test of design defect, but does it really? What role does risk/utility balancing play in the *Potter* Court's version of the consumer expectations test?

2   In a jurisdiction that uses the consumer expectations test for design defect, what would be the result in a case where the typical consumer would expect a design that would actually *increase* the danger of the product?

3   The Court here considered and rejected requiring a showing of feasible alternative design, opting instead to retain the consumer expectations test. Does one test or the other favor either plaintiffs or defendants? In answering this question, consider the court's decision in the following case.

. . . Armour of America, Inc. (Armour) appeals a judgment based on a jury verdict in favor of the widow and children of Jimmy Linegar, a Missouri State Highway Patrol trooper who was killed in the line of duty. The jury found that the bullet-resistant vest manufactured by Armour and worn by Linegar at the time of the murder was defectively designed, and it awarded his family $1.5 million in damages. We reverse.

On April 15, 1985, as part of a routine traffic check, Linegar stopped a van with Nevada license plates near Branson, Missouri. The van's driver produced an Oregon operator's license bearing the name Matthew Mark Samuels. Linegar ascertained from the Patrol dispatcher that the name was an alias for David Tate, for whom there was an outstanding warrant on a weapons charge. Linegar did not believe the driver matched the description the dispatcher gave him for Tate, so he decided to investigate further.

A fellow trooper, Allen Hines, who was working the spot check with Linegar, then approached the passenger's side of the van while Linegar approached the driver's side. After a moment of questioning, Linegar asked the driver to step out of the van. The driver, who was in fact David Tate, brandished an automatic weapon and fired at the troopers first from inside and then from outside the van. By the time Tate stopped firing, Hines had been wounded by three shots and Linegar, whose body had been penetrated by six bullets, lay dead or dying. . . . None of the shots that hit the contour-style, concealable protective vest Linegar was wearing – there were five such shots – penetrated the vest or caused injury. The wounds Linegar suffered all were caused by shots that struck parts of his body not protected by the vest.

The Missouri State Highway Patrol issued the vest to Linegar when he joined the Patrol in 1981. The vest was one of a lot of various sizes of the same style vest the Patrol purchased in 1979 directly from Armour. The contour style was one of several different styles then on the market. It provided more protection to the sides of the body than the style featuring rectangular panels in front and back, but not as much protection as a wrap-around style. The front and back panels of the contour vest, held together with Velcro closures under the arms, did not meet at the sides of the wearer's body, leaving an area along the sides of the body under the arms exposed when the vest was worn. This feature of the vest was obvious to the Patrol when it selected this vest as standard issue for its troopers and could only have been obvious to any trooper who chose to wear it. The bullet that proved fatal to Linegar entered between his seventh and eighth ribs, approximately three-and-one-fourth inches down from his armpit, and pierced his heart.

The theory upon which Linegar's widow and children sought and won recovery from Armour was strict liability in tort based on a design defect in the vest. On appeal, Armour challenges . . . the sufficiency of the evidence to make a submissible case of strict liability in tort . . . .

Under Missouri products liability law, plaintiff potentially had available to her three theories of recovery: negligence, strict liability, and breach of warranty. . . . In 1969, the Missouri Supreme Court adopted section 402A of the Restatement (Second) of Torts, which imposes strict liability in tort upon sellers and manufacturers for selling "any product in a defective condition unreasonably dangerous to the user or consumer" that results in injury to the user or consumer. . . . Although here the first amended complaint stated claims against Armour on all of Missouri's products liability theories, . . . plaintiff later elected to dismiss all claims except Count I, strict liability for defective design . . . , and the case was submitted to the jury only on that theory.

To recover under a theory of strict liability in tort for defective design, Missouri law requires that a party prove the following elements:

1. [the] defendant sold the product in the course of its business;

2. the product was then in a defective condition unreasonably dangerous when put to a reasonably anticipated use;

3. the product was used in a manner reasonably anticipated;

4. [the] plaintiff was damaged as a direct result of such defective condition as existed when the product was sold.

. . . The jury instructions in this case tracked the applicable law. . . .

While there is some dispute between the parties over various of the elements, we predicate our reversal on the dearth of plaintiff's evidence of element (2). We conclude that, as a matter of law, the contour vest Trooper Linegar was wearing when he was murdered was not defective and unreasonably dangerous. . . .

The Missouri cases leave the meaning of the phrase "unreasonably dangerous" largely a matter of common sense, the court's or the jury's. . . . The conditions under which a bullet-resistant vest will be called upon to perform its intended function most assuredly will be dangerous, indeed life-threatening, and Armour surely knew that. It defies logic, however, to suggest that Armour reasonably should have anticipated that anyone would wear its vest for protection of areas of the body that the vest obviously did not cover.

Courts applying Missouri law also have applied what has become known as the "consumer expectation" test for unreasonable dangerousness: "The article sold must be dangerous to an extent beyond that which would be contemplated by the ordinary consumer who purchases it, with the ordinary knowledge common to the community as to its characteristics." Restatement (Second) of Torts § 402A comment i (1965) . . . .

The consumer expectation test focuses attention on the vest's wearer rather than on its manufacturer. The inherent limitations in the amount of coverage offered by Armour's contour vest were obvious to this Court, observing a demonstration from the bench during oral argument, as they would be to anyone with ordinary knowledge, most especially the vest's wearer. A person wearing the vest would no more expect to be shielded from a shot taken under the arm than he would expect the vest to deflect bullets aimed at his head or neck or lower abdomen or any other area not covered by the vest.

Plaintiff insists that the user's expectations should not be considered by us . . . . We disagree. . . . Here, the vest's purported dangerous defect – its lack of closure at the sides – could not have been more open and obvious. An otherwise completely effective protective vest cannot be regarded as dangerous, much less unreasonably so, simply because it leaves some parts of the body obviously exposed. . . .

We have no difficulty in concluding as a matter of law that the product at issue here was neither defective nor unreasonably dangerous. Trooper Linegar's protective vest performed precisely as expected and stopped all of the bullets that hit it. No part of the vest nor any malfunction of the vest caused Linegar's injuries. . . . The vest was designed to prevent the penetration of bullets where there was coverage, and it did so; the amount of coverage was the buyer's choice. The Missouri Highway Patrol could have chosen to buy, and Armour could have sold the Patrol, a vest with more coverage; no one contests that. But it is not the place of courts or juries to set specifications as to the parts of the body a bullet-resistant garment must cover. A manufacturer is not obliged to market only one version of a product, that being the very safest design possible. If that were so, automobile manufacturers could not offer consumers sports cars, convertibles, jeeps, or compact cars. All boaters would have to buy full life vests instead of choosing a ski belt or even a flotation cushion. Personal safety devices, in particular, require personal choices, and it is beyond the province of courts and juries to act as legislators and preordain those choices.

In this case, there obviously were trade-offs to be made. A contour vest like the one here in question permits the wearer more flexibility and mobility and allows better heat dissipation and sweat evaporation, and thus is more likely to be worn than a more confining vest. It is less expensive than styles of vests providing more complete coverage. If manufacturers like Armour are threatened with economically devastating litigation if they market any vest style except that offering maximum coverage, they may decide, since one can always argue that more coverage is possible, to get out of the business altogether. Or they may continue to market the vest style that, according to the latest lawsuit, affords the "best" coverage. Officers who find the "safest" style confining or uncomfortable will either wear it at risk to their mobility or opt not to wear it at all. . . . Law enforcement agencies trying to work within the confines of a budget may be forced to purchase fewer vests or none at all. How "safe" are those possibilities? . . . We are firmly convinced that to allow this verdict to stand would run counter to the law's purpose of promoting the development of safe and useful products, and would have an especially pernicious effect on the development and marketing of equipment designed to make the always-dangerous work of law enforcement officers a little safer.

The death of Jimmy Linegar by the hand of a depraved killer was a tragic event. We keenly feel the loss that this young trooper's family has suffered, and our sympathies go out to them. But we cannot allow recovery from a blameless defendant on the basis of sympathy for the plaintiffs. To hold Armour liable for Linegar's death would cast it in the role of insurer for anyone shot while wearing an Armour vest, regardless of whether any shots penetrated the vest. That a manufacturer may be cast in such a role has been soundly rejected by courts applying Missouri law. . . .

The judgment of the District Court is reversed. The District Court shall enter a final judgment in favor of Armour.

(2) RISK-BENEFIT TEST

The Restatement (Third) of Torts: Products Liability, Section 2 would do away with the consumer expectations test of design defect and would instead test the defectiveness of a design by comparing the additional costs of a theoretical feasible alternative design to the risk reduction garnered through the alternative design – in essence, this is an application of the Learned Hand forumula in the design defect context:

> *f. Design defects: factors relevant in determining whether the omission of a reasonable alternative design renders a product not reasonably safe.* Subsection (b) states that a product is defective in design if the omission of a reasonable alternative design renders the product not reasonably safe. A broad range of factors may be considered in determining whether an alternative design is reasonable and whether its omission renders a product not reasonably safe. The factors include, among others, the magnitude and probability of the foreseeable risks of harm, the instructions and warnings accompanying the product, and the nature and strength of consumer expectations regarding the product, including expectations arising from product portrayal and marketing. *See* Comment g. The relative advantages and disadvantages of the product as designed and as it alternatively could have been designed may also be considered. Thus, the likely effects of the alternative design on production costs; the effects of the alternative design on product longevity, maintenance, repair, and esthetics; and the range of consumer choice among products are factors that may be taken into account. A plaintiff is not necessarily required to introduce proof on all of these factors; their relevance, and the relevance of other factors, will vary from case to case. Moreover, the factors interact with one another. For example, evidence of the magnitude and probability of foreseeable harm may be offset by evidence that the proposed alternative design would reduce the efficiency and the utility of the product. On the other hand, evidence that a proposed alternative design would increase production costs may be offset by evidence that product portrayal and marketing created substantial expectations of performance or safety, thus increasing the probability of foreseeable harm. Depending on the mix of these factors, a number of variations in the design of a given product may meet the test in Subsection (b). On the other hand, it is not a factor under Subsection (b) that the imposition of liability would have a negative effect on corporate earnings or would reduce employment in a given industry.
>
> When evaluating the reasonableness of a design alternative, the overall safety of the product must be considered. It is not sufficient that the alternative design would have reduced or prevented the harm suffered by the plaintiff if it would also have introduced into the product other dangers of equal or greater magnitude.
>
> While a plaintiff must prove that a reasonable alternative design would have reduced the foreseeable risks of harm, Subsection (b) does not require the plaintiff to produce expert testimony in every case. Cases arise in which the feasibility of a reasonable alternative design is obvious and understandable to laypersons and therefore expert testimony is unnecessary to support a finding that the product should have been designed differently and more safely. For example, when a manufacturer sells a soft stuffed toy with hard plastic buttons that are easily

removable and likely to choke and suffocate a small child who foreseeably attempts to swallow them, the plaintiff should be able to reach the trier of fact with a claim that buttons on such a toy should be an integral part of the toy's fabric itself (or otherwise be unremovable by an infant) without hiring an expert to demonstrate the feasibility of an alternative safer design. Furthermore, other products already available on the market may serve the same or very similar function at lower risk and at comparable cost. Such products may serve as reasonable alternatives to the product in question.

In many cases, the plaintiff must rely on expert testimony. Subsection (b) does not, however, require the plaintiff to produce a prototype in order to make out a prima facie case. Thus, qualified expert testimony on the issue suffices, even though the expert has produced no prototype, if it reasonably supports the conclusion that a reasonable alternative design could have been practically adopted at the time of sale.

The requirements in Subsection (b) relate to what the plaintiff must prove in order to prevail at trial. This Restatement takes no position regarding the requirements of local law concerning the adequacy of pleadings or pretrial demonstrations of genuine issues of fact. It does, however, assume that the plaintiff will have the opportunity to conduct reasonable discovery so as to ascertain whether an alternative design is practical.

A test that considers such a broad range of factors in deciding whether the omission of an alternative design renders a product not reasonably safe requires a fair allocation of proof between the parties. To establish a prima facie case of defect, the plaintiff must prove the availability of a technologically feasible and practical alternative design that would have reduced or prevented the plaintiff's harm. Given inherent limitations on access to relevant data, the plaintiff is not required to establish with particularity the costs and benefits associated with adoption of the suggested alternative design.

In sum, the requirement of Subsection (b) that a product is defective in design if the foreseeable risks of harm could have been reduced by a reasonable alternative design is based on the commonsense notion that liability for harm caused by product designs should attach only when harm is reasonably preventable. For justice to be achieved, Subsection (b) should not be construed to create artificial and unreasonable barriers to recovery.

The necessity of proving a reasonable alternative design as a predicate for establishing design defect is, like any factual element in a case, addressed initially to the courts. Sufficient evidence must be presented so that reasonable persons could conclude that a reasonable alternative could have been practically adopted. Assuming that a court concludes that sufficient evidence on this issue has been presented, the issue is then for the trier of fact. This Restatement takes no position regarding the specifics of how a jury should be instructed. So long as jury instructions are generally consistent with the rule of law set forth in Subsection (b), their specific form and content are matters of local law.

MICALLEF V. MIEHLE CO.
348 N.E.2D 571 (N.Y. 1976)

. . .

Paul Micallef, plaintiff, was employed by Lincoln Graphic Arts at its Farmingdale plant as a printing-press operator. For eight months he had been assigned to operate a photo-offset press, model RU 1, manufactured and sold by defendant Miehle-Goss Dexter, Inc., to his employer. . . . Then, while working on January 22, 1969, plaintiff discovered that a foreign object had made its way onto the plate of the unit. Such a substance, known to the trade as a "hickie," causes a blemish or imperfection on the printed pages. Plaintiff informed his superior of the problem and told him he was going to "chase the hickie," whereupon the foreman warned him to be careful. "Chasing a hickie" consisted of applying, very lightly, a piece of plastic about eight inches wide to the printing plate, which is wrapped around a circular plate cylinder which spins at high speed. The revolving action of the plate against the plastic removes the "hickie." Unsuccessful in his first removal attempt, plaintiff started anew but this time the plastic was drawn into the nip point between the plate cylinder and an ink-form roller along with his hand. The machine had no safety guards to prevent such occurrence. Plaintiff testified that while his hand was trapped he reached for a shut-off button but couldn't contact it because of its location.

Plaintiff was aware of the danger of getting caught in the press in "chasing hickies." However, it was the custom and usage in the industry to "chase hickies on the run," because once the machine was stopped, it required at least three hours to resume printing and, in such event, the financial advantage of the high speed machine would be lessened. Although it was possible to have "chased the hickie" from another side of the machine, such approach would have caused plaintiff to be in a leaning position and would have increased the chances of scratching the plate. Through its representatives and engineers, defendant had observed the machine in operation and was cognizant of the manner in which "hickies were chased" by Lincoln's employees.

Samuel Aidlin, a professional engineer, had inspected the machine subsequent to the mishap. In his opinion, based upon the custom in the printing industry, it would have been good custom and practice to have placed guards near the rollers where plaintiff's hand entered the machine, the danger of human contact being well known. Moreover, he testified that at least three different types of guards were available, two for over 30 years, that they would not have impeded the practice of "chasing hickies," and that these guards would have protected an employee from exposure to the risk. . . .

Plaintiff sought damages by alleging two causes of action, one couched in negligence in the design of the machinery and the other premised upon the breach of an implied warranty. Since the time of trial, a third independent cause of action, one in strict products liability, has been recognized by this court . . . .

. . . [D]efendant asserts . . . that the action must be dismissed because the danger created by the absence of safeguards on the machine was open and obvious and, therefore, as the manufacturer it was under no duty to protect plaintiff from such a patent defect. . . .

A casting of increased responsibility upon the manufacturer, who stands in a superior position to recognize and cure defects, for improper conduct in the placement of finished products into the channels of commerce furthers the public interest. To this end, we hold that a manufacturer is obligated to exercise that degree of care in his plan or design so as to avoid any unreasonable risk of harm to anyone who is likely to be exposed to the danger when the product is used in the manner for which the product was intended . . . , as well as an unintended yet reasonably foreseeable use . . . .

This does not compel a manufacturer to clothe himself in the garb of an insurer in his dealings . . . nor to supply merchandise which is accident proof . . . . It does require, however, that legal responsibility, if any, for injury caused by machinery which has possible dangers incident to its use should be shouldered by the one in the best position to have eliminated those dangers.

. . . [T]he patent-danger doctrine should not, in and of itself, prevent a plaintiff from establishing his case. That does not mean, however, that the obviousness of the danger as a factor in the ultimate injury is thereby eliminated . . . . Rather, the openness and obviousness of the danger should be available to the defendant on the issue of whether plaintiff exercised that degree of reasonable care as was required under the circumstances. . . .

DAWSON V. CHRYSLER CORP.
630 F.2D 950 (3RD CIR. 1980)

This appeal from a jury verdict and entry of judgment in favor of the plaintiffs arises out of a New Jersey automobile accident in which a police officer was seriously injured. . . .

I. FACTUAL BACKGROUND

On September 7, 1974, Richard F. Dawson, while in the employ of the Pennsauken Police Department, was seriously injured as a result of an automobile accident that occurred in Pennsauken, New Jersey. As Dawson was driving on a rain-soaked highway, responding to a burglar alarm, he lost control of his patrol car a 1974 Dodge Monaco. The car slid off the highway, over a curb, through a small sign, and into an unyielding steel pole that was fifteen inches in diameter. The car struck the pole in a backwards direction at a forty-five degree angle on the left side of the vehicle; the point of impact was the left rear wheel well. As a result of the force of the collision, the vehicle literally wrapped itself around the pole. The pole ripped through the body of the car and crushed Dawson between the seat and the "header" area of the roof, located just above the windshield. The so-called "secondary collision" of Dawson with the interior of the automobile dislocated Dawson's left hip and ruptured his fifth and sixth cervical vertebrae. As a result of the injuries, Dawson is now a quadriplegic. He has no control over his body from the neck down, and requires constant medical attention.

Dawson, his wife, and their son brought suit in the Court of Common Pleas of Philadelphia against the Chrysler Corporation, the manufacturer of the vehicle in which Dawson was injured. . . . The plaintiffs' claims were based on theories of strict products liability and breach of implied warranty of fitness. They alleged that the patrol car was defective because it did not have a full, continuous steel frame extending through the door panels, and a cross-member running through the floor board between the posts located between the front and rear doors of the vehicle. Had the vehicle been so designed, the Dawsons alleged, it would have "bounced" off the pole following relatively slight penetration by the pole into the passenger space.

Expert testimony was introduced by the Dawsons to prove that the existing frame of the patrol car was unable to withstand side impacts at relatively low speed, and that the inadequacy of the frame permitted the pole to enter the passenger area and to injure Dawson. The same experts testified that the improvements in the design of the frame that the plaintiffs proposed were feasible and would have prevented Dawson from being injured as he was. According to plaintiffs' expert witnesses, a continuous frame and cross-member would have deflected the patrol car away from the pole after a minimal intrusion into the passenger area and, they declared, Dawson likely would have emerged from the accident with only a slight injury.

In response, Chrysler argued that it had no duty to produce a "crashproof" vehicle, and that, in any event, the patrol car was not defective. Expert testimony for Chrysler established that the design and construction of the 1974 Dodge Monaco complied with all federal vehicle safety standards, . . . and that deformation . . . of the body of the vehicle is desirable in most crashes because it absorbs the impact of the crash and decreases the rate of deceleration on the occupants of the vehicle. Thus, Chrysler's experts asserted that, for most types of automobile accidents, the design offered by the Dawsons would be less safe than the existing design. They also estimated that the steel parts that would be required in the model suggested by the Dawsons would have added between 200 and 250 pounds to the weight, and approximately $300 to the price of the vehicle. It was also established that the 1974 Dodge Monaco's unibody construction was stronger than comparable Ford and Chevrolet vehicles.

After all testimony had been introduced, Chrysler moved for a directed verdict, which the district judge denied. The jury thereupon returned a verdict in favor of the plaintiffs. In answers to a series of special interrogatories, the jurors concluded that (1) the body structure of the 1974 Dodge Monaco was defective and unreasonably dangerous; (2) Chrysler breached its implied warranty that the vehicle would be fit for use as a police car; (3) as a result of the defective design and the breach of warranty, Dawson sustained more severe injuries than he would have incurred had Chrysler used the alternative design proposed by Dawsons expert witnesses; (4) the defective design was the proximate cause of Dawson's enhanced injuries; and (5) Dawson's failure to use a seatbelt was not a proximate cause of his injuries. The jury awarded Mr. Dawson $2,064,863.19 for his expenses, disability, and pain and suffering, and granted Mrs. Dawson $60,000.00 for loss of consortium and loss of services. After the district court entered judgment, . . . Chrysler moved for judgment notwithstanding the verdict or, alternatively for a new trial. The court denied both motions. . . .

On appeal, Chrysler . . . [contends that t]he evidence presented by the Dawsons was insufficient to establish that the patrol car was defective and unreasonably dangerous or that Chrysler breached an implied warranty of fitness. . . .

We affirm.

II. DISCUSSION

At the outset, it is important, indeed crucial, to point out, that the substantive issues of this diversity case are controlled by the law of New Jersey.

A. Judgment Notwithstanding the Verdict

Dawsons' claims are premised on two legal theories strict tort liability and breach of an implied contractual warranty. . . . [U]nder the law of New Jersey, the governing principles of strict liability and the implied warranty theory are identical. . . . Accordingly, we proceed with the adjudication of this appeal pursuant to the rubric of strict liability.

Under New Jersey law, . . . a jury in a strict liability action must decide two factual questions: (1) whether the product at issue was defective; and (2) whether the defective product was a proximate cause of the plaintiff's injuries. . . . With these guidelines in mind, we turn to the contentions set forth by Chrysler in its appeal from the denial of its motion for judgment notwithstanding the verdict. . . .

2. Defective Product

Thus, the controlling issue in the case is whether the jury could be permitted to find, under the law of New Jersey, that the patrol car was defective. In *Suter*, the New Jersey Supreme Court summarized its state's law of strict liability as follows:

> If at the time the seller distributes a product, it is not reasonably fit, suitable and safe for its intended or reasonably foreseeable purposes so that users or others who may be expected to come in contact with the product are injured as a result thereof, then the seller shall be responsible for the ensuing damages.

81 N.J. at 169, 406 A.2d at 149 (footnote omitted). The court, in adopting this test, specifically rejected the requirement of the Restatement (Second) of Torts s 402A that the defect must cause the product to be "unreasonably dangerous to the user or consumer.". . . In the court's view, "the Restatement language may lead a jury astray for "(i)t may suggest an idea like ultra-hazardous, or abnormally dangerous, and thus give rise to the impression that the plaintiff must prove that the product was unusually or extremely dangerous.' " 81 N.J. at 175, 406 A.2d at 151 (quoting Wade, *On the Nature of Strict Liability for Products*, 44 Miss.L.J. 825, 832 (1973)).

The determination whether a product is "reasonably fit, suitable and safe for its intended or reasonably foreseeable purposes" is to be informed by what the New Jersey Supreme Court has termed a "risk/utility analysis." . . . Under this approach, a product is defective if "a reasonable person would conclude that the magnitude of the scientifically perceivable danger *as it is proved to be at the time of trial* outweighed the benefits of the way the product was so designed and marketed." *Id.* at 172-73, 386 A.2d at 826 (quoting Keeton, *Products Liability and the Meaning of Defect*, 5 St. Mary's L.J. 30, 37-38 (1973) (emphasis in original)). The court in *Cepeda*, relying heavily on the article by Dean John Wade, referred to in *Suter*, identified seven factors that might be relevant to this balancing process:

1. The usefulness and desirability of the product—its utility to the user and to the public as a whole.

2. The safety aspects of the product—the likelihood that it will cause injury, and the probable seriousness of the injury.

3. The availability of a substitute product which would meet the same need and not be as unsafe.

4. The manufacturer's ability to eliminate the unsafe character of the product without impairing its usefulness or making it too expensive to maintain its utility.

5. The user's ability to avoid danger by the exercise of care in the use of the product.

6. The user's anticipated awareness of the dangers inherent in the product and their avoidability, because of general public knowledge of the obvious condition of the product, or of the existence of suitable warnings or instructions.

7. The feasibility, on the part of the manufacturer, of spreading the loss by setting the price of the product or carrying liability insurance.

Id. at 173-74, 386 A.2d at 826-27 (quoting Wade, *On the Nature of Strict Tort Liability for Products*, 44 Miss.L.J. 825, 837-38 (1973). The court suggested that the trial judge first determine whether a balancing of these factors precludes liability as a matter of law. If it does not, then the judge is to incorporate into the instructions any factor for which there was presented specific proof and which might be deemed relevant to the jury's consideration of the matter. *Id.*

Chrysler maintains that, under these standards, the district court erred in submitting the case to the jury because the Dawsons failed, as a matter of law, to prove that the patrol car was defective. Specifically, it insists that the Dawsons did not present sufficient evidence from which the jury reasonably might infer that the alternative design that they proffered would be safer than the existing design, or that it would be cost effective, practical, or marketable. In short, Chrysler urges that the substitute design would be less socially beneficial than was the actual design of the patrol car. . . .

Our examination of the record persuades us that the district court did not err in denying Chrysler's motion for judgment notwithstanding the verdict. The Dawsons demonstrated that the frame of the 1974 Dodge Monaco was noncontinuous that is, it consisted of a front portion that extended from the front of the car to the middle of the front passenger seat, and a rear portion that ran from the middle of the rear passenger seat to the back end of the vehicle. Thus, there was a gap in the seventeen-inch side area of the frame between the front and rear seats. The plaintiffs also proved that, after colliding with the pole, the car slid along the left side portion of the rear frame until it reached the gap in the frame. At that point, the pole tore through the body of the vehicle into the passenger area and proceeded to push Dawson into the header area above the windshield.

Three experts—a design analyst, a mechanical engineer, and a biochemical engineer—also testified on behalf of the Dawsons. These witnesses had examined the patrol car and concluded that it was inadequate to withstand side impacts. They testified that there was an alternative design available which, had it been employed in the 1974 Monaco, would have prevented Dawson from sustaining serious injuries. . . . According to these witnesses, this design was known in the industry well before the accident and had been tested by a number of independent testing centers in 1969 and in 1973.

The mechanical engineer conducted a number of studies in order to ascertain the extent to which the alternative design would have withstood the crash. On the basis of these calculations, he testified that the pole would have penetrated only 9.9 inches into the passenger space, and thus would not have crushed Dawson. Instead, the engineer stated, the car would have deflected off the pole and back into the highway. Under these circumstances, according to the biochemical engineer, Dawson would have been able to "walk away from the accident" with but a bruised shoulder.

Also introduced by the Dawsons were reports of tests conducted for the United States Department of Transportation, which indicated that, in side collisions with a fixed pole at twenty-one miles per hour, . . . frame improvements similar to those proposed by the experts presented by the Dawsons reduced intrusion into the passenger area by fifty percent, from sixteen inches to eight inches. The study concluded that the improvements, "in conjunction with interior alterations, demonstrated a dramatic increase in occupant protection." . . . There was no suggestion at trial that the alternative design recommended by the Dawsons would not comply with federal safety standards. On cross-examination, Chrysler's attorney did get the Dawsons' expert witnesses to acknowledge that the alternative design would add between 200 and 250 pounds to the vehicle and would cost an additional $300 per car. The Dawsons' experts also conceded that the heavier and more rigid an automobile, the less able it is to absorb energy upon impact with a fixed object, and therefore the major force of an accident might be transmitted to the passengers. Moreover, an expert for Chrysler testified that, even if the frame of the patrol car had been designed in conformity with the plaintiffs' proposals, Dawson would have sustained injuries equivalent to those he actually incurred. Chrysler's witness reasoned that Dawson was injured, not by the intrusion of the pole into the passenger space, but as a result of being thrown into the header area of the roof by the vehicle's initial contact with the pole that is, prior to the impact of the pole against the driver's seat.

On the basis of the foregoing recitation of the evidence presented respectively by the Dawsons and by Chrysler, we conclude that the record is sufficient to sustain the jury's determination, in response to the interrogatory, that the design of the 1974 Monaco was defective. The jury was not required to ascertain that all of the factors enumerated by the New Jersey Supreme Court in *Cepeda* weighed in favor of the Dawsons in order to find the patrol car defective. . . . Rather, it need only to have reasonably concluded, after balancing these factors, that, at the time Chrysler distributed the 1974 Monaco, the car was "not reasonably fit, suitable and safe for its intended or reasonably foreseeable purposes."*Suter*, 81 N.J. at 169, 406 A.2d at 149. Moreover, our role in reviewing the record for purposes of determining whether a trial judge erred in denying a motion for a directed verdict or for judgment notwithstanding the verdict is necessarily a limited one. . . .

III. CONCLUSION

Although we affirm the judgment of the district court, we do so with uneasiness regarding the consequences of our decision and of the decisions of other courts throughout the country in cases of this kind.

As we observed earlier, . . . Congress, in enacting the National Traffic and Motor Vehicle Safety Act, provided that compliance with the Act does not exempt any person from liability under the common law of the state of injury. The effect of this provision is that the states are free, not only to create various standards of liability for automobile manufacturers with respect to design and structure, but also to delegate to the triers of fact in civil cases arising out of automobile accidents the power to determine whether a particular product conforms to such standards. In the present situation, for example, the New Jersey Supreme Court has instituted a strict liability standard for cases involving defective products, has defined the term "defective product" to mean any such item that is not "reasonably fit, suitable and safe for its intended or reasonably foreseeable purposes," and has left to the jury the task of determining whether the product at issue measures up to this standard.

The result of such arrangement is that while the jury found Chrysler liable for not producing a rigid enough vehicular frame, a factfinder in another case might well hold the manufacturer liable for producing a frame that is too rigid. Yet, as pointed out at trial, in certain types of accidents head-on collisions it is desirable to have a car designed to collapse upon impact because the deformation would absorb much of the shock of the collision, and divert the force of deceleration away from the vehicle's passengers. In effect, this permits individual juries applying varying laws in different jurisdictions to set nationwide automobile safety standards and to impose on automobile manufacturers conflicting requirements. It would be difficult for members of the industry to alter their design and production behavior in response to jury verdicts in such cases, because their response might well be at variance with what some other jury decides is a defective design. Under these circumstances, the law imposes on the industry the responsibility of insuring vast numbers of persons involved in automobile accidents.

Equally serious is the impact on other national social and economic goals of the existing case-by-case system of establishing automobile safety requirements. . . .

In sum, this appeal has brought to our attention an important conflict that implicates broad national concerns. Although it is important that society devise a proper system for compensating those injured in automobile collisions, it is not at all clear that the present arrangement of permitting individual juries, under varying standards of liability, to impose this obligation on manufacturers is fair or efficient. Inasmuch as it was the Congress that designed this system, and because Congress is the body best suited to evaluate and, if appropriate, to change that system, we decline today to do anything in this regard except to bring the problem to the attention of the legislative branch.

Bound as we are to adjudicate this appeal according to the substantive law of New Jersey, and because we find no basis in that law to overturn the jury's verdict, the judgment of the district court will be affirmed.

(3) HYBRID TEST

SOULE V. GENERAL MOTORS CORP.
882 P.2D 298 (CAL. 1994)

Plaintiff's ankles were badly injured when her General Motors (GM) car collided with another vehicle. She sued GM, asserting that defects in her automobile allowed its left front wheel to break free, collapse rearward, and smash the floorboard into her feet. GM denied any defect and claimed that the force of the collision itself was the sole cause of the injuries. Expert witnesses debated the issues at length. Plaintiff prevailed at trial, and the Court of Appeal affirmed the judgment. . . .

We reach the following conclusions: The trial court erred by giving an "ordinary consumer expectations" instruction in this complex case. . . .

FACTS

On the early afternoon of January 16, 1984, plaintiff was driving her 1982 Camaro in the southbound center lane of Bolsa Chica Road . . . . There was a slight drizzle, the roadway was damp, and apparently plaintiff was not wearing her seat belt. A 1972 Datsun, approaching northbound, suddenly skidded into the path of plaintiff's car. The Datsun's left rear quarter struck plaintiff's Camaro in an area near the left front wheel. Estimates of the vehicles' combined closing speeds on impact vary from 30 to 70 miles per hour. . . .

The collision bent the Camaro's frame adjacent to the wheel and tore loose the bracket that attached the wheel assembly (specifically, the lower control arm) to the frame. As a result, the wheel collapsed rearward and inward. The wheel hit the underside of the "toe pan"-the slanted floorboard area beneath the pedals-causing the toe pan to crumple, or "deform," upward into the passenger compartment.

Plaintiff received a fractured rib and relatively minor scalp and knee injuries. Her most severe injuries were fractures of both ankles, and the more serious of these was the compound compression fracture of her left ankle. This injury never healed properly. In order to relieve plaintiff's pain, an orthopedic surgeon fused the joint. As a permanent result, plaintiff cannot flex her left ankle. She walks with considerable difficulty, and her condition is expected to deteriorate. . . .

Plaintiff sued GM for her ankle injuries, asserting a theory of strict tort liability for a defective product. She claimed the severe trauma to her ankles was not a natural consequence of the accident, but occurred when the collapse of the Camaro's wheel caused the toe pan to crush violently upward against her feet. Plaintiff attributed the wheel collapse to a manufacturing defect, the substandard quality of the weld attaching the lower control arm bracket to the frame. She also claimed that the placement of the bracket, and the configuration of the frame, were defective designs because they did not limit the wheel's rearward travel in the event the bracket should fail.

The available physical and circumstantial evidence left room for debate about the exact angle and force of the impact and the extent to which the toe pan had actually deformed. The issues of defect and causation were addressed through numerous experts produced by both sides in such areas as biomechanics, metallurgy, orthopedics, design engineering, and crash-test simulation.

Plaintiff submitted the results of crash tests, and also asserted the similarity of another real-world collision involving a 1987 Camaro driven by Dana Carr. According to plaintiff's experts, these examples indicated that Camaro accidents of similar direction and force do not generally produce wheel bracket assembly failure, extensive toe pan deformation, or severe ankle injuries such as those plaintiff had experienced. These experts opined that without the deformation of the toe pan in plaintiff's car, her accident could not have produced enough force to fracture her ankles.

A metallurgist testifying on plaintiff's behalf examined the failed bracket from her car. He concluded that its weld was particularly weak because of excess "porosity" caused by improper welding techniques. Plaintiff's experts also emphasized the alternative frame and bracket design used by the Ford Mustang of comparable model years. They asserted that the Mustang's design, unlike the Camaro's, provided protection against unlimited rearward travel of the wheel should a bracket assembly give way.

GM's metallurgist disputed the claims of excessive weakness or porosity in the bracket weld. Expert witnesses for GM also countered the assertions of defective design. GM asserted that the Camaro's bracket was overdesigned to withstand forces in excess of all expected uses. According to expert testimony adduced by GM, the Mustang's alternative frame and bracket configuration did not fit the Camaro's overall design goals and was not distinctly safer for all collision stresses to which the vehicle might be subjected. Indeed, one witness noted, at least one more recent Ford product had adopted the Camaro's design. . . .

The court instructed the jury that a manufacturer is liable for "enhanced" injuries caused by a manufacturing or design defect in its product while the product is being used in a foreseeable way. Over GM's objection, the court gave the standard design defect instruction without modification. (*See* BAJI No. 9.00.5 (7th ed. 1986).) This instruction advised that a product is defective in design "if it fails to perform as safely as an ordinary consumer would expect when used in an intended or reasonably foreseeable manner *or if there is a risk of danger inherent in the design* which outweighs the benefit of the design." (Italics added.)

The jury was also told that in order to establish liability for a design defect under the "ordinary consumer expectations" standard, plaintiff must show (1) the manufacturer's product failed to perform as safely as an ordinary consumer would expect, (2) the defect existed when the product left the manufacturer's possession, (3) the defect was a "legal cause" of plaintiff's "enhanced injury," and (4) the product was used in a reasonably foreseeable manner. . . .

In a series of special findings, the jury determined that the Camaro contained a defect (of unspecified nature) which was a "legal cause" of plaintiff's "enhanced injury." The jury further concluded that although plaintiff was guilty of comparative fault, her conduct was not a legal cause of her enhanced injuries. Plaintiff received an award of $1.65 million.

GM appealed. Among other things, it argued that the trial court erred by instructing on ordinary consumer expectations in a complex design-defect case . . . .

We granted review.

DISCUSSION

1. Test for design defect.

A manufacturer, distributor, or retailer is liable in tort if a defect in the manufacture or design of its product causes injury while the product is being used in a reasonably foreseeable way. (*Cronin v. J.B.E. Olson Corp.* (1972) 8 Cal.3d 121, 126-130, 104 Cal.Rptr. 433, 501 P.2d 1153 [*Cronin*]; *Greenman v. Yuba Power Products, Inc.* (1963) 59 Cal.2d 57, 62, 27 Cal.Rptr. 697, 377 P.2d 897 [*Greenman*].) Because traffic accidents are foreseeable, vehicle manufacturers must consider collision safety when they design and build their products. Thus, whatever the cause of an accident, a vehicle's producer is liable for specific collision injuries that would not have occurred but for a manufacturing or design defect in the vehicle. (*Cronin, supra*, 8 Cal.3d at p. 126, 104 Cal. Rptr. 433, 501 P.2d 1153.)

In *Cronin, supra*, a bread van driver was hurt when the hasp retaining the bread trays broke during a collision, causing the trays to shift forward and propel him through the windshield. He sued the van's producer, alleging that the hasp had failed because of the defective metal used in its manufacture. The court instructed that the driver could recover if he proved a defect, unknown to him, which caused injury while the van was being used as intended or designed. The manufacturer appealed the subsequent damage award. It urged the court should have instructed that liability could not be imposed unless the defect rendered the product "unreasonably dangerous."

We rejected this contention, holding that the "unreasonably dangerous" test derived from the Restatement (*see* Rest.2d Torts, § 402A) is inapplicable in California. As we observed, the Restatement defines "unreasonably dangerous" as "dangerous to an extent beyond that which would be contemplated by the ordinary consumer who purchases it, *with the ordinary knowledge common to the community as to its characteristics."* (*Id.*, com. i, p. 352, italics added.) The original purpose of this formula, we explained, was to make clear that common products such as sugar, butter, and liquor are not defective simply because they pose inherent health risks well known to the general public. However, *Cronin* indicated, the formula had been applied so as to force injured persons to prove both an actual defect and "unreasonable" danger. (8 Cal.3d at pp. 132-133, 104 Cal.Rptr. 433, 501 P.2d 1153.)

This "double burden," *Cronin* reasoned, ran contrary to the purpose of *Greenman, supra,* to relieve persons injured by defective products from proof of elements that ring of negligence. Instead, *Cronin* concluded, an injured plaintiff should recover so long as he proves that the product was defective, and that the defect caused injury in reasonably foreseeable use. (*Cronin, supra,* 8 Cal.3d at pp. 133-134, 104 Cal.Rptr. 433, 501 P.2d 1153.)

In *Barker v. Lull Engineering Co., supra,* 20 Cal.3d 413, 143 Cal.Rptr. 225, 573 P.2d 443 (*Barker*), the operator of a high-lift loader sued its manufacturer for injuries he received when the loader toppled during a lift on sloping ground. The operator alleged various design defects which made the loader unsafe to use on a slope. In a pre- *Cronin* trial, the court instructed that the operator could recover only if a defect in the loader's design made the machine "'unreasonably dangerous for its intended use.'" (*Id.*, at p. 417, 143 Cal.Rptr. 225, 573 P.2d 443.) The operator appealed the defense verdict, citing the "unreasonably dangerous" instruction as prejudicial error.

The manufacturer responded that even if the "unreasonably dangerous" test was inappropriate for manufacturing defects, such as the substandard fastener material in *Cronin*, it should be retained for design defects. This rule would not produce the undue double burden that concerned us in *Cronin*, the manufacturer insisted, because unreasonable danger is part of the definition of design defect, not an additional element of strict product liability. Without this limitation, the manufacturer contended, juries would lack guidance when determining if a defect had sprung not from a mistake in supply or assembly, but from a flaw in the product's specifications.

The *Barker* court disagreed. It reasoned as follows: Our concerns in *Cronin* extended beyond double-burden problems. There we also sought to avoid the danger that a jury would deny recovery, as the Restatement had intended, "so long as the product did not fall below the ordinary consumer's expectations as to [its] safety...." (*Barker, supra,* 20 Cal.3d at p. 425, 143 Cal.Rptr. 225, 573 P.2d 443, fn. omitted.) This danger was particularly acute in design defect cases, where a manufacturer might argue that because the item which caused injury was identical to others of the same product line, it must necessarily have satisfied ordinary consumer expectations. (*Id.*, at p. 426, 143 Cal.Rptr. 225, 573 P.2d 443.)

Despite these difficulties, *Barker* explained, it is possible to define a design defect, and the expectations of the ordinary consumer are relevant to that issue. At a minimum, said *Barker*, a product is defective in design if it does fail to perform as safely as an ordinary consumer would expect. This principle, *Barker* asserted, acknowledges the relationship between strict tort liability for a defective product and the common law doctrine of warranty, which holds that a product's presence on the market includes an implied representation "'that it [will] safely do the jobs for which it was built.'" (20 Cal.3d at p. 430, 143 Cal.Rptr. 225, 573 P.2d 443, quoting *Greenman, supra*, 59 Cal.2d at p. 64, 27 Cal.Rptr. 697, 377 P.2d 897.) "Under this [minimum] standard," *Barker* observed, "an injured plaintiff will frequently be able to demonstrate the defectiveness of the product *by resort to circumstantial evidence, even when the accident itself precludes identification of the specific defect at fault.* [Citations.]" (20 Cal.3d at p. 430, 143 Cal.Rptr. 225, 573 P.2d 443, italics added.)

However, *Barker* asserted, the Restatement had erred in proposing that a violation of ordinary consumer expectations was necessary for recovery on this ground. "As Professor Wade has pointed out, ... the expectations of the ordinary consumer cannot be viewed as the exclusive yardstick for evaluating design defectiveness because '[i]n many situations ... *the consumer would not know what to expect,* because he would have *no idea* how safe the product could be made.' " (20 Cal.3d at p. 430, 143 Cal.Rptr. 225, 573 P.2d 443, quoting Wade, *On the Nature of Strict Tort Liability for Products* (1973) 44 Miss.L.J. 825, 829, italics added.)

Thus, *Barker* concluded, "a product may be found defective in design, even if it satisfies ordinary consumer expectations, if through hindsight the jury determines that the product's design embodies 'excessive preventable danger,' or, in other words, if the jury finds that the risk of danger inherent in the challenged design outweighs the benefits of such design. [Citations.]" (20 Cal.3d at p. 430, 143 Cal.Rptr. 225, 573 P.2d 443, fn. omitted.) *Barker* held that under this latter standard, "a jury may consider, among other relevant factors, the gravity of the danger posed by the challenged design, the likelihood that such danger would occur, the mechanical feasibility of a safer alternative design, the financial cost of an improved design, and the adverse consequences to the product and to the consumer that would result from an alternative design. [Citations.]" (*Id.*, at p. 431, 143 Cal.Rptr. 225, 573 P.2d 443.) . . .

Barker also made clear that when the ultimate issue of design defect calls for a careful assessment of feasibility, practicality, risk, and benefit, the case should not be resolved simply on the basis of ordinary consumer expectations. As *Barker* observed, "past design defect decisions demonstrate that, as a practical matter, in many instances it is simply impossible to eliminate the balancing or weighing of competing considerations in determining whether a product is defectively designed or not...." (20 Cal.3d at p. 433, 143 Cal.Rptr. 225, 573 P.2d 443.) . . .

In *Barker*, we offered two alternative ways to prove a design defect, each appropriate to its own circumstances. The purposes, behaviors, and dangers of certain products are commonly understood by those who ordinarily use them. By the same token, the ordinary users or consumers of a product may have reasonable, widely accepted minimum expectations about the circumstances under which it should perform safely. Consumers govern their own conduct by these expectations, and products on the market should conform to them.

In some cases, therefore, "ordinary knowledge ... as to ... [the product's] characteristics" (Rest.2d Torts, *supra*, § 402A, com. i., p. 352) may permit an inference that the product did not perform as safely as it should. If the facts permit such a conclusion, and if the failure resulted from the product's design, a finding of defect is warranted without any further proof. The manufacturer may not defend a claim that a product's design failed to perform as safely as its ordinary consumers would expect by presenting expert evidence of the design's relative risks and benefits.[3]

However, as we noted in *Barker*, a complex product, even when it is being used as intended, may often cause injury in a way that does not engage its ordinary consumers' reasonable minimum assumptions about safe performance. For example, the ordinary consumer of an automobile simply has "no idea" how it should perform in all foreseeable situations, or how safe it should be made against all foreseeable hazards. (*Barker, supra*, 20 Cal.3d at p. 430, 143 Cal.Rptr. 225, 573 P.2d 443.)

An injured person is not foreclosed from proving a defect in the product's design simply because he cannot show that the reasonable minimum safety expectations of its ordinary consumers were violated. Under *Barker*'s alternative test, a product is still defective if its design embodies "excessive preventable danger" (20 Cal.3d at p. 430, 143 Cal.Rptr. 225, 573 P.2d 443), that is, unless "the benefits of the ... design outweigh the risk of danger inherent in such design" (*id.*, at p. 432, 143 Cal.Rptr. 225, 573 P.2d 443). But this determination involves technical issues of feasibility, cost, practicality, risk, and benefit (*id.*, at p. 431, 143 Cal.Rptr. 225, 573 P.2d 443) which are "impossible" to avoid (*id.*, at p. 433, 143 Cal.Rptr. 225, 573 P.2d 443). In such cases, the jury must consider the manufacturer's evidence of competing design considerations (*id.*, at pp. 433-434, 143 Cal.Rptr. 225, 573 P.2d 443), and the issue of design defect cannot fairly be resolved by standardless reference to the "expectations" of an "ordinary consumer."

As we have seen, the consumer expectations test is reserved for cases in which the everyday experience of the product's users permits a conclusion that the product's design violated minimum safety assumptions, and is thus defective regardless of expert opinion about the merits of the design. It follows that where the minimum safety of a product is within the common knowledge of lay jurors, expert witnesses may not be used to demonstrate what an ordinary consumer would or should expect. Use of expert testimony for that purpose would invade the jury's function (*see* Evid.Code, § 801, subd. (a)), and would invite circumvention of the rule that the risks and benefits of a challenged design must be carefully balanced whenever the issue of design defect goes beyond the common experience of the product's users.[4]

---

3   For example, the ordinary consumers of modern automobiles may and do expect that such vehicles will be designed so as not to explode while idling at stoplights, experience sudden steering or brake failure as they leave the dealership, or roll over and catch fire in two-mile-per-hour collisions. If the plaintiff in a product liability action proved that a vehicle's design produced such a result, the jury could find forthwith that the car failed to perform as safely as its ordinary consumers would expect, and was therefore defective.

4   Plaintiff insists that manufacturers should be forced to design their products to meet the "objective" safety demands of a "hypothetical" reasonable consumer who is fully informed about what he or she should expect. Hence, plaintiff reasons, the jury may receive expert advice on "reasonable" safety expectations for the product. However, this function is better served by the risk-benefit prong of *Barker*. There, juries receive expert advice, apply clear guidelines, and decide accordingly whether the product's design is an acceptable compromise of competing considerations. On the other hand, appropriate use of the consumer expectations test is not necessarily foreclosed simply because the product at issue is only in specialized use, so that the general public may not be familiar with its safety characteristics. If the safe performance of the product fell below the reasonable, widely shared minimum expectations of those who do use it, perhaps the injured consumer should not be forced to rely solely on a technical comparison of risks and benefits. By the same token, if the expectations of the product's limited group of ordinary consumers are beyond the lay experience common to all jurors, expert testimony on the limited subject of what the product's actual consumers do expect may be proper. (*See, e.g., Lunghi v. Clark Equipment Co., supra*, 153 Cal.App.3d 485, 496, 200 Cal.Rptr. 387.)

By the same token, the jury may not be left free to find a violation of ordinary consumer expectations whenever it chooses. Unless the facts actually permit an inference that the product's performance did not meet the minimum safety expectations of its ordinary users, the jury must engage in the balancing of risks and benefits required by the second prong of *Barker*.

Accordingly, as *Barker* indicated, instructions are misleading and incorrect if they allow a jury to avoid this risk-benefit analysis in a case where it is required. (20 Cal.3d at p. 434, 143 Cal.Rptr. 225, 573 P.2d 443.) Instructions based on the ordinary consumer expectations prong of *Barker* are not appropriate where, as a matter of law, the evidence would not support a jury verdict on that theory. Whenever that is so, the jury must be instructed solely on the alternative risk-benefit theory of design defect announced in *Barker*. . . .

GM argues at length that the consumer expectations test is an "unworkable, amorphic, fleeting standard" which should be entirely abolished as a basis for design defect. In GM's view, the test is deficient and unfair in several respects. First, it defies definition. Second, it focuses not on the objective condition of products, but on the subjective, unstable, and often unreasonable opinions of consumers. Third, it ignores the reality that ordinary consumers know little about how safe the complex products they use can or should be made. Fourth, it invites the jury to isolate the particular consumer, component, accident, and injury before it instead of considering whether the whole product fairly accommodates the competing expectations of all consumers in all situations (*see Daly v. General Motors Corp., supra*, 20 Cal.3d 725, 746-747, 144 Cal.Rptr. 380, 575 P.2d 1162). Fifth, it eliminates the careful balancing of risks and benefits which is essential to any design issue.

In its amicus curiae brief, the Product Liability Advisory Council, Inc. (Council) makes similar arguments. The Council proposes that all design defect claims be resolved under a single risk-benefit analysis geared to "reasonable safety."

We fully understand the dangers of improper use of the consumer expectations test. However, we cannot accept GM's insinuation that ordinary consumers lack any legitimate expectations about the minimum safety of the products they use. In particular circumstances, a product's design may perform so unsafely that the defect is apparent to the common reason, experience, and understanding of its ordinary consumers. In such cases, a lay jury is competent to make that determination.

Nor are we persuaded by the Council's proposal. In essence, it would reinvest product liability claims with the requirement of "unreasonable danger" that we rejected in *Cronin* and *Barker*.

When use of the consumer expectations test is limited as *Barker* intended, the principal concerns raised by GM and the Council are met. Within these limits, the test remains a workable means of determining the existence of design defect. We therefore find no compelling reason to overrule the consumer expectations prong of *Barker* at this late date, and we decline to do so. . . .

Applying our conclusions to the facts of this case, however, we agree that the instant jury should not have been instructed on ordinary consumer expectations. Plaintiff's theory of design defect was one of technical and mechanical detail. It sought to examine the precise behavior of several obscure components of her car under the complex circumstances of a particular accident. The collision's exact speed, angle, and point of impact were disputed. It seems settled, however, that plaintiff's Camaro received a substantial oblique blow near the left front wheel, and that the adjacent frame members and bracket assembly absorbed considerable inertial force.

An ordinary consumer of automobiles cannot reasonably expect that a car's frame, suspension, or interior will be designed to remain intact in any and all accidents. Nor would ordinary experience and understanding inform such a consumer how safely an automobile's design should perform under the esoteric circumstances of the collision at issue here. Indeed, both parties assumed that quite complicated design considerations were at issue, and that expert testimony was necessary to illuminate these matters. Therefore, injection of ordinary consumer expectations into the design defect equation was improper.

We are equally persuaded, however, that the error was harmless, because it is not reasonably probable defendant would have obtained a more favorable result in its absence. . . .

CONCLUSION

The trial court erred when it instructed on the consumer expectations test for design defect, and when it refused GM's special instruction on causation. However, neither error caused actual prejudice. Accordingly, the judgment of the Court of Appeal, upholding the trial court judgment in favor of plaintiff, is affirmed. . . .

(4) PRODUCT CATEGORY LIABILITY

O'BRIEN V. MUSKIN CORP.
463 A.2D 298 (N.J. 1983)

Plaintiff, Gary O'Brien, seeks to recover in strict liability for personal injuries sustained because defendant, Muskin Corporation, allegedly marketed a product, an above-ground swimming pool, that was defectively designed and bore an inadequate warning. . . .

O'Brien sued to recover damages for serious personal injuries sustained when he dove into a swimming pool . . . . At the close of the plaintiff's case, the trial court determined that he had failed to prove a design defect in the pool. Accordingly, at the close of the entire case, the court refused to charge the jury on design defect. Instead, the court submitted the case to the jury solely on the adequacy of the warning. . . .

[T]he jury found that O'Brien was guilty of contributory negligence, and allocated fault for the injury as 15% attributable to Muskin and 85% attributable to O'Brien. Thus, under New Jersey's comparative negligence statute, O'Brien was barred from recovery. . . .

On appeal, the Appellate Division found that the trial court erred in removing from the jury the issue of design defect. Consequently, that court reversed the judgment against Muskin and remanded the matter for a new trial. . . .

I

Muskin, a swimming pool manufacturer, made and distributed a line of above-ground pools. Typically, the pools consisted of a corrugated metal wall, which the purchaser placed into an oval frame assembled over a shallow bed of sand. This outer structure was then fitted with an embossed vinyl liner and filled with water.

In 1971, Arthur Henry bought a Muskin pool and assembled it in his backyard. The pool was a twenty-foot by twenty-four-foot model, with four-foot walls. An embossed vinyl liner fit within the outer structure and was filled with water to a depth of approximately three and one-half feet. At one point, the outer wall of the pool bore the logo of the manufacturer, and below it a decal that warned "DO NOT DIVE" in letters roughly one-half inch high.

On May 17, 1974, O'Brien, then twenty-three years old, arrived uninvited at the Henry home and dove into the pool. A fact issue exists whether O'Brien dove from the platform by the pool or from the roof of the adjacent eight-foot high garage. As his outstretched hands hit the vinyl-lined pool bottom, they slid apart, and O'Brien struck his head on the bottom of the pool, thereby sustaining his injuries.

In his complaint, O'Brien alleged that Muskin was strictly liable for his injuries because it had manufactured and marketed a defectively designed pool. In support of this contention, O'Brien cited the slippery quality of the pool liner and the lack of adequate warnings.

At trial, both parties produced experts who testified about the use of vinyl as a pool liner. One of the plaintiff's witnesses, an expert in the characteristics of vinyl, testified that wet vinyl was more than twice as slippery as rubber latex, which is used to line in-ground pools. The trial court, however, sustained an objection to the expert's opinion about alternative kinds of pool bottoms, specifically whether rubber latex was a feasible liner for above-ground pools. The expert admitted that he knew of no above-ground pool lined with a material other than vinyl, but plaintiff contended that vinyl should not be used in above-ground pools, even though no alternative material was available. A second expert testified that the slippery vinyl bottom and lack of adequate warnings rendered the pool unfit and unsafe for its foreseeable uses.

Muskin's expert testified that vinyl was not only an appropriate material to line an above-ground pool, but was the best material because it permitted the outstretched arms of the diver to glide when they hit the liner, thereby preventing the diver's head from striking the bottom of the pool. Thus, he concluded that in some situations, specifically those in which a diver executes a shallow dive, slipperiness operates as a safety feature. Another witness, Muskin's customer service manager, who was indirectly in charge of quality control, testified that the vinyl bottom could have been thicker and the embossing deeper. A fair inference could be drawn that deeper embossing would have rendered the pool bottom less slippery.

At the close of the entire case, the trial court instructed the jury on the elements of strict liability, both with respect to design defects and the failure to warn adequately. The court, however, then limited the jury's consideration to the adequacy of the warning. That is, the court took from the jury the issue whether manufacturing a pool with a vinyl liner constituted either a design or manufacturing defect.

II

Strict liability law, a relatively recent but rapidly growing legal phenomenon, has received uneven treatment from scholars, legislatures and courts. Underlying the various responses is a shared concern about the allocation of the risk of loss upon manufacturers, distributors and others in the stream of commerce for injuries sustained by the public from unsafe products.

One of the policy considerations supporting the imposition of strict liability is easing the burden of proof for a plaintiff injured by a defective product, a policy that is achieved by eliminating the requirement that the plaintiff prove the manufacturer's negligence. . . . Generally speaking, a plaintiff has the burden of proving that (1) the product was defective; (2) the defect existed when the product left the hands of the defendant; and (3) the defect caused injury to a reasonably foreseeable user. . . . Proof that the product was defective requires more than a mere showing that the product caused the injury. The necessity of proving a defect in the product as part of the plaintiff's *prima facie* case distinguishes strict from absolute liability, and thus prevents the manufacturer from also becoming the insurer of a product. . . .

Fundamental to the determination of a products liability case, including one predicated on a defective design or inadequate warning, is the duty of the manufacturer to foreseeable users. The duty includes warning foreseeable users of the risks inherent in the use of that product, . . . and not placing defective products on the market. . . . *see* Restatement (Second) of Torts §402A (1965). A manufacturer who breaches these duties is strictly liable to an injured party. That liability reflects the policy judgment that by marketing its product, a manufacturer assumes responsibility to members of the public who are injured because of defects in that product. Restatement (Second) of Torts §402A comment c (1965).

In determining whether a manufacturer has breached its duty, we focus on the product. . . . Under strict liability, a manufacturer that produces defective products is liable even if those products are carefully produced. Thus, the legal standard for evaluating whether a product is defective becomes the touchstone of strict liability.

Critical, then, to the disposition of products liability claims is the meaning of "defect." The term is not self-defining and has no accepted meaning suitable for all strict liability cases. Implicit in the term "defect" is a comparison of the product with a standard of evaluation; something can be defective only if it fails to measure up to that standard. . . . Speaking generally, defects may be classified as design defects or manufacturing defects. In cases alleging manufacturing defects, as distinguished from design defects, defining the standard, and thus the meaning of "defect," is relatively easy. For example, the injury-causing product may be measured against the same product as manufactured according to the manufacturer's standards. If the particular product used by the plaintiff fails to conform to those standards or other units of the same kind, it is defective. An apt illustration is a mass-produced product that comes off the assembly line missing a part. The question in those cases becomes whether the product as produced by the manufacturer conformed to the product as intended. . . .

The considerations are more subtle when a plaintiff alleges that a product is defective due to any feature of its design, including the absence or inadequacy of accompanying warnings.

In design defect or failure-to-warn cases, the product has been manufactured as intended and cannot be "defective" by comparison to a standard set by the manufacturer. . . . Rather, the standard to measure the product reflects a policy judgment that some products are so dangerous that they create a risk of harm outweighing their usefulness. From that perspective, the term "defect" is a conclusion rather than a test for reaching that conclusion. . . .

Although the appropriate standard might be variously defined, one definition, based on a comparison of the utility of the product with the risk of injury that it poses to the public, has gained prominence. To the extent that "risk-utility analysis," as it is known, implicates the reasonableness of the manufacturer's conduct, strict liability law continues to manifest that part of its heritage attributable to the law of negligence. . . .

Another standard is the consumer expectations test, which recognizes that the failure of the product to perform safely may be viewed as a violation of the reasonable expectations of the consumer. . . . In this case, however, the pool fulfilled its function as a place to swim. The alleged defect manifested itself when the pool was used for diving.

. . . [S]ome factors relevant in risk-utility analysis are:

1. The usefulness and desirability of the product – its utility to the user and to the public as a whole.

2. The safety aspects of the product – the likelihood that it will cause injury, and the probable seriousness of the injury.

3. The availability of a substitute product which would meet the same need and not be as unsafe.

4. The manufacturer's ability to eliminate the unsafe character of the product without impairing its usefulness or making it too expensive to maintain its utility.

5. The user's ability to avoid danger by the exercise of care in the use of the product.

6. The user's anticipated awareness of the dangers inherent in the product and their avoidability, because of general public knowledge of the obvious condition of the product, or of the existence of suitable warnings or instructions.

7. The feasibility, on the part of the manufacturer, of spreading the loss by setting the price of the product or carrying liability insurance.

By implication, risk-utility analysis includes other factors such as the "state-of-the-art" at the time of the manufacture of the product. . . . The "state-of-the-art" refers to the existing level of technological expertise and scientific knowledge relevant to a particular industry at the time a product is designed. . . .

The assessment of the utility of a design involves the consideration of available alternatives. If no alternatives are available, recourse to a unique design is more defensible. The existence of a safer and equally efficacious design, however, diminishes the justification for using a challenged design.

The evaluation of the utility of a product also involves the relative need for that product; some products are essentials, while others are luxuries. A product that fills a critical need and can be designed in only one way should be viewed differently from a luxury item. Still other products, including some for which no alternative exists, are so dangerous and of such little use that under the risk-utility analysis, a manufacturer would bear the cost of liability of harm to others. That cost might dissuade a manufacturer from placing the product on the market, even if the product has been made as safely as possible. Indeed, plaintiff contends that above-ground pools with vinyl liners are such products and that manufacturers who market those pools should bear the cost of injuries they cause to foreseeable users.

A critical issue at trial was whether the design of the pool, calling for a vinyl bottom in a pool four feet deep, was defective. The trial court should have permitted the jury to consider whether, because of the dimensions of the pool and slipperiness of the bottom, the risks of injury so outweighed the utility of the product as to constitute a defect. In removing that issue from consideration by the jury, the trial court erred. To establish sufficient proof to compel submission of the issue to the jury for appropriate fact-finding under risk-utility analysis, it was not necessary for plaintiff to prove the existence of alternative, safer designs. Viewing the evidence in the light most favorable to plaintiff, even if there are no alternative methods of making bottoms for above-ground pools, the jury might have found that the risk posed by the pool outweighed its utility.

In a design-defect case, the plaintiff bears the burden of both going forward with the evidence and of persuasion that the product contained a defect. To establish a *prima facie* case, the plaintiff should adduce sufficient evidence on the risk-utility factors to establish a defect. With respect to above-ground swimming pools, for example, the plaintiff might seek to establish that pools are marketed primarily for recreational, not therapeutic purposes; that because of their design, including their configuration, inadequate warnings, and the use of vinyl liners, injury is likely; that, without impairing the usefulness of the pool or pricing it out of the market, warnings against diving could be made more prominent and a liner less dangerous. It may not be necessary for the plaintiff to introduce evidence on all those alternatives. Conversely, the plaintiff may wish to offer proof on other matters relevant to the risk-utility analysis. It is not a foregone conclusion that plaintiff ultimately will prevail on a risk-utility analysis, but he should have an opportunity to prove his case. . . .

Our concurring and dissenting colleague, Justice Schreiber, disagrees with the majority opinion in several respects. His opinion begins with the correct statement that the imposition of strict liability in a products liability case requires proof of a defect in the product. We depart from our colleague, however, because he believes that proof of a defect through risk-utility analysis is tantamount to absolute, not strict, liability. . . .

A second difference between the two opinions is that Justice Schreiber would find that no matter how dangerous a product may be, if it bears an adequate warning, it is free from design defects if there is no known alternative. Under that hypothesis, manufacturers, merely by placing warnings on their products, could insulate themselves from liability regardless of the number of people those products maim or kill. By contrast, the majority concludes that the judicial, not the commercial, system is the appropriate forum for determining whether a product is defective with the resultant imposition of strict liability upon those in the commercial chain. . . .

We modify and affirm the judgment of the Appellate Division reversing and remanding the matter for a new trial. . . .

SCHREIBER, J., concurring and dissenting.

Until today, the existence of a defect was an essential element in strict product liability. This no longer is so. Indeed, the majority has transformed strict product liability into absolute liability and delegated the function of making that determination to a jury. I must dissent from that conclusion because the jury will not be cognizant of all the elements that should be considered in formulating a policy supporting absolute liability, because it is not satisfactory to have a jury make a value judgment with respect to a type or class of product, and because its judgment will not have precedential effect.

Our Court adopted the principle in the Restatement (Second) of Torts § 402A (1965) that the seller of a product in a "defective condition unreasonably dangerous" (we have substituted the language not reasonably safe) is subject to liability for harm to the ultimate user or consumer. . . . A plaintiff had to prove that the chattel that caused his injury was *defective*. There had to be something wrong with it. . . .

What is a defect? Defects fall within three categories. A flaw in the particular product, such as an improper weld, is one class. A second group consists of design defects. Here there must be a showing that there was an alternative, technologically feasible design available at the time the product was designed. . . . The third class, which is closely analogous to the second, involves inadequate warnings and instructions. In a technical sense this does not involve a defect in the product. However, in the absence of reasonable warnings of the dangers of the product and instructions on its use to avoid dangerous consequences, the product is not reasonably safe. The failure to include adequate literature is functionally equivalent to a failure to design properly in that an alternative adequate warning could have been given.

In design defect and inadequate warning cases the product is produced as intended by the manufacturer, but is wanting in another respect. . . .

In addition to establishing that the product was defective because of the flaw, design, or inadequate warning, the plaintiff has the burden of proving that the product with its defect was not reasonably safe, fit and proper. One way this burden can be met is by proving a failure to measure up to consumer expectations.

In deciding whether a case should be submitted to the jury, a court must engage in a risk-utility analysis. . . .

Risk-utility factors to be considered by the court may be summarized as follows: usefulness of the product, likelihood it will cause injury and seriousness of the injury; availability of safer substitutes; manufacturer's ability to eliminate the danger; user's ability to avoid the danger; user's knowledge of the danger; and feasibility of risk spreading. . . .

The purpose of strict product liability is to hold a manufacturer responsible for damages attributable to a failure of the product to perform with reasonable safety. It is not to make the manufacturer an insurer against all losses. . . . The strict liability policy of encouraging manufacturers to market a safer product is generally inapplicable where the product is unavoidably unsafe. Strict liability arose in part because of a basic presumption that persons not abusing products are not usually injured unless the manufacturer failed in some respect in designing, manufacturing or marketing the product. The strict liability theory was designed to facilitate redress for the injured user or consumer because of the difficulty in proving negligence. This policy is not advanced when imposing absolute liability. . . .

It is conceivable that a court could decide that a manufacturer should have absolute liability for a defect-free product where as a matter of policy liability should be imposed. Suppose a manufacturer produced toy guns for children that emitted hard rubber pellets – an obviously dangerous situation. A court could reasonably conclude that the risks (despite warnings) outweighed the recreational value of the toy, that the manufacturer should bear the costs and that there should be absolute liability to a child injured by the toy. . . .

It is important to note that the risk-utility analysis is *not* submitted to the jury for the purpose of determining absolute liability for a class or type of product. Dean Wade has explained that when a whole group or class or type of a product may be unsafe, "the policy issues become very important and the factors [the seven listed in the risk-utility analysis] must be collected and carefully weighed. It is here that the court – whether trial or appellate – does consider these issues in deciding whether to submit the case to the jury." 44 Miss.L.J. at 838. . . .

When the case is submitted to the jury in strict liability, the jury must decide whether the product is defective and reasonably safe, not whether as a matter of policy the manufacturer should be absolutely liable. In determining questions of defectiveness and safety, *some* of the same risk-utility factors may be pertinent. However, reference to any one of the factors is to be made only when it is relevant and may be of assistance in deciding whether the product is defective and whether it is not reasonably safe. . . .

Now the Court . . . decides that a jury may speculate that, though there is no manufacturing flaw, the duty to warn has been satisfied and the manufacturer could not possibly have designed the item in a safer manner, the manufacturer can be absolutely liable because the jury finds that the risk outweighs the product's usefulness. It is not appropriate to foresake uniformity of treatment of a class or type of product by permitting juries to decide these questions. Nor is it appropriate for a jury to make this value judgment in addition to resolving factual issues. . . .

The majority holds that the jury should have been permitted to decide whether the risks of above-ground swimming pools with vinyl bottoms exceed their usefulness despite adequate warnings and despite unavailability of any other design. The plaintiff had the burden of proving this proposition. . . . Yet he adduced no evidence on many of the factors bearing on the risk-utility analysis. . . .

These factors should be given some consideration when deciding the policy question of whether pool manufacturers and, in the final analysis, consumers should bear the costs of accidents arising out of the use of pools when no fault can be attributed to the manufacturer because of a flaw in the pool, unavailability of a better design, or inadequate warning. If this Court wishes to make absolute liability available in product cases and not leave such decisions to the Legislature, it should require that trial courts determine in the first instance as a matter of law what products should be subject to absolute liability. In that event the court would consider all relevant factors including those utilized in the risk-utility analysis.

The difference between absolute and strict liability is not one of semantics. . . . Strict liability is imposed where there is a defect in a product due to an individual product flaw, an improper design or an inadequate warning. . . . Absolute liability is imposed where, on the basis of policy considerations including risk-spreading, it is determined that a manufacturer or other seller should bear the cost of injuries he causes to foreseeable users, regardless of the presence or absence of any defect. In some circumstances a manufacturer may be liable though a product is free from defects.

The majority's view of "strict liability" encompasses both strict liability and absolute liability. Although the majority and I adopt the same formulaic statement that strict liability is imposed only where there is a "defect," . . . the majority uses the term to include not only individual product flaw, improper design and inadequate warning cases, but also a fourth category of cases in which the jury decides that the risks outweigh the utility of the product. It follows from the majority's rationale that a jury may be permitted to find that there is a "defect" whenever there is an accident involving a product.

I join in the result, however. There was proof that the pool liner was slippery and that the vinyl bottom could have been thicker and the embossing deeper. As the majority states, a "fair inference could be drawn that deeper embossing would have rendered the pool bottom less slippery." . . . The plaintiff's theory was that the dangerous condition was the extreme slipperiness of the bottom. Viewing the facts favorably from the plaintiff's frame of reference, I would agree that he had some proof that the pool was incorrectly designed and therefore was defective. This issue, together with causation, should have been submitted to the jury.

Other than as stated herein, I join in the majority's opinion and concur in the judgment reversing and remanding the matter for a new trial.

c. WARNING DEFECT

MACDONALD V. ORTHO PHARMACEUTICAL CORP.
475 N.E.2D 65 (MASS. 1985)

This products liability action raises the question of the extent of a drug manufacturer's duty to warn consumers of dangers inherent in the use of oral contraceptives. The plaintiffs brought suit against the defendant, Ortho Pharmaceutical Corporation (Ortho), for injuries allegedly caused by Ortho's birth control pills, and obtained a jury verdict in their favor. The defendant moved for a judgment notwithstanding the verdict. The judge concluded that the defendant did not owe a duty to warn the plaintiffs, and entered judgment for Ortho. The plaintiffs appealed. We transferred the case to this court on our own motion and reinstate the jury verdict. . . .

We summarize the facts. In September, 1973, the plaintiff Carole D. MacDonald (MacDonald), who was twenty-six years old at the time, obtained from her gynecologist a prescription for Ortho-Novum contraceptive pills, manufactured by Ortho. As required by the then effective regulations promulgated by the United States Food and Drug Administration (FDA), the pill dispenser she received was labeled with a warning that "oral contraceptives are powerful and effective drugs which can cause side effects in some users and should not be used at all by some women," and that "[t]he most serious known side effect is abnormal blood clotting which can be fatal." . . . The warning also referred MacDonald to a booklet which she obtained from her gynecologist, and which was distributed by Ortho pursuant to FDA requirements. The booklet contained detailed information about the contraceptive pill, including the increased risk to pill users that vital organs such as the brain may be damaged by abnormal blood clotting. . . . The word "stroke" did not appear on the dispenser warning or in the booklet.

MacDonald's prescription for Ortho-Novum pills was renewed at subsequent annual visits to her gynecologist. The prescription was filled annually. On July 24, 1976, after approximately three years of using the pills, MacDonald suffered an occlusion of a cerebral artery by a blood clot, an injury commonly referred to as a stroke. . . . The injury caused the death of approximately twenty per cent of MacDonald's brain tissue, and left her permanently disabled. She and her husband initiated an action . . . against Ortho, seeking recovery for her personal injuries and his consequential damages and loss of consortium.

MacDonald testified that, during the time she used the pills, she was unaware that the risk of abnormal blood clotting encompassed the risk of stroke, and that she would not have used the pills had she been warned that stroke is an associated risk. . . . The case was submitted to a jury on the plaintiffs' theories that Ortho was negligent in failing to warn adequately of the dangers associated with the pills and that Ortho breached its warranty of merchantability. These two theories were treated, in effect, as a single claim of failure to warn. The jury returned a special verdict, finding no negligence or breach of warranty in the manufacture of the pills. The jury also found that Ortho adequately advised the gynecologist of the risks inherent in the pills; . . . the jury found, however, that Ortho was negligent and in breach of warranty because it failed to give MacDonald sufficient warning of such dangers. The jury further found that MacDonald's injury was caused by Ortho's pills, that the inadequacy of the warnings to MacDonald was the proximate cause of her injury, and that Ortho was liable to MacDonald and her husband. . . .

After the jury verdict, the judge granted Ortho's motion for judgment notwithstanding the verdict, concluding that, because oral contraceptives are prescription drugs, a manufacturer's duty to warn the consumer is satisfied if the manufacturer gives adequate warnings to the prescribing physician, and that the manufacturer has no duty to warn the consumer directly.

The narrow issue, on appeal, is whether, as the plaintiffs contend, a manufacturer of birth control pills owes a direct duty to the consumer to warn her of the dangers inherent in the use of the pill. We conclude that such a duty exists under the law of this Commonwealth.

1. *Extent of duty to warn.* Ordinarily, "a manufacturer of a product, which the manufacturer knows or should know is dangerous by nature or is in a dangerous condition," is under a duty to give warning of those dangers to "persons who it is foreseeable will come in contact with, and consequently be endangered by, that product." *H.P. Hood & Sons* v. *Ford Motor Co.*, 370 Mass. 69, 75 (1976). The element of privity being long discarded, a manufacturer's warning to the immediate purchaser will not, as a general matter, discharge this duty. However, "there are limits to that principle." *Carter* v. *Yardley & Co.*, 319 Mass. 92, 98 (1946). Thus, "a manufacturer may be absolved from blame because of a justified reliance upon . . . a middleman." *Id.* at 99. This exception is applicable only in the limited instances in which the manufacturer's reliance on an intermediary is reasonable. . . . In such narrowly defined circumstances, the manufacturer's immunity from liability if the consumer does not receive the warning is explicable on the ground . . . that, because it is unreasonable in such circumstances to expect the manufacturer to communicate with the consumer, the manufacturer has no duty directly to warn the consumer. . . . Restatement (Second) of Torts, *supra* at § 452 comment f.

The rule in jurisdictions that have addressed the question of the extent of a manufacturer's duty to warn in cases involving prescription drugs is that the prescribing physician acts as a "learned intermediary" between the manufacturer and the patient, and "the duty of the ethical drug manufacturer is to warn the doctor, rather than the patient, [although] the manufacturer is directly liable to the patient for a breach of such duty." *McEwen* v. *Ortho Pharmaceutical Corp.*, 270 Or. 375, 386-387 (1974). Oral contraceptives, however, bear peculiar characteristics which warrant the imposition of a common law duty on the manufacturer to warn users directly of associated risks. Whereas a patient's involvement in decision making concerning use of a prescription drug necessary to treat a malady is typically minimal or nonexistent, the healthy, young consumer of oral contraceptives is usually actively involved in the decision to use "the pill," as opposed to other available birth control products, and the prescribing physician is relegated to a relatively passive role. . . .

Furthermore, the physician prescribing "the pill," as a matter of course, examines the patient once before prescribing an oral contraceptive and only annually thereafter. . . . At her annual checkup, the patient receives a renewal prescription for a full year's supply of the pill. . . . Thus, the patient may only seldom have the opportunity to explore her questions and concerns about the medication with the prescribing physician. . . .

Last, the birth control pill is specifically subject to extensive Federal regulation. The FDA has promulgated regulations designed to ensure that the choice of "the pill" as a contraceptive method is informed by comprehensible warnings of potential side effects. . . .

The oral contraceptive thus stands apart from other prescription drugs in light of the heightened participation of patients in decisions relating to use of "the pill"; the substantial risks affiliated with the product's use; the feasibility of direct warnings by the manufacturer to the user;

the limited participation of the physician (annual prescriptions); and the possibility that oral communications between physicians and consumers may be insufficient or too scanty standing alone fully to apprise consumers of the product's dangers at the time the initial selection of a contraceptive method is made as well as at subsequent points when alternative methods may be considered. We conclude that the manufacturer of oral contraceptives is not justified in relying on warnings to the medical profession to satisfy its common law duty to warn, and that the manufacturer's obligation encompasses a duty to warn the ultimate user. Thus, the manufacturer's duty is to provide to the consumer written warnings conveying reasonable notice of the nature, gravity, and likelihood of known or knowable side effects, and advising the consumer to seek fuller explanation from the prescribing physician or other doctor of any such information of concern to the consumer. . . .

2. *Adequacy of the warning.* Because we reject the judge's conclusion that Ortho had no duty to warn MacDonald, we turn to Ortho's separate argument, not reached by the judge, that the evidence was insufficient to warrant the jury's finding that Ortho's warnings to MacDonald were inadequate. Ortho contends initially that its warnings complied with FDA labeling requirements, and that those requirements preempt or define the bounds of the common law duty to warn. We disagree. The regulatory history of the FDA requirements belies any objective to cloak them with preemptive effect. In response to concerns raised by drug manufacturers that warnings required and drafted by the FDA might be deemed inadequate by juries, the FDA commissioner specifically noted that the boundaries of civil tort liability for failure to warn are controlled by applicable state law. . . . Although the common law duty we today recognize is to a large degree coextensive with the regulatory duties imposed by the FDA, we are persuaded that, in instances where a trier of fact could reasonably conclude that a manufacturer's compliance with FDA labeling requirements or guidelines did not adequately apprise oral contraceptive users of inherent risks, the manufacturer should not be shielded from liability by such compliance. . . . We therefore concur with the plaintiffs' argument that even if the conclusion that Ortho complied with FDA requirements were inescapable, an issue we need not decide, the jury nonetheless could have found that the lack of a reference to "stroke" breached Ortho's common law duty to warn.

The common law duty to warn, like the analogous FDA "lay language" requirement, necessitates a warning "comprehensible to the average user and . . . convey[ing] a fair indication of the nature and extent of the danger to the mind of a reasonably prudent person." *Ortho Pharmaceutical Corp.* v. *Chapman*, 180 Ind. App. 33, 49 (1979), quoting *Spruill* v. *Boyle-Midway, Inc.*, 308 F.2d 79, 85 (4th Cir. 1962). Whether a particular warning measures up to this standard is almost always an issue to be resolved by a jury; few questions are "more appropriately left to a common sense lay judgment than that of whether a written warning gets its message across to an average person." *Ferebee* v. *Chevron Chem. Co.*, 552 F. Supp. 1293, 1304 (D.D.C. 1982). . . . A court may, as a matter of law, determine "whether the defendant has conformed to that standard, in any case in which the jury may not reasonably come to a different conclusion,"

Restatement (Second) of Torts § 328B (d) and comment g (1965), but judicial intrusion into jury decision making in negligence cases is exceedingly rare. . . .

Ortho argues that reasonable minds could not differ as to whether MacDonald was adequately informed of the risk of the injury she sustained by Ortho's warning that the oral contraceptives could cause "abnormal blood clotting which can be fatal" and further warning of the incremental likelihood of hospitalization or death due to blood clotting in "vital organs, such as the brain." We disagree. . . . We cannot say that this jury's decision that the warning was inadequate is so unreasonable as to require the opposite conclusion as a matter of law. . . . The jury may well have concluded, in light of their common experience and MacDonald's testimony, that the absence of a reference to "stroke" in the warning unduly minimized the warning's impact or failed to make the nature of the risk reasonably comprehensible to the average consumer. Similarly, the jury may have concluded that there are fates worse than death, such as the permanent disablement suffered by MacDonald, and that the mention of the risk of death did not, therefore, suffice to apprise an average consumer of the material risks of oral contraceptive use. . . .

We reverse the judgment, which the judge ordered notwithstanding the verdict, and remand the case . . . for the entry of judgment for the plaintiffs.

So ordered. . . .

NOTES AND QUESTIONS

1 *Causation.* How did the MacDonalds make out a *prima facie* case that a defect in the product caused plaintiff's injury? In *Ayers v. Johnson & Johnson,* a fifteen-month old infant took baby oil from a container in his teenage sister's purse and aspirated it when his mother shouted, startling the infant. The baby had trouble breathing and suffered cardiac arrest during treatment, resulting in brain damage. The baby oil included no warning about the hazard of aspiration. An important causation issue in the case was whether plaintiff proved by a preponderance of the evidence that things would have been different if the product had included an aspiration warning. Would plaintiffs like the *Ayers* family have been likely to change their behavior in response to a warning on a baby oil container that the oil is dangerous if aspirated? If so, how? Is it likely that the *Ayers* plaintiffs were unaware that baby oil could be very dangerous in the lungs? Note that whether the judge believes that plaintiffs likely would have behaved differently is not the question – the question is whether there was sufficient evidence from which a jury could reasonably conclude that a warning would have changed things. Plaintiffs' testimony in *Ayers* supported the jury's finding that plaintiffs would have heeded a warning if given, and a majority of the court found this evidence to be sufficient.

2 *Heeding presumption.* Many courts have held that plaintiffs are entitled to the presumption that they would have heeded a warning if given. How would a defendant go about rebutting such a presumption?

3 *Information overload.* Notice that in the warnings context sometimes less can be more. A warning may be found sufficient even though it left out some information if the information was left out to to avoid the problem of information overload. Conversely, a warning may be inadequate because of information overload.

4 Sometimes a danger should be designed against, if possible, instead of warned against. Under the comments to section 402A, the manufacturer was entitled to assume that the consumer would "read and heed" warnings and instructions so that a product's defectiveness would be considered under that assumption. The Restatement Third requires the manufacturer to design away reasonably avoidable risk instead of merely warning against it.

5   *Warning v. instruction. MacDonald* is an example of a claim that a product is defective because of inadequate
warnings. It is important to distinguish between warnings and instructions. Instructions are intended to allow
a consumer to use a product so as to avoid or minimize risks that might attend the product's use. Warnings, by
contrast, do not make use of the product any safer – they simply alert the consumer to the inherent risk of the
product so that the consumer then can make a rational choice about whether to encounter that risk. The duty to
warn is especially common with regard to drugs and toxic substances. Because of the nature of the duty to warn,
there is no duty to warn against open and obvious risks – if the risk already is obvious, then the consumer has had
the opportunity to consider that risk when deciding whether to use the product. But there may well be a duty to
instruct concerning an obvious risk if instructions can help to mitigate the inherent risk.

VASSALLO V. BAXTER HEALTHCARE CORP.
696 N.E.2D 909 (MASS. 1998)

. . . Florence Vassallo claimed that the defendants . . . were liable to her for damages because silicone breast implants, . . . which had been implanted in her, were . . . accompanied by negligent
product warnings, . . . with the consequence that she was injured. . . . We conclude . . . that we
should change our products liability law to conform to the clear majority rule regarding what
has to be shown to recover in a . . . claim for failure to warn of risks associated with a product
. . . .

In February, 1977, at the age of forty-eight, Mrs. Vassallo underwent breast implantation
surgery. The silicone gel breast implants that Mrs. Vassallo received were manufactured . . . in
October, 1976. . . . In 1992, Mrs. Vassallo underwent a mammogram after complaining of chest
pains that extended up under her left armpit. The mammogram revealed that her breast implants
might have ruptured. The silicone gel implants were subsequently removed in April, 1993, and
were replaced with saline implants. During the course of the explant surgery, the surgeon noted
severe, permanent scarring of Mrs. Vassallo's pectoral muscles which she attributed to the silicone gel. The implants themselves were encapsulated in scar tissue with multiple nodules of
silicone granulomas. Dissection of the scar tissue capsules revealed that the left implant had
ruptured, releasing free silicone gel, while the right implant was intact, but had several pinholes
through which silicone gel could escape.

The plaintiff's pathology expert, Dr. Douglas Shanklin, indicated that, based on the cellu-
lar responses shown in the pathology slides of Mrs. Vassallo's breast tissue taken at the time
of explant, the rupture had been longstanding, perhaps for several years. According to Dr.
Shanklin, Mrs. Vassallo's pathology slides showed silicone granulomas, giant cells, lympho-
cytes, and macrophages, all of which indicated a chronic immunological and inflammatory reaction to the silicone implants. Dr. Shanklin also identified deposits of silica and lymphocytic
vasculitis, which, he testified, were evidence that Mrs. Vassallo suffered from an autoimmune
disease caused by the silicone gel.

Doctor Christopher Batich, professor of materials science and engineering at the University
of Florida, testified for the plaintiffs on the effects of silicone in the body. He discussed animal
studies that demonstrated migration of silicone to various organs both from ruptured gel

implants and after intramuscular injection of "radio-labeled" liquid silicone. Doctor Batich also . . . explained that the use of silicone gel in breast implants was unreasonably dangerous "because the material can get out of the implant, it can break up into small particles, it can travel through the body, and it can undergo chemical transformation into things that have biochemical effects."

Doctor Bruce Freundlich, chief of rheumatology at Graduate Hospital in Philadelphia and an associate professor of medicine at the University of Pennsylvania, indicated that silicone gel breast implants can cause atypical connective tissue disease with a variety of symptoms that can include joint pain, dry eyes and mouth, difficulty sleeping leading to chronic fatigue, breast pain, fever, reduced sensation in the hands and feet, hair loss, itching, problems swallowing, and heartburn. Doctor Freundlich also offered his opinion that Mrs. Vassallo was suffering from atypical autoimmune disease, based on a review of her medical records and a physical examination that revealed the following symptoms: "tobacco pouch mouth," or a tightening of the face around the mouth which has been associated with scleroderma or mixed connective tissue disease; puffy fingers; an ulceration on one finger; thickening of the skin on her face and neck; telangiectasia, or small red blood vessels, of the nose; hyperreflexia; nocturnal myophonic jerking; dry eyes; elevated levels of antinuclear antibodies and IGA immunoglobin antibodies . . . ; numbness and tingling in her hands; chronic fatigue; hair loss; difficulty swallowing; and problems with memory loss. According to Dr. Freundlich, Mrs. Vassallo's problems were related to her exposure to silicone gel, and her future was "guarded."

Doctor Eric Gershwin, chief of the division of rheumatology, immunology and allergy at the University of California at Davis School of Medicine, discussed his own clinical research, and internal Dow Corning studies, to support his conclusion that silicone gel acts as an adjuvant to stimulate the body's immune system. . . . Based on his research and treatment of more than 700 women with silicone gel breast implants, Dr. Gershwin stated that there is a unique constellation of symptoms seen in approximately five per cent of women with silicone breast implants, and that these symptoms, taken together, constitute an atypical autoimmune disease. Doctor Gershwin also reviewed Mrs. Vassallo's medical records and concluded that her symptoms were consistent with this atypical autoimmune disease and were caused by her ruptured silicone gel breast implant.

There was also extensive testimony as to knowledge, attributable to the defendants, of the risks of silicone gel breast implants up to the time of Mrs. Vassallo's implant surgery in 1977. According to [the manufacturer's] own internal correspondence, the company was aware of a "Talk Paper," issued by the United States Food and Drug Administration in 1976, that documented migration to the brain, lungs, and heart, and death following injections of liquid silicone into the human body. In 1976, [the manufacturer] received a report of an animal study, partially funded by [the manufacturer] and conducted using miniature silicone gel implants supplied by [the manufacturer], that documented migration of gel from ruptured implants to the surrounding connective tissues and local inflammatory responses with fibroblastic activity and giant cell formation. The authors of the study stated: "The present tendency by manufacturers of breast implants towards ever thinner envelopes and a filler that is getting further away from gel and closer to silicone liquid must be looked at in the light of these experimental findings, and the question must be asked whether the possible advantages of these changes outweigh the disadvantages." [The manufacturer] was also aware that some of their implants were rupturing, having received 129 complaints of ruptured gel implants in 1976. In fact, the president of [the manufacturer] had written in 1975 that "presently, mammary implants have been designed to be increasingly fragile in response to plastic surgeons' demand for softness, realistic feel and mobility." As a result, [the manufacturer] knew that its implants were "not consistent as far as durability or destructibility is concerned." The encapsulation of the implant, and the viscous nature of the silicone gel, made it difficult to detect that a rupture had occurred, allowing the silicone to leak into the body for long periods before explantation. By 1975, [the manufacturer] also knew that, even without a rupture of the implant shell, the silicone gel could leak (known as "gel bleed") through to the exterior surface of the implant and possibly produce "detrimental effect[s]" in the body.

Despite this knowledge of the possible adverse long-term consequences of leaking silicone in the body, [the manufacturer] conducted few animal, and no clinical, studies to document the safety and efficacy of its silicone gel implants. When [the manufacturer] began using silicone gel manufactured by Dow Corning in 1976, they relied primarily on the animal testing conducted by Dow Corning, despite the observations of a [the manufacturer] scientist that "the data . . . [did] not answer questions concerning migration," and "was lacking in quality and left many questions unanswered." [the manufacturer] did conduct toxicity testing on the Dow Corning gel; the gel passed the seven-day and thirty-day toxicity tests, but failed the ninety-day toxicity test based on the microscopic tissue evaluation that showed considerably greater fibrous tissue reaction and inflammation to the silicone gel than to the control material. There is no indication in the record that [the manufacturer] ever repeated this ninety-day toxicity test, and the company continued to use the Dow Corning gel in the manufacture of their silicone gel breast implants.

[The manufacturer] did furnish warnings to physicians concerning their silicone gel implants in a product insert data sheet (PIDS). The 1976 version of the PIDS that accompanied Mrs. Vassallo's implants included warnings that the implant shell could be easily cut or ruptured by excessive stresses, and that [the manufacturer] could not guarantee gel containment in the case of a rupture. The warnings did not address the issue of gel bleed, the fact that a rupture could result from normal stresses and could persist undetected for a significant time period, or the consequences of gel migration in the body. The PIDS also contained a list of potential complications associated with breast implants, but this list did not address the risks of chronic inflammation, permanent tissue scarring, or possible effects on the immune system. Proposed revisions to the PIDS, which would have included "a warning to the effect that uncontained silicone gel may have untoward consequences," and complications of "migration of the silicone, with mild to severe consequences, including reduction of breast size and absorption of the silicone by the blood and lymph systems, resulting in damage to the liver and kidneys," were rejected by [the manufacturer]'s president in March, 1976. The president did issue a letter to doctors dated August 23, 1976, which stated that "if a shell is torn[] with time and normal stresses the gel will migrate," and that "mild inflammation and polynuclear giant cell response characterized as mild foreign body reaction" had been associated with the silicone gel implants. Once again, this letter did not completely address the potential effects of silicone migration on the body's immune system. Mrs. Vassallo stated that, if she had known that the implants could cause permanent scarring, chronic inflammation, and problems with her immune system, she would not have gone ahead with the implantation procedure. We now turn to the issues appropriate for discussion. . . .

Our current law, regarding the duty to warn . . . presumes that a manufacturer was fully informed of all risks associated with the product at issue, regardless of the state of the art at the time of the sale, and amounts to strict liability for failure to warn of these risks. . . . This rule has been justified by the public policy that a defective product, "unreasonably dangerous due to lack of adequate warning[s], [is] not fit for the ordinary purposes for which [it is] used regardless of the absence of fault on [a defendant's] part." *Id.*

At trial, the defendants requested a jury instruction that a manufacturer need only warn of risks "known or reasonably knowable in light of the generally accepted scientific knowledge available at the time of the manufacture and distribution of the device." The judge declined this request, and instead gave an instruction using language taken almost verbatim from that in *Hayes, supra.* While the judge's instruction was a correct statement of our law, we recognize that we are among a distinct minority of States that applies a hindsight analysis to the duty to warn. . . .

The majority of States, either by case law or by statute, follow the principle expressed in Restatement (Second) of Torts §402A comment j (1965), which states that "the seller is required to give warning against [a danger], if he has knowledge, or by the application of reasonable, developed human skill and foresight should have knowledge, of the . . . danger." . . . Restatement (Third) of Torts: Products Liability, Reporters' Note to comment m, at 104 (1998) ("An overwhelming majority of jurisdictions supports the proposition that a manufacturer has a duty to warn only of risks that were known or should have been known to a reasonable person"). At least three jurisdictions that previously applied strict liability to the duty to warn in a products liability claim have reversed themselves, either by statute or by decision, and now require knowledge, or reasonable knowability as a component of such a claim. . . .

The thin judicial support for a hindsight approach to the duty to warn is easily explained. The goal of the law is to induce conduct that is capable of being performed. This goal is not advanced by imposing liability for failure to warn of risks that were not capable of being known. . . .

The Restatement (Third) of Torts: Products Liability §2 (c) (1998), recently approved by the American Law Institute, reaffirms the principle expressed in Restatement (Second) of Torts, *supra* at §402A comment j, by stating that a product "is defective because of inadequate instructions or warnings when the foreseeable risks of harm posed by the product could have been reduced or avoided by the provision of reasonable instructions or warnings . . . and the omission of the instructions or warnings renders the product not reasonably safe." The rationale behind the principle is explained by stating that "unforeseeable risks arising from foreseeable product use . . . by definition cannot specifically be warned against." Restatement (Third) of Torts: Products Liability, *supra* at §2 comment m, at 34. However, comment m also clarifies the manufacturer's duty "to perform reasonable testing prior to marketing a product and to discover risks and risk-avoidance measures that such testing would reveal. A seller is charged with knowledge of what reasonable testing would reveal." *Id.* . . .

We have stated that liability under the implied warranty of merchantability in Massachusetts is "congruent in nearly all respects with the principles expressed in Restatement (Second) of Torts § 402A." *Commonwealth v. Johnson Insulation*, 425 Mass. 650, 653-654, 682 N.E.2d 1323 (1997), quoting *Back v. Wickes Corp.*, 375 Mass. 633, 640, 378 N.E.2d 964 (1978). The main difference has been our application of a hindsight approach to the duty to warn of (and to provide adequate instructions regarding) risks associated with a product. . . . In recognition of the clear judicial trend regarding the duty to warn in products liability cases, and the principles stated in Restatement (Third) of Torts: Products Liability, *supra* at §2 (c) and comment m, we hereby revise our law to state that a defendant will not be held liable . . . for failure to warn or provide instructions about risks that were not reasonably foreseeable at the time of sale or could not have been discovered by way of reasonable testing prior to marketing the product. A manufacturer will be held to the standard of knowledge of an expert in the appropriate field, and will remain subject to a continuing duty to warn (at least purchasers) of risks discovered following the sale of the product at issue. . . .

4. DAMAGES

For the most part, compensatory damages analysis in a strict liability case is essentially similar to damages issues that arise in an ordinary negligence action. However, when the theory of recovery is breach of warranty, contract limitations on damages come into play, including the economic loss doctrine. Also, punitive damages ordinarily will not be recoverable in a products liability case without a showing of defendant's fault.

5. PLAINTIFF'S CONDUCT

Consider the following hypothetical scenario: Jeb and his son Jethro are out in the woods "shootin' at some food." Jeb draws a bead on a fat juicy possum, but as he squeezes the trigger, the barrel on his gun explodes, and Jeb and Jethro are struck by flying shrapnel. The expert metallurgist hired by Jeb's lawyer determines that the barrel exploded due to an unusual impurity in the metal of the barrel that compromised its strength. Is this a case of strict liability against gun manufacturer? Would it make any difference to the outcome of Jeb's suit if the defect in the barrel were quite noticeable, but Jeb never bothered to inspect his weapon? Would Jeb's failure to inspect be a defense under Restatement (Second) Section 402A?

What if Jeb notices the defect about the same time that he spots the possum and knows that there is a good chance that the barrel will explode, but he is so hungry that he blasts away anyway? Does the gun manufacturer have a defense now, if the gun barrel explodes?

Now assume that Jeb draws down on a fat juicy ground hog, not knowing that Jethro is in the line of fire behind a bush answering nature's call. When Jethro is struck by Jeb's bullet, Jethro's lawyer sues the gun manufacturer arguing that the product is unreasonably dangerous because it can propel a lead slug at speeds sufficient to penetrate flesh and bone. Is this a case of strict products liability?

[As a post script, Jeb won his products liability suit and was awarded $1,000,000 in compensatory damages and $10,000,000 in punitive damages by a West Virginia jury. In post-trial interviews, individual jurors said that they thought the punitive damages were warranted because the gun manufacturer's failure violated the sacred relationship between a man and his gun.]

DALY V. GENERAL MOTORS CORP.
575 P.2D 1162 (CAL. 1978)

The most important of several problems which we consider is whether the principles of comparative negligence expressed by us in *Li v. Yellow Cab Co.* (1975) . . . apply to actions founded on strict products liability. We will conclude that they do. . . .

The Facts And The Trial

Although there were no eyewitnesses, the parties agree, generally, on the reconstruction of the accident in question. In the early hours of October 31, 1970, decedent Kirk Daly, a 36-year-old attorney, was driving his Opel southbound on the Harbor Freeway . . . . The vehicle, while travelling at a speed of 50-70 miles per hour, collided with and damaged 50 feet of metal divider fence. After the initial impact between the left side of the vehicle and the fence the Opel spun counterclockwise, the driver's door was thrown open, and Daly was forcibly ejected from the car and sustained fatal head injuries. It was equally undisputed that had the deceased remained in the Opel his injuries, in all probability, would have been relatively minor.

Plaintiffs, who are decedent's widow and three surviving minor children, sued General Motors Corporation, Boulevard Buick, Underwriter's Auto Leasing, and Alco Leasing Company, the successive links in the Opel's manufacturing and distribution chain. The sole theory of plaintiffs' complaint was strict liability for damages allegedly caused by a defective product, namely, an improperly designed door latch claimed to have been activated by the impact. It was further asserted that, but for the faulty latch, decedent would have been restrained in the vehicle and, although perhaps injured, would not have been killed. Thus, the case involves a so-called "second collision" in which the "defect" did not contribute to the original impact, but only to the "enhancement" of injury. . . .

Over plaintiffs' objections, defendants were permitted to introduce evidence indicating that: (1) the Opel was equipped with a seat belt-shoulder harness system, and a door lock, either of which if used, it was contended, would have prevented Daly's ejection from the vehicle; (2) Daly used neither the harness system nor the lock; (3) the 1970 Opel owner's manual contained warnings that seat belts should be worn and doors locked when the car was in motion for "accident security"; and (4) Daly was intoxicated at the time of collision, which evidence the jury was advised was admitted for the limited purpose of determining whether decedent had used the vehicle's safety equipment. After relatively brief deliberations the jury returned a verdict favoring all defendants, and plaintiffs appeal from the ensuing adverse judgment.

Strict Products Liability And Comparative Fault

In response to plaintiffs' assertion that the "intoxication-nonuse" evidence was improperly admitted, defendants contend that the deceased's own conduct contributed to his death. Because plaintiffs' case rests upon strict products liability based on improper design of the door latch and because defendants assert a failure in decedent's conduct, namely, his alleged intoxication and nonuse of safety equipment, without which the accident and ensuing death would not have occurred, there is thereby posed the overriding issue in the case, should comparative principles apply in strict products liability actions?

It may be useful to refer briefly to certain highlights in the historical development of the two principles – strict and comparative liability. Tort law has evolved from a legal obligation initially imposed without "fault," to recovery which, generally, was based on blameworthiness in a moral sense. For reasons of social policy and because of the unusual nature of defendants' acts, liability without fault continued to be prescribed in a certain restricted area, for example, upon keepers of wild animals, or those who handled explosives or other dangerous substances, or who engaged in ultrahazardous activities. Simultaneously, and more particularly, those who were injured in the use of personal property were permitted recovery on a contract theory if they were the purchasers of the chattel or were in privity. Subsequently, liability was imposed in negligence upon the manufacturer of personalty in favor of the general consumer. . . . Evolving social policies designed to protect the ultimate consumer soon prompted the extension of legal responsibility beyond negligence to express or implied warranty. . . .

General dissatisfaction continued with the conceptual limitations which traditional tort and contract doctrines placed upon the consumers and users of manufactured products, this at a time when mass production of an almost infinite variety of goods and products was responding to a myriad of ever-changing societal demands stimulated by wide-spread commercial advertising. From an historic combination of economic and sociological forces was born the doctrine of strict liability in tort.

We, ourselves, were perhaps the first court to give the new principle judicial sanction. In *Greenman* v. *Yuba Power Products, Inc.* (1963) . . . , confronted with injury to an ultimate consumer caused by a defective power tool, we fastened strict liability on a manufacturer who placed on the market a defective product even though both privity and notice of breach of warranty were lacking. We rejected both contract and warranty theories, express or implied, as the basis for liability. Strict liability, we said, did not rest on a consensual foundation but, rather, on one created by law. The liability was created judicially because of the economic and social need for the protection of consumers in an increasingly complex and mechanized society, and because of the limitations in the negligence and warranty remedies. . . . Subsequently, the *Greenman* principle was incorporated in section 402A of the Restatement Second of Torts, and adopted by a majority of American jurisdictions. . . .

From its inception, however, strict liability has never been, and is not now, *absolute* liability. As has been repeatedly expressed, under strict liability the manufacturer does not thereby become the insurer of the safety of the product's user. . . . On the contrary, the plaintiff's injury must have been caused by a "defect" in the product. Thus the manufacturer is not deemed responsible when injury results from an unforeseeable use of its product. . . . Furthermore, we have recognized that though most forms of contributory negligence do not constitute a defense to a strict products liability action, plaintiff's negligence is a complete defense when it comprises assumption of risk. . . . As will thus be seen, the concept of strict products liability was created and shaped judicially. In its evolution, the doctrinal encumbrances of contract and warranty, and the traditional elements of negligence, were stripped from the remedy, and a new tort emerged which extended liability for defective product design and manufacture beyond negligence but short of absolute liability.

In *Li* v. *Yellow Cab Co., supra,* . . . we introduced the other doctrine with which we are concerned, comparative negligence. We examined the history of contributory negligence, the massive criticism directed at it because its presence in the slightest degree completely barred plaintiff's recovery, and the increasing defection from the doctrine. . . . Concluding that none of the obstacles was insurmountable, we announced in *Li* the adoption of a "pure" form of comparative negligence which, when present, reduced but did not prevent plaintiff's recovery. . . . We held that the defense of assumption of risk, insofar as it is no more than a variant of contributory negligence, was merged into the assessment of liability in proportion to fault. . . .

We stand now at the point of confluence of these two conceptual streams . . . . Those counseling against the recognition of comparative fault principles in strict products liability cases vigorously stress, perhaps equally, not only the conceptual, but also the semantic difficulties incident to such a course. The task of merging the two concepts is said to be impossible, that "apples and oranges" cannot be compared, that "oil and water" do not mix, and that strict liability, which is not founded on negligence or fault, is inhospitable to comparative principles. The syllogism runs, contributory negligence was only a defense to negligence, comparative negligence only affects contributory negligence, therefore comparative negligence cannot be a defense to strict liability. . . . While fully recognizing the theoretical and semantic distinctions between the twin principles of strict products liability and traditional negligence, we think they can be blended or accommodated. . . .

Furthermore, the "apples and oranges" argument may be conceptually suspect. It has been suggested that the term "contributory negligence," one of the vital building blocks upon which much of the argument is based, may indeed itself be a misnomer since it lacks the first element of the classical negligence formula, namely, a duty of care owing to another. . . .

We pause at this point to observe that where, as here, a consumer or user sues the manufacturer or designer alone, technically, neither fault nor conduct is really compared functionally. The conduct of one party in combination with the product of another, or perhaps the placing of a defective article in the stream of projected and anticipated use, may produce the ultimate injury. In such a case, as in the situation before us, we think the term "equitable apportionment or allocation of loss" may be more descriptive than "comparative fault."

Given all of the foregoing, we are, in the wake of *Li*, disinclined to resolve the important issue before us by the simple expedient of matching linguistic labels which have evolved either for convenience or by custom. Rather, we consider it more useful to examine the foundational reasons underlying the creation of strict products liability in California to ascertain whether the purposes of the doctrine would be defeated or diluted by adoption of comparative principles. We imposed strict liability against the manufacturer and in favor of the user or consumer in order to relieve injured consumers "from problems of proof inherent in pursuing negligence [and warranty] remedies. . . ." [A]s we have noted, we sought to place the burden of loss on manufacturers rather than ". . . injured persons *who are powerless to protect themselves . . . .*"

The foregoing goals, we think, will not be frustrated by the adoption of comparative principles. Plaintiffs will continue to be relieved of proving that the manufacturer or distributor was negligent in the production, design, or dissemination of the article in question. Defendant's liability for injuries caused by a defective product remains strict. The principle of protecting the defenseless is likewise preserved, for plaintiff's recovery will be reduced *only* to the extent that his own lack of reasonable care contributed to his injury. The cost of compensating the victim of a defective product, albeit proportionately reduced, remains on defendant manufacturer, and will, through him, be "spread among society." However, we do not permit plaintiff's own conduct relative to the product to escape unexamined, and as to that share of plaintiff's damages which flows from his own fault we discern no reason of policy why it should, following *Li*, be borne by others. Such a result would directly contravene the principle announced in *Li*, that loss should be assessed equitably in proportion to fault.

We conclude, accordingly, that the expressed purposes which persuaded us in the first instance to adopt strict liability in California would not be thwarted were we to apply comparative principles. What would be forfeit is a degree of semantic symmetry. However, in this evolving area of tort law in which new remedies are judicially created, and old defenses judicially merged, impelled by strong considerations of equity and fairness we seek a larger synthesis. If a more just result follows from the expansion of comparative principles, we have no hesitancy in seeking it, mindful always that the fundamental and underlying purpose of *Li* was to promote the equitable allocation of loss among all parties legally responsible in proportion to their fault.

A second objection to the application of comparative principles in strict products liability cases is that a manufacturer's incentive to produce safe products will thereby be reduced or removed. While we fully recognize this concern we think, for several reasons, that the problem is more shadow than substance. First, of course, the manufacturer cannot avoid its continuing liability for a defective product even when the plaintiff's own conduct has contributed to his injury. The manufacturer's liability, and therefore its incentive to avoid and correct product defects, remains; its exposure will be lessened only to the extent that the trier finds that the victim's conduct contributed to his injury. Second, as a practical matter a manufacturer, in a particular case, cannot assume that the user of a defective product upon whom an injury is visited will be blameworthy. Doubtless, many users are free of fault, and a defect is at least as likely as not to be exposed by an entirely innocent plaintiff who will obtain full recovery. In such cases the manufacturer's incentive toward safety both in design and production is wholly unaffected. Finally, we must observe that under the present law, which recognizes assumption of risk as a complete defense to products liability, the curious and cynical message is that it profits the manufacturer to make his product so defective that in the event of injury he can argue that the user had to be aware of its patent defects. To that extent the incentives are inverted. We conclude, accordingly, that no substantial or significant impairment of the safety incentives of defendants will occur by the adoption of comparative principles.

In passing, we note one important and felicitious result if we apply comparative principles to strict products liability. This arises from the fact that under present law when plaintiff sues in negligence his own contributory negligence, however denominated, may diminish but cannot wholly defeat his recovery. When he sues in strict products liability, however, his "assumption of risk" *completely bars* his recovery. Under *Li*, as we have noted, "assumption of risk" is merged into comparative principles. . . . The consequence is that after *Li* in a negligence action, plaintiff's conduct which amounts to "negligent" assumption of risk no longer defeats plaintiff's recovery. Identical conduct, however, in a strict liability case acts as a complete bar under rules heretofore applicable. Thus, strict products liability, which was developed to free injured consumers from the constraints imposed by traditional negligence and warranty theories, places a consumer plaintiff in a worse position than would be the case were his claim founded on simple negligence. This, in turn, rewards adroit pleading and selection of theories. The application of comparative principles to strict liability obviates this bizarre anomaly by treating alike the defenses to both negligence and strict products liability actions. In each instance the defense, if established, will reduce but not bar plaintiff's claim.

A third objection to the merger of strict liability and comparative fault focuses on the claim that, as a practical matter, triers of fact, particularly jurors, cannot assess, measure, or compare plaintiff's negligence with defendant's strict liability. We are unpersuaded by the argument and are convinced that jurors are able to undertake a fair apportionment of liability. . . .

We note that the majority of our sister states which have addressed the problem, either by statute or judicial decree, have extended comparative principles to strict products liability. . . .

Moreover, we are further encouraged in our decision herein by noting that the apparent majority of scholarly commentators has urged adoption of the rule which we announce herein. . . .

Having examined the principal objections and finding them not insurmountable, and persuaded by logic, justice, and fundamental fairness, we conclude that a system of comparative fault should be and it is hereby extended to actions founded on strict products liability. In such cases the separate defense of "assumption of risk," to the extent that it is a form of contributory negligence, is abolished. While, as we have suggested, on the particular facts before us, the term "equitable apportionment of loss" is more accurately descriptive of the process, nonetheless, the term "comparative fault" has gained such wide acceptance by courts and in the literature that we adopt its use herein.

In *Li*, we announced a system of pure comparative negligence "the fundamental purpose of which shall be to assign responsibility and liability for damage in direct proportion to the amount of negligence of each of the parties." (13 Cal.3d, at p. 829.) Those same underlying considerations of policy which moved us judicially in *Li* to rescue blameworthy plaintiffs from a 100-year-old sanction against *all* recovery persuade us now to extend similar principles to the strict products liability area. Legal responsibility is thereby shared. We think that apportioning tort liability is sound, logical and capable of wider application than to negligence cases alone. . . . We reiterate that our reason for extending a full system of comparative fault to strict products liability is because it is fair to do so. The law consistently seeks to elevate justice and equity above the exact contours of a mathematical equation. We are convinced that in merging the two principles what may be lost in symmetry is more than gained in fundamental fairness. . . .

For the guidance of trial courts, we . . . note the existence . . . of a form of special verdict tailored to cases applying the maritime doctrine of strict liability for unseaworthiness . . . . Under this form, the jury is first required to answer "yes" or "no" to a series of questions setting forth possible bases for a finding that vessel unseaworthiness was a proximate cause of the plaintiff's injuries. If the jury indicates that unseaworthiness was a contributing cause, it then moves on to a second group of similar questions seeking to determine whether, and in what particulars, the plaintiff's own negligence was also a contributing factor. If the answers to these questions establish a finding of contributory negligence, the jury is told to "state in percentage the extent to which the plaintiff's own negligence contributed to his injuries. (%)." Finally, the jury is instructed to indicate the amount of plaintiff's damages *without reference* to his own negligence. The *court* then reduces the damage award by the percentage figure the jury has supplied. . . . We cite this form as illustrative of one technique by which the court and jury may approach the task of apportionment. . . .

Conclusion

It is readily apparent that the foregoing broad expressions of principle do not establish the duties of the jury with that fixed precision which appeals to minds trained in law and logic. . . . By extending and tailoring the comparative principles announced in *Li, supra,* to the doctrine of strict products liability, we believe that we move closer to the goal of the equitable allocation of legal responsibility for personal injuries. . . . In making liability more commensurate with fault we undermine neither the theories nor the policies of the strict liability rule. In *Li* we took "a first step in what we deem to be a proper and just direction . . ." (13 Cal.3d at p. 826.) We are convinced that the principles herein announced constitute the next appropriate and logical step in the same direction.

The judgment is reversed.

1   Product Misuse. Consider the following hypothetical scenario: Mr. Misuse experiences an interruption in his natural gas service, but his electricity service still is available. To heat some water for household use, Mr. Misuse fills his bathtub with water, plugs in his "Mr. Coffee," and immerses it in the tub, suffering an electric shock. Is the manufacturer of the coffee maker strictly liable under 402A? Why or why not? Would it make any difference if Mr. Misuse could prove that the thermal fuse in the coffee maker was defective so that the product carried an unreasonable risk of overheating and fire when used in a foreseeable manner? Would it affect the liability calculus if Mr. Misuse had carefully read the instructions and knew that immersing his coffee maker in water created a risk of electric shock, but did it anyway? Changing the scenario a bit, what if Mr. Misuse knew that it was not recommended to leave the coffee maker plugged in, turned on, and unattended, but, while using the coffeemaker to make coffee, he ran outside when he heard his neighbor screaming "Help" "Help"? Assume that he paused for a split second before running to his neighbor's aid and thought about turning off the coffee maker but decided not to take time the time to turn it off? What if Mr. Misuse left the coffee maker plugged in, turned on, and unattended for an entire week while he was on vacation and it overheated and caught fire? What if Mr. Misuse failed to notice a slight crack in the carafe that an ordinarily prudent consumer would have noticed and was cut by flying glass when the carafe suddenly shattered?

LEWIS V. BRUNSWICK CORP.
107 F.3D 1494 (11TH CIR. 1997)

Gary and Vicky Lewis appeal the district court's grant of summary judgment in favor of Brunswick Corporation ("Brunswick") on the Lewises' state common law negligence, product liability, and fraudulent misrepresentation claims. The Lewises sued Brunswick to recover damages for the death of their daughter, who died after she fell or was thrown from a boat and then struck by a Brunswick engine propeller. According to the Lewises, the Brunswick engine involved in their daughter's death was defective because it lacked a propeller guard. Upon Brunswick's motion for summary judgment, the district court held that the Lewises' claims were preempted by the Federal Boat Safety Act, 46 U.S.C. §§ 4301-4311 ("the FBSA" or "the Act"). We affirm. . . .

I. FACTS AND PROCEDURAL HISTORY

On June 6, 1993, Kathryn Lewis was spending the day with her boyfriend's family in a boat on Strom Thurmond Lake in Georgia. While the boat was pulling Kathryn's boyfriend on an inner tube, the driver made a right-hand turn. Kathryn fell or was thrown from the left side of the boat. Once in the water, Kathryn was struck repeatedly in the head and body by the propeller of an engine designed and manufactured by Brunswick. The engine did not have a propeller guard. Kathryn died instantly.

The Lewises filed suit against Brunswick in Georgia state court, alleging that the lack of a propeller guard made the Brunswick engine a defective product. They also claim that Brunswick committed negligence by failing to install a propeller guard on the engine. . . .

Brunswick removed this case to federal district court on diversity grounds and moved for summary judgment. In its summary judgment motion, Brunswick contended that all of the Lewises' claims were preempted by the FBSA. The district court agreed and granted summary judgment in favor of Brunswick. The Lewises appeal. . . .

III. THE FEDERAL BOAT SAFETY ACT

The FBSA was enacted in 1971 in part "to improve boating safety by requiring manufacturers to provide safer boats and boating equipment to the public through compliance with safety standards to be promulgated by the Secretary of the Department in which the Coast Guard is operating--presently the Secretary of Transportation." *P.L. 92-75, Federal Boat Safety Act of 1971,* S.Rep. No. 92-248, *reprinted in* 1971 U.S.C.C.A.N. 1333. To implement that goal, the Act grants authority to the Secretary of Transportation to prescribe regulations establishing minimum safety standards for recreational boats. *See* 46 U.S.C. § 4302 (West Supp.1995). The Secretary of Transportation has delegated rulemaking authority under the FBSA to the United States Coast Guard. . . .

The FBSA requires the Coast Guard to follow certain guidelines and procedures when promulgating a regulation under 46 U.S.C. §4302. . . .

IV. COAST GUARD CONSIDERATION OF A PROPELLER GUARD REGULATION

In 1988, the Coast Guard directed the Advisory Council to examine the feasibility and potential safety advantages and safety disadvantages of propeller guards. In response, the Advisory Council appointed a Propeller Guard Subcommittee "to consider, review and assess available data concerning the nature and incidence of recreational boating accidents in which persons in the water are struck by propellers." National Boating Safety Advisory Council, Report of the Propeller Guard Subcommittee 1 (1989). The Advisory Council also asked the Subcommittee to consider whether "the Coast Guard [should] move towards a federal requirement for some form of propeller guard." *Id.* at Appendix A.

The Advisory Council Subcommittee held hearings on three occasions and received information from a variety of individuals and groups interested in the topic of propeller guards. . . . One of the matters on which the Subcommittee received information was propeller guard litigation, and the Subcommittee devoted a section of its report to the topic. *Id.* at 4. That section states that, at the time of the hearings, propeller guard advocates were petitioning federal and state legislators to mandate propeller guards. According to the Subcommittee Report, a legislative or administrative mandate "would necessarily be predicated on the feasibility of guards and establish prima facie manufacturer liability in having failed to provide them"; therefore, feasibility was an important question before the Subcommittee. *Id.* at 5. The report also discusses the theories of liability that were being asserted by propeller guard victims and the defenses used by manufacturers. . . . Immediately following that discussion, the report notes that "manufacturers are opposed to mandatory propeller guards." *Id.* at 5.

The Subcommittee also considered the technical issues posed by propeller guards. After reviewing the available scientific data and testimony, the Subcommittee found that propeller guards affect boat operation adversely at speeds greater than 10 miles per hour. . . . Further, the Subcommittee found that propeller guards would not increase overall safety, because they increase the chances of contact between a blunt object and a person in the water. . . . The Subcommittee Report states:

> Injuries/fatalities caused by underwater impacts result from a person coming into contact with the propeller or any part of the propulsion unit (i.e., lower unit, skeg, torpedo, anti-ventilation plate, etc.) and even the boat itself. Currently reported accidents make it obvious that all such components are involved in the total picture, and that the propeller itself is the sole factor in only a minority of impacts. The development and use of devices such as "propeller guards" can, therefore, be counter-productive and can create new hazards of equal or greater consequence.... Although the controversy which currently surrounds the issue of propeller guarding is, by its very nature, highly emotional and has attracted a great deal of publicity, there are no indications that there is a generic or universal solution currently available or foreseeable in the future. The boating public must not be misled into thinking there is a "safe" device which would eliminate or significantly reduce such injuries or fatalities.

Id. at 23-24. The report also states that:

> boats and motors should be designed to incorporate technologically feasible safety features to avoid or minimize the consequences of inexperienced or negligent operation, without at the same time (a) creating some other hazard, (b) materially interfering with normal operations, or (c) being at economic costs disproportionate to the particular risk. . . .

Id. at 20. In its conclusion, the Advisory Council Subcommittee Report recommends that "the U.S. Coast Guard should take no regulatory action to require propeller guards." *Id.* at 24.

The Subcommittee presented its report to the entire Advisory Council, which accepted the report and adopted the recommendations of the Subcommittee. . . . The Advisory Council then forwarded the report and recommendations to the Coast Guard. The Coast Guard adopted each of the Advisory Council's recommendations, giving explanations of the Coast Guard's position on each matter. *See* Letter from Robert T. Nelson, Rear Admiral, U.S. Coast Guard, Chief, Office of Navigation, Safety and Waterway Services to A. Newell Garden, Chairman, National Boating Safety Advisory Council (Feb. 1, 1990). The Coast Guard's position on propeller guards, which is set out in that letter, is as follows:

> The regulatory process is very structured and stringent regarding justification. Available propeller guard accident data do not support imposition of a regulation requiring propeller guards on motorboats. Regulatory action is also limited by the many questions about whether a universally acceptable propeller guard is available or technically feasible in all modes of boat operation.

Additionally, the question of retrofitting millions of boats would certainly be a major economic consideration

The Coast Guard will continue to collect and analyze data for changes and trends; and will promote increased/improved accident reporting . . . . The Coast Guard will also review and retain any information made available regarding development and testing of new propeller guard devices or other information on the state of the art.

Id. at 1.

V. POSITIONS OF THE PARTIES

The Lewises contend that the FBSA does not expressly or impliedly preempt state law tort claims based on the absence of a propeller guard on a boat engine. According to the Lewises, common law claims are expressly saved from preemption by the Act's savings clause. Furthermore, the Lewises argue, the Act does not preempt any state law, regulation, or claims until the Coast Guard issues a formal regulation on the matter. There being no regulation on propeller guards, the Lewises assert they may proceed with their case.

In response, Brunswick argues that the FBSA expressly preempts any state regulation, including regulation through common law claims, that conflicts with a Coast Guard regulation or regulatory position. Brunswick contends that the Coast Guard has made a regulatory decision that propeller guards cannot be required. For that reason, Brunswick says, the Lewises' claims are expressly preempted by the Act. Furthermore, even if the Lewises' claims are not expressly preempted, Brunswick argues that the claims conflict with the Coast Guard's position that propeller guards should not be required. For that reason, Brunswick contends, the claims are preempted by implication.

VI. AN OVERVIEW OF PREEMPTION DOCTRINE

Any state law that conflicts with federal law is preempted by the federal law and is without effect under the Supremacy Clause of the Constitution. *Cipollone v. Liggett Group, Inc.,* 505 U.S. 504 . . . (1992). State regulation established under the historic police powers of the states is not superseded by federal law unless preemption is the clear and manifest purpose of Congress. *Id.* Accordingly, the intent of Congress is the touchstone of preemption analysis. *See id.*

Congressional intent to preempt state law may be revealed in several ways: (1) "express preemption," in which Congress defines explicitly the extent to which its enactments preempt state law; (2) "field preemption," in which state law is preempted because Congress has regulated a field so pervasively, or federal law touches on a field implicating such a dominant federal interest, that an intent for federal law to occupy the field exclusively may be inferred; and (3) "conflict preemption," in which state law is preempted by implication because state and federal law actually conflict, so that it is impossible to comply with both, or state law "stands as an obstacle to the accomplishment and execution of the full purposes and objectives of Congress." *Teper v. Miller*, 82 F.3d 989, 993 (11th Cir.1996) (citations omitted).

By including an express preemption clause in the FBSA, Congress has demonstrated its intent that the Act preempt at least some state law. . . . Therefore, the issue in this case is not whether Congress intended for the FBSA to have any preemptive effect, but the intended scope of preemption—the extent to which the FBSA preempts state law. . . . In areas traditionally regulated by the states through their police powers, we apply a presumption in favor of a narrow interpretation of an express preemption clause. . . .

VII. EXPRESS PREEMPTION

Brunswick contends that the Lewises' claims fall within the scope of the FBSA's express preemption clause, which provides:

> Unless permitted by the Secretary under section 4305 of this title, a State or a political subdivision of a State may not establish, continue in effect, or enforce a law or regulation establishing a recreational vessel or associated equipment performance or other safety standard or imposing a requirement for associated equipment (except insofar as the State or political subdivision may, in the absence of the Secretary's disapproval, regulate the carrying or use of marine safety articles to meet uniquely hazardous conditions or circumstances within the State) that is not identical to a regulation prescribed under section 4302 of this title.

46 U.S.C.A. § 4306 (West Supp.1995). According to Brunswick, the Lewises' claims, if successful, would result in a regulation imposing a propeller guard requirement. That regulation would not be identical to—in fact, it would be in conflict with—the Coast Guard's position that propeller guards should not be required. In Brunswick's view, the Coast Guard's position is equivalent to a "regulation prescribed under section 4302," which preempts state law. Following this reasoning, Brunswick argues that the Lewises' claims are preempted by the express terms of the FBSA preemption clause.

In response, the Lewises contend that the phrase "law or regulation" does not reach common law claims, because Congress did not mention "common law" specifically in the preemption clause. According to the Lewises, Congress' decision not to specify "common law" in the preemption clause demonstrates congressional intent to save common law claims. As Brunswick points out, however, the omission of the phrase "common law" in the preemption clause is not determinative, because "law" and "regulation" may be read to include state tort actions. *See Cipollone*, 505 U.S. at 520-30 . . . (1992) (plurality opinion) (holding that the phrase "State law" in the Federal Cigarette Labeling and Advertising Act was intended to include common law claims) . . . . In fact, the overwhelming majority of courts have held that common law claims fall within the scope of "laws" and "regulations" expressly preempted by the FBSA. . . .

We agree that the terms "law" and "regulation" evidence an intent to include common law claims. However, we stop short of concluding that common law claims are expressly preempted by the FBSA, because another provision in the Act pulls us away from that conclusion. As the Lewises point out, Congress included a savings clause in the Act, which seems to save common law claims from preemption. That clause, which is found within the section of the Act entitled "Penalties and Injunctions," provides: "Compliance with this chapter or standards, regulations, or orders prescribed under this chapter does not relieve a person from liability at common law or under State law." 46 U.S.C.A. § 4311(g) (West Supp.1995).

Because the FBSA preempts an area (safety) that historically has been regulated by the states through their police powers, we must construe the Act's preemption clause narrowly. *See Medtronic, . . .* 116 S. Ct. at 2250. The preemption clause easily could be read to cover common law claims, but because the savings clause indicates that at least some common law claims survive express preemption, we cannot give the preemption clause that broad reading. Instead, we must resolve doubts in favor of the narrower interpretation of the preemption clause and conclude that the express preemption clause does not cover common law claims. We hold that those claims are not expressly preempted.

The Lewises urge us to go further and hold that the savings clause demonstrates clear congressional intent to save common law claims from preemption. We find congressional intent to be less than clear, given the conflicting language in the preemption and savings clauses. Just as the conflict between those provisions prevents us from concluding that the Lewises' claims are expressly preempted, so also does that conflict prevent us from concluding that those claims are expressly saved. . . . The express terms of the FBSA simply fail to answer the question of whether Congress intended to preempt common law claims. As a result, our decision about preemption depends on whether the Lewises' claims are impliedly preempted by federal law. . . .

VIII. IMPLIED CONFLICT PREEMPTION

The Lewises' claims are preempted impliedly by the FBSA to the extent that those claims conflict with the "accomplishment and execution of the full purposes and objectives of Congress." *See Freightliner Corp. v. Myrick,* 514 U.S. 280, 115 S. Ct. 1483, 1487, 131 L. Ed. 2d 385 (1995). In other words, the Lewises' claims are preempted if they prevent or hinder the FBSA from operating the way Congress intended it to operate. In deciding whether the Lewises' claims conflict with the purposes of the FBSA, we do not apply a presumption against preemption, even though common law tort claims are a mechanism of the police powers of the state. . . .

According to Brunswick, the Lewises' claims are preempted by implication because those claims would interfere with the regulatory scheme enacted by Congress in the FBSA. Brunswick argues that the Coast Guard has the last say on whether a safety feature on boats or associated equipment should be required. Where the Coast Guard believes that a safety feature should not be required, Brunswick argues that states may not require the feature, even through common law claims. . . .

The Lewises argue that . . . Congress did not intend for a mere decision not to regulate to have preemptive effect under the FBSA. In the Lewises' view, any state regulation on boat and equipment safety standards is permissible, unless the Coast Guard promulgates a regulation that conflicts with the state regulation. As the Lewises understand the FBSA regulatory scheme, a Coast Guard position not to impose a safety standard on a matter leaves room for states to impose safety standards on that matter. There being no regulation on propeller guards, the Lewises argue that their claims are not affected by the Coast Guard's position. For support, they point to *Freightliner Corp. v. Myrick,* 514 U.S. 280, 115 S. Ct. 1483, 131 L. Ed. 2d 385 (1995), a case in which the Supreme Court concluded that an absence of regulation on a safety matter did not preempt state common law claims imposing such standards.

In *Freightliner,* the Supreme Court considered whether common law claims based on the failure to install antilock brakes were expressly or impliedly preempted by the Vehicle Safety Act. . . . The preemption clause in the Vehicle Safety Act provided:

> Whenever a Federal motor vehicle safety standard established under this subchapter is in effect,
> no State or political subdivision of a State shall have any authority either to establish, or to con-
> tinue in effect, with respect to any motor vehicle or item of motor vehicle equipment any safety
> standard applicable to the same aspect of performance of such vehicle or item of equipment
> which is not identical to the Federal standard.

15 U.S.C.A. §1392(d) (West 1982) (repealed 1994). The defendants in *Freightliner* argued that the failure-to-install claims were preempted, because the relevant agency had indicated its intent to regulate braking systems by promulgating a regulation on that matter. That regulation was struck down by an appellate court, but the defendants in *Freightliner* believed it still had pre-emptive effect, because it demonstrated the agency's intent to forbid state regulation on braking systems. . . .

The Supreme Court rejected that argument. First, the Court explained, there was no evidence that the Vehicle Safety Act gave the relevant federal agency exclusive authority to issue safety standards. . . . In fact, the preemption clause in that act clearly implied that states could impose safety standards on auto manufacturers, until the federal government came forward with a different standard. Therefore, under the Vehicle Safety Act regulatory scheme, the absence of regulation failed to have preemptive effect . . . ; instead, the agency's failure to put into effect a valid regulation left the state common law intact. . . .

In contrast to the Vehicle Safety Act, the FBSA was intended to give its regulatory agency —the Coast Guard—exclusive authority to issue safety standards:

> This section [containing the preemption clause] provides for federal preemption in the issuance
> of boat and equipment safety standards. This conforms to the long history of preemption in
> maritime safety matters and is founded on the need for uniformity applicable to vessels moving
> in interstate commerce. In this case it also assures that manufacture for the domestic trade
> will not involve compliance with widely varying local requirements. At the same time, it was
> recognized that there may be serious hazards which are unique to a particular locale and which
> would justify variances at least with regard to the carriage or use of marine safety articles on
> boats. Therefore, the section does permit individual States to impose requirements with respect

to carrying or using marine safety articles which go beyond the federal requirements when necessary to meet uniquely hazardous local conditions or circumstances. A right of disapproval, however, is reserved to the Secretary to insure that indiscriminate use of state authority does not seriously impinge on the basic need for uniformity.

The section does not preempt state law or regulation directed at safe boat operation and use, which was felt to be appropriately within the purview of state or local concern.

S.Rep. No. 92-248, *reprinted in* 1971 U.S.C.C.A.N. at 1341. . . . While an absence of regulation under the Vehicle Safety Act does not prevent states from regulating motor vehicle safety standards, an absence of federal regulation under the FBSA means that no regulation, state or federal, is appropriate. *Freightliner* is distinguishable for that reason.

Also in contrast to *Freightliner,* the relevant agency here, the Coast Guard, *did* make an affirmative decision to refrain from regulating propeller guards. Unlike the agency in *Freightliner,* the Coast Guard did not try to promulgate a regulation, and then fail, under a statutory scheme that would leave state law intact in the absence of federal regulatory action. Instead, under a statutory scheme that forbids any state standard or regulation "not identical to" a federal regulation, the Coast Guard decided not to issue a regulation. After consulting with the Advisory Council and reviewing the available data, the Coast Guard reached a carefully considered decision that "available propeller guard accident data do not support imposition of a regulation requiring propeller guards on motorboats."

The Coast Guard decided not only that a federal regulation would be inappropriate, but that the scientific data counseled against any regulation requiring propeller guards. Given that Congress intended for the FBSA to create a uniform system of regulation, and that the Coast Guard has determined that propeller guards should not be required, the Coast Guard's position mandates an absence of both federal and state propeller guard requirements. . . . *Freightliner* does not require that we hold otherwise.

But the Lewises contend that even if *Freightliner* is not controlling here, we cannot find an implied conflict between their claims and the Act, because we know from the savings clause that Congress expected some common law claims to be brought in this area. About the savings clause, the Senate report says:

This section is a Committee amendment and is intended to clarify that compliance with the Act or standards, regulations, or orders promulgated thereunder, does not relieve any person from liability at common law or under State law. The purpose of the section is to assure that in a product liability suit mere compliance by a manufacturer with the minimum standards promulgated under the Act will not be a complete defense to liability. Of course, depending on the rules of evidence of the particular judicial forum, such compliance may or may not be admissible for its evidentiary value.

S.Rep. No. 92-248, *reprinted in* 1971 U.S.C.C.A.N. at 1352.

From the savings clause, we know that Congress understood at least some product liability claims to be consistent with the FBSA regulatory scheme. In order to decide which claims, we must determine when product liability claims can be brought without upsetting the overall scheme Congress intended. Addressing that question, several courts have held that the only claims which do not present a conflict with the FBSA regulatory scheme are product liability claims based on the defective design or installation of products that are already installed, as opposed to claims based on the failure to install a certain safety device. . . . Permitting product liability claims against manufacturers for negligent or defective design of products required by the Coast Guard, or for products provided voluntarily by manufacturers, simply requires manufacturers to comply with FBSA regulations, and to do any additional manufacturing, in a non-negligent and non-defective manner. Permitting such claims is consistent with the FBSA scheme, which is designed to ensure that boats and associated equipment are safe.

By contrast, claims based on the failure to install a product that the Coast Guard has decided should not be required would conflict with the regulatory uniformity purpose of the FBSA. Without doubt, the Lewises' product liability claims seek to impose a propeller guard requirement. . . . That requirement conflicts with the FBSA's grant of exclusive regulatory authority to the Coast Guard, and for that reason those claims are in conflict with and are therefore preempted by the Act.

The Lewises argue that their fraud claim should be treated differently from their other claims, because it would not create a propeller guard requirement beyond FBSA requirements. We disagree. If the Lewises succeeded with their fraud claim, a jury could impose liability upon Brunswick for attempting to persuade the Coast Guard and others that propeller guards are unsafe. The necessary element of causation in any such claim would be that but for the wrongful conduct of Brunswick, propeller guards would have been required by the Coast Guard. Such a judgment would conflict with the Coast Guard's position that propeller guards should not be required. Thus, the fraud claim is impliedly preempted by the Coast Guard's position and the preemptive effect given that position by the FBSA.

Regulatory fraud claims of this nature are impliedly preempted for fundamental, systemic reasons. Permitting such claims would allow juries to second-guess federal agency regulators through the guise of punishing those whose actions are deemed to have interfered with the proper functioning of the regulatory process. If that were permitted, federal regulatory decisions that Congress intended to be dispositive would merely be the first round of decision making, with later more important rounds to be played out in the various state courts. Virtually any federal agency decision that stood in the way of a lawsuit could be challenged indirectly by a claim that the industry involved had misrepresented the relevant data or had otherwise managed to skew the regulatory result. Ironically, such circumvention of the regulatory scheme likely would be more pronounced where, as here, Congress mandated more extensive industry input into the regulatory process. . . . Congress could not have intended for the process it so carefully put in place to be so easily and thoroughly undermined. . . .

In sum, we conclude that because Congress has made the Coast Guard the exclusive authority in the area of boat and equipment safety standards, its position rejecting a propeller guard requirement takes on the character of a ruling that no such requirement may be imposed. That position impliedly preempts state law requirements of propeller guards, even in the form of common law claims. It also prevents plaintiffs from bringing fraud claims intended to demonstrate that the Coast Guard would have reached a different conclusion on the matter of propeller guards but for alleged industry manipulation or subversion of the federal regulatory process. We hold that each of the Lewises' claims is preempted by implication because it conflicts with the Coast Guard's position on propeller guards and would interfere with the FBSA regulatory process designed by Congress.

IX. CONCLUSION

The district court's grant of summary judgment to Brunswick is AFFIRMED.

NOTES AND QUESTIONS

1 The Federal Boat Safety Act ("FBSA") expressly preempts all state laws or regulations that are not identical to federal regulations, but the FBSA also includes a "savings clause." The common law standard proposed by the plaintiff, which the *Lewis* court held was a "law or regulation" within the meaning of the preemption clause, was pretty clearly non-identical to the federal standard. Is there any way to reconcile the express preemption clause with the savings clause?

2 Would plaintiffs' claim conflict with the FBSA?

3 Critique the following argument: Here the state would not require a boat with a propeller guard. The manufacturers are free, if they choose, to design only to the regulations prescribed by federal law. Nobody will be thrown into jail. Defendants merely will be required to pay damages for harm caused.

VIII.

While tort remedies can include injunction and restitution, money damages is the standard tort remedy. While damages are recoverable in all tort actions, they play a special role in the negligence cause of action – proof of actual damages is a required element of plaintiff's *prima facie* case in a negligence suit. The finder of fact determines the amount of damages necessary. Three types of damages may be recoverable: "Nominal" damages are a very small sum awarded as a token indicating that plaintiff's rights were violated. "Compensatory" damages are intended to compensate plaintiff for a loss – to make the plaintiff whole. "Punitive" damages are intended to punish and deter the defendant.

A. COMPENSATORY DAMAGES

"Compensatory" damages are the core concept of recoverable damages – they are designed to make the plaintiff "whole." This idea of restoring plaintiff to the *status quo ante* is at the heart of the "corrective justice" vision of tort liability. Of course, it often is not literally possible to make the injured plaintiff whole again, but an appropriate award of money damages usually is as close as our tort system can come to restoring the injured plaintiff.

The category of compensatory damages can be sub-divided in a variety of ways. One way to divide compensatory damages is between property damage and personal injury. Property damage is physical injury to or dispossession of real or personal property. Usually, property damage is measured by the difference between the market value of the property before and after defendant's tort. The court might also issue an injunction prohibiting defendant from intermeddling with plaintiff's property in the future. Personal injury damages generally consist of medical expenses, lost wages, and pain and suffering.

Another way to sub-divide compensatory damages is between "general" (noneconomic) damages and "special" (economic) damages. Usually, property damage is "special" damage item while personal injury is "general." General damages are intangible losses resulting from a personal injury. Because there is not and cannot be a market for the losses compensated by a general damages award, placing a dollar value on such losses is less certain than valuing special damages. Moreover, because money is far from a perfect substitute for the losses compensated by general damages, the idea that money damages restores the victim to the *status quo ante*, always a fictional concept, is especially so with regard to general damage losses.

Special damages are actual pecuniary losses, sometimes called "out-of-pocket" losses. In a personal injury case, special damages usually consist primarily of medical expenses and lost wages (past and future). Reasonably certain future damages also are recoverable, but recovery for future economic losses requires a reasonable prediction of future losses that entails a level of complexity not present when determining past economic losses. The distinction between general and special damages is illustrated by the following Virginia Model Jury Instruction. The damage items listed as (1) – (4) are "general" damages, and the items listed as (5) – (8) are more in the nature of "special" damages.

I-9 VIRGINIA MODEL JURY INSTRUCTIONS – CIVIL 9.000

General Personal Injury and Property Damage

If you find your verdict for the plaintiff, then in determining the damages to which he is entitled, you shall consider any of the following which you believe by the greater weight of the evidence was caused by the negligence of the defendant:

1. any bodily injuries he sustained and their effect on his health according to their degree and probable duration;

2. any physical pain [and mental anguish] he suffered in the past [and any that he may be reasonably expected to suffer in the future];

3. any disfigurement or deformity and any associated humiliation or embarrassment;

4. any inconvenience caused in the past [and any that probably will be caused in the future];

5. any medical expenses incurred in the past [and any that may be reasonably expected to occur in the future];

6. any earnings he lost because he was unable to work at his calling;

7. any loss of earnings and lessening of earning capacity, or either, that he may reasonably be expected to sustain in the future;

8. any property damage he sustained.

Your verdict shall be for such sum as will fully and fairly compensate the plaintiff for the damages sustained as a result of the defendant's negligence.

1. GENERAL DAMAGES: PAIN AND SUFFERING

Damages recoverable for non-economic harm usually are described as "pain and suffering." The words "pain and suffering" sometimes are thought to describe two different elements of recoverable non-economic loss. "Pain" refers to actual physical pain caused by an injury. "Suffering" refers to "mental anguish" experienced by the injured party.

Plaintiffs may recover for both past and future pain and suffering, but determining the appropriate award for such non-pecuniary losses is notoriously difficult. After all, unlike most elements of pecuniary loss, there is not market for "pain and suffering." The following well-known case illustrates the nature of damages for pain and suffering.

MCDOUGALD V. GARBER
536 N.E.2D 372 (N.Y. 1989)

This appeal raises fundamental questions about the nature and role of nonpecuniary damages in personal injury litigation. By nonpecuniary damages, we mean those damages awarded to compensate an injured person for the physical and emotional consequences of the injury, such as pain and suffering and the loss of the ability to engage in certain activities. Pecuniary damages, on the other hand, compensate the victim for the economic consequences of the injury, such as medical expenses, lost earnings and the cost of custodial care.

The specific questions raised here deal with the assessment of nonpecuniary damages and are (1) whether some degree of cognitive awareness is a prerequisite to recovery for loss of enjoyment of life and (2) whether a jury should be instructed to consider and award damages for loss of enjoyment of life separately from damages for pain and suffering. We answer the first question in the affirmative and the second question in the negative. . . .

On September 7, 1978, plaintiff Emma McDougald, then 31 years old, underwent a Caesarean section and tubal ligation at New York Infirmary. Defendant Garber performed the surgery; defendants Armengol and Kulkarni provided anesthesia. During the surgery, Mrs. McDougald suffered oxygen deprivation which resulted in severe brain damage and left her in a permanent comatose condition. This action was brought by Mrs. McDougald and her husband, suing derivatively, alleging that the injuries were caused by the defendants' acts of malpractice.

A jury found all defendants liable and awarded Emma McDougald a total of $9,650,102 in damages, including $1,000,000 for conscious pain and suffering and a separate award of $3,500,000 for loss of the pleasures and pursuits of life. The balance of the damages awarded to her were for pecuniary damages—lost earnings and the cost of custodial and nursing care. Her husband was awarded $1,500,000 on his derivative claim for the loss of his wife's services. On defendants' post-trial motions, the Trial Judge reduced the total award to Emma McDougald to $4,796,728 by striking the entire award for future nursing care ($2,353,374) and by reducing the separate awards for conscious pain and suffering and loss of the pleasures and pursuits of life to a single award of $2,000,000. Her husband's award was left intact. On cross appeals, the Appellate Division affirmed and later granted defendants leave to appeal to this court. . . .

We note at the outset that the defendants' liability for Emma McDougald's injuries is unchallenged here . . . . Also unchallenged are the awards in the amount of $770,978 for loss of earnings and $2,025,750 for future custodial care . . . .

What remains in dispute, primarily, is the award to Emma McDougald for nonpecuniary damages. . . . The parties and the trial court agreed that Mrs. McDougald could not recover for pain and suffering unless she were conscious of the pain. Defendants maintained that such consciousness was also required to support an award for loss of enjoyment of life. The court, however, accepted plaintiffs' view that loss of enjoyment of life was compensable without regard to whether the plaintiff was aware of the loss. Accordingly, because the level of Mrs. McDougald's cognitive abilities was in dispute, the court instructed the jury to consider loss of enjoyment of life as an element of nonpecuniary damages separate from pain and suffering. . . .

We conclude that the court erred, both in instructing the jury that Mrs. McDougald's awareness was irrelevant to their consideration of damages for loss of enjoyment of life and in directing the jury to consider that aspect of damages separately from pain and suffering.

We begin with the familiar proposition that an award of damages to a person injured by the negligence of another is to compensate the victim, not to punish the wrongdoer. The goal is to restore the injured party, to the extent possible, to the position that would have been occupied had the wrong not occurred. To be sure, placing the burden of compensation on the negligent party also serves as a deterrent, but purely punitive damages – that is, those which have no compensatory purpose – are prohibited unless the harmful conduct is intentional, malicious, outrageous, or otherwise aggravated beyond mere negligence.

Damages for nonpecuniary losses are, of course, among those that can be awarded as compensation to the victim. This aspect of damages, however, stands on less certain ground than does an award for pecuniary damages. An economic loss can be compensated in kind by an economic gain; but recovery for noneconomic losses such as pain and suffering and loss of enjoyment of life rests on "the legal fiction that money damages can compensate for a victim's injury" (Howard v Lecher, 42 NY2d 109, 111). We accept this fiction, knowing that although money will neither ease the pain nor restore the victim's abilities, this device is as close as the law can come in its effort to right the wrong. We have no hope of evaluating what has been lost, but a monetary award may provide a measure of solace for the condition created.

Our willingness to indulge this fiction comes to an end, however, when it ceases to serve the compensatory goals of tort recovery. When that limit is met, further indulgence can only result in assessing damages that are punitive. The question posed by this case, then, is whether an award of damages for loss of enjoyment of life to a person whose injuries preclude any awareness of the loss serves a compensatory purpose. We conclude that it does not.

Simply put, an award of money damages in such circumstances has no meaning or utility to the injured person. An award for the loss of enjoyment of life "cannot provide [such a victim] with any consolation or ease any burden resting on him . . . . He cannot spend it upon necessities or pleasures. He cannot experience the pleasure of giving it away" *(Flannery v United States*, 718 F2d 108, 111, *cert denied* 467 U.S. 1226).

We recognize that, as the trial court noted, requiring some cognitive awareness as a prerequisite to recovery for loss of enjoyment of life will result in some cases "in the paradoxical situation that the greater the degree of brain injury inflicted by a negligent defendant, the smaller the award the plaintiff can recover in general damages." The force of this argument, however – the temptation to achieve a balance between injury and damages – has nothing to do with meaningful compensation for the victim. Instead, the temptation is rooted in a desire to punish the defendant in proportion to the harm inflicted. However relevant such retributive symmetry may be in the criminal law, it has no place in the law of civil damages, at least in the absence of culpability beyond mere negligence.

Accordingly, we conclude that cognitive awareness is a prerequisite to recovery for loss of enjoyment of life. We do not go so far, however, as to require the fact finder to sort out varying degrees of cognition and determine at what level a particular deprivation can be fully appreciated. With respect to pain and suffering, the trial court charged simply that there must be "some level of awareness" in order for plaintiff to recover. We think that this is an appropriate standard for all aspects of nonpecuniary loss. No doubt the standard ignores analytically relevant levels of cognition, but we resist the desire for analytical purity in favor of simplicity. A more complex instruction might give the appearance of greater precision but, given the limits of our understanding of the human mind, it would in reality lead only to greater speculation. We turn next to the question whether loss of enjoyment of life should be considered a category of damages separate from pain and suffering.

There is no dispute here that the fact finder may, in assessing nonpecuniary damages, consider the effect of the injuries on the plaintiff's capacity to lead a normal life. Traditionally, . . . this aspect of suffering has not been treated as a separate category of damages; instead, the plaintiff's inability to enjoy life to its fullest has been considered one type of suffering to be factored into a general award for nonpecuniary damages, commonly known as pain and suffering.

Recently, however, there has been an attempt to segregate the suffering associated with physical pain from the mental anguish that stems from the inability to engage in certain activities, and to have juries provide a separate award for each.

Some courts have resisted the effort, primarily on the ground that duplicative and therefore excessive awards would result. Other courts have allowed separate awards, noting that the types of suffering involved are analytically distinguishable. Still other courts have questioned the propriety of the practice but held that, in the particular case, separate awards did not constitute reversible error . . . .

We do not dispute that distinctions can be found or created between the concepts of pain and suffering and loss of enjoyment of life. If the term "suffering" is limited to the emotional response to the sensation of pain, then the emotional response caused by the limitation of life's activities may be considered qualitatively different. But suffering need not be so limited – it can easily encompass the frustration and anguish caused by the inability to participate in activities that once brought pleasure. Traditionally, by treating loss of enjoyment of life as a permissible factor in assessing pain and suffering, courts have given the term this broad meaning.

If we are to depart from this traditional approach and approve a separate award for loss of enjoyment of life, it must be on the basis that such an approach will yield a more accurate evaluation of the compensation due to the plaintiff. We have no doubt that, in general, the total award for nonpecuniary damages would increase if we adopted the rule. That separate awards are advocated by plaintiffs and resisted by defendants is sufficient evidence that larger awards are at stake here. But a larger award does not by itself indicate that the goal of compensation has been better served.

The advocates of separate awards contend that because pain and suffering and loss of enjoyment of life can be distinguished, they must be treated separately if the plaintiff is to be compensated fully for each distinct injury suffered. We disagree. Such an analytical approach may have its place when the subject is pecuniary damages, which can be calculated with some precision. But the estimation of nonpecuniary damages is not amenable to such analytical precision and may, in fact, suffer from its application. Translating human suffering into dollars and cents involves no mathematical formula; it rests, as we have said, on a legal fiction. The figure that emerges is unavoidably distorted by the translation. Application of this murky process to the component parts of nonpecuniary injuries (however analytically distinguishable they may be) cannot make it more accurate. If anything, the distortion will be amplified by repetition.

Thus, we are not persuaded that any salutary purpose would be served by having the jury make separate awards for pain and suffering and loss of enjoyment of life. We are confident, furthermore, that the trial advocate's art is a sufficient guarantee that none of the plaintiff's losses will be ignored by the jury.

. . . Accordingly, the order of the Appellate Division, insofar as appealed from, should be modified, with costs to defendants, by granting a new trial on the issue of nonpecuniary damages of plaintiff Emma McDougald, and as so modified, affirmed.

Titone, J. (dissenting).

The majority's holding represents a compromise position that neither comports with the fundamental principles of tort compensation nor furnishes a satisfactory, logically consistent framework for compensating nonpecuniary loss. Because I conclude that loss of enjoyment of life is an objective damage item, conceptually distinct from conscious pain and suffering, I can find no fault with the trial court's instruction authorizing separate awards and permitting an award for "loss of enjoyment of life" even in the absence of any awareness of that loss on the part of the injured plaintiff. Accordingly, I dissent. . . .

The capacity to enjoy life – by watching one's children grow, participating in recreational activities, and drinking in the many other pleasures that life has to offer – is unquestionably an attribute of an ordinary healthy individual. The loss of that capacity as a result of another's negligent act is at least as serious an impairment as the permanent destruction of a physical function, which has always been treated as a compensable item under traditional tort principles. Indeed, I can imagine no physical loss that is more central to the quality of a tort victim's continuing life than the destruction of the capacity to enjoy that life to the fullest.

Unquestionably, recovery of a damage item such as "pain and suffering" requires a showing of some degree of cognitive capacity. Such a requirement exists for the simple reason that pain and suffering are wholly subjective concepts and cannot exist separate and apart from the human consciousness that experiences them. In contrast, the destruction of an individual's capacity to enjoy life as a result of a crippling injury is an objective fact that does not differ in principle from the permanent loss of an eye or limb. As in the case of a lost limb, an essential characteristic of a healthy human life has been wrongfully taken, and, consequently, the injured party is entitled to a monetary award as a substitute, if, as the majority asserts, the goal of tort compensation is "to restore the injured party, to the extent possible, to the position that would have been occupied had the wrong not occurred" (majority opn, at 254).

Significantly, this equation does not suggest a need to establish the injured's awareness of the loss. The victim's ability to comprehend the degree to which his or her life has been impaired is irrelevant, since, unlike "conscious pain and suffering," the impairment exists independent of the victim's ability to apprehend it. Indeed, the majority reaches the conclusion that a degree of awareness must be shown only after injecting a new element into the equation. Under the majority's formulation, the victim must be aware of the loss because, in addition to being compensatory, the award must have "meaning or utility to the injured person." . . . This additional requirement, however, has no real foundation in law or logic. . . .

Moreover, the compensatory nature of a monetary award for loss of enjoyment of life is not altered or rendered punitive by the fact that the unaware injured plaintiff cannot experience the pleasure of having it. The fundamental distinction between punitive and compensatory damages is that the former exceed the amount necessary to replace what the plaintiff lost. As the Court of Appeals for the Second Circuit has observed, "[the] fact that the compensation [for loss of enjoyment of life] may inure as a practical matter to third parties in a given case does not transform the nature of the damages" (*Rufino v United States*, 829 F2d 354, 362).

Ironically, the majority's expressed goal of limiting recovery for nonpecuniary loss to compensation that the injured plaintiff has the capacity to appreciate is directly undercut by the majority's ultimate holding, adopted in the interest of "simplicity," that recovery for loss of enjoyment of life may be had as long as the injured plaintiff has "some level of awareness," however slight . . . . Manifestly, there are many different forms and levels of awareness, particularly in cases involving brain injury. Further, the type and degree of cognitive functioning necessary to experience "pain and suffering" is certainly of a lower order than that needed to apprehend the loss of the ability to enjoy life in all of its subtleties. Accordingly, the existence of "some level of awareness" on the part of the injured plaintiff says nothing about that plaintiff's ability to derive some comfort from the award or even to appreciate its significance. Hence, that standard does not assure that loss of enjoyment of life damages will be awarded only when they serve "a compensatory purpose," as that term is defined by the majority.

In the final analysis, the rule that the majority has chosen is an arbitrary one, in that it denies or allows recovery on the basis of a criterion that is not truly related to its stated goal. In my view, it is fundamentally unsound, as well as grossly unfair, to deny recovery to those who are completely without cognitive capacity while permitting it for those with a mere spark of awareness, regardless of the latter's ability to appreciate either the loss sustained or the benefits of the monetary award offered in compensation. In both instances, the injured plaintiff is in essentially the same position, and an award that is punitive as to one is equally punitive as to the other. Of course, since I do not subscribe to the majority's conclusion that an award to an unaware plaintiff is punitive, I would have no difficulty permitting recovery to both classes of plaintiffs.

Having concluded that the injured plaintiff's awareness should not be a necessary precondition to recovery for loss of enjoyment of life, I also have no difficulty going on to conclude that loss of enjoyment of life is a distinct damage item which is recoverable separate and apart from the award for conscious pain and suffering. The majority has rejected separate recovery, in part because it apparently perceives some overlap between the two damage categories and in part because it believes that the goal of enhancing the precision of jury awards for nonpecuniary loss would not be advanced. However, the overlap the majority perceives exists only if one assumes, as the majority evidently has, that the "loss of enjoyment" category of damages is designed to compensate only for "*the emotional response* caused by the limitation of life's activities" and "*the frustration and anguish caused by* the inability to participate in activities that once brought pleasure" (emphasis added), both of which are highly *subjective* concepts.

In fact, while "pain and suffering compensates the victim for the physical and mental discomfort caused by the injury; . . . loss of enjoyment of life compensates the victim for the limitations on the person's life created by the injury", a distinctly *objective* loss *(Thompson v National R. R. Passenger Corp., supra,* at 824). In other words, while the victim's "emotional response" and "frustration and anguish" are elements of the award for pain and suffering, the "limitation of life's activities" and the "inability to participate in activities" that the majority identifies are recoverable under the "loss of enjoyment of life" rubric. Thus, there is no real overlap, and no real basis for concern about potentially duplicative awards where, as here, there is a properly instructed jury.

Finally, given the clear distinction between the two categories of nonpecuniary damages, I cannot help but assume that permitting separate awards for conscious pain and suffering and loss of enjoyment of life would contribute to accuracy and precision in thought in the jury's deliberations on the issue of damages. . . . In light of the concrete benefit to be gained by compelling the jury to differentiate between the specific objective and subjective elements of the plaintiff's nonpecuniary loss, I find unpersuasive the majority's reliance on vague concerns about potential distortion owing to the inherently difficult task of computing the value of intangible loss. My belief in the jury system, and in the collective wisdom of the deliberating jury, leads me to conclude that we may safely leave that task in the jurors' hands.

For all of these reasons, I approve of the approach that the trial court adopted in its charge to the jury. Accordingly, I would affirm the order below affirming the judgment.

NOTES AND QUESTIONS

1 *Pain and Suffering.* Why are damages for so-called "non-pecuniary losses" such as pain and suffering appropriate at all? Can money remedy chronic pain or the permanent loss of the ability to enjoy certain aspects of life? The standard answer is that even if money cannot truly "remedy" pain and suffering, if defendant were not made to compensate plaintiff for pain and suffering caused, plaintiff would be undercompensated, and defendant would be allowed to "externalize" a significant cost of defendant's risky activity.

2 *Valuing Pain and Suffering.* Even assuming that money can, to some extent, remedy pain and suffering, it is not at all clear that it is possible to put an accurate dollar value on such pain and suffering. Is it possible to put an accurate dollar value on pain and suffering? How? Would it be appropriate for the jury to consider comparable awards in other cases? Most courts do not allow this.

3 Most jurisdictions allow plaintiffs' counsel to argue to the jury the *per diem* rule whereby the jury is encouraged to gauge the value of pain and suffering for a shorter period, such as a day or an hour, and then to multiply that appropriately to arrive at a total award for pain and suffering. Such arguments sometimes are accompanied by a so-called "day in the life" video presentation, which is designed to dramatize the difficulties that plaintiff faces on a daily basis due to her injuries. Does this approach help? Some jurisdictions do not allow such arguments to be made to the jury. One argument that generally is disallowed is the so-called "golden rule" argument in which plaintiff's counsel asks the jury to estimate how much they would accept to trade places with the plaintiff.

4 *Inconsistency.* Not surprisingly, despite tools such as those discussed in the preceding Note, jury awards for non-economic damages tend to be highly variable.

5 The *McDougald* court's opinion suggests that a plaintiff must be conscious to recover for lost pleasures and pursuits because money cannot compensate in any way if the plaintiff is not conscious of the loss (or, more importantly, of the compensation). Assuming that the court is right that there is no compensatory purpose to be served by damages for lost pleasures and pursuits when the plaintiff is unconscious, does this argument prove too much? How does money palliate the suffering of an unconscious plaintiff for anything, including conscious pain and suffering? The *McDougald* decision probably represents the majority position, that plaintiffs may recover for "lost pleasures and pursuits" only if conscious of the loss, but some recent cases have allowed recovery for the lost pleasure itself, even if plaintiff is not and will never be conscious of the loss.

6 In those jurisdictions that permit recovery for "lost pleasures and pursuits" (sometimes called "hedonic" damages), courts tend to distinguish between the negative experience of pain and the absence of the positive experience of pleasure. Even the *McDougald* majority "did not dispute that distinctions can be found or created between the concepts of pain and suffering and loss of enjoyment of life." The majority further expressed "no doubt that, in general, the total award for nonpecuniary damages would increase" if separate awards were allowed for pain and suffering and loss of enjoyment. Why should this be so?

7 *Contingent Fees.* Perhaps the person most interested in the plaintiff's recovery for pain and suffering is her attorney. Almost all personal injury cases are handled on a "contingent fee" basis – plaintiff's lawyer's fee is contingent on plaintiff's recovery and measured by a percentage of the recovery. Without pain and suffering awards, special

damages alone frequently would not be sufficient to support a contingent fee award that would make many personal injury cases financially worth pursuing by plaintiff's attorney.

8   *Statutory Caps.* Most American jurisdictions have enacted some sort of cap on compensatory damages awards. Several of those jurisdictions have placed statutory limits on the amount of recoverable non-economic damages. These "caps" often are part of a "tort reform" effort designed to minimize the cost and maximize the availability of liability insurance.

9   *Remittitur and Additur.* Courts generally will defer to the jury's damage award unless the award "shocks the conscience." The process that courts use to control jury discretion in damage awards is called "remittitur" and "additur." All states use remittitur, but only some states permit additur. In either case, the court conditionally grants a motion for a new trial unless the beneficiary of the excessive or inadequate award agrees to a reduction or increase (as the case may be) of the unreasonable award.

2. SPECIAL DAMAGES: ECONOMIC LOSSES

PROVERBS 27:1

Boast not thyself of tomorrow; for thou knowest not what a day may bring forth.

Economic or "special" damages are actual out-of-pocket dollar losses suffered by the plaintiff. Special damages usually consist primarily of medical expenses and lost earnings, both past and future. The recoverability of future expenses and losses requires the estimate of future expenses and earnings, but, as the proverb quoted above emphasizes, it is impossible for people to know the future with any reasonable degree of certainty, and this is especially true of future earnings. This uncertainty leads to some recurring issues concerning the recoverability of future losses, such as whether lost future wages must be discounted to present value.

O'SHEA V. RIVERWAY TOWING CO.
677 F.2D 1194 (7TH CIR. 1982)

. . . We are called upon to decide . . . the question . . . whether, and if so how, to account for inflation in computing lost future wages. On the day of the accident, Margaret O'Shea was coming off duty as a cook on a towboat plying the Mississippi River . . . and while getting off the boat she fell and sustained the injury complained of. The district judge found Riverway negligent and Mrs. O'Shea free from contributory negligence, and assessed damages in excess of $150,000. Riverway appeals only . . . from the part of the damage award that was intended to compensate Mrs. O'Shea for her lost future wages. . . .

Mrs. O'Shea's job as a cook paid her $40 a day, and since the custom was to work 30 days consecutively and then have the next 30 days off, this comes to $7200 a year although, as we shall see, she never had earned that much in a single year. She testified that when the accident occurred she had been about to get another cook's job on a Mississippi towboat that would have paid her $60 a day ($10,800 a year). She also testified that she had been intending to work as a boat's cook until she was 70 – longer if she was able. An economist who testified on Mrs. O'Shea's behalf used the foregoing testimony as the basis for estimating the wages that she lost because of the accident. He first subtracted federal income tax from yearly wage estimates based on alternative assumptions about her wage rate (that it would be either $40 or $60 a day); assumed that this wage would have grown by between six and eight percent a year; assumed that she would have worked either to age 65 or to age 70; and then discounted the resulting lost-wage estimates to present value, using a discount rate of 8.5 percent a year. These calculations, being based on alternative assumptions concerning starting wage rate, annual wage increases, and length of employment, yielded a range of values rather than a single value. The bottom of the range was $50,000. This is the present value, computed at an 8.5 percent discount rate, of Mrs. O'Shea's lost future wages on the assumption that her starting wage was $40 a day and that it would have grown by six percent a year until she retired at the age of 65. The top of the range was $114,000, which is the present value (again discounted at 8.5 percent) of her lost future wages assuming she would have worked till she was 70 at a wage that would have started at $60 a day and increased by eight percent a year. The judge awarded a figure – $86,033 – near the midpoint of this range. He did not explain in his written opinion how he had arrived at this figure, but in a preceding oral opinion he stated that he was "not certain that she would work until age 70 at this type of work," although "she certainly was entitled to" do so and "could have earned something"; and that he had not "felt bound by (the economist's) figure of eight per cent increase in wages" and had "not found the wages based on necessarily a 60 dollar a day job." If this can be taken to mean that he thought Mrs. O'Shea would probably have worked till she was 70, starting at $40 a day but moving up from there at six rather than eight percent a year, the economist's estimate of the present value of her lost future wages would be $75,000.

There is no doubt that the accident disabled Mrs. O'Shea from working as a cook on a boat. . . . But Riverway argues that Mrs. O'Shea (who has not worked at all since the accident, which occurred two years before the trial) could have gotten some sort of job and that the wages in that job should be deducted from the admittedly higher wages that she could have earned as a cook on a boat. The question is not whether Mrs. O'Shea is totally disabled in the sense . . . that there is no job in the American economy for which she is medically fit. . . . It is whether she can by reasonable diligence find gainful employment, given the physical condition in which the accident left her. . . . Here is a middle-aged woman, very overweight, badly scarred on one arm and one leg, unsteady on her feet, in constant and serious pain from the accident, with no education beyond high school and no work skills other than cooking, a job that happens to require standing for long periods which she is incapable of doing. It seems unlikely that someone in this condition could find gainful work at the minimum wage. True, the probability is not zero; and a better procedure, therefore, might have been to subtract from Mrs. O'Shea's lost future wages as a boat's cook the wages in some other job, discounted (i.e., multiplied) by the probability – very low – that she would in fact be able to get another job. But the district judge cannot be criticized for having failed to use a procedure not suggested by either party. . . .

Riverway argues next that it was wrong for the judge to award damages on the basis of a wage not validated, as it were, by at least a year's employment at that wage. Mrs. O'Shea had never worked full time, had never in fact earned more than $3600 in a full year, and in the year preceding the accident had earned only $900. But previous wages do not put a cap on an award of lost future wages. If a man who had never worked in his life graduated from law school, began working at a law firm at an annual salary of $35,000, and was killed the second day on the job, his lack of a past wage history would be irrelevant to computing his lost future wages. The present case is similar if less dramatic. Mrs. O'Shea did not work at all until 1974, when her husband died. She then lived on her inheritance and worked at a variety of part-time jobs till January 1979, when she started working as a cook on the towboat. According to her testimony, which the trial judge believed, she was then working full time. It is immaterial that this was her first full-time job and that the accident occurred before she had held it for a full year. Her job history was typical of women who return to the labor force after their children are grown or, as in Mrs. O'Shea's case, after their husband dies, and these women are, like any tort victims, entitled to damages based on what they would have earned in the future rather than on what they may or may not have earned in the past.

If we are correct so far, Mrs. O'Shea was entitled to have her lost wages determined on the assumption that she would have earned at least $7200 in the first year after the accident and that the accident caused her to lose that entire amount by disabling her from any gainful employment. And since Riverway neither challenges the district judge's (apparent) finding that Mrs. O'Shea would have worked till she was 70 nor contends that the lost wages for each year until then should be discounted by the probability that she would in fact have been alive and working as a boat's cook throughout the damage period, we may also assume that her wages would have been at least $7200 a year for the 12 years between the date of the accident and her seventieth birthday. . . .

We come at last to the most important issue in the case, which is the proper treatment of inflation in calculating lost future wages. Mrs. O'Shea's economist based the six to eight percent range which he used to estimate future increases in the wages of a boat's cook on the general pattern of wage increases in service occupations over the past 25 years. During the second half of this period the rate of inflation has been substantial and has accounted for much of the increase in nominal wages in this period; and to use that increase to project future wage increases is therefore to assume that inflation will continue, and continue to push up wages. Riverway argues that it is improper as a matter of law to take inflation into account in projecting lost future wages. Yet Riverway itself wants to take inflation into account – one-sidedly, to reduce the amount of the damages computed. For Riverway does not object to the economist's choice of an 8.5 percent discount rate for reducing Mrs. O'Shea's lost future wages to present value, although the rate includes an allowance – a very large allowance – for inflation.

To explain, the object of discounting lost future wages to present value is to give the plaintiff an amount of money which, invested safely, will grow to a sum equal to those wages. So if we thought that but for the accident Mrs. O'Shea would have earned $7200 in 1990, and we were computing in 1980 (when this case was tried) her damages based on those lost earnings, we would need to determine the sum of money that, invested safely for a period of 10 years, would grow to $7200. Suppose that in 1980 the rate of interest on ultra-safe (i.e., federal government) bonds or notes maturing in 10 years was 12 percent. Then we would consult a table of present values to see what sum of money invested at 12 percent for 10 years would at the end of that time have grown to $7200. The answer is $2318. But a moment's reflection will show that to give Mrs. O'Shea $2318 to compensate her for lost wages in 1990 would grossly under-compensate her. People demand 12 percent to lend money risklessly for 10 years because they expect their principal to have much less purchasing power when they get it back at the end of the time. In other words, when long-term interest rates are high, they are high in order to compensate lenders for the fact that they will be repaid in cheaper dollars. In periods when no inflation is anticipated, the risk-free interest rate is between one and three percent. . . . Additional percentage points above that level reflect inflation anticipated over the life of the loan. But if there is inflation it will affect wages as well as prices. Therefore to give Mrs. O'Shea $2318 today because that is the present value of $7200 10 years hence, computed at a discount rate – 12 percent – that consists mainly of an allowance for anticipated inflation, is in fact to give her less than she would have been earning then if she was earning $7200 on the date of the accident, even if the only wage increases she would have received would have been those necessary to keep pace with inflation.

There are (at least) two ways to deal with inflation in computing the present value of lost future wages. One is to take it out of both the wages and the discount rate-to say to Mrs. O'Shea, "we are going to calculate your probable wage in 1990 on the assumption, unrealistic as it is, that there will be zero inflation between now and then; and, to be consistent, we are going to discount the amount thus calculated by the interest rate that would be charged under the same assumption of zero inflation." Thus, if we thought Mrs. O'Shea's real (i.e., inflation-free) wage rate would not rise in the future, we would fix her lost earnings in 1990 as $7200 and, to be consistent, we would discount that to present (1980) value using an estimate of the real interest rate. At two percent, this procedure would yield a present value of $5906. Of course, she would not invest this money at a mere two percent. She would invest it at the much higher prevailing interest rate. But that would not give her a windfall; it would just enable her to replace her lost 1990 earnings with an amount equal to what she would in fact have earned in that year if inflation continues, as most people expect it to do. (If people did not expect continued inflation, long-term interest rates would be much lower; those rates impound investors' inflationary expectations.)

An alternative approach, which yields the same result, is to use a (higher) discount rate based on the current risk-free 10-year interest rate, but apply that rate to an estimate of lost future wages that includes expected inflation. Contrary to Riverway's argument, this projection would not require gazing into a crystal ball. The expected rate of inflation can, as just suggested, be read off from the current long-term interest rate. If that rate is 12 percent, and if as suggested earlier the real or inflation-free interest rate is only one to three percent, this implies that the market is anticipating 9-11 percent inflation over the next 10 years, for a long-term interest rate is simply the sum of the real interest rate and the anticipated rate of inflation during the term.

Either approach to dealing with inflation is acceptable (they are, in fact, equivalent) and we by no means rule out others; but it is illogical and indefensible to build inflation into the discount rate yet ignore it in calculating the lost future wages that are to be discounted. That results in systematic undercompensation, just as building inflation into the estimate of future lost earnings and then discounting using the real rate of interest would systematically overcompensate. The former error is committed, we respectfully suggest, by those circuits . . . that refuse to allow inflation to be used in projecting lost future earnings but then use a discount rate that has built into it a large allowance for inflation. . . . We align ourselves instead with those circuits (a majority . . .) . . . that require that inflation be treated consistently in choosing a discount rate and in estimating the future lost wages to be discounted to present value using that rate. . . .

Applying our analysis to the present case, we cannot pronounce the approach taken by the plaintiff's economist unreasonable. He chose a discount rate – 8.5 percent – well above the real rate of interest, and therefore containing an allowance for inflation. Consistency required him to inflate Mrs. O'Shea's starting wage as a boat's cook in calculating her lost future wages, and he did so at a rate of six to eight percent a year. If this rate had been intended as a forecast of purely inflationary wage changes, his approach would be open to question, especially at the upper end of his range. For if the estimated rate of inflation were eight percent, the use of a discount rate of 8.5 percent would imply that the real rate of interest was only .5 percent, which is lower than most economists believe it to be for any substantial period of time. But wages do not rise just because of inflation. Mrs. O'Shea could expect her real wages as a boat's cook to rise as she became more experienced and as average real wage rates throughout the economy rose, as they usually do over a decade or more. It would not be outlandish to assume that even if there were no inflation, Mrs. O'Shea's wages would have risen by three percent a year. If we subtract that from the economist's six to eight percent range, the inflation allowance built into his estimated future wage increases is only three to five percent; and when we subtract these figures from 8.5 percent we see that his implicit estimate of the real rate of interest was very high (3.5-5.5 percent). This means he was conservative, because the higher the discount rate used the lower the damages calculated.

If conservative in one sense, the economist was most liberal in another. He made no allowance for the fact that Mrs. O'Shea, whose health history quite apart from the accident is not outstanding, might very well not have survived – let alone survived and been working as a boat's cook or in an equivalent job – until the age of 70. The damage award is a sum certain, but the lost future wages to which that award is equated by means of the discount rate are mere probabilities. If the probability of her being employed as a boat's cook full time in 1990 was only 75 percent, for example, then her estimated wages in that year should have been multiplied by .75 to determine the value of the expectation that she lost as a result of the accident; and so with each of the other future years. . . . The economist did not do this, and by failing to do this he overstated the loss due to the accident.

But Riverway does not make an issue of this aspect of the economist's analysis. Nor of another: the economist selected the 8.5 percent figure for the discount rate because that was the current interest rate on Triple A 10-year state and municipal bonds, but it would not make sense in Mrs. O'Shea's federal income tax bracket to invest in tax-free bonds. If he wanted to use nominal rather than real interest rates and wage increases (as we said was proper), the economist should have used a higher discount rate and a higher expected rate of inflation. But as these adjustments would have been largely or entirely offsetting, the failure to make them was not a critical error.

Although we are not entirely satisfied with the economic analysis on which the judge, in the absence of any other evidence of the present value of Mrs. O'Shea's lost future wages, must have relied heavily, we recognize that the exactness which economic analysis rigorously pursued appears to offer is, at least in the litigation setting, somewhat delusive. Therefore, we will not reverse an award of damages for lost wages because of questionable assumptions unless it yields an unreasonable result – especially when, as in the present case, the defendant does not offer any economic evidence himself and does not object to the questionable steps in the plaintiff's economic analysis. We cannot say the result here was unreasonable. If the economist's method of estimating damages was too generous to Mrs. O'Shea in one important respect it was, as we have seen, niggardly in another. Another error against Mrs. O'Shea should be noted: the economist should not have deducted her entire income tax liability in estimating her future lost wages. . . . While it is true that the damage award is not taxable, the interest she earns on it will be (a point the economist may have ignored because of his erroneous assumption that she would invest the award in tax-exempt bonds), so that his method involved an element of double taxation.

If we assume that Mrs. O'Shea could have expected a three percent annual increase in her real wages from a base of $7200, that the real risk-free rate of interest (and therefore the appropriate discount rate if we are considering only real wage increases) is two percent, and that she would have worked till she was 70, the present value of her lost future wages would be $91,310. This figure ignores the fact that she did not have a 100 percent probability of actually working till age 70 as a boat's cook, and fails to make the appropriate (though probably, in her bracket, very small) net income tax adjustment; but it also ignores the possibility, small but not totally negligible, that the proper base is really $10,800 rather than $7200.

So we cannot say that the figure arrived at by the judge, $86,033, was unreasonably high. But we are distressed that he made no attempt to explain how he had arrived at that figure, since it was not one contained in the economist's testimony though it must in some way have been derived from that testimony. Unlike many other damage items in a personal injury case, notably pain and suffering, the calculation of damages for lost earnings can and should be an analytical rather than an intuitive undertaking. . . . We do not consider this reversible error, because our own analysis convinces us that the award of damages for lost future wages was reasonable. But for the future we ask the district judges in this circuit to indicate the steps by which they arrive at damage awards for lost future earnings.

JUDGMENT AFFIRMED.

NOTES AND QUESTIONS

1   *Future Earnings.* If Mrs. O'Shea had died in the accident, would an award of lost future wages be appropriate then? Why or why not? Are lost future wages in a wrongful death case different from lost pleasures of life? How?

If the victim does not survive, she does not need the money. Would this not be like the comatose plaintiff in the *McDougald* case, who could not recover for lost pleasures and pursuits unless she was conscious of the loss? If the estate in a wrongful death suit is awarded damages for lost future wages, should defendant then get a set-off for the living expenses avoided by the deceased plaintiff?

2   *Lost Earning Capacity.* What if Mrs. O'Shea had had no present or future plans to work at all when she was injured? How should her damages have been measured then? If she never intended to work, has she lost anything now that she cannot work? Plaintiffs generally may recover for their "lost earning capacity." While estimating the lost earning capacity of very young plaintiffs can be particularly difficult, most courts will allow a plaintiff with no wage history to recover for lost earning capacity. Is lost earning capacity a pecuniary loss or a non-pecuniary loss?

3   *Lump Sum and Discount to Present Value.* As this case illustrates, when a plaintiff successfully tries a case to judgment, all damages, including future damages, typically are awarded presently in one lump sum. (Of course, most cases are settled before trial, and the parties sometimes will agree to a "structured settlement" that is paid out over time.) The typical practice of awarding one lump sum for all damages past, present, and future, raises the issue of "discounting" awards of future earnings to present value. "Discounting" merely recognizes the time value of money. If a court desires to award plaintiff a sum that will replace $40,000 of income expected to be received at some time in the future, giving plaintiff $40,000 now will over-compensate the plaintiff because plaintiff can invest that sum to obtain a larger sum by the time that the income is to be replaced. Therefore, once the sum to be replaced in the future is determined, that future sum is "discounted" to a present sum that, if invested conservatively, would grow into the desired sum by the time the income is expected to be lost. In 1997, the United States Treasury Department began releasing "inflation-indexed" bonds designed to give a specified yield and a preservation of principal adjusted for inflation. Some courts treat the interest rate on such bonds as strong evidence of the time value of money. Generally, pecuniary losses are discounted to present value, but awards for non-pecuniary losses are not. The "flipside" of discounting to present value is adjusting future damages elements upward to take into account likely inflation in the interim between the award and the loss. Sometimes, the inflation effect and the discounting to present value and create a sort of wash.

4   *Taxes on Future Earnings.* Notice that plaintiff's expert deducted taxes from his future wage calculation. Why? The Internal Revenue Code excludes from income compensatory personal injury awards, including awards for past and future earnings. Most courts do not permit the jury to take tax consequences into account when determining damages awards.

5   *Pre-judgment Interest.* In many, perhaps most jurisdictions, including in federal courts exercising federal question jurisdiction, prejudgment interest is available. In some jurisdictions, such as in Virginia, and in federal question cases, whether plaintiff recovers pre-judgment interest is within the court's discretion.

6   *Eggshell Skull Rule.* What if Mrs. O'Shea had been a popular entertainer so that her lost future earnings ran into the hundreds of millions? Courts generally have held such damages recoverable using the maxim that defendant "takes his victim as he finds him." Note that this rule is perfectly consonant with the compensatory purpose of damages.

7   *Workers' Compensation.* Today, when an employer is legally responsible for an employee's workplace injury, compensation typically is handled through a workers' compensation system. Compensation levels tend to be lower under the workers' compensation system, but the employee is freed from the obligation to prove employer fault. Injuries typically are compensated using a fixed schedule. Recovery of many elements of general damage is not allowed.

B. MITIGATION

Plaintiffs generally are under a duty to take reasonable steps to mitigate their damages. Frequently, the duty to mitigate damages involves seeking reasonable medical treatment for injuries caused by defendant. As illustrated by the following two cases, this duty can give rise to some sticky questions concerning what steps in mitigation of damages are "reasonable."

MCGINLEY V. UNITED STATES
329 F. SUPP. 62 (E.D. PA. 1971)

This is an action . . . in which plaintiff, Charles Joseph McGinley is suing the United States of America for injuries which he sustained while working aboard the SS CITADEL VICTORY. Liability having been admitted, the instant action involves solely the issue of damages. . . .

FINDINGS OF FACT

1. On February 11, 1968, plaintiff, Charles Joseph McGinley, presently 45 years of age, was employed by Northern Metal Company as head stevedore foreman. . . .

3. As plaintiff descended a vertical steel ladder into the No. 2 hold, he had his feet on one of the rungs of the lower tween deck ladder and held the bottom rung of the upper tween deck ladder with his right hand.

4. As he exerted a pull on this rung, it came loose in his hand, causing him to fall from the ladder. . . .

11. On April 15, 1968, plaintiff was admitted to Pennsylvania Hospital by Dr. Langfitt who surgically removed a herniated cervical disc. . . .

13. Plaintiff attempted to return to work on or about July 8, 1968, but was unable to work because of pains in his low back. . . .

14. Plaintiff again returned to work on or about September 3, 1968, but was able to work only until November 6, 1968, at which time he left because of pains in his back. . . .

15. On November 6, 1968, plaintiff was admitted to University of Pennsylvania Hospital for approximately twenty days, during which time a second myelogram was performed and plaintiff underwent various treatments. . . .

16. After plaintiff was discharged from the hospital he continued to receive outpatient physiotherapy. . . .

18. Plaintiff returned to work on March 31, 1969, and continued to work until on or about September 4, 1969. . . .

19. On or about September 4, 1969, while talking to a co-worker, plaintiff felt a sharp pain in his low back which caused him to collapse. . . .

21. Plaintiff has not worked since September 4, 1969. . . .

24. If plaintiff is suffering from arachnoiditis, an inflammation of the covering of the spinal cord, . . . an operation would not improve his condition. . . .

25. Further surgery could worsen plaintiff's condition. . . .

27. Plaintiff is permanently disabled from performing his former duties as head stevedore foreman. . . .

28. Plaintiff is unable to engage in any activity which requires protracted walking, climbing, lifting or bending. He is also unable to remain seated for any extensive period of time. . . .

30. In order to obtain employment as a checker or a dispatcher, it would be necessary for plaintiff, who attended one year of high school, to complete his high school education, receive additional vocational training and obtain membership in the appropriate union. Plaintiff would have difficulty performing such a job because of his pain. . . .

31. There is a very poor record of success in placing in indoor work a person who has worked outdoors all of his life as plaintiff has done. . . .

32. There is no evidence of any employment which plaintiff, considering his condition, working background and education, can obtain. . . .

34. Plaintiff has been deprived of ten years' future income because of the injuries which he suffered aboard the SS CITADEL VICTORY.

35. Plaintiff earned $14,640 in 1966 and $16,208 in 1967. His average income for those two years is $15,424. . . .

36. Plaintiff's future loss of earnings, based on an income of $15,424 per year and reduced to present worth, totals $117,222. . . .

37. Plaintiff's earnings for 1968 and 1969 were $13,278 and $8,809 respectively. . . .

38. Plaintiff's past loss of earnings to June 1, 1971, based on an income of $15,424 per year, totals $30,610.

39. Plaintiff's medical expenses total $7,367.49. There is no evidence of continuing medical expenses.

40. Plaintiff's present life expectancy is 27.4 years. . . .

41. As a result of plaintiff's injuries, he has undergone two operations. He has had two myelograms and two electromyograms performed on him. He has been admitted to the hospital on four separate occasions and has spent at least twenty days in traction. He has also been forced to wear a Knight spinal brace since July, 1968.

42. Plaintiff has suffered constant severe pain as a result of his accident and will continue to suffer such pain.

43. Plaintiff continues to suffer instances in which he feels a sudden intense pain in his lower back which causes him to collapse. . . .

44. Plaintiff has a severe limp and is able to move around only with great pain.

45. A reasonable compensation for plaintiff's past pain and suffering is $50,000.

46. A reasonable compensation for plaintiff's future pain and suffering is $150,000.

DISCUSSION

This case presents several issues of damages which require discussion. The first is whether we should reduce the amount of plaintiff's recovery because of his failure to undergo further surgery in an attempt to alleviate the pain in his low back. We conclude that his recovery should not be so reduced.

It is, of course, settled law that if injuries may be cured or alleviated by a simple and safe surgical operation, then refusal to submit thereto should be considered in mitigation of damages. . . . This is not true, however, where the operation is a serious one, or one attended by grave risk of death or failure. . . . A plaintiff has a duty to submit to reasonable medical treatment and the test of reasonableness is to be determined by the triers of fact. . . .

The record in this instant case clearly demonstrates that plaintiff has continuously submitted to reasonable medical treatment since he first sustained his injuries. He has already undergone two operations, one for the removal of a herniated cervical disc and the other an exploratory operation on his spine. Moreover he has never refused to submit to further surgery. His physician, Dr. Langfitt, while testifying that another exploratory operation to locate and remove a possible herniated disc might alleviate plaintiff's condition, also testified that he had never, prior to trial, advised plaintiff to have another operation. Consequently this is not a case where a plaintiff has refused to follow the advice of his physician. . . .

The evidence also indicates that the proposed operation is of highly questionable value. In the first instance, such an operation would have only a 60 to 70% chance of being successful. . . . Moreover, it would relieve his disc problem only at the L/5 level of the spine, and the likelihood exists that further surgery would be necessary in a few years to relieve disc problems at other levels of his spine. . . . It is also not inconceivable that further surgery at this time could worsen plaintiff's condition. . . . Finally, an operation such as the one described would obviously be successful only in the event that plaintiff does, in fact, have a herniated disc. If, however, he is suffering from arachnoiditis, as appears likely, such an operation would not relieve his condition. . . . Under these circumstances we do not find it unreasonable for plaintiff to decline to undergo further surgery.

Defendants have also attempted to show that plaintiff, although permanently disabled from his former occupation as head stevedore foreman, can mitigate his damages by obtaining other employment. It has been demonstrated that plaintiff, because of his condition and employment background is unsuitable for indoor employment. Defendants maintain, however, that he could obtain employment as a checker on the waterfront.

The law requires of an injured party a reasonable effort to mitigate his damages. . . . This includes a duty to seek reasonable alternative employment. . . . We believe that the course which defendants would have plaintiff follow oversteps the bounds of reasonableness.

We have found no case which holds that a disabled plaintiff has a duty not only to obtain alternative employment which he is capable of performing, but also to prepare himself educationally for a job which he is not capable of performing at the time of his injury. Nor do we feel that such a rule is appropriate, especially in a case such as this where the plaintiff has been out of school for approximately thirty years and the amount of time that it would take him to complete the necessary schooling would be extensive. Accordingly, we conclude that plaintiff has no duty to obtain employment as a checker. . . .

NOTE

1   Like the comparative responsibility rule, the doctrine of avoidable consequences imposes on plaintiff a duty to take reasonable care for plaintiff's own protection, but the two doctrines function in different ways. Comparative responsibility reduces the damages for which defendant is responsible based on plaintiff's relative percentage of fault. The avoidable consequences analysis, by contrast, is causal – that is defendant avoids responsibility for the discrete part of plaintiff's injury caused by plaintiff's own failure to take reasonable steps to mitigate the loss. It is not necessary to determine a "percentage" of plaintiff's fault or to calculate the effect of that fault on plaintiff's recovery for an indivisible injury. Thus, in "modified" comparative responsibility jurisdictions, even when plaintiff's failure to mitigate has caused the lion's share of plaintiff's loss, defendant still would be responsible for the loss

that plaintiff would have suffered even if plaintiff had taken reasonable mitigation steps. Nevertheless, some courts have merged the plaintiff's duty to mitigate damages into the comparative responsibility analysis.

2   The defendant bears the burden to plead and prove plaintiff's failure to take reasonable care to mitigate damages.

MUNN V. ALGEE
924 F.2D 568 (5TH CIR. 1991)

Plaintiff Ray James Munn asserts that his and his deceased wife's adherence to the Jehovah's Witnesses faith was used improperly to impair his ability to recover compensation for their injuries. Finding no reversible error, we affirm.

I. Facts.

On Christmas morning 1986, vehicles driven by Munn and defendant Trudy Algee collided in Tunica County, Mississippi. Elaine Munn, Munn's wife and a passenger in his car, was transported to the Regional Medical Center in Memphis, Tennessee, arriving approximately three hours after the accident. Doctors identified a variety of injuries, including multiple rib and pelvic fractures, a lacerated chest artery, and a retroperitoneal hematoma.

Upon arrival at the hospital, Mrs. Munn informed doctors that she was a Jehovah's Witness and thus would not accept blood transfusions. Responding to her deteriorating condition, doctors unsuccessfully sought Munn's permission later in the day to perform a blood transfusion on his wife. Munn also refused to allow doctors to transfuse Mrs. Munn's own blood back into her.

Mrs. Munn died on the operating table from a loss of blood. Elaine and Ray James Munn incurred medical expenses in the amounts of $10,411.67 and $241.44, respectively.

II. Procedural History.

Munn brought suit against Algee in three separate capacities: (1) individually for his own injuries; (2) as administrator of his deceased spouse's estate; and (3) on behalf of his children, who, along with Mr. Munn, are the wrongful death beneficiaries under the Mississippi wrongful death statute . . . . The district court granted Algee's motion for partial summary judgment, thereby precluding Munn from establishing what his wife's damages would have been had she consented to the blood transfusions and survived. The court granted a directed verdict in favor of plaintiffs on the question of liability.

After a trial, the jury awarded Munn $241.44 for his own medical expenses. It also returned a verdict for Munn in the amount of $20,411.67 to compensate Mrs. Munn's estate for her medical bills ($10,411.67) and her pain and suffering ($10,000.00). With respect to the wrongful death claim, the jury concluded that Mrs. Munn would not have died had she accepted blood transfusions and thus awarded the wrongful death beneficiaries no damages.

Munn moved for a new trial, asserting that the court erred in (1) admitting evidence of Jehovah's Witnesses' beliefs; (2) allowing Algee to invoke the avoidable consequences doctrine; (3) refusing to allow Munn to show what his wife's damages would have been had she accepted blood and lived; (4) refusing to apply the eggshell skull doctrine; (5) entering judgment on allegedly inconsistent answers to jury interrogatories; and (6) its instructions to the jury. Munn also argued that the verdict was against the great weight of the evidence and that the damage award was inadequate. The court denied the motion for new trial, . . . and Munn now appeals. . . .

III. Admission of Evidence of Religious Beliefs.

Over Munn's objection, the district court allowed Algee's counsel to question him about many aspects of the Jehovah's Witnesses faith, including, inter alia, the following beliefs and practices: (1) Christ's physical return to earth in 1914; (2) the eternal damnation of all those not adhering to the faith; (3) the non-existence of hell; (4) the non-existence of souls; (5) refusal to "do service to their country"; and (6) refusal to salute the flag. Algee's counsel further questioned Munn about his and his wife's adherence vel non to the faith's prohibition on premarital cohabitation. . . .

A. Admissibility.

. . . Algee asserts that the fact of consequence of which this testimony is probative is the sincerity of the Munns' adherence to their faith. . . . One might plausibly argue that sincerity is a fact of consequence in that a decision sincerely motivated by a religious belief is more reasonable [4] than an otherwise inexplicable action. However, only the discussion of the Munns' adherence to the prohibition on premarital cohabitation reflects upon their sincerity. Simply inquiring otherwise into whether the Jehovah's Witnesses faith incorporates certain beliefs does not reveal anything about whether the Munns sincerely adhered to them.

Nor were these questions directly probative of the reasonableness of Mrs. Munn's decision to refuse blood. Algee fails to demonstrate how Jehovah's Witnesses' beliefs unrelated to blood transfusions reveal the reasonableness of her adherence to one particular article of the faith.[5] . . .

---

[4] The reasonableness of Mrs. Munn's decision is most definitely a fact of consequence, for Algee invoked the doctrine of avoidable consequences, which precludes recovery for injuries that an injured plaintiff might *reasonably* have avoided. *See infra* part IV.

[5] Algee may have sought to imply that, in her view, because the entire religion is unreasonable, any decision made in accordance therewith is per se unreasonable. However, *United States v. Ballard*, 322 U.S. 78, 87, 64 S. Ct. 882, 886, 88 L. Ed. 1148(1944), which bars adjudication of a religion's reasonableness, forbids a jury from relying upon this argument.

B. Reversible or Harmless Error.

... After reviewing the record, we conclude – although it is a close question – that the admission of Munn's testimony did not adversely influence the jury. Munn failed to articulate any substantial right affected by this evidence's admission, ... and no prejudice is reflected in the jury's verdict. First, Munn cannot plausibly argue that the amount of damages for pain and suffering awarded to Elaine Munn's estate demonstrates prejudice. For approximately eight hours of pain and suffering, the jury awarded $10,000.00, an amount not so small as to arouse suspicion as to the jury's motives. Second, the jury's failure to award Munn any damages for his own pain and suffering most likely reflects the relatively minor nature of his injuries. ... He incurred only $241.44 in medical expenses and by his own admission suffered only "bruises and contusions."

The jury's failure to award any wrongful death damages is the most plausible expression of any prejudice caused by the erroneous admission of this evidence. However, the jury most likely refused to compensate the wrongful death beneficiaries because it believed that Mrs. Munn would have lived had she taken blood transfusions. A number of doctors testified as to whether blood transfusions would have saved Mrs. Munn's life, ... and although their testimony was conflicting, the evidence was such that in deciding the cause of Mrs. Munn's death, there is no indication that the jury was using her refusal to take blood as a pretext for expressing its possible distaste for Jehovah's Witnesses. ...

Thus we hold that the erroneous admission of Munn's testimony did not affect any substantial right. In this regard we affirm the denial of the motion for new trial.

IV. The First Amendment and the Avoidable Consequences Doctrine.

In an effort to avoid liability for Mrs. Munn's death, Algee argued that Mrs. Munn's refusal to accept blood transfusions was unreasonable and thus that the doctrine of avoidable consequences[9] precluded any recovery. Munn now asserts that application of this doctrine violated the first amendment's free exercise and establishment clauses, arguing that the rule burdened his wife's exercise of the Jehovah's Witnesses faith and invited the jury to consider the reasonableness of that religion.

Munn cites a published article to support his argument that application of this doctrine violates the first amendment. *See* Comment, *Medical Care, Freedom of Religion, and Mitigation of Damages*, 87 Yale L.J. 1466 (1978). The comment writer accurately identifies two judicial approaches to religiously motivated refusals to mitigate tort damages. *Id.* at 1467. The first, labelled the "objective" approach, holds that religion may not justify an otherwise unreasonable failure to mitigate. The second, termed the "case-by-case" approach, attempts to accommodate religious beliefs by allowing the jury to consider the plaintiff's religious beliefs in determining

---

9   Under Mississippi law, an injured plaintiff may not recover for damages that he did not take reasonable efforts to avoid. . . . Courts frequently use the phrases "avoidance of consequences" and "mitigation of damages" interchangeably.

whether his or her failure to mitigate was reasonable. . . . In the instant case, the court applied the case-by-case approach, attempting to accommodate Mrs. Munn's religious beliefs.[10]

Without identifying the court's approach, Munn argues that its application of the avoidable consequences doctrine violated both first amendment clauses. He accordingly desires . . . that we recognize a special exemption from the doctrine's application for religiously motivated failures to mitigate damages. We decline to do so, as we conclude that proper application of the avoidable consequences doctrine does not violate the first amendment.

A. Free Exercise Concerns.

Munn contends that applying the mitigation of damages principle to this case violates the first amendment because it incidentally affects Mrs. Munn's exercise of her religion. This argument is foreclosed by Supreme Court cases holding that generally applicable rules imposing incidental burdens on particular religions do not violate the free exercise clause. . . . Accordingly, we hold that the application of the mitigation of damages doctrine, under either of the two approaches, does not violate the free exercise clause of the first amendment. . . .

E. Jury Instructions.

. . . During the jury instruction conference, Munn's counsel urged the court to direct the jury to ask what a reasonable Jehovah's Witness would have done in Mrs. Munn's situation. The court refused to adopt this instruction, instead instructing the jury in a way that defies easy categorization as "objective" or "subjective":

> In determining whether or not Elaine Munn's decision to refuse the blood transfusion was unreasonable, you may consider that the blood transfusions were medically recommended. But, you may also consider her religious beliefs and related teachings, together with the known risks of blood transfusions, if you find that to be a factor in her decision.

Both parties blithely conclude that this language reflects an "objective" standard of reasonableness. However, this standard is not purely objective; it does not ask the jury whether reasonable people would have done what Mrs. Munn did. It contains a subjective component, allowing the jury to "consider her religious beliefs and related teachings."

. . . Mississippi cases considering the avoidable consequences doctrine do not prohibit this instruction. . . . Some cases do apply a standard of reasonableness that is "subjective" in the sense that the nature of the plaintiff is taken into account. In Henderson, the plaintiff sought damages

---

10   The court stated that "the jury is going to be called upon to determine the reasonableness of their beliefs considering their religion as one of the factors." Later in the proceedings the court similarly declared that "one of the issues for the jury to decide is the reasonableness of the deceased, presumably Mr. Munn's decision, based on their belief in the Jehovah's Witness doctrine."

for his continuing physical disability, even though surgery would have enabled him to return to work and thus mitigate his damages. The plaintiff argued that he was unable to pay for the operation, and the defendant responded by asserting that the plaintiff's financial condition was not relevant to the reasonableness of his failure to mitigate damages.

The Mississippi Supreme Court rejected this position, stating that the mitigation of damages rule is "one of reason, and, if the injured person be powerless to take the needed step, reasonableness has become exhausted and the applicability of the rule is at an end."[8] 177 So. at 530. Although Henderson effectively jettisons the notion that Mississippi has a purely objective standard of reasonableness, . . . it does not render erroneous the district court's instruction, which did not contain a purely objective standard. The instruction allowed the jury to consider factors unique to the decedent, such as "her religious beliefs and related teachings." Hence, because the instruction comported with Mississippi law, the district court's judgment in this regard is affirmed. . . .

The judgment of the district court is in all respects AFFIRMED. . . .

ALVIN B. RUBIN, Circuit Judge, dissenting:

The personal-injury and wrongful-death claims of two black Jehovah's Witnesses from Tennessee were being tried before a predominantly white jury in Clarksdale, Mississippi. Judge Smith correctly finds that the trial court erred in admitting irrelevant evidence that was calculated to evoke the jury's prejudices, but concludes that this inflammatory effort by counsel and error by the trial court did not affect a substantial right of the plaintiffs. In my opinion, this commits a legal error both because it equates effect on a substantial right with the likelihood that a different verdict would have been reached had the evidence been excluded and by substituting a judge's personal view of the effect of the evidence for the evaluation of its possible impact in this case before this jury: it minimizes the potential consequences of the deliberate appeal to religious prejudice and to chauvinism permitted by the trial court. . . . I therefore respectfully dissent.

I

The majority opinion carefully relates most of the facts. It recites some, however, in bland generality. The record contains the following specifics: Ray James Munn and his wife, both blacks, were residents of Tennessee. Ms. Munn was critically injured in an automobile accident in Mississippi by a vehicle driven by Trudy Algee, a white resident of Mississippi. After Ms. Munn's death, her husband could file suit only in Mississippi because Algee, an individual, was a resident of that state and did not do business in Tennessee. Instead of suing in state court, he invoked the constitutional and statutory grants of diversity jurisdiction, designed to protect nonresidents from the possible prejudice of state courts, to file suit in the United States District

---

18   Incidentally, Munn could argue that Mrs. Munn was "powerless" to mitigate her damages. However, she was not "powerless" to accept blood transfusions in the sense that the plaintiff in *Henderson* was "powerless" to pay for the operation. There is a difference between hard choices and physical impossibility.

Court for Northern District of Mississippi, on his behalf and on behalf of Ms. Munn's three children.

Algee admitted liability, so the trial was only to determine damages. The case was tried before a jury of six; five of the jurors were white, one was black. Algee used all three of her peremptory challenges to exclude blacks. . . .

Munn testified both on direct and on cross-examination that he and his wife were Jehovah's Witnesses, that his wife had refused to take a blood transfusion because of her religious beliefs; that, after she lost consciousness, he rejected a transfusion because she and he both believed that, "even if it meant dying, you would not take that risk [of a blood transfusion] however small it was;" and that, "We don't waiver in our faith."

Counsel for the defendant then proceeded to cross examine him not on his or his wife's personal beliefs or faith, or on reasonableness of their opposition to transfusions, but on the general beliefs of those who profess to be Jehovah's Witnesses. Part of the cross-examination follows:

Q. Let me ask you this. Isn't it true that the Jehovah Witnesses' faith adheres to the belief that Christ returned to earth in 1914 and has invisibly ruled since that time through the Watchtower?

A. Through the organization here.

Q. The organization is the Watchtower?

A. Well, not the Watchtowser. It's the one, the governing body of the Jehovah's Witnesses – of where the magazines come from.

Q. It is the belief in accordance with that of Jehovah's Witnesses that since Christ returned in 1914 there will not be a resurrection but there will be ultimately Armageddon and after Armageddon Christ will begin his ruling of the millennium and the Jehovah's Witnesses will be spared that and all others will be eternally damned; isn't that the belief of the Jehovah's Witnesses?

A. You stated that well.

Q. Is it the belief of the Jehovah's Witnesses that there is no hell for the wicked; the wicked will merely be annihilated?

A. That's what the scripture [sic] say.

Q. It is the belief of the Jehovah's Witnesses that man has no soul, and when man dies that the soul was merely a manifestation for the body during life; isn't that true?

A. Well, the soul is the breath and the life force combined along with it.

Q. It is the belief of the Jehovah's Witnesses that followers of Jehovah's Witnesses are not members of any earthly kingdom?

A. Well, you didn't state that correct.

Q. How would you state it?

A. There is – we – it's not an earthly kingdom. Christ is his invisible presence from the Scriptures ruled from the heaven, the heavenly kingdom, not an earthly kingdom.

Q. Is it based on that premise that Jehovah's Witnesses are, for instance, conscientious objectors toward service to their country; isn't that true?

A. Say that again.

Q. It is based on that premise of followers of this religion not being servants to any earthly kingdom upon which Jehovah's Witnesses base their belief that they are conscientious objectors and therefore do not do service to their country, like going to war?

A. No, we don't go to war. . . .

Q. Is my statement correct?

A. Right. We don't go to war.

Q. It is on that same premise, or stated differently, that Jehovah's Witnesses, for instance, don't salute the flag because that would be ascribing salvation to the flag; isn't that true?

A. Right. We don't salute the flag. . . .

Counsel for Algee also delved into another matter: . . .

Q. Included in the material that you have brought into court and that you referred to yesterday on direct examination, if you will turn to the page that I have the yellow tab on, please, sir. It is also the beliefs and teachings of Jehovah's Witness faith that a man and woman do not live together prior to marriage, isn't it?

A. That's right.

Q. But you and Mrs. Munn lived together prior to marriage, didn't you, in violation of the Scriptures and your teachings?

A. At the time I met her –

Q. Go ahead and answer yes or no, first, and then you may explain.

A. Yes, we did. Now, let me explain. When I met her she was not in the organization. As I explained to you earlier how someone is disciplined for certain things and if they show no sign of repentance, at that time they're disfellowshipped, she had left the organization when I met her. And I was not in the organization, didn't know anything about the organization. For a short period of time we did live together, but she did repent and go back into the organization. And I, myself, became a Jehovah's Witness.

Q. Are you saying that at the time you met her she had been disfellowshipped for some other transgression?

A. She had.

Counsel for Algee was careful to remind the jury of the Munns' sinful conduct in his closing argument. None of this, of course, had any probative value whatever as to any issue before the jury.

II

Judge Smith agrees with me that the admission of this testimony was error. Indeed, considering who the parties were, the time and place of the trial, and the patent irrelevance both of the beliefs of other members of Munn's faith and the Munns' premarital relations, the error was in my opinion egregious. He concludes, however, that the effect of this evocation of patriotic passion, religious prejudice, and bias against premarital sexual conduct is completely dissipated because its admission did not affect a substantial right of the Munns.

. . . [S]ome would contend that, given the conditions under which this case was tried, errors like those committed in this trial warrant reversal per se. . . . Ms. Algee had admitted her liability. The jury was called upon to decide only the damages due Mr. Munn and his wife's children. In doing so, the jurors were asked to make four necessarily subjective determinations: (1) Whether Ms. Munn's refusal to take blood was reasonable; (2) What portion of Ms. Munn's damages were attributable to her unreasonable refusal to take blood; (3) What amount of damages would compensate Ms. Munn's estate for her pain and suffering; and (4) What amount of damages would compensate Mr. Munn for his pain and suffering. The jury's sympathy for or antipathy to the Munns might substantially affect their decision on each of these issues. I therefore see no way that a reviewing court could be "sure" – other than by substituting its own views for those of the jury or by inventing some post-hoc rationalization for the verdict – that Algee's appeal to the jury's religious prejudice and nationalism "had but slight effect" on the verdict. In this case, however, we need not go so far as to find error per se. Under the traditional analysis, this error could not have been harmless.

III

The interrogatories submitted to the jury with respect to Ms. Munn and the jury's answers follow:

1. What amount of damages do you find plaintiff has proven by a preponderance of the evidence to have been incurred by Elaine Munn up to the time of her death for pain and suffering and mental anguish?
     $ 10,000.00.

2. Do you find that defendant proved by a preponderance of the evidence that Elaine Munn would have survived had she accepted the blood transfusions?
     Yes.

3. Do you find that defendant has proved by a preponderance of the evidence that Elaine Munn's refusal of blood transfusions was unreasonable?

> Yes.

4. Do you find that the original injuries sustained by Elaine Munn combined with her unreasonable refusal of blood to cause her death?

> Yes.

If your answer to this interrogatory is "Yes," what percentage did Elaine Munn's unreasonable refusal of blood contribute to her death?

> 100 percent.

No special interrogatories concerning Mr. Munn were submitted to the jury.

I do not understand the statement that "Munn failed to articulate any substantial right affected by this evidence's admission." . . . I cannot imagine a more explicit articulation than Munn's claim that the evidence "poisoned the minds of the jury [sic] from the outset," thus preventing him from obtaining an impartial assessment of the damages due. The inquiry, then, must focus on whether there was any realistic possibility that counsel for Algee succeeded in his calculated effort to "poison" the minds of the jurors and to affect their verdict through the erroneously admitted evidence.

Patently, it seems to me, the jury's view of whether Ms. Munn and her husband were honest, sincere, and responsible members of the community might have affected the amount of damages it awarded for Ms. Munn's pain and suffering before death, its view that her refusal of blood transfusions was or was not reasonable, and its evaluation of the conflicting testimony concerning whether her refusal to accept a transfusion was either the sole or even a cause of death. Judge Smith does not even intimate a different view. Instead, because he finds the verdict to be within what he considers a reasonable range, he grants absolution for the error.

Apparently, neither of my brothers accepts the view that any lawyer who has tried personal injury cases considers fundamental: the sympathy or disaffection the jury has for the victim affects the amount of damages. . . .

Instead of asking whether, absent the tainted testimony the jury might have awarded more, Judge Smith observes that the error did not result in an absurdly low verdict. "For approximately eight hours of pain and suffering, the jury awarded $10,000.00, an amount not so small as to arouse suspicion as to the jury's motives." . . . Yet the jury might have awarded a much larger amount. Apart from whether her death might have been averted, Ms. Munn suffered for eight hours from severe injuries. Her pelvis was fractured in two places. Her ribs were broken. She was bleeding profusely internally and suffered extensive internal bruising. Her physicians inserted a tube in her chest. They cut open her abdomen to insert lavage fluid. They cut open her chest and spread her ribs eight inches apart to clamp a lacerated artery. . . .

In like fashion, Judge Smith concludes that awarding Munn nothing for his own pain and suffering "most likely" reflects the relatively minor nature of his injuries. This conjectural determination of probability takes no account of the other possibility that I consider likely and with which I think most lawyers would agree: that a jury who considered Munn a patriotic, moral, sensible, and sympathetic person might well have awarded him thousands of dollars for the same infliction. None of us who sit on this court are virgins at the bar. We have all seen, and some of us have affirmed, substantial verdicts for "bruises and contusions." Indeed, I can conceive of no reason but general dislike of the plaintiff for a jury to award medical expenses against an admittedly liable defendant, but to award nothing for pain and suffering when the uncontroverted evidence was that Munn suffered pain and general discomfort from his "bruises and contusions" for several months. . . .

Justice Frankfurter said that we as judges should not be ignorant of what we know as men. . . . Nor should we disregard what we know as experienced lawyers. We know that persuading the jury of the good character of the plaintiffs is likely to enhance their verdict, and that portraying them unfavorably tends to decrease it. Anecdote has it that the late Sammy Davis Jr., when about to play golf, was asked, "What is your handicap?" He replied, "I'm black, one-eyed and Jewish, and you still want to know my handicap?!" The Munns were quadruply handicapped – black nonresidents adhering to an unpopular faith, some of whose members were unpatriotic, trying a case before a north Mississippi jury, five of whose six members were white.

Judge Smith concludes that inducing this predominantly white Mississippi jury to believe or at least to infer that the Munns believed that Christ returned to earth in 1914 and has invisibly ruled since that time, that there will not be a resurrection but that the jury (like all others ever on earth save Jehovah's Witnesses) will be eternally damned, that Munn believes man has no soul, that Munn is a conscientious objector who will not expose himself to the dangers inherent in military service even when the nation is threatened, that the Munns even refuse to salute the flag, and that they lived together in adultery prior to their marriage all likely had no effect on the Munns' substantial rights. . . . This to me, with all respect . . . , is contrary to the universal knowledge and experience of trial lawyers and judges, and to the human disposition to favor those we like and to discountenance those we disfavor. Algee's lawyer deliberately threw the proverbial skunk of inadmissible evidence into the jury box. No amount of conjecture that the jury might not have smelled the stink can undo the odor that, even now, permeates the record. I therefore respectfully dissent.

C. WRONGFUL DEATH AND LOSS OF CONSORTIUM

1. WRONGFUL DEATH/SURVIVAL ACTIONS

At common law, an injured plaintiff could recover for wrongful injury, but not for wrongful death. All causes of action between two parties were personal and extinguished upon the death of either. Survivors had no cognizable cause of action for the tortious death of a loved one.

This situation has been changed by statute in all fifty states. Wrongful death is not so much an independent cause of action as it is a statement of particular types of compensable harm that result to survivors from death of a near relative and that arise from another established cause of action. A major difference among the American jurisdictions is whether the near relatives who may recover in a wrongful death action are limited to recovering economic losses or whether they may also recover general damages.

Almost all jurisdictions now also have a survival statute, providing that the decedent's cause of action for recovery of damages for the harms suffered by the decedent, and for which he would have been able to recover had he not died, "survives" his death. The word "survival" in the phrase "survival statute" refers to the survival of the action, not to the survival of the decedent. Damages recoverable include precisely what the decedent could have recovered had he survived. "Survival statutes" also provide for the survival of causes of action against the decedent's estate.

The Virginia Wrongful Death and Survival statutes, which are not exceptional, are set out below. Such statutes typically establish who recovers in a wrongful death action, what types of harm are compensable, and how the damages are measured. In Virginia, for example, the surviving spouse, children, grandchildren, or any dependent relative who lived in decedent's household are those who recover. Other statutes are not so clear about who may recover, leaving some room for judicial interpretation.

VA. CODE § 8.01-50 (2003)

Action for death by wrongful act; how and when to be brought
   A. Whenever the death of a person shall be caused by the wrongful act, neglect,
      or default of any person or corporation, or of any ship or vessel, and the act,
      neglect, or default is such as would, if death had not ensued, have entitled
      the party injured to maintain an action . . . and to recover damages in respect
      thereof, then, and in every such case, the person who, or corporation or ship or
      vessel which, would have been liable, if death had not ensued, shall be liable to
      an action for damages . . . , notwithstanding the death of the person injured . . . .

B. Every such action under this section shall be brought by and in the name of the personal representative of such deceased person . . . .

C. If the deceased person was an infant who was in the custody of a parent pursuant to an order of court or written agreement with the other parent, administration shall be granted first to the parent having custody; however, that parent may waive his right to qualify in favor of any other person designated by him. If no such parent or his designee applies for administration within thirty days from the death of the infant, administration shall be granted as in other cases.

VA. CODE § 8.01-53(A) (2003)

The damages awarded pursuant to § 8.01-52 shall be distributed as specified under § 8.01-54 to (i) the surviving spouse, children of the deceased and children of any deceased child of the deceased or (ii) if there be none such, then to the parents, brothers and sisters of the deceased, and to any other relative who is primarily dependent on the decedent for support or services and is also a member of the same household as the decedent or (iii) if the decedent has left both surviving spouse and parent or parents, but no child or grandchild, the award shall be distributed to the surviving spouse and such parent or parents or (iv) if there are survivors under clause (i) or clause (iii), the award shall be distributed to those beneficiaries and to any other relative who is primarily dependent on the decedent for support or services and is also a member of the same household as the decedent or (v) if no survivors exist under clause (i), (ii), (iii), or (iv), the award shall be distributed in the course of descents as provided for in § 64.1-1. Provided, however, no parent whose parental rights and responsibilities have been terminated by a court of competent jurisdiction or pursuant to a permanent entrustment agreement with a child welfare agency shall be eligible as a beneficiary under this section. For purposes of this section, a relative is any person related to the decedent by blood, marriage, or adoption and also includes a stepchild of the decedent.

VA. CODE § 8.01-25 (2003)

Survival of causes of action

Every cause of action whether legal or equitable, which is cognizable in the Commonwealth of Virginia, shall survive either the death of the person against whom the cause of action is or may be asserted, or the death of the person in whose favor the cause of action existed, or the death of both such persons. Provided that in such an action punitive damages shall not be awarded after the death of the party liable for the injury. . . .

As used in this section, the term "death" shall include the death of an individual or the termination or dissolution of any other entity.

O'GRADY V. BROWN
654 s.w.2d 904 (mo. 1983)

In January of 1979, appellant Terri O'Grady was nine months pregnant with an expected delivery date of January 25, 1979. During her pregnancy she had been under the care of respondent doctors Robert Brown and Robert Slickman; her prenatal course was uneventful. On January 15, 1979, appellant began experiencing severe back pains. She spoke with one of her physicians by telephone and then proceeded to St. Joseph Hospital where she was admitted shortly after midnight. . . . During the course of the 24 hours following Terri O'Grady's admission, her uterus ruptured and the fetus was delivered stillborn.

Appellants contend that Terri O'Grady was not properly monitored, observed, or treated by respondents and that her injuries and the death of the fetus were the direct result of respondents' negligence. Appellants filed a petition in three counts, seeking recovery in Count I for personal injuries to Terri O'Grady, in Count II for loss of consortium suffered by Kevin O'Grady, and in Count III for damages suffered by both parents by reason of the wrongful death of their unborn child. Respondents filed motions to dismiss or in the alternative for summary judgment. The trial court sustained respondents' motions to dismiss Count III of the petition . . . . Counts I and II were voluntarily dismissed by appellants without prejudice, and the trial court certified its order dismissing Count III as a final and appealable order. . . .

Appellants urge us to reconsider our ruling in *State ex rel. Hardin v. Sanders*, 538 S.W.2d 336 (hereinafter *Hardin*), in which we held that an action for the wrongful death of an unborn fetus could not be maintained under the provisions of § 537.080 RSMo 1969. In *Hardin* we held that a fetus was not a "person" within the meaning of the statute, observing that "if there had been an intention to create such an action it would have been specifically so stated." 538 S.W.2d at 339. In support of this conclusion, we noted in *Hardin* that the United States Supreme Court in *Roe v. Wade*, 410 U.S. 113, 93 S.Ct. 705, 35 L.Ed.2d 147 (1973), has stated that a fetus is not a "person" within the protection of the Fourteenth Amendment. We interpreted § 537.080 as requiring the deceased "person" to "be entitled to maintain an action at the time the injury was sustained and not at some later time," 538 S.W.2d at 340 (emphasis added), and then concluded it was "obvious" that a fetus could not meet this standard.

Appellants argue that the rule announced in *Hardin* should be reconsidered because it is unduly harsh and not in accord with the result reached in the majority of jurisdictions which have recently considered the issue. Respondents counter that the reasoning of *Hardin* is sound and should not be overruled. They further maintain that the issue presented is one of public policy which would be more appropriately decided in the legislature rather than the courts. The Missouri Hospital Association and the Missouri State Medical Association were granted leave to file briefs as amici curiae and their briefs supported the arguments advanced by respondents.

Because the action for wrongful death is statutory, we must first examine the pertinent language of the present Missouri statute, §§ 537.080 to 537.100, RSMo 1978 (1982 Supp.). . . .

Section 537.080 provides, in part, that:

Whenever the death of a person results from any act, conduct, occurrence, transaction, or circumstance which, if death had not ensued, would have entitled such person to recover damages in respect thereof, the person or party who, or the corporation which, would have been liable if death had not ensued shall be liable in an action for damages, notwithstanding the death of the person injured, which damages may be sued for [by certain classes of plaintiffs which are enumerated here.] Provided further that only one action may be brought under this section against any one defendant for the death of any one person.

Section 537.090 provides that:

In every action brought under Section 537.080, the trier of the facts may give to the party or parties entitled thereto such damages as the trier of the facts may deem fair and just for the death and loss thus occasioned, having regard to the pecuniary losses suffered by reason of the death, funeral expenses, and the reasonable value of the services, consortium, companionship, comfort, instruction, guidance, counsel, training, and support of which those on whose behalf suit may be brought have been deprived by reason of such death and without limiting such damages to those which would be sustained prior to attaining the age of majority by the deceased or by the person suffering any such loss. In addition, the trier of the facts may award such damages as the deceased may have suffered between the time of injury and the time of death and for the recovery of which the deceased might have maintained an action had death not ensued. The mitigating or aggravating circumstances attending the death may be considered by the trier of the facts, but damages for grief and bereavement by reason of the death shall not be recoverable.

This language is a significant change from the prior Section 537.090, which provided only for such damages as would "fairly and justly compensate" the plaintiff. *See* Note, 45 Mo.L.Rev. 476 at 482. The earlier provision "was construed to allow recovery only for 'pecuniary' losses. In other words, no recovery was permitted for loss of companionship, society or comfort as a result of the death." (Footnotes omitted). *Id.*, citing *Acton v. Shields*, 386 S.W.2d 363 (Mo.1965). In *Acton* we denied recovery for the wrongful death of a fetus on the ground that the plaintiffs in that case (who were grandparents, aunts and uncles of the unborn child) were unable to show "a reasonable probability of pecuniary benefit" from the continued life of the child. 386 S.W.2d at 366. The new statute explicitly declares the legislature's intention that damages in wrongful death actions should include compensation for the loss of "consortium, companionship, comfort, instruction, guidance, counsel, training, and support." § 537.090 RSMo 1978 (1982 Supp.).

Respondents assert that this statute must be "strictly construed" because it is "in derogation of the common law." We do not agree. The wrongful death statute is not, strictly speaking, in "derogation" of the common law. Derogation is defined as "[t]he partial abrogation or repeal of a law, contract, treaty, legal right, etc." or as a "lessening, weakening, curtailment, ... impairment," detraction or taking away of a power or authority. 3 *Oxford English Dictionary* 232 (1933). Wrongful death acts do not take away any common law right;3 they were designed to mend the fabric of the common law, not to weaken it. Remedial acts are not strictly construed although they do change a rule of the common law. *Steggal v. Morris*, 363 Mo. 1224, 258 S.W.2d 577, 582 (1953). We must therefore apply the statutory language "with a view to promoting the apparent object of the legislative enactment." *United Airlines v. State Tax Commission of Missouri*, 377 S.W.2d 444, 451 (Mo. banc 1964).

This principle was recently enunciated in a unanimous opinion authored by Justice Harlan in *Moragne v. States Marine Lines, Inc.*, 398 U.S. 375, 90 S.Ct. 1772, 26 L.Ed.2d 339 (1970). In this case a widow of a deceased longshoreman brought an action for his wrongful death contending that although the common law did not provide for wrongful death, the general maritime law did permit such a remedy. She sought reversal of a previous Supreme Court decision which held that [in the] absence of a specific statute there is no action for wrongful death and a declaration that the general maritime laws incorporate a wrongful death action.

Justice Harlan in analyzing the trend of federal and state legislative enactments looked at it for guidance. In doing so the Court stated: "These numerous and broadly applicable statutes, taken as a whole, make it clear that there is no present public policy against allowing recovery for wrongful death .... This legislative establishment of policy carries significance beyond the particular scope of each of the statutes involved. The policy thus established has become itself a part of the law, to be given its appropriate weight not only in matters of statutory construction but also in those of decisional law," *Id.* p. 390–391, 90 S.Ct. p. 1782. The court then concluded that, "this appreciation of the broader role played by legislation in the development of the law reflects the practices of common law courts from the most ancient times. As Professor Landis has said, "much of what is ordinarily regarded as 'common law' finds its source in legislative enactment." Landis, *Statutes and the Sources of Law*, Harvard Legal Essays, 213, 214 (1934). It has always been the duty of the common law court to perceive the import of major legislative innovations and to interweave the new legislative policies with the inherited body of common law principles." *Id.* p. 392, 90 S.Ct. p. 1783.

Our first task, therefore, is to consider whether it would be consistent with the purpose of the statute to permit a cause of action for the wrongful death of an unborn child.

The manifest purpose of our statute is clearly to provide, for a limited class of plaintiffs, compensation for the loss of the "companionship, comfort, instruction, guidance, counsel, ... and support" of one who would have been alive but for the defendants' wrong. § 537.090. Appellants point out that the loss suffered by parents of an unborn child is in every respect a substantial and genuine loss, which is not distinguishable from the loss suffered when the child dies shortly after birth. To deny recovery based on the arbitrary requirement of live birth would work an injustice, in appellants' view. Furthermore, the wrongful death statute evidences a legislative intent to place the cost of "unsafe" activities upon the actors who engage in them, and thereby provide a deterrent to tortious conduct. The timing of the tortious conduct does not affect either the extent of the child's injuries or the desirability of the defendant's conduct. Comment, *Preconception tort as a basis for recovery*, 60 Wash. U.L.Q. 275, 279 (1982). Appellant suggests that there is no substantial reason why a tortfeasor who causes prenatal death should be treated more favorably than one who causes prenatal injury, with the death of the child following its birth. This would simply perpetuate the much-criticized rule of the common law which made it "more profitable for the defendant to kill the plaintiff than to scratch him." Prosser, *Law of Torts* § 127 (4th ed. 1971). As Justice Cardozo aptly stated:

> Death statutes have their roots in dissatisfaction with the archaisms of the [common-law rule of no liability] .... It would be a misfortune if a narrow or grudging process of construction were to exemplify and perpetuate the very evils to be remedied. There are times when uncertain words are to be wrought into consistency and unity with a legislative policy which is itself a source of law, a new generative impulse transmitted to the legal system.

Van Beeck v. Sabine Towing Co., 300 U.S. 342, 350–51, 57 S.Ct. 452, 456, 81 L.Ed. 685, 690 (1937), quoted in *Weitl v. Moes*, 311 N.W.2d 259, 276 (Iowa 1981) (Larson, J. dissenting).

Permitting appellant to maintain a wrongful death action for the death of a viable fetus would, therefore, be consistent with the broad purpose for which the statute was passed. Nothing in the language of the statute prevents this conclusion.

Respondents maintain that a fetus cannot be viewed as a "person" within the meaning of § 537.080. We do not agree. We note that the term "person" is used in many disparate senses in common speech, in philosophy, psychology, and in the law; it has no "plain and ordinary meaning" which we can apply. The term must therefore be construed in light of purpose for which this statute was passed. *See generally* Sutherland, *Statutory Construction*, § 71.05. The relevant inquiry is whether the death of a human fetus is the type of loss for which the legislature intended to establish a remedy. We can discern three basic objectives behind the statute: to provide compensation to bereaved plaintiffs for their loss, to ensure that tortfeasors pay for the consequences of their actions, and generally to deter harmful conduct which might lead to death. It should be clear that these reasons apply with equal force whether the deceased is born or unborn. Parents clearly have an interest in being protected against or compensated for the loss of a child they wish to have. The fetus itself has an interest in being protected from injury before birth. *See Steggall v. Morris*, 363 Mo. 1224, 258 S.W.2d 577. It follows logically that it should be protected against fatal injuries as well.

The United States Supreme Court in *Roe v. Wade*, 410 U.S. 113, 150, 93 S.Ct. 705, 725, 35 L.Ed.2d 147, 175 (1973), recognized a legitimate societal interest in providing legal protection to the fetus: "in assessing the state's interest recognition may be given to the ... claim that as long as potential life is involved, the state may assert interests beyond the protection of the pregnant woman alone." Fetal interests are presently recognized in several areas of the law. Missouri criminal law, for instance, provides that "[t]he willful killing of an unborn quick child, by any injury to the mother of such child, which would be murder if it resulted in the death of such mother, shall be deemed manslaughter." § 565.026 RSMo 1978. The Missouri abortion statute, § 188.030(3) RSMo 1979 (1982 Supp.) recognizes a state interest in protecting the life and health of a viable fetus. Some state courts have held that the fetus is a "child" for purposes of child neglect statutes. *Matter of Baby X*, 97 Mich.App. 111, 293 N.W.2d 736, 738 (1980); *Hoener v. Bertinato*, 67 N.J.Super. 517, 171 A.2d 140 (1961). A guardian ad litem may be appointed to protect the interests of an unborn child. *Wainwright v. Moore*, 374 So.2d 586 (Fla.App.1979); *Hatch v. Riggs National Bank*, 284 F.Supp. 396 (D.D.C.1968); *contra, Brady v. Doe*, 598 S.W.2d 338 (Tex.Civ.App.1980). And it is widely recognized that an unborn child has property rights which are entitled to legal protection. *Steggall v. Morris*, 363 Mo. 1224, 258 S.W.2d 577; *see also,* §§ 442.520 and 474.050, RSMo 1978; Note, *The Law and the Unborn Child: The Legal and Logical Inconsistencies,* 46 Notre Dame Lawyer 349 (1971). *Roe v. Wade*, while holding that the fetus is not a "person" for purposes of the 14th amendment, does not mandate the conclusion that the fetus is a legal nonentity. "The abortion issue involves the resolution of the mother's rights as against the child when the two are in conflict. Whatever may be the determination of the rights in that context, this special relation gives a third-party tortfeasor no comparable rights." Note, *Torts-Wrongful Death-Unborn Child* 70 Mich.L.Rev. 729, 746–747 (1972).

We conclude that the term "person" as used in 537.080 includes the human fetus en ventre sa mere. To hold otherwise would frustrate the remedial purpose for which the statute was intended. This conclusion is supported by a strong positive trend among other jurisdictions holding that the fetus is a "person," "minor," or "minor child" within the meaning of their particular wrongful death statutes. Recent decisions include *Dunn v. Rose Way Inc.*, 333 N.W.2d 830 (Iowa 1983); *Volk v. Baldazo*, 103 Idaho 570, 651 P.2d 11 (1982); *Danos v. St. Pierre*, 402 So.2d 633 (La.1981); *Salazar v. St. Vincent Hospital*, 95 N.M. 150, 619 P.2d 826 (App.1980); *Vaillancourt v. Medical Center Hospital*, 139 Vt. 138, 425 A.2d 92 (1980). *See generally* cases cited in Speiser, 1 *Recovery for Wrongful Death* 2d § 4:35 et seq.; Anno. 15 A.L.R.3d 992; Kader, *The Law of Tortious Prenatal Death since Roe v. Wade*, 45 Mo.L.Rev. 639 (1980).

Further examining the language of the statute, it is also necessary for us to consider whether the fetus would have been "entitled ... to recover damages" from the defendant "if death had not ensued." § 537.080. Prior to the 1979 amendment, the statute used the phrase "entitled to maintain an action and recover damages." The *Hardin* decision interpreted this language to require that the injured party be able to "maintain an action" at the time the injury was sustained. 538 S.W.2d at 340. As authority for this statement, the *Hardin* decision cited *Lawrence v. Craven Tire Co.*, 210 Va. 138, 169 S.E.2d 440 (1969), and *Carroll v. Skloff*, 415 Pa. 47, 202 A.2d 9 (1964). Both of those cases held that the critical factor was the deceased person's ability to maintain an action at the time of death, not at the time of the injury. Neither rule, in our opinion, reflects a proper interpretation of the phrase "if death had not ensued" as used in § 537.080. The interpretation announced in *Hardin* is in direct conflict with the result reached in *Steggal v. Morris*, 363 Mo. 1224, 258 S.W.2d 577. The deceased person in *Steggal* sustained injuries while still in the womb, was born alive and subsequently died. Recovery was allowed on the basis that the child clearly had the right to maintain a tort action after his birth. 258 S.W.2d at 581. The deceased could not have "maintained an action" at the time of his injury (since he was still in the womb). The rule announced in *Hardin* is similarly not supported by the cases cited in that decision. *Lawrence v. Craven Tire Co.* applied Virginia law which treats the wrongful death action as a survival action. *Carroll v. Skloff* applied Pennsylvania law which similarly conditions availability of a wrongful death action upon qualification under that state's survival statute. Missouri law has emphatically rejected this approach. "The wrongful death act creates a new cause of action where none existed at common law and did not revive a cause of action belonging to the deceased." (Citations omitted). *State ex rel. Jewish Hospital v. Buder*, 540 S.W.2d 100, 104 (Mo.App.1976). The right of action thus created is neither a transmitted right nor a survival right. The plain language of the statute itself does not condition recovery upon the existence of a right to sue at either the time of the injury or the time of death. Instead, it permits an action "[w]henever the death of a person results from any act ... which, if death had not ensued, would have entitled such person to recover damages in respect thereof ...." § 537.080. We interpret this provision to mean that a cause of action for wrongful death will lie whenever the person injured would have been entitled to recover from the defendant but for the fact that the injury resulted in death. Appellants here have alleged that respondents' negligence resulted in the death of their unborn child. But for the fact that the injuries resulted in death, the child would have been born and "entitled to recover" from respondents. We conclude that the cause of action asserted by appellants does fall within the terms of our statute.

We have examined the decisions of jurisdictions which deny recovery and are not persuaded by their reasoning. *See generally* Speiser, 1 *Recovery for Wrongful Death* 2d § 4.35 et seq.; Kader, 45 Mo.L.Rev. 639. Some of these decisions are based on statutes which, unlike § 537.080, limit recovery to pecuniary losses, or which are essentially survival statutes. Other decisions reason that proof of causation would be too difficult and too speculative in such cases. As a general principle, we think it unwise for courts to refuse to entertain suits simply because the plaintiff would have difficulty in proving his case. *Steggal v. Morris*, 258 S.W.2d at 580. This reasoning may have been compelling in an era when medical science knew little about fetal development, health, and treatment, but it is untenable in the light of modern knowledge. *See* Note, *The Impact of Medical Knowledge on the Law Relating to Prenatal Injuries.* 110 U.Pa.L.Rev. 554 (1962); King, *The Jurisdictional Status of the Fetus: A Proposal for Legal Protection of the Unborn*, 77 Mich.L.Rev. 1647 (1979); Speiser, 1 *Recovery for Wrongful Death* 2d § 4.38.

Finally, we must consider respondents' contention that the issue before us is properly one for the legislature and not the courts. Respondents maintain that the legislature has indicated its satisfaction with the *Hardin* decision by amending the statute without replacing or redefining the term "person." We are unwilling to speculate concerning the reasons for the legislature's inaction on this issue, and do not find this reasoning persuasive. We note, however, that the legislature did change the focus of the statute by permitting recovery for loss of society and companionship. Presumably the legislature intended that the courts would construe the statute in a manner which would give effect to this declared purpose. Furthermore, it is significant that the legislature has continued to incorporate common law principles of liability into the statute as the basis of entitlement to an action for wrongful death. This patently indicates that the legislature did not intend to occupy this field of law entirely, leaving no room for judicial development of wrongful death remedies. *Compare Justus v. Atchison*, 19 Cal.3d 564, 565 P.2d 122, 139 Cal.Rptr. 97 (1977). Instead the drafters expected the statutory cause of action to keep pace with developments in the common law. *O'Neill v. Morse*, 385 Mich. 130, 188 N.W.2d 785, 786 (1971). "Any legislative intent to foreclose ... traditional judicial activity should require positive expression." *Justus v. Atchison*, 565 P.2d at 129, 139 Cal.Rptr. at 104 (Tobriner, J., concurring in result). "If the statute carries no such implication, the court has the inherent power to apply the principles announced in the statute." R. Dickerson, *The Interpretation and Application of Statutes* 201 (1975), quoted in Note, *Wrongful Death and the Stillborn Fetus: A Common Law solution to a Statutory Dilemma*, 43 U.Pa.L.Rev. 809, 833 (1982). The issue presented to us is, therefore, properly a matter for judicial decision.

We hold, therefore, that § 537.080 does provide a cause of action for the wrongful death of a viable fetus. *State ex rel. Hardin v. Sanders*, 538 S.W.2d 336 (Mo. banc 1976), is hereby overruled. We limit our holding in this case to the facts presented and do not decide whether the same action would lie for the death of a nonviable fetus. The decision below is therefore reversed and the cause remanded to the trial court for further proceedings not inconsistent with this opinion. Reversed and remanded.

MURPHY V. MARTIN OIL CO.
308 N.E.2D 583 (ILL. 1974)

The plaintiff, Charryl Murphy, as administratrix of her late husband, Jack Raymond Murphy, and individually, and as next friend of Debbie Ann Murphy, Jack Kenneth Murphy and Carrie Lynn Murphy, their children, filed a complaint in the circuit court of Cook County against the defendants, Martin Oil Company and James Hocker. Count I of the complaint claimed damages for wrongful death under the Illinois Wrongful Death Act and count II sought damages for conscious pain and suffering, loss of wages and property damage. The circuit court allowed the defendants' motion to strike the second count of the complaint on the ground that it failed to state a cause of action. When the court further ordered that there was no just reason for delaying enforcement or appeal from this order the plaintiffs then appealed the dismissal under Rule 304 (50 Ill.2d R. 304) to the appellate court. That court affirmed the dismissal of count II of the complaint as to its allegations of pain and suffering and reversed the judgment as to its allegations of loss of wages and property damage. The cause was remanded with directions to reinstate as much of count II as related to loss of wages and property damage. (4 Ill.App.3d 1015, 283 N.E.2d 243.) We granted the plaintiff's petition for leave to appeal.

The first count set out the factual background for the complaint. It alleged that on June 11, 1968, the defendants owned and operated a gasoline station in Oak Lawn, Cook County, and that on that date the plaintiff's decedent, Jack Raymond Murphy, while having his truck filled with gasoline, was injured through the defendants' negligence in a fire on the defendants' premises. Nine days later he died from the injuries. Damages for wrongful death were claimed under the Illinois Wrongful Death Act. (Ill.Rev.Stat.1971, ch. 70, pars. 1 and 2.) The language of section 1 of the statute is:

> Whenever the death of a person shall be caused by wrongful act, neglect or default, and the
> act, neglect or default is such as would, if death had not ensued, have entitled the party injured
> to maintain an action and recover damages in respect thereof, then and in every such case the

person who or company or corporation which would have been liable if death had not ensued, shall be liable to an action for damages, notwithstanding the death of the person injured, and although the death shall have been caused under such circumstances as amount in law to felony.

The second count of the complaint asked for damages for the decedent's physical and mental suffering, for loss of wages for the nine-day period following his injury and for the loss of his clothing worn at the time of injury. These damages were claimed under the common law and under our survival statute, which provides that certain rights of action survive the death of the person with the right of action. (Ill.Rev.Stat.1971, ch. 3, par. 339.) The statute states:

In addition to the actions which survive by the common law, the following also survive: actions of replevin, actions to recover damages for an injury to the person (except slander and libel), actions to recover damages for an injury to real or personal property or for the detention or conversion of personal property, actions against officers for misfeasance, malfeasance, or nonfeasance of themselves or their deputies, actions for fraud or deceit, and actions provided in Section 14 of Article VI of 'An Act relating to alcoholic liquors', approved January 31, 1934, as amended.

On this appeal we shall consider: (1) whether the plaintiff can recover for the loss of wages which her decedent would have earned during the interval between his injury and death; (2) whether the plaintiff can recover for the destruction of the decedent's personal property (clothing) at the time of the injury; (3) whether the plaintiff can recover damages for conscious pain and suffering of the decedent from the time of his injuries to the time of death.

This State in 1853 enacted the Wrongful Death Act and in 1872 enacted the so-called Survival Act (now section 339 of the Probate Act). This court first had occasion to consider the statutes in combination in 1882 in *Holton v. Daly*, 106 Ill. 131. The court declared that the effect of the Wrongful Death Act was that a cause of action for personal injuries, which would have abated under the common law upon the death of the injured party from those injuries, would continue on behalf of the spouse or the next of kin and would be 'enlarged to embrace the injury resulting from the death.' (106 Ill. 131, 140.) In other words, it was held that the Wrongful Death Act provided the exclusive remedy available when death came as a result of given tortious conduct. In considering the Survival Act the court stated that it was intended to allow for the survival of a cause of action only when the injured party died from a cause other than that which caused the injuries which created the cause of action. Thus, the court said, an action for personal injury would not survive death if death resulted from the tortious conduct which caused the injury.

This construction of the two statutes persisted for over 70 years. . . . Damages, therefore, under the Wrongful Death Act were limited to pecuniary losses, as from loss of support, to the surviving spouse and next of kin as a result of the death. (*Ohnesorge v. Chicago City Ry. Co.* (1913), 259 Ill. 424, 102 N.E. 819.) Under the survival statute damages recoverable in a personal injury action, as for conscious pain and suffering, loss of earnings, medical expenses and physical disability, could be had only if death resulted from a cause other than the one which gave rise to the personal injury action.

This court was asked in 1941 to depart from its decision in *Holton v. Daly* and to permit, in addition to a wrongful death action, an action for personal injuries to be brought, though the injuries had resulted in the death of the injured person. This court acknowledged that there had been other jurisdictions which held contrary to *Holton v. Daly* and permitted the bringing of both actions, but the court said that any change in the rule in *Holton* must come from the legislature. (*Susemiehl v. Red River Lumber Co.* (1941), 376 Ill. 138, 33 N.E.2d 211.) In 1960, however, in *Saunders v. Schultz*, 20 Ill.2d 301, 170 N.E.2d 163, this court noted the absence of legislative action and permitted a widow to recover for funeral and medical expenses in an action which was independent of and in addition to an action brought by her for damages under the Wrongful Death Act. . . .

This disfavoring of abatement and enlarging of survival statutes has been general. In Prosser, *Handbook of the Law of Torts* (4th ed. 1971), at page 901, it is said:

> (T)he modern trend is definitely toward the view that tort causes of action and liabilities are as fairly a part of the estate of either plaintiff or defendant as contract debts, and that the question is rather one of why a fortuitous event such as death should extinguish a valid action. Accordingly, survival statutes gradually are being extended; and it may be expected that ultimately all tort actions will survive to the same extent as those founded on contract.

And at page 906 Prosser observes that where there have been wrongful death and survival statutes the usual holding has been that actions may be concurrently maintained under those statutes. The usual method of dealing with the two causes of action, he notes, is to allocate conscious pain and suffering, expenses and loss of earnings of the decedent up to the date of death to the survival statute, and to allocate the loss of benefits of the survivors to the action for wrongful death.

As the cited comments of Prosser indicate, the majority of jurisdictions which have considered the question allow an action for personal injuries in addition to an action under the wrongful death statute, though death is attributable to the injuries. Recovery for conscious pain and suffering is permitted in most of these jurisdictions. . . .

We consider that those decisions which allow an action for fatal injuries as well as for wrongful death are to be preferred to this court's holding in *Holton v. Daly* that the Wrongful Death Act was the only remedy available when injury resulted in death.

The holding in *Holton* was not compelled, we judge, by the language or the nature of the statutes examined. The statutes were conceptually separable and different. The one related to an action arising upon wrongful death; the other related to a right of action for personal injury arising during the life of the injured person.

The remedy available under *Holton* will often be grievously incomplete. There may be a substantial loss of earnings, medical expenses, prolonged pain and suffering, as well as property damage sustained, before an injured person may succumb to his injuries. To say that there can be recovery only for his wrongful death is to provide an obviously inadequate justice. Too, the result in such a case is that the wrongdoer will have to answer for only a portion of the damages he caused. Incongruously, if the injury caused is so severe that death results, the wrongdoer's liability for the damages before death will be extinguished. It is obvious that in order to have a full liability and a full recovery there must be an action allowed for damages up to the time of death, as well as thereafter. Considering "It is more important that the court should be right upon later and more elaborate consideration of the cases than consistent with previous declarations" (*Barden v. Northern Pacific R.R. Co.* (1894), 154 U.S. 288, 322, 14 S.Ct. 1030, 1036, 38 L.Ed. 992, 1000), we declare *Holton* and the cases which have followed it overruled. . . .

For the reasons given, the judgment of the appellate court is affirmed insofar as it held that an action may be maintained by the plaintiff for loss of property and loss of wages during the interval between injury and death, and that judgment is reversed insofar as it held that the plaintiff cannot maintain an action for her decedent's pain and suffering.

Affirmed in part; reversed in part.

2. LOSS OF CONSORTIUM

A claim for loss of "consortium" refers to the loss of benefits that plaintiff would have expected to receive from the injured party. Damages for loss of consortium are much like wrongful death damages – but in the case of loss of consortium, the victim need not die. Unfortunately, the phrase "loss of consortium" is not always used consistently – it sometimes also means non-pecuniary damages in wrongful death cases.

At early common law, a husband could claim loss of consortium when his wife was injured, but the wife could not make the same claim when her husband was injured. That asymmetry as been corrected for the better part of a century now so that both spouses can recover for loss of consortium. Several, but still a minority of, American jurisdictions permit children to recover loss of consortium when their parents are injured. Somewhat fewer states permit parents to recover when children are injured.

FERRITER V. DANIEL O'CONNELL'S SONS, INC.
413 N.E.2D 690 (MASS. 1980)

The plaintiffs, Judith A. Ferriter and her minor children, Jason R. and Leah N., filed a complaint . . . on June 7, 1979 . . . . The complaint alleged that the plaintiffs' husband and father, Michael Ferriter, was seriously injured as a result of the negligent . . . conduct of the defendant, Daniel O'Connell's Sons, Inc. (O'Connell). The complaint alleges that . . . the plaintiffs . . . have suffered loss of consortium and society. . . . On July 5, 1979, the defendants moved for summary judgment. . . . On October 3, a judge of the Superior Court denied the motion on the claims for loss of consortium and society, but granted the defendant's motion on the claims for mental anguish and impaired health. . . . We granted the plaintiffs' application for direct appellate review. . . .

According to the statement of agreed facts, the plaintiffs are the wife and two children, aged five and three, of Michael Ferriter. While working as a carpenter for the defendant, Michael was seriously injured on May 18, 1979. A one-to-two-hundred pound load of wood beams, which was hoisted in a nylon sling from the boom of a crane, fell fifty feet, and at least one beam struck Michael on the neck. The persons hoisting the lumber, operating the crane, monitoring site safety, and supervising the work were O'Connell employees. The defendant also supplied the materials and equipment used. . . . Since the accident, Michael Ferriter has been hospitalized and paralyzed from the neck down. . . .

The employer does not assert that the wife's and children's counts for loss of consortium and society fail to state a claim upon which relief can be granted. Although a wife's right to recover for loss of consortium is well established, . . . a child's right to recover for loss of a parent's society and companionship through a defendant's negligence is problematic. . . . The question whether a child can recover for loss of a parent's companionship and society caused by a defendant's negligence is a matter of first impression in Massachusetts. . . . We are skeptical of any suggestion that the child's interest in this setting is less intense than the wife's.

. . . [T]o take the measure of the present action, we consider this question in the perspective of the common law. Under the doctrine of paterfamilias, an injury to the family was an injury to the father. Neither children nor wives could bring actions in their own names to recover for personal injury. The action and any damages obtained belonged to the father. . . . The law also furnished the father with various actions to protect family relationships. . . .

A father has traditionally had actions for abduction and seduction of his child. . . . Both causes were founded upon an analogy with a master's action for enticement of his servant. . . . In order to prevail, the father had to show actual loss of his child's services. . . . With time, a doctrine of constructive loss of services developed. If the child was a minor and the father had a right to his or her services the child was presumed to be his servant. . . . Thus, loss of services became a technical requirement, an acknowledged fiction. . . . Once the parent established that the defendant's act made the child mentally or physically incapable of rendering services, the court could award damages for emotional harm done the parent. . . . In abduction cases, the father could recover for loss of the child's society. . . . Such recovery appears also to have been available in seduction cases. . . .

In addition to the actions for abduction and seduction, our cases recognized a further consequence of the master-servant analogy. . . . A third person's tortious infliction of injury upon a child gave the parent . . . a cause of action for loss of services. Even a negligent act would suffice. . . . Moreover, the parent could recover for labor performed and expenses reasonably incurred in the child's care. . . . As in actions for abduction and seduction, the requirement of actual loss of services withered, becoming a mere fiction. . . . However, it does not appear that damages for the parent's mental suffering or for loss of the child's society were available when the gravamen of the parent's claim was physical injury to the child. . . .

These cases supply analogous precedent for a child's right to recover for loss of a parent's society resulting from the defendant's negligence. The common law has traditionally recognized a parent's interest in freedom from tortious conduct harming his relationship with his child.

As in husband-wife relations, albeit to a more limited extent, our law has compensated parents for sentimental as well as economic injuries. . . . If the common law sometimes protects a parent's sentiments in the parent-child relationship, we might expect similar protection for the fledgling needs of the child. But the common law has been nearly silent concerning a child's right to recover damages for loss of parental society. Perhaps because courts would not stand the master-servant analogy on its head, with the child as master, . . . the question of the child's action does not appear in our cases until 1931. . . .

We hold that the Ferriter children have a viable claim for loss of parental society if they can show that they are minors dependent on the parent, Michael Ferriter. This dependence must be rooted not only in economic requirements, but also in filial needs for closeness, guidance, and nurture. . . . As claims for injuries to other relationships come before us, we shall judge them according to their nature and their force. . . .

Over sixty years ago, Dean Pound said, "As against the world at large a child has an interest . . . in the society and affection of the parent, at least while he remains in the household. But the law has done little to secure these interests . . . . It will have been observed that legal securing of the interests of children falls far short of what general considerations would appear to demand." Pound, *Individual Interests in the Domestic Relations*, 14 Mich.L.Rev. 177, 185-186 (1916). We meet part of that demand today.

D. "WRONGFUL" LIFE

GRECO V. UNITED STATES
893 P.2D 345 (NEV. 1995)

. . . In July 1989, appellant . . . Sundi A. Greco, mother of co-appellant Joshua Greco, ("Joshua") filed suit individually, and on Joshua's behalf, against respondent, the United States of America. Sundi Greco and Joshua alleged that Sundi Greco's doctors at the Nellis Air Force Base in Nevada committed several acts of negligence in connection with Sundi Greco's prenatal care and delivery and that, as a result, both Sundi and Joshua are entitled to recover money damages. . . . The United States moved to dismiss the suit on the ground that the complaint failed to state a cause of action.

The Grecos, mother and child, in this case seek to recover damages from the United States arising out of the negligence of physicians who, they claim, negligently failed to make a timely diagnosis of physical defects and anomalies afflicting the child when it was still in the mother's womb. Sundi Greco asserts that the physicians' negligence denied her the opportunity to terminate her pregnancy and thereby caused damages attendant to the avoidable birth of an unwanted and severely deformed child. On Joshua's behalf, Sundi Greco avers that the physicians' negligence and the resultant denial of Joshua's mother's right to terminate her pregnancy caused Joshua to be born into a grossly abnormal life of pain and deprivation.

These kinds of tort claims have been termed "wrongful birth" when brought by a parent and "wrongful life" when brought on behalf of the child for the harm suffered by being born deformed.

THE CHILD'S CAUSE OF ACTION: "WRONGFUL LIFE"

We decline to recognize any action by a child for defects claimed to have been caused to the child by negligent diagnosis or treatment of the child's mother. The Grecos' argument is conditional and narrowly put, so: if this court does not allow Sundi Greco to recover damages for Joshua's care past the age of majority, it should allow Joshua to recover those damages by recognizing claims for "wrongful life." Implicit in this argument is the assumption that the child would be better off had he never been born. These kinds of judgments are very difficult, if not impossible, to make. Indeed, most courts considering the question have denied this cause of action for precisely this reason. . . . Recognizing this kind of claim on behalf of the child would require us to weigh the harms suffered by virtue of the child's having been born with severe handicaps against "the utter void of nonexistence"; this is a calculation the courts are incapable of performing. . . . The New York Court of Appeals framed the problem this way:

> Whether it is better never to have been born at all than to have been born with even gross deficiencies is a mystery more properly to be left to the philosophers and the theologians. Surely the law can assert no competence to resolve the issue, particularly in view of the very nearly uniform high value which the law and mankind has placed on human life, rather than its absence.

Becker v. Schwartz, 46 N.Y.2d 401, 413 N.Y.S.2d 895, 900, 386 N.E.2d 807, 812 (1978). We conclude that Nevada does not recognize a claim by a child for harms the child claims to have suffered by virtue of having been born.

THE MOTHER'S CAUSE OF ACTION

With regard to Sundi Greco's claim against her physician for negligent diagnosis or treatment during pregnancy, we see no reason for compounding or complicating our medical malpractice jurisprudence by according this particular form of professional negligence action some special status apart from presently recognized medical malpractice or by giving it the new name of "wrongful birth." . . . Sundi Greco either does or does not state a claim for medical malpractice; and we conclude that she does. . . . Medical malpractice, like other forms of negligence, involves a breach of duty which causes injury. To be tortiously liable a physician must have departed from the accepted standard of medical care in a manner that results in injury to a patient. . . . In the case before us, we must accept as fact that Sundi Greco's physicians negligently failed to perform prenatal medical tests or performed or interpreted those tests in a negligent fashion and that they thereby negligently failed to discover and reveal that Sundi Greco was carrying a severely deformed fetus. As a result of such negligence Sundi Greco claims that she was denied the opportunity to terminate her pregnancy and that this denial resulted in her giving birth to a severely deformed child.

It is difficult to formulate any sound reason for denying recovery to Sundi Greco in the case at hand. Sundi Greco is saying, in effect, to her doctors:

> If you had done what you were supposed to do, I would have known early in my pregnancy that I was carrying a severely deformed baby. I would have then terminated the pregnancy and would not have had to go through the mental and physical agony of delivering this child, nor would I have had to bear the emotional suffering attendant to the birth and nurture of the child, nor the extraordinary expense necessary to care for a child suffering from such extreme deformity and disability.

The United States advances two reasons for denying Sundi Greco's claim: first, it argues that she has suffered no injury and that, therefore, the damage element of negligent tort liability is not fulfilled; second, the United States argues that even if Sundi Greco has sustained injury and damages, the damages were not caused by her physicians. To support its first argument, the United States points out that in *Szekeres v. Robinson*, 102 Nev. 93, 715 P.2d 1076 (1986), this court held that the mother of a normal, healthy child could not recover in tort from a physician who negligently performed her sterilization operation because the birth of a normal, healthy child is not a legally cognizable injury. . . . The United States argues that no distinction can be made between a mother who gives birth to a healthy child and a mother who gives birth to a child with severe deformities and that, therefore, *Szekeres* bars recovery.

Szekeres can be distinguished from the instant case. Unlike the birth of a normal child, the birth of a severely deformed baby of the kind described here is necessarily an unpleasant and aversive event and the cause of inordinate financial burden that would not attend the birth of a normal child. The child in this case will unavoidably and necessarily require the expenditure of extraordinary medical, therapeutic and custodial care expenses by the family, not to mention the additional reserves of physical, mental and emotional strength that will be required of all concerned. Those who do not wish to undertake the many burdens associated with the birth and continued care of such a child have the legal right, under *Roe v. Wade* and codified by the voters of this state, to terminate their pregnancies. . . . Sundi Greco has certainly suffered money damages as a result of her physician's malpractice.

We also reject the United State's second argument that Sundi Greco's physicians did not cause any of the injuries that Sundi Greco might have suffered. We note that the mother is not claiming that her child's defects were caused by her physicians' negligence; rather, she claims that her physicians' negligence kept her ignorant of those defects and that it was this negligence which caused her to lose her right to choose whether to carry the child to term. The damage Sundi Greco has sustained is indeed causally related to her physicians' malpractice.

Sundi Greco's claim here can be compared to one in which a physician negligently fails to diagnose cancer in a patient. Even though the physician did not cause the cancer, the physician can be held liable for damages resulting from the patient's decreased opportunity to fight the cancer, and for the more extensive pain, suffering and medical treatment the patient must undergo by reason of the negligent diagnosis. . . . The "chance" lost here, was Sundi Greco's legally protected right to choose whether to abort a severely deformed fetus. . . . If we were to deny Sundi Greco's claim, we would, in effect, be groundlessly excepting one type of medical malpractice from negligence liability. We see no reason to treat this case any differently from any other medical malpractice case. Sundi Greco has stated a prima facie claim of medical malpractice under Nevada law.

DAMAGE ISSUES

The certified question requires us to decide specifically what types of damages the mother may recover if she succeeds in proving her claim. Courts in these cases have struggled with what items of damages are recoverable because, unlike the typical malpractice claim, claims such as Sundi Greco's do not involve a physical injury to the patient's person. We consider each of Sundi Greco's claimed items of damage separately.

Extraordinary Medical and Custodial Expenses

This claim for damages relates to the medical, therapeutic and custodial costs associated with caring for a severely handicapped child. There is nothing exceptional in allowing this item of damage. It is a recognized principle of tort law to "afford compensation for injuries sustained by one person as the result of the conduct of another." W. Page Keeton, et al., *Prosser and Keeton on the Law of Torts*, § 2 at 6 (5th ed. 1984). . . . Extraordinary care expenses are a foreseeable result of the negligence alleged in this case, and Sundi Greco should be allowed to recover those expenses if she can prove them. This leads us to the question of how to compensate for these kinds of injuries.

Sundi Greco correctly observes that Nevada law requires the parents of a handicapped child to support that child beyond the age of majority if the child cannot support itself. . . . Nevada recognizes the right of a parent to recover from a tortfeasor any expenses the parent was required to pay because of the injury to his or her minor child. . . . Accordingly, Sundi Greco claims the right to recover damages for these extraordinary costs for a period equal to Joshua's life expectancy. Other states which require parents to care for handicapped children past the age of majority allow plaintiffs to recover these types of damages for the lifetime of the child or until such time as the child is no longer dependent on her or his parents. . . . We agree with these authorities and conclude that Sundi Greco may recover extraordinary medical and custodial expenses associated with caring for Joshua for whatever period of time it is established that Joshua will be dependent upon her to provide such care. . . .

Loss of Services and Companionship

The United States contends that Sundi Greco should not be allowed to recover any damages for the services of her child lost due to the child's handicap, because Sundi Greco claims that but for the negligence of her physician she would never have carried her pregnancy to term. It follows then, that if the child had not been born, Sundi Greco would have had far less in terms of service and companionship than what she can currently expect from her handicapped child. Amicus NTLA attempts to rebut the United States' argument by analogizing Sundi Greco's situation to that of the wife in *General Electric Co. v. Bush*, 88 Nev. 360, 498 P.2d 366 (1972). In that case a wife was permitted to recover damages from a tortfeasor for loss of the services and companionship of her husband, who was still alive but had become a permanent invalid. The General Electric case exemplifies the problems relating to Sundi Greco's request for these sorts of damages in the instant case. In General Electric, the wife lost the services of a healthy, productive individual; here, the crux of Sundi Greco's claim is that she would have aborted the fetus had she been given the opportunity to do so. In that case, she would have had no services or companionship at all. We thus conclude that Sundi Greco may not recover for lost services or companionship.

Damages for Emotional Distress

Sundi Greco asserts that she is suffering and will continue to suffer tremendous mental and emotional pain as a result of the birth of Joshua. Several jurisdictions allow plaintiffs such as Sundi Greco to recover such damages. . . . In line with these cases, we agree that it is reasonably foreseeable that a mother who is denied her right to abort a severely deformed fetus will suffer emotional distress, not just when the child is delivered, but for the rest of the child's life. . . . Consequently, we conclude that the mother in this case should have the opportunity to prove that she suffered and will continue to suffer emotional distress as a result of the birth of her child.

We reject the United States' argument that this court should follow an "offset" rule with regard to damages for emotional distress. *Cf. Blake v. Cruz*, 108 Idaho 253, 258, 698 P.2d 315, 320 (1984) (requiring damages for emotional distress to be offset by "the countervailing emotional benefits attributable to the birth of the child"). Any emotional benefits are simply too speculative to be considered by a jury in awarding emotional distress damages. As Dean Prosser observes:

> In the case of the wrongful birth of a severely impaired child, it would appear that the usual joys of parenthood would often be substantially overshadowed by the emotional trauma of caring for the child in such a condition, so that application of the benefit rule would appear inappropriate in this context.

Prosser and Keeton on the Law of Torts, supra, § 55 at 371 n. 48 (citations omitted). . . . Moreover, it would unduly complicate the jury's task to require it to weigh one intangible harm against another intangible benefit.

CONCLUSION

We conclude that a mother may maintain a medical malpractice action under Nevada law based on her physicians' failure properly to perform or interpret prenatal examinations when that failure results in the mother losing the opportunity to abort a severely deformed fetus. Sundi Greco should be given the right to prove that she has suffered and will continue to suffer damages in the form of emotional or mental distress and that she has incurred and will continue to incur extraordinary medical and custodial care expenses associated with raising Joshua. We decline to recognize the tort sometimes called "wrongful life."

E. COLLATERAL SOURCE

In modern American society, the civil tort action makes up a very small part of the safety net that protects people from the effects of accidental injury. A much larger part of that net is formed by insurance and government programs. What effect, if any, should resources available to the injured plaintiff from such "collateral sources" have on plaintiff's ability to recover damages from defendant in a private tort action?

HELFEND V. SOUTHERN CALIFORNIA RAPID TRANSIT DISTRICT
465 P.2D 61 (CAL. 1970)

Defendants appeal from a judgment of the Los Angeles Superior Court entered on a verdict in favor of plaintiff, Julius J. Helfend, for $16,400 in general and special damages for injuries sustained in a bus-auto collision that occurred on July 19, 1965, in the City of Los Angeles. . . .

1. The facts.

Shortly before noon on July 19, 1965, plaintiff drove his car in central Los Angeles . . . . While traveling in the second lane from the curb, plaintiff observed an automobile driven by Glen A. Raney, Jr., stopping in his lane and preparing to back into a parking space. Plaintiff put out his left arm to signal the traffic behind him that he intended to stop; he then brought his vehicle to a halt so that the other driver could park.

At about this time Kenneth A. Mitchell, a bus driver for the Southern California Rapid Transit District, pulled out of a bus stop . . . and headed in the same direction as plaintiff. Approaching plaintiff's and Raney's cars which were stopped in the second lane from the curb, Mitchell pulled out into the lane closest to the center of the street in order to pass. The right rear of the bus sideswiped plaintiff's vehicle, knocking off the rearview mirror and crushing plaintiff's arm, which had been hanging down at the side of his car in the stopping signal position . . . .

Plaintiff filed a tort action against the Southern California Rapid Transit District, a public entity, and Mitchell, an employee of the transit district. At trial plaintiff claimed slightly more than $2,700 in special damages, including $921 in doctor's bills, a $336.99 hospital bill, and about $45 for medicines. . . . Defendant requested permission to show that about 80 percent of the plaintiff's hospital bill had been paid by plaintiff's Blue Cross insurance carrier and that some of his other medical expenses may have been paid by other insurance. The superior court . . . concluded that the judgment should not be reduced to the extent of the amount of insurance payments which plaintiff received. The court ruled that defendants should not be permitted to show that plaintiff had received medical coverage from any collateral source.

After the jury verdict in favor of plaintiff in the sum of $16,300, defendants appealed, raising only two contentions: (1) The trial court committed prejudicial error in refusing to allow the introduction of evidence to the effect that a portion of the plaintiff's medical bills had been paid from a collateral source. (2) The trial court erred in denying defendant the opportunity to determine if plaintiff had been compensated from more than one collateral source for damages sustained in the accident. . . .

2. The collateral source rule.

The Supreme Court of California has long adhered to the doctrine that if an injured party receives some compensation for his injuries from a source wholly independent of the tortfeasor, such payment should not be deducted from the damages which the plaintiff would otherwise collect from the tortfeasor. . . . Although the collateral source rule remains generally accepted in the United States, nevertheless many other jurisdictions . . . have restricted . . . or repealed it. In this country most commentators have criticized the rule and called for its early demise. . . .

The collateral source rule as applied here embodies the venerable concept that a person who has invested years of insurance premiums to assure his medical care should receive the benefits of his thrift. The tortfeasor should not garner the benefits of his victim's providence.

The collateral source rule expresses a policy judgment in favor of encouraging citizens to purchase and maintain insurance for personal injuries and for other eventualities. Courts consider insurance a form of investment, the benefits of which become payable without respect to any other possible source of funds. If we were to permit a tortfeasor to mitigate damages with payments from plaintiff's insurance, plaintiff would be in a position inferior to that of having bought no insurance, because his payment of premiums would have earned no benefit. Defendant should not be able to avoid payment of full compensation for the injury inflicted merely because the victim has had the foresight to provide himself with insurance. . . .

[I]nsurance policies increasingly provide for either subrogation or refund or benefits upon a tort recovery, and such refund is indeed called for in the present case. . . . Hence, the plaintiff receives no double recovery; the collateral source rule simply serves as a means of by-passing the antiquated doctrine of non-assignment of tortious actions and permits a proper transfer of risk from the plaintiff's insurer to the tortfeasor by way of the victim's tort recovery. The double shift from the tortfeasor to the victim and then from the victim to his insurance carrier can normally occur with little cost in that the insurance carrier is often intimately involved in the initial litigation and quite automatically receives its part of the tort settlement or verdict.

. . . .

If we consider the collateral source rule as applied here in the context of the entire American approach to the law of torts and damages, we find that the rule presently performs a number of legitimate and even indispensible functions. Without a thorough revolution in the American approach to torts and the consequent damages, the rule at least with respect to medical insurance benefits has become so integrated within our present system that its precipitous judicial nullification would work hardship. In this case the collateral source rule lies between two systems for the compensation of accident victims: the traditional tort recovery based on fault and the increasingly prevalent coverage based on non-fault insurance. Neither system possesses such universality of coverage or completeness of compensation that we can easily dispense with the collateral source rule's approach to meshing the two systems. . . . The reforms which many academicians propose cannot easily be achieved through piecemeal common law development; the proposed changes, if desirable, would be more effectively accomplished through legislative reform. In any case, we cannot believe that the judicial repeal of the collateral source rule, as applied in the present case, would be the place to begin the needed changes.

. . . We therefore reaffirm our adherence to the collateral source rule in tort cases in which the plaintiff has been compensated by an independent collateral source-such as insurance, pension, continued wages, or disability payments-for which he had actually or constructively . . . paid or in cases in which the collateral source would be recompensed from the tort recovery through subrogation, refund of benefits, or some other arrangement. Hence, we concluded that in a case in which a tort victim has received partial compensation from medical insurance coverage entirely independent of the tortfeasor the trial court properly followed the collateral source rule and foreclosed defendant from mitigating damages by means of the collateral payments. . . .

NOTE AND QUESTIONS

1   Is the result in this case fair? Should plaintiff get a double recovery? Would the equities differ if part of plaintiff's expenses from the injury had been paid by a very close family friend instead of by an insurance carrier?

2   Some have pointed out that the collateral source rule does not usually result in a "double recovery" by the plaintiff. First, plaintiff has to compensate her attorneys. Second, general damages typically are not covered by insurance. Third, insurance coverage frequently involves limitations such as deductibles and co-payments. Fourth, insurance policies usually include subrogation clauses that give the insurance carrier an interest in any recovery.

3   Most jurisdictions have abrogated or altered the collateral source rule by statute.

F. PUNITIVE DAMAGES

EXODUS 22:7-9

If a man shall deliver unto his neighbour money or stuff to keep, and it be stolen out of the man's house; if the thief be found, let him pay double. If the thief be not found, then the master of the house shall be brought unto the judges, to see whether he have put his hand unto his neighbour's goods. For all manner of trespass, whether it be for ox, for ass, for sheep, for raiment, or for any manner of lost thing, which another challengeth to be his, the cause of both parties shall come before the judges; and whom the judges shall condemn, he shall pay double unto his neighbour.

"Punitive" damages (sometimes called "exemplary" or "vindictive"damages) are fundamentally different from compensatory damages. While the purpose of compensatory damages is to come as close as possible to making the plaintiff whole, the purpose of punitive damages is not about the injured plaintiff at all. The purpose of punitive damages is not to compensate the victim but rather, as the name suggests, to punish the defendant whose conduct toward the plaintiff has been particularly aggravated. Therefore, the focus of the analysis of punitive damages is completely different from that of compensatory damages. While compensatory damages focus on the loss to the victim, punitive damages focus on the culpability or blameworthiness of the defendant and on what measure of damages is required to punish the defendant sufficiently.

While actual punitive damages awards are relatively rare, theories used to justify punitive damage awards abound. Punitive damages can be justified under a utilitarian deterrence theory, a retributive theory, under a compensation theory, or under any combination of the three. Under a deterrence theory of punitive damages, extra damages (beyond compensatory damages) are necessary for optimal deterrence because not all tortfeasors will be caught and held responsible. This theory operates independent of the "wrongfulness," in any moral sense, of defendant's conduct.

Others justify punitive damages on the basis that defendant "deserves" the punitive damages. It is thought that justice demands that wrongdoing be punished. This theory is closely aligned with the immorality of defendant's conduct. Under this theory, punitive damages appear to be, at best, a ham-handed way of meting out punishment.

Still others see punitive damages as not punitive at all, but rather as an extra "dollop" (to borrow a term from Judge Posner, *see infra*) of compensation, just to make sure that plaintiff is fully compensated. Because American courts do not routinely shift attorneys' fees to the loser, even the fully compensated "winning" plaintiff still usually loses, at least to the extent of her attorneys' fees – punitive damages can correct this by compensating her more fully. This theory does not accord with what courts have said about punitive damages over the years. However, punitive damages certainly look more like compensation than punishment in one very important way – they are paid to the plaintiff, although a few jurisdictions now direct at least some damages to someone other than the plaintiff.

Whether to award punitive damages generally is considered a jury question. All jurisdictions require the plaintiff who would recover punitive damages to prove something more than the defendant's simple negligence. Punitive damages generally are potentially available in cases of intentional tort. But courts take various approaches to what lesser showing will suffice. Some permit a recovery of punitive damages on a mere showing of "gross negligence." Others require even higher levels of proven wrongdoing for the recovery of punitive damages. With increasing frequency, punitive damages are used to "punish" large corporations for something like putting profits ahead of avoiding massive harms threatened by the scale of their operations.

Punitive damages have been around since the birth of the American republic, and American courts and commentators long have noted the incongruities arising from a system of punishment implemented by requiring the wrongdoer to pay extra damages to the victim of a private wrong. For one thing, the plaintiff who obtains a punitive damage award far larger than the harm that he suffered seems to get a windfall. Moreover, the availability of huge damages awards, without regard to the actual harm done, has given rise to a relatively recent surge in filings where the principle sum sought is punitive rather than compensatory. Some suspect that the rise in punitive damages claims may be driven by "entrepreneurial" plaintiffs' counsel, who have a one-third stake in the outcome. Some of the difficulties with punitive awards are discussed in the immediately following opinion.

MURPHY V. HOBBS
5 P. 119 (COLO. 1884)

This is a civil action, brought to recover damages for malicious prosecution and false imprisonment. Plaintiff procured a verdict, and judgment was duly entered thereon. Defendant prosecutes this appeal, and assigns in support thereof numerous errors. The most important of these assignments is one which relates to the measure of damages adopted in the court below. Upon this subject the following instruction was there given:

> That the measure of damages in an action for malicious prosecution is not confined alone to
> actual pecuniary loss sustained by reason thereof; but if it is believed, from the evidence, that
> the arrest and imprisonment stated in the complaint were without probable cause, then the jury
> may award damages to plaintiff to indemnify him for the peril occasioned to him in regard to
> personal liberty, feelings, and reputation, and *as a punishment to defendant* in such further sense
> as they shall deem just.

By the assignment of error and argument challenging the correctness of this instruction we are called upon to consider the following question . . . : Can damages *as a punishment* be recovered in cases like this? The rule allowing under certain circumstances in civil actions based upon torts, exemplary, punitive, or vindictive damages, for the purpose of *punishing* the defendant, has taken deep root in law. . . . Were this subject now presented to the various courts of the country for the first time, we have little doubt as to what the verdict would be. The propriety of adhering exclusively to the rule of compensation appears upon careful investigation with striking clearness. . . .

Perhaps the most impressive objection to allowing damages as a punishment in cases like the one at bar, is that which relates to dual prosecutions for a single tort. Our state constitution declares that no one shall be twice put in jeopardy for the same offense. A second criminal prosecution for the same act after acquittal, or conviction and punishment therefor, is something which no English or American lawyer would defend for a moment. But here is an instance where, practically, this wrong is inflicted. The fine awarded as a punishment in the civil action does not prevent indictment and prosecution in a criminal court. On the other hand, it has been held that evidence of punishment in a criminal suit is not admissible even in mitigation of exemplary damages in a civil action. . . . Courts attempt to explain away the apparent conflict with the constitutional inhibition above mentioned; they say that the language there used refers exclusively to criminal procedure, and cannot include civil actions. . . . But this position amounts to a complete surrender of the evident spirit and intent of that instrument. When the convention framed and when the people adopted the constitution both understood the purpose of this clause to be the prevention of double prosecutions for the same offense. Yet, under the rule allowing exemplary damages, not only may two prosecutions, but also two convictions and punishments, be had. What difference does it make to the accused, so far as this question is concerned, that one prosecution takes the form of a civil action, in which he is called defendant? He is practically harassed with two prosecutions and subjected to two convictions; while no hypothesis, however ingenious, can cloud in his mind the palpable fact that for the same tort he suffers two punishments. . . .

A second weighty objection to the rule under discussion relates to procedure. It is doubtful if another instance can be found within the whole range of English or American jurisprudence where the distinctions between civil and criminal procedure are so completely ignored. Plaintiff sues for damages arising from the injury done to *himself.* His complaint or declaration is framed with a view to compensation for a purely private wrong. It need not be under oath, and does not inform defendant that he is to be tried for a public offense. The summons makes no mention of punishment; it simply commands defendant to appear and answer in damages for the private injury inflicted upon plaintiff. When the cause is called for trial, no issue upon a public criminal charge is fairly presented by the pleadings. A trial and conviction are had, and punishment by fine is inflicted, without indictment or sworn information. The rules of evidence peculiarly applicable in criminal prosecutions are rejected. The doctrine of reasonable doubt is replaced by the rule controlling in civil actions, and a mere preponderance in the weight of testimony warrants conviction. Defendant is compelled to testify against himself, and such forced testimony may produce the verdict under which he is punished. Depositions may be read against him, and thus the right of meeting adverse witnesses face to face be denied.

The law fixes a maximum punishment for criminal offenses, and in this state the presiding judge determines the extent thereof, where a discretion is given; but under the rule we are considering the jury are entirely free from control, except through the court's power—always unwillingly exercised—to set aside the verdict; they may, for an offense which is punishable under criminal statutes by $100 fine at most, award as a punishment many times that sum. And finally, when the defendant has been punished in the civil action, he is denied the privilege of pleading such expiation in bar of a criminal prosecution for the same offense. He can hope for no executive clemency in the civil suit; and, if imprisoned upon the second conviction, under the authorities *habeas corpus* does not lie to aid him.

The incongruities of this proceeding are not confined to the criminal branch of the law. Civil actions are instituted for the purpose of redressing private wrongs; it is the aim of civil jurisprudence to mete out as nearly exact justice as possible between contending litigants. There ought to be no disposition to take from the defendant or give to the plaintiff more than equity and justice require. Yet under this rule of damages these principles are forgotten, and judicial machinery is used for the avowed purpose of giving plaintiff that to which he has no shadow of right. He recovers full compensation for the injury to his person or property; for all direct and proximate losses occasioned by the tort; for the physical pain, if any, inflicted; for his mental agony, lacerated feelings, wounded sensibilities; and then, in addition to the foregoing, he is allowed damages which are awarded as a punishment of defendant and example to others. Who will undertake to give a valid reason why plaintiff, after being fully paid for all the injury inflicted upon his property, body, reputation, and feelings, should still be compensated, above and beyond, for a wrong committed against the public at large? The idea is inconsistent with sound legal principles, and should never have found a lodgment in the law.

The reflecting lawyer is naturally curious to account for this "heresy" or "deformity," as it has been termed. Able and searching investigations made by both jurist and writer disclose the following facts concerning it . . . : That it was entirely unknown to the civil law; that it never obtained a foothold in Scotland; that it finds no real sanction in the writings of Blackstone, Hammond, Comyns, or Rutherforth; that it was not recognized in the earliest English cases; that the supreme courts of New Hampshire, Massachusetts, Indiana, Iowa, Nebraska, Michigan, and Georgia have rejected it in whole or in part; that of late other states have falteringly retained it because "committed" so to do; that a few years ago it was correctly said, "at last accounts the court of queen's bench was still sitting hopelessly involved in the meshes of what Mr. Justice QUAIN declared to be 'utterly inconsistent propositions,'" and that the rule is comparatively modern, resulting in all probability from a misconception of impassioned language and inaccurate expressions used by judges in some of the earlier English cases.

. . . The words "smart money," and also the following adjectives, have been used to designate this class of damages: "speculative," "imaginary," "presumptive," "exemplary," "vindictive," and "punitive" or "punitory." The literal meaning of all but the last three is easily reconcilable with the idea of compensation: they were so used in the first place; and even as to the excepted ones, there are many cases wherein it is evident they were employed without any intentional reference to punishment. These words all came into use through the beneficent design of courts to distinguish between private wrongs with and those without an evil intent, and to extend the right of recovery in the former case to injuries excluded from computation in the latter.

Mr. Justice FOSTER concludes a discussion of the expression "smart money," as used by Grotius, and jurists contemporary with that author, in the following language:

> It is interesting, as well as instructive, to observe that one hundred and twenty years ago the term "smart money" was employed in a manner entirely different from the modern signification which it has obtained, being then used as indicating compensation for the smarts of the injured person, and not, as now, money required by way of punishment, and to make the wrong-doer smart.

Fay v. Parker, supra.

So long as the jury are considering the material pecuniary injury, direct or approximate, shown by the evidence, and the physical pain, their inquiry relates to what are *termed* actual damages; but, when authorized by a vicious intent of the wrong-doer, they turn to the realm of mental anguish, public indignity, wounded sensibility, etc. The damages awarded may more appropriately be described as "presumptive," "speculative," or "imaginary." The injury in the latter case is no less actual or real than in the former, but it is less tangible. Compensation therefor is more a matter of judgment, less a result of computation. A misapprehension seems sometimes to exist as to the word "compensatory" when used in this connection. Under the rule limiting them to compensatory damages, juries will, with proper instruction, recognize a broad distinction between a tort unaccompanied by malice, or circumstances of aggravation or disgrace, and one producing equal direct pecuniary damage, where either of these conditions exists. In the former case they consider only the actual injury to the person or property, including expenses, loss of time, bodily pain, etc., occasioned by the wrongful act. In the latter, they allow such additional sum as, in their judgment, is warranted by the circumstances of contumely, anguish, or oppression; but in both instances the damages are awarded as "compensation." The additional sum is given to the individual as a recompense for the mental suffering or wounded sensibilities, as the case may be. It often happens that this constitutes the principal element of the recovery. If, upon a crowded thoroughfare, one maliciously assaults me with blows and epithets, five dollars may fully compensate the injury inflicted to my person and clothing; but $500 may be utterly inadequate to requite the sense of insult, the personal indignity, the public disgrace and humiliation. The extra $500 exacted may operate indirectly as a punishment. It may constitute an example to others, and also deter my assailant himself from repetitions of the offense in future. In law, however, it is simply compensation for the private wrong,—a kind of indemnity which, probably, no court has ever refused to allow when warranted by the circumstances. But, under the doctrine of exemplary damages, as announced by the instruction given in this case, the jury are not required to stop with the five dollars for material injury and $500 for lacerated feelings; they may turn to the domain of criminal law, and consider the public wrong, and they may add $1,000 more as a punishment to my assailant. The arrangement is highly satisfactory to me, since I have the pleasure of pocketing the additional $1,000 to which I am not entitled; but, as we have already seen, it hardly comports with correct legal principles.

The case at bar furnishes a good illustration of the doctrine under discussion. The jury are told that if they find certain facts to exist they may award damages to plaintiff for (1) the actual pecuniary loss sustained; (2) the peril occasioned in regard to personal liberty; (3) the injury to his person and liberty; (4) injury to his feelings and reputation; (5) the punishment of defendant. The first four items comprise all the injuries for which plaintiff ought to recover; they all rest upon the theory of compensation for the private wrong, and are therefore in perfect harmony with the principles and procedure in civil actions; they furnish ample ground for discrimination by the jury should they find the prosecution and imprisonment to have been malicious. Why not remit the punishment of defendant to a criminal forum? The jury returned a verdict for $2,780. How much of this sum was given as a punishment? Perhaps $1,000, perhaps more; yet, under our Criminal Code, $500 would have been the maximum. When defendant is on trial in the criminal court he cannot plead in bar payment of this penalty. He must, if convicted, discharge the additional fine assessed, or go to jail, if such be the sentence. Whatever may be the technical distinctions, he is, in fact, twice prosecuted, twice convicted, and twice punished for the same offense. And one of these prosecutions, convictions, and punishments is had without any regard for the leading principles obtaining in criminal procedure. . . .

We deem no further argument necessary to show that the question is one of weighty importance; that it affects the fundamental distinctions between civil and criminal procedure; that it bears directly upon the legal rights, and in many cases, also, upon the constitutional rights of the citizen. . . . It is not unlikely that courts will, in the course of time, generally condemn the practice of blending the interests of the individual with those of society, using a purely private action to redress a public wrong. . . . But it is sufficient for us to say that in the case at bar the objections to double prosecutions and punishments for the same offense are decisive. . . . It makes but little difference what adjective or expression is used to designate the damages beyond those termed "actual" which may be awarded by the jury for injury to the feelings when the wrong is accompanied by malice, provided the instructions clearly indicate the proper limitation. But it is believed safer not to employ the words "exemplary," "vindictive," "punitory," or either of them, as there is danger of misapprehension growing out of their literal meaning, notwithstanding the accompanying explanations of the court.

It has been with no little reluctance that we have arrived at the foregoing conclusion as to the doctrine of punitive or exemplary damages. The persuasive reasons and strong array of authorities in support of the rule, the corresponding convictions of a large part of the bench and bar of the state, and the confusion that may exist for a time, have impelled us to the most careful and conservative deliberation. But we feel that the doctrine of compensation, as explained, is more in consonance with the reason, the logic, the science of the law; that it is more in harmony with the dictates of equity and justice; and that the tendency of the courts and writers is favorable to its exclusive adoption,—more correctly speaking, "readoption." We deem it wiser to accept and declare the rule now than to resist for a time, and ultimately be compelled to do so, when the confusion produced would be tenfold greater than at present is possible.

. . . In view of the uncontradicted evidence in behalf of the plaintiff below, now before us, we do not consider the verdict excessive. Under a correct rule of damages it would not be disturbed on account of the sum awarded. But we cannot say that a portion thereof was not given for the purpose of punishing appellant. The judgment is reversed, and the cause remanded for a new trial.

One unique and surprising aspect of punitive damages is that the consideration of what measure of punitive damages might be appropriate makes inquiry into defendant's wealth relevant, as illustrated by the following case.

KEMEZY V. PETERS
79 F.3D 33 (7TH CIR. 1996)

POSNER, *Chief Judge.*

Jeffrey Kemezy sued a Muncie, Indiana policeman named James Peters . . . claiming that Peters had wantonly beaten him with the officer's nightstick in an altercation in a bowling alley where Peters was moonlighting as a security guard. The jury awarded Kemezy $10,000 in compensatory damages and $20,000 in punitive damages. Peters' appeal challenges only the award of punitive damages, and that on the narrowest of grounds: that it was the plaintiff's burden to introduce evidence concerning the defendant's net worth for purposes of equipping the jury with information essential to a just measurement of punitive damages.

Two courts have adopted the position that Peters advocates. . . . But the majority view is opposed . . . . [W]e think the majority rule, which places no burden of production on the plaintiff, is sound, and we take this opportunity to make clear that it is indeed the law of this circuit.

The standard judicial formulation of the purpose of punitive damages is that it is to punish the defendant for reprehensible conduct and to deter him and others from engaging in similar conduct. This formulation is cryptic, since deterrence is a purpose of punishment, rather than, as the formulation implies, a parallel purpose, along with punishment itself, for imposing the specific form of punishment that is punitive damages. An extensive academic literature, however, elaborates on the cryptic judicial formula, offering a number of reasons for awards of punitive damages. A review of the reasons will point us toward a sound choice between the majority and minority views.

1. Compensatory damages do not always compensate fully. Because courts insist that an award of compensatory damages have an objective basis in evidence, such awards are likely to fall short in some cases, especially when the injury is of an elusive or intangible character. If you spit upon another person in anger, you inflict a real injury but one exceedingly difficult to quantify. If the court is confident that the injurious conduct had no redeeming social value, so that "overdeterring" such conduct by an "excessive" award of damages is not a concern, a generous award of punitive damages will assure full compensation without impeding socially valuable conduct.

2. By the same token, punitive damages are necessary in such cases in order to make sure that tortious conduct is not underdeterred, as it might be if compensatory damages fell short of the actual injury inflicted by the tort.

These two points bring out the close relation between the compensatory and deterrent objectives of tort law, or, more precisely perhaps, its rectificatory and regulatory purposes. Knowing that he will have to pay compensation for harm inflicted, the potential injurer will be deterred from inflicting that harm unless the benefits to him are greater. If we do not want him to balance costs and benefits in this fashion, we can add a dollop of punitive damages to make the costs greater.

3. Punitive damages are necessary in some cases to make sure that people channel transactions through the market when the costs of voluntary transactions are low. We do not want a person to be able to take his neighbor's car and when the neighbor complains tell him to go sue for its value. We want to make such expropriations valueless to the expropriator and we can do this by adding a punitive exaction to the judgment for the market value of what is taken. This function of punitive damages is particularly important in areas such as defamation and sexual assault, where the tortfeasor may, if the only price of the tort is having to compensate his victim, commit the tort because he derives greater pleasure from the act than the victim incurs pain.

4. When a tortious act is concealable, a judgment equal to the harm done by the act will underdeter. Suppose a person who goes around assaulting other people is caught only half the time. Then in comparing the costs, in the form of anticipated damages, of the assaults with the benefits to him, he will discount the costs (but not the benefits, because they are realized in every assault) by 50 percent, and so in deciding whether to commit the next assault he will not be confronted by the full social cost of his activity.

5. An award of punitive damages expresses the community's abhorrence at the defendant's act. We understand that otherwise upright, decent, law-abiding people are sometimes careless and that their carelessness can result in unintentional injury for which compensation should be required. We react far more strongly to the deliberate or reckless wrongdoer, and an award of punitive damages commutes our indignation into a kind of civil fine, civil punishment.

Some of these functions are also performed by the criminal justice system. Many legal systems do not permit awards of punitive damages at all, believing that such awards anomalously intrude the principles of criminal justice into civil cases. Even our cousins the English allow punitive damages only in an excruciatingly narrow category of cases. But whether because the

American legal and political cultures are unique, or because the criminal justice system in this country is overloaded and some of its functions have devolved upon the tort system, punitive damages are a regular feature of American tort cases, though reserved generally for intentional torts, including the deliberate use of excess force as here. This suggests additional functions of punitive damages:

6. Punitive damages relieve the pressures on the criminal justice system. They do this not so much by creating an additional sanction, which could be done by increasing the fines imposed in criminal cases, as by giving private individuals—the tort victims themselves—a monetary incentive to shoulder the costs of enforcement.

7. If we assume realistically that the criminal justice system could not or would not take up the slack if punitive damages were abolished, then they have the additional function of heading off breaches of the peace by giving individuals injured by relatively minor outrages a judicial remedy in lieu of the violent self-help to which they might resort if their complaints to the criminal justice authorities were certain to be ignored and they had no other legal remedy.

What is striking about the purposes that are served by the awarding of punitive damages is that none of them depends critically on proof that the defendant's income or wealth *exceeds* some specified level. The more wealth the defendant has, the smaller is the relative bite that an award of punitive damages not actually geared to that wealth will take out of his pocketbook, while if he has very little wealth the award of punitive damages may exceed his ability to pay and perhaps drive him into bankruptcy. To a very rich person, the pain of having to pay a heavy award of damages may be a mere pinprick and so not deter him (or people like him) from continuing to engage in the same type of wrongdoing. What in economics is called the principle of diminishing marginal utility teaches, what is anyway obvious, that losing $1 is likely to cause less unhappiness (disutility) to a rich person than to a poor one. . . . But rich people are not famous for being indifferent to money, and if they are forced to pay not merely the cost of the harm to the victims of their torts but also some multiple of that cost they are likely to think twice before engaging in such expensive behavior again. Juries, rightly or wrongly, think differently, so plaintiffs who are seeking punitive damages often present evidence of the defendant's wealth. The question is whether they *must* present such evidence—whether it is somehow unjust to allow a jury to award punitive damages without knowing that the defendant really is a wealthy person. The answer, obviously, is no. A plaintiff is not required to seek punitive damages in the first place, so he should not be denied an award of punitive damages merely because he does not present evidence that if believed would persuade the jury to award him even more than he is asking.

Take the question from the other side: if the defendant is not as wealthy as the jury might in the absence of any evidence suppose, should the plaintiff be required to show this? That seems an odd suggestion too. The reprehensibility of a person's conduct is not mitigated by his not being a rich person, and plaintiffs are never required to apologize for seeking damages that if awarded will precipitate the defendant into bankruptcy. A plea of poverty is a classic appeal to the mercy of the judge or jury, and why the plaintiff should be required to make the plea on behalf of his opponent eludes us.

The usual practice with respect to fines is not to proportion the fine to the defendant's wealth, but to allow him to argue that the fine should be waived or lowered because he cannot possibly pay it. . . . Given the close relation between fines and punitive damages, this is the proper approach to punitive damages as well. The defendant who cannot pay a large award of punitive damages can point this out to the jury so that they will not waste their time and that of the bankruptcy courts by awarding an amount that exceeds his ability to pay. . . .

Since, moreover, information about net worth is in the possession of the person whose net wealth is in issue, the normal principles of pleading would put the burden of production on the defendant—which, as we have been at pains to stress, is just where defendants as a whole would want it. . . .

AFFIRMED.

NOTES AND QUESTIONS

1   Is the *Kemezy* defendant's wealth relevant to a compensatory damages award? If not, then why is defendant's wealth relevant to the punitive damages question at all? Are there any dangers to permitting the jury to consider the defendant's wealth?

2   While the wealth of the defendant generally is viewed as relevant to the proper measure of a punitive award, it is not seen as the most important factor. The reprehensibility of defendant's conduct usually is identified as most important to a punitive award.

3   While the recovery of punitive damages in a civil case was once a controversial idea, every state in the United States now permits an award of punitive damages under certain circumstances. Many states govern the availability of punitive damages by statute. For example, Va. Code Ann. § 8.01-38.1 provides that "the total amount awarded for punitive damages against all defendants found to be liable shall be determined by the trier of fact. In no event shall the total amount awarded for punitive damages exceed $350,000. The jury shall not be advised of the limitation prescribed by this section. However, if a jury returns a verdict for punitive damages in excess of the maximum amount specified in this section, the judge shall reduce the award and enter judgment for such damages in the maximum amount provided by this section." Virginia's statute is an example of the growing minority of states that cap punitive damage awards.

4   Some states provide that punitive damages awards be paid into the state's general revenue fund. Does it ever make sense for a punitive damages award to be paid over to plaintiff?

5   It has sometimes been held that liability insurance policies covering punitive damages are void as against public policy.

For the last couple decades, the Supreme Court of the United States has been in the business of policing punitive damages awards on Constitutional grounds. In *Pacific Mut. Life Ins. Co. v. Haslip*, 499 U.S. 1 (1991), the Court held that the Due Process Clause of the Fourteenth Amendment required certain procedural safeguards when awarding punitive damages. The Court twice expanded on this holding until finally, in *BMW of North America, Inc. v. Gore*, 517

U.S. 559 (1996) the Court held that Due Process limits the size of punitive damages awards. The Court has twice expanded on its holding in *BMW v. Gore*.

STATE FARM MUT. AUTO. INS. CO. V. CAMPBELL
538 U.S. 408 (2003)

JUSTICE KENNEDY delivered the opinion of the Court.

We address once again the measure of punishment, by means of punitive damages, a State may impose upon a defendant in a civil case. The question is whether, in the circumstances we shall recount, an award of $145 million in punitive damages, where full compensatory damages are $1 million, is excessive and in violation of the Due Process Clause of the Fourteenth Amendment to the Constitution of the United States.

I

In 1981, Curtis Campbell (Campbell) was driving with his wife, Inez Preece Campbell, in Cache County, Utah. He decided to pass six vans traveling ahead of them on a two-lane highway. Todd Ospital was driving a small car approaching from the opposite direction. To avoid a head-on collision with Campbell, who by then was driving on the wrong side of the highway and toward oncoming traffic, Ospital swerved onto the shoulder, lost control of his automobile, and collided with a vehicle driven by Robert G. Slusher. Ospital was killed, and Slusher was rendered permanently disabled. The Campbells escaped unscathed.

In the ensuing wrongful death and tort action, Campbell insisted he was not at fault. Early investigations did support differing conclusions as to who caused the accident, but "a consensus was reached early on by the investigators and witnesses that Mr. Campbell's unsafe pass had indeed caused the crash." Campbell's insurance company, petitioner State Farm Mutual Automobile Insurance Company (State Farm), nonetheless decided to contest liability and declined offers by Slusher and Ospital's estate (Ospital) to settle the claims for the policy limit of $50,000 ($25,000 per claimant). State Farm also ignored the advice of one of its own investigators and took the case to trial, assuring the Campbells that "their assets were safe, that they had no liability for the accident, that [State Farm] would represent their interests, and that they did not need to procure separate counsel." To the contrary, a jury determined that Campbell was 100 percent at fault, and a judgment was returned for $185,849, far more than the amount offered in settlement.

At first State Farm refused to cover the $135,849 in excess liability. Its counsel made this clear to the Campbells: "You may want to put for sale signs on your property to get things moving." Nor was State Farm willing to post a supersedeas bond to allow Campbell to appeal the judgment against him. Campbell obtained his own counsel to appeal the verdict. During the pendency of the appeal, in late 1984, Slusher, Ospital, and the Campbells reached an agreement whereby Slusher and Ospital agreed not to seek satisfaction of their claims against the Campbells. In exchange the Campbells agreed to pursue a bad faith action against State Farm and to be represented by Slusher's and Ospital's attorneys. The Campbells also agreed that Slusher and Ospital would have a right to play a part in all major decisions concerning the bad faith action. No settlement could be concluded without Slusher's and Ospital's approval, and Slusher and Ospital would receive 90 percent of any verdict against State Farm.

In 1989, the Utah Supreme Court denied Campbell's appeal in the wrongful death and tort actions. . . . State Farm then paid the entire judgment, including the amounts in excess of the policy limits. The Campbells nonetheless filed a complaint against State Farm alleging bad faith, fraud, and intentional infliction of emotional distress. The trial court initially granted State Farm's motion for summary judgment because State Farm had paid the excess verdict, but that ruling was reversed on appeal. On remand State Farm moved *in limine* to exclude evidence of alleged conduct that occurred in unrelated cases outside of Utah, but the trial court denied the motion. At State Farm's request the trial court bifurcated the trial into two phases conducted before different juries. In the first phase the jury determined that State Farm's decision not to settle was unreasonable because there was a substantial likelihood of an excess verdict. Before the second phase of the action against State Farm we decided *BMW of North America, Inc.* v. *Gore,* 517 U.S. 559 . . . (1996), and refused to sustain a $2 million punitive damages award which accompanied a verdict of only $4,000 in compensatory damages. Based on that decision, State Farm again moved for the exclusion of evidence of dissimilar out-of-state conduct. The trial court denied State Farm's motion.

The second phase addressed State Farm's liability for fraud and intentional infliction of emotional distress, as well as compensatory and punitive damages. The Utah Supreme Court aptly characterized this phase of the trial:

> State Farm argued during phase II that its decision to take the case to trial was an "honest mistake" that did not warrant punitive damages. In contrast, the Campbells introduced evidence that State Farm's decision to take the case to trial was a result of a national scheme to meet corporate fiscal goals by capping payouts on claims company wide. This scheme was referred to as State Farm's "Performance, Planning and Review," or PP & R, policy. To prove the existence of this scheme, the trial court allowed the Campbells to introduce extensive expert testimony regarding fraudulent practices by State Farm in its nation-wide operations. Although State Farm moved prior to phase II of the trial for the exclusion of such evidence and continued to object to it at trial, the trial court ruled that such evidence was admissible to determine whether State Farm's conduct in the Campbell case was indeed intentional and sufficiently egregious to warrant punitive damages.

Evidence pertaining to the PP&R policy concerned State Farm's business practices for over 20 years in numerous States. Most of these practices bore no relation to third-party automobile insurance claims, the type of claim underlying the Campbells' complaint against the company. The jury awarded the Campbells $2.6 million in compensatory damages and $145 million in punitive damages, which the trial court reduced to $1 million and $25 million respectively. Both parties appealed.

The Utah Supreme Court sought to apply the three guideposts we identified in *Gore*, . . . and it reinstated the $145 million punitive damages award. Relying in large part on the extensive evidence concerning the PP&R policy, the court concluded State Farm's conduct was reprehensible. The court also relied upon State Farm's "massive wealth" and on testimony indicating that "State Farm's actions, because of their clandestine nature, will be punished at most in one out of every 50,000 cases as a matter of statistical probability," and concluded that the ratio between punitive and compensatory damages was not unwarranted. Finally, the court noted that the punitive damages award was not excessive when compared to various civil and criminal penalties State Farm could have faced, including $10,000 for each act of fraud, the suspension of its license to conduct business in Utah, the disgorgement of profits, and imprisonment. We granted certiorari.

II

We recognized in *Cooper Industries, Inc.* v. *Leatherman Tool Group, Inc.,* 532 U. S. 424 (2001), that in our judicial system compensatory and punitive damages, although usually awarded at the same time by the same decisionmaker, serve different purposes. . . . Compensatory damages "are intended to redress the concrete loss that the plaintiff has suffered by reason of the defendant's wrongful conduct." *Ibid.* . . . By contrast, punitive damages serve a broader function; they are aimed at deterrence and retribution. . . .

While States possess discretion over the imposition of punitive damages, it is well established that there are procedural and substantive constitutional limitations on these awards. The Due Process Clause of the Fourteenth Amendment prohibits the imposition of grossly excessive or arbitrary punishments on a tortfeasor. The reason is that "[e]lementary notions of fairness enshrined in our constitutional jurisprudence dictate that a person receive fair notice not only of the conduct that will subject him to punishment, but also of the severity of the penalty that a State may impose." . . . To the extent an award is grossly excessive, it furthers no legitimate purpose and constitutes an arbitrary deprivation of property. . . .

Although these awards serve the same purposes as criminal penalties, defendants subjected to punitive damages in civil cases have not been accorded the protections applicable in a criminal proceeding. This increases our concerns over the imprecise manner in which punitive damages systems are administered. We have admonished that "[p]unitive damages pose an acute danger of arbitrary deprivation of property. Jury instructions typically leave the jury with wide discretion in choosing amounts, and the presentation of evidence of a defendant's net worth creates the potential that juries will use their verdicts to express biases against big businesses, particularly those without strong local presences." Our concerns are heightened when the decisionmaker is presented, as we shall discuss, with evidence that has little bearing as to the amount of punitive damages that should be awarded. Vague instructions, or those that merely inform the jury to avoid "passion or prejudice," do little to aid the decisionmaker in its task of assigning appropriate weight to evidence that is relevant and evidence that is tangential or only inflammatory.

In light of these concerns, in *Gore*, . . . we instructed courts reviewing punitive damages to consider three guideposts: (1) the degree of reprehensibility of the defendant's misconduct; (2)

the disparity between the actual or potential harm suffered by the plaintiff and the punitive damages award; and (3) the difference between the punitive damages awarded by the jury and the civil penalties authorized or imposed in comparable cases. We reiterated the importance of these three guideposts in *Cooper Industries* and mandated appellate courts to conduct *de novo* review of a trial court's application of them to the jury's award. . . .

III

Under the principles outlined in *BMW of North America, Inc.* v. *Gore*, this case is neither close nor difficult. It was error to reinstate the jury's $145 million punitive damages award. We address each guidepost of *Gore* in some detail.

A

"[T]he most important indicium of the reasonableness of a punitive damages award is the degree of reprehensibility of the defendant's conduct." *Gore, supra,* at 575. We have instructed courts to determine the reprehensibility of a defendant by considering whether: the harm caused was physical as opposed to economic; the tortious conduct evinced an indifference to or a reckless disregard of the health or safety of others; the target of the conduct had financial vulnerability; the conduct involved repeated actions or was an isolated incident; and the harm was the result of intentional malice, trickery, or deceit, or mere accident. The existence of any one of these factors weighing in favor of a plaintiff may not be sufficient to sustain a punitive damages award; and the absence of all of them renders any award suspect. It should be presumed a plaintiff has been made whole for his injuries by compensatory damages, so punitive damages should only be awarded if the defendant's culpability, after having paid compensatory damages, is so reprehensible as to warrant the imposition of further sanctions to achieve punishment or deterrence.

. . . While we do not suggest there was error in awarding punitive damages based upon State Farm's conduct toward the Campbells, a more modest punishment for this reprehensible conduct could have satisfied the State's legitimate objectives, and the Utah courts should have gone no further.

This case, instead, was used as a platform to expose, and punish, the perceived deficiencies of State Farm's operations throughout the country. The Utah Supreme Court's opinion makes explicit that State Farm was being condemned for its nationwide policies rather than for the conduct direct toward the Campbells. . . .

A State cannot punish a defendant for conduct that may have been lawful where it occurred. Nor, as a general rule, does a State have a legitimate concern in imposing punitive damages to punish a defendant for unlawful acts committed outside of the State's jurisdiction. Any proper adjudication of conduct that occurred outside Utah to other persons would require their inclusion, and, to those parties, the Utah courts, in the usual case, would need to apply the laws of their relevant jurisdiction. . . .

For a more fundamental reason, however, the Utah courts erred in relying upon this and other evidence: The courts awarded punitive damages to punish and deter conduct that bore no relation to the Campbells' harm. A defendant's dissimilar acts, independent from the acts upon which liability was premised, may not serve as the basis for punitive damages. A defendant should be punished for the conduct that harmed the plaintiff, not for being an unsavory individual or business. Due process does not permit courts, in the calculation of punitive damages, to adjudicate the merits of other parties' hypothetical claims against a defendant under the guise of the reprehensibility analysis, but we have no doubt the Utah Supreme Court did that here. Punishment on these bases creates the possibility of multiple punitive damages awards for the same conduct; for in the usual case nonparties are not bound by the judgment some other plaintiff obtains.

The same reasons lead us to conclude the Utah Supreme Court's decision cannot be justified on the grounds that State Farm was a recidivist. Although "[o]ur holdings that a recidivist may be punished more severely than a first offender recognize that repeated misconduct is more reprehensible than an individual instance of malfeasance," *Gore, supra,* at 577, in the context of civil actions courts must ensure the conduct in question replicates the prior transgressions.

The Campbells have identified scant evidence of repeated misconduct of the sort that injured them. Nor does our review of the Utah courts' decisions convince us that State Farm was only punished for its actions toward the Campbells. Although evidence of other acts need not be identical to have relevance in the calculation of punitive damages, the Utah court erred here because evidence pertaining to claims that had nothing to do with a third-party lawsuit was introduced at length. . . . The reprehensibility guidepost does not permit courts to expand the scope of the case so that a defendant may be punished for any malfeasance, which in this case extended for a 20-year period. In this case, because the Campbells have shown no conduct by State Farm similar to that which harmed them, the conduct that harmed them is the only conduct relevant to the reprehensibility analysis.

B

Turning to the second *Gore* guidepost, we have been reluctant to identify concrete constitutional limits on the ratio between harm, or potential harm, to the plaintiff and the punitive damages award. . . . We decline again to impose a bright-line ratio which a punitive damages award cannot exceed. Our jurisprudence and the principles it has now established demonstrate, however, that, in practice, few awards exceeding a single-digit ratio between punitive and compensatory damages, to a significant degree, will satisfy due process. In *Haslip*, in upholding a punitive damages award, we concluded that an award of more than four times the amount of compensatory damages might be close to the line of constitutional impropriety. . . . The Court further referenced a long legislative history, dating back over 700 years and going forward to today, providing for sanctions of double, treble, or quadruple damages to deter and punish. . . . While these ratios are not binding, they are instructive. They demonstrate what should be obvious: Single-digit multipliers are more likely to comport with due process, while still achieving the State's goals of deterrence and retribution . . . .

Nonetheless, because there are no rigid benchmarks that a punitive damages award may not surpass, ratios greater than those we have previously upheld may comport with due process where "a particularly egregious act has resulted in only a small amount of economic damages." . . . The converse is also true, however. When compensatory damages are substantial, then a lesser ratio, perhaps only equal to compensatory damages, can reach the outermost limit of the due process guarantee. The precise award in any case, of course, must be based upon the facts and circumstances of the defendant's conduct and the harm to the plaintiff.

In sum, courts must ensure that the measure of punishment is both reasonable and proportionate to the amount of harm to the plaintiff and to the general damages recovered. In the context of this case, we have no doubt that there is a presumption against an award that has a 145-to-1 ratio. The compensatory award in this case was substantial; the Campbells were awarded $1 million for a year and a half of emotional distress. This was complete compensation. The harm arose from a transaction in the economic realm, not from some physical assault or trauma; there were no physical injuries; and State Farm paid the excess verdict before the complaint was filed, so the Campbells suffered only minor economic injuries for the 18-month period in which State Farm refused to resolve the claim against them. The compensatory damages for the injury suffered here, moreover, likely were based on a component which was duplicated in the punitive award. Much of the distress was caused by the outrage and humiliation the Campbells suffered at the actions of their insurer; and it is a major role of punitive damages to condemn such conduct. Compensatory damages, however, already contain this punitive element. . . .

C

The third guidepost in *Gore* is the disparity between the punitive damages award and the "civil penalties authorized or imposed in comparable cases." *Id.,* at 575. We note that, in the past, we have also looked to criminal penalties that could be imposed. The existence of a criminal penalty does have bearing on the seriousness with which a State views the wrongful action. When used to determine the dollar amount of the award, however, the criminal penalty has less utility. Great care must be taken to avoid use of the civil process to assess criminal penalties that can be imposed only after the heightened protections of a criminal trial have been observed, including, of course, its higher standards of proof. Punitive damages are not a substitute for the criminal process, and the remote possibility of a criminal sanction does not automatically sustain a punitive damages award.

Here, we need not dwell long on this guidepost. The most relevant civil sanction under Utah state law for the wrong done to the Campbells appears to be a $10,000 fine for an act of fraud, an amount dwarfed by the $145 million punitive damages award. The Supreme Court of Utah speculated about the loss of State Farm's business license, the disgorgement of profits, and possible imprisonment, but here again its references were to the broad fraudulent scheme drawn from evidence of out-of-state and dissimilar conduct. This analysis was insufficient to justify the award.

IV

An application of the *Gore* guideposts to the facts of this case, especially in light of the substantial compensatory damages awarded (a portion of which contained a punitive element), likely would justify a punitive damages award at or near the amount of compensatory damages. The punitive award of $145 million, therefore, was neither reasonable nor proportionate to the wrong committed, and it was an irrational and arbitrary deprivation of the property of the defendant. The proper calculation of punitive damages under the principles we have discussed should be resolved, in the first instance, by the Utah courts.

The judgment of the Utah Supreme Court is reversed, and the case is remanded for proceedings not inconsistent with this opinion.

It is so ordered.

JUSTICE SCALIA, dissenting.

I adhere to the view expressed in my dissenting opinion in *BMW of North America, Inc.* v. *Gore,* 517 U. S. 559,598-99 (1996), that the Due Process Clause provides no substantive protections against "excessive" or "unreasonable" awards of punitive damages. I am also of the view that the punitive damages jurisprudence which has sprung forth from *BMW* v. *Gore* is insusceptible of principled application; accordingly, I do not feel justified in giving the case *stare decisis* effect. . . . I would affirm the judgment of the Utah Supreme Court.

JUSTICE THOMAS, dissenting.

I would affirm the judgment below because "I continue to believe that the Constitution does not constrain the size of punitive damages awards." *Cooper Industries, Inc.* v. *Leatherman Tool Group, Inc.,* 532 U. S. 424, 443 (2001) (*Thomas,* J., concurring) . . . . Accordingly, I respectfully dissent.

JUSTICE GINSBURG, dissenting.

. . . It was not until 1996, in *BMW of North America, Inc.* v. *Gore,* 517 U. S. 559 (1996), that the Court, for the first time, invalidated a state-court punitive damages assessment as unreasonably large. . . .

In *Gore,* I stated why I resisted the Court's foray into punitive damages "territory traditionally within the States' domain." 517 U. S., at 612 (dissenting opinion). I adhere to those views . . . .

I

The large size of the award upheld by the Utah Supreme Court in this case indicates why damage-capping legislation may be altogether fitting and proper. Neither the amount of the award nor the trial record, however, justifies this Court's substitution of its judgment for that of Utah's competent decisionmakers. In this regard, I count it significant that, on the key criterion "reprehensibility," there is a good deal more to the story than the Court's abbreviated account tells....

II

The Court dismisses the evidence describing and documenting State Farm's PP&R policy and practices as essentially irrelevant, bearing "no relation to the Campbells' harm." ... It is hardly apparent why that should be so. What is infirm about the Campbells' theory that their experience with State Farm exemplifies and reflects an overarching underpayment scheme, one that caused "repeated misconduct of the sort that injured them," *ante*, at 13? The Court's silence on that score is revealing: Once one recognizes that the Campbells did show "conduct by State Farm similar to that which harmed them," *ante*, at 14, it becomes impossible to shrink the reprehensibility analysis to this sole case, or to maintain, at odds with the determination of the trial court ....

Evidence of out-of-state conduct, the Court acknowledges, may be "probative [even if the conduct is lawful in the state where it occurred] when it demonstrates the deliberateness and culpability of the defendant's action in the State where it is tortious...." "Other acts" evidence concerning practices both in and out of State was introduced in this case to show just such "deliberateness" and "culpability." ...

III

When the Court first ventured to override state-court punitive damages awards, it did so moderately. The Court recalled that "[i]n our federal system, States necessarily have considerable flexibility in determining the level of punitive damages that they will allow in different classes of cases and in any particular case." *Gore*, 517 U. S., at 568. Today's decision exhibits no such respect and restraint.... Moreover, the Court adds, when compensatory damages are substantial, doubling those damages "can reach the outermost limit of the due process guarantee." ... In a legislative scheme or a state high court's design to cap punitive damages, the handiwork in setting single-digit and 1-to-1 benchmarks could hardly be questioned; in a judicial decree imposed on the States by this Court under the banner of substantive due process, the numerical controls today's decision installs seem to me boldly out of order.

I remain of the view that this Court has no warrant to reform state law governing awards of punitive damages. ... Even if I were prepared to accept the flexible guides prescribed in *Gore*, I would not join the Court's swift conversion of those guides into instructions that begin to resemble marching orders. For the reasons stated, I would leave the judgment of the Utah Supreme Court undisturbed.

1   Justice Scalia filed the following dissenting opinion in *BMW of North America v. Gore*, 517 U.S. 559 (1996):

Today we see the latest manifestation of this Court's recent and increasingly insistent "concern about punitive damages that 'run wild.'" *Pacific Mut. Life Ins. Co. v. Haslip*, 499 U.S. 1 . . . (1991). Since the Constitution does not make that concern any of our business, the Court's activities in this area are an unjustified incursion into the province of state governments.

In earlier cases that were the prelude to this decision, I set forth my view that a state trial procedure that commits the decision whether to impose punitive damages, and the amount, to the discretion of the jury, subject to some judicial review for "reasonableness," furnishes a defendant with all the process that is "due." *See TXO Production Corp. v. Alliance Resources Corp.*, 509 U.S. 443, 470 . . . (1993) (SCALIA, J., concurring in judgment); . . . I do not regard the Fourteenth Amendment's Due Process Clause as a secret repository of substantive guarantees against "unfairness" – neither the unfairness of an excessive civil compensatory award, nor the unfairness of an "unreasonable" punitive award. What the Fourteenth Amendment's procedural guarantee assures is an opportunity to contest the reasonableness of a damages judgment in state court; but there is no federal guarantee a damages award actually *be* reasonable. . . .

Because today's judgment represents the first instance of this Court's invalidation of a state-court punitive assessment as simply unreasonably large, I think it a proper occasion to discuss these points at some length.

I

. . . *Haslip* and *TXO* revived the notion, moribund since its appearance in the first years of this century, that the measure of civil punishment poses a question of constitutional dimension to be answered by this Court. Neither of those cases, however, nor any of the precedents upon which they relied, actually took the step of declaring a punitive award unconstitutional simply because it was "too big."

At the time of adoption of the Fourteenth Amendment, it was well understood that punitive damages represent the assessment by the jury, as the voice of the community, of the measure of punishment the defendant deserved. . . . Today's decision, though dressed up as a legal opinion, is really no more than a disagreement with the community's sense of indignation or outrage expressed in the punitive award of the Alabama jury, as reduced by the State Supreme Court. It reflects not merely, as the concurrence candidly acknowledges, "a judgment about a matter of degree," . . . ; but a judgment about the appropriate degree of indignation or outrage, which is hardly an analytical determination.

There is no precedential warrant for giving our judgment priority over the judgment of state courts and juries on this matter. The only support for the Court's position is to be found in a handful of errant federal cases, bunched within a few years of one other, which invented the notion that an unfairly severe civil sanction amounts to a violation of constitutional liberties. . . .

II

One might understand the Court's eagerness to enter this field, rather than leave it with the state legislatures, if it had something useful to say. In fact, however, its opinion provides virtually no guidance to legislatures, and to state and federal courts, as to what a "constitutionally proper" level of punitive damages might be.

We are instructed at the outset of Part II of the Court's opinion – the beginning of its substantive analysis – that "the federal excessiveness inquiry . . . begins with an identification of the state interests that a punitive award is designed to serve." . . . As Part II of the Court's opinion unfolds, it turns out to be directed, not to the question "How much punishment is too much?" but rather to the question "Which acts can be punished?" "Alabama does not have the power," the Court says, "to punish BMW for conduct that was lawful where it occurred and that had no impact on Alabama or its residents." . . . That may be true, though only in the narrow sense that a person cannot be *held liable to be punished* on the basis of a lawful act. But if a person has been held subject to punishment because he committed an *un*lawful act, the *degree* of his punishment assuredly *can* be increased on the basis of any other conduct of his that displays his wickedness, unlawful or not. . . . Why could the Supreme Court of Alabama not consider lawful (but disreputable) conduct, both inside and outside Alabama, for the purpose of assessing just how bad an actor BMW was?

The Court follows up its statement that "Alabama does not have the power . . . to punish BMW for conduct that was lawful where it occurred" with the statement: "Nor may Alabama impose sanctions on BMW in order to deter conduct that is lawful in other jurisdictions." . . . The Court provides us no citation of authority to support this proposition – other than the barely analogous cases cited earlier in the opinion . . . – and I know of none.

These significant issues pronounced upon by the Court are not remotely presented for resolution in the present case. There is no basis for believing that Alabama has sought to control conduct elsewhere. The statutes at issue merely permit civil juries to treat conduct such as petitioner's as fraud, and authorize an award of appropriate punitive damages in the event the fraud is found to be "gross, oppressive, or malicious," Ala. Code § 6-11-20(b)(1) (1993). To be sure, respondent did invite the jury to consider out-of-state conduct in its calculation of damages, but any increase in the jury's initial award based on that consideration is not a component of the remitted judgment before us. As the Court several times recognizes, in computing the amount of the remitted award the Alabama Supreme Court – whether it was constitutionally required to or not – "expressly disclaimed any reliance on acts that occurred in other jurisdictions." . . . (internal quotation marks omitted) . . . Thus, the only question presented by this case is whether that award, limited to petitioner's Alabama conduct and viewed in light of the factors identified as properly informing the inquiry, is excessive. The Court's sweeping (and largely unsupported) statements regarding the relationship of punitive awards to lawful or unlawful out-of-state conduct are the purest dicta.

III

In Part III of its opinion, the Court identifies "three guideposts" that lead it to the conclusion that the award in this case is excessive: degree of reprehensibility, ratio between punitive award and plaintiff's actual harm, and legislative sanctions provided for comparable misconduct. . . . The legal significance of these "guideposts" is nowhere explored, but their necessary effect is to establish federal standards governing the hitherto exclusively state law of damages. Apparently (though it is by no means clear) all three federal "guideposts" can be overridden if "necessary to deter future misconduct," . . . – a loophole that will encourage state reviewing courts to uphold awards as necessary for the "adequat[e] protect[ion]" of state consumers . . . . By effectively requiring state reviewing courts to concoct rationalizations – whether within the "guideposts" or through the loophole – to justify the intuitive punitive reactions of state juries, the Court accords neither category of institution the respect it deserves.

Of course it will not be easy for the States to comply with this new federal law of damages, no matter how willing they are to do so. In truth, the "guideposts" mark a road to nowhere; they provide no real guidance at all. As to "degree of reprehensibility" of the defendant's conduct, we learn that "'nonviolent crimes are less serious than crimes marked by violence or the threat of violence,'" . . . and that "'trickery and deceit'" are "more reprehensible than negligence," . . . . As to the ratio of punitive to compensatory damages, we are told that a "'general concer[n] of reasonableness . . . enter[s] into the constitutional calculus,'" . . . -- though even "a breathtaking 500 to 1" will not necessarily do anything more than "'raise a suspicious judicial eyebrow,'" . . . . And as to legislative sanctions provided for comparable misconduct, they should be accorded "'substantial deference,'" . . . . One expects the Court to conclude: "To thine own self be true."

These criss-crossing platitudes yield no real answers in no real cases. And it must be noted that the Court nowhere says that these three "guideposts" are the *only* guideposts; indeed, it makes very clear that they are not – explaining away the earlier opinions that do not really follow these "guideposts" on the basis of *additional* factors, thereby "reiterating our rejection of a categorical approach." . . . In other words, even these utter platitudes, if they should ever happen to produce an answer, may be overridden by other unnamed considerations. The Court has constructed a framework that does not genuinely constrain, that does not inform state legislatures and lower courts – that does nothing at all except confer an artificial air of doctrinal analysis upon its essentially ad hoc determination that this particular award of punitive damages was not "fair." . . .

For the foregoing reasons, I respectfully dissent.

PHILIP MORRIS USA V. WILLIAMS
549 U.S. 346 (2007)

Justice BREYER delivered the opinion of the Court.

The question we address today concerns a large state-court punitive damages award. We are asked whether the Constitution's Due Process Clause permits a jury to base that award in part upon its desire to punish the defendant for harming persons who are not before the court (e.g., victims whom the parties do not represent). We hold that such an award would amount to a taking of "property" from the defendant without due process.

I

This lawsuit arises out of the death of Jesse Williams, a heavy cigarette smoker. Respondent, Williams' widow, represents his estate in this state lawsuit for negligence and deceit against Philip Morris, the manufacturer of Marlboro, the brand that Williams favored. A jury found that Williams' death was caused by smoking; that Williams smoked in significant part because he thought it was safe to do so; and that Philip Morris knowingly and falsely led him to believe that this was so. The jury ultimately found that Philip Morris was negligent (as was Williams) and that Philip Morris had engaged in deceit. In respect to deceit, the claim at issue here, it awarded compensatory damages of about $821,000 (about $21,000 economic and $800,000 noneconomic) along with $79.5 million in punitive damages.

The trial judge subsequently found the $79.5 million punitive damages award "excessive," *see, e.g., BMW of North America, Inc. v. Gore*, 517 U.S. 559 ... (1996), and reduced it to $32 million. Both sides appealed. The Oregon Court of Appeals rejected Philip Morris' arguments and restored the $79.5 million jury award. Subsequently, Philip Morris sought review in the Oregon Supreme Court (which denied review) and then here. We remanded the case in light of *State Farm Mut. Automobile Ins. Co. v. Campbell*, 538 U.S. 408 ... (2003). The Oregon Court of Appeals adhered to its original views. And Philip Morris sought, and this time obtained, review in the Oregon Supreme Court.

Philip Morris then made two arguments relevant here. First, it said that the trial court should have accepted, but did not accept, a proposed "punitive damages" instruction that specified the jury could not seek to punish Philip Morris for injury to other persons not before the court. In particular, Philip Morris pointed out that the plaintiff's attorney had told the jury to "think about how many other Jesse Williams in the last 40 years in the State of Oregon there have been. ... In Oregon, how many people do we see outside, driving home ... smoking cigarettes? ... [C]igarettes ... are going to kill ten [of every hundred]. [And] the market share of Marlboros [i.e., Philip Morris] is one-third [i.e., one of every three killed]." App. 197a, 199a. In light of this argument, Philip Morris asked the trial court to tell the jury that "you may consider the extent of harm suffered by others in determining what [the] reasonable relationship is" between any punitive award and "the harm caused to Jesse Williams" by Philip Morris' misconduct, "[but] you are not to punish the defendant for the impact of its alleged misconduct on other persons, who may bring lawsuits of their own in which other juries can resolve their claims ...." *Id.,* at 280a. The judge rejected this proposal and instead told the jury that "[p]unitive damages are awarded against a defendant to punish misconduct and to deter misconduct," and "are not intended to compensate the plaintiff or anyone else for damages caused by the defendant's conduct." *Id.*, at 283a. In Philip Morris' view, the result was a significant likelihood that a portion of the $79.5 million award represented punishment for its having harmed others, a punishment that the Due Process Clause would here forbid.

Second, Philip Morris pointed to the roughly 100-to-1 ratio the $79.5 million punitive damages award bears to $821,000 in compensatory damages. Philip Morris noted that this Court in *BMW* emphasized the constitutional need for punitive damages awards to reflect (1) the "reprehensibility" of the defendant's conduct, (2) a "reasonable relationship" to the harm the plaintiff (or related victim) suffered, and (3) the presence (or absence) of "sanctions," e.g., criminal penalties, that state law provided for comparable conduct, 517 U.S., at 575-585 . . . . And in *State Farm*, this Court said that the longstanding historical practice of setting punitive damages at two, three, or four times the size of compensatory damages, while "not binding," is "instructive," and that "[s]ingle-digit multipliers are more likely to comport with due process." 538 U.S., at 425 . . . . Philip Morris claimed that, in light of this case law, the punitive award was "grossly excessive." *See TXO Production Corp. v. Alliance Resources Corp.*, 509 U.S. 443, 458 . . . (1993) (plurality opinion); *BMW, supra*, at 574-575 . . .; *State Farm, supra*, at 416-417 . . . .

The Oregon Supreme Court rejected these and other Philip Morris arguments. In particular, it rejected Philip Morris' claim that the Constitution prohibits a state jury "from using punitive damages to punish a defendant for harm to nonparties." 340 Or. 35, 51-52, 127 P.3d 1165, 1175 (2006). And in light of Philip Morris' reprehensible conduct, it found that the $79.5 million award was not "grossly excessive." *Id.*, at 63-64, 127 P.3d, at 1181-1182.

Philip Morris then sought certiorari. It asked us to consider, among other things, (1) its claim that Oregon had unconstitutionally permitted it to be punished for harming nonparty victims; and (2) whether Oregon had in effect disregarded "the constitutional requirement that punitive damages be reasonably related to the plaintiff's harm." Pet. for Cert. (I). We granted certiorari limited to these two questions.

For reasons we shall set forth, we consider only the first of these questions. We vacate the Oregon Supreme Court's judgment, and we remand the case for further proceedings.

II

This Court has long made clear that "[p]unitive damages may properly be imposed to further a State's legitimate interests in punishing unlawful conduct and deterring its repetition." *BMW, supra*, at 568, 116 S.Ct. 1589. *See also Gertz v. Robert Welch, Inc.*, 418 U.S. 323, 350, 94 S.Ct. 2997, 41 L.Ed.2d 789 (1974); *Newport v. Fact Concerts, Inc.*, 453 U.S. 247, 266-267, 101 S.Ct. 2748, 69 L.Ed.2d 616 (1981); *Pacific Mut. Life Ins. Co. v. Haslip*, 499 U.S. 1, 22, 111 S.Ct. 1032, 113 L.Ed.2d 1 (1991). At the same time, we have emphasized the need to avoid an arbitrary determination of an award's amount. Unless a State insists upon proper standards that will cabin the jury's discretionary authority, its punitive damages system may deprive a defendant of "fair notice ... of the severity of the penalty that a State may impose," *BMW, supra*, at 574, 116 S.Ct. 1589; it may threaten "arbitrary punishments," i.e., punishments that reflect not an "application of law" but "a decision-maker's caprice," *State Farm, supra*, at 416, 418, 123 S.Ct. 1513 (internal quotation marks omitted);

and, where the amounts are sufficiently large, it may impose one State's (or one jury's) "policy choice," say as to the conditions under which (or even whether) certain products can be sold, upon "neighboring States" with different public policies, *BMW, supra,* at 571-572, 116 S.Ct. 1589.

For these and similar reasons, this Court has found that the Constitution imposes certain limits, in respect both to procedures for awarding punitive damages and to amounts forbidden as "grossly excessive." *See Honda Motor Co. v. Oberg,* 512 U.S. 415, 432, 114 S.Ct. 2331, 129 L.Ed.2d 336 (1994) (requiring judicial review of the size of punitive awards); *Cooper Industries, Inc. v. Leatherman Tool Group, Inc.,* 532 U.S. 424, 443, 121 S.Ct. 1678, 149 L.Ed.2d 674 (2001) (review must be de novo); *BMW, supra,* at 574-585, 116 S.Ct. 1589 (excessiveness decision depends upon the reprehensibility of the defendant's conduct, whether the award bears a reasonable relationship to the actual and potential harm caused by the defendant to the plaintiff, and the difference between the award and sanctions "authorized or imposed in comparable cases"); *State Farm, supra,* at 425, 123 S.Ct. 1513 (excessiveness more likely where ratio exceeds single digits). Because we shall not decide whether the award here at issue is "grossly excessive," we need now only consider the Constitution's procedural limitations.

III

In our view, the Constitution's Due Process Clause forbids a State to use a punitive damages award to punish a defendant for injury that it inflicts upon nonparties or those whom they directly represent, i.e., injury that it inflicts upon those who are, essentially, strangers to the litigation. For one thing, the Due Process Clause prohibits a State from punishing an individual without first providing that individual with "an opportunity to present every available defense." *Lindsey v. Normet,* 405 U.S. 56, 66, 92 S.Ct. 862, 31 L.Ed.2d 36 (1972) (internal quotation marks omitted). Yet a defendant threatened with punishment for injuring a nonparty victim has no opportunity to defend against the charge, by showing, for example in a case such as this, that the other victim was not entitled to damages because he or she knew that smoking was dangerous or did not rely upon the defendant's statements to the contrary.

For another, to permit punishment for injuring a nonparty victim would add a near standardless dimension to the punitive damages equation. How many such victims are there? How seriously were they injured? Under what circumstances did injury occur? The trial will not likely answer such questions as to nonparty victims. The jury will be left to speculate. And the fundamental due process concerns to which our punitive damages cases refer-risks of arbitrariness, uncertainty and lack of notice-will be magnified. *State Farm,* 538 U.S., at 416, 418, 123 S.Ct. 1513; *BMW,* 517 U.S., at 574, 116 S.Ct. 1589.

Finally, we can find no authority supporting the use of punitive damages awards for the purpose of punishing a defendant for harming others. We have said that it may be appropriate to consider the reasonableness of a punitive damages award in light of the potential harm the defendant's conduct could have caused. But we have made clear that the potential harm at issue was harm potentially caused the plaintiff. *See State Farm, supra,* at 424, 123 S.Ct. 1513 ("[W]e have been reluctant to identify concrete constitutional limits on the ratio between harm, or potential harm, *to the plaintiff* and the punitive damages award" (emphasis added)). *See also TXO*, 509 U.S., at 460-462, 113 S.Ct. 2711 (plurality opinion) (using same kind of comparison as basis for finding a punitive award not unconstitutionally excessive). We did use the term "error-free" (in *BMW*) to describe a lower court punitive damages calculation that likely included harm to others in the equation. 517 U.S., at 568, n. 11, 116 S.Ct. 1589. But context makes clear that the term "error-free" in the *BMW* footnote referred to errors relevant to the case at hand. Although elsewhere in *BMW* we noted that there was no suggestion that the plaintiff "or any other BMW purchaser was threatened with any additional potential harm" by the defendant's conduct, we did not purport to decide the question of harm to others. *Id.*, at 582, 116 S.Ct. 1589. Rather, the opinion appears to have left the question open.

Respondent argues that she is free to show harm to other victims because it is relevant to a different part of the punitive damages constitutional equation, namely, reprehensibility. That is to say, harm to others shows more reprehensible conduct. Philip Morris, in turn, does not deny that a plaintiff may show harm to others in order to demonstrate reprehensibility. Nor do we. Evidence of actual harm to nonparties can help to show that the conduct that harmed the plaintiff also posed a substantial risk of harm to the general public, and so was particularly reprehensible-although counsel may argue in a particular case that conduct resulting in no harm to others nonetheless posed a grave risk to the public, or the converse. Yet for the reasons given above, a jury may not go further than this and use a punitive damages verdict to punish a defendant directly on account of harms it is alleged to have visited on nonparties.

Given the risks of unfairness that we have mentioned, it is constitutionally important for a court to provide assurance that the jury will ask the right question, not the wrong one. And given the risks of arbitrariness, the concern for adequate notice, and the risk that punitive damages awards can, in practice, impose one State's (or one jury's) policies (e.g., banning ciga-rettes) upon other States-all of which accompany awards that, today, may be many times the size of such awards in the 18th and 19th centuries, *see id.*, at 594-595, 116 S.Ct. 1589 (BREYER, J., concurring)-it is particularly important that States avoid procedure that unnecessarily deprives juries of proper legal guidance. We therefore conclude that the Due Process Clause requires States to provide assurance that juries are not asking the wrong question, i.e., seeking, not simply to determine reprehensibility, but also to punish for harm caused strangers.

IV

Respondent suggests as well that the Oregon Supreme Court, in essence, agreed with us, that it did not authorize punitive damages awards based upon punishment for harm caused to nonpar-ties. We concede that one might read some portions of the Oregon Supreme Court's opinion as focusing only upon reprehensibility. *See, e.g.*, 340 Ore., at 51, 127 P.3d, at 1175 ("[T]he jury could consider whether Williams and his misfortune were merely exemplars of the harm that Philip Morris was prepared to inflict on the smoking public at large"). But the Oregon court's opinion elsewhere makes clear that that court held more than these few phrases might suggest.

The instruction that Philip Morris said the trial court should have given distinguishes between using harm to others as part of the "reasonable relationship" equation (which it would allow) and using it directly as a basis for punishment. The instruction asked the trial court to tell the jury that "you may consider the extent of harm suffered by others in determining what [the] reasonable relationship is" between Philip Morris' punishable misconduct and harm caused to Jesse Williams, " [but] you are not to punish the defendant for the impact of its alleged misconduct on other persons, who may bring lawsuits of their own in which other juries can resolve their claims ...." App. 280a (emphasis added). And as the Oregon Supreme Court explicitly recognized, Philip Morris argued that the Constitution "prohibits the state, acting through a civil jury, from using punitive damages to punish a defendant for harm to nonparties." 340 Ore., at 51-52, 127 P.3d, at 1175.

The court rejected that claim. In doing so, it pointed out (1) that this Court in *State Farm* had held only that a jury could not base its award upon "dissimilar" acts of a defendant. 340 Ore., at 52-53, 127 P.3d, at 1175-1176. It added (2) that "[i]f a jury cannot punish for the conduct, then it is difficult to see why it may consider it at all." *Id.*, at 52, n. 3, 127 P.3d, at 1175, n. 3. And it stated (3) that "[i]t is unclear to us how a jury could 'consider' harm to others, yet withhold that consideration from the punishment calculus." *Ibid.*

The Oregon court's first statement is correct. We did not previously hold explicitly that a jury may not punish for the harm caused others. But we do so hold now. We do not agree with the Oregon court's second statement. We have explained why we believe the Due Process Clause prohibits a State's inflicting punishment for harm caused strangers to the litigation. At the same time we recognize that conduct that risks harm to many is likely more reprehensible than conduct that risks harm to only a few. And a jury consequently may take this fact into account in determining reprehensibility. *Cf., e.g., Witte v. United States*, 515 U.S. 389, 400, 115 S.Ct. 2199, 132 L.Ed.2d 351 (1995) (recidivism statutes taking into account a criminal defendant's other misconduct do not impose an "'additional penalty for the earlier crimes,' but instead ... 'a stiffened penalty for the latest crime, which is considered to be an aggravated offense because a repetitive one' " (quoting *Gryger v. Burke*, 334 U.S. 728, 732, 68 S.Ct. 1256, 92 L.Ed. 1683 (1948))).

The Oregon court's third statement raises a practical problem. How can we know whether a jury, in taking account of harm caused others under the rubric of reprehensibility, also seeks to punish the defendant for having caused injury to others? Our answer is that state courts cannot authorize procedures that create an unreasonable and unnecessary risk of any such confusion occurring. In particular, we believe that where the risk of that misunderstanding is a significant one-because, for instance, of the sort of evidence that was introduced at trial or the kinds of argument the plaintiff made to the jury-a court, upon request, must protect against that risk. Although the States have some flexibility to determine what kind of procedures they will implement, federal constitutional law obligates them to provide some form of protection in appropriate cases.

V

As the preceding discussion makes clear, we believe that the Oregon Supreme Court applied the wrong constitutional standard when considering Philip Morris' appeal. We remand this case so that the Oregon Supreme Court can apply the standard we have set forth. Because the application of this standard may lead to the need for a new trial, or a change in the level of the punitive damages award, we shall not consider whether the award is constitutionally "grossly excessive." We vacate the Oregon Supreme Court's judgment and remand the case for further proceedings not inconsistent with this opinion.

It is so ordered.

Justice STEVENS, dissenting.

The Due Process Clause of the Fourteenth Amendment imposes both substantive and procedural constraints on the power of the States to impose punitive damages on tortfeasors. *See State Farm Mut. Automobile Ins. Co. v. Campbell*, 538 U.S. 408, 123 S.Ct. 1513, 155 L.Ed.2d 585 (2003); *Cooper Industries, Inc. v. Leatherman Tool Group, Inc.*, 532 U.S. 424, 121 S.Ct. 1678, 149 L.Ed.2d 674 (2001); *BMW of North America, Inc. v. Gore*, 517 U.S. 559, 116 S.Ct. 1589, 134 L.Ed.2d 809 (1996); *Honda Motor Co. v. Oberg*, 512 U.S. 415, 114 S.Ct. 2331, 129 L.Ed.2d 336 (1994); *TXO Production Corp. v. Alliance Resources Corp.*, 509 U.S. 443, 113 S.Ct. 2711, 125 L.Ed.2d 366 (1993). I remain firmly convinced that the cases announcing those constraints were correctly decided. In my view the Oregon Supreme Court faithfully applied the reasoning in those opinions to the egregious facts disclosed by this record. I agree with Justice GINSBURG's explanation of why no procedural error even arguably justifying reversal occurred at the trial in this case. *See post*, p. 1068-1069.

Of greater importance to me, however, is the Court's imposition of a novel limit on the State's power to impose punishment in civil litigation. Unlike the Court, I see no reason why an interest in punishing a wrongdoer "for harming persons who are not before the court," ante, at 1060, should not be taken into consideration when assessing the appropriate sanction for reprehensible conduct.

Whereas compensatory damages are measured by the harm the defendant has caused the plaintiff, punitive damages are a sanction for the public harm the defendant's conduct has caused or threatened. There is little difference between the justification for a criminal sanction, such as a fine or a term of imprisonment, and an award of punitive damages. *See Cooper Industries*, 532 U.S., at 432, 121 S.Ct. 1678. In our early history either type of sanction might have been imposed in litigation prosecuted by a private citizen. *See Steel Co. v. Citizens for Better Environment*, 523 U.S. 83, 127-128, 118 S.Ct. 1003, 140 L.Ed.2d 210 (1998) (STEVENS, J., concurring in judgment). And while in neither context would the sanction typically include a pecuniary award measured by the harm that the conduct had caused to any third parties, in both contexts the harm to third parties would surely be a relevant factor to consider in evaluating the reprehensibility of the defendant's wrongdoing. We have never held otherwise.

In the case before us, evidence attesting to the possible harm the defendant's extensive deceitful conduct caused other Oregonians was properly presented to the jury. No evidence was offered to establish an appropriate measure of damages to compensate such third parties for their injuries, and no one argued that the punitive damages award would serve any such purpose. To award compensatory damages to remedy such third-party harm might well constitute a taking of property from the defendant without due process, *see cf.* at 1060. But a punitive damages award, instead of serving a compensatory purpose, serves the entirely different purposes of retribution and deterrence that underlie every criminal sanction. *State Farm*, 538 U.S., at 416, 123 S.Ct. 1513. This justification for punitive damages has even greater salience when, as in this case, *see* Ore.Rev.Stat. § 31.735(1) (2003), the award is payable in whole or in part to the State rather than to the private litigant. . . .

While apparently recognizing the novelty of its holding, *ante*, at 1065, the majority relies on a distinction between taking third-party harm into account in order to assess the reprehensibility of the defendant's conduct-which is permitted-and doing so in order to punish the defendant "directly"-which is forbidden. Ante, at 1064. This nuance eludes me. When a jury increases a punitive damages award because injuries to third parties enhanced the reprehensibility of the defendant's conduct, the jury is by definition punishing the defendant-directly-for third-party harm. . . . A murderer who kills his victim by throwing a bomb that injures dozens of bystanders should be punished more severely than one who harms no one other than his intended victim. Similarly, there is no reason why the measure of the appropriate punishment for engaging in a campaign of deceit in distributing a poisonous and addictive substance to thousands of cigarette smokers statewide should not include consideration of the harm to those " bystanders" as well as the harm to the individual plaintiff. The Court endorses a contrary conclusion without providing us with any reasoned justification.

It is far too late in the day to argue that the Due Process Clause merely guarantees fair procedure and imposes no substantive limits on a State's lawmaking power. *See, e.g., Moore v. East Cleveland*, 431 U.S. 494, 544, 97 S.Ct. 1932, 52 L.Ed.2d 531 (1977) (White, J., dissenting); *Poe v. Ullman*, 367 U.S. 497, 540-541, 81 S.Ct. 1752, 6 L.Ed.2d 989 (1961) (Harlan, J., dissenting); *Whitney v. California*, 274 U.S. 357, 373, 47 S.Ct. 641, 71 L.Ed. 1095 (1927) (Brandeis, J., concurring). It remains true, however, that the Court should be "reluctant to expand the concept of substantive due process because guideposts for responsible decisionmaking in this unchartered area are scarce and open-ended." *Collins v. Harker Heights*, 503 U.S. 115, 125, 112 S.Ct. 1061, 117 L.Ed.2d 261 (1992). Judicial restraint counsels us to "exercise the utmost care whenever we are asked to break new ground in this field." *Ibid.* Today the majority ignores that sound advice when it announces its new rule of substantive law.

Essentially for the reasons stated in the opinion of the Supreme Court of Oregon, I would affirm its judgment.

Justice THOMAS, dissenting.

I join Justice GINSBURG's dissent in full. I write separately to reiterate my view that "'the Constitution does not constrain the size of punitive damages awards.' " *State Farm Mut. Automobile Ins. Co. v. Campbell,* 538 U.S. 408, 429-430, 123 S.Ct. 1513, 155 L.Ed.2d 585 (2003) (THOMAS, J., dissenting) (quoting *Cooper Industries, Inc. v. Leatherman Tool Group, Inc.,* 532 U.S.

424, 443, 121 S.Ct. 1678, 149 L.Ed.2d 674 (2001) (THOMAS, J., concurring)). It matters not that the Court styles today's holding as "procedural" because the "procedural" rule is simply a confusing implementation of the substantive due process regime this Court has created for punitive damages. *See Pacific Mut. Life Ins. Co. v. Haslip*, 499 U.S. 1, 26-27, 111 S.Ct. 1032, 113 L.Ed.2d 1 (1991) (SCALIA, J., concurring in judgment) ("In 1868 ... punitive damages were undoubtedly an established part of the American common law of torts. It is ... clear that no particular procedures were deemed necessary to circumscribe a jury's discretion regarding the award of such damages, or their amount"). Today's opinion proves once again that this Court's punitive damages jurisprudence is "insusceptible of principled application." *BMW of North America, Inc. v. Gore*, 517 U.S. 559, 599, 116 S.Ct. 1589, 134 L.Ed.2d 809 (1996) (SCALIA, J., joined by THOMAS, J., dissenting).

Justice GINSBURG, with whom Justice SCALIA and Justice THOMAS join, dissenting.

The purpose of punitive damages, it can hardly be denied, is not to compensate, but to punish. Punish for what? Not for harm actually caused "strangers to the litigation," ante, at 1063, the Court states, but for the reprehensibility of defendant's conduct, ante, at 1063-1064. "[C]onduct that risks harm to many," the Court observes, "is likely more reprehensible than conduct that risks harm to only a few." Ante, at 1065. The Court thus conveys that, when punitive damages are at issue, a jury is properly instructed to consider the extent of harm suffered by others as a measure of reprehensibility, but not to mete out punishment for injuries in fact sustained by nonparties. Ante, at 1063-1065. The Oregon courts did not rule otherwise. They have endeavored to follow our decisions, most recently in *BMW of North America, Inc. v. Gore*, 517 U.S. 559, 116 S.Ct. 1589, 134 L.Ed.2d 809 (1996), and *State Farm Mut. Automobile Ins. Co. v. Campbell*, 538 U.S. 408, 123 S.Ct. 1513, 155 L.Ed.2d 585 (2003), and have "deprive[d] [no jury] of proper legal guidance," ante, at 1064. Vacation of the Oregon Supreme Court's judgment, I am convinced, is unwarranted.

The right question regarding reprehensibility, the Court acknowledges, ante, at – 8, would train on "the harm that Philip Morris was prepared to inflict on the smoking public at large." *Ibid.* (quoting 340 Or. 35, 51, 127 P.3d 1165, 1175 (2006)). *See also* 340 Ore., at 55, 127 P.3d, at 1177 ("[T]he jury, *in assessing the reprehensibility of Philip Morris's actions*, could consider evidence of similar harm to other Oregonians caused (or threatened) by the same conduct." (emphasis added)). The Court identifies no evidence introduced and no charge delivered inconsistent with that inquiry.

The Court's order vacating the Oregon Supreme Court's judgment is all the more inexplicable considering that Philip Morris did not preserve any objection to the charges in fact delivered to the jury, to the evidence introduced at trial, or to opposing counsel's argument. The sole objection Philip Morris preserved was to the trial court's refusal to give defendant's requested charge number 34. *See id.*, at 54, 127 P.3d, at 1176. The proposed instruction read in pertinent part:

"If you determine that some amount of punitive damages should be imposed on the defendant, it will then be your task to set an amount that is appropriate. This should be such amount as you believe is necessary to achieve the objectives of deterrence and punishment. While there is no set formula to be applied in reaching an appropriate amount, I will now advise you of some of the factors that you may wish to consider in this connection.

"(1) The size of any punishment should bear a reasonable relationship to the harm caused to Jesse Williams by the defendant's punishable misconduct. Although you may consider the extent of harm suffered by others in determining what that reasonable relationship is, you are not to punish the defendant for the impact of its alleged misconduct on other persons, who may bring lawsuits of their own in which other juries can resolve their claims and award punitive damages for those harms, as such other juries see fit.

.....

"(2) The size of the punishment may appropriately reflect the degree of reprehensibility of the defendant's conduct-that is, how far the defendant has departed from accepted societal norms of conduct." App. 280a.

Under that charge, just what use could the jury properly make of "the extent of harm suffered by others"? The answer slips from my grasp. A judge seeking to enlighten rather than confuse surely would resist delivering the requested charge.

The Court ventures no opinion on the propriety of the charge proposed by Philip Morris, though Philip Morris preserved no other objection to the trial proceedings. Rather than addressing the one objection Philip Morris properly preserved, the Court reaches outside the bounds of the case as postured when the trial court entered its judgment. I would accord more respectful treatment to the proceedings and dispositions of state courts that sought diligently to adhere to our changing, less than crystalline precedent.

* * *

For the reasons stated, and in light of the abundant evidence of "the potential harm [Philip Morris'] conduct could have caused," ante, at 1063 (emphasis deleted), I would affirm the decision of the Oregon Supreme Court.

IX.

DEFAMATION

PSALM 34:12-14

What man is he that desireth life, and loveth many days, that he may see good? Keep thy tongue from evil, and thy lips from speaking guile. Depart from evil, and do good; seek peace, and pursue it.

A. INTRODUCTION

The law of defamation protects a person's reputation. This area of the law is something of a confusing jumble consisting of two somewhat independent, overlapping areas of the law. First there were the common law torts of libel and slander, which protected the plaintiff's reputation against false statements. Over the common law tort doctrine has been layered constitutional doctrines protecting freedom of expression.

While there were differences between libel (written defamation) and slander (oral defamation), the common law cause of action for defamation consisted of three main elements: (1) a defamatory communication, (2) "published" to a third party, (3) which statement was "concerning" the plaintiff. No showing of fault was required, and damages frequently were presumed. Truth was a defense. Other privileges eventually arose as well.

Much of this common law doctrine was been displaced by more recent constitutional case-law, beginning with *New York Times v. Sullivan*. First, we will look at the cause of action as it existed at common law. Then we will layer on that basic understanding the constitutional jurisprudence that has developed since the United States Supreme Court decided in 1964 that defamation can be constitutionally protected.

B. THE COMMON LAW TORT

1. DEFAMATORY STATEMENTS

YOUSSOUPOFF V. METRO-GOLDWYN-MAYER PICTURES, LTD
50 T.L.R. 581 (C.A. 1934)

LORD JUSTICE SCRUTTON - An English company called Metro-Goldwyn-Mayer Pictures, Limited, which produces films circulated to the cinemas in this country, and which, according to its solicitor and chairman, is controlled by a firm of similar name in America, produced in this country a film which dealt with the alleged circumstances in which the influence of a man called Rasputin, an alleged monk, on the Czar and Czarina brought about the destruction of Russia. The film also dealt with the undoubted fact that Rasputin was ultimately murdered by persons who conceived him to be the evil genius of Russia.

In the course of that film a lady who had relations of affection with the person represented as the murderer was represented as having also had relations, which might be either relations of seduction or relations of rape, with the man Rasputin, a man of the worst possible character. When the film was produced in this country the plaintiff alleged that reasonable people would understand that she was the woman who was represented as having had these illicit relations. The plaintiff is a member of the Russian Royal House, Princess Irina Alexandrovna of Russia, and she was married after the incidents in question to a man who undoubtedly was one of the persons concerned in the killing of Rasputin. She issued a writ for libel against the English company. The English company declined to stop presenting the film. The action for libel proceeded. It was tried before one of the most experienced Judges on the Bench and a special jury, the constitutional tribunal for trying actions of libel, and, after several days' hearing, and after the jury had twice gone to see the film itself, they returned a verdict for the plaintiff with £25,000 damages.

The defendants now appeal from that verdict, and, as I understand the argument put before us . . . for the defendants, it falls under three heads. First-of all, they say that there was no evidence on which a jury, properly directed, could find that reasonable people would understand the Princess Natasha of the film to be Princess Irina, the plaintiff. That was the first point-the question of identification. Secondly, they say that if we are to take the Princess Natasha of the film to be identified with the Princess Irina, the plaintiff, there was no evidence on which a jury, reasonably directed, could find the film to be defamatory of the plaintiff. Thirdly, they say: "Assuming both of those points are decided against us, the damages were excessive. They were such as no jury, properly directed, could give in the circumstances of the case."

I deal with each of those three points in turn. First-of-all, there is the question of identification. . . . In *Hulton and Co., Limited v. Jones* . . . a Manchester paper published by Messrs. Hulton published what was supposed to be an amusing article about a gentleman named Artemus

Jones, who, on one side of his life, was a blameless churchwarden at Peckham and, on the other side of his life, indulged in wild careers unfitted for such a churchwarden at Le Touquet. A Mr. Artemus Jones – there may be several – conceived that that article was a libel upon him, and he brought an action for libel. The editor and proprietors of the paper said, rightly or wrongly, that they had never heard of Mr. Artemus Jones as an existing being, and that they had not the slightest intention of libeling him. There was some unfortunate doubt whether the gentleman who wrote the article had not a personal grudge against the real Mr. Artemus Jones, but, at any rate, the proprietors and publishers of the paper said: "We are innocent of any intention to injure Mr. Artemus Jones, of whom we never heard."

The . . . House of Lords unanimously came to the conclusion which is expressed in the first lines of the headnote in this way: "In an action for libel it is no defence to show that the defendant did not intend to defame the plaintiff, if reasonable people would think the language to be defamatory of the plaintiff"; and the Lord Chancellor quoted in his judgment this passage from the summing up. "The real point upon which your verdict must turn is, ought or ought not sensible and reasonable people reading this article to think that it was a mere imaginary person such as I have said-Tom Jones, Mr. Pecksniff as a humbug, Mr. Stiggins, or any of that sort of names that one reads of in literature used as types? If you think any reasonable person would think that -that is to say, that it wits mere type and did not mean anybody"it is not actionable at all. If, on the other hand, you do not think that, but think that people would suppose it to mean same real person-those who did not know the plaintiff of course would not know who the real person was, but those who did know of the existence of the plaintiff would think that it was the plaintiff-then the action is maintainable." . . . [W]e follow the law that though the person who writes and publishes the libel may not intend to libel a particular person and, indeed, has never heard of that particular person, the plaintiff, yet, if evidence is produced that reasonable people knowing some of the circumstances, not necessarily all, would take the libel complained of to relate to the plaintiff, an action for libel will lie.

That, therefore, was the class of evidence put before the jury in this case. On the one side, various people, some of them representatives of England in Russia at the time of these occurrences, some of them people who had been merely reading books about Russia and thought they knew something about it, were called to say that they saw the film, and they understood it to relate to the present plaintiff, the Princess Irina. On the other side, other people who knew something about Russia, or who did not know anything about Russia, were called to say that they saw the film, that they did not think it related to the plaintiff, and they gave their views as to whom they did think the characters in the film related.

There was evidence each side. I think counsel for the defendants agree that it would have been impossible for the jury to have stopped the case because the film was not capable of a defamatory meaning, and the jury, who are a tribunal particularly suited to try an action for libel, for the reason that I am going to allude to under the second head, came to the view that reasonable people would take the film to relate to the plaintiff in the action. It is not my business to express an opinion on the matter. It was the jury's business, and the only question for me is whether there was evidence on which the jury might come to the conclusion to which they have come. That being my position, I can quite see that there is a great deal of evidence on which the jury might take the view that the plaintiff was identified reasonably with the Princess Natasha.

Therefore, on the first point, I come to the conclusion that we cannot possibly interfere with the verdict of the jury, who are the constitutional tribunal, when they think, as they obviously have thought, that reasonable people, not all reasonable people but many reasonable people, would take the film representing Princess Natasha as also representing and referring to the plaintiff in the action, the Princess Irina. They would undoubtedly be helped to that by the defendants' own description of the film "This concerns the destruction of an Empire brought about by the mad ambition of one man," obviously Rasputin. There is a list of eight principal characters given: "A few of the characters are still alive; the rest met death by violence." Of the eight characters mentioned above the Czar, Czarina, Rasputin, the Czarevitch, and the Grand Duke Igor did meet death by violence. The rest are "still alive." The rest are Prince Chegodieff, Princess Natasha and Dr. Remezov. Part of the defence in the action seems really to be: "It is quite that the defendants said that this is a story of fact, buts really all a fiction. We ought to have used, if we described it properly, the formula which is now put at the beginning of most novels: 'All circumstances in this novel are imaginary, and none of the characters are in real life.'" Of course, that would not have fitted in with a representation that it was really a representation of the relations of the Royal Family with Rasputin and the people who killed Rasputin. But the film is so far from the real facts in some cases that one regrets that it was represented at all as being any genuine representation of the facts which had happened. However that may be, on the first point, whether there was evidence on which the jury could reasonably find that a considerable number of reasonable people who saw the film would identify the Princess Natasha of the film with the Princess Irina of Russia, I think that there was such evidence.

Now the second point is this, and it takes some courage to argue it, I think: suppose that the jury are right in treating Princess Irina, the plaintiff, as the Princess Natasha in real life, the film does not contain anything defamatory of her. There have been several formula for describing what is defamation. The learned Judge at the trial uses the stock formula "calculated to bring into hatred, ridicule, or contempt," and because it has been clearly established some time ago that that is not exhaustive because there may be things which are defamatory which have nothing to do with hatred, ridicule, or contempt he adds the words "or causes them to be shunned or avoided." . . .

I understand the principal thing argued by the defendants is this: "This procedure, as it contains some spoken words, is slander and not libel. Slanders are not as a rule actionable unless you prove special damage. No special damage was proved in this case. Consequently, the plaintiff must get within the exceptions in which slander is actionable without proof of special damage." One of those exceptions is the exception which is amplified in the Slander of Women Act, 1891-namely, if the slander imports unchastity or adultery to a woman-and this is the argument as I understand it: "To say of a woman that she is raped does not impute unchastity." From that we get to this, which was solemnly put forward, that to say of a woman of good character that she has been ravished by a man of the worst possible character is not defamatory. . . . That, really, as I understand it, is the argument upon which is based the contention that no reasonable jury could come to the conclusion that to say of a woman that she had been ravished by a man of very bad character when as a matter of fact she never saw the man at all and was never near him is not defamatory of the woman.

I really have no language to express my opinion of that argument. I therefore come, on the second point, to the view that there is no ground for interfering with the verdict of the jury (assuming the identification to stand, as I have assumed), that the words and the pictures in the film are defamatory of the lady whom they have found to be Princess Irina.

For these reasons, in my opinion, this appeal should be dismissed, with costs.

LORD Justice Greer –

After hearing the arguments on both sides in this case, I have come to the same conclusion.

So far as the case raises questions of liability, the questions raised in this appeal are quite simple and very easy to deal with. If anyone printed and published the following words, "The lady who was engaged to Prince Youssoupoff had had sexual relations with the mad monk Rasputin," nobody could suggest that that was not a libel which ought to meet with serious consequences. The question as to the liability of the defendants in this case was: Did they say it? I do not think myself that this case has any similarity to cases like . . . *Hulton and Co., Limited v. Jones* . . . because here, if the jury are right in their identification, although the defendants did not use the name of the plaintiff, they used a description of her that could apply to no one but the plaintiff. If anyone says, for example, that the Prime Minister of Ruritania is a fraudulent thief and there is evidence that the plaintiff is the Prime Minister of Ruritania, that is quite clearly a case in which he can recover, though his name has never been mentioned. If the jury come, as they may, to the conclusion that what has been said in the course of this film by means that amount to libel rather than slander is that the lady who was at one time betrothed to Prince Youssoupoff is a lady who had sexual relations with Rasputin, there is no answer, and there could be no real answer, to a claim, for damages for libel brought by her.

For these reasons I agree that this appeal should be dismissed, with costs.

LORD JUSTICE SLESSER –

This action is one of libel and raises at the outset an interesting and difficult problem which, I believe, to be a novel problem, whether the product of the combined photographic and talking instrument which produces these modern films does, if it throws upon the screen and impresses upon the ear defamatory matter, produce that which can be complained of as libel or as slander.

In my view, this action, as I have said, was properly framed in libel. There can be no doubt that, so far as the photographic part of the exhibition is concerned, that is a permanent matter to be seen by the eye, and is the proper subject of an action for libel, if defamatory. I regard the speech which is synchronized with the photographic reproduction and forms part of one complex, common exhibition as an ancillary circumstance, part of the surroundings explaining that which is to be seen.

Sir William Jowitt complained that different standards were applied at different times, some of the witnesses being professors, some being friends of the plaintiff, and yet others being readers of Russian books. When the question is as propounded in *Hulton and Co., Limited v. Jones . . .* and later cases, what persons of a reasonable class might think about a matter, I can see no objection to the fact that it is sought to be proved that persons who read Russian books, persons versed in Russian history, and friends of the plaintiff all conceived this imaginary Princess Natasha to be the plaintiff. The fact that the matter was approached from several angles and that different persons from different points of view took the same view seems to strengthen and not to weaken her case, because, from all these angles, these persons came and all said, some with certainty, some with comparative doubt, but at any rate in the end, that sooner or later in the film they made up their minds that this was meant to represent the plaintiff. Nor does it seem to me at all material that other persons came into Court and said the contrary. I imagine in *Hulton and Co., Limited v. Jones (supra)* that, if all the persons who had not connected Mr. Artemus Jones, the plaintiff, with the person mentioned in the article had been called, the case would have gone on for very many days, but that did not prevent him from being successful when he had satisfied the jury that a substantial and reasonable number of persons had connected him with the person mentioned in the article.

That being so, and it being established to the jury's satisfaction on sufficient evidence, what remains of this case from the appellants' point of view other than the question of damages? To my mind, nothing. I, for myself, cannot see that from the plaintiff's point of view it matters in the least whether this libel suggests that she has been seduced or ravished. The question whether she is or is not the more or the less moral seems to me immaterial in considering this question whether she has been defamed, and for this reason, that, as has been frequently pointed out in libel, not only is the matter defamatory if it brings the plaintiff into hatred, ridicule, or contempt by reason of some moral discredit on her part, but also if it treads to make the plaintiff be shunned and avoided and that without any moral discredit on her past. It is for that reason that persons who have been alleged to have been insane, or to be suffering from certain diseases, and other cases where no direct moral responsibility could be placed upon them, have been held to be entitled to bring an action to protect their reputation and their honour.

One may, I think, take judicial notice of the fact that a lady of whom it has been said that she has been ravished, albeit against her will, has suffered in social, reputation and in opportunities of receiving respectful consideration from the world. It is to shut one's eyes to realities to make these nice distinctions, but in this case I see no reason to suppose that this jury did come to a conclusion on this film that the imaginary lady depicted in the film, the Princess Natasha, was ravished and not seduced. I have looked at the pictures carefully, I have read the language, and it seems to me perfectly consistent with either view, and to assume at the outset that this film does represent a ravishment and not a seduction seems to me itself to assume that which the jury might have refused to assume at all. More particularly am I disinclined to take any view on this subject, because I have not seen the film and the jury have, and, as Sir Patrick Hastings has told us, they have seen it more than once. If it be the case that the jury may have thought the lady was seduced, of course the whole of this argument falls to the ground for want of any foundation of fact.

BELLI V. ORLANDO DAILY NEWSPAPERS, INC.
389 F.2D 579 (5TH CIR. 1967)

This action for damages for libel and slander is based on a false statement relating to Mr. Melvin Belli. Belli, an attorney of national prominence, is well known in the legal profession for his pioneering in the development of demonstrative evidence as a trial tactic and his success in obtaining large judgments for plaintiffs in personal injury suits. He is well known to the general public because of his representation of Jack Ruby and others in the public eye.

In March 1964 Mr. Leon Handley, an attorney in Orlando, Florida, in a conversation with Miss Jean Yothers, a columnist for the Orlando Evening Star, repeated a story he had heard concerning Belli. Handley told Yothers that the Florida Bar Association had invited Belli to serve as a member of one of the panels on the program of the Association at its 1955 Convention in Miami Beach. Belli agreed, with the understanding that "since there were no funds provided in the budget for payment per se for his contribution as a lawyer to the program the Florida Bar instead would pick up the hotel tab for himself and his wife during their stay." According to Handley, after Mr. and Mrs. Belli left Florida, the Association discovered that the Bellis "ran up a bunch of [clothing] bills" which they charged to their hotel room. The derogatory portion of the story was admittedly false: the Bellis had not charged any purchases to their hotel account. Unfortunately for all, Jean Yothers reported, with embellishments, this nine-year old story in her gossip column in the Orlando Evening Star for March 19, 1964. She commented, in part: "Oops . . . the plan backfired on the Florida Bar. [Mr. Belli and 'his well-dressed wife' had charged] clothing bills amounting to hundreds . . . to their hotel rooms. . . . The Florida Bar had been taken. . . . After all, that was the plan!"

On these facts, Belli brought this diversity action. . . . The district court dismissed Belli's complaint for failure to state a claim upon which relief could be granted. . . . We reverse and remand. . . .

Historically, libel, as generally distinguishable from slander, was actionable without the necessity of pleading or proving that the plaintiff had suffered any damages as a result of it. That is the accepted rule today in England [4] and in many jurisdictions in the United States both as to libel per se and libel per quod. A libel per se is one that is defamatory on its face, including a publication that is susceptible of several meanings, one of which is defamatory; it is actionable without proof of special harm. A libel per quod is one in which the defamatory meaning, or innuendo, is not apparent on the face of the publication, but must be established by proof of extrinsic facts. Here the district court held, correctly, that the Belli claim "must be determined

---

4   *Youssoupoff v. Metro-Goldwyn-Mayer Pictures*, 1934, 50 T.L.R. 581.

solely on the basis of whether it sufficiently alleges a publication which is libelous per se" —
since, as is evident from the complaint, the plaintiff did not allege defamation by extrinsic facts
or plead special damages. . . .

In its opinion below the court recognized that there are four categories of defamatory impu-
tations which traditionally have been considered actionable without proof of harm. As set out
in the Restatement of Torts, Second, Tentative Draft 12, Section 569, these are statements which
impute to another "(1) a criminal offense, (2) a loathsome disease, (3) matter incompatible with
his business, trade, profession or office, and (4) unchastity on the part of a woman plaintiff."
Such defamatory statements, whether the publication is in the form of libel or in the form of
slander, are regarded as especially likely to cause harm to the reputation of the person defamed,
although such harm is not and perhaps cannot be proved. . . .

Libel per se is not limited to these four categories: Courts use a stock formula to describe a
general class of per se libel (but not per se slander). The Restatement's formula is:

> One who publishes defamatory matter is subject to liability without proof of special harm or loss
> of reputation if the defamation is
> (a) Libel whose defamatory innuendo is apparent from the publication itself without reference to
> extrinsic facts by way of inducement.

Restatement, Second, Tentative Draft 12, Section 569.

In Florida and in many states the rubric runs: a libel per se is "any publication which exposes
a person to distrust, hatred, contempt, ridicule, obloquy". . . . There is no dispute between the
parties as to these fundamental principles. The dispute centers about the district court's conclusion that "whether a given writing is or is not libelous per se is a question of law for the Court
to determine." . . . We find that the general law and Florida law are in agreement with Dean
Prosser's conclusion: "It is for the court *in the first instance* to determine whether the words
are reasonably capable of a particular interpretation, or whether they are necessarily so; it is
then for the jury to say whether they were in fact understood as defamatory. If the language
used is open to two meanings . . . it is for the jury to determine whether the defamatory sense
was the one conveyed." (Emphasis added.) Prosser, *Law of Torts* §106, at 765 (1963). Similarly the
Restatement, Second, Tentative Draft 12, Section 614, expresses the rule as follows:

1. The Court determines
   (a) Whether a communication is capable of bearing a particular meaning, and
   (b) Whether that meaning is defamatory.
2. The jury determines whether a communication, capable of a defamatory meaning,
   was so understood by its recipient.

Section 615 states:

1. The Court determines

(a) Whether the defamatory meaning of libel is apparent from the publication itself without reference to extrinsic facts, and

(b) Whether an imputation of crime or disease or of unchastity to a woman, is of such a character as to make libel or slander actionable without proof of special harm.

2. Subject to the control of the court whenever the issue arises, the jury determines whether language imputes to another conduct, characteristics or a condition incompatible with the proper conduct of his business, trade, profession or office.

Both judge and jury play a part in determining whether language constitutes libel. The Supreme Court has delineated these roles in *Washington Post Co. v. Chaloner*, 1919, 250 U.S. 290 . . . :

> A publication claimed to be defamatory must be read and construed in the sense in which the readers to whom it is addressed would ordinarily understand it. * * * When thus read, if its meaning is so unambiguous as to reasonably bear but one interpretation, it is for the judge to say whether that signification is defamatory or not. If, upon the other hand, it is capable of two meanings, one of which would be libelous and actionable and the other not, it is for the jury to say, under all the circumstances surrounding its publication, including extraneous facts admissible in evidence, which of the two meanings would be attributed to it by those to whom it is addressed or by whom it may be read.
>
> . . .

The defendants argue that the article did not "hurt" Belli as an attorney, did not imply that he was "losing his touch with demonstrative evidence," did not affect his ability to "obtain those 'more adequate awards' for seamen and railroad workers for which he is so justly famous." In effect, so the argument runs, the article was nothing more than caustic comment on the acuteness of the Florida Bar Association. Belli simply "showed the Florida lawyers that their agreement was somewhat more favorable to him that they – in their naivete – contemplated." In its harshest sense, they say, "the article implies no more than that Mr. Belli 'put one over' on the Florida Bar," which is "not quite the same as conning a destitute widow out of her homestead." In short, Mr. Belli just got "a little more out of the agreement than the Bar Association contemplated."

The defendants make a case – just barely – for the view that the article is capable of being reasonably interpreted as non-defamatory. But since the article on its face is also capable of carrying a defamatory meaning, it is for the jury to decide whether the words were in fact so understood.

The plaintiff contends, in his brief, "No person reading the headline and the article *sub judice* . . . could conclude other than that Melvin Belli, both as a lawyer and as a private citizen is grasping, conniving, contemptible, dishonest; a cheat, swindler, trickster, deceiver, defrauder; a person to be avoided, shunned and distrusted." Without benefit of the defendants' cavalier reading of the article or the plaintiff's retort hyperbolic, we consider that the bare bones of the article are capable of carrying the meaning that Belli tricked and deceived the Florida Bar Association out of hundreds of dollars worth of clothes.

The story alleges: (1) Belli knew that the Florida Bar Association's budget would enable him to be reimbursed only for his hotel bill; (2) subject to this limitation he agreed to participate in a panel discussion; (3) he deliberately planned to "take" the Association for hundreds of dollars by charging clothing purchases to his hotel bill; (4) he and his well-dressed wife left Miami before the Association found out about their purchases; (5) the Association, to its embarrassment, had to pick up the tab. "The Florida Bar had been taken. * * * After all that was the plan."

The author's comment seems intended to insure the common reader's understanding of what purportedly happened. The common reader is likely to understand "take", just as Miss Yothers must have understood it. A recent dictionary defines it: "To cheat, deceive;" . . . other dictionaries agree with this definition. . . . The man in the street is likely to understand that hotel expenses do not include "hundreds of dollars worth of clothing." But any doubts the reader might have as to what purportedly happened are likely to be resolved by the reference to Belli's "plan" to "take" the Florida Bar. We hold that a jury might reasonably conclude that the conduct imputed to Belli was incompatible with the standards of an ethical lawyer and as such violated one of the four traditional categories of libel per se. A jury might also conclude that such conduct subjected Belli to contempt and ridicule humiliating him socially and injuring him professionally.

The Court has some doubt whether the publication in question carries a non-defamatory meaning. The Court has very little doubt that it carries a defamatory meaning. The Court has concluded however that the final determination of the issue of defamation should be made by a jury. . . .

Historically, the action for written defamation (libel) developed as a criminal action in the Star Chamber; the separate action for spoken defamation (slander) developed in the ecclesiastical courts. For the crime of libel, it was necessary to show harm only to the reputation; to recover on slander it was necessary to show pecuniary loss. The strict requirements for a slander action were rationalized on the ground that since libel is in a relatively permanent form and has a wider potential audience, pecuniary harm is so probable as to be presumed. . . .

With slander, as with libel, certain defamatory words are actionable without proof of any actual damage to the plaintiff. These fall into the same categories of libel per se. . . . Any allegedly slanderous statements not falling within any of these categories may constitute slander per quod but are actionable only upon a showing of special damages. . . . Belli has not complained of special damage by reason of Handley's statement. . . .

2. PUBLICATION

"Publication," in the defamation context, means simply to communicate the defamatory statement to at least one person other than the plaintiff. Publication is required because no reputational harm occurs unless someone other than plaintiff hears the defamatory statement.

ECONOMOPOULOS V. A. G. POLLARD CO.
105 N.E. 896 (MASS. 1914)

. . . There was evidence that a clerk of defendant stated in English to plaintiff, a Greek, that he had stolen a handkerchief, and that a Greek clerk stated to plaintiff in Greek that plaintiff had stolen a handkerchief. There was nothing to show that third persons heard the charge . . . . We do not find it necessary to decide whether the two statements relied on by the plaintiff could have been found to be accusations of larceny. If it be assumed that such a finding could have been made the judge was right in directing the jury to find a verdict for the defendant because there was no evidence of publication of either of them. . . . There was no evidence that anybody but the plaintiff was present when Carrier spoke to the plaintiff in English. There was no publication of this statement made in English, because on the evidence the words could not have been heard by anyone but the plaintiff. . . . Nor was there any evidence of publication of the Greek words spoken by Miralos, for although there was evidence that they were spoken in the presence of others, there was no evidence that any one understood them but the plaintiff. . . .

PUBLICATION HYPOTHETICALS

1. Would it have made a difference if some Greek speakers had been around when the defamatory statement was made in Greek?

2. What if defendant had written a defamatory letter in Latin, knowing that plaintiff does not know Latin but also knowing that plaintiff shares office space with a Latin expert?

3. What if defendant had written a defamatory letter and locked the letter in his desk without sending it and a thief broke in and stole and read the letter?

4. What if defendant had written a defamatory accusation in a letter and carelessly left the letter on defendant's desk where it could easily be seen by numerous passers-by, and some do see and read it?

5. What if defendant had written a defamatory letter and tacked it on plaintiff's door and a passer-by read it?

6. What if defendant had written a defamatory letter and sent it to plaintiff and a third party opened and read plaintiff's mail?

7. What if defendant had written and sent the letter knowing that plaintiff frequently was away and that his secretary opened his mail in his absence?

8. What if defendant, intending to send the letter to plaintiff, carelessly placed the letter in an envelope addressed to a third-party, who opened and read it?

9. What if defendant had written the letter and plaintiff received and read it and indignantly showed it to his son, who also read it?

ZERAN V. AMERICA ONLINE, INC.
129 F.3D 327 (11TH CIR. 1997)

Kenneth Zeran brought this action against America Online, Inc. ("AOL"), arguing that AOL unreasonably delayed in removing defamatory messages posted by an unidentified third party, refused to post retractions of those messages, and failed to screen for similar postings thereafter. . . . Much of the information transmitted over its network originates with the company's millions of subscribers. They may transmit information privately via electronic mail, or they may communicate publicly by posting messages on AOL bulletin boards, where the messages may be read by any AOL subscriber.

. . . On April 25, 1995, an unidentified person posted a message on an AOL bulletin board advertising "Naughty Oklahoma T-Shirts." The posting described the sale of shirts featuring offensive and tasteless slogans related to the April 19, 1995, bombing of the Alfred P. Murrah Federal Building in Oklahoma City. Those interested in purchasing the shirts were instructed to call "Ken" at Zeran's home phone number in Seattle, Washington. As a result of this anonymously perpetrated prank, Zeran received a high volume of calls, comprised primarily of angry and derogatory messages, but also including death threats. Zeran could not change his phone number because he relied on its availability to the public in running his business out of his home. Later that day, Zeran called AOL and informed a company representative of his predicament. The employee assured Zeran that the posting would be removed from AOL's bulletin board . . . . . The parties dispute the date that AOL removed this original posting from its bulletin board.

On April 26, the next day, an unknown person posted another message advertising additional shirts with new tasteless slogans related to the Oklahoma City bombing. Again, interested buyers were told to call Zeran's phone number, to ask for "Ken," and to "please call back if busy" due to high demand. The angry, threatening phone calls intensified. Over the next four days, an unidentified party continued to post messages on AOL's bulletin board, advertising additional items including bumper stickers and key chains with still more offensive slogans. During this time period, Zeran called AOL repeatedly and was told by company representatives that the individual account from which the messages were posted would soon be closed. . . . By April 30, Zeran was receiving an abusive phone call approximately every two minutes.

Meanwhile, an announcer for Oklahoma City radio station KRXO received a copy of the first AOL posting. On May 1, the announcer related the message's contents on the air, attributed them to "Ken" at Zeran's phone number, and urged the listening audience to call the number. After this radio broadcast, Zeran was inundated with death threats and other violent calls from Oklahoma City residents. Over the next few days, Zeran talked to both KRXO and AOL representatives. . . . By May 14, after an Oklahoma City newspaper published a story exposing the shirt advertisements as a hoax and after KRXO made an on-air apology, the number of calls to Zeran's residence finally subsided to fifteen per day.

Zeran first filed suit on January 4, 1996, against radio station KRXO in the United States District Court for the Western District of Oklahoma. On April 23, 1996, he filed this separate suit against AOL in the same court. . . . AOL answered Zeran's complaint and interposed 47 U.S.C. § 230 as an affirmative defense. AOL then moved for judgment on the pleadings pursuant to Fed. R. Civ. P. 12(c). The district court granted AOL's motion, and Zeran filed this appeal. . . .

Because § 230 was successfully advanced by AOL in the district court as a defense to Zeran's claims, we shall briefly examine its operation here. Zeran seeks to hold AOL liable for defamatory speech initiated by a third party. He argued to the district court that once he notified AOL of the unidentified third party's hoax, AOL had a duty to remove the defamatory posting promptly, to notify its subscribers of the message's false nature, and to effectively screen future defamatory material. . . . [AOL] claimed that Congress immunized interactive computer service providers from claims based on information posted by a third party.

The relevant portion of § 230 states: "No provider or user of an interactive computer service shall be treated as the publisher or speaker of any information provided by another information content provider." 47 U.S.C. § 230(c)(1). By its plain language, § 230 creates a federal immunity to any cause of action that would make service providers liable for information originating with a third-party user of the service. Specifically, §230 precludes courts from entertaining claims that would place a computer service provider in a publisher's role. Thus, lawsuits seeking to hold a service provider liable for its exercise of a publisher's traditional editorial functions – such as deciding whether to publish, withdraw, postpone or alter content – are barred.

The purpose of this statutory immunity is not difficult to discern. Congress recognized the threat that tort-based lawsuits pose to freedom of speech in the new and burgeoning Internet medium. The imposition of tort liability on service providers for the communications of others represented, for Congress, simply another form of intrusive government regulation of speech. Section 230 was enacted, in part, to maintain the robust nature of Internet communication and, accordingly, to keep government interference in the medium to a minimum. . . .

None of this means, of course, that the original culpable party who posts defamatory messages would escape accountability. While Congress acted to keep government regulation of the Internet to a minimum, it also found it to be the policy of the United States "to ensure vigorous enforcement of Federal criminal laws to deter and punish trafficking in obscenity, stalking, and harassment by means of computer." *Id.* § 230(b)(5). Congress made a policy choice, however, not to deter harmful online speech through the separate route of imposing tort liability on companies that serve as intermediaries for other parties' potentially injurious messages.

Congress' purpose in providing the §230 immunity was thus evident. Interactive computer services have millions of users. . . . The amount of information communicated via interactive computer services is therefore staggering. The specter of tort liability in an area of such prolific speech would have an obvious chilling effect. It would be impossible for service providers to screen each of their millions of postings for possible problems. Faced with potential liability for each message republished by their services, interactive computer service providers might choose to severely restrict the number and type of messages posted. Congress considered the weight of the speech interests implicated and chose to immunize service providers to avoid any such restrictive effect.

. . . For the foregoing reasons, we affirm the judgment of the district court.

AFFIRMED

NOTE

1   *Republication.* Notice that the radio station became a defendant even though it merely repeated what had been posted to AOL's bulletin board. The common law rule is that, unless privileged, one who merely repeats the defamatory statement of another also is a publisher of the defamation.

3. FAULT

E. HULTON & CO. V. JONES
[1910] A.C. 20 (HOUSE OF LORDS)

. . . The appellants published in the *Sunday Chronicle* an article defamatory of a person described as "Artemus Jones." . . . [F]riends of the respondent gave evidence that they had read the libel and believed it to refer to the respondent. The evidence of the author of the article and of the editor of the *Sunday Chronicle* that they did not know of the existence of the respondent was accepted as true by the respondent's counsel. The jury found a verdict for the plaintiff . . . , and judgment was entered for him. . . .

LORD LOREBURN L.C. . . . A question in regard to the law of libel has been raised which does not seem to me to be entitled to the support of your Lordships. Libel is a tortious act. What does the tort consist in? It consists in using language which others knowing the circumstances would reasonably think to be defamatory of the person complaining of the injury by it. A person charged with libel cannot defend himself by shewing that he intended in his own breast not to defame, or that he intended not to defame the plaintiff, if in fact he did both. He has none the less imputed something disgraceful and has none the less injured the plaintiff. A man in good faith may publish a libel believing it to be true, and it may be found by the jury that he acted in good faith believing it to be true, and reasonably believing it to be true, but that in fact the statement was false. Under those circumstances he has no defence to the action, however excellent his intention. If the intention of the writer be immaterial in considering whether the matter written is defamatory, I do not see why it need be relevant in considering whether it is defamatory of the plaintiff. The writing, according to the old form, must be malicious, and it must be of and concerning the plaintiff. Just as the defendant could not excuse himself from malice by proving that he wrote it in the most benevolent spirit, so he cannot shew that the libel was not of and concerning the plaintiff by proving that he never heard of the plaintiff. His intention in both respects equally is inferred from what he did. His remedy is to abstain from defamatory words.

It is suggested that there was a mis-direction by the learned judge in this case. I see none. He lays down in his summing up the law as follows: "The real point upon which your verdict must turn is, ought or ought not sensible and reasonable people reading this article to think that it was a mere imaginary person . . . that one reads of in literature used as types? If you think any reasonable person would think that, it is not actionable at all. If, on other hand, you do not think that, but think that people would suppose it to mean some real person—those who did not know the plaintiff of course would not know who the real person was, but those who did know of the existence of the plaintiff would think that it was the plaintiff—then the action is maintainable, subject to such damages as you think under all the circumstances are fair and right to give to the plaintiff."

I see no objection in law to that passage. . . . I think your Lordships ought to remember . . . . the jury were entitled to say this kind of article is to be condemned. . . . If they think that the license is not fairly used and that the tone and style of the libel is reprehensible and ought to be checked, it is for the jury to say so; and for my part, . . . I am not prepared to advise your Lordships to interfere . . . with the verdict. . . .

LORD SHAW OF DUNFERMLINE. My Lords, I concur in the observations which have been made by the Lord Chancellor, but for my own part I should desire in terms to adopt certain language which I will now read from the judgment of the Lord Chief Justice: "The question, if it be disputed whether the article is a libel upon the plaintiff, is a question of fact for the jury, and in my judgment this question of fact involves not only whether the language used of a person in its fair and ordinary meaning is libelous or defamatory, but whether the person referred to in the libel would be understood by persons who knew him to refer to the plaintiff."

My Lords, with regard to this whole matter I should put my propositions in a threefold form . . . . In the publication of matter of a libelous character, that is matter which would be libelous if applying to an actual person, the responsibility is as follows: In the first place there is responsibility for the words used being taken to signify that which readers would reasonably understand by them; in the second place there is responsibility also for the names used being taken to signify those whom the readers would reasonably understand by those names; and in the third place the same principle is applicable to persons unnamed but sufficiently by designation or description.

My Lords, I demur to the observation so frequently made in the argument that these principles are novel. Sufficient expression is given to the same principles by Abbott C.J. in *Bourke* v. *Warren* . . . , in which that learned judge says: "The question for your consideration is whether you think the libel designates the plaintiff in such a way as to let those who knew him understand that he was the person meant. It is not necessary that all the world should understand the libel; it is sufficient if those who know the plaintiff can make out that he is the person meant." I think it is out of the question to suggest that the means "meant in the mind of the writer" or of the publisher; it must mean "meant by the words employed." The late Lord Chief Justice Coleridge dealt similarly with the point in *Gibson* v. *Evans*, when in the course of the argument he remarked: "It does not signify what the writer meant; the question is whether the alleged libel was so published by the defendant that the world would apply it to the plaintiff."

NOTE

1   *Strict Liability. Hulton v. Jones* illustrates that defamation was, at common law, a strict liability tort. Some courts now require a showing of negligence, and the U.S. Constitution has been found to require proof of fault under some circumstances.

4. LIBEL AND SLANDER

At common law, it was important to distinguish libel from slander. The cleanest, although not entirely accurate, dividing line between libel and slander is that libel is written and slander is oral. Libel is more serious and permanent – usually a written defamation. For example, *Youssoupoff* involved libel because the defamatory statement was reduced to a physical form. Publication by sight generally will be considered libel, as will radio broadcasts. Merely oral defamatory communications usually will be considered slander.

The practical significance of the common law distinction between libel and slander is that general damages were presumed and could be recovered for libel, but to recover for slander, plaintiff had to prove actual pecuniary (special) damages. While the slander victim usually had to plead and prove actual pecuniary damages to recover, several categories of "slander *per se*" were treated as so serious that no special damages need be shown: (1) imputation of crime; (2) imputation of loathsome disease; (3) imputation of unchastity or adultery; (4) imputation of unfitness or incompetence in plaintiff's office, profession, calling, trade, or business.

Another layer of complexity is added in some jurisdictions, which distinguish between libel *per se* and libel *per quod*. Libel *per se* is libel on the face of it. Libel *per quod* requires information from outside the publication either to identify the victim (sometimes called "colloquium") (as in *Yousoupoff*) or to understand the defamatory nature of the statement ("inducement"). Again using *Yousoupoff* as an example, this would be a case of libel *per quod* because to appreciate the defamatory nature of the statement (sometimes called *innuendo*), the audience must bring some extrinsic information to the statement itself. The significance of the distinction in those jurisdictions that observe it is that victims of libel *per quod* were not entitled to the usual presumption of general damages accorded to libel *per se*. They had to plead and prove special damages, just like ordinary slander victims.

BIONDI V. NASSIMOS
692 A.2D 103 (N.J. SUPER. 1997)

This appeal involves the "slander per se" doctrine. At the time of the alleged slander, plaintiff Thomas J. Biondi was Chairman of the New Jersey Board of Examiners of Master Plumbers (the Board). Defendant Antoine Nassimos regularly attended the Board's public meetings, apparently acting as a liaison between the New Jersey Society of Professional Energy and Environmental Contractors (NJSPEEC) and the Board. On September 23, 1993, Nassimos attended a public meeting at which the Board announced a decision that Joseph Fichner, Jr., a licensed master plumber and member of the NJSPEEC, had committed various acts of occupational misconduct, fraud and misrepresentation. . . . Later in the meeting when the public was given the opportunity to speak, Nassimos charged the Board with improperly releasing information about its decision in the Fichner matter prior to taking official action. Nassimos also charged that it was improper for plaintiff, as a member of the Board, to be affiliated with the New Jersey Association of Plumbing, Heating & Cooling Contractors. According to plaintiff, Nassimos then said "words to the effect of: 'I have information that the Chairman, Mr. Biondi, has mob connections and that if I don't stop complaining against him and the Board, he will order a hit on me.'" In response, plaintiff said to Nassimos: "I think you've overstepped your bounds. I might have to consult an attorney."

On November 3, 1993, plaintiff filed this action against Nassimos and the NJSPEEC. Plaintiff's complaint alleged that Nassimos' statement that plaintiff "has mob connections" and would "order a hit" on him was "intended by Mr. Nassimos and were understood by the listeners to indicate and designate someone as a member of organized crime, as the perpetrator of uncounted serious crimes, as one who makes his living through a life of crime, as one who directs others to commit crimes, . . . and as one who is involved in crimes including, but not limited to murder, extortion, gambling and bribery of public officials." . . . [P]laintiff's counsel conceded that he did not have any "special damages" and was "stuck with a slander per se case." . . . [T]he court granted defendants' motion, concluding that a statement that a person has "connections with [the] mafia" does not constitute an allegation of criminal activity and therefore does not constitute slander per se. Plaintiff appeals from the summary judgment dismissing his complaint. . . . We affirm.

At the outset, we note that the issue presented in this appeal is not whether Nassimos' statements that plaintiff has "mob connections" and may "order a hit" upon him are defamatory but rather whether they constitute "slander per se." We have no doubt that a jury could find these statements to be defamatory, that is, as "tend[ing] so to harm the reputation of another as to lower him in the estimation of the community or to deter third persons from associating or dealing with him." *Ward v. Zelikovsky*, 136 N.J. 516, 529, 643 A.2d 972 (1994) (quoting Restatement (Second) of Torts § 559 (1977)) . . . . In fact, it is possible that such statements could be found to be defamatory per se, that is, to so clearly denigrate a person's reputation that a court could decide that the statements are defamatory without submitting the issue to the jury. . . . However, plaintiff cannot prevail merely by showing that Nassimos' statements were defamatory because he has not offered any evidence of the type of damages generally required to establish a cause of action for slander. To establish a slander claim under the common law, a plaintiff is required to show "special damages," which is defined as "harm of a material or pecuniary nature." *Ward v. Zelikovsky, supra*, 136 N.J. at 540, 643 A.2d 972. Plaintiff admittedly has no evidence that he suffered such "special damages" as a result of Nassimos' statements. . . . Plaintiff testified at his deposition that when he attended a meeting of the New Jersey Association of Plumbing, Heating and Cooling Contractors, other members referred to him as "Don Thomasso" and "Godfather," asked whether they had to "kiss [his] ring," and insisted that he sit at the head of the table. However, plaintiff did not show the kind of damage to reputation ordinarily required to establish a cause of action for defamation, because he did not present evidence that anyone had refused to associate with him or that any of his business or personal relationships had been "seriously disrupted." *Sisler v. Gannett Co., Inc., supra*, 104 N.J. at 281, 516 A.2d 1083 . . . . Therefore, his claim is maintainable only if Nassimos' statements constituted slander per se.

The slander per se doctrine is limited to defamatory statements which impute to another person (1) a criminal offense; (2) a loathsome disease; (3) conduct, characteristics or a condition that is incompatible with his business, trade or office; or (4) serious sexual misconduct. Restatement (Second) of Torts §§ 570-574 (1977) . . . . If a defamatory statement constitutes slander per se, a plaintiff may establish a cause of action not only without proving "special damages," that is, damages of a pecuniary nature, but without proving any form of actual damage to reputation. . . . This is sometimes referred to as the "presumed damages" doctrine. . . . The slander per se doctrine has been severely criticized by scholarly commentators, who recommend the elimination of both the "presumed damages" rule applicable to slander per se cases and the "special damages" rule applicable to all other slander cases. *Anderson, supra*, 25 Wm. & Mary L.Rev. at 749, 774-78 . . . . The commentators conclude that these archaic common law rules should be replaced by a single uniform rule that a plaintiff must prove actual damage to reputation, either pecuniary or non-pecuniary, to establish any cause of action for defamation. . . . Missouri and Kansas have eliminated slander per se and the corollary "presumed damages" rule. Consequently, these states now require a showing of actual damage to reputation to establish any cause of action for defamation. . . .

We also note that the First Amendment precludes an award of presumed damages for a defamatory statement involving an "issue of public concern." *See Dun & Bradstreet, Inc. v. Greenmoss Builders, Inc.*, 472 U.S. 749, 757-61, 105 S.Ct. 2939, 2944-46, 86 L.Ed.2d 593, 601-04 (1985); *Gertz v. Robert Welch, Inc.*, 418 U.S. 323, 348-50, 94 S.Ct. 2997, 3011-12, 41 L.Ed.2d 789, 810-11 (1974). However, defendants have not argued that Nassimos' statements about plaintiff involved any "issue of public concern."

Plaintiff argues that Nassimos' statements that he has "mob connections" and would "order a hit" upon Nassimos unless Nassimos stopped complaining about plaintiff and the Board constituted slander per se because they implied that he had committed a crime. The Restatement of Torts describes this category of slander per se as follows:

One who publishes a slander that imputes to another conduct constituting a criminal offense is subject to liability to the other without proof of special harm if the offense imputed is of a type which, if committed in the place of publication, would be

    a.   punishable by imprisonment in a state or federal institution, or

    b.   regarded by public opinion as involving moral turpitude.

[Restatement (Second) of Torts § 571 (1977).]

However, it does not constitute slander per se "to suggest that another is capable of committing a crime" or "to charge another with a criminal intention or design, if no criminal act is charged." Restatement (Second) of Torts § 571 cmt. c (1977).

We are satisfied that a statement that a person has "mob connections" does not constitute an assertion that he has committed a crime. It is not uncommon for the mass media to report that an entertainer or other celebrity has "mob ties" or "mob connections." The ordinary understanding of such a story is not that the celebrity himself has committed crimes but rather that he associates with criminals. Consequently, even though a statement that a person has "mob connections" may be defamatory, it is not slander per se because it does not allege the commission of a crime. . . .

Nassimos' further alleged comment that he had information plaintiff would "order a hit on me" if Nassimos did not "stop complaining against him and the Board" is not slander per se because it merely alleges plaintiff's intention to commit a crime sometime in the future rather than a past criminal act. *See* Restatement (Second) of Torts, § 571 cmt. c. Although plaintiff argues that this comment implied that he was a member of an ongoing criminal enterprise because only such a person could "order a hit," we believe that such a comment could be just as easily construed to mean that plaintiff would ask his "mob connections" to kill Nassimos as a favor or in exchange for the payment of money. . . . The circumstance that Nassimos' comment was uttered in the midst of a heated personal attack upon plaintiff, as Chairman of the Board, for allegedly leaking information about a decision in a pending disciplinary matter, reduces the possibility that the audience reasonably could have understood Nassimos was asserting that plaintiff had committed a crime. . . . In view of the disfavor with which the slander per se doctrine is currently held, courts should not permit speculative inferences regarding the possible meaning of an alleged defamatory statement to support a verdict in favor of a plaintiff who is unable to show any actual damage to his reputation.

Affirmed.

ELLSWORTH V. MARTINDALE-HUBBELL LAW DIRECTORY, INC.
280 N.W. 879 (N.D. 1938)

This is an action for libel. . . . The case has been here before. . . . On the former appeal we held that the alleged defamatory matter on which the action was predicated, was actionable, but that it was not libelous per se, and that therefore the complaint was bad because it failed to plead special damages and a defamatory understanding.

On the instant appeal it is conceded that the amended complaint sufficiently pleads a defamatory understanding. But the defendant insists that the special damages are not well pleaded and so the complaint is bad on that account. The eleventh paragraph of the complaint, having to do with . . . damages, . . . reads as follows:

And plaintiff further alleges, that the publication of his name with its attached marking in said 1929 Edition of Martindale's American Law Directory by said Defendant, was untrue and false . . . . That by reason of the printing and insertion by Defendant . . . of said false and malicious, libelous and defamatory "rating" against his name and the publication of said volume by said Defendant and the wide circulation and distribution of the same by said Defendant throughout the United States and Canada, and the understanding of the 12,000 or more attorneys, and business people who received and read said volume of said derogatory marking and meaning of the same, Plaintiff has been defamed, minimized, and derogated in his professional reputation, and injured in his business and practice in particulars as follows to wit: Certain persons whose names are unknown at this time, residing in Plaintiff's locality have spoken of and treated him in a contemptuous manner by reason of such publication, alleging of Plaintiff, "That he has no business;" others have alleged that, "Whatever his ability and reputation as a lawyer, he is shunned and avoided in a business way;" others have gone to clients of Plaintiff and urged them to employ another lawyer as according to the statement Plaintiff was now without influence with the Court, and was worthless for business purposes; further than this many business men, former clients of Plaintiff, since and after the publication of Plaintiff's name with the alleged "rating" in said Directory for 1929 have withdrawn their business and replaced it elsewhere; also, certain business men of other localities who had no acquaintance with attorneys in Jamestown, or its locality, and have important business to place there, after consulting and examining said Directory for the purpose of placing said business have given Plaintiff's name no consideration whatever, and have placed the business elsewhere owing to such publication. That on account of the contempt, scorn, and obloquy, given to Plaintiff, and his name by said publication and its understanding by persons who read said Directory Plaintiff has been deprived of much valuable business proceeding from people whose names he cannot give at this time. That on account of said publication and its wide circulation Plaintiff has been brought into contempt, ridicule, and obloquy throughout the professional ranks of the Bar, in the United States and Canada, and generally among the business men in all places in which said Directory was and has been circulated. That in the year 1928 the gross professional income of Plaintiff was $4,171.06. That in the year 1929 as one of the direct results of the libel of Plaintiff by the Defendant through such publication and the distribution of its Directory, as aforesaid, the income of Plaintiff reduced to $2,958.55. In the year 1930 for like reasons it was $3,047.20, in the year 1931 it reduced further for like reasons to $2,784.65. In the year 1932 for like reasons it was $1,704.40. That these reductions in income on Plaintiff's part were caused by reason of the said libelous statement of Defendant published and distributed against Plaintiff's name in its issue of Martindale's American Law Directory for the years of 1928, and 1929 and that Plaintiff believes and has every reason to believe and alleges amount to more than the sum of $2,500.

The sole question on this appeal is as to whether this amended paragraph sufficiently sets forth the special damages claimed to have been suffered. The defendant contends that it does not. That it fails to set out the names of the clients lost by the plaintiff because of the publication of the alleged defamatory matter, and that it does not specify particularly the origin, character, and amount of the business the plaintiff has been deprived of because of its publication.

In substance, the amended complaint alleges that the plaintiff has been engaged in the practice of law for many years; that he has always borne a good reputation as a man and as a lawyer; that he has had a substantial law business that came to him largely from forwarders through a widely spread foreign territory; that he was personally unacquainted with such forwarders; that the defendant's publication in which the alleged defamatory matter was published, was circulated generally throughout such territory and among those who forwarded business to the plaintiff; that, as a consequence of the circulation of such matter and immediately following such publication and circulation, his practice decreased in the manner and to the extent as set out in that portion of the complaint hereinbefore quoted.

In *Ellsworth v. Martindale-Hubbell Law Directory, supra,* we held that in actions for libel, where the defamatory matter was not libelous per se, special damages must be pleaded. This rule, however, applies not only in libel actions but in all cases where a recovery is sought for special damages. . . . The rule is predicated on the character of special damages which are the natural and proximate but not the necessary consequence of the wrong complained of. General damages, on the other hand, are such as naturally and necessarily result. So general damages are implied by law while special damages are not. Accordingly, the latter must be stated in order that it may appear that they are the legal, natural, and proximate, if not the necessary consequence of such wrong . . . and also to give notice to the defendant and prevent surprise at the trial. . . . In libel actions, special damages "refer to a special pecuniary loss that may have been sustained on account of the peculiar circumstances and condition of the party injured, but are not such a necessary result that they will be inferred by law from the character of the words used." *Meyerle v. Pioneer Pub. Co.* 45 N.D. 568, 178 N.W. 792.

While the rule with respect to the pleading of special damages is universally recognized, apparent contradictions have arisen in its application to particular states of fact. And nowhere is this application more difficult than in actions for defamation. . . . In any event, in the instant case, it seems to us that both right and reason are on the side of the plaintiff and that his amended complaint must be held sufficient. . . . [Plaintiff] alleges that he had a fairly lucrative law business that came to him from foreign territory through forwarders with whom he was not and from the nature of things could not be personally acquainted; that such business came because of the personal and professional reputation and standing which he enjoyed; that because of the defamatory publication of which he complains, this reputation and standing was disparaged in the minds of those who sent business to him and, consequently, his business fell off. From the nature of the circumstances as disclosed by the pleading the plaintiff cannot describe the particular items of business which he has lost or given the names of particular individuals who would have become his clients had it not been for the publication. But he does show a diminution of his business and of the income therefrom by pleading what that business amounted to prior to the publication and what it was after the publication, and as a result thereof. As to whether he can make proof in support of the allegations contained in his pleading is another matter with which we are not now concerned. . . .

The order must be and it is affirmed.

MILLER, Dist. J., I dissent.

In the former opinion herein . . . , this court held that the published statement complained of was not libelous per se and that in such case plaintiff must allege special damages and a defamatory understanding of the statement. Special damages were also defined and several cases cited quoting the rule that such damages must be alleged with certainty and precision. This is the general rule. . . .

With reference to a "defamatory understanding" it was held in such opinion that since the publication was not slanderous per se it cannot be presumed to be understood in a defamatory sense. Such understanding of the reader must be pleaded and proved.

It is alleged in the amended complaint that the readers of the statement had such an understanding, but it is also alleged that the plaintiff does not know the names of such people. If this is the case, and the plaintiff so states in his complaint, he cannot know what understanding any reader had of the rating, and his allegation to the contrary is not sufficient.

A pleading should be liberally construed, but the allegations of such pleading disclose that no cause of action exists as a matter of law, and to hold otherwise is placing the defendant in the same position he would be were the statement libelous per se, i.e., it would be presuming that certain prospective clients had read the statement, understood its defamatory character and by reason thereof refused to send him business, to his pecuniary loss.

The demurrer should be sustained.

5. DAMAGES

FAULK V. AWARE, INC.
244 N.Y.S.2D 259 (N.Y. APP. DIV. 1963)

This action is in libel. At the time of the alleged libel the plaintiff was a radio and television performer. He had his own show known as the "John Henry Faulk Show," . . . . In addition he made guest appearances on other radio and television programs. There is no question but that he was widely known by the public and in his profession. The defendant, Aware, Inc., is a "membership corporation whose purpose is to combat Communism in the entertainment and communication industries". . . .

The plaintiff charges that the defendants conspired to defame him through the issuance of libelous articles with the express malicious intent of destroying his career in television and radio and that through the issuance of such libelous articles they succeeded in so doing. Chief among these articles was a special bulletin issued and published by the defendant, Aware . . . . It is charged by the plaintiff that it was distributed not only to the membership of Aware, Inc., but to its entire mailing list of about 2,000 names. The mailing was designed to and did reach every source or possible source of plaintiff's employment – radio and television stations, advertising agencies, sponsors of programs and advertisers, newspapers and columnists [sic], and particularly the station employing the plaintiff and the sponsors supporting his program. . . .

The plaintiff was extremely successful in his suit, the jury bringing in a verdict of $1,000,000 as compensatory damages as against all three defendants, and $1,250,000 as punitive damages against each of the defendants . . . . The proof in support of the plaintiff's case was overwhelming. He conclusively established that the defendants planned to destroy his professional career through the use of the libelous publications directed to the places where they would do him the most harm. He proved that they succeeded in doing so. The proof established that the libelous statements were not made recklessly but rather that they were made deliberately. The acts of the defendants were proven to be as malicious as they were vicious. The defendants were not content merely with publishing the libelous statements complained of knowing that injury to the plaintiff must follow such publication. They pursued the plaintiff with the libel making sure that its poison would be injected directly into the wellsprings of his professional and economic existence. They did so with deadly effect. He was professionally destroyed, his engagements were cancelled and he could not gain employment in his field despite every effort on his part. . . .

The appellants urge . . . that the judgment be reversed because, among other reasons, "the testimony regarding 'blacklisting' was so prejudicial as to amount to reversible error." Blacklisting, as its name implies, was the practice prevalent in the entertainment industry of listing those entertainers who were accused of being Communists, or of having communistic affiliations. Such listing invariably resulted in the cancellation of the engagements of one so listed and generally rendered him unemployable. That the defendants used the libelous material to effect the blacklisting of plaintiff was made quite clear. The plaintiff charged that his blacklisting flowed from the publication of the libelous articles, and that because of it he lost his employment and became unemployable. . . .

We are greatly concerned, however, with the size of the verdict – both as to compensatory and punitive damages. True, fixing the amount of damage is primarily in the province of the jury . . . . The court, if possible, should try to avoid invading that field. However, a court may not stand by idly when it is apparent that a verdict is shockingly excessive. A jury's verdict must have some relation to reality and it is the court's duty to keep it so. We find the verdict to be grossly excessive and most unrealistic – even in the field of entertainment.

The plaintiff's prior earnings are an important factor in assessing the damage suffered when his earnings are cut off. His damage need not be limited to the level of his actual earnings at the time of the libel. His potential earnings may be taken into consideration when there is evidence to enable a jury to assess those potentialities . . . . In this case, the plaintiff's potential earnings were fixed by his witnesses in amounts ranging from $100,000 to $1,000,000 a year. The larger figure was arrived at by reference to the earnings of those who had reached the very top of the profession. . . . While the plaintiff's experts testified that the plaintiff would, without doubt, be among the "chosen," it seems that none of these experts, although in the entertainment field, was perceptive enough to contract for his services even though his earnings were never more than about $35,000 a year.

Those who testified to potential earnings of between $100,000 and $250,000 arrived at that estimate based upon what comparable performers were receiving. Yet they gave no explanation as to why the plaintiff's earnings were so comparatively low. In short, the testimony of the experts left plenty of room for speculation.

Upon that testimony, the jury was justified in its obvious conclusion that the plaintiff's prospects for advancement in his profession were extremely good and that his income would rise correspondingly. Despite that however, there is hardly enough justification for the finding of compensatory damages in the amount of $1,000,000, even making allowance for his mental pain and suffering. It is interesting to note that at current savings bank interest rates, his yearly income for life would exceed the best of his past earnings. We believe that the compensatory damages should be fixed at a figure no higher than $400,000. . . .

We now consider the amount of punitive damages awarded. . . . It is the duty of the court to keep a verdict for punitive damages within reasonable bounds considering the purpose to be achieved as well as the *mala fides* of the defendant in the particular case. In observance of such duty we conclude that the awards made for punitive damages in this case are grossly excessive.

The jury awarded the sum of $1,250,000 against each of the two appellants. . . . It is our considered opinion that the maximum sum that should have been awarded against Aware, by way of punitive damages, is $50,000, and as against Hartnett, who by far was the more guilty of the two, the sum of $100,000. . . .

Accordingly, the judgment should be reversed, on the law, on the facts and in the exercise of discretion, without costs, and a new trial ordered unless the plaintiff consents to a reduction of the amount of compensatory damages to $400,000 and punitive damages as against Aware to the sum of $50,000 and as against Hartnett to the sum of $100,000, in which event the judgment as modified, should be affirmed, without costs. . . .

6. DEFENSES

a. TRUTH

AUVIL V. CBS "60 MINUTES"
67 F.3D 816 (9TH CIR. 1995)

Grady and Lillie Auvil et al., suing on behalf of themselves and other similarly situated Washington State apple growers ("growers"), appeal from the district court's summary judgment in favor of CBS "60 Minutes" ("CBS"). . . .

BACKGROUND

On February 26, 1989, CBS's weekly news show "60 Minutes" aired a segment on daminozide, a chemical growth regulator sprayed on apples. . . . The broadcast was based largely on a Natural Resources Defense Council ("NRDC") report, entitled Intolerable Risk: Pesticides in Our Children's Food ("*Intolerable Risk*"), which outlined health risks associated with the use of a number of pesticides on fruit, especially the risks to children. "'A' is for Apple" focused on the NRDC report's findings concerning daminozide, as well as the EPA's knowledge of daminozide's carcinogenity. Scientific research had indicated that daminozide, more commonly known by its trade name, Alar, breaks down into unsymmetrical dimethylhydrazine (UDMH), a carcinogen. . . .

The segment opened with the following capsule summary from Ed Bradley, a "60 Minutes" commentator:

> The most potent cancer-causing agent in our food supply is a substance sprayed on apples to keep them on the trees longer and make them look better. That's the conclusion of a number of scientific experts. And who is most at risk? Children, who may someday develop cancer from this one chemical called daminozide. Daminozide, which has been sprayed on apples for more than 20 years, breaks down into another chemical called UDMH.

During the broadcast, Bradley garnered a number of viewpoints on the Alar issue. Those interviewed included an Environmental Protection Agency ("EPA") administrator, an NRDC attorney, a U.S. congressman, a professor of pediatrics at Harvard Medical School, and a scientist from the Consumers Union, which publishes *Consumer Reports* magazine. After Bradley's opening synopsis, the broadcast segment began with the EPA administrator's admission that the EPA had known of cancer risks associated with daminozide for sixteen years, but that EPA regulations had hampered the removal of the chemical from the market. . . . The broadcast segment continued with testimonials from the NRDC attorney, who discussed the findings published in *Intolerable Risk*, focusing on the cancer risks to children from ingestion of apples treated with daminozide. The NRDC's findings were corroborated both by the EPA administrator and the Harvard pediatrician. The broadcast ended with the statements of a Consumers Union scientist, who revealed that most manufacturers of apple products said they no longer use apples treated with daminozide but that the manufacturers were unsuccessful in keeping daminozide completely out of their products.

Following the "60 Minutes" broadcast, consumer demand for apples and apple products decreased dramatically. The apple growers and others dependent upon apple production lost millions of dollars. Many of the growers lost their homes and livelihoods.

In November 1990, eleven Washington State apple growers, representing some 4,700 growers in the Washington area, filed a complaint . . . against CBS, local CBS affiliates, the NRDC, and Fenton Communications, Inc., a public relations firm used by the NRDC in 1989. . . . After discovery, which was limited to the question of the falsity of the CBS broadcast, the growers moved . . . for partial summary judgment on the question of falsity. CBS also moved for summary judgment on the question of falsity. The district court denied the growers' motions but granted summary judgment to CBS because the growers did not produce evidence sufficient to create a triable issue of fact as to the falsity of the broadcast. . . . The growers appeal the district court's summary judgment ruling that they failed to offer evidence sufficient to present a genuine issue of fact for trial on the falsity of the CBS broadcast.

DISCUSSION

. . . To establish a claim of product disparagement, also known as trade libel, a plaintiff must allege that the defendant published a knowingly false statement harmful to the interests of another and intended such publication to harm the plaintiff's pecuniary interests. Restatement (Second) of Torts § 623A. Accordingly, for a product disparagement claim to be actionable, the plaintiff must prove, *inter alia,* the falsity of the disparaging statements. *See* Restatement (Second) of Torts §§ 623A, 651(1)(c).

Existing case law on product disparagement provides little guidance on the falsity prong. Nonetheless, as a tort whose actionability depends on the existence of disparaging speech, the tort is substantively similar to defamation. Therefore, we reference defamation cases to arrive at a decision in the instant matter.

"'A' is for Apple" was based on *Intolerable Risk,* a scientific report disseminated by the NRDC. The report discussed the findings of cancer research studies on various chemicals used on fruit and questioned the EPA's hesitance in removing Alar from the market. . . . The broadcast contained a number of factual assertions, several of which are pointed out by the growers to support their claim that the broadcast falsely disparaged their product. . . . On the subject of daminozide's cancer-causing potential, the growers point to the following statements:

> The most potent cancer-causing agent in our food supply is a substance sprayed on apples to keep them on the trees longer and make them look better.
>
> We know that [daminozide and other chemicals] do cause cancer.
>
> Just from these eight pesticides, what we're finding is that the risk of developing cancer is approximately 250 times what EPA says is an acceptable level of cancer in our population.
>
> [The EPA administrator] took another look at the evidence and decided to start the process of banning daminozide after all. But the process could take five years. So we returned to Washington to ask him why he doesn't just declare daminozide an imminent hazard, and suspend it right away . . . .

The growers offered evidence showing that no studies have been conducted to test the relationship between ingestion of daminozide and incidence of cancer in *humans.* Such evidence, however, is insufficient to show a genuine issue for trial regarding the broadcast's assertions that daminozide is a potent carcinogen. Animal laboratory tests are a legitimate means for assessing cancer risks to humans. . . .

The growers provide no other challenge to the EPA's findings, nor do they directly attack the validity of the scientific studies. All of the statements referenced above are factual assertions made by the interviewees, based on the scientific findings of the NRDC. These findings were corroborated by the EPA administrator and a Harvard pediatrician. The EPA, which often relies on the results of animal studies, acknowledged that it knew of the cancer risks associated with ingestion of daminozide and, in August 1985, classified daminozide as a "probable human carcinogen." Indeed, the EPA estimated that the dietary risk to the general population from UDMH, a metabolite of daminozide, was fifty times an acceptable risk and ultimately concluded that daminozide posed an unreasonable risk to the general population. . . .

The growers' only challenge to the scientific studies is their claim that animal studies cannot be relied on to indicate cancer risk for humans. Because animal studies can be relied upon, their evidence that no studies have been conducted on the effects of daminozide on humans does not create a genuine issue for trial on the falsity of the broadcast's assertions regarding daminozide's carcinogenicity.

On the subject of cancer risks to children from the use of daminozide on apples, the growers point to the following factual assertions to support their falsity claim:

> What we're talking about is a cancer-causing agent used on food that EPA knows is going to cause cancer for thousands of children over their lifetime.
>
> The Natural Resources Defense Council[ ] has completed the most careful study yet on the effect of daminozide and seven other cancer-causing pesticides on the food children eat.
>
> Over a lifetime, one child out of every 4,000 or so of our preschoolers will develop cancer just from these eight pesticides.
>
> [The NRDC study] says children are being exposed to a pesticide risk several hundred times greater than what the agency says is acceptable.

The growers offered evidence showing that no scientific study has been conducted on cancer risks to children from the use of pesticides. However, CBS based its statements regarding cancer and children on the NRDC's findings that the daminozide found on apples is more harmful to children because they ingest more apple products per unit of body weight than do adults. The growers have provided no affirmative evidence that daminozide does not pose a risk to children. The fact that there have been no studies conducted specifically on the cancer risks to children from daminozide does nothing to disprove the conclusion that, if children consume more of a carcinogenic substance than do adults, they are at higher risk for contracting cancer. The growers' evidence, therefore, does not create a genuine issue as to the falsity of the broadcast's assertion that daminozide is more harmful to children.

Despite their inability to prove that *statements* made during the broadcast were false, the growers assert that summary judgment for CBS was improper because a jury could find that the broadcast contained a provably false *message,* viewing the broadcast segment in its entirety. They further argue that, if they can prove the falsity of this implied message, they have satisfied their burden of proving falsity.

The growers' contentions are unavailing. Their attempt to derive a specific, implied message from the broadcast as a whole and to prove the falsity of that overall *message* is unprecedented and inconsistent with Washington law. No Washington court has held that the analysis of falsity proceeds from an implied, disparaging message. It is the statements themselves that are of primary concern in the analysis. . . . The defamatory character of the language must be apparent from the words themselves. . . .

The Washington courts' view finds support in the Restatement, which instructs that a product disparagement plaintiff has the burden of proving the "falsity of the *statement*." Restatement (Second) of Torts § 651(1)(c) (emphasis added). This standard refers to individual statements and not to any overall message. Therefore, we must reject the growers' invitation to infer an overall message from the broadcast and determine whether that message is false.

We also note that, if we were to accept the growers' argument, plaintiffs bringing suit based on disparaging speech would escape summary judgment merely by arguing, as the growers have, that a jury should be allowed to determine both the overall message of a broadcast and whether that overall message is false. Because a broadcast could be interpreted in numerous, nuanced ways, a great deal of uncertainty would arise as to the message conveyed by the broadcast. Such uncertainty would make it difficult for broadcasters to predict whether their work would subject them to tort liability. Furthermore, such uncertainty raises the spectre of a chilling effect on speech. . . .

CONCLUSION

Because the growers have failed to raise a genuine issue of material fact regarding the falsity of statements made during the broadcast of "'A' is for Apple," the district court's decision granting CBS's motion for summary judgment is
AFFIRMED.

QUESTIONS

1   The Court of Appeals here upheld the summary judgment for defendant because plaintiffs failed to raise a genuine issue whether the CBS broadcast was false. Plaintiffs had alleged, among other things, that the broadcast falsely stated that apples cause cancer in humans, but the Court of Appeals held that defendant had a reasonable basis upon which to make that assertion because of animal studies showing a link between Alar and cancer in animals. Would it have made any difference if the CBS broadcast had said that human studies conclusively prove that Alar causes cancer?

2   What if the broadcast had said, without the benefit of even the animal studies, that Alar causes cancer?

3   What if broadcast said, "We have reviewed all of the evidence and are of the opinion that Alar causes cancer"?

b. QUALIFIED PRIVILEGES

Once plaintiff has carried the burden of making out a *prima facie* case of defamation, it is defendant's burden to prove the defense of an applicable privilege. A defendant generally is privileged to make a defamatory communication if he has a legal, moral, or social right or duty to communicate the defamatory facts. Such privileged communications fall into three categories: communications to protect the interest of a third party, communications to protect the self-interest of the speaker, and communications to protect a common interest between the speaker and recipient. *See* Restatement Secs. 594-595. The privilege to publish defamatory information to protect the interests of the recipient or a third party is more limited than the privilege to protect the publisher's own interests. *See* Restatement Sec. 595(1)(b). The following case illustrates the scope of these qualified privileges and how the privilege can be exceeded.

WATT V. LONGSDON
1 K.B. 130 (C.A. 1930)

. . . The Scottish Petroleum Co., which carried on business, among other places in Morocco, had in Casablanca . . . a manager named Browne, and a managing director named Watt. The company had in England a chairman named Singer . . . and also another director, Longsdon . . . . . The latter had been in Morocco in business and in friendly relations with Watt and Browne, and was a friend of Mrs. Watt . . . . In April, 1928, Mrs. Watt was in England, and her husband in Casablanca. . . . Longsdon, in England, received a letter at the beginning of May from Browne in Casablanca stating that Watt had left for Lisbon, . . . that he had left a bill . . . for whisky unpaid, and that he had been for two months in immoral relations with his housemaid, who was now publicly raising claims against him for money matters. The woman was described as an old woman, stone deaf, almost blind, and with dyed hair. A number of details were given which Browne said Watt's cook had corroborated. The information was mixed up with an allegation that Watt had been scheming to compromise or seduce Mrs. Browne. The letter concluded:

> From a letter shown to me by Mr. Watt I know how bitterly disappointed Mrs. Watt is, and how very much troubled she is. It would therefore perhaps be better not to show her this letter as it could only increase most terribly her own feelings in regard to her husband. These awful facts might be the cause of a breakdown to her, and I think she has enough to cope with at present. Mr. Singer, however, should perhaps know.

On May 5 Longsdon, without making inquiries, sent Browne's letter on to Singer, the chairman of the board of directors. . . . On May 5 Longsdon wrote a long letter to Browne, in which he said that he had long suspected Watt's immorality, but had no proof, that he thought it wicked and cruel that Mrs. Watt, a very old friend of the writer's, should be in the dark when Watt might return to her—did not Browne agree?, that he (Longsdon) would not speak until he had a sworn statement in his possession, "and only with such proof would I speak, for an interferer between husband and wife nearly always comes off worst." Could Browne get a sworn statement? . . . Londgsdon's letter describes the woman who was to make this sworn statement as "a prostitute all her life," a description not contained in Browne's letter. Watt returned to England in May, and, without waiting for the sworn statement, on May 12 Longsdon sent the letter to Mrs. Watt. Mr. and Mrs. Watt separated, and Mrs. Watt instituted proceedings for divorce, which, apparently, are still pending.

Mr. Watt then instituted proceedings against Longsdon for libel, namely: (i) the publication of Browne's letter to Singer; (ii) the publication of the same letter to Mrs. Watt; (iii) Longsdon's letter of May 5 to Browne. . . . The defendant . . . pleaded privilege. The case was tried before HORRIDGE, J., and a jury. The learned judge held all three publications to be privileged, and that there was no evidence of malice fit to be left to the jury. He, therefore, entered judgment for the defendant. The plaintiff appeals.

The learned judge appears to have taken the view that the authorities justify him in holding that if there is an obvious interest in the person to whom a communication is made which causes him to be a proper recipient of a statement, even if the party making the communication had no moral or social duty to the party to whom the communication is made, the occasion is privileged. . . . He has, therefore, found in the present case that the occasion of each of the three communications, to Singer, to the wife, and to Browne, was privileged, and that there is no evidence of excess of communication or of malice to be left to the jury. . . .

By the law of England there are occasions on which a person may make defamatory statements about another which are untrue without incurring any legal liability for his statements. These occasions are called privileged occasions. A reason frequently given for this privilege is that the allegation that the speaker has "unlawfully and maliciously published" is displaced by proof that the speaker had either a duty or an interest to publish, such duty or interest conferring the privilege. But communications made on these occasions may lose their privilege. (i) They may exceed the privilege of the occasion by going beyond the limits of the duty or interest, or (ii) they may be published with express malice, so that the occasion is not being legitimately used, but abused. . . . The question whether the occasion was privileged is for the judge, and so far as "duty" is concerned, the question is: Was there a duty, legal, moral or social, to communicate? As to legal duty, the judge should have no difficulty; the judge should know the law. But as to moral or social duties of imperfect obligation, the task is far more troublesome. The judge had no evidence as to the view which the community takes of moral or social duties. . . . Is the judge merely to give his own view of moral and social duty, though he thinks a considerable portion of the community holds a different opinion, or is he to endeavour to ascertain what view "the great mass of right-minded men" would take? It is not surprising that with such a standard both judges and text-writers treat the matter as one of great difficulty in which no definite line can be drawn.

. . . [E]xcept in the case of communications based on common interest, the principle is that there must be either interest in the recipient, and a duty to communicate in the speaker, or an interest to be protected in the speaker, and a duty to protect it in the recipient. Except in the case of common interest justifying intercommunication, the correspondence must be between duty and interest; there may, in the common interest cases, be also a common or reciprocal duty. It is not every interest which will create a duty in a stranger or volunteer.

But that does not settle the question, for it is necessary to consider, in the present case, whether there was, as to each communication, a duty to communicate, and an interest in the recipient. First, as to the communication between Longsdon and Singer, I think the case must proceed on the admission that at all material times Watt, Longsdon, and Browne were in the employment of the same company, and the evidence of the answer to the interrogatory put in by the plaintiff that Longsdon honestly believed the statements in Browne's letter. In my view, on these facts, there was a duty, moral and business, on Longsdon to communicate the letter to Singer, the chairman of his company, who, apart from questions of present employment, might be asked by Watt for a testimonial to a future employer. Equally, I think Longsdon receiving the letter from Browne, might discuss the matter with him, and ask for further information, on the ground of a common interest in the affairs of the company, and to obtain further information for his chairman. . . . As to the communications to Singer and Browne, in my opinion, the appeal should fail, but, as both my brethren take the view that there was evidence of malice which should be left to the jury, there must, of course, be a new trial as to the claim on these two publications.

The communication to Mrs. Watt stands on a different footing. I have no intention of writing an exhaustive treatise on the circumstances when a stranger or a friend should communicate to husband or wife information he receives as to the conduct of the other party to the marriage. I am clear that it is impossible to say that he is always under a moral or social duty to do so; it is equally impossible to say that he is never under such a duty. It must depend on the circumstances of each case, the nature of the information, and the relation of speaker and recipient. It cannot, on the one hand, be the duty even of a friend to communicate all the gossip the friend hears at men's clubs or women's bridge parties to one of the spouses affected. On the other hand, most men would hold that it was the moral duty of a doctor who attended his sister-in-law, and believed her to be suffering from a miscarriage, for which an absent husband could not be responsible to communicate that fact to his wife and the husband. . . . Using the best judgment I can in the difficult matter, I have come to the conclusion that there was not a moral or social duty in Longsdon to make this communication to Mrs. Watt such as to make the occasion privileged, and that there must be a new trial so far as it relates to the claim for publication of a libel to Mrs. Watt. The communications to Singer and Browne being made on a privileged occasion, there must be a new trial of the issue as to malice defeating the privilege. There must also be a new trial of the complaint as to publication to Mrs. Watt, the occasion being held not to be privileged. . . .

GREER, L.J.—Assuming that the defendant has no common interest with the person to whom the libel is published, and it is necessary that there should be some moral or social duty to make the communication, what is the test by which duty is to be determined? . . . Opinions may easily differ as to whether the circumstances are such as to make the communication a moral or social duty. Similar questions of degree arise in many cases, and are left to the determination of a jury.

In negligence cases, what the average reasonably careful man would do is left to be determined by a jury whenever it is a question in which opinions may differ. But it is well settled that whether an occasion be privileged or not is a question for the judge, though he may ask the jury to determine any particular facts that are in dispute. . . .

In my judgment, no right-minded man in the position of the defendant, a friend of the plaintiff and of his wife, would have thought it right to communicate the horrible accusations contained in Mr. Browne's letter to the plaintiff's wife. The information came to Mr. Browne from a very doubtful source, and, in my judgment, no reasonably right-minded person could think it his duty, without obtaining some corroboration of the story, and without first communicating with the plaintiff, to pass on these outrageous charges of marital infidelity of a gross kind, and drunkenness and dishonesty, to the plaintiff's wife. As regards the publication to the plaintiff's wife, the occasion was not privileged, and it is unnecessary to consider whether there was evidence of express malice. As regards the publication to the chairman of the company, who owned nearly all the shares, and to Mr. Browne, I think on the facts as pleaded there was, between the defendant and the recipients of the letters, a common interest which would make the occasion privileged, but I also think there is intrinsic evidence in the letter to Browne, and evidence in the hasty and unjustifiable communication to the plaintiff's wife, that would be sufficient to entitle the plaintiff to ask for a verdict on these publications on the ground of express malice. . . . Malice is a state of mind . . . . A man may believe in the truth of a defamatory statement, and yet when he published it will be reckless whether his belief be well founded or not. His motive for publishing a libel on a privileged occasion may be an improper one, even though he believes the statement to be true. He may be moved by hatred or dislike, or a desire to injure the subject of the libel, and may be using the occasion for that purpose, and if he is doing so the publication will be maliciously made, even though he may believe the defamatory statements to be true. . . .

I think the defendant's conduct in disseminating the gross charges that he did to the plaintiff's wife, and to Mr. Singer, and repeating, and to some extent adding to them, in his letter to Mr. Browne, and his offer to provide funds for procuring the evidence of the two women in Casablanca, affords some evidence of malice which ought to have been left to the jury. It is not for us to weigh the evidence. It will be for the jury to decide whether they are satisfied that in publishing the libels the defendant was, in fact, giving effect to his malicious, or otherwise improper, feelings towards the plaintiff, and was not merely using the occasion for the protection of the interests of himself and his two correspondents. . . .

QUESTIONS

1   Should the analysis of the defendant's asserted privilege differ if the wife had come to defendant and asked whether defendant had heard anything about plaintiff's extra-marital activities?

2   Should the analysis of the defendant's asserted privilege differ if defendant had learned and communicated that plaintiff had contracted the AIDS virus? Why or why not?

3   Should the analysis of the defendant's asserted privilege differ if defendant had made up some handbills describing the information and passed them out in front of the parties' common place of employment?

4 *Malice.* Assuming that defendant has a right or duty to communicate what he has heard, at least to the chairman of the company, should the privilege protect defendant if he communicates information that he knows to be false? What if the defendant believes the information to be true, but communicates it to the chairman, not because he is concerned for the good of the company, but because he dislikes plaintiff?

ERICKSON V. MARSH & MCLENNAN CO.
569 A.2D 793 (N.J. 1990)

. . . Plaintiff John Erickson claims he was the victim of sexual discrimination in that his employer, defendant Marsh & McLennan Co., Inc. (M & M) discharged him because of a romantic consensual relationship between his supervisor and a female employee. This appeal also addresses whether an employer, in responding to inquiries from prospective employers concerning a former employee, has a qualified privilege protecting it from a libel action.

I

On November 2, 1981, M & M hired Erickson as an "at-will" employee and assigned him to the company's Morristown Office as an account representative in the Major Accounts Casualty Department. In May 1982, the company transferred Erickson to the Commercial Accounts Department as an account executive. Erickson asserts that this transfer was a promotion because an account executive enjoys a higher job category than account representative. Several executives from M & M, however, testified that Erickson had been unilaterally transferred from the largest and most prestigious department to a smaller and less prestigious department, at the same salary, because he had failed to grasp certain technical aspects of his job.

In his new position, Erickson's supervisor was Angela Kyte, an Assistant Vice President and the Manager of Commercial Accounts. Kyte's supervisor was Frank Hayes, a Vice-President and Operations Manager of the Morristown Office. Erickson was the "team leader" of Karen Niedhammer, an account representative, and Stuart Torbert, an insurance assistant.

The events leading to the lawsuit began in February 1983. On February 8, 1983, Niedhammer and a colleague, Kelly Lennan, met with Kyte in her office. Niedhammer reluctantly reported that on several occasions Erickson had sexually harassed her. . . .

The following Monday, February 14, 1983, Kyte and Hayes met to discuss Niedhammer's allegations. Kyte prepared a memorandum regarding that meeting:

[Hayes] wants to know what I plan to do about it. [I] told him I was not sure, but had planned to talk to John about it and cool him off. Frank called [Ed] Pazicky, [Richard] Mikulak, personnel for advice. Pazicky said do something fast and either fire or give threat of firing if actions continue.

After the meeting, Hayes instructed Kyte to question other female employees discreetly to determine whether Erickson had ever sexually harassed them. Two women reported that Erickson had previously made improper gestures and comments to them.

The next day, Kyte met with Erickson to discuss the allegations made against him. According to Kyte, Erickson admitted the acts but stated that he had intended them only as a joke. A memorandum that Kyte wrote to Erickson recounted the meeting:

> John, confirming our discussions of this morning, your behavior towards your subordinate, Karen Niedhammer, and other female members of the department has included incidents, actions and comments which are unprofessional in nature and can only be interpreted as a form of sexual harassment.
>
>   * * *
>
> I have expressly instructed you to stop any such conduct as physical contact and suggestive comments, whether joking or not, and to avoid and prevent any situations which can be interpreted as sexual harassment in the future. Further, you are not in any way to mention this matter to Karen or bring it up to her in any way.
>
>   * * *
>
> Should there be any further incidents of this nature or breach of the above ban it will be considered grounds for termination.
>
>   A copy of this memo is being entered in your personnel file.

After receiving the memorandum, Erickson consulted an attorney. His lawyer, Michael Critchley, sent a letter dated March 10, 1983 to Kyte stating that Erickson denied every accusation and wished to discuss the matter. According to Kyte, she had not been aware that Erickson was contesting the sexual-harassment allegations until she received Critchley's letter.

Kyte referred Critchley's letter to Hayes, who forwarded it to Frank Cooper, Assistant Vice President and Manager of M & M's Employee and Government Relations Department in New York. After reviewing the matter, Cooper sent Critchley a letter dated March 31, 1983, stating: "We recognize the seriousness and sensitivity of the issue and assure you that as long as there are no further thematic recurrences attributable to your client and he complies with the proscriptions of Ms. Kyte's February 15th memorandum, the matter is closed."

He also advised Critchley that all documents concerning the sexual harassment charge would be kept separate from Erickson's personnel file. In an April 18, 1983 letter to Cooper, Critchley reiterated his request for a conference and specifically requested "an opportunity to confront Ms. Niedhammer for the purposes of refuting the validity of her charges and thereafter having the matter closed." Cooper denied this request in a letter to Critchley of May 3, 1983:

> I see no benefit to be derived from the confrontation you suggest. Furthermore, in our view such an undertaking would be disruptive to the working environment. Consequently, I ask you to encourage your client to put this matter behind him as we have, and go forward with the work at hand.

Cooper also advised Critchley that he had asked the Morristown Office to forward all documentation concerning the matter to him so that he could store it in his confidential file. Cooper explained that putting the document in that file, which would not be available to management, would "virtually reduce to zero the probability of anyone drawing negative inferences in the future from a review of Mr. Erickson's file."

On May 2, 1983, Kyte prepared a formal appraisal of Erickson in which she evaluated his performance as falling between "acceptable" and "inadequate." She did not, however, recommend his discharge. On May 9, 1983, Erickson responded to Kyte's appraisal report:

> I am very distressed over the contents of this report and I am in total disagreement with it. I do not view this report as an objective assessment of my knowledge and skills, but a prejudicial view which is motivated as a result of my response to the recent allegations brought against me.
>
> The alleged deficiencies contained within the report were never brought to my attention since the inception of my employment with Marsh and McLennan, Inc. Further, nowhere within the report is there any mention, nor is it implied, that I had been previously advised of said alleged deficiencies.
>
> I find it highly coincidental that such allegations are forthcoming at this time. Surely, my knowledge, skills and abilities have not dissipated since I began my employment with Marsh & McLennan and, most certainly, not since my retention of legal counsel became known to Marsh and McLennan in March of 1983.

After receiving the response, Kyte concluded that Erickson's unwillingness to acknowledge his deficiencies would prevent him from responding favorably to her "constructive criticism." According to a memo prepared by Kyte, Erickson's response was the "final catalyst which convinced me once and for all that no amount of critique or constructive criticism was going to be acted upon for the benefit of improving John Erickson's work performance."

Subsequently Kyte consulted with Hayes and recommended Erickson's termination. Hayes then communicated with the head of the New Jersey operation, Roger Egan, of the New York Office. Having worked with Erickson in the past, Egan had criticized his work on a project in which Kyte had to rewrite an entire report. Egan, Hayes and Kyte agreed that Erickson should be discharged, and on May 20, 1983, Hayes fired Erickson. Niedhammer did not replace Erickson.

After his termination, Erickson sought employment with other insurance-brokerage firms. Howard James Insurance Services, Inc., and Joseph L. Iraci Insurance Agency asked M & M for references. Howard James Insurance Services, Inc. stated that the job for which they were considering Erickson "entails a general knowledge of all lines of insurance along with general abilities to deal with the public and a strong organization ability." They inquired whether M & M would recommend Erickson for such a position and the reason for his discharge.

In response to this inquiry, Kyte wrote: "John left our operation because his level of expertise and areas of interest in insurance did not match the depth required for the proper service of [M & M] clients." She added, however, that "John does possess a general knowledge of commercial insurance and is well known among the insurance markets. If these are qualities you are seeking for your Account Executive position, we would recommend John Erickson to you."

Kyte's response to Joseph L. Iraci Insurance Agency's inquiry for "any information" regarding Erickson's past history and performance was similar to her response to Howard James Insurance Services, Inc. In August 1983 Erickson accepted employment with another insurance agency.

Later that month Erickson sued M & M for various wrongful acts committed during and after his term of employment. . . . Specifically, he . . . charged that Kyte's responses to his prospective employers had been libelous. A jury found M & M liable of . . . libel. . . .

IV

With respect to the libel claim, the trial court ruled that a qualified privilege extended to Kyte's responses to the inquiries of Erickson's prospective employers. The trial court instructed the jury that to overcome that privilege, Erickson must demonstrate by a preponderance of the evidence that Kyte had acted with actual malice when sending the letters. Without reaching the issue of the appropriate burden of proof, the Appellate Division held that the evidence did not support a finding of abuse of privilege. . . . We agree that a qualified privilege extends to an employer who responds in good faith to the specific inquiries of a third party regarding the qualifications of an employee. Because the trial court incorrectly charged the jury on the burden of proof necessary to overcome a qualified privilege, however, we reverse so much of the Appellate Division's judgment as affects the libel claim and remand for a new proceeding. . . .

Although defamatory, a statement will not be actionable if it is subject to an absolute or qualified privilege. A statement made in the course of judicial, administrative, or legislative proceedings is absolutely privileged and wholly immune from liability. . . . That immunity is predicated on the need for unfettered expression critical to advancing the underlying government interest at stake in those settings. . . . A qualified privilege, on the other hand, enjoys a lesser degree of immunity and is overcome on a showing of actual malice. . . .

This qualified or conditional privilege is based on the public policy "that it is essential that true information be given whenever it is reasonably necessary for the protection of one's own interests, the interests of third persons or certain interests of the public." Introductory Note, Restatement (Second) of Torts, § 592A, at 258 (1965) (Restatement (Second)).

In order to protect those interests, both public and private, we have recognized the utility of a qualified privilege in a variety of settings. . . . We recognize that Erickson does not dispute that Kyte's communications to his prospective employers are subject to a qualified privilege. . . . [W]e hold that a qualified privilege extended to Kyte for the statements she made to Erickson's prospective employers. Her publication was made in response to inquiries of those employers and was not simply volunteered. Additionally, those prospective employers had a legitimate and obvious interest in the professional qualifications, skill, and experience of Erickson, including the reasons for his termination. Moreover, the information Kyte offered specifically addressed the questions posed by those employers; her publication was directly relevant to their inquiry. *Supra* at 797-98. Thus, a qualified privilege appropriately shielded her responses. . . .

Having ruled that a qualified privilege protected Kyte's letters, we now turn to the standards for determining whether that privilege was abused. At general common law a qualified privilege could be overcome only by a showing of "ill motive or malice in fact." . . . We recognize that if the letters were true, Erickson's claim fails because truth is a defense to charge of libel. . . . Likewise, if Kyte believed in good faith that the charges were true, the claim fails because she was not acting with actual malice. . . .

c. ABSOLUTE PRIVILEGES

KENNEDY V. CANNON
182 A.2D 54 (MD. 1962)

This appeal questions whether the trial court erred in directing a verdict for the defendant, an attorney, in a suit for slander on the grounds that the allegedly slanderous statement was privileged as part of the defendant's duty as counsel to his client, and that no malice on the part of the defendant had been shown.

The appellee, Robert Powell Cannon (defendant below), was summoned to the Wicomico County jail . . . at the request of Charles L. Humphreys, . . . who had been arrested early that morning and charged with the rape of the appellant, Jane Linton Kennedy, a . . . married woman. After conferring with the prisoner, appellee made a telephone call to Richard L. Moore, managing editor of the Salisbury Times, a daily newspaper published in Salisbury, with a circulation of about 23,000. He inquired concerning any information the newspaper might have received in regard to the charge against Humphreys and was informed by Mr. Moore that "we had talked to the authorities and had gotten a story together, and the story said that Humphreys had signed a statement admitting intercourse with the woman who was involved." Mr. Moore told the appellee that the information had been given by the State's Attorney. Thereupon, the appellee proceeded to tell Mr. Moore everything that Humphreys had related to him, including an assertion by Humphreys that Mrs. Kennedy had consented to the intercourse. When informed that it would be impossible to print matter of that type, and at such great length, appellee agreed, with some reluctance, to the publication as part of the news article of additional material quoting the appellee as to Humphreys' claim. The article which was published that afternoon included in the information furnished by the State's Attorney the identity of the appellant, . . . the fact that she had accused Humphreys . . . of raping her, and a statement that Humphreys had signed an admission of the intercourse. The article then quoted appellee as having said, "He [Humphreys] emphatically denies the charge. He says that the woman submitted to his advances willingly." As a result of the publication of the statement appellant alleged she suffered humiliation and harassment by annoying phone calls from unknown persons and eventually was forced to move with her family out of the community and the State. She instituted a suit against appellee alleging that the words spoken by him to the newspaper charged her with the crime of adultery, were slanderous *per se* . . . , and were not privileged.

The appellee admitted on the witness stand that the newspaper article correctly quoted his statement to the editor. He sought to justify its publication on the ground that the physical safety of his client required it. He stated he feared the possibility of a lynching if only the material released by the State's Attorney were published. Recalling a lynching which had occurred in Salisbury under similar circumstances some 25 years previously, he said he felt that the account should include a denial of the charge based upon his client's claim of consent by the woman. At the conclusion of the testimony before a jury, the trial court granted appellee's motion for a directed verdict, expressing the opinion that when the State had undertaken to publish a statement about the case damaging to his client, the appellee was justified and privileged in replying as he did. Appellant appeals from the judgment for costs entered in favor of appellee. The question raised here is . . . whether a recovery by appellant is barred because the statement was privileged. Words of the nature involved here have been held to be slanderous *per se*. . . .

The privilege afforded an attorney in a judicial proceeding and its rationale are discussed in the leading case of *Maulsby v. Reifsnider*, 69 Md. 143 . . . (1888), where this Court stated . . . :

> All agree, that counsel are privileged and protected to a certain extent, at least, for defamatory words spoken *in a judicial proceeding*, and words thus spoken are not actionable, which would in themselves be actionable, if spoken elsewhere. He is obliged in the discharge of a professional duty to prosecute and defend the most important rights and interests, the life it may be, or the liberty or the property of his client, and it is absolutely essential to the administration of justice that he should be allowed the widest latitude in commenting on the character, the conduct and motives of parties and witnesses and other persons directly or remotely connected with the subject-matter in litigation. And to subject him to actions of slander by everyone who may consider himself aggrieved, and to the costs and expenses of a harassing litigation, would be to fetter and restrain him in that open and fearless discharge of duty which he owes to his client, and which the demands of justice require. Not that the law means to say, that one, because he is counsel in the trial of a cause, has the right, abstractly considered, deliberately and maliciously to slander another, but it is the fear that if the rule were otherwise, actions without number might be brought against counsel who had not spoken falsely and maliciously. It is better therefore to make the rule of law so large that counsel acting *bona fide* in the discharge of duty, shall never be troubled, although by making it so large, others who have acted *mala fide* and maliciously, are included. The question whether words spoken by counsel were spoken maliciously or in good faith, are, and always will be, open questions, upon which opinion may differ, and counsel, however innocent, would be liable if not to judgments, to a vexatious and expensive litigation. The privilege thus recognized by law is not the privilege merely of counsel, but the privilege of clients, and the evil, if any, resulting from it must be endured for the sake of the greater good which is thereby secured. But this privilege is not an absolute and unqualified privilege, and cannot be extended beyond the reason and principles on which it is founded.

(Emphasis added.) The Court went on to hold that the words, to be privileged, must also be relevant to the judicial proceeding in which they were spoken.

The statement just quoted reflects the view of a majority of the jurisdictions in this country . . . . What was characterized in that case as a qualified privilege for communications, conditioned on their being pertinent or relevant to a judicial proceeding, without regard to the motive of the speaker, is referred to by modern text writers and in case law as an absolute privilege. . . . This absolute immunity extends to the judge as well as to witnesses and parties to the litigation, for defamatory statements uttered in the course of a trial or contained in pleadings, affidavits, depositions, and other documents directly related to the case. . . . An absolute privilege is distinguished from a qualified privilege in that the former provides immunity regardless of the purpose or motive of the defendant, or the reasonableness of his conduct, while the latter is conditioned upon the absence of malice and is forfeited if it is abused. . . .

Appellee in this case contends that . . . his statement was absolutely privileged. It is not disputed that the statement was relevant to the criminal proceeding. The essential question to be answered is whether it was published in – that is, as part of – a "judicial proceeding."

The term "judicial proceeding" is broad enough to cover all steps in a criminal action, so that when Humphreys was arrested and charged with rape it would be a valid conclusion that the judicial proceeding had commenced. . . . However, this does not necessarily mean that every statement made by an attorney after the inception of a judicial proceeding will be privileged.

Appellee cites the oft quoted rule from 3 Restatement, Torts, §586: "An attorney at law is absolutely privileged to publish false and defamatory matter of another in communications preliminary to a proposed judicial proceeding, or in the institution of, or during the course and as a part of a judicial proceeding in which he participates as counsel, if it has some relation thereto."

However, the extension of this absolute privilege to statements not made in the judicial proceeding itself is limited both by the comments on the rule of the Restatement itself, and by the decisions. The scope of the privilege is restricted to communications such as those made between an attorney and his client, or in the examination of witnesses by counsel, or in statements made by counsel to the court or jury. . . . Appellee cites no authorities which would extend the privilege beyond a communication to one actually involved in the proceeding, either as judge, attorney, party or witness. On the other hand, it has been held that such absolute privilege will not attach to counsel's extra-judicial publications, related to the litigation, which are made outside the purview of the judicial proceeding. . . . Nor will the attorney be privileged for actionable words spoken before persons in no way connected with the proceeding. . . . We hold that appellee had no absolute privilege in regard to the statement made by him to the newspaper.

However, the argument is made (and the language of the trial court's opinion shows that it was persuasive there) that the forum had been chosen by the State's Attorney, and not by appellee, and that he had a right, perhaps even a duty to his client, to publish the statement in question. This argument raises indirectly the contention that because of the attorney-client relationship, at least a qualified privilege existed in the absence of a showing of malice or abuse of the privilege.

There may well be a qualified privilege based upon an attorney-client relationship which would justify an otherwise slanderous communication to certain other persons, to protect the rights of society or one to whom a legal or moral duty is owed. However, the communication *must be made in a proper manner and to proper parties only*, i.e., to parties having a corresponding interest or duty. . . . It may be conceded that appellee indeed had a duty to act upon the information he had gained as to the statement given by the State's Attorney to the newspaper, particularly in light of Humphreys' statement to him. However, the means he chose to fulfill that duty were not proper, nor did he release the communication to a party having a corresponding interest or duty in the matter; and it cannot be said that his action was within the scope of his professional acts as an attorney in a pending case. . . . Other steps . . . were open to appellee. He could have requested the transfer of Humphreys to the jail of another jurisdiction for safekeeping until trial. He could have sought to have the objectionable matter, contained in the proposed article, kept out of publication. Even if this attempt were unsuccessful, other tactics were possible to the attorney who eventually defended the case, e.g., a request for change of venue, *voir dire* examination of prospective jurors in regard to the article, and preservation of the question of the prejudicial effect of the article, for appellate review.

The solicitude of appellee for his client is understandable, and the initial act of the State's Attorney in releasing his statement to the press must be disapproved. Nevertheless, as we have stated, appellee's legal duty in no way justified the publication of his defamatory reply statement. To hold otherwise would open the door to the universally condemned "trial by press," a procedure forbidden to counsel and subversive of the fair and orderly conduct of judicial proceedings. . . .

We hold that as a matter of law appellee had neither an absolute nor a qualified privilege in regard to the defamatory statement. Since the words spoken were slanderous *per se* they required no proof of special damage and carried the implication of malice. However, even though appellee was not reasonably entitled to believe in the existence of privilege, since none existed at law under the circumstances of this case, the trier of facts, on retrial, may consider his testimony, if reoffered, that he acted in good faith and without actual malice, on the question of mitigation of damages. . . .

For the reasons stated, the granting of a directed verdict for appellee was erroneous and the case should have been submitted to the jury.

Judgment reversed and case remanded for a new trial; the costs of this appeal to be paid by appellee.

BROWN & WILLIAMSON TOBACCO CORP. V. JACOBSON
713 F.2D 262 (7TH CIR. 1983)

POSNER, Circuit Judge.
. . . In 1975, Ted Bates, the advertising agency that had the Viceroy account, hired the Kennan market-research firm to help develop a new advertising strategy for Viceroy. Kennan submitted

a report which stated that for "the young smoker," "a cigarette, and the whole smoking process, is part of the illicit pleasure category. . . . In the young smoker's mind a cigarette falls into the same category with wine, beer, shaving, wearing a bra (or purposely not wearing one), declaration of independence and striving for self-identity. For the young starter, a cigarette is associated with introduction to sex life, with courtship, with smoking 'pot' and keeping late studying hours. . . ." The report recommended, therefore, the following pitches to "young smokers, starters": "Present the cigarette as part of the illicit pleasure category of products and activities. . . . To the best of your ability, (considering some legal constraints), relate the cigarette to 'pot', wine, beer, sex, etc. *Don't* communicate health or health-related points." Ted Bates forwarded the report to Brown & Williamson. According to the allegations of the complaint, which on this appeal we must accept as true, Brown & Williamson rejected the "illicit pleasure strategy" proposed in the report, and fired Ted Bates primarily because of displeasure with the proposed strategy.

Years later the Federal Trade Commission conducted an investigation of cigarette advertising, and in May 1981 it published a report of its staff on the investigation. The FTC staff report discusses the Kennan report, correctly dates it to May 1975, and after quoting from it the passages we have quoted states that "B&W adopted many of the ideas contained in this report in the development of a Viceroy advertising campaign." In support of this assertion the staff report quotes an internal Brown & Williamson document on "Viceroy Strategy," dated 1976, which states, "The marketing efforts must cope with consumers' attitudes about smoking and health, either providing them a *rationale* for smoking a full flavor VICEROY or providing a means of *repressing* their concerns about smoking a full flavor VICEROY." The staff report then quotes a description of three advertising strategies. Although the description contains no reference to young smokers or to "starters," the staff report states: "B&W documents also show that it translated the advice [presumably from the Kennan report] on how to attract young 'starters' into an advertising campaign featuring young adults in situations that the vast majority of young people probably would experience and in situations demonstrating adherence to a 'free and easy, hedonistic lifestyle.'" The interior quotation is from another 1976 Brown & Williamson document on advertising strategy.

On November 4, 1981, a reporter for WBBM-TV called Brown & Williamson headquarters and was put in touch with a Mr. Humber in the corporate affairs department. The reporter told Mr. Humber that he was preparing a story on the tobacco industry for Walter Jacobson's "Perspective" program and asked him about the part of the FTC staff report that dealt with the Viceroy advertising strategy. Humber replied that Brown & Williamson had rejected the proposals in the Kennan report and had fired Ted Bates in part because of dissatisfaction with those proposals.

Walter Jacobson's "Perspective" on the tobacco industry was broadcast on November 11 and rebroadcast on November 12 and again on March 5, 1982. In the broadcast, Jacobson, after stating that "pushing cigarettes on television is prohibited," announces his theme: "Television is off limits to cigarettes and so the business, the killer business, has gone to the ad business in New York for help, to the slicksters on Madison Avenue with a billion dollars a year for bigger and better ways to sell cigarettes. Go for the youth of America, go get 'em guys. . . . Hook 'em while they are young, make 'em start now – just think how many cigarettes they'll be smoking when they grow up." Various examples of how cigarette marketing attempts "to addict the children to poison" are given. The last and longest concerns Viceroy.

> The cigarette business insists, in fact, it will swear up and down in public, it is not selling cigarettes to children, that if children are smoking, which they are, more than ever before, it's not the fault of the cigarette business. "Who knows whose fault it is?" says the cigarette business. That's what Viceroy is saying, "Who knows whose fault it is that children are smoking? It's not ours."
>
> Well, there is a confidential report on cigarette advertising in the files of the Federal Government right now, a Viceroy advertising, the Viceroy strategy for attracting young people, starters they are called, to smoking – "FOR THE YOUNG SMOKER . . . . A CIGARETTE FALLS INTO THE SAME CATEGORY WITH WINE, BEER, SHAVING OR WEARING A BRA. . . ." says the Viceroy strategy – "A DECLARATION OF INDEPENDENCE AND STRIVING FOR SELF-IDENTITY." Therefore, an attempt should be made, says Viceroy, to ". . . PRESENT THE CIGARETTE AS AN INITIATION INTO THE ADULT WORLD," to ". . . PRESENT THE CIGARETTE AS AN ILLICIT PLEASURE . . . A BASIC SYMBOL OF THE GROWING-UP, MATURING PROCESS." An attempt should be made, says the Viceroy slicksters, "TO RELATE THE CIGARETTE TO 'POT', WINE, BEER, SEX. DO NOT COMMUNICATE HEALTH OR HEALTH-RELATED POINTS." That's the strategy of the cigarette slicksters, the cigarette business which is insisting in public, "We are not selling cigarettes to children."
>
> They're not slicksters, they're liars.

While Jacobson is speaking these lines the television screen is showing Viceroy ads published in print media in 1980. Each ad shows two packs of Viceroys alongside a golf club and ball.

The complaint charges that the broadcast made statements about Brown & Williamson that the defendants knew to be false and that not only were libelous per se and injurious to Brown & Williamson but also wrongfully interfered with Brown & Williamson's business relations . . . .

Under traditional principles, a finding of libel per se ("per se" in defamation law meaning just that pecuniary damage – "special damage" – need not be proved) requires only that the defamatory character of the statement alleged to be libelous be apparent on the face of the statement, or in other words that "extrinsic facts" not be necessary to make the statement defamatory. (If the statement was that Mrs. Jones had given birth on January 11, 1939, the extrinsic fact necessary to complete the libel might be that Mrs. Jones had married the child's father the previous month.) The defendants admitted at oral argument that the fact that Walter Jacobson's broadcast did not mention Brown & Williamson by name was not an extrinsic fact in this sense. . . . The reason for distinguishing between statements that are and statements that are not libelous on their face is that the impact of an apparently innocuous statement will be limited to the presumably small group of readers who know additional facts, so damage cannot be presumed but must be proved. The Jacobson broadcast was not innocuous on its face, and the fact that Brown & Williamson was not mentioned by name is relevant not to whether the broadcast was libel per se but to the distinct question whether it would be understood as referring to Brown & Williamson rather than to someone else. The defendants do not deny it would be.

So the broadcast is libel per se in the traditional sense – unless the aspersions that it casts on Brown & Williamson's corporate character cannot be considered defamatory at all, which is hardly tenable. . . . Slander per se unlike libel per se depends on the character as well as completeness of the defamatory statement. Under traditional principles, an utterance is slander per se only if it imputes to the plaintiff (1) crime, (2) unchastity (if the plaintiff is female), (3) a loathsome disease, or (4) anything likely to discredit the plaintiff in his trade or business. . . .

Jacobson's broadcast fits the fourth category. The defendants argue that since a cigarette company cannot survive in the long run if young people do not take up smoking, the broadcast will be understood in the business community as complimenting Brown & Williamson for its aggressive efforts to hook the young on smoking. But we doubt that a cigarette company could survive in the short run and thus be around to enjoy the long run if it flouted the strong public policy against encouraging children to smoke . . . .

Obviously it would have been grossly defamatory for Walter Jacobson to have accused Brown & Williamson of poisoning children; yet that is what he did in effect – indeed in those words, though used figuratively rather than literally. It is irrelevant that some unreconstructed businessmen might approve of what Walter Jacobson accused Brown & Williamson of doing. . . .

Under contemporary as under traditional Illinois law, Jacobson's broadcast is libelous per se. Accusing a cigarette company of what many people consider the immoral strategy of enticing children to smoke – enticing them by advertising that employs themes exploitive of adolescent vulnerability – is likely to harm the company. It may make it harder for the company to fend off hostile government regulation and may invite rejection of the company's product by angry parents who smoke but may not want their children to do so. These harms cannot easily be measured, but so long as some harm is highly likely the difficulty of measurement is an additional reason, under the modern functional approach of the Illinois courts, for finding libel per se rather than insisting on proof of special damage. . . . The libel in the present case falls in one of the new as well as old per se categories – it prejudices the plaintiff in its trade – and it also has the required gravity.

. . . The defendants also argue and the district court also found that the libel was privileged as a fair and accurate summary of the Federal Trade Commission staff's report on cigarette advertising. The parties agree as they must that Illinois recognizes a privilege for fair and accurate summaries of, or reports on, government proceedings and investigations. . . . They agree that the privilege extends to a public FTC staff report on an investigation. But they disagree over whether Jacobson's summary of the FTC staff report was "fair," that is, whether the overall impression created by the summary was no more defamatory than that created by the original. *See* Restatement (Second) of Torts § 611, Comment f (1977). . . .

Although the FTC report (and the Kennan report from which it quotes) refers to the targets of the Viceroy advertising campaign as "young smokers" and "starters," not as children, the broadcast implies that the campaign is aimed at children; for after quoting from the Kennan report as quoted by the FTC staff, Jacobson comments: "That's the strategy of the cigarette slicksters, the cigarette business which is insisting in public, 'We are not selling cigarettes to children.' They're not slicksters, they're liars." Also, although the quotations in the broadcast are from the Kennan report rather than from any document written inside Brown & Williamson, and this is clearly indicated in the FTC staff report, the broadcast implies that they are quotations from Brown & Williamson. For example, Jacobson states that "an attempt should be made, says Viceroy" – and there follow quotations from the Kennan report without identification of the true source. This is misleading. True, the FTC staff report does state that Brown & Williamson "adopted many of the ideas in" the Kennan report, and does not say which these were. But its quotations from Brown & Williamson's "Viceroy Strategy" paper imply that they were the ideas of repressing any concerns about the health hazards of smoking and of attracting young smokers by an advertising campaign associating smoking with a "free and easy, hedonistic lifestyle"; there is no suggestion that Brown & Williamson adopted Kennan's specific proposal, quoted by Jacobson, "to relate the cigarette to 'pot', wine, beer, sex," or to "wearing a bra." Jacobson also deleted the qualification, "considering some legal constraints," and omitted mention of the fact that the Kennan report had been written six years before and that the advertising campaign which the FTC staff thought based in part on that report had been conducted five years before. The omission was misleading because the juxtaposition of the audio portion of the broadcast with current Viceroy advertising implied that Viceroy was continuing to employ the disreputable methods recommended by the Kennan report (though the connection between golf and a strategy of enticing children is obscure).

The fact that there are discrepancies between a libel and the government report on which it is based need not defeat the privilege of fair summary. Unless the report is published verbatim it is bound to convey a somewhat different impression from the original, no matter how carefully the publisher attempts to summarize or paraphrase or excerpt it fairly and accurately. An unfair summary in the present context is one that amplifies the libelous effect that publication of the government report verbatim would have on a reader who read it carefully – that carries a "greater sting," . . . . The FTC staff report conveys the following message: six years ago a market-research firm submitted to Brown & Williamson a set of rather lurid proposals for enticing young people to smoke cigarettes and Brown & Williamson adopted many of its ideas (though not necessarily the specific proposals quoted in the report) in an advertising campaign aimed at young smokers which it conducted the following year. The Jacobson broadcast conveys the following message: Brown & Williamson currently is advertising cigarettes in a manner designed to entice children to smoke by associating smoking with drinking, sex, marijuana, and other illicit pleasures of youth. So at least a rational jury might interpret the source and the summary, and if it did it would be entitled to conclude that the summary carried a greater sting and was therefore unfair.

Brown & Williamson argues that even if the Jacobson broadcast fairly summarized the FTC staff report the defendants forfeited the privilege of fair summary because they knew that the staff report was false in a crucial particular – the assertion that Brown & Williamson had adopted many of the ideas in the Kennan report. The defendants reply that the mere fact that Brown & Williamson told their reporter that the assertion was false does not either make it false or mean they knew it was false. This is correct but we must assume for purposes of this appeal that Brown & Williamson can prove that the defendants knew the assertion to be false. The question is whether this would save the defamation count if the jury found that the broadcast was a fair summary after all.

. . . The truth is that Illinois law is in disarray on the question whether actual malice defeats the privilege of fair summary. This is not surprising; it is a difficult question. . . .

Suppose instead that a newspaper merely publishes without comment the daily transcript of a sensational criminal trial. The transcript includes scurrilous accusations against the defendant which the newspaper's staff believes to be false and which are in fact false, as shown by the fact that not only is the defendant acquitted but the prosecutor later apologizes for having prosecuted an innocent man. It is unclear that the privilege of republishing government documents (which a trial transcript is, in effect) in fair and accurate fashion would be forfeited in such a case. The trial would be newsworthy and the newspaper could reasonably believe that its readers ought to be allowed to form their own conclusions regarding the truth of the accusations. . . . But we need not decide on this appeal whether or when the privilege to republish government reports is forfeited by proof of actual malice. The issue will become moot if the jury finds that the Jacobson broadcast was not a fair summary of the FTC staff report, as well it may. . . .

The judgment dismissing Count I of the complaint (defamation) is reversed and the case is remanded for further proceedings consistent with this opinion. . . .

NOTES

1   *Legislative privilege.* Absolute privilege protects legislators for statements made during legislative discussions.
2   *Executive privilege.* Absolute privilege also extends to representatives of the executive branch of government.

C. CONSTITUTIONAL LIMITATIONS

PROVERBS 22:1

A GOOD name is rather to be chosen than great riches, and loving favour rather than silver and gold.

DISCUSSION QUESTIONS

1   "Sticks and stones." Why should our tort system protect reputational interests? What limits, if any, should there be on that protection? Is there any value to permitting some defamation to go uncompensated?
2   Is our society too quick to protect reputation or too willing to countenance the savaging of reputation?

The United States was not always as solicitous of defamatory falsehood as it is today. From the founding of the United States until 1964, the universal rule throughout the country was that defamation was not constitutionally protected. Accordingly, the tort law of some states allowed plaintiffs to be quite aggressive in protecting their reputations against false and defamatory statements. But the Supreme Court of the United States changed all that beginning in 1964.

1. PUBLIC OFFICIALS

NEW YORK TIMES CO. V. SULLIVAN
376 U.S. 254 (1964)

Justice BRENNAN delivered the opinion of the Court.

We are required in this case to determine for the first time the extent to which the constitutional protections for speech and press limit a State's power to award damages in a libel action brought by a public official against critics of his official conduct.

Respondent L. B. Sullivan is one of the three elected Commissioners of the City of Montgomery, Alabama. . . . He brought this civil libel action against . . . petitioner the New York Times Company . . . . [An Alabama jury] awarded him damages of $500,000, the full amount claimed, against all the petitioners, and the Supreme Court of Alabama affirmed. . . .

Respondent's complaint alleged that he had been libeled by statements in a full-page advertisement . . . in the New York Times . . . . Entitled "Heed Their Rising Voices," the advertisement began by stating that "As the whole world knows by now, thousands of Southern Negro students are engaged in widespread non-violent demonstrations in positive affirmation of the right to live in human dignity as guaranteed by the U.S. Constitution and the Bill of Rights." It went on to charge that "in their efforts to uphold these guarantees, they are being met by an unprecedented wave of terror by those who would deny and negate that document which the whole world looks upon as setting the pattern for modern freedom. . . ." Succeeding paragraphs purported to illustrate the "wave of terror" by describing certain alleged events. . . .

Of the 10 paragraphs of text in the advertisement, the third and a portion of the sixth were the basis of respondent's claim of libel. They read as follows:

Third paragraph:

In Montgomery, Alabama, after students sang "My Country, 'Tis of Thee" on the State Capitol steps, their leaders were expelled from school, and truckloads of police armed with shotguns and tear-gas ringed the Alabama State College Campus. When the entire student body protested to state authorities by refusing to re-register, their dining hall was padlocked in an attempt to starve them into submission.

Sixth paragraph:

Again and again the Southern violators have answered Dr. King's peaceful protests with intimidation and violence. They have bombed his home almost killing his wife and child. They have assaulted his person. They have arrested him seven times – for "speeding," "loitering" and similar "offenses." And now they have charged him with "perjury" – a *felony* under which they could imprison him for *ten years*. . . .

Although neither of these statements mentions respondent by name, he contended that the word "police" in the third paragraph referred to him as the Montgomery Commissioner who supervised the Police Department, so that he was being accused of "ringing" the campus with police. He further claimed that the paragraph would be read as imputing to the police, and hence to him, the padlocking of the dining hall in order to starve the students into submission. As to the sixth paragraph, he contended that since arrests are ordinarily made by the police, the statement "They have arrested [Dr. King] seven times" would be read as referring to him; [and] that the "They" who did the arresting would be equated with the "They" who committed the other described acts and with the "Southern violators." Thus, he argued, the paragraph would be read as accusing the Montgomery police, and hence him, of answering Dr. King's protests with "intimidation and violence," bombing his home, assaulting his person, and charging him with perjury. Respondent and six other Montgomery residents testified that they read some or all of the statements as referring to him in his capacity as Commissioner.

It is uncontroverted that some of the statements contained in the two paragraphs were not accurate descriptions of events which occurred in Montgomery. . . . The campus dining hall was not padlocked on any occasion, and the only students who may have been barred from eating there were the few who had neither signed a preregistration application nor requested temporary meal tickets. Although the police were deployed near the campus in large numbers on three occasions, they did not at any time "ring" the campus, and they were not called to the campus in connection with the demonstration on the State Capitol steps, as the third paragraph implied. . . . On the premise that the charges in the sixth paragraph could be read as referring to him, respondent was allowed to prove that he had not participated in the events described. Although Dr. King's home had in fact been bombed twice when his wife and child were there, both of these occasions antedated respondent's tenure as Commissioner, and the police were not only not implicated in the bombings, but had made every effort to apprehend those who were. . . .

Respondent made no effort to prove that he suffered actual pecuniary loss as a result of the alleged libel. One of his witnesses, a former employer, testified that if he had believed the statements, he doubted whether he "would want to be associated with anybody who would be a party to such things that are stated in that ad," and that he would not re-employ respondent if he believed "that he allowed the Police Department to do the things that the paper say he did." But neither this witness nor any of the others testified that he had actually believed the statements in their supposed reference to respondent.

The cost of the advertisement was approximately $4800, and it was published by the Times upon an order from a New York advertising agency acting for the signatory Committee. The agency submitted the advertisement with a letter from A. Philip Randolph, Chairman of the

Committee, certifying that the persons whose names appeared on the advertisement had given their permission. Mr. Randolph was known to the Times' Advertising Acceptability Department as a responsible person, and in accepting the letter as sufficient proof of authorization it followed its established practice. There was testimony that the copy of the advertisement which accompanied the letter listed only the 64 names appearing under the text, and that the statement, "We in the south . . . warmly endorse this appeal," and the list of names thereunder, which included those of the individual petitioners, were subsequently added when the first proof of the advertisement was received. Each of the individual petitioners testified that he had not authorized the use of his name, and that he had been unaware of its use until receipt of respondent's demand for a retraction. The manager of the Advertising Acceptability Department testified that he had approved the advertisement . . . because he knew nothing to cause him to believe that anything in it was false, and because it bore the endorsement of "a number of people who are well known and whose reputation" he "had no reason to question." Neither he nor anyone else at the Times made an effort to confirm the accuracy of the advertisement, either by checking it against recent Times news stories relating to some of the described events or by any other means. . . .

The trial judge submitted the case to the jury under instructions that the statements in the advertisement were "libelous per se" and were not privileged, so that petitioners might be held liable if the jury found that they had published the advertisement and that the statements were made "of and concerning" respondent. The jury was instructed that, because the statements were libelous per se, "the law . . . implies legal injury from the bare fact of publication itself," "falsity and malice are presumed," "general damages need not be alleged or proved but are presumed," and "punitive damages may be awarded by the jury even though the amount of actual damages is neither found nor shown." . . . Once "libel per se" has been established, the defendant has no defense as to stated facts unless he can persuade the jury that they were true in all their particulars. . . . Unless he can discharge the burden of proving truth, general damages are presumed, and may be awarded without proof of pecuniary injury. . . .

The question before us is whether this rule of liability, as applied to an action brought by a public official against critics of his official conduct, abridges the freedom of speech and of the press that is guaranteed by the First and Fourteenth Amendments.

Respondent relies heavily . . . on statements of this Court to the effect that the Constitution does not protect libelous publications. Those statements do not foreclose our inquiry here. None of the cases sustained the use of libel laws to impose sanctions upon expression critical of the official conduct of public officials. . . .

The general proposition that freedom of expression upon public questions is secured by the First Amendment has long been settled by our decisions. . . . Thus we consider this case against the background of a profound national commitment to the principle that debate on public issues should be uninhibited, robust, and wide-open, and that it may well include vehement, caustic, and sometimes unpleasantly sharp attacks on government and public officials. The present advertisement, as an expression of grievance and protest on one of the major public issues of our time, would seem clearly to qualify for the constitutional protection. The question is whether it forfeits that protection by the falsity of some of its factual statements and by its alleged defamation of respondent.

Authoritative interpretations of the First Amendment guarantees have consistently refused to recognize an exception for any test of truth – whether administered by judges, juries, or administrative officials – and especially one that puts the burden of proving truth on the speaker. . . . As Madison said, "Some degree of abuse is inseparable from the proper use of everything; and in no instance is this more true than in that of the press." 4 *Elliot's Debates on the Federal Constitution* (1876), p. 571. In *Cantwell* v. *Connecticut*, 310 U.S. 296, 310, the Court declared:

> In the realm of religious faith, and in that of political belief, sharp differences arise. In both fields the tenets of one man may seem the rankest error to his neighbor. To persuade others to his own point of view, the pleader, as we know, at times, resorts to exaggeration, to vilification of men who have been, or are, prominent in church or state, and even to false statement. But the people of this nation have ordained in the light of history, that, in spite of the probability of excesses and abuses, these liberties are, in the long view, essential to enlightened opinion and right conduct on the part of the citizens of a democracy.

[E]rroneous statement is inevitable in free debate, and . . . it must be protected if the freedoms of expression are to have the "breathing space" that they "need . . . to survive," *N.A.A.C.P.* v. *Button*, 371 U.S. 415, 433 . . . .

If neither factual error nor defamatory content suffices to remove the constitutional shield from criticism of official conduct, the combination of the two elements is no less inadequate. This is the lesson to be drawn from the great controversy over the Sedition Act of 1798, which first crystallized a national awareness of the central meaning of the First Amendment. That statute made it a crime, punishable by a $5,000 fine and five years in prison, "if any person shall write, print, utter or publish . . . any false, scandalous and malicious writing or writings against the government of the United States, or either house of the Congress . . . , or the President . . . , with intent to defame . . . or to bring them, or either of them, into contempt or disrepute; or to excite against them, or either or any of them, the hatred of the good people of the United States." The Act allowed the defendant the defense of truth, and provided that the jury were to be judges both of the law and the facts. Despite these qualifications, the Act was vigorously condemned as unconstitutional in an attack joined in by Jefferson and Madison. . . .

Although the Sedition Act was never tested in this Court, the attack upon its validity has carried the day in the court of history. Fines levied in its prosecution were repaid by Act of Congress on the ground that it was unconstitutional. . . . Jefferson, as President, pardoned those who had been convicted and sentenced under the Act and remitted their fines . . . . The invalidity of the Act has also been assumed by Justices of this Court. These views reflect a broad consensus that the Act, because of the restraint it imposed upon criticism of government and public officials, was inconsistent with the First Amendment. . . .

What a State may not constitutionally bring about by means of a criminal statute is likewise beyond the reach of its civil law of libel. The fear of damage awards under a rule such as that invoked by the Alabama courts here may be markedly more inhibiting than the fear of prosecution under a criminal statute. . . . The state rule of law is not saved by its allowance of the defense of truth. . . . A rule compelling the critic of official conduct to guarantee the truth of all his factual assertions – and to do so on pain of libel judgments virtually unlimited in amount – leads to . . . "self-censorship." Allowance of the defense of truth, with the burden of proving it on the defendant, does not mean that only false speech will be deterred.[19] Even courts accepting this defense as an adequate safeguard have recognized the difficulties of adducing legal proofs that the alleged libel was true in all its factual particulars. Under such a rule, would-be critics of official conduct may be deterred from voicing their criticism, even though it is believed to be true and even though it is in fact true, because of doubt whether it can be proved in court or fear of the expense of having to do so. . . . The rule thus dampens the vigor and limits the variety of public debate. It is inconsistent with the First and Fourteenth Amendments.

The constitutional guarantees require, we think, a federal rule that prohibits a public official from recovering damages for a defamatory falsehood relating to his official conduct unless he proves that the statement was made with "actual malice" – that is, with knowledge that it was false or with reckless disregard of whether it was false or not. . . .

We hold today that the Constitution delimits a State's power to award damages for libel in actions brought by public officials against critics of their official conduct. Since this is such an action, the rule requiring proof of actual malice is applicable. While Alabama law apparently requires proof of actual malice for an award of punitive damages, where general damages are concerned malice is "presumed." Such a presumption is inconsistent with the federal rule. . . . Since the trial judge did not instruct the jury to differentiate between general and punitive damages, it may be that the verdict was wholly an award of one or the other. But it is impossible to know, in view of the general verdict returned. Because of this uncertainty, the judgment must be reversed and the case remanded.

Since respondent may seek a new trial, we deem that considerations of effective judicial administration require us to review the evidence in the present record to determine whether it could constitutionally support a judgment for respondent. This Court's duty is not limited to the elaboration of constitutional principles; we must also in proper cases review the evidence to make certain that those principles have been constitutionally applied. . . . [W]e consider that the proof presented to show actual malice lacks the convincing clarity which the constitutional standard demands, and hence that it would not constitutionally sustain the judgment for respondent under the proper rule of law. . . .

Finally, there is evidence that the Times published the advertisement without checking its accuracy against the news stories in the Times' own files. The mere presence of the stories in the files does not, of course, establish that the Times "knew" the advertisement was false, since the state of mind required for actual malice would have to be brought home to the persons in the Times' organization having responsibility for the publication of the advertisement. With respect to the failure of those persons to make the check, the record shows that they relied

---

19 Even a false statement may be deemed to make a valuable contribution to public debate, since it brings about "the clearer perception and livelier impression of truth, produced by its collision with error." Mill, On Liberty . . . .

upon their knowledge of the good reputation of many of those whose names were listed as sponsors of the advertisement, and upon the letter from A. Philip Randolph, known to them as a responsible individual, certifying that the use of the names was authorized. . . . We think the evidence against the Times supports at most a finding of negligence in failing to discover the misstatements, and is constitutionally insufficient to show the recklessness that is required for a finding of actual malice. . . .

Justice BLACK, with whom Justice DOUGLAS joins, concurring.

. . . I base my vote to reverse on the belief that the First and Fourteenth Amendments not merely "delimit" a State's power to award damages to "public officials against critics of their official conduct" but completely prohibit a State from exercising such a power. . . . Unlike the Court, therefore, I vote to reverse exclusively on the ground that the Times and the individual defendants had an absolute, unconditional constitutional right to publish in the Times advertisement their criticisms of the Montgomery agencies and officials. . . .

In my opinion the Federal Constitution has dealt with this deadly danger to the press in the only way possible without leaving the free press open to destruction – by granting the press an absolute immunity for criticism of the way public officials do their public duty. . . . We would, I think, more faithfully interpret the First Amendment by holding that at the very least it leaves the people and the press free to criticize officials and discuss public affairs with impunity. . . To punish the exercise of this right to discuss public affairs or to penalize it through libel judgments is to abridge or shut off discussion of the very kind most needed. This Nation, I suspect, can live in peace without libel suits based on public discussions of public affairs and public officials. But I doubt that a country can live in freedom where its people can be made to suffer physically or financially for criticizing their government, its actions, or its officials. "For a representative democracy ceases to exist the moment that the public functionaries are by any means absolved from their responsibility to their constituents; and this happens whenever the constituent can be restrained in any manner from speaking, writing, or publishing his opinions upon any public measure, or upon the conduct of those who may advise or execute it."[5] An unconditional right to say what one pleases about public affairs is what I consider to be the minimum guarantee of the First Amendment. . . .

Justice GOLDBERG, with whom Justice DOUGLAS joins, concurring in the result.

The Court today announces a constitutional standard which prohibits "a public official from recovering damages for a defamatory falsehood relating to his official conduct unless he proves that the statement was made with 'actual malice' – that is, with knowledge that it was false or with reckless disregard of whether it was false or not." . . . The Court thus rules that the Constitution gives citizens and newspapers a "conditional privilege" immunizing nonmalicious misstatements of fact regarding the official conduct of a government officer. . . .

---

5   1 Tucker, Blackstone's Commentaries (1803), 297 (editor's appendix); cf. Brant, Seditious Libel: Myth and Reality, 39 N. Y. U. L. Rev. 1.

In my view, the First and Fourteenth Amendments to the Constitution afford to the citizen and to the press an absolute, unconditional privilege to criticize official conduct despite the harm which may flow from excesses and abuses. . . . It necessarily follows that in a case such as this, where all agree that the allegedly defamatory statements related to official conduct, the judgments for libel cannot constitutionally be sustained.

QUESTIONS

1   *Public Officials.* The holding in *New York Times v. Sullivan* covers only those statements about public officials relating to official conduct, but who is a public official? Are all government employees public officials? If not, why should the Montgomery City Commissioner be considered a public official? Would an ordinary police offer be considered a "public official"? If not, what is the difference?

2   Is the constitutional privilege announced here qualified or absolute?

3   *Actual malice.* This holding does not protect statements that are knowingly false or made with "reckless disregard." Was there any evidence here of reckless disregard for truth? If the facts of this case are insufficient to satisfy the "actual malice" standard, can you imagine any case when a public official would be able to vindicate her reputation against published defamatory falsehoods?

2. PUBLIC FIGURES

CURTIS PUBLISHING CO. V. BUTTS
388 U.S. 130 (1967)

JUSTICE HARLAN announced the judgments of the Court and delivered an opinion in which JUSTICE CLARK, JUSTICE STEWART, and JUSTICE FORTAS join. . . .

. . . We brought these two cases here . . . to consider the impact of [*New York Times v. Sullivan*] on libel actions instituted by persons who are not public officials, but who are "public figures" and involved in issues in which the public has a justified and important interest. . . .

I.

No. 37, *Curtis Publishing Co. v. Butts*, stems from an article . . . which accused respondent of conspiring to "fix" a football game between the University of Georgia and the University of Alabama . . . . At the time of the article, Butts was the athletic director of the University of Georgia and had overall responsibility for the administration of its athletic program. . . . Butts had previously served as head football coach of the University and was a well-known and respected figure in coaching ranks. He had maintained an interest in coaching and was negotiating for a position with a professional team at the time of publication.

The article was entitled "The Story of a College Football Fix" and prefaced by a note from the editors stating: "Not since the Chicago White Sox threw the 1919 World Series has there been a sports story as shocking as this one. . . . Before the University of Georgia played the University of Alabama . . . Wally Butts . . . gave [to its coach] . . . ." The text revealed that one George Burnett, an Atlanta insurance salesman, had accidentally overheard, because of electronic error, a telephone conversation between Butts and the head coach of the University of Alabama, Paul Bryant, which took place approximately one week prior to the game. . . .

The evidence showed that Burnett had indeed overheard a conversation between Butts and the Alabama coach, but the content of that conversation was hotly disputed. It was Butts' contention that the conversation had been general football talk and that nothing Burnett had overheard would have been of any particular value to an opposing coach. . . . The evidence on the preparation of the article, on which we shall focus in more detail later, cast serious doubt on the adequacy of the investigation underlying the article. It was Butts' contention that the magazine had departed greatly from the standards of good investigation and reporting and that this was especially reprehensible, amounting to reckless and wanton conduct, in light of the devastating nature of the article's assertions. . . .

The jury returned a verdict for $60,000 in general damages and for $3,000,000 in punitive damages. The trial court reduced the total to $460,000 by remittitur. . . . For reasons given below, we would affirm.

II.

No. 150, *Associated Press* v. *Walker*, arose out of the distribution of a news dispatch giving an eyewitness account of events on the campus of the University of Mississippi on the night of September 30, 1962, when a massive riot erupted because of federal efforts to enforce a court decree ordering the enrollment of a Negro, James Meredith, as a student in the University. The dispatch stated that respondent Walker, who was present on the campus, had taken command of the violent crowd and had personally led a charge against federal marshals sent there to effectuate the court's decree and to assist in preserving order. It also described Walker as encouraging rioters to use violence and giving them technical advice on combating the effects of tear gas.

Walker was a private citizen at the time of the riot and publication. He had pursued a long and honorable career in the United States Army before resigning to engage in political activity, and had, in fact, been in command of the federal troops during the school segregation confrontation at Little Rock, Arkansas, in 1957. He was acutely interested in the issue of physical federal intervention, and had made a number of strong statements against such action which had received wide publicity. Walker had his own following, the "Friends of Walker," and could fairly be deemed a man of some political prominence.

Walker initiated this libel action in the state courts of Texas, seeking a total of $2,000,000 in compensatory and punitive damages. . . .

A verdict of $500,000 compensatory damages and $300,000 punitive damages was returned. The trial judge, however, found that there was "no evidence to support the jury's answers that there was actual malice" and refused to enter the punitive award. . . . For reasons given below, we would reverse. . . .

IV.

. . . We note that the public interest in the circulation of the materials here involved, and the publisher's interest in circulating them, is not less than that involved in *New York Times*. And both Butts and Walker commanded a substantial amount of independent public interest at the time of the publications; both, in our opinion, would have been labeled "public figures" under ordinary tort rules. Butts may have attained that status by position alone and Walker by his purposeful activity amounting to a thrusting of his personality into the "vortex" of an important public controversy, but both commanded sufficient continuing public interest and had sufficient access to the means of counterargument to be able "to expose through discussion the falsehood and fallacies" of the defamatory statements. *Whitney* v. *California*, 274 U.S. 357, 377 (Brandeis, J., dissenting).

These similarities and differences between libel actions involving persons who are public officials and libel actions involving those circumstanced as were Butts and Walker . . . lead us to the conclusion that libel actions of the present kind cannot be left entirely to state libel laws, unlimited by any overriding constitutional safeguard, but that the rigorous federal requirements of *New York Times* are not the only appropriate accommodation of the conflicting interests at stake. We consider and would hold that a "public figure" who is not a public official may also recover damages for a defamatory falsehood whose substance makes substantial danger to reputation apparent, on a showing of highly unreasonable conduct constituting an extreme departure from the standards of investigation and reporting ordinarily adhered to by responsible publishers. . . .

CHIEF JUSTICE WARREN, concurring in the result.

. . . To me, differentiation between "public figures" and "public officials" and adoption of separate standards of proof for each have no basis in law, logic, or First Amendment policy. . . . Our citizenry has a legitimate and substantial interest in the conduct of such persons, and freedom of the press to engage in uninhibited debate about their involvement in public issues and events is as crucial as it is in the case of "public officials." The fact that they are not amenable to the restraints of the political process only underscores the legitimate and substantial nature of the interest, since it means that public opinion may be the only instrument by which society can attempt to influence their conduct.

I therefore adhere to the *New York Times* standard in the case of "public figures" as well as "public officials." . . .

3. ACTUAL MALICE

ST. AMANT V. THOMPSON
390 U.S. 727 (1968)

... [P]etitioner St. Amant, a candidate for public office, made a televised speech in Baton Rouge, Louisiana. In the course of this speech, St. Amant read a series of questions which he had put to J. D. Albin, a member of a Teamsters Union local, and Albin's answers to those questions. The exchange concerned the allegedly nefarious activities of E. G. Partin, the president of the local, and the alleged relationship between Partin and St. Amant's political opponent. One of Albin's answers concerned his efforts to prevent Partin from secreting union records; in this answer Albin referred to Herman A. Thompson, an East Baton Rouge Parish deputy sheriff and respondent here:

> Now, we knew that this safe was gonna be moved that night, but imagine our predicament, knowing of Ed's connections with the Sheriff's office through Herman Thompson, who made recent visits to the Hall to see Ed. We also knew of money that had passed hands between Ed and Herman Thompson .... We also knew of his connections with State Trooper Lieutenant Joe Green. We knew we couldn't get any help from there and we didn't know how far that he was involved in the Sheriff's office or the State Police office through that, and it was out of the jurisdiction of the City Police.

Thompson promptly brought suit for defamation, claiming that the publication had "impute[d] gross misconduct" and "infer[red] conduct of the most nefarious nature." . . . The trial judge ruled in Thompson's favor and awarded $5,000 in damages. . . .

Purporting to apply the *New York Times* malice standard, the Louisiana Supreme Court ruled that St. Amant had broadcast false information about Thompson recklessly, though not knowingly. Several reasons were given for this conclusion. St. Amant had no personal knowledge of Thompson's activities; he relied solely on Albin's affidavit although the record was silent as to Albin's reputation for veracity; he failed to verify the information with those in the union office who might have known the facts; he gave no consideration to whether or not the statements defamed Thompson and went ahead heedless of the consequences; and he mistakenly believed he had no responsibility for the broadcast because he was merely quoting Albin's words.

These considerations fall short of proving St. Amant's reckless disregard for the accuracy of his statements about Thompson. "Reckless disregard," it is true, cannot be fully encompassed in one infallible definition. . . . Our cases, however, have furnished meaningful guidance for the further definition of a reckless publication. . . . [R]eckless conduct is not measured by whether a reasonably prudent man would have published, or would have investigated before publishing. There must be sufficient evidence to permit the conclusion that the defendant in fact entertained serious doubts as to the truth of his publication. Publishing with such doubts shows reckless disregard for truth or falsity and demonstrates actual malice.

It may be said that such a test puts a premium on ignorance, encourages the irresponsible publisher not to inquire, and permits the issue to be determined by the defendant's testimony that he published the statement in good faith and unaware of its probable falsity. Concededly the reckless disregard standard may permit recovery in fewer situations than would a rule that publishers must satisfy the standard of the reasonable man or the prudent publisher. But *New York Times* and succeeding cases have emphasized that the stake of the people in public business and the conduct of public officials is so great that neither the defense of truth nor the standard of ordinary care would protect against self-censorship and thus adequately implement First Amendment policies. Neither lies nor false communications serve the ends of the First Amendment, and no one suggests their desirability or further proliferation. But to insure the ascertainment and publication of the truth about public affairs, it is essential that the First Amendment protect some erroneous publications as well as true ones. We adhere to this view and to the line which our cases have drawn between false communications which are protected and those which are not.

The defendant in a defamation action brought by a public official cannot, however, automatically insure a favorable verdict by testifying that he published with a belief that the statements were true. The finder of fact must determine whether the publication was indeed made in good faith. Professions of good faith will be unlikely to prove persuasive, for example, where a story is fabricated by the defendant, is the product of his imagination, or is based wholly on an unverified anonymous telephone call. Nor will they be likely to prevail when the publisher's allegations are so inherently improbable that only a reckless man would have put them in circulation. Likewise, recklessness may be found where there are obvious reasons to doubt the veracity of the informant or the accuracy of his reports.

By no proper test of reckless disregard was St. Amant's broadcast a reckless publication about a public officer. Nothing referred to by the Louisiana courts indicates an awareness by St. Amant of the probable falsity of Albin's statement about Thompson. Failure to investigate does not in itself establish bad faith. . . . Closer to the mark are considerations of Albin's reliability. However, the most the state court could say was that there was no evidence in the record of Albin's reputation for veracity, and this fact merely underlines the failure of Thompson's evidence to demonstrate a low community assessment of Albin's trustworthiness or unsatisfactory experience with him by St. Amant.

Other facts in this record support our view. St. Amant made his broadcast in June 1962. He had known Albin since October 1961, when he first met with members of the dissident Teamsters faction. St. Amant testified that he had verified other aspects of Albin's information and that he had affidavits from others. Moreover Albin swore to his answers, first in writing and later in the presence of newsmen. According to Albin, he was prepared to substantiate his charges. St. Amant knew that Albin was engaged in an internal struggle in the union; Albin seemed to St. Amant to be placing himself in personal danger by publicly airing the details of the dispute.

Because the state court misunderstood and misapplied the actual malice standard which must be observed in a public official's defamation action, the judgment is reversed and the case remanded for further proceedings not inconsistent with this opinion.

Reversed and remanded.

Mr. Justice BLACK and Mr. Justice DOUGLAS concur in the judgment of the Court for the reasons set out in their concurring opinions in *New York Times Co.* v. *Sullivan*, 376 U.S. 254, 293 (1964) . . . .

Mr. Justice FORTAS, dissenting.

I do not believe that petitioner satisfied the minimal standards of care specified by *New York Times Co.* v. *Sullivan*, 376 U.S. 254 (1964). The affidavit that petitioner broadcast contained a seriously libelous statement directed against respondent. . . . Petitioner's casual, careless, callous use of the libel cannot be rationalized as resulting from the heat of a campaign. Under *New York Times*, this libel was broadcast by petitioner with "actual malice" – with reckless disregard of whether it was false or not. . . .

The First Amendment is not so fragile that it requires us to immunize this kind of reckless, destructive invasion of the life, even of public officials, heedless of their interests and sensitivities. The First Amendment is not a shelter for the character assassinator . . . . The occupation of public officeholder does not forfeit one's membership in the human race. The public official should be subject to severe scrutiny and to free and open criticism. But if he is needlessly, heedlessly, falsely accused of crime, he should have a remedy in law. *New York Times* does not preclude this minimal standard of civilized living.

Petitioner had a duty here to check the reliability of the libelous statement about respondent. If he had made a good-faith check, . . . he should be protected even if the statement were false, because the interest of public officials in their reputation must endure this degree of assault. But since he made no check, . . . *New York Times* does not prohibit recovery.

I would affirm.

NOTE

1 Because of plaintiff's burden to prove "actual malice," the defendant who publishes a defamatory falsehood opens her investigatory and editorial policies to searching discovery and careful scrutiny.

4. PRIVATE PLAINTIFFS

GERTZ V. ROBERT WELCH, INC.
418 U.S. 323 (1974)

Mr. Justice POWELL delivered the opinion of the Court. . . .

In 1968 a Chicago policeman named Nuccio shot and killed a youth named Nelson. The state authorities prosecuted Nuccio for the homicide and ultimately obtained a conviction for murder in the second degree. The Nelson family retained petitioner Elmer Gertz, a reputable attorney, to represent them in civil litigation against Nuccio.

Respondent publishes American Opinion, a monthly outlet for the views of the John Birch Society. Early in the 1960's the magazine began to warn of a nationwide conspiracy to discredit local law enforcement agencies and create in their stead a national police force capable of supporting a Communist dictatorship. . . . [T]o alert the public to this assumed danger, the managing editor of American Opinion commissioned an article on the murder trial of Officer Nuccio. . . . In March 1969 respondent published the resulting article under the title "FRAME-UP: Richard Nuccio And The War On Police." The article purports to demonstrate that the testimony against Nuccio at his criminal trial was false and that his prosecution was part of the Communist campaign against the police.

In his capacity as counsel for the Nelson family in the civil litigation, petitioner attended the coroner's inquest into the boy's death and initiated actions for damages, but neither discussed Officer Nuccio with the press nor played any part in the criminal proceeding. Notwithstanding petitioner's remote connection with the prosecution of Nuccio, respondent's magazine portrayed him as an architect of the "frame-up." According to the article, the police file on petitioner took "a big, Irish cop to lift." The article stated that petitioner had been an official of the "Marxist League for Industrial Democracy, originally known as the Intercollegiate Socialist Society, which has advocated the violent seizure of our government." It labeled Gertz a "Leninist" and a "Communist-fronter." It also stated that Gertz had been an officer of the National Lawyers Guild, described as a Communist organization that "probably did more than any other outfit to plan the Communist attack on the Chicago police during the 1968 Democratic Convention."

These statements contained serious inaccuracies. The implication that petitioner had a criminal record was false. Petitioner had been a member and officer of the National Lawyers Guild some 15 years earlier, but there was no evidence that he or that organization had taken any part in planning the 1968 demonstrations in Chicago. There was also no basis for the charge that petitioner was a "Leninist" or a "Communist-fronter." And he had never been a member of the "Marxist League for Industrial Democracy" or the "Intercollegiate Socialist Society."

The managing editor of American Opinion made no effort to verify or substantiate the charges against petitioner. Instead, he appended an editorial introduction stating that the author had "conducted extensive research into the Richard Nuccio Case." . . . Respondent placed the issue of American Opinion containing the article on sale at newsstands throughout the country and distributed reprints of the article on the streets of Chicago.

. . . The jury awarded $50,000 to petitioner. . . .

The principal issue in this case is whether a newspaper or broadcaster that publishes defamatory falsehoods about an individual who is neither a public official nor a public figure may claim a constitutional privilege against liability for the injury inflicted by those statements. . . .

We begin with the common ground. Under the First Amendment there is no such thing as a false idea. However pernicious an opinion may seem, we depend for its correction not on the conscience of judges and juries but on the competition of other ideas. But there is no constitutional value in false statements of fact. Neither the intentional lie nor the careless error materially advances society's interest in "uninhibited, robust, and wide-open" debate on public issues. *New York Times Co.* v. *Sullivan*, 376 U.S., at 270. . . .

Although the erroneous statement of fact is not worthy of constitutional protection, it is nevertheless inevitable in free debate. . . . And punishment of error runs the risk of inducing a cautious and restrictive exercise of the constitutionally guaranteed freedoms of speech and press. Our decisions recognize that a rule of strict liability that compels a publisher or broadcaster to guarantee the accuracy of his factual assertions may lead to intolerable self-censorship. Allowing the media to avoid liability only by proving the truth of all injurious statements does not accord adequate protection to First Amendment liberties. . . . The First Amendment requires that we protect some falsehood in order to protect speech that matters.

The need to avoid self-censorship by the news media is, however, not the only societal value at issue. If it were, this Court would have embraced long ago the view that publishers and broadcasters enjoy an unconditional and indefeasible immunity from liability for defamation. Such a rule would, indeed, obviate the fear that the prospect of civil liability for injurious falsehood might dissuade a timorous press from the effective exercise of First Amendment freedoms. Yet absolute protection for the communications media requires a total sacrifice of the competing value served by the law of defamation.

The legitimate state interest underlying the law of libel is the compensation of individuals for the harm inflicted on them by defamatory falsehood. We would not lightly require the State to abandon this purpose . . . . Some tension necessarily exists between the need for a vigorous and uninhibited press and the legitimate interest in redressing wrongful injury. . . .

Theoretically, of course, the balance between the needs of the press and the individual's claim to compensation for wrongful injury might be struck on a case-by-case basis. . . . But this approach would lead to unpredictable results and uncertain expectations, and it could render our duty to supervise the lower courts unmanageable. Because an *ad hoc* resolution of the competing interests at stake in each particular case is not feasible, we must lay down broad rules of general application. Such rules necessarily treat alike various cases involving differences as well as similarities. Thus it is often true that not all of the considerations which justify adoption of a given rule will obtain in each particular case decided under its authority.

With that caveat we have no difficulty in distinguishing among defamation plaintiffs. The first remedy of any victim of defamation is self-help – using available opportunities to contradict the lie or correct the error and thereby to minimize its adverse impact on reputation. Public officials and public figures usually enjoy significantly greater access to the channels of effective communication and hence have a more realistic opportunity to counteract false statements than private individuals normally enjoy. Private individuals are therefore more vulnerable to injury, and the state interest in protecting them is correspondingly greater.

More important . . . , there is a compelling normative consideration underlying the distinction between public and private defamation plaintiffs. An individual who decides to seek governmental office must accept certain necessary consequences of that involvement in public affairs. He runs the risk of closer public scrutiny than might otherwise be the case. And society's interest in the officers of government is not strictly limited to the formal discharge of official duties. . . .

Those classed as public figures stand in a similar position. Hypothetically, it may be possible for someone to become a public figure through no purposeful action of his own, but the instances of truly involuntary public figures must be exceedingly rare. For the most part those who attain this status have assumed roles of special prominence in the affairs of society. Some occupy positions of such persuasive power and influence that they are deemed public figures for all purposes. More commonly, those classed as public figures have thrust themselves to the forefront of particular public controversies in order to influence the resolution of the issues involved. In either event, they invite attention and comment.

Even if the foregoing generalities do not obtain in every instance, the communications media are entitled to act on the assumption that public officials and public figures have voluntarily exposed themselves to increased risk of injury from defamatory falsehood concerning them. No such assumption is justified with respect to a private individual. He has not accepted public office or assumed an "influential role in ordering society." He has relinquished no part of his interest in the protection of his own good name, and consequently he has a more compelling call on the courts for redress of injury inflicted by defamatory falsehood. Thus, private individuals are not only more vulnerable to injury than public officials and public figures; they are also more deserving of recovery.

For these reasons we conclude that the States should retain substantial latitude in their efforts to enforce a legal remedy for defamatory falsehood injurious to the reputation of a private individual. . . .

We hold that, so long as they do not impose liability without fault, the States may define for themselves the appropriate standard of liability for a publisher or broadcaster of defamatory falsehood injurious to a private individual. This approach provides a more equitable boundary between the competing concerns involved here. It recognizes the strength of the legitimate state interest in compensating private individuals for wrongful injury to reputation, yet shields the press and broadcast media from the rigors of strict liability for defamation. . . .

Our accommodation of the competing values at stake in defamation suits by private individuals allows the States to impose liability on the publisher or broadcaster of defamatory falsehood on a less demanding showing than that required by *New York Times*. This conclusion is not based on a belief that the considerations which prompted the adoption of the *New York Times* privilege for defamation of public officials and its extension to public figures are wholly inapplicable to the context of private individuals. Rather, we endorse this approach in recognition of the strong and legitimate state interest in compensating private individuals for injury to reputation. But this countervailing state interest extends no further than compensation for actual injury. For the reasons stated below, we hold that the States may not permit recovery of presumed or punitive damages, at least when liability is not based on a showing of knowledge of falsity or reckless disregard for the truth.

The common law of defamation is an oddity of tort law, for it allows recovery of purportedly compensatory damages without evidence of actual loss. Under the traditional rules pertaining to actions for libel, the existence of injury is presumed from the fact of publication. Juries may award substantial sums as compensation for supposed damage to reputation without any proof that such harm actually occurred. The largely uncontrolled discretion of juries to award damages where there is no loss unnecessarily compounds the potential of any system of liability for defamatory falsehood to inhibit the vigorous exercise of First Amendment freedoms. Additionally, the doctrine of presumed damages invites juries to punish unpopular opinion rather than to compensate individuals for injury sustained by the publication of a false fact. More to the point, the States have no substantial interest in securing for plaintiffs such as this petitioner gratuitous awards of money damages far in excess of any actual injury.

We would not, of course, invalidate state law simply because we doubt its wisdom, but here we are attempting to reconcile state law with a competing interest grounded in the constitutional command of the First Amendment. It is therefore appropriate to require that state remedies for defamatory falsehood reach no farther than is necessary to protect the legitimate interest involved. It is necessary to restrict defamation plaintiffs who do not prove knowledge of falsity or reckless disregard for the truth to compensation for actual injury. We need not define "actual injury," as trial courts have wide experience in framing appropriate jury instructions in tort actions. Suffice it to say that actual injury is not limited to out-of-pocket loss. Indeed, the more customary types of actual harm inflicted by defamatory falsehood include impairment of reputation and standing in the community, personal humiliation, and mental anguish and suffering. Of course, juries must be limited by appropriate instructions, and all awards must be supported by competent evidence concerning the injury, although there need be no evidence which assigns an actual dollar value to the injury.

We also find no justification for allowing awards of punitive damages against publishers and broadcasters held liable under state-defined standards of liability for defamation. In most jurisdictions jury discretion over the amounts awarded is limited only by the gentle rule that they not be excessive. Consequently, juries assess punitive damages in wholly unpredictable amounts bearing no necessary relation to the actual harm caused. And they remain free to use their discretion selectively to punish expressions of unpopular views. Like the doctrine of presumed damages, jury discretion to award punitive damages unnecessarily exacerbates the danger of media self-censorship, but, unlike the former rule, punitive damages are wholly irrelevant to the state interest that justifies a negligence standard for private defamation actions. They are not compensation for injury. Instead, they are private fines levied by civil juries to punish reprehensible conduct and to deter its future occurrence. In short, the private defamation plaintiff who establishes liability under a less demanding standard than that stated by *New York Times* may recover only such damages as are sufficient to compensate him for actual injury. . . .

Notwithstanding our refusal to extend the *New York Times* privilege to defamation of private individuals, respondent contends that we should affirm the judgment below on the ground that petitioner is either a public official or a public figure. There is little basis for the former assertion. Several years prior to the present incident, petitioner had served briefly on housing committees appointed by the mayor of Chicago, but at the time of publication he had never held any remunerative governmental position. Respondent admits this but argues that petitioner's appearance at the coroner's inquest rendered him a "de facto public official." Our cases recognize no such concept. Respondent's suggestion would sweep all lawyers under the *New York Times* rule as officers of the court and distort the plain meaning of the "public official" category beyond all recognition. We decline to follow it.

Respondent's characterization of petitioner as a public figure raises a different question. That designation may rest on either of two alternative bases. In some instances an individual may achieve such pervasive fame or notoriety that he becomes a public figure for all purposes and in all contexts. More commonly, an individual voluntarily injects himself or is drawn into a particular public controversy and thereby becomes a public figure for a limited range of issues. In either case such persons assume special prominence in the resolution of public questions.

Petitioner has long been active in community and professional affairs. He has served as an officer of local civic groups and of various professional organizations, and he has published several books and articles on legal subjects. Although petitioner was consequently well known in some circles, he had achieved no general fame or notoriety in the community. None of the prospective jurors called at the trial had ever heard of petitioner prior to this litigation, and respondent offered no proof that this response was atypical of the local population. We would not lightly assume that a citizen's participation in community and professional affairs rendered him a public figure for all purposes. Absent clear evidence of general fame or notoriety in the community, and pervasive involvement in the affairs of society, an individual should not be deemed a public personality for all aspects of his life. It is preferable to reduce the public-figure question to a more meaningful context by looking to the nature and extent of an individual's participation in the particular controversy giving rise to the defamation.

In this context it is plain that petitioner was not a public figure. He played a minimal role at the coroner's inquest, and his participation related solely to his representation of a private client. He took no part in the criminal prosecution of Officer Nuccio. Moreover, he never discussed either the criminal or civil litigation with the press and was never quoted as having done so. He plainly did not thrust himself into the vortex of this public issue, nor did he engage the public's attention in an attempt to influence its outcome. We are persuaded that the trial court did not err in refusing to characterize petitioner as a public figure for the purpose of this litigation.

We therefore conclude that the *New York Times* standard is inapplicable to this case and that the trial court erred in entering judgment for respondent. Because the jury was allowed to impose liability without fault and was permitted to presume damages without proof of injury, a new trial is necessary. We reverse and remand for further proceedings in accord with this opinion.

It is so ordered.

. . .

MR. CHIEF JUSTICE BURGER, dissenting.

The doctrines of the law of defamation have had a gradual evolution primarily in the state courts. In *New York Times Co.* v. *Sullivan*, 376 U.S. 254 (1964), and its progeny this Court entered this field.

Agreement or disagreement with the law as it has evolved to this time does not alter the fact that it has been orderly development with a consistent basic rationale. In today's opinion the Court abandons the traditional thread so far as the ordinary private citizen is concerned and introduces the concept that the media will be liable for negligence in publishing defamatory statements with respect to such persons. . . .

The petitioner here was performing a professional representative role as an advocate in the highest tradition of the law, and under that tradition the advocate is not to be invidiously identified with his client. The important public policy which underlies this tradition – the right to counsel – would be gravely jeopardized if every lawyer who takes an "unpopular" case, civil or criminal, would automatically become fair game for irresponsible reporters and editors who might, for example, describe the lawyer as a "mob mouthpiece" for representing a client with a serious prior criminal record, or as an "ambulance chaser" for representing a claimant in a personal injury action. . . .

MR. JUSTICE DOUGLAS, dissenting.

The Court describes this case as a return to the struggle of "[defining] the proper accommodation between the law of defamation and the freedoms of speech and press protected by the First Amendment." It is indeed a struggle, once described by Mr. Justice Black as "the same quagmire" in which the Court "is now helplessly struggling in the field of obscenity." *Curtis Publishing Co.* v. *Butts*, 388 U.S. 130, 171 (concurring opinion). I would suggest that the struggle is a quite hopeless one, for, in light of the command of the First Amendment, no "accommodation" of its freedoms can be "proper" except those made by the Framers themselves.

Unlike the right of privacy which, by the terms of the Fourth Amendment, must be accommodated with reasonable searches and seizures and warrants issued by magistrates, the rights of free speech and of a free press were protected by the Framers in verbiage whose proscription seems clear. I have stated before my view that the First Amendment would bar Congress from passing any libel law. . . . This was the view held by Thomas Jefferson . . . and it is one Congress has never challenged through enactment of a civil libel statute. The sole congressional attempt at this variety of First Amendment muzzle was in the Sedition Act of 1798 – a criminal libel act never tested in this Court and one which expired by its terms three years after enactment. As President, Thomas Jefferson pardoned those who were convicted under the Act, and fines levied in its prosecution were repaid by Act of Congress. . . . The general consensus was that the Act constituted a regrettable legislative exercise plainly in violation of the First Amendment. . . .

With the First Amendment made applicable to the States through the Fourteenth, I do not see how States have any more ability to "accommodate" freedoms of speech or of the press than does Congress. This is true whether the form of the accommodation is civil or criminal since "[what] a State may not constitutionally bring about by means of a criminal statute is likewise beyond the reach of its civil law of libel." *New York Times Co.* v. *Sullivan*, 376 U.S. 254, 277. Like Congress, States are without power "to use a civil libel law or any other law to impose damages for merely discussing public affairs." *Id.*, at 295 (Black, J., concurring). . . .

Continued recognition of the possibility of state libel suits for public discussion of public issues leaves the freedom of speech honored by the Fourteenth Amendment a diluted version of First Amendment protection. This view is only possible if one accepts the position that the First Amendment is applicable to the States only through the Due Process Clause of the Fourteenth, due process freedom of speech being only that freedom which this Court might deem to be "implicit in the concept of ordered liberty." . . . But the Court frequently has rested state free speech and free press decisions on the Fourteenth Amendment generally . . . rather than on the Due Process Clause alone. The Fourteenth Amendment speaks not only of due process but also of "privileges and immunities" of United States citizenship. I can conceive of no privilege or immunity with a higher claim to recognition against state abridgment than the freedoms of speech and of the press. In our federal system we are all subject to two governmental regimes, and freedoms of speech and of the press protected against the infringement of only one are quite illusory. The identity of the oppressor is, I would think, a matter of relative indifference to the oppressed.

There can be no doubt that a State impinges upon free and open discussion when it sanctions the imposition of damages for such discussion through its civil libel laws. Discussion of public affairs is often marked by highly charged emotions, and jurymen, not unlike us all, are subject to those emotions. It is indeed this very type of speech which is the reason for the First Amendment since speech which arouses little emotion is little in need of protection. The vehicle for publication in this case was the American Opinion, a most controversial periodical which disseminates the views of the John Birch Society, an organization which many deem to be quite offensive. The subject matter involved "Communist plots," "conspiracies against law enforcement agencies," and the killing of a private citizen by the police. With any such amalgam of controversial elements pressing upon the jury, a jury determination, unpredictable in the most neutral circumstances, becomes for those who venture to discuss heated issues, a virtual roll of the dice separating them from liability for often massive claims of damage.

It is only the hardy publisher who will engage in discussion in the face of such risk, and the Court's preoccupation with proliferating standards in the area of libel increases the risks. It matters little whether the standard be articulated as "malice" or "reckless disregard of the truth" or "negligence," for jury determinations by any of those criteria are virtually unreviewable. This Court, in its continuing delineation of variegated mantles of First Amendment protection, is, like the potential publisher, left with only speculation on how jury findings were influenced by the effect the subject matter of the publication had upon the minds and viscera of the jury. The standard announced today leaves the States free to "define for themselves the appropriate standard of liability for a publisher or broadcaster" in the circumstances of this case. This of course leaves the simple negligence standard as an option, with the jury free to impose damages upon a finding that the publisher failed to act as "a reasonable man." With such continued erosion of First Amendment protection, I fear that it may well be the reasonable man who refrains from speaking.

Since in my view the First and Fourteenth Amendments prohibit the imposition of damages upon respondent for this discussion of public affairs, I would affirm the judgment below.

MR. JUSTICE BRENNAN, dissenting.

I agree with the conclusion, expressed in Part V of the Court's opinion, that, at the time of publication of respondent's article, petitioner could not properly have been viewed as either a "public official" or "public figure" . . . . I cannot agree, however, that free and robust debate – so essential to the proper functioning of our system of government – is permitted adequate "breathing space," *NAACP* v. *Button*, 371 U.S. 415, 433 (1963), when, as the Court holds, the States may impose all but strict liability for defamation if the defamed party is a private person and "the substance of the defamatory statement 'makes substantial danger to reputation apparent.'" *Ante*, at 348. . . . I adhere to my view . . . that we strike the proper accommodation between avoidance of media self-censorship and protection of individual reputations only when we require States to apply the *New York Times Co.* v. *Sullivan*, 376 U.S. 254 (1964), knowing-or-reckless-falsity standard in civil libel actions concerning media reports of the involvement of private individuals in events of public or general interest.

The Court does not hold that First Amendment guarantees do not extend to speech concerning private persons' involvement in events of public or general interest. It recognizes that self-governance in this country perseveres because of our "profound national commitment to the principle that debate on *public issues* should be uninhibited, robust, and wide-open." *Id.*, at 270 (emphasis added). . . .

Although acknowledging that First Amendment values are of no less significance when media reports concern private persons' involvement in matters of public concern, the Court refuses to provide, in such cases, the same level of constitutional protection that has been afforded the media in the context of defamation of public persons. The accommodation that this Court has established between free speech and libel laws in cases involving public officials and public figures – that defamatory falsehood be shown by clear and convincing evidence to have been published with knowledge of falsity or with reckless disregard of truth – is not apt, the Court holds, because the private individual does not have the same degree of access to the media to rebut defamatory comments as does the public person and he has not voluntarily exposed himself to public scrutiny. . . .

Since petitioner failed, after having been given a full and fair opportunity, to prove that respondent published the disputed article with knowledge of its falsity or with reckless disregard of the truth, . . . I would affirm the judgment of the Court of Appeals.

MR. JUSTICE WHITE, dissenting.

For some 200 years – from the very founding of the Nation – the law of defamation and right of the ordinary citizen to recover for false publication injurious to his reputation have been almost exclusively the business of state courts and legislatures. Under typical state defamation law, the defamed private citizen had to prove only a false publication that would subject him to hatred, contempt, or ridicule. Given such publication, general damage to reputation was presumed, while punitive damages required proof of additional facts. The law governing the defamation of private citizens remained untouched by the First Amendment because until relatively recently, the consistent view of the Court was that libelous words constitute a class of speech wholly unprotected by the First Amendment, subject only to limited exceptions carved out since 1964.

But now, using that Amendment as the chosen instrument, the Court, in a few printed pages, has federalized major aspects of libel law by declaring unconstitutional in important respects the prevailing defamation law in all or most of the 50 States. That result is accomplished by requiring the plaintiff in each and every defamation action to prove not only the defendant's culpability beyond his act of publishing defamatory material but also actual damage to reputation resulting from the publication. Moreover, punitive damages may not be recovered by showing malice in the traditional sense of ill will; knowing falsehood or reckless disregard of the truth will now be required. . . .

Lest there be any mistake about it, the changes wrought by the Court's decision cut very deeply. In 1938, the Restatement of Torts reflected the historic rule that publication in written form of defamatory material – material tending "so to harm the reputation of another as to lower him in the estimation of the community or to deter third persons from associating or dealing with him" – subjected the publisher to liability although no special harm to reputation was actually proved. . . . Truth was a defense, and some libels were privileged; but, given a false circulation, general damage to reputation was presumed and damages could be awarded by the jury, along with any special damages such as pecuniary loss and emotional distress. At the very least, the rule allowed the recovery of nominal damages for any defamatory publication actionable *per se* . . .

If the defamation was not libel but slander, it was actionable *per se* only if it imputed a criminal offense; a venereal or loathsome and communicable disease; improper conduct of a lawful business; or unchastity by a woman. . . . To be actionable, all other types of slanderous statements required proof of special damage other than actual loss of reputation or emotional distress, that special damage almost always being in the form of material or pecuniary loss of some kind. . . .

At the heart of the libel-and-slander-*per-se* damage scheme lay the award of general damages for loss of reputation. . . . Proof of actual injury to reputation was itself insufficient proof of that special damage necessary to support liability for slander not actionable *per se*. But if special damage in the form of material or pecuniary loss were proved, general damages for injury to reputation could be had without further proof. . . . The right to recover for emotional distress depended upon the defendant's otherwise being liable for either libel or slander. . . . Punitive damages were recoverable upon proof of special facts amounting to express malice. . . .

Preparations in the mid-1960's for Restatement (Second) of Torts reflected what were deemed to be substantial changes to the law of defamation, primarily a trend toward limiting *per se* libels to those where the defamatory nature of the publication is apparent on its face, i.e., "where the defamatory innuendo is apparent from the publication itself without reference to extrinsic facts by way of inducement." Restatement (Second) of Torts [Sec.] 569, p. 29 (Tent. Draft No. 12, Apr. 27, 1966). Libels of this sort and slanders *per se* continued to be recognized as actionable without proof of special damage or injury to reputation. All other defamations would require proof of special injury in the form of material or pecuniary loss. . . .

Unquestionably, state law continued to recognize some absolute, as well as some conditional, privileges to publish defamatory materials, including the privilege of fair comment in defined situations. But it remained true that in a wide range of situations, the ordinary citizen could make out a prima facie case without proving more than a defamatory publication and could recover general damages for injury to his reputation unless defeated by the defense of truth.

The impact of today's decision on the traditional law of libel is immediately obvious and indisputable. No longer will the plaintiff be able to rest his case with proof of a libel defamatory on its face or proof of a slander historically actionable *per se*. In addition, he must prove some further degree of culpable conduct on the part of the publisher, such as intentional or reckless falsehood or negligence. And if he succeeds in this respect, he faces still another obstacle: recovery for loss of reputation will be conditioned upon "competent" proof of actual injury to his standing in the community. This will be true regardless of the nature of the defamation and even though it is one of those particularly reprehensible statements that have traditionally made slanderous words actionable without proof of fault by the publisher or of the damaging impact of his publication. The Court rejects the judgment of experience that some publications are so inherently capable of injury, and actual injury so difficult to prove, that the risk of falsehood should be borne by the publisher, not the victim. Plainly, with the additional burden on the plaintiff of proving negligence or other fault, it will be exceedingly difficult, perhaps impossible, for him to vindicate his reputation interest by securing a judgment for nominal damages, the practical effect of such a judgment being a judicial declaration that the publication was indeed false. Under the new rule the plaintiff can lose, not because the statement is true, but because it was not negligently made.

So too, the requirement of proving special injury to reputation before general damages may be awarded will clearly eliminate the prevailing rule, worked out over a very long period of time, that, in the case of defamations not actionable *per se*, the recovery of general damages for injury to reputation may also be had if some form of material or pecuniary loss is proved. Finally, an inflexible federal standard is imposed for the award of punitive damages. No longer will it be enough to prove ill will and an attempt to injure.

These are radical changes in the law and severe invasions of the prerogatives of the States. They should at least be shown to be required by the First Amendment or necessitated by our present circumstances. Neither has been demonstrated.

Of course, *New York Times Co.* v. *Sullivan*, 376 U.S. 254 (1964); *Rosenblatt v. Baer*, 383 U.S. 75 (1966), and *Curtis Publishing Co.* v. *Butts* and *Associated Press v. Walker*, 388 U.S. 130 (1967), have themselves worked major changes in defamation law. Public officials and public figures, if they are to recover general damages for injury to reputation, must prove knowing falsehood or reckless disregard for the truth. The States were required to conform to these decisions. . . .

The Court does not contend, and it could hardly do so, that those who wrote the First Amendment intended to prohibit the Federal Government, within its sphere of influence in the Territories and the District of Columbia, from providing the private citizen a peaceful remedy for damaging falsehood. At the time of the adoption of the First Amendment, many of the consequences of libel law already described had developed, particularly the rule that libels and some slanders were so inherently injurious that they were actionable without special proof of damage to reputation. . . .

Scant, if any, evidence exists that the First Amendment was intended to abolish the common law of libel, at least to the extent of depriving ordinary citizens of meaningful redress against their defamers. . . .

The Court evinces a deep-seated antipathy to "liability without fault." But this catch-phrase has no talismanic significance and is almost meaningless in this context where the Court appears to be addressing those libels and slanders that are defamatory on their face and where the publisher is no doubt aware from the nature of the material that it would be inherently damaging to reputation. He publishes notwithstanding, knowing that he will inflict injury. With this knowledge, he must intend to inflict that injury, his excuse being that he is privileged to do so – that he has published the truth. But as it turns out, what he has circulated to the public is a very damaging falsehood. Is he nevertheless "faultless"? Perhaps it can be said that the mistake about his defense was made in good faith, but the fact remains that it is he who launched the publication knowing that it could ruin a reputation.

In these circumstances, the law has heretofore put the risk of falsehood on the publisher where the victim is a private citizen and no grounds of special privilege are invoked. The Court would now shift this risk to the victim, even though he has done nothing to invite the calumny, is wholly innocent of fault, and is helpless to avoid his injury. I doubt that jurisprudential resistance to liability without fault is sufficient ground for employing the First Amendment to revolutionize the law of libel, and in my view, that body of legal rules poses no realistic threat to the press and its service to the public. The press today is vigorous and robust. To me, it is quite incredible to suggest that threats of libel suits from private citizens are causing the press to refrain from publishing the truth. I know of no hard facts to support that proposition, and the Court furnishes none.

The communications industry has increasingly become concentrated in a few powerful hands operating very lucrative businesses reaching across the Nation and into almost every home. . . . Neither the industry as a whole nor its individual components are easily intimidated, and we are fortunate that they are not. Requiring them to pay for the occasional damage they do to private reputation will play no substantial part in their future performance or their existence.

In any event, if the Court's principal concern is to protect the communications industry from large libel judgments, it would appear that its new requirements with respect to general and punitive damages would be ample protection. Why it also feels compelled to escalate the threshold standard of liability I cannot fathom, particularly when this will eliminate in many instances the plaintiff's possibility of securing a judicial determination that the damaging publication was indeed false, whether or not he is entitled to recover money damages. Under the Court's new rules, the plaintiff must prove not only the defamatory statement but also some degree of fault accompanying it. The publication may be wholly false and the wrong to him unjustified, but his case will nevertheless be dismissed for failure to prove negligence or other fault on the part of the publisher. I find it unacceptable to distribute the risk in this manner and force the wholly innocent victim to bear the injury; for, as between the two, the defamer is the only culpable party. It is he who circulated a falsehood that he was not required to publish.

It is difficult for me to understand why the ordinary citizen should himself carry the risk of damage and suffer the injury in order to vindicate First Amendment values by protecting the press and others from liability for circulating false information. . . .

Not content with escalating the threshold requirements of establishing liability, the Court abolishes the ordinary damages rule, undisturbed by *New York Times* and later cases, that, as to libels or slanders defamatory on their face, injury to reputation is presumed and general damages may be awarded along with whatever special damages may be sought. Apparently because the Court feels that in some unspecified and unknown number of cases, plaintiffs recover where they have suffered no injury or recover more than they deserve, it dismisses this rule as an "oddity of tort law." The Court thereby refuses in *any* case to accept the fact of wide dissemination of a *per se* libel as prima facie proof of injury sufficient to survive a motion to dismiss at the close of plaintiff's case.

I have said before, but it bears repeating, that even if the plaintiff should recover no monetary damages, he should be able to prevail and have a judgment that the publication is false. But beyond that, courts and legislatures literally for centuries have thought that in the generality of cases, libeled plaintiffs will be seriously shortchanged if they must prove the extent of the injury to their reputations. Even where libels or slanders are not on their face defamatory and special damage must be shown, when that showing is made, general damages for reputation injury are recoverable without specific proof. . . .

The new rule with respect to general damages appears to apply to all libels or slanders, whether defamatory on their face or not, except, I gather, when the plaintiff proves intentional falsehood or reckless disregard. Although the impact of the publication on the victim is the same, in such circumstances the injury to reputation may apparently be presumed in accordance with the traditional rule. Why a defamatory statement is more apt to cause injury if the lie is intentional than when it is only negligent, I fail to understand. I suggest that judges and juries who must live by these rules will find them equally incomprehensible.

With a flourish of the pen, the Court also discards the prevailing rule in libel and slander actions that punitive damages may be awarded on the classic grounds of common-law malice, that is, "'[actual] malice' in the sense of ill will or fraud or reckless indifference to consequences." C. McCormick, *Law of Damages* § 118, p. 431 (1935). In its stead, the Court requires defamation plaintiffs to show intentional falsehood or reckless disregard for the truth or falsity of the publication. . . . But I see no constitutional difference between publishing with reckless disregard for the truth, where punitive damages will be permitted, and negligent publication where they will not be allowed. It is difficult to understand what is constitutionally wrong with assessing punitive damages to deter a publisher from departing from those standards of care ordinarily followed in the publishing industry, particularly if common-law malice is also shown. . . .

I fail to see how the quality or quantity of public debate will be promoted by further emasculation of state libel laws for the benefit of the news media. . . . If anything, this trend may provoke a new and radical imbalance in the communications process. . . . It is not at all inconceivable that virtually unrestrained defamatory remarks about private citizens will discourage them from speaking out and concerning themselves with social problems. This would turn the First Amendment on its head. . . .

Freedom and human dignity and decency are not antithetical. Indeed, they cannot survive without each other. Both exist side-by-side in precarious balance, one always threatening to overwhelm the other. Our experience as a Nation testifies to the ability of our democratic institutions to harness this dynamic tension. One of the mechanisms seized upon by the common law to accommodate these forces was the civil libel action tried before a jury of average citizens. And it has essentially fulfilled its role. . . .

For the foregoing reasons, I would reverse the judgment of the Court of Appeals and reinstate the jury's verdict.

DUN & BRADSTREET, INC. V. GREENMOSS BUILDERS, INC.
472 U.S. 749 (1985)

JUSTICE POWELL announced the judgment of the Court and delivered an opinion, in which JUSTICE REHNQUIST and JUSTICE O'CONNOR joined.

In *Gertz* v. *Robert Welch, Inc.*, 418 U.S. 323 (1974), we held that the First Amendment restricted the damages that a private individual could obtain from a publisher for a libel that involved a matter of public concern. More specifically, we held that in these circumstances the First Amendment prohibited awards of presumed and punitive damages for false and defamatory statements unless the plaintiff shows "actual malice," that is, knowledge of falsity or reckless disregard for the truth. The question presented in this case is whether this rule of *Gertz* applies when the false and defamatory statements do not involve matters of public concern.

I

Petitioner Dun & Bradstreet, a credit reporting agency, provides subscribers with financial and related information about businesses. . . . On July 26, 1976, petitioner sent a report to five subscribers indicating that respondent, a construction contractor, had filed a voluntary petition for bankruptcy. This report was false and grossly misrepresented respondent's assets and liabilities. That same day, while discussing the possibility of future financing with its bank, respondent's president was told that the bank had received the defamatory report. He immediately called petitioner's regional office, explained the error, and asked for a correction. . . .

After determining that its report was indeed false, petitioner issued a corrective notice on or about August 3, 1976, to the five subscribers who had received the initial report. The notice stated that one of respondent's former employees, not respondent itself, had filed for bankruptcy and that respondent "continued in business as usual." Respondent told petitioner that it was dissatisfied with the notice, and it again asked for a list of subscribers who had seen the initial report. Again petitioner refused to divulge their names.

Respondent then brought this defamation action in Vermont state court. It alleged that the false report had injured its reputation and sought both compensatory and punitive damages. The trial established that the error in petitioner's report had been caused when one of its employees, a 17-year-old high school student paid to review Vermont bankruptcy pleadings, had inadvertently attributed to respondent a bankruptcy petition filed by one of respondent's former employees. Although petitioner's representative testified that it was routine practice to check the accuracy of such reports with the businesses themselves, it did not try to verify the information about respondent before reporting it.

After trial, the jury returned a verdict in favor of respondent and awarded $50,000 in compensatory or presumed damages and $300,000 in punitive damages. Petitioner moved for a new trial. It argued that in *Gertz* v. *Robert Welch, Inc., supra,* at 349, this Court had ruled broadly that "the States may not permit recovery of presumed or punitive damages, at least when liability is not based on a showing of knowledge of falsity or reckless disregard for the truth," and it argued that the judge's instructions in this case permitted the jury to award such damages on a lesser showing. . . .

III

In *New York Times Co.* v. *Sullivan, supra,* the Court for the first time held that the First Amendment limits the reach of state defamation laws. . . . In *Gertz* v. *Robert Welch, Inc.,* 418 U.S. 323 (1974), . . . we held that the fact that expression concerned a public issue did not by itself entitle the libel defendant to the constitutional protections of *New York Times.* These protections, we found, were not "justified solely by reference to the interest of the press and broadcast media in immunity from liability." 418 U.S., at 343. Rather, they represented "an accommodation between [First Amendment] [concerns] and the limited state interest present in the context of libel actions brought by public persons." *Ibid.* In libel actions brought by private persons we found the competing interests different. Largely because private persons have not voluntarily exposed themselves to increased risk of injury from defamatory statements and because they generally lack effective opportunities for rebutting such statements, *id.,* at 345, we found that the State possessed a "strong and legitimate . . . interest in compensating private individuals for injury to reputation." *Id.,* at 348-349. Balancing this stronger state interest against the same First Amendment interest at stake in *New York Times,* we held that a State could not allow recovery of presumed and punitive damages absent a showing of "actual malice." Nothing in our opinion, however, indicated that this same balance would be struck regardless of the type of speech involved. . . .

IV

We have never considered whether the *Gertz* balance obtains when the defamatory statements involve no issue of public concern. To make this determination, we must employ the approach approved in *Gertz* and balance the State's interest in compensating private individuals for injury to their reputation against the First Amendment interest in protecting this type of expression. This state interest is identical to the one weighed in *Gertz.* There we found that it was "strong and legitimate." 418 U.S., at 348. A State should not lightly be required to abandon it,

> for, as Mr. Justice Stewart has reminded us, the individual's right to the protection of his own
> good name "reflects no more than our basic concept of the essential dignity and worth of every
> human being – a concept at the root of any decent system of ordered liberty. The protection
> of private personality, like the protection of life itself, is left primarily to the individual States

under the Ninth and Tenth Amendments. . . ." *Rosenblatt* v. *Baer*, 383 U.S. 75, 92 (1966) (concurring opinion).

Id., at 341.

The First Amendment interest, on the other hand, is less important than the one weighed in *Gertz*. We have long recognized that not all speech is of equal First Amendment importance. . . . It is speech on "'matters of public concern'" that is "at the heart of the First Amendment's protection." *First National Bank of Boston* v. *Bellotti*, 435 U.S. 765, 776 (1978), citing *Thornhill* v. *Alabama*, 310 U.S. 88, 101 (1940). . . . In contrast, speech on matters of purely private concern is of less First Amendment concern. *Id.*, at 146-147. . . .

While such speech is not totally unprotected by the First Amendment, . . . its protections are less stringent. In *Gertz*, we found that the state interest in awarding presumed and punitive damages was not "substantial" in view of their effect on speech at the core of First Amendment concern. 418 U.S., at 349. This interest, however, *is* "substantial" relative to the incidental effect these remedies may have on speech of significantly less constitutional interest. The rationale of the common-law rules has been the experience and judgment of history that "proof of actual damage will be impossible in a great many cases where, from the character of the defamatory words and the circumstances of publication, it is all but certain that serious harm has resulted in fact." W. Prosser, Law of Torts § 112, p. 765 (4th ed. 1971) . . . . As a result, courts for centuries have allowed juries to presume that some damage occurred from many defamatory utterances and publications. Restatement of Torts § 568, Comment *b*, p. 162 (1938) (noting that Hale announced that damages were to be presumed for libel as early as 1670). This rule furthers the state interest in providing remedies for defamation by ensuring that those remedies are effective. In light of the reduced constitutional value of speech involving no matters of public concern, we hold that the state interest adequately supports awards of presumed and punitive damages – even absent a showing of "actual malice." . . .

V

The only remaining issue is whether petitioner's credit report involved a matter of public concern. In a related context, we have held that "[whether] . . . speech addresses a matter of public concern must be determined by [the expression's] content, form, and context . . . as revealed by the whole record." *Connick* v. *Myers, supra*, at 147-148. These factors indicate that petitioner's credit report concerns no public issue. . . . It was speech solely in the individual interest of the speaker and its specific business audience. . . . This particular interest warrants no special protection when – as in this case – the speech is wholly false and clearly damaging to the victim's business reputation. . . . There is simply no credible argument that this type of credit reporting requires special protection to ensure that "debate on public issues [will] be uninhibited, robust, and wide-open." *New York Times Co.* v. *Sullivan*, 376 U.S., at 270.

In addition, the speech here, like advertising, is hardy and unlikely to be deterred by incidental state regulation. . . . It is solely motivated by the desire for profit, which, we have noted, is a force less likely to be deterred than others. . . . In any case, the market provides a powerful incentive to a credit reporting agency to be accurate, since false credit reporting is of no use to creditors. Thus, any incremental "chilling" effect of libel suits would be of decreased significance. . . .

VI

We conclude that permitting recovery of presumed and punitive damages in defamation cases absent a showing of "actual malice" does not violate the First Amendment when the defamatory statements do not involve matters of public concern. . . .

CHIEF JUSTICE BURGER, concurring in the judgment.

In *Gertz* v. *Robert Welch, Inc.*, 418 U.S. 323 (1974), contrary to well-established common law prevailing in the states, a divided Court held that a private plaintiff in a defamation action cannot recover for a published falsehood unless he proves that the defendant was at least negligent in publishing the falsehood. The Court further held that there can be no "presumed" damages in such an action and that the private plaintiff cannot receive "punitive" damages unless it is established that the publication was made with "actual malice," as defined in *New York Times Co.* v. *Sullivan*, 376 U.S. 254 (1964). . . .

The single question before the Court today is whether *Gertz* applies to this case. The plurality opinion holds that *Gertz* does not apply because, unlike the challenged expression in *Gertz*, the alleged defamatory expression in this case does not relate to a matter of public concern. I agree that *Gertz* is limited to circumstances in which the alleged defamatory expression concerns a matter of general public importance, and that the expression in question here relates to a matter of essentially private concern. I therefore agree with the plurality opinion to the extent that it holds that *Gertz* is inapplicable in this case for the two reasons indicated. No more is needed to dispose of the present case. . . .

JUSTICE WHITE, concurring in the judgment.

Until *New York Times Co.* v. *Sullivan*, 376 U.S. 254 (1964), the law of defamation was almost exclusively the business of state courts and legislatures. Under the then prevailing state libel law, the defamed individual had only to prove a false written publication that subjected him to hatred, contempt, or ridicule. Truth was a defense; but given a defamatory false circulation, general injury to reputation was presumed; special damages, such as pecuniary loss and emotional distress, could be recovered; and punitive damages were available if common-law malice were shown. General damages for injury to reputation were presumed and awarded because the judgment of history was that "in many cases the effect of defamatory statements is so subtle and indirect that it is impossible directly to trace the effects thereof in loss to the person defamed." Restatement of Torts § 621, Comment *a*, p. 314 (1938). The defendant was permitted to show that there was no reputational injury; but at the very least, the prevailing rule was that at least nominal damages were to be awarded for any defamatory publication actionable *per se*. . . .

New York Times Co. v. *Sullivan* was the first major step in what proved to be a seemingly irreversible process of constitutionalizing the entire law of libel and slander. Under the rule announced in that case, a public official suing for libel could no longer make out his case by proving a false and damaging publication. He could not establish liability and recover any damages, whether presumed or actually proved, unless he proved "malice," which was defined as a knowing falsehood or a reckless disregard for the truth. 376 U.S., at 280. . . .

[I]n *Gertz* v. *Robert Welch, Inc.*, 418 U.S. 323 (1974), the Court . . . dealt with defamation actions by private individuals, for the first time holding that such plaintiffs could no longer recover by proving a false statement, no matter how damaging it might be to reputation. They must, in addition, prove some "fault," at least negligence. *Id.*, at 347, 350. Even with that proof, damages were not presumed but had to be proved. *Id.*, at 349. Furthermore, no punitive damages were available without proof of *New York Times* malice. 418 U.S., at 350. This decision, which again purported to implement First Amendment values, seemingly left no defamation actions free from federal constitutional limitations.

. . . The question before us is whether *Gertz* is to be applied in this case. For either of two reasons, I believe that it should not. First, I am unreconciled to the *Gertz* holding and believe that it should be overruled. Second, as JUSTICE POWELL indicates, the defamatory publication in this case does not deal with a matter of public importance. Consequently, I concur in the Court's judgment. . . .

PHILADELPHIA NEWSPAPERS, INC. V. HEPPS
475 U.S. 767 (1986)

JUSTICE O'CONNOR delivered the opinion of the Court.

This case requires us once more to "[struggle] . . . to define the proper accommodation between the law of defamation and the freedoms of speech and press protected by the First Amendment." *Gertz* v. *Robert Welch, Inc.*, 418 U.S. 323, 325 (1974). In *Gertz*, the Court held that a private figure who brings a suit for defamation cannot recover without some showing that the media defendant was at fault in publishing the statements at issue. *Id.*, at 347. Here, we hold that, at least where a newspaper publishes speech of public concern, a private-figure plaintiff cannot recover damages without also showing that the statements at issue are false.

I

Maurice S. Hepps is the principal stockholder of General Programming, Inc. (GPI), a corporation that franchises a chain of stores – known at the relevant time as "Thrifty" stores – selling beer, soft drinks, and snacks. Mr. Hepps, GPI, and a number of its franchisees are the appellees here. . . . Appellant Philadelphia Newspapers, Inc., owns the Philadelphia Inquirer (Inquirer). The Inquirer published a series of articles, authored by appellants William Ecenbarger and William Lambert, containing the statements at issue here. The general theme of the five articles, which appeared in the Inquirer between May 1975 and May 1976, was that appellees had links to organized crime and used some of those links to influence the State's governmental processes, both legislative and administrative. . . . The stories reported that federal "investigators have found connections between Thrifty and underworld figures," *id* ., at A65; that "the Thrifty Beverage beer chain . . . had connections . . . with organized crime," *id.*, at A80; and that Thrifty had "won a series of competitive advantages through rulings by the State Liquor Control Board," *id.*, at A65. A grand jury was said to be investigating the "alleged relationship between the Thrifty chain and known Mafia figures," and "[whether] the chain received special treatment from the [state Governor's] administration and the Liquor Control Board." *Id.*, at A68.

Appellees brought suit for defamation against appellants in a Pennsylvania state court. Consistent with *Gertz, supra,* Pennsylvania requires a private figure who brings a suit for defamation to bear the burden of proving negligence or malice by the defendant in publishing the statements at issue. . . . As to falsity, Pennsylvania follows the common law's presumption that an individual's reputation is a good one. Statements defaming that person are therefore presumptively false, although a publisher who bears the burden of proving the truth of the statements has an absolute defense. . . . After all the evidence had been presented by both sides, the trial court concluded that Pennsylvania's statute giving the defendant the burden of proving the truth of the statements violated the Federal Constitution. . . . The trial court therefore instructed the jury that the plaintiffs bore the burden of proving falsity. . . . The jury ruled for appellants and therefore awarded no damages to appellees.

Pursuant to Pennsylvania statute, . . . the appellees here brought an appeal directly to the Pennsylvania Supreme Court. That court viewed *Gertz* as simply requiring the plaintiff to show fault in actions for defamation. It concluded that a showing of fault did not require a showing of falsity, held that to place the burden of showing truth on the defendant did not unconstitutionally inhibit free debate, and remanded the case for a new trial. . . . We noted probable jurisdiction, 472 U.S. 1025 (1985), and now reverse.

II

In *New York Times Co.* v. *Sullivan*, 376 U.S. 254 (1964), the Court "[determined] for the first time the extent to which the constitutional protections for speech and press limit a State's power to award damages in a libel action brought by a public official against critics of his official conduct." *Id.*, at 256. . . . The jury found for the plaintiff and made an award of damages that did not distinguish between compensatory and punitive damages. *Id.*, at 262. . . . This Court reversed, holding that . . . the Constitution

> prohibits a public official from recovering damages for a defamatory falsehood relating to his official conduct unless he proves that the statement was made with "actual malice" – that is, with knowledge that it was false or with reckless disregard of whether it was false or not.

Id., at 279-280. . . .

A decade after *New York Times*, the Court examined the constitutional limits on defamation suits by private-figure plaintiffs against media defendants. *Gertz, supra.* The Court concluded that the danger of self-censorship was a valid, but not the exclusive, concern in suits for defamation . . . . Any analysis must also take into account the "legitimate state interest underlying the law of libel [in] the compensation of individuals for the harm inflicted on them by defamatory falsehood." *Gertz, supra,* at 341. . . . In light of that interest, and in light of the fact that private figures have lesser access to media channels useful for counteracting false statements and have not voluntarily placed themselves in the public eye, *Gertz, supra,* at 344-345, the Court held that the Constitution "allows the States to impose liability on the publisher or broadcaster of defamatory falsehood on a less demanding showing than that required by *New York Times*," 418 U.S., at 348: "[So] long as they do not impose liability without fault, the States may define for themselves the appropriate standard of liability for a publisher or broadcaster of defamatory falsehood injurious to a private individual." *Id.,* at 347. Nonetheless, even when private figures are involved, the constitutional requirement of fault supersedes the common law's presumptions as to fault and damages. In addition, the Court in *Gertz* expressly held that, although a showing of simple fault sufficed to allow recovery for actual damages, even a private-figure plaintiff was required to show actual malice in order to recover presumed or punitive damages. *Id.,* at 348-350.

The Court most recently considered the constitutional limits on suits for defamation in *Dun & Bradstreet, Inc.* v. *Greenmoss Builders, Inc.,* 472 U.S. 749 (1985). In sharp contrast to *New York Times, Dun & Bradstreet* involved not only a private-figure plaintiff, but also speech of purely private concern. 472 U.S., at 751-752. A plurality of the Court in *Dun & Bradstreet* was convinced that, in a case with such a configuration of speech and plaintiff, the showing of actual malice needed to recover punitive damages under either *New York Times* or *Gertz* was unnecessary:

> In light of the reduced constitutional value of speech involving no matters of public concern,
> we hold that the state interest [in preserving private reputation] adequately supports awards of
> presumed and punitive damages – even absent a showing of "actual malice."

472 U.S., at 761 (opinion of POWELL, J.) (footnote omitted). . . .

One can discern in these decisions two forces that may reshape the common-law landscape to conform to the First Amendment. The first is whether the plaintiff is a public official or figure, or is instead a private figure. The second is whether the speech at issue is of public concern. When the speech is of public concern and the plaintiff is a public official or public figure, the Constitution clearly requires the plaintiff to surmount a much higher barrier before recovering damages from a media defendant than is raised by the common law. When the speech is of public concern but the plaintiff is a private figure, as in *Gertz,* the Constitution still supplants the standards of the common law, but the constitutional requirements are, in at least some of their range, less forbidding than when the plaintiff is a public figure and the speech is of public concern. When the speech is of exclusively private concern and the plaintiff is a private figure, as in *Dun & Bradstreet,* the constitutional requirements do not necessarily force any change in at least some of the features of the common-law landscape.

Our opinions to date have chiefly treated the necessary showings of fault rather than of falsity. Nonetheless, as one might expect given the language of the Court in *New York Times, see supra*, at 772-773, a public-figure plaintiff must show the falsity of the statements at issue in order to prevail in a suit for defamation. . . . Here, as in *Gertz*, the plaintiff is a private figure and the newspaper articles are of public concern. In *Gertz*, as in *New York Times*, the common-law rule was superseded by a constitutional rule. We believe that the common law's rule on falsity – that the defendant must bear the burden of proving truth – must similarly fall here to a constitutional requirement that the plaintiff bear the burden of showing falsity, as well as fault, before recovering damages.

There will always be instances when the fact finding process will be unable to resolve conclusively whether the speech is true or false; it is in those cases that the burden of proof is dispositive. Under a rule forcing the plaintiff to bear the burden of showing falsity, there will be some cases in which plaintiffs cannot meet their burden despite the fact that the speech is in fact false. The plaintiff's suit will fail despite the fact that, in some abstract sense, the suit is meritorious. Similarly, under an alternative rule placing the burden of showing truth on defendants, there would be some cases in which defendants could not bear their burden despite the fact that the speech is in fact true. Those suits would succeed despite the fact that, in some abstract sense, those suits are unmeritorious. Under either rule, then, the outcome of the suit will sometimes be at variance with the outcome that we would desire if all speech were either demonstrably true or demonstrably false.

This dilemma stems from the fact that the allocation of the burden of proof will determine liability for some speech that is true and some that is false, but *all* of such speech is *unknowably* true or false. Because the burden of proof is the deciding factor only when the evidence is ambiguous, we cannot know how much of the speech affected by the allocation of the burden of proof is true and how much is false. In a case presenting a configuration of speech and plaintiff like the one we face here, and where the scales are in such an uncertain balance, we believe that the Constitution requires us to tip them in favor of protecting true speech. To ensure that true speech on matters of public concern is not deterred, we hold that the common-law presumption that defamatory speech is false cannot stand when a plaintiff seeks damages against a media defendant for speech of public concern.

In the context of governmental restriction of speech, it has long been established that the government cannot limit speech protected by the First Amendment without bearing the burden of showing that its restriction is justified. . . . It is not immediately apparent from the text of the First Amendment, which by its terms applies only to governmental action, that a similar result should obtain here: a suit by a private party is obviously quite different from the government's direct enforcement of its own laws. Nonetheless, the need to encourage debate on public issues that concerned the Court in the governmental-restriction cases is of concern in a similar manner in this case involving a private suit for damages: placement by state law of the burden of proving truth upon media defendants who publish speech of public concern deters such speech because of the fear that liability will unjustifiably result. . . . Because such a "chilling" effect would be antithetical to the First Amendment's protection of true speech on matters of public concern, we believe that a private-figure plaintiff must bear the burden of showing that the speech at issue is false before recovering damages for defamation from a media defendant. . . .

We recognize that requiring the plaintiff to show falsity will insulate from liability some speech that is false, but unprovably so. Nonetheless, the Court's previous decisions on the restrictions that the First Amendment places upon the common law of defamation firmly support our conclusion here with respect to the allocation of the burden of proof. In attempting to resolve related issues in the defamation context, the Court has affirmed that "[the] First Amendment requires that we protect some falsehood in order to protect speech that matters." *Gertz*, 418 U.S., at 341. Here the speech concerns the legitimacy of the political process, and therefore clearly "matters." *See Dun & Bradstreet*, 472 U.S., at 758-759 (speech of public concern is at the core of the First Amendment's protections). To provide "'breathing space,'" *New York Times, supra*, at 272 (quoting *NAACP* v. *Button*, 371 U.S., at 433), for true speech on matters of public concern, the Court has been willing to insulate even *demonstrably* false speech from liability, and has imposed additional requirements of fault upon the plaintiff in a suit for defamation. . . . We therefore do not break new ground here in insulating speech that is not even demonstrably false.

We note that our decision adds only marginally to the burdens that the plaintiff must already bear as a result of our earlier decisions in the law of defamation. The plaintiff must show fault. A jury is obviously more likely to accept a plaintiff's contention that the defendant was at fault in publishing the statements at issue if convinced that the relevant statements were false. As a practical matter, then, evidence offered by plaintiffs on the publisher's fault in adequately investigating the truth of the published statements will generally encompass evidence of the falsity of the matters asserted. . . .

For the reasons stated above, the judgment of the Pennsylvania Supreme Court is reversed, and the case is remanded for further proceedings not inconsistent with this opinion.

It is so ordered.

X

While "privacy" is a very current social topic, it is a relative youngster on the social landscape. The legal concept of invasion of privacy was essentially "invented" in a famous 1890 article, *The Right to Privacy*, published in the Harvard Law Review and written by attorney Samuel Warren and his law partner, Louis Brandeis, who later would become a Justice of the United States Supreme Court. While the newly-suggested right of privacy was not immediately accepted, one-by-one, courts gradually came to adopt one form or another of Warren and Brandeis' new right.

Perhaps not surprisingly, the cases tended at first to be all over the map until William Prosser drafted an article organizing the cases into four causes of action: (1) unreasonable intrusion upon seclusion; (2) appropriation of name or likeness; (3) unreasonable public disclosure of private facts; (4) placing another in a false light before the public. Prosser later included these categories in The Restatement (Second) of Torts, Sec. 652, which gained general acceptance. Some confusion persists – these four categories of invasion of privacy cover a lot of varied and, to some extent, overlapping territory, not all of which fits comfortably under the title "privacy," and not all jurisdictions have adopted all of the theories.

STIEN V. MARRIOTT OWNERSHIP RESORTS, INC.
944 P.2D 374 (UTAH CT. APP. 1997)

Plaintiff Cassedy Stien appeals the dismissal, on summary judgment, of her complaint for invasion of privacy growing out of the screening of a tasteless video at a company party. We affirm.

FACTS . . .

At the center of this case is a videotape for which defendants are responsible, in which seventeen employees of defendant Marriott Ownership Resorts, Inc. (Marriott) . . . describe in detail a household chore they hate doing. The video includes appearances by nine men and eight women, including plaintiff's husband, Brad Bauman. The video does not identify any of the employees by name, job title, or employment task.

Unbeknownst to Mr. Bauman, and apparently unbeknownst to the other sixteen participants, the videotape was edited to make it appear as if the employees were answering the question, "What's sex like with your partner?" The video, about five minutes and twenty seconds long, was then shown at a formal company Christmas party for the amusement of some 200 Marriott employees and their guests, including Bauman and plaintiff.

The video opens with a close up of a picturesque pond, with classical music playing in the background. After a second or two, a female voice serenely states: "Recently, we asked a collection of people what they thought and felt about having sex with their partner. Let's listen to their comments."

Following this introduction, the video presents edited clips of the employees' earlier descriptions of a household chore. Each employee-participant appearing in the video is seated in a chair behind what appears to be a conference room table. A caption appears for the first few minutes at the side of the participant, reading: "What's sex like with your partner?" The first employee appearing on the video is male and comments: "Having to carry this huge thing down some stairs; and it's heavy and it smells real bad." Similarly, another male employee states that he "hate[s] doing it because it involves so much time and energy." A female employee states that "[i]t's one of those greasy grimy things that you just have to do at least once a year whether you want to or not." Still another female employee states that she "hate[s] something that has to be done every day." Not all of the comments were negative. For instance, one female employee stated that she was "very tall" and therefore was "good at it."

Interspersed throughout the video are comments made by Bauman. His statements and descriptions are as follows:

The smell. The smell, the smell. And then you go with the goggles. You have to put on the goggles. And then you get the smell through the nose. And as you get into it things start flying all over the place. And the smell. And you get covered in these things.

....

And you have to do it and you have to enjoy doing it. And you cannot-you can't-get into the idea that this is something that you don't want to do.

....

But the smell gets worse and then it gets worse and then it gets worse.

....

And then your biggest problem is you forget to remove this smell from the house and then you leave it there and then you come back and your wife uncovers the smell.

....

But I've found that the goggles work very well because eye protection is a very important item.

. . .

Once the employees' comments are concluded, the video returns to the scenic pond and accompanying background music which opened the video. . . .

Plaintiff did not appear in the video, nor is she ever mentioned by name, either by her husband, Mr. Bauman, or by any other participant. Nonetheless, plaintiff was not amused by the video. She and Bauman filed this lawsuit against Marriott and various individuals who had a hand in making the video, alleging that her privacy was invaded. Specifically, plaintiff alleged that defendants intruded upon her seclusion, appropriated her name and likeness for the benefit of Marriott, publicized private facts regarding plaintiff, and placed her in a false light. All defendants subsequently moved for summary judgment, which the court granted. In so doing, the trial court ruled, as a matter of law, that the elements constituting the four distinct torts of invasion of privacy could not be established by plaintiff. This appeal, pursued by plaintiff Cassedy Stien only, followed. . . .

INVASION OF PRIVACY IN GENERAL

"[T]he law of privacy is a relatively recent phenomenon." *Crump v. Beckley Newspapers, Inc.*, 173 W.Va. 699, 320 S.E.2d 70, 81 (1984). Even so, it has developed over the years into a widely accepted area of tort law, providing a remedy independent of other tort theories protecting reputation and peace of mind, including defamation and intentional infliction of emotional distress. *See generally* Samuel D. Warren & Louis D. Brandeis, *The Right to Privacy*, 4 Harv. L.Rev. 193 (1890) (discussing concept of privacy giving rise to independent tort remedy).

The current formulation of privacy law has been influenced to a large degree by Dean William L. Prosser, who illuminated the law of privacy in a 1960 law review article. *See* William L. Prosser, *Privacy*, 48 Cal. L.Rev. 383 (1960). Instead of just one tort, Dean Prosser wrote, the law of privacy

> comprises four distinct kinds of invasion of four different interests of the plaintiff, which are tied together by the common name, but otherwise have almost nothing in common except that each represents an interference with the right of the plaintiff, in the phrase coined by Judge Cooley, "to be let alone."

Id. at 389 (footnote omitted).

According to Dean Prosser, the four privacy torts are: (1) intrusion upon the plaintiff's seclusion or solitude, or into plaintiff's private affairs, (2) appropriation, for the defendant's advantage, of the plaintiff's name or likeness, (3) public disclosure of embarrassing private facts about the plaintiff, and (4) publicity which places the plaintiff in a false light in the public eye. *See id.* This characterization of the privacy torts was later adopted by the Restatement, *see* Restatement (Second) of Torts §§ 652A-652E (1977), as well as by a number of states. . . .

FIRST BRANCH: INTRUSION UPON SECLUSION

... [I]n order to establish a claim of intrusion upon seclusion, the plaintiff must prove two elements by a preponderance of the evidence: (1) that there was "an intentional substantial intrusion, physically or otherwise, upon the solitude or seclusion of the complaining party," and (2) that the intrusion "would be highly offensive to the reasonable person." This holding comports with the view expressed in the Restatement. *See* Restatement (Second) of Torts § 652B (1977). ...

SECOND BRANCH: APPROPRIATION OF NAME OR LIKENESS

The second invasion of privacy tort alleged by plaintiff is the tort of appropriation of name or likeness for the benefit of another. This privacy tort was examined by the Utah Supreme Court in *Cox v. Hatch*, 761 P.2d 556 (Utah 1988). *Cox* requires the plaintiff to establish three elements: (1) appropriation, (2) of another's name or likeness that has some "intrinsic value," (3) for the use or benefit of another. *Id.* at 564. ...

THIRD BRANCH: PUBLICITY GIVEN TO PRIVATE FACTS

The third of the privacy torts is that of publicity given to private facts. Dean Prosser synthesized from the case law three elements for this tort:

1. the disclosure of the private facts must be a public disclosure and not a private one;

2. the facts disclosed to the public must be private facts, and not public ones; and

3. the matter made public must be one that would be highly offensive and objectionable to a reasonable person of ordinary sensibilities.

W. Page Keeton et al., *Prosser and Keeton on the Law of Torts* § 117, at 856-57 (5th ed.1984) (footnote omitted). The Restatement added to these requirements the notion that the public must not have a legitimate interest in having the information made available. *See* Restatement (Second) of Torts § 652D (1977). ...

FOURTH BRANCH: FALSE LIGHT

The "false light" privacy tort provides that one is subject to liability to another for invasion of privacy if (1) he or she

> gives publicity to a matter concerning another that places the other before the public in a false
> light[; (2)] the false light in which the other was placed would be highly offensive to a reasonable

person[;] and [(3)] the actor ha[d] knowledge of or acted in reckless disregard as to the falsity of the publicized matter and the false light in which the other would be placed.

Russell v. Thomson Newspapers, Inc., 842 P.2d 896, 907 (Utah 1992) (quoting Restatement (Second) of Torts § 652E (1977)).

A false light claim is "closely allied" with an action for defamation, and "the same considerations apply to each." *Cibenko v. Worth Publishers, Inc.*, 510 F.Supp. 761, 766-67 (D.N.J.1981). . . .

CONCLUSION

Plaintiff's invasion of privacy claims fail as a matter of law. Plaintiff's claim of intrusion upon seclusion fails because, as a matter of law, the alleged intrusion upon her private life with her husband is not highly offensive. Because plaintiff did not appear in the video by name or likeness, her claim of appropriation must likewise fail. Further, plaintiff has not shown that the statements disclosed on the video were factual and that the video could have been understood by a reasonable person to be something other than a joke or spoof. Therefore, plaintiff's claims of publicity given to private facts and of portrayal in a false light must also fail. Accordingly, the judgment appealed from is affirmed.

NOTES AND QUESTIONS

1   *Privacy rights of Corporations.* While a corporation is a "person" that can sue and be sued, tort recovery for the invasion of the right of privacy is limited to natural persons.

2   While all American jurisdictions have adopted some form of the cause of action for invasion of privacy, not all jurisdictions have adopted all four branches of the tort.

3   *Constitutional Right to Privacy.* This course deals with the tort of one person's invasion of another's protected legal interest in privacy. When a government oversteps its bounds and intrudes inappropriately into the life of a person or an association of people such as a family, this also is sometimes referred to as the invasion of the "right to privacy." This, however, is a matter of constitutional law, beyond the scope of this course.

4   Because the concept of privacy applies naturally to people and not to corporations, the tort of invasion of privacy does not extend to corporate plaintiffs, but think about whether each of Prosser's four categories of "invasion of privacy" actually involves the right to privacy at all. If not, is there any unifying concept to these four torts? Do not some of the categories apply in the corporate context?

A. INTRUSION UPON SECLUSION

This branch of invasion of privacy law, unlike some of the others, fits quite well with common conceptions of what constitutes an invasion of pricacy. The tort of intrusion upon seclusion protects plaintiff's right to a certain zone of personal space. However, unlike the real property owner's right to exclude, which is protected by the tort of trespass, no bright line delineates precisely when a defendant has intruded into plaintiff's protected space.

NADER V. GENERAL MOTORS CORP.
255 N.E.2D 765 (N.Y. 1970)

. . . The plaintiff, an author and lecturer on automotive safety, has, for some years, been an articulate and severe critic of General Motors' products from the standpoint of safety and design. According to the complaint – which, for present purposes, we must assume to be true – the appellant, having learned of the imminent publication of the plaintiff's book "Unsafe at Any Speed," decided to conduct a campaign of intimidation against him in order to "suppress plaintiff's criticism of and prevent his disclosure of information" about its products. To that end, the appellant authorized and directed the other defendants to engage in a series of activities which, the plaintiff claims in his first two causes of action, violated his right to privacy. Specifically, the plaintiff alleges that the appellant's agents (1) conducted a series of interviews with acquaintances of the plaintiff, "questioning them about, and casting aspersions upon [his] political, social * * * racial and religious views * * *; his integrity; his sexual proclivities and inclinations; and his personal habits"; (2) kept him under surveillance in public places for an unreasonable length of time; (3) caused him to be accosted by girls for the purpose of entrapping him into illicit relationships; (4) made threatening, harassing and obnoxious telephone calls to him; (5) tapped his telephone and eavesdropped, by means of mechanical and electronic equipment, on his private conversations with others; and (6) conducted a "continuing" and harassing investigation of him. . . .

Quite obviously, some intrusions into one's private sphere are inevitable concomitants of life in an industrial and densely populated society, which the law does not seek to proscribe even if it were possible to do so. . . . The classic article by Warren and Brandeis . . . was premised, to a large extent, on principles originally developed in the field of copyright law. . . . Their principal concern appeared to be not with a broad "right to be let alone" but, rather, with the right to protect oneself from having one's private affairs known to others and to keep secret or intimate facts about oneself from the prying eyes or ears of others. . . .

It should be emphasized that the mere gathering of information about a particular individual does not give rise to a cause of action under this theory. Privacy is invaded only if the information sought is of a confidential nature and the defendant's conduct was unreasonably intrusive. Just as a common-law copyright is lost when material is published, so, too, there can be no invasion of privacy where the information sought is open to public view or has been voluntarily revealed to others. In order to sustain a cause of action for invasion of privacy, therefore, the plaintiff must show that the appellant's conduct was truly "intrusive" and that it was designed to elicit information which would not be available through normal inquiry or observation.

. . . At most, only two of the activities charged to the appellant are, in our view, actionable as invasions of privacy . . . . Turning, then, to the particular acts charged in the complaint, we cannot find any basis for a claim of invasion of privacy . . . in the allegations that the appellant, through its agents or employees, interviewed many persons who knew the plaintiff, asking questions about him and casting aspersions on his character. Although those inquiries may have uncovered information of a personal nature, it is difficult to see how they may be said to have invaded the plaintiff's privacy. Information about the plaintiff which was already known to others could hardly be regarded as private to the plaintiff. Presumably, the plaintiff had previously revealed the information to such other persons, and he would necessarily assume the risk that a friend or acquaintance in whom he had confided might breach the confidence. If, as alleged, the questions tended to disparage the plaintiff's character, his remedy would seem to be by way of an action for defamation, not for breach of his right to privacy.

Nor can we find any actionable invasion of privacy in the allegations that the appellant caused the plaintiff to be accosted by girls with illicit proposals, or that it was responsible for the making of a large number of threatening and harassing telephone calls to the plaintiff's home at odd hours. Neither of these activities, howsoever offensive and disturbing, involved intrusion for the purpose of gathering information of a private and confidential nature.

As already indicated, it is manifestly neither practical nor desirable for the law to provide a remedy against any and all activity which an individual might find annoying. On the other hand, where severe mental pain or anguish is inflicted through a deliberate and malicious campaign of harassment or intimidation, a remedy is available in the form of an action for the intentional infliction of emotional distress . . . . But the elements of such an action are decidedly different from those governing the tort of invasion of privacy, and . . . we should be wary of any attempt to rely on the tort of invasion of privacy as a means of avoiding the more stringent pleading and proof requirements for an action for infliction of emotional distress.

Apart, however, from the foregoing allegations which we find inadequate to spell out a cause of action for invasion of privacy . . . , the complaint contains allegations concerning other activities by the appellant or its agents which do satisfy the requirements for such a cause of action. The one which most clearly meets those requirements is the charge that the appellant and its codefendants engaged in unauthorized wiretapping and eavesdropping by mechanical and electronic means. . . . In point of fact, the appellant does not dispute this, acknowledging that, to the extent the two challenged counts charge it with wiretapping and eavesdropping, an actionable invasion of privacy has been stated.

There are additional allegations that the appellant hired people to shadow the plaintiff and keep him under surveillance. In particular, he claims that, on one occasion, one of its agents followed him into a bank, getting sufficiently close to him to see the denomination of the bills he was withdrawing from his account. From what we have already said, it is manifest that the mere observation of the plaintiff in a public place does not amount to an invasion of his privacy. But, under certain circumstances, surveillance may be so "overzealous" as to render it actionable. Whether or not the surveillance in the present case falls into this latter category will depend on the nature of the proof. A person does not automatically make public everything he does merely by being in a public place, and the mere fact that Nader was in a bank did not give anyone the right to try to discover the amount of money he was withdrawing. On the other hand, if the plaintiff acted in such a way as to reveal that fact to any casual observer, then, it may not be said that the appellant intruded into his private sphere. In any event, though, it is enough for present purposes to say that the surveillance allegation is not insufficient as a matter of law.

Since, then, the first two causes of action do contain allegations which are adequate to state a cause of action for invasion of privacy . . . , the courts below properly denied the appellant's motion to dismiss those causes of action. . . . We would but add that the allegations concerning the interviewing of third persons, the accosting by girls and the annoying and threatening telephone calls, though insufficient to support a cause of action for invasion of privacy, are pertinent to the plaintiff's third cause of action – in which those allegations are reiterated – charging the intentional infliction of emotional distress. However, as already noted, it will be necessary for the plaintiff to meet the additional requirements prescribed by the law . . . for the maintenance of a cause of action under that theory.

The order appealed from should be affirmed, with costs, and the question certified answered in the affirmative.

NOTES AND QUESTIONS

1 What alleged conduct by GM did Nader contend invaded his privacy? Which of these alleged actions by GM did the Court hold to be potentially actionable? What is the distinction between those actions that are potential invasions of privacy and those that are not?

2 Would Nader have alleged a cause of action if he had alleged that the investigators had repeatedly walked into Nader's back yard and knocked on the door? If so, how is this allegation different from the allegation of the harassing phone calls?

3 The court held that GM's alleged tapping of Nader's phone stated a cause of action but that interviewing Nader's acquaintances did not. What if the wiretap had picked up only non-personal, non-embarrassing information? Why were the interviews not an invasion? How is using a wiretap to obtain conversations with third parties more intrusive than obtaining those conversations by interviewing the third parties?

4 The Court also held that GM's alleged surveillance of Nader stated a cause of action. How is this more intrusive into his privacy or seclusion than the alleged interviewing of acquaintances, which the Court held not to state a cause of action?

B. APPROPRIATION OF NAME OR LIKENESS

Especially with reference to celebrities (in which context the interest invaded frequently is called the "right of publicity"), this branch of the law of invasion of privacy sometimes does not involve what the average person probably thinks of as a "privacy" interest at all. What interest is protected by this tort? Does it really fit with the "privacy" concept?

WHITE V. SAMSUNG ELECTRONICS AMERICA, INC.
971 F.2D 1395 (9TH CIR. 1992)

. . . Plaintiff Vanna White is the hostess of "Wheel of Fortune," one of the most popular game shows in television history. . . . Capitalizing on the fame which her participation in the show has bestowed on her, White markets her identity to various advertisers.

The dispute in this case arose out of a series of advertisements prepared for Samsung by Deutsch. The series ran in at least half a dozen publications with widespread, and in some cases national, circulation. Each of the advertisements in the series followed the same theme. Each depicted a current item from popular culture and a Samsung electronic product. Each was set in the twenty-first century and conveyed the message that the Samsung product would still be in use by that time. By hypothesizing outrageous future outcomes for the cultural items, the ads created humorous effects. For example, one lampooned current popular notions of an unhealthy diet by depicting a raw steak with the caption: "Revealed to be health food. 2010 A.D." Another depicted irreverent "news"-show host Morton Downey Jr. in front of an American flag with the caption: "Presidential candidate. 2008 A.D."

The advertisement which prompted the current dispute was for Samsung video-cassette recorders (VCRs). The ad depicted a robot, dressed in a wig, gown, and jewelry which Deutsch consciously selected to resemble White's hair and dress. The robot was posed next to a game board which is instantly recognizable as the Wheel of Fortune game show set, in a stance for which White is famous. The caption of the ad read: "Longest-running game show. 2012 A.D." Defendants referred to the ad as the "Vanna White" ad. Unlike the other celebrities used in the campaign, White neither consented to the ads nor was she paid. . . .

White . . . argues that the district court erred in granting summary judgment to defendants on White's common law right of publicity claim. In *Eastwood v. Superior Court*, 198 Cal. Rptr. 342 (1983), the California court of appeal stated that the common law right of publicity cause of action "may be pleaded by alleging (1) the defendant's use of the plaintiff's identity; (2) the appropriation of plaintiff's name or likeness to defendant's advantage, commercially or otherwise; (3) lack of consent; and (4) resulting injury." The district court dismissed White's claim for failure to satisfy *Eastwood*'s second prong, reasoning that defendants had not appropriated White's "name or likeness" with their robot ad. We agree that the robot ad did not make use of White's name or likeness. However, the common law right of publicity is not so confined. . . .

The "name or likeness" formulation referred to in *Eastwood* originated not as an element of the right of publicity cause of action, but as a description of the types of cases in which the cause of action had been recognized. The source of this formulation is Prosser, *Privacy*, 48 Cal.L.Rev. 383, 401-07 (1960), one of the earliest and most enduring articulations of the common law right of publicity cause of action. In looking at the case law to that point, Prosser recognized that right of publicity cases involved one of two basic factual scenarios: name appropriation, and picture or other likeness appropriation. *Id.*

Even though Prosser focused on appropriations of name or likeness in discussing the right of publicity, he noted that "it is not impossible that there might be appropriation of the plaintiff's identity, as by impersonation, without the use of either his name or his likeness, and that this would be an invasion of his right of privacy." *Id.* at 401, n.155. At the time Prosser wrote, he noted however, that "no such case appears to have arisen."

Since Prosser's early formulation, the case law has borne out his insight that the right of publicity is not limited to the appropriation of name or likeness. . . . These cases teach not only that the common law right of publicity reaches means of appropriation other than name or likeness, but that the specific means of appropriation are relevant only for determining whether the defendant has in fact appropriated the plaintiff's identity. The right of publicity does not require that appropriations of identity be accomplished through particular means to be actionable. . . . It is not important *how* the defendant has appropriated the plaintiff's identity, but *whether* the defendant has done so. . . . A rule which says that the right of publicity can be infringed only through the use of nine different methods of appropriating identity merely challenges the clever advertising strategist to come up with the tenth.

Indeed, if we treated the means of appropriation as dispositive in our analysis of the right of publicity, we would not only weaken the right but effectively eviscerate it. The right would fail to protect those plaintiffs most in need of its protection. Advertisers use celebrities to promote their products. The more popular the celebrity, the greater the number of people who recognize her, and the greater the visibility for the product. The identities of the most popular celebrities are not only the most attractive for advertisers, but also the easiest to evoke without resorting to obvious means such as name, likeness, or voice.

Consider a hypothetical advertisement which depicts a mechanical robot with male features, an African-American complexion, and a bald head. The robot is wearing black hightop Air Jordan basketball sneakers, and a red basketball uniform with black trim, baggy shorts, and the number 23 (though not revealing "Bulls" or "Jordan" lettering). The ad depicts the robot dunking a basketball one-handed, stiff-armed, legs extended like open scissors, and tongue hanging out. Now envision that this ad is run on television during professional basketball games. Considered individually, the robot's physical attributes, its dress, and its stance tell us little. Taken together, they lead to the only conclusion that any sports viewer who has registered a discernible pulse in the past five years would reach: the ad is about Michael Jordan.

Viewed separately, the individual aspects of the advertisement in the present case say little. Viewed together, they leave little doubt about the celebrity the ad is meant to depict. The female-shaped robot is wearing a long gown, blond wig, and large jewelry. Vanna White dresses exactly like this at times, but so do many other women. The robot is in the process of turning a block letter on a game-board. Vanna White dresses like this while turning letters on a game-board but perhaps similarly attired Scrabble-playing women do this as well. The robot is standing on what looks to be the Wheel of Fortune game show set. Vanna White dresses like this, turns letters, and does this on the Wheel of Fortune game show. She is the only one. Indeed, defendants themselves referred to their ad as the "Vanna White" ad. We are not surprised.

Television and other media create marketable celebrity identity value. Considerable energy and ingenuity are expended by those who have achieved celebrity value to exploit it for profit. The law protects the celebrity's sole right to exploit this value whether the celebrity has achieved her fame out of rare ability, dumb luck, or a combination thereof. We decline Samsung and Deutch's invitation to permit the evisceration of the common law right of publicity through means as facile as those in this case. Because White has alleged facts showing that Samsung and Deutsch had appropriated her identity, the district court erred by rejecting, on summary judgment, White's common law right of publicity claim. . . .

In remanding this case, we hold only that White has pleaded claims which can go to the jury for its decision.

ALARCON, Circuit Judge, concurring in part, dissenting in part:

. . . I must dissent from the majority's holding on Vanna White's right to publicity claim. The district court found that, since the television commercial did not show a "likeness" of Vanna White, Samsung did not improperly use the plaintiff's identity. The majority asserts that the use of a likeness is not required under California common law. According to the majority, recovery is authorized if there is an appropriation of one's "identity." I cannot find any holding of a California court that supports this conclusion. Furthermore, the record does not support the majority's finding that Vanna White's "identity" was appropriated. . . . All of the California cases that my research has disclosed hold that a cause of action for appropriation of the right to publicity requires proof of the appropriation of a name or likeness. . . .

No reasonable juror could confuse a metal robot with Vanna White.

The majority contends that "the individual aspects of the advertisement . . . viewed together leave little doubt about the celebrity the ad is meant to depict." . . . It derives this conclusion from the fact that Vanna White is "the only one" who "dresses like this, turns letters, and does this on the Wheel of Fortune game show." *Id.* In reaching this conclusion, the majority confuses Vanna White, the person, with the role she has assumed as the current hostess on the "Wheel of Fortune" television game show. A recognition of the distinction between a performer and the part he or she plays is essential for a proper analysis of the facts of this case. As is discussed below, those things which Vanna White claims identify her are not unique to her. They are, instead, attributes of the *role* she plays. The representation of those attributes, therefore, does not constitute a representation of Vanna White. . . .

Vanna White is a one-role celebrity. She is famous solely for appearing as the hostess on the "Wheel of Fortune" television show. There is nothing unique about Vanna White or the attributes which she claims identify her. Although she appears to be an attractive woman, her face and figure are no more distinctive than that of other equally comely women. She performs her role as hostess on "Wheel of Fortune" in a simple and straight-forward manner. Her work does not require her to display whatever artistic talent she may possess.

The majority appears to argue that because Samsung created a robot with the physical proportions of an attractive woman, posed it gracefully, dressed it in a blond wig, an evening gown, and jewelry, and placed it on a set that resembles the Wheel of Fortune layout, it thereby appropriated Vanna White's identity. But an attractive appearance, a graceful pose, blond hair, an evening gown, and jewelry are attributes shared by many women, especially in Southern California. These common attributes are particularly evident among game-show hostesses, models, actresses, singers, and other women in the entertainment field. They are not unique attributes of Vanna White's identity. Accordingly, I cannot join in the majority's conclusion that, even if viewed together, these attributes identify Vanna White and, therefore, raise a triable issue as to the appropriation of her identity.

The only characteristic in the television commercial that is not common to many female performers or celebrities is the imitation of the "Wheel of Fortune" set. This set is the only thing which might possibly lead a viewer to think of Vanna White. The Wheel of Fortune set, however, is not an attribute of Vanna White's identity. It is an identifying characteristic of a television game show, a prop with which Vanna White interacts in her role as the current hostess. To say that Vanna White may bring an action when another blond female performer or robot appears on such a set as a hostess will, I am sure, be a surprise to the owners of the show. . . .

The record shows that Samsung recognized the market value of Vanna White's identity. No doubt the advertisement would have been more effective if Vanna White had appeared in it. But the fact that Samsung recognized Vanna White's value as a celebrity does not necessarily mean that it appropriated her identity. When Samsung and White could not agree on an appropriate compensation to induce her to participate in the television commercial, Samsung dressed a robot in a costume usually worn by television game-show hostesses. A blond wig, and glamorous clothing are not characteristics unique to the current hostess of Wheel of Fortune. This evidence does not support the majority's determination that the advertisement was meant to depict Vanna White. The advertisement was intended to depict a robot, playing the role Vanna White currently plays on the Wheel of Fortune. I quite agree that anyone seeing the television commercial would be reminded of Vanna White. *Any* performance by another female celebrity as a game-show hostess, however, will also remind the viewer of Vanna White because Vanna White's celebrity is so closely associated with the role. But the fact that an actor or actress became famous for playing a particular role has, until now, never been sufficient to give the performer a proprietary interest in it. I cannot agree with the majority that the California courts, which have consistently taken a narrow view of the right to publicity, would extend law to these unique facts. . . .

The protection of intellectual property presents the courts with the necessity of balancing competing interests. On the one hand, we wish to protect and reward the work and investment of those who create intellectual property. In so doing, however, we must prevent the creation of a monopoly that would inhibit the creative expressions of others. We have traditionally balanced those interests by allowing the copying of an idea, but protecting a unique expression of it. Samsung clearly used the idea of a glamorous female game show hostess. Just as clearly, it avoided appropriating Vanna White's expression of that role. Samsung did not use a likeness of her. The performer in the television commercial is unmistakably a lifeless robot. Vanna White has presented no evidence that any consumer confused the robot with her identity. Indeed, no reasonable consumer could confuse the robot with Vanna White or believe that, because the robot appeared in the advertisement, Vanna White endorsed Samsung's product.

I would affirm the district court's judgment in all respects.

1   Apparently, the tort of appropriation of name or likeness, at least in its celebrity form of "the right of publicity,"
has little or nothing to do with "privacy" – it protects a purely commercial interest. This really is an intellectual
property case.

ZACCHINI V. SCRIPPS-HOWARD BROADCASTING CO.

433 U.S. 562 (1977)

MR. JUSTICE WHITE delivered the opinion of the Court.

Petitioner, Hugo Zacchini, is an entertainer. He performs a "human cannonball" act in which
he is shot from a cannon into a net some 200 feet away. Each performance occupies some 15
seconds. In August and September 1972, petitioner was engaged to perform his act on a regular
basis at the Geauga County Fair in Burton, Ohio. He performed in a fenced area, surrounded by
grandstands, at the fairgrounds. Members of the public attending the fair were not charged a
separate admission fee to observe his act.

On August 30, a free-lance reporter for Scripps-Howard Broadcasting Co., the operator of a
television broadcasting station and respondent in this case, attended the fair. He carried a small
movie camera. Petitioner noticed the reporter and asked him not to film the performance. The
reporter did not do so on that day; but on the instructions of the producer of respondent's daily
newscast, he returned the following day and videotaped the entire act. This film clip, approximately 15 seconds in length, was shown on the 11 o'clock news program that night, together with
favorable commentary. . . .

Petitioner then brought this action for damages, alleging that he is "engaged in the entertainment business," that the act he performs is one "invented by his father and . . . performed
only by his family for the last fifty years," that respondent "showed and commercialized the film
of his act without his consent," and that such conduct was an "unlawful appropriation of plaintiff's professional property." . . . Respondent answered and moved for summary judgment, which
was granted by the trial court. The Court of Appeals of Ohio reversed. . . .

[T]he Supreme Court of Ohio rested petitioner's cause of action under state law on his "right
to publicity value of his performance." 47 Ohio St. 2d 224, 351 N.E. 2d 454, 455 (1976). The opinion
syllabus, to which we are to look for the rule of law used to decide the case, . . . declared first that
one may not use for his own benefit the name or likeness of another, whether or not the use or
benefit is a commercial one, and second that respondent would be liable for the appropriation,
over petitioner's objection and in the absence of license or privilege, of petitioner's right to the
publicity value of his performance. . . . The court nevertheless gave judgment for respondent
because, in the words of the syllabus:

> A TV station has a privilege to report in its newscasts matters of legitimate public interest which
> would otherwise be protected by an individual's right of publicity, unless the actual intent of the

TV station was to appropriate the benefit of the publicity for some non-privileged private use, or unless the actual intent was to injure the individual.

Ibid.

We granted certiorari, 429 U.S. 1037 (1977), to consider an issue unresolved by this Court: whether the First and Fourteenth Amendments immunized respondent from damages for its alleged infringement of petitioner's state-law "right of publicity." . . . Insofar as the Ohio Supreme Court held that the First and Fourteenth Amendments of the United States Constitution required judgment for respondent, we reverse the judgment of that court. . . . The Ohio Supreme Court held that respondent is constitutionally privileged to include in its newscasts matters of public interest that would otherwise be protected by the right of publicity, absent an intent to injure or to appropriate for some non-privileged purpose. If under this standard respondent had merely reported that petitioner was performing at the fair and described or commented on his act, with or without showing his picture on television, we would have a very different case. But petitioner is not contending that his appearance at the fair and his performance could not be reported by the press as newsworthy items. His complaint is that respondent filmed his entire act and displayed that film on television for the public to see and enjoy. This, he claimed, was an appropriation of his professional property. The Ohio Supreme Court agreed that petitioner had "a right of publicity" that gave him "personal control over commercial display and exploitation of his personality and the exercise of his talents." . . . This right of "exclusive control over the publicity given to his performances" was said to be such a "valuable part of the benefit which may be attained by his talents and efforts" that it was entitled to legal protection. It was also observed, or at least expressly assumed, that petitioner had not abandoned his rights by performing under the circumstances present at the Geauga County Fair Grounds.

The Ohio Supreme Court nevertheless held that the challenged invasion was privileged, saying that the press "must be accorded broad latitude in its choice of how much it presents of each story or incident, and of the emphasis to be given to such presentation. No fixed standard which would bar the press from reporting or depicting either an entire occurrence or an entire discrete part of a public performance can be formulated which would not unduly restrict the 'breathing room' in reporting which freedom of the press requires." 47 Ohio St. 2d, at 235, 351 N.E. 2d, at 461. Under this view, respondent was thus constitutionally free to film and display petitioner's entire act. . . .

The broadcast of a film of petitioner's entire act poses a substantial threat to the economic value of that performance. As the Ohio court recognized, this act is the product of petitioner's own talents and energy, the end result of much time, effort, and expense. Much of its economic value lies in the "right of exclusive control over the publicity given to his performance"; if the public can see the act free on television, it will be less willing to pay to see it at the fair. . . . The effect of a public broadcast of the performance is similar to preventing petitioner from charging an admission fee. "The rationale for [protecting the right of publicity] is the straight-forward one of preventing unjust enrichment by the theft of good will. No social purpose is served by having the defendant get free some aspect of the plaintiff that would have market value and for which he would normally pay." Kalven, *Privacy in Tort Law - Were Warren and Brandeis Wrong?*, 31 Law & Contemp. Prob. 326, 331 (1966). Moreover, the broadcast of petitioner's entire performance, unlike the unauthorized use of another's name for purposes of trade or the incidental use of a name or picture by the press, goes to the heart of petitioner's ability to earn a living as an entertainer. Thus, in this case, Ohio has recognized what may be the strongest case for a "right of publicity" - involving, not the appropriation of an entertainer's reputation to enhance the attractiveness of a commercial product, but the appropriation of the very activity by which the entertainer acquired his reputation in the first place.

Of course, Ohio's decision to protect petitioner's right of publicity here rests on more than a desire to compensate the performer for the time and effort invested in his act; the protection provides an economic incentive for him to make the investment required to produce a performance of interest to the public. This same consideration underlies the patent and copyright laws long enforced by this Court. . . . There is no doubt that entertainment, as well as news, enjoys First Amendment protection. It is also true that entertainment itself can be important news. . . . But it is important to note that neither the public nor respondent will be deprived of the benefit of petitioner's performance as long as his commercial stake in his act is appropriately recognized. Petitioner does not seek to enjoin the broadcast of his performance; he simply wants to be paid for it. Nor do we think that a state-law damages remedy against respondent would represent a species of liability without fault contrary to the letter or spirit of *Gertz v. Robert Welch*, Inc., 418 U.S. 323 (1974). Respondent knew that petitioner objected to televising his act but nevertheless displayed the entire film.

We conclude that although the State of Ohio may as a matter of its own law privilege the press in the circumstances of this case, the First and Fourteenth Amendments do not require it to do so.

Reversed.

NOTE

1   Usually creative works are protected by copyright law, but that protection did not extend to this case because plaintiff had not "fixed" his act in tangible form.

FACTORS ETC., INC. V. PRO ARTS, INC.
579 F.2D 215 (2D CIR. 1978)

Plaintiffs-Appellees, Factors Etc., Inc. (Factors) and Boxcar Enterprises, Inc. (Boxcar), sued Defendants-Appellants, Pro Arts, Inc. (Pro Arts) and Stop and Shop Companies, Inc. (Stop and Shop), for injunctive relief and damages based upon defendants' alleged misappropriation and unauthorized use of the name and likeness of Elvis Presley (Presley). The trial court granted the plaintiffs' preliminary injunction upon its findings that the exclusive right to market Presley memorabilia survived the death of Presley, and the Presley poster printed by defendants allegedly in derogation of this right was not privileged as the publication of a newsworthy event. This is an interlocutory appeal . . . .

Because the facts are not in dispute, we need not describe them in detail. During Presley's career as an entertainer, Colonel Tom Parker (Parker) served as his close friend, mentor and personal manager. This professional relationship between the two parties began on March 26, 1956, with the execution of the first contract between them. Parker immediately began the task of creating the "Elvis persona." In so doing, both he and Presley capitalized upon the marketing of merchandise bearing the Elvis name and likeness. Parker directed this effort until Presley's death, a task reflected by the numerous extensions of the contract between the two parties. . . . Boxcar Enterprises, a Tennessee corporation controlled by Presley and Parker, . . . was the vehicle through which the commercial Elvis Presley rights were marketed. Boxcar sublicensed other companies to do the actual manufacturing and distributing of each specific item, receiving royalties from the sales. . . .

On August 16, 1977, Elvis Presley died suddenly and unexpectedly. His father, Vernon Presley, was appointed executor of his estate. On August 18, 1977, two days after Presley's death, Boxcar granted Factors the exclusive license to exploit commercially the name and likeness of Elvis Presley. Factors paid Boxcar $100,000 on execution of the agreement against a guarantee of $150,000. Vernon Presley, as executor of the estate, signed the agreement licensing Factors, at the same time warranting that Boxcar was the sole and exclusive owner of the commercial Elvis Presley rights. . . . The agreement was also approved by Parker.

Immediately following Presley's death, Pro Arts decided that it too wanted a share in the market for Elvis Presley memorabilia. It purchased the copyright in the photograph of Presley from a staff photographer of the Atlanta (Georgia) Journal. On August 19, 1977, three days after his death, Pro Arts published a poster using the photograph and filed an application for registration of copyright. The poster is entitled "IN MEMORY" and below the photograph of Presley the poster bears the dates "1935-1977."

On the same day that the poster was published, Pro Arts began to market it. One of its first customers was co-defendant Stop and Shop Companies, which thereafter sold the poster through its Bradlees Stores Division . . . . On August 24, 1977, five days after its poster was placed on the market, Pro Arts notified Boxcar Enterprises that it was offering "a memorial 'Elvis' poster to meet the public demand." When Factors was informed of the letter, it replied to Pro Arts claiming the exclusive right to manufacture, sell and distribute all merchandise utilizing the name and likeness of Elvis Presley. Factors also warned Pro Arts that if it did not discontinue sale of the poster, it would be subject to a lawsuit for injunctive relief, damages and an accounting. . . .

On October 13, 1977, the New York court filed an opinion and order of preliminary injunction against Pro Arts. The injunction restrained Pro Arts during the pendency of the action from manufacturing, selling or distributing (1) any more copies of the poster labeled "IN MEMORY . . . 1935-1977," (2) any other posters, reproductions or copies containing any likeness of Elvis Presley, and (3) utilizing for commercial profit in any manner or form the name or likeness of Elvis Presley. The order also denied Pro Arts' motion to dismiss, stay or transfer. Pro Arts has duly perfected this interlocutory appeal from the order. . . .

In concluding that Factors would likely prevail on the merits at trial, the court found that Elvis Presley exercised his right of publicity during his lifetime by giving Parker the exclusive authority to exploit his image through Boxcar Enterprises. This exclusive authority survived Presley's death, after which it was validly assigned to Factors. For this reason Pro Arts was enjoined from manufacturing, distributing, selling or otherwise profiting from merchandise bearing the name or likeness of the late Elvis Presley.

On appeal, Pro Arts alleges two errors of law on the part of the trial court. According to Pro Arts, the trial court erred first in concluding that the right of publicity could survive the death of the celebrity. Second, Pro Arts argues that even if the right did so survive, Pro Arts was privileged, as a matter of law, in printing and distributing its "memorial poster" of Presley, because the poster celebrated a newsworthy event.

The first issue, the duration of the so-called "right of publicity," is one of state law, more specifically the law of the State of New York. . . . As the district court noted, much confusion shrouds the so-called "right of publicity," largely because it has often been discussed under the rubric "right of privacy." As Dean Prosser has stated, the right of privacy embraces "four distinct kinds of invasion of four different interests of the plaintiff, which are tied together by the common name, but otherwise have almost nothing in common except that each represents an interference with the right of the plaintiff 'to be let alone.'" W. PROSSER, TORTS 804 (4th ed. 1971). Prosser has classified the four species of this tort as (1) intrusion upon the plaintiff's physical solitude or seclusion, *id.* at 807, (2) public disclosure of private facts, *id.* at 809, (3) false light in the public eye, *id.* at 812, and (4) appropriation of plaintiff's name or likeness for defendant's benefit, *id.* at 804.

The fourth type, appropriation of plaintiff's name or likeness for defendant's benefit, has in recent years acquired the label, "right of publicity." The distinguishing feature of this branch of the tort is that it involves the use of plaintiff's protected right for defendant's direct commercial advantage. The nature of the remedy also separates the right of publicity from the other three species of the tort. To protect his interest with respect to the first three, the injured party attempts to minimize the intrusion or publication of the damaging matter. In contrast, the right of publicity plaintiff does not necessarily object to the commercial exploitation - so long as the exploitation is at his behest and he is receiving the profits. This point was recently underscored by the Supreme Court in *Zacchini v. Scripps-Howard Broadcasting Co.*, 433 U.S. 562 . . . (1977). According to the Court, the interest protected: "is closely analogous to the goals of patent and copyright law, focusing on the right of the individual to reap the reward of his endeavors and having little to do with protecting feeling or reputation." *Id.* at 573. . . .

There can be no doubt that Elvis Presley assigned to Boxcar a valid property right, the exclusive authority to print, publish and distribute his name and likeness. In so doing, he carved out a separate intangible property right for himself, the right to a certain percentage of the royalties which would be realized by Boxcar upon exploitation of Presley's likeness and name. The identification of this exclusive right belonging to Boxcar as a transferable property right compels the conclusion that the right survives Presley's death. The death of Presley, who was merely the beneficiary of an income interest in Boxcar's exclusive right, should not in itself extinguish

Boxcar's property right. Instead, the income interest, continually produced from Boxcar's exclusive right of commercial exploitation, should inure to Presley's estate at death like any other intangible property right. To hold that the right did not survive Presley's death, would be to grant competitors of Factors, such as Pro Arts, a windfall in the form of profits from the use of Presley's name and likeness. At the same time, the exclusive right purchased by Factors and the financial benefits accruing to the celebrity's heirs would be rendered virtually worthless. . . . In sum, we hold that Boxcar's exclusive right to exploit the Presley name and likeness, because exercised during Presley's life, survived his death. . . . The right was therefore validly transferred to Factors following Presley's death.

Pro Arts' final argument is that even if Factors possesses the exclusive right to distribute Presley memorabilia, this right does not prevent Pro Arts from publishing what it terms a "memorial poster" commemorating a newsworthy event. In support of this argument, Pro Arts cites *Paulsen v. Personality Posters, Inc.*, 59 Misc. 2d 444, 299 N.Y.S.2d 501 (Sup. Ct. 1968), a case arising out of the bogus presidential candidacy of the television comedian Pat Paulsen. Paulsen sued defendant for publishing and distributing a poster of Paulsen with the legend "FOR PRESIDENT." The court refused to enjoin sale of the poster because Paulsen's choice of the political arena for satire made him "newsworthy" in the First Amendment sense. We cannot accept Pro Arts contention that the legend "IN MEMORY . . ." placed its poster in the same category as one picturing a presidential candidate, albeit a mock candidate. We hold, therefore, that Pro Arts' poster of Presley was not privileged as celebrating a newsworthy event.

In conclusion we hold that the district court did not abuse its discretion in granting the injunction since Factors has demonstrated a strong likelihood of success on the merits at trial. Factors possesses the exclusive right to print and distribute Elvis Presley memorabilia, a right which was validly transferred to it from Boxcar following Presley's death. Pro Arts infringed this right by printing and distributing the Elvis Presley poster, a poster whose publication was not privileged as a newsworthy event.

We affirm the action of the district court and remand for further proceedings.

QUESTIONS

1   If, in an effort to sell VCR's, Samsung had published an advertisement including a photo of Vanna White, has Samsung improperly appropriated White's name or likeness? Are these hypothetical facts materially different from the facts of *White v. Samsung*?

2   If, in an effort to sell magazines, Star magazine published a story about Vanna White and published White's photo on the cover of the magazine, has Star magazine improperly appropriated White's name or likeness? Are these hypothetical facts materially different from the facts assumed in Question 1 above?

3   Are the facts of *Zacchini* materially different from the hypothetical facts in Question 2 above?

4   Are the facts of *Factors v. Pro Arts* materially different from the hypothetical facts in Question 2 above?

C. PUBLIC DISCLOSURE OF PRIVATE FACTS

PROVERBS 11:13

A talebearer revealeth secrets: but he that is of a faithful spirit concealeth the matter.

This tort clearly implicates what most Americans probably would identify as a "privacy" interest. It has a very "personal" rather than the "commercial" flavor of the most common applications of the misappropriation tort. At least part of the nineteenth century basis of this tort was the idea that gossip is corrosive to society.

COX BROADCASTING CORP. V. COHN
420 U.S. 469 (1975)

... In August 1971, appellee's 17-year-old daughter was the victim of a rape and did not survive the incident. Six youths were soon indicted for murder and rape. Although there was substantial press coverage of the crime and of subsequent developments, the identity of the victim was not disclosed pending trial.... In April 1972, some eight months later, the six defendants appeared in court....

In the course of the proceedings that day, appellant Wassell, ... a reporter covering the incident for his employer, learned the name of the victim from an examination of the indictments which were made available for his inspection in the courtroom.... That the name of the victim appears in the indictments and that the indictments were public records available for inspection are not disputed.... Later that day, Wassell broadcast ... a news report concerning the court proceedings. The report named the victim of the crime and was repeated the following day....

In May 1972, appellee brought an action for money damages against appellants, ... claiming that his right to privacy had been invaded by the television broadcasts giving the name of his deceased daughter. Appellants admitted the broadcasts but claimed that they were privileged under ... the First and Fourteenth Amendments. The trial court, rejecting appellants' constitutional claims ..., granted summary judgment to appellee as to liability, with the determination of damages to await trial by jury....

Georgia stoutly defends ... the State's common-law privacy action challenged here. Its claims are not without force, for powerful arguments can be made, and have been made, that however it may be ultimately defined, there *is* a zone of privacy surrounding every individual, a zone within which the State may protect him from intrusion by the press, with all its attendant publicity.... Indeed, the central thesis of the root article by Warren and Brandeis, *The Right to Privacy*, 4 Harv. L. Rev. 193, 196 (1890), was that the press was overstepping its prerogatives by publishing essentially private information and that there should be a remedy for the alleged abuses....

More compellingly, the century has experienced a strong tide running in favor of the so-called right of privacy. In 1967, we noted that "[it] has been said that a 'right of privacy' has been recognized at common law in 30 States plus the District of Columbia and by statute in four States." *Time, Inc.* v. *Hill*, 385 U.S. 374, 383 n. 7. We there cited the 1964 edition of Prosser's Law of Torts. The 1971 edition of that same source states that "[in] one form or another, the right of privacy is by this time recognized and accepted in all but a very few jurisdictions." W. Prosser, Law of Torts 804 (4th ed.) (footnote omitted). Nor is it irrelevant here that the right of privacy is no recent arrival in the jurisprudence of Georgia, which has embraced the right in some form since 1905 when the Georgia Supreme Court decided the leading case of *Pavesich* v. *New England Life Ins. Co.*, 122 Ga. 190, 50 S.E. 68.

These are impressive credentials for a right of privacy, . . . but we should recognize that we do not have at issue here an action for the invasion of privacy involving the appropriation of one's name or photograph, a physical or other tangible intrusion into a private area, or a publication of otherwise private information that is also false although perhaps not defamatory. The version of the privacy tort now before us – termed in Georgia "the tort of public disclosure," 231 Ga., at 60, 200 S.E.2d, at 130 – is that in which the plaintiff claims the right to be free from unwanted publicity about his private affairs, which, although wholly true, would be offensive to a person of ordinary sensibilities. Because the gravamen of the claimed injury is the publication of information, whether true or not, the dissemination of which is embarrassing or otherwise painful to an individual, it is here that claims of privacy most directly confront the constitutional freedoms of speech and press. The face-off is apparent, and the appellants urge upon us the broad holding that the press may not be made criminally or civilly liable for publishing information that is neither false nor misleading but absolutely accurate, however damaging it may be to reputation or individual sensibilities.

It is true that in defamation actions, where the protected interest is personal reputation, the prevailing view is that truth is a defense; . . . and the message of *New York Times Co.* v. *Sullivan*, 376 U.S. 254 (1964); . . . *Curtis Publishing Co.* v. *Butts*, 388 U.S. 130 (1967), and like cases is that the defense of truth is constitutionally required where the subject of the publication is a public official or public figure. What is more, the defamed public official or public figure must prove not only that the publication is false but that it was knowingly so or was circulated with reckless disregard for its truth or falsity. Similarly, where the interest at issue is privacy rather than reputation and the right claimed is to be free from the publication of false or misleading information about one's affairs, the target of the publication must prove knowing or reckless falsehood where the materials published, although assertedly private, are "matters of public interest." *Time, Inc.* v. *Hill, supra*, at 387-388. . . . The Court has nevertheless carefully left open the question whether the First and Fourteenth Amendments require that truth be recognized as a defense in a defamation action brought by a private person as distinguished from a public official or public figure. . . .

In this sphere of collision between claims of privacy and those of the free press, the interests on both sides are plainly rooted in the traditions and significant concerns of our society. Rather than address the broader question whether truthful publications may ever be subjected to civil or criminal liability consistently with the First and Fourteenth Amendments, or to put it another way, whether the State may ever define and protect an area of privacy free from unwanted publicity in the press, it is appropriate to focus on the narrower interface between press and privacy that this case presents, namely, whether the State may impose sanctions on the accurate publication of the name of a rape victim obtained from public records – more specifically, from judicial records which are maintained in connection with a public prosecution and which themselves are open to public inspection. We are convinced that the State may not do so.

In the first place, in a society in which each individual has but limited time and resources with which to observe at first hand the operations of his government, he relies necessarily upon the press to bring to him in convenient form the facts of those operations. Great responsibility is accordingly placed upon the news media to report fully and accurately the proceedings of government, and official records and documents open to the public are the basic data of governmental operations. Without the information provided by the press most of us and many of our representatives would be unable to vote intelligently or to register opinions on the administration of government generally. With respect to judicial proceedings in particular, the function of the press serves to guarantee the fairness of trials and to bring to bear the beneficial effects of public scrutiny upon the administration of justice. . . .

Appellee has claimed in this litigation that the efforts of the press have infringed his right to privacy by broadcasting to the world the fact that his daughter was a rape victim. The commission of crime, prosecutions resulting from it, and judicial proceedings arising from the prosecutions, however, are without question events of legitimate concern to the public and consequently fall within the responsibility of the press to report the operations of government.

The special protected nature of accurate reports of judicial proceedings has repeatedly been recognized. . . . Thus even the prevailing law of invasion of privacy generally recognizes that the interests in privacy fade when the information involved already appears on the public record. The conclusion is compelling when viewed in terms of the First and Fourteenth Amendments and in light of the public interest in a vigorous press. The Georgia cause of action for invasion of privacy through public disclosure of the name of a rape victim imposes sanctions on pure expression – the content of a publication – and not conduct or a combination of speech and nonspeech elements that might otherwise be open to regulation or prohibition. . . . The publication of truthful information available on the public record contains none of the indicia of those limited categories of expression, such as "fighting" words, which "are no essential part of any exposition of ideas, and are of such slight social value as a step to truth that any benefit that may be derived from them is clearly outweighed by the social interest in order and morality." . . .

By placing the information in the public domain on official court records, the State must be presumed to have concluded that the public interest was thereby being served. Public records by their very nature are of interest to those concerned with the administration of government, and a public benefit is performed by the reporting of the true contents of the records by the media. The freedom of the press to publish that information appears to us to be of critical importance to our type of government in which the citizenry is the final judge of the proper conduct of public business. In preserving that form of government the First and Fourteenth Amendments command nothing less than that the States may not impose sanctions on the publication of truthful information contained in official court records open to public inspection.

We are reluctant to embark on a course that would make public records generally available to the media but forbid their publication if offensive to the sensibilities of the supposed reasonable man. Such a rule would make it very difficult for the media to inform citizens about the public business and yet stay within the law. The rule would invite timidity and self-censorship and very likely lead to the suppression of many items that would otherwise be published and that should be made available to the public. At the very least, the First and Fourteenth Amendments will not allow exposing the press to liability for truthfully publishing information released to the public in official court records. If there are privacy interests to be protected in judicial proceedings, the States must respond by means which avoid public documentation or other exposure of private information. Their political institutions must weigh the interests in privacy with the interests of the public to know and of the press to publish. . . . Once true information is disclosed in public court documents open to public inspection, the press cannot be sanctioned for publishing it. In this instance as in others reliance must rest upon the judgment of those who decide what to publish or broadcast. . . . Appellee has not contended that the name was obtained in an improper fashion or that it was not on an official court document open to public inspection. Under these circumstances, the protection of freedom of the press provided by the First and Fourteenth Amendments bars the State of Georgia from making appellants' broadcast the basis of civil liability. . . .

NOTE AND QUESTIONS

1   Is this case distinguishable from *Doe v. Mills, infra*?
2   The Supreme Court in *Florida Star v. B.J.F.* extended constitutional protection to all truthful, lawfully-obtained information of public interest absent a state interest of "the highest order."
3   How would Cohn's case have fared under a defamation analysis?

HAYNES V. ALFRED A. KNOPF, INC.
8 F.3D 1222 (7TH CIR. 1993)

POSNER, *Chief Judge.*

Luther Haynes and his wife, Dorothy Haynes nèe Johnson, appeal from the dismissal on the defendants' motion for summary judgment of their suit against Nicholas Lemann, the author of a highly praised, best-selling book of social and political history called *The Promised Land: The Great Black Migration and How It Changed America* (1991), and Alfred A. Knopf, Inc., the book's publisher. The plaintiffs claim that the book libels Luther Haynes and invades both plaintiffs' right of privacy. . . .

Between 1940 and 1970, five million blacks moved from impoverished rural areas in the South to the cities of the North in search of a better life. Some found it, and after sojourns of shorter or greater length in the poor black districts of the cities moved to middle-class areas. Others, despite the ballyhooed efforts of the federal government, particularly between 1964 and 1972, to erase poverty and racial discrimination, remained mired in what has come to be called the "urban ghetto." *The Promised Land* is a history of the migration. It is not history as a professional historian, a demographer, or a social scientist would write it. Lemann is none of these. He is a journalist and has written a journalistic history, in which the focus is on individuals whether powerful or representative. In the former group are the politicians who invented, executed, or exploited the "Great Society" programs. In the latter are a handful of the actual migrants. Foremost among these is Ruby Lee Daniels. Her story is the spine of the book. . . .

When we meet her, it is the early 1940s and she is a young woman picking cotton on a plantation in Clarksdale, Mississippi. . . . Ruby had married young, but after her husband had been inducted into the army on the eve of World War II she had fallen in love with a married man, by whom she had had a child. The man's wife died and Ruby married him, but they broke up after a month. Glowing reports from an aunt who had moved to Chicago persuaded Ruby Daniels to move there in 1946. She found a job doing janitorial work, but eventually lost the job and went on public aid. She was unmarried, and had several children, when in 1953 she met "the most important man in her life." Luther Haynes, born in 1924 or 1925, a sharecropper from Mississippi, had moved to Chicago in an effort to effect a reconciliation with his wife. The effort had failed. When he met Ruby Daniels he had a well-paying job in an awning factory. They lived together, and had children. But then "Luther began to drink too much. When he drank he got mean, and he and Ruby would get into ferocious quarrels. He was still working, but he wasn't always bringing his paycheck home." Ruby got work as a maid. They moved to a poorer part of the city. The relationship went downhill. "It got to the point where [Luther] would go out on Friday evenings after picking up his paycheck, and Ruby would hope he wouldn't come home, because she knew he would be drunk. On the Friday evenings when he did come home—over the years Ruby developed a devastating imitation of Luther, and could re-create the scene quite vividly—he would walk into the apartment, put on a record and turn up the volume, and saunter into their bedroom, a bottle in one hand and a cigarette in the other, in the mood for love. On one such night, Ruby's last child, Kevin, was conceived. Kevin always had something wrong with him—he was very moody, he was scrawny, and he had a severe speech impediment. Ruby was never able to find out exactly what the problem was, but she blamed it on Luther; all that alcohol must have gotten into his sperm, she said."

Ruby was on public aid, but was cut off when social workers discovered she had a man in the house. She got a night job. Luther was supposed to stay with the children while she was at work, especially since they lived in a dangerous neighborhood; but often when she came home, at 3:00 a.m. or so, she would "find the older children awake, and when she would ask them if Luther had been there, the answer would be, 'No, ma'am.'" Ruby's last aid check, arriving providentially after she had been cut off, enabled the couple to buy a modest house on contract—it "was, by a wide margin, the best place she had ever lived." But "after only a few months, Luther ruined everything by going out and buying a brand-new 1961 Pontiac. It meant more to him than the house did, and when they couldn't make the house payment, he insisted on keeping the car" even though she hadn't enough money to buy shoes for the children. The family was kicked out of the house. They now moved frequently. They were reaching rock bottom. At this nadir, hope appeared in the ironic form of the Robert Taylor Homes, then a brand-new public housing project, now a notorious focus of drug addiction and gang violence. Ruby had had an application for public housing on file for many years, but the housing authority screened out unwed mothers. Told by a social worker that she could have an apartment in the Taylor Homes if she produced a marriage license, she and Luther (who was now divorced from his first wife) were married forthwith and promptly accepted as tenants. "The Haynes family chose to rejoice in their good fortune in becoming residents of the Robert Taylor Homes. As Ruby's son Larry, who was twelve years old at the time, says, 'I thought that was the beautifullest place in the world.'"

Even in the halcyon days of 1962, the Robert Taylor Homes were no paradise. There was considerable crime, and there were gangs, and Ruby's son Kermit joined one. Kermit was not Luther's son and did not recognize his authority. The two quarreled a lot. Meanwhile Luther had lost his job in the awning factory "that he had had for a decade, and then bounced around a little. He lost jobs because of transportation problems, because of layoffs, because of a bout of serious illness, because of his drinking, because he had a minor criminal record (having been in jail for disorderly conduct following a fight with Ruby), and because creditors were after him." He resumed "his old habit of not returning from work on Fridays after he got his paycheck." One weekend he didn't come home at all. In a search of his things Ruby discovered evidence that Luther was having an affair with Dorothy Johnson, a former neighbor. "Luther was not being particularly careful; he saw in Dorothy, who was younger than Ruby, who had three children compared to Ruby's eight, who had a job while Ruby was on public aid, the promise of an escape from the ghetto, and he was entranced." The children discovered the affair. Kermit tried to strangle Luther. In 1965 Luther moved out permanently, and eventually he and Ruby divorced. . . . After divorcing Ruby, Luther Haynes married Dorothy Johnson. He is still married to her, "owns a home on the far South Side of Chicago, and has worked for years as a parking-lot attendant; only recently have he and Ruby found that they can speak civilly to each other on the phone." . . .

The major claim in the complaint, and the focus of the appeal . . . is invasion of the right of privacy. In tort law the term "right of privacy" covers several distinct wrongs. Using a celebrity's (or other person's) name or picture in advertising without his consent. . . . Harassing a celebrity by following her too closely, albeit on a public street. . . . Casting a person in a false light by publicizing details of the person's life that while true are so selected or highlighted as to convey a misleading impression of the person's character. . . . Publicizing personal facts that while true and not misleading are so intimate that their disclosure to the public is deeply embarrassing to the person thus exposed and is perceived as gratuitous by the community. . . . The last, the publicizing of personal facts, is the aspect of invasion of privacy charged by the Hayneses.

Even people who have nothing rationally to be ashamed of can be mortified by the publication of intimate details of their life. Most people in no wise deformed or disfigured would nevertheless be deeply upset if nude photographs of themselves were published in a newspaper or a book. They feel the same way about photographs of their sexual activities, however "normal," or about a narrative of those activities, or about having their medical records publicized. . . . The desire for privacy illustrated by these examples is a mysterious but deep fact about human personality. It deserves and in our society receives legal protection. The nature of the injury shows, by the way, that the defendants are wrong to argue that this branch of the right of privacy requires proof of special damages. . . .

But this is not the character of the depictions of the Hayneses in *The Promised Land*. Although the plaintiffs claim that the book depicts their "sex life" and "ridicules" Luther Haynes's love-making (the reference is to the passage we quoted in which the author refers to Ruby's "devastating imitation" of Luther's manner when he would come home Friday nights in an amorous mood), these characterizations are misleading. No sexual act is described in the book. No intimate details are revealed. Entering one's bedroom with a bottle in one hand and a cigarette in the other is not foreplay. Ruby's speculation that Kevin's problems may have been due to Luther's having been a heavy drinker is not the narration of a sexual act.

. . . The branch of privacy law that the Hayneses invoke in their appeal is not concerned with, and is not a proper surrogate for legal doctrines that are concerned with, the accuracy of the private facts revealed. It is concerned with the propriety of stripping away the veil of privacy with which we cover the embarrassing, the shameful, the tabooed, truths about us. . . . The revelations in the book are not about the intimate details of the Hayneses' life. They are about misconduct, in particular Luther's. (There is very little about Dorothy in the book, apart from the fact that she had had an affair with Luther while he was still married to Ruby and that they eventually became and have remained lawfully married.) The revelations are about his heavy drinking, his unstable employment, his adultery, his irresponsible and neglectful behavior toward his wife and children. So we must consider cases in which the right of privacy has been invoked as a shield against the revelation of previous misconduct.

Two early cases illustrate the range of judicial thinking. In *Melvin v. Reid,* 297 P. 91 (Cal. App. 1931), the plaintiff was a former prostitute, who had been prosecuted but acquitted of murder. She later had married and (she alleged) for seven years had lived a blameless respectable life in a community in which her lurid past was unknown—when all was revealed in a movie about the murder case which used her maiden name. The court held that these allegations stated a claim for invasion of privacy. The Hayneses' claim is similar although less dramatic. They have been a respectable married couple for two decades. Luther's alcohol problem is behind him. He has steady employment as a doorman. His wife is a nurse, and in 1990 he told Lemann that the couple's combined income was $60,000 a year. He is not in trouble with the domestic relations court. He is a deacon of his church. He has come a long way from sharecropping in Mississippi and public housing in Chicago and he and his wife want to bury their past just as Mrs. Melvin wanted to do and in *Melvin v. Reid* was held entitled to do. . . . In Luther Haynes's own words, from his deposition, "I know I haven't been no angel, but since almost 30 years ago I have turned my life completely around. I stopped the drinking and all this bad habits and stuff like that, which I deny, some of [it] I didn't deny, because I have changed my life. It take me almost 30 years to change it and I am deeply in my church. I look good in the eyes of my church members and my community. Now, what is going to happen now when this public reads this garbage which I didn't tell Mr. Lemann to write? Then all this is going to go down the drain. And I worked like a son of a gun to build myself up in a good reputation and he has torn it down."

But with *Melvin v. Reid* compare *Sidis v. F-R Publishing Corp.,* 113 F.2d 806 (2d Cir. 1940), another old case but one more consonant with modern thinking about the proper balance between the right of privacy and the freedom of the press. A child prodigy had flamed out; he was now an eccentric recluse. The *New Yorker* ran a "where is he now" article about him. The article, entitled "April Fool," did not reveal any misconduct by Sidis but it depicted him in mocking tones as a comical failure, in much the same way that the report of Ruby's "devastating imitation" of the amorous Luther Haynes could be thought to have depicted him as a comical failure, albeit with sinister consequences absent from Sidis's case. The invasion of Sidis's privacy was palpable. But the publisher won. No intimate physical details of Sidis's life had been revealed; and on the other side was the undoubted newsworthiness of a child prodigy, as of a woman prosecuted for murder. Sidis, unlike Mrs. Melvin, was not permitted to bury his past.

Evolution along the divergent lines marked out by *Melvin* and *Sidis* continued—until *Cox Broadcasting Corp. v. Cohn,* 420 U.S. 469 (1975), which may have consigned the entire Melvin line to the outer darkness.... [T]he implications of [*Cox* and *Florida Star*] for the branch of the right of privacy that limits the publication of private facts are profound, even for a case such as this in which, unlike *Melvin v. Reid,* the primary source of the allegedly humiliating personal facts is not a public record. (The primary source is Ruby Daniels.) The Court must believe that the First Amendment greatly circumscribes the right even of a private figure to obtain damages for the publication of newsworthy facts about him, even when they are facts of a kind that people want very much to conceal. To be identified in the newspaper as a rape victim is intensely embarrassing. And it is not invited embarrassment. No one asks to be raped; the plaintiff in *Melvin v. Reid* did not ask to be prosecuted for murder (remember, she was acquitted, though whether she actually was innocent is unknown); Sidis did not decide to be a prodigy; and Luther Haynes did not aspire to be a representative figure in the great black migration from the South to the North. People who do not desire the limelight and do not deliberately choose a way of life or course of conduct calculated to thrust them into it nevertheless have no legal right to extinguish it if the experiences that have befallen them are newsworthy, even if they would prefer that those experiences be kept private. The possibility of an involuntary loss of privacy is recognized in the modern formulations of this branch of the privacy tort, which require not only that the private facts publicized be such as would make a reasonable person deeply offended by such publicity but also that they be facts in which the public has no legitimate interest. *Restatement (Second) of Torts* § 652D(b).

The two criteria, offensiveness and newsworthiness, are related. An individual, and more pertinently perhaps the community, is most offended by the publication of intimate personal facts when the community has no interest in them beyond the voyeuristic thrill of penetrating the wall of privacy that surrounds a stranger. The reader of a book about the black migration to the North would have no legitimate interest in the details of Luther Haynes's sex life; but no such details are disclosed. Such a reader does have a legitimate interest in the aspects of

Luther's conduct that the book reveals. For one of Lemann's major themes is the transposition virtually intact of a sharecropper morality characterized by a family structure "matriarchal and elastic" and by an "extremely unstable" marriage bond to the slums of the northern cities, and the interaction, largely random and sometimes perverse, of that morality with governmental programs to alleviate poverty. Public aid policies discouraged Ruby and Luther from living together; public housing policies precipitated a marriage doomed to fail. No detail in the book claimed to invade the Hayneses' privacy is not germane to the story that the author wanted to tell, a story not only of legitimate but of transcendent public interest.

The Hayneses question whether the linkage between the author's theme and their private life really is organic. They point out that many social histories do not mention individuals at all, let alone by name. That is true. Much of social science, including social history, proceeds by abstraction, aggregation, and quantification rather than by case studies; the economist Robert Fogel has won a Nobel prize for his statistical studies of economic history, including, not wholly unrelated to the subject of Lemann's book, the history of Negro slavery in the United States. But it would be absurd to suggest that cliometric or other aggregative, impersonal methods of doing social history are the only proper way to go about it and presumptuous to claim even that they are the best way. Lemann's book has been praised to the skies by distinguished scholars, among them black scholars covering a large portion of the ideological spectrum . . . . Lemann's methodology places the individual case history at center stage. If he cannot tell the story of Ruby Daniels without waivers from every person who she thinks did her wrong, he cannot write this book.

Well, argue the Hayneses, at least Lemann could have changed their names. But the use of pseudonyms would not have gotten Lemann and Knopf off the legal hook. The details of the Hayneses' lives recounted in the book would identify them unmistakably to anyone who has known the Hayneses well for a long time (members of their families, for example), or who knew them before they got married; and no more is required for liability either in defamation law or in privacy law. Lemann would have had to change some, perhaps many, of the details. But then he would no longer have been writing history. He would have been writing fiction. The nonquantitative study of living persons would be abolished as a category of scholarship, to be replaced by the sociological novel. That is a genre with a distinguished history punctuated by famous names, . . . but we do not think that the law of privacy makes it (or that the First Amendment would permit the law of privacy to make it) the exclusive format for a social history of living persons that tells their story rather than treating them as data points in a statistical study. . . .

The Promised Land does not afford the reader a titillating glimpse of tabooed activities. The tone is decorous and restrained. Painful though it is for the Hayneses to see a past they would rather forget brought into the public view, the public needs the information conveyed by the book, including the information about Luther and Dorothy Haynes, in order to evaluate the profound social and political questions that the book raises. Given the *Cox* decision, moreover, all the discreditable facts about the Hayneses that are contained in judicial records are beyond the power of tort law to conceal; and the disclosure of those facts alone would strip away the Hayneses' privacy as effectively as *The Promised Land* has done. . . .

Does it follow, as the Hayneses' lawyer asked us rhetorically at oral argument, that a journalist who wanted to write a book about contemporary sexual practices could include the intimate details of named living persons' sexual acts without the persons' consent? Not necessarily, although the revelation of such details in the memoirs of former spouses and lovers is common enough and rarely provokes a lawsuit even when the former spouse or lover is still alive. The core of the branch of privacy law with which we deal in this case is the protection of those intimate physical details the publicizing of which would be not merely embarrassing and painful but deeply shocking to the average person subjected to such exposure. The public has a legitimate interest in sexuality, but that interest may be outweighed in such a case by the injury to the sensibilities of the persons made use of by the author in such a way. *Restatement (Second) of Torts, supra,* § 652D, comment h. At least the balance would be sufficiently close to preclude summary judgment for the author and publisher. . . .

AFFIRMED.

NOTE AND QUESTIONS

1   Notice that the meaning of the word "publication" in the publication of private facts is different from its meaning in defamation law. Publication for defamation purposes requires sharing the information with only one person. In the invasion of privacy context, publication means wide publicity.

2   Recall the facts of *Watt v. Longsdon.* Could the plaintiff in *Watt* state a valid cause of action for public disclosure of private facts?

DOE V. MILLS
536 N.W.2D 824 (MICH. CT. APP. 1995)

PER CURIAM.

. . . Plaintiffs, using pseudonyms to protect their identity, commenced this action against defendants Lynn Mills, Sister Lois Mitoraj, and Mitoraj's religious order, The Felician Sisters of O.S.F. of Livonia, for the torts of invasion of privacy and intentional infliction of emotional distress. According to plaintiffs' complaint, defendants Mills and Mitoraj (hereinafter defendants), while protesting outside the Women's Advisory Center in Livonia, displayed the real names of plaintiffs Jane Doe and Sally Roe on "large signs" that were "held up for public view." The signs indicated that Doe and Roe were about to undergo abortions and implored them, inter alia, not to "kill their babies." Plaintiffs alleged that they did not give defendants permission to publicize the fact of their abortions. To the contrary, it was plaintiffs' intent to "keep the fact of their abortions private, confidential, and free from any publicity."

Plaintiffs alleged two different theories of invasion of privacy. Count II was labeled "public disclosure of private facts" and count III was labeled "intrusion upon seclusion." In addition, plaintiffs brought a claim for intentional infliction of emotional distress.

Defendants Mills and Mitoraj brought a motion for summary disposition . . . . The motion was supported by the affidavits of Robert Thomas, a nonparty, and defendant Mills. Thomas stated in his affidavit that he went to the Women's Advisory Center on June 1, 1991, at approximately 10:30 p.m., and climbed into a refuse dumpster that was located in the parking lot. Inside the dumpster, Thomas found a piece of paper indicating that plaintiffs Doe and Sally Roe were about to undergo abortions. Thomas gave this information to Mills the following day. Mills stated in her affidavit that she and Mitoraj went to the Women's Advisory Center on June 8, 1991, believing that Doe and Sally Roe would be arriving that day to have an abortion. Mills claimed that it was her intent to persuade both Doe and Sally Roe not to have an abortion and, therefore, she placed their names on two separate signs in order to "capture [their] attention." Mills took one sign and Mitoraj the other, and then both of them held the signs up for public view while positioned at the entrance to the Women's Advisory Center's parking lot.

In opposition to defendants' motion, plaintiffs submitted a portion of Mills' deposition testimony wherein Mills admitted that, before displaying the signs, she was aware that Thomas had obtained the information concerning plaintiffs from the garbage at the Women's Advisory Center. Plaintiffs did not submit any evidence indicating that either defendant was involved along with Thomas in obtaining the information from the garbage.

In an opinion dated November 9, 1993, the trial court granted defendants summary disposition of each of the two claims of invasion of privacy as well as the claim for intentional infliction of emotional distress. Plaintiffs appeal. . . .

Plaintiffs first argue that the trial court erred in dismissing their two claims of invasion of privacy.

The tort of invasion of privacy is based on a common-law right to privacy, which is said to protect against four types of invasion of privacy: (1) intrusion upon the plaintiff's seclusion or solitude, or into his private affairs; (2) public disclosure of embarrassing private facts about the plaintiff; (3) publicity that places the plaintiff in a false light in the public eye; and (4) appropriation, for the defendant's advantage, of the plaintiff's name or likeness. . . . Only the first two types of claims are involved in this case. We find that the trial court erred in dismissing plaintiffs' claim for public disclosure of embarrassing private facts, but that summary disposition of the claim regarding intrusion upon seclusion was proper.

A. Public Disclosure of Embarrassing Private Facts

A cause of action for public disclosure of embarrassing private facts requires (1) the disclosure of information, (2) that is highly offensive to a reasonable person, and (3) that is of no legitimate concern to the public. . . . Plaintiffs meet the first element of this action because they allege that defendants, while protesting in public, disclosed information publicizing their decision to have an abortion.

Regarding the second element, the trial court stated:

The words on the placards that were carried by the defendants conveyed the message that plaintiffs were contemplating and or scheduling an abortion. This is the disclosed information. Would plaintiffs seriously suggest or argue that one who contemplates or schedules an abortion has committed an act that is highly offensive to a reasonable person?

We disagree with the trial court to the extent it suggested the disclosure of the information was not actionable as a matter of law.

In analyzing a claim of invasion of privacy, courts generally have embraced the provisions of the Restatement of Torts describing that tort. . . . The Restatement of Torts describes the type of publicity that will give rise to an action for public disclosure of embarrassing private facts:

The rule stated in this Section gives protection only against unreasonable publicity, of a kind highly offensive to the ordinary reasonable man. . . . It is only when the publicity given to him is such that a reasonable person would feel justified in feeling seriously aggrieved by it that the cause of action arises.

Restatement Torts, 2d, § 652D, comment c . . . .

Whether a public disclosure involves "embarrassing private facts" has been held to be a question of fact for the jury. . . . Here, plaintiffs allege that defendants publicized the fact of their abortions despite their intent to keep this matter "private, confidential, and free from any publicity." Plaintiffs further allege that the publicity given by defendants was highly offensive and was deliberately calculated to embarrass and humiliate them, which it allegedly did. We cannot say that a reasonable person would not be justified in feeling seriously aggrieved by such publicity. Rather, we find that plaintiffs' allegations are sufficient to constitute a question for the jury regarding whether embarrassing private facts were involved in a public disclosure.

In order to satisfy the final element of an action for public disclosure of embarrassing private facts, the information disclosed must concern the individual's private life. Liability will not be imposed for giving publicity to matters that are already of public record or otherwise open to the public. . . . In describing those matters that will support an action for public disclosure of private facts, the Restatement of Torts states:

Every individual has some phases of his life and his activities and some facts about himself that he does not expose to the public eye, but keeps entirely to himself or at most reveals only to his family or to close personal friends. Sexual relations, for example, are normally entirely private matters.

Restatement Torts, 2d, § 652D, comment b . . . . Matters concerning a person's medical treatment or condition are also generally considered private. . . .

In this case, the trial court observed that the subject of abortion is one of public interest and, for that reason, intimated that plaintiffs could not satisfy the final element:

It is this court's opinion that abortion, no matter how one views this subject, is unquestionably a matter of great public concern.... Because abortions are so controversial in our society, events surrounding abortions do attract considerable public attention, witness the heavy picketing of abortion clinics and the extensive amount of publicity the subject of abortion receives. So, it is doubtful that plaintiffs could ever establish the third element of this cause of action because plaintiffs were involved in an event that attracts public attention.

We disagree with the trial court's reasoning.

The fact that [persons] engage in an activity in which the public can be said to have a general interest does not render every aspect of their lives subject to public disclosure. Most persons are connected with some activity, vocational or avocational, as to which the public can be said as a matter of law to have a legitimate interest or curiosity. To hold as a matter of law that private facts as to such persons are also within the area of legitimate public interest could indirectly expose everyone's private life to public view.

Winstead, supra at 674, 517 N.W.2d 874, quoting *Virgil v. Time, Inc.,* 527 F.2d 1122, 1131 (CA 9, 1975).

The Missouri Court of Appeals applied this principle in *Y.G. & L.G., supra.* In that case, the plaintiffs sued a television station for invasion of privacy after the station filmed the plaintiffs' participation in a hospital's in vitro fertilization program without the plaintiffs' consent. The Missouri Court of Appeals agreed that a private matter was involved, notwithstanding the public's interest in in vitro fertilization:

The *in vitro* program and its success may well have been matters of public interest, but the identity of the plaintiffs participating in the program was, we conclude, a private matter. It did concern matters of procreation and sexual relations as well as medical treatment—all private matters. The *in vitro* fertilization program participation was certainly not a matter of public record nor did it become of public concern due to any of the ordinary incidents of public concern.

795 S.W.2d at 500.

Likewise, in this case, plaintiffs' complaint alleges a private matter. The alleged disclosure concerns the plaintiffs' decisions to have an abortion. We have no hesitancy in concluding that such an allegation involves a matter that a reasonable person would consider private. Indeed, abortion concerns matters of sexual relations and medical treatment, both of which are regarded as private matters. Furthermore, even though the abortion issue may be regarded as a matter of public interest, the plaintiffs' identities in this case were not matters of legitimate public concern, nor a matter of public record, but, instead, were purely private matters. We conclude, therefore, that plaintiffs' allegations are sufficient to meet the minimum prima facie showing necessary to establish that the information disclosed must concern a private matter. . . . Accordingly, we find that plaintiffs have alleged a prima facie case of public disclosure of embarrassing private facts, thereby making summary disposition for the defendants . . . improper.

The trial court ruled that, even if plaintiffs had alleged a cause of action for public disclosure of embarrassing private facts, summary disposition was still warranted . . . given that the undisputed facts showed that defendants had learned of each plaintiff's decision to have an abortion from a document that was obtained from the trash at the Women's Advisory Center. Relying on cases construing the scope of protection under the Fourth Amendment of the United States Constitution, . . . the trial court ruled that, because information concerning plaintiffs' decisions to have an abortion had been discarded into the trash, plaintiffs had lost their right of privacy with respect to that information. The flaw in the trial court's analysis is that plaintiffs' action is not based on a constitutional right of privacy, but on a right of privacy under the common law. . . . . Furthermore, while the aim of the Fourth Amendment is to provide "protect[ion of] individual privacy against certain kinds of governmental intrusion," *Katz, supra* at 350, 88 S.Ct. at 510, an action for public disclosure of embarrassing private facts is concerned, not with governmental intrusions, but with protecting a person's common-law right to be free of unreasonable or unnecessary publicity of one's private matters, *Beaumont, supra* at 104-105, 257 N.W.2d 522.

We conclude, therefore, that the trial court erred in relying on cases construing the Fourth Amendment as a basis for concluding that plaintiffs had somehow lost their common-law privacy rights.

Although it is possible for the right of privacy to be waived or lost by a course of conduct that estops its assertion, . . . the facts of this case do not establish any waiver. It has been said that "'[t]here can never be a waiver of the right of privacy, in the absence of knowledge and consent of the person entitled to waive.'" *Id.*, quoting 77 CJS, *Right of Privacy*, § 6, p. 414. Moreover, an implied waiver requires a "clear, unequivocal, and decisive act of the party showing such a purpose." 62A Am.Jur.2d, *Privacy*, § 226, p. 836.

According to the undisputed facts in this case, a nonparty learned of plaintiffs' decisions to have an abortion from a document that had been discarded into the trash. There is no evidence that either plaintiff personally discarded the document or had knowledge that the document was discarded. Moreover, even if plaintiffs had discarded the document, such an act does not demonstrate consent to having information in that document publicly disclosed. Therefore, the facts do not establish a waiver of plaintiffs' common-law privacy rights.

Defendants also maintain that the undisputed facts show that they did not give publicity to a private matter because the Women's Advisory Center is located in a public place and plaintiffs' "comings and goings to the clinic were acts exposed to the public eye." The information disclosed, however, concerned an activity that took place within the private confines of the clinic, a matter which was not "exposed to the public eye." Also, merely because plaintiffs' "comings and goings" may have been visible to members of the public does not mean that the public was aware of the precise purpose of those "comings and goings." Moreover, we agree with the court in *Y.G. & L.G., supra,* which held, in a similar context, that the plaintiffs there did not lose their privacy rights with respect to their participation in an in vitro fertilization program merely because they attended the program at a public hospital. . . .

Therefore, for the reasons stated, we reverse the trial court's judgment granting the defendants' motion for summary disposition of plaintiffs' claim for public disclosure of embarrassing private facts.

B. Intrusion Upon Seclusion

An action for intrusion upon seclusion focuses on the manner in which information is obtained, not its publication; it is considered analogous to a trespass. . . . In this case, the alleged wrongful actions that form the basis of plaintiffs' claim of intrusion relate only to the publication of information, not to any wrongful intrusion. Specifically, plaintiffs' complaint alleges: "Defendants intentionally intruded upon the private affairs of the Plaintiffs by *publicizing* the fact that Jane Doe and Sally Roe intended to undergo abortions." [Emphasis added.]

In *Tobin*, our Supreme Court noted that an action for intrusion does not exist where "[t]he only aspect of the contemplated disclosure offensive to the plaintiffs is the fact of disclosure, not the method by which it was obtained." *Tobin, supra* at 674, 331 N.W.2d 184. That is exactly the situation in this case. Therefore, because plaintiffs' complaint alleges only the fact of disclosure and does not allege any offensive intrusion, we conclude that summary disposition of plaintiffs' intrusion claim was proper . . . .

Although not specifically alleged, plaintiffs argue that a cause of action for intrusion exists because the evidence shows that the information about plaintiffs was obtained from a garbage dumpster at the Women's Advisory Center. . . . The trial court rejected this argument, however, noting that, even if the search of the garbage could be considered a wrongful intrusion, the undisputed facts showed that the search was conducted by Robert Thomas, a nonparty, and there was no evidence showing that either defendant was involved along with Thomas in obtaining the information from the garbage.

Plaintiffs insist, however, that liability still may be imposed under an intrusion theory because defendant Mills admitted in her deposition that she was aware of the source of the information before publicizing it. We disagree. Mills' mere receipt of the information from Thomas, even with knowledge of its source, is insufficient to subject her to liability under an intrusion theory.

Accordingly, we conclude that summary disposition of plaintiffs' claim of intrusion upon seclusion was proper. . . . Affirmed in part, reversed in part, and remanded for further proceedings. . . .

D. FALSE LIGHT

Because this tort involves giving publicity to false information about the plaintiff instead of true information, the constitutional and policy implications of liability are not as significant in the false light context as they are when the tort is for publicizing embarrassing but true private facts.

TIME, INC. V. HILL
385 U.S. 374 (1967)

MR. JUSTICE BRENNAN delivered the opinion of the Court.

The question in this case is whether appellant, publisher of Life Magazine, was denied constitutional protections of speech and press by the application . . . of the New York Civil Rights Law . . . to award appellee damages on allegations that Life falsely reported that a new play portrayed an experience suffered by appellee and his family.

The article appeared in Life in February 1955. It was entitled "True Crime Inspires Tense Play," with the subtitle, "The ordeal of a family trapped by convicts gives Broadway a new thriller, 'The Desperate Hours.'" The text of the article reads as follows:

> Three years ago Americans all over the country read about the desperate ordeal of the James Hill family, who were held prisoners in their home outside Philadelphia by three escaped convicts. Later they read about it in Joseph Hayes's novel, *The Desperate Hours*, inspired by the family's experience. Now they can see the story re-enacted in Hayes's Broadway play based on the book, and next year will see it in his movie, which has been filmed but is being held up until the play has a chance to pay off.
>
> The play, directed by Robert Montgomery and expertly acted, is a heart-stopping account of how a family rose to heroism in a crisis.

LIFE photographed the play during its Philadelphia tryout, transported some of the actors to the actual house where the Hills were besieged. On the next page scenes from the play are re-enacted on the site of the crime.

The pictures on the ensuing two pages included an enactment of the son being "roughed up" by one of the convicts, entitled "brutish convict," a picture of the daughter biting the hand of a convict to make him drop a gun, entitled "daring daughter," and one of the father throwing his gun through the door after a "brave try" to save his family is foiled.

The James Hill referred to in the article is the appellee. He and his wife and five children involuntarily became the subjects of a front-page news story after being held hostage by three escaped convicts in their suburban, Whitemarsh, Pennsylvania, home for 19 hours on September 11-12, 1952. The family was released unharmed. In an interview with newsmen after the convicts departed, appellee stressed that the convicts had treated the family courteously, had not molested them, and had not been at all violent. The convicts were thereafter apprehended in a widely publicized encounter with the police which resulted in the killing of two of the convicts. Shortly thereafter the family moved to Connecticut. The appellee discouraged all efforts to keep them in the public spotlight through magazine articles or appearances on television.

In the spring of 1953, Joseph Hayes' novel, The Desperate Hours, was published. The story depicted the experience of a family of four held hostage by three escaped convicts in the family's suburban home. But, unlike Hill's experience, the family of the story suffer violence at the hands of the convicts; the father and son are beaten and the daughter subjected to a verbal sexual insult.

The book was made into a play, also entitled The Desperate Hours, and it is Life's article about the play which is the subject of appellee's action. The complaint sought damages . . . on allegations that the Life article was intended to, and did, give the impression that the play mirrored the Hill family's experience, which, to the knowledge of defendant ". . . was false and untrue." Appellant's defense was that the article was "a subject of legitimate news interest," "a subject of general interest and of value and concern to the public" at the time of publication, and that it was "published in good faith without any malice whatsoever . . . ."

The jury awarded appellee $50,000 compensatory and $25,000 punitive damages. . . .

The New York Court of Appeals affirmed . . . . We reverse and remand the case to the Court of Appeals for further proceedings not inconsistent with this opinion.

I.

. . . The guarantees for speech and press are not the preserve of political expression or comment upon public affairs, essential as those are to healthy government. One need only pick up any newspaper or magazine to comprehend the vast range of published matter which exposes persons to public view, both private citizens and public officials. Exposure of the self to others in varying degrees is a concomitant of life in a civilized community. The risk of this exposure is an essential incident of life in a society which places a primary value on freedom of speech and of press. . . . We have no doubt that the subject of the Life article, the opening of a new play linked to an actual incident, is a matter of public interest. . . . Erroneous statement is no less inevitable in such a case than in the case of comment upon public affairs, and in both, if innocent or merely negligent, ". . . it must be protected if the freedoms of expression are to have the 'breathing space' that they 'need . . . to survive' . . . ." New York Times Co. v. Sullivan, supra, at 271-272. . . . We create a grave risk of serious impairment of the indispensable service of a free press in a free society if we saddle the press with the impossible burden of verifying to a certainty the facts associated in news articles with a person's name, picture or portrait, particularly as related to nondefamatory matter. Even negligence would be a most elusive standard, especially when the content of the speech itself affords no warning of prospective harm to another through falsity. A negligence test would place on the press the intolerable burden of guessing how a jury might assess the reasonableness of steps taken by it to verify the accuracy of every reference to a name, picture or portrait.

In this context, sanctions against either innocent or negligent misstatement would present a grave hazard of discouraging the press from exercising the constitutional guarantees. Those guarantees are not for the benefit of the press so much as for the benefit of all of us. A broadly defined freedom of the press assures the maintenance of our political system and an open society. Fear of large verdicts in damage suits for innocent or merely negligent misstatement, even fear of the expense involved in their defense, must inevitably cause publishers to "steer . . . wider of the unlawful zone," *New York Times Co.* v. *Sullivan*, 376 U.S., at 279 . . . .

But the constitutional guarantees can tolerate sanctions against *calculated* falsehood without significant impairment of their essential function. We held in *New York Times* that calculated falsehood enjoyed no immunity in the case of alleged defamation of a public official concerning his official conduct. Similarly, calculated falsehood should enjoy no immunity in the situation here presented us. . . .

We find applicable here the standard of knowing or reckless falsehood, not through blind application of *New York Times Co.* v. *Sullivan*, relating solely to libel actions by public officials, but only upon consideration of the factors which arise in the particular context of the application of the New York statute in cases involving private individuals. This is neither a libel action by a private individual nor a statutory action by a public official. Therefore, although the First Amendment principles pronounced in *New York Times* guide our conclusion, we reach that conclusion only by applying these principles in this discrete context. It therefore serves no purpose to distinguish the facts here from those in *New York Times*. Were this a libel action, the distinction which has been suggested between the relative opportunities of the public official and the private individual to rebut defamatory charges might be germane. And the additional state interest in the protection of the individual against damage to his reputation would be involved. . . . Moreover, a different test might be required in a statutory action by a public official, as opposed to a libel action by a public official or a statutory action by a private individual. . . .

II.

Turning to the facts of the present case, the proofs reasonably would support either a jury finding of innocent or merely negligent misstatement by Life, or a finding that Life portrayed the play as a re-enactment of the Hill family's experience reckless of the truth or with actual knowledge that the portrayal was false. . . .

The jury might reasonably conclude from this evidence – particularly that the New York Times article was in the story file, that the copy editor deleted "somewhat fictionalized" after the research assistant questioned its accuracy, and that Prideaux admitted that he knew the play was "between a little bit and moderately fictionalized" – that Life knew the falsity of, or was reckless of the truth in, stating in the article that "the story re-enacted" the Hill family's experience. On the other hand, the jury might reasonably predicate a finding of innocent or only negligent misstatement on the testimony that a statement was made to Prideaux by the free-lance photographer that linked the play to an incident in Philadelphia, that the author Hayes cooperated in arranging for the availability of the former Hill home, and that Prideaux thought beyond doubt that the "heart and soul" of the play was the Hill incident. . . .

III.

We do not think, however, that the instructions confined the jury to a verdict of liability based on a finding that the statements in the article were made with knowledge of their falsity or in reckless disregard of the truth. The jury was instructed . . . that a verdict of liability could rest only on findings that (1) Life published the article, "not to disseminate news, but was using plaintiffs' names, in connection with a fictionalized episode as to plaintiffs' relationship to The Desperate Hours"; the Court variously restated this "fictionalization" requirement in terms such as whether appellant "altered or changed the true facts concerning plaintiffs' relationship to The Desperate Hours, so that the article, as published, constituted substantially fiction or a fictionalized version . . . ," whether the article constituted "fiction," or was "fictionalized"; and that (2) the article was published to advertise the play or "for trade purposes." This latter purpose was variously defined as one "to amuse, thrill, astonish or move the reading public so as to increase the circulation of the magazine or for some other material benefit," "to increase circulation or enhance the standing of the magazine with its readers," and "for the publisher's profits through increased circulation, induced by exploitation of the plaintiffs." . . .

Appellee argues that the instructions to determine whether Life "altered or changed" the true facts, and whether, apart from incidental errors, the article was a "substantial fiction" or a "fictionalized version" were tantamount to instructions that the jury must find that Life knowingly falsified the facts. We do not think that the instructions bear that interpretation . . . . The element of "knowingly" is mentioned only in the instruction that punitive damages must be supported by a finding that Life falsely connected the Hill family with the play "knowingly or through failure to make a reasonable investigation." . . .

IV.

The appellant argues that the statute should be declared unconstitutional on its face if construed by the New York courts to impose liability without proof of knowing or reckless falsity. . . . Such a declaration would not be warranted even if it were entirely clear that this had previously been the view of the New York courts. The New York Court of Appeals, as the *Spahn* opinion demonstrates, has been assiduous in construing the statute to avoid invasion of the constitutional protections of speech and press. We, therefore, confidently expect that the New York courts will apply the statute consistently with the constitutional command. Any possible difference with us as to the thrust of the constitutional command is narrowly limited in this case to the failure of the trial judge to instruct the jury that a verdict of liability could be predicated only on a finding of knowing or reckless falsity in the publication of the Life article.

The judgment of the Court of Appeals is set aside and the case is remanded for further proceedings not inconsistent with this opinion.

It is so ordered.

MR. JUSTICE BLACK, with whom MR. JUSTICE DOUGLAS joins, concurring.

I concur in reversal of the judgment in this case based on the grounds and reasons stated in the Court's opinion. I do this, however, in order for the Court to be able at this time to agree on an opinion in this important case based on the prevailing constitutional doctrine expressed in *New York Times Co. v. Sullivan*, 376 U.S. 254. The Court's opinion decides the case in accordance with this doctrine, to which the majority adhere. In agreeing to the Court's opinion, I do not recede from any of the views I have previously expressed about the much wider press and speech freedoms I think the First and Fourteenth Amendments were designed to grant to the people of the Nation. *See, e.g., New York Times Co. v. Sullivan*, 376 U.S., at 293 (concurring opinion) . . . .

MR. JUSTICE HARLAN, concurring in part and dissenting in part.

While I find much with which I agree in the opinion of the Court, I am constrained to express my disagreement with its view of the proper standard of liability to be applied on remand. Were the jury on retrial to find negligent rather than, as the Court requires, reckless or knowing "fictionalization," I think that federal constitutional requirements would be met. . . .

MR. JUSTICE FORTAS, with whom THE CHIEF JUSTICE and MR. JUSTICE CLARK join, dissenting.

The Court's holding here is exceedingly narrow. It declines to hold that the New York "Right of Privacy" statute is unconstitutional. I agree. The Court concludes, however, that the instructions to the jury in this case were fatally defective because they failed to advise the jury that a verdict for the plaintiffs could be predicated only on a finding of knowing or reckless falsity in the publication of the Life article. Presumably, the appellee is entitled to a new trial. If he can stand the emotional and financial burden, there is reason to hope that he will recover damages for the reckless and irresponsible assault upon himself and his family which this article represents. But he has litigated this case for 11 years. He should not be subjected to the burden of a new trial without significant cause. This does not exist. Perhaps the purpose of the decision here is to indicate that this Court will place insuperable obstacles in the way of recovery by persons who are injured by reckless and heedless assaults provided they are in print, and even though they are totally divorced from fact. If so, I should think that the Court would cast its decision in constitutional terms. Short of that purpose, with which I would strongly disagree, there is no reason here to order a new trial. The instructions in this case are acceptable even within the principles today announced by the Court. . . .

The courts may not and must not permit either public or private action that censors or inhibits the press. But part of this responsibility is to preserve values and procedures which assure the ordinary citizen that the press is not above the reach of the law – that its special prerogatives, granted because of its special and vital functions, are reasonably equated with its needs in the performance of these functions. For this Court totally to immunize the press – whether forthrightly or by subtle indirection – in areas far beyond the needs of news, comment on public persons and events, discussion of public issues and the like would be no service to freedom of the press, but an invitation to public hostility to that freedom. This Court cannot and should not refuse to permit under state law the private citizen who is aggrieved by the type of assault which we have here and which is not within the specially protected core of the First Amendment to recover compensatory damages for recklessly inflicted invasion of his rights.

Accordingly, I would affirm.

MISREPRESENTATION

EXODUS 20:16

Thou shalt not bear false witness against thy neighbour.

The unifying element of the law of misrepresentation is defendant's false statement. This area of the law can be divided into two parts: 1) intentional misrepresentation (aka fraud or deceit) and 2) negligent misrepresentation (limited to commercial cases).

A. DECEIT/FRAUD

LAIDLAW V. ORGAN
15 U.S. 178 (1817)

[Defendant, Organ, was a New Orleans merchant. Plaintiff, Laidlaw, was a tobacco seller. Organ knew, but did not reveal to Laidlaw, that the Treaty of Ghent had been signed, ending the War of 1812 between the United States and Britain. The end of the war would result in the lifting of the British blockade of New Orleans, which blockade had prevented tobacco from shipping out of New Orleans, resulting in excess local supply and driving down the price of tobacco.]

Mr. Chief Justice MARSHALL delivered the opinion of the court.

The question in this case is, whether the intelligence of extrinsic circumstances, which might influence the price of the commodity, and which was exclusively within the knowledge of the vendee, ought to have been communicated by him to the vendor? The court is of opinion that he was not bound to communicate it. It would be difficult to circumscribe the contrary doctrine within proper limits, where the means of intelligence are equally accessible to both parties. But at the same time, each party must take care not to say or do any thing tending to impose upon the other. . . .

1. FALSE STATEMENT OF FACT, CONCEALMENT, AND NON-DISCLOSURE

The beginning place for causes of action both for intentional and negligent misrepresentation is the false statement.

SWINTON V. WHITINSVILLE SAVINGS BANK
42 N.E.2D 808 (MASS. 1942)

The declaration alleges that on or about September 12, 1938, the defendant sold the plaintiff a house in Newton to be occupied by the plaintiff and his family as a dwelling; that at the time of the sale the house "was infested with termites, an insect that is most dangerous and destructive to buildings"; that the defendant knew the house was so infested; that the plaintiff could not readily observe this condition upon inspection; that, "knowing the internal destruction that these insects were creating in said house," the defendant falsely and fraudulently concealed from the plaintiff its true condition; that the plaintiff at the time of his purchase had no knowledge of the termites, exercised due care thereafter, and learned of them about August 30, 1940; and that, because of the destruction that was being done and the dangerous condition that was being created by the termites, the plaintiff was put to great expense for repairs and for the installation of termite control in order to prevent the loss and destruction of said house.

There is no allegation of any false statement or representation, or of the uttering of a half truth which may be tantamount to a falsehood. There is no intimation that the defendant by any means prevented the plaintiff from acquiring information as to the condition of the house. There is nothing to show any fiduciary relation between the parties, or that the plaintiff stood in a position of confidence toward or dependence upon the defendant. So far as appears the parties made a business deal at arm's length. The charge is concealment and nothing more; and it is concealment in the simple sense of mere failure to reveal, with nothing to show any peculiar duty to speak. The characterization of the concealment as false and fraudulent of course adds nothing in the absence of further allegations of fact. . . .

If this defendant is liable on this declaration every seller is liable who fails to disclose any nonapparent defect known to him in the subject of the sale which materially reduces its value and which the buyer fails to discover. Similarly it would seem that every buyer would be liable who fails to disclose any nonapparent virtue known to him in the subject of the purchase which materially enhances its value and of which the seller is ignorant. . . . The law has not yet, we believe, reached the point of imposing upon the frailties of human nature a standard so idealistic as this. That the particular case here stated by the plaintiff possesses a certain appeal to the moral sense is scarcely to be denied. . . . But the law . . . can hardly attempt to determine liability according to the varying probabilities of the existence and discovery of different possible defects in the subjects of trade. . . . The order sustaining the demurrer is affirmed, and judgment is to be entered for the defendant. . . .

So ordered.

GRIFFITH V. BYERS CONSTR. CO. OF KANSAS, INC.
510 P.2D 198 (KAN. 1973)

The purchasers of new homes in Woodlawn East Addition, City of Wichita, Kansas, brought separate actions for damages because of the saline condition of the soil of their homesites. These actions . . . were brought against the developer. This appeal is from an order granting summary judgments in favor of the developer, Byers Construction Co. of Kansas, Inc. (Byers).

The petitions allege that Byers developed and advertised the addition . . . . Prior to the time of development the addition was part of an abandoned oil field which contained salt water disposal areas which Byers knew or should have known would not sustain vegetation because of the saline content of the soil. It was alleged that Byers graded and developed the whole addition for homesites in such a manner that it became impossible for a purchaser to discover the presence of these salt areas. It further appears . . . that each of the plaintiffs selected a homesite which was located within a salt water disposal area. After houses were constructed attempts to landscape the homesites failed. Grass, shrubs and trees were planted and died because of the saline content of the soil. . . .

Each prospective homeowner contracted with a separate building contractor to construct a home on a homesite to be chosen by the owner. . . . When a homesite was chosen the respective building contractor then purchased the lot. The contractors obtained warranty deeds from Byers. When the houses were completed in accordance with specifications titles were transferred and the homeowners then received deeds to the improved homesites. No inquiry was made and no assurance was given by Byers on soil fertility. . . . The saline content of the soil of these homesites does not affect the structural qualities of the homes. The allegations of the petitions . . . indicate that landscaping is either impossible or highly expensive.

. . . [W]e do not believe the record conclusively establishes the inability of the appellants to support their charges of fraud nor did the trial court dispose of the motion on that ground. It is true the appellants and the builders stated in their depositions they had talked to no one who said the appelle Byers knew the soil of the lots was incapable of growing vegetation. However, this does not mean they had no evidence to support their claim of fraud. It was alleged in the petitions that appellee Byers developed the area and at that time the salt water disposal areas were apparent, that Byers knew or should have known of their nature and presence, that it graded the whole addition and the areas thereafter became latent, and that appellee was guilty of fraud in failing to disclose the presence of the salt areas to appellants. . . . The allegations of fraud appear to be viable issues for trial if nondisclosure of a known material defect in the lots constitutes actionable fraud as to the appellants.

This court has held that the purchaser may recover on the theory of fraud from a vendor-builder for nondisclosure of defects. In *Jenkins v. McCormick*, 184 Kan. 842, 339 P.2d 8, it is stated:

> Where a vendor has knowledge of a defect in property which is not within the fair and reasonable reach of the vendee and which he could not discover by the exercise of reasonable diligence, the silence and failure of the vendor to disclose the defect in the property constitutes actionable fraudulent concealment. . . .

This *Jenkins* rule approximates that stated in Restatement, Second, Torts, s 551:

1. One who fails to disclose to another a thing which he knows may justifiably induce the other to act or refrain from acting in a business transaction is subject to the same liability to the other as though he had represented the nonexistence of the matter which he has failed to disclose, if, but only if, he is under a duty to the other to exercise reasonable care to disclose the matter in question.

2. One party to a business transaction is under a duty to disclose to the other before the transaction is consummated.

* * *

e. Facts basic to the transaction, if he knows that the other is about to enter into the transaction under a mistake as to such facts, and that the other, because of the relationship between them, the customs in the trade, or other objective circumstances, would reasonably expect a disclosure of such facts.

. . . We see no reason why the rule in *Jenkins* should not be extended in the present case to a developer of residential lots. . . . Under the alleged facts of our present case, accepting the same in the light most favorable to the appellants, we must assume the appellee, Byers, had knowledge of the saline content of the soil of the lots it placed on the market. After the grading and development of the area this material defect in the lots was not within the fair and reasonable reach of the vendees, as they could not discover this latent defect by the exercise of reasonable care. The silence of the appellee, Byers, and its failure to disclose this defect in the soil condition to the purchasers could constitute actionable fraudulent concealment . . . . One who makes a fraudulent misrepresentation or concealment is subject to liability for pecuniary loss to the persons or class of persons whom he intends or has reason to expect to act or to refrain from action in reliance upon the misrepresentation or concealment.

Of course, the fraudulent concealment to be actionable has to be material to the transaction. A matter is material if it is one to which a reasonable man would attach importance in determining his choice of action in the transaction in question. (Restatement, Second, Torts, s 538.) There is little doubt in this case a prospective purchaser of a residential building site would consider the soil condition a material factor in choosing a lot on which to build his home. It materially affected the value and acceptability of the homesite.

. . . [T]he order of the district court entering summary judgment in favor of the appellee is . . . reversed as to the alternative claims based on fraud, and these cases are remanded with instructions to proceed in accordance with the views expressed herein.

1 *Failure to disclose v. concealment.* A mere failure to disclose is not a misrepresentation unless there is a duty to disclose; however, affirmative acts of concealment are tantamount to a misrepresentation.

2. SCIENTER

The state of mind required for a cause of action for intentional misrepresentation is quite different from the state of mind required for negligent misrepresentation.

DERRY V. PEEK
14 APP. CAS. 337 (1889)

. . . "This action is one which is commonly called an action of deceit, a mere common-law action." This is the description of it given by Cotton, L.J., in delivering judgment. . . . In an action of deceit, . . . it is not enough to establish misrepresentation alone; it is conceded on all hands that something more must be proved to cast liability upon the defendant, though it has been a matter of controversy what additional elements are requisite. . . .

I think· the authorities establish the following propositions: First, in order to sustain an action of deceit there must be proof of fraud, and nothing short of that will suffice. Secondly, fraud is proved when it is shown that a false representation has been made (1) knowingly, or (2) without belief in its truth, or (3) recklessly, careless whether it be true or false. Although I have treated the second and third as distinct cases, I think the third is but an instance of the second, for one who makes a statement under such circumstances can have no real belief in the truth of what he states. To prevent a false statement being fraudulent there must, I think, always be an honest belief in its truth. And this probably covers the whole ground, for one who knowingly alleges that which is false has obviously no such honest belief. . . . In my opinion making a false statement through want of care falls far short of, and is a very different thing from, fraud, and the same may be said of a false representation honestly believed though on insufficient grounds.

At the same time I desire to say distinctly that when a false statement has been made the questions whether there were reasonable grounds for believing it, and what were the means of knowledge in the possession of the person making it, are most weighty matters for consideration. The ground upon which an alleged belief was founded is a most important test of its reality. I can conceive of many cases where the fact that an alleged belief was destitute of all reasonable foundation would suffice of itself to convince the Court that it was not really entertained, and that the representation was a fraudulent one. So, too, although means of knowledge are . . . a very different thing from knowledge, if I thought that a person making a false statement had shut his eyes to the facts, or purposely abstained from inquiring into them I should hold that honest belief was absent, and that he was just as fraudulent as if he had knowingly stated that which was false. . . .

I quite admit that the statements of witnesses as to their belief are by no means to be accepted blindfolded. The probabilities must be considered. Whenever it is necessary to arrive at a conclusion as to the state of mind of another person, and to determine whether his belief under given circumstances was such as he alleges, we can only do so by applying the standard of conduct which our own experience of the ways of men has enabled us to form; by asking ourselves whether a reasonable man situated as the defendants were, with their knowledge and means of knowledge, might well believe what they state they did believe, and consider that the representations made were substantially true. . . .

3. JUSTIFIABLE RELIANCE

WILLIAMS V. RANK & SON BUICK, INC.
170 N.W.2D 807 (WIS. 1969)

[R]espondent and his brother went to appellant's used car lot where they examined a 1964 Chrysler Imperial automobile. While doing so, they were approached by a salesman who permitted them to take the car for a test run. They drove the car for approximately one and one-half hours before returning the car to the appellant's lot. During that time they tested the car's general handling as well as its radio and power windows. According to the respondent, however, it was not until several days after he had purchased the car that he discovered that the knobs marked 'AIR' were for ventilation and that the car was not air-conditioned.

At the trial the respondent testified that while examining the car he discussed its equipment with the salesman and was told that it was air-conditioned. He also testified that he relied upon both this representation and an advertisement which read: "64 CHRYSLER Imperial 2 door hardtop; silver mist with black vinyl interior; full power, including FACTORY AIR CONDITIONING: there aren't many around like this. See, drive, you'll buy. * * * $1,559." The appellant's salesman denied making any representations concerning air conditioning . . . . An examination of the record discloses that the advertisement introduced into evidence was dated March 21, 1968, whereas the sales contract signed by both parties was dated March 19, 1968. Upon these facts the trial court found that the respondent had proven fraud on the part of the appellant and awarded him $150 in damages. The appellant appeals from a circuit court order affirming that judgment . . . .

In order to establish that a representation was fraudulent one must establish, first, that the statement of fact is untrue; second, that it was made with intent to defraud and for the purpose of inducing the other party to act upon it; and third, that he did in fact rely upon it and was thereby induced to act, to his injury or damage. . . . As to the first element there is no question that the advertisement and the alleged oral representation of the salesman were false. The automobile in question was simply not equipped with air conditioning. . . .

In regard to the alleged oral misrepresentations of the appellant's salesman, there is, of course, conflict in testimony. Despite denial by the salesman, however, there is sufficient evidence upon which the trial court could find that such statements were made and that they were made with intent to defraud the respondent.

Appellant's counsel argues that there was no reliance by the respondent and that therefore there was no fraud. . . . Many previous decisions of this court have held that one cannot justifiably rely upon obviously false statements. In *Jacobsen v. Whitely* (1909), 138 Wis. 434, 436, 437, 120 N.W. 285, 286, the court said:

> * * * It is an unsavory defense for a man who by false statements, induces another to act to assert
> that if the latter had disbelieved him he would not have been injured. * * * Nevertheless courts
> will refuse to act for the relief of one claiming to have been misled by another's statements who
> blindly acts in disregard of knowledge of their falsity or with such opportunity that by the exercise of ordinary observation, not necessarily by search, he would have known. He may not close
> his eyes to what is obviously discoverable by him. * * *

It is apparent that the obviousness of a statement's falsity vitiates reliance since no one can rely upon a known falsity. Were the rule otherwise a person would be free to enter into a contract with no intent to perform under the contract unless it ultimately proved profitable. On the other hand, a party who makes an inadvertent slip of the tongue or pencil would continually lose the benefit of the contract.

The question is thus whether the statement's falsity could have been detected by ordinary observation. Whether the falsity of a statement could have been discovered through ordinary care is to be determined in light of the intelligence and experience of the misled individual. Also to be considered is the relationship between the parties. . . . In several cases this court has held that the above factors negated the opportunity to inspect and the obviousness of the statement's falsity. . . .

In the instant case, however, no such negating factors exist. The respondent specifically testified that, being a high school graduate, he was capable of both reading and writing. It is also fair to assume that he possessed a degree of business acumen in that he and his brother operated their own business. No fiduciary relationship existed between the parties. They dealt with each other at arms' length. The appellant made no effort to interfere with the respondent's examination of the car, but, on the contrary, allowed him to take the car from the premises for a period of one and one-half hours.

Although the obviousness of a statement's falsity is a question of fact, this court has decided some such questions as a matter of law. . . . In the instant case the respondent had ample opportunity to determine whether the car was air-conditioned. He had examined the car on the lot and had been allowed to remove the car from the lot unaccompanied by a salesman for a period of approximately one and one-half hours. This customers were normally not allowed to do.

No great search was required to disclose the absence of the air conditioning unit since a mere flip of a knob was all that was necessary. If air conditioning was, as stated by the respondent, the main reason he purchased the car, it is doubtful that he would not try the air conditioner. . . . We conclude that as a matter of law the respondent under the facts and circumstances was not justified in relying upon the oral representation of the salesman. This is an action brought in fraud and not an action for a breach of warranty. . . .

Order reversed.

WILKIE, Justice (dissenting).

. . . [T]he respondent was an individual bargaining with a large car dealership. There is no evidence to show that the respondent was familiar with auto air-conditioning systems. The false advertisement said that the air-conditioning unit in the car was factory equipment. Thus, it can be inferred that there would be no box-type unit under the dashboard which would be readily apparent upon entering the car. Presumably, a factory equipped unit would be housed under the hood of the car. Similarly, the fact that the car was purchased in March rather than in the midst of a heat wave would tend to reduce the significance of respondent's failure to test the air conditioning before purchase. . . .

Here, I would hold that the falsity of the representation was not so obvious that it could be held as a matter of law that the respondent had no right to rely on it. It was for the finder of fact and by finding reliance the trial court, by implication, found respondent had a right to rely thereon. . . . I would affirm.

I am authorized to state the BEILFUSS and HEFFERNAN, JJ., join in this dissent.

SAXBY V. SOUTHERN LAND CO.
63 S.E. 423 (VA. 1909)

More than two years after the transaction here involved had been consummated between the parties thereto, this action was brought by the plaintiffs in error against . . . the Southern Land Company . . . to recover damages for alleged false and fraudulent representations made in regard to the sale of a certain farm known as "Winslow." . . .

The second and third grounds of fraud alleged are that the farm contained at least 150 acres of pine timber, of which about 20 acres had been burned over; whereas, there was about 120 acres in timber, of which about 60 acres had been burned over.

It is well settled that a misrepresentation, the falsity of which will afford ground for an action for damages, must be of an existing fact, and not the mere expression of an opinion. The mere expression of an opinion, however strong and positive the language may be, is no fraud. Such statements are not fraudulent in law, because . . . they do not ordinarily deceive or mislead. Statements which are vague and indefinite in their nature and terms, or are merely loose, conjectural or exaggerated, go for nothing, though they may not be true, for a man is not justified in placing reliance upon them. An indefinite representation ought to put the person to whom it is made on inquiry. . . .

The declaration states that the farm in question contained 444 acres, 1 rood, and 26 poles. It is manifest that the vendor was not asserting a fact in stating the number of acres in timber and the number burned over, but was merely expressing his opinion from appearances. The declaration does not charge him with saying more than that there was about 150 acres in timber and about 20 acres burned over. These expressions indicate that the defendant in error was not making statements of ascertained facts, but was merely expressing his opinion of the acreage in timber and the portion thereof which was burned over. The statements were sufficiently indefinite to have put the plaintiffs in error on their guard to make further inquiry if they regarded the matter as material.

The last two grounds of fraud alleged are that the defendant in error stated that the timber, when cut into cordwood, would readily sell at the local stations on the railroad for $4 per cord, whereas, it could be sold only for a much smaller price, and that the land was specially adapted to potato culture, and would by the use of fertilizer yield 100 bushels of potatoes to the acre, whereas, by actual experiment the land failed to produce anything like that yield by the use of fertilizers.

There is no allegation that the land had produced 100 bushels of potatoes to the acre, or that cordwood had brought $4 per cord at local stations. The production of land in the future and the price of cordwood in the future are dependent upon so many conditions that no assertion of an existing fact could be made with respect thereto.

The statements relied on as grounds of fraud cannot be regarded otherwise than as speculative expressions of opinion-mere trade talk-with respect to matters of an essentially uncertain nature. . . .

We are of opinion that the demurrer to the declaration was properly sustained. The judgment complained of must, therefore, be affirmed.

VULCAN METALS CO. V. SIMMONS MFG. CO.
248 F. 853 (2D CIR. 1918)

[Based upon Simmons' representations concerning the quality of its vacuum cleaners and that Simmons had not tried to sell them, Vulcan bought the vacuum manufacturing business from Simmons.]

LEARNED HAND, District Judge. The first question is of the misrepresentations touching the quality and powers of the patented machine. These were general commendations, or, in so far as they included any specific facts, were not disproved; e.g., that the cleaner would produce 18 inches of vacuum with 25 pounds water pressure. They raise, therefore, the question of law how far general "puffing" or "dealers' talk" can be the basis of an action for deceit.

The conceded exception in such cases has generally rested upon the distinction between "opinion" and "fact"; but that distinction has not escaped the criticism it deserves. An opinion is a fact, and it may be a very relevant fact; the expression of an opinion is the assertion of a belief, and any rule which condones the expression of a consciously false opinion condones a consciously false statement of fact. When the parties are so situated that the buyer may reasonably rely upon the expression of the seller's opinion, it is no excuse to give a false one. . . . And so it makes much difference whether the parties stand "on an equality." For example, we should treat very differently the expressed opinion of a chemist to a layman about the properties of a composition from the same opinion between chemist and chemist, when the buyer had full opportunity to examine. The reason of the rule lies, we think, in this: There are some kinds of talk which no sensible man takes seriously, and if he does he suffers from his credulity. If we were all scrupulously honest, it would not be so; but, as it is, neither party usually believes what the seller says about his own opinions, and each knows it. Such statements, like the claims of campaign managers before election, are rather designed to allay the suspicion which would attend their absence than to be understood as having any relation to objective truth. It is quite true that they induce a compliant temper in the buyer, but it is by a much more subtle process than through the acceptance of his claims for his wares.

So far as concerns statements of value, the rule is pretty well fixed against the buyer. . . . It has been applied more generally to statements of quality and serviceability. . . . But this is not always so. . . . Cases of warranty present the same question and have been answered in the same way. . . .

In the case at bar, since the buyer was allowed full opportunity to examine the cleaner and to test it out, we put the parties upon an equality. It seems to us that general statements as to what the cleaner would do, even though consciously false, were not of a kind to be taken literally by the buyer. As between manufacturer and customer, it may not be so; but this was the case of taking over a business, after ample chance to investigate. Such a buyer, who the seller rightly expects will undertake an independent and adequate inquiry into the actual merits of what he gets, has no right to treat as material in his determination statements like these. The standard of honesty permitted by the rule may not be the best; but, as Holmes, J., says in *Deming v. Darling*, 148 Mass. 504, 20 N.E. 107, 2 L.R.A. 743, the chance that the higgling preparatory to a bargain may be afterwards translated into assurances of quality may perhaps be a set-off to the actual wrong allowed by the rule as it stands. We therefore think that the District Court was right in disregarding all these misrepresentations.

As respects the representation that the cleaners had never been put upon the market or offered for sale, the rule does not apply; nor can we agree that such representations could not have been material to Freeman's decision to accept the contract. The actual test of experience in their sale might well be of critical consequence in his decision to buy the business, and the jury would certainly have the right to accept his statement that his reliance upon these representations was determinative of his final decision. We believe that the facts as disclosed by the depositions of the Western witnesses were sufficient to carry to the jury the question whether those statements were false. It is quite true, as the District Judge said, that the number of sales was small, perhaps not 60 in all; but they were scattered in various parts of the Mountain and Pacific States, and the jury might conclude that they were enough to contradict the detailed statements of Simmons that the machines had been kept off the market altogether.

The Simmons Manufacturing Company insists that there was no evidence that Simmons, who was the only party authorized to speak for that company, knew that the goods had ever been put on sale, and it is quite true that there was no such direct evidence. It is at least arguable whether the evidence was sufficient to allow a jury to say that Simmons had known of these efforts. The results of the sales seem to have come to the knowledge only of the local agents, but we think a jury might say that the fact of their sale and the decision of the agents to sell them might have been authorized by the home office, and that Simmons might have known of both. While, therefore, if the case turned only upon Simmons' knowledge of the failure of the machines upon sale, we should hardly think the evidence sufficient to justify any inference that he did know, yet, since the fraud alleged was of the fact of sale alone, the evidence did not justify a directed verdict. Such a misrepresentation might have been material to Freeman in the execution of the contract, since, if he did learn that they had been on sale, he might well have insisted that the results of those sales should be disclosed before he proceeded. Sweetland's testimony to the contrary only discredits Freeman's statements; it cannot be itself the basis of any recovery. . . .

Judgment in the action of deceit reversed, and new trial ordered. . . .

B. NEGLIGENT MISREPRESENTATION

INTERNATIONAL PRODUCTS CO. V. ERIE R.R. CO.
155 N.E. 662 (N.Y. 1927)

ANDREWS, J.

Early in August, 1921, the plaintiff was expecting a valuable shipment consigned to it to arrive in New York on the steamer Plutarch. It was an importer selling the goods received to other customers. Consequently, it was necessary that such goods should be stored until resold, either in ordinary warehouses or in one maintained by some carrier, who might in turn send them over its lines to the ultimate consumer. The plaintiff . . . inquired of the defendant what its prices would be, and arranged, while no definite contract was executed, that the goods when they arrived should be stored at the railroad company's warehouse docks.

The Plutarch was to dock in Brooklyn. There the Erie would receive the goods . . . , transfer them to New Jersey, and then ship them on upon the order of the plaintiff. Both parties must have understood that at some period a bill of lading was to be issued, but certainly there would be some delay. It could hardly be issued simultaneously with the receipt of the goods . . . , and the custom seems to have been that, after the goods were stored by the railroad company in its warehouse, a notice of their receipt was to be given to the plaintiff, who then prepared a bill of lading in the usual form, signed it, sent it to the defendant, who in turn signed it and returned it to the plaintiff.

Here then were the parties both understanding that, when the goods arrived in Brooklyn, they were to be taken by the defendant to its docks, and there stored for a certain price, and that thereafter the ordinary bill of lading would be executed.

The Plutarch reached Brooklyn between August 10th and August 15th, and was unloaded in three or four days. The goods in question were covered by insurance until they reached the warehouse. Naturally the plaintiff was desirous of protecting itself from that time forward, and to protect itself it was essential that the particular warehouse in which they were stored should be made known to the insurer. Therefore, on August 17th, giving this reason for its question, it inquired of the defendant where the goods would be stored. The latter, taking time to obtain the required information, replied they were docked at dock F, Weekawken. From this reply the plaintiff had the right to infer that the goods were already received and stored. It immediately thereafter obtained its insurance, giving the same information to the insurer.

The answer was erroneous. In fact, the goods were not received from the steamer by the defendant until August 27th and August 31st. The plaintiff's officer, however, having charge of the transaction, did not know but what the representation was true, nor did the plaintiff itself know that it was not . . . . We have then the false assurance as to an existing fact, given by one who had arranged to become, and who in fact subsequently did become, bailee of these goods, to the owner, to enable it to obtain valid insurance thereon, and in reliance upon which the owner acted.

One-half of the goods were in fact stored when they arrived, not on dock F, but on dock D; both docks belonging to the defendant. When the formal bill of lading prepared by the defendant some time later was returned to it early in September, a close examination of certain stamps impressed upon it would have revealed the truth. It was not discovered, however. In November dock D with the goods stored thereon was destroyed by fire. The plaintiff could obtain no insurance because of the misdescription in the policy. It therefore seeks to recover the insurance it would have been entitled to had it not given the misdescription in reliance on the statement of the defendant. The defendant denies liability on any theory, either of tort or of contract. . . .

Confining ourselves to the issues before us, we eliminate any theory of fraud or deceit. . . . We come to the vexed question of liability for negligent language. In England the rule is fixed. "Generally speaking, there is no such thing as liability for negligence in word as distinguished from act." *Pollock on Torts* (12th Ed.) p. 565 . . . . Dicta to the contrary may be found in earlier cases. . . . But since *Derry v. Peek*, L. R. 14 App. Cas. 337, although what was said was not necessary to the decision, the law is clearly to the effect "that no cause of action is maintainable for a mere statement, although untrue, and although acted upon to the damage of the person to whom the statement is made, unless the statement be false to the knowledge of the person making it". . . , or, as said elsewhere, "we have to take it as settled that there is no general duty to use any care whatever in making statements in the way of business or otherwise, on which other persons are likely to act" . . . .

These cases have not been without criticism. The denial, under all circumstances, of relief because of the negligently spoken or written word, is, it is said, a refusal to enforce what conscience, fair dealing, and the usages of business require. The tendency of the American courts has been towards a more liberal conclusion. The searcher of a title employed by one who delivers his abstract to another to induce action on the faith of it must exercise care. . . . So must a physician who assures a wife that she may safely treat the infected wound of her husband . . ., or, hired by another, examines a patient, and states the result of his diagnosis . . . . So of a telegraph company, stating that a telegram was delivered when in fact it was not. . . . And the liability of such a company to the receiver for the erroneous transcription of a telegram has also sometimes been placed on this ground. . . .

In New York we are already committed to the American as distinguished from the English rule. In some cases a negligent statement may be the basis for a recovery of damages. In . . . *Glanzer v. Shepard*, 135 N. E. 275[, a] public weigher, hired by the seller to weigh goods, realizing that the buyer would rely on his certificate in paying therefor, was held liable for erroneous statements contained therein.

. . . [R]ecovery was placed on the ground of negligence. The weigher was to weigh and certify. There was, so far as appeared, no negligence in the act of weighing. The negligence was inferred from the issuance of a false certificate. That was the wrong for which a recovery was allowed. "Diligence was owing, not only to him who ordered, but to him also who relied."

Obviously, however, the rule we have adopted has its limits. Not every casual response, not every idle word, however damaging the result, gives rise to a cause of action. . . . Liability in such cases arises only where there is a duty, if one speaks at all, to give the correct information. And that involves many considerations. There must be knowledge, or its equivalent, that the information is desired for a serious purpose; that he to whom it is given intends to rely and act upon it; that, if false or erroneous, he will because of it be injured in person or property. Finally, the relationship of the parties, arising out of contract or otherwise, must be such that in morals and good conscience the one has the right to rely upon the other for information, and the other giving the information owes a duty to give it with care. . . . An inquiry made of a stranger is one thing; of a person with whom the inquirer has entered, or is about to enter, into a contract concerning the goods which are, or are to be, its subject, is another. Even here the inquiry must be made as the basis of independent action. We do not touch the doctrine of caveat emptor. But in a proper case we hold that words negligently spoken may justify the recovery of the proximate damages caused by faith in their accuracy.

When such a relationship as we have referred to exists may not be precisely defined. All that may be stated is the general rule. In view of the complexity of modern business, each case must be decided on the peculiar facts presented. The same thing is true, however, in the usual action for personal injuries. There whether negligence exists depends upon the relations of the parties, the thing done or neglected, its natural consequences, and many other considerations. No hard and fast line may be drawn.

Here, as we view the facts, the duty to speak with care, if it spoke at all, rested on the defendant. We have it about to become the bailee of the plaintiff's goods; the inquiry made by him with whom it was dealing for the purpose as it knew of obtaining insurance; the realization that the information it gave was to be relied upon, and that, if false, the insurance obtained would be worthless. We have an inquiry such as might be expected in the usual course of business made of one who alone knew the truth. We have a negligent answer, untrue in fact, actual reliance upon it, and resulting proximate loss. True, the answer was not given to serve the purposes of the defendant itself. This we regard as immaterial. . . .

The judgment appealed from should be affirmed, with costs.

Table of Cases

Index

National Highway & Transportation Safety Administration (NHTSA), 3

Necessity: public, 158-161; private, 154-158

Negligence: breach, 237; causation as element of, 196,389-450; contrasted to strict liability, 175; early definition of, 168; elements of, 195-196,198; duty as element of, 200-202; failure to warn, 217-225; fault, as, 195; foundations for, 167-168; introduction to, 195; judge-made rules for, 294-302; meaning of word, 195; misfeasance, and, 200; *per se*, 282-302; premises liability, 225; reasonably prudent person, 198; rebuttable presumptions of, 288-290; *res ipsa loquitur*, 302-308; strict liability, versus, 268; violations of statute, as, 282-294; volitional act, requiring, 196-197; warn, failure to, 217-225

Negligence *per se*, 282-302: legislative intent, and, 286; rebuttable presumptions, and, 288; Restatement, and, 286; violation of statute, 282-294

Negligent misrepresentation, 751-753

Nonfeasance, no duty for, 200,205-207,229

Nuisance, 87-105: causation, and, 103; coming to, as defense, 92; control, and, 103; damages for, 93-96; injunctions against, 93-99; lead paint, as, 104-105; nature of liability, 87-93; *per se*, 90; private, 87-99; private distinguished from public, 87,103; public, 99-105; public right, interference with, 102; remedies for, 93-96; unreasonable interference, and, 102

Nurses, malpractice of, 279

Objective standards, 26,127,240

Ordinary care, 171

Parental responsibility, 10: statutory liability, 10

Preemption of products liability, 533-541: express, 536-537; implied conflict preemption, 537-541

Premises liability: activities, 229; assumption of risk, and, 232; categories for, 225; changing categories, 229; children, 232-233; common hazards, 233; common law, 226; conditions versus activities, 229; duties, 225; firefighter's rule, 233; invitee, 225-228; licensee, 225-228; misfeasance, 229; natural conditions, 232; outside the propery, harm, 237; ownership; 229; possession, 229; recreational-use statutes, and, 237; Restatement (Third), standard under, 237; social guests, 227; trespasser, duty to, 225,228-232; unitary standard for, 234-237

Presumptions, rebuttable, violation of statute creating, 288-290

Prima facie case: definition of, 105

Privacy, right to and invasion of, 703-740: appropriation form, 710-720; forms of claim, distinguished, 703,705-707; false light, 736-740; intrusion-on-seclusion form, 707-710; public disclosure of private facts, 721-735

Private necessity, 154-158: cause of action, as, 155; damages despite, 157; duty to rescue, 155; incomplete

privilege, 157

Private nuisance, 87-99: coming to, as defense, 92; nature of liability, 87-93; *per se*, 90

Privilege: absolute, against defamation claim, 661-669; incomplete, private necessity as, 157; judicial proceeding, in, 663; malice as defeating qualified, 657; qualified, against defamation claim, 652-661; *see also* Defenses

Privity, contract theories, and, 455-462

Probable cause for detention of suspected shoplifter, 42,47

Products liability, 451-542: contract theories for, 455-462; damages, and, 525; development of, 451; federal preemption, and, 533-541; negligence theories for, 470; plaintiff's conduct, and, 525-532; preemption, and, 533-541; privity, abolition of, as requirement for, 451-455; product misuse, and, 532; *res ipsa loquitur*, and, 470; strict liability theories for, 466-542; warranty theories, 455,457-465; *see also* Strict products liability

Professional malpractice, 273-282: custom standard of care, 277; expert testimony, need for, 277; informed consent, 279-282; locality rule for, 278; modified locality rule for, 278; negligence, distinguished from, 277; non-medical practitioners, and, 279; nurses, and, 279; *prima facie* case of, 277; reasonable care, and, 277; specialists, and, 279; standard of care for, 277

Proximate cause, 413-450: approaches to, 414; causal link, 414-423; defined, 413; direct-cause test for, 423-426; duty versus, 436; eggshell-skull rule, and, 440; foreseeability test for, 426-444; intervening force, and, 447; introduction to, 414-423; question of fact, as, 436; scope-of-the-risk test for, 426-444; superceding cause, and, 444-450; thin-skulled plaintiff rule, 440

Public disclosure of private facts, 721-735: constitutional protection against claim of, 722-724; elements of, 731; publication element, 730; Restatement, and, 732

Public necessity, 158-161: government destruction of private property, immunity for, 160; just compensation, 161

Public nuisance, 99-105: causation, and, 103; control, and, 103; lead paint, as, 104-105; public right, interference with, 102; Restatement definition of, 101; unreasonable interference, and, 102

Public officials, defamation claims by, 669-676: actual-malice requirement, 679-681

Public figures, defamation claims by, 676-679: actual-malice requirement, 679-681

Punitive damages, 594-623: civil penalties, relationship to, as measure of, 609-610; compensatory damages, ratio to, 608-609; compensatory damages, relationship to, 600; constitutional limits on, 603-623; defined, 594; difficulties of, 595-599; history of, 595; insurance for, as void, 603; jury question, as, 595; measure of, 600-603; purpose of, 594; ratio to compensatory damages, 608-609; rationale for, 594; reasonableness of, 607; receipt by state, of, 603; statutes governing, 603; wealth as measure of, 602-603

Quantitative analysis, 265
Question of fact, 267,436: proximate cause, as to, 436

Reasonable-person standard, 238-240: knowledge of reasonable person, 240; mental illness, 241-243
Rebuttable presumptions, violation of statute creating, 288-290
Recreational-use statutes, 237
Release, 327: contribution, effect of, on, 361
Religious beliefs: affecting duty to mitigate damages, 563-572; standards in consequence of, 253-258
Rescue, duty to, 155,203
Respondeat superior, 373-377: detour, and, 377; frolic, and, 377
Remedies: damages, 93-96; injunctions, 93-99; nominal damages, 110; nuisance, for, 93-96
Res ipsa loquitur, 302-308: effects of doctrine, 307-308; *prima facie* case, and, 302
Restatement of Torts, 6,10
Right to privacy, invasion of, 703-740: appropriation form, 710-720; forms of claim, distinguished, 703,705-707; false light, 736-740; intrusion-on-seclusion form, 707-710; public disclosure of private facts, 721-735

Self-defense, 130-143: danger of attack, 143-144; deadly force, 141-143; police officers, 143
Several liability, 356-358
Sexual advance: as intentional infliction of emotional distress, 66-69
Sexual affair: as obviating consent to relations, 113-114
Sexual relations: consent to, obviated by fraud, 113-114; STD from, 114
Shopkeepers: privilege to recapture chattels, 153; probable cause to restrain customer, 42; recovery of chattels, and, 40-42
Shoplifters: false imprisonment of, 40-47; recapture of chattels, 151-153; statute for detention of, 43, unreasonable delay in releasing, 46
Sovereign immunity, 160
Special verdict, 40
Special verdict form, 326
Standard of care: adult activities, children, by, 245-246; children, 244-246; emergencies, in, 250-253; informed consent, 127; intellectual disability, for, 239; negligence, flowering of standard for, 171; objective, 26,127,240; ordinary care, 171; physical disabilities, and, 247-249; premises liability, for, 225-237; reasonable person, 239; reasonable physician, 125; religious belief, and, 253-258; rendering aid, 216; special skill, and, 249-250; unitary, premises liability, for, 234-237
Strict liability: abnormally dangerous activities, for, 175-180,187-190; animals, 180-184; blasting, for, 190; contract theories, under, 455; contributory negligence, not a

defense to, 186; defenses to, 190; domesticated animals, 184; fencing-out statutes, and, 184; foundations for, 167; negligence versus, 268; traditional, 175; vicious animals, 185; wild animals, 184
Strict products liability, 466,542: adoption of, 466-473; books, for, 481-483; breach, product defects and, 483-484; categories of product defects, 484; commercial seller, of, 473-476; consumer-expectations test for, 485-492; defects in product, 483-484; design defect, 485; distributor liability for, 473; duty, and, 473; factors for, 493-494; failure to warn, 516-525; feasible alternative design, 489; hybrid test for, 502-509; manufacturing defect, 484-485; negligence theories for, 470; pharmacy, liability of, 476-481; product category liability, 509; product defects, 481,483-484; proper defendants for, 473; *res ipsa loquitur*, and, 470; Restatement (Second), and, 472; Restatement (Third), and, 473,476,493; retailer liability for, 473-476; risk-benefit test for, 493; risk-utility analysis for, 512-515; seven-factor test for, 499,512; state of the art, and, 512; unintended product uses, 496; unreasonably dangerous, defined, 472; warning defect, 516-525
Superceding cause, 444-450: intervening force, and, 447; Restatement factors for, 445; scope of the risk, and, 445
Survival actions, 574,581-584

Thin-skulled plaintiff rule, 440,558
Third party, duty to warn, 217-225
Threats: assault and, 32; false imprisonment and, 39
Tort: definition of, 2; direct compensation for, 3
Tort law: case method, and, 6; common law, and, 5; corrective-justice vision of, 543; development of, 167-168; direct regulation, contrasted with, 3; function of, 5; practice skills, 6; questions of fact, and, 6; rationale for, 5; *stare decisis*, and, 5,6
Tort liability, development of, 167-168
Tort reform, 552
Torts, categories of, 167
Transferred intent, 23-24
Trespass on the case, 167
Trespass to chattels, 74-79: Restatement definition of, 78
Trespass to land, 82-87: causing entry, and, 83; intent, and, 83-84,86; nuisance, and, 85-86; particulate matter, and, 82-86; Restatement definition of, 83,85-86
Trespassers: assumption of risk by, 232; attractive nuisance, and, 232; children, 232; discovered, 225; duty to, 225,228-232; reason to know of, 232; tolerated, 225
Trespassing livestock, 184

Ultrahazardous activities, 189,194
Unavoidable accidents, 171

Vicarious liability, 25,372-388: bailments, for, 387-388; direct liability, versus, 377; independent contractors, and, 377-383; joint enterprise, of, 383-387; motor vehicles, consensual use of, 388; *respondeat superior*,

CPSIA information can be obtained
at www.ICGtesting.com
Printed in the USA
LVHW060426170820
663362LV00006B/54